The International Encyclopedia of Media Literacy

The Wiley Blackwell-ICA International Encyclopedias of Communication

Series Editor-in-Chief: Wolfgang Donsbach (1949–2015), Technische Universität Dresden, Germany

This series of newly commissioned, subdisciplinary international encyclopedias of communication builds on the success of the existing 12-volume Wiley Blackwell-ICA *International Encyclopedia of Communication* (Donsbach, 2008) and is closely linked to it in content and usage. These A–Z encyclopedias represent the major subfields and areas of communication studies and provide state-of-the-art research for scholars in a highly interactive and accessible format. Available simultaneously online and in print, each work will aim to serve and inform experts in their respective fields with the most up-to-date and definitive research available. In keeping with the goals of the International Communication Association (ICA), authors, editors, and the nature of the content are global in scope.

This series builds a resource that will become the first and foremost location on the web for all those needing scholarly, authoritative information about the field – a gateway to communication research for generations of students and scholars all over the world.

Published

The International Encyclopedia of Digital Communication and Society
Edited by Robin Mansell and Peng Hwa Ang
The International Encyclopedia of Language and Social Interaction
Edited by Karen Tracy
The International Encyclopedia of Political Communication
Edited by Gianpietro Mazzoleni
The International Encyclopedia of Interpersonal Communication
Edited by Charles R. Berger and Michael E. Roloff
The International Encyclopedia of Communication Theory and Philosophy
Edited by Klaus Bruhn Jensen and Robert T. Craig
The International Encyclopedia of Organizational Communication
Edited by Craig R. Scott and Laurie Lewis
The International Encyclopedia of Media Effects
Edited by Patrick Rössler
The International Encyclopedia of Communication Research Methods
Edited by Jörg Matthes
The International Encyclopedia of Intercultural Communication
Edited by Young Yun Kim
The International Encyclopedia of Strategic Communication
Edited by Robert L. Heath and Winni Johansen
The International Encyclopedia of Media Literacy
Edited by Renee Hobbs and Paul Mihailidis

Forthcoming

The International Encyclopedia of Journalism Studies
Edited by Tim P. Vos and Folker Hanusch
The International Encyclopedia of Gender, Media, and Communication
Edited by Karen Ross
The International Encyclopedia of Media Psychology
Edited by Jan van den Bulck
The International Encyclopedia of Health Communication
Edited by Vish Viswanath

The International Encyclopedia of Media Literacy

Volume I
A–Media Literacy in Austria

Editors-in-Chief

Renee Hobbs
Paul Mihailidis

Associate Editors

Gianna Cappello
Maria Ranieri
Benjamin Thevenin

WILEY Blackwell

This edition first published 2019

Registered Office
John Wiley & Sons, Inc., 111 River Street, Hoboken, NJ 07030, USA

Editorial Office
101 Station Landing, Medford, MA 02155, USA

For details of our global editorial offices, customer services, and more information about Wiley products visit us at www.wiley.com.

Wiley also publishes its books in a variety of electronic formats and by print-on-demand. Some content that appears in standard print versions of this book may not be available in other formats.

Library of Congress Cataloging-in-Publication Data

Names: Hobbs, Renee, editor. | Mihailidis, Paul, 1978- editor.
Title: The international encyclopedia of media literacy / editors-in-chief, Renee Hobbs, Paul Mihailidis.
Description: Hoboken, NJ : Wiley-Blackwell, 2019. | Series: The Wiley Blackwell-ICA international encyclopedias of communication | Includes bibliographical references and index.
Identifiers: LCCN 2018050991 | ISBN 9781118978245 (hardcover)
Subjects: LCSH: Media literacy–Encyclopedias. | Mass media–Encyclopedias.
Classification: LCC P96.M4 I58 2019 | DDC 302.2303–dc23 LC record available at https://lccn.loc.gov/2018050991

Cover Design: Wiley
Cover Image: © Rawpixel.com / Shutterstock

Set in 10.5/13pt MinionPro by SPi Global, Chennai, India
Printed in Singapore by C.O.S. Printers Pte Ltd

10 9 8 7 6 5 4 3 2 1

Contents

The International Communication Association

The International Communication Association (ICA) is an academic association for scholars interested in the study, teaching, and application of all aspects of human and mediated communication. ICA began more than 50 years ago as a small association of US researchers and is now a truly international association, with more than 4,500 members in 80 countries. Since 2003, ICA has been officially associated with the United Nations as a nongovernmental association. The ICA has partnered with Wiley Blackwell to publish the 12-volume *International Encyclopedia of Communication* (Donsbach 2008, www.communicationencyclopedia.com) and the series of subdisciplinary international encyclopedias of communication of which the present work is a part.

Encyclopedia Series Advisory Board

About the Editors

Editors-in-Chief

Renee Hobbs is a professor of communication studies and Director of the Media Education Lab at the Harrington School of Communication and Media at the University of Rhode Island. Her research examines the conditions of media literacy education in elementary and secondary schools and she has authored eight books and over 150 scholarly and professional articles. She has offered professional development programs in media literacy on four continents. She is the founding editor of the *Journal of Media Literacy Education*, an open-access, peer-review journal sponsored by the National Association for Media Literacy Education.

Paul Mihailidis is an associate professor of civic media and journalism in the school of communication at Emerson College in Boston, MA, where he teaches media literacy, civic media, and community activism. He is founding program director of the MA in Media Design, senior fellow of the Emerson Engagement Lab, and faculty chair and director of the Salzburg Academy on Media and Global Change. He has published widely on the nexus of media, community activism, and civic voices. His work has been featured by the *New York Times*, the *Washington Post, Slate* magazine, the Nieman Foundation, *USA Today*, CNN, and others. He coedits the *Journal of Media Literacy Education* and sits on the advisory board for iCivics. He earned his PhD from the Phillip Merrill College of Journalism at the University of Maryland, College Park.

Associate Editors

Gianna Cappello is an associate professor at the University of Palermo (Italy) where she teaches undergraduate and graduate courses in digital media sociology and media education. She's cofounder and current president of MED (the Italian Association of Media Education, https://www.medmediaeducation.it). She is codirector of MED's journal *Media Education-Studi, Ricerche e Buone Pratiche* (http://riviste.erickson.it/med/). She's cofounder and current vice president of IAME (the International Association of Media Education, https://iame.education). Her research addresses issues in critical media theory, sociology of childhood, media literacy education, and digital media sociology.

Maria Ranieri is an associate professor of educational methods and technology. Her main research areas include theory and methodology relating to media and technology in education. She has also worked on educational practices aimed at tackling different forms of intolerance, especially online hate speech and digital discrimination, through the promotion of critical media literacy skills. On these topics she has published several books and articles and coordinated European projects.

Benjamin Thevenin is an assistant professor of media arts at Brigham Young University. His studies focus on the relationships between youth, media and politics, and in particular how we can better prepare young people to become thoughtful citizens, consumers, and creators of media. Thevenin teaches classes on creativity, children's media, new media, and media education. He serves on the Leadership Council of the National Association of Media Literacy Education. Benjamin lives with his wife Emily and three boys in the beautiful Wasatch mountains.

Contributors

Ignacio Aguaded University of Huelva, Spain

Leopoldo Abad Alcalá Universidad CEU San Pablo, Spain

Jinnat Ali Western Sydney University, Australia

Donna E. Alvermann University of Georgia, USA

Irene Andriopoulou EKOME SA – National Centre of Audiovisual Media & Communication, Greece

Seth Ashley Boise State University, USA

Erica W. Austin Washington State University, USA

Robert J. Baron Austin Peay State University, USA

Valentina Baú University of New South Wales, Australia

Richard Beach University of Minnesota, USA

Tomás Durán Becerra Autonomous University of Barcelona, Spain

Olga M. Belikov Brigham Young University, USA

Amy Bellmore University of Wisconsin-Madison, USA

Matthias Berg University of Bremen, Germany

Rahul Bhargava MIT Media Lab, USA

Ibrar Bhatt Queen's University Belfast, UK

Melinda C. Bier University of Missouri, St. Louis, USA

James Alex Bonus The Ohio State University, USA

David L. Bruce University at Buffalo, USA

Morgan Brummer University of Wisconsin-Madison, USA

Moniek Buijzen Radboud University, The Netherlands

Sahara Byrne Cornell University, USA

Enrico Calandro Research ICT Africa, South Africa

Angela Calvin University of Wisconsin-Madison, USA

Julie S. Cannon Cornell University, USA

Gianna Cappello University of Palermo, Italy

Patrick Carmichael University of Bedfordshire, UK

Andrés Castillo Universidad Iberoamericana, Mexico

Filippo Ceretti Free University of Bozen-Bolzano, Italy

Maria F. Cervera Gutierrez Independent scholar, USA

Denise N.J. Chapman Monash University, Australia

Yvonnes Chen University of Kansas, USA

C.K. Cheung University of Hong Kong, China

Lana Ciboci Edward Bernays University College, USA

Jamie Cohen Molloy College, USA

Jonathan S. Comer Florida International University, USA

Angela Cooke-Jackson California State University, Los Angeles, USA

Jayne Cubbage Bowie State University, USA

Catherine D'Ignazio Emerson College, USA

Ingrid Hu Dahl Capital One, USA

Nicole Damico University of Central Florida, USA

Belinha S. De Abreu Sacred Heart University, USA

Lies De Kimpe University of Antwerp, Belgium; Ghent University, Belgium

Agueda Delgado-Ponce University of Huelva, Spain

Michael Dezuanni Queensland University of Technology, Australia

Sarah E. Domoff Central Michigan University, USA; University of Michigan, USA

Emily Drabinski Long Island University, Brooklyn, USA

Alexander Fedorov Rostov State University of Economics, Russia

Deborah A. Fields Utah State University, USA

Stephanie A. Flores-Koulish Loyola University Maryland, USA

Michael Forsman Södertörn University, Sweden

Arielle Friedman Oranim Academic College of Education, Israel

Elizaveta Friesem Temple University, USA

Yonty Friesem Columbia College Chicago, USA

Megan Fromm Colorado Mesa University, USA

Katherine G. Fry Brooklyn College of the City University of New York, USA

Linda M. Gallant Emerson College, USA

Roman Gerodimos Bournemouth University, UK

Jason P. Goldston Austin Peay State University, USA

Eric Gordon Emerson College, USA

Erhardt Graeff MIT Media Lab, USA

Silke Grafe University of Würzburg, Germany

Vanessa E. Greenwood Montclair State University, USA

Rosanna E. Guadagno University of Texas, Dallas, USA

Clarice Gualberto Universidade Federal de Minas Gerais, Brasil

Manuel Alejandro Guerrero Universidad Iberoamericana, Mexico

Pallavi Guha Towson University, USA

Claudia Haines Homer Public Library, USA

Frances Jacobson Harris University of Illinois at Urbana-Champaign, USA

Alicia Haywood Independent scholar

Haixia He Ningxia University, China

Troy Hicks Central Michigan University, USA

Christina Hicks-Goldston Austin Peay State University, USA

Brigitte Hipfl University of Klagenfurt, Austria

Garry Hoban University of Wollongong, Australia

Renee Hobbs University of Rhode Island, USA

Erica Hodgin University of California, Riverside, USA

Michael Hoechsmann Lakehead University, Canada

Theo Hug University of Innsbruck, Austria

Gabriella Huggins Spy Hop Productions, USA

Mizuko Ito University of California, Irvine, USA

Sophie Jehel Université Paris 8, France

Amy Petersen Jensen Brigham Young University, USA

Hyeon-Seon Jeong Gyeongin National University of Education, South Korea

Jan Jirák Metropolitan University Prague, Czech Republic; Charles University, Czech Republic

Tessa Jolls Center for Media Literacy, USA

Yasmin B. Kafai University of Pennsylvania, USA

Igor Kanižaj University of Zagreb, Croatia

Jill R. Kavanaugh Boston Children's Hospital, USA

Douglas Kellner University of California, Los Angeles, USA

Ted Kesler Queens College, CUNY, USA

Sadia Khan University of South Carolina, USA

Amie Kim Gyeonggi Institute of Education, South Korea

Amanda M. Kimbrough University of Texas, Dallas, USA

Royce Kimmons Brigham Young University, USA

Heather L. Kirkorian University of Wisconsin-Madison, USA

Tibor Koltay Eszterházy Károly University, Hungary

Sirkku Kotilainen University of Tampere, Finland

Gunther Kress University College London, UK

Daniel G. Krutka University of North Texas, USA

Keval J. Kumar Mudra Institute of Communications, India

Janis B. Kupersmidt Innovation Research & Training, USA

Reijo Kupiainen University of Tampere, Finland; Norwegian University of Science and Technology, Norway

Danijel Labaš University of Zagreb, Croatia

Patricia G. Lange California College of the Arts, USA

Diane Lapp San Diego State University, USA

Kristelle Lavallee Boston Children's Hospital, USA

Geoff Lealand University of Waikato, New Zealand

Christopher Leeder Rutgers University, USA

Dafna Lemish Rutgers University, USA

Anastasia Levitskaya Taganrog Institute of Management and Economics, Russia

Rachael Liberman University of Denver, USA

Kristin J. Lieb Emerson College, USA

Sun Sun Lim Singapore University of Technology and Design, Singapore

Michelle Linford EPIK Deliberate Digital, USA

Sonia Livingstone London School of Economics and Political Science, UK

Renae Sze Ming Loh Utrecht University, The Netherlands

Antonio López John Cabot University, Italy

Marta Lysik University of Wroclaw, Poland

Juan D. Machin-Mastromatteo Universidad Autónoma de Chihuahua, Mexico

Adam Maksl Indiana University Southeast, USA

Christina V. Malik Innovation Research & Training, USA

Marie-Louise Mares University of Wisconsin-Madison, USA

Crystle Martin El Camino College, USA

Lance E. Mason Indiana University Kokomo, USA

Agustín García Matilla Universidad de Valladolid, Spain

Jody Lynn McBrien University of South Florida, Sarasota-Manatee, USA

Kimberly Walsh McDermott University of California, Santa Barbara, USA

Julian McDougall Bournemouth University, UK

Siân A. McLean Victoria University, Australia; La Trobe University, Australia

Sara G. McNeil University of Houston, USA

Kelly Mendoza Common Sense Education, USA

Gustavo S. Mesch University of Haifa, Israel

Scott Alan Metzger Penn State University, USA

Joshua Meyrowitz University of New Hampshire, USA

Ellen Middaugh San José State University, USA

Paul Mihailidis Emerson College, USA

Stefania Milan University of Amsterdam, The Netherlands

Shin Mizukoshi University of Tokyo, Japan

Susan D. Moeller University of Maryland, USA

David Cooper Moore Independent scholar

Gabriel Mugar Emerson College, USA

Kyoko Murakami Hosei University, Japan

Annamaria Neag Bournemouth University, UK

Russell Newman Emerson College, USA

Joanna Nurmis University of Maryland, College Park, USA

W. Ian O'Byrne College of Charleston, USA

Jennifer L. O'Flynn Northeastern University, USA

Brian O'Neill Dublin Institute of Technology, Ireland

Elaine J. O'Quinn Appalachian State University, USA

Chelsea Olson University of Wisconsin-Madison, USA

Suzanna J. Opree Erasmus University Rotterdam, The Netherlands

Leali Osmančević Catholic University of Croatia, Croatia

Joris Van Ouytsel University of Antwerp, Belgium; University of Texas Medical Branch, USA

Rose Pacatte Pauline Center for Media Studies, USA

Luci Pangrazio Deakin University, Australia

Alberto Parola University of Turin, Italy

Susan J. Paxton La Trobe University, Australia

Tina L. Peterson Rice University, USA

Kwame Phillips John Cabot University, Italy

Mari Pienimäki University of Tampere, Finland

Joy Pierce University of Utah, USA

Bruce E. Pinkleton Washington State University, USA

Karolien Poels University of Antwerp, Belgium

Koen Ponnet Ghent University, Belgium

Joan Ferrés Prats University Pompeu Fabra, Spain

Brian A. Primack University of Pittsburgh School of Medicine, USA

Grzegorz Ptaszek AGH University of Science and Technology, Poland

Jenny S. Radesky University of Michigan, USA

Srividya Ramasubramanian Texas A&M University, USA

Holly Randell-Moon Charles Sturt University, Australia

Maria Ranieri University of Florence, Italy

Isabella Rega Bournemouth University, UK

Vítor Reia-Baptista University of Algarve, Portugal

Mark Reid British Film Institute, UK

Eva van Reijmersdal University of Amsterdam, The Netherlands

Felice Resnik University of Wisconsin-Madison, USA

Rebecca B. Reynolds Rutgers University, USA

Colin Rhinesmith Simmons University, USA

Michael Rich Boston Children's Hospital, USA; Harvard Medical School, USA; Harvard T.H. Chan School of Public Health, USA

Judith E. Riddell Queen's University Belfast, UK

Claudia Riesmeyer Ludwig-Maximilians-University of Munich, Germany

Ryan M. Rish University at Buffalo (SUNY), USA

Jessica Roberts Universidade Católica Portuguesa, Portugal

Bernard R. Robin University of Houston, USA

Rachel F. Rodgers Northeastern University, USA

Esther Rozendaal Radboud University, The Netherlands

Rachel Kaminski Sanders University of Georgia, USA

Hagit Sasson University of Haifa, Israel

Denise L. Sauerteig KQED, USA

Molly Sauter McGill University, Canada

Erica Scharrer University of Massachusetts Amherst, USA

Hans C. Schmidt Pennsylvania State University, USA

Alexander Schmoelz University of Vienna, Austria

Tracy M. Scull Innovation Research & Training, USA

Kristin A. Searle Utah State University, USA

Laras Sekarasih Universitas Indonesia, Indonesia

Neil Selwyn Monash University, Australia

Jeff Share University of California, Los Angeles, USA

Moses Shumow Florida International University, USA

Julie Smith Webster University, USA

Alexandra Sousa Texas A&M University, USA

Lucie Stastna Institute of Communication Studies and Journalism, Czech Republic

Christian J. Swertz University of Vienna, Austria

Lynde Tan Western Sydney University, Australia

Javier Tarango Universidad Autónoma de Chihuahua, Mexico

Mirian Nogueira Tavares University of Algarve, Portugal

Jeff R. Temple University of Texas Medical Branch, USA

Eamon Tewell Long Island University, Brooklyn, USA

Benjamin Thevenin Brigham Young University, USA

Vitor Tomé CIAC—Algarve University, Portugal

José Manuel Pérez Tornero Autonomous University of Barcelona, Spain

Brit Toven-Lindsey California State University East Bay, USA

Gerhard Tulodziecki University of Paderborn, Germany

Ornat Turin Gordon College of Education, Israel

Michel Walrave University of Antwerp, Belgiums

Guofang Wan University of West Florida, USA

Emily Bailin Wells Columbia University, USA

Eleanor H. Wertheim La Trobe University, Australia

Dennis M. West Brigham Young University, USA

Rebekah Willett University of Wisconsin-Madison, USA

Carolyn Wilson Western University, Canada

Thomas DeVere Wolsey American University in Cairo, Egypt

Ashley Woodfall Bournemouth University, UK

Michelle S. Woods University of Pittsburgh Center for Research on Media, Technology, and Health, USA

Amanda Wortman University of California, Irvine, USA

Yin Wu Zhejiang University of Media and Communications, China

Ellen Yeh Columbia College Chicago, USA

Melda N. Yildiz New York Institute of Technology, USA

Jiwon Yoon Northwest University, USA

Sarah Zaidan Emerson College, USA

Arezou Zalipour Auckland University of Technology, New Zealand

Brahim Zarouali University of Antwerp, Belgium

Marketa Zezulkova Charles University, Czech Republic

Michelle Zoss Georgia State University, USA

Alphabetical List of Entries

Thematic List of Entries

Community, Democracy, and Policy

History, Theory, and Foundations

Literacy, Education, and Technology

Media, Children, and Youth

Editors' Introduction

Media literacy stands at the intersections of media studies and education as one of the "applied" fields of communication. Media literacy scholarship embraces the potential of active audiences who access, analyze, evaluate, and communicate, as individuals who engage in reflection and take civic, social, and political action in responding to mass media, popular culture, and digital media. In both formal and informal learning contexts, media literacy educators develop innovative pedagogies that enable children, youth, and people of all ages to be full participants in contemporary culture. Media literacy education emphasizes a lifelong process of self-development that connects the individual to society, technology, media, and culture.

Today the rapid changes brought about by the Internet and the rise of digital culture are increasing the variety of stakeholders who recognize the need for media literacy education as means to address a variety of inequalities of knowledge, skills, competencies, and habits of mind. Among members of the discourse community of media literacy are a diverse array of scholars with interests in participatory culture and digital learning; socialization and civic engagement; the impact of media on children; sociocultural, economic, and political dimensions of literacy education; issues of representation, stereotyping, and the role of media in shaping personal and social identity; activism and empowered producers and audiences; the use of technology for teaching and learning; and the role of media in shaping health behavior.

We are sanguine about the potential of media literacy education as it contributes to social progress, democratic participation, a deepening respect for the arts and humanities, and a focus on student-centered learning. This two-volume encyclopedia, with 200 entries and 680,000 words, reveals the depth and breadth of the global community of scholars and practitioners from fields including communication, media studies, education, human development, sociology, and other fields.

How We Built These Volumes

The editors have spent 6 years developing this project. During this time, the topic of media literacy was an especially fast-growing topic and we struggled to keep up with the rapid growth of scholarship in the field. For example, in 2014, a Google search on the phrase "media literacy" revealed 1.3 million results but by 2018, the same search yielded 3.4 million results. For comparison purposes, consider that this is nearly three times as many as the phrase "media effects" (which yielded 1 million results). Between 2010 and 2019, there were more than 3,100 dissertations written that included the keyword "media literacy," according to a search of the ProQuest dissertation database. Clearly, people from many walks of life are considering the panoply of competencies needed to thrive in an increasingly digital world.

By defining the vocabulary and key concepts that have shaped the trajectory of the field, this two-volume subdisciplinary encyclopedia offers a perspective on the past, present, and future of media literacy around the world. As this encyclopedia reveals, media literacy continues to be a term that is generative and dynamic in its formulation, relevant to scholarship in the humanities, social sciences as well as the professional fields of education, communication, and public health.

We designed *The International Encyclopedia of Media Literacy* with students, teachers, scholars, and practitioners of media literacy in mind. People with interests in media literacy come from a wide range of academic and professional fields, with diverse backgrounds and life experiences. While we expect that most readers are new to the field, some bring expertise as researcher and others will explore the volume to understand the state of knowledge, research, and practice in this multiperspectival field.

We were fortunate to assemble a group of nearly 200 global experts who contributed entries to this volume. Thanks to their talent and expertise, the encyclopedia offers a comprehensive and multidisciplinary reference to the theory and practice of media literacy. In developing *The International Encyclopedia of Media Literacy*, we aimed to be inclusive with respect to both geography and disciplinarity. We wanted to validate a variety of research trajectories, especially those that are underrepresented in academic scholarship or rooted in the worlds of practitioners and activists, whose work has contributed much to the knowledge base of the field. We wanted to include the perspectives of scholars, researchers, media professionals, and media activists as well as people with experience with government policymaking, K-12 or higher education, the arts, social services, or technology. For these reasons, we ensured the inclusion of a variety of epistemological perspectives, including those with a transnational and transtheoretical perspective.

Authors from a variety of countries helped us become more sensitive to the particularities of how knowledge in media literacy scholarship is rooted to the contexts in which research, scholarship, and practice develop. No one scholar has a solid understanding of the full diversity of global media literacy practice, that is for certain. We all have much to learn from the entries in this volume. *The International Encyclopedia of Media Literacy* offers country-specific reviews of research to address the specific situational contexts in which media literacy has developed around the world. Other articles address media literacy practices across geographic contexts. Although the field is far too young and multifaceted for a canonical perspective that identifies the most significant authors, research agendas, and practice developments, we aimed to acknowledge, wherever possible, the growing theoretical and pedagogical areas of consensus that are emerging across the diverse scholarly perspectives in the field.

To create this volume, we first developed a framework that encompassed our best understanding of the depth and breadth of the field. Expert reviewers offered feedback that shaped the design and strategy of this work. *The International Encyclopedia of Media Literacy* features four broad themes. We used these themes to generate headwords and reflect the interdisciplinary nature of the field. Gianna Cappello led the editorial review of entries aligned with History, Theory, and Foundations. Maria Ranieri led the review of entries on the theme of Literacy, Education, and Technology. Renee Hobbs led the review of entries on Children, Media, and Youth, and Paul Mihailidis and Benjamin Thevenin led the review of themed work on the topic of Community, Democracy, and Policy. We aimed for a pluralistic stance on media literacy as articulated from these four distinctive themes which each offer unique theoretical, conceptual, methodological, and global perspectives.

We generated a list of headwords to reflect key ideas in the field and invited the three Associate Editors to review, add, and edit the headwords and to suggest potential authors with expertise relevant to each specific concept. With their feedback and with support from the International Communication Association, we refined this list and assigned entries to nearly 200 authors from nearly 30 countries. Upon receiving manuscripts, editors reviewed them for quality. During this process, we were delighted to see the creativity with which authors approached the task. Authors were gracious in responding to our feedback and in revising their work to address our queries. We learned much from the insights of the authors of these volumes.

Aware of the different formulations and conceptualizations of media literacy, we balanced the perspectives of scholars from across the generations, inviting younger and more senior scholars to contribute their interpretation of the headwords in relation their own particular areas of expertise. We also sought out a variety of methodological perspectives in creating this encyclopedia. Some entries explore a topic from a single methodological vantage point, for example, by focusing primarily on knowledge gained from observations, interviews, or focus groups. Other entries examine social scientific ways of developing new knowledge in media literacy through the use of experiments, surveys, and questionnaires. Still others rely on historical and analytic approaches to knowledge generation.

Whatever the terms or disciplinary traditions, it is clear that many scholars, policymakers, and educators are eager to identify and share a set of useful practices for examining how media and technology intersect with culture and values. We hope this project contributes to the development of new knowledge and strategies for developing productive competencies, knowledge, and skills to help people be socially responsible and civically engaged in a world full of media and technology. We invite readers to explore the volumes to observe how our current understanding of media literacy is shaped by the range of epistemological and methodological strategies used by scholars and practitioners to advance new knowledge in the field.

Acknowledgements

We are grateful to Professor Wolfgang Donsbach who first invited us to contribute to the Wiley Blackwell and International Communication Association series in 2014, just 1 year before his untimely death in 2015. He graciously communicated to us the idea that media literacy had indeed finally arrived as a unique subdiscipline of the field of communication and that the opportunity to shape a two-volume encyclopedia focused on media literacy would help to inspire young scholars and advance new knowledge in the field. His leadership in imagining these volumes is a continued inspiration to us. We have also appreciated the leadership of Sonia Livingstone and Amy Jordan, former presidents of the International Communication Association, whose interest in media literacy encouraged us. At Wiley Blackwell, editors Elizabeth Swayze, Haze Humbert, Zachary Gillan, Beth Stapleton, and Shahzadi Asra have supported the editorial process tirelessly and with professionalism. In addition, the freelance team comprised copy-editors Giles Flitney, Manuela Tecusan, and Fionnguala Sherry-Brennan, proofreaders Jo Pyke and Felicity Watts, revised-proof checker Janey Fisher, indexer Neil Manley, and project manager Nik Prowse. We are grateful to them all.

As we share the project with you, our readers, we are humbly aware of the limitations of these volumes, despite their breadth and depth. Readers with interests in media literacy may search for particular topics of interest and not find exactly what they are looking for. Some readers may recognize the bias and point of view embedded in all the works, since despite our effort to offer an authoritative stance on these topics, we recognize that all media messages are selective and incomplete. We invite our readers to identify the big themes that connect across these diverse topics of interest and to identify gaps in the knowledge to be found in these pages. Your attentive inquiry will ensure that media literacy continues to develop and advance in the decades ahead.

Renee Hobbs, Editor-in-Chief
Paul Mihailidis, Editor-in-Chief
Gianna Cappello, Associate Editor
Maria Ranieri, Associate Editor
Benjamin Thevenin, Associate Editor

Acceptable Use Policies

W. IAN O'BYRNE
College of Charleston, USA

As access to the Internet and other technologies become a mandatory requirement of working in a connected society, networks need to protect against misuse of access to the web. Throughout each working day, organizations ranging from corporations to schools and libraries need to prepare for possible misuse by users. Users can be a wide-ranging term that includes employees of a business, students in a school, or patrons of an organization such as a library. The challenge faced by all of these organizations is how exactly should they address these challenges of possible misuse by users.

The standard method of addressing these situations is to create and disseminate an acceptable use policy (AUP) that strives to avoid network misuse, while identifying consequences for breaking the rules of this contract. The goal is to develop and promote AUPs within organizations and institutions that are progressive, responsive to changes in the Internet, while not negatively impacting morale and productivity. The challenge behind these documents and policies is that they often differ in terms of purpose and implementation. Furthermore, the actual impact of these policies may be quite different for each institution across multiple fields. This is further exacerbated as individuals engage in media literacy practices in and out of school environments, and across multiple digital tools, platforms, and spaces. These policies and the expectations and limitations they place on Internet usage have an impact on use and acquisition of media literacy. This has implications for educators, researchers, and practitioners as they encounter AUPs in their everyday work.

What is an acceptable use policy?

Generally, an AUP is defined as a set of "strategies that allow school districts to notify technology users of expected behavior and set forth the consequences of misuse"

The International Encyclopedia of Media Literacy. Renee Hobbs and Paul Mihailidis (Editors-in-Chief), Gianna Cappello, Maria Ranieri, and Benjamin Thevenin (Associate Editors).

(Conn, 2002, p. 91). In application, there is much more at stake in the implementation of AUPs. Wikipedia defines an AUP as a set of rules applied by the owner, creator, or administrator of a network, website, or service. This AUP is sometimes identified as an acceptable usage policy, or a fair use policy. These policies are meant to restrict the ways in which the network, website, or system may be used and establish guidelines for usage. AUPs are documents written for organizations (e.g., corporations, businesses, universities, schools, libraries, Internet service providers, website owners).

These documents (i.e., AUPs), are an integral piece of the information security policies of an organization. The information security policy may include monitoring, active blocking of specific materials (e.g., blocking keywords or URLs), or applying bandwidth caps to usage. As users (e.g., employees, students, patrons, visitors of a website, users of service) are given access to the network, website, or service, they are often asked to sign an AUP before they are given access. There are instances where this AUP is agreed to by the user through clicking through, or checking a box, as they are given access.

AUPs and related documents are loosely referred to as legal documents as it relates to their tone and structure. The document is meant to be written in a manner that is clear, concise, and not confusing to the user. AUPs usually include details about the philosophy of the organization providing the service or product. The AUP will also include a detailed "code of conduct" that includes the important details about what a user is allowed to do, and not allowed to do, with the technology service. The AUP should also clearly detail the sanctions that will be applied if a user does not follow the terms detailed in the document. It is important to note that an AUP is only as strong as it is enforced by the administrators of a network, website, or service.

AUPs are similar to the terms of service (ToS), terms of use (ToU), or End-user License Agreement (EULA) documents that technology companies and developers include with their products or services. There are slight differences between these documents (i.e., ToS, ToU, EULA) and AUPs. AUPs cover large computing resources, such as websites or networks. AUPs emphasize etiquette and respect for fellow users (presumably not applicable to single-user programs or other computer services). One key difference is that ToS and ToU usually detail how they will interact with the user, and provide little guidance as to how to use the product or service.

The role of AUPs in and out of educational settings

Educators, researchers, and practitioners face many challenges as they interact with AUPs in their own work, and as they protect and prepare students for current and future environments. AUPs may dictate usage of apps, networks, and Internet access at work, home, or the library for individuals. To some extent, our everyday interactions in a web and media literacy environment are dictated by a blanket of documents and agreements constructed from AUPs as well as other ToS or ToU. Educators, researchers, and practitioners not only have to be aware of their own rights and privileges under these documents, but also educate and advocate for students as they use these tools and services.

Within educational contexts, AUPs are evidence of a policy that outlines how a school, district, or institution expects its members to behave in regard to the usage of technology. The usage of technology is typically written broadly and includes hardware, information systems or databases, as well as the Internet, and associated networking capabilities. AUPs in education typically identify acceptable and unacceptable behaviors in their documents. Unacceptable behaviors may include issues of plagiarism, copyright violations, piracy, visitation of inappropriate materials and websites.

It is suggested that the AUP in educational contexts should contain the standards for acceptable use as well as outline the consequences for specific types of violations (Rader, 2002). Complicating the implementation of this is that these indicated "standards" may mean different things for different schools and districts. In general, an AUP in educational settings should describe four things in detail (Conn, 2002):

- The district's expectation that district computing facilities will be used exclusively for educational purposes.
- The district's expectations that students and teachers will use educationally appropriate speech and expression when using the Internet and other technological tools.
- Users' responsibilities to avoid copyright violations; or users' reasonable expectations (or lack of such expectations) of privacy in any and all uses of district technology resources.
- Users' responsibilities to avoid substantial and material disruption of the educational process for the school community (p. 93).

Educational systems also face challenges as they decide how to develop policies to address students and parents that refuse to agree to the terms defined in an AUP. Many schools dictate that the AUP is required for access to the school and Internet networks (Taylor, Whang, Tettegah, 2006). The challenge in these policies is that pedagogy in our current media-literate environment should include access to digital, networked texts (Greenhow, Robelia, & Hughes, 2009). This enforcement of policy is also problematic as it does not take into account the ubiquitous access to digital texts that individuals may already bring into learning spaces due to their own devices (Leander, Phillips, & Taylor, 2010). This is especially true as learning moves into hybrid and blended spaces (Pytash & O'Byrne, 2014), or in systems that espouse bring your own device policies (Ghosh, Gajar, & Rai, 2013).

We must also acknowledge that new digital texts and tools are being produced at a much faster rate than AUPs can be updated to guide use of these tools. Educators and researchers are in a race to better understand and modify pedagogies and the literacy practices necessary to best utilize these texts and tools. As noted, AUPs are also working in concert or competition with ToS and ToU provided by the developers of these products and services. The rise of cloud computing exacerbates these complexities as it is shortsighted to view use of digital technologies as only existing in or out of classroom settings. Cloud computing uses the Internet for the application and delivery of software and services as opposed to storing these materials on a computer's hard drive. The rise of social networks also requires that AUPs "acknowledge both the risks and benefits" (Osborne, 2011, p. 6) of these spaces and have users understand and accept the guidelines. These circumstances create a ubiquitous opportunity to learn and engage in literacy practices anywhere, not just within the walls of a brick and mortar classroom.

This influences the use of digital tools and infusion of media literacy into pedagogy as school district AUPs may ultimately force educators, researchers, and students into more risky online behaviors (Osborne, 2011). Due to this influx of new digital texts and tools, AUPs are frequently not routinely audited and revised. Network filters, lack of interest, and formal or district policies are often cited as key reasons for the lack of integration of digital media tools and literacies in instruction (Simkins & Schultz, 2010). Educators may choose to use or avoid digital tools and spaces that learners may need to use in current or future endeavors (Tinnerman, Johnson, & Grimes, 2010). To deepen learning through authentic, real-world learning experiences, AUPs need to offer more flexibility and freedom as they utilize these networks and tools (Collins & Halverson, 2009). Educators, researchers, and students need to be provided opportunities to make decisions on their use of networks, websites, or services (Hengstler, 2013). By reducing the restrictions placed upon integration of digital texts and tools in instruction while not reducing safety and privacy, tool use may increase exponentially (Light & Polin, 2010).

Developing an AUP

Development of an AUP should begin with an understanding of the culture and philosophy of the service and the group that will utilize the networks, websites, or services. Existing AUPs and templates can be identified from a number of sources online; however, these should only be used as a starting point for discussion. Osborne (2011) suggests that groups create a social media policy to guide discussion and come to consensus about appropriate conduct online. This discussion, and subsequent revisions about the social media guidelines, should include stakeholders that will need to agree to, and enforce, these policies. In a school district or building, this may include school administrators, parents, and students.

The AUP, or documents related to expected online behaviors (e.g., social media policies), should be easy to comprehend, detailed, and focus on the complexities required to be web- and media-literate (Taylor et al., 2006). The development of an AUP should also take into account existing policies that dictate expected behaviors and literacy practices (Russo, 2013). As an example, if there are already policies in place that dictate appropriate discourse and speech, perhaps it is not necessary to duplicate these policies in a new document. Many school districts also curtail their AUP as they contemplate the need for a new statement that indicates how they comply with existing policies (e.g., bullying), state or national telecommunication rules and regulations, as well as fair use and other intellectual property laws (Ahrens, 2012; Brooks-Young, 2010; Marwick, Murgia-Diaz, & Palfrey, 2010).

Finally, the language of the AUP should be easy to read and understand by not only the parties agreeing to the terms, but also the groups enforcing the document. AUPs, ToS, ToU, and EULA documents are often too long, too complex, and not transparent (Fiesler, Lampe, & Bruckman, 2016). The end result is that the document is not easy to read, understand, or enforce. Media and web literacy instruction should include guidance not only for the development of AUPs, but also the comprehension of these documents. More transparency is needed for these documents (i.e., AUPs, ToS, ToU, EULA) to ensure that they are written in a manner that is easy to understand and follow.

Conclusion

Digital networks, websites, and services are a necessary component of the toolset required to build and utilize digital and media literacies. Appropriate policies, procedures, and guidelines are necessary to protect the developers and administrators of these texts and tools, as well as the users of these spaces. These documents often fail to provide users with the freedom needed to expand their skills, while still creating safe and appropriate boundaries for use of the Internet and all it has to offer. To prepare individuals to be digitally savvy, media-literate citizens, there is a need for guidelines, discussions, and agreed upon policies that emphasize successful practice and define the suitable use of the technology and tools being used.

SEE ALSO: Adolescent Literacy in a Digital World; Apps for Children, Regulatory Issues; Authorship and Participatory Culture; CIPA/Internet Filtering; Communication; Copyright and Fair Use; Data Literacy; Digital Literacy; Internet Safety; Literacy, Technology, and Media; Media and Adolescent Identity Development; Participation through Public Media: Improving Media Literacy among Vulnerable Youth; Social Networking Skills

References

Ahrens, D. (2012). Schools, cyberbullies, and the surveillance state. *American Criminal Law Review, 49*, 1669.

Brooks-Young, S. (2010). *Teaching with the tools kids really use: Learning with web and mobile technologies*. Corwin Press.

Collins, A., & Halverson, R. (2009). *Rethinking education in the age of technology: The digital revolution and schooling in America*. New York, NY: Teachers College Press. Retrieved from http://llk.media.mit.edu/courses/readings/Collins-Rethinking-Education.pdf

Conn, K. (2002). *The internet and the law: What educators need to know*. Alexandria, VA: ASCD.

Fiesler, C., Lampe, C., & Bruckman, A.S. (2016). Reality and perception of copyright terms of service for online content creation. In *Proceedings of the 19th ACM Conference on Computer-Supported Cooperative Work & Social Computing* (pp. 1450–1461). ACM.

Ghosh, A., Gajar, P.K., & Rai, S. (2013). Bring your own device (BYOD): Security risks and mitigating strategies. *International Journal of Global Research in Computer Science (UGC Approved Journal), 4*(4), 62–70.

Greenhow, C., Robelia, B., & Hughes, J.E. (2009). Learning, teaching, and scholarship in a digital age—Web 2.0 and classroom research: What path should we take now? *Educational Researcher, 38*(4), 246–259.

Hengstler, J. (2013). *A K-12 primer for British Columbia teachers posting students' work online*. Educational technologies & more. Retrieved from http://etec.ctlt.ubc.ca/510wiki/images/2/2b/Primer_on_Posting_Minor_Students_Final.pdf

Leander, K.M., Phillips, N.C., & Taylor, K.H. (2010). The changing social spaces of learning: Mapping new mobilities. *Review of Research in Education, 34*(1), 329–394.

Light, D., & Polin, K. (2010). *Integrating web 2.0 tools into the classroom: Changing the culture of learning*. New York, NY: EDC Center for Children and Technology. Retrieved from http://cct.edc.org/sites/cct.edc.org/files/publications/Integrating Web2.0.PDF

Marwick, A.E., Murgia-Diaz, D., & Palfrey, J.G. (2010). Youth, privacy and reputation. *Berkman Center for Internet and Society at Harvard University*. Retrieved from https://dmlcentral.net/wp-content/uploads/files/YouthPrivacyReputationBERKMAN.pdf

Osborne, N. (2011). Using social media in education, part 1: Opportunity, risk, and policy. *IBM Developer Works*. Retrieved from http://www.ibm.com/developerworks/library/wa-ind-educ-social-media1/

Pytash, K.E., & O'Byrne, W.I. (2014). Research on literacy instruction and learning in virtual, blended and hybrid environments. In R.E. Ferdig & K. Kennedy (Eds.), *Handbook of research on K-12 online and blended learning* (pp. 179–200). Pittsburgh, PA: Carnegie Mellon University, ETC Press.

Rader, M.H. (2002). Strategies for teaching internet ethics. *INSTITUTION Delta Pi Epsilon Society, Little Rock, AR.*, 116.

Russo, D.L. (2013). The necessity of developing responsible use policies: Advocacy for use of web 2.0 tools in a comprehensive school computing program. (Doctoral dissertation, Foster G. McGaw Graduate School). Retrieved from https://digitalcommons.nl.edu/cgi/viewcontent.cgi?referer=https://duckduckgo.com/&httpsredir=1&article=1000&context=pa

Simkins, M., & Schultz, R. (2010). Using web 2.0 tools at school. *Leadership, 39*(3), 12–38.

Taylor, R.K., Whang, W.E., & Tettegah, S.Y. (2006). Acceptable use policies in school districts: Myth or reality? In S.Y. Tettegah & R.C. Hunter (Eds.), *Technology and education: Issues in administration, policy, and applications in K12 schools* (pp. 115–123). Bingley, England: Emerald Group Publishing Limited.

Tinnerman, L., Johnson, J., & Grimes, R. (2010). Technology assisted collaborative and project-based learning; of blogs, wikis, and networking. *i-Manager's Journal on School Educational Technology, 6*(1), 1.

Further reading

Holcomb, L., Brady, K., & Smith, B. (2010). The emergence of "educational networking": Can noncommercial, education-based social networking sites really address the privacy and safety concerns of educators? *MERLOT Journal of Online Learning and Teaching, 6*(2). Retrieved from http://jolt.merlot.org/vol6no2/holcomb_0610.pdf

Rodgers, D., & Garcia, P. (2013). The social media dilemma in education: Policy design, implementation and effects. Los Angeles, CA: USC Libraries. Retrieved from http://digitallibrary.usc.edu/cdm/ref/collection/p15799coll3/id/53189

W. Ian O'Byrne is an educator, researcher, and speaker. He is Assistant Professor of literacy education at the College of Charleston. His research investigates the literacy practices of individuals as they read, write, and communicate in online spaces. Ian has been involved in initiatives ranging from online and hybrid coursework, integrating technology in the classroom, digital badges, and supporting marginalized students in literacy practices.

Access

VÍTOR REIA-BAPTISTA and MIRIAN NOGUEIRA TAVARES
University of Algarve, Portugal

Access is a term that, in the English language, has undergone variations of meaning throughout the centuries. Of Latin origin, the term *accessus* was first used to designate a sudden access of fever (ca. 14th century). Later it related to the idea of *an approach*, whose meaning derives directly from Latin—a coming to, an approach, way of approach, entrance. Etymologically, the sense of access as *an entrance* registers itself from the 16th century and is what has carried through to the present. In the 1960s, the term became part of the universe of new technologies whose center was the machines that would revolutionize the world: computers.

To access is to enter somewhere; to have the ability to access something or someone. In the case of computers, it concerns contents. The user, through the access, enters the machine, either on its hard or soft face. For literacy studies the term is fundamental because it is believed that access is only available to someone whose capacity for apprehending or understanding is enough to be able to decode the signs before them, be they concrete, physical, or symbolic and virtual.

We therefore try to understand the possible meanings of the term access in the field of literacy. We delimit its meaning, first and foremost, as something concrete that concerns the socioeconomic, and even territorial, capacity to have access to the machine and the network, either in the symbolic sense that is to perceive, or decode, the contents correctly, mainly for the purpose of creating an *active audience*—one of the principal purposes of literacy in any field.

Access in the knowledge society

It might be argued that anyone can become media-literate, without formal media education, by being exposed to the media. It could be suggested that all exposure to the media acts as media pedagogy of which one is simply not aware. Yet, more specific media education processes may indeed become important in achieving a higher order of media literacy, both for media readers and media makers.

To develop formal and informal media education strategies for school environments, for home, and, necessarily, professional media environments, effectively means to grant access to information. Since the media industries are usually almost completely closed to such pedagogical approaches, this would mean concentrating efforts on academic environments for media training, that is, universities and other media training centers.

From this perspective, besides journalism, other fields of major importance that are concerned with media education and media literacy are film, videogames, music, advertising, and, because all tend to converge towards it, the Internet—probably the most eclectic, syncretic of all media. Internet literacy is often required to make coherent sense of all its elements.

To think about the Internet universe is equivalent to thinking about the concept of the information or knowledge society. This has generated one of the greatest contemporary fallacies, namely that everyone everywhere at every time has access to information—and, consequently, to knowledge. First, access to information demands the means, supports, and basic physical conditions that a significant part of the world population may neither possess nor take for granted. According to recent data presented by the ITU (International Telecommunications Union) (ITU, 2016) 3.7 billion people in the world still have no Internet access.

The *ICT Facts & Figures 2016* report demonstrates that the Internet reaches 81% of the population in developed countries, 40% in developing countries, and 15% in the poorest areas. The percentage of individuals using the Internet represents 79.1% in Europe, 65% in the Americas, and 66.6% in the countries of the Commonwealth. Numbers are lower in the Asia/Pacific area (41.9%), in the Arab States (41.6%), and in Africa—with the world's lowest percentage (25.1%). The relevance of this report by the United Nation's specialized agency for information and communication technologies is undeniable. It demonstrates that despite the significant increase in access to mobile devices all over the world, in the poorest countries such access does not correspond to network connections.

Thus, to think about the concept of access means first to consider the idea supporting it—that we live in an information society, which, according to the statistics above, is not a given. The economist Fritz Machlup was one of the first specialists to develop the concept of the information society. His work resulted in the 1962 cornerstone *The Production and Distribution of Knowledge in the United States*, in which he reflected upon a topic that became increasingly contemporary—the problem of technology and of its role in society nowadays. The information society—also designated as the knowledge society, or new economy—still originates in the term globalization. The term information society is still developing and expanding, since it is supported by a mode of social and economic development in which information as a means of knowledge creation plays a fundamental role in the production of riches and in the contribution toward the well-being and quality of citizens' lives. This begs the question of whether conditions are being met for the advancement of an information society which is based on the possibility that everyone can access information and communication technologies (ICT) present in our daily lives—requisite devices for personal, work, and leisure communication.

Reading images

Besides the socioeconomic conditions making it either difficult or impossible to access information (and, therefore, knowledge) there are yet other, symbolic topics limiting the understanding of contents to those who daily access the world through different media. A significant part of the material transmitted by the media is based on visual language, which demands accurate reading capacities to correctly understand the message, and to make sure consumers are not at risk of manipulation—for the belief is still strong that visual images faithfully reproduce reality.

The world of images is also the world of seduction and recognition. It is above all a constructed, ideological world. Artists in the early 20th century aimed at demystifying the role of the Renaissance perspective, and to demonstrate that, just like everything else in the arts, linear perspective was generated from construction and abstraction. It was by no means the only or the correct mode of representing the world. When considering the process of creating artistic images in the West, one encounters the Greek–Roman ideal of representation, which is taken as the "ideal model" and has become canonical. This western canon, it is observed, is politically and ideologically constructed. Such a model has been predominant in history for apparently being the most natural and/or mimetic mode of representing the world. Images are thus seen as the result of awareness about a given reality added to the wish to render or make it immortal. From the moment it is crystallized the image becomes visible and shareable. The creation of a model of representation in the western world led to the appearance of an ideal model of humankind itself. The mimetic idea of Greek–Roman images invaded the collective mind and became a mirror, the predominance of which repelled any other model that did not correspond to it. The ones which did not fit that model (such as those from the rest of the world) were then seen as *the other*. Alterity granted to those not sharing the western representational mode, however, was not limited to the field of images: it became as vast as transforming a culture, or cultural model, into the only desirable canon.

Film and audiovisual literacy

As the paradigm of the world of images we refer to in the process of creation and fruition of images of and in films, the language of film takes on a vital role in the processes of communicative and educational evolution as a vehicle of collective communication and education. That is, as a factor for an in-depth learning of the most varied domains of human knowledge. It is therefore also important that the evolution of the pedagogical dimensions of audiovisual communication in general, and cinematographic education in particular, are examined as true starting points for an entire cultural repository that can neither be neglected nor ignored—lest we run the risk of casting into oblivion some of the most important traits of western cultural identity which are by nature so often fragile.

The anthropologist Massimo Canevacci explores the relationship between film and the human psyche by way of Gregory Bateson's double bind thesis. "The object of the double bind theory establishes an interwoven tissue of messages that only have meaning because of context" (Canevacci, 1990, p. 41). Message in film exists within a context which can be amplified up to the point of a *metacontext* resulting in the "film effect," the structure of the film direction reproducing the mechanisms of the human perception system. Furthermore, the association of film—since its beginning—to photography furnished projected images with an idea of reality. In context, recognition of the dramatic structure can be referred to, a process which has undergone little variation since the cinematic grammar was brought about by D.W. Griffith. Similarly, the *embodiment* evoked by the vision of bodies on-screen can also be recognized. The spectator thus recognizes the mechanical, formal, and dramatic structure of films and can therefore develop a double bind with them.

According to the theory presented by Canevacci, cinema is the perfect means to experience Bateson's double bind model, since the spectator experiences as their own image the images appearing on the screen, while they are aware that they are not reality but rather some form of existence not belonging to them, and which would hardly happen within their social space. The studies developed by Bateson, at the Palo Alto School, with schizophrenics and with dolphins were later used to analyze relations within families, namely within the mother–child pair. The child, often receiving ambiguous messages, is bound to the mother who issues two orders, "one of which annulling the other" (Canevacci, 1990, p. 39). To avoid the feeling of loss brought about by the first interpretation, the child chooses to be wrong and to wrongly discriminate the signs emitted by the mother. In extreme cases—the schizophrenics—the child loses the capacity to "communicate about communication," therefore becoming "incapable of determining the true meaning of what others say and of expressing what s/he understands" (p. 40).

In cinema, the spectator takes the place of the child cheating itself to obtain pleasure from the film and stop feeling the frustration of not understanding that what stands before them is clearly a lie and an impossibility. By recognizing the context they thus respond positively to the "cinema effect" and let themselves be entangled in the emotion simulated on-screen and experienced among the audience. As stated by Jacques Lacan, the unconscious is structured as a language—the language of film helps to build and to reorganize reality, one further active element in the daily established game to attempt to install and inscribe new meanings.

Notwithstanding the fact that one recognizes the double bind of cinema images, that which one sees seems to rest on an ontological status of pre-thought: I see, therefore I am. However, one cannot forget that the Cartesian *cogito, ergo sum* still dominates the sphere of world apprehension as well as of that which is produced in the world, which is the case of images. I see but my "seeing" is already impregnated with what I think about what I see. That which is given us as organic, acquired, or natural—the capacity to recognize images and representations of the world is indeed part of a complex process. Even the physiological ace of seeing is not neutral, since one does not see with the eyes but rather with the mind—which means what one sees results from a physical-chemical-psychological-affective process. Images are not neutral—not as pure rendering themselves to sight, and not as representation.

Just like Bateson's child, the spectator suffers for realizing that what they see does not exist except in the realm of possibilities, for it seems real because it mimetically reproduces the bodies. And all cinema, whether documentary, or fiction, is a document of a body that has been photographed or somehow recorded, and which has been at some point in the presence of the camera that recorded it. Just like in the Batesonian double bind thesis, the spectator recognizes and rejects the lack of bodily density of the image; however, they cannot but wish to see themselves represented by that shadow projected on-screen. That is to say the contemporary spectator, hit by a diversity of images, often would rather feel represented, or feel part of a social collective, than interpret or realize that which lies before them.

Access in the era of complexity

The second half of the 20th century was defined by the Great War, and by the instability of the relations of the world to its environment that war brought about. The conflict also gave greater visibility to the means of production and propagation of culture, the arts, and science, and, above all, of communication. Theories such as cybernetics were created in an attempt to give some answers to the complexification of the relationships between people and their surrounding universe. Cybernetics is based on the following principle: to offer knowledge about the whole through the relations within it. The word cybernetics derives from the Greek verb *kybernein* (to govern a ship), that is, it points to the art of piloting a ship well. Plato added one further meaning to the phrase: to steer not only the course of ships but also that of the whole society: to govern. In 1886, the Scottish physicist James Clerk Maxwell used the phrase to refer to the artifacts that control machines, and in the 1940s Norbert Wiener adapted the word to designate *the full command of communication theory, and control and communication in the animal and the machine.*

Wiener uses the phrase to honor Maxwell's work: control over machines is fundamental, and he assures that the activity reproduces—at a different scale—the technique of pilots and the art of governing. One should note that when it comes to the universe of technology, everything connects with everything. The so-called information society did not start with the appearance of computers and networks: it came by much earlier, at the onset of modern science. To know is above all to control knowledge, to produce it, and to propagate it. Mathematics has been granted a major role in the 17th and 18th centuries: it was considered a model for reason and useful action. Science only accepted that which could be counted and measured. Mathematics offered a democratic and shareable model of knowledge, since numbers are, from the start, and unlike human languages, universal.

In the 17th century, Gottfried Wilhelm Leibniz declared that knowledge could manifest itself in the interior of a machine. He then elaborated on a binary arithmetic intent on simplifying and compressing knowledge, making it accessible and decodable. Leibniz's project, like that of others such as Francis Bacon, reveals a new attitude toward time and space. Velocity becomes part of the logic of daily life. Leibniz proposed the creation of an ecumenical language which would allow communication among all peoples.

Thus, the need to understand the system as a whole, and the world as a village, may be well represented by the problem of the black box: only by knowing the whole is it possible to understand its functioning, as well as the causes and consequences of the operated connections.

One is therefore obliged to delve into the media, channels, technologies, and language that have been developed for over a century in order to add clarity to the collective creativity and necessities of the artistic and documentary narration that represents us and enables us to reflect on our human condition. Strange though it may seem, though, societies, sciences, and technologies within which these narratives develop can suffer memory loss just as individuals can be forgetful and unable to regenerate the hetero-recognition mechanisms (sometimes not even self-recognition), or cannot distance themselves sufficiently from the prevailing knowledge and narratives in order to gain a more holistic, universal, and reflective perspective. Not because artists, scientists, or pedagogues, as other human beings, have "short memory," but because the arts, sciences, and technologies, and their languages are closed off and isolated within their own particular spaces, sometimes even separated from knowledge, application, and dissemination. This can happen in any branch of the arts or sciences, even when the fundamental principles of languages belong to education or communication, in itself a strong contradiction. Thus, the technological and communicative supports of the records of the individual and collective production of knowledge turn inwards in their apparent self-sufficiency from the standpoint of the evolution of communication. That is, taking into account the technological and linguistic development of the past century, which has shown itself to be redundant as well as a reducing agent that erroneously and inefficiently conserved the procedural knowledge of construction and communication of scientific or cultural learning. If memory loss causes damage, albeit unconscious, of sometimes tragic consequence to the individual, which is often impossible to recover in terms of personal and cultural identity, the possible loss of collective memory in societies amounts to an unimaginable level. Consequently, one is obliged to analyze the possible risks of losing this collective property, often incredibly substantial, and even more valuable for that. To do so, one must also conserve, articulate, and systematize some of the main features of the processes of cultural communication as phenomena of collective memorization and learning. As so many scientists and researchers have stated over the years in the exercise of their scientific irreverence and theoretical restlessness, scientists are hardly ever able to take a step backwards and view science in space and time, in a way that they can see it move—*e pur si muove* (and yet it moves). As for art, various languages and certain technological supports can help us to simultaneously conserve a factual record of events and approach all these events and the phenomena that surround them in an inclusive and holistic way. In this sense, the richness and diversity of the language, technique, and technologies of film are seen as instruments of great importance, from the primitive films of the Lumière brothers and of Georges Mélies to the most sophisticated virtual inserts in YouTube. Their role as vehicles of artistic and documentary narratology, and as factors in authentic literacy, acquires an unquestionable importance in any society that calls itself a knowledge and information society.

SEE ALSO: Critical Information Literacy; Film Education in Europe; Media Literacy as Contemporary Rhetoric; Policy Issues in European Media Literacy; Visual Literacy

References

Canevacci, M. (1990). *Anthropology of visual communication*. São Paulo, Brazil: Brasiliense.

ITU. (2016). *ICT facts and figures 2016*. Retrieved from http://www.itu.int/en/ITU-D/Statistics/Documents/facts/ICTFactsFigures2016.pdf

Further reading

Baudry, J.-L. (1974–1975). Ideological effects of the basic cinematographic apparatus. *Film Quarterly, 28*(2).

Comolli, J.-L. (2007). *Ver y poder – la inocencia perdida: cine, televisión, ficción, documental* [See and power – lost innocence: film, television, fiction, documentary]. Buenos Aires, Argentina: Aurelia Rivera.

Díez-Gutiérrez, E., & Díaz-Nafría, J. (2018). Ubiquitous learning ecologies for a critical cybercitizenship [Ecologías de aprendizaje ubicuo para la ciberciudadanía crítica]. *Comunicar, 54*, 49–58. doi: 10.3916/C54-2018-05.

Friesem, Y. (2017). Beyond accessibility: How media literacy education addresses issues of disabilities. *Journal of Media Literacy Education, 9*(2), 1–16. doi: 10.23860/JMLE-2019-09-02-01. Retrieved from http://digitalcommons.uri.edu/jmle/vol9/iss2/1

Nogueira, M.E. (2010). Understanding cinema: The avant-gardes and the construction of film discourse [Comprender el cine: las vanguardias y la construcción del texto fílmico]. *Comunicar, 35*, 43–51. doi: 10.3916/C35-2010-02-04

Reia, V. (2010). Film languages in the European collective memory [Lenguajes fílmicos en la memoria colectiva de Europa]. *Comunicar, 35*, 10–13. doi: 10.3916/C35-2010-02-00

Tomé, V., Reia-Baptista, V., & Bévort, E. (2015). *Research on social media: A glocal view*. Lisbon, Portugal: RVJ Editores.

Vítor Reia-Baptista (PhD in communication studies) is a Coordinator Professor at the University of Algarve, where he was the director of the communication sciences course and the coordinator of the department of communication, art, and design. He has developed projects and studies in film literacy at the universities of Lund – Sweden, Barcelona, Huelva, and Algarve. He was a founding member of the steering group of the European charter for media literacy and a member of the European Union counseling group for media literacy. He has also been a consortium member in collaboration with the British Film Institute for the European projects: Framework for Film Education and Screening Film Literacy. He was also a co-founder of the CIAC – the Research Centre for the Arts and Communication at the University of Algarve.

Mirian Nogueira Tavares is an Associate Professor at the University of Algarve. With academic studies in communication sciences, semiotics, and cultural studies (PhD in communication and contemporary culture, from the Federal University of Bahia/UNL, New University of Lisbon) she has developed research work and theoretical production in fields related to cinema, literature, and other arts, as well as artistic and aesthetic film studies. As a lecturer at the University of Algarve, she has participated in the development of the visual arts degree, the master's programs in communication, culture and arts, and cultural management, and the PhD programs in communication, culture and arts, and digital media and arts. She is the current coordinator of CIAC (Arts and Communication Research Centre), funded by FCT.

Active Audiences

GIANNA CAPPELLO
University of Palermo, Italy

The concept of the active audience has been one of the most fruitful and provocative ones in the field of media literacy as it has brought media educators to seriously question the traditional ways of defining both their students' involvement with the media and the effects they supposedly produce on them.

Defining the audience (whether as passive or active) has probably been "the" milestone question of all media theory. The idea of a passive audience is historically linked to the advent of mass communications in the early 20th century, which coincided with the negative connotations of the "mass" that crowded the large industrialized cities. As communication research established itself as a new field of study, a differentiation between a normative paradigm and an interpretative one emerged, that was fundamental for defining the concept of the "active audience." The first, long-dominant one, inspired by a behaviorist stimulus–response approach, gives the media a strong power of influence in determining or conditioning certain behaviors in the audience. The second paradigm, opposed to the first, is characterized instead by an attention to the media not so much in terms of effects and behavior, but as social production of meaning. The second, interpretative paradigm connects to the turning point made in the field of social sciences and communication research by currents such as symbolic interactionism and ethnomethodology that focus on the microprocesses of communication and interpretation/construction of meaning from actors placed within specific social contexts. If in the normative theories the social system is central and the objective is that of explaining social phenomena "from the outside," in the interpretative approach the subject is central and therefore the objective is to analyze social phenomena "from the inside," that is, from the point of view of the subject itself. Furthermore, each of these two paradigms is linked to a different conception of the communication process: linear–transmissive in the first case, based on the metaphor of transport/passage of contents/signals; ritual–expressive in the second case, based on the notion of the polysemic text and the metaphor of exchange, sharing, and participation. Finally, from a strictly methodological point of view, while the normative paradigm adopts experimental and laboratory techniques to measure media effects on the audience and produces an infinite number of quantitative studies of media content through content analysis, the interpretative paradigm adopts either an ethnographic approach using techniques such as participant observation and in-depth interviews, or a textual one, using techniques such as conversational analysis, discourse analysis, and textual analysis.

It is because of this interpretative turn that we start talking about active audiences and the polysemic content of the media. The causes and effects of media consumption are no longer the main focus of interest, but rather a more precise definition of the consumption process itself, and the specific ways, contexts, and practices it produces. Indeed, precisely all that normative research had taken for granted.

Table 1 Two paradigms in media audiences and communication research.

	Objects of study	*Audience*	*Concept of communication*	*Methodology*
Normative paradigm	Behaviors Content Effects Influence processes	Mass	Linear–transmissive model	Quantitative approach Content analysis Experimental studies
Interpretative paradigm	Meanings Social production of meanings Interpretative processes Polysemic texts Subcultures	Micro-groups	Ritual–expressive model	Ethnography Participant observation In-depth interviews Conversational analysis Discourse analysis Textual analysis

Source: Author originated.

Schematically, these two paradigms are represented in Table 1.

From the different approaches that have variously been used to study the active audience, some common characteristics have emerged (Biocca, 1988): the first one is *selectivity*, that is the capacity audiences have to select the media they want or need to use. The second characteristic is *utilitarianism*, that is the fact audiences use the media according to a certain level of rational choice to "gratify" particular needs and goals. The third is *intentionality*, that is the cognitive processing and structuring of media information, as a result of which media consumption "bear[s] the clear imprint of the audience member's motivation, personality, and individual cognitive processing structure" (Biocca, 1988, p. 53). The fourth is individual and collective *involvement*, both emotional and at the level of social interaction and discourses originating from media products. The last characteristic is *impervious to influence*, that is the capacity of the audiences to resist and/or redefine media meanings through different "decodings."

Two theoretical orientations preceded and prepared the affirmation of the interpretative paradigm and the notion of active audience: the "uses and gratifications" approach and cultural studies. The former, grafting onto the functionalist tradition, especially since the 1970s in the USA, has made a breakthrough in the tradition of research on media effects and overturned the classic question "what the media do to people" to "what people do with the media" (Blumler & Katz, 1974). The basic assumption is that the media are used with precise functional aims responding to personal and subjective needs, therefore producing differentiated gratifications (Rosengren, 1985). The influence of the media is no longer linked to the manipulating power of content but is rather mediated by individual needs and uses. In other words, the "uses and gratifications" approach, emphasizing the use of media as aimed at a gratifying purpose, configures the audience as actively selecting what to enjoy and therefore capable of "resisting" media influence. Several criticisms of this approach have been advanced, starting from its bracketing out of the more general social dimension, which brings it to consider individual and psychological aspects sufficient to explain media consumption practices, regardless of the structural and systemic aspects that inevitably influence consumption choices in the first place. Moreover, the audience is considered too "rational" and purpose-oriented in pursuing the aim of satisfying certain needs by selecting the appropriate content. As ethnographic audience studies have shown, media consumption often takes place as a ritual, out of habit, so to speak, as an unreflective daily routine and therefore without a specific purpose. Finally, a methodological limit derives from the assumption that people are "authentic" sources of information about their needs. This ignores the fact that choices are also determined either by structural conditions of living or unconsciously, so that answers given may be vitiated by the so-called "social desirability bias," that is, the tendency of respondents to give answers that overreport good behaviors and underreport bad ones, hence making them look better to the interviewer's eyes.

These limits have in part been overcome due to cultural studies, and in particular to Stuart Hall's encoding/decoding model (Hall, 1980). The general objective of the Center for Contemporary Cultural Studies, founded at the end of the 1950s at the University of Birmingham, UK, consists of the study of contemporary popular culture based on a broad notion of culture that includes not only meanings and values, but also the practices that express them. Culture is not defined as an esthetic product but as a "whole way of life", as Raymond Williams puts it (Williams, 1977), thus giving a cultural value to all the meanings produced in the course of the most diverse daily social practices. The main elements of this "culturalist" perspective are: (i) focus on the ideological function of the media moving away from a generic notion of content and adopting instead a more complex notion of text in its discursive, linguistic, and psychoanalytic implications, (ii) revision of the communicative model with the adoption of a more ritual–expressive vision, (iii) attention to the processes of signification enacted in specific social contexts of daily life and therefore, (iv) a more articulated conception of the audience composition and media consumption practices.

Hall's encoding/decoding model represents a milestone in the active audience studies. Drawing from structuralist semiotics, on the one hand, and the Marxist model of production and reproduction of culture, on the other, Hall overcomes the linearity of the sender/message/receiver model and includes it within a more complex and articulated model redefined in terms of production/circulation/distribution/consumption/reproduction; a model that sees communication as a discourse, that is, a social construction of meaning expressed in signs and codes. The focus here is on the text and at the same time on the subjects placed at opposite poles of the process of meaning production and communication. At the encoding pole, the production of meaning as incorporated into the text by the sender according to a hierarchy of "dominant or preferred" meanings that reproduces and feeds into the "hegemonic" social order, in Gramscian terms. At the decoding pole, the production of meaning is deconstructed and reconstructed by the receiver according to three different modes of reading or interpretation: from the most aligned to the dominant encoding (*preferred reading*) to the most alternative (*oppositional reading*), passing through a *negotiated reading* that, although generally aligned with dominant meanings, adapts them on the basis of contextualized and subjective interpretations. In short, both the "uses and gratifications" approach and cultural studies move away from the Marxist-Frankfurtian notion of the passive and manipulated/alienated audience. However, according to the cultural studies perspective, the specific and situated readings of the active audience are not modeled only by psycho-cognitive variables but also by the social context as well as by the broader discursive "hegemonic" structures operating within it.

These two currents—the "uses and gratifications" approach and cultural studies—are the two antecedents that paved the way to the audience studies tradition that, from the 1980s, started to fully explore the notion of the active audience. The general aim of these studies is to describe and analyze the multifaceted phenomenology of the media consumer experience. Using ethnographic techniques, they define media consumption as a social practice enacted by specific groups within specific social contexts (Ang, 1985; Lull, 1991; Morley, 1980, 1986, 1992). As such, it is no longer conceived as a deterministic or behaviorist act, but rather as a complex and articulated process situated in (and influenced by) specific structural conditions of living (age, gender, socioeconomic status). The vision of the audience as an undifferentiated mass is then overcome, and the mediation of the social context is emphasized in guiding certain types of media use and interpretation. The subjects, seen as socially situated actors, manifest different types of interpretative activity and use of the media, although this activity is always connected to more general social contexts, to certain cultural competences, to their belonging to certain groups or subcultures. Another interesting line of investigation that we can trace back to the audience studies tradition is reception theory and reader response criticism, both sharing an interest in deconstructing the complex relationship that originates between texts and readers from a semiotic or textual point of view rather than an ethnographic one (Iser, 1974; Tompkins, 1980).

With the advent of the Internet and social networking sites in particular, the notion of the active audience has a new twist as it no longer simply refers to the activity of interpreting or resisting media messages but to the possibility users have for producing and sharing content, as the expression user-generated content (UGC) suggests. Being part of the active audience in the era of Web 2.0 means to be active within the so-called "participatory culture," as defined by Henry Jenkins as:

> a culture with relatively low barriers to artistic expression and civic engagement, strong support for creating and sharing creations, and some type of informal mentorship whereby experienced participants pass along knowledge to novices. In a participatory culture, members also believe their contributions matter and feel some degree of social connection with one another (at the least, members care about others' opinions of what they have created). (2009, p. xi)

However, it is precisely the notion of participatory culture that amplifies and at the same time seriously questions the "activism" of Web 2.0 users. In order to be active on Web 2.0, it is necessary to acquire diverse media literacy competencies: to maximize the benefits and opportunities offered by the Internet and at the same minimize and govern the risks and problems that may hamper its potential as a new powerful "public sphere" for the full development of culture, democracy, participation, freedom of expression, and so on. Thanks to these competencies, users will be able to critically analyze media content, produce their own content, and be aware of and responsible for the consequences of their choices as media-makers. Jenkins (2009) posits three significant concerns with respect to participatory culture that in a way reinforce the critical stance intrinsic to the media literacy tradition: the "participation gap," the "transparency problem," and the "ethics challenge." The first addresses the problem of the digital divide redefining it not only in terms of unequal access to technology but also, and more radically, in terms of the unequally distributed ability to use technology in a significant, effective, creative, and responsible way. The "transparency problem" addresses the issue of the pressure or influence media exert on people both in ideological and economic terms. The "ethics challenge" draws attention to the fact that, although in participatory culture all users have the possibility to produce their own content, they may not have the ethical standards to act responsibly. As traditional forms of media professional training and socialization are being bypassed by UGC spread and shared on social media platforms and services, the problem arises of preparing (young) people to adopt some fundamental ethical norms and values "for their increasingly public roles as media makers and community participants" (Jenkins, 2009, p. xiii). Indeed, the call for media literacy commitment—public and private, individual and collective—has never been so urgent!

SEE ALSO: Authorship and Participatory Culture; Civic Activism; Critical Theory Applied to Media Literacy

References

Ang, I. (1985). *Watching "Dallas."* London, England: Methuen.

Biocca, F. (1988). Opposing conceptions of the audience: The active and passive hemispheres of mass communication theory. *Communication Yearbook, 11*, 51–80.

Blumler, J.G., & Katz, E. (Eds.). (1974). *The uses of mass communications: Current perspectives on gratifications research.* Beverly Hills, CA: SAGE.

Hall, S. (1980). Encoding/decoding. In Centre for Contemporary Cultural Studies (Ed.), *Culture, media, language: Working papers in cultural studies, 1972–79* (pp. 128 138). London, England: Hutchinson.

Iser, W. (1974). *The Implied Reader*. Baltimore, MA: Johns Hopkins University Press.

Jenkins, H. (with Purushotma, R., Weigel, M., Clinton, J., & Robison, A.J.). (2009). *Confronting the challenges of participatory culture media education for the 21st century.* Cambridge, MA: MIT Press.

Lull, J. (1991). *Inside family viewing*. London, England: Routledge.

Morley, D. (1980). *The nationwide audience*. London, England: British Film Institute.

Morley, D. (1986). *Family television*. London, England: Comedia.

Morley, D. (1992). *Television, audience and cultural studies.* London, England: Routledge.

Rosengren, K.E. (1985). Growth of a research tradition. In K.E. Rosengren, L.A. Wenner, & P. Palmgreen (Eds.), *Media gratifications research.* Beverly Hills, CA: SAGE.

Tompkins, J. (Ed.). (1980). *Reader response criticism.* Baltimore, MA: Johns Hopkins University Press.

Williams, R. (1977). *Marxism and literature.* Oxford, England: Oxford University Press.

Further reading

Abercrombie, N., & Longhurst, B. (1998). *Audiences: A sociological theory of performance and imagination*. Thousand Oaks, CA: SAGE.
Fiske, J. (1987). *Television culture*. London, England: Methuen.
McQuail, D. (1997). *Audience analysis*. Thousand Oaks, CA: SAGE.
Sullivan, J.L. (2013). *Media audiences: Effects, users, institutions, power*. Thousand Oaks, CA: SAGE.

Gianna Cappello is an Associate Professor at the University of Palermo (Italy) where she teaches undergraduate and graduate courses in digital media sociology and media education. She is cofounder and current president of MED (the Italian Association of Media Education, https://www.medmediaeducation.it), codirector of MED's journal *Media Education-Studi, Ricerche e Buone Pratiche* (http://riviste.erickson.it/med/), and cofounder and current vice president of IAME (the International Association of Media Education (https://iame.education). Her research addresses issues in critical media theory, sociology of childhood, media literacy education, and digital media sociology.

Adolescent Literacy in a Digital World

DONNA E. ALVERMANN and RACHEL KAMINSKI SANDERS
University of Georgia, USA

Today's adolescents, commonly referred to as the 12- to 18-year-old segment of the world's population, have never known a time in which information was not created, stored, retrieved, and synchronized through an electronic spectrum we call the Internet. This is not, however, a claim that supports coining the term "digital natives" to describe today's adolescents. Growing up in a digital age in which technology is prevalent does not amount to having achieved mastery over the complex skill sets required for full participation in a 21st-century world. The fallacy of referring to adolescents as digital natives is further evidenced by a digital divide that continues to widen for young people living in households whose earnings fall at or below the poverty line (Bennett, Maton, & Kervin, 2008; Jenkins, Ito, & boyd, 2016).

At the same time, it would not be too much of an overstatement to claim that contemporary youths' literacies are for the most part digitally inspired, or at least significantly mediated by the Internet. This electronic communication network is filled with young people's digital footprints that document in visual, linguistic, and aural modes the many-faceted ways they come to know, construct, and share information. In fact, a growing body of research demonstrates that adolescents use a range of web-based resources and digital literacy skills to construct their online identities. For example, boyd (2014) found in her extensive interview study that today's teens are successful at participating in several networked places simultaneously. In a "selfie"-driven society, holding multiple online identities is among the more common practices of youth culture.

While such practices have been shown to connect in numerous and concrete ways with students' offline lives (Alvermann et al., 2012), the field of literacy teacher education has yet to embrace fully the relevancy of digital literacies in preparing youth to be contributing members of society. Alvermann (2012) points out that "children growing up today are experiencing a world that is increasingly less dominated by print-centric texts than the world their teachers experienced a mere decade ago" (pp. 219–220). This is reflected in the term *new literacies*—not new, as in a replacement metaphor, but new in the sense that social, economic, cultural, intellectual, and institutional changes are continually at work—even speeded up in a world of fast-changing technologies (Lankshear & Knobel, 2011).

Instructionally, these changes are reflected in the degree to which teacher educators and classroom teachers have welcomed them (or not) as a result of questioning the assumptions underlying two competing models of literacy: specifically, the autonomous and the ideological models, both of which coexist and are instrumental in shaping literacy instruction as it is currently practiced in the United States. The autonomous model views reading and writing as neutral processes that are largely explained by individual variations in cognitive and physiological functioning. It is a view that assumes a universal set of reading and writing skills for decoding and encoding printed text.

Shortly after Street's (1995) critique of the autonomous model of literacy and within a decade of Gee's (1990) seminal publication *Social Linguistics and Literacies: Ideology in Discourses*, the New London Group (1996) published its treatise on multiliteracies. This latter work drew attention to the need for an integration of communication modes (e.g., language, still and moving images, speech, sound, gesture, and movement) and content in the context of a culturally and linguistically diverse world, grown significantly more attached to new and ever-changing communication technologies.

Digital media, when viewed as content (print and nonprint) that has been digitized and is thus potentially ready for dissemination on the Internet, are integral to adolescents' construction of digital identities in both formal and informal spaces. Because literacies are social practices (Gee, 1990; Street, 1995), they are also closely associated with how people negotiate their identities as readers and writers. An individual can identify with a number of digital literacy practices (or not) at any one time. Sometimes an act of identifying lasts a short period of time; at other times it may signal a long-term identification with a particular digital literacy practice (e.g., blogging).

As defined in this entry, identity is a theoretical concept that, while socially constructed, is not exempt from an individual's pushing back or resisting society's labels (e.g., blogger)—especially when such labeling conflicts with that individual's self-perceptions and lived experiences. Being recognized as having a particular identity (e.g., blogger) in a certain kind of discourse community (e.g., online digital communication) does not commit a person to operating solely within the boundaries of that group. Instead, digital identities are deemed fluid, in that they frequently change over time in different contexts and for different purposes. It is this fluidity that adds to the attractiveness of digital literacy practices among adolescents.

Adolescents want to create a public identity that connects them beyond the confines of their bedroom walls and puts them on the social map as they begin to figure out who they want to be. They want to be seen and heard but, most importantly, feel as if what they do is relevant, what they do really matters. Rather than waiting to be a part of society by becoming an adult, adolescents are participating with the world in which they live through their electronic devices. When provided access to high-speed Internet and the appropriate hardware and software needed for producing media online, young people have become technology experts in their own right. This fact makes it imperative that their digital identities be welcomed in classrooms where digital knowledge and interest in communicating meet up with formal approaches to critical thinking, reading, and writing. For it is critical thinking rather than mere technical competence that is key to becoming digitally literate.

Society's use of technological devices has individuals in today's culture reading and writing more than ever, affecting both the structuring of traditional textbook assignments and the literacy practices used in comprehending and responding to them. For instance, in the Norwegian context, a survey study (Blikstad-Balas, 2015) of older adolescents at the upper secondary level provided evidence of their widespread use of the online encyclopedia Wikipedia in completing their work. Although the students in the study indicated that they trusted Wikipedia the least as far as credibility was concerned, they nonetheless reported using it most often. The anonymous authorship of Wikipedia was not a deterrent, especially if it gave them quick and easily obtained information that, in their judgment, was good enough for finishing the task at hand (e.g., everyday school assignments, except when studying for a test).

Digital spaces that support young people's interests in comics, gaming, and media fandom—which in turn have the potential to connect complex patterns of learning required for living in a technologically driven culture—are vital to developing literacy practices valued both in and out of school. A growing body of research (Hagood, 2008; Guzzetti & Lesley, 2016) attempts to explain how adolescents thrive individually as producers and consumers of digital media while simultaneously sharing their work in the larger world community. Young people want to have choice in their adventures and the freedom to fail. They need to tinker and play, design and create in order to make sense of the world around them. They want to grab hold and see where the moment takes them.

Bringing forms of popular culture such as fandom, comics, and gaming into the classroom is an invitation to adolescents to make important connections between formal learning spaces and their personal lives (Sanders, 2016). This invitation comes with a call for interactivity and moment-to-moment media relationships that students crave in present-day society. Young people are eager to engage with digital literacy practices in spaces that afford what they view as authentic learning opportunities. Rather than replace or remove required instructional content, pop culture becomes the vehicle through which they explore that content both critically and in light of their own lived experiences.

With the Internet, communication happens in a matter of seconds and across numerous platforms. Information no longer flows in a linear direction from one point to the next; rather, communication is diffused throughout numerous points that make multiple connections simultaneously. This enables adolescents who have adequate access to technology, tools, and media texts to exercise their interest in making connections across social networks in seemingly endless ways—in effect affording them the opportunity to be in more than one place at a time.

At the same time, a lack of access to high-speed Internet creates a digital divide that largely thwarts efforts aimed at encouraging adolescents to become part of the participatory digital culture that defines 21st-century learning. This divide also defeats expectations among young people that the necessary technology and related resources will be available for accomplishing the kinds of content they are interested in producing. While limited access in the past has mainly been attributed to socioeconomic factors, Hargittai's (2003) research would suggest that inequalities in Internet use are also dependent on the "quality of equipment, autonomy of use, the presence of social support networks, experience, and online skill" (p. 823). Hargittai's more nuanced approach to the digital divide calls for developing an awareness, among school administrators and policymakers, of the potential for investing in professional growth opportunities aimed at improving teachers' online skills—the assumption being that their students will benefit in the end.

In addition to those logistical concerns, there are issues of access that stem from inadequate exposure to what Lankshear and Knobel (2011) termed the right "ethos stuff"—or the set of conditions known to foster participatory and collaborative online learning. When school- or district-wide policies restrict what teachers (who perhaps are themselves high-end users of technoliteracies) can provide in the way of digital learning opportunities, then students with limited Internet access at home fall even further behind their more advantaged peers.

The literacies of today are not the literacies of tomorrow; nor are they the literacies of yesterday. Constant change that somewhat ironically preserves the status quo—in keeping with the old adage that the more things change the more they stay the same—cannot be ignored. In the face of contradictions that stem from political and socioeconomic maneuverings, the need for questioning, dissecting, and critically assessing all digital media formats—whether linguistic, visual, aural, or performative—has never been greater. A parallel need is research that makes use of specially designed methods for studying adolescents' use of digital literacies and the changes wrought by such use. Deep inquiries are needed into how multiliteracies, multimodal texts, and game-based literacy instruction have the potential to change what counts as adolescent literacy in a 21st-century digital world. Such inquiries might also uncover anomalies or misfits within the existing literacy instruction paradigm that are indicative of the conditions necessary for a full-blown paradigm shift.

Meanwhile, adolescents' present level of engagement with digital media resources suggests a range of literacy aptitudes and skills that are fast becoming the cultural and symbolic capital necessary for harnessing the high-tech world in which they live (Guzzetti & Lesley, 2016). From selfies on Instagram to cryptic messages on Twitter to videos on YouTube, teens are discovering online spaces in which to belong and feel connected. Their engagement in these spaces could be thought of as ongoing efforts to try on social identities that are creatively compatible with the digitally resourced world around them.

Rather than view such spaces as trivializing or corrupting influences on young people's lives, literacy scholars from around the world are increasingly advocating for classrooms in which digitally produced popular media and games work alongside age-old methods for supporting adolescents' active identity construction (Dezuanni, 2016). Encouraging youths' engagement in an open-ended approach to learning is as essential in the classroom as it is in the everyday world outside of school. In a nutshell, to ignore the potential of 21st-century digital literacy practices and popular media texts is to sabotage young people's motivation for learning.

SEE ALSO: Connected Learning; Digital Literacy; Game Media Literacy; Media and Adolescent Identity Development; Media Literacy Education and 21st Century Teacher Education; Social Media as Media Literacy

References

Alvermann, D.E. (2012). Is there a place for popular culture in curriculum and classroom instruction? In A.J. Eakle (Ed.), *Curriculum and instruction* (Vol. 2, pp. 214–220, 227–228). Thousand Oaks, CA: SAGE.

Alvermann, D.E., Marshall, J.D., McLean, C.A., Huddleston, A.P., Joaquin, J., & Bishop, J. (2012). Adolescents' web-based literacies, identity construction, and skill development. *Literacy Research and Instruction, 51*(3), 179–195.

Bennett, S.J., Maton, K.A., & Kervin, L.K. (2008). The "digital natives" debate: A critical review of the evidence. *British Journal of Educational Technology, 39*(5), 775–786.

Blikstad-Balas, M. (2015). "You get what you need": A study of students' attitudes towards using Wikipedia when doing school assignments. *Scandinavian Journal of Educational Research, 60*(6), 594–608. Retrieved from https://www.researchgate.net/publication/281305503_You_get_what_you_need_A_study_of_students'_attitudes_towards_using_Wikipedia_when_doing_school_assignments/stats.

boyd, d. (2014). *It's complicated: The social lives of networked teens*. New Haven, CT: Yale University Press.

Dezuanni, M. (2016). Digital media literacy: Connecting young people's identities, creative production, and learning about video games. In D.E. Alvermann (Ed.), *Adolescents' online literacies: Connecting classrooms, digital media, and popular culture* (rev. ed., pp.145–164). New York, NY: Peter Lang.

Gee, J.P. (1990). *Social linguistics and literacies: Ideology in discourses*. London, England: Falmer.

Guzzetti, B., & Lesley, M. (Eds.) (2016). *Handbook of research on the societal impact of digital media*. Hershey, PA: IGI Global.

Hagood, M.C. (2008). Intersections of popular culture, identities, and new literacies research. In J. Coiro, M. Knobel, C. Lankshear, & D.J. Leu (Eds.), *Handbook of research on new literacies* (pp. 531–551). New York, NY: Lawrence Erlbaum.

Hargittai, E. (2003). The digital divide and what to do about it. In D.C. Jones (Ed.), *New economy handbook* (pp. 821–839). Amsterdam, Netherlands: Elsevier Science.

Jenkins, H., Ito, M., & boyd, d. (Eds.) (2016). *Participatory culture in a networked era*. Malden, MA: Polity.

Lankshear, C., & Knobel, M. (2011). *New literacies* (3rd ed.). Berkshire, England: Open University Press.
New London Group (1996). A pedagogy of multiliteracies: Designing social futures. *Harvard Educational Review, 66*, 60–93.
Sanders, R.K. (2016). Fandom: Exploring adolescent pop culture through multiple literacies. In D.E. Alvermann (Ed.), *Adolescents' online literacies: Connecting classrooms, digital media, and popular culture* (rev. ed., pp. 77–108). New York, NY: Peter Lang.
Street, B.V. (1995). *Social literacies: Critical approaches to literacy in development, ethnography and education*. London, England: Longman.

Further reading

Albers, P., Holbrook, T., & Flint, A.S. (2014). *New methods of literacy research*. New York, NY: Routledge.
Brandt, D. (2015). *The rise of writing: Redefining mass literacy*. Cambridge, England: Cambridge University Press.
Cope, B., & Kalantzis, M. (2000). *Multiliteracies: Literacy learning and the design of social futures*. New York, NY: Routledge.
Hobbs, R. (Ed.). (2016). *Exploring the roots of digital and media literacy through personal narrative*. Philadelphia, PA: Temple University Press.
Mills, K.A. (2016). *Literacy theories for the digital age: Social, critical, multimodal, spatial, material and sensory lenses*. Buffalo, NY: Multilingual Matters.
Turner, K.H., & Hicks, T. (2015). *Connected reading: Teaching adolescent readers in a digital world*. Urbana, IL: National Council of Teachers of English.

Donna E. Alvermann, University of Georgia Appointed Distinguished Research Professor of Language and Literacy Education, studies young people's digital literacies and uses of popular media. She has edited *Adolescents and Literacies in a Digital World* (2002) and *Adolescents' Online Literacies: Connecting Classrooms, Digital Media, and Popular Culture* (2nd ed., 2010) and coedited *Reconceptualizing the Literacies in Adolescents' Lives* (with Kathleen Hinchman; 3rd ed., 2012). Author of over 150 articles and chapters, she co-designed a website (with Crystal L. Beach and Joe Johnson) that collects data on how a community of researchers disrupt boundaries imposed by social media.

Rachel Kaminski Sanders received her doctoral degree from the Language and Literacy Education Department at the University of Georgia. Her research interests include adolescent as well as digital literacies, specifically in pop culture, and multigenre. Rachel teaches undergraduate courses focusing on adolescent reading and writing. She is teacher consultant for the Upstate Writing Project and has provided professional development to school districts throughout South Carolina. Previously, Rachel served as teacher in residence for the College Ready Writers Program, involving a grant with the National Writing Project. Before that, Rachel taught writing to seventh graders at a public school.

Advertising Literacy

BRAHIM ZAROUALI, MICHEL WALRAVE, and KAROLIEN POELS
University of Antwerp, Belgium

KOEN PONNET
Ghent University, Belgium

In the current online media era, advertisements are increasingly embedded within informative and entertaining content (e.g., on a website, in an online game, etc.). Therefore, being able to recognize and understand these advertisements becomes really challenging, not least for young and unexperienced consumers. Children are, unlike adults, considered to be particularly vulnerable to advertising as they are less aware of the commercial intent of these persuasive messages. It has been argued that they are more likely to be "unfairly" influenced by advertising than adults because they have considerably less knowledge of the true purpose of advertising (i.e., to persuade and sell). The latter has led to heightened public and regulatory concerns and heated debates over the past few decades. With his seminal review back in the 1990s (entitled *Television Advertising and Children*), Brian Young (1990) therefore proposed a research agenda with respect to some important issues on children and advertising, such as whether or not children are able to understand advertising, how and when they develop this advertising-related knowledge, and how educational programs might enhance children's understanding of advertising. Hence, he paved the way for investigating what has been called "advertising literacy." These important issues, among others, will lie at the heart of this entry.

Children as a target group

For many marketers, children are considered an important and lucrative consumer market for multiple reasons (see Buckingham, 2009). First and foremost, they are an important *primary* target group for companies as they buy specific products and services with their own pocket money. As economic actors in their own right, they can decide to spend their savings on what they find personally relevant, attractive, or popular among their peer group. Second, advertisers may target children to reach their parents. As young people have some say in a family's buying decisions, young consumers are targeted with a view to them requesting from or recommending to their parents a brand or product. Thus, to influence children actually means to influence the entire family's buying patterns. This influence does not only occur directly (e.g., children that explicitly ask their parents for certain products), but also indirectly, as parents often take product and brand preferences of their children into account when making purchase decisions. Therefore, next to children's direct impact on their parents' purchases, a more subtle influence can occur as well. Finally, for many advertisers, children represent a long-term "market potential." Advertisers may seek to develop brand loyalty at a very young age, in the expectation that this will eventually pay off in the future. Children are considered the next generation of consumers, so if advertisers succeed in assuring that children have positive experiences with their brands, they may become loyal customers for the rest of their lives. In this regard, adults remain loyal to brands they have discovered as a child, as those particular brands may have good memories for them.

Advertising literacy: a battle of perspectives

Importantly, ever since children were recognized as a lucrative and important target audience (see previous section), the topic of advertising and children has been the subject of major debate (for an excellent account about this, see Rozendaal, Buijzen, & Valkenburg, 2010). In this respect, two main perspectives can be distinguished: the stakeholders in favor of advertising to children, and those against. On the one hand, critics of advertising to children (e.g., policymakers, parents, educators, etc.) hold the view that children are inexperienced critical consumers who are less able to defend themselves against advertising (as compared to adults) due to a lack of cognitive skills. This perspective is fueled by empirical research showing that advertising exposure is related to harmful effects on children's well-being (e.g., unhealthy eating habits, materialistic values, and parent–child conflicts). This has raised some serious questions regarding the fairness and appropriateness of advertising directed to children. On the other hand, proponents of child-targeted advertising (e.g., marketers and manufacturers of child products) argue that children are able to critically understand advertising. These actors claim that advertising can help children make informed choices and, moreover, is important to prepare the child (in an early stage) for the world of consumption they are going to face in adulthood. Put differently, they portray it as being part and parcel of consumer socialization.

Inspired by this debate, scientists from different disciplines have investigated whether children are able to recognize and understand different types of advertisements, that is, their *advertising literacy* (Young, 1990). This concept is heavily built upon the tenets of the persuasion knowledge model (Friestad & Wright, 1994), which refers to consumers' theories of persuasion attempts and includes beliefs about marketers' motives, strategies, and tactics. More precisely, advertising literacy is limited to advertising in particular, thereby excluding other sources of persuasion. This knowledge develops throughout life, starting from early childhood, and continues through early adulthood. It has generally been argued that advertising literacy consists of two major aspects: (i) *advertising recognition*, which refers to people's ability to identify a message as advertising, and (ii) *advertising understanding*, which refers to their abilities to understand advertising's commercial intent (Rozendaal et al., 2010). Advertising understanding further consists of two important dimensions: (i) understanding of the *selling intent*, which refers to realizing that advertising aims to sell products for profitable reasons, and (ii) understanding of the *persuasive intent*, which refers to the fact that advertising aims to change someone's opinions about a product (e.g., advertising wants you to like a product). In addition, other components of *advertising understanding* have been identified as well, yet studied less frequently (e.g., *understanding persuasive tactics*, *understanding the source of advertising*, and *identifying advertisers' target audiences*) (Rozendaal, Lapierre, van Reijmersdal, & Buijzen, 2011).

Wright, Friestad, and Boush (2005) stress the importance of focusing on how these aspects of children's advertising literacy differ from adult-like advertising knowledge, considering the latter as a benchmark. However, this does not mean that adults are never influenced by advertising. Advertising does influence adult consumers (otherwise marketers would not allocate great shares of their media budgets to advertising), but at least they are able to interpret the real underlying intentions of advertisers (as compared to children, who are not). So if adults are persuaded to buy advertised products, their advertising literacy usually prevents them from being unfairly exploited (Gunter, Oates, & Blades, 2005). Obviously, the latter does not apply to children. Therefore, Wright et al. (2005) questioned what it is that children have not yet learned, or do not do as efficiently and effectively as adults in coping with advertising directed at them. In answering this question, many researchers used cognitive development and socialization theories to determine when children learn or acquire the required skills and beliefs to recognize and understand advertising. The point of departure here is that as children's socialization and cognitive development unfolds, their advertising literacy increases until it reaches adult-like levels. This will be discussed in the next section.

Development of advertising literacy

Inspired by Piaget's cognitive development theory, John (1999) developed a consumer socialization theory that discerned several phases in children's competence to understand advertising. Until about the age of 7, children are considered limited processors, as their competence to process information is not fully developed. This phase is further divided in a sensorimotor stage (until more or less the age of 2), where children use their senses to touch and taste, and a preoperational phase (from about 2 to 7), where children learn to discern reality from fiction. Due to their limited cognitive capacities, children under the age of 5 are often not able to discern advertising from other media content. In this regard, ads are just perceived as another form of entertainment. Starting from the age of 5, a lot of children are able to discern (TV) advertising from other media content. However, this does not imply they are capable of understanding its commercial intent, nor which strategies and techniques advertisers use to influence consumers. Between the ages of 7 and 11 (the concrete operational stage of cognitive development), children are able to reason based on concrete events and objects. They discern the difference between advertising and other content, but they usually need a specific cue to do so. Therefore, children in this stage are called "cued processors."

Around the age of 8 years, children start to understand advertising's *selling intent*. However, it is only around the age of 11–12 that children understand the *persuasive intent* of advertising. Insight into advertising's persuasive intent is cognitively more complex than the straightforward purpose of the selling intent and, therefore, takes more time to develop. Based on the latter, researchers have assumed that by the age of 12, children's advertising literacy should be similar to that of adults. From this point on, differences in persuasion effects between children and adults are said to be more likely the result of different experiences, rather than the consequence of different levels of advertising literacy (Gunter et al., 2005). However, a study conducted by Rozendaal and colleagues (2010) revealed that by the age of 12, children have not yet reached an adult-like advertising literacy. By comparing children (aged 12) to adults (18–30), they found that children did not have a similar level of understanding of advertising's selling and persuasive intent to that of adults. They concluded that advertising literacy has not matured at the age of 12, but continues to develop through adolescence and (young) adulthood as well.

Factors influencing the development of advertising literacy

Notwithstanding the abovementioned (i.e., the age-related developments in advertising literacy), the development of children's advertising literacy also depends on their social environment. In this regard, two important influences have to be discerned: *parents* and *peers*. First, parents can educate and teach their children the functioning of advertising, which positively influences the development of advertising literacy. Although parents play an important role in their children's socialization as consumers, they were found to address traditional forms of advertising but were mostly unaware of newer, more embedded marketing content (e.g., advertising on websites, advergames, etc.) (Newman & Oates, 2014). This proves that even adults have difficulties at times in recognizing and understanding advertising, especially when these persuasive messages are embedded in digital media. They harbor a poor conception of the subtle ways advertisements can influence people through newer media. Therefore, adults might be vulnerable to covert persuasion influences, despite their developed critical thinking about advertising (Gunter et al., 2005). But despite this, they are still a crucial factor in assisting children with acquiring the necessary skills to critically engage with advertising.

Second, interactions with peers can also influence the development of one's advertising literacy. Children can communicate with their peers about consumption matters, which can be perceived as an important source in their advertising learning process. Peers can provide information about advertisements, testify about their experiences with certain products, give advice about which products to buy, and so on. Therefore, they are considered an influential source contributing to the development of advertising literacy.

Advertising literacy: an overview of traditional and nontraditional formats

Having addressed the development of children's advertising literacy in general, the focus will now switch to children's advertising literacy level for specific advertising formats. Recently, the embeddedness of advertising in an entertaining digital context has raised new questions concerning the development of advertising literacy. As children are avid users of digital media, they frequently come across covert forms of advertising, such as product placement and advergames (see below for more information about these formats). This subtle integration of commercial messages in entertaining media environments poses new challenges to young consumers in terms of recognizing and understanding the nature of these ad formats. A recent study has established that children have significantly more difficulties in recognizing interactive and nontraditional forms of advertising compared to traditional mass media advertising (Owen, Lewis, Auty, & Buijzen, 2013). To illustrate this, a concise overview will be given of children's advertising literacy regarding traditional (TV commercials) and nontraditional (e.g., advergames, product placement, banners, etc.) advertising formats.

TV commercials

Television has long been the most dominant medium that advertisers have chosen to allocate their largest budget shares for marketing purposes aimed at children. Since the early 1970s, this practice has heightened public and academic concern, raising the question of whether children are able to critically recognize and understand TV commercials. Ever since, innumerous studies have been devoted to children's knowledge and skills with regards to TV advertising (Vanwesenbeeck et al., 2016). Recognizing a TV commercial is an early achievement among children: at the age of 5, they are already able to distinguish TV commercials from TV programs. Their early success in making the distinction between advertising and TV content largely depends on perceptual and contextual features that are typically associated with commercials, such as the duration, pace, and jingles (Zarouali, Walrave, Poels, Ponnet, & Vanwesenbeeck, 2016). Although children are already able to recognize commercials at a young age, the understanding of the selling intent comes later. Once children have reached the age of 8 years, they begin to understand the selling intention of advertising, but a thorough understanding of the persuasive intent of TV commercials only develops around the age of 12 years. All in all, children perform reasonably well in recognizing and understanding commercials at a young age. However, this conclusion only holds for *traditional* TV advertising. Children have much greater difficulties with hybrid forms of online advertising. These advertising formats will be addressed in the following paragraphs.

Advergames

Advergames are basically games that are created with the purpose of promoting a company's brand or product. It is a format that gives the opportunity to the advertiser to benefit from interactive game technology to promote a brand. Advergames often promote unhealthy food products that are low in nutritional value and contain high levels of sugar. Exposure to these advergames has been associated with an unhealthy lifestyle among children, which could eventually lead to obesity. Therefore, a considerable amount of academic attention has been paid to children's advertising literacy toward advergames. In this regard, studies have shown that children have a hard time recognizing the commercial purpose of advergames because the persuasive content is not clearly separated from the game itself (Vanwesenbeeck et al., 2016). In other words, this technique integrates a persuasive message into highly entertaining game content, resulting in blurred boundaries between advertising and entertainment. This makes it difficult for children to activate their advertising literacy. Moreover, an advergame is also characterized as a highly interactive format, which makes it even more challenging for inexperienced consumers such as children to distinguish advertising from other content, in this case the game. Therefore, it has been argued that children are very susceptible and vulnerable to the (negative) advertising effects of advergames.

In-game advertising

In the case of in-game advertising, advertisers pay the developers to place brands or products in the game. This can occur with different intensities. The product or brand can be integrated in the background of the game (e.g., a billboard in a racing game) or integrated in the story line (e.g., the gamer interacts with the product in the game) (Terlutter & Capella, 2013). In-game advertising has an important advantage for many advertisers: games are often played repeatedly, resulting in a long average game playtime. Consequently, children are exposed to the commercial messages more often and for a longer period of time compared to advertising in other media. Another advantage of in-game advertising is that it is embedded in a highly interactive, involving, and immersive environment. It then follows that children are usually exposed to commercial content in an unconscious manner (as they are fully focused on the interactive and involving game play). Because of this, studies have shown that children's recognition and understanding of in-game advertising develops considerably later than for traditional TV advertising (Owen et al., 2013). Therefore, children have a hard time grasping this format as being commercial content.

Online banners

Banners are omnipresent on the Internet and are still one of the most used online advertising formats. They appear as ads on almost all websites, usually in the form of small buttons, rectangles (rectangular images on the page), or skyscrapers (narrow and high banners). Although one is inclined to think that online banners should be an easily distinguishable ad format because of their specific form on websites, the literature surprisingly points toward the opposite direction. A study reveals that the recognition of advertising represents an exercise that is not effortless for children aged 10–12 years (Zarouali et al., 2016). However, it should be noted that only a couple of studies have dealt with advertising literacy in the context of online banners. Therefore, researchers must be careful with formulating powerful conclusions as solid empirical ground generally lacks in this regard. Nevertheless, one can witness the tendency that even in the case of online banners, children seem to experience difficulties, even when they reach the age of 12.

Product placement

Product placement is a popular example of embedded advertising where advertisers pay the creators of a movie or TV program to incorporate their product or brand in the media content. So in this regard it is quite similar to in-game advertising. Because of the integration of marketing stimuli in programming, it makes it more difficult for children to activate their advertising literacy and identify the persuasive intent while watching TV content. The viewer's attention is aimed at carefully following the story line and, therefore, he or she hardly considers product placements as advertising since they cleverly fit with the scenario. Indeed, studies suggest that young consumers find it difficult to recognize product placements as persuasive attempts originating from a commercial agent. It has been revealed that product placements are truly a form of "hidden" persuasion that influences children, slipping under the radar of consciousness (Matthes & Naderer, 2015). Even as children get older (emerging into adolescence), they still seem to be unable to adequately protect themselves against product placements in a critical way. Therefore, this particular advertising technique has greatly heightened public and regulatory concern, leading to the decision that it needs to be closely regulated in order to avoid unwanted and unconscious persuasion among children.

Social media advertising

Exposure to social media advertising is an issue that is particularly relevant among older children, as some important existing social network sites (SNSs) only allow participation from the age of 13 onward (e.g., Facebook and Instagram). Most of these SNSs are free of cost because they earn their revenues mainly through advertising. SNSs have one important asset in serving online ads: they have compiled an unprecedented database of personal information about their users. They allow companies to use this database to target advertising at specific people. Advertisers can choose their target audience based on many features, such as age, gender, profession, likes, interests, hobbies, and relationship status. Next to targeted ads, companies can also build a presence on SNSs by creating a free brand page. Users can then subscribe to this brand page by hitting the "like" or "follow" button. Although this is a relatively new research area, there are indications that children are not fully aware of the persuasive content that circulates in a social networking environment (Lawlor, Dunne, & Rowley, 2016). They have a hard time understanding the commercial motives that advertisers hold with branded pages and targeted advertising. Therefore, based on this reasoning, children's advertising literacy on social media should be considered as underdeveloped.

Conclusion

As the previous paragraphs illustrate, children are dealing these days with a media environment full of different advertising formats (most of which have been addressed here, but there are still many others). With the exception of traditional TV advertising, their advertising literacy is rather poor when it comes to recognizing and understanding (newer) embedded advertising formats. Put differently, children are not (yet) fully experienced consumers who reflect upon the content and purpose of covert advertising in a critical way. Therefore, a call has been spread to help children in acquiring the necessary advertising literacy skills. Based on this, certain initiatives have been suggested in order to improve children's advertising knowledge. Two initiatives will be discussed: *disclosures* and *advertising literacy programs.*

Improving advertising literacy

Disclosures

One of the important initiatives to improve children's advertising literacy is disclosures. The rationale behind these cues is rather straightforward. It is generally assumed that children do not automatically use their advertising literacy during a persuasive exposure but must be triggered or cued to do so (John, 1999). In other words, children can be stimulated to use their advertising literacy if they are helped and encouraged to think about the advertisements they see and why they see them. Presenting them with a disclosure cue is one way to do this. Such a cue can take various forms. Cues may be pre-warnings (e.g., an announcement at the beginning of the commercial break), a (single or multiple) sentence cue that indicates the presence of advertising (e.g., "this is advertising" on a website), icons or symbols (e.g., PP-logo in Belgium to announce product placement, PEGI-ratings on video games, etc.), or overlays in online content that warn consumers that the content they are about to watch is commercially loaded.

Academic research devoted to the effect of disclosures in stimulating the advertising literacy of children is, surprisingly enough, rather limited. However, there is some scarce evidence to argue that children do not engage in critical thinking about advertising unless a disclosure is present to activate their advertising literacy. In other words, only with a cue to trigger their advertising literacy are children able to generate critical thoughts and counterarguments about advertising. Moreover, some studies have also investigated the effect of disclosures on children's susceptibility to advertising, and found that these cues can succeed in reducing (undesired) persuasion effects (An & Stern, 2011). However, academic research on this topic remains underdeveloped, certainly for new and interactive advertising formats. Consequently, it is important to gain a wider base of empirical knowledge on the effectiveness of these disclosure cues in activating children's advertising literacy.

Advertising literacy programs

Another important intervention that has been suggested in order to improve children's processing of advertising is an advertising literacy program. This consists of school-based educational and didactical packages aimed at developing children's knowledge about the commercial purpose of advertising, thereby increasing their advertising literacy. Schools are important outlets to reach a large number of children. Consequently, school-based education programs make it possible to teach children on a large scale how to reflect on advertising and how to deal with the negative consequences of advertising exposure. In the end, the overall goal of an advertising literacy program is to teach children the critical and skeptical elaboration of commercial messages in different media environments. By this means, they can become more experienced consumers who are able to make well-informed and thoughtful decisions about advertised products and services.

In the academic community, advertising literacy education has long been proposed as a necessary intervention to protect young consumers from the negative impact of persuasive communication (Eagle, 2007). However, surprisingly, scant knowledge is available about the role of educational programs in the context of advertising literacy. A limited body of research indicates that an educational intervention can make a difference by enhancing children's comprehension and knowledge of advertising. Yet, these studies mainly focus on advertising in traditional media, while nowadays (online) embedded advertising formats are taking the lead. Quite recently, scholars started investigating the impact of educational interventions on advertising literacy with regards to embedded advertising. Although these results look very promising in terms of increasing advertising literacy, more research is still needed to draw solid and sound conclusions on the effectiveness of such educational interventions. Therefore, this issue certainly deserves a high-priority position on the public agenda in the years to come.

On a practical level, these promising results resulted in educational tools that have been initiated in some European countries and elsewhere. These programs have mostly been developed by the advertising industry. A well-known example is the Media Smart program. Media Smart was launched back in 2002 in the United Kingdom as a media literacy intervention that specifically focuses on enhancing children's critical advertising knowledge (Eagle, 2007). More precisely, Media Smart UK provides educational materials to primary schools that teach children to think critically about advertising in their daily lives. In addition, apart from literacy programs aimed at children, it could also prove to be important to provide parents the necessary advertising training. A study conducted by Hindin, Contento, and Gussow (2004) revealed that a 4-week media literacy education curriculum resulted in a better understanding of the persuasive techniques of advertising among 35 American parents. As parents usually discuss and evaluate advertising with their children, their children will most likely also benefit from these media literacy programs aimed at parents.

New challenges and future directions

In conclusion, some future areas of research will be provided. First, while it is assumed that enhancing consumers' advertising literacy may work as a cognitive defense mechanism against the possible effects of advertising, results of scientific research are not unequivocal. Studies on the influence of children's advertising literacy on advertising effects yielded mixed results, and therefore, future research may untangle these relationships to offer a clearer picture. In this regard, taking the individual characteristics and the social context of children into account can be relevant. Second, more research is needed on the effectiveness of disclosures and advertising literacy programs. By providing solid empirical proof, these initiatives can be very important tools to improve children's advertising literacy. Third, the advertising landscape is evolving rapidly and is continuously introducing new advertising formats. Therefore, it will be important for advertising researchers to keep pace with the rapid innovations made in digital marketing. It is essential to investigate how new, hybrid forms of advertising are processed by young consumers. Finally, research may also take an intergenerational approach. As digital natives grow up with several new forms of advertising, they may differ in how they perceive and react to these persuasive messages, in comparison with older age groups.

SEE ALSO: Children's Understanding of Persuasion; EU Kids Online; Game Media Literacy; Health Literacy; Internet Safety; Parental Mediation

References

An, S., & Stern, S. (2011). Mitigating the effects of advergames on children. *Journal of Advertising, 40*(1), 43–56. doi: 10.2753/JOA0091-3367400103

Buckingham, D. (2009). *The impact of the commercial world on children's wellbeing*. London, England: Department for Children, Schools and Families / Department for Culture Media and Sport.

Eagle, L. (2007). Commercial media literacy: What does it do, to whom – and does it matter? *Journal of Advertising, 36*(2), 101–110. doi: 10.2753/JOA0091-3367360207

Friestad, M., & Wright, P. (1994). The persuasion knowledge model: How people cope with persuasion attempts. *Journal of Consumer Research, 21*(1), 1–31. doi: 10.1086/209380

Gunter, B., Oates, C., & Blades, M. (2005). *Advertising to children on TV: Content, impact, and regulation*. Mahwah, NJ: Lawrence Erlbaum.

Hindin, T.J., Contento, I.R., & Gussow, J.D. (2004). A media literacy nutrition education curriculum for head start parents about the effects of television advertising on their children's food requests. *Journal of the American Dietetic Association, 104*(2), 192–198. doi: 10.1016/j.jada.2003.11.006

John, D.R. (1999). Consumer socialization of children: A retrospective look at twenty-five years of research. *Journal of Consumer Research, 26*(3), 183–213.

Lawlor, M.-A., Dunne, Á., & Rowley, J. (2016). Young consumers' brand communications literacy in a social networking site context. *European Journal of Marketing, 50*(11), 2018–2040. doi: 10.1108/EJM-06-2015-0395

Matthes, J., & Naderer, B. (2015). Children's consumption behavior in response to food product placements in movies. *Journal of Consumer Behaviour, 14*(2), 127–136. doi: 10.1002/cb.1507

Newman, N., & Oates, C.J. (2014). Parental mediation of food marketing communications aimed at children. *International Journal of Advertising, 33*(3), 579–598. doi: 10.2501/IJA-33-3-579-598

Owen, L., Lewis, C., Auty, S., & Buijzen, M. (2013). Is children's understanding of nontraditional advertising comparable to their understanding of television advertising? *Journal of Public Policy & Marketing, 32*(2), 195–206. doi: 10.1509/jppm.09.003

Rozendaal, E., Buijzen, M., & Valkenburg, P. (2010). Comparing children's and adults' cognitive advertising competences in the Netherlands. *Journal of Children and Media, 4*(1), 77–89. doi: 10.1080/17482790903407333
Rozendaal, E., Lapierre, M.A., van Reijmersdal, E.A., & Buijzen, M. (2011). Reconsidering advertising literacy as a defense against advertising effects. *Media Psychology, 14*(4), 333–354. doi: 10.1080/15213269.2011.620540
Terlutter, R., & Capella, M.L. (2013). The gamification of advertising: Analysis and research directions of in-game advertising, advergames, and advertising in social network games. *Journal of Advertising, 42*(2–3), 95–112. doi: 10.1080/00913367.2013.774610
Vanwesenbeeck, I., De Wolf, R., Lambrecht, I., Hudders, L., Cauberghe, V., Adams, B., ... & Walrave, M. (2016). *Minors' advertising literacy in relation to new advertising formats: Identification and assessment of the risks.* Flanders, Belgium: AdLit SBO project.
Wright, P., Friestad, M., & Boush, D.M. (2005). The development of marketplace persuasion knowledge in children, adolescents, and young adults. *Journal of Public Policy & Marketing, 24*(2), 222–233. doi: 10.1509/jppm.2005.24.2.222
Young, B.M. (1990). *Television advertising and children.* Oxford, England: Clarendon Press.
Zarouali, B., Walrave, M., Poels, K., Ponnet, K., & Vanwesenbeeck, I. (2016). Online reclamewijsheid bij kinderen [Online advertising literacry in children]. *Tijdschrift Voor Communicatiewetenschap, 44*(1), 24–45.

Further reading

Blades, M., Oates, C., Blumberg, F., & Gunter, B. (2014). *Advertising to children: New directions, new media.* Basingstoke, England: Palgrave Macmillan.
Kunkel, D., Wilcox, B.L., Cantor, J., Palmer, E., Linn, S., & Dowrick, P. (2004). *Report of the APA task force on advertising and children.* Washington, DC: APA.
Clarke, B., & Svanaes, S. (2012). *Digital marketing and advertising to children: A literature review.* The Advertising Education forum. Retrieved from http://www.aeforum.org/gallery/8612144.pdf

Brahim Zarouali (MSc, University of Antwerp) is a PhD candidate at the Department of Communication Studies of the University of Antwerp. His research focuses on how adolescents deal with advertising persuasion on social networking sites.

Michel Walrave is a professor at the Department of Communication Studies of the University of Antwerp and Chairman of the research group MIOS (Media and ICT in Organisations and Society). His research is centered around online self-disclosure and privacy. He investigates adolescents' and adults' online disclosure of personal information to other individuals or companies, and related opportunities and risks.

Koen Ponnet is a professor at Ghent University (imec-mict). His main research interests are the determinants of risk and problem behavior of adolescents and adults, both offline and online.

Karolien Poels (PhD, Ghent University) is an associate professor at the Department of Communication Studies of the University of Antwerp. She studies how and why individuals use information and communication technology (ICT) and applies these insights to the study of ICT for persuasive purposes (e.g., online advertising, persuasive technology, etc.).

Alternative Media

GABRIEL MUGAR
Emerson College, USA

Alternative media can be described as a response to a deficit in democratic participation. Participation in a democracy requires having voice, and voices are amplified through various media practices. Voices seeking representation in the democratic process have particular impact in the context of mass media, however access to mass media is reserved primarily for the rich and powerful. How then do those who do not have access to mass media participate and influence public conversations and civic processes? This is one question that we can use to frame the urgency and role of alternative media in society. More broadly, alternative media can be defined as the tactics and strategies for generating media that carve out and hold space for the perspectives and issues that exist outside of the agenda defined by those who own mass media systems.

Publics, counterpublics, and the purpose of alternative media

The idea of the public sphere offers a productive starting point for understanding what alternative media are responding to. Jürgen Habermas proposes that civil society can be described as a relationship between the private interests of individuals and business and the policy making power of the state (Habermas, 1989). This relationship plays out in part through public conversations, both in-person and through conversations in various media channels (e.g., newspapers).

In his description of the public sphere, Habermas is critiqued for describing a space for public conversation that is highly idealized, bracketing out concerns for the challenges faced by marginalized groups that are unable to participate in public life openly or have their voices heard (Fraser, 1990). Fraser's critique highlights both cultural and structural challenges to the idea of a single, all encompassing arena for public expression and action around personal interests. She points out that biases and exclusions from public life were based not only on gender and class, but were also compounded by the structural exclusion stemming from high capital costs required to start, own, and operate major media outlets. For example, one cannot start a newspaper with a wide-scale distribution without access to a significant amount of capital. Therefore, the conversations of private and economic interests that appear in large media outlets often reflect the interests of the rich and powerful (Fraser, 1990).

Because of the cultural and economic exclusions from participation in public life, Fraser notes that members of marginalized social groups have created alternative publics, or counterpublics; "discursive arenas where members of subordinated social groups invent and circulate counter discourses" (Fraser, 1990, p. 67). Fraser points out that such counterpublics are essential to democracies because they expand discursive spaces, ensuring that the concerns and issues of marginalized groups can come together and be heard.

It is in this definition of counterpublics that we find the urgency and purpose of alternative media. Because discursive spaces are reliant on media to circulate and represent ideas at scale, looking at the media production and distribution strategy of counterpublics is important to understanding how they are achieved. Media production and distribution in the contexts of counterpublics can therefore be understood as alternative media, or that which offers the "means for democratic communication to people who are normally excluded from media production" (Atton, 2002, p. 11).

Three characteristics of alternative media

To define alternative media, I offer three distinct modalities (infrastructure, perspective, and agency) in the media ecosystem that alternative media are responding to. While all three are interrelated, their individual treatment here highlights distinct and important features for the content and practice of alternative media.

Infrastructure

The high-cost to produce and distribute content on the scale of mass media makes it prohibitive for anyone that does not have the financial capital required to participate. For this reason, affluent people have exclusive control over determining the priorities of media systems, leaving those without the financial means outside the sphere of influence (McChesney, 2004). Similarly, in his analysis of the art world, Howard Becker (2008) points out that art movements and popular esthetics are shaped by the owners of galleries and other systems of distribution. Infrastructure in the context of the above examples can be understood as the technology (both physical and digital) and the social agreements that stabilize and perpetuate the production of specific content. Infrastructures of distributions and production that stabilize large-scale media models are one of the distinct modalities of media ecosystems that alternative media respond to.

Focusing on what she describes as the enclosure of media production and distribution created by corporations, Stefania Milan (2016) unpacks the concept of emancipatory communication practices, or distinct technological tactics and strategies for bypassing mass media models of production and distribution. Such practices create "alternative spaces of communication where freedom of expression, participation, and self organization are practiced independently of social norms and legislation" (Milan, 2016, p. 109).

Milan points to such examples as Indy Media, which originated during the protests of the 1999 World Trade Organization (WTO) meeting in Seattle as a means to cover the work of the global justice movement that was not being featured in mainstream press. Indy Media, or the Independent Media Center, started in Seattle using an online open publishing platform to share reports and content generated by activists and journalists on the frontline of the WTO protests. Indy Media is now a global network of local centers that use the shared platform to share content globally, with each center acting as a clearing house for the news.

Another example of emancipatory media practices can be seen in community media infrastructure. As Colin Rhinesmith points out in his historical account of community media, local access cable platforms have been the natural allies of civic organizations and community groups. "Civic and community groups understood that public access television provided a space where ordinary citizens could engage with other local residents to raise awareness about the important issues of the day" (Rhinesmith, 2016, p. 484).

Examples like IndyMedia and public access stations define the objective of alternative media to offer low cost methods of production and distribution. While platforms like Facebook and Twitter offer such opportunities as well, they are private entities beholden to shareholders and incentives models that do not necessarily align with the interests of all users. As such, infrastructures for alternative media cannot rely solely on such platforms and must also look to infrastructures defined by principles of self-determination and collective action.

Perspective

Advertising as a revenue generating model for television and news requires that shows have a broad appeal so that advertisers can be sure to reach their target demographic (McChesney, 2004). Creating content that is appealing across a population requires avoiding topics that are relevant to smaller subsets of the population. Compounding this restriction to content that has a wide appeal is that content often aligns with the interests of media owners and their allies. Citing research by the Glasgow University Media Group, Atton notes that "An élite of experts and pundits tends to have easier and more substantial access to a platform for their ideas than do dissidents, protesters, minority groups and even 'ordinary people'" (Atton, 2002, p. 17).

As a result of these defining constraints, social issues, interests, and perspectives that do not have a popular following are often left out of the content of mass media. Underrepresented issues and perspectives are a key modality of the media ecosystem that alternative media respond to, working free of constraints to ensure the free flow of ideas and perspectives that are missing from mass media (Atton, 2002).

Historically, alternative media has played a critical role in bringing attention to societal issues that eventually gained mainstream attention. For example, alternative publications covered the topic of rape and sexual violence years before major newspapers and publishers took on the issue (Schuman, 1982).

A salient example of alternative media publications that cover perspectives outside of the mainstream are Zines (short for magazines). Zines are self-published and have a small circulation. Because the topics may have a small audience, the objective of the Zine is to advance an idea or perspective rather than make profit. Zines have covered a range of topics, from fanfiction related to various cultural phenomena to the publication of social theory. Inasmuch as Zines make underrepresented cultural and ideological trends the object of their attention, they are also understood as reflections of the writer's experience with such topics, inviting others to see themselves in the writing and build community around interests and ideas that may not have popular or accessible venues for dialogue (Atton, 2002). Perspectives in alternative media therefore go beyond simply representing ideas and content outside of the mainstream. Perspectives in alternative media are often an invitation for a conversation that needs to be had (e.g., social justice) or personal identities looking for affinity groups.

Agency

Compared to the infrastructures of mass media, alternative media infrastructure supports greater agency for individuals and communities to represent perspectives on issues and ideas that are important to them. Here, agency can be understood as the opportunity to take action in a media ecosystem. While there is indeed a wide range of alternative media content, spanning from serious political content to humorous fanfiction, two distinct spaces of content production that highlight why agency is an important feature when defining alternative media are suggested.

The first is agency as it pertains to democratic participation, in particular agency to participate in the democratic sphere of conversation outside the constraints of state or corporate controlled media. Returning to the concept of publics and counterpublics provided earlier, democratic processes are reliant on discursive opportunities, where people are able to freely circulate, articulate, and act on issues. By removing the financial and cultural constraints of mass media, alternative media hold space and give agency to marginalized issues, addressing the democratic participation deficit described earlier by ensuring possibilities for such issues to enter into discursive spaces. Alternative media also give agency to marginalized actors by allowing for more rapid response to issues. Where mass media will only represent issues that have wide appeal, alternative media can address emergent issues that are not yet known to a wider public.

The second feature of alternative media and agency is that of marginalized groups reclaiming how they are represented in mass media. Atton (2002) points out that there are countless studies that examine how mass media characterizes various social groups as being the source of societal challenges and unrest. Often, such groups are not able to counteract such narratives as they don't have access to influence mass media outlets. In such cases, alternative media gives agency to groups that are the targets of attacks and mischaracterization to generate content that offers a counterpoint to narratives pushed through mass media.

Conclusion

Fraser's response to Habermas's historical account of the public sphere suggests that it overlooks the cultural and economic factors that excluded marginalized groups from dominant discursive space for democratic activity. To address this exclusion, Fraser describes how such groups created counterpublics, or spaces where they were free of constraints and could circulate "counter discourses." Drawing on Fraser's definition of counterpublics, alternative media are defined here as a response to the constraints that mass media place on inclusive democratic participation. The high costs to engage in a mass media ecosystem coupled with its narrow focus on issues that exclude the interests of marginalized communities demonstrate that mass media outlets cannot be the sole space for discursive activity.

The components of alternative media are described here as consisting of infrastructure that offers low cost opportunities to create and distribute content, content that offers perspectives that do not adhere to the lowest common denominator principle of mass media, and agency for people to circulate ideas and issues that are important to them as well as defend how they are represented in mass media narratives.

SEE ALSO: Civic Media; Emancipatory Communication; Local Public Access Centers; Political Economy; Representation

References

Atton, C. (2002). *Alternative media.* Thousand Oaks, CA: SAGE.

Becker, H.S. (2008). *Art worlds.* Oakland, CA: University of California Press.

Fraser, N. (1990). Rethinking the public sphere: A contribution to the critique of actually existing democracy. *Social Text, 25/26*, 56–80.

Habermas, J. (1989). *The structural transformation of the public sphere: An inquiry into a category of bourgeois society.* (T. Burger, Trans.). Cambridge, MA: MIT Press.

McChesney, R. (2004). *The problem of the media: U.S. communication politics in the 21st century.* New York, NY: Monthly Review Press.

Milan, S. (2016). Liberated technology: inside emancipatory communication activism. In E. Gordon & P. Mihailidis (Eds.), *Civic media: Technology, design, and practice.* Cambridge, MA: MIT Press.

Rhinesmith, C. (2016). Community media infrastructure as civic engagement. In E. Gordon & P. Mihailidis (Eds.), *Civic media: Technology, design, practice.* Cambridge, MA: MIT Press.

Schuman, P.G. (1982). Libraries and alternatives. In J.P. Danky & E. Shore (Eds.), *Alternative materials in libraries* (pp. 1–5). Metuchen, NJ: Scarecrow Press.

Gabriel Mugar is a research associate and affiliate faculty member at the Emerson College Engagement Lab. His research focuses on digital participatory platforms and the production of civic media.

Amateur—Professional

TIBOR KOLTAY
Eszterházy Károly University, Hungary

Amateurs are persons who love to be engaged in a specific activity and have a particular self-identity, which is often different from that of professionals. They may be knowledgeable about their subject but do not possess credentials, owing to not having received any formal training or not having access to important tools or knowledge (or both). Sometimes they act just for the sake of amusing themselves and, as a rule, do not make a living out of their field of interest. While this last condition remains true of the majority of amateurs, some earn money through the production of various types of content.

Professionals are members of a profession or persons who earn their living from a specified professional activity. Professionals' preparation is based on standards of education and training that enable them to become members of a prestigious profession by acquiring the particular knowledge and skills that characterize it. They learn and usually follow the rules and codes of conduct that are necessary for the performance of their specific role within that profession, typically agreed upon by and maintained through professional associations.

Amateurs are involved in a wide variety of activities. Thus we can encounter amateur filmmakers, theater performers, musicians, technical editors, astronomers, or journalists, and the act of separating them from professionals is valid not only in media literacy but in digital and information literacy as well.

The division between amateurs and professionals and the perception that they produce artifacts that are distinct from the ones created by professionals have existed as long as professionals have been around. On the other hand, the question of whether this distinction carries more weight in the era when Web 2.0 and social media (new media) enable and encourage readers to become producers has been a subject of debate.

The prevalence of user-generated content is welcomed and in some cases celebrated by many, who accentuate its potential to empower people and democratize media production. It is also underlined that user-generated contents contribute to the emergence of a nonhierarchical model of organization and distribution.

On the other hand, ideas of democratization as well as the deliberating and empowering capacity of social media are regularly criticized on the grounds that these amateurs sell their labor as a commodity. Hence, critics argue, the nonhierarchical organization and distribution are an illusion. Critical voices also contend that the augmented productivity of amateurs is prompted by the constant and forced expectation of novelty that characterizes social media. Moreover, it is frequently underlined that the social media environment fosters superficiality to an increasing degree, as social networks do not encourage or even impede critical comparison and contrast between different views; thus discretion and selectivity do not characterize them. In consequence, amateurs are regularly accused of being superficial.

No matter how we appreciate the nature of this environment, the lines between work and leisure, between consumption and production are becoming increasingly blurred, as social media seem to enable amateurs to accomplish increasingly complex tasks. It has become difficult to discern the difference between professional and amateur media. Amateurs can be placed between laypersons and professionals because the limits of authorship broaden as a result of the diminishing power of those institutions that provide credentials for professionals and drive nonprofessionals out of business.

The relationship between amateurs and professionals is riddled with controversies, even though it is defined by convergence and divergence concurrently. This is because self-staging and self-stylization, and even self-thematization, are now increasingly present on the web.

Determining the identity and value of the amateur is also complicated by the fact that professionalism affects individuals' identity, their location and worth within the economic system. Hence the apparent threat to professionals' status through the proliferation of amateur activities: supplanting professionals is both an abstract concept and a real attack on professional individuals' livelihoods (Brabham, 2012).

There is a view that amateurs have reflective capacities different from the ones of the professionals. It is undoubtedly not by accident that many brilliant inventions were conceived by amateurs, as the outcome of their practices shows innovativeness and productivity. Moreover, in many cases, virtually the same demands and standards are set against amateurs and professionals. This implies that amateurs are not necessarily inferior to their professional counterparts.

Accordingly, under the circumstances of today's economy, especially regarding amateurs and professionals who work in creative industries, the distinction between them may be better explained along a continuum of work relationships between the individual and the organization, as a number of amateurs achieve professional status (Brabham, 2012).

The prevalence of video-sharing websites and the easiness of producing videos also result in porous and elastic borders, which occasionally help amateur videos reach the level of professional ones. The easy production of music videos, in particular, changes the relationship between amateur and professional musicians and audiences. Nevertheless, the experience is that professionals repeatedly separate themselves from amateurs and there is a tangible distance between professionals and amateurs, though amateur contents are both accommodated by professional ones and set apart from them at the same time.

The participation of amateurs in journalistic activities vividly exemplifies the complex relationship between amateur and professional approaches and contents—which, somewhat contradictorily, consists of cooperation and opposition. In general, the strong presence of social media in this arena has influenced and diversified views about the nature of good journalism.

There is a multitude of terms to cover the journalistic activities of social media users who produce content online and publish it themselves. However, *citizen journalist* seems to be the prevailing term, as it emphasizes the (perceived) accomplishment of important democratic functions. Not infrequently, citizen journalism is regarded as competing with professional journalism, and citizen journalists are said to challenge the hierarchical, top-down structure of traditional journalism through their journalistic content. Citizen journalism involves a personal and generally subjective stance that is free of the constraints of objective journalism, in some cases representing a fundamental break with professional journalistic practice.

The centrality of user-generated content, particularly in the form of photographs and videos, has increased with the invention and spread of social media. Amateur photographs regularly appear in the news, when professional images and reports are not available or are inadequate; this happens quite often in local and global crises. In the news media, amateur photographs are frequently treated as raw, additional material, which has to be translated into professional content. This view and the corresponding practice show that professionals maintain their authority over amateur photographs in much the same way as quotations from bystanders are used in written journalism (Schmieder, 2015). In other words, rooted in the disparity between professional journalists and amateurs, journalistic discourses generally emphasize the continued need for professional skills and stress that user-generated contents (which are normally separated from professional ones, and rarely co-opted) have to be turned into polished and trustworthy contributions by professionals (Compton & Benedetti, 2010).

When speaking about citizen journalists, one should not neglect that the contents they generate—just like other user-generated content—are not a product of unmediated agency, since the producers are members of the consumer society. Even more, a number of current or former professional journalists are involved in citizen journalism. This implies that news production that relies on amateur citizens is not able to supersede professional journalism. On the other hand, the increasing importance of amateur content may change the ways of knowing and determining what counts as truth; thus professional journalists can adopt the strategy of taking on board, or even actively inviting, amateur contributions to mainstream media outlets (Wahl-Jörgensen, 2015).

The results of an Internet survey that investigated some features of photojournalism show that amateurs and professionals hold similar photojournalism values and agree about them for the most part. Citizen photojournalists are well versed in the techniques needed. There are no significant differences between the two groups when it comes to amateur photography values, and citizen photojournalists may seek to model themselves on professionals. Nonetheless, citizen photojournalists do not conform to all of the characteristics of an amateur, while professionals are less resistant to some amateur values than it might be expected. Still, even though professionals and amateurs have very different views on some values, this is not the case in this field, where the work the two parties perform is quite similar (Mortensen, 2014).

The example of *citizen science* is also instructive. In recent decades, an increased demand has emerged for openness and public scrutiny in research. It is also true that the divide between professionals and amateurs is being blurred in this field by the participation of members of the public in research programs, which means that citizen scientists, in other words amateur researchers, entered the scene. It is, however, usually recognized that several areas of scientific research require skills and understanding that go beyond the capabilities of most people without a proper professional education, although there is the example of astronomy, where the cooperation between amateurs and professionals is famed for its fruitfulness.

On the one hand, we see valid arguments that social media may change the nature of scholarly work. On the other hand, this influence has been rather limited so far, mainly because the processes of change in scholarly environments are slow. As a result, the existence and importance of academic credentials and authorship have remained relatively unquestioned. Another reason is that professionals—that is, individual researchers and learned societies—are attached to authenticity, trustworthiness, authority, and reliability and also continually scrutinize their attainment.

A particular case, yet one that relates to a symptomatic view on amateurism, is that of translation: besides the ongoing shift to digital culture, widespread lay assumptions allow nonprofessional translators and interpreters to advance. It is believed that being bilingual makes someone into a translator and that translation is essentially an extension of communicative abilities that most monolingual persons possess (Pérez-González & Susam-Saraeva, 2012).

As the boundaries between amateurs and professionals are vague, a number of intermediate categories have appeared around them and resulted in hybrid identities. Some of these categories have existed already before the appearance of social media.

Hobbyists differ from amateurs, because they act outside the "professional–amateur–public" system of functionally interdependent relationships. However, this does not mean that they are not serious about their pursuits (see Stebbins, 1980).

Among the "genuinely" intermediate categories, *professional amateurs* (pro-ams) have to be mentioned. They are also called "self-trained experts" or labeled "educated amateurs." They make their contribution to significant innovations and discoveries in a wide range of fields by making use of the Internet.

Produsers are volunteer social media participants who easily switch from using mediated messages to producing them in a more or less unplanned manner. These messages cannot be conceptualized as fixed and complete products in the industrial meaning of the term and the resulting artifacts may be unfinished, because the processes of achieving the goals of produsage projects are usually less focused in defining their goals.

Produsers may move then to professional (semiprofessional) employment. Therefore it is often difficult to tell whether they are amateurs in the general sense or they belong in the ranks of educated amateurs (Bruns, 2008).

The nature of contemporary amateurism is well exemplified by the frequent participation of amateurs in *crowdsourcing* projects. The discourse around crowdsourcing is characterized by the prevalent idea of its power to democratize production, which suggests that participants in such projects are more empowered because they are more in control of the products and media they consume. Crowdsourcing undoubtedly shows democratic features at the level of participation. This is exemplified by the fact that a crowd dissatisfied with a crowdsourcing organization can abandon a given project anytime. Nonetheless, crowdsourcing lacks the apparatus of professionalism that safeguards authority and prestige and has the autonomy to protect and serve members of the profession through unions and other organizations, or through professional ethical codes. In reality, these (allegedly amateur) participants are outsourced professionals, who produce content that is created no more democratically than any other product and sold not much differently from it (Brabham, 2012). Therefore Frechette's (2016) warning seems to be valid, when she states that crowdsourcing the news by using amateur spectators' material does not necessarily lead to accurate and representative citizen journalism.

In general, the wisdom of the crowd may be a powerful tool. However, its value system is questioned by many, because people who gather somewhere and are together are not necessarily wiser than the individuals who constitute this crowd. Irresponsibility and lack of expertise in the crowd may cause a lack of ability to correct errors and mistakes and to filter out rubbish and misinformation or erroneous interpretations.

The contradiction between furthering democratic ideals by providing a potential for more voices and perspectives and the frequent lack of critical analysis may characterize not only citizen journalism, but also practically all kinds of amateur media production. Therefore media literacy education has to target amateurs and inspire them to be critical, without forgetting that they need to be encouraged to leverage networked technology and infrastructures.

SEE ALSO: Alternative Media; Authorship and Participatory Culture; Citizen Journalism; Civic Media; Creative Works; Critical Information Literacy; Digital News; Media Competence; Media Literacy and Visual Culture; News Literacies; Understanding Media Literacy and DIY Creativity in Youth Digital Productions; Visual Literacy

References

Brabham, D. (2012). The myth of amateur crowds: A critical discourse analysis of crowdsourcing coverage. *Information, Communication & Society, 15*(3), 394–410.

Bruns, A. (2008). *Blogs, wikipedia, second life, and beyond: From production to produsage.* New York, NY: Peter Lang.

Compton, J.R., & Benedetti, P. (2010). Labour, new media and the institutional restructuring of journalism. *Journalism Studies, 11*(4), 487–499.

Frechette, J. (2016). From print newspapers to social media: News literacy in a networked environment. *Journalism Education, 5*(1), 45–60.

Mortensen, T.M. (2014). Blurry and centered or clear and balanced? Citizen photojournalists and professional photojournalists' understanding of each other's visual values. *Journalism Practice, 8*(6), 704–725.

Pérez-González, L., & Susam-Saraeva, Ş. (2012). Non-professionals translating and interpreting: Participatory and engaged perspectives. *Translator, 18*(2), 149–165.

Schmieder, K. (2015). Amateur photographs as visual quotes: Does the rise of amateur photography lead to fundamental changes in the news media? *Journalism Practice, 9*(4), 580–596.

Stebbins, R.A. (1980). "Amateur" and "hobbyist" as concepts for the study of leisure problems. *Social Problems, 27*(4), 413–417.

Wahl-Jörgensen, K. (2015). Resisting user-generated epistemologies content? Cooptation, segregation and the boundaries of journalism. In M. Carlson & S. Lewis (Eds.), *Shaping inquiry in culture, communication and media studies: Boundaries of journalism: Professionalism, practices and participation* (pp. 169–185). London, England: Routledge.

Further reading

Keen, A. (2011). *The cult of the amateur: How blogs, MySpace, YouTube and the rest of today's user generated media are killing our culture and economy.* London, England: Nicholas Brealey.

Vodanovic, L. (2013). The new art of being amateur: Distance as participation. *Journal of Visual Art Practice, 12*(2), 169–179.

Tibor Koltay is professor of library and information science and chairs the Institute of Learning Technologies at Eszterházy Károly University in Jászberény, Hungary. His professional interests include examining the relationship between information literacy, media literacy, and digital literacy. He also published papers about information overload and data literacy.

Apps for Children, Regulatory Issues

CLAUDIA HAINES
Homer Public Library, USA

Children are recognized as particularly vulnerable to online safety concerns including issues around privacy and misuse of personal data. Yet, the widespread use of digital technology, including use of the Internet and mobile apps, allows children and teens new, unprecedented opportunities for participation in societal conversations and debates. Government regulation of apps for children provides some protection for children's privacy, but its focus is considered by some to be limited in terms of media literacy value.

Apps and the mobile devices that run them have experienced rapid adoption rates since the release of Apple's iPad tablet in 2010, and not only by adults. Kids and teens have become avid users of the iPhone and iPad and also of the plethora of other smartphones and tablets that followed. Children in the United States under the age of 8 almost universally have access to mobile media such as smartphones or tablets in their homes (Rideout, 2017), and a growing number of young children have their own tablet. Similarly, the majority of American tweens and teens ages 8–18 have access to a mobile device within their family environment, but they are also more likely to own smartphones themselves (Lenhart, 2015). Children in Europe, Africa, Asia, and the Middle East are also adopting mobile technology quickly, including the use of smartphones. Kids, teens, and their families use these mobile devices and the apps downloaded on to them for communication, learning, and entertainment.

The term "apps" is short for applications and typically refers to the small, limited software programs that run on Apple, Android, and Windows mobile devices such as smartphones and tablets. They are designed to be easy to use and run on smaller screens. Apps are downloaded via the Internet and some share data online as part of the game, activity, or purpose. Some apps are free and some are paid for, but in general they are less expensive than their more robust relatives that run on desktop and laptop computers. Children and teens use apps to talk, text, watch television and movies, read, take pictures, make videos, blog, listen to and create music, and play video games. They do all of this using some of the more than 6.7 million apps that exist on the Apple, Google, Amazon, and Microsoft app stores.

The app market is vast and varied, with content designed specifically for kids, adults, or a general audience. The apps available vary in quality, purpose, cost, and appropriateness for the intended age group. Because of the wide variety of apps available, and concerns about content and personal details being collected by the apps' developers, the US and other governments have implemented regulations designed to protect kids.

Government regulations pertaining to children's media actually began long before the introduction of the smartphone and tablet. Regulations currently in place include both amended versions of long-standing media legislation that dates back to a time when television for children was new and more recent rules drafted with the beginning of widespread Internet use. In both cases, the regulations are intended to anticipate and address the rapidly changing technology used by children and their families. These regulations are designed as preemptive measures to protect children's privacy and prevent their access to content deemed harmful to children. They were drafted in response to the massive amount of information shared on the Internet, including via mobile devices, and the unique vulnerability of children, especially those under 13 years of age, who may be less aware of their rights and the risks, consequences, and safeguards.

Major regulations: overview

Children's Online Privacy Protection Act

The US Children's Online Privacy Protection Act (COPPA), which aims to protect children's online privacy, first took effect in 2000 and was then updated in 2013. The regulation asserts that controlling online privacy helps children and adults prevent unwanted sharing of their personal information, whether that information is an embarrassing photo, a home address, a school name, or a credit card number.

COPPA, enforced by the Federal Trade Commission (FTC), compels operators and creators of websites, gaming platforms, apps, social networks, and voice-over-Internet services *directed at kids* to require verifiable consent from a parent or legal guardian before they may collect, record, use, or disclose personally identifiable information about users under the age of 13. In addition to requiring consent, the act requires easily findable disclosures of collected information, limits data that can be collected, and requires that parents or guardians can remove a child's personal information at any time. Content from third-party websites, ad networks, and app plug-ins that targets children is also included within the media regulated by COPPA.

Personal information as defined by COPPA includes: first and last name, home or other physical address, online contact information, screen or user name that acts as contact information, telephone number, social security number, photograph, video or audio file, persistent identifier, and geolocation information or information that can be used combined with an identifier (Federal Trade Commission, 2013). However, the FTC recently announced a decision not to consider apps and devices that record children's voices, convert that audio to text, and then immediately delete the audio file without seeking parents' consent, out of compliance with COPPA (FTC, 2017). This decision is in response to the type of activity that might occur when a child uses the popular "connected" toys or devices that allow pre-readers to search content with an audio command instead of the child typing text which requires a high level of proficiency in reading and writing.

Children's Internet Protection Act

The US Children's Internet Protection Act (CIPA) was enacted in the United States in 2000 also, but this legislation, enforced by the Federal Communications Commission (FCC), focuses on content accessed by minors. Considering the vast amount of information available on the Internet, CIPA aims to protect children's safety in electronic communications, prevent unlawful online activities by minors, and block unauthorized use and dissemination of personal information (Federal Communications Commission, 2017a). As a result of legal challenges to CIPA which resulted in a Supreme Court clarification, minors are legally defined as anyone 16 years of age and younger (American Library Association, 2003).

Instead of targeting website operators or app creators, CIPA regulates schools and libraries that provide Internet access and receive E-rate discounts, valuable discounts on telecommunication services. CIPA requires that in order for schools and libraries to receive E-rate discounts, they must enact policies that restrict access to content that includes *visual depictions* of obscenity, child pornography, and material "harmful to minors." What is considered "harmful to minors" is not defined in the regulation language, but schools and libraries must make a "good faith" effort to filter the content in question. The FCC requires these entities to certify that CIPA-compliant policies are in place before receiving the discounts. Additionally, schools must include monitoring of minors' online activity in their CIPA compliance policies and must offer education about cyberbullying and appropriate online behavior: both required by the Protecting Children in the 21st Century Act. The FCC and FTC websites both include a link to the resource OnGuardOnline (Federal Trade Commission, n.d.), which includes information for educators and parents about children's privacy and online safety.

For compliance, schools and libraries often use server-based Internet filtering software and security software, provided by private companies, to determine inappropriate content and restrict children's access. However, there are no rules about what kind of software is used or what specifically is filtered beyond online content that is obscene, contains child pornography, or is considered "harmful to minors" (American Library Association, 2003).

Library Services and Technology Act

The US Libraries Library Services and Technology Act (LSTA) is a federal funding program administered by the Institute of Museum and Library Services (IMLS) exclusively for libraries. Grants are provided to each state through the appropriate state library and, along with a state match, projects are funded at public, school, academic, and research libraries for all ages. While LSTA grants do not specifically target children or Internet access, LSTA funds often provide access to important digital resources, and libraries that receive LSTA funds, many of which serve children, are subject to CIPA compliance (American Library Association, 2017).

Family Educational Rights and Privacy Act

The US Family Educational Rights and Privacy Act (FERPA) is a US law that gives parents certain rights to their child's educational records. In regards to FERPA, parental rights extend until a child reaches 18 years of age or enrolls in a school beyond high school. As part of FERPA, schools are not allowed to disclose personally identifiable information about a student beyond what is considered their directory record (name, phone number, email) without parental permission, including information to third-party, educational apps. There are exceptions that do allow schools to set up online educational services, such as apps, which use some personal information and metadata. If the apps require personal data, schools may need to require parental consent, often received on an annual basis, or use of the app must qualify as a FERPA exception. Exceptions cover services that are under the direct control of the school or district, perform a service that would normally be done by a school or district employee, or involve an app that uses records only for authorized purposes where the personal information is not disclosed beyond the authorized use (Department of Education, 2014).

General Data Protection Regulation

The European Union's General Data Protection Regulation (GDPR) took effect in May of 2018. It replaces the European Union's Data Protection Directive and is designed to protect people's data privacy and sync data protection laws across Europe. The regulation pertains to all personal data that is processed by automated means either in whole or in part. The regulation may apply to many US-based apps because it emphasizes where the user lives, not where the operator is based, and the Internet by design allows operators and users to connect across geographical and political boundaries.

While GDPR is designed to protect the privacy of both adults and children, its protection of children's data is similar to that of COPPA in the United States (Macenaite & Kosta, 2017). GDPR requires that consent to process personal data be obtained from the adult who is the holder of parental responsibilities when a child is using online services. While the GDPR's provisions to protect the personal data in general are robust, the regulation provides minimal specifics on how parental consent must be obtained and it leaves the responsibility of compliance primarily up to the operator. The GDPR considers children to be anyone under 16 years of age. European Union member states may reduce the age at which parental consent is required to 13 years, but not lower (European Union, 2016).

Net neutrality

While not targeting children's privacy or digital media use specifically, the broader issue of net neutrality, or network neutrality, also impacts children and teens. Net neutrality is the principle that all lawful data on the Internet be treated the same and that broadband providers and the government cannot treat or charge content differently. Net neutrality prevents broadband providers from "throttling" (the intentional speeding up or slowing down of service), charging content providers for faster speeds and any kind of prioritization (Federal Communications Commission, 2017b).

In 2015, the FCC passed the Open Internet Order and the Internet was reclassified as an essential public utility, similar to the telephone service. Prior to the order, Internet access via broadband (cable, digital subscriber line or DSL) was not regulated the same as voice telephony and dial-up access and left an opening for throttling and other disparities (American Library Association, 2017). The District of Columbia District Court of Appeals declared that this reclassification was necessary in order for the FCC to be able to require that broadband providers provide access to all lawful online content, like websites and apps, at equal speeds.

As more and more information and essential services are found online, access to the Internet for school, entertainment, civic engagement, and lifelong learning has become essential for all ages. The Internet has allowed people from diverse geographic locations and with a range of viewpoints, backgrounds, and ideas to communicate and share information.

While many larger content providers would be able to afford paid prioritization, ultimately passing on the cost to consumers, supporters of net neutrality fear that individuals and content creators with smaller budgets—libraries, for example—would be limited in their ability to connect with other Internet users. Internet users' access to information may be controlled by which operator's site is prioritized. For consumers, especially those who are the most vulnerable, net neutrality and the regulation of broadband providers as utility companies equates to equal access to content, freedom of expression, and the ability to participate in civic dialogue (Woodruff, Ploeg, Cooper, & Schwartz, 2017).

Industry self-regulation

Along with the variety of government regulations, the app industry has responded to public concern by instituting measures addressing child safety. Self-regulation programs like the Entertainment Software Rating Board (ESRB), which assigns age and content ratings to video games, are certified by the FTC as "safe harbor" provisions which allow developers to comply with program requirements and avoid FTC enforcement.

The most widely applied industry initiative is app store ratings. These ratings, or categories, organize apps according to audience age and, in theory, help parents find apps suitable for children. An app's audience is declared by the developer, but its placement in a "kids" or "families" category implies that it complies with appropriate regulations. However, ratings are sometimes inconsistent across platforms, and surveys have revealed that in some cases parents find the ratings "too lenient" (Jordan, 2008).

Additional features may also be required for apps to be placed into these categories. For example, children's apps in Apple's App Store must include a "parental gate," a tool that requires users to perform an "adult-level" task. Parental gates are used to prevent young children from accessing specific parts of an app intended for adults.

Regulation issues

While these regulations may reduce both the quantity of children's personal data which is shared online and access to content deemed "harmful," the regulations have recognized limits, both for the app developer and the families who use the apps.

Compliance

Each of the regulations focuses on a particular aspect of media use, and compliance can be difficult to navigate. Regulations intended for one type of children's media—television, for example—do not necessarily apply to newer forms of media and do not take into account new ways of using media. Regulations for new media require regular clarification and amendments. Even the most conscientious developers of apps for kids—high-quality educational resources, for example—can find the rules vague and out of touch with the rapidly changing technology. Compliance can be difficult as new features develop or innovations are introduced that support children's use of new technology.

Compliance with privacy regulations can be costly and the increased expense may drive developers away from the children's app market, reducing the diversity of content designed for kids. The most appealing, or trendy, apps may be instead designed for a general audience, minus the restrictive extras, pushing kids to access content not intended for them and defeating the purpose of the regulation.

Teens not included

While teens, ages 13–17, are not protected under regulations like COPPA, they are also not technically old enough to enter into legally binding contracts, including app privacy policies. Teens, also vulnerable to violent and obscene content and behavioral advertising, are typically accessing an even wider range of content than their younger counterparts, for both educational and entertainment purposes, yet these regulations do little to protect them online or help them understand how to control their online privacy and select high-quality content.

Definitions

Some regulations include vague definitions, making compliance difficult. In the case of CIPA, what is considered obscene is not clearly defined in the regulation language. Instead it relies on the Miller test, a standard often used to determine if a photo, video, or image is obscene.

Based on the 1973 US Supreme Court case of Miller vs. California, the three-part standard offers some guidelines for what is generally considered obscene, but in reality, teachers, administrators, and librarians are ultimately left to decide what is obscene in order to comply. Watching over children's shoulders can be time-consuming and nonproductive, so filtering content is often left up to private filtering companies and computer programs in order to meet CIPA rules.

These filters have been criticized for blocking access to informative and educational content deemed obscene or otherwise inappropriate according to CIPA. The American Library Association (ALA) unsuccessfully argued against the effectiveness of Internet filtering and the constitutionality of CIPA in United States vs. ALA (2003). Opponents of CIPA complain that parents are not afforded the control or guidance to help children evaluate digital content. Instead visual content is blocked based on keywords or phrases that may or may not keep up with the rapidly changing nature of the Internet.

Consumer education

Online regulations are meant to be preemptive, protecting children and focusing on preconsumption measures. These regulations do little in the way of informing and educating families about issues related to privacy and harmful content. While multiple regulations mention educating children about online behavior, the focus of the actual regulations is enforcement. Few media literacy tools are available for children, parents, or educators within the information provided. For example, the FTC mentions the resource OnGuardOnline, but goes no further, leaving the education aspect of media use to nonregulatory organizations.

Politics

The political nature of legislation, even in regards to children's apps, does not depend solely on the most current research or the latest innovations, but also on the input of politicians, advocacy groups, academics, and lobbyists. And while organizations like the FCC and FTC are charged with oversight and enforcement, all three branches of government—judicial, executive, and legislative—are ultimately involved with writing regulations that effect children's media use (Jordan, 2008). Regulations may be drafted or amended based on the political platform of the party currently in power or at the whim of the lobbying group with the most influence, instead of based on what we know about children's media, its use, and child development.

Current app regulations may restrict children's rights of expression, including the right to access and create information, affirmed by the widely ratified United Nation's Convention on the Rights of the Child (United Nations, 1989). The United States is one of only three member countries that have not adopted (ratified) the Convention. While the US ambassador signed the Convention, the United States is not legally bound by the document.

Children's use of apps

Regulations in both the United States and the European Union specifically target digital media intended for children. However, children are increasingly accessing not only child-specific digital media but also apps with no specific audience or intended age group, social media platforms in particular. In these cases, compliance with the regulations previously discussed does not apply, and these sites do not necessarily authenticate age. These apps are required to make attempts to identify the age of users if an account is created, but kids and teens often circumvent this process, or the apps make content available without an account or age declaration requirement. Children are creating accounts, accessing a wide range of content with limited or no filtering, and sharing their personal data with the media creators and other users, often unknowingly or with little knowledge of the repercussions, with or without parental permission.

Blocking access

Current regulations may inhibit kids' and teens' access to valuable apps and information. In some cases, apps and digital media that do not meet COPPA or GDPR guidelines, for example, may attract an audience with a wide age range because they offer the most current information available, for example in the case of rapidly evolving societal events such as natural disasters or political situations. Some apps not specifically designed for children under 13, and thus not necessarily regulation compliant, can provide information in a format that meets a specific learning or physical disability. Other apps may make accessible important information only available in a digital format, and their developers may not spend resources to be compliant.

Multiple issues have arisen around the implementation of these regulations and the access they restrict. Court decisions, like the United States vs. ALA (2003) Supreme Court case, have been necessary to clarify whether or not regulations pertaining to online information restrict children's constitutionally protected freedoms. Court challenges have also clarified important definitions on which the regulations are based.

Self-regulation

While industry-initiated standards and self-regulation attempt to offer additional measures to help parents choose apps for kids, some categories have vague definitions that have been considered confusing and inconsistent across platforms, and even within these categories, selecting an app for a child can be daunting for parents. For example, each of the app stores has also created "Education" categories, in addition to either a "Kids" or "Family" category. Educational apps, however, have minimal requirements to qualify as "educational" and are geared for a range of ages, not specifically children. What is deemed educational varies and is based on, sometimes unsubstantiated, claims by the developer. Finding educational apps for children may be difficult within the app store's interface. Parents and educators must evaluate each app to determine its educational value with limited resources from regulation text or industry support.

Evolving media landscape

Where and how children access apps can bring new questions to the current regulations. Apps and online media are being used in school for educational purposes, and some of these apps require parental permission to be compliant. While some districts seek parental permission with annual acknowledgments signed by parents, there may be circumstances that require a more agile approach to app use. In these cases, schools are providing consent on behalf of parents as a practicality, yet this may not align with the regulations' intended outcomes: parental involvement in the app use (Herold, 2017).

Youths are increasingly selecting, creating, and producing content on devices they own, with or without the help of adults (Jordan, 2008). They are participating in important civic engagement that occurs either simultaneously or exclusively online. Regulations governing apps and other digital media may restrict kids' and teens' ability to contribute to the societal conversations happening across the globe. Some contend that regulations may even impact children's and teens' freedom of speech and freedom of expression. Rapidly changing technology, including the popularity of apps and mobile devices, has redefined how a child's right to freedom of expression

(United Nations, 1989) is articulated. Using apps to voice stories, articulate ideas, and communicate opinions is part of "participatory culture" (Jenkins, 2006), in which users of mobile and digital technology create and produce content, and the participation of kids and teens is growing.

Regulations often distinguish between platforms or are drafted around specific media, but the rapidly changing nature of technology merges platforms. Shows on television may be held to different standards than shows in an app designed for general audiences, for example (Jordan, 2008, p. 248). TV stations face restrictions on content and advertising that do not translate to apps that stream shows, like Netflix or YouTube. The latter may be in compliance with regulations, and include industry-created age ratings for content, but children can still access content deemed "harmful" to some because the app is intended for a general audience.

Guidelines and recommendations

Several organizations have published guidelines and other materials to help families understand the important issues related to app use and recommendations for developers making apps for children. These guidelines, and the connected resources, play a significant role in educating families about not just app regulations but the impetus behind the regulations. Families and professionals who work with children can use these organizations' resources to learn what online privacy means, what children's rights are, and what high-quality, age-appropriate children's apps are and where to find them. Additionally, professional organizations are identifying and training individuals as media mentors to support and guide families using apps and other new media with children and teens.

Children and Adolescents and Digital Media

In 2016, the American Academy of Pediatrics (AAP) released their updated media use recommendations for children and adolescents, *Children and Adolescents and Digital Media*. The recommendations for digital media use rely on current research to identify practices that address safety, privacy, advertising, learning, entertainment, equitable access to information, and civic engagement in regards to digital media such as apps. The AAP committee also provides some recommendations for the children's digital media industry in support of high-quality digital media for children. The report was published at the same time as the organization launched the Family Media Use Plan, a digital tool designed to inform families and help them navigate children's digital media use.

Technology and Interactive Media as Tools in Early Childhood Programs Serving Children from Birth through Age 8

In 2012, the National Association for the Education of Young Children (NAEYC) and the Fred Rogers Center for Early Learning and Children's Media at Saint Vincent

College published a joint position statement on technology use with young children, *Technology and Interactive Media as Tools in Early Childhood Programs Serving Children from Birth through Age 8*. This statement, released early in the evolution of widespread app use by children, includes several key messages for professionals who work with young children. The recommendations address: intentional use of technology appropriate for children 8 and under; potential benefits of technology for dual language learners and of assistive technology for kids with special needs; age-appropriate content and use of technology; digital citizenship; equitable digital access; and the need for ongoing research. The NAEYC/Fred Rogers Position Statement continues to be referenced by educators and policymakers.

Guidelines for Industry on Child Online Protection

The United Nations International Children's Emergency Fund (UNICEF) defends children's rights around the world. In 2015, they published *Guidelines for Industry on Child Online Protection*, a document that applies internationally recognized rights for children to the Internet and digital media such as apps. The document is based on five principles that recommend integration of children's rights into corporate policies and practices, development of processes to handle content that deals with child sexual assault, creation of age-appropriate content, educating families about online safety and responsible use of digital media, and promotion of digital media as a tool for civic engagement. These guidelines emphasize family education about app use and online activity alongside the development of industry standards related to children's well-being.

Media Mentorship in Libraries Serving Youth

The ALA's Association for Library Service to Children (ALSC) adopted the white paper *Media Mentorship in Libraries Serving Youth* in 2015 to help guide library staff working with families. Children, teens, and adults use libraries to access a wide range of resources, including books, magazines, online databases, e-books, and apps. Not only do libraries provide free WiFi, public access to computers, and digital device lending, but librarians teach children and families how to use the equipment, find the information they need, and create content during one-on-one interactions in programs like storytime and in afterschool homework help or maker clubs. Librarians share information about privacy, digital citizenship, online safety, and healthy digital media use in person and through publicity campaigns.

The authors of the ALSC white paper curated the latest research, examples of current practices, and other considerations that librarians acting as media mentors would need to support children and their families in their media decisions and use. Librarians have used the white paper as a starting point for educating themselves on the issues and skills they need to support families in the digital age.

SEE ALSO: CIPA/Internet Filtering; EU Kids Online; Network Neutrality

References

American Academy of Pediatrics. (2016). *Children and adolescents and digital media*. Retrieved from http://pediatrics.aappublications.org/content/pediatrics/early/2016/10/19/peds.2016-2593.full.pdf

American Library Association. (2003). Children's Internet Protection Act (CIPA) legal FAQ. Retrieved from http://www.ala.org/advocacy/advleg/federallegislation/cipa/cipalegalfaq

American Library Association. (2017). Library Services and Technology Act (LSTA). Retrieved from http://www.ala.org/advocacy/advleg/federallegislation/lsta

Association for Library Service to Children. (2015). *Media mentorship in libraries serving youth*. Retrieved from http://www.ala.org/alsc/sites/ala.org.alsc/files/content/Media%20Mentorship%20in%20Libraries%20Serving%20Youth_FINAL_no%20graphics.pdf

Department of Education. (2014). Protecting student privacy while using online educational services: Requirements and best practices. Retrieved from https://tech.ed.gov/wp-content/uploads/2014/09/Student-Privacy-and-Online-Educational-Services-February-2014.pdf

European Union. (2016). General Data Protection Regulation. Retrieved from https://gdpr-info.eu/art-2-gdpr/

Federal Communications Commission. (2017a). Children's Internet Protection Act (CIPA). Retrieved from https://www.fcc.gov/consumers/guides/childrens-internet-protection-act

Federal Communications Commission. (2017b). The open Internet. Retrieved from https://www.fcc.gov/document/fcc-releases-open-internet-order

Federal Trade Commission. (2013). Children's Online Privacy Protection Rule. Retrieved from https://www.ecfr.gov/cgi-bin/text-idx?SID=4939e77c77a1a1a08c1cbf905fc4b409&node=16%3A1.0.1.3.36&rgn=div5#se16.1.312_15

Federal Trade Commission. (2017). Enforcement policy statement regarding the applicability of the COPPA rule to the collection and use of voice recordings. Retrieved from https://www.ftc.gov/system/files/documents/public_statements/1266473/coppa_policy_statement_audiorecordings.pdf

Federal Trade Commission. (n.d.). OnGuardOnline. Retrieved from https://www.consumer.ftc.gov/features/feature-0038-onguardonline

Herold, B. (2017, July 28). COPPA and schools: The (other) federal student privacy law, explained. *Education Week*. Retrieved from https://www.edweek.org/ew/issues/childrens-online-privacy-protection-act-coppa/index.html

Jenkins, H. (2006). *Confronting the challenges of participatory culture: Media education for the 21st century*. Chicago, IL: The John D. and Catherine T. Macarthur Foundation.

Jordan, A.S. (2008). Children's media policy. *Future Child, 18*(1), 235–253. Retrieved from https://files.eric.ed.gov/fulltext/EJ795865.pdf

Lenhart, A. (2015, April 9). Teen, social media and technology overview *2015*. Retrieved from http://www.pewinternet.org/2015/04/09/teens-social-media-technology-2015/

Macenaite, M., & Kosta, E. (2017). Consent for processing children's personal data in the EU: Following in US footsteps? *Information & Communications Technology Law, 26*(2), 146–197. doi: 10.1080/13600834.2017.1321096

National Association for the Education of Young Children & Fred Rogers Center for Early Learning and Children's Media. (2012). *Technology and interactive media as tools in early childhood programs serving children from birth through age 8*. Retrieved from https://www.naeyc.org/sites/default/files/globally-shared/downloads/PDFs/resources/topics/PS_technology_WEB.pdf

Rideout, V. (2017). *The Common Sense census: Media use by kids age zero to eight*. San Francisco, CA: Common Sense Media.

United Nations. (1989). Convention on the Rights of the Child. Retrieved from http://www.ohchr.org/EN/ProfessionalInterest/Pages/CRC.aspx

United Nations International Children's Emergency Fund. (2015). *Guidelines for industry on child online protection*. Retrieved from https://www.unicef.org/csr/files/COP_Guidelines_English.pdf

Woodruff, S., Ploeg, L.V., Cooper, K., & Schwartz, D. (Producers). (2017). *To the point*. Retrieved from http://www.kcrw.com/news-culture/shows/to-the-point/fccs-plan-to-roll-back-net-neutrality

Further reading

boyd, d. (2014). *It's complicated*. New Haven, CT: Yale University Press.

Common Sense Media. (n.d). Digital citizenship. Retrieved from https://www.commonsense.org/education/digital-citizenship

Donohue, C. (Ed.). (2014). *Technology and digital media in the early years: Tools for teaching and learning*: New York, NY: Routledge.

Haines, C., Campbell, C., & Association for Library Service to Children. (2016). *Becoming a media mentor: A guide for working with children and families*. Chicago, IL: American Library Association.

Claudia Haines leads storytimes, hosts maker programs, and gets great media of all kinds into the hands of kids and teens as the Youth Services Librarian and media mentor at the Homer Public Library (Alaska). She trains other librarians as media mentors and serves on both local and national committees that support families and literacy. She is the coauthor of the Association for Library Service to Children's white paper on media mentorship and the book *Becoming a Media Mentor: A Guide for Working with Children and Families* (2016).

Arts Education with iPads

MICHAEL DEZUANNI
Queensland University of Technology, Australia

Intellectual and social context

Since 2010, the iPad and other touchscreen mobile devices have disrupted how many children and young people use computers for entertainment, learning, and creativity. Access to popular culture and media has changed and there have been significant shifts in how children and young people create their own media and develop literacies. This has significant implications for media literacy. Educational policymakers, media literacy and arts education advocates, and scholars in general have aimed to find ways to recognize the opportunities and challenges presented by touchscreen mobile devices.

Media literacy has evolved to keep pace with rapid technological change and media industry volatility in the digital era. Desktop and laptop computers became relevant to media literacy in the 1990s, when they enabled media activities such as desktop publishing, graphic design, and video editing, along with access to media content via the Internet. When faster Internet and social media services became available during the first decade of the 21st century, the nature of "media" began to change and digital disruption of the media industries significantly altered how people could access and share media.

The arrival of the iPad in 2010 both symbolized and catalyzed a shift from old to new ways of interacting with the media. Suddenly a screen for viewing newspaper text, TV content, videos, and films could be held in one hand. In addition, the iPad was a powerful computer that allowed users to search the Internet for information and to interact with social media. The second-generation iPad also contained a camera, which significantly changed how individuals could create and circulate their own media.

The iPad was, and remains, central to what Henry Jenkins (2006) has called a "convergence culture." The contemporary digital media ecology at the center of convergence culture is made up of personal, educational, and professional practices where iPads and similar devices are used alongside TV screens, gaming consoles, desktop and laptop computers, digital audio players and smart phones.

Major dimensions of the topic

The iPad has disrupted media practice in ways that potentially change our expectations for both media literacy and arts education by drawing attention to new opportunities and challenges for creative practice and conceptual thinking in the classroom.

Creative practice

The iPad disrupts media literacy and creativity because it facilitates media production during the earliest years of schooling. It challenges what we imagine young children can achieve with media production and potentially transforms students' learning experiences. Even very young children are able to use iPads so as to combine digital materials for the purpose of communicating ideas, and thus begin to develop media literacy knowledge. The building blocks of digital media literacy are developed as children begin to tell stories for various purposes by combining images, sound, and digital text (Dezuanni, 2015).

The iPad's touchscreen interface, simple applications (apps), and "hidden" file management system change how individuals interact with the "computer"; and this in turn disrupts our usual expectations for media literacy and creative practice. As a computer, the iPad has a low entry point for participation. The absence of a peripheral keyboard and mouse or trackpad makes interaction with the device much easier for young children, novice adult computer users, and users with disabilities. In addition, the file management systems of Windows and Macintosh computer operating systems are replaced by a hidden file management system on the iPad, which simplifies the process of accessing and saving files, storing them inside projects in apps rather than in separate folders.

Finally, the apps themselves are typically easy to use, often with a very simple menu system that requires only three or four actions. The iPad's affordances have made it a popular choice for schools, and the iPad has increasingly been used for media production, literacy development, and creative expression with young children (Marklund & Dunkels, 2016).

Conceptual thinking

As children become content creators who are able to reach real audiences through the circulation of their own content, opportunities to develop conceptual thinking emerge. Media literacy "key concepts" such as "audience," "institution," "representation," "genre and convention," and "technologies" can be explored through practical application using iPads. As students use the iPads and associated apps to make content, they may also respond to a range of questions designed to assist with critical reflection, for example: Who are they making content for and why? What choices might they make in order to represent people, places, or ideas? How will they arrange their ideas in conventional ways? And what technological affordances may assist them to communicate most effectively? Also, consideration of concepts such as accuracy, fairness, and bias is more meaningful when children and young people are able to reflect on their own communication and creative practices. The immediacy of media production with touch screen devices potentially makes these questions relevant on a daily basis.

The iPad is a device that makes it easy to remix existing media so as to recast material in order to create new meanings and to comment on media through creative practice. In this sense, young people are able to directly interact with the existing media, and this fact extends opportunities for developing a critical relationship with media content.

Although iPads are highly sophisticated communication devices, the affordances of some apps may potentially limit students' conceptual thinking. For instance, many creative apps rely on templates that provide a small number of predetermined choices, making it difficult for students to make personal choices and therefore to develop conceptual thinking. Media literacy educators are often required to account for these limitations in the development of learning experiences.

Changes over time

Media literacy advocates have long promoted educational strategies that aim to impact positively on children's and young people's out-of-school media use (Buckingham, 2003; Martens, 2010). The arrival of the iPad in 2010 represented a significant point in the evolution of children's and young people's media culture and in scholarly thinking about how to intervene in media literacy education in formal environments.

The early years of the decade 2000–2010 saw the emergence of post-broadcast TV culture, with the uptake of cable and subscription television and, later, of handheld devices (Turner & Tay, 2009). TV viewing became less communal and more personal, as highly segmented content became available on mobile devices (Given, Brealey, & Gray, 2015). There has been a dissipation of the notion of "the audience" with the availability of vastly more screen content and choice.

Even where children access relatively traditional sources of entertainment such as TV programs through established broadcasters or cable TV outlets, they may be doing this through an app on an iPad that presents "on demand" choice and variety. The British Broadcasting Corporation's iPlayer Kids App, the Australian Broadcasting Corporation's ABC Kids iView App, the Public Broadcasting Service's PBS Kids Video App, and the Disney Channel App all provide significant amounts of choice for children. Indeed, Apple's App store and Google's Play store have vast arrays of choice for children's entertainment on iPads and other touchscreen devices across games, interactive stories, video entertainment, and information.

Touchscreen devices have also led to greater consumption of content on new media platforms. YouTube content became highly popular with children and young people during the 2010s, with the emergence of new genres of entertainment such as Let's Play videos and Unboxing videos. The YouTube "Let's Player" StampyLonghead, who makes Minecraft videos for children and young people, has 8 million subscribers and his videos have been watched 5.5 billion times. Unboxing videos in which a YouTuber unboxes a toy and comments on the experience are also highly popular with children (Marsh, 2016).

The iPad has also emerged as a significant gaming platform for children and young people. For instance, the Pocket Edition of Minecraft (for phones and tablets) has sold more copies in North America, Europe, and Asia than copies of the PC and console versions of the game (Mojang, 2016). Bearing in mind that Minecraft is the second most popular game in history, this suggests that many young people around the world play Minecraft on the iPad. Children's and young people's media experiences have become highly differentiated and the iPad is a central technological platform for the delivery, consumption, and production of the content they use.

Current emphases in work on the topic in research and theory

Current scholarship on children's and young people's use of touchscreen devices for literacy and creativity has two main focuses: changes in children's and young people's play and creative practices; and the use of these devices in the classroom for teaching and learning.

Rapid changes in children's culture in postindustrial societies include play across digital and nondigital environments. Edwards refers to this as "converged play," which crosses traditional, nondigital play and play associated with popular culture and digital media (Edwards, 2013). To give just one example, there are several touchscreen Lego apps available that allow children to complement their physical, nondigital block play with digital block play experiences. In addition, there is a multitude of ways to interact with Lego themed stories: through film, television, game play, literature, and costume play. Significant scholarship aims to better understand converged play practices (Ito, et al. 2010; Clark, 2013; Willett, Richards, Marsh, Burn, & Bishop, 2013).

The idea of converged play has implications for creative practice because children and young people are likely to be creative using both digital and nondigital materials.

For instance, children living digital lives are likely to draw using pencils on both paper and the glass screen of a tablet computer (Knight & Dooley, 2015). Material experiences with digital technologies may be considered embodied, sensory experiences that are just as "real" as nondigital experiences. Within arts education, it has long been considered important for children and young people to be creative with wet paint, clay, traditional music instruments, or their own bodies (Sinclair, Jeanneret, & O'Toole, 2012); and there is increasing recognition of the need for children to be creative with digital images, sound, and text (ACARA, 2016).

In schools, it is becoming more common for students to be asked to use touch-screen devices to record images and video explanations of ideas and concepts across the curriculum. This is particularly true in schools that have introduced "bring your own device" (BYOD) schemes. As a result, there is increasing scholarly focus on multimodal communication in the classroom (see Mills, Stornaiuolo, Smith, & Pandya, 2018). The availability of a high-quality camera and microphone on the iPad cancels the need to organize separate digital still cameras, microphones, and audio recorders and the complex process of moving digital files onto a computer. The production process and the workflow are much simpler on an iPad. In some cases, students complete quite complex editing tasks using apps like iMovie.

Future directions in research, theory, and methodology

As research in this field emerges, scholars need to better understand how children use digital media in their daily lives. Media literacy and arts education too often continue to be informed by predigital practices (Livingstone, 2004). It is now much less common for children and young people to have similar viewing experiences than was the case in the 1980s and 1990s, when many watched after-school block televising programming on free-to-air TV networks. For instance, in a book titled *The Class*, which reports on ethnographic research in London, Livingstone and Sefton-Green (2016) show how one class of lower secondary students had widely varying home media experiences. Application in a range of contexts of the type of ethnographic work developed by Livingstone and Sefton-Green would enhance our understanding of the complexity and variety of media practices that children and young people participate in in the 2010s. Jenkins (2006) shows how young people living in a digitally mediated "convergence culture" interact with media that involve them in digital participation in ways that were not possible before the emergence of low-cost computer technologies. We need a much better understanding of these new home-based media literacy practices to understand how to develop appropriate media literacy interventions in schools.

In school contexts, an expanded understanding of media literacy and creative practice would improve understanding of how media literacy may be implemented in classrooms. In contexts where every student has a personal device, which gets used at home for a variety of daily purposes, it is necessary to consider how media literacy might become more "everyday" or "vernacular" in classroom contexts. The use of images and sound for general communication may be investigated as an aspect of media literacy development even where it does not explicitly address communications media. Just as the everyday use of spoken and written literacy is at the center of traditional literacy practice and education, media communication is at the center of media literacy.

It remains important that media literacy involves analysis and evaluation of the texts and contexts of media production and use; but media literacy advocates should not underestimate the importance of the normalization of communication with images and recorded sound. Every time a student is asked to record a video about his or her understanding of a concept in an arts, literacy, or science class, there is an opportunity for that student to rehearse framing, shot size, audio manipulation, and lighting. Such students may also be asked to think about their audience and about the choices they make to represent a process or an idea. Therefore, as digital media production with touchscreen technologies becomes common in schools, media literacy scholarship will need to address how to best incorporate both creative and critical elements of media literacy education.

SEE ALSO: Apps for Children, Regulatory Issues; Arts Literacies; Children's Culture; Creative Works; Creativity and Media Production in Schools; Literacy, Technology, and Media; Media Arts; Youth Digital Culture

References

ACARA. (2016). *Australian curriculum, the arts: Media arts.* Australian Curriculum, Assessment and Reporting Authority, Sydney. Retrieved from https://www.australiancurriculum.edu.au/f-10-curriculum/the-arts/media-arts

Buckingham, D. (2003). *Media education: Literacy, learning and contemporary culture.* Cambridge, England: Polity.

Clark, L.S. (2013). *The parent app: Understanding families in the digital age.* London, England: Oxford University Press.

Dezuanni, M. (2015). The building blocks of digital media literacy: Socio-material participation and the production of media knowledge. *Journal of Curriculum Studies, 47*(3), 416–419.

Edwards, S. (2013). Post-industrial play: Understanding the relationship between traditional and converged forms of play in the early years. In A. Burke & J. Marsh (Eds.), *Children's virtual play worlds: Culture, learning and participation* (pp. 10–25). New York, NY: Peter Lang.

Given, J., Brealey, M., & Gray, C. (2015). *Television 2025: Rethinking small screen media in Australia.* Spreading Fictions: Distributing Stories in the Online Age, No. 3. Retrieved November 9, 2016 from http://researchbank.swinburne.edu.au/vital/access/manager/Repository/swin:43725

Ito, M., Baumer, S., Bittanti, M., boyd, d., Cody, R., Herr-Stephenson, B., … Yardi S. (2010). *Hanging out, messing around and geeking out: Kids living and learning with new media.* Boston, MA: MIT Press.

Jenkins, H. (2006). *Convergence culture: Where old and new media collide.* New York, NY: NYU Press.

Knight, L.M., & Dooley, K.T. (2015). Drawing and writing on the screen. In M. Dezuanni, K. Dooley, S. Gattenhof, & L. Knight (Eds.), *iPads in the early years: Developing literacy and creativity* (pp. 150–162). New York, NY: Routledge.

Livingstone, S. (2004). Media literacy and the challenge of new information and communication technologies. *Communication Review, 7*(1), 3–14.

Livingstone, S., & Sefton-Green, J. (2016). *The class: Living and learning in the digital age.* New York, NY: NYU Press.

Marklund, L., & Dunkels, E. (2016). Digital play as a means to develop children's literacy and power in the Swedish preschool. *Early Years, 36*(3), 289–304.
Marsh, J. (2016). "Unboxing" videos: Co-construction of the child as cyberflâneur. *Discourse: Studies in the Cultural Politics of Education, 37*(3). doi: 10.1080/01596306.2015.1041457
Martens, H. (2010). Evaluating media literacy education: Concepts, theories and future directions. *Journal of Media Literacy Education, 2*, 1–22.
Mills, K.A., Stornaiuolo, A., Smith, A., & Pandya, J.Z. (Eds.). (2018). *Handbook of writing, literacies and education in digital cultures*. New York, NY: Routledge.
Mojang. (2016). Minecraft. Retrieved from https://mojang.com/2016/06/weve-sold-minecraft-many-many-times-look
Sinclair, C., Jeanneret, N., & O'Toole, J. (2012). Education in the arts (2nd ed.). Melbourne, Australia: Oxford University Press.
Turner, G., & Tay, J. (2009). *Television studies after TV: Understanding television in the post-broadcast era*. London, England: Routledge.
Willett, R., Richards, C., Marsh, J., Burn, A., & Bishop, J.C. (2013). *Children, media and playground cultures*. London, England: Palgrave Macmillian.

Further reading

Dezuanni, M.L., Dooley, K., Gattenhof, S., & Knight, L. (2015). *iPads in the early years: Developing literacy and creativity*. Routledge Research in Early Childhood Education. London, England: Routledge.

Michael Dezuanni undertakes research and teaching in the field of digital cultures and education, which includes film and media education, digital literacies, and arts education. He is appointed by the Film, Television and Animation Discipline in the Creative Industries Faculty and is a member of the Queensland University of Technology's Digital Media Research Centre. Michael explores the most effective, productive, and meaningful ways for individuals to use and understand the media and technologies in their lives.

Arts Literacies

AMY PETERSEN JENSEN
Brigham Young University, USA

A theoretical context for arts literacies: new literacies and multimodality

Ideas about artistic literacies were first formed when the concept of multimodality was introduced into education conversations. In 2000, literacy education theorists began to actively discuss what meaningful talk, texts, tools, and technologies might look like in a 21st-century classroom. Education scholars argued for progressive educational frameworks, which further expanded notions of what students should know and be able to do as readers and writers. Literacy educators explored and adopted ideas about multimodal literacies (Gee, 2001; Kress, 2003; New London Group, 2000). Notably the prominent theorist Gunther Kress describes the study of multimodal literacies as a shift from a world that solely values the written (printed) word as text to a world in which gestures, images, and technologies make up the discourse produced across various meaning-making platforms.

Kress outlines this construct of multimodality in two parts. He first defines modes (printed, aural, linguistic, spatial, visual, etc.) for his purposes. These are "socially and culturally shaped resources [designed] for making meaning" (Kress & Van Leeuwen, 2001, p. 79). He then makes clear that the various modes of communication are "shaped by both the intrinsic characteristics and potentialities of the medium and by the requirements, histories and values of societies and their cultures." These modes of meaning-making therefore have strengths and weaknesses inherent to their unique design. They are also historically and socially situated (Barton & Hamilton, 2000; Gee, 2004).

The development of scholarship about multimodal literacies changed how teachers and teacher educators thought about texts and literacies. Multimodal literacy theories expanded the notion of texts and literacies to include more than the printed word. Content area literacy experts began thinking beyond the traditional literacy discourse. While the study of reading and writing as associated with print texts was still valued, many literacy experts began to describe a broader notion of texts and literacies.

This rethinking of literacy fostered the further development of the rationale around arts literacies as well as digital media literacy, information literacy, and other disciplinary literacies. It also provided educators within the various disciplines a means through which they could reimagine the literacies associated with each unique content area instruction within educational settings.

The major dimensions of arts literacies

Arts (dance, media, music, theatre, visual arts) literacies comprise the knowledge and the skills necessary to learn in the arts. Educational constructs that build arts literacies provide opportunities for students and teachers to participate in the specialized discourse of each unique art form. Rich arts literacy environments also encourage authentic disciplinary practice in which study and creation are shaped by an understanding of (i) arts texts, (ii) artistic processes, and (iii) arts contexts.

Arts texts

In current literature, arts texts are broadly defined (Albers & Sanders, 2010; Draper, Broomhead, Jensen, Nokes, & Siebert, 2010; Jensen & Draper, 2015). While artists may work with printed texts occasionally, it is more likely that an arts text might be the human body, a digital image, a musical instrument, choreography, or paint applied to a canvas. A good definition of arts texts would be "texts that are essential to each arts discipline" (Jensen & Draper, 2015). Successful reading, viewing, and creating using these texts would therefore require an understanding of the specialized discourse of that art form. For example, a theatre artist and a media artist would each utilize a different vocabulary when they described bodies interacting and performing. Understanding theatre or digital media language would aid the creator or viewer in communicating with other disciplinary artists or explaining their work in cross-disciplinary settings.

Artistic processes

Artistic processes within educational settings are the "processes whereby something new is created as young people and teachers use imagination, investigation, construction, and reflection in arts environs" (Jensen & Draper, 2015, p. 9).

The National Core Arts Standards for Media Arts (State Education Agency Directors of Arts Education [SEADAE], 2014) identify four common artistic processes through which artists work as they are making art:

- Creating: conceiving and developing new artistic ideas and work;
- Producing: realizing and presenting artistic ideas and work;
- Responding: understanding and evaluating how the arts convey meaning;
- Connecting: relating artistic ideas and work with personal meaning and external context.

It is important to note that these processes do not work in isolation and do not necessarily build one to the next. Instead, the processes are integrated and iterative. For example, a team of visual artists working to assemble a media projection wall might conceive of and produce something and receive ongoing response to the work from peers while in the development and presenting phases of the project.

Arts contexts

Arts contexts are the social, cultural, and historical lenses through which art is created and viewed. Contexts often grow out of the subject or content of a work of art. Understanding arts contexts might aid creators to explore meanings, ideas, and beliefs. In the study of arts contexts one may also consider how the environment or time period in which the work was made or received impacts understanding.

Arts literacies that include a new understanding about arts texts, processes, and contexts underpin the development of the National Core Arts Standards for Media Arts (SEADAE, 2014), which have now been adopted or adapted in most states.

Challenges to the development of arts literacies within media literacy education

Content area literacies discussions included the media literacy education community in the larger discussions about new literacies, which was critically important. Media literacy education is situated well in the description of new literacies. Like information and technology literacies, media literacy was a new form of literacy that had come to the fore during a period of growth in digital technologies. Media literacy education scholars have successfully added their voice to those interested in the broader fields of information technology and education (e.g., Coiro, 2003; Hobbs, 2007; Leu, Kinzer, Coiro, & Cammack, 2004).

The integrated study of information and technology literacies and media literacy education is vital to the continued growth of media literacy education. Both fields acknowledge the changing nature of childhood because of new media environments (Leu et al., 2004; Livingston, 2002). Each field has a desire to restructure educational settings to match the needs of different students. The two fields both have an interest in designing educative experiences that empower young people to engage with technologies (see Cope & Kalantzis, 2003; Gee, 2004; Lankshear & Knobel, 2006). Additionally, the information and technology education community is successfully situated within schools. Career and technology education courses are thought of as part of the core curriculum in most US schools. The International Society for Technology in Education has great lobbying power, and because of this, significant school resources are dedicated to technology education.

However, it is important to note that a challenge to the further development of arts literacies within media literacy education is precisely this wholesale adoption of the media literacy education community into the information and technology literacy community. While it is important to continue leveraging the intersections between the media literacy education community and the information and technology community, it is also valuable to remember that historically two sets of issues impacted media literacy education: "(1) media literacy's relationship to the integration of educational technology into the K-12 curriculum and (2) the relationship between media literacy education and the humanities, arts, and sciences" (Hobbs & Jensen, 2009). Because the philosophical underpinnings of media literacy education are grounded in both of these philosophical camps it is imperative that educators think about creating as well as consuming. Through this type of work, the humanities, arts, and sciences might differently impact media literacy education as a whole.

Future directions in theory and methodology: media literacy education, arts literacies, and technologies

The media literacy education community and the media arts education community could increase and strengthen students' media literacy opportunities in the arts and humanities through purposeful conversations among the two groups. National media art standards invite "media arts educators and media literacy advocates to develop curricula, time, and space within public schools that encourages media arts and critical media literacy learning" (Jensen, 2013, p. 122). This conversation between arts educators and media literacy educators is nascent but has potential to benefit young people.

One place that those interested in beginning a conversation might start is with a statement made by media arts standards writers who say that their hope to aid students in cultivating "both artistic abilities and a technological aptitude" (Olsen et al., 2014). Conversations between arts educators and media literacy advocates could begin with this notion and build from there. Other emerging theories address how arts literacies and media literacies might be used in art, theatre, dance, and music classrooms (Jensen, 2016; Rogers, Winters, & Perry, 2014; Thevenin, 2015). Importantly, this work in arts classrooms can benefit from media literacy. Conversely media literacy is strengthened when it borrows from the rich making processes embedded in the arts.

With this beginning, media literacy and arts educators might provide young people with opportunities to more fully develop as actively engaged creators and consumers.

SEE ALSO: Critical Pedagogy; Esthetics in Media Literacy; Media Arts

References

Albers, P., & Sanders, J. (Eds.), (2010). *Literacies, the arts and multimodality*. Urbana, IL: National Council of Teachers of English.

Barton, D., & Hamilton, M. (2000). Literacy practices. In D. Barton, M. Hamilton, & R. Ivanic (Eds.), *Situated literacies: Reading and writing in context* (pp. 7–15). New York, NY: Routledge.

Coiro, J. (2003). Exploring literacy on the Internet: Reading comprehension on the Internet: Expanding our understanding of reading comprehension to encompass new literacies. *The Reading Teacher, 56*(5), 458–464.

Cope, B., & Kalantzis, M. (Eds.). (2000). *Multiliteracies: Literacy learning and the design of social futures*. New York, NY: Routledge.

Draper, R.J., Broomhead, P., Jensen, A.P., Nokes, J.D., & Siebert, D. (Eds.). (2010). *(Re)imagining content-area literacy instruction*. New York, NY: Teachers College Press.

Gee, J.P. (2001). Reading as situated language: A sociocognitive perspective. *Journal of Adolescent and Adult Literacy, 44*(8), 714–725. doi: 10.1598/JAAL.44.8.3

Gee, J.P. (2004). *Situated language and learning: A critique of traditional schooling*. New York, NY: Routledge.

Hobbs, R. (2007). *Reading the media: Media literacy in high school English*. New York, NY: Teachers College Press.

Hobbs, R., & Jensen, A. (2009). The past, present, and future of media literacy education. *Journal of Media Literacy Education, 1*(1). Retrieved from http://digitalcommons.uri.edu/jmle/vol1/iss1/1/

Jensen, A.P. (2013). Why media arts curriculum standards could improve media arts and critical media literacy in K-12 settings. In B.S. De Abreu & P. Mihailidis (Eds.), *Media literacy education in action: Theoretical and pedagogical perspectives* (pp. 116–122). New York, NY: Routledge. doi: 10.1080/10632913.2016.1187970

Jensen, A.P. (2016). A technological, pedagogical, arts knowledge framework. *Arts Education Policy Review, 117*(3), 153–158.

Jensen, A.P., & Draper, R.J. (2015). *Arts education and literacy*. New York, NY: Routledge.

Kress, G. (2003). *Literacy in the new media age*. London, England: Routledge.

Kress, G., & Van Leeuwen, T. (2001). *Multimodal discourse: The modes and media of contemporary communication*. London, England: Arnold.

Lankshear, C., & Knobel, M. (2006). *New literacies* (2nd ed.). Maidenhead, England: Open University Press.

Leu, D.J., Jr., Kinzer, C.K., Coiro, J., & Cammack, D. (2004). Toward a theory of new literacies emerging from the Internet and other information and communication technologies. In R.B. Ruddell & N. Unrau (Eds.), *Theoretical models and processes of reading* (5th ed., pp. 1568–1611). Newark, DE: International Reading Association.

Livingston, S. (2002). *Young people and new media: Childhood and the changing media environment*. London, England: SAGE.

New London Group. (2000). A pedagogy of multiliteracies: Designing social futures. In B. Cope & M. Kalantzis (Eds.), *Multiliteracies: Literacy learning and the design of social futures* (pp. 9–37). New York, NY: Routledge.

Olsen, D., Davis, J., Hockman, R.S., Holien, J., Kornfeld, A., Macklin, C., … & Stokes, N. (2014). Preface to media arts standards. Retrieved from http://www.mediaartseducation.org/media-arts-standards/

Rogers, T., Winters, K., & Perry, M. (2014). *Youth critical literacies and civic engagement*. New York, NY: Routledge.

State Education Agency Directors of Arts Education on behalf of NCCAS. (2014). Core standards for media arts. Retrieved from http://www.mediaartseducation.org/wp-content/uploads/2014/06/Media-Arts-Standards-6-4-14.pdf

Thevenin, B. (2015). Connecting. In A.P. Jensen & R.J. Draper, *Arts education and literacy* (pp. 174–181). New York, NY: Routledge.

Further reading

Kress, G. (2010). *Multimodality: A social semiotic approach to contemporary communication*. New York, NY: Routledge.

National Coalition for Core Arts Standards (NCCAS). (2012). National core arts standards: A conceptual framework for arts learning. Retrieved from http://www.nationalartsstandards.org/

Amy Petersen Jensen is a professor and associate dean over faculty in the College of Fine Arts and Communications at Brigham Young University. She is a faculty member in the Theatre and Media Arts Department where she formerly served as department chair. Amy teaches courses in theatre and media education. Amy is the coeditor (with Roni Jo Draper) of *Arts Education and Literacies* (2015). She has served as the coeditor (with Renee Hobbs) of the *Journal of Media Literacy Education* and as the general editor of the *Youth Theatre Journal*. Amy has served as a board member of the National Association for Media Literacy Education and the American Alliance for Theatre and Education. She was a leader in the development of the National Core Art Standards in 2014, which include media arts standards for the first time.

Authorship and Participatory Culture

BENJAMIN THEVENIN
Brigham Young University, USA

Media literacy and authorship

Since media education's beginnings, scholars and educators have included in their conceptualization of media literacy an engagement with authorship. The Center for Media

Literacy's (CML) core concepts include examinations of the origins ("Who created this message?") and intentions ("Why is this message being sent?") of media texts (Thoman & Jolls, 2008). These questions encourage the public to understand (i) that media messages are constructed, and (ii) that the individuals, institutions, and intentions behind this construction contribute to the meaning of these messages.

Given that media literacy is a diverse field, drawing from different interpretive traditions and utilizing different analytical and practical approaches, particular engagements with the idea of authorship and its relationship to media literacy vary widely.

For example, media arts approaches and youth media programs discuss authorship in terms of authorial intention; media creators making deliberate esthetic decisions to tell a story, express an emotion, or communicate a theme. Deliberately or not, these programs draw upon the understandings of authorship that developed out of traditions including film studies, art history, and literary criticism. In these perspectives, an understanding of the intentions of the author/artist/creator is paramount; not simply as a means of effectively engaging with a text, but also to allow one to effectively produce one's own art and express one's self.

Messaris (1998) describes the importance of *visual literacy*, and the value of not only understanding authorship but also becoming authors of media, as follows: "In a world as permeated by attempts at visual manipulation as ours is, these findings point to one possible avenue for increasing viewers' awareness of intent: training in production" (p. 183). As noted by Messaris, these approaches to media education address issues of authorship both through encouraging analyses of the intentions of media creators and through affording individuals the opportunity to produce their own media.

Next, scholars and educators coming from the perspective of critical media literacy often draw from studies of propaganda, the culture industries, and the political economy of media, and, in so doing, approach authorship through a different lens (see Hammer, 2006; Kellner & Share, 2005, 2007a, 2007b; Lewis & Jhally, 1998; McChesney, 1998). This approach addresses authorship, not in terms of authorial intention or self-expression, but rather in relation to institutional interests and media's role in maintaining political, economic, and social relations. Kellner and Share (2007a) write:

> Critical media literacy also encourages students to consider the question of why the message was sent and where it came from. … [K]nowing what sort of corporation produces a media artifact, or what sort of system of production dominates given media, will help to critically interpret biases and distortions in media texts. (pp. 15–16)

And last, a large segment of the field has drawn upon the tradition of cultural studies to determine how media literacy education can helpfully inform how the public makes meanings of media messages. This tradition—effectively articulated in Johnson's (1986) model of cultural analysis—discusses the *production* of a media text in relation to other "moments" of the meaning-making process, including *readings*, *lived cultures*, and *texts*. Each of these "moments" is understood as dependent "upon the others and is indispensable to the whole" (p. 46).

Consequently, media literacy education that draws from this tradition encourages an understanding of the production of media messages as including individual intentions and imperatives of industry, and seeks to situate authorship in relation to audiences, and creative production within the context of broader cultural and social practices.

Ultimately, while each of these segments of the field approach authorship from different directions, the combination of these frameworks helps the public understand:

- the *constructedness* of media texts,
- the intentions and interests behind the creation of media texts, and
- the relationship between production, text, and reception in the meaning-making process.

Contextualizing authorship

While media literacy scholars and educators acknowledge the importance of examining media *production*, they are also careful to contextualize these discussions of authorship within larger conversations about media culture.

Perhaps the greatest limitation of examining media through the lens of authorship is the potential for this approach to eclipse other valid, and even arguably more productive, understandings of media. Wimsatt and Beardsley's (1954) discussion of the *intentional fallacy* argues that cultural texts should not be understood or evaluated according to the author's intentions. So, while CML's first "key question" of media literacy might address the source of a particular media message, this question is accompanied by others which address other "moments" within the meaning-making process.

Questioning the place of privilege that the author has traditionally held in culture, Barthes (2001) emphasizes the active role that the audience plays, famously arguing that "the birth of the reader must be ransomed by the death of the Author" (p. 6). This conception of the *active audience* has since been explored by scholars in the cultural studies tradition (perhaps most famously by Hall, 1980) and integrated into the key frameworks of media literacy. For example, the National Association for Media Literacy Education (NAMLE) includes among its central concepts that "People use their individual skills, beliefs and experiences to construct their own meanings from media messages" (NAMLE, 2007, p. 3). Thus, while scholars and educators recognize how media literacy necessarily includes an engagement with the concept of authorship, these issues are carefully situated in relation to a myriad of other aspects of media culture.

Participatory culture and authorship

In his essay "What is an Author?" (1977) Foucault emphasizes that while, since the Enlightenment, authorship has played an important role in how we have understood culture, "the 'author-function' is not universal or constant in all discourse" (p. 125). The historical and cultural contingency of the conception of the author that Foucault emphasizes is important to remember in an age with such dramatic changes in media technologies and cultural practices. Not only are our definitions of authorship changing, but so must our critical frameworks for analyzing media production.

The concept of *participatory culture*—introduced by Jenkins (2006, 2012) in his examinations of fan communities—is used to characterize the changing landscape of today's media culture. It emphasizes: (i) the shift in relations between producers and consumers, authors and audiences that has occurred in the past few decades; and (ii) that these changes correlate with the increased availability of digital, networked, and mobile media technologies to the public, allowing audiences to author their own media and share them with others.

Scholars Jenkins, Ito, and boyd (2016) have further explored the concept of *participatory culture*, writing:

> For us, participation is not an absolute: it's defined in opposition to the dominant structures of institutionalized power. In the 1980s, it was about fans resisting and appropriating forms of commercial media. Today, it is about people finding voice, agency, and collective intelligence within the corporate-maintained structures of Web 2.0 platforms. (p. 184)

The type of participation that these scholars describe not only includes the idea of active audiences constructing their own meanings from the media they consume, but also using newly accessible media technologies to create and communicate themselves. Due to these changes in contemporary culture, media literacy education must, now more than ever, address authorship both as a framework for media analysis as well as preparation for the public to become aware of how their posting and sharing, modding, and remixing makes them authors.

Emerging media and authorship

While a discussion of this shift in understandings and practices of cultural production could examine fan-communities, citizen journalism, or "memes," this entry focuses on video games to explore issues of authorship in participatory culture. Video games provide a particularly productive object of study when considering authorship and participatory culture because they demonstrate:

1. The role that digital, interactive, and networked media technologies play in the production of media and the benefit of using materialist approaches to studying media in considerations of authorship.
2. The increasingly blurred distinction between producers and consumers, as evidenced in technically savvy game audiences who augment their gameplay and author their own experiences.
3. The opportunity that the increased accessibility of media authoring technologies has provided individuals who have been historically marginalized to create their own media and share their experiences and perspectives.

4. The rise of "indie" and "alternative" media encourages an understanding of authorship that challenges the Enlightenment-era understanding of the author as an individual and emphasizes the role of communities in creative production.

While each of these concepts will be illustrated using examples from video games, they are equally applicable in understanding how authorship is changing in other areas of contemporary media culture.

Manovich (2002) notes that "new media culture [including video games] brings with it a number of new models of authorship which all involve different forms of collaboration." He notes that new media—like cathedrals, symphonies, and films before them—are created by teams of collaborators, which challenges traditional conceptions of the single author. But perhaps even more significant is that these media require a new perspective on authorship, one that involves both humans and computers. Manovich writes:

> [W]e can say that all authorship that uses electronic and computer tools is a collaboration between the author and these tools that make possible certain creative operations and certain ways of thinking while discouraging others. (2002)

Video games, like all media texts, are constructed, but not just by their creators; in this case, game developers work with software programs that operate with specific protocols and algorithms, exercising their own type of agency on the creation of the game.

As a result, digital media literacy in the age of participatory culture must include what Bogost and Montfort call *platform studies*, defined as "new focus for the study of digital media, a set of approaches which investigate the underlying computer systems that support creative work" (2009). In order for audiences to understand the role of authors in the development of a video game, they must be able to examine the affordances and limitations that a particular software or system presents to the creative process.

Shaw (2014) provides a particularly interesting example of how this analysis of platforms can enrich media analysis. Discussing the process by which Nintendo designed its famous hero Mario, Shaw emphasizes the role of the system as coauthor:

> [Mario's] pudgy features, colorful costume, large nose, and bushy mustache—characteristics subsequently read as signifying his Italianness—were all designed to make the most of the limited graphics of early arcade machines and Nintendo consoles. The hat saved programmers from having to make animated hair. The bushy mustache and large nose gave him character despite the low resolution, limited animations, and small size of the sprite. His bright-red costume helped distinguish him from the dark background of the Donkey Kong game in which he made his original appearance … *The logics by which the world got to know the now decades-old, goomba stomping hero are unique to the particularities of 1980s game design processes.* (p. 23, italics added)

This emphasis on materialist media analysis does not, however, indicate an abandonment of the cultural studies approaches that have so informed media studies in general and media literacy in particular. In fact, this new conception of the system/software as author provides helpful insights into emerging media practices in participatory culture.

For example, studies like Ito et al.'s (2009) examination of *augmented game play*—which looks at the creation of peripheral media texts including mods, hacks, machinima, and game remixes—explores how communities of "amateurs" use their knowledge of the systems and software used by developers to create their own versions of video games. As Ito et al. observe:

> This orientation toward remaking and customizing media is in many ways a hallmark of the digital era and a key training ground for learning critical engagement with media; it is also a pathway into various forms of creative production … (p. 241)

Practices such as *augmented game play* are examples of how ideas of authorship—as well as the critical frameworks used to understand media's *constructedness*—are developing in the age of digital media and participatory culture.

Shifting our focus to the ways in which participatory culture influences the role of authors in the meaning-making process, this entry uses video games to demonstrate some of these changes and suggests some directions for media literacy education. Bogost (2015) notes that in the case of video games, it is often difficult to identify the role that particular individuals' intentions or institutional interests play in the creation of video games. The role of the author (or author*s*) is hard to pin down:

> In part, it's because games are more highly industrialized even than film, and aesthetic headway is often curtailed by commercial necessity. And in part, it's because games are so tightly coupled to consumer electronics that technical progress outstrips aesthetic progress in the public imagination. (p. 11)

While an examination of the commercial and technological pressures experienced within the video game industry provide a particular understanding of how authorship functions within contemporary media culture, this perspective is limited in that it does not adequately account for the individual creators' interests, ideologies, and esthetics nor the social, political, and cultural contexts in which media texts—in this case, video games—are being made. However, certain developments within the game industry provide potentially productive sites to examine these often overlooked aspects of authorship.

For example, the increased accessibility of game-making software and the proliferation of "indie games" is evidence of a (gradual but not insignificant) decentralization of the video game industry. And the increased accessibility of these means of production has allowed a new and diverse range of voices to join the conversation. These new game developers—often representing populations traditionally marginalized within the video game industry and game culture—are not only sharing new perspectives, but also developing new ways of making and understanding games.

One interesting example is the increased representation of LGBTQ+ developers (and characters) in games, and in particular within text-based interactive narratives called Twine games. The game industry, which has historically operated under the (false) assumption that most gamers are straight, adolescent males, has very rarely attempted to represent diverse perspectives or reach wider audiences. In response to this lack of diversity, indie developers like Anna Anthropy, Porpentine, and Lydia Neon (among many others) have authored Twine games that address various struggles faced by the LGBTQ+ community (Hudson, 2014).

This development within video games is interesting to media literacy scholars and educators because it provides an excellent example of the powers at play in both the media industry and the meaning-making process: audiences-turned-authors are challenging the industry imperatives by developing games in alternative platforms with alternative perspectives. This is precisely the type of alternative media production that critical media literacy scholars have championed; taking on the role of author and creating media that "challenges media texts and narratives that appear natural and transparent" (Kellner & Share, 2007a, p. 4).

Last, these subtle shifts in power relations within video game industry and culture also point to an idea of authorship that is less concerned with individuals, or even industries, and more about communities. Celebrating the increased accessibility of game-design tools and the subsequent flood of new voices in games, Anthropy (2012) discusses her hopes for the future of game creation:

> … what I want from video games is a plurality of voices. I want games to come from a wider set of experiences and present a wider range of perspectives. I can imagine—you are invited to imagine with me—a world in which digital games are not manufactured by publishers for the same small audience, but one in which games are authored by you and me for the benefit of our peers. (p. 8)

Today's media consumers are sharing, spreading, collaborating, and curating on social media and the web, and they are engaging in these acts of creation and communication as communities. boyd highlights the significance of this shift, writing "participatory culture requires us to move beyond a focus on individualized personal expression; it is about an ethos of 'doing it together' in addition to 'doing it yourself'" (Jenkins et al. 2015, p. 181).

This entry has offered new ideas about how we might understand and practice authorship as media consumers, creators, scholars, and educators. It has explored how advances in media technologies and cultural practices require new ways of seeing the construction of media texts, the interests and intentions that influence media production, and the meaning-making process. And it anticipates that this conversation will continue and new perspectives on the relationship between media literacy, authorship, and participatory culture will emerge.

SEE ALSO: Active Audiences; Amateur—Professional; Coding as Literacy; Creative Works; Curation; Digital Storytelling; Documentary Analysis and Production in Media Literacy; Esthetics in Media Literacy; Game Design in Media Literacy Education; Game Media Literacy; Media Arts; Media Education Research and Creativity; Production in the Pedagogic Project of Media Literacy; Remix Culture; Understanding Media Literacy and DIY Creativity in Youth Digital Productions; Video Games as Education

References

Anthropy, A. (2012). *Rise of the video game zinesters: How freaks, normal, amateurs, artists, dreamers, drop-outs, queers, housewives, and people like you are taking back an art form*. New York, NY: Seven Stories Press.

Barthes, R. (2001). The death of the author. *Contributions in Philosophy, 83*, 3–8.

Bogost, I. (2015). *How to talk about video games*. Minnesota, MN: University of Minnesota Press.

Bogost, I., & Montfort, N. (2009). *Platform studies: Frequently questioned answers*. Digital Arts and Culture. Retrieved from http://nickm.com/if/bogost_montfort_dac_2009.pdf

Foucault, M. (1977). What is an author? In D. Bouchard (Ed.), *Language, counter-memory, practice: Selected essays and interviews*. Ithaca, NY: Cornell University Press.

Hall, S. (1980). Encoding/decoding. In S. Hall, D. Hobson, A. Love, & P. Willis, (Eds.), *Culture, media, language*. London, England: Hutchinson.

Hammer, R. (2006). Teaching critical media literacies: Theory, praxis and empowerment. *Interactions: UCLA Journal of Education and Information Studies, 2*(1).

Hudson, L. (2014, November 19). Twine, the video-game technology for all. *New York Times*. Retrieved from http://www.nytimes.com/2014/11/23/magazine/twine-the-video-game-technology-for-all.html?_r=1

Ito, M., Baumer, S., Bittanti, M., Cody, R., Stephenson, B.H., Horst, H.A., … Tripp, L. (2009). *Hanging out, messing around, and geeking out: Kids living and learning with new media*. Cambridge, MA: MIT Press.

Jenkins, H. (2006). *Convergence culture: Where old and new media collide*. New York, NY: NYU Press.

Jenkins, H. (2012). *Textual poachers: Television fans and participatory culture*. New York, NY: Routledge.

Jenkins, H., Ito, M., & boyd, d. (2015). *Participatory culture in a networked era: A conversation on youth, learning, commerce and politics*. Malden, MA: Polity Press.

Johnson, R. (1986). What is cultural studies anyway? *Social Text*, 16, 38–80.

Kellner, D., & Share, J. (2005). Toward critical media literacy: Core concepts, debates, organizations, and policy. *Discourse: Studies in the Cultural Politics of Education, 26*(3), 369–386.

Kellner, D., & Share, J. (2007a). Critical media literacy, democracy, and the reconstruction of education. *Media Literacy: A Reader*, 3–23.

Kellner, D., & Share, J. (2007b). Critical media literacy is not an option. *Learning Inquiry, 1*(1), 59–69.

Lewis, J., & Jhally, S. (1998). The struggle over media literacy. *Journal of Communication, 48*(1).

Manovich, L. (2002). *Models of authorship in new media*. Retrieved from http://manovich.net/index.php/projects/models-of-authorship-in-new-media

McChesney, R. (1998). Making media democratic. *Boston Review*. Retrieved from https://bostonreview.net/archives/BR23.3/mcchesney.html

Messaris, P. (1998). Visual aspects of media literacy. *Journal of Communication, 48*(1).

NAMLE (National Association of Media Literacy Education). (2007). *The core principles of media literacy education in the United States*. Retrieved from http://namle.net/publications/core-principles/

Shaw, A. (2014). *Gaming at the edge: Sexuality and gender at the margins of gamer culture*. Minnesota, MN: University of Minnesota Press.

Thoman, E., & Jolls, T. (2008). *Literacy for the 21st century: An overview and orientation guide to media literacy education. Theory CML MedicaLit Kit*. Center for Media Literacy.

Wimsatt, W., & Beardsley, M. (1954). The intentional fallacy. In *The verbal icon: Studies in the meaning of poetry*. Lexington, KY: University of Kentucky Press.

Benjamin Thevenin is an assistant professor of media arts at Brigham Young University. His studies focus on the relationships between youth, media, and politics, and in particular, how we can better prepare young people to become thoughtful citizens, consumers, and creators of media. Thevenin teaches classes on creativity, children's media, new media, and media education. He serves on the Leadership Council of the National Association of Media Literacy Education (NAMLE).

Awareness

DOUGLAS KELLNER and JEFF SHARE
University of California, Los Angeles, USA

We don't know who discovered water, but we're certain it wasn't a fish.

Attributed to John Culkin in Carpenter, 1970
(unnumbered page titled "The Islander")

In the 21st century, media are as ubiquitous and ever-present as the air we breathe, enveloping us like fish swimming in water; we are so accustomed to their presence that we seldom consider their influence. We have become dependent on social media for our relationships, on informational media for our work and school life, and on entertainment media for our pleasures; yet, with its synergy that bundles, interconnects, and remixes our worlds, there is seldom separation between these forms and functions.

The influential role media play in organizing, shaping, and disseminating information, ideas, and values is creating a powerful *public pedagogy* (Giroux, 1999; Luke, 1997) that shapes and validates dominant ideas and discourses. While new information communication technologies (ICTs) have created potent tools for sharing information and connecting people across the planet, they have also concentrated access to and control of information and produced digital divides and information inequalities. Further, today's dominant storytellers are enormous transnational corporations merging and expanding internationally to almost every corner of the globe and, domestically, to every nook and cranny they can reach. Only a handful of corporations own the majority of the world's media, creating a small group of wealthy people with tremendous power to decide who and what will be represented and what lessons will be taught by the largest cultural industry the world has ever known (McChesney & Nichols, 2016).

When a small group of people has the power to create and disseminate enormous amounts of information, the diversity of ideas shrinks as the potential for abuse increases. Media consolidation is especially problematic when the majority of the audience perceives the messages as neutral and transparent. This positivist perspective promotes an unproblematic relationship with media in which the messages are rarely questioned or challenged, especially when they are considered entertainment. Awareness through critical inquiry, therefore, becomes an essential requirement for literacy in the 21st century. Changes in technology, media, and society require the development of critical media literacy (CML) to empower students and citizens to critically read media messages and produce media themselves in order to be active participants in a democratic society. This requires awareness of how media function in everyday life and developing critical literacies to decode crucial meanings, messages, and effects. Much of the daily public pedagogy that mass media teach about race, gender, class, sexuality, consumption, fear, morals, and the like reflects corporate profit motives and hegemonic ideologies that dominate at the expense of social concerns necessary for a healthy and vibrant democracy.

Since traditional education does little to help students recognize and counteract these influences, we need a new type of literacy, which *expands* critical consciousness and awareness so as to encompass new ICTs, media, and popular culture and *deepens* pedagogical practices by taking them to more complex levels in order to question the relationships between power and information.

Critical awareness is akin to what Paulo Freire (1970) calls *conscientização*, a revolutionary critical consciousness that involves perception as well as action against oppression. Critical awareness in CML involves seeing, analyzing, and criticizing media that promote representations or narratives involving racism, sexism, classism, homophobia, and other forms of bias that further oppression of targeted social groups.

Through this horizontal expansion of literacy and vertical deepening of critical inquiry and awareness, CML aims to challenge popular assumptions that frame media as unproblematic windows to the world. An essential concept of media literacy is the social construction of knowledge and the ramifications of that understanding, which aim to disrupt positivist misconceptions (Kellner & Share, 2007). This critical pedagogical approach to literacy offers the dual possibility of building awareness of media domination through critical analysis and empowering individuals to create alternative media for counterhegemonic expression. CML pedagogy offers students and teachers an opportunity to embrace the changes in society and technology, not as threats to education, but as opportunities to rethink teaching and learning as political acts of consciousness-raising and empowerment.

A framework of conceptual understandings

While media education has sprung from many disciplines, an important arena of theoretical work for CML is the multidisciplinary field of cultural studies. This is a field of critical inquiry that developed from the work of researchers from the Frankfurt School, the Birmingham School, feminism, queer theory, critical race theory, and critical indigenous theory, as well as from researchers who examine the impact of the culture industries. These scholars have expanded the concept of ideology to include gender, race, sexuality, and other forces of identity and oppression in addition to class, while proposing a sophisticated understanding of the audience as active makers of meaning. Applying concepts from semiotics, feminism, multiculturalism, postmodernism, a dialectical understanding of political economy, textual analysis, and audience theory, CML has evolved into a practice of analyzing media and popular culture as dynamic discourses that reproduce dominant ideologies as well as entertain, educate, and offer possibilities for counterhegemonic alternatives (Kellner, 1995).

In the 1980s, cultural studies research began to enter the educational arena. After the publication of Masterman's (1985/2001) *Teaching the Media*, educators in various parts of the world embraced media education more as a framework of *conceptual understandings* (Buckingham, 2003) than as a specific body of knowledge or set of skills. While many media literacy organizations have their own lists of essential ideas, these lists tend to coincide with a handful of basic elements; and we have adapted these elements into a framework with six CML conceptual understandings (see Funk, Kellner, & Share, 2016), presented here as follows:

1. Who are all the possible people who made choices that helped create this text?
   Social constructivism: all information is co-constructed by individuals and/or groups of people who make choices within social contexts.
2. How was this text constructed and delivered or accessed?
   Languages/Semiotics: each medium has its own language, with a specific grammar and semantics.
3. How could this text be understood differently?
   Audience/Positionality: individuals and groups understand media messages similarly and/or differently depending on multiple contextual factors.
4. What values, points of view, and ideologies are represented or missing from this text, or are influenced by the medium?
   Politics of representation: media messages and the medium through which they travel always have a bias and support and/or challenge dominant hierarchies of power, privilege, and pleasure.
5. Why was this text created and/or shared?
   Production/Institutions: all media texts have a purpose (often commercial or governmental) that is shaped by the creators and/or systems within which they operate.
6. Whom does this text advantage and/or whom does it disadvantage?
   Social and environmental justice: media culture is a terrain of struggle that perpetuates or challenges positive and/or negative ideas about people, groups, and issues; it is never neutral.

These conceptual understandings promote an awareness of the ubiquity of media in our lives; of who produces the media and what interests, values, and narratives these serve; of how media texts are constructed and appropriated by audiences; and of how media can be produced and used to combat dominant hierarchies of power in the realms of class, race, gender and sexuality, as well as to reproduce and naturalize these hierarchies. Critical awareness of the many dimensions of media in our lives and of the need to receive, read, decode, critique, and transmit media critically is an important part of CML, just as awareness in general is a mark of an informed and reflective life, which sees media as an important component of society.

Rethinking literacy through a sociological lens

The traditional model of reading and writing that is common in schools around the world is based on a psychological model that frames literacy as individual cognitive skills. This paradigm needs to evolve into a deeper sociological understanding of literacy as a social practice "tied up in the politics and power relations of everyday life in literate cultures" (Luke & Freebody, 1997, p. 185). On the basis of their work in Australia, Luke and Freebody (1997, 1999) developed *the four resources model*, a dynamic understanding of literacy as social practices where critical competence is one of the necessary practices. Luke and Freebody (1999) explain that effective literacy requires four basic competencies, namely competencies that allow learners to "break the code … participate in understanding and composing … use texts functionally … [and] critically analyze and transform texts by acting on knowledge that texts are not ideologically natural or neutral." This sociological perspective on literacy as a *family of practices* fits well into a multiperspectival approach to CML.

Lewis and Jhally (1998) express concern "that media education in the United States will flounder if it cannot locate media texts in a broad set of social realities" (p. 3). They argue that, when media literacy focuses on the text at the expense of the context, it ignores important questions of ideology, power, political economy, production, and reception. They do not call for replacing a text-centered approach with a contextual approach but, more in the manner of Luke and Freebody (1997), suggest the infusion of a sociological perspective into psychological and cognitive ideas that are most common in literacy education.

The four resources model has been used by Pandya and Aukerman (2014) as a lens in analyzing technology in the Common Core State Standards (CCSS). Through their research, these authors explain the dearth of critical competence in the language of the new standards. They describe critical competence in its relation to technology as "the ability to critique and analyze texts, and to redesign new print and digital texts (sometimes as part of that critique); the knowledge that texts are never neutral but always embody particular points of view" (p. 429). Pandya and Aukerman caution that, if teachers do not give specific attention "to building children's *critical competencies*, we suspect that both children and teachers will remain focused on interpreting, creating, and sharing (digital) texts at the expense of analyzing and critiquing the power relations that underlie and are formed by texts" (p. 432). Students today need the skills and the disposition to engage with messages in many ways, especially if they are to play a role in shaping democracy. It is because of this sociological understanding of literacy that media education needs to have a critical dimension that values a contextual approach and an inquiry process.

Understanding the role of context is an essential part of reading and writing the world and the word. When a text, whether it involves printed words, an image, a video, a song, or a T-shirt, is taken out of context, re-presented, and remixed, the variety of meanings that readers will make of the message is likely to increase. The different understandings of the message will vary because of the different contexts that readers bring with them, their prior knowledge, beliefs, and experiences, as well as the contexts in which the message is constructed and the politics of representation (the subjectivities of the people who construct the message, the bias of those who share the information, the qualities of the medium through which the information is distributed, and the codes and conventions of the text). The context always influences messages, regardless of whether the listeners, readers, or viewers are aware of it or not. No message can be neutral and no technology can represent a message without in some way affecting that message (McLuhan, 1997). Therefore a skill that students need in order to make sense of new information is the reflexive ability to question the construction and context of a text. This is the same challenge as being aware of and analyzing the bias and accuracy of news reports, music, movies, video games, and social media. The task can be more difficult when the information is taken out of context, as often happens for mediated and networked publics, where the information is often shared, sampled, and "mashed up" (boyd, 2014). Rather than searching for a single "truth" and making evaluations accordingly, students should learn to search for different perspectives and for evidence that enables them to triangulate the findings and evaluate the information from multiple sources. This should make them more aware and more discerning consumers, users, and producers of media.

Students also need to understand how ideology functions to maintain dominant ideas and ways of making sense of the world. Ferguson (1998) states: "'Ideology' is not directly visible, but can only be experienced and/or comprehended. What is visible is a range of social and representational manifestations which are rooted in relationships of power and subordination" (p. 43). Through the process of *naturalizing* power relations, ideology removes from view their social and historical construction. Hall (2003) explains: "Ideologies tend to disappear from view into the taken-for-granted 'naturalised' world of common sense" (p. 90). Developing a critical awareness is essential, because what one does not see one rarely questions. Therefore CML encourages students to explore questions that can reveal structures, history, and social contexts that are too often obscured from view by the hegemonic ideology. Ferguson (1998) asserts: "The relationship of consciousness to ideology is not psychological or moralistic in character, but 'structural and epistemological.' This means that it has to do with the ways in which knowledge and understanding are constructed and defended" (p. 44).

CML provides critical media awareness by engaging students, through the use of media, technology, and popular culture, to question the interconnections of power and information, providing a lens and a process for analyzing and creating meanings through multiple media and technology. Morrell (2012) explains that this perspective "also enlightens students to the potential that they have, as media producers, to shape the world they live in, to help turn it into the world they imagine" (p. 302). Although CML is rooted in a rich history of cultural studies, CML pedagogy is not a content area to be siloed within the domain of media studies or communication. CML belongs in every classroom, from preschool to university; it invites educators to teach through inquiry and to question "commonsense" assumptions as they are reading and writing the word and the world (Freire & Macedo, 1987; Vasquez, 2014).

SEE ALSO: Critical Pedagogy; Educommunication; Representation of Race

References

boyd, d. (2014). *It's complicated: The social lives of networked teens*. New Haven, CT: Yale University Press.

Buckingham, D. (2003). *Media education: Literacy, learning and contemporary culture*. Cambridge, England: Polity.

Carpenter, E. (1970). *They became what they beheld.* New York, NY: Outerbridge & Dienstfrey/Ballantine Books.
Ferguson, R. (1998). *Representing "race": Ideology, identity and the media.* New York, NY: Oxford University Press.
Freire, P. (1970). *Pedagogy of the oppressed.* New York, NY: Seabury Press.
Freire, P., & Macedo, D. (1987). *Literacy: Reading the word and the world.* Westport, CT: Bergin & Garvey.
Funk, S., Kellner, D., & Share, J. (2016). Critical media literacy as transformative pedagogy. In M.N. Yildiz & J. Keengwe (Eds.), *Handbook of research on media literacy in the digital age* (pp. 1–30). Hershey, PA: IGI Global.
Giroux, H. (1999). *The mouse that roared: Disney and the end of innocence.* Boulder, CO: Rowman & Littlefield.
Hall, S. (2003). The whites of their eyes: Racist ideologies and the media. In G. Dines & J.M. Humez (Eds.), *Gender, race, and class in media* (2nd ed., pp. 89–93). Thousand Oaks, CA: SAGE.
Kellner, D. (1995). *Media culture: Cultural studies, identity and politics between the modern and the postmodern.* New York, NY: Routledge.
Kellner, D., & Share, J. (2007). Critical media literacy, democracy, and the reconstruction of education. In D. Macedo & S.R. Steinberg (Eds.), *Media literacy: A reader* (pp. 3–23). New York, NY: Peter Lang.
Lewis, J., & Jhally, S. (1998). The struggle over media literacy. *Journal of Communication, 48*(1), 1–8.
Luke, A., & Freebody, P. (1997). Shaping the social practices of reading. In S. Muspratt, A. Luke, & P. Freebody (Eds.), *Constructing critical literacies: Teaching and learning textual practice* (pp. 185–225). Sydney, Australia: Allen & Unwin, and Cresskill, NJ: Hampton Press.
Luke, A., & Freebody, P. (1999). Further notes on the four resources model. Reading Online. Retrieved February 12, 2006, from http://www.readingonline.org/research/lukefreebody.html
Luke, C. (1997). *Technological literacy.* Melbourne, Australia: National Languages & Literacy Institute.
Masterman, L. (1985/2001). *Teaching the media.* New York, NY: Routledge.
McChesney, R., & Nichols, J. (2016). *People get ready: The fight against a jobless economy and a citizenless democracy.* New York, NY: Nation Books.
McLuhan, M. (1997). *Understanding media: Extensions of man.* Cambridge, MA: MIT Press.
Morrell, E. (2012). 21st-century literacies, critical media pedagogies, and language arts. *Reading Teacher, 66*(4), 300–302. doi: 10.1002/TRTR.01125
Pandya, J.Z., & Aukerman, M. (2014). A four resources analysis of technology in the CCSS. *Language Arts, 91*(6), 429–435.
Vasquez, V. (2014). *Negotiating critical literacies with young children.* New York, NY: Routledge.

Douglas Kellner is George Kneller Chair in the Philosophy of Education at the University of California, Los Angeles and author of many books on social theory, politics, history, and culture. His website contains several of his books and many articles.

Jeff Share has worked as a photojournalist, elementary school teacher, and curriculum designer and trainer. He is currently a faculty advisor in the Teacher Education Program at the University of California, Los Angeles. In 2015 he published the second edition of his book *Media Literacy Is Elementary: Teaching Youth to Critically Read and Create Media.*

B

Boomerang Effects

JULIE S. CANNON and SAHARA BYRNE
Cornell University, USA

Media literacy interventions refer to organized attempts to promote pro-social effects of media and reduce antisocial effects. Media literacy intervention effects should be proactive (intentional), positive, and apply to a broad variety of audiences and contexts. An optimistic theme emerges from the desired goals and effects of media literacy; however, this outcome is not always realistic. Media literacy interventions are vulnerable to the same failures as any strategic communication attempt. There are a wide variety of potential unintended consequences of interventions, including perhaps the most disappointing and potentially harmful, when the inverse of the desired outcome occurs. The terms "contradictory," "paradoxical," "unintended," "backfire," and "boomerang" are often used interchangeably in reference to harmful effects of media literacy interventions.

Documented boomerang effects in media literacy interventions

Boomerang effects are not limited by the context or theoretical foundations of an intervention. These effects have been documented in diverse contexts including efforts to reduce the negative effects of media on health behaviors, risk behaviors, body consciousness, stereotyping, and aggression.

The potentially harmful effects of media violence on the healthy development of children and young adults provide one of the most substantial bodies of work on both media literacy and boomerang effects. Media literacy boomerang effects among children have been documented since the 1980s, and more recently, Byrne (2009) designed an intervention that demonstrated this type of effect. The media literacy intervention she designed included a "basic condition" with a lesson about violence in media, and

The International Encyclopedia of Media Literacy. Renee Hobbs and Paul Mihailidis (Editors-in-Chief), Gianna Cappello, Maria Ranieri, and Benjamin Thevenin (Associate Editors).

an "activity condition" using the same violence in media lesson with the addition of a cognitive activity. Both groups viewed and responded to media clips. Children who received the basic intervention, without the cognitive activity, reported higher likelihood of aggression over time within subjects, as well as in comparison to the control group. The results indicate that long-term effects of a curricula including video clips seemed to exist on a continuum of harm, as opposed to being pro-social. Comparably, Bickham and Slaby (2012) evaluated the effectiveness of an intervention to reduce verbal aggression. The program itself was integrated into the fifth-grade curriculum over 6 weeks, in health and art classes, combining analytical and production components. The study found potential verbal aggression increased among participants in the treatment condition. The researchers suggest the boomerang effect may have been a result of priming via an activity in which participants rewrote a bullying scene. In all of these cases, the boomerang effect was reported, but potential causal attributions were not tested. Note, neither sex of participant nor format of intervention appear to be decisive indicators of why these effects occur.

Boomerang effects are not isolated to media violence interventions. Ramasubramanian and Oliver (2007) define media literacy operationally as deterring viewers from making generalizations based on bias. The researchers situate their work in realistic conflict theory and the stereotype conflict model. They analyzed reactions to either stereotypical or nonstereotypical news stories about African Americans or Asian Indians, following a media literacy video. The media literacy intervention increased stereotyped perceptions of African Americans (Ramasubramanian & Oliver, 2007). Possible reasons provided for the unintended effect are that attitudes toward African Americans are less malleable than those toward Asian Indians in the United States; alternatively, the media literacy lesson may have been too authoritative, or mentioning generalization may have primed for stereotypes (Ramasubramanian & Oliver, 2007).

Choma, Foster, and Radford (2007) argued that paradoxical or contradictory findings may not be inherently bad. Their study investigated the potential for a boomerang effect on state self-objectification, alongside other more desirable effects like improved self-esteem. The results are described as contradictory – the video intervention resulted in both positive effects and increased state self-objectification. The researchers suggest that the negative emotions that accompany a sense of empowerment are reflective of the construction of a feminist identity (Choma et al., 2007). Choma et al. (2007) also propose a reconsideration of what constitutes a successful media literacy intervention, arguing that some effects that appear negative initially may actually be related to other, positive outcomes. Thus, understanding the mechanisms and relationships that underlie unintended effects is imperative to progressing media literacy curricular design.

The aforementioned examples are illustrative, not exhaustive. It is difficult to locate examples of boomerang effect in intervention literature, likely because these effects are often viewed as indicative of intervention failure. However, to best understand these effects, several overarching theories of why messages go wrong have been advanced.

Theorizing the boomerang effect

At the time that media literacy interventions and curricula are designed, it is possible to carefully examine the stimuli for specific elements with the potential to have nuanced effects of activating both intended and unintended constructs. Byrne and Hart (2009) structure their boomerang effect framework around a synthesis of theorized explanations for such effects. According to this framework, message failure can occur at either the competitive processing or the effects decision phase.

At the competitive processing phase, intended and unintended elements compete for salience. The winning element becomes more accessible. Additionally, when ability to process the message is low, the easiest elements to process will take precedence. If the unintended elements are easier to process then constructs related to that element activate in the mind of the viewer. In the event that a receiver comprehends unintended elements of a message, boomerang effects can emerge from a cost–benefit assessment of the behaviors linked to unintended constructs and those linked to intended constructs. For example, Byrne, Linz, and Potter (2009) investigated psychological reactance and media priming as underlying mechanisms of a boomerang effect among the participation of elementary school students in anti-violence media literacy intervention. Byrne et al. (2009) explain that priming via violent clips emerged from analysis as a predictor of the boomerang effect. As more boomerang effects are documented, the move toward understanding those effects is gaining momentum.

When participants do focus on the elements of an intervention designed for pro-social outcomes, there is a chance for the desired effect to take place. However, a risk of null or boomerang effects is still a possibility. When a message is comprehended as intended, unintended effects may still occur via ironic processing, engaging in fear control, freedom- or commodity-based values, or reactance. Ramasubramanian and Oliver (2007) suggested the authoritarian tone of their intervention may have produced boomerang effect. This attribution exemplifies the idea of participant reactance.

Another helpful theory on why messages don't always work is fuzzy-trace theory (FTT). Mills, Reyna, and Estrada (2008) contend that FTT may help explain instances where risk perception has a paradoxical effect on risk-taking. The theory posits that at one level of processing the more qualitative, "gist" view of avoiding risk is enacted, while in other instances a cost–benefit analysis occurs wherein the risk may be perceived as "worth it." According to FTT, verbatim mental representations of information emphasize exactitude, whereas gist representations provide qualitative, less exact, contextual elements of meaning to information through retrieved knowledge, beliefs, and values (Reyna, 2008). When considering a risk behavior, people generally rely on gist representations, especially as they gain expertise and experience, which tends to correlate with age (Reyna, 2008). Specific cues to memories may promote the more quantitative style of representation.

Conceptually, this theory maps well onto the failures of some logistic and fact-oriented media literacy curricula. For example, Nathanson (2004) argued that ease of processing, emphasis on social norms, and guidance in how to interpret the factual elements of violent media production support the notion that evaluative mediation would be more successful than factual mediation. Not only was evaluative mediation more effective lighter viewing, older children may have been harmed by the factual mediation condition. Additionally, Peter, Sobowale, and Ekeanyanwu (2013) sought to educate groups of Nigerian students between the ages of 13 and 18 about the harmful media influence on alcohol consumption behaviors. The researchers designed a curricular intervention that incorporated homework, parental sessions, and formal intervention over 5 weeks with the goal of improved critical analysis of media content. They reported that increased understanding of how authors produce targeted messages designed for profit increased participants' positive impressions of the consequences of drinking alcohol (Peter et al., 2013). These studies demonstrate the risk in relying on verbatim representations associated with an intervention.

Additionally, the goal of an FTT-based intervention is to better understand *why* a behavior is risky (Reyna, 2008). The *why* element of behavior is derived from the meaning-making that occurs in gist representation and processing. One of the principles of media literacy is the development of a critical understanding of why media may be harmful. To this end, FTT, traditionally applied in health contexts of risk behavior research (Reyna, 2008), offers an interesting alternative to Byrne and Hart's (2009) explanation for unintended effects, especially among adolescents (Mills et al., 2008). Similar to Byrne and Hart (2009), Reyna (2008) discusses how "people can get the facts right, and still not derive proper meaning" (p. 850); however, Reyna proposes the underlying mechanism is processing interference associated with base rate neglect and category confusion associated with decision-making.

To avoid unintended effects, several scholars across the contexts of public health and media literacy emphasize the need for formative evaluations in the design phase of interventions (Cho & Salmon, 2007; Salmon, Byrne, & Fernandez, 2014). Dark logic models (Bonell, Jamal, Melendez-Torres, & Cummins, 2015) situated in established theory may offer techniques for circumventing potential ill-effects of public health intervention. Bonell et al.'s (2015) proposal to develop dark logic models was inspired by boomerang effects of a UK-based public health intervention designed to reduce teen pregnancy rates. Dark logic models would outline the potential causal pathways of negative effects of intervention should they be developed in tandem with the desired effect models for intervention. Bonell et al. (2015) propose using what has been learned through frameworks like that proposed by Byrne and Hart (2009) to preclude boomerang effects. Taken in conjunction, these perspectives on interventions support the notion that research regarding formative evaluations and unintended effects in the public health sector may be useful in theorizing boomerang effects in media literacy.

SEE ALSO: Health Media Literacy; Media Literacy and Smoking; Teaching about Media Violence

References

Bickham, D.S., & Slaby, R.G. (2012). Effects of a media literacy program in the US on children's critical evaluation of unhealthy media messages about violence, smoking, and food. *Journal of Children and Media*, 6(2), 255–271. doi: 10.1080/17482798.2012.662031

Bonell, C., Jamal, F., Melendez-Torres, G.J., & Cummins, S. (2015). "Dark logic": Theorising the harmful consequences of public health interventions. *Journal of Epidemiology and Community Health, 69*(1), 95–98. doi: 10.1136/jech-2014-204671

Byrne, S. (2009). Media literacy interventions: What makes them boom or boomerang? *Communication Education, 58*(1), 1–14. doi: 10.1080/03634520802226444

Byrne, S., & Hart, P.S. (2009). The boomerang effect: A synthesis of findings and a preliminary theoretical framework. *Annals of the International Communication Association, 33*(1), 3–37. doi: 10.1080/23808985.2009.11679083

Byrne, S., Linz, D., & Potter, W.J. (2009). A test of competing cognitive explanations for the boomerang effect in response to the deliberate disruption of media-induced aggression. *Media Psychology, 12*(3), 227–248. doi: 10.1080/15213260903052265

Cho, H., & Salmon, C.T. (2007). Unintended effects of health communication campaigns. *Journal of Communication, 57*(2), 293–317. doi: 10.1111/j.1460-2466.2007.00344.x

Choma, B.L., Foster, M.D., & Radford, E. (2007). Use of objectification theory to examine the effects of a media literacy intervention on women. *Sex Roles, 56*(9), 581–590. doi: 10.1007/s11199-007-9200-x

Mills, B., Reyna, V.F., & Estrada, S. (2008). Explaining contradictory relations between risk perception and risk taking. *Psychological Science, 19*(5), 429–433. doi: 10.1111/j.1467-9280.2008.02104.x

Nathanson, A.I. (2004). Factual and evaluative approaches to modifying children's responses to violent television. *Journal of Communication, 54*(2), 321–336. doi.10.1111/j.1460-2466.2004.tb02631.x

Peter, A.S., Sobowale, I.A., & Ekeanyanwu, N.T. (2013). Theory of planned behavior: Measuring adolescents' media literacy and alcohol drinking expectancies. *Covenant Journal of Communication, 1*(2), 118–129. http://eprints.covenantuniversity.edu.ng/9021/1/Alcohol%20Advertising%20Literacy.pdf

Ramasubramanian, S., & Oliver, M.B. (2007). Activating and suppressing hostile and benevolent racism: Evidence for comparative media stereotyping. *Media Psychology, 9*(3), 623–646. doi: 10.1080/15213260701283244

Reyna, V.F. (2008). A theory of medical decision making and health: Fuzzy trace theory. *Medical Decision Making, 28*(6), 850–865. doi: 10.1177/0272989X08327066

Salmon, C.T., Byrne, S., & Fernandez, L. (2014). Exploring unintended consequences of risk communication messages. In J. Arvai & L.I. Rivers (Eds.), *Effective risk communication*. New York, NY: Routledge.

Further reading

Austin, E.W., & Pinkleton, B.E. (2016). The viability of media literacy in reducing the influence of misleading media messages on young people's decision-making concerning alcohol, tobacco, and other substances. *Current Addiction Reports, 3*(2), 1–7. doi: 10.1007/s40429-016-0100-4

Byrne, S., & Lee, T. (2011). Toward predicting youth resistance to Internet risk prevention strategies. *Journal of Broadcasting & Electronic Media, 55*(1), 90–113. doi: 10.1080/08838151.2011.546255

Cantor, J., & Wilson, B.J. (2003). Media and violence: Intervention strategies for reducing aggression. *Media Psychology, 5*(4), 331–403. doi: 10.1207/S1532785XMEP0504_03

Julie S. Cannon is a doctoral student at Cornell University. She holds an MA from Purdue University in media, society, and health.

Sahara Byrne is an associate professor in the Department of Communication at Cornell University. Her research examines persuasion and unintended effects, more specifically youth resistance to pro-social campaigns, with an emphasis on health interventions and messaging. Her recent work in these areas has been published in *Health Communication* and the *Journal of Computer-Mediated Communication*.

Celebrity Culture

HOLLY RANDELL-MOON
Charles Sturt University, Australia

A celebrity is an individual who is ascribed or considered to have innate talents and exceptional charisma, which makes them widely known or famous. While scholars who study celebrity have a broad consensus as to how to define and recognize one, their research is predominantly focused on what makes someone a celebrity. They focus on the social, cultural, economic, and media factors that lead to the creation of and possibility for celebrity in contemporary society. This is what can be termed "celebrity culture," a set of social and media structures that accommodate the elevation of certain individuals to celebrity status above others. Celebrities can be found in different societies and historical periods. Often celebrities are distinctive because their achievements are tied to particular forms of social valorization that are recognized in some cultures but not others. Celebrities require recognition and, in contemporary society, media cultures and technologies provide the exposure and management for the creation of celebrity. This entry will provide a definition of celebrity, discuss some of the common explanations for the existence of celebrities, and give a brief outline of the media industrial context to celebrity culture. The entry will conclude by outlining the permeation of celebrity culture into everyday life through the self-promotion and identity management encouraged by late capitalism and social media platforms.

Celebrity culture and its attendant topics related to fame, charisma, and personality management and branding have been studied within a number of disciplines such as sociology, cultural studies, social anthropology, media and communications, history, and marketing. A relatively recent and interdisciplinary field of inquiry known as celebrity studies investigates the social meanings, media practices, and formation of celebrity, understood in its broadest terms. Within this field, different definitions of celebrity are offered based on the specific economic, media, and cultural circumstances which produce celebrities. According to cultural studies scholar Graeme Turner (2014), celebrities are given recognition that seems "disproportionate" to

The International Encyclopedia of Media Literacy. Renee Hobbs and Paul Mihailidis (Editors-in-Chief), Gianna Cappello, Maria Ranieri, and Benjamin Thevenin (Associate Editors).

their talents. They exemplify personality-based traits deemed desirable at a particular cultural moment, they are individuals whose private life is publicized as extraordinary, and while they present a relatable personality to audiences, they also possess an exceptional and out-of-reach set of talents or physical appearance. Celebrities may become famous because of these traits, but they are not dependent on them for sustaining their notoriety. Celebrities' fame often exceeds the initial achievement or event that produced prominence. Conversely, an individual can achieve fame for an event or accomplishment, but that does not make them a celebrity.

Sociologist Chris Rojek categorizes celebrity in three ways: "ascribed," "achieved," or "attributed" (2001). Ascribed celebrity occurs when an individual inherits a position of renown, for instance as a member of the British royal family. Celebrity can be achieved through success as an actor, for instance in the case of model and Bollywood star Aishwarya Rai. Celebrity can also be attributed when the media, through news or entertainment programs, label a personality or individual famous, such as the Australian bushranger Ned Kelly. Celebrities also tend to emerge in specific industries, for instance sport and media entertainment. These defining attributes of celebrity draw attention to the external processes that produce celebrity rather than positioning celebrity as derived from the inherent or innate qualities of a person.

Celebrities are cultivated through practices of recognition, meaning they emerge in industries that are tied to high media visibility. Sociologist Olivier Driessens suggests that mediatization is a precondition for celebrity formation (2012). Mediatization refers to the media's role in shaping social practices and identities for audience consumption (making content or ideas presentable for a media audience). Not all forms of celebrity are media-driven. Literary or academic celebrities, for instance, owe their fame to personality or achievement rather than media visibility. Most celebrities, though, emerge from industries that are highly mediatized. For this reason, celebrity studies scholars view celebrities as a historical product of modernity coinciding with the introduction of media cultures and technologies, such as film and visual print media. In a contemporary cross- or multiplatform media culture, where media personalities can work across different media such as film or print publishing, the ability for celebrities to diversify their talents and move into other fields is another way in which celebrity fame is sustained. Celebrity culture can be understood as an industrial process that cultivates celebrity most prominently in, but not limited to, different media according to the requirements of those industries.

Within sociological modes of inquiry, celebrities are viewed as serving a para-social function. This approach falls broadly within a functionalist perspective that sees society made up of systems, with individuals and institutions serving a function or purpose intended to achieve an overall social equilibrium. Approached in this way, celebrities enable forms of social and community identification that can otherwise not be achieved within an individual's own social sphere. Turner suggests celebrities can fill an "affective deficit in modern life" (2014, p. 6) by providing an emotional or social outlet for bonding with others and a common means of sharing personal experiences and desires. Some scholars view fans' relationship to celebrities as facilitating a productive mode of integration for socially excluded or marginalized individuals into a broader society or community (see Cinque & Redmond, 2016; Shiau, 2014).

A large area of research on celebrity culture and civil society concerns the public mourning of the British royal family member Diana, Princess of Wales. This research argues that Diana was an example of celebrity mobilizing social and communal bonding, which enabled members of the British public to express emotions and feelings about the monarchy, their country, motherhood, and death (Shome, 2014). This intense engagement with celebrity figures has also been viewed by some scholars as producing problematic behavior associated with hysteria and an inability to distinguish fantasy from social reality (see Gamson, 1994, p. 9; McCutcheon, Ashe, Houran, & Maltby, 2003; McCutcheon, Lange, & Houran, 2002). A similar line of inquiry suggests that celebrity culture contributes to the "dumbing down" of media and public discourse because of the apparent superficiality of entertainment and gossip. It is important to note that topics considered worthy of news attention and public debate can be gendered and can reinforce perceptions that celebrity culture is "feminine" and therefore trivial to important social and political concerns (see McRobbie, 2009).

The elevation of certain individuals to celebrity status is not simply a one-sided process orchestrated by media industries. Not all prominent or talented individuals become celebrities. Active engagement with the media content and personality of celebrities by audiences plays a significant role in bringing celebrities into public and civic culture. As with the case of Princess Diana, the transformation of prominent individuals into celebrity figures by fans and audiences is exemplary of broader cultural, political, and gender ideals about the kind of society we live in. What makes someone a celebrity in a particular historical context reflects the social and cultural values that are publicly affirmed at that time. The study of celebrity culture is insightful precisely because, as Turner notes, an understanding of how a figure becomes famous is "not only a story of the professional cultivation of her persona as a star, but also of the discursive and ideological context within which that persona could develop" (2014, p. 7).

Because celebrity culture is tied to the ways in which audiences publicly identify important social values, when celebrities from marginalized backgrounds become famous they can challenge the parameters of what is socially acceptable or normal in terms of appearance, personal history, and identity. This is often why celebrities who are members of the lesbian, gay, bisexual, and transgender (LGBT) community or people of color can occasion media and political discourse about their ostensibly "harmful" effects on audiences, fans, and the public at large. For instance, the North American singer-songwriter Beyoncé was criticized by media commentators for incorporating elements of the history of Black civil rights and anarchist groups into her music videos and performances. Conversely, she was also celebrated for emphasizing the importance of Black civil rights histories to African American identity. Celebrities, then, can have a socially transformative and political effect on the inclusion of marginalized communities within the representational practices of media and society more broadly. Celebrity culture can also work to reinforce dominant forms of embodiment and identity. A subfield of celebrity studies scholarship examines how the predominance of white celebrities in Western European contexts reinforces the centrality of white people to representation, entertainment, and the media (Osuri, 2008; Randell-Moon, 2017; Redmond, 2007).

Another functionalist view of celebrities is that they enable a secular form of worship that has replaced what was once the social function of religion. Chris Rojek has argued that "religiosity permeates the production, exchange and consumption of celebrity culture" (2012, p. 121) and that the attribution of celebrity is based on religious discourses of personality. This can be evidenced most obviously in the discourse and framing of celebrities as icons, stars, and heavenly figures (see Dyer, 2007a). He continues, "The modern meaning of the term *celebrity* actually derives from the fall of the gods, and the rise of democratic governments and secular societies" (Rojek, 2001, p. 9). In this reading of the formation of celebrity culture, celebrities owe their cult of personality and brand management to earlier royal court society rituals where there was an emphasis on publicity and presentation as a means of securing power. Modern forms of celebrity have also been viewed as displacing the symbolic and civic role of monarchy and royal families as part of the secularization of Western European countries where religious sources of authority are viewed as declining.

Finally, there is a spatial dimension to celebrity culture in terms of particular countries or places being connected to the realization and production of celebrity. Being placed in a location with high prominence and mediatization, such as Paris or Tokyo, makes the elevation of talented or conspicuous individuals more readily achievable. Space and the management of bodily boundaries also reinforce a social hierarchy between ordinary and extraordinary people within celebrity culture. The ability of the former to touch or speak with the latter is carefully managed by celebrity handlers. Being touched by celebrities is often discursively likened to a form of contact with religious saints or being blessed. Celebrity culture is implicated in the circulation and formation of ideas and norms about personal space, proximity, emotion, sense, and touch (see Redmond, 2014, 2016).

Through these different definitions of and explanations for the existence of celebrities, celebrity studies scholarship argues that celebrity is not self-generated nor is it "a property of specific individuals" (Turner, 2014, p. 8). The view of celebrity as self-generated has several ideological effects with respect to "consumer capitalism, democracy and individualism" (p. 27). Celebrity culture circulates values and ideas regarding the importance of a capitalist system and individualism. These ideas emphasize the moral and social worth of individuals even as celebrity positions these figures within a social hierarchy. This focus on individualism maintains the cultural and political belief in the democratic possibility for individual success. Thus the ideological effect of believing that celebrities have "earned" their success makes it seem as though fans and audiences elect and reward celebrities for their innate personality. A reading of celebrity culture as reinforcing hegemony, the manufacturing of consent for hierarchies, explores how the popularity and engagement with celebrities and celebrity culture works to encourage audiences and fans to consent to the unequal construction of fame and its attendant benefits as socially desirable (see Alberoni, 2007).

The branding and presentation of celebrities as innately famous and charismatic reaffirms the ideologies of capitalism and its attendant inequalities in the distribution of success and wealth. The ideology of individualism is crucial to smoothing over and explaining these inequalities within a democratic culture as the result of individual achievement (see Marshall, 1997). The construction and management of fame is enabled through media processes of individualizing celebrity figures. Film scholar Richard Dyer's research on celebrity explains how stars were created through personas, or personality types, that actors would embody and perform under the Classic Hollywood Studio system during the early to middle part of the 20th century (2007b). Personality management within this system was tightly controlled. The star could not do anything publicly to disrupt their image, as they would then compromise their fame and economic position within the studio and agency they were signed to. Cultivating a particular look was also integral to a star's persona. Dyer argues that stars and celebrities can be read as cultural texts, embodying semiotic signs that audiences are encouraged to decode through intertextual association with other media-created characters and genres of representation. Sociologist Joshua Gamson also suggests that the semiotic currency of stars is based on the face and its distribution through media content (1994). The focus on stars' faces, as embodying a unique and distinctive look, is premised on distancing these figures from the ordinary person in the audience.

The Hollywood system of star-making had an undesired effect which was that personas and publicity centered on an individual style (however generic and recycled this was) established an actor's fame independent of the films they starred in. For instance, as North American Hollywood actor Marilyn Monroe became popular regardless of the films she starred in, she could begin to command more autonomy over her working conditions. What this example illustrates is that celebrities can establish relationships with fans and the public without needing to star in films or be under contract to studios. Once they attain fame, this gives celebrities greater economic and industrial power. Referred to as "star power," this describes a star's ability to make media content commercially successful through name-association. Audiences will then consume media content featuring this star on the basis that the star provides a guarantee of quality entertainment. Fans and audiences are key to this process, since their engagement with stars and consumption of their media can influence the industrial practices of film production and marketing. The ideology of individualism, and individual success, underpins both the creation of celebrities and the mode of engagement with them by audiences. Because the celebrity is positioned as the intermediary between media content and the audience, this can both reinforce and undermine practices of media control and management.

Transformations in media production and information and communication technologies (ICT) have, in turn, changed the industrial and promotional components of celebrity culture. Broadly speaking, media industries previously concerned with managing and creating celebrities focused on cultivating their client's distance from the ordinary (emphasizing how extraordinary they are). Contemporary celebrity industries contend with "ordinary" individuals becoming famous through DIY (do-it-yourself) media platforms such as YouTube and reality television, scripted documentary television shows focused on capturing the "everyday" lives of its stars, or the orchestration of a talent competition. Rojek labels the performers on these shows and platforms "celetoids," drawing attention to the fleeting nature of their fame (2001). An ideological reading of these figures is that they democratize celebrity by making it seem attainable to a broader audience. However, it is important to remember that the representational strategies employed in all media involve the cultivation and management of its subjects for entertainment purposes. As Turner notes, "celebrity still remains a systematically hierarchical and exclusive category, no matter how much it proliferates" (2006, p. 157). He points out that contestants on reality programming already have considerable skills and experience with personality management, performance, and talent agencies before they enter a reality TV contest. Their celebrity is also temporary and they generally do not sustain their fame as compared with celebrities from the acting and sporting professions. If their fame does continue it is because they have successfully transitioned from an "amateur" to "professional" status, thereby reaffirming industrial standards. The notoriety of celetoids does not exemplify celebrity as such but rather the rapid labor turnover required for this type of TV programming and a general tightening of production costs for entertainment in general.

While the boundaries between ordinary and talented amateurs and their professional and elite counterparts still prevail, the contemporary domination of the film industry by North American stars in Hollywood is waning. The production of films in this industry is no longer reliant on star power but on preexisting properties and franchises. For this reason, a successful film and media franchise such as *Harry Potter* may generate more fame and renown for its fictional characters than for the actors who play them. Moreover, the diversification and fragmentation of audiences and media platforms has also transformed the promotional and branding influence of celebrities. Traditional media such as print newspapers or broadcast television attempted to reach the largest heterogeneous audience possible through the same media content. Within this media, the value of a known star or celebrity was tied to their ability to reach this audience. With the proliferation of new media platforms, where audiences can choose what to consume and when, media producers have to try to reach as many niche markets as possible across media.

As a result, the emergence of microcelebrities or DIY stars shifts the promotional flow of media so that influence on style, communication, and branding emerges from outside the dominant spheres of publicity (see Khamis, Ang, & Welling, 2017). For instance, Xiaxue, the pseudonym adopted by Singaporean blogger Wendy Cheng, began self-producing media on YouTube which involved her commenting on clothes and other items she purchased. The popularity of her videos allowed her to integrate sponsored advertising content into her media and transition to producing such content as a full-time profession and source of income. What this example illustrates is how DIY media personalities can parlay their capacity for attention to other media and promotional interests. These microcelebrities have also facilitated the creation of ancillary media industries based on managing Internet and ICT branding.

The phenomenon of microcelebrities is tied to the shifts in communicative practices related to labor and the knowledge economy which require personality management and promotion of the self. The knowledge economy emerges within a postindustrial economy, where services and ideas rather than manufacturing drive growth. Within this economy and the proliferation of media platforms, the attention economy (the capacity to garner attention) becomes the primary source of revenue generated through media content. Such media transformations involve the extension of the promotion and publicity professions into everyday life as ICT users are encouraged to treat themselves and their lives as projects to sell. The role of personality and working on the self are connected to the individualization of work and culture (see Beck, 2004) under late capitalism or neoliberalism where the state withdraws from individual and collective well-being in favor of market forces.

Celebrities are connected to this process of individualization and monetization of the self under a knowledge economy because they popularize individualization and personality management. As noted earlier, scholars have argued that celebrities have always played a role in affirming capitalism and class hierarchies as desirable. Celebrities would not exist without a capitalist economy that relies on forms of persuasion to buy items that are surplus to our needs. Celebrities enhance the economic value of products and brands through social capital, the renown or name-recognition associated with the celebrity. But celebrities can encourage forms of activism or critiques of capitalism through their prominence and media attention. For instance, in Aotearoa New Zealand, film and TV actor Lucy Lawless uses her star power to draw attention to environmental issues. With the social capital gained through personality management and their labor on the self, to enhance their capacity for media attention, celebrities epitomize a consumer and neoliberal economy premised on individualization.

Under late capitalism, the role of celebrity has altered from a professional to a promotional one. Famous actors, for example, may now make more money from endorsements than from the films they star in; in other words, not from the profession from which their fame is derived. Driessens's definition of celebritization (2012) is a useful way of explaining how identity, labor, and the broader public culture under late capitalism parallel processes of celebrity personality management and communication. The practices of working on the self, viewing ourselves as the site of labor or monetization, practicing how we narrate our life biography and experiences, involves a celebritization of culture.

Importantly, this process is not the same thing as celebrification, which is how someone becomes famous. Celebritization explains "how celebrity moulds the cultures we live in" and its effects on "power relations, expectations, identity formation and self-presentation (online as well)" (Driessens, 2012, p. 653). Celebrity culture influences contemporary communicative practices in a range of spaces that are not just confined to celebrity industries. In this economic incitement to adopt the communicative practices of celebritization in order to achieve success, "neoliberal ideologies of market meritocracy … use the rhetoric of equality of opportunity to disguise and sustain massive inequality" (Tyler & Bennett, 2010, p. 379). The flow of celebrity into work, identity, and public culture can be explained by the individualization of economic practices associated with the knowledge economy that stress identity management to create distinction and attention. Related to this economic valorization of the self and its presentability through media is a process identified as the feminization of late capitalism. Scholars have suggested that women are more advantageously positioned to benefit from the identity formation potentials of new media (see Yue, 2012). This is because they have been traditionally assigned to the private and domestic spheres and are socialized into modes of identity that emphasize attention to the self and appearance.

The study of celebrity culture is concerned with the social, economic, and political contexts that create celebrity and make certain kinds of celebrity possible. Celebrities have been studied in a range of disciplines and fields of inquiry where social formation and hierarchy are tied to representational practices. An interdisciplinary field of inquiry known as celebrity studies brings these disciplines and scholarship together. The many different definitions and explanations for celebrity cohere around the central insight that celebrities are manufactured through representational and media practices rather than being elevated to a high economic and social status by innate personal qualities. There are particular ideological effects that result from a democratic contradiction that emphasizes equality of opportunity while also valorizing exceptional and elite figures. The role of celebrities in reaffirming capitalism as well as social norms of identity, particularly in relation to gender, sexuality, and race, reveals how celebrities make our culture and society intelligible in certain ways. Celebrity culture has undergone transformations that coincide with the transition from traditional to niche and multiplatform media. In contemporary celebrity industries, there is an emphasis less on known personalities and instead more on the cultivation of influence through the adoption of personality management and branding. While star power may be in decline in terms of its media and economic utility, celebrity culture nevertheless has an ongoing influence on modes of communicating work, identity, and social relationships in contemporary media cultures.

SEE ALSO: Active Audiences; Learning about Materialism and Consumer Culture; Social Semiotics; Understanding Media Literacy and DIY Creativity in Youth Digital Productions

References

Alberoni, F. (2007). The powerless "elite": Theory and sociological research on the phenomenon of the stars. In S. Redmond & S. Holmes (Eds.), *Stardom and celebrity: A reader* (pp. 65–77). London, England: SAGE.

Beck, U. (2004). *Risk society: Towards a new modernity*. London, England: SAGE.

Cinque, T., & Redmond, S. (2016). Lazarus rises: Storying the self in the migrant fandom of David Bowie. *iaspm@journal, 6*(1), 7–24. doi: 10.5429/2079-3871(2016)v6i1.2en

Driessens, O. (2012). The celebritization of society and culture: Understanding the structural dynamics of celebrity culture. *International Journal of Cultural Studies, 16*(6), 641–657. doi: 10.1177/1367877912459140

Dyer, R. (2007a). Heavenly bodies. In S. Redmond & S. Holmes (Eds.), *Stardom and celebrity: A reader* (pp. 85–89). London, England: SAGE.

Dyer, R. (2007b). Stars. In S. Redmond & S. Holmes (Eds.), *Stardom and celebrity: A reader* (pp. 78–83). London: SAGE.

Gamson, J. (1994). *Claims to fame: Celebrity in contemporary America*. Berkeley: University of California Press.

Khamis, S., Ang, L., & Welling, R. (2017). Self-branding, "micro-celebrity" and the rise of social media influencers. *Celebrity Studies, 8*(2), 191–208. doi: 10.1080/19392397.2016.1218292

Marshall, P.D. (1997). *Celebrity and power: Fame in contemporary culture*. Minneapolis: University of Minnesota Press.

McCutcheon, L.E., Ashe, D.D., Houran, J., & Maltby, J. (2003). A cognitive profile of individuals who tend to worship celebrities. *The Journal of Psychology Interdisciplinary and Applied, 137*(4), 309–322. doi: 10.1080/00223980309600616
McCutcheon, L.E., Lange, R., & Houran, J. (2002). Conceptualization and measurement of celebrity worship. *British Journal of Psychology, 93*(1), 67–87. doi: 10.1348/000712602162454
McRobbie, A. (2009). *The aftermath of feminism: Gender, culture, and social change*. London, England: SAGE.
Osuri, G. (2008). Ash-coloured whiteness: The transfiguration of Aishwarya Rai. *South Asian Popular Culture, 6*(2), 109–123. doi: 10.1080/14746680802365212
Randell-Moon, H. (2017). Thieves like us: The British monarchy, celebrity and settler colonialism. *Celebrity Studies, 8*(3), 393–408. doi: 10.1080/19392397.2017.1299019
Redmond, S. (2007). The whiteness of stars. In S. Redmond & S. Holmes (Eds.), *Stardom and celebrity: A reader* (pp. 263–274). London, England: SAGE.
Redmond, S. (2014). *Celebrity and the media*. Basingstoke, England: Palgrave Macmillan.
Redmond, S. (2016). Sensing celebrities. In P.D. Marshall & S. Redmond (Eds.), *A companion to celebrity* (pp. 385–400). Oxford, England: Wiley Blackwell.
Rojek, C. (2001). *Celebrity*. London, England: Reaktion.
Rojek, C. (2012). *Fame attack: The inflation of celebrity and its consequences*. London, England: Bloomsbury.
Shiau, H.-C. (2014). The use of celebrity scandals and sensational news for identity negotiations: Analyzing gossip among the queers within Taiwanese families. *Chinese Journal of Communication, 7*(2), 230–250. doi: 10.1080/17544750.2014.905866
Shome, R. (2014). *Diana and beyond: White femininity, national identity, and contemporary media culture*. Urbana: University of Illinois Press.
Turner, G. (2006). The mass production of celebrity: "Celetoids," reality TV and the "demotic turn." *International Journal of Cultural Studies, 9*(2), 153–165. doi: 10.1177/1367877906064028
Turner, G. (2014). *Understanding celebrity* (2nd ed.). London, England: SAGE.
Tyler, I., & Bennett, B. (2010). "Celebrity chav": Fame, femininity and social class. *European Journal of Cultural Studies, 13*(3), 375–393. doi: 10.1177/1367549410363203
Yue, A. (2012). Female individualization and illiberal pragmatics: Blogging and new life politics in Singapore. In Y. Kim (Ed.), *Women and the media in Asia: The precarious self* (pp. 237–254). Basingstoke, England: Palgrave Macmillan.

Further reading

Celebrity studies (2010–). Retrieved from https://www.tandfonline.com/loi/rcel20
Turner, G. (2014). *Understanding celebrity* (2nd ed.). London, England: SAGE.

Holly Randell-Moon is a senior lecturer in the School of Indigenous Australian Studies, Charles Sturt University, Australia. She has published widely on media representations of race, religion, and Indigeneity in the journals *Social Semiotics*, *Critical Race and Whiteness Studies*, *borderlands*, and *Celebrity Studies*. Her publications on popular culture, biopower, and gender and sexuality have appeared in the edited book collection *Television Aesthetics and Style* (2013) as well as the journals *Feminist Media Studies* and *Refractory*. Along with Ryan Tippet, she is the editor of *Security, Race, Biopower: Essays on Technology and Corporeality* (2016).

Children and Media as a Discipline

DAFNA LEMISH
Rutgers University, USA

The field of children and media can be understood to be a microcosm of the media studies discipline as a whole. It encompasses all the major domains of inquiry that media researchers explore. The first key area is concerned with the *institutions and organizations* that create media contents, their history and structures, the way they are managed, supervised, and controlled. This area also requires investigating the political economy that guides the functioning of the institutions and organizations in question and the cultural contexts in which they are grounded. The second major area of inquiry relates to the *content* of the various media channels. It explores the messages they convey, the ideologies they perpetuate, the power relationships in society they unveil, and the dynamics they foster of mirroring as well as cultivating worldviews. The third area focuses on the nature of the *technologies*, independently or in interaction with the content they convey. This area studies how the ever changing media technologies shape everyday lives, human relationships, cognitive processes, family structures, schooling, work, and leisure. Finally, there is the major area of study that focuses on *audiences*. This area studies what, when, where, how, and why children use media, the various roles that media play in their everyday lives, the meaning-making processes in which they engage, and their individual and collective tastes and pleasures.

It is in the audience dimension that we find the major difference between the subdiscipline of children, adolescents, and media and other areas of media studies. What is more, this dimension determines the unique prism of inquiry that characterizes the field. Indeed, the same questions are addressed, but with specific consideration of the unique nature of the young audience segment. An underlying assumption of audience-oriented studies is that, given their lack of cognitive, social, emotional, and physical maturity, children and youths are more vulnerable to media effects. They have limited experience in general, and with media more specifically. Thus they are prone to being less aware of the risks and potential harms of some forms of media engagement. They need caring, sometimes protective, and responsible adults to socialize them so that they mature into productive, healthy, and happy adults. For this reason, the adults' responsibility for their young carries over to media use, just as it does to schooling, health, nutrition, and all aspects of children's well-being.

As in media studies in general, the exponential growth in the field of media and children since the mid-20th century is due to a large degree to the infiltration of television and to the growing impact of mediatization. For example, *institutional* studies have been concerned with media policies that seek to protect children from harms of violence and sex, from exploitation through advertising for financial gain, or from exposure to age-inappropriate websites. *Content-focused* studies have examined gender and racial stereotypes in children's media, instructional and educational content, content modeling, and the promotion of antisocial and prosocial behaviors. The focus on *technology* led researchers to ask, for example, about the effects of television on the attention span and on the ability to delay gratifications; about relationships between the amount of time spent in front of screens and childhood obesity; or about how having a computer and a mobile phone in the bedroom can disrupt sleep patterns. When it comes to children as an *audience*, studies explored usage habits as children grow up; how development is related to the roles media have in their private, familial, and social lives; and media contributions to identity construction (Lemish, 2015).

In addition, children and media as a discipline is a microcosm of the whole field, because it has employed the entire toolbox of scholarly and methodological approaches adopted from the social sciences, humanities, and health professions. These include a variety of quantitative methods such as surveys, experimental designs, content analyses, and the use and analysis of big data sets, as well as qualitative and critical methods such as participant observation, interviews, and semiotic analyses of verbal, audio, and visual texts. This noted, the unique characteristics of young audiences require an adaptation of methods to their abilities and skills. This is particularly true for younger audiences, whose linguistic outputs do not necessarily represent the children's inner world fully or accurately. Young children may have difficulties expressing themselves verbally in ways that are accessible to adults, but they may be able to convey meanings through their artwork, free play, or choice of toys and bedroom decorations (Lemish, 2018).

Mapping the field

As a highly interdisciplinary area of study, the field of media and children brings together scholarship from media studies, developmental psychology, cultural studies, education, health, sociology of childhood, gender studies, technology, arts, policy, globalization, and law—among other disciplines. Hence the challenge of mapping the main areas of investigation has produced a wide range of options (e.g., Lemish, 2015; Strasburger, Wilson, & Jordan, 2014; Valkenburg & Piotrowski, 2017). One widely applied approach organizes the field through *life-cycle developmental stages*, each stage being characterized by unique features and challenges. For example, studies of babies and toddlers focus on media, cognitive development, and language acquisition. Research interests shift to the more general learning of attitudes and behaviors and to the ability to process narratives, along with school preparedness in the case of preschool and kindergarten children. Competition between school and leisure culture, the learning of antisocial behaviors, and gradual risk-taking with media are phenomena investigated in relation to children's primary school years. Studies of media and adolescents focus on identity development, the roles of media in sexual activities and attitudes and in substance abuse, and, more recently, the roles of social media in networking and social life.

An alternative approach maps the field via *key topics of interest* to scholars and persons involved in public policy. For example, ongoing studies of media involvement in children's exposure to violence and sex have created an extensive body of research in which effects of media on violent behaviors and attitudes, desensitization to human suffering, and fearful and anxious reactions are studied. Similarly, researchers explore effects of media on early sexual experiences, promiscuity, attitudes towards sexuality, and risky sexual behaviors. Consumer culture and advertising, too, are central topics of inquiry; included here are questions about understanding the persuasive intent of advertising, about vulnerability to manipulative strategies, and about the contribution of commercialism to personal dissatisfaction, lower self-image, eating disorders, and family conflict. Another example is scholarship that investigates the roles of media in formal and informal learning, for example in learning social perceptions of self and others and in the development of stereotypes, worldviews, political socialization, and civic participation.

Integrated mapping employs four main *ecologies* of children's lives, starting from *home and family contexts* and encompassing family communication patterns and families' mediation strategies of media use and content. The *school context* is the second field; here there is particular focus on how media are integrated into or compete with educational goals. Third comes *peer culture* and the centrality of various media forms and contents as children's interests, needs, and abilities change. Finally, there is *society at large*—the society in which children grow up, which contains public discourse around media, the activities of policymakers and advocacy groups, globalization and localization forces, and the political economy of media in general.

Finally, a *media-centered* approach studies the unique characteristics of each medium and the opportunities and challenges they bring to the lives of children and youth. Such is, for example, the growing interest in children's activism and creativity on the web, the roles of social networks in children's identity construction and social lives, the centrality of audio media in mood management, the role of the mobile phone for immigrant youths who want to keep in touch with their homeland in terms of family, friends, language, and culture, or the bonding potential, for the family, of a TV set located in the center of the home.

Notably, these four approaches are far from being mutually exclusive, and most overviews "mix and match" them, devoting chapters to many of these topics in each collection. In addition, most of these discussions lead to questions about responsibility and include calls for interventions to minimize negative media effects and to optimize the positive potential of media.

Furthermore, given these shared characteristics, it is no wonder that the field of children and media grew, to a large extent, hand in hand with the interest in *media literacy*. For example, the "effects" tradition was dominant throughout most of the early decades of media research and continues to be so, particularly in North American scholarship. Effects studies focus on the vulnerability of children—mostly to the negative effects of media on their behaviors, attitudes, health, and safety. Here we see a pattern in which public expressions of "moral panic" occur (Drotner, 1992) with the introduction of each new medium into young people's lives; these are followed by public and political pressure around concerns for children's well-being, which leads to an infusion of funds into research (Wartella & Reeves, 1985). For example, grant benefactors currently draw proposals for investigating various aspects of the roles of digital media in children's lives. This interest is also visible in the headlines and news coverage of health-related negative media effects that attract public attention (Bickham, Kavanaugh, & Rich, 2016).

Findings from studies of media and young people are employed in public and political advocacy efforts. Their discourse targets four stakeholders that have the potential to make a difference in children's lives: family, media industry, policymakers, and educational systems. The family, and particularly parents, are stakeholders, owing to their function as primary socializers of children's media use and as role models and mediators of media use at home. The media industry produces media content and makes it available to children. The public expectation is that it acts responsibly regarding the content it produces and makes accessible to children. Policymakers are stakeholders, owing to their role of regulating media industries and of providing safeguards when the voluntary action expected of these industries is insufficient. Finally, educational systems were originally expected to embrace media literacy in an effort to "inoculate" children against the negative effects of media use, to make them develop "resistance" to tempting messages, to refine their tastes and media choices, and to help them become "critical media users." While some public groups' advocacy efforts assign most of the responsibility to one or another of these stakeholders, scholars among others often argue for a combination of approaches. Recent such discussions have emphasized bridge building and collaboration among various stakeholders concerned with the well-being of children and youth as main strategies in advancing significant social change (Patriarche et al., 2014). More specifically, media literacy is often acclaimed by scholars as well as by advocacy groups as one of the main strategies that could be employed in confronting challenges posed by the media to young people today and as one of the pillars of the kind of education that is required for citizenship in our time.

While there would seem to be a natural bond between study of children and media and advocacy for media literacy, historically these two endeavors remain largely separate and, indeed, often treat each other's scholarly territory with suspicion and critique, as a result of divergence of interests.

On the one hand, educators and citizen advocates are concerned with defining the learning goals and objectives of various media literacy interventions, developing appropriate teacher training, and applying appropriate pedagogical and evaluation methods in advancing a successful implementation of this or that media literacy program.

On the other hand, social scientists studying children and media are often most interested in testing the effectiveness of various media literacy curricula. Commonly such studies are conducted through experimental designs. Here children are "pretested," that is, tested before exposure to an educational intervention, and then "posttested," that is, tested again after exposure, in order for the researcher to examine the degree of effectiveness of that particular media literacy intervention. An alternative—the cultural and critical studies approach to media and children—focuses on major cultural and ideological forces that impact children's media use, as well as on ways to empower children and young people to resist them.

In addition, many researchers have chosen to dissociate themselves from citizen advocacy groups that promote media literacy. Their main reason for taking this stance is related to an *objectivist* approach to scholarship as a result of which they do not want to be associated with the advocates' drive to attain visibility in public discourse, with media appearances for the sake of raising awareness, and with fundraising—all perceived by scholars as nonscientific and thus less credible. Historically, then, there have been limited attempts to foster intergroup understanding between media studies and education scholars, or assessments of their mutual value and contributions. Emerging efforts by engaged scholars worldwide may well succeed in developing an integrated paradigm that will facilitate dialogue across interests, stakeholders, endeavors, and ecological contexts.

School and leisure learning

At the core of these complex interrelationships are studies of children's and youths' experiences and learning in schools versus leisure activities. In general, it is important to understand the precise differences, interests, and complicated relationships between formal school institutions and the learning that takes place through leisure use of media. More specifically, these relationships are key to understanding media literacy initiatives.

On the one hand, schools have been established with specific educational goals in mind. They have structures in place and hierarchies of authority and curricula that require following a largely linear progression from one level to another. They expect from pupils an investment of hard work sustained over long periods of time; and they operate on a system of rewards, punishments, and expectations of self-discipline. Schools are also heavily reliant on verbal language skills and traditional literacies (reading, writing, arithmetic).

Leisure media use, on the other hand, is often viewed as an alternative, competitive "school" in terms of its effectiveness for users' learning of information, behaviors, attitudes, values, aspirations, stereotypes. It offers a very different type of learning environment. Its goals are mainly to entertain and please, it is nonhierarchical, has nonlinear characteristics, and is mostly voluntary. Furthermore, it requires little investment of hard work and little delay of gratification, and it is dominated by audiovisual language.

To a large extent, the advent of digital media challenges the school-based dependency on "unity of place and time"—the fact that all students of a certain grade meet in a specific location, at a set hour, for a specific lesson. Instead, students can participate from all over the world, at any time, networking with whoever may be available. While many exceptions to this schematic description exist, nevertheless the learning environments of school and media seem quite distinct, with perceived advantages, from the perspective of the learner, for leisure forms of "schooling."

In terms of their mutual views and interrelationships, schools for the most part ignore, dismiss, or disregard leisure media culture through an inclusive overgeneralization according to which this is simply popular, low-level entertainment. As a result, there is limited discussion (if any at all) of leisure culture in school curricula globally. This approach has placed significant obstacles on any possible collaboration between the study of children and media, on the one hand, and, on the other, media literacy scholarly, advocacy, and intervention efforts.

Findings from studies of the negative effects of leisure media use on school performance contributed directly to this situation. Several hypotheses have been offered about the presumed negative relationship between media consumption and school performance. While these hypotheses were developed in relation to television viewing (Neuman, 1991), they can be applied to digital media as well. One hypothesis argues that media use displaces school-related activities (e.g., reading, completing homework, getting enough sleep) and thus results in unsatisfactory performance in school. A second hypothesis argues that the cognitive processes required for hours of screen culture are fundamentally different from those developed by verbal school-based and print-based learning. Therefore leisure media use by children and youths comes at the expense of developing appropriate information-processing skills required for success in school. A third hypothesis posits that heavy media use affects children's expectations of constant stimulation and entertaining education, reduces their tolerance for delay of gratification, affects their attention span, and thus sets them on a path of boredom, impatience, and intolerance of schooling. Finally, there is an oppositional hypothesis according to which media exposure can enrich children's lives and stimulate interest in discipline-based as well as in new areas of study.

Understanding children

Expansion of the study of children and media that led to the development of alternative approaches to the dominant "effects" scholarly and methodological tradition was inspired, among other reasons, by the recognition that childhood is socially constructed and its meaning is grounded in social–cultural–political contexts. This understanding has contributed in significant ways to the study of the role media have in children's lives and the way they impact their developing identities, aspirations, and understanding of themselves and of the world around them. For example, nuanced approaches to the concept of childhood led to the recognition that age is an insufficient marker of distinction in and of itself. Five-year-old children can have very different experiences if they are a Chinese immigrant child living in Los Angeles, a street child in Rio de Janeiro, or a member of a middle-class family living in Amsterdam. Similarly, the experiences of a 14-year-old girl can differ significantly if she is married and living in Bangladesh, living with her family in a suburb in Madrid, or working in the Las Vegas sex industry.

A second important distinction between approaches is that the *developmental* approach views the child as a person in the process of "becoming" an adult, while the cultural studies approach accepts the child as "being" in his/her own right.

More specifically, the "becoming" approach assumes that children are incomplete and deficient. They lack the abilities, skills, experiences, and knowledge possessed by adults. As essentially a psychological view, this approach has well-delineated stages by which children move from complete deficiency and vulnerability to successful adulthood, in areas such as cognitive, moral, and emotional development. Accordingly, media-related research compares children to the "ideal" or mature adult. This can be illustrated by prototypical research questions, such as the following: Are children able to distinguish between reality and fantasy? Are they more likely to be manipulated by advertising directed to create desire for something they may not need, or that is even harmful to them? Are they naïve, too trusting, and thus vulnerable to predators lurking on the web? Various research methods, such as experimental designs, enabled researchers to determine, for example, that children acquire the ability to distinguish between media fantasy and reality, to understand the internal motivations of media characters, and to be less dependent on audiovisual cues in reacting fearfully to scary content somewhere around the age of seven to eight.

The "being" approach focuses on the here and now of the child. While it recognizes that children are different from adults, it assumes childhood to be a form of "being" in its own right. In consequence, researchers and educators encourage children to express themselves authentically and to be listened to respectfully. Thus a preschooler's deep sadness over Bambi's loss of his mother is understood to be the expression of a healthy, natural attachment reaction of a young child, rather than an inability to understand that it is "only a movie." A teenager's constant posting on her Facebook page is not judged to be wasteful nonsense of a narcissistic adolescent who does not appreciate the values of time and productivity, but experimentation with identity building and social location within a network.

The "being" approach's interest in children's voice received two significant and related boosts, which enrich our understanding of media and children—first, through the advent of the interactive abilities of digital media and the opportunities they provide for children's participation and creativity; and, second, through globalization and global access. Thus we have a richer understanding of adolescent media use through studies of youth-made media around the world (Fisherkeller, 2011) and of various forms of the participatory cultures of youths (Jenkins, Shersthova, Gamber-Thompson, Kligler-Vilenchik, & Zimmerman, 2016; Mazzarella, 2010). These studies explored how young people use the media at their disposal to explore their many identities (e.g., gender, racial, class, religious), to test boundaries, to share their interests, and to connect and stay connected to others. Whether texting on their mobile devices, engaging in various forms of social networking, uploading YouTube videos, or organizing petitions, they experiment with creativity, relationship building, and self-exploration. Some of these activities may be empowering and facilitate very positive experiences, such as finding an online support group of gay youths or sharing photos of a sustainability workshop with a wider network. In contrast, other uses can be harmful and even devastating, for example engagement in bullying peers or in sexting (i.e., the distribution of sexual images of self and/or friends), or participation in "pro-ana" (pro-anorexia) groups.

The global perspective has also played an important role in rethinking the basic assumptions that motivate scholarship in the field through the discourse of children's rights, as defined originally in the UN Convention on the Rights of the Child (UN, 1989), which is enjoying a revival of interest following the 25th anniversary events. The Convention is specifically concerned with the role communication plays in improving the lives of children worldwide: the rights to be heard and to be taken seriously, to free speech and to information, to maintain privacy, to develop cultural identity, and to be proud of one's heritage and beliefs. Considering these rights in the digital age raises a host of issues for scholars to study: complexities related to the diversity of the contexts in which children are raised; the relationships between rights and the responsibilities that come with them; and how communication rights themselves, such as the right to privacy, are being reconfigured (Livingstone, 2016).

It is not surprising, then, that media literacy definitions and discussions surrounding its mission have also been expanded to recognize the importance of participation in the mediated world beyond focus on the abilities to access, analyze, evaluate, and communicate messages. For example, verbal capability to "communicate messages" has grown to include all forms of media participation, educational curricula recognizing the need to devote significantly more efforts to the production side of media education. Similarly, the tilting of research interests toward the study of digital media and the declining focus on television as the central medium in children's lives are also noticeable in debates about digital literacy as distinct from, complementary with, or even redundant in relation to media literacy (Buckingham, 2009; Livingstone, 2008).

Overall, regardless of the approach taken, scholars of media and children are largely in agreement that media can be both positive and negative forces in children's lives. Books, movies, radio, television, the Internet, mobile phones, game consoles are not inherently good or bad for children but rather can be used in positive or negative ways. To a large degree, the impact of media in children's lives is highly dependent on the three Cs (Lemish, 2015): the characteristics of the *child*, the *content* with which the child is engaged, and the *context* within which these activities are grounded. With this in mind, the discipline of children and media has grown to recognize the differential susceptibility of children to media effects and the need for a personalized approach that inquires about individual children's characteristics, circumstances, and relationships with the media (Valkenburg, 2015).

A second area of agreement among scholars is that the field of children and media, as a subdiscipline, continues to grow and change as it evolves with technological developments, the expansion of research methods, and growing interest in a wide range of media and nonmedia disciplines. Its reciprocal relationship with media literacy remains highly desirable, yet complicated and often contested. It is the interdisciplinary nature of this field as well as the focus on the well-being of children that promise to strengthen this relationship as we continue to explore the mediatization of childhood worldwide.

SEE ALSO: Children's Culture; Children's Judgment of Reality and Fantasy; Children's Understanding of Persuasion; EU Kids Online; Girl Culture and Their Literacies; Parental Mediation

References

Bickham, D.S., Kavanaugh, J.R., & Rich, M. (2016). Media effects as health research: How pediatricians have changed the study of media and child development. *Journal of Children and Media, 10*(2), 191–199.

Buckingham, D. (2009). The future of media literacy in the digital age: Some challenges for policy and practice. In P. Verniers (Ed.), *Media literacy in Europe: Controversies, challenges and perspectives* (pp. 13–24). Brussels, Belgium: EuroMeduc. Retrieved from http://www.medienimpulse.at/articles/view/143

Drotner, K. (1992). Modernity and media panics. In M. Skovmand & K.C. Schrøder (Eds.), *Media cultures: Reappraising transnational media* (pp. 42–62). London, England: Routledge.

Fisherkeller, J. (Ed.). (2011). *International perspectives on youth media: Cultures of production and education*. New York, NY: Peter Lang.

Jenkins, H., Shersthova, S., Gamber-Thompson, L., Kligler-Vilenchik, N., & Zimmerman, A.M. (2016). *By any media necessary: The new youth activism*. New York, NY: NYU Press.

Lemish, D. (2015). *Children and media: A global perspective*. Oxford, England: Wiley Blackwell.
Lemish, D. (2018). How do researchers study young people and the media? In S.R. Mazzarella and N. Bryant (Eds.), *Kid stuff: 20 questions about youth and the media* (2nd ed.) (pp. 87–97). New York, NY: Peter Lang.
Livingstone, S. (2008). Engaging with media: A matter of literacy? *Communication, Culture & Critique, 1*(1), 51–62.
Livingstone, S. (2016). Reframing media effects in terms of children's right in the digital age. *Journal of Children and Media, 10*(1), 4–12.
Mazzarella, S. (Ed.). (2010). *Girl Wide Web2.0: Revisiting girls, the Internet, and the negotiation of identity*. New York, NY: Peter Lang.
Neuman, S.B. (1991). *Literacy in the television age*. Norwood, NJ: Ablex.
Patriarche, G., Bilandzic, H., Carpentier, N., Ponte, C., Schrøder, K.C., & Zeller, F. (Eds.). (2014). *Building bridges: Pathways to a greater societal significance for audience research*. Brussels, Belgium: COST Action ISO906.
Strasburger, V., Wilson, B., & Jordan, A. (2014). *Children, adolescents, and the media* (3rd ed.). Thousands Oak, CA: SAGE.
UN. (1989). Convention on the Rights of the Child. Retrieved from http://www.ohchr.org/en/professionalinterest/pages/crc.aspx
Valkenburg, P. (2015). The limited informativeness of meta-analysis of media effects. *Perspectives in Psychological Science, 10*(5), 680–682.
Valkenburg, P.M., & Piotrowski, J.T. (2017). *Plugged in: Psychological perspectives on youth and media*. New Haven, CT: Yale University Press.
Wartella, E., & Reeves, B. (1985). Historical trends in research on children and the media: 1900–1960. *Journal of Communication, 35*(2), 118–133.

Further reading

boyd, d. (2014). *It's complicated: The social lives of networked teens*. New Haven, CT: Yale University Press.
Calvert, S., & Wilson, B. (Eds.). (2008). *The handbook of media and child development*. New York, NY: Blackwell.
Drotner, K., & Livingstone, S. (2008). *The international handbook of children, media, and culture*. Los Angeles, CA: SAGE.
Lemish, D. (Ed.). (2015). *The Routledge international handbook of children, adolescents and media*. New York, NY: Routledge.
Livingstone, S., & Sefton-Green, J. (2016). *The class: Living and learning in the digital age*. New York, NY: NYU Press.
Singer, D.G., & Singer, J.L. (Eds.). (2012). *Handbook of children and media*. Thousand Oaks, CA: SAGE.

Dafna Lemish earned her PhD at Ohio State University in 1982. She is associate dean of programs and professor at the School of Communication and Information at Rutgers University in New Jersey. Before this she was dean of the College of Mass Communication and Media Arts at Southern Illinois University Carbondale. She is the founding editor of the *Journal of Children and Media*. She is author of numerous books and articles on children, media, and gender representations, most recently *Children and Media: A Global Perspective* (2015) and *Screening Gender on Children's Television: The*

Views of Producers around the World (2010), and has edited and coedited *Beyond the Stereotypes?: Images of Boys and Girls, and Their Consequences* (with Maya Götz; 2017), *The Routledge International Handbook on Children, Adolescents and Media* (2013) and *Sexy Girls, Heroes and Funny Losers: Gender Representations in Children's TV around the World* (with Maya Götz; 2012). She is fellow of the International Communication Association (ICA), the first recipient of the Teresa Award for the Advancement of Feminist Scholarship, and the inaugural recipient of the Senior Researcher Award of Children, Adolescents and Media Division of ICA.

Children and News

MEGAN FROMM
Colorado Mesa University, USA

JULIE SMITH
Webster University, USA

Children represent a complicated news audience. On one hand, the vast audiences of young people engaging in news consumption through myriad technologies have the potential to become empowered citizens, who then transition into adulthood as active members of their local and global community. However, different age groups, especially young children, require special care and education as they learn to consume and interact with news. Education, specifically from a media literacy focus, helps parents, educators, and children themselves choose content that is developmentally appropriate while also equipping children and young people with the necessary skills for using news media productively. While anyone under the age of 18 could be considered a child, it is more useful to consider age groups when discussing children and the news. Educators, scholars, and advocacy groups often divide young people into groups representing ages under 3 (sometimes labeled "pre-kindergarten"), ages 4 to 8 (often labeled "children"), ages 9 through 12 (often called "pre-teen"), and ages 13 through 18 (or, "teenagers").

The world of children and news engagement includes a complex web of issues including content concerns, policy and regulations, technological changes, parental involvement and controls, advertising, socialization and habituation effects, and the role of media education in introducing young people to news content and programming.

Habits and practices

Children are more likely to be exposed to news media through radio or television first because these technologies are more accessible thanks to their visual and auditory components. In these cases, news media engagement is more likely to be opportunistic than intentional. Younger children watch what their parents watch until they are allowed to choose for themselves or possess the necessary motor skills to change the channel. Textual sources of news, such as magazines, newspapers, and the Internet, often do not find a place in children's habits until their reading skills are strong enough to facilitate such use. Parents, educators, and health practitioners have long been concerned with what habits are engendered when children engage in heavy media consumption, and news engagement is often a corollary discussion. Because younger children may have difficulty discerning fact from fiction, unsupervised news media consumption may not be in the best interest of the child. Many experts recommend family media plans that take into account both the educational and the entertainment needs of children aged 5 to 18. Co-viewing, or viewing with children, has been shown to be beneficial to a child's news consumption and interpretation, especially for children still developing those cognitive functions that help them distinguish between reality and fantasy. Watching TV news with children can enable a parent to ask questions, provide context, and help the child process what is happening on the screen as it happens. Additionally, both legal and policy restraints exist in many countries to limit children's exposure to potentially harmful content.

Advocacy groups such as Common Sense Media have developed guidelines to help parents establish healthy news habits for children. While the organization does not recommend direct news consumption for children under age 7, guidelines for ages 8 through 12 encourage parents to filter news and keep children from seeing repetitive coverage, which can make events—especially crisis news—seem more prominent, threatening, or damaging than they may actually be. For teenagers, Common Sense Media encourages parents to check in with their young adults to hear about what information they are consuming and to offer ideas or alternative interpretations of news coverage.

Policy, law, and ratings systems

In America, broadcast news programming is not regulated in the same way entertainment TV or cable programming is. As a result, children may be exposed to content on news broadcasts that is inappropriate for their age or cognitive development. Even channels which are regulated, mainly for time and audience considerations, could contain advertisements or sports programming that may not be specifically vetted for a young audience. Television, as a platform for many types of content, has more significant restrictions designed to protect children than other media such as newspapers, magazines, or books. In the United States, the Federal Communications Commission (FCC) regulates how much advertising content can run during children's programming and restricts such content to no more than 10.5 minutes of commercial content per hour of children's programming on weekends. Up to 12 minutes of commercial content per hour of children's programming is allowed during the week. These restrictions only apply to programming produced and broadcast for children aged 12 years or younger. As a result, news programming is not considered children's programming, and advertisements broadcast during a news segment are not subject to these restrictions.

Technology has made it easier for parents to ensure children are only exposed to developmentally appropriate material. The "V-chip" is a generic name for a device that blocks TV programming with certain ratings that are not child-friendly. The device works in the United States, Canada, and Brazil, although other countries have similar mechanisms for helping parents safeguard their children from mature content. V-chips use parental ratings to filter out content, and those ratings take into account whether shows have excessive violence, sex, death, mature themes, and mature language. In the United States, parental ratings indicate whether a program is suitable for the following audiences: all children, older children, older children due to fantasy violence themes, general audience, parental guidance suggested, parents strongly cautioned, or mature audiences only.

While the 1990 Children's Television Act required broadcast carriers to increase the amount of educational programming they offer for children, the act made no recommendations or requirements for whether such programming should contain news content.

Age-specific programming and publications

Over time, many different types of news content and publications have been produced strictly for a young audience. Channel One News offers daily newscasts for grades 3 to 5 and a separate broadcast for grades 6 through 12, both available online. In 2016, Channel One News' daily newscast reached 6 million students in classrooms around the United States. Time for Kids is a weekly classroom news magazine with different editions for kindergarten through fifth grade. Scholastic News Online is aimed at students in kindergarten through sixth grade and provides prepackaged news stories that explore news through science, technology, sports, and art, among other topics. CNN Student News, the network's longest-running show that began in 1989, transitioned in early 2017 to CNN 10, a 10-minute show aimed at a more global audience. Perhaps the most well-known news media initiative aimed at children is the Newspapers in Education program, created by the *New York Times*, which provides resources and funding to schools that use journalism and news as a learning tool. The *New York Times* has its own educational subscription offered to classroom teachers and provides an online component, The Learning Network, with teacher resources. Many states offer their own Newspapers in Education program via sponsorships with local or regional media, and similar programs exist internationally. Programs like these, especially those linked to an educational setting, are often the first introduction of news into a child's daily routine.

Researching children and the news

As exposure to news has become more pervasive thanks to mobile technology and news engagement efforts, children are more likely to come across news content than ever before. While this may pose some distinct benefits to children, researchers also study whether certain news engagement practices might be harmful to children. However, studying how children engage with not only news content but other media in general is an important but potentially hazardous practice. Researchers, in accordance with their own institutions' research guidelines and ethics, must be careful not to put study participants in harm's way. This ethical mandate can make it difficult, for example, to conduct a study on whether watching, hearing, or reading news consistently would make 10- to 12-year-olds more afraid of the world around them. Simply tracking children's media habits is a bit less problematic, and scholars believe children spend more time with media of all types than ever before. Some studies put media use for children between ages 8 and 18 as high as almost 8 hours per day, the same amount of time an adult might spend at work (Strasburger, Wilson, & Jordan, 2014). Understanding how these habits might affect children today and in their future adult lives is of utmost importance. Today's research on children and media, including children and news, tends to focus on issues of exposure, technology used, and the effects of news and media engagement, especially on issues of habituation or socialization.

Exposure and technology

How much time, and through what devices, children spend engaging in media is a concern for parents, educators, and researchers. Psychological, behavioral, physical, and cognitive problems can result from too much media use or from extensive exposure to content that is developmentally inappropriate. Attention and sleep problems linked to media use are among the primary concerns for parents. In the United States, the American Academy of Pediatrics recommends no screen time for children under the age of 2, so most studies on news and media use focus on children aged 3 and older. Studies focusing on news and media exposure often delineate outcomes based on age and platform used, which could include video games, smartphones, movies, laptops, televisions, radios, MP3 players, electronic readers, and educational games.

Audience studies/effects

One of the primary concerns for researchers is how news exposure, particularly to sensitive, violent, or criminal content, affects young viewers and readers. For example, researchers who studied the effects of coverage of the Oklahoma bombing on middle school students living 100 miles from the scene of the bombing found a correlation between traditional media use and posttraumatic stress symptoms (Pfefferbaum et al., 2003). Even youths who do not directly experience disaster or violent crime may exhibit emotional distress that is related to media use and news content detailing the event. Best practices for youth media viewing and reading suggest adult supervision or co-practice, allowing an adult figure to engage in news consumption with youths in order to monitor and support emotional reactions. New media, specifically social media, allow greater access to live and potentially traumatic news media coverage. Because social media and the Internet allow vast, seemingly endless, access to myriad types of coverage, the potential for children and young adults to view age- or developmentally-inappropriate material is higher than for traditional media. As such, experts recommend families monitor children's social media use by using technological controls, limiting time on the Internet, or placing devices for access in communal family areas. The interactive nature of social media, namely, the expected right or obligation to comment, reply, share, or "like," also means adults should recognize that children who encounter news via social media may not be merely passively receiving information. Instead, they may be engaging with others in discussion or even argument. Researchers believe adults should provide support and context for discussion during this process instead of merely censoring or prohibiting engagement with news media in this way.

On the other end of the spectrum, some researchers examine the positive impacts on children and young adults of disaster and trauma news coverage. Such media coverage can be normative, helping children and young adults to understand the processes in place to help others recover, to provide assistance, and to ensure safety for a given community. Displays of empathy are often central to such coverage, which could positively impact children and young adults who consume crisis news media.

News habituation

Researchers have used intergenerational panel testing to examine what factors contributed to news consumption in children and young adults and found that parental news habits have complex and lasting effects on their children's news behaviors. Between the ages of 11 and 18, child and young adult news usage is somewhat rare, the researchers found (York & Scholl, 2015). However, usage was found to be a positive predictor of news engagement 7 years later. In other words, kids who engaged with the news (in the case of this study, print newspapers) at a young age were more likely to do so in later years. The authors additionally found a link between observed parental news behavior and later modeling or adopting of that behavior in young adults. Central to children's media habits were, among others, discussion of the potential for cyberbullying and the development of negative media habits, such as sexting.

Research has shown that the frequency with which parents read or watch news has lasting effects on the news consumption habits of their offspring. If children grow up in a news-consuming household, they are more likely to consume news as they grow older. Likewise, if children grow up in homes without a significant amount of news consumption, they are less likely to care about the news. The role of parents in exposing children to news as well as using it as a basis for family discussion and bonding cannot be understated.

Societal perceptions

While it is not uncommon for children and young adults to consume news, especially through television, less common is a scholarly consensus on the effects of this consumption in regards to how children and young adults come to view the world around them. Representation of race, lifestyle, religion, and other social or demographic facets through news coverage is an important consideration. For example, some researchers have found that African American children find entertainment content on television more representative of their race than news media content. Similarly, how news media cover children and children's issues is a significant point of research. Scholars have found that coverage of children's issues is less prominent for children of color, and what coverage does exist is more likely to cover African American children than other races. White missing children, for example, are more likely to be overrepresented in news coverage than children of color. Beyond issues of race or class, news media can act as a socialization agent for political perceptions, as well. While some scholars view the news media as a secondary socializing mechanism (that is, news media may affect socialization but only in response to or as a successor to initial, existing dispositions), others are finding the news media to be more important in shaping children and young adults' political views than ever before. Researchers have found that young adults' news media use and knowledge of political systems are an important determining factor for political participation.

Participatory culture

While there are areas of concern regarding how young children consume media, especially content that includes violence, preteens and young adults can use news media engagement as means toward more participatory behavior in their civic and social lives. Early engagement with news media can help preteens and teenagers develop a sense of agency within their community as well as a greater connection to global issues. When accompanied by education and guidance on active media literacy engagement, news consumption can also propel young adults to take ownership in the world around them and connect with their peers through digital technology. In this way, child and young adult news engagement is a meaningful precursor to developing civic awareness and global empathy. What's more, teaching children and young adults how to use news and entertainment media in a healthy, productive way can help mitigate the effects of commercial advertising, which often commodifies childhood and makes young people nothing more than a target audience.

Democracy

Whether children develop healthy news habits that follow them into adulthood is a central concern for educators and policymakers. Informed citizenship through news media engagement can mean people are more aware of issues of power, social justice, equality, and economics. This informed citizenship is generally a habit that must be cultivated over time, so early patterns of news engagement can be important cues for how a person will use news media in later stages of life. Educators and scholars have linked news consumption not only to markers of engaged, active citizenship but also to perceptions of journalism as a necessary Fourth Estate. Sustained, early engagement with news could help young adults learn to value journalism as a necessary watchdog for democracy. On the other hand, ingrained distrust for news media could teach young people to dismiss journalism and news as unimportant or even unnecessary. How children and young adults are taught to interact with and seek out news media could be an integral motivator for how young people view news.

Teaching children news

Children who are exposed to media literacy education are more likely to learn how to analyze different news forms and functions. Rather than teaching children what to think about news, media literacy education can provide a lens through which news is viewed and analyzed. For example, children simultaneously exposed to news and media literacy education would learn to consider the source of information, how word choice shapes the message, and how to evaluate the secondary content that accompanies news stories, such as headlines and captions. More specifically, a media literacy approach would encourage children and young adults to compare the same news story from two different sources and look for story placement, photo choices, or use of connotative words. Since many children and young adults receive news from their mobile devices instead of television (primarily still used by the adult generation), young people can learn to evaluate how the form of the news system affects the content. Television, for example, is a visual medium and will concentrate on stories with accompanying video while newspapers are a textual medium, so the use of visual images is less important. Media literacy for children and young adults emphasizes how the form can affect the content of the story or even which stories are covered. A media literacy approach to news consumption would advocate parents or adults asking specific questions during and after consumption. For example, parents could ask children about the purpose of a news segment: What is the message this news segment is designed to send? Who created this message? Who is the intended audience? Where could we go for more information? What information is omitted? Who profits from this message? How might others interpret this story?

Likewise, educating children as they learn to become news consumers should require helping them to understand the commercial aspects of news systems. Most American news outlets are subsidiaries of large, multinational conglomerates. News in America is typically profit-based and privately held, which means sources are more likely to cater to audiences with affirming, entertaining messages in order to increase ratings and profit rather than providing messages the audience might actually need to hear. One challenge scholars have identified in teaching children about media literacy is to not create consumers who are cynics about news, but rather to create critical thinkers who routinely ask questions about the content, source, and validity of news messages. This critical approach would help children and young adults tackle the preponderance of fake news or misleading viral news content that travels so quickly via social media.

Selection and specialization

Innovations in news, both in content and in delivery, have made it easier for young people and children to connect to news, but those same innovations have limitations and drawbacks that could negatively affect how children and young adults come to perceive and engage with news. Most preteens and teenagers receive news content via their social media feeds, including Facebook, Instagram, Twitter, and Tumblr. These feeds are curated and personalized by their friends, computer algorithms, and prior use habits. Called a "filter bubble," what most people—children and young adults included—see on their social media sites is content and advertising specifically and painstakingly specialized to each user. This means that important news or diverse opinions likely never make it through a computer or news feed's algorithmic filter unless the user intentionally goes looking for them. The rise of social media as a news source has led to other outcomes for children and young adults, including the rise of "pulled news" rather than "pushed news" and the effect of "affirmation bubbles." With thousands of news sources, young people can choose the sources they want to engage with based on the subject and perspective of the message rather than having news sources pushed on them. In doing so, media users are more likely to select information that affirms ideas they already believe to be true. This selective exposure can keep children and young adults from ever hearing or reading a point of view different from their own.

In addition, a growing distrust for mainstream media among young people, namely digital natives, means children can be habituated through their media use to disregard reliable news and information simply because it comes from a legacy media or mainstream source. As a result, preteens and young adults especially use alternative forms of news to become more informed on issues. These forms may include late night news shows, Snapchat stories, or even a heavier reliance on citizen journalism and curation sites like Reddit and Storify. These technologies, especially news curation sites, allow children and young adults to contribute to news as it develops by recording their own observations and perceptions. Additionally, the very act of watching satirical news (whether in person or on the other side of a screen) encourages young people to engage by laughing, booing, or otherwise responding to the content presented. The disregard for reliable news and interest in alternative forms can occasionally lead children and young adults to place credibility in media products that do not meet a high news standard: Internet memes, viral photos, and suspicious websites. With few if any gatekeepers, these sources of news and information place the onus upon the receiver to identify noncredible, false, and misleading content. Children and young adults who are not educated about the processes of news and journalism may not recognize how different these alternative content forms truly are, so they may conflate the importance or authority of this content—and even content created by their peers—as on par with neutral, fact-checked journalistic news.

SEE ALSO: Adolescent Literacy in a Digital World; Authorship and Participatory Culture; Children and Media as a Discipline; Children's Judgment of Reality and Fantasy; Children's Understanding of Persuasion; Educational Media, History; Emancipatory Communication; Family Strategies for Managing Media in the Home; Informal Learning on YouTube; Internet Safety; Media Addiction among Children and Youths; Media and Adolescent Identity Development; Media Literacy Foundations; Media Literacy in the Primary Grades; Mobile Media and Parenting; Preschool Children and Media; Representation; Sexting

References

Pfefferbaum, B., Seale, T.W., Brandt, Jr., E.N., Pfefferbaum, R.L., Doughty, D.E., & Rainwater, S.M. (2003). Media exposure in children one hundred miles from a terrorist bombing. *Annals of Clinical Psychology, 15*(1), 1–8.

Strasburger, V., Wilson, B., & Jordan, A. (2014). *Children, adolescents, and the media* (3rd ed.). Thousand Oaks, CA: SAGE.

York, C., & Scholl, R.M. (2015). Youth antecedents to news media consumption. *Journalism & Mass Communication Quarterly, 92*(3), 681–699. doi: 10.1177/1077699015588191

Further reading

Bilton, N. (2010). *I live in the future & here's how it works.* New York, NY: Crown Business.

Bleakley, A., Jordan, A.B., & Hennessy, M. (2013). The relationship between parents' and children's television viewing. *Pediatrics, 132*(2), e364–e371. doi: 10.1542/peds.2012-3415

Chaffee, S.H., McLeod, J.M., & Atkin, C.K. (1971). Parental influences on adolescent media use. *The American Behavioral Scientist, 14*(3), 323–340. doi: 10.1177/000276427101400304

Chen, P., Kunkel, D., Miller, P., & Children Now, O.C. (1999). *The news media's picture of children: A five-year update and a focus on diversity.* Oakland, CA: Children Now. Retrieved from https://files.eric.ed.gov/fulltext/ED436236.pdf

Children Now, O.C. (1998). *A different world: Children's perceptions of race and class in the media. A series of focus groups and a national poll of children.* Oakland, CA: Children Now. Retrieved from https://files.eric.ed.gov/fulltext/ED436234.pdf

Conway, M.M., Wyckoff, M.L., Feldbaum, E., & Ahern, D. (1981). The news media in children's political socialization. *Public Opinion Quarterly, 45*(2), 164–178. doi: 10.1086/268648

Gerbner, G., Gross, L., Morgan, M., Signorielli, N., & Shanahan, J. (2002). Growing up with television: Cultivation processes. In J. Bryant & D. Zillmann (Eds.), *Media effects: Advances in theory and research* (2nd ed., pp. 43–68). Mahwah, NJ: Lawrence Erlbaum.

Houston, J.B., Pfefferbaum, B., & Reyes, G. (2008). Experiencing disasters indirectly: How traditional and new media disaster coverage impacts youth. *Prevention Researcher, 15*(3), 14–17.

Kovach, B., & Rosenstiel, T. (2010). *Blur: How to know what's true in the age of information overload.* New York, NY: Bloomsbury.

Rushkoff, D. (2014). *Present shock: When everything happens now.* New York, NY: Current.

Megan Fromm, PhD, is an assistant professor at Colorado Mesa University. She is also a faculty member for the Salzburg Academy on Media & Global Change. Fromm is coauthor of the textbook *Student Journalism and Media Literacy* (2014). Her work, including book chapters, journal articles, and curriculum, focuses on journalism education, media literacy, and scholastic press freedom.

Julie Smith, MS, is an instructor at Webster University in St. Louis. She is the coauthor, with Art Silverblatt, of *Media Literacy: Keys to Interpreting Media Messages* (2014) and the author of *Master the Media: How Teaching Media Literacy Can Save our Plugged-In World* (2015). She is a board member of the Gateway Media Literacy Partners and on the Leadership Council of the National Association for Media Literacy Education. Julie's writings and presentations focus on media literacy, validating online information, and classroom engagement.

Children's Culture

ASHLEY WOODFALL
Bournemouth University, UK

MARKETA ZEZULKOVA
Charles University, Czech Republic

Culture means many things to many people and similarly children's culture can be, and is, interpreted in multiple ways. In encompassing shared behavior, characteristics, values, interactions, constructs, and understandings culture is such a generic, many-faced, loose, and malleable concept that it could perhaps be seen to be of limited analytical utility. Even though slightly "uncertain" of (the myth of?) culture (Bhabha, 1994), children's culture is mobilized here as the shared values, beliefs, and artifacts of children's lived experience, and recognizes "culture" primarily from the cultural studies perspective as a circuit of social meaning-making and remaking; culture as encoding, store, conduit, transmission, and learning of social practices and beliefs. Culture attaches meaning to our existence, and encompasses "the everyday thought, emotions and actions with which we 'spin' our lives" and can be understood as developing "through interaction and confrontation with the products, media, places, events, excerpts from reality and so on to which people ascribe meaning" (Hengst, 2005, p. 22). It should not be difficult to argue for children as having some measure of agency within the production of their own culture, yet the adult still acts as agent to much children's cultural meaning-making. As this entry illustrates, this meaning-making does not happen in isolation, but in a social, cultural, and historical context. Rather than trying to hem understanding in to something finite and fixed, the text rejects the attempts to universally define and position children's culture. It sketches the parameters of children's culture in the broadest sense: instead of being discipline-, platform-, or practice-bound, it should be seen as interdisciplinary, free, and as part of everyday life.

The amorphousness of culture may actually be its strength. Drawing upon Kidd (2002), the vagueness of culture and its "wide range of designation" (p. 146) might ultimately allow for an understanding of culture, and in turn *children's* culture, that can include the material and immaterial. In this way children's culture can usefully be said to encompass the toys, books, food, clothes, and other physical devices, spaces, and artifacts of a child's lived experience, as well as music, literature, film, television, and other cultural practices, constructs, and content. Castells (1998) described media as "expression of our culture, and our culture works primarily with the materials provided by the media" (p. 365). Media are key "tools" through which people think and speak, and in the creation and maintenance of children's culture, and culture more broadly. Children's culture is media made and maintained, and mediatized.

Children's culture "invented"

Children's culture is difficult to address in isolation from the sociocultural construction of childhood itself. The appearance of what one recognizes as children's culture only comes into being with the "invention" of childhood. Understandings of childhood differ quite substantially across premodern and nonwestern societies, and even within modern western society, which tends toward the gendered heteronormative, there are many childhoods at play, whether due to ethnicity, class, beliefs, age, and so forth. Children operate not only within one cultural space that adults do not, but two, the second of which is the child's gendered one. Here rebellious "backyard and blue" boy culture is held apart from social "bedroom pink" girl culture. The independent boy and the interdependent girl. The "hero" and the "princess." Yet these dualistic (mis)readings ignore the realities of children's lives. Children sit within and across multiple, ever shifting, hybrid cultural spaces, and one cannot address children's culture without acknowledging the complexity of the very idea of what constitutes a child, and, in turn, how children are understood by and positioned within society.

Like children's culture, childhood can be interpreted in many ways. There are telling arguments that childhood was only "invented" within the past few hundred years, or at least childhood as it might be recognized today (Postman, 1982). Ariès (on interpreting historical artwork), for example, suggests that "in medieval society the idea of childhood did not exist" (1962, p. 125), and children were simply seen as small adults; to Ariès it was just in infancy that a young person was seen to be substantially distinct from the rest of society. It was possibly only in the 19th century, when the lives of young people in the West shifted from being centered around work, to being centered around education, that childhood, and a recognizable children's culture, came into focus. With children taken out of one industrial space, as shared with adults, and moved in to another, the school, Postman argues that childhood was ultimately a by-product of the printing press, the spread of literacy, and, in turn, the need for education, and it would be "quite possible for a culture to exist without a social idea of children" (1982, p. xi).

The visions of a childhood "invented" are perhaps flawed (for concentrating on artwork alone in Ariès' case, or being too western facing in the case of Postman), but they do usefully highlight how childhood and children's culture are historically and culturally contextual. Childhood has been understood differently, often distinctly so, across history, and "always relates to a particular cultural setting" (Jenks, 1996, p. 7). The "ideal child" in the West, for example, came to the fore within 18th-century romanticism. The stage was set by Locke's turn against "original sin" and Rousseau's "un-corrupted" child, and childhood as a construct was shepherded in through works by the likes of Blake, whose "vision" of *The Chimney Sweep*, *Little Boy Lost*, and so forth (in the *Songs of Innocence and Experience*, 1789) was of a society inhumane in its treatment of children.

In the 19th century children's "innocence" came further into focus with Dickens' writings, and in the works of Carroll (*Alice in Wonderland*, 1865), Twain (*The Adventures of Tom Sawyer/Huckleberry Finn*, 1876/1884), and later Barrie (*Peter Pan*, 1902) where children's culture was created by those escaping from a troubling present. Children's culture was forged by those who rejected "growing up" and held fast to a nostalgic, ideal, and regressed childhood. From a romantic sensibility the child could serve as a symbol of dissatisfaction with a society in the process of harsh and swift transition: "In a world given increasingly to utilitarian values and the Machine, the child could become the symbol of Imagination and Sensibility, a symbol of Nature set against the forces abroad in society actively de-naturing humanity" (Coveney, 1967, p. 31). In light of this "ideal," childhood became a worthy project, one that set out to preserve and protect children (from time, from adults, from each other) and through a steady march toward universal educationalism as well as state and policy oversight (as later expressed in the United Nations' Convention on the Rights of the Child (UNCRC; United Nations, 1989), childhood eventually became the one recognized today in the West.

Childhoods

When looking at how conceptions of childhood have changed across time and place, one realizes that the child, or childhood, cannot be pinned down to just one definition. This is, however, something adults readily appear to do. The United Nations (UN), under the Convention on the Rights of the Child (United Nations, 1989), has, for example, arbitrarily defined anyone under the age of 18 as a child, as if adulthood can be achieved and childhood left behind with a single tick of the clock. This essentializing act alerts us to the predominantly adult construction of childhood, and the temporality of its status; whilst it also highlights the ways in which, as conceptualizations of childhood shift, the actual lived experience of being a child is also affected.

Although childhood may offer an interpretive frame to the early years of human life, it could also be addressed as "a social artefact, not a biological necessity" (Postman, 1982, p. 143). Unlike infancy, it is historically and socially constructed, yet childhood is neither natural nor universal; there are as many childhoods as lived, and as many childhoods as conceptualized. When addressing the child adults tend to:

> divide up the life course in different ways, and have vastly differing expectations of the abilities of, for example, a six-year-old. Such expectations often contrast with western categorisations of age and highlight that they are not natural or fixed, but are, in fact, a very particular cultural construction. (Lucy, 2005, p. 56)

This ambiguity cautions us against uncritically accepting any vision of a universalized child that "captures" everyone under a certain age, because a universalized childhood would fail to address the ways in which children at different times, within different cultures, develop different competencies. Serpell (1979), for example, found that Zambian children surpassed British children in their abilities in creating 3D wire models, whilst British children surpassed Zambian children when drawing (with there being no noticeable difference between the two groups when modeling with plasticine). Serpell interpreted these results not in light of universal developmental markers, but instead as reflecting the manner whereby the context of a child's everyday lived experience helps shape development. Highlighting the spatiality of childhood and children's cultures reminds us that when one speaks of "western" childhoods one speaks for less than 10% of those under 18 on the planet.

Children, however, wherever they are, increasingly exist within a media culture that can span continents as easily as it can platforms. Children have become aware of and are actively engaging with other children's global lives; often introduced by the hand of media organizations, but also through self-directed cultural appropriation, as with much western children's engagement with Japanese manga and anime. A child that may once have been isolated from other children's cultures is now likely to be aware of and interact with a diversity of childhoods. Paradoxically this interaction may simultaneously be softening the edges of that diversity, with cultural cross-talk and hybridization at play, as well as potential marginalization and overwriting (as recognizable in the dominant cultural interplay between the US and other English language countries). Here it is worth reminding ourselves that children come with many voices, and any understanding of children's culture acts to privilege the experiences and perspectives of certain children over others.

"Incomplete" child and subordinate culture

Discussion has touched on the cultural and temporal specificity of childhood, and that beyond certain biological "markers" childhood may be shaped, and understood, relationally. Yet one must be alert to the many ways in which the concept of childhood, and of children's culture, can be defined and interpreted, and how conflations and reifications across these concepts can feedback in structuring ways. The child, simplistically put, is a physiologically immature human, whilst childhood denotes the "general state of being a child" that operates in binary with adulthood (Gittins, 2009, p. 37). We share the experience of having been a child, and thus claim some knowledge of what childhood is, or *was*, and perhaps we then also share an understanding that as a "totalizing concept" (Jenks, 1996, p. 6) a child is unlikely to be able to step out of it to any great extent. The constructed delineation (particularly when one notes the contemporary structural requirement for schooling, for example) is not easily challenged, even if actual boundaries as lived may be ambiguous.

Childhood and children's culture is something we "grow out of" (Jenks, 1996); with acting like a child often recognized in disparaging ways. This dismissiveness or "disregard" positions childhood as little more than a time of physical growth and socialization can be said to operate in light of an adult "dominant culture." Indeed Durkheim saw children as separate and incomplete, and childhood as a time where "the individual, in both the physical and moral sense, does not yet exist" (1979, p. 150). In this scenario the child is "not a complete work or finished product—but *a becoming*, an incipient being, a person in the process of formation" (italics in original). If recognized in this way, it is no wonder that childhood brings with it connotations of "dependency, powerlessness and inferiority" (Gittins, 2009, p. 37) and that children's culture occupies a position that is subordinate and marginalized.

Childhood may have been invented by adults to help them make sense of their world, yet children are trapped within the consequences. As a malleable concept childhood has been constructed through separation and othering from adulthood, even if paradoxically some of the traits of adulthood only come in to focus with that construct. This leaves child and adult, childhood and adulthood, children's culture and adult culture, separate yet interdependent. The ways in which the adult–child binary polarizes cultural practices (like play or work) must be viewed critically, as should the psychological costs to children of living within a sentimentalized, prolonged, and education-led construct that is intimately woven into the fabric of consumer society.

Children's *own* culture?

Children's culture can be seen as that produced *for* children and that produced *by* children, with culture produced for children making up the structuring mass, whilst children's "own" culture is more marginal, appropriative, transgressive, and ephemeral. Children's culture is predominately as much something done to children, as it is something of itself. It is a positioning, ideological, and comes loaded with purpose; even nursery rhymes (as recorded and disseminated by adults) deliver cultural messages.

Children are of course creative meaning-makers, often on their own terms, but rather than acting to create afresh, tabula rasa if you will, a child's cultural palette is handed to them; "what might be taken for children's culture has always been primarily a matter of culture produced for and urged upon children" (Kline, 1998, p. 5). Children are predominantly acting within a cultural play space made for them, participating "in cultural routines in which information is first mediated by adults" (Corsaro, 2015, p. 148), and even a child's humor and physical play are shaped from a repertoire offered by others (Kline, 1998). Significantly, this children's culture shaped by adults is widely addressed and understood from a rarely questioned "adultism" (Speier, 1976), leaving children short of agency in shaping *their* culture, and with even less agency in defining and critiquing it.

Children's culture is of course not just a product of adult culture, children actively create meaning within their lived experience, but this is predominately through appropriation of adult culture. Corsaro (2015), with a particular interest in children's peer cultures, illustrates this with the example of children bringing small (adult produced) toys into the classroom, even though the school has explicitly banned them, with this collective practice subverting the adult order and reinforcing peer culture. The toys and classroom are part of the structuring adult construct; the play and subversion are what children do with it. Similarly in her discussion on the way children can subvert adult ordained or approved food intake through diet "dis-ordering," James suggests that "children create for themselves considerable room for movement within the limits imposed on them by adult society" (2001, p. 74), and that aspects of children's culture can flourish largely unnoticed and beyond the control of adults.

Children's *own* culture is predominantly an act of appropriation and reordering, and occasionally direct transgression, rejection, and rebellion against adultism. Children are well versed in actively claiming sometimes limited opportunities for agency as they coproduce children's culture through a series of negotiations with adults, and their peers. They inhabit multiple overlapping shared geographies, in different ways, with their lived experience spanning domestic and school culture, as well as other spaces of childhood. These spaces can operate both under the oversight of adults, and outside of that oversight, with these "adult free" cultural spaces, some of them heterotopic, being a cause of anxiety to adults. Children's culture can be seen to be "predicated on middle-class ideals of child rearing; ideals that stressed the need to maintain power hierarchies between generations and to keep children innocent of adult secrets" (Spigel, 1998, p. 111). Yet children's entertainment is partly grounded in "the transgression of generational roles" and, in a Bakhtinian carnivalesque subversion of power relations, it offers equal voice to all, but more so acts as temporary pressure "release valve." Within children's culture, "perceived" acts of rebellion are often fleeting and swiftly reversed come bedtime.

Children may have *a measure* of say in the creation and maintenance of children's culture, but in the context of media, children are far from creative center-stage. Consider, for example, the media that children can make and co-opt in relation to the corporate weight of a media franchise like *Harry Potter*. Similarly consider the institutions of education and parental power in relation to the marginal auto-didactic edge of learning. Even consider the discussion on children's culture within this entry. The voice of children is heard, but secondhand, re-framed, and attenuated at best.

Children's culture may broadly operate under the oversight of adults, but in recent times there have been technological and wider cultural shifts that have allowed more room for children's *own* culture to develop. Drawing on the affordances of "new" and "social" media, children can now inhabit, shape, and embellish cultural spaces in ways that often appear unmappable and impenetrable to adults. Adults look on with some anxiety as children reshape their cultural landscape. These cultural assertions, although liberating perhaps for children, can be said to have triggered a reassertion of adult oversight under the cover of children's Internet safety. Jenkins is optimistic for children's cultural agency within these technological shifts, but he is blinkered to "the power relations between child and adult" and even though he celebrates children as active participants in creating their own culture he does caution us to the ways in which they are joining "these interactions from positions of unequal power" (1998, p. 4).

It is persuasive to read children's culture within a simplistic adult–child binary, but in acknowledging an ideological adultism one should also consider a reading of "mass culture" in which those that have (cultural) capital, knowingly or otherwise, impose their value system over others through establishing that value system as the natural order of things. This is an accusation made of corporate capitalism, whereby according to Horkheimer and Adorno (2002/1944) the media organizations that shape the "culture industry" dominate mass culture, and block out any other ideological perspective. Rather than there being a deliberate project, however, the effectiveness of the culture industry is not secured through "a deceptive ideology, but by the removal from the consciousness of the masses of any alternative to capitalism" (Stevenson, 1995, p. 53). Returning to children's culture, this ideology-led reading can be mapped on to the lack of an alternative to "childhood"; it is positioned as absolute, universal, and timeless, even though childhood as illustrated here is itself a predominantly modern western construct.

Children's culture owned?

It is difficult to envisage contemporary children's culture disconnected from consumer culture. In simply focusing on one organization, like Disney, one could trace a presence across near innumerable material and immaterial interactions with children, and even in addressing just one example, it would be difficult to picture a girl's cultural landscape without some engagement with a media franchise like *Frozen* (2003). Kline (1998) saw the spread of television in particular as promoting a (global) consumer culture that has helped shape and define children's culture, and one can now see the practice of contemporary media organizations that make media for children as well versed in drawing children in to consumption practices.

Discussion could more optimistically be framed in light of active fandoms in which children potentially exploit media texts for their own purposes; co-opting and using media in socially connected ways. In this way fans may indeed be able to resist the culture industry/cultural hegemony, having the potential to take control of their cultural "taste," interpretation, and production (Bourdieu, 1984). Taking culture as made for children and appropriating it, both in line with original intent and transgressing that intent, children can re-work and re-context consumer culture for their own, often social, purposes. By means of example a young fan of the boyband *One Direction*, can be seen to actively engage with other fans through Twitter, rather than engage with the Tweets of actual band members themselves. Through "playful and productive identity work" (boyd, 2014, p. 41) this fan played a part in creating her own "separate context" (p. 40) and "third space" cultural meaning-making. For all the optimistic, sometime near-utopian, readings of children's agency within their culture, the majority of children, however, are not fully active "fans," with there being notable disparities in terms of resources and opportunities to engage in cultural creation. And even though there are children active within fandoms, much like children's culture itself, children's fandom is often an adult (nostalgic and/or transgressive) construction.

The adult anxieties that surround a child's agency within children's culture are echoed within a wider anxiety about the suitability of children's media and their lives more generally. From early fears for the effects of books, comics, television, and cinema, through to more recent anxiety surrounding video gaming and social media, there has been recurring adult unease for the potentially negative influence of children's media culture, with, for example, popular disclosure regularly turning to the effect violent media might have on children. A direct cause and effect reading triggers us to ask, what will engaging with this media "change" in a child, or more portentously, will children's lives be damaged by this advancing technology? Adult anxieties are as much shaped around platform as they are on any particular content, and it is possible to recognize the ways whereby newer media technologies, like the Internet or mobile phones, can be swept up within a society's concerns. There is much causal confusion aired, with the US Surgeon General's call to action on "Childhood Overweight and Obesity Prevention" (2008), for example, directly implicating television viewing, computer use, and video games in childhood obesity. Clear distinctions between adult and children's culture are made, and in terms of children's entertainment the adult population strives "to keep these distinctions intact" (Spigel, 1998, p. 111). There are ongoing negotiations between parent and state on the suitability, or otherwise, of media for children; notably, however, negotiation rarely features the voices of children, as adults fail to validate children's say in *their* culture.

Conclusion

Addressing children and their lived experience through children's culture and the "construct" of childhood allows us to address the socially situated cultural world that children inhabit. Adult and child cultures are binary to each other, and yet intricately woven together. As every culture is a hybrid and "draws on diverse sources [and] depends on borrowings" (Kuper, 1999, p. 13), children's cultures are plural and far from hermetically sealed from adult culture, with the borders of children's culture being permeable and in flux. Children's culture has been positioned within this entry as something predominately done to children, with children broadly speaking at the whim of adult and consumer culture; children are seen to have some agency within children's culture, however limited it may be at times. Children's culture was recognized here in its widest sense as a circuit of social meaning-making and remaking, and through wielding their cultural "tools" children can make sense of their lived experience and find their place in the world:

> As children express children's culture, a collective system of meaning, they become competent actors in their world and thus generate at the same time the framework which makes it possible for them to be competent in the adult world. (Honig, 2016, p. 64)

This entry acknowledges the social construction of childhood and challenges any tendency to universalize. Ultimately children are seen here as cultural actors, being as competent as adults, and under these readings childhood and children's culture should be valued for their own qualities, rather than a way-stage to something else.

SEE ALSO: Active Audiences; Girl Culture and Their Literacies; Internet Safety; Learning about Materialism and Consumer Culture

References

Ariès, P. (1962). *Centuries of childhood*. London, England: Jonathan Cape.

Bhabha, H.K. (1994). *The location of culture*. Abingdon, England: Routledge.

Bourdieu, P. (1984). *Distinction: A social critique of the judgement of taste*. Abingdon, England: Routledge.
boyd, d. (2014). *It's complicated: The social lives of networked teens*. New Haven, CT: Yale University Press.
Castells, M. (1998). *The rise of the network society*. Oxford, England: Blackwell.
Corsaro, W.A. (2015). *The sociology of childhood*. London, England: SAGE.
Coveney, P. (1967). *The image of childhood*. Harmondsworth, England: Penguin Books.
Durkheim, E. (1979). Childhood. In W.S.F. Pickering (Ed.), *Emile Durkheim: Selected writings on education. Volume I: Durkheim: Essays of morals and education*. London, England: Routledge.
Galson, S.K. (2008). Childhood overweight and obesity prevention. *Public Health Reports, 123*(3), 258–259. doi: 10.1177/003335490812300302.
Gittins, D. (2009). The historical construction of childhood. In M.J. Kehily (Ed.), *An introduction to childhood studies* (2nd ed.). Maidenhead, England: Open University Press.
Hengst, H. (2005). Complex interconnections: The global and local in children's minds and everyday worlds. In J. Qvortrup (Ed.), *Studies in modern childhood: Society, agency, culture*. Basingstoke, England: Palgrave Macmillan.
Honig, M.-S. (2016). How is the child constituted in childhood studies? In J. Qvortrup, W.A. Corsaro, & M.-S. Honig (Eds.), *The Palgrave handbook of childhood studies*. Basingstoke, England: Palgrave Macmillan.
Horkheimer, M., & Adorno, T.W. (2002/1944). *Dialectic of enlightenment*. Stanford, CA: Stanford University Press.
James, A. (2001). Confections, concoctions and conceptions. In D. Miller (Ed.), *Consumption: Objects, subjects and mediations in consumption*. London, England: Routledge.
Jenkins, H. (1998). *The children's culture reader*. New York, NY: NYU Press.
Jenks, C. (1996). *Childhood*. London, England: Routledge.
Kidd, K. (2002). Children's culture, children's studies and the ethnographic imaginary. *Children's Literature Association Quarterly, 27*(3), 146–155.
Kline, S. (1998). The making of children's culture. In H. Jenkins (Ed.), *The children's culture reader*. New York, NY: NYU Press.
Kuper, A. (1999). *Culture: The anthropologists' account*. Cambridge, MA: Harvard University Press.
Lucy, S. (2005). The archaeology of age. In M. Díaz-Andreu, S. Lucy, S. Babić, & D.N. Edwards (Eds.), *Archaeology of identity* (pp. 43–66). Abingdon, England: Routledge.
Postman, N. (1982). *The disappearance of childhood*. New York, NY: Vintage Books.
Serpell, R. (1979). How specific are perceptual skills? A cross-cultural study of pattern reproduction. *British Journal of Psychology, 70*(3), 365–380.
Speier, M. (1976). The adult ideological viewpoint in studies of childhood. In A. Skolnick (Ed.), *Rethinking childhood*. Boston, MA: Little Brown.
Spigel, L. (1998). Seducing the innocent: Childhood and television in postwar America. In H. Jenkins (Ed.), *The children's culture reader*. New York, NY: NYU Press.
Stevenson, N. (1995). *Understanding media culture*. London, England: SAGE.
United Nations. (1989). Convention on the Rights of the Child. Retrieved from http://www.ohchr.org/en/professionalinterest/pages/crc.aspx

Further reading

Cunningham, H. (2006). *The invention of childhood*. London, England: BBC Books.
Drotner, K., & Livingstone, S. (Eds.). (2008). *International handbook of children, media and culture*. London, England: SAGE.

James, A., Jenks, C., & Prout, A. (1998). *Theorizing childhood*. Cambridge, England: Polity Press.
Woodfall, A., & Zezulkova, M. (2016). What "children" experience and "adults" may overlook: Phenomenological approaches to media practice, education and research. *Journal of Children and Media, 10*(1), 98–106.

Ashley Woodfall worked within UK children's television production for many years before joining the research and teaching community at Bournemouth University. He is a fellow of the Royal Society of Arts and the Higher Education Academy, lectures in media theory and production, and is co-convener of the *Children's Media Foundation* academic advisory board. His primary research focus is on children and cross-platform media.

Marketa Zezulkova is Assistant Professor in the Institute of Communication Studies and Journalism at Charles University (Czech Republic) and an affiliated faculty of Media Education Lab (USA). She holds a PhD in philosophy of media education from Bournemouth University and her main interest is in intercultural and interdisciplinary research exploring preschool and primary school children's media learning and experience. Marketa has been involved in several related EU and UN initiatives and in organizing the annual media education summit. She is an assistant editor of *Media Education Research Journal* and a fellow of the Higher Education Academy.

Children's Judgment of Reality and Fantasy

MARIE-LOUISE MARES
University of Wisconsin-Madison, USA

JAMES ALEX BONUS
The Ohio State University, USA

Research suggests that children are sometimes confused about fantasy–reality distinctions. How easily their errors can be corrected depends in part on whether the correction contradicts strongly held intuitions and on who makes the correction. By age 6, children consider adults better sources of reality information than other children, but they also take into account how reliable the adults have been in the past, and whether they seem to have relevant expertise. As children learn about physical properties and processes, they are less likely to make reality–fantasy mistakes.

Young children in western cultures report believing in various fantasy creatures, such as Santa Claus, the Easter Bunny, and dragons. In one study, researchers had 3- and 5-year-olds sort pictures into "real," "pretend," or "not sure" piles. For real entities (e.g., clowns, knights, Michael Jordan), 3-year-olds were guessing at chance levels, but 5-year-olds were right the majority of the time. For the fantastical entities, both groups were performing at chance levels overall, indicating high levels of errors. However, among the 5-year-olds, the main mistakes involved misclassifying Santa Claus and the Easter Bunny as real. Unlike younger children, they tended to say that fairies, monsters, Superman, and dragons weren't real.

One reason that children believe in fantasy creatures, including Santa Claus, is that parents and other adults often tell children that these creatures are real, and often provide "evidence" that seems to support their reality, such as presents arriving under the Christmas tree, or money from "the tooth fairy." In fact, research suggests that older preschoolers and elementary school children are even more influenced than younger children by the appearance of evidence.

In a famous experiment, Woolley, Boerger, and Markman (2004) assigned 3- to 5-year-old preschoolers to two groups: half were taught about the "Candy Witch" (a witch who would bring them a toy in exchange for their Halloween candy) and half were not taught about her. When Halloween came, parents of children in the experimental group pretended that they were making a phone call to the Candy Witch, inviting her to come to their house. Some parents also switched their child's Halloween candy for a toy when the child was asleep. When interviewed later, 66% of children said the Candy Witch was real, and they gave similar ratings of reality to the Candy Witch as to pictures of a cat and a teacher. Older preschoolers were more likely to say they believed in her if they actually got a toy (i.e., apparent evidence), but for younger children the presence or absence of evidence made relatively little difference to their judgment.

There is some indication that desire to believe, or the emotional tone of the object/event, plays a role in children's judgments. In the Candy Witch study, older children (but not younger children) who preferred toys to candy were more likely to say they believed in the Candy Witch, presumably because desire to believe affects the tendency to pay attention to confirming evidence. Finally, in some studies, children who tended to engage in more fantasy play (e.g., have imaginary friends) performed better than those who engaged in less fantasy play at categorizing fantasy and real objects and events, perhaps because they spent more time thinking about this distinction.

Fantasy–reality in storybooks

Research suggests that preschool-aged children are sometimes confused about what is real versus pretend, and what is possible and impossible, in storybooks. In one study, researchers asked 3- to 5-year-olds about events and characters in fantasy, realistic, or religious stories. Across the three story types, 37% of 3-year-olds mistakenly said that the main character was a real person and/or could come play with them, compared to 21% of 4-year-olds and 15% of 5-year-olds. That is, they were showing signs of confusing fantasy for reality. The more common error, though, was to say that possible things were impossible: 72% of 3-year-olds, 62% of 4-year-olds, and 42% of 5-year-olds said the key events in realistic stories (e.g., a boy learning to dance) could not possibly happen, and over half the children denied that someone like the main character could exist in real life. Some researchers have argued that children's skepticism about possible or even realistic events in stories (like a boy learning to dance) may reflect children's lack of awareness about how little they know and have experienced.

Children's judgments of reality for storybook pictures depend both on the child's age and on the emotional tone of the images. In a series of studies, 3- to 5-year-olds were shown storybook pictures that were either fantastical or realistic (e.g., a giant vs. a mother and son), and that were happy, sad, or frightening (e.g., giant laughing with people, bunny crying, or giant scaring children). When asked "can this happen in real life?" the 5-year-olds were more accurate than the 3- and 4-year-olds in saying that things in fantastical pictures couldn't happen and those in realistic pictures could happen. However, children overall were more likely to say that things in happy pictures could happen than things in scary pictures (with sad pictures falling in between). Like in the Candy Witch study described earlier, children may have based their judgments on what they would like to be real or not real.

Some research suggests children are less likely to learn and use information from picture books with fantasy elements than from books without such elements. Other research suggests that children's learning and use may actually increase with the addition of fantasy. It is possible that it depends on the amount and type of fantasy content, but that remains unclear.

In a series of experiments, Richert and Smith (2011) read 3- to 6-year-olds picture books that showed the characters solving physical or social problems (e.g., using a blanket to carry apples, helping people as a way of making friends) with either fantastical or realistic characters. When children were then asked what people could do in a similar situation, or when they themselves were given a similar task (e.g., trying to carry a lot of marbles), they were less likely to use the depicted strategies if they had heard about them in the fantasy version than if they had heard the realistic version.

However, in another study, preschoolers in low-income classrooms were taught 20 new words over the course of two weeks, using either somewhat realistic storybooks and toys (e.g., about farming, though featuring talking animals) or more fantastical storybooks and toys (e.g., about dragons). Children who heard new words in the more fantastical stories were better at explaining what those words meant than those who heard new words in more realistic stories.

Fantasy–reality in screen media

Fantasy–reality judgments may be more difficult for TV, film, and other forms of video content (rather than for everyday life, picture books, etc.), given that unrealistic and even impossible events can be shown occurring.

One aspect of screen reality that seems to puzzle 3- to 5-year-olds (and even some 6- and 7-year-olds) is whether characters and objects depicted on-screen are literally inside the television or computer. In some studies, preschool-aged viewers tended to agree that characters on *Sesame Street* could hear and see them, or that characters from animated programs such as *Dora the Explorer* could hear them answering their questions. Observational data also indicates that young viewers often respond to TV character prompts (e.g., "Can you point to the star?") by pointing and answering questions as if they believe that the character can see and hear them.

Another type of confusion concerns the ongoing reality of fictional characters. One study found that 3- to 6-year-olds (but not older children) tended to say that fictional characters on familiar shows continued living their lives as depicted (e.g., together as a family) even after each episode was over. In another study, researchers asked 5- and 7-year-olds whether the characters on their favorite show rehearsed their lines before going on television and whether they performed their depicted job in real life. The 5-year-olds were significantly more likely than the 7-year-olds to say that their favorite show was not rehearsed and were somewhat more likely to say the characters held their job in real life, but even 7-year-olds sometimes made these mistakes.

A third type of reality confusion concerns fantastical elements within fictional programming. The use of special effects and animation may make it extra difficult for young viewers to distinguish fantasy from realistic/possible content. In one study, researchers showed Chinese 4- to 6-year-olds brief TV clips that were either animated or live action, and that depicted either realistic or impossible events (e.g., two men talking; a man suddenly growing a third arm). The 4-year-olds (but not the 6-year-olds) were confused by the live action fantasy events, saying that roughly half were possible, though they were much more accurate for the animated fantasy events. Mares and Sivakumar (2014) studied US 3- to 5-year-olds' interpretations of the fantasy elements (e.g., talking backpacks) in animated educational programs like *Dora the Explorer*. Roughly half of the 3-year-olds (and even 18% of 5-year-olds) said these elements were real rather than pretend.

Finally, young children also make the opposite type of error of dismissing realistic and/or educational TV content as just pretend. In the study of Chinese 4- and 6-year-olds watching brief clips of realistic or fantastical events, the 4-year-olds judged roughly 30% of the realistic events to be impossible, regardless of whether they were depicted in cartoons or live action. In the Mares and Sivakumar (2014) study of children's responses to animated educational TV programs, over half the 3-year-olds (and 20% of 5-year-olds) said that the Spanish or Chinese traditions depicted in the episodes were just pretend, and that the Spanish and Chinese words used on the show were just made up for the show.

Some scholars have suggested that young children's confusions about video reality are partly a reflection of their limited, emerging understanding of genre. However, most studies have found little evidence that general TV exposure or prior exposure to particular TV programs predict the accuracy of children's reality judgments of video content. Other research suggests that children's increasing ability to reason about evidence from their own experiences may help them figure out what is real and fantasy on television.

Most studies examining the relationship between children's reality judgments and their learning from screens have concluded that video content is more educationally effective when children endorse the material as realistic.

Early studies found that school-aged children recalled more of TV characters' emotions when they judged events in TV programs to be factual (e.g., the events happened to a real family) rather than when they judged them as pretend, and they recalled more actions and events from the program if they thought that material was realistic (e.g., the characters are like people they know in real life) than when they judged it as fantasy. Similarly, in the Mares and Sivakumar (2014) study of *Dora the Explorer* and similar programs, 3- to 5-year-olds learned more of the Spanish or Chinese words when they perceived those words as real rather than made up for the show.

Children's reality judgments also affect whether they subsequently use the information they have learned. In one study, 3- to 5-year-olds who learned about fiestas from watching *Sesame Street* (e.g., what food and dances are "perfect") were more likely to use that information one week later to plan a real fiesta if they had said that it was real rather than pretend. In another study, 7- to 9-year-olds were only likely to use career information from fictional clips if they understood that the representations were realistic.

Although reality judgments affect learning and use of information, some fantasy content may help learning by attracting children's attention to key moments. A recent study found that preschoolers were generally willing to apply information about engineering that they learned from animated science programs to new, real-world problems even if it included some fantasy material (i.e., animated characters, talking animals). However, they were more likely to do so when the fantasy material was relevant to the educational lesson (i.e., while characters modeled the correct solution) than when it was irrelevant (i.e., during non-educational portions of the clip), and when they correctly judged the fantasy material as unrealistic.

Fantasy–reality and children's fright reactions to media

Research suggests that young children are often frightened by grotesque, fantastical creatures depicted in media content, and that they are often not comforted by being told that the content is not real. In several surveys, parents of preschool-aged children were more likely than parents of older children to report that their child had been frightened by a fantastical media character (e.g., a witch or a monster); parents of older children were more likely to report that their child had been frightened by realistic or news content. However, even adolescents and adults can be intensely scared by horror with fantasy elements, particularly those that seem very realistic apart from the central fantastical element (e.g., ghosts, aliens).

Younger children tend to be frightened by a fantasy character's appearance and/or sound, rather than by their actions. In a classic study, Sparks and Cantor (1986) found that 3- to 5-year-olds were afraid when the Incredible Hulk (a somewhat monster-like, huge green man) appeared on screen, even though he was actually being heroic.

In other studies, the researchers found that the most effective strategies for reducing preschool-aged children's fright responses (for both fantastical or realistic threats) included hugs and pleasant distractions, rather than verbal reassurances that something was not real or was unlikely to happen. Older children (and adults) benefited from distraction, but also benefited from verbal reassurances and explanations.

Fantastical thinking and beliefs decrease from childhood to adulthood, as individuals learn about physical properties and processes. Nonetheless, some fantastical beliefs may remain (e.g., roughly 20% of teens and adults say they believe in ghosts and hauntings). Moreover, research indicates that adults sometimes engage in magical thinking, particularly when they are anxious or when they want something to happen or not happen. Superstitious behaviors sometimes reflect such thinking.

SEE ALSO: Children and News; Learning from Media; Parental Mediation; Preschool Children and Media

References

Mares, M.L., & Sivakumar, G. (2014). "Vámonos means go, but that's made up for the show": Reality confusions and learning from educational TV. *Developmental Psychology, 50*(11), 2498. doi: 10.1037/a0038041

Richert, R.A., & Smith, E.I. (2011). Preschoolers' quarantining of fantasy stories. *Child Development, 82*(4), 1106–1119. doi: 10.1111/j.1467-8624.2011.01603.x

Sparks, G.G., & Cantor, J. (1986). Developmental differences in fright responses to a television program depicting a character transformation. *Journal of Broadcasting & Electronic Media, 30*(3), 309–323. doi: 10.1080/08838158609386626

Woolley, J.D., Boerger, E.A., & Markman, A.B. (2004). A visit from the Candy Witch: Factors influencing young children's belief in a novel fantastical being. *Developmental Science, 7*(4), 456–468. doi: 10.1111/j.1467-7687.2004.00366.x

Further reading

Hopkins, E.J., & Weisberg, D.S. (2016). The youngest readers' dilemma: A review of children's learning from fictional sources. *Developmental Review, 43*, 48–70. doi: 10.1016/j.dr.2016.11.001

Woolley, J.D., & Cox, V. (2007). Development of beliefs about storybook reality. *Developmental Science, 10*(5), 681–693. doi: 10.1111/j.1467-7687.2007.00612.x

Woolley, J.D., & Ghossainy, M. (2013). Revisiting the fantasy–reality distinction: Children as naïve skeptics. *Child Development, 84*, 1496–1510. doi: 10.1111/cdev.12081

Wright, J.C., Huston, A.C., Reitz, A.L., & Piemyat, S. (1994). Young children's perceptions of television reality: Determinants and developmental differences. *Developmental Psychology, 30*(2), 229–239. doi: 10.1037/0012-1649.30.2.229

Marie-Louise Mares is a professor in the Department of Communication Arts at University of Wisconsin-Madison. Her research covers life-span developmental changes in media uses and interpretations. Her research on children focuses on responses to educational and pro-social media content.

James Alex Bonus is an assistant professor in the School of Communication at The Ohio State University. His research focuses on children's responses to and learning from educational media, as well as positive media experiences in adulthood.

Children's Understanding of Persuasion

ESTHER ROZENDAAL and MONIEK BUIJZEN
Radboud University, The Netherlands

EVA VAN REIJMERSDAL
University of Amsterdam, The Netherlands

Children's sensitivity to advertising has been the subject of social and political debate for many years. Besides concerns over the negative side effects of advertising on the well-being of children, there are also concerns about the honesty of advertising targeted at children. The biggest concern is that children are not yet capable of critically assessing advertising. In comparison with adults, children are thought to be more vulnerable when confronted with advertising and, consequently, more sensitive to its impact. The rationale behind this common assumption is that the understanding of persuasion has not fully developed in children, and that therefore they are less capable of recognizing the temptations of advertising. In the children and advertising literature, understanding of persuasion is often referred to as persuasion knowledge (or advertising literacy).

Development of children's persuasion knowledge

An extensive and long-established body of research has focused on the development of children's persuasion knowledge (for reviews, see John, 1999; Kunkel et al., 2004, Wright, Friestad, & Boush, 2005). Most of these studies have concentrated on two of its components: recognition of advertising and understanding of its intent. Recognition of advertising is generally defined as the ability to distinguish commercial content from noncommercial content. For example, it has been shown that before about 5 years of age, children still have difficulty distinguishing commercials from TV programs and, thus, view advertising primarily as entertainment. However, around the age of 7, the majority of children are able to recognize the difference between TV advertising and programs. However, in comparison with TV commercials, children find it far more difficult to recognize digital advertising formats such as brand placements in games as a form of persuasion. The most significant explanation for this is that these forms of advertising are integrated into editorial content (e.g., on a website) or entertainment (e.g., in a game), whereas this is not the case with TV commercials. An advertising banner on a website is on screen at the same time as editorial content of that website. In games, the commercial message is in general entirely woven into the game itself. There are, therefore, far fewer identifiable commercial characteristics, and consequently children find it more difficult to recognize these forms of advertising.

Around the age of 8, children demonstrate an increasing understanding of the intent of advertising. Studies have consistently shown that more than three quarters of all children understand advertising's selling intent around this age. From the age of 8 onwards, children understand that commercials are not shown on television as a handy toilet break, but that they are designed to sell products. This insight develops further as children get older. Around the age of 11 they understand that advertisers are trying to persuade them to buy a certain brand or product by influencing their thoughts and opinions about that brand or product. They also increasingly gain insight into the tactics that are deployed by advertisers to tempt them. What these studies show is that children develop the understanding of the *persuasive* intent of advertising noticeably later than the understanding of its *selling* intent. This is in line with Moses and Baldwin's (2005) assumption that it is easier for children to understand that advertisers try to change their behavior (i.e., selling intent) than to understand that they try to change their mental states (i.e., persuasive intent). That is, to understand the persuasive intent of advertising, children have to be able to put themselves into the position of the advertiser, and apply their reasoning. This way of reasoning is necessary to make a link between the use of certain temptation techniques (for instance, "when an advertisement is very funny … ") and a certain desired impact (" … that's because the advertisers want me to like the advertisement"). From the age of 10, children are increasingly capable of doing so.

In comparison with TV commercials children find it far more difficult to understand the commercial nature of more integrated forms of advertising, primarily because they don't recognize it as a commercial message. In particular younger children (8 years and below) view the integrated forms of advertising primarily as entertainment.

Increasing children's persuasion knowledge

A way to increase children's persuasion knowledge is through media literacy education in schools (Livingstone & Helsper, 2006). Over the past few years, a number of educational programs specifically focusing on advertising have been implemented, varying from multiple-hour in-class curricula (e.g., www.mediasmart.uk.com), to educational games (e.g., www.admongo.gov), and short training sessions as part of larger media literacy curricula (e.g., www.mediaeducationlab.com). The purpose of these programs, generally, is to develop children's knowledge about the purpose and tactics of advertising, and to provide critical thinking skills and coping mechanisms. Despite calls for research (Wright et al., 2005) research focusing on the development and testing of advertising education programs is still scarce (see for an overview Jeong, Cho, & Hwang, 2012). The handful of studies that did focus on advertising education effectiveness indeed showed that these programs can be effective in enhancing children's persuasion knowledge. For example, a field study by Nelson (2016) showed that just a few hours of training could result in significant increases in several aspects of persuasion knowledge, including understanding of selling intent, understanding of persuasive tactics, and awareness of the commercial source and target audience.

Persuasion knowledge and advertising susceptibility

As children develop and grow older, they are increasingly able to recognize and understand the persuasive tactics and intent of both traditional and contemporary advertising formats. However, this does not necessarily mean that older children are less influenced by advertising than are younger children. In debates about children and advertising it is often assumed that persuasion knowledge can make children less susceptible to the influence of advertising, and hence that older children are less easily persuaded. However, research shows that adolescents are not less affected by advertising than are younger children, even though the former have better persuasion knowledge (see Livingstone & Helsper, 2006). An explanation for this is that insight into the persuasive intent and tactics of advertising does not automatically result in increased resistance (Rozendaal, Lapierre, Van Reijmersdal, & Buijzen, 2011). Children who understand that advertising is aimed at selling are influenced to the same degree as children who do not understand this. This implies that, in contrast with what has often been assumed, media education programs focusing on increasing children's persuasion knowledge are not necessarily effective in reducing children's advertising susceptibility.

There are significant reasons to doubt the notion that persuasion knowledge makes children more immune to the impact of advertising. That is, it is very plausible that children do not use this knowledge at all when they come into contact with advertising. Due to the nature of contemporary advertising, combined with children's immature cognitive skills, children have major difficulty activating and using their previously stored persuasion knowledge spontaneously when confronted with advertising. Specifically, to activate and use their persuasion knowledge, children need to have the cognitive control to stop and shift their attention away from the emotionally appealing advertisement and then enact a cognitive script to help evaluate the advertisement critically. This process is also referred to as the "stop-and-think response" (Rozendaal et al., 2011) and is closely linked to children's executive functions. Executive functions refer to a set of mental processes that aid in the monitoring and control of emotion, thought, and action, and do not reach adult levels until late adolescence.

Thus, in order to increase children's ability to defend against the effect of advertising, it is not enough to increase their understanding of persuasion. Children also need to be stimulated to activate and use their persuasion knowledge. For example, research found that children who were asked to think aloud when they watched a commercial on television were much more critical about the commercial and the product being advertised (Rozendaal, Buijzen, & Valkenburg, 2012). This means that susceptibility to advertising in children can be reduced by encouraging children to think about what they see and hear in a commercial. Making a remark about the commercial at the time they are watching it (e.g., "This commercial wants to sell you something. The makers want you to ask your parents for this toy") has the same effect. Making the comment causes the child to become more aware of the fact that they are watching a commercial, and to think about it more.

Another way to increase children's advertising defenses is to give a warning alongside the advertising message. Advertising warnings are assumed to empower children because they may activate their awareness and knowledge of the commercial nature of advertised media content. Specifically, the warning can facilitate recognition of the commercial message and trigger children to think about the purpose of the advertised media content. When they realize that this is to persuade, children may adopt a more critical attitude, which helps them to make more deliberate and autonomous decisions.

A pioneering study by An and Stern (2011) on the effectiveness of advertising forewarnings among children has shown that the presence of a warning in an advergame ("Advertisement: the game and other activities on this website contain messages about the products sold by Kraft") made children more resistant to its effects; more specifically, the children who played an advergame in which the warning was present showed less desire for the advertised product. It is important to note that the warning did not cause the children to understand the persuasive intent of the game better. This indicates that an advertisement warning in an advergame makes children less susceptible to the advertising message of the game itself, without them being aware of the commercial nature. This finding is interesting. It demonstrates that resistance to advertising does not need to be a conscious process, but that children can also resist the influence of advertising at a subconscious level.

SEE ALSO: Advertising Literacy; Learning about Materialism and Consumer Culture

References

An, S., & Stern, S. (2011). Mitigating the effects of advergames on children. *Journal of Advertising, 40*(1), 43–56. doi: 10.2753/JOA0091-3367400103

Jeong, S.H., Cho, H., & Hwang, Y. (2012). Media literacy interventions: A meta-analytic review. *Journal of Communication, 62*(3), 454–472. doi: 10.1111/j.1460-2466.2012.01643.x

John, D.R. (1999). Consumer socialization of children: A retrospective look at twenty-five years of research. *Journal of Consumer Research, 26*(3), 183–213. doi: 10.1086/209559

Kunkel, D., Wilcox, B.L., Cantor, J., Palmer, E., Linn, S., & Dowrick, P. (2004). *Report of the APA Task Force on advertising and children.* Washington, DC: American Psychological Association.

Livingstone, S., & Helsper, E.J. (2006). Does advertising literacy mediate the effects of advertising on children? A critical examination of two linked research literatures in relation to obesity and food choice. *Journal of Communication, 56*(3), 560–584. doi: 10.1111/j.1460-2466.2006.00301.x

Moses, L.J., & Baldwin, D.A. (2005). What can the study of cognitive development reveal about children's ability to appreciate and cope with advertising? *Journal of Public Policy & Marketing, 24*(2), 186–201. doi: 10.1509/jppm.2005.24.2.186

Nelson, M.R. (2016). Developing persuasion knowledge by teaching advertising literacy in primary school. *Journal of Advertising, 45*(2), 169–182. doi: 10.1080/00913367.2015.1107871

Rozendaal, E., Buijzen, M., & Valkenburg, P.M. (2012). Think-aloud method superior to thought-listing in increasing children's advertising defenses. *Human Communication Research, 38*(2), 198–220. doi: 10.1111/j.1468-2958.2011.01425.x

Rozendaal, E., Lapierre, M.A., Van Reijmersdal, E.A., & Buijzen, M. (2011). Reconsidering advertising literacy as a defense against advertising effects. *Media Psychology, 14*(4), 333–354. doi: 10.1080/15213269.2011.620540

Wright, P., Friestad, M., & Boush, D.M. (2005). The development of marketplace persuasion knowledge in children, adolescents, and young adults. *Journal of Public Policy & Marketing, 24*(2), 222–233. doi: 10.1509/jppm.2005.24.2.222

Further reading

Buijzen, M., Van Reijmersdal, E.A., & Owen, L.H. (2010). Introducing the PCMC model: An investigative framework for young people's processing of commercialized media content. *Communication Theory, 20*(4), 427–450. doi: 10.1111/j.1468-2885.2010.01370.x

Friestad, M., & Wright, P. (1994). The persuasion knowledge model: How people cope with persuasion attempts. *Journal of Consumer Research, 21*(1), 1–31. doi: 10.1086/209380

Hudders, L., Cauberghe, V., & Panic, K. (2015). How advertising literacy training affect children's responses to television commercials versus advergames. *International Journal of Advertising, 35*(6), 909–931. doi: 10.1080/02650487.2015.1090045

Nairn, A., & Fine, C. (2008) Who's messing with my mind? The implications of dual-process models for ethics of advertising to children. *International Journal of Advertising, 27*(3), 447–470. doi: 10.2501/S0265048708080062

Esther Rozendaal is Associate Professor of Communication at the Behavioural Science Institute at Radboud University. Her research addresses youth-directed communication and marketing, with a specific focus on children's advertising literacy. She has published in leading journals, such as *Human Communication Research*, *Media Psychology*, and *Journal of Children & Media*. Her work has been recognized with awards from the National Communication Association, the International Communication Association, and the *International Journal of Advertising*. She also co-initiated Bitescience.com, a website presenting academic knowledge on young people's media and consumer behavior in bitesize portions.

Eva van Reijmersdal is Associate Professor of Marketing Communication at the Amsterdam School of Communication Science at the University of Amsterdam. Her research focuses on the effect of subtle forms of advertising (advergames, advertorials, sponsored blogs, and brand placement) on children and adolescents. She has been published in many journals including *Journal of Youth and Adolescents*, *Journal of Advertising Research*, and *Psychology & Marketing*. Her work has received awards from the European Advertising Academy, the International Communication Association, and the Dutch Flanders Communication Association.

Moniek Buijzen is Professor and Chair of Communication Science at the Behavioural Science Institute at Radboud University. Her research focuses on young (media) consumers, striving to apply insights to communication processes to improve child and adolescent well-being. Her work has been recognized with awards from the International Communication Association, the Netherlands Organisation for Scientific Research, and the European Research Council. She co-initiated Bitescience.com, a website presenting academic knowledge on young people's media and consumer behavior in bitesize portions.

CIPA/Internet Filtering

FRANCES JACOBSON HARRIS
University of Illinois at Urbana-Champaign, USA

As the Internet expanded during the 1990s and took on ever greater importance in American life, lawmakers looked for ways to protect children from exposure to harmful material online. The result was the Children's Internet Protection Act of 2000 (CIPA), which requires US schools and public libraries that are recipients of federal government Internet E-rate funding to install a "technology protection measure" (filtering software) that "blocks or filters Internet access to visual depictions that are (1) obscene; (2) child pornography; or (3) harmful to minors." In practice, the effectiveness of filtering technology has proven problematic. The technology itself is imperfect, allowing in some content that should be prohibited and blocking permissible content. Further, implementation at the local level typically overreaches the requirements of the law by blocking a much wider range of information and media than the three prescribed categories of visual depiction. This reduced access inhibits students' ability to assess the credibility of online media and information as well as educators' efforts to deliver information and media literacy education. It also raises concerns among librarians regarding issues of censorship and intellectual freedom.

Background

CIPA was the last in a series of attempts to protect children from harmful online content. The Communications Decency Act of 1996, the Child Online Protection Act of 1998 (COPA), and the Child Pornography Prevention Act of 1996 (CPPA) all failed as a result of court challenges. In each case, restrictions on content providers were ruled as being overly broad and therefore unconstitutional. With successful passage of the Children's Internet Protection Act in 2000, Congress put the focus on controlling access at the receiving end – on the nation's schools and libraries – rather than on the content creators. The law is not a universal mandate. It only applies to schools and libraries that receive the Universal Service Discount (E-rate) for their Internet technology. As noted, these institutions are required to have an Internet safety policy that includes a "technology protection measure" designed to block visual depictions that are obscene, child pornography, or harmful to minors. The policy must also address other topics, such as unlawful online activity and the safety and security of minors while using email or other means of direct communication. But the sole function of the technology protection provision is to block those specific categories of visual content.

Filtering in practice

Despite the relatively focused requirements of the law's technology protection measure clause, the vast majority of K-12 schools, both public and private, have installed

Internet filtering software that blocks a great deal more content than the visual depictions specified by the law (Batch, 2014). Using a combination of keyword algorithms, content categories, domain blacklists, and web protocols, commercial filtering products have the technical capability of blocking a wide range of content and web services. Content categories can include such topics as terrorism and extremism, hate and discrimination, sex and sexuality, occult and New Age, religion, and guns and weaponry. Blocked web services can range from blogs and "personal" pages to social networking, gaming, online chat and messaging, streaming media, and even collaborative web services like Google Drive and wikis. In a longitudinal survey of school library programs, the American Association of School Librarians (2012) found that 88% of schools blocked social networks, 74% blocked instant messaging and online chat clients, 69% blocked online games, and 66% blocked video services. None of these services, as a class, is included in the protection requirements mandated by CIPA.

In the case of public libraries, authorized staff members are allowed to disable the filter to allow Internet access for lawful purposes by adults aged 17 or older. In fact, public libraries must do so in order to avoid unconstitutionally blocking access to legally protected content. Minors in public libraries can only request to have specific legal sites unblocked, a prospect that can be daunting for a young person. In the case of school settings, the situation is quite different. Filtering software is typically installed with a wide variety of blocked categories enabled, including legally protected content. This practice is common even in schools that do not utilize federal E-rate funding and are exempt from the technology protection requirement.

There are many reasons for this status quo in schools. Community standards and expectations about appropriate use in the school environment have great influence on how online information is ultimately accessed and used by minors at the local level. Educators have understandable concerns about controlling exposure to inappropriate content by younger children. Teachers and administrators want to protect students from cyberbullying and minimize opportunities for student participation in undesirable or illegal activities. Blocking social network services and other interactive media makes classroom management easier. Administrators, technology staff, school boards, and even school district lawyers misunderstand or misapply the actual requirements of the law. Filtering decisions may be driven more by technology than by pedagogy; the technology makes it easy for installers to simply check off categories of content for restriction. The unintended consequence is that teachers and librarians often have little input or control over how filtering decisions are made.

Impact of filtering on media and information literacy

Young people generally experience a very different Internet at school from the one they experience outside of school and on their personal devices. It is difficult to teach students to evaluate content they are blocked from accessing in the classroom or school library. A common compensating strategy employed by educators is the use of purpose-built websites created for teaching media and information literacy. These include sites such as a debate on the use of the chemical dihydrogen monoxide (www.dhmo.org), a campaign to save the Pacific Northwest Tree Octopus (http://zapatopi.net/treeoctopus), and an introduction to explorers for elementary school students (http://allaboutexplorers.com). While the pedagogical role of these sites can be very effective, particularly at the elementary level, reliance on such strategies can mislead students into thinking that the only "bad" site is a fake site. In contrast, the website of the Institute for Historical Review (IHR) (http://ihr.org), a very real anti-Semitic Holocaust denial organization, is often blocked at schools due to its hate content. Learners have no guided opportunity to analyze the IHR's sophisticated persuasion tactics, such as interspersing its central news feed with hand-picked articles from mainstream press sources, including Jewish and Israeli ones.

With CIPA-mandated filtering, parents, administrators, and other stakeholders are led to assume students only see "good" or "safe" content while at school. A central paradox of filtering is that while most (but certainly not all) obscene material is blocked, inaccurate and substandard content is allowed through. Filters do not teach students to discern sponsored content, identify editorial material, or assess authority and credibility. There is concern that filters prevent children and young adults from seeking a variety of perspectives, thus harming their potential for intellectual development (Radom, 2007). And without access to a "real" Internet, educators have concerns that schools are ceding important teaching responsibilities to commercial providers whose products merely mask some of the Internet's undesirable content.

Changes over time in the topic and its treatment

To date, our understanding of the impact of CIPA and Internet filtering on media literacy is somewhat limited because the topic, as a subject of scholarly research, is in its relative infancy. Even so, it could be argued that there is a greater paucity of research than one would expect for a topic that has had an impact on so many.

Initial and continuing research on the impact of CIPA and filtering has focused primarily on two areas: (i) the effectiveness and accuracy of filters in blocking targeted content, and (ii) principles of intellectual freedom and minors' First Amendment rights. The latter topic hasn't been so much the subject of scholarly research as it has been a topic of discussion and concern in the fields of library science and information and media literacy.

Effectiveness and accuracy of filters

Aware of the limitations of a software solution, the American Library Association published the *Statement on Library Use of Filtering Software* (2000) cautioning parents that libraries employing filters could not fulfill an implied contract that their children would not be able to access material their parents would not wish them to read or view.

In fact, commercial filtering software products were almost immediately shown to both under-block content that should be restricted as well as over-block content that should be permitted. In filter accuracy studies from 2001 to 2008, the average accuracy success rate for text content was 78.347% (Houghton-Jan, 2010). Only one study was conducted during that time that examined filtering efficacy on images, which is of concern since the only specific CIPA-prohibited category is visual imagery. These studies confirmed fears that reliance on commercial filtering products was giving educators and parents a false sense of security about the kind of content their children could access at school and in libraries.

A study on the retrieval of health information conducted by the Kaiser Family Foundation shortly after the law was enacted found that filter settings made a difference. Filters set at a more restrictive level resulted in a significant increase in blocked health sites, yet yielded only a marginal increase in effectiveness at blocking pornography (Rideout, Richardson, & Resnick, 2002). The percentage of health sites blocked increased from 1.4 to 24%, while the percentage of pornography sites blocked only increased from 87 to 91%. Even on the least restrictive settings, search terms made a difference in the retrieval of results. Sexual health sites retrieved from searches using terms such as "safe sex" or "condoms" were much more likely to be blocked than sites that resulted from search terms such as "birth control," "STD," or "herpes." To wit, 28% of health sites from a search on "condom" were blocked at intermediate blocking levels, compared to 5% of sites from a search on "birth control" being blocked. A more recent study (Peterson, Oltmann, & Knox, 2017) examined the interaction of market factors (e.g., how content categories are defined) and the complex network of actors involved in configuring products at the local level. These variables produce inconsistencies in filtering implementation that greatly compound any "errors" in software.

Intellectual freedom

There was and continues to be a great deal of concern from the library community about CIPA and preserving principles of intellectual freedom for minors. This concern focuses on two problematic outcomes of filtering: (i) limiting or blocking access to legally protected information, and (ii) favoring information that is biased or reflective of particular points of view. Bias is difficult to establish due to the proprietary nature of filtering software. Educators have no access to lists of content blocked by individual products. Determinations must be made by inference or triangulation of independently collected data. Radom (2007) used a data set that identified Internet filtering companies with religious affiliations and found that in 2005 at least 15.9% of Indiana public libraries used filters with connections to conservative religious groups. She concluded that this situation posed an ethical dilemma for librarians, who would then be placed in the unwitting position of promoting a particular religious ideology from within a public institution and would be in conflict with the American Library Association's Library Bill of Rights (1996), which states that materials should not be proscribed or removed because of partisan or doctrinal disapproval.

Through frontline experience, Tennessee school librarian Karyn Storts-Brinks (2010) discovered that Education Networks of America (ENA), the filtering system used by the Knox County, Tennessee, school district, blocked LGBTQ-friendly websites such as the Human Rights Campaign (www.hrc.org) (HRC) and the Gay Lesbian Straight Education Network (www.glsen.org) (GLSEN). ENA did not, however, block "reparative therapy" sites, such as People Can Change (now known as Brothers on a Road Less Traveled) (www.brothersroad.org) and other anti-gay websites. In seeking to have access to the HRC and GLSEN sites restored, she was informed by her director of technology that CIPA required such sites to be filtered, a clear misinterpretation of the law on the part of the district. Ultimately, Storts-Brinks enlisted the help of the Tennessee chapter of the American Civil Liberties Union (ACLU), which filed suit and was successful in requiring the district to unblock the LGBTQ-friendly sites.

The ACLU also represented the organization Parents, Families, and Friends of Lesbians and Gays (PFLAG) in the case of a Rhode Island school district in which LGBT-positive sites were often blocked because of a "sexuality" filter, while anti-LGBT sites were allowed because they were typically placed in a "religion" category (PFLAG v. Camdenton R-III School District, 2012). The Court found that the district was discriminating based on viewpoint, and, furthermore, that the URL blacklist it employed still failed to block 30% of material intended to be restricted by CIPA. Because the district had a choice to either reconfigure its own system to achieve viewpoint neutrality or use another filtering product that would at least maintain, if not improve, its effectiveness at blocking CIPA-regulated content, the Court concluded that the district continued to use their URL blacklist as its primary filter because it discriminated against websites that discuss LGBT from a positive viewpoint. The Court also determined that allowing students to request the unblocking of specific websites was an insufficient remedy because the unblocking procedure in place was not certain to protect student anonymity, burdened a particular viewpoint, and had a stigmatizing effect on the students making the requests.

Recourse

Timely recourse to over-blocking has been problematic at best. CIPA permits schools and libraries to unblock legal content for adults and when specific content is demonstrated not to prove harmful to minors. In practice, particularly in school settings, unblocking has proven to be a difficult and time-consuming process, most often made at the district level rather than by the educators working directly with youth. In 2012, only 27% of school librarians reported their unblocking requests were addressed immediately or within a few hours, while 35% reported these requests taking one to two days (American Association of School Librarians, 2012). One in five (20%) said it took more than a week to unblock a site. A study of postings on a national school librarian email discussion list found that school librarians and teachers often gave up on making active objections, regarding the issue an externally imposed limitation over which they had no control (Harris, 2009). In some cases, educators actively facilitated limited access owing to personal beliefs about the appropriateness of certain types of content in school settings.

Current and future directions

Current scholarship and discussion is focused on issues of equity, the impact of CIPA and filtering on 21st-century learning, and on the role school librarians can play in mitigating that impact.

Equity

Concerns about equitable access to the Internet have been a constant since the first days of consumer access to online information. The *digital divide* was initially defined in terms of equal access to computers and the Internet in the home and at school. More recently, discussions regarding equity have shifted to a focus on the availability of broadband access and to meaningful instructional opportunities. For minors in low-income communities and rural areas, schools and libraries often serve as the only locations for broadband access and trained help.

CIPA has also had a disproportionate impact on equity. Batch (2014) notes that Internet filtering effectively creates two classes of students – an advantaged class with unfiltered access at home and a disadvantaged class with only filtered access at school. Smartphones and other WiFi-enabled mobile devices further widen the divide. Youth with these mobile devices are able to access anything they search for online, wherever they are, regardless of filters. They do so outside of school networks and without meaningful instruction or coaching from educators. These advantaged young people are also able to participate fully in social media and online communities, where they learn skills and develop connections in a way their more disadvantaged counterparts cannot.

Even when schools provide mobile devices, such devices are generally configured in a restrictive manner. The Los Angeles Unified School District's 2013 iPad rollout has become a case study of how disastrous this locked-down approach can be (Schwartz, 2015). Because the iPads did not allow open searching of the Internet, nor the use of social media, resourceful students learned to unlock the devices to make full use of their capabilities. The backlash was swift; the students were labeled hackers and delinquents by the press and the public. For their part, the students were disappointed the district did not trust them to access educational material as well as other content online and to learn on their own to negotiate distractions. The experiment was quickly called to a halt and the iPads were retrieved.

Impact on 21st-century learning

The Office of Educational Technology national technology plan (2016) calls for students to engage in the core 21st-century competencies of critical thinking, complex problem-solving, collaboration, and multimedia communication in all subject areas. Hobbs (2010) recommends that success in building such competencies will only be possible if educators and decision-makers avoid a tool-based focus in their teaching, noting that mastery of technology tools does not translate into the acquisition of critical thinking skills about media. More simply put, many students can conduct a Google search, but cannot identify the author of a website or identify misleading information. In the public mind, student access to technology is often conflated with the skills to use it effectively. Yet filtering has been demonstrated to hamper efforts to meet the needs of 21st-century learning by impeding access to technology-delivered media (Batch, 2014). School librarians and teachers have fewer options for teaching evaluation skills in an organic manner, one which allows their students to encounter – while in a supported environment – the complex and challenging content of a real-life Internet. Some filtering systems even direct students to already vetted sites, effectively creating a generation of students who are never given the opportunity to learn to discern fact from fiction online.

Social media and collaborative web tools also play a strong role in the lives of 21st-century learners, who will need them for future educational and professional pursuits. Filtering practices have created an environment in which educators have few opportunities to help their students create and maintain positive digital footprints because these tools are often blocked in schools due to safety and classroom management concerns. Though Internet safety has become a curriculum staple in many districts, even a legal requirement, the instruction is necessarily decontextualized because the real-life services it addresses are blocked. Hobbs (2010) argues that digital literacy education should include both empowerment and protection components, and exploit the transformative social potential of today's online environment in the context of child and adolescent development.

Some mainstream educators are making pedagogical arguments for incorporating educational uses of social media services. Maguth and Harshman (2013) described the benefits of using social media to teach citizenship in the social studies classroom. In an era when so much of public policy discussion, government business, citizen activism, and political discourse takes place on social media, it doesn't make sense to bar students from studying these phenomena at school merely because of their mechanism of delivery. Research by the Stanford History Education Group (2016) revealed that many high school students couldn't distinguish between a real and a fake news source on Facebook and that most college students didn't suspect potential bias in a tweet from an advocacy organization. This research, along with a growing reliance by the general population on social media for civic information, points to the benefits of incorporating social media in credibility assessment and media literacy curricula.

Role of school librarians

The school librarian serves all curriculum areas and is well situated to observe curricular problem areas that affect a wide swath of students. In their role, librarians have a unique awareness of the impact of CIPA and filtering on teaching and learning. Valenza and Stephens (2015) point out that when web resources are heavily blocked, it is likely to be the school librarian who "waves the intellectual freedom banner," calling it a professional mandate to do so. School librarians also call attention to issues of equity, noting that when there is overattention on issues of online safety and privacy independent of economic situations, schools reinforce entrenched disparities in learning opportunities.

In the American Association of School Librarians (AASL) longitudinal survey (2012), 52% of respondents reported that filters impeded student research when students conducted topic or key word searches, and 42% responded that filtering discounted the social aspects of learning. AASL has since broadened recognition of censorship issues in the digital realm by devoting one day of its long-standing Banned Books Week to an initiative called Banned Websites Awareness Day (American Association of School Librarians, 2018), a day in which "AASL asks school librarians and other educators to promote an awareness of how overly restrictive filtering affects student learning." As a profession, school librarians represent the perspective that filtering websites is detrimental to the next generation of digital citizens, who must develop skills to evaluate information from all types of sources and in multiple formats and "containers." Included in these containers are online social networking sites, from Facebook and Twitter to Instagram and YouTube, which are part of the communication fabric of today's world and are important to incorporate into authentic assignments in the school setting.

Teaching information literacy in all domain areas has long been in the school librarian's toolkit and is ideally taught as a reiterative process – during search, analysis, synthesis, and content creation phases, and throughout a young person's formal education (Kuhlthau, 2004). Starting with sharing and discussing picture books with the youngest students, school librarians partner with classroom teachers on the research process and introduce students to analysis of a variety of media, from political cartoons and campaign ads to clips from television shows and corporate press releases. They teach the deconstruction of media messages, how to discern between editorial content and impartial reporting, and they assist students in creating their own digital media, including artifacts such as digital storytelling and infographics as products of inquiry (Valenza & Stephens, 2015). Hobbs (2010) urges educators not to just teach *with* digital media, but to teach *about* it. School librarians do so by teaching the search process as a media literacy, leading students to understand how search algorithms work, how to trace content back to its original container, how to identify sponsored content, and to understand the impact of the "filter bubble" on an individual's search results.

Recommendations for further research

Batch's (2014) policy brief for the American Library Association represents the first substantive examination of the impacts of the Children's Internet Protection Act on student learning. The study team conducted an extensive review of the literature, held interviews with public and school librarians, and convened a national symposium with more than 30 experts and practitioners from diverse disciplines. Though the study clearly demonstrates that CIPA and filtering have had a negative impact on media literacy, the education community at large does not appear to be cognizant of the relationship. For example, the National Council for the Social Studies (2016) issued a strong position statement on media literacy that calls for teaching the ability to analyze, evaluate, and produce communication, including "the forms of communication that dominate the lives of our students." Yet the statement makes no mention of the fact that today's students are prohibited by school filters from accessing much of the content and communication they are expected to study. The aforementioned National Education Technology Plan (Office of Educational Technology, 2016) only mentions CIPA in the context of protecting student privacy and educating students about appropriate online behavior, and does not address the disconnect between the law's actual requirements and the over-blocking practices of most school districts.

Further research is needed on the impact of CIPA and filtering on media literacy. The following is a partial list of research questions that could be addressed to shed further light on this topic:

- Filters do not block substandard content, including fake news sites and advertisement-driven, low-quality "content mills." Do today's students ascribe the same measure of credibility to substandard sites as they do to reputable sites on the same topic, simply because the filter does not block them?
- The education technology market has seen a rise in the number of self-contained, subscription-based information products designed to meet the research and study needs of students by providing pre-packaged content that is purported to be safe and reliable (Attick & Boyles, 2016). Most of the systems include online spaces for student–teacher communication and student content creation. As closed information platforms, or "walled gardens," they bypass filters and even a need for students to access the open Internet. Research is needed to understand more about the relationship between products of this type and the requirements of CIPA, as well as about the impact of such products on student ability to assess credibility of information and analyze media on the open Internet.
- In addition to the filtering required by CIPA, search technology drives de facto filtering in other forms. Peterson, Oltmann, and Knox (2017) point out that certain information is made more or less visible through a variety of agents, including social media and other networked information intermediaries. Search engines and social network sites track user searches and behavior, customizing search results, and creating a "filter bubble" that sorts and selects the information users see and of which they are not always aware. Proprietary filtering products installed by schools generally inform the user when a site is being blocked; a search engine does not. Developments in net neutrality laws levy another potential form of filtering. Though these other types of filtering have no direct connection to CIPA, they have an impact on youth and exposure to media, thus on media literacy. When regarded in the aggregate, what do we know about their impact?
- What are the long-term impacts of CIPA and filtering on media literacy? Little is known about the relationship between implementation of the law and post-high school graduation adult media literacy in the United States.

Clearly, much work remains to be done to raise awareness among educators of the impact of CIPA and filtering on media literacy. In its webpage on filters and filtering, the American Library Association (2017) advises libraries and schools to "implement policies and procedures that mitigate the negative effects of filtering to the greatest extent possible," and that Internet safety for children and adults is best addressed through education and teaching consumers how to find and evaluate information of all types. Unless public policy changes, following this advice and conducting further research is the best course of action.

SEE ALSO: Digital Divide; Digital Divide and Web-Use Skills; Digital Literacy; Internet Safety; Media Literacy in the Social Studies NCSS

References

American Association of School Librarians. (2012). *School libraries count! National longitudinal survey of school library programs: Supplemental report on filtering*. Chicago, IL: American Library Association. Retrieved from http://www.ala.org/aasl/sites/ala.org.aasl/files/content/researchandstatistics/slcsurvey/2012/AASL-SLC-filtering-2012-WEB.pdf

American Association of School Librarians. (2018). Banned websites awareness day. Chicago: American Library Association. Retrieved from http://www.ala.org/aasl/advocacy/bwad

American Library Association. (1996). Library bill of rights. Chicago, IL: American Library Association. Retrieved from http://www.ala.org/advocacy/intfreedom/librarybill

American Library Association. (2000). Statement on library use of filtering software. Chicago, IL: American Library Association. Retrieved from http://www.ala.org/advocacy/intfreedom/statementspols/statementlibrary

American Library Association. (2017). Filters and filtering. Chicago, IL: American Library Association. Retrieved from http://www.ala.org/advocacy/intfreedom/filtering

Attick, D., & Boyles, D. (2016). Pearson Learning and the ongoing corporatization of public education. *Journal of Thought, 50*(1 & 2), 5–19. Retrieved from http://journalofthought.com/wp-content/uploads/2016/07/06attickboyles.pdf

Batch, K.R. (2014). *Fencing out knowledge: Impacts of the Children's Internet Protection Act 10 years later* (Policy Brief No. 5). Office for Information Technology Policy and Office for Intellectual Freedom, Chicago, IL: American Library Association. Retrieved from http://www.ala.org/advocacy/sites/ala.org.advocacy/files/content/advleg/pp/pub/policy/cipa_report.pdf

Children's Internet Protection Act. *Public Law 106-554*, 2000.

Harris, F.J. (2009). Challenges to teaching evaluation of online information: A view from LM_NET. *School Library Media Research, 12*. Retrieved from http://www.ala.org/aasl/sites/ala.org.aasl/files/content/aaslpubsandjournals/slr/vol12/SLMR_ChallengesTeaching_V12.pdf

Hobbs, R. (2010). *Digital and media literacy: A plan of action. A white paper on the digital and media literacy recommendations of the Knight Commission on the Information Needs of Communities in a Democracy*. Washington, DC: The Aspen Institute Communications and Society Program. Retrieved from https://assets.aspeninstitute.org/content/uploads/files/content/docs/Digital_and_Media_Literacy.pdf

Houghton-Jan, S. (2010). Internet filtering. *ALA TechSource, 8*, 25–33. Retrieved from https://journals.ala.org/ltr/article/view/4713/5611

Kuhlthau, C.C. (2004). *Seeking meaning: A process approach to library and information services* (2nd ed.). Westport, CT: Libraries Unlimited.

Maguth, B.M., & Harshman, J.R. (2013). Social networking and the social studies for citizenship education. *Journal of the Research Center for Educational Technology, 9*(1), 192–201.

National Council for the Social Studies. (2016). Media literacy: NCSS position statement. *Social Education, 80*(3), 183–185. Retrieved from http://www.socialstudies.org/publications/socialeducation/may-june2016/media-literacy

Office of Educational Technology, US Department of Education. (2016). *Future ready learning: Reimagining the role of technology in education. 2016 National Education Technology Plan*. Retrieved from http://tech.ed.gov/files/2015/12/NETP16.pdf

Peterson, C., Oltmann, S.M., & Knox, E.J.M. (2017). The inconsistent work of web filters: Mapping information access in Alabama public schools and libraries. *International Journal of Communication, 11*, 4583–4609. Retrieved from http://ijoc.org/index.php/ijoc/article/view/6944/2182

PFLAG v. Camdenton R-III School District, 853 F.Supp.2d 888 (W.D. Mo. 2012).

Radom, R. (2007). Internet filtering companies with religious affiliations in the context of Indiana public libraries. *LIBRES: Library and Information Science Research Electronic Journal, 17*(2). Retrieved from http://www.libres-ejournal.info/wp-content/uploads/2014/06/Vol17_I2_Radom.pdf

Rideout, V., Richardson, C., & Resnick, P. (2002). *See no evil: How Internet filters affect the search for online health information* [Executive summary]. Menlo Park, CA: The Henry J. Kaiser Family Foundation. Retrieved from http://kff.org/other/report/see-no-evil-how-internet-filters-affect

Schwartz, K. (2015). How students uncovered lingering hurt from LAUSD iPad rollout. *KQED Mind/Shift*. Retrieved from http://ww2.kqed.org/mindshift/2015/06/01/how-students-uncovered-lingering-hurt-from-lausd-ipad-rollout

Stanford History Education Group. (2016). *Evaluating information: The cornerstone of civic online reasoning* [Executive summary]. Retrieved from https://sheg.stanford.edu/upload/V3LessonPlans/Executive%20Summary%2011.21.16.pdf

Storts-Brinks, K. (2010). Censorship online: One school librarian's journey to provide access to LGBT resources. *Knowledge Quest, 39*(1), 22–28. Retrieved from http://www.ala.org/aasl/sites/ala.org.aasl/files/content/aaslpubsandjournals/knowledgequest/docs/KQ_39_1_SeptOct10.pdf

Valenza, J.K., & Stephens, W.S. (2015). Challenging channels: School librarians and evolving literacies. *Journal of Media Literacy, 62*(3 & 4), 28–38. Retrieved from http://frankwbaker.com/mlc/wp-content/uploads/2015/12/jml-ccs.pdf

Further reading

Batch, K.R. (2014). *Fencing out knowledge: Impacts of the Children's Internet Protection Act 10 years later* (Policy brief no. 5). Office for Information Technology Policy and Office for Intellectual Freedom, Chicago, IL: American Library Association. Retrieved from http://www.ala.org/advocacy/sites/ala.org.advocacy/files/content/advleg/pp/pub/policy/cipa_report.pdf

Magi, T. (Ed.), & Garnar, M. (Asst. Ed.) (2015). *Intellectual Freedom Manual* (9th ed.). Office for Intellectual Freedom, Chicago, IL: American Library Association.

Valenza, J.K., & Stephens, W.S. (2015). Challenging channels: School librarians and evolving literacies. *Journal of Media Literacy, 62*(3 & 4), 28–38. Retrieved from http://frankwbaker.com/mlc/wp-content/uploads/2015/12/jml-ccs.pdf

Frances Jacobson Harris, Professor Emerita of Library Administration, University Library, University of Illinois at Urbana-Champaign, served as the librarian at University of Illinois Laboratory High School for 27 years. In that capacity, she team-taught a required computer literacy course for eighth- and ninth-grade students covering information literacy and Internet ethics components. She is the author of *I Found It on the Internet: Coming of Age Online* (2nd ed., 2011) and has presented and published widely on topics related to young adults, Internet ethics, and digital information.

Citizen Journalism

JESSICA ROBERTS
Universidade Católica Portuguesa, Portugal

Citizen journalism is a term used to describe the involvement of nonprofessionals in the creation, analysis, and dissemination of news and information in the public interest. It has been applied variously to the activities of individual citizens sharing information on blogs, social networks, and online forums, participatory media projects organized and run by professional news organizations or civic groups, and social media users commenting on, tagging, "liking," and sharing news stories and other content. Advocates praise the democratizing potential of citizen involvement in these processes, while critics question the quality of the information produced, the evenness of participation, and the effect on professional journalism's financial viability. The growth of social media and the migration of many citizen journalist activities to social media sites have increased the involvement of users, but also complicated the labels applied to various kinds of audience participation. Media literacy can be a key factor in distinguishing between general social media activities and citizen journalism.

Context

Citizen journalism has been the object of much study for the past two decades, and while the attention of scholars on the subject peaked between 2005 and 2010, the definition remains somewhat unclear, fluid, and applied somewhat inconsistently to describe a wide range of activities. Citizen journalism is often combined or conflated with civic journalism, public journalism, social media, crowdsourcing, and participatory media. Such portmanteaus as produsage and prosumption were also created to attempt to describe the dual role of users in producing and using or consuming online content. Many researchers cite Jay Rosen's 2006 statement: "When the people formerly known as the audience employ the press tools they have in their possession to inform one another, that's citizen journalism."

Of course, there are a variety of contexts within which this participation can take place, ranging from citizens sharing content as part of a project coordinated by professional journalists or through a site with professional editors filtering content, to linking to content produced by professional journalists, to individual blog posts or personal posts on social media that may only be of interest to a limited audience. Citizen involvement in information-sharing can be radical, representing opposition to the mainstream press, or conventional and subject to the filters and processes of professional journalism. Most researchers emphasize the participatory nature of citizen journalism and the different opportunities it presents to audiences, as well as the additional demands it places on them. Many are concerned with the degree to which citizen journalism compares—or competes—with professional journalism, or how and when its practices or practitioners are adopted by professional journalism organizations.

Generally, definitions of citizen journalism are based on the description of 20th-century professional journalists and the content they provide and the role they play in the information ecology. A key part of the definition of citizen journalism is the fact that the activity is done by a "citizen," meant to distinguish it from the work done by a professional journalist. Although the word "citizen" is problematic given that not every participant in information-sharing online in a particular context is a citizen—the word "netizen," coined by Michael Hauben in 1997 and used commonly in English-language media in China may be more appropriate—it is nonetheless the standard term in much of the scholarship on the phenomenon.

Citizen journalism includes everything from a spontaneous, one-time act based on a citizen's presence at a newsworthy event or as witness of police misconduct, to regular efforts to inform others through a blog, Twitter feed, or other medium. Commenting on news stories and tagging or rating content are perhaps the lowest-stakes ways of participating in the process. The activities of citizens in creating, sharing, and commenting on information can be considered in terms of variation across several axes: the degree of independence from professional media (from a blogger who created their own site to someone sharing information with or through a newspaper), the extent or duration of involvement (from a one-time recording of police brutality to a blog updated regularly), the degree of coordination with others (from individual to mass crowdsourced), and the level of effort required (from simply rating comments posted by others to seeking out original information, examining documents, etc.).

Social media refer to a variety of media and social-networking sites that serve as platforms for people to connect with other users and share information. Much citizen journalism takes place on social media, but not all information shared on social media is citizen journalism. Some social media sites are more likely to include the sharing and discussion of news, such as Twitter, while others, such as Instagram, are more often used for sharing personal information.

Civic journalism and *public journalism* describe a particular orientation of journalists that rejects the professional value of objectivity in favor of actively seeking to serve the public interest. Civic journalism is a label applied to journalism that adopts this approach, while public journalism is the name of a movement in the 1990s that encouraged professional journalists having an active interest in the needs of their communities and in fostering citizen involvement in civic life, taking steps to determine community needs in cooperation with citizens, and using their skills to provide information related to the issues raised by citizens. Public journalism was adopted as practice by at least a few journalists at several city newspapers, but was largely rejected by professional journalists, many of whom expressed concern that it would compromise their objectivity or detachment. Citizen journalism, meanwhile, may be perceived to serve the public interest simply by engaging all citizens in the creation of public information and therefore the construction of meaning and the determination of the public agenda, as if engagement alone were sufficient.

Participatory journalism generally refers to journalism that invites participation from a group of citizens in the creation of content. The term may cover those activities that simply allow citizens to comment on or contribute to information created by professionals, or collaborative projects initiated by either citizens or professionals. There is a difference between those projects organized by professionals who offer a topic and even material for examination (crowdsourced reporting), and platforms that simply provide the opportunity and space to create collaborative information but require users to self-organize or contribute. It is sometimes used in place of "citizen journalism" by researchers who want to deemphasize the citizen–professional dichotomy.

History

Interest in citizen journalism grew as the awareness of citizen journalists' contributions to public information increased, and those contributions increased as access to tools to record (home video cameras, digital cameras, and finally camera phones) and share (the Internet, but especially easy to use blogging sites, photo-sharing sites, and later social media) extended to a broader portion of the public through advances in technology that lowered cost and made tools easier to use and easier to carry, so that citizens were more likely to have them at hand. The widespread adoption of smartphones made this even more common, connecting the increasingly high-quality cameras in phones to the Internet immediately, and even constantly, in the case of apps such as Periscope.

The case often identified as the earliest example of citizen journalism is Los Angeles resident George Holliday's recording of Los Angeles police officers beating Rodney King in 1991. Holliday recorded the video with his home video camera and gave the tape to local news station KTLA, which aired an edited version of the tape. The process was somewhat different from what many citizen journalists do today, as Holliday submitted his recording to a professional news organization, which maintained its gatekeeping role, deciding when and how to broadcast the video, in what context, and even what parts of it were shown. The video did not result in convictions for the officers brought to trial, but it did provoke public outrage at the perceived injustice, leading to riots in Los Angeles. This incident inspired the creation of several organizations dedicated to monitoring the police and recording their interactions with citizens in order to prevent police brutality. The international not-for-profit organization WITNESS was founded in 1992 to train and support people to use video to record human rights abuses. Nearly 20 years later, when Oscar Grant was shot by a BART (Bay Area Rapid Transit) police officer in Oakland in 2009, several citizens recorded videos and shared them with news organizations, but also posted them on social media sites, such as YouTube. This practice has become so ubiquitous as to be expected when accusations of police brutality are made. Part of the appeal of citizen journalism may be the authenticity of the amateur or the nonprofessional account, at a time when public confidence or trust in the news media is very low. A grainy, poorly framed video may be perceived as more credible, because it comes from a person on the scene, and has not been manipulated in any professional sense to convey a particular message.

Citizen journalism reached the height of its popularity among scholars in the 2000s, when citizen sharing of photos and other news content was becoming increasingly common. Books such as Dan Gillmor's (2004) *We the Media* and Scott Gant's (2007) *We're All Journalists Now* argued that the increased ability of citizens to contribute to news was a sign of a more fluid process of information creation, one that included not just professional gatekeepers, but possibly every citizen. Blogging was growing at a fast pace, and citizen journalists played an important role in capturing tragic events such as natural disasters (the 2004 tsunami in Southeast Asia) and terrorist attacks (the 2005 London bombings, the 2007 mass shooting at Virginia Tech University, and the 2013 Boston marathon bombing) as people now armed with the tools to record and share pictures and video or personal reports captured events as they unfolded, before professional journalists were able to reach the scene. As the value of these witnesses became clear, professional journalists also sought to engage them by inviting their contributions, as *The Guardian* (UK) did following the 2005 terrorist attacks in London, England. Several professional journalism sites introduced curated Twitter feeds during real-time coverage of events.

By the end of that decade, many of the ideals had become practically possible with the mass adoption of smartphones that allowed users to record information and share it immediately, and the growth of social media sites where that information was collected and shared. Sue Robinson (2011) called the increased contribution of nonprofessionals to professional news media, "journalism as process," suggesting that journalists are no longer creating definitive accounts, but rather beginning processes that are continued by readers who comment and share and further shape stories through their contributions.

The study of citizen journalism lost some steam in part due to a growing interest in social media, and in part because the concept was so heavily focused on how citizens could fit their contributions in the existing paradigm of professional journalism. In many ways, citizen journalism was subsumed into the vast amounts of sharing that takes place on social media, where citizens sharing information has become commonplace. Perhaps the death knell of citizen journalism was the retiring of CNN's iReport site 9 years after its launch in 2006, and the transfer to a new version of the site that sources stories from social media via a hashtag.

Social media and professional journalists' interest in using social media to engage audiences led to increased opportunities for citizens to participate in engaging with public information in a variety of ways, from liking and commenting on stories to sharing stories with their circles. This allowed citizens to influence the news agenda more than standard "letters to the editor" or other forms of feedback permitted prior to digital media. News organizations sought this participation both as part of their civic responsibility and in hopes of increasing profit margins. At the same time, citizens were increasingly sharing information among themselves, without the participation or filter of professional journalists. With their increased activity on social media, citizens gained even more power to shape the media agenda. News organizations frequently report on trends that originate in social media, including political statements as hashtags, such as #blacklivesmatter and #yesallwomen, and increasingly conversations about news take place on social media, where citizens can comment publicly, countering or adding to the information disseminated by journalists.

Current study

Advocates and proponents of citizen journalism (see e.g., Gant, Gillmor, Rosen, Bruns, Benkler) have lauded the democratizing potential of increased participation by nonprofessionals in the creation of news content and the ability to exert more influence in the construction of the public agenda, determining what news is discussed, and how it is framed. In some cases, social media have allowed this kind of influence, not only through the use of hashtag campaigns to tell stories (#yesallwomen), but also responses to shift the conversation and subvert the intended message of powerful institutions, such as in the case of #myNYPD, when citizens responded to a New York Police Department Twitter account invitation to post photos with their favorite officers by posting hundreds of photos of police brutality. This activity has the potential to threaten the role journalists had developed as gatekeepers.

Some proponents argue that self-representation is an empowering experience that is offered by participation in citizen journalism and social media. Self-representation as empowerment has been promoted for much longer than citizen journalism has existed in its current form, but social media have provided more opportunities for it. Several organizations specifically seek to foster these opportunities, believing that it is important for otherwise disenfranchised individuals and groups to tell their own stories and present their own narratives to the rest of society through these media. This is particularly powerful when groups feel the professional media have ignored or misrepresented them or their interests. The existing power dynamics in other news media are not easily erased through the use of social media, as news media organizations (newspapers, cable news channels, etc.) can use known brand names and established audiences to garner huge numbers of followers on social media, for example, to a degree that is much more difficult for citizens or even NGOs to achieve. However, social media at least offer the possibility for individual citizens to create or contribute to a conversation about issues that might otherwise be left out. Several researchers have found users experience emotional and social benefits as a result of participation in collaborative information-sharing.

The rise of social media, both in terms of the number of sites and number of people participating, has contributed to the glut of information in an already information-heavy digital age. Much of that information, of course, is not of interest to the broader public and does not address common issues or experiences, but is intended for a small social circle. It may be that social media will require a redefinition of "news" to consider the varying sizes and relative distance from each other of audiences sharing and receiving information. For example, to friends, news of the birth of a child is interesting and relevant, but to an international audience, it may not be news. Yet the collective experiences of several families having children may be news if they indicate a trend. In this way, individuals sharing with each other outside the gates of professional journalists may be able to construct a news story collaboratively.

Citizen journalism also provides citizens with an opportunity to be more actively involved in the process of acquiring information, which might be viewed as a crucial part of the democratic process. James Carey argued that the development of a professional press had placed American citizens in a much more passive role regarding information, making them consumers who relied on the press to determine what information was of public interest and put that information in context. Citizen participation in information-sharing means that not only are citizens distributing information and potentially shaping the public agenda, but also representing themselves rather than relying on professional journalists to represent them and their interests. Social media have also provided opportunities for using loose ties and low barriers to share political positions, resulting in "hashtag campaigns" that are most effective in simply raising awareness about issues. Critics have noted that this may result in so-called "slacktivism," in which users exert very little effort to "like" or "share" a post on social media, and make no concurrent effort offline, as they may feel satisfied, as if they have already taken some action, but those online actions lack the power of in-person demonstrations and other actions that require more effort. Other critics suggest that participation alone is not sufficient, and note that not all participation is equal, simply liking a news story may not reflect real engagement, and posting uninformed comments may be more damaging to the process of informing citizens.

These information-sharing activities may also place an increased burden on citizens in terms of greater demands on their time and energy without compensation. Citizen journalism relies on unpaid volunteers to produce most of the content and also consume it, while their attention online is sold to advertisers, allowing multibillion-dollar corporations such as Facebook and Google (which claim more than 50% of advertising online) to profit from the labor of their users. The labor performed by citizens on social media sites, which generate huge profits for multibillion-dollar media companies such as Facebook, is particularly problematic. Social media users often agree to end-user license agreements without reading the terms and conditions, or fully understanding their rights or how much ownership of content the site claims, yet all the content on the sites comes from users.

Another concern about citizen journalism is the extent to which participation is evenly distributed across the population. Despite enthusiasm about upending traditional power structures, the increased power to the audience does not mean all parts of the audience benefit equally. Gender inequality in participatory media remains a concern. Wikipedia, for instance, has a dramatic imbalance in the gender of contributors, as some surveys show as much as 90% of the site's editors are male. The broader digital divide affecting access to and use of digital media means that potential participants in citizen journalism activities are more likely to come from the educated and economically advantaged. The involvement of citizens in the news-creation process may place a greater burden on citizens to be media-literate as well, exacerbating existing inequalities in education and access to information. Besides the gender gap in participatory media and the digital divide, the overall rate of participation is not as high as it is often touted to be. The 89–10–1 rule, identified by van Mierlo (2014) suggests that the vast majority of users in any given community simply consume rather than create content, while 10% edit, tag, or modify, and only 1% create content.

However, this rule has not been measured on social media sites, or the Internet more broadly.

Much of the research on citizen journalism has focused on the distinction between professionals and citizens, and the paradigm on which those distinctions are based. Since journalists in the United States are not required to obtain a degree or license, the differences between a citizen or amateur and a professional are the compensation (or lack thereof) for their work, the institutional hierarchy (or, again, lack thereof) within which they work, and the adherence to particular routines or practices. Some research has examined the responses of professional journalists to citizen journalism, using paradigm repair theory and boundary work to describe how professional journalists distinguish themselves and their work from nonprofessionals, and the basis on which they do so. Many journalism professionals have been overly concerned about the activities of citizen journalists, and discredited citizen journalism and information shared on social media. These distinctions can be problematic because they often rely on a definition of professional journalism that is based on particular communication technologies or work routines used, or institutional hierarchies in place, rather than an ethical framework or public service orientation of the people gathering and disseminating the information. Increasingly this distinction is also problematic because professional journalists share information or comment on social media sites and in other ways blur the lines between what they do as employees of news media organizations and what they do as individual citizens with access to social media.

Other studies have considered how the digital environment, in which the role and authority of journalists may be diminished, may undermine the news industry. Citizen journalism has been viewed as a threat to the economic model of professional news organizations, since the content produced and disseminated for free by amateurs competes with their work, or at the very least contributes to an expectation that information is free. Central to these concerns is often the assumption that an informed citizenry is essential to the proper functioning of a democracy, and that journalists serve a special role in informing the public.

Critics argue that citizen journalists lack the ethics, skills, or accountability of professional journalists, and that their activities may contribute to the failure of the economic model and ultimately the disappearance of professional news media organizations. While acknowledging the potential for citizens to be empowered by representing themselves, critics point out that many citizens lack the skills or media literacy to do so effectively, and may place themselves at risk of attack online, as not all participation online is positive or productive. Social media are also used for bullying, hate speech, and, in the most extreme cases, recruiting by terrorist groups such as Daesh (the Islamic State).

Another concern is that the growth of citizen journalism may dilute legal protections for professional journalists, or, on the other side, that citizen journalists will not receive the same protections provided to professional journalists. The current test to determine the right to claim journalistic privilege is the Madden test, established by the Third Circuit Court of Appeals in 1998, which distinguishes a journalist on the basis of activity, content, and intent, but specifically does not require employment at a professional news media organization.

In response to concerns about accuracy, objectivity, and credibility, some scholars, such as Axel Bruns (2008) have suggested that a new framework is necessary to understand the work of a participatory audience. Primary among these is the rejection of the problematic objectivity norm in journalism, in favor of a kind of objectivity that is achieved through a multitude of diverse contributors. Proponents have lauded this as an opportunity for citizens to advocate for their interests without a concern for objectivity, and to freely express opinions. Bruns suggested that in the produsage process, accuracy will be achieved through a diversity of contributors and ongoing corrections, rather than through the objective stance of an individual journalist working under a few editors. Objectivity is one of the main dividing lines between citizen or civic journalism and professional journalists. This ideal-typical value became so vaunted during the development of the professional press and ethical ideals of professional journalists that journalists are criticized for any perceived opinion.

Lacking thus far in the study of citizen journalism is a clear understanding of the motivations of users who post various kinds of content online, whether an internal system of ethics or perception of justice motivates citizens to record and share videos of police brutality, or the desire to satisfy other needs (status, entertainment, etc.) that motivates those behaviors, and also the sharing of selfies or "liking" Facebook posts. Also not yet fully understood is the extent to which citizens are able to inform each other successfully to serve the information needs they have as citizens of a democracy, or whether, in a global society, citizens have even greater needs, and how those might be met.

The role of media literacy

Media literacy can be the differentiating factor between everyday user-generated content (including most activity on social media) and citizen journalism: the intentional sharing of information of public interest to educate, inform, debate, or engage with fellow citizens. Citizens who are aware of their ability to contribute to public information, armed with the technical skills to capture and share that information with their fellow citizens, and conscious of the potential impact and ethical implications of their actions, will be able to make productive and important contributions to the public good. Media literacy enables users to consume, produce, share, and engage with information with greater self-efficacy.

Media literacy is crucial to citizen journalists in a world where they play a role in informing each other about issues of critical importance. Citizens who possess media analysis skills to judge information content they encounter before passing it on to others will produce more accurate citizen journalism. Citizens who understand social and political issues will have a better ability to judge what information or events they observe may be of interest or use to others, and in what context. Citizens educated about the ethical responsibilities of users sharing information online will engage with others in a more productive way, creating an environment of productive and more egalitarian engagement online, rather than one that is threatening or intimidating to users. This will facilitate a democratic system in which all citizens are fully able to engage in civic life through discussion of public ideas and information.

Media literacy is also crucial to an audience that is presented with a huge amount of information, much of it from sources that vary in terms of their ethical understanding, accountability, and work practices. Media consumers must understand both the value and potential risks of information from citizen journalists, just as they must understand the value and potential risks of information from professional sources. They need to understand the social, political, and economic influences on media content created by social media users just as they need to understand influences on professional media content.

SEE ALSO: Active Audiences; Alternative Media; Authorship and Participatory Culture; Civic Media; Social Action and Advocacy

References

Bruns, A. (2008). *Blogs, Wikipedia, Second Life, and beyond*. New York, NY: Peter Lang.

Gant, S. (2007). *We're all journalists now: The transformation of the press and reshaping of the law in the Internet age*. New York, NY: Free Press.

Gillmor, D. (2004). *We the media: Grassroots journalism by the people, for the people*. Sebastopol, CA: O'Reilly Media.

Hauben, M., & Hauben, R. (1997). *Netizens: On the history and impact of usenet and the internet*. New York, NY: Wiley.

Robinson, S. (2011). Journalism as process: The organizational implications of participatory online news. *Journalism & Communication Monographs, 13*(3), 137–210.

Rosen, J. (2006, June 27). The people formerly known as the audience. [Blog post]. *PressThink*. Retrieved from http://archive.pressthink.org/2006/06/27/ppl_frmr.html

van Mierlo, T. (2014). The 1% rule in four digital health social networks: An observational study. *Journal of Medical Internet Research, 16*(2).

Further reading

Allan, S. (2009). *Citizen journalism: Global perspectives*. New York, NY: Peter Lang.

Benkler, Y. (2006). *The wealth of networks: How social production transforms markets and freedom*. New Haven, CT: Yale University Press.

Haas, T. (2007). *The pursuit of public journalism: Theory, practice, and criticism*. New York, NY: Routledge.

Jenkins, H., Ito, M., & boyd, d. (2015). *Participatory culture in a networked era: A conversation on youth, learning, commerce, and politics*. Cambridge, England: Polity.

Jessica Roberts is an assistant professor of communication studies in the School of Human Sciences, Universidade Católica Portuguesa, in Lisbon. Her research interests are in journalism and new media, examining ways citizens contribute to and shape public information, including through the use of alternative models such as WikiLeaks and through social media. Her recent work has been published in *Journalism* and the *International Journal of Communication*, and she is coauthor of the 2018 book *American Journalism and Fake News: Examining the Facts.*

Civic Activism

PAUL MIHAILIDIS
Emerson College, USA

Contemporary discussions about the outcomes of media literacy pedagogies and practices often incorporate what forms of engagement learners should be positioned to act upon in daily life. Media literacy pedagogies have traditionally emphasized that a focus on critical thinking about media messages necessarily dictates increased knowledge and awareness of the intentions of media messages and increased engagement with media texts (Bulger & Davison, 2018). This orientation has offered productive dialogues around how young people can be best prepared to leverage media literacy skills for active and inclusive participation in civic life. While a host of studies show that media literacies lead to increased awareness and knowledge (Hobbs, Donnelly, Friesem, & Moen, 2013; Kahne & Bowyer, 2016; Mihailidis, 2015), there is less clarity as to what constitutes media literacy practice support for active participation in daily life (Mihailidis, 2018). Constraints on media literacies that support activism include the political nature of the term "activism" and the hesitancy of formal schooling to engage in this type of teaching. Media literacies practitioners often lack the time and resources to prioritize civic activism as an outcome of their practices. And media literacy pedagogies often do not agree on what forms of activism should be prioritized as an outcome of media literacy experiences.

Civic activism emerges from a long tradition in social science research that explores citizen involvement in public life. The International Institute for Social Studies defines civic activism as "the social norms, organizations, and practices which facilitate greater citizen involvement in public policies and decisions. These include access to civic associations, participation in the media, and the means to participate in civic activities such as nonviolent demonstration or petition" (International Institute of Social Studies, n.d.). Action-taking is often seen as the last step in the media literacy process, signifying a direct form of engagement in public life. Where engagement definitions often incorporate a broader set of motivations, knowledge sets, and skills used to participate in daily life (Ehrlich, 2000), activism is directly connected to the ways in which people intervene in support of a cause, or in defiance of oppressive policies and institutions that marginalize.

Action-taking in civic life emerges from larger discussions about how people choose to participate, a topic that incorporates how people use voice and exercise agency in society. Voice, Zuckerman (2016, p. 69) writes, "is how people signal their affiliations, their priorities, and the issues they care sufficiently about that they share them with friends in the hope of influencing their actions." Voice embodies the process of engagement, whereby people opt in a collective space by revealing, sharing, and evoking empathy. Jenkins, Shresthova, Gamber-Thompson, & Zimmerman (2016, p. 300) see voice as a precursor to action-taking, whereby people develop a "capacity to imagine alternatives to current social, political or economic conditions." To acquire voice, Bandura (1989) argues that individuals need first to believe in their ability to have a voice and then to locate the structures and approaches where "people can generate novel ideas and innovative actions that transcend their past experiences."

Couldry (2010) puts forward a set of principles for voice to flourish as a space for active engagement in contemporary society. Couldry positions voice as value; it moves beyond giving an "account of oneself" and toward a mechanism where it can be used to advocate for certain social norms that push back against the dominant discriminating structures of contemporary life. Couldry (2010, pp. 7–10) advances properties for voice as a value that is socially grounded, represents a form of reflexive agency, is an embodied process and a material form (individual, collective, distributive), and is undermined by rationalities that take no account of voice and by practices that exclude voice or undermine forms for its expression and position voice as value-driven practice.

Voice that incorporates an activist agenda embraces agency. Agency incorporates a set of capacities that people employ as they actively strive to make a difference in the world (Frost, 2006). Agency emerges from what Hannah Arendt understands as the relational ways in which individuals act in public. Arendt (1958) believes that people must feel free and empowered to act in public, but they also must have public spaces that are open, free, and allow people to reveal themselves to the world. This revealing relies on building relations with others in order to recognize a shared or common pursuit. Voice becomes agentive when the discrete acts of expression can be connected and put into the world, against the structures that both allow people to act and resist their acting. Arendt's work speaks closely to Giddens's *structuration theory*, in which he understands human agency as dependent on the structures and norms that humans must live in, abide by, and reform through action-taking. Agency, to Giddens (1984), focuses on how social norms, laws, and institutions are reformed by civic actors, not through their intentions but through the actions they take to achieve outcomes.

Jenkins (2017, p. 4) defines agency as having to do with "issues of self-representation and self-determination within the contested spaces that shape our everyday lives." This process is both "personal (how much control do I have over how I perceive and act upon the world) and collective (how much power do I gain by joining forces with others to pursue shared interests)." Jenkins builds on the work of Bandura (2009, p. 504), who advances the concept of human agency to explore how individuals exert influence on events: "humans can visualize futures that act on the present; construct, evaluate, and modify alternative courses of action to gain valued outcomes; and override environmental influences." Agency in this sense relies not only on individual voice, but also on the proximal: the ways in which our choices impact those around us, and what types of interactions and interdependencies must exist for agency to be meaningful and impactful. Buckingham (2017) positions agency as implying both activity and power. These factors denote a focus on making a difference in the world and a process that embraces this difference. Buckingham (2017, p. 12) notes that structures "shape and constrain" the potential of agency in the world, and often determine the actions that individuals take.

The result of agency, within these constraints, is action-taking or participation in the world. Jenkins, Purushotma, Weigel, Clinton, and Robison (2009, p. 3) advance the concept of a participatory culture, which embraces "relatively low barriers to artistic expression and civic engagement, strong support for creating and sharing one's creations, and some type of informal mentorship whereby what is known by the most experienced is passed along to novices." In a participatory culture, "members believe their contributions matter, and feel some degree of social connection with one another" (Jenkins et al., 2009, p. 3). Carpentier (2012, p. 174) understands participation not as a fixed set of circumstances, but rather as something "deeply embedded within our political realities, and thus … the object of long-lasting and intense ideological struggles." Carpentier distinguishes between minimalist and maximalist participation: minimalist participation succumbs to the power relations embedded in contemporary society, and maximalist participation is seen as equalizing the decision-making capacity of all actors in a deliberating body. Maximalist participation, Carpentier argues, has been far less present in contemporary society, as power negotiations often fail to scale to such levels of equitable engagement.

Bennett and Segerberg (2016, p. 91) explore how people participate in digital culture in both connective and collective contexts. They differentiate connective and collective forms of action-taking; in their view, connective action involves "taking public action or contributing to a common good; … an act of personal expression and recognition of self-validation achieved by sharing ideas and actions in trusted relationships." This form of action-taking embraces digital culture, where platforms and loosely affiliated groups can share, interact, and take actions in support of causes or ideas they believe in. Collective action, they argue, requires more effort and resources, at the individual and structural levels, to become impactful.

Civic activism, in contemporary digital culture, embraces the complex relationships that emerge between voice, agency, and participation and, in doing so, positions young people to take the role of active agents in the process of meaning-making (Deuze, 2006). Activism should not be seen as an absolute position but as one that contextually emerges and shifts in relation to the structures, publics, and intentions of the immediate circumstances. One particular area that helps explain how we think about effective action-taking in digital culture is Zuckerman's (2013) application of a two-dimensional matrix (see Figure 1), where he distinguishes thin from thick, and symbolic from impactful engagement.

On the *y* axis, Zuckerman sees thin engagement as requiring little effort on the part of the citizen and thick engagement as requiring sincere effort in the form of active resources—time, effort, and capital—to support action-taking. On the *x* axis, symbolic action-taking describes public affiliation with, or opposition to, a cause, whereas instrumental action-taking supports specific outcome change and articulatable impacts that promote tangible outputs (Zuckerman, 2013).

Similar forms of scaling activism are articulated by Shirky's (2008) engagement ladder. The lowest rung of the ladder is *sharing*, where loosely formed groups exchange meaningful bits of information. The next rung is *cooperation*, where groups opt into

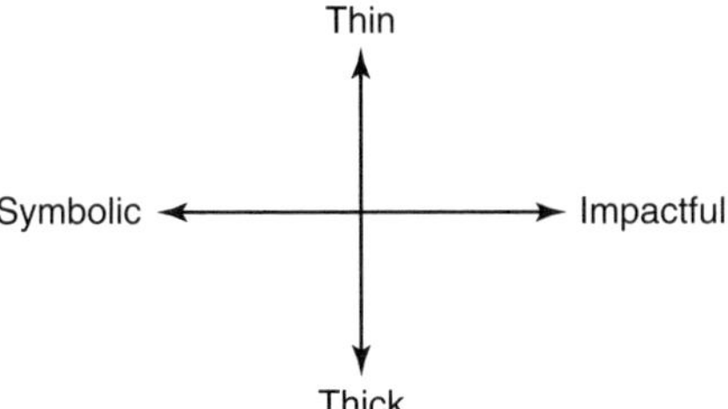

Figure 1 Civic engagement matrix. Source: Zuckerman (2013). Reproduced by permission of Ethan Zuckerman.

networked spaces and actively cooperate around problem-solving. The final step on the ladder is *collective action*, where action-taking moves from online to physical and involves significant resources from the participants (Shirky, 2008). In Shirky's ladder, the investment of resources in action-taking increases as one moves along the ladder.

In spite of the potential for robust forms of civic activism through new types of digital culture, this kind of action-taking has also been critiqued. Gladwell (2010) believes that "social networks are effective at increasing *participation*—by lessening the level of motivation that participation requires." Morozov (2012, 2013) has also been openly critical about the ability of technologies to create a sense of civic responsibility and activism when such technologies automate engagement and prioritize transactional approaches to civic participation. These critiques are further justified by recent research that exposes the negative ways in which social technologies have impacted civic activism, favoring data extraction and advertising over relational voice, meaningful engagement, and impactful activism (Tufekci, 2017; Cohen, forthcoming).

Media literacies of civic activism

Contemporary media literacy models have increasingly incorporated "acting" as an end goal of media literacy interventions. Early media literacy scholarship promoted media production as a form of activism (Aufderheide & Firestone, 1993; Buckingham, 2003; Bulger & Davison, 2018) but, as the barriers for production have lessened and production technologies have become more accessible, the pedagogies that inform media literacy have focused increasingly on civic action-taking as a core outcome (Ito, 2009). Hobbs (2010) presents a framework for media and digital literacy that moves creation to the middle of a media literacy pedagogy process and integrates reflection and acting as core outcomes (see Table 1). In this model, we see a shift in the traditional media literacy experience to encourage problem-solving, knowledge sharing, and participation. While these concepts integrate themes across the media literacy spectrum, they focus on action-taking in the world.

A recent report by Bulger and Davison (2018) argues for media literacy interventions that more squarely focus on action-taking and positive engagement with media as core attributes of an effective media literacy pedagogy. They propose a shift away from interpretation-centered media literacy approaches and toward approaches that

Table 1 Essential components of digital and media literacy.

1. Access	Finding and using media and technology tools skillfully and sharing appropriate and relevant information with others
2. Analyze and Evaluate	Comprehending messages and using critical thinking to analyze message quality, veracity, credibility, and point of view, while considering potential effects or consequences of messages
3. Create	Composing or generating content using creativity and confidence in self-expression, with awareness of purpose, audience, and composition techniques
4. Reflect	Applying social responsibility and ethical principles to one's own identity and lived experience, communication behavior and conduct
5. Act	Working individually and collaboratively to share knowledge and solve problems in the family, the workplace and the community, and participating as a member of a community at local, regional, national and international levels

Source: Hobbs (2010).

embrace participation and engagement in local issues. In support of media literacies that prioritize activism, Allen and Light (2015, p. 294) write that "deep knowledge about civic agency and civic relationships, about communication and action, and about how these are all changing is necessary to understand the pathways along which we might pursue [egalitarian participatory democracy] as an ideal." Costanza-Chock, Schweilder, Basilio, McDermott, and Lo (2016, p. 44) request that media literacies be community-focused and positioned so as to "transform consciousness, skills and creative capacity." It is these new approaches that media literacy now embraces as core to outcomes focused on voice, agency, and participation and that respond meaningfully to the realities of a digital culture.

In *Confronting the Challenges of Participatory Culture*, Jenkins et al. (2009, p. 4) argue that media literacies in support of a participatory culture "[shift] the focus of literacy from one of individual expression to community involvement. The new literacies almost all involve social skills developed through collaboration and networking." Allen (2017) developed a guide for young people who want to use the media to lead or foster active change-making processes in the world. Her Changemaker Initiative maps a process through which people employ voice, agency, and participation in a media-driven activism process. The questions Allen puts forward scale from the personal—How much should I share? How do I make it more than about myself?—to the collective—How do we make it easy and engaging for others to join? How do we get wisdom from crowds? How can we find allies?—and conclude in questions with direct implications for action—How do we get from voice to change? Are we pursuing voice or influence or both? This process marks media literacy as a space in which people may become civic actors in the world and understand the use of civic media as fundamental to their role in the world and to their position as participants in civic life.

Media literacy practices have come to embrace civic activism as a key drive for participation in contemporary digital culture. As digital culture is further integrated into daily life, media literacy will continue to evolve around the kind of pedagogical intervention it should result in. The move has been from awareness and production to voice, agency, and participation. Action-taking, while complex and still developing, is now situated as a core mechanism for media literacy practice.

SEE ALSO: Civic Media; Emancipatory Communication; Media Access and Activism; Media Activism and Action-Oriented Learning; Mediatization; Participatory Action Research; Understanding Media Literacy and DIY Creativity in Youth Digital Productions

References

Allen, D. (2017). Danielle Allen on civic agency in a digital age. Youth Participatory Politics Research Network, Harvard University. Retrieved from https://yppactionframe.fas.harvard.edu/danielle-allens-talk-10-questions-changemakers

Allen, D., & Light, J.S. (Eds.). (2015). *From voice to influence: Understanding citizenship in a digital age*. Chicago, IL: University of Chicago Press.

Arendt, H. (1958). *The human condition*. Chicago, IL: University of Chicago Press.

Aufderheide, P., & Firestone, C.M. (1993). *Media literacy: A report of the national leadership conference on media literacy*. Cambridge, England: Polity.

Bandura, A. (1989). Human agency in social cognitive theory. *American Psychologist, 44*(9), 1175–1184.

Bandura, A. (2009). Social cognitive theory goes global. In M. Guha (Ed.), *Encyclopedia of the life course and human development* (pp. 504–506). Detroit, MI: Gale.

Bennett, L., & Segerberg, A. (2016). The logic of connective action. In E. Gordon & P. Mihailidis (Eds.), *Civic media: Technology, design, practice* (pp. 77–100). Cambridge, MA: MIT Press.

Buckingham, D. (2003). *Media education: Literacy, learning and contemporary culture*. Cambridge, England: Polity.

Buckingham, D. (2017). Media theory 101: Agency. *Journal of Media Literacy, 64*(1/2), 12–16.

Bulger, M., & Davison, P. (2018). The promises, challenges, and futures of media literacy. Data & Society. Retrieved from https://datasociety.net/output/the-promises-challenges-and-futures-of-media-literacy

Carpentier, N. (2012). The concept of participation: If they have access and interact, do they really participate? *Revista Fronteiras: Estudos midiáticos, 14*(2), 164–177.

Cohen, J. (forthcoming). Exploring echo-systems: A digital media literacy approach to algorithms. *Journal of Media Literacy Education*.

Costanza-Chock, S., Schweilder, C., Basilio, T., McDermott, M., & Lo, P. (2016). Towards transformative media organizing: LGBTQ and two-spirit media work in the United States. In V. Pickard & G. Yang (Eds.), *Media activism in the digital age* (pp. 28–48). London, England: Routledge.

Couldry, N. (2010). *Why voice matters: Culture and politics after neoliberalism*. London, England: SAGE.

Deuze, M. (2006). Participation, remediation, bricolage: Considering principal components of a digital culture. *Information Society, 22*(2), 63–75.

Ehrlich, T. (Ed.). (2000). *Civic responsibility and higher education*. Westport, CT: Greenwood Publishing Group.

Frost, D. (2006). The concept of "agency" in leadership for learning. *Leading and Managing, 12*(2), 19–28.

Giddens, A. (1984). *The constitution of society: Outline of the theory of structuration*. Berkeley: University of California Press.

Gladwell, M. (2010). Small change. *New Yorker*, October 4. Retrieved from https://www.newyorker.com/magazine/2010/10/04/small-change-malcolm-gladwell

Hobbs, R. (2010). Digital and media literacy: A plan of action. White paper on the digital and media literacy recommendations of the Knight Commission on the Information Needs of Communities in a Democracy. Washington, DC: Aspen Institute. Retrieved from https://www.knightfoundation.org/media/uploads/publication_pdfs/Digital_and_Media_Literacy_A_Plan_of_Action.pdf

Hobbs, R., Donnelly, K., Friesem, J., & Moen, M. (2013). Learning to engage: How positive attitudes about the news, media literacy, and video production contribute to adolescent civic engagement. *Educational Media International, 50*(4), 231–246.

International Institute of Social Studies. (n.d.). Civic activism. Retrieved from http://www.indsocdev.org/civic-activism.html

Ito, M. (2009). *Living and learning with new media: Summary of findings from the digital youth project*. Cambridge, MA: MIT Press.

Jenkins, H. (2017). An interview with Henry Jenkins. *Journal of Media Literacy, 64*(1/2), 4–11.

Jenkins, H., Purushotma, R., Weigel, M., Clinton, K., & Robison, A.J. (2009). *Confronting the challenges of participatory culture: Media education for the 21st century*. Cambridge, MA: MIT Press.

Jenkins, H., Shresthova, S., Gamber-Thompson, L., & Zimmerman, A. (2016). Superpowers to the people! How young activists are tapping the civic imagination. In E. Gordon & P. Mihailidis (Eds.), *Civic media: Technology, design, practice* (pp. 295–320). Cambridge, MA: MIT Press.

Kahne, J., & Bowyer, B. (2016). Educating for democracy in a partisan age: Confronting the challenges of motivated reasoning and misinformation. *American Educational Research Journal, 54*(1), 3–34.

Mihailidis, P. (2015). Digital curation and digital literacy: Evaluating the role of curation in developing critical literacies for participation in digital culture. *E-learning and Digital Media, 12*(5–6), 443–458.

Mihailidis, P. (2018). Civic media literacies: Re-imagining engagement for civic intentionality. *Learning, Media and Technology, 43*(2), 152–164. doi: 10.1080/17439884.2018.1428623

Morozov, E. (2012). *The net delusion: The dark side of Internet freedom*. New York, NY: Public Affairs.

Morozov, E. (2013). *To save everything, click here: The folly of technological solutionism*. New York, NY: Public Affairs.

Shirky, C. (2008). *Here comes everybody: The power of organizing without organizations*. New York, NY: Penguin.

Tufekci, Z. (2017, September). We're building a dystopia just to make people click on ads. TED Talk presented at the TED Talk, New York City. Retrieved from https://www.ted.com/talks/zeynep_tufekci_we_re_building_a_dystopia_just_to_make_people_click_on_ads

Zuckerman, E. (2013). Beyond "the crisis in civics": Notes from my 2013 DML talk. Retrieved from http://www.ethanzuckerman.com/blog/2013/03/26/beyond-the-crisis-in-civics-notes-from-my-2013-dml-talk

Zuckerman, E. (2016). Effective civics. In E. Gordon & P. Mihailidis (Eds.), *Civic media: Technology, design, practice* (pp. 49–76). Cambridge, MA: MIT Press.

Further Reading

Bandura, A. (2006). Toward a psychology of human agency. *Perspectives on Psychological Science, 1*(2), 164–165.

Bennett, L., & Segerberg, A. (2012). *The logic of connective action: Digital media and the personalization of contentious politics*. Cambridge, England: Cambridge University Press.
Jenkins, H., Shresthova, S., Gamber-Thompson, L., Kligler-Vilenchik, N., & Zimmerman, A. (2016). *By any media necessary: The new youth activism*. New York, NY: NYU Press.
Levine, P. (2015). *We are the ones we have been waiting for: The promise of civic renewal in America*. New York, NY: Oxford University Press.
Mihailidis, P. (2018). *Civic media literacies: Re-imagining voice, agency and participation for a digital culture*. New York, NY: Routledge.
Vivienne, S. (2016). *Digital identity and everyday activism: Sharing private stories with networked publics*. London, England: Palgrave Macmillan.

Paul Mihailidis is associate professor of civic media and journalism in the School of Communication at Emerson College in Boston, MA, where he teaches media literacy, civic media, and community activism. He is founding program director of the MA in Civic Media: Art & Practice, principal investigator of the Emerson Engagement Lab, and faculty chair and director of the Salzburg Academy on Media and Global Change. His research focuses on the nexus of media, education, and civic voices. The newest books authored by him (*Civic Media Literacies*, 2018; *Media Literacy and the Emerging Citizen*, 2014) and edited by him (*Civic Media: Technology, Design, Practice*, coedited with Eric Gordon, 2016) outline effective practices for participatory citizenship and engagement in digital culture. His work has been featured in the *New York Times*, the *Washington Post*, the *Slate* Magazine, and in programs of the Nieman Foundation, USA Today, CNN, and other broadcasting corporations. He coedits the *Journal of Media Literacy Education* and sits on the advisory board for iCivics. Mihailidis holds a visiting professorship at Bournemouth University in England. He earned his PhD from the Phillip Merrill College of Journalism at the University of Maryland, College Park.

Civic Media

ERIC GORDON and GABRIEL MUGAR
Emerson College, USA

In the introduction to the edited collection *Civic Media: Technology, Design, Practice*, Gordon and Mihailidis define civic media as "any mediated practice that enables a community to imagine themselves as being connected, not through achieving, but through striving for common good" (2016, p. 2). There are two important aspects of this definition: (i) "striving for" suggests process over product, and (ii) "common good" suggests a clear set of negotiated values driving the work. In this sense, there is a clear distinction between what is called civic media, and other more established terms such as civic technology, community, or activist media. "Civic technology," or "civic tech," typically refers to novel tools for civic problem-solving, both within and outside of government. Within government, this includes anything from transit apps that make public transportation data usable for commuters to entire offices in city government devoted to building and sourcing new technologies. Outside of government, it refers to tech start-ups focused on government services, nonprofit organizations using social media, all the way to news organizations experimenting with new methods of packaging stories. The term is broad-ranging and has been productive over the past several years in its ability to label a set of tools within a common domain. But as more and more organizations rush to build civic tech, with various intentions and desired outcomes, the term has failed to capture the underlying public value that drives much of the work. Likewise, community, alternative, and activist media are a set of practices and texts that create space for marginalized voices in power structures and in some cases challenge and alter such structures (Atton, 2001; Lievrouw, 2011; Milan, 2016). Civic media does not refer to specific outcomes, technologies, or genres of media, but rather a specific set of intentions regarding the process of media-making. Civic media describes a set of media practices that seek to challenge the norms of the institutions that mediate civic life, including government, the press, and civil society.

This is important because the institutions which these media practitioners are working in or alongside are experiencing a trust deficit. In 2017, Pew reported that only 20% of Americans trust in the federal government to do what's right "just about always" (4%) or "most of the time" (16%) (Pew Research Center, 2017). Trust in the medical establishment and organized religion is also waning (Edelman, 2017). And at the same time, there is deep distrust of "the media," a flame fanned by the president of the United States with his cries of "fake news." While startlingly obvious now, the trend is nothing new. Narrowcasting and ideological extremes have catered to distinct factions in the media since the start of cable television in the 1970s and certainly with the rise of the web in the 1990s, contributing to what the sociologist Robert Putnam colloquially described as "bowling alone" (Putnam, 2000). As the analogy goes, we are still bowling but we're not joining leagues. We are still consuming politics and media, but we're doing it alone or in ad hoc networks. Media technologies play a role in this shift, but they're not the whole story. Political scandals, social upheavals, and increasing inequality have all contributed to waning trust. Importantly, it is not simply a distrust in one's city government, but in the very philosophy of governance; or not simply a distrust of the *New York Times*, but of the moral obligations of the news. This distrust represents a slippage between the institution and the organization (which implements its values).

One response might be to reject institutions all together and attempt to make media from the outside. But according to philosopher Hugh Heclo, this anti-institutionalist thinking is a bit of a fallacy. What he calls a "postmodern stance" rejects all inherited values as cultural oppressions and believes that "meaning is to be found only in self-creation, not faithful reception of something beyond oneself" (2008, pp. 100–101). Heclo argues this position mistakes the organization for the institutional values that underlie it. Operating outside of a government organization does not reflect any necessary freedom from the moral framework that structures government. MSNBC correspondent Chris Hayes represents the opposite perspective in his rather dark and prescient portrayal of American politics, where he draws a clear distinction between institutionalism and insurrectionism, arguing that political action either supports institutional values or rejects them (2012). Media scholar Ethan Zuckerman (2015) applies this perspective specifically to media practice, advocating strongly that "civic media" needs to be situated in the insurrectionist mode. But Heclo provides a useful nuance to this perspective. So as not to fall into that "postmodern stance," wherein a false binary is created between self and institution, he introduces the concept of "thinking institutionally," which "is to enter and participate in a world of larger, self-transcendent meanings" (2008, p. 107). Thinking institutionally rests outside of institutionalism and insurrectionism. It is not a matter of supporting or rejecting existing institutional logics, but of thinking through (either critically or otherwise) the values or moral obligations that undergird institutions and the way these morals and values are performed.

Media and an ethics of care

The term media connotes the built constraints around how we communicate. Well beyond media industries (television, radio, film, etc.), media is any mechanism designed for people to communicate with each other. The term civic connotes the work of people coming together to achieve a shared objective, a practice that can be associated with an *ethics of care*.

Caring is a "species of activity that includes everything that we do to maintain, continue, and repair our 'world' so that we can live in it as well as possible" (Fisher & Tronto, 1990). For the political philosopher Joan Tronto (1993), care is more than a private moral value; it is an essential part of citizenship in a democracy, orienting people toward an understanding that citizenship is the practice of how we work with others to take care of the world in which we live. Within this context, Tronto asks: "How can people claim to live in a democracy if their fears and insecurities begin to override their abilities to act for the common good?" (2013). She associates acting for a common good with the act of caring for others, and she argues that democracy is about assigning caring responsibilities. Tronto defines a hierarchy of caring responsibilities, from caring about, which suggests an attentiveness to a person or issue, to caring for, which implies a relation and reciprocity, care giving, which implies the actual action, and care receiving, which is the response to the action. And she proposes a fifth stage that she calls caring with. "The final phase of care requires that caring needs and the ways in which they are met need to be consistent with democratic commitments to justice, equality and freedom for all" (p. 23). She explains further that this feminist democratic care ethic "is relational." By this view, "the world consists not of individuals who are the starting point for intellectual reflection, but of humans who are always in relation with others" (p. 36). This position is a speculative and normative proposition, as it increasingly runs counter to hegemonic values. Political scientist Yascha Mounk (2017) asserts that the very notion of responsibility in the United States has transformed since the start of the Cold War. Shared responsibility for others has slowly morphed into personal accountability, where one's responsibility for oneself takes precedence over any sense of common good. The care ethic, therefore, is positioned as a counter-value to dominant institutional logics. And civic media is its manifestation in practice.

By aligning civic media practice with the care ethic, the argument builds on Hugh Heclo's call to "think institutionally," attending to the ideas and moral obligations that motivate and inform institutions. As such, it is possible to understand civic media as an emerging institution, a practice that has identifiable routines and behaviors that are aligned with distinct, widely understood, and desired objectives related to the ethics of care. Civic media is a conceptual framework meant to identify and amplify an emergent practice field both within and outside of legacy organizations, so an independent media activist group can engage in civic media practice, just as a unit within a city government can adopt these practices.

Civic media as process

The following description of civic media practice is derived from analysis of over 40 interviews with media practitioners working at the edges of civic institutions in Boston, Chicago, and Oakland. The interviews are in no way representative of any particular organization or industry, but they represent a commonality of practice across a diversity of domains. In this analysis, three dimensions of civic media practice have been identified: social infrastructure, objective, and time. Civic media can be assessed, over time, as it strives for a negotiated concept of common good through caring practice.

Figure 1 provides a way to visualize civic media practice. All media projects begin with some level of social infrastructure, which can be plotted along the horizontal context line. Social infrastructure is defined as the "people, places, and institutions that foster cohesion and support" (Klinenberg, 2012). Social infrastructure presents itself as the opportunities for encounter, sharing, embeddedness, persistence, and collaboration. It takes different shapes depending on the specific project, including relationships with community groups and leaders, deep and valued knowledge of a community, or access to shared spaces. If a group has strong existing relationships with a community, they will be on the right side of the plot. If they are brand new to a community, they will be on the left.

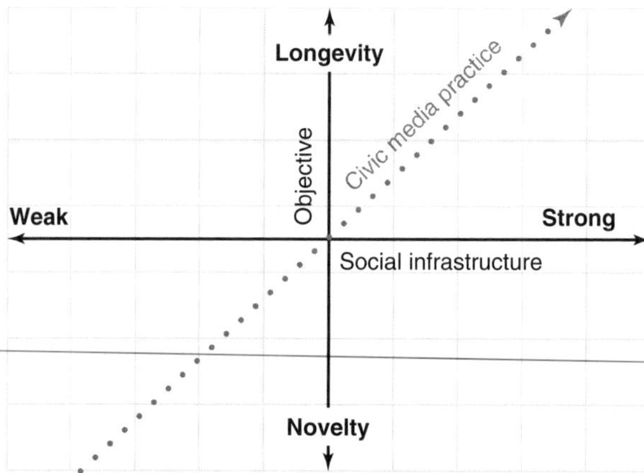

Figure 1 Civic media practice takes place over time across two dimensions.

The second dimension of civic media practice is the objective. In other words, how one thinks about the impact of one's work on a temporal scale (i.e., impact in the short term or long term). Some projects are designed with novelty in mind (i.e., a social media campaign designed to garner quick attention), and some with longevity in mind (i.e., a publicly designed mural on a community center). The former would be plotted on the bottom, the latter on the top. Every project begins in one of the four quadrants, and over time, through practice, moves in some direction. Civic media practice, we argue, is always pushing toward the top right quadrant. It doesn't need to begin there, but it needs to strive to get there. Civic media is the work of interfacing with power and negotiating with existing institutional logics. Embodying these values in practice, however, can be a complicated proposition, often revealing distinct boundaries within and across communities of practice that present themselves as obstacles that must be attended to.

Caring practice

Regardless of where a project starts, it can be assessed by its caring practice and its progress toward the upper right-hand quadrant of the graph. Below we outline two modes of civic media practice that move civic media projects along the axis of social infrastructure and the axis of objectives, respectively. As a project moves along these axes, practitioners negotiate various boundaries that reflect distinct interests and practice, pushing a project toward strong social infrastructure and long-term impact.

Working toward strong social infrastructure

Civic media practitioners work in or strive to create strong bonds with the community where they work. Before a project begins, many practitioners seek out and rely on access to *informal gathering spaces* that support encounters between stakeholders and allow people to identify critical mass around local social issues as well as explore possible approaches for taking on particular challenges. These sorts of encounters, whether on- or offline, further enable opportunities for sharing experiences and knowledge.

In the same way that practitioners have access to conversations about ongoing challenges and tactics, they rely on *proximity to the problem space*, where sharing is accomplished without significant loss or fidelity of representation of key constituents. For example, for journalists covering local neighborhood politics, there is recognition of the importance of being embedded within that context for an extended period of time. This prioritizes the authority of situated knowledge, where having access to such authority is predicated on long-standing trusting relationships.

In some cases where practitioners are not directly embedded in a problem space, sharing of experience happens through tight-knit *social networks*. For practitioners who are not directly embedded in a problem space, approaching and becoming sensitized to the issues occurs through long-term engagement with collaborators and colleagues that have closer proximity to the issues. This strategy yields different results depending on the tactics used to engage their network. For example, depending on the physical location of the conversations held with partners, different constituencies in their network will be activated, yielding unique perspectives that define the shape of the emergent civic media practice in different ways.

In addition to the spatial proximity to issues, temporal proximity, or *persistence*, is also crucial to understanding issues. Civic media practitioners understand the context of their issues by not simply asking people what they think, but doing so from a position of stability, continuity, and trust, asking once, and then being in the same place to ask again. This persistence is reflected in long-term relationships between civic media practitioners and the communities they work in. This practice of understanding the problem through persistent relationships is not only what motivates the design of a particular story or project, it is the value driving the entire practice.

By being embedded for extended periods of time in a unique problem space, the work of developing new civic media practices is less a question of identifying an issue to address as it is a question of building solidarity around an issue. One such starting point for building solidarity is *acknowledging the intersectionality* of constituent identity, attending to how the dimensions of race, class, and gender shape the characteristics of an issue (Crenshaw, 1991). While collaborating civic media practitioners and target constituencies may not exhibit a direct overlap and agreement on the intersectional features of an issue, building solidarity for the motivating values of civic media work was described by many practitioners as essential to the foundation of what they do.

Working toward long-term impact

Civic media practitioners view the long-term possibilities of the work as being built around a clearly established *relationship of mutual benefit*. For example, journalists working within a vulnerable underserved population prioritize being both sensitive and responsive to the needs of the community where they work, bringing light to issues that are important to the residents. In making this work part of their daily practice, the journalists achieve relevance by demonstrating a clear value proposition to the residents, ideally becoming part of the fabric of the community they work in.

The presence of mutually beneficial relationships also supports possibilities for the *stewardship* of nascent media practice, positioning the constituents of a problem space to take it over and further define its characteristics. For one civic arts organization, the link between mutually beneficial relationships and stewardship appeared when consensus was reached between the artist and neighborhood residents about the objectives of the work, clearly articulating a shared value proposition for everyone who was or may have been involved with the work. Stewardship can also come about when there are clearly defined pathways of participation, actively welcoming stakeholders to take the reins of the practice, guiding them from peripheral low-impact activities to more essential jobs that sustain the practice at its core (Lave & Wenger, 1991).

Expertise would not seem to be a hurdle, but in civic media practice where authenticity is premised on coproduction and relationships, the power asymmetry that comes with expertise can be quite detrimental. For example, a grassroots community-led storytelling initiative supported by an academic research lab may require the academic researchers to take a position of humility, placing their assumptions and expertise aside and letting community members take the lead in shaping the project. Being mindful of this potential asymmetry is sometimes addressed through a process of co-design, where expertise is distributed to different stakeholders occupying varying positions of power as a means to create a more equitable and coproduced outcome. The co-design process through which many of the civic media practitioners did their work, is an explicit *allocation of expertise across all stakeholders* and a clear process for providing input.

Finally, the work of *cultivating a nurturing relationship* is probably the most significant negotiation required by the civic media practitioner, in that existing institutional values often prioritize efficiency of transaction over the inefficiency of relationships. Returning to the example of a community-led storytelling initiative partnering with an academic research lab, getting access to vulnerable communities should be reciprocated with, for example, providing people with the mental health support needed after interacting with researchers. In this case, the civic media practitioners may end up pushing up against the institutional constraints of the university, which is set up to do traditional research but is not positioned for long-term nurturing relationships with a community. This is not so much a value clash as it is a negotiation between institutional cultures and is one of the significant hurdles we see in civic media practice within larger organizations.

Conclusion

Civic media practice is shaped by ongoing negotiation across various boundaries of interests. Through the constant negotiation of boundaries, a civic media project will journey over time across the different quadrants, ideally moving toward the upper right-hand quadrant defined by strong social infrastructure and longevity. The care ethic is the practice of working with others to take care of the world in which we live (Tronto, 1993). In this orientation toward caring for others, a civic media practitioner works to create conditions in which all voices and interests are represented, accounted for, and involved in shaping the outputs and effects of the media practice.

Civic media is a normative model of media practice. It is not a genre, a suite of technologies, or even a set of best practices; it describes an approach to media-making that sits in direct opposition to the logics and actions that have perpetuated deep-seated distrust in institutions. As media and technology dominate social life and the everyday interfacing between people and institutions, the establishment of the institution of civic media, whereby caring practice over time generates longevity and strong social infrastructure, has taken on enhanced urgency.

Civic media needs to be understood in the context of civic institutions lacking legitimacy among the public or direct constituents. The work of civic media then is to "think institutionally" in order to reshape institutional logics such that we invent more "authentic" ways of representing and connecting that, for example, could inform governance or journalism.

Civic media is not about new business models; it's about new value models. By focusing on and operationalizing moral obligations that undergird institutions, civic media practitioners work toward creating novel media practices that fly in the face of disruption, seeking instead to reimagine and reconfigure models of social production for the long term.

SEE ALSO: Civic Activism; Community Media; Emancipatory Communication; Mediated Communities; Representation

References

Atton, C. (2001). *Alternative media*. Thousand Oaks, CA: SAGE.

Crenshaw, K. (1991). Mapping the margins: Intersectionality, identity politics, and violence against women of color. *Stanford Law Review, 43*(6), 1241–1299. doi: 10.2307/1229039

Edelman. (2017). *Trust Barometer – 2017 annual global study*. Retrieved from www.edelman.com/

Fisher, B., & Tronto, J. (1990). Toward a feminist theory of caring. In E. Abel & M. Nelson (Eds.), *Circles of care: Work and identity in women's lives* (pp. 35–62). New York, NY: SUNY Press.

Gordon, E., & Mihailidis, P. (2016). Introduction. In E. Gordon & P. Mihailidis (Eds.), *Civic media: Technology, design, practice* (pp. 1–26). Cambridge, MA: MIT Press.

Hayes, C. (2012). *Twilight of the elites: America after meritocracy*. New York, NY: Crown.

Heclo, H. (2008). *On thinking institutionally*. New York, NY: Oxford University Press.

Klinenberg, E. (2012). *Going solo: The extraordinary rise and surprising appeal of living alone*. New York, NY: Penguin Press.

Lave, J., & Wenger, E. (1991). *Situated learning: Legitimate peripheral participation*. Cambridge, England: Cambridge University Press.

Lievrouw, L. (2011). *Alternative and activist new media*. Malden, NY: Polity Press.

Milan, S. (2016). Liberated technology: Inside emancipatory communication activism. In E. Gordon & P. Mihailidis (Eds.), *Civic media: Technology, design, and practice* (pp. 107–124). Cambridge, MA: MIT Press.

Mounk, Y. (2017). *The age of responsibility: Luck, choice, and the welfare state*. Cambridge, MA: Harvard University Press.

Pew Research Center. (2017, May 3). Public trust in government remains at near historic lows as partisan attitudes shift. Retrieved from http://www.people-press.org/2017/05/03/public-trust-in-government-remains-near-historic-lows-as-partisan-attitudes-shift/

Putnam, R.D. (2000). *Bowling alone*. New York, NY: Simon & Schuster.

Tronto, J.C. (1993). *Moral boundaries: A political argument for an ethic of care*. New York, NY: Routledge.

Tronto, J.C. (2013). *Caring democracy: Markets, equality, and justice*. New York, NY: NYU Press.

Zuckerman, E. (2015, October 19). Insurrectionist civics in the age of mistrust. *My Heart's in Accra*. Retrieved from http://www.ethanzuckerman.com/blog/2015/10/19/insurrectionist-civics-in-the-age-of-mistrust/

Further reading

Arendt, H. (2013). *The human condition*. Chicago, IL: University of Chicago Press.

Fisher, B., & Tronto, J. (1990). Toward a feminist theory of caring. In E. Abel & M. Nelson (Eds.), *Circles of care: Work and identity in women's lives* (pp. 35–62). New York, NY: SUNY Press.

Gordon, E., & Mihailidis, P. (2016). Introduction. In E. Gordon & P. Mihailidis (Eds.), *Civic media: Technology, design, practice* (pp. 1–26). Cambridge, MA: MIT Press.

Jenkins, H. (2007, October 2). What is civic media? *Confessions of an Aca-Fan*. Retrieved from http://henryjenkins.org/2007/10/what_is_civic_media_1.html

Karpf, D. (2016). The partisan technology gap. In E. Gordon & P. Mihailidis (Eds.), *Civic media: Technology, design, and practice* (pp. 199–216). Cambridge, MA: MIT Press.

Milan, S. (2016). Liberated technology: Inside emancipatory communication activism. In E. Gordon & P. Mihailidis (Eds.), *Civic media: Technology, design, and practice* (pp. 107–124). Cambridge, MA: MIT Press.

Zuckerman, E. (2016). Effective civics. In E. Gordon & P. Mihailidis (Eds.), *Civic media: Technology, design, practice* (pp. 49–76). Cambridge, MA: MIT Press.

Eric Gordon is a professor of media arts at Emerson College and the executive director of the Engagement Lab. He is the author, along with Adriana de Souza e Silva, of *Net Locality: Why Location Matters in a Networked World* (2011), and editor, along with Paul Mihailidis, of *Civic Media: Technology, Design, Practice* (2016).

Gabriel Mugar is a design researcher at IDEO and an affiliate faculty member at the Engagement Lab at Emerson College. He received his PhD from the Syracuse University School of Information Studies, where his dissertation examined how participatory media platforms define opportunities for volunteer contributions and how volunteers negotiate, resist, and repurpose such opportunities.

Civic Media Literacies

PAUL MIHAILIDIS
Emerson College, USA

In contemporary digital culture, media literacies are increasingly seen as responses to current crises of credibility in media, and as solutions positioned to help people navigate an increasingly complex and abundant media landscape. Media literacy as a form of "solutionism" is an attractive proposition, as it positions an educational narrative that provides a concrete set of practices to employ. Positioning media literacy in this way has faced some pushback from scholars (see Buckingham, 2017; Mihailidis, 2018; Rogow, 2016), and ignited a larger discussion about media literacy's role in contemporary digital culture (boyd, 2017).

One key attribute emerging from this space is the notion that media literacies take on a more intentionally civic focus. This focus responds to a landscape where citizens have a more direct role in information flow and dissemination through connective social networks (Van Dijck, 2013), and where alternative media platforms have emerged as viable alternatives to mainstream news outlets (Marwick & Lewis, 2017; Tripodi, 2018). It is important to understand the emergence of fake news within these specific technological realities. Morozov (2017) writes that fake news is a direct product of digital capitalism, where unregulated economic structures of the web incentivize a culture of clicks for money at all cost. These large advertising infrastructures are unregulated, transcend borders and economic structures, and have enabled a new type of market-driven political persuasion. The new factors emergent in this market are described by Titcomb and Carson (2016) as:

- *Distribution and cost:* The costs of publishing (via WordPress) and distributing (via social networks) approached zero.
- *Audiences and trust*: Given these much lower costs, reputations are far more expendable.
- *Laws and regulation:* With much lower costs, far more operators were involved in exchanging information. The trickle of regulated (at least by law) information exchange through the gate became a tidal wave, and one that is impossible to regulate in full.

Such new technological advancements have supported the growth of a media industry where truth and fact, credibility and trust, and reliability and validity have all been put in question. And while large-scale new media platforms have contributed to the infrastructure of fake news and a crisis of trust, it is important to recognize the historical antecedents of this current trend. Hamilton and Tworek (2018) detail early advances in fake news that American media outlets engaged in to increase subscriptions, advertising revenue, and political favor. "Institutional fake news," they write, "has been neither random nor errant. It has been an established feature of news throughout history" (Hamilton & Tworek, 2018, p. 3).

In the present day, new legacy media organizations continue to focus on the use of salacious and spectacle-based stories to perpetuate a system where fake stories, personal missives, and the spectacular are integrated into the daily news and information feeds of citizens. Taplin (2017) details the extent to which the new media conglomerates—Apple, Google (now referred to as Alphabet), Microsoft, Amazon, and Facebook—increasingly profit from demanding the presence of users. Their methods for engagement range in scope and substance, but collectively they perpetuate what Rushkoff (2013) calls *digiphrenia*—"*digi* for digital, and *phrenia* for disordered condition of mental activity" (p. 75). As companies demand extended presence, they continue to find ways to stimulate their users, who Taplin (2017) refers to as *human products*: "as the phrase goes, if you are not paying for it, you are not the customer, you are the product" (p. 150).

One result of the demand for presence is the reemergence of spectacle in the daily media environment. Popularized by French critical theorist Guy Debord (1967) in the mid-20th century, spectacle reflected a culture where images create a representation that reduces the complexities of society into simple and coherent narratives, that in turn work to unify through general discord, distrust, and the need to perpetuate engagement with the spectacle itself.

In the current media age, Kellner (2010) applied spectacle to a more abundant media ecosystem, where "media constructs that are out of the ordinary and habitual daily routine become special media spectacles … They are highly public social events, often taking a ritualistic form to celebrate society's highest values" (p. 76). Kellner applies spectacle to a mass media culture, where media are designed to bring together distant groups through the manicured and curated "events" that reflect and perpetuate a dominant political, cultural, economic, or social reality. The competitive aspect, Kellner argues, works to create a sense of wonder and constant engagement in the act itself.

A culture of spectacle is bound with that of extractive data practices. As more users are asked to show their affiliations with texts through likes, shares, and comments, engagement is tracked by large digital media conglomerates to further target advertisements, exploit personal data for political gains, and maintain user presence in the platform. Jenkins, Ford, and Green (2013) describe the concept of spreadable media—"the potential—both technical and cultural—for audiences to share content for their own purposes, sometimes with the permission of rights holders, sometimes against their wishes" (p. 3)—to explore the ways in which audiences participate in the sharing of information with peer communities.

A spreadable culture provides a strong infrastructure for spectacle, as people are often prone to share more salacious, spectacular, and loud information. Spreadable media is further supported by social networks that are designed for peer validation: like-minded individuals are more likely to be connected around similar content, and placed in groups where similar ideas, opinions, values, and ideologies align. In these networks, peer support through likes, shares, and retweets can propel information to spread further, wider, and faster, without the need for mainstream media, furthering the crisis of credibility, and seeding distrust of media institutions. A recent study by Edelman (2017) on trust in public institutions across 28 countries found that media were the least trusted entity compared to other public institutions (government, nongovernmental organizations) and had experienced the largest decline in trust comparatively over the past decade.

Declining trust emerges from a digital culture that promotes spectacle and provides avenues where people can find a sense of trust and connectivity through their peers. Sundar (2017) describes findings from research that show citizens prioritizing peer affirmation and information that aligns with personal viewpoints over that which is credible and fact-based. Sundar points to the number of layers that sources are buried under in online spaces and the amount of trust that readers place in peers as the main reasons for a growing culture of distrust.

It is within this contemporary landscape that media literacies have been positioned by policymakers, scholars, and funders as spaces for responsive pedagogies and practices. Media literacies have been oriented traditionally toward a focus on skill attainment, interpretation, deconstruction, and creation of media texts. While this orientation has provided a strong infrastructure for media literacy approaches in formal classrooms, and in teaching foundational analysis and critical thinking skills with regards to media texts, they have focused less on the environment that supports media ecosystems and the place of platforms and human behaviors that guide media ecosystems in the first place.

Media literacy practices have to date prioritized critical thinking and skill attainment over value-based approaches to media literacy practice. While these approaches are highly valued and incorporate a range of skills and dispositions, they often necessitate a set of approaches that may not hold direct relevance to the current digital and media landscape. Embedded in media literacy pedagogies and practices that teach skills of critical analysis, interpretation, deconstruction, and creation are a set of norms that enable such inquiries to be made. These norms—*critical distance*, *transactionality*, *deficit-focus*, *content orientation*, and *individual responsibility*—allow for a focus on skill attainment, critical inquiry, and critical production. These norms also prioritize deep engagement with media texts and have been associated with increased media deconstruction skills, knowledge of media and news systems, and political knowledge (Ashley, Maksl, & Craft, 2013; Hobbs, Donnelly, Friesem, & Moen, 2013; Kahne & Bowyer, 2016; Mihailidis, 2009). At the same time, however, the norms embedded in contemporary media literacy practice have been slower to respond to new media landscapes and ecosystems, and the ways in which digital realities have impacted the relationship between media cultures and civic cultures.

It is with this gap that civic constraints emerge. A gap between skill attainment and civic outcomes is apparent in the lack of action-taking or civic participation embedded in media literacy practices. These constraints emerge from school systems that avoid political dialogue in schools, and that lack time and resources to move student learning from beyond the classroom into the communities, an approach to learning that has been seen as effective, but mostly exists outside of formal learning structures (Costanza-Chock, Schweilder, Basilio, McDermott, & Lo, 2017; Ito et al., 2015).

Human connection in the age of the platform

The emergence of the *platform* as the central organizing infrastructure for information and communication flows online has further propelled media literacy approaches to consider digital realities and youth learner engagement. Platforms—Facebook, Google, Amazon, Microsoft, and beyond—have emerged alongside new models for advertising and digital economies that have fundamentally changed the ways in which people interact with information, and one another (Srnicek, 2017). While platforms have enabled widespread communicative and collaborative infrastructures (Shirky, 2010; Surowiecki, 2005), they have also been associated with digital economies that contribute to greater inequality, fewer resources for the poor, and further exploitation of workers (Eubanks, 2018), and exploiting the connection of users for economic gain (Van Dijck, 2013).

The embedding of platforms into the daily lives of young people has further complicated the ways in which media literacies can respond. Cohen (2018) writes about the algorithm as a central principle of the platform, and the lack of attention that media literacies pay in response. Cohen writes of "ambivalent machines" where algorithms are thought of as neutral actors in the platform media landscape. Cohen (2018) reminds us that, in their quest to quantize their users, machines are in no way ambivalent: "Algorithms are pieces of code that are written by coders, human operators who imbue their intellect and talent into the program. Code is assumed to be structurally cold, but is actually imbued with the agenda, biases, and drawbacks of the coder" (p. 8).

A significant implication of platforms in daily life has been the ways in which people forge meaningful human connections. Rushkoff (2016) argues that the web has worked to "dehumanize" society, and that unregulated technologies have commoditized human behaviors through isolation. Turkle (2015) writes, "without conversation, studies show that we are less empathetic, less concerned, less creative and fulfilled" (p. 13). Sloman and Fernbach (2017), in their text on the need for collaboration in learning environments, argue that "contributions we make as individuals depend more on our ability to work with others than on our individual mental horsepower. Individual intelligence is overrated. It also means that we learn best when we're thinking with others" (p. 18). They focus on the potential of collaborative technologies in the present to leverage greater knowledge production and sharing, but state that their "intelligence doesn't come from a deep understanding of the best way to reason or through immense computing power. Their intelligence derives from making use of the community" (p. 147).

The core media literacy issue in platform culture concerns how platforms impact our ability to meaningfully connect. Rushkoff (2016) believes that "there are ways to change our real-world behavior and approaches that can easily compensate for the dehumanization of the web, the corporate surveillance of our every action, and the mockery of the democratic process. They require us to be more conscious—more human." One of the central barriers to making technologies more human is their impact on the value systems by displacing a sense of belonging with others in the world. Bugeja (2018) argues that the increasing centrality of technology in all aspects of private and public life, from home to school to work, has altered our value systems. As a result, "we have forgotten how to cope with the rigors of the human condition" (p. 10).

Media literacies, as response mechanisms to contemporary digital culture, must embrace what Sloman and Fernbach (2017) call *intentionality*: "Machines are intelligent enough that we rely on them as a central part of our community of knowledge. Yet no machine has that singular ability so central to human activity: no machine can share *intentionality*" (p. 141). Intentionality signifies a focus on the human and value-driven elements of technologies, and how they are applied in civic life. The work of intentionality in media literacy supports a human-centered approach, where technologies support gathering, and where the focus of media literacies embraces the values of being in the world together toward civic betterment.

Civic media literacies: a value-driven approach

Media literacies that prioritize human connections, and the values that support being in the world together toward a common good, embrace a civic intentionality. Civic media literacies are the ways in which media literacy processes and practices are designed to bring people together and support media critique and creation that is intentional in its design toward civic impact. This approach to media literacy emerges from scholarship in civic media, which Gordon and Mihailidis (2016) define as "the technologies, designs, and practices that produce and reproduce the sense of being in the world with others toward common good" (p. 3). In their argument for a common good, Gordon and Mihailidis highlight the "dramatic increase in the [media] channels available to

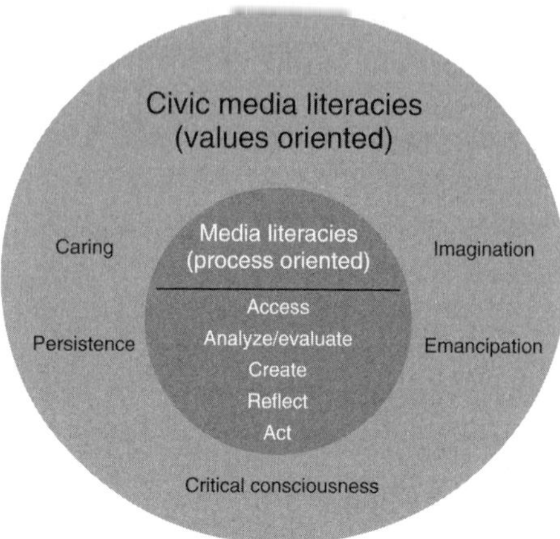

Figure 1 Civic media literacies.

people to participate in what we now call civic life" (p. 2). They believe this has necessitated a specific focus on the practices and processes that motivate media use toward a common good. Common good, while subjective in nature, refers to "invoking the good of the commons, or actions taken that benefit a public outside of the actor's intimate sphere" (p. 4). In this way, media literacies must embrace new value models that support, or add to, traditional practices. Media literacies have long supported outcomes associated with common good, but have rarely prioritized the values and dispositions needed to embrace such outcomes.

The values that comprise civic media literacies (see Figure 1) have an intentional focus on constructs that bring people together. These value constructs provide a front door for media literacy practices where deep investigation, interpretation, and application can be framed in an intentionally civic way. Each value construct supports an agentive approach to media literacy practice. Agency in this context concerns the relations needed for people to act meaningfully in the world. Arendt (1958) describes this form of agency as revealing ourselves in public with others, and acting as a way to enact relation in the world. Revealing ourselves necessitates a sense of self-efficacy, where individuals have the ability to see themselves as impactful actors in the world, and where self-efficacy becomes collective as they engage with other actors in the world (Bandura, 1989).

A *caring* ethic focuses on how we embrace relations with others in the world. Noddings (1984) describes the phenomenon of care as "how, in general, we should meet and treat one another" (p. 11). She develops a caring ethic, which she defines as "a state of being in relation, characterized by receptivity, relatedness and engrossment" (Noddings, 1984, p. 11). Noddings differentiates *caring about* from *caring for*: where caring about is transactional and individually focused to the point that it absolves us from deep relational engagement. Caring for, on the other hand, is a collective process in which we build deep, meaningful, and relational approaches to being in the world with one another. A caring ethic in media literacy supports practices and processes that prioritize relation, embeddedness, and presence. They forefront media inquiries by asking how we care for, how that is enacted in our relation to the world, and in what ways media use supports a caring ethic.

Critical consciousness, developed by Paolo Freire in his work with marginalized populations in Brazil, focuses on a form of media literacy pedagogy that promotes transformation, and "learning to perceive social, political and economic contractions and to take action against the oppressive elements of reality" (Freire, 1973, p. 4). Critical consciousness promotes education as a practice of freedom (hooks, 1994), where pedagogies focus on a reinvention of the future, and through criticality challenge the existing oppressions that define societies. Civic media literacies focus on the ways in which critical consciousness can promote responsiveness in the real world. Dewey (1897) wrote about social consciousness as a form of reconstruction in society, and education was a means of striving for such consciousness. Civic media literacies are designed in a way to intentionally focus on responsiveness, transgression, and education as reform, freedom, and transformation.

Imagination focuses on the capacity for media literacies to pursue "the capacity to imagine alternatives to current social, political or economic conditions" (Jenkins, Shresthova, Gamber-Thompson, & Zimmerman, 2016, p. 300). In this scenario, young people learn to embrace and build alternative worlds, remix existing content, and build creative exercises that are focused on experimentation, play, and wonder. Imagination embraces what Gordon and Walter (2016) term *meaningful inefficiencies*, an approach to playful engagement in the world that moves from seriousness and outcomes to one that embraces finding creativity and connected approaches to reinventing current systems. An imagination frame also opens up avenues for expression and collaboration that are beyond the bounds of conventional political communication, which is something from which young people often feel alienated. Civic media literacies that focus on imagination embrace the exploration of alternative realities, where young people can imagine and subvert conventional media systems through wonder, play, and creativity.

Persistence is a value construct that responds to the demands of digital presence and a current media environment that promotes shallow engagements and consistent pivoting from pursuit to pursuit, idea to idea, issue to issue. A persistent mindset builds from the scholarship of Duckworth, Peterson, Matthews, and Kelly (2007) on the concept of *grit*, which Duckworth defines as "working strenuously toward challenges, maintaining effort and interest over years despite failure, adversity, and plateaus in progress" (p. 1087). In this formulation, young people develop the capacity to employ consistent effort to advocate for a position or on behalf of an issue, and continue to do so when faced with challenges and hurdles in their pursuit. Civic media literacies embrace persistence as a way to connect knowledge to action, to bring a sense of self-efficacy and agency to the learner, and to help them find fulfillment in the pursuit of media reforms that require consistent effort and engagement over time.

Emancipation positions media literacies as a practice of reform and rejuvenation. Here we position media literacy as the potential to liberate, and to build communication practices that help build self-determination and empowerment. Milan (2016) writes about the power of such practices to develop a sense of active response to social oppression and marginalization, positioning media practice as a form of liberation.

Civic media literacy practices that focus on emancipation are designed to interrogate the structures and institutions that build and control information and communication. This approach also allows media literacy skills to be developed to question voice, participation, and active engagement in digital culture.

Civic media literacies are presented here to advocate for media practices and processes that embrace the values of human connection. They support what Levine (2013) has termed "civic renewal," where people take control of their media environments and collaborate to improve social conditions. These value constructs are positioned to support existing media literacy practices, and to build into them a civic focus based on the values of being in the world together and the processes that support a common good.

Acknowledgment

This entry is adapted from *Civic Media Literacies: Re-Imagining Human Connection in an Age of Digital Abundance*, by Paul Mihailidis (2018). Reproduced by permission of Taylor and Francis Group, LLC, a division of Informa plc.

SEE ALSO: Citizen Journalism; Civic Activism; Civic Media; Connected Learning; Emancipatory Communication; Media Activism and Action-Oriented Learning; Mediatization; Participatory Politics and the Civic Dimensions of Media Literacy

References

Arendt, H. (1958). *The human condition*. Chicago, IL: University of Chicago Press.

Ashley, S., Maksl, A., & Craft, S. (2013). Developing a news media literacy scale. *Journalism & Mass Communication Educator, 68*(1), 7–21. doi: 10.1177/1077695812469802

Bandura, A. (1989). Human agency in social cognitive theory. *American Psychologist, 44*(9), 1175. doi: 10.1037/0003-066X.44.9.1175

boyd, d. (2017). Did media literacy backfire? *Data & Society*. Retrieved from https://points.datasociety.net/did-media-literacy-backfire-7418c084d88d

Buckingham, D. (2017). Media theory 101: Agency. *Journal of Media Literacy, 64* (1 & 2), 12–16.

Bugeja, M.J. (2018). *Interpersonal divide in the age of the machine*. Oxford, England: Oxford University Press.

Cohen, J. (2018). Exploring echo-systems: A digital media literacy approach to algorithms. *Journal of Media Literacy Education*, forthcoming.

Costanza-Chock, S., Schweilder, C., Basilio, T., McDermott, M., & Lo, P. (2017). Towards transformative media organizing: LGBTQ and two-spirit media work in the United States. In V. Pickard & G. Yang (Eds.), *Media activism in the digital age* (pp. 28–48). New York, NY: Taylor & Francis.

Debord, G. (1967). *Society of the spectacle*. Orlando, FL: Bread and Circuses.

Dewey, J. (1897). *My pedagogic creed*. New York, NY: E.L. Kellogg.

Duckworth, A.L., Peterson, C., Matthews, M.D., & Kelly, D.R. (2007). Grit: Perseverance and passion for long-term goals. *Journal of Personality and Social Psychology, 92*(6), 1087–1101. doi: 10.1037/0022-3514.92.6.1087

Edelman. (2017). Trust barometer. Retrieved from https://www.edelman.com/trust2017/

Eubanks, V. (2018). *Automating inequality: How high-tech tools profile, police, and punish the poor*. New York, NY: St. Martin's Press.

Freire, P. (1973). *Education for critical consciousness*. London, England: Bloomsbury.

Gordon, E., & Mihailidis, P. (2016). *Civic media: Technology, design, practice*. Cambridge, MA: MIT Press.

Gordon, E., & Walter, S. (2016). Meaningful inefficiencies: Resisting the logic of technological efficiency in the design of civic systems. In E. Gordon & P. Mihailidis (Eds.), *Civic media: Technology, design, practice*. Cambridge, MA: MIT Press.

Hamilton, J., & Tworek, H. (2018). Fake news: A modern history. Working Paper presented at the 2018 John Breaux Symposium on the Anatomy of Fake News, Washington, DC.

Hobbs, R., Donnelly, K., Friesem, J., & Moen, M. (2013). Learning to engage: How positive attitudes about the news, media literacy, and video production contribute to adolescent civic engagement. *Educational Media International, 50*(4), 231–246. https://doi.org/10.1080/09523987.2013.862364

hooks, b. (1994). Teaching to transgress: Education as the practice of freedom. *Journal of Engineering Education, 1*: 126–138.

Ito, M., Soep, E., Kligler-Vilenchik, N., Shresthova, S., Gamber-Thompson, L., & Zimmerman, A. (2015). Learning connected civics: Narratives, practices, infrastructures. *Curriculum Inquiry, 45*(1), 10–29. https://www.tandfonline.com/doi/ref/10.1080/03626784.2014.995063?scroll=top

Jenkins, H., Ford, S., & Green, J. (2013). *Spreadable media: Creating value and meaning in a networked culture*. New York, NY: NYU Press.

Jenkins, H., Shresthova, S., Gamber-Thompson, L., & Zimmerman, A. (2016). Superpowers to the people! How young activists are tapping the civic imagination. In E. Gordon & P. Mihailidis (Eds.), *Civic media: Technology, design, practice* (pp. 295–320). Cambridge, MA: MIT Press.

Kahne, J., & Bowyer, B. (2016). Educating for democracy in a partisan age: Confronting the challenges of motivated reasoning and misinformation. *American Educational Research Journal, 54*(1), 3–34. https://doi.org/10.3102/0002831216679817

Kellner, D. (2010). Media spectacle and media events: Some critical reflections. In N. Couldry, A. Hepp, & F. Krotz (Eds.), *Media events in a global age* (pp. 76–92). London, England: Routledge.

Levine, P. (2013). *We are the ones we have been waiting for: The promise of civic renewal in America*. New York, NY: Oxford University Press.

Marwick, A., & Lewis, R. (2017). Media manipulation and disinformation online. Data & Society Research Institute. Retrieved from https://datasociety.net/pubs/oh/DataAndSociety_MediaManipulationAndDisinformationOnline.pdf

Mihailidis, P. (2009). Beyond cynicism: Media education and civic learning outcomes in the university. *International Journal of Media and Learning, 1*(3), 1–13. doi: 10.1162/ijlm_a_00027

Mihailidis, P. (2018). Civic media literacies: re-Imagining engagement for civic intentionality. *Learning, Media and Technology, 42*(2), 152–164. https://doi.org/10.1080/17439884.2018.1428623

Milan, S. (2016). Liberated technology: Inside emancipatory communication activism. In E. Gordon & P. Mihailidis (Eds.), *Civic media: Technology, design, practice* (pp. 107–124). Cambridge, MA: MIT Press.

Morozov, E. (2017) Moral panic over fake news hides the real enemy – the digital giants. *The Guardian*. Retrieved from https://www.theguardian.com/commentisfree/2017/jan/08/blaming-fake-news-not-the-answer-democracy-crisis

Noddings, N. (1984). *Caring: A relational approach to ethics and moral education*. Berkeley, CA: University of California Press.

Rogow, F. (2016, December 4). "If everyone were media literate, would Donald Trump be president?" Retrieved from https://medialiteracyeducationmaven.edublogs.org/2016/12/04/if-everyone-was-media-literate-would-donald-trump-be-president/

Rushkoff, D. (2013). *Present shock: When everything happens now*. New York, NY: Penguin Books.
Rushkoff, D. (2016). The economy needs to be more human: A chat with Douglas Rushkoff. By Alex Pasternak. *Motherboard*. Retrieved from https://motherboard.vice.com/en_us/article/qkjwa3/douglas-rushkoff-team-human-podcast
Shirky, C. (2010). *Cognitive surplus: Creativity and generosity in a connected age*. London, England: Penguin Books.
Sloman, S., & Fernbach, P. (2017). *The knowledge illusion: Why we never think alone*. New York, NY: Penguin Books.
Srnicek, N. (2017). *Platform capitalism*. Oxford, England: Wiley.
Sundar, S.S. (2017). There's a psychological reason for the appeal of fake news. *New Republic*. Retrieved from https://newrepublic.com/article/139230/theres-psychological-reason-appeal-fake-news
Surowiecki, J. (2005). *The wisdom of crowds*. New York: NY: Anchor.
Taplin, J. (2017). *Move fast and break things: How Facebook, Google, and Amazon cornered culture and undermined democracy*. Newport Beach, CA: Back Bay Books.
Titcomb, J., & Carson, J. (2016). Fake news: What exactly is it and how can you spot it? *The Telegraph*. Retrieved from http://www.telegraph.co.uk/technology/0/fake-news-origins-grew-2016/
Tripodi, F. (2018). Searching for alternative facts: Analyzing scriptural inference in conservative news practices. Data & Society Research Institute. Retrieved from https://datasociety.net/wp-content/uploads/2018/05/Data_Society_Searching-for-Alternative-Facts.pdf
Turkle, S. (2016). *Reclaiming conversation: The power of talk in a digital age*. New York, NY: Penguin Books.
Van Dijck, J. (2013). *The culture of connectivity: A critical history of social media*. Oxford, England: Oxford University Press.

Further reading

Dahlgren, P. (2009). *Media and political engagement*. Cambridge, England: Cambridge University Press.
Gordon, E., & Mihailidis, P. (Eds.). (2016). *Civic media: Technology, design, practice*. Cambridge, MA: MIT Press.
Gordon, E., & Mugar, G. (2018). *Civic media practice: Identification and evaluation of media and technology that facilitates democratic process*. Engagement Lab White Paper. Retrieved from https://elab.emerson.edu/projects/civic-media-practice
Milner, H. (2002). *Civic literacy: How informed citizens make democracy work*. Lebanon, NH: University Press of New England.
Schudson, M. (1998). *The good citizen: A history of American civic life*. New York, NY: Free Press.
Silverstone, R. (2007). *Media and morality*. Cambridge, England: Polity Press.

Paul Mihailidis is an associate professor of civic media and journalism in the school of communication at Emerson College in Boston, MA, where he teaches media literacy, civic media, and community activism. He is founding Program Director of the MA in Civic Media: Art & Practice, Principle Investigator of the Emerson Engagement Lab, and Faculty Chair and Director of the Salzburg Academy on Media and Global Change. His research focuses on the nexus of media, education, and civic voices. His most recent books, *Civic Media Literacies* (2018) and *Civic Media: Technology, Design,*

Practice (2016, with Eric Gordon), outline effective practices for engagement and action taking in daily civic life. His work has been featured in the *New York Times*, the *Washington Post*, *Slate Magazine*, the Nieman Foundation, *USA Today*, CNN, and others. Mihailidis holds a visiting professorship at Bournemouth University in England. He coedits the *Journal of Media Literacy Education*, and sits on the advisory board for *iCivics*. He earned his PhD from the Phillip Merrill College of Journalism at the University of Maryland, College Park.

Coding as Literacy

CRYSTLE MARTIN
El Camino College, USA

Coding has been hailed as the 21st-century need-to-know skill. This is partly because of the ever growing tech sector, which requires more and more people who have coding skills to meet its demand. A second reason is that learning to code teaches you more than just how to make an app or a game. It also helps you understand how to solve problems and think. It has become such a foundational part of learning that it has been called a form of literacy. Computational thinking, the conceptual underpinning of coding, has been described as an integral part of understanding how the technologically driven world works, since coding infiltrates nearly every part of it. This entry explores what coding is, why it is important, and what about it makes it a form of literacy.

What is coding?

Coding is the act of using code, short pieces of predetermined language, to write a program. Code is the building block to all digital things. Code, like all languages, comes in many forms. For example, Javascript is used for coding websites; Python is designed to emphasize code readability through clear and expressive syntax; SQL is used to interact with databases; PHP produces dynamic web pages.

You do not need to be a computer programmer or a computer scientist to understand the basics of coding or to access the benefits that coding has to offer. Instead, learning the basics and the logic behind coding can offer a lot of benefits. This is because coding has both a code side and a logic side. The logic or the thought process behind coding is often called "computational thinking" or "computational literacy."

Why is coding important?

Coding is what makes it possible to create software, apps, and websites. It is a process that begins with a computing problem and ends with an executable computer program.

The popular press has extolled the virtues of coding and the need for coding as part of youth education (Crow, 2014; Dishman, 2016; Kohli, 2015; Mims, 2015; Missio, 2015). President Obama launched the Coding for All initiative, which made coding a national education priority. Understanding how coding works helps explain the world. Coding is not only related to computer science positions but concerns all fields of expertise. It is a complete way of thinking. Computing is involved in all aspects of life. Learning to code develops problem-solving, creativity, digital literacy, and computational thinking skills (Brennan & Resnick, 2012; Wing, 2011). Jobs in software development are projected to grow 17% between 2014 and 2024, as reported by the Bureau of Labor Statistics (2016). But coding is used by more than just those in software development: it is used in many professions such as research, web design, and art.

Increasing diversity in participation is important to the improvement of computer science. Studies have shown that increased diversity improves problem-solving (Ashcraft & Blithe, 2010; Barker & Aspray, 2006; Papastergiou, 2008; Wulf, 1999). Many barriers, as described by the National Center for Women & Information Technology (2012) in its "Girls in IT" report, remain for reaching equity in coding: unequal opportunities, lack of role models, computing curriculum disconnected from interest and environment, and computing portrayed in popular media as masculine and geeky.

What is literacy?

The term "literacy" has changed over time. Although deceptively simple on the surface, literacy is both complex and dynamic. It is continually being redefined as times change. The notion of what it is like to be literate and what constitutes literacy is influenced by academic research, institutional agendas, national context, cultural values, policy, and personal experience. Historically, in English, *being literate* means being well educated or learned. But starting in the 19th century it also began to refer to a person's ability to read and write text, quite apart from designating one's being educated in a given field. From the mid-20th century on, scholars started to spend more time defining literacy.

UNESCO's report *Education for All* (Preston, 2006) breaks down the debate on literacy into four discrete units of understandings that cover nearly all theoretical conceptions of literacy:

- literacy as an autonomous set of skills;
- literacy as applied, practiced, and situated;
- literacy as a learning process;
- literacy as text.

Literacy has changed from being a simple process of acquiring basic cognitive skills to being a complex process of using these skills so as to contribute to socioeconomic growth and development and to social awareness and critical reflection as a basis for personal and social change.

Literacy has come to be conceived of as based on skills; and it has diversified. The most common skill set of literacy would be reading, writing, and oral skills. These are generally what people think of when they think of literacy. They are often considered to be at the core of both language and being educated. Numeracy is also a very common skill. It usually consists of the ability to process, interpret, and communicate numerical, quantitative, spatial, statistical, and even mathematical information in contextually appropriate ways. Information literacy is considered skills-based literacy that describes how people find, evaluate, and use information. Over time, these skills-based approaches have been seen as limited; and a set of applied and situated literacies has been explored. The change took place as researchers argued that literacy practice is changed by social and cultural context; and this idea gave rise to new literacy studies.

As the perception of literacy has changed, literacy came to be viewed as a learning process. Experiential learning cycles are necessary for the development of literacy. This learning strategy means that there is no final state of literacy, but only a state of continual learning. People are always able to develop literacy in better ways; they can also develop many literacies at once or multiple literacies. This approach makes coding a perfect candidate for being considered a form of literacy.

The framing of coding as a literacy and its connection to other frameworks

In the past two decades coding has been ascribed to various types of literacies. Digital literacy and traditional literacy are two of these. There are some who feel that coding is just part of larger digital literacy. Digital literacy does incorporate a much larger literacy, which covers a variety of activities, from basic computing to web development. So coding could be considered part of digital literacy, but if the two should be connected coding could be a subliteracy of digital literacy, still recognized on its own.

Being able to edit photos is not the same as being able to code; coding is about the skill and the understanding—the literacy.

Is coding a literacy?

The discussion of coding's being a literacy is not new; it has been around for over 50 years. The first person on record as arguing that programming is a skill widely applicable outside computer science is Alan Perlis. During a forum at MIT in 1961, he described an undergraduate computer class that looked very similar to the standard first-year writing course (Perlis, 1962). Perlis highlighted the fact that contact with computers should happen early on in one's education, should be analytical, not purely descriptive, and the course should develop an operational literacy. Perlis attempted to demonstrate how coding should be treated as any other foundational course and should be part of an experiential approach to learning.

This discussion about coding being a form of literacy continues. One major question is whether coding, being fundamental, should function outside computer science.

Some, such as Annette Vee, say "yes." If coding is a literacy and is fundamental to students, then it needs to be available to all and not contained inside computer science. Annette Vee (2013) describes the potential impact of everyone who learns to code as a way to restructure law and representative government. Vee feels that this literacy, like other literacies, has the potential to be transformative at a societal level. Coding is an everyday activity, on a par with reading and writing, because code makes many devices we interact with on a daily basis. It should be treated as an ordinary activity, not as a special or strange phenomenon.

In an article titled "Is Coding the New Literacy?" Tasneem Raja (2014) describes an ongoing feeling about the importance of coding and its being as essential as reading and writing. Raja stresses that computational thinking cannot be limited to the elite. Raja emphasizes the importance of producing tech-savvy citizens in every public-school classroom, and ends by saying that coding literacy is essential to getting a good job. Coding, when seen as a literacy, is considered essential. This creates the need to understand how coding as a literacy can be identified. Computational thinking is one way to do this.

Computational thinking

Computational thinking is essentially described as the way programmers think. It focuses on problem-solving, experimentation, and critical thinking. Annette Vee is of the view that you must understand how a computer solves problems in order to be able to ask useful questions and get the truly desired answer. Computational thinking is the process of recognizing aspects of computation in the surrounding world and of applying tools and techniques from computer science to understand and reason about both natural and artificial systems and process, as described by Furber (2012). A similar definition is presented by the ITEST Working Group on Computational Thinking. The group described computational thinking as sharing commonalities with other types of thinking such as algorithmic thinking, engineering thinking, and mathematical thinking. In 2012, a report of the British Royal Society titled *Shut Down or Restart: The Way Forward for Computing in UK Schools* asserted that computational thinking offers insights into information operation in natural and engineered systems (Furber, 2012). The Center for Computational Thinking at Carnegie Mellon University describes computational thinking as a way to solve problems that involves abstraction, algorithmic thinking, and other computer science concepts.

To go back to the beginning, Jeanette Wing coined the term "computational thinking." She created it as a way to highlight the pervasiveness of computing in all aspects of contemporary life and understanding. She wanted to highlight how computer science offers more than software and hardware artifacts; it is also an intellectual framework for thinking. Computational thinking is a thought process used in formulating a problem and in expressing its solutions. It encompasses problem formulation as well as problem solution. Using abstraction and the automation of computer science, more complex systems can be created, allowing for scaling. Wing has a grand vision of computational thinking being integrated as a regular part of the K-12 curriculum (primary and secondary education in the United States), on a par with reading, writing, and mathematics. Computational thinking helps not only with understanding the systems of technology, but also with the collection and production of data—through instruments, experiments, simulations, and crowdsourcing. Wing (2014) describes computational thinking as not solely focused on computer science, but as offering educational and intellectual benefits across domains. Wing's (2008) article "Computational Thinking and Thinking about Computing" stresses the pervasiveness of computational thinking and seeks a "deeper" version of it. She posits that deeper computational thinking will support the modeling of more and more complex systems and the analysis of the vast amounts of data we produce.

Wing (2008) describes a set of challenges that the educational community will have to tackle as computational thinking becomes more and more integrated into everyday life.

1. What are effective ways of learning (teaching) computational thinking by (to) children? What are the elemental concepts of computational thinking? What would be an effective ordering of concepts in teaching children, as their learning ability progresses over the years? How should we best integrate the tool with teaching the concepts?
2. How do we make our technology and the wealth of its applications accessible to all? How do we balance openness with privacy?

One method for having more people with access to computational thinking is for them to develop it through block-based coding. Examples of such coding would be Scratch (http://scratch.mit.edu), App Inventor, Alice (http://www.alice.org), and Google's Blockly. Visually designing applications and programs allows all to learn the underlying logic of coding, that being computational thinking. Because block-based coding is visual and offers immediate feedback, it creates opportunities for problem-driven learning and motivational potential, both of which foster opportunities for computational thinking development.

One place where one can see computational thinking in action on a large scale is Scratch. Scratch is an online visual coding language and online community, with over 20 million members, developed by MIT's Lifelong Kindergarten Group, which is led by Mitch Resnick. It was created as a place for youths to develop computational thinking through interest. Scratch designers use a constructionist approach to learning that is based on the work of Seymour Papert; and they attempt to place the learning of computational thinking in a social context. Papert was an early pioneer in programming languages for kids, developing the Logo programming languages, which used turtle graphics, where commands for movement and drawing produced graphic lines either virtually or physically, with the use of a robot called a turtle.

Karen Brennan and Mitch Resnick (2012), in a paper originally presented at the American Education Research Association conference in Vancouver in 2012, have broken computational thinking into computational concepts, computational practices, and computational perspectives. Computational concepts are common across most programming languages. Brennan and Resnick have identified seven concepts that are highly useful and transfer across programming languages. These are sequences, loops, parallelism, events, conditionals, operators, and data. Sequences specify that a certain set of coding or programming instructions should elicit a particular behavior or action. Loops indicate that a particular sequence of code should be run a designated number of times. Events are actions or activities that cause something else to happen. Parallelism is a situation where two sets of instructions happen at the same time. Conditionals are pieces of code that cause certain outcomes on the basis of particular conditions. Operators provide support for mathematical, logical, and string manipulations. Data involve storing, retrieving, and updating values. Computational practices cover the process of thinking and learning, incorporating how learning occurs, not just what was learned. Computational practices cover four main areas: being incremental and interactive; testing and debugging; reusing and remixing; and abstracting and modularization. Being incremental and iterative illustrates the adaptive process needed when designing a project and implementing it in code. Testing and debugging are strategies for dealing with and fixing problems, and include strategies like trial and error. Reusing and remixing constitute the process of using one's own or others' code to develop new projects. Abstracting and modularizing represent the development of large programs through the assemblage of smaller pieces. Computational perspectives describe the shift of those who learn to code, namely a shift in how they see themselves. Computational perspectives consist of expressing, connecting, and questioning, expressing a situation where a computational thinker uses computation and coding for design and self-expression. Connecting describes a situation where a computational thinker understands the social practices that accompany computational thinking and the learning that goes with it. Questioning indicates that a computational thinker sees the integration of technology into his or her surroundings; it gives that thinker the ability to negotiate the realities of the technological world. Brennan and Resnick take this comprehensive view, which focuses on computational thinking as a whole mental system, as a literacy, through which one can interpret the power that coding offers.

Coding as literacy

A report released by the Girl Scouts of America titled *Generation STEM* (Modi, Schoenberg, & Salmond, 2012) indicates that girls who have participated in hands-on science activities, gone to science and tech museums, and engaged in extracurricular science, technology, engineering, and math (STEM) activities are more likely to be interested in STEM and in the potential of STEM careers. Exposure to coding with the intention to embark on a future career path is a great opportunity, but coding offers more than career opportunities: as a literacy, it opens a host of possibilities for understanding and solving problems in the 21st century.

SEE ALSO: Adolescent Literacy in a Digital World; Connected Learning; Critical Information Literacy; Digital Literacy; Game Design in Media Literacy Education; Literacy, Technology, and Media

References

Ashcraft, C., & Blithe, S. (2010). *Women in IT: The facts.* Boulder, CO: National Center for Women & Information Technology.

Barker, L.J., & Aspray, W. (2006). The state of research on girls and IT. In J.M. Cohoon & W. Aspray (Eds.), *Women and information technology: Research on underrepresentation* (pp. 3–54). Cambridge, MA: MIT Press.

Brennan, K., & Resnick, M. (2012). New frameworks for studying and assessing the development of computational thinking. In *Proceedings of the American Educational Research Association annual conference* (n.p.). Retrieved from http://scratched.gse.harvard.edu/ct/files/AERA2012.pdf

Bureau of Labor Statistics. (2016). *Occupational outlook handbook 2016–17 edition.* Washington, DC: US Department of Labor. Retrieved http://www.bls.gov/ooh/computer-and-information-technology/software-developers.htm

Crow, D. (2014). *Why every child should learn to code.* Retrieved from https://www.theguardian.com/technology/2014/feb/07/year-of-code-dan-crow-songkick

Dishman, L. (2016). *Why coding is the job skill of the future for everyone.* Retrieved from http://www.fastcompany.com/3060883/the-future-of-work/why-coding-is-the-job-skill-of-the-future-for-everyone

Furber, S. (2012). *Shut down or restart? The way forward for computing in UK schools.* London, England: Royal Society.

Kohli, S. (2015). *The economic importance of teaching coding to teens.* Retrieved from http://www.theatlantic.com/education/archive/2015/05/the-economic-importance-of-teaching-coding-to-teens/393263

Mims, C. (2015). *Why coding is your child's key to unlocking the future.* Retrieved from http://www.wsj.com/articles/why-coding-is-your-childs-key-to-unlocking-the-future-1430080118

Missio, L. (2015). *Why kids should learn to code and how to get them started.* Retrieved from http://www.cbc.ca/parents/learning/view/why-kids-should-learn-to-code-and-how-to-get-them-started

Modi, K., Schoenberg, J., & Salmond, K. (2012). *Generation STEM: What girls say about science, technology, engineering, and math: A report from the Girl Scout Research Institute.* New York, NY: Girl Scouts of the USA.

National Center for Women and Information Technology (NCWIT). (2012). *Girls in IT: The facts.* Retrieved https://www.ncwit.org/sites/default/files/resources/girlsinit_thefacts_fullreport2012.pdf

Papastergiou, M. (2008). Are computer science and information technology still masculine fields? High school students' perceptions and career choices. *Computers & Education, 51*(2), 594–608.

Perlis, A. (1962). The computer in the university. In M. Greenberger (Ed.), *Computers and the world of the future* (pp. 180–219). Cambridge, MA: MIT Press.

Preston, R. (2006). *Education for all: Global monitoring report, 2005.* Paris, France: UNESCO.

Raja, T. (2014). Is coding the new literacy? Why America's schools need to train a generation of hackers. *Mother Jones, 39*, 28–35.

Vee, A. (2013). *Is coding the new literacy everyone should learn? Moving beyond yes or no.* Retrieved from http://www.annettevee.com/blog/2013/12/11/is-coding-the-new-literacy-everyone-should-learn-moving-beyond-yes-or-no

Wing, J. (2008). Computational thinking and thinking about computing. *Philosophical Transactions of the Royal Society of London, A: Mathematical, Physical and Engineering Sciences, 366*(1881), 3717–3725.

Wing, J. (2011). Research notebook: Computational thinking: What and why? *Link Magazine*, Spring. Retrieved from https://www.cs.cmu.edu/link/research-notebook-computational-thinking-what-and-why

Wing, J. (2014). Computational thinking benefits society. *40th Anniversary Blog of Social Issues in Computing*. Retrieved from http://socialissues.cs.toronto.edu/index.html%3Fp=279.html

Wulf, W. (1999). *Testimony to the Commission on the Advancement of Women and Minorities in Science, Engineering, and Technology Development*. National Academy of Engineering. Retrieved from https://www.nae.edu/MediaRoom/SpeechesandRemarks/TestimonytotheCommissionontheAdvancementofWomenandMinoritiesinScienceEngineeringandTechnologyDevelopment.aspx

Further reading

Cummings, R.E. (2006). Coding with power: Toward a rhetoric of computer coding and composition. *Computers and Composition, 23*(4), 430–443.

Falkner, K. (2015). Computational thinking as the "new literacy": Professional development opportunities. *Curriculum & Leadership Journal, 13*(9). Retrieved from http://www.curriculum.edu.au/leader/computational_thinking_as_the_new_literacy,38197.html?issueID=13005

Lankshear, C., & Knobel, M. (2003). *New literacies: Changing knowledge and classroom learning*. Buckingham, England: Open University Press.

Monson, R. (2016). Natural language proficiency and computational thinking: Two linked literacies of the 21st century. In *33rd International Conference of* [sic] *Innovation, Practice and Research in the Use of Educational Technologies in Tertiary Education* (pp. 434–439). University of South Australia, Adelaide, Australia.

Papert, S. (1980). *Mindstorms: Children, computers, and powerful ideas*. New York, NY: Basic Books.

Papert, S., & Harel, I. (Eds.). (1991). *Constructionism: Research reports and essays, 1985–1990, by the Epistemology and Learning Research Group, the Media Lab, Massachusetts Institute of Technology*. Norwood, NJ: Ablex Publishing.

Vee, A. (2013). Understanding computer programming as a literacy. *Literacy in Composition Studies, 1*(2), 42–64.

Vee, A. (2017). *Coding literacy: How computer programming is changing writing*. Cambridge, MA: MIT Press.

White House. (2015). *Fact sheet: President Obama announces Computer Science for All initiative*. Retrieved from https://www.whitehouse.gov/the-press-office/2016/01/30/fact-sheet-president-obama-announces-computer-science-all-initiative-0

Wing, J. (2006). Computational thinking. *Communications of the ACM, 49*(3), 33–35.

Crystle Martin, PhD, is director of library and learning resources at El Camino College, California. Her research addresses youth learning and information literacy development in informal learning spaces. She focuses on the role that interest plays in helping persevere in the acquisition of new information and in developing new skills. She has studied communities for World of Warcraft, Professional Wrestling, and Scratch, a visual coding language. Dr. Martin has published books and articles for education and library and information science audiences.

Communication

ANTONIO LÓPEZ
John Cabot University, Italy

Communication is often simply defined as the act of sending and receiving messages or the exchange of information. More complex definitions refer to it as symbolic communication, which is described as the process of encoding and decoding meaning with signs, images, and language. But communication is not a static term nor simplistic; it can be understood as a culturally constructed concept that has evolved over time, especially as it corresponds to the development of media technology and prevailing views of media effects and society in the past 150 years. Subsequently, at different points in time diverse models of communication have evolved to reflect the media landscape, ranging from one-way models of communication based on traditional broadcast or print media (one-to-many) to interactive views of media based on computer information technology (CIT) and mobile media (many-to-many, many-to-few, and few-to-few). It is further complicated by how communication can be differentiated as either face-to-face, mediated, or extended, and by medium (such as the way a song communicates differently than a photograph, or a newspaper differently than a painting).

Broadly, media literacy educators have been primarily concerned with electronic media, visual media, and print communication (as opposed to interpersonal communication). As such, Joshua Meyrowitz (1998) identified three dimensions of communication that permeate media research and media literacy: content elements (representation, ideas, topics, ideology, etc.), grammar variables (languages specific to medium, such as film/television, print, photography, radio, comics), and medium environments (sensory experience on the individual or societal level). Historically, media literacy practices have mostly focused on content elements. The reason for this pre-dates media education, and relates to the evolution and legacy of communication theory. For this reason, it is necessary to closely examine the focus of much communication theory: the "thing" that is being communicated. Most common definitions of communication include either the concept of a "message" that is sent and received or "information" that is transacted. While the concept of a message might seem self-evident, it is in fact a metaphor and has different meanings according to usage and context. A message can be a literal text (such as a note posted on a door, a text message, or a voicemail), or something implied, such as conveying something with body language, tone of voice, gestures, or emoticons. Neurolinguists George Lakoff and Mark Johnson (1980) identified "message" as a "container metaphor," which means that in everyday language, we think of messages as containers of ideas or information. For example, when we say, "I'm trying to give you a message" or "he is not getting the message," we imply that the message is something that moves through space from one person to another, and that the message itself contains information that can be unpacked like a package.

Everyday usage of the message metaphor reinforces the belief that messages are vessels of ideas or information, and this has been reflected in major communication theories, such as the Shannon–Weaver model, which had tremendous impact on media and communication studies in the 20th century. According to the Shannon–Weaver model, which was developed to improve telephone engineering, a message is coded and then transmitted from sender to receiver on a linear pathway through a channel, encountering noise along the way that could impact the ability of the message to be received clearly. Noise in this sense is literally interference, such as static, that makes it difficult to receive a completed message. "Successful" communication was thought of purely on technical terms, and communication "failure" was seen as rare and a problem of human error or technical problems. Meaning was seen as free of distortion and fully conveyable. Concurrently, early media effects theories also drew upon container metaphors. For example, the hypodermic needle theory (also called magic bullet and conveyor belt theory) popularized in the 1930s by behaviorists is a container metaphor that implied mass media could communicate uniformly with low feedback. The belief was that media messages (including propaganda) could "shoot" or "inject" people with beliefs or ideology. In current media literacy practice, this assumption tends to align with protectionist media literacy proponents who view media as harmful, and therefore promote some kind of protective remedy or "inoculation" against media effects (such as violence).

Historically, the message-as-container metaphor also is linked with the transmission model of communication. According to James Carey (2009), the transmission model is grounded in a 19th-century conception of communication in which messages were transported through space. Before the telegraph, communication was divided between forms of symbolic communication (language, text) and physical communication afforded by travel (roads, boats, airlines, trains, etc.). The invention of the telegraph led to the conflation of these two meanings so that symbolic communication was viewed as something that moved through space (despite the fact that the telegraph converged space and time). According to Carey, terms that associate communication with transmission include "transmitting," "imparting," "sending," and "giving information to others." Alternately, Carey proposed a more interactive model of communication based on a ritual definition in which reality is constantly produced, maintained, and updated *in time* as opposed to *across space*. Here he tied communication to related words, such as "sharing," "participation," "association," "fellowship," and "the possession of a common faith," rooted in the words that derive from the same linguistic origins, such as "commonness," "communion," and "community." Indeed, the meaning of communication from 15th-century usage was "to make common." Communication-as-transmission loses the sense of sharing attributed to original usage. In addition, the ritual framework situates communication as taking place within the context of particular social practices and technological environments. The difference between transmission and ritual concepts of communication is not limited to media, but also corresponds with teaching methods. A traditional classroom environment where the teacher lectures to students with little interaction is a small-scale form of transmission-based communication. Interactive and dialogical approaches to teaching are in alignment with ritual forms of communication.

Stuart Hall's (2001) model of encoding/decoding recognized that communication is inseparable from social, economic, and political structures. According to Hall, when communication takes place, meaning is socially produced when it is coded and decoded; but senders and receivers can be positioned differently and may or may not accept or agree on the same codes. A communicator will encode a media text with a certain intended outcome, but the receiver could respond ("read") in three different ways: either a preferred reading that agrees with and shares the dominant codes; a negotiated response in which the codes are not entirely agreed upon or clearly understood; or an oppositional reading in which the codes are understood but are contested. This model entails a semiotic approach to analysis that involves analyzing how communication is coded, not just in terms of language, but also technically. For example, a live TV news bulletin does not just communicate with information, but also with visual and technical cues that indicate "this is news" (professionally dressed presenters, discursive style, technology in the studio, on-screen text, colors, lighting, etc.). Thus, an encoding/decoding media literacy approach would not just study the information component of news, but also take into consideration the social practices and semiotic conventions used to produce news. Cultural studies has incorporated this theory into the "circuit of culture" model of communication in which an object (like a technological gadget or media text) is examined from multiple dimensions that feed back on themselves. From this approach, communication is seen as a highly complex, iterative process that is constantly negotiated between individuals, institutions (government and private), and society.

Just as "message" has variable meanings, the concept of "information" is widely interpreted according to discipline (i.e., information literacy, information science, information theory, information society, physics, semiotics, etc.), ranging from the concept of fact, to information systems, to sensory input. Greggory Bateson (2000) proposed information be defined as a "difference that makes a difference." So rather than be a container of facts, information was envisioned by Bateson as dynamically shifting according to emerging, new information in an iterative circuit. His example was the lumberjack chopping down a tree. Every blow to the tree produces new information that causes him or her to adjust and calibrate the next swing; information is constantly changing and updated as part of a larger "thinking system"; it is not static or a thing, but rather is dynamic and constantly in flux. In this instance, information is an iterative concept functioning within a communicative ecosystem. Likewise, Mikhail Bakhtin theorized communication as inherently dialogic, occurring in a chain of "utterances" that constantly reference other "utterances" (a clear example of this is in the practice of remix and intertextuality). Etienne Wenger proposed that communication is situated through the interaction of "boundary objects" within social contexts. Boundary objects are texts that have mutually agreed upon properties (such as an insurance claim form or passport), but will have different meanings according to their perceived value in a particular context. For example, the insurance claim form has a different meaning and purpose according to the claimant, postal worker who delivers it, claims processor, or insurance company manager in charge of claims policy.

These examples demonstrate that communication can be ecological in the sense that it occurs within broader environments and systems that are constantly interacting and adjusting through feedback and changing contexts. Subsequently, ecology as an alternative metaphor for communication has gained traction in recent years. For example, the information ecology model proposes that communication is conditioned by information ecosystems that have specific social practices (such as libraries, schools, copy centers, or hospitals). Places where media literacy is practiced, be they school computer labs, classrooms, youth centers, or alternative media centers, can also be considered information ecologies in which communication is situated and conditioned by those environments. With the prevalence of CITs and mobile phones in learning spaces and general media use, communication can be considered as part of the convergence culture model where electronic media entails increasing interaction, participation, affective economics, collective intelligence, and transmedia storytelling.

Dialogic approaches of communication also correspond with nonwestern perspectives on communication ethics. A growing body of scholarship from Africa, Asia, and Latin America recognizes the importance of the right to be heard, the practice of listening, the role of meaning construction as a communal act, the social nature of language and identity, and the role of communication in the encounter with the Other. Nonwestern approaches to communication highlight the needs of minority communities to be heard and recognize that communication is inherently linked to the interdependence of people across cultures. For example, empathy and love are aspects of communication that are ignored by western models. Moreover, they argue that human rights are fundamentally grounded in the equality of communication. Additionally, many indigenous and ancient cultures viewed communication as "alive," and not inert as traditional communications models suggest. This view is reflected in the Buddhist precept that one should refrain from harmful speech in order to avoid the repercussions that speech acts can evoke.

Meyrowitz proposed that communication theory move from the study of messages to communication technologies as social environments. This approach is largely influenced by the media ecology movement that emerged from the work of Marshall McLuhan and Neil Postman. As McLuhan famously said, the medium is the message. From this perspective, how technology shapes communication is much more important than the actual content of communication. For example, with the telephone the actual content of phone calls is not what has changed society, but the use of the phone itself. In terms of media literacy education, this is a very underdeveloped area of practice and pedagogy. Some media literacy approaches treat content (such as violence) as uniform, regardless of whether it is in a film, comics, or video games, without regard to how the medium shapes the content. Meyrowitz suggested that in order to explore the importance of medium, students could compare communication from different media environments, such as email messages vs. phone calls, debates on television vs. radio, news on television vs. newspapers, and so on.

For media literacy educators, how one approaches or defines communication can affect pedagogy. For some media educators, communication is related to the rhetorical arts, that is, mastering public speaking and verbal, written, and multimedia skills. Those that concentrate on the technical aspects of teaching media, such as video production, tend to focus more on form and media grammar. By understanding the complexity and diversity of perspectives on communication – and the history of the concept – media educators can better situate and orient their practices. Many of the examples in this entry demonstrate that communication is not merely the sending and receiving of messages that contain information; it is a concept constructed through language and is situational in terms of meaning, practice, and discipline. Whether media literacy approaches are often based on reflective practices (such as decoding or deconstructing media messages around issues of content, representation, and ideology), producing media content (to learn how to better develop communication "skills"), or interactive media, it is necessary to examine what texts communicate in terms of content, but also how they communicate in terms of form and medium. Future research and curriculum development can focus on an expanded definition of communication that explores holistically the three broad categories defined by Meyrowitz (content, grammar, and environment).

SEE ALSO: Civic Media Literacies; Computer Labs in Primary and Secondary Education; Emancipatory Communication; Knowledge Structures; Literacy, Technology, and Media; Meaning-Making; Media Literacy for the 21st Century Teacher; Media Literacy in Communication Education; Medium Theory; News Literacies; Political Economy

References

Bateson, G. (2000). *Steps to an ecology of mind.* Chicago, IL: University of Chicago Press.
Carey, J.T. (2009). *Communication as culture: Essays on media and society* (Rev. ed.). New York, NY: Routledge.
Hall, S. (2001). Encoding/decoding. In M.G. Durham & D. Kellner (Eds.), *Media and cultural studies: Keyworks* (Rev. ed., pp. xxxviii, 755). Oxford, England: Blackwell.
Lakoff, G., & Johnson, M. (1980). *Metaphors we live by.* Chicago, IL: University of Chicago Press.
Meyrowitz, J. (1998). Multiple media literacies. *Journal of Communication, 48*(1), 96–108. doi: 10.1111/j.1460-2466.1998.tb02740.x

Further reading

Christians, C.G., & Nordenstreng, K. (Eds.). (2014). *Communication theories in a multicultural world.* New York, NY: Peter Lang.
Holmes, D. (2011). *Communication theory: Media, technology, society.* London, England: SAGE.
McQuail, D. (2002). *McQuail's reader in mass communication theory* (6th ed.). London, England: SAGE.
Nardi, B.A., & O'Day, V. (2000). *Information ecologies: Using technology with heart.* Cambridge, MA: MIT Press.
Reddy, M.J. (1979). The conduit metaphor: A case of frame conflict in our language about language. In A. Ortony (Ed.), *Metaphor and thought* (pp. 284–324). Cambridge, England: Cambridge University Press.

Antonio López, PhD, has a research focus on bridging sustainability with media literacy. He has written numerous academic articles and essays linking sustainability and environmental issues with media literacy, as well as three books: *Mediacology: A Multicultural Approach to Media Literacy in the 21st Century* (2008), *The Media Ecosystem: What Ecology Can Teach Us About Responsible Media Practice* (2012), and

Greening Media Education: Bridging Media Literacy with Green Cultural Citizenship (2014). He is currently Associate Professor of Communications and Media Studies at John Cabot University in Rome, Italy.

Community Informatics

LINDA M. GALLANT
Emerson College, USA

Community informatics is the practice of using information and communication technologies to empower communities and to facilitate community engagement. Technology is used as a focal point and organizing tool. Informatics is the process of turning digital data into information. In turn, communities can leverage this process to augment and extend civic engagement beyond time-bound meetings and physical locations. Community informatics is steeped in an action-oriented and problem-solving perspective with a core social-value proposition to improve people's lives in community contexts (Stillman & Denison, 2014).

Its pragmatic focus is often criticized as having a weak theoretical base (Goodwin, 2012; Stillman & Denison, 2014; Stillman & Linger, 2009). Historically, community informatics develops from two action-based research streams: traditional and online studies of communities; and computer-supported cooperative work (CSCW) and groupware.

The inception of group and community goal-oriented work through computer-mediated communication started in the 1970s with CSCW and groupware; then in the early 1990s, with increasing public access to the Internet, virtual communities and electronic bulletin boards sought to strengthen social ties and civic goals (De Cindio, 2015). Community is the core social form of community informatics.

A community has three integral components: interaction; identification; and shared locality. Interaction is primarily direct in communities where cooperation is a prominent civic practice with decision-making as a problem-solving characteristic. The decision-making authority of the community brings about the matter of the problem-solving ability. Interaction patterns follow socially developed norms. Identification unites people and can provide measurable boundaries around which those people are integrated into communities. A sense of community identification can be intangible; it can also be geographical or functional. The losses of territoriality with urban groups lead to the emergence of functional communities. Shared locality allows community members to interact. Communities must have information-intensive centers or institutions such as government buildings, religious centers, town squares, cafes, bars, and other official and unofficial places to share information in order to create and maintain community life. Shared locality or spaces that facilitate social interaction can occur online.

As traditional communities take advantage of online tools and social media, it is important to emphasize that community informatics research and practice are grounded in communities online and not in online communities. "An online community may be loosely defined as a group of people who interact in cyberspace together over time. A community online, however, is a community that exists offline, and which uses cyberspace as part of community 'life'" (Lawson, 2004, p. 128). Civically engaged geographic and functional communities can use online communication platforms to supplement face-to-face meetings and communication.

As an approach, community informatics advocates participatory design (Gurstein, 2003). This means that the design and application of information and communications technology (ICT) systems in communities must take into consideration the social context and must provide effective use that is based on a system's users. Moreover, community informatics must adopt ICTs to facilitate problem-solving and achieve community empowerment (Stillman & Denison, 2014). To fully engage the community, an inclusive approach must be secured. Access can be addressed by applying practices from research and guidelines on universal access, the digital divide, and digital disparities.

Universal access must be a guiding principle for policy on the use of ICTs for civic engagement. Access should extend to people with physical disabilities, and also to people affected by other barriers, such as limited literacy and outdated technology (Warschauer & Newhart, 2016). Communities must address concerns related to the digital divide and digital disparities in order to remedy any problems of access and usage that their members may face and allow them to engage civically. The digital divide is generally categorized as an inequality in access to the technology that enables users to physically connect to the Internet. The digital divide is a set of "gaps in access to computers and the Internet based on ethnicity, education, and household income" (Rains, 2008, p. 283). Access to ICTs for civic engagement and citizenship is a public policy issue. Post-access disparities occur when people have access to the Internet but may not have adequate language skills, user skills, or content available that relates to their cultural or language needs (Gallant, Irizarry, Boone, & Ruiz-Gordon, 2010; Morey, 2007).

With an ecosystem of tools, communities must choose the technologies that are best suited to their needs and goals. ICT choices may include civic engagement platforms provided by institutional partners or by sponsors, such as civic learning games; effective use of open-source community technologies such as E-forums, listservs, and E-bulletin boards; and commercial social platforms such as Facebook and Twitter. Matching the ICT with the community profile is critical for a community informatics strategy.

Stillman and Denison (2014) emphasize that the focus of community informatics is on collective community well-being as opposed to networked individualism, the basis of social media platforms. Social media platforms such as Facebook, Instagram, and Twitter build on individual profiles. Individuals build social media networks often on lifestyle demographics, which may not correlate with local community concerns. While little research exists as to the extent to which local governments are actually using social media, researchers and practitioners advocate the use of social media platforms as a communication tool, in order to advance open and participatory forms of local civic engagement between citizens and government (Avery & Graham, 2013). Urban planning is a focal point of community informatics practice.

In an example of urban planning, Bryer (2013) provides research that suggests that social media can be used as a collaborative tool between a local government and its citizens. The City of Los Angeles used Facebook and Twitter to communicate with citizens about a Metropolitan Transit Authority (MTA) project. Guidelines for interaction such as comments should be on topic and any defamatory comments should be deleted in order to encourage community engagement. Moreover, appropriately managing community interaction through social media tools takes resources. "A full-time staff member is required to implement and serve as convener and facilitator of the social media space. The tools can be transformational, but if cities are not prepared to implement them fully and strategically, it may be better to not implement them at all" (Bryer, 2013, p. 50).

Increasingly, platforms are being specifically designed for civic engagement. Such platforms include Textizen, Neighborland, Placehood.org, Voterheads, PlaceSpeak, Outline.com, Community PlanIt, and Open Town Hall (Government Technology, 2013). The tools can target a particular population or area of local government, such as public schools. For instance, Chicago Public School administrators who encountered problems in collecting parent feedback employed Textizen, which simplified the process via text messaging. Other platforms, for example Community PlanIt, use gamification techniques for civic engagement by augmenting face-to-face interaction at community meetings with digital role-play.

Beyond collaborative government and civic engagement, social justice is another area researchers in community informatics have explored. Ensuring access to ICTs for all individuals and community members is a core social justice principle in an information society (Gurstein, 2003; Stillman & Denison, 2014; Stoecker, 2005). Social justice promotion in community informatics is especially evident in educational projects and library science disciplines. For instance, educational access programs using Inquire-Based Learning to engage local youth have adopted community informatics to design and implement programs (Montague, 2015). Educational literacy programs connecting schools, libraries, and communities are an established area of community informatics research and practice (Ritzo, Nam, & Bruce, 2009).

Community informatics combines social knowledge of community interaction with ICTs to advance community goals in government planning, civic engagement, and access to education. Community support for community members' access to ICTs, so that they may be able to participate fully in community informatics programming, is a fundamental ethical principle. As studies are mostly action-oriented, researchers are seeking to strengthen the theoretical development of community informatics.

SEE ALSO: Civic Media; Community Media; Digital Divide; Social Action and Advocacy

References

Avery, E.J., & Graham, M.W. (2013). Political public relations and the promotion of participatory, transparent government through social media. *International Journal of Strategic Communication, 7*(4), 274–291. doi: 10.1080/1553118X.2013.824885

Bryer, T.A. (2013). Designing social media strategies for effective citizen engagement: A case example and model. *National Civic Review, 102*(1), 43–50. doi: 10.1002/ncr.21114

De Cindio, F. (2015). Community and technologies, community informatics: Tensions and challenges. *The Journal of Community Informatics*. Retrieved from http://ci-journal.net/index.php/ciej/article/view/1156/1149; doi: 10.4018/9781878289698.ch010

Gallant, L.M., Irizarry, C., Boone, G.M., & Ruiz-Gordon, B. (2010). Spanish content on hospital websites: An analysis of US hospitals' in concentrated Latino communities. *Journal of Computer Mediated Communication, 15*(4), 552–574. doi: 10.1111/jcmc.2010.15.issue-2

Goodwin, I. (2012). Theorizing community as discourse in community informatics: "Resistant identities" and contested technologies. *Communication and Critical/Cultural Studies, 9*(1), 47–66. doi: 10.1080/14791420.2011.645214

Government Technology. (2013). Introducing the 21st-century city hall. *Government Technology*. Retrieved from http://www.govtech.com/e-government/Introducing-the-21st-Century-City-Hall.html; doi: 10.1080/03003938508433207

Gurstein, M. (2003). Effective use: A community informatics strategy beyond the digital divide. *First Monday, 8*(12). Retrieved from http://firstmonday.org/ojs/index.php/fm/article/view/1107/1027; doi: 10.5210/fm.v8i12.1107

Lawson, K. (2004). Libraries in the USA as traditional and virtual "third places." *New Library World, 105*(1198/1199), 125–130. doi: 10.1108/03074800410526758

Montague, R.A. (2015). Mix it up! A blending of community informatics and youth services librarianship to further social justice in library and information. *Library Trends, 64*(2), 444–457. doi: 10.1353/lib.2015.0049

Morey, O. (2007). Health information ties: Preliminary findings on the health information seeking behaviour of an African-American community. *Information Research, 12*(2), paper 297. Retrieved from http://InformationR.net/ir/12-2/paper297.html11.1.2008

Rains, S.A. (2008). Health at high speed: Broadband Internet access, health communication, and the digital divide. *Communication Research, 35*(3), 283–297. doi: 10.1177/0093650208315958

Ritzo, C., Nam, C., & Bruce, B. (2009). Building a strong web: Connecting information spaces in schools and communities. *Library Trends, 58*(1), 82–94. doi: 10.1353/lib.0.0068.

Stillman, L., & Denison, D. (2014). The capability approach community informatics. *Information Society, 30*(3), 200–211. doi: 10.1080/01972243.2014.896687

Stillman, L., & Linger, H. (2009). Community informatics and information systems: Can they be better connected? *Information Society, 25*(4), 255–264. doi: 10.1080/01972240903028706

Stoecker, R. (2005). Is community informatics good for communities? Questions confronting an emerging field. *Journal of Community Informatics, 1*(3). Retrieved from http://www.ci-journal.net/index.php/ciej/article/view/183/129

Warschauer, M., & Newhart, V.A. (2016). Broadening our concepts of universal access. *Universal Access in the Information Society, 15*(2), 183–188. doi: 10.1007/s10209-015-0417-0

Further reading

Day, P. (2010). A brief introduction to the history of community informatics. *AI & Society, 25*(3), 259–263. doi: 10.1007/s00146-010-0286-2

Shin, Y., & Shin, D.H. (2012). Community informatics and the new urbanism: Incorporating information and communication technologies into planning integrated urban communities. *Journal of Urban Technology, 19*(1), 23–42. doi: 10.1080/10630732.2012.626698

Sproull, L., & Arriaga, M. (2007). Online communities. In H. Bidogli (Ed.), *The handbook of computer networks* (Vol. 3, pp. 898–914). Hoboken, NJ: John Wiley & Sons, Inc. doi: 10.1002/9781118256107.ch58

Linda M. Gallant, PhD, is associate professor and graduate program director for the MA in public relations at Emerson College, Boston, Massachusetts. Her research focuses on how web-based technology and social media impact communication. She has published in the *Journal of Computer-Mediated Communication*, *Personal and Ubiquitous Computing*, *First Monday*, the *Journal of Participatory Medicine*, and the *e-Service Journal*.

Community Media

COLIN RHINESMITH
Simmons University, USA

Media literacy scholars have identified five essential competencies that support digital and media literacy: these are the abilities to access, analyze, create, reflect, and act (Hobbs, 2011). While these core competencies are often advanced through community media practice, few studies have made explicit connections between media literacy education and the community media sector. Presented here is an overview of the ways in which community media support these essential competencies; attention will be paid to community media's role in promoting access, participation, diversity, and empowerment as key drivers of media literacy education. This entry highlights youth media as a form of media literacy education within the community media sector. It includes a discussion of the social, cultural, and political contexts that are critical to understanding how community media support fundamental media literacy goals.

What are community media?

Community media facilitate access to the tools, skills, and knowledge needed to participate in media production activities within local social settings. The purpose is to advance the communications needs and interests *of* a particular community rather than *for* the community (Berrigan, 1979). Community media initiatives are often led by community-based organizations or civil society groups, which represent a unique sector of media production activities outside the market and the state. Traditional forms of community media include cable access television, low-power radio, community arts and music initiatives, zines, and street newspapers. In more recent years, community media researchers have sought to understand how the Internet has enabled new forms of community media practice (Breitbart, Glaisyer, Ninan, & Losey, 2011; Fuentes-Bautista, 2014; Johnson, 2007; Rennie, 2006; Rhinesmith, 2016). Community media projects also play a critical role in promoting media diversity and empowerment, often in the form of aboriginal, diasporic, ethnic, and indigenous media practice (Fuller, 2007, 2011; Howley, 2013; Rennie, 2013). These initiatives often connect to community development efforts that work to advance self-determination among underrepresented and historically marginalized populations, including youths.

Community media are often described in relation to what they are not—mainstream commercial media. "Alternative," "citizen," "grassroots," "independent," and "radical" media are closely aligned terms. All are concerned with ensuring that individuals and groups in geographic communities have at least some degree of ownership and control over their local communications landscape. This approach is often emphasized as a response to the concentration of commercial media ownership, which has been portrayed as a threat to democracy. Issues of ownership and control extend beyond the media production channels, training, and facilities, to the underlying infrastructure for community media that makes free speech possible in many places around the globe (Breitbart et al., 2011; Halleck, 2002; Rhinesmith, 2016). Conversations about infrastructure also allow constituents to connect their local community media engagement to state, federal, and global media policy debates.

Funding for these initiatives is as diverse as the types of community media themselves. Community media initiatives receive their support through diverse funding models, from national government policies to private foundation funding to small-scale cooperative approaches. In consequence, discussions about funding for community media are often connected to broader public policy debates. For example, in the United States, where funding for cable access television has been under attack in recent years, the local cable franchising model established through the Cable Communications Policy Act of 1984 has provided individuals and groups in local communities with an opportunity to engage in local communication policy debates connected to state and federal legislation. In this way, community media not only open an opportunity for individual self-expression, but represent a way for private citizens to enter into public life and for youth to engage in media production activities that connect to democratic processes.

Media literacy

Education has always played a critical role in supporting community media (Berrigan, 1979; Higgins, 1999; King & Mele, 1999). In fact, participation in community media production entails media literacy on account of the tools, skills, and knowledge needed to critique and respond to dominant media narratives, symbols, and messages within popular culture (King & Mele, 1999). Such educational initiatives support the empowerment goals within the community media sector. Here Freire's (1970/1993) pedagogical philosophies and techniques are often called upon to differentiate the educational outcomes of community media from commercial media industry-focused trainings. Berrigan (1979), for example, highlighted community media's consciousness-raising focus with Freire's approach, which seeks to break down the "banking model" of education, where knowledge is deposited in a one-way manner into the minds of students. This strategy has been widely embraced by community media practitioners, particularly those who work with youth to support their learning through digital media and civic engagement.

Youth media programs exemplify community media's core values, which focus on local media access, participation, diversity, and empowerment. Scholars have described community media's empowerment orientation as a key media literacy strategy designed to promote learning to gain a civic voice in media culture, to articulate media bias, to engage in media and politics, and to understand commodity culture—among other objectives (Johnson, 2007). Many community media organizations offer educational programs, both during and after school, which serve youths through media literacy and production activities. In the United States, for example, cable-access television has played an important role in promoting media literacy through youth media projects. These initiatives have shown the value and benefits of teaching people to use technology as a means to promote community dialogue while strengthening community ties (Haywood, 2008). Many of these efforts have supported youths in learning how to create media using both traditional (e.g., radio and television) and emerging media forms enabled by networked technologies. Rather than seen as something entirely new, the Internet has changed the ways in which youths access and participate in media, which community media scholars have argued is perhaps "making all media more like community media" (Rennie, 2007, p. 27).

Building on the traditional broadcast, over-the-airwaves model of media engagement through television and radio, youth media activities have clearly extended into online spaces. YouTube and other video-sharing platforms have enabled local community media projects to broaden their reach beyond their local area, into global spaces. Such initiatives have created the potential to elicit empathy and new understandings across cultures and to allow young people to experience what is common across disparate communities around the world. For example, Youth Channel at the Manhattan Neighborhood Network in New York City was among the first TV channels to promote access and participation particularly among disadvantaged, low-income, and minority youths (Johnson, 2007). The station also provides Internet streaming of its youth media content. Many other community media centers in the US provide similar opportunities for young people to benefit from media literacy education through their engagement with both traditional and digital media formats.

Digital storytelling has also been a popular media literacy technique for youth media practitioners. Enabled by digital technologies and online video-sharing platforms, digital storytelling has been used by artists and educators to explore the ways in which digital media can be used to empower personal storytelling (StoryCenter, 2016). This approach has also made it easier for youths and adults to create and share their own stories through community media. Storytelling is powerful because it can combat alienation and isolation by allowing people to both express themselves and develop a sense of empathy (Johnson, 2007). This process also allows individuals and groups from marginalized communities to share their stories with others within a specific geographic area, which can become part of a process of deliberation to advance local community-development goals. These evolving forms of media literacy education offer exciting potential for community media to move forward. However, as digital media access and participation enabled by networked technologies reflect community media production on the surface, questions about how to create a distinct space that is separate from the market and the state continue to remain relevant for the community media sector in the digital age.

Challenges and future directions

There are many social, political, and cultural challenges facing the community media sector. Many are rooted in a lack of funding and support for community media at a time when online engagement is becoming monopolized by commercialized Internet spaces. Part of this challenge stems from ongoing misconceptions surrounding community media in the Internet age. One misconception is that all online amateur media are community media; another is that, because online media occur "naturally," they do not require funding (Rennie, 2007). As long as society embraces these technologically deterministic perspectives, there will continue to be confusion about community media's role in bridging the digital divide, in promoting inclusive media engagement, and in supporting media literacy education for everyone, regardless of race, class, gender, sexuality, and ability. Public libraries suffer from similar misconceptions about the Internet's impact on access to information. Public libraries, like the community media sector, need ongoing funding to support an ever evolving digital media landscape—one that requires sophisticated digital and media literacy strategies to enhance its democratizing potential.

Community media scholars have also pointed to the need for the field to develop histories of community media (Howley, 2013). This approach has significant value in showing the historical developments and connections between community media practice and technological innovations. Work in this area could also help demonstrate how media literacy education has evolved as the technologies of community media have transitioned. Historical perspectives might in turn inform future community media research, practice, and public policy by helping researchers, practitioners, and policymakers learn from the past. In addition, historical investigations of the types of infrastructure that have supported community media practice would be helpful for understanding the various public policy mechanisms that have been leveraged around the world. The community media sector is unique in that it provides people with the opportunity to create and distribute their own media, while at the same time allowing people to make decisions about how the wires, cables, and other mundane aspects of community media infrastructure can be used to promote public access and participation in community media. This history of community media infrastructure as a form of civic engagement might also introduce a new element to thinking about how community media enable participation both in media production and in civic life.

These future directions highlight opportunities for the fields of community media and media literacy to jointly examine how community media, and in particular youth media, create new methods of participation in digital culture (Rennie, 2006). Such an examination includes a focus on the ways in which community media can embrace a multiplatform approach made possible through broadband infrastructure and applications, including community wireless networks, as well as strong community benefits agreements designed to support digital inclusion activities (Breitbart et al., 2011; Johnson, 2007; Rhinesmith, 2016). Community media policy must focus on broadband infrastructure as a key element of its future and development. Community-owned broadband networks offer an exciting opportunity to extend media literacy's core competencies (i.e., access, analyze, create, reflect, and act) into areas that include ownership and control of community media infrastructure. Regardless of the technology, the community media sector must champion its strong human and social networks as part of this broader strategy of moving forward.

SEE ALSO: Access; Citizen Journalism; Civic Media; Community Informatics; Critical Pedagogy; Digital Storytelling; Local Public Access Centers; Media Access and Activism; Media Arts; Youth Media

References

Berrigan, F.J. (1979). *Community communications: The role of community media in development*. Retrieved from http://unesdoc.unesco.org/images/0004/000440/044035eo.pdf

Breitbart, J., Glaisyer, T., Ninan, B., & Losey, J. (2011). *Full spectrum community media: Expanding public access to communications infrastructure*. Retrieved from http://newamerica.net/publications/policy/full_spectrum_community_media

Freire, P. (1970/1993). *Pedagogy of the oppressed*. New York, NY: Continuum.

Fuentes-Bautista, M. (2014). Rethinking localism in the broadband era: A participatory community development approach. *Government Information Quarterly, 31*(1), 65–77.

Fuller, L. (Ed.). (2007). *Community media: International perspectives*. Basingstoke, England: Palgrave Macmillan.

Fuller, L. (Ed.). (2011). *The power of global community media*. Basingstoke, England: Palgrave Macmillan.

Halleck, D. (2002). *Hand-held visions: The impossible possibilities of community media*. New York, NY: Fordham University Press.

Haywood, A. (2008). Access television and youth media: Building partnerships, saving voices and strengthening our communities. *Youth Media Reporter, 2*(1–6), 58–65.

Higgins, J.W. (1999). Community television and the vision of media literacy, social action and empowerment. *Journal of Broadcasting & Electronic Media, 43*(4), 625–644.

Hobbs, R. (2011). *Digital and media literacy: Connecting culture and the classroom*. London, England: Corwin.

Howley, K. (2013). Community media studies: An overview. *Sociology Compass, 7*(10), 818–828.

Johnson, F. (2007). *What's going on in community media?* Washington: Benton Foundation.

King, D.L., & Mele, C. (1999). Making public access television: Community participation, media literacy and the public sphere. *Journal of Broadcasting & Electronic Media, 43*(4), 603–623.

Rennie, E. (2006). *Community media: A global introduction*. Lanham, MD: Rowman & Littlefield.

Rennie, E. (2007). Community media in the prosumer era. *3C Media: Journal of Community, Citizen's and Third Sector Media and Communication, 3*, 25–32.

Rennie, E. (2013). Co-creative media in remote Indigenous communities. *Cultural Science, 6*(1), 22–36.

Rhinesmith, C. (2016). Community media infrastructure as civic engagement. In E. Gordon & P. Mihailidis (Eds.), *Civic media: Technology, design, practice* (pp. 481–500). Cambridge, MA: MIT Press.

StoryCenter. (2016). *Our story*. Retrieved from http://www.storycenter.org/press

Further reading

Howley, K. (2005). *Community media: People, places, and communication technologies*. Cambridge, England: Cambridge University Press.
Howley, K. (2010). *Understanding community media*. Los Angeles, CA: SAGE.
Jankowski, N.W., & Prehn, O. (Eds.). (2002). *Community media in the information age: Perspectives and prospects*. Cresskill, NJ: Hampton Press.
Lewis, P., & Jones, S. (Eds.). (2006). *From the margins to the cutting edge: Community media and empowerment*. New York, NY: Hampton Press.
Stein, L., Kidd, D., & Rodriguez, R. (2009). *Making our media: National and global movements for democratic communication*. Cresskill, NJ: Hampton Press.

Colin Rhinesmith is assistant professor of library and information science at Simmons University, USA. His research and teaching interests are focused on the social, community, and policy aspects of information and communication technology, particularly in areas related to digital inclusion and broadband adoption. Rhinesmith's work has appeared in the following scholarly journals: *Information, Communication & Society*; *Government Information Quarterly*; *International Journal of Communication*; *Telecommunications Policy*; the *Journal of Community Informatics*; the *Journal of Education for Library and Information Science*; and the *Journal of Research on Libraries and Young Adults*.

Computer Labs in Primary and Secondary Education

PATRICK CARMICHAEL
University of Bedfordshire, UK

Many schools have computers and other resources located in computer laboratories or learning resource hubs, although their design and purpose, and patterns of teacher and learner access to them, may vary. This variation reflects wider debates about the place of digital technologies in schools, their role in the curriculum, and the contributions they are intended or expected to make to learning.

The establishment of school computer laboratories has been justified, even in the face of increasing home computer ownership, Internet access, and personal technology use, on the grounds that they enable focused instruction, either about technologies, or in relation to other curriculum content, and guarantee some form of access where personal technology ownership remains uneven. At the same time, this has raised concerns about the educational implications of localizing digital technologies within particular curriculum areas (for example, mathematics and sciences), within school timetables (so that teachers cannot easily integrate computer use with other activities), or in specific locations within school premises. These are particular concerns in primary-level schooling where integrated, cross-curricular work is the norm; Seymour Papert (cited in Kyle, 2000) famously asked what the implications would be for the teaching and learning of writing if children had to go, at a set time, once a week, to a specially designated "pencil room." These concerns aside, there are pragmatic reasons for maintaining a central resource in order that high-value resources, including robotics equipment, printers, and other specialized hardware and software, can be centrally managed and maintained.

There have been significant changes in the digital technologies that enable school computer laboratories to function: not only those immediately evident, such as computers, printers, and interface devices, but also Internet connections, internal networking, and learner monitoring, content management, and Internet filtering systems. Educational software has also developed significantly, taking advantage of the availability of faster network connections and implementing richer web content, hypermedia, and the gamification of educational content.

Two broad traditions in the history of school computer laboratories may be identified: the first emphasizes direct instruction and individual learning, the second, collaborative participation in design projects. Each of these has distinct views as to the role of digital technologies, and the variability in the design and use of school computer laboratories may be understood as material enactments of differences in broader pedagogical theory and practice. This may present teachers and learners with challenges as they attempt to use or repurpose spaces configured for a specific style of instruction to which they do not ascribe, or which is no longer employed in the educational setting in which they are working. The task of the teacher may, therefore, be to try to reconcile sometimes conflicting pedagogical commitments with the physical environment and the available technological resources. These tensions and challenges are reflected in research into technologically rich learning environments; issues that might once have been seen primarily as pedagogical and technological have increasingly been explored in terms of sociomaterial theory which explores the interactions between all the human and nonhuman elements in complex learning environments (Fenwick & Edwards, 2010), or in terms of "ecologies of resources" (Luckin, 2010).

The first tradition in the design and use of school computer laboratories positions technologies as means of delivering or enabling highly focused instruction, often coupled with summative, diagnostic, or adaptive assessment. This can be traced back to Skinner's programmed learning using "teaching machines" (1961, 1965); through the introduction of computer-based instruction systems such as the PLATO (Programmed Logic for Automatic Teaching Operations) system developed at the University of Illinois (Smith & Sherwood, 1976); and then into Internet-based managed learning systems such as Pearson's SuccessMaker (Thrall & Tingey, 2003), which offer adaptive and highly targeted interventions for individual learners.

The computer laboratories developed as part of such initiatives have tended to replicate conventional classrooms in some respects, with fixed computer terminals in rows, supplemented by large screens and, later, interactive whiteboards, for whole-class instruction. Even when programmed learning is not being implemented, this dominant design paradigm has been based on an assumption that learners would interact with digital content through terminals or networked computers primarily on an individual basis. With a shift toward the teaching of information and communications technology

(ICT) as a discrete subject in secondary schools and the establishment of curricula designed to develop techno-literacies (such as use of industry-standard office tools, information retrieval, use of the World Wide Web, web design, and online safety), these too have tended to be taught in formal laboratory settings which may, of course, originally have been designed in support of programmed learning initiatives.

In primary schools, different configurations of space and technologies broadly reflect distinctive pedagogical approaches: where computer laboratories or computer rooms do exist, they may reflect a more integrated, topic-based approach. Computers are typically arranged around the periphery of the available space, and other fixtures and furniture allow group work, discussion, or teacher-led activities; but interaction between learners and technology tends to be individual, and personalization forms an important part of the rhetoric that accompanies the introduction of learning technologies.

The second tradition in the design of computer laboratories reflects a different set of pedagogical principles and practices; namely, the social constructivist and constructionist approaches to the use of learning technologies associated with, among others, Papert, Harel, and Resnick. Papert and Harel (1991) describe how design projects in which knowledge is built through the construction of public and shared entities (software programs, devices, media productions) can be integrated with, and enhance, more formal instruction. This approach also undermines the primacy of screen-based interaction, instead encouraging a "closeness to objects," both digital and physical, which are explored, designed, constructed, and then in turn become a focus for experimentation, evaluation, and potential redesign. The development of the LOGO programming language, for example, has been part of a broader pedagogical program in which learners are able to experiment in "microworlds," not only onscreen and in design projects (using, for example, robotics equipment such as Lego Mindstorms or Arduino), but in which the computer laboratory itself becomes a space for experimentation, prototyping, and collaborative knowledge construction (Papert, 1993).

The archetype for this model of the school computer laboratory was realized in the "Computer Clubhouse" developed originally by the Media Laboratory at the Massachusetts Institute of Technology (MIT) and the Computer Museum in Boston, Massachusetts, where the purpose was, according to Resnick and Rusk (1996, p. 432), not just to teach computer skills but that participants learned to express themselves fluently with new technology, becoming motivated and confident learners in the process. As well as imbuing confidence, the clubhouse was intended to allow young people to become designers and creators, not just consumers, of computer-based products, creating their own artwork, animations, simulations, multimedia presentations, virtual worlds, musical creations, websites, and robotic constructions. The clubhouse model is often invoked as a model of how school computer laboratories might work, and examples from clubhouse initiatives are often cited as evidence of the benefits of technology-enhanced learning and technology-rich learning environments. However, as might be expected, such an approach may be difficult to implement in schools where curriculum frameworks, lack of resources, and the demands of high-stakes assessment combine with physical spaces configured for direct instruction or individual learning.

The availability of networked portable devices (laptops, tablet computers, and smartphones) has led to the role of the school computer laboratories being called into question, as the need for centralized technology resources and the management and monitoring functions that accompany them has been challenged. This has been compounded by changing patterns of personal technology ownership, and, in particular, smartphones, although the "bring your own device" philosophy has impacted less in schools than in higher education. However, schools have begun to acknowledge that such devices can be integrated into teaching and learning activities, and while concerns about management of network access, security, and equity remain, there is evidence that the use of personal technologies is becoming more accepted, for example in performance review in sports; in the collection of environmental data, images, and interviews; and in creative subjects such as art, dance, and music. Against this background, the school computer laboratory additionally becomes a hub where digital data collected or generated on personal devices are downloaded, aggregated, and managed, and where access to specialist software for data analysis, image manipulation, and video editing is provided.

Two further recent developments have suggested that the computer laboratory, in some form, still has a place in schools. The first of these is a new emphasis on learning to code as an important contributor to individual employability and national competitiveness, leading to computer coding becoming part of political rhetoric and thence being established as an important aspect of school curricula (Williamson, 2016). This is not without its challenges, however, as this leaves educational decision-makers at national, regional, and school level having to decide whether this is best addressed through training programs and direct instruction (aligning with the first tradition outlined above) or whether learning to code is something that is more effectively supported through integrated design projects in learning environments following the constructionist "clubhouse" model. Interestingly, several of the core technologies that are recommended for use in learn-to-code initiatives (the Lego Mindstorms construction kits and the Scratch visual programming environment) emerged from the MIT Media Lab, but this has not precluded their being incorporated wholesale into formal curricula which prioritize skills acquisition over creative problem-solving and design projects.

The second recent development builds on the second, constructivist/constructionist tradition in educational technology as well as the recent appearance of "makerspaces" (also called "hackerspaces" and "fablabs"). Makerspaces are often described as "studio environments," many being based on the working environments of artists, media professionals, architects, or engineers. They typically contain a wide range of technologies including computers and media production equipment, but these are supplemented with tools and materials for prototyping, repair, assembly, disassembly, and tinkering. A key development that has led to increased public interest in and engagement with makerspaces has been the progressively lower costs of three-dimensional printing and other computer-controlled fabrication equipment. While these might still be beyond individuals' budgets, they are now realistic purchases for community organizations, not-for-profits and, critically, schools. Some of the same arguments that drove and sustained the implementation of the first computer laboratories in schools (access to shared but high-cost resources and expertise, management and maintenance, and security) are now being applied to these new kinds of learning environments. Computers still have a role to play, supporting research, envisioning, design, control of equipment, and coding, and the products that emerge from makerspaces may be digital as well as physical artifacts, but the design project paradigm predominates.

There are exciting prospects both for schools to reenvision computer laboratories in the image of makerspaces, and also, by doing so, to establish themselves as a new form of technology hub in which teachers and learners work together with members of local communities, or where links between schools and higher education may be forged. Britton (2012) and Holman (2015) highlight how makerspaces can encourage technological and pedagogical experimentation; revitalize public services such as libraries and museums; and address broader concerns about sustainability and lifelong learning. Ultimately, what may emerge is a model where some form of school laboratory space exists long into the future, providing training and retraining in skills and techno-literacies, but also addressing authentic and pressing social and design challenges.

SEE ALSO: Connected Learning; Digital Divide and Web-Use Skills; Educational Media, History; Internet Safety

References

Britton, L. (2012, October 1). The makings of maker spaces. *Library Journal.* Retrieved from http://www.thedigitalshift.com/.../the-makings-of-maker-spaces-part-1-space-for-creation-not-just-consumption/

Fenwick, T., & Edwards, R. (2010). *Actor-network theory in education.* Abingdon, England: Routledge.

Holman, W. (2015, November). Makerspace: Towards a new civic infrastructure. *Places Journal.* Retrieved from https://placesjournal.org/article/makerspace-towards-a-new-civic-infrastructure

Kyle, B. (2000, March 30). Acute pencil shortage strikes state lawmakers. *Bangor Daily News.* Retrieved from http://www.papert.org/articles/laptops/acute_pencil_shortage.html

Luckin, R. (2010). *Re-designing learning contexts: Technology-rich, learner-centred ecologies.* Abingdon, England: Routledge.

Papert, S. (1993). *The children's machine: Rethinking school in the age of the computer.* New York, NY: Basic Books.

Papert, S., & Harel, I. (1991). Situating constructionism. In *Constructionism* (pp. 193–206). New York, NY: Ablex.

Resnick, M., & Rusk, M. (1996). The Computer Clubhouse: Preparing for life in a digital world. *IBM Systems Journal, 35*(3–4), 431–440. doi: 10.1147/sj.353.0431

Skinner B.F. (1961). Teaching machines. *Scientific American, 205*(5), 90–112. Retrieved from https://www.scientificamerican.com/magazine/sa/1961/11-01/

Skinner, B.F. (1965). *The technology of teaching.* Des Moines, IA: Meredith.

Smith, S., & Sherwood, B. (1976). Educational uses of the PLATO computer system. *Science, 192*(4237), 344–352. doi: 10.1126/science.769165

Thrall, T., & Tingey, B. (2003). SuccessMaker® motion: A research summary (Technical Note TN030409). Pearson Education. Retrieved from https://www.pearsoned.com/wp-content/uploads/dc2-successmaker-motion-a-research-summary.pdf

Williamson, B. (2016). Political computational thinking: Policy networks, digital governance and "learning to code." *Critical Policy Studies, 10*(1), 39–58. doi: 10.1080/19460171.2015.1052003

Patrick Carmichael is Professor Emeritus of Education at the University of Bedfordshire, UK. He has conducted and published research on a range of learning and media technologies including digital archives, online community platforms, semantic web technologies, and automated assessment systems. He is particularly interested in the interplay between learning environments and pedagogy, and in the cross-disciplinary discourses that these provoke.

Connected Learning

AMANDA WORTMAN and MIZUKO ITO
University of California, Irvine, USA

Connected learning is learning that is interest-driven, supported by peers and mentors, and connected to academic, economic, and civic opportunities. The model is based on evidence and ongoing research that the most resilient learning involves: learner-centered interests; social support for these interests from peers, mentors, and the broader community; and learning that is directed toward opportunity and recognition. Connected learning was conceived of by an interdisciplinary network of researchers, designers, and practitioners for the purpose of advancing an evidence-driven approach to learning, the design of learning environments that support this learning, and an educational reform that addresses the ongoing issues of educational inequity.

Young people can have diverse pathways into connected learning. Schools, homes, afterschool programs, religious institutions, community centers, and the parents, teachers, friends, mentors, and coaches whom young people encounter at these diverse locations all potentially have a role in guiding youths to connected learning. The connected learning framework recognizes the unique value and opportunity for online and digital media to broaden access to specialized and interest-driven learning, but the model is not limited to technology-enhanced learning. Examples of learning environments that integrate the spheres of peers, interests, and academic pursuits include school-sponsored athletics, arts and civic engagement programs, and interest-driven academic programs such as chess teams, academic decathlon, and robotics competition. While connected learning can apply to all ages, the model grew out of research with young adults and adolescents. This is a pivotal developmental period, when individuals form identities and interests that are often leveraged in their future educational and career explorations.

Connected learning is an educational reform agenda created and situated in the digital age, and is responsive to the immense opportunities afforded by networked and digital media, as well as to the risks associated with new media. Rooted in the tradition of sociocultural learning theory, connected learning is not simply a technique for improving individual educational outcomes but seeks to support communities and collective capacities for learning and opportunity. In the sections that follow,

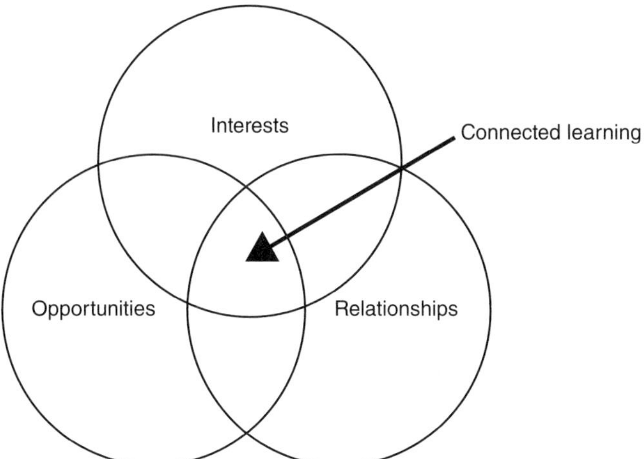

Figure 1 Connecting the spheres of learning. Created by author.

the properties, guiding principles, outcomes, and current emphases of the connected learning approach will be explored.

Situating the discussion of connected learning

In the United States and many other countries in the Global North, educational institutions are struggling to fulfill their mission of providing pathways to opportunity for all youths. Even worse, educational systems may be doing more to perpetuate and increase inequality than to expand opportunities (Duncan & Murnane, 2011). The connected learning model recognizes the tension between current approaches to education and schooling and the world that youths will inhabit. Conventional pathways through schooling toward stable, successful careers are an option for fewer and fewer young people; currently, schools only deliver real opportunity to a declining proportion of youths.

Today's youths are entering a labor market markedly different from that of earlier generations. In the "golden age of capitalism" of the fifties and sixties, the middle class was expanding and returns on education were high; high school, college, and professional degrees all provided reliable stepping stones toward quality careers (Marglin & Schor, 1992). Over the past decade, the doubling of the global labor market and the economic downturn have created a chronic shortage of jobs in relation to job seekers (Freeman, 2008). Coupled with higher rates of unemployment, rising income inequality has also contributed to a decline in the working and middle classes. Youths have suffered from these trends more than older generations, and find themselves disproportionately in lower quality jobs with stagnated wages (Mishel, Bivens, Gould, & Shierholz, 2012). A college degree has become a prerequisite for most quality jobs, but is no longer a guarantee of obtaining one. Wages for both men and women who are entry-level college graduates have fallen over the past decade (Mishel et al., 2012). At the same time, the cost of higher education has risen 2.6 times by comparison to what it was in 1980 (National Center for Education Statistics, 2016).

Much has been discussed about adapting to these market changes and where the future of quality work resides. Many have argued that creative work is where future job security will be, and the current educational system must produce students with creative and critical thinking skills to fill these jobs (Florida, 2002). In contrast, others believe that job growth will be concentrated in low-skill work in the service sector and conclude that creative jobs will be a privilege for only a fraction of the labor force (Brown, Lauder, & Ashton, 2010). Regardless of which forecast comes true, the future of heightened competition for quality jobs and a reduction in the wage premium gained by education is here. Connected learning seeks to address this growing inequity by looking to education as a way of building capacity and meaningful networks rather than as a pipeline to a dwindling set of opportunities.

Disparities in access to educational, economic, and civic opportunity have become bleaker and continue to be tied to race and ethnicity in troubling ways. Many studies have documented the achievement gap between white and Asian students on the one hand and African American and Latinx students on the other. This gap is at risk of expanding as the proportion of nonwhite youths in the United States continues to grow. These educational and demographic indicators point to growing populations of nondominant youths who are being denied pathways to opportunity. While much research has been conducted on this achievement gap, there is little consensus among scholars, as some focus on cultural factors, peer dynamics, punitive practices in schools, financial and institutional hurdles, or home environments. Duncan and Murnane's (2011) work and, previously, Lareau's (2003) work shed light on the high levels of investment that upper- and middle-class families make in out-of-school enrichment activities. Duncan and Murnane (2011) found that money spent on enrichment activities among upper-class families nearly tripled in the years from 1972 to 2006, while at the same time remaining flat among lower-income households. Rideout and collaborators also found in a recent survey that highly educated households are turning their gaze to, and have begun to value more, popular and digital media, in contrast to previous generations, where limiting popular media use was considered a marker of good parenting (Rideout, Foehr, & Roberts, 2010). These studies show that educationally privileged youths with supportive learning environments at home are the ones who are best able to leverage the new learning opportunities of the digital world and to convert these opportunities to academic and career achievement and success.

Complicating these issues is the fact that young people are increasingly immersed in media. The *Common Sense Census* (Common Sense Media Inc., 2015) reported that American teenagers average roughly nine hours of entertainment media use per day, not including use for school or homework. The *Census* also shows marked differences in the amount of time young people spend with media on the basis of household income, parent education, and race/ethnicity. For example, teens from lower-income families spend on average two hours and 45 minutes more time with media than those from higher-income households. This immersive media landscape has caused some scholars to argue that, as media have become more personalized and individualized, people gravitate toward sources that suit their interests and perspectives. This can lead to a polarization of political discourse and a growing equity gap between those who have a well-rounded view of culture and current events, and those who do not (Prior, 2007). An abundance of media choice also adds to the disconnect between classroom learning and the everyday lives and interests of young people. Collins and Halverson (2009) describe a culture gap between educational institutions designed in the industrial age and the emerging learning practices of the knowledge age. Today's economic, social, and technological trends in the United States and other postindustrial settings present a host of challenges to those who seek to transform educational systems and create opportunities for more youths. The connected learning approach is situated within this historically specific set of circumstances.

Defining connected learning

Connected learning recognizes the unique opportunities for change that accompany the shift to digital and networked media. While today's digitally mediated environment presents youths with new risks, it also offers unparalleled opportunities in making interest-driven, engaging, and meaningful learning accessible to more young people. Networked media, when linked to youth-centered interests and community contribution, provide new entry points into learning, opportunity, achievement, and civic participation. Unlike other approaches to educational technology, connected learning is not defined by particular technologies, techniques, or institutional contexts but by a set of values, an orientation to social change, and a philosophy of lifelong learning.

In examining the role of networked and new media in young people's lives, the connected learning model considers a broader "ecology" of learning settings and their interconnections. The notion of a learning ecology positions the young person in meanings, practices, structures, and institutions contextualized by family, neighborhood, culture, and global contexts (Barron, 2006). Learning can and does happen in all of these contexts. The connected learning model points out that all of these sites of learning are increasingly supported by digital media technologies. For today's youths and for many adults alike, their media and learning ecology does not just encompass the world of leisure and entertainment but has become infrastructural, more like the distribution of electricity or water. This idea of media ecology better informs our understanding of the digital media landscape by focusing, not on the learning potential of individual media, but on how youths' actions, individually and collectively, intersect with key institutions in their lives and with a wider array of media and communication possibilities open to them (Ito et al., 2013).

Unlike previous educational reform efforts that focused on specific technology deployments or institutional changes, connected learning takes a networked approach to social change that aligns with an ecological perspective. Systemic educational shift requires linked efforts across different sites of learning and connecting similar reform efforts across sectors of home, popular culture, technology, and educational institutions. Connected learning posits that today's networked technologies offer a unique opportunity to build open and scalable networks in the service of educational reform across diverse sites of learning—homes, schools, communities, popular culture, online communities, and informal learning institutions. A large body of previous research on technology innovation, design of educational environments, and learning informs the development of the connected learning model.

Learning approach

Connected learning draws from approaches to learning that stress how learning and development are embedded within social relationships and cultural contexts. This body of work focuses on understanding people's everyday activities instead of focusing exclusively on formal educational systems and academic subjects. The development of the connected learning model is guided by three key findings that have emerged from this body of learning research: a disconnect between classroom and everyday learning, the meaningful nature of learning that is embedded in valued relationships, practice and culture, and the need for learning contexts that bring together in-school and out-of-school learning (Ito et al., 2013).

1. *Formal education is often disconnected and lacking in relevance.* In-school learning is often disconnected from the settings where young people find meaning and social connection. School subjects are thought to impart knowledge and skills that are transferable to everyday life and future work, but these connections have been difficult to prove among learning scholars. A recent report by the National Academies concluded: "Over a century of research on transfer has yielded little evidence that teaching can develop general cognitive competencies that are transferable to any new discipline, problem, or context, in or out of school" (National Research Council, 2012).
2. *Learning is meaningful when it is part of valued relationships, shared practice, culture, and identity.* Research on lifelong learning and on learning that occurs as part of everyday social life, work, and other purposeful activity has shown that learning is highly relational and tied to shared purpose and activity. Drawing on this body of work, the connected learning model emphasizes that, when youth are pursuing shared interests and goals with peers and adults, learning is meaningful, relevant, and resilient. The connected learning framework identifies specific supports and outcomes of learning that are embedded in joint activity and shared purpose.
3. *Young people need connection and translation between in-school and out-of-school learning.* Connected learning builds on the idea that youths need to form stronger connections between different sites of learning and that networked and digital technologies can play a role in fostering these connections. Learning is oriented toward shared practices that emerge from horizontal knowledge and from connections across the domains of experience in and out of school. In order to realize meaningful and resilient learning, youths need concrete and sustained social networks, relationships, institutional links, shared activities, and communication infrastructures that connect their social, academic, and interest-driven learning (Ito et al., 2013). This is in contrast to purely cognitive and individual models of transfer, which

expect youths to apply knowledge to varied settings but do it "in their head," without social, institutional, and cultural supports that connect across these settings.

Connecting the spheres of learning

Connected learning seeks to integrate three spheres of learning that are often disconnected and at odds with one another in young people's lives: interests, peer culture, and academic, civic, and career opportunity.

1. *Interest-driven.* Young people's interests and affinities run the gamut of hobbies, sports, popular culture, academic and artistic pursuits. Research on interest development indicates a complex interaction between personal dispositions and the discovery and cultivation of interests within social and cultural contexts (Hidi and Renninger, 2006; Crowley, Barron, Knutson, & Martin, 2015). The connected learning model recognizes how learning that grows out of a personal interest is both motivating and meaningful. When situated within a group or community that shares that interest, with high standards and metrics for knowledge and expertise, this interest-driven learning is tied to higher-order and resilient learning outcomes. This learning can also be subcultural or quite different from what is valued by local peers, teachers, or academic institutions and can provide youths with a safe space for developing varied identities and affinities.
2. *Peer-supported.* Young people's peer culture typically centers on status negotiations over popularity, romantic relationships, and hanging out with friends and is generally tied to their school or community social networks. In school, where youths are segregated by age rather than by interests, peer culture does not necessarily reward knowledge, expertise, or specialization, and those with deep interests are often labeled "weird," "nerds," or "geeks." In contrast, when peer cultures are centered on and supportive of interests, they can drive expertise development and intergenerational relationships.

   Connected learning environments foreground the social support of peer and friendship networks centered on shared purpose, projects, and interests. When young people are engaged with peers in these shared contexts, they learn fluidly from each other by giving and receiving feedback and sharing knowledge in timely and task-specific ways. Seeking recognition and validation from peers also provides the social motivation for acquiring skills and expertise.
3. *Opportunity-oriented.* The other major sphere of activity in young people's lives is driven by adult-defined achievement and future-oriented goals, for instance academic achievement, civic and political engagement, and the cultivation of career-relevant skills. When describing young people's learning, the connected learning model has often focused on academic orientation, as most young people are primarily focused on immediate future-directed goals and success in school.

   Educational institutions and academic achievement play a critically important role in providing access to societal opportunity more broadly. At the same time, the connected learning model recognizes varied pathways to civic and economic opportunity that might not be mediated and brokered by educational institutions and pathways. The emphasis here is on the fact that young people need connections to and recognition from institutions that provide access to social, civic, and economic opportunity.

Many young people experience their learning in the three spheres as being disconnected; they themselves have no exposure or support to explore what interests them. Youths' interest-driven activities are often pursued in siloed institutions, peer groups, or communities of practice that do not cut across the worlds of home, school, after-school, peer culture, and online activities. Connected learning is an effort to link these spheres of learning more purposefully. The goal is not to fully integrate these spheres, but to build connections, entry points, brokering opportunities, and sites of translation that reach youths where they are.

Supporting and designing connected learning environments

Connected learning environments can emerge organically through youth affinity groups, community organizing, or programs sponsored by educational institutions. They can also be explicitly designed, supported, and engineered by individuals and organizations. Design principles for fostering connected learning environments include properties that characterize environments that foster connected learning, guidelines for educators and designers to consider, and ways of leveraging technology.

These principles are both social and technical in nature and address platforms and spaces for learning, the production of learning resources, and the creation of social norms and policies. Although connected learning experiences and environments do not require new technology, the networked and digital world of today afford expanded access to information, communities of interest, and connections across settings, lowering barriers of access. The following design principles are also interconnected—it is in the relationship among and between principles that the opportunities for connected learning arise. Further, the design of connected learning environments is distributed and evolving work, where educators share authority and ownership with youth, technology makers, and cultural creators in developing shared infrastructure, norms, and practices (Ito et al., 2013).

Properties of connected learning environments

Environments that can effectively join these spheres of learning are characterized by similar properties: a focus on production, shared purpose, and open networks.

1. *Production-centered.* Connected learning environments provide tools and opportunities for learners to produce, curate, circulate, and give feedback on materials created within the community and beyond. The hands-on nature of production-centered communities draws on the long-standing creative traditions of learning through doing.

Media creation has become more widely accessible through digital tools, and social media provide myriad opportunities for circulating, publicizing, and commenting on media works. The power of production and performance is extended through digital and networked tools in that it allows (i) increased access to high-quality, and often free, digital production tools; (ii) the ability to remix and curate digital content, which is often seen as a valuable stepping-stone to creativity; and (iii) a window into visibility and circulation in the form of blogs, podcasts, and video- and image-sharing sites.

2. *Shared purpose.* In contrast to some classroom learning, everyday learning out of school usually occurs in contexts where individuals work together, share knowledge, and engage in joint inquiry. When learning is part of a purposeful activity, embedded in meaningful social relationships and practices, it is engaging and resilient. In these settings, there is little need to assess and mark individual work and knowledge: it is more important that collective goals be accomplished.

   Connected learning environments draw together youths and adult participants in joint activities that are defined by a shared purpose, goals, and collaborative production. Through shared purpose, communities provide opportunities for intergenerational and cross-cultural communication centered on learning activities. Such communities create an atmosphere in which the role of expert and that of novice are based on experience, with little bias toward age, whereas in traditional settings the role of expert is typically held by those who are older. Connected learning environments leverage the idea of shared purpose through projects with collective goals, collaborations and competitions, and cross-generational leadership and ownership.

3. *Openly networked.* Today's digital networks afford new opportunities for learners to access a wide range of resources and knowledge across the boundaries of home, school, and after-school settings. They also allow learners to make their work and achievements visible across these settings. Digital media greatly expand opportunities to connect learning experiences across the often fragmented settings of a young person's life (Ito et al., 2013).

   The infrastructure of connected learning environments is based on ideas of openness, accessibility, and transparency designed to keep barriers to entry and participation low. In online spaces, this amounts to maintaining open standards that allow for people and institutions to connect across diverse settings (home, school, community, and work) and platforms (PC, mobile, game devices, traditional media). In physical space, this means maintaining an open and welcoming environment and using online infrastructures to extend work and learning beyond the physical boundaries of the space.

Open networks can be leveraged to expand learning opportunities in the following ways:

Cross-institutional networks. Openly networked environments link institutions and groups across various sectors, including popular culture, educational institutions, home, and interest communities. Digital networks provide opportunities for producers to make their work visible across settings and for learners to more easily access this content and community.

MULTIPLE POINTS OF ENTRY AND OUTREACH. Youths and adults can enter connected learning environments through multiple channels, including those centered on peers and friendships, interests, or school and work. There is no one single pipeline for participants to learn about and join the group, and the space is attractive and accessible to diverse participants.

OPEN ASSESSMENT, RECOGNITION, AND CERTIFICATIONS. Connected learning environments strive to recognize learning and achievement that happens in self-directed, informal, and unstructured ways and makes that learning visible and recognizable to parents, educators, learning institutions, and potential workplaces.

OPEN ACCESS AND IP. Resources, tools, and materials can be accessible and visible across settings and available through open, networked platforms and policies that protect the collective right to circulate and access knowledge and culture.

Guiding principles

In addition to a set of common properties, connected learning environments are guided by shared values and principles.

1. *Everyone can participate.* A key design principle of connected learning environments centers on the idea that everyone participates. Experiences are built around the notion that everyone is invited to participate and contribute, and barriers to entry and access are low. Many and varied opportunities to participate and contribute and a diversity of voices and cultural capital are valued elements. A diverse set of resources supports both teaching and mentoring activities.
2. *Learning happens by doing.* Connected learning is punctuated by participatory and experiential learning. Connected learning environments are committed to ensuring that learners have access to robust mechanisms for discoverability; tools and resources are easy to find, diverse, and easily sharable across networks (Ito et al., 2013). Learners collaborate in many different ways and can explore different roles or identities related to an area of interest, or an area in which they want to develop expertise.
3. *Challenge is constant.* In connected learning environments, an interest or its cultivation creates both a need to know and a need to share. Learners are motivated to take up challenges either because the problem itself is engaging or because it relates to an existing interest or affinity. Structures that pose challenges or obstacles to overcome offer opportunities for advancement, and these opportunities can lead to occasions for building social and cultural capital. A mixture of competitive and collaborative elements in the service of problem discovery and solving are important components of connected learning environments.
4. *Everything is interconnected.* Participants in connected learning environments are provided with multiple learning contexts for engaging in connected learning—contexts in which they receive immediate feedback on progress, have access to tools for planning and reflection, and are given opportunities for the

mastery of specialist language and practices. Infrastructures that encourage youths to share their work, skills, and knowledge with others across networks, groups, and communities enhance learning and social connectivity (Ito et al., 2013). Diverse forms of recognition and assessment might take the form of online portfolios, prizes, badges, ratings, reviews, and credential and mentoring systems. Educators, mentors, and outside experts act as translators and bridge builders for learners across domains in these environments.

Connected learning and new media

Connected learning experiences and environment do not require technology, though today's digital and networked technologies expand the accessibility and potential reach of these experiences. Use of new media has the potential to expand the level of engagement, accessibility, social support, and diversity of connected learning experiences. The connected learning model's key innovation is not that it uses new media to extend school learning into the home or into after-school spaces. Rather it is in a focus on the creation of social, cultural, and technological supports that enable youths to link, integrate, and translate their interests across academic, civic, and career-relevant domains (Ito et al., 2013).

1. *Fostering engagement and self-expression.* Today's new media have the potential to support more engaged, creative, and self-directed forms of learning. Interactive, immersive, and personalized technologies can provide responsive feedback, support a diversity of learning styles and literacy, and pace the learning process according to individual needs. Researchers have suggested that today's complex media environment requires new forms of literacy, collaboration, and cognitive skills that are more agile and adaptive than those of previous eras. Games, for example, can be a medium for engaged social learning, and digital writing tools can be tied to media literacy programs that focus on participatory approaches to creative production and self-expression.
2. *Accessibility to knowledge and learning experiences.* Online networks reduce the barriers of access to media and information in that information and niche communities can be accessed from multiple devices and in diverse locations, for instance at home, in school, in the community, and while mobile. In the connected learning model, this accessibility has the potential to connect the learning that happens separately in the spheres of peer culture, interests, and academic institutions.

   For many young people who have interests that are more specialized or stigmatized, it can be next to impossible to find local support for these interests. The online world and the networks that youths can connect to have begun to change this dynamic. These online communities or affinity groups can support intellectual and creative identities and expertise that are not supported in academic institutions or peer culture; they can also provide new opportunities for intergenerational connection and mentoring. In this way, new media enable youths to seek out and find new communities and safe havens for their learning and identity development.

3. *Expanding social supports for interests.* The advent of social media has made it more possible for young people to form relationships with peers and caring adults that are centered on interests, expertise, and future opportunities. Unlike in online social networks such as Facebook, interest-driven activity (whether online or offline) is often intergenerational: fellow hobbyists, leaders, experts, and mentors of all ages are included (Ito et al., 2010). The presence of these caring adults who are tied to areas of authentic interest has the potential to reorient and transform a young person's identities and academic and economic opportunities in the more distant future.
4. *Expanding diversity and building capacity.* Today's open and social networks serve a democratizing function, where nondominant and marginalized forms of knowledge, culture, and value gain visibility and where communities can build capacity from the ground up. The costs of publicity, circulation, and organization have declined rapidly in recent years and are key to the equity agenda of connected learning. Entry points, pathways, and linkages need to be developed in ways that respect and support cultures and practice within youth-driven and nondominant contexts. It is important to recognize that these sites can be generative of learning rather than places to colonize with mainstream and adult-driven ideas of achievement and success (Ito et al., 2013).

Scholars see opportunity in the fact that black and Latinx youths are engaging in new media and in mobile media at high rates and that engagement with popular media is increasing across class divides. The connected learning model aims to build more contexts that leverage the engagement of nondominant youths in new media and to use that engagement so as to extend knowledge, expertise, and participation in community life.

Connected learning outcomes

Scholars often frame learning outcomes in terms of individual skills, competencies, and dispositions. Here again, connected learning takes a more ecological approach, by placing both individual and collective outcomes at the core of the model. Outcomes must be viewed not only in terms of individual success and competitiveness, but in relation to the health of the groups, communities, and institutions that support connected learning environments. Most classrooms and schools focus on standardized metrics and individual competitiveness (as manifest, for instance, in grades and test scores), which don't explicitly seek to elevate culture at large or to expand and improve social capital beyond the classroom walls. In contrast, connected learning environments often have a very different dynamic, where individual growth and achievement are tied to collective goals and community development. Often there are ample opportunities for individual contributions that are in the service of community goals and shared practice.

Individual outcomes

The connected learning framework acknowledges the importance of 21st-century skills, while at the same time proposing a set of proximate outcomes that are more specific to interest-driven and connected learning: depth and breadth of interests, learning supports, and academic orientation.

1. *Twenty-first-century skills*. Educators, policymakers, and researchers have been increasingly recognizing the importance of metacognitive and social skills—such as systems thinking, information literacy, creativity, adaptability, persistence, intellectual openness, and self-regulation and evaluation—under the banner of "21st-century skills" (National Research Council, 2012). This label includes new media literacies that are associated with participation in new media practices and communities (Jenkins, Purushotma, Weigel, Clinton, & Robison, 2009). The connected learning approach is well suited to developing these metacognitive capacities, social skills, and new media literacies thanks to its emphasis on problem-solving, self-expression, and civic engagement within authentic and technology-enhanced communities of practice.
2. *Greater depth and breadth of interests*. Learning scholars have pointed out that, even from an early age, youths develop "islands of expertise" around topics such as dinosaurs and roller coasters and share and display this knowledge to others (Palmquist & Crowley, 2007). An outcome of connected learning seeks to link this type of deep, vertical expertise to other cultural domains and interests. This process of building connections, or branching out, to other areas of expertise from the base of a core interest is central to the connected learning model.
3. *Peer, adult, and institutional learning supports*. Another outcome of connected learning is increasing social capital in areas of interest, expertise, and opportunity. Social supports can include similar-age peers with shared interests, adult peers and mentors, and institutional relationships that tie areas of interest to achievement. In the connected learning model, youth should feel agency to rely on these communities of interest for help, feedback, and mentorship. Development of new peer and adult relationships centered on shared interests is a key proximate outcome of connected learning, in that these socially driven learning networks can help youths acquire and refine new skills and shape their future identities by broadening the adult role models that youths can draw from.
4. *Greater academic orientation*. A key indicator of connected learning is a positive disposition to academics, programs, and institutions, as well as to civic and career opportunities. The connected learning model seeks to leverage the everyday cultural practices of youths to design environments intended to build more of these positive feelings.

Societal outcomes

Connected learning aims to effect change in collective outcomes as well as in individual ones. When people are pursuing interests and meaningful social relationships in the service of academic, civic, and workplace institutions, the connected learning model suggests this will lead to broader societal outcomes: high-quality culture and knowledge products, civically oriented collectives, and diverse and equitable pathways to opportunity (Ito et al., 2013).

1. *High standards for knowledge and creative production.* The connected learning model recognizes that one key component of high-functioning interest groups is the presence of effective support and recognition for learning and expertise development. Connected learning environments draw on like-minded peers to provide expert knowledge, support, and feedback, and this feedback loop feeds into status systems that allow for recognition and demonstrations of skill.
2. *Civically oriented and politically activated collectives.* In the connected learning model, high value is placed on joint activity and participation in civic and political outcomes. By contributing to their communities, connected learners build civic collectives while also developing capacities that can function as gateways to more traditional civic and political engagement. Groups like the Harry Potter Alliance are a good example of the ways in which peer-driven activity in an interest area can lead to civic and political engagement (Ito et al., 2015; Jenkins, Shresthova, Gamber-Thompson, Kligler-Vilenchik, & Zimmerman, 2016).
3. *Diverse and equitable pathways for recognition and contribution.* A core motivation of connected learning is to promote a more equitable set of entry points and pathways to educational and economic lifelong opportunity. Connected learning seeks greater societal equity by expanding the range of cultural institutions and organizations that can be entry points and pathways to educational opportunity. Environments that exemplify connected learning are often characterized by low barriers to entry, and a multitude of roles, ways of participating, and improving and getting expertise.

An evolving model

The theory, the research, and the design principles that encompass the connected learning framework are a work in progress. They continue to be refined, revised, and revisited as part of a collective research, design, and implementation effort. Rather than centering on a top-down design of a specific product, technology, or curriculum, connected learning environments are a complex mix of designed and emergent elements in a process of experimentation and flux. The connected learning framework is presented in this spirit of experimentation and iteration (Ito et al., 2013).

Connected learning in educational practice

Since the introduction of the connected learning framework in 2011, educators and practitioners seeking new ways to support the learning lives of their students have taken up the banner and principles of connected learning. For example, a national network of educators, the National Writing Project, has launched a new initiative called Educator Innovator, where educators have the opportunity to participate in connected learning events that encourage them to take a step toward creating a connected learning environment in their own classrooms or after-school programs. The Educator Innovator network hosts an ongoing webinar series on connected learning and an online community intended to inspire educators to incorporate connected learning into their practice. The network has also produced a report that highlights how writing teachers have adopted connected learning (Garcia et al., 2014).

A range of other educational organizations and networks have incorporated connected learning into their mission and approach. The Mozilla Foundation supports the spread of the Hive Learning Networks, regional professional networks of informal educators dedicated to connected learning approaches. Hives have been established in Chicago, New York City, Pittsburgh, and Toronto; and more are spinning up in other cities. One member of the Hive, the Quest to Learn school in New York City, was also informed by a connected learning approach (Salen, Torres, Wolozin, Rufo-Tepper, & Shapiro, 2011). The Consortium for School Networking has adopted connected learning as a core focus area (visit http://www.cosn.org/ConnectedLearning). The Tang Institute at Phillips Academy is also dedicated to the principles of connected learning (visit http://tanginstitute.andover.edu). A network of faculty members in higher education have been advocating for connected learning approaches in their practices (visit http://connectedcourses.net). Connected Camps, a start-up founded by connected learning researchers Ito and Salen, offers online summer camps in the game of Minecraft.

Connected learning has also found a home among librarians and informal educators involved in museums and after-school programs. The Young Adult Library Services Association (YALSA) (2016) has adopted connected learning as a cornerstone of its 2016–2018 three-year strategic plan. Connected learning has also been part of a growing movement for youth learning labs and makerspaces in libraries and museums across the United States. After the success of the YOUmedia youth digital makerspace in the Harold Washington Library in Chicago, which opened its doors in 2009, the MacArthur Foundation and the Institute for Museum and Library Services jointly funded the start-up of 24 additional YOUMedia learning labs based on the connected learning approach (Urban Libraries Council and Association of Science–Technology Centers, 2014). These spaces provide new opportunities for young people to connect with peers and mentors through interest-driven project-based learning.

Research themes

The connected learning approach continues to guide research in the Connected Learning Research Network as well as among a growing network of researchers around the world. While the range of research and research topics being pursued in relation to connected learning is wide, a few themes have emerged as areas of shared inquiry.

1. *Online learning and affinity networks.* An ongoing focus has been the study of how online communities and affinity networks can support connected learning. Research has documented the important role that new, open online learning resources can contribute to interest-driven and connected learning (Carfagna, 2014). Ito's research team has focused on case studies of online affinity networks that are centered around diverse youth interests, which could in principle connect to academic settings. The sense of belonging and bonding in these affinity networks is a powerful driver of participation and learning, as young people get

recognized by others who "get it" and share similar culture and values. However, the subcultural qualities and the compartmentalized nature of the relationships in online affinity networks mean that most of the learning in online affinity networks is not connected to local settings and communities and is difficult to translate into cultural referents that are relevant to academic and career advancement. This suggests an important missed opportunity, which could be addressed through intentionally designed educational programs that connect to these youth networks (Ito et al., 2018).

2. *Brokering.* A related theme that has emerged across a range of studies is the importance of brokering connections across different learning settings. This brokering, or productive network building, requires the agency and interest of the learner, as well as the collective efforts of those invested in developing learning environments and opportunities. Youth-centered research has indicated the lack of connection between many youth interests and academic opportunity. Although some young people are able to advocate for their interests and translate them into opportunity in school and career, the vast majority need the support of local programs, mentors, and parents with the relevant social capital to broker these connections. If this process continues to play out as a private, market-driven one, the growth of informal online learning will exacerbate the equity gap, making it less and less likely that lower-income youth are able to pursue higher education and career opportunities in areas that they are genuinely interested in and passionate about.

   Research with youth-serving educators has also documented the important role that educators play in connecting young people to opportunities outside a particular program. Even when young people develop interests and skills within the context of a youth program, they can productively build on this learning only if they are able to connect it to a next set of opportunities and relationships (Ching, Santo, Hoadley, & Peppler, 2016).

3. *Social capital and affinity based mentoring.* A range of studies have demonstrated the importance of concrete relational support in developing, deepening, and persisting in specialized interest areas such as in science, technology, engineering, and mathematics (STEM) and in the arts. In particular, relationships with peers and adults with shared interests and affinities are closely tied to these positive outcomes. For example, findings from the Longitudinal Study of Connected Learning (part of the Connected Learning Research Network) indicate that youths who have strong relationships and rapport with peers and mentors in their target field are much more likely to persist and deepen their interests. A meta-analysis of youth mentoring programs also shows that, when young people are matched with mentors with shared interests, they are much more likely to have positive outcomes (Dubois, Portillo, Rhodes, Silverthorn, & Valentine, 2011). These studies suggest the powerful role that affinity-based mentorship and peer support can play in sustaining interest-driven learning and in addressing equity gaps. Jean Rhodes, a member of the Connected Learning Research Network, has expanded on these findings to study whether programs that help young people recruit mentors whom they identify with can support these forms of positive relationship building (Schwartz, Rhodes, Spencer, & Grossman, 2013).

4. *Equity*. Perhaps the most pressing and cross-cutting theme of connected learning research has been centered on seeking a deeper understanding of how these new approaches can result in more equitable outcomes. Novel educational approaches tend to be adopted more quickly and more effectively among more privileged groups. This risk is especially acute with technology-enhanced learning and enrichment activities that are often fee-based and offered in out-of-school settings. A common theme across research on connected learning is understanding these underlying dynamics, as well as the forms of intervention that can mitigate these risks. By focusing on the needs of less privileged learners and by stressing the importance of culturally relevant and relationally focused approaches, connected learning research aims to hone in on mechanisms that address some of the inherent inequities in our educational system.

These themes represent a few shared topics among a growing body of research that expands on, and refines, the connected learning model, extending its relevance and efficacy in diverse learning settings. Because the connected learning approach, by definition, spans a wide range of settings and disciplinary approaches, its questions, methods, and research themes are diverse and constantly evolving.

SEE ALSO: Digital Divide; Digital Literacy; Youth Digital Culture; Youth Media

References

Barron, B. (2006). Interest and self-sustained learning as catalysts of development: A learning ecology perspective. *Human Development, 49*(4), 193–224.

Brown, P., Lauder, H., & Ashton, D. (2010). *The global auction: The broken promises of education, jobs, and incomes*. New York, NY: Oxford University Press.

Carfagna, L. (2014). *Beyond learning-as-usual: Connected learning among open learners*. Irvine, CA: Digital Media and Learning Research Hub.

Ching, D., Santo, R., Hoadley, C., & Peppler, K. (2016). Not just a blip in someone's life: Integrating brokering practices into out-of-school programming as a means of supporting youth futures. *On the Horizon, 24*(3), 296–312.

Collins, A., & Halverson, R. (2009). *Rethinking education in the age of technology: The digital revolution and schooling in America*. New York, NY: Teachers College Press.

Common Sense Media Inc. (2015). *The common sense census: Media use by tweens and teens*. San Francisco, CA. Retrieved from http://static1.1.sqspcdn.com/static/f/1083077/26645197/1446492628567/CSM_TeenTween_MediaCensus_FinalWebVersion_1.pdf

Crowley, K., Barron, B., Knutson, K., & Martin, C. K. (2015). Interest and the development of pathways to science. In K.A. Renninger, M. Nieswandt, & S. Hidi (Eds.), *Interest in mathematics and science learning* (pp. 297–313). Washington, DC: AERA.

Dubois, D.L., Portillo, N., Rhodes, J.E., Silverthorn, N., & Valentine, J.C. (2011). How effective are mentoring programs for youth? A systematic assessment of the evidence. *Psychological Science in the Public Interest, 12*. Retrieved from http://www.rhodeslab.org/files/DuBoisetalMeta.pdf

Duncan, G.J., & Murnane, R.J. (2011). *Whither opportunity? Rising inequality, schools, and children's life chances*. New York, NY: Russell Sage Foundation. Retrieved from https://www.russellsage.org/publications/whither-opportunity

Florida, R. (2002). *The rise of the creative class: And how it's transforming work, leisure, community and everyday life*. New York, NY: Basic Books.

Freeman, R.B. (2008). The new global labor market. *Focus, 26*(1), 1–6. Retrieved from http://www.irp.wisc.edu/publications/focus/pdfs/foc261.pdf

Garcia, A., Cantrill, C., Filipiak, D., Hunt, B., Lee, C., Mirra, N., & Peppler, K. (2014). *Teaching in the connected learning classroom*. Irvine, CA: Digital Media and Learning Research Hub.

Hidi, S., & Renninger, K.A. (2006). The four-phase model of interest development. *Educational Psychologist, 41*(2), 111–127.

Ito, M., Baumer, S., Bittanti, M., boyd, d., Cody, R., Herr-Stephenson, B., … Tripp, L. (2010). *Hanging out, messing around, and geeking out: Kids living and learning with new media*. Cambridge, MA: MIT Press.

Ito, M., Gutiérrez, K., Livingstone, S., Penuel, B., Rhodes, J., Salen, K., … Craig Watkins, S. (2013). *Connected learning: An agenda for research and design*. Irvine, CA: Digital Media and Learning Research Hub. Retrieved from http://dmlhub.net/publications/connected-learning-agenda-research-and-design

Ito, M., Martin, C., Cody-Pfister, R., Rafalow, M., Salen, K., & Wortman, A. (2018). *Affinity online: How connection and shared interest fuel learning*. New York, NY: NYU Press.

Ito, M., Soep, E., Kligler-Vilenchik, N., Shresthova, S., Gamber-Thompson, L., & Zimmerman, A. (2015). Learning-connected civics: Narratives, practices, infrastructures. *Curriculum Inquiry, 45*(1), 10–29.

Jenkins, H., Purushotma, R., Weigel, M., Clinton, K., & Robison, A.J. (2009). *Confronting the challenges of participatory culture: Media education for the 21st century*. Cambridge, MA: MIT Press.

Jenkins, H., Shresthova, S., Gamber-Thompson, L., Kligler-Vilenchik, N., & Zimmerman, A. (2016). *By any media necessary: The new youth activism*. New York, NY: NYU Press.

Lareau, A. (2003). *Unequal childhoods: Class, race and family life*. Los Angeles: University of California Press.

Marglin, S.A., & Schor, J.B. (Eds.). (1992). *The golden age of capitalism: Reinterpreting the postwar experience*. New York, NY: Oxford University Press.

Mishel, L., Bivens, J., Gould, E., & Shierholz, H. (2012). *The state of working America*. Ithaca, NY. Retrieved from http://www.epi.org/state-of-working-america-12th-edition-preview

National Center for Education Statistics. (2016). *Digest of education statistics, 2014 (NCES 2016–006)*. National Center for Education Statistics. Retrieved from http://nces.ed.gov/fastfacts/display.asp?id=76

National Research Council. (2012). *Education for life and work: Developing transferable knowledge and skills in the 21st century*. Washington, DC. Retrieved from http://www7.nationalacademies.org/BOTA/Education_for_Life_and_Work_report_brief.pdf

Palmquist, S., & Crowley, K. (2007). Studying dinosaur learning on an island of expertise. In R. Goldman, R. Pea, B. Barron, & S.J. Derry (Eds.), *Video research in the learning sciences* (pp. 271–286). Mahwah, NJ: Lawrence Erlbaum.

Prior, M. (2007). *Post-broadcast democracy: How media choice increases inequality in political involvement and polarizes elections*. Cambridge, England: Cambridge University Press.

Rideout, V.J., Foehr, U.G., & Roberts, D.R. (2010). *Generation M2: Media in the lives of 8- to 18-year-olds* (Report). Washington, DC: Kaiser Family Foundation.

Salen, K., Torres, R., Wolozin, L., Rufo-Tepper, R., & Shapiro, A. (2011). *Quest to learn: Developing the school for digital kids*. Cambridge, MA: MIT Press.

Schwartz, S.E.O., Rhodes, J.E., Spencer, R., & Grossman, J.B. (2013). Youth initiated mentoring: Investigating a new approach to working with vulnerable adolescents. *American Journal of Community Psychology, 52*(1–2), 155–169. doi: 10.1007/s10464-013-9585-3

Urban Libraries Council and Association of Science–Technology Centers. (2014). *Learning labs in libraries and museums: Transformative spaces for teens.* Washington, DC. Retrieved from https://www.imls.gov/sites/default/files/legacy/assets/1/AssetManager/LearningLabsReport.pdf

Young Adult Library Services Association. (2016). 3-year organizational plan, 2016–2018. Retrieved from http://www.ala.org/yalsa/aboutyalsa/strategicplan

Further reading

Bruce, M., & Bridgeland, J. (2014). *The mentoring effect: Young people's perspectives on the outcomes and availability of mentoring.* Retrieved from http://www.mentoring.org/new-site/wp-content/uploads/2015/09/The_Mentoring_Effect_Full_Report.pdf

Maltese, A.V., & Tai, R.H. (2010). Eyeballs in the fridge: Sources of early interest in science. *International Journal of Science Education, 32*(5), 669–685. doi: 10.1080/09500690902792385

Amanda Wortman is research manager of the Digital Media and Learning Research Hub on the campus of University of California, Irvine. She serves as the project manager for the Connected Learning Research Network (MacArthur Foundation), and Capturing Connected Learning in Libraries project (Institute of Museum and Library Services).

Mizuko Ito is a cultural anthropologist and Research Director of the Digital Media and Learning Research Hub. She is also Professor in Residence and John D. and Catherine T. MacArthur Foundation Chair in Digital Media and Learning at the University of California, Irvine, with appointments in the University of California Humanities Research Institute, the Department of Anthropology, and the Department of Informatics.

Copyright and Fair Use

RENEE HOBBS
University of Rhode Island, USA

Human creativity is boundless and it shapes every aspect of social, cultural, and economic life. And although many people know that copyright law protects the professional media and entertainment industries, including book publishing, filmed entertainment, music, and video games, many do not understand how important copyright law is to creativity, education, the arts, and culture. For creative people as well as teachers and students, copyright supports creative expression and the critical analysis of mass media, popular culture, and digital media. In many ways, media literacy would be impossible without the protections offered by copyright law.

Although people recognize that copyright protects the rights of creators, those rights are balanced against the rights of readers, viewers, and users of copyrighted materials, protecting the public interest in accessing creative work. Originating in 1710 when, in England, the Statute of Anne gave authors the legal right to disseminate their work for fixed terms, the copyright laws of each nation have served to protect and empower both authors and users. Copyright law protects all stakeholders in the circulation of ideas and information, as the purpose of copyright is to promote creativity and innovation by contributing to the spread of knowledge.

However, copyright laws vary from country to country, with some important general similarities but many unique and specific differences. There is no such thing as an international copyright that automatically protects an author's works throughout the entire world. Protection depends on the national laws of each country, and international agreements, treaties, and conventions have greatly simplified international copyright. Still, the World Intellectual Property Organization notes that, in some countries, copyright law protects authors in unique ways. For example, in European nations, authors hold *moral rights* that enable them to prevent distorted reproductions of the work. US copyright law does not include this specific provision. Although this encyclopedia entry primarily uses examples from US copyright law as it applies to the theory and practice of media literacy education, most conceptual and legal elements described here are relevant to the laws of other nations around the world.

Author rights

An understanding of the scope of rights and responsibilities under copyright is essential knowledge for a media-literate individual. An author (and this term applies to all forms of human creative expression, including photographers, filmmakers, poets, dancers, performers, teachers, musicians, architects, vidders, etc.) has legal rights and responsibilities under copyright. Copyright legislation is part of the wider body of law known as intellectual property (IP) which refers broadly to the creations of the human mind. Many forms of human creativity are copyrighted, including literary, artistic, and scientific works. Books, music, paintings, maps, lyrics, poems, illustrations, photos, sculptures, films, videos, computer programs, and databases—and more—are fully protected by copyright. Patent law protects inventions including scientific discoveries and industrial designs, and trademarks protect commercial names and other symbols involved in business.

Many people are not aware that copyright is declaratory. This means that a created work is automatically protected by copyright. As soon as the ink is dry on the drawing or you've pressed "save" on your computer, your work is protected by the full force of copyright law. There is no need to fill out paperwork or pay any fees. A work does not need to have the little copyright symbol (©) in order to be protected. Authors of any age are protected by copyright, which means that students' creative work is copyrighted.

Copyright law provides strong economic protection to copyright holders. In general, these rights include the ability to: (i) make copies of the work and (ii) distribute, sell, or lend them; (iii) perform or display the work; (iv) prepare adaptations or derivative works based upon the original work; and (v) authorize others to exercise any of these rights through licensing or sale. Authors are free to share their work with others, without payment or permission, if they choose. They can set up contracts called licensing agreements, which give users permission to use material with some limitations.

With this strong bundle of rights, under copyright law, the author of an original work also has the right to stop unauthorized persons from copying or otherwise using the work. But there are no copyright police; copyright holders themselves are responsible for identifying unauthorized uses, where a user is reproducing, distributing, or using without permission or payment. It's important to note that some unauthorized uses are legal and some are considered illegal, or an infringement of copyright law.

Copyright protects expressions, not ideas. Ideas cannot be copyrighted. Only particular expressions of ideas in fixed and tangible form can be copyrighted. For example, a stand-up comedy performance cannot be copyrighted, but an audio or video recording of that comedy performance is automatically copyrighted.

An author is anyone who creates writing, images, graphic designs, music, books, films, software, animations, podcasts, academic research, and many other forms of creative expression. In a knowledge economy, much creative work is copyrighted by the companies who pay people to create work, not the actual authors themselves. In "work for hire" arrangements, the author is not considered to be the individual who actually created the work. For example, when an author sends out a work to be translated into a foreign language, the author maintains copyright over the translated work. When writers are hired to produce writing, a contract or memorandum of understanding should specify whether the author or the company owns the copyright. Sadly, even in educational contexts, some teachers are considered to be in a "work for hire" relationship with their employers and, thus, the curriculum materials they create are not legally owned by them. An author may choose to transfer copyrights to another individual or institution in exchange for a royalty or other payment. As a result, an author may or may not be the copyright holder. Although the terms author and copyright holder are sometimes used interchangeably, they are distinct (and sometimes) separate entities (Russell, 2004).

The author is responsible for identifying potential copyright infringements. When an author discovers an unauthorized use of their materials, a legal process may be initiated. At the first stage of the process, a *cease-and-desist* letter may be sent. This letter demands that the user stop using the copyrighted content. If the user believes that his or her usage of copyrighted material is likely to be protected under the law, then lawyers representing the author and lawyers representing the user prepare evidence and develop legal arguments. Judges ultimately determine whether infringement has occurred, applying a legal rule of reason. If a judge determines that infringement has occurred, penalties for copyright may include fines from $200 up to $150 000 for each work infringed. In the United States, willful copyright infringement can even lead to imprisonment of up to 5 years.

Although copyright law is designed to protect authors for a limited time, in order that creative work circulates widely to benefit society, the law's terms have been extended since 1790 to protect authors (and their heirs) for a very long period after the work has been created (Hyde, 2010). For works created after 1978, a copyright lasts for the life of the author plus 70 years after the author's death. If the work is a joint work with multiple

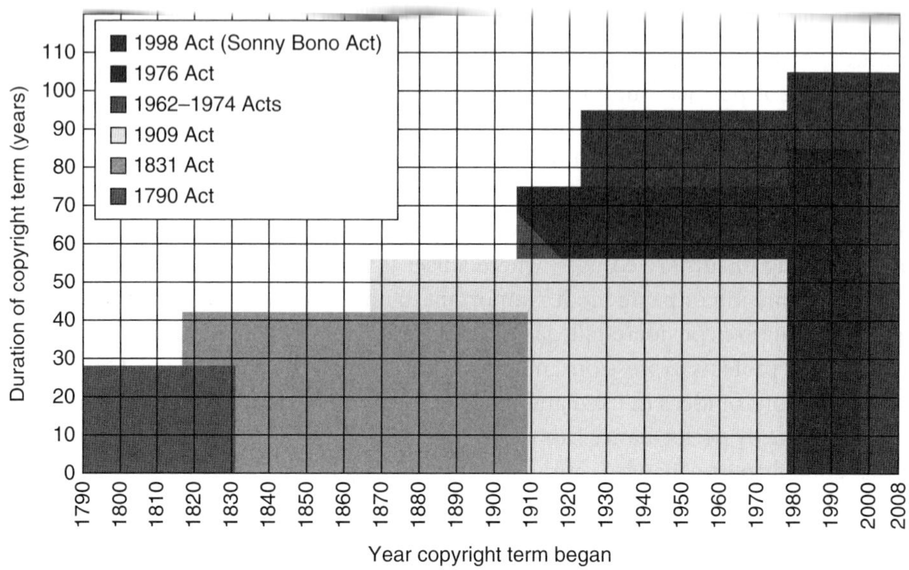

Figure 1 Term extensions to copyright in the United States.

authors, the term lasts for 70 years after the last surviving author's death. Figure 1 shows how laws have extended copyright protections over time. For these reasons, lawyers say that copyright law is "long and strong."

Authors have built a flexible array of licensing models in order to prevent copyright law from stifling innovation. Lawrence Lessig (2004) spearheaded the development of a new model of licensing creative works called Creative Commons. Creative Commons promotes itself as a "best-of-both-worlds" way for creators to protect their works while encouraging certain uses of them.

The Creative Commons model allows creators to specify exactly how they want their work to be used by others; in other words, they can declare "some rights reserved.'" Creative Commons was developed in order to counteract the problems with the current copyright system; namely, the fact that large copyright holders were exercising a disproportionate amount of power that made it hard for new content creators to distribute their work. Lessig has publicly condemned the "permission culture" that is evident in the current copyright system.

As the value of intellectual property grew to be the second-largest export sector in the United States, a shift in attitudes about copyright became noticeable. By the early 1990s, a culture of fear was well in place and social norms had developed in the worlds of music, publishing, and film that payment and permission was needed for even the tiniest use of a clip, quotation, or excerpt. Educators who had previously never thought twice to use a newspaper article, book chapter, or off-air recording in the classroom became more uncertain about the right to use such content. In his 2004 book *Free Culture* (published under a Creative Commons license and available free online), he writes: "The law's response to the Internet, when tied to changes in the technology of the Internet itself, has massively increased the effective regulation of creativity in America. To build upon or critique the culture around us one must ask, Oliver Twist-like, for permission first … Permission is, of course, often granted—but it is not often granted to the critical or the independent" (pp. 10–11).

In response, the Creative Commons license offers many alternatives to this permission culture with new types of licenses for creators who wish to share their work. There are different types of licenses that offer more or less freedom to users in sharing, repurposing, or revising their work. There are also searchable indexes for users who are looking to find work that is freely available. While Lessig and other scholars argue that Creative Commons provides a useful copyright alternative, the model has received some criticism. For example, some critics have argued that the Creative Commons model fuels the same corporate system as copyright. Others claim that Creative Commons is providing unnecessary licenses, and that some of the Creative Commons licensing options are incompatible with one another. Finally, others argue that Creative Commons licenses actually diminish users' rights, by promoting a system of licensing options instead of the doctrine of fair use.

User rights

In part because of the long and strong protection of owner rights, *limitations and exceptions* have always been a part of copyright law, providing the necessary balance to ensure that copyright law fulfill its mandate to promote creativity, innovation, and the spread of knowledge. Among the many exceptions, for example, librarians can make copies of works for archival purposes (Russell, 2004) and they can digitize films and videos under some conditions (Kemp, 2016). Users also have the right to resell, distribute, or even destroy a legally acquired copy, known as the *first sale* doctrine. It is beyond the scope of this entry to include all such limitations and exceptions, but the ones most relevant to media literacy and media education are described below.

First, let us consider why users' rights are protected under copyright law. Protecting users ensures the continuation of authorship, because all authors draw upon preexisting works in the process of creating new ones. In US copyright law, this protection comes from the doctrine of fair use, Section 107 of the 1976 Copyright Act, which enables creative people to use copyrighted content in their own creative work if they meet the fair use standard applying a four-factor analysis, considering the author's purpose in using the copyrighted material, the nature of the copyrighted work, the amount used, and the potential effect of the particular use on the market.

Explicitly stated in the law, "the fair use of a copyrighted work … for purposes such as criticism, comment, news reporting, teaching (including multiple copies for classroom use), scholarship, or research, is not an infringement of copyright." Some people mistakenly believe that only these named uses are fair use exceptions, but courts have found a wide variety of other uses to be fair uses by applying the rule of reason and considering the context and situation of the use.

An important case articulating the benefits of fair use to authorship was Campbell v. Acuff-Rose Music, Inc, where the copyright holder for the well-known Roy Orbison song "Pretty Woman" sued Luther Campbell and his rap group 2 Live Crew for their identically named song. The rap song drew upon the lyrics and melody of the original in a parody version of the song. Campbell had asked for permission to make transformative use of the song and although they were refused, they produced the song anyway. In deciding the infringement case, the Supreme Court recognized Campbell's use as a fair use, noting that of course, as a genre, parody needs to mimic an original to make its point. The Court also explained that fair use exemptions are essential for future authorship, in order to prevent copyright law from stifling the very creativity which the law is designed to promote.

The flexibility of the doctrine of fair use can be applied to new forms of expression and communication as they arise. For example, noncommercial user-generated content is becoming a more and more important part of contemporary culture, but few countries have a specific exception to allow remixes and mash-ups, even though this is a now common form of creative expression. The doctrine of fair use is easily applied to these media forms and any other forms and genres that develop as a result of human creativity in the future.

Obviously, then, limitations and exceptions to copyright law are important to promote social, educational, and cultural goals. Most countries have copyright rules that enable the use of copyrighted materials in the course of face-to-face teaching in non-profit educational institutions. Special formats of works can be created so that disabled persons can have access to them.

Educators have broad protection to use any copyrighted work in face-to-face teaching and learning contexts. Under US copyright law, Section 110(a) of the Copyright Act of 1976 enables educators to use any copyrighted content in face-to-face teaching and learning contexts and even empowers them to make copies for classroom use. A more recently created law, Section 110(b), which is sometimes called the "Teach Act," includes educational use provisions for distance learning (Crews, 2002). Although this law was designed to support online learning, it defined the concept so narrowly that the numerous provisions and highly detailed limitations have not proven to be relevant to the fast-changing innovations in educational technology or the variety of learning environments that now exist. As a result, when it comes to the use of new forms of audiovisual distribution like streaming, some institutions of higher education engaged in online learning have preferred to use the more flexible fair use standard instead (Adams & Holland, 2017).

Section 107 of the Copyright Law is the doctrine of fair use, and it protects all users, not just educators. Because fair use is contextual and situational and relatively simple to apply, fair use is a concept that ordinary people can understand. Instead of having to read a long list of exceptions to find one that arguably applies to the specific activity in which they are engaged, people can apply fair use reasoning to their particular situation through asking some basic questions. This is especially important in supporting certain forms of creative expression, including appropriation, fanfiction, mash-ups and remixes, and other cultural practices where copyrighted material is reused.

In recent years, the concept of *transformativeness* has been particularly useful to educators with interests in media education. In an influential law review article, Judge Pierre Leval (1990) introduced the concept, which is not explicitly mentioned in the Copyright Act, as a way to assess the first statutory fair use factor, the purpose and character of the use. To be transformative, Leval noted, the use must contribute to new work and must use copyrighted material in a different manner or for a different purpose from the original. If the new work adds value to the original—"if the quoted matter is used as raw material, transformed in the creation of new information, new aesthetics, new insights and understandings—this is the very type of activity that the fair use doctrine intends to protect for the enrichment of society" (p. 1111).

To apply the transformativeness standard, when people create work using the copyrighted work of others, they can ask themselves the following.

1. Did my use of the copyrighted work "transform" the original by using it for a new purpose or in a new context?
2. Did I use only the amount needed to accomplish my purpose in ways that could not be a substitute for the original?

Although transformativeness is an important concept, it isn't the whole story when it comes to the doctrine of fair use. Copying is a time-honored method of learning and it's an important part of the creative process. Many Enlightenment-era writers learned to compose original sentences by first copying sentences directly, and then modifying their content while preserving the structure. Elementary educators recognize that copying can also support a writer's skills by allowing opportunity for careful analysis and close imitation of the text. As learners study the text, they "try it out" by modeling their creative work upon the work of the author. For example, a learner may focus on a genre like "blackout poetry," reading the poetry of Austin Kleon, who creates poems by taking newspaper articles and removing words using a black magic marker. The words he does not erase become poetic expression. By copying this approach to composing poetry, student learning occurs.

Copying as an exception to copyright law also fosters the public interest in gaining access to information, which is a prerequisite for the democratic process of self-governance. Tushnet (2004) points out that copying serves a broad variety of First Amendment goals. She points out, "Copies can still serve free speech purposes when their culture-altering and culture-constituting effects aren't distilled into some new derivative work but remain in a viewer's mind or appear in her conversation—when their power derives from their content and not from a second comer's modifications." And consider this point by legal scholar Pamela Samuelson (2015): "Whenever an author forgoes the opportunity to reuse portions of another author's work out of fear that the use might be challenged as infringing, there is a loss not only to that author, but also to the public. The public cannot benefit from the insights that the second author's reuse of a first author's work would have enabled. There is, moreover, some loss to freedom of expression and to access to information when lawful reuses are forgone. Losses to the public may be more substantial when news is not reported or publications on matters of public concern are suppressed because of copyright concerns."

Thus, copyright limitations and exceptions are essential for the free expression of ideas. The strong value placed on the public interest also explains why courts have ruled that data mining of copyrighted works can be considered to be a fair use. Data mining occurs after copyrighted works have been digitized and indexed, and are then analyzed by specialized software programs. In one case, high school students sued a software company for infringement because the company made copies of their term papers and processed the copies using a computer program designed to detect plagiarism. The court ruled that the digitization of high school papers was a fair use, because the copying and processing of the papers was for the purpose of assessing whether the papers were original or plagiarized, thus promoting a public interest in education and scholarship.

Limitations and exceptions to copyright law also protect personal autonomy and individual rights. Copying for personal use is protected under fair use. In Sony Corporation of America v. Universal City Studios, the question was whether Betamax video tape recorders could be sold to the public, since they could enable people to make copies of Hollywood movies that were aired on broadcast television. The Supreme Court ruled that time-shift copying of television programs qualified as fair use. Private noncommercial copying should be presumed to be fair, the courts declared.

Over time, it is evident that the Sony decision had many important benefits to advance technological innovation. For example, the case helped establish a *safe harbor* for technologies that provide substantial access to noninfringing uses of copyrighted material. A safe harbor insulates a technology creator from infringement lawsuits. Such protection has been an important shield against liability for the makers of many forms of information technologies and digital platforms like Facebook and YouTube. The Sony case also laid the legal groundwork to enable the mass digitization of books from research library collections to make a full-text searchable database available on the Internet.

Communities of practice advance user rights

Educators and learners have broad rights to use copyrighted content for educational purposes, but for many the topic of copyright can be "scary," and often it simply comes from simply not knowing one's rights and responsibilities under the law. Today, some educators want to do more than use copyrighted material as a vehicle for transmitting content in face-to-face learning environments. They may want students to critique or comment on excerpted media texts as a media literacy practice. They may want students to memorialize their personal encounters with media texts, as a way to promote personal reflection or increase awareness of media's role in daily life. They may want to use film clips as a stimulus for charged discussions about how technology and media affects cultural participation or identity development, or reproduces social and political power. Today, learners themselves can express their learning in a wide variety of ways, using images, language, sound, and multimedia to create infographics, podcasts, blogs, vlogs, and screencasts, just to name a few (Hobbs, 2017).

To create and share ideas with colleagues, some educators want to create curriculum materials that employ excerpts, clips, and examples of copyrighted works. To promote professional development, others want to distribute samples of student work to inspire and motivate educators and show what students can do in various types of learning environments.

But without a solid understanding of how fair use applies to this work, all these valuable instructional practices are less likely to occur. In some schools and communities, a culture of copyright confusion can limit the practice of media literacy education. Fear, uncertainty, and doubt about what is legal have increased due to the ease of online copying and downloading as well as the drumbeat of fear-inducing messages from the film, music, and publishing industries. These industries even created curriculum materials designed to introduce copyright law to learners where they equated all forms of copying with stealing and simultaneously either ignored fair use or claimed that it was vague and unreliable (Hobbs, 2010).

When fear of copyright infringement was affecting the quality of documentary filmmakers work, they decided to take action. As a result of the high costs and complicated process of clearing rights to use copyrighted images, texts, or sounds in their work, documentary filmmakers were avoiding making films that addressed certain topics. They also changed sound, images, and locations in order to avoid copyright problems. Each facet of documentary production comes with its own hurdles: images, text, art, graphics, and music are copyrighted by the original creators; soundtracks are copyrighted separately from the film; and promotional materials can be copyrighted and trademarked at both the federal and state levels. At American University in Washington, DC, Patricia Aufderheide and Peter Jaszi helped filmmakers develop their own clearly articulated consensus about what is fair and reasonable under the law, in a document called the *Documentary Filmmakers' Statement of Best Practices*, which articulated the ways that documentary filmmakers needed to apply fair use to create nonfiction films.

To address the copyright confusion within the community, media literacy activists and educators then began exploring copyright education with the support of a collaboration between Peter Jaszi, Patricia Aufderheide, and Renee Hobbs, then at Temple University. Together, they worked with the community to develop a "best practices" model for media literacy educators in 2007, with support from the John D. and Catherine T. MacArthur Foundation. Groups of educators from higher education, K-12 (primary and secondary) settings, and youth media organizations in 10 cities across the United States came together for day-long meetings to develop a set of consensus principles. The resulting document, the *Code of Best Practices in Fair Use for Media Literacy Education* (Media Education Lab, Program on Information Justice and Intellectual Property, Center for Media and Social Impact, 2007), was rigorously reviewed by a team of legal experts and adopted by several national membership organizations, including the National Association for Media Literacy Education (NAMLE), the Action Coalition for Media Education (ACME), the Visual Communication Studies Division of the International Communication Association (ICA), the Media Education Foundation, and the Association of College and Research Libraries (ACRL). Significantly, the 60 000-member National Council of Teachers of English (NCTE) also adopted the Code as its official policy in November 2008, replacing an earlier policy from 1980. Academic librarians have also been leaders in advancing their knowledge of copyright law and helping educators and learners to understand it (Disclafani & Hall, 2012).

The Code identifies five principles, each with limitations, representing the community's current consensus about acceptable practices for the fair use of copyrighted materials. As Table 1 shows, educators and learners have broad rights to copy, use, and share copyrighted materials for the purpose of media literacy education; they can sell and distribute works that contain copyrighted content.

Table 1 Five principles from the *Code of Best Practices in Fair Use for Media Literacy Education*

Educators can:

1. make copies of newspaper articles, TV shows, and other copyrighted works, and use them and keep them for educational use;
2. create curriculum materials and scholarship with copyrighted materials embedded; and
3. share, sell, and distribute curriculum materials with copyrighted materials embedded.

Learners can, under some circumstances:

1. use copyrighted works in creating new material;
2. distribute their works digitally if they meet the transformativeness standard.

At a time when online digital technologies are enabling educators and learners to create and share an ever widening array of texts, sounds, still and moving images, music, and graphic art, communities of practice have discovered how to work collaboratively to promote the use of digital media as tools for teaching and learning media literacy. Knowledge of the law and its application to digital learning have increased as a result of participation in communities of practice. With support from the Center for Media and Social Impact at American University, codes of best practice have been created with and for online video producers, academic librarians, dance educators, and many other creative communities.

The doctrine of fair use can only be applied by considering the social practices within creative communities. Artists, teachers, architects, TV producers, and poets all have social norms, established by the traditions within each professional group, for what's appropriate in using copyrighted materials. These social norms exist side by side with the marketplace model for disseminating information and entertainment. Because copyright law includes a provision for fair use that is flexible and contextual, it can be responsive to the social norms of many different creative communities. As Aufderheide (2018) writes, "A proven way to lower perceived risk, bring risk assessment into the realm of reality, and permit educators, learners and creators to do their work has been to create codes of best practices in fair use at the level of professional practice. A community of practitioners expresses their collective judgment about appropriate interpretation of fair use given their cultural and creative practices."

Takedown notices and ripping clips: Digital Millennium Copyright Act

Technology changes the ways we use media and the law follows more slowly in its footsteps. Copyright issues enter into the online space in a variety of ways and they enter our living rooms, too. In this section we consider the Digital Millennium Copyright Act of 1998, the law that once made ripping DVDs (digital video discs) illegal and which also protects Internet service providers (ISPs) from copyright infringement via the automatic takedown process and criminalizing the sale of technologies designed to circumvent access control devices protecting copyrighted material from unauthorized copying or use.

Nearly every YouTuber is familiar with the practice of "takedowns." If your video includes some copyrighted music or film clips, your video might get taken down. This is now called a Content ID claim, and they are issued automatically by the content companies that own music, movies, TV shows, video games, or other copyright-protected material. Content owners can block material, allow the video to remain live on YouTube, mute the music on your video, track the viewing statistics, or block your video from being seen on certain devices, apps, or websites. Most importantly, under the YouTube Terms of Service, they can even choose to monetize your content with ads. Advertising revenue earned from views on your creative work goes to the copyright owners of the claimed content.

Where did Content ID come from and how does it help Google (owner of YouTube)? When Congress crafted legislation in order to harmonize US copyright with the World Intellectual Property Organization (WIPO), they granted special protections to copyright holders, far more protection than the WIPO required. The 1998 Digital Millennium Copyright Act created protections for those companies and businesses who find themselves accused of infringement; in this case, the platform companies like Google and Facebook. The safe harbor provision of the law allows platforms to avoid culpability for copyright violations by third parties. Content owners may legally use automatic takedown software to search for and find content across the Internet that may be infringing and send withdrawal requests to platform companies, which must automatically take down content under the law (Cobia, 2008). Thus, digital rights management (DRM) software handles copyright matters automatically.

But many fair uses of copyrighted content cannot be determined through DRM tools because of the flexibility of fair use, and its sensitivity to context and situation. Media-literate individuals know how to analyze whether a particular use of copyrighted material is a fair use. They understand the concept of transformativeness and can conduct a four-factor analysis with sensitivity to context and situation. Those on YouTube also know how to file a counternotification when their work has received copyright claim. By completing an online form, you offer reasons why your use of copyrighted content is a fair use, and within 48 hours a decision is made and in many cases the video is restored.

In 2017, Renee Hobbs uploaded a short video to YouTube which included an excerpt from a Discovery Channel documentary about human development. She wanted to demonstrate the practice of critical analysis of media. To explore the concept of point of view, the video uses her voice-over to introduce a media literacy activity where students are divided into two teams: one team writes a voice-over from the point of view of the baby, while the other team writes the voice-over from the point of view of the parent. Figure 2 shows what a completed YouTube counternotification looks like when completed. Media literacy educators are expected to be familiar with the process of filing takedown counternotifications and should help learners understand how to use the process when needed.

Copyright law continues to change in response to changing technologies and cultural norms, and the content industries have used their political and economic power to restructure the technological landscape in relation to copying media. Gillespie (2007) has chronicled the early history of DRM, which involves a complex balancing act

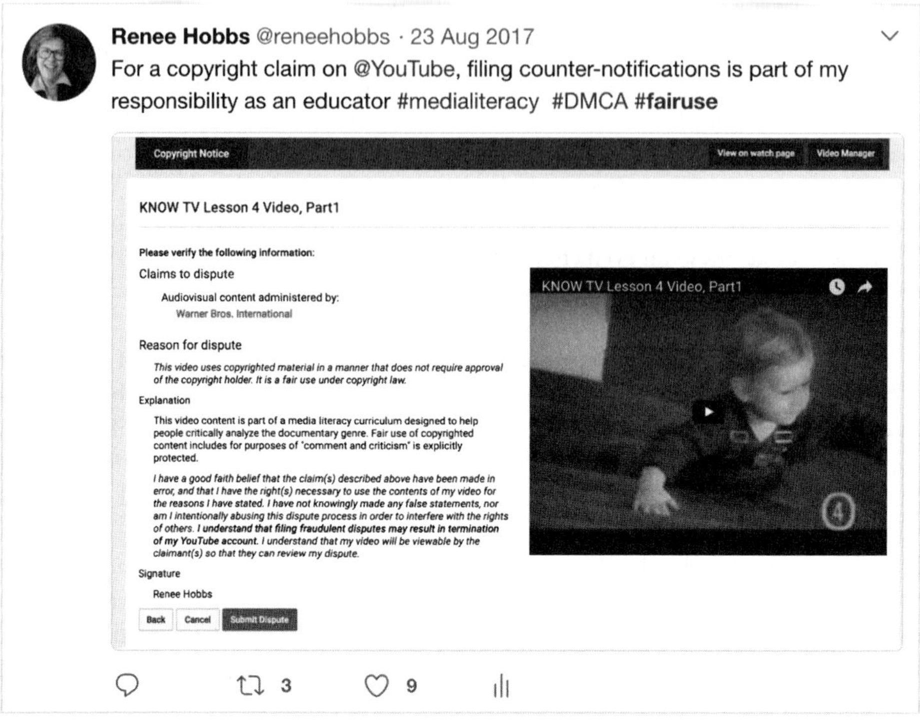

Figure 2 The counternotification process shared on Twitter.

between businesses, government, and citizens through laws, licenses, and cultural ideas. He explains how DVD players and other technology are built without the capacity to make copies, thanks to an act from Congress. By making copying technically impossible, the music and movie industries have used pressure and the force of law to impose strong and complex limitations on manufacturers. Hollywood movies on DVD are encrypted with a code that prevents them from being copied. The Content Scrambling System (CSS) licensing ensures that the manufacturers of playback devices prevent copying, creating a system of "lock and license."

If you're old enough to remember renting VHS (Video Home System) tapes at Blockbuster, you may remember the warnings placed at the front of the videos and shown right before the film began: they had official-looking logos and warned of a $250 000 fine for unauthorized copying. These warnings were intended to deter those who might violate copyright law. But warnings can be ignored and codes and locks can be broken. Bypassing the copy-protection systems on DVDs (called "ripping") has been around for a long time. In 1999, hackers in Norway developed DeCSS, enabling people to "rip" copy-protected DVDs. Since then, thousands of other hackers have continued to develop special software to bypass encryption.

Why do people want to break encryption? After people buy a DVD, they sometimes want to make a back-up copy to watch at their summer house at the lake. They might want to make a copy to watch on a tablet or other digital device. They might want to upload a copy of the digital file to a peer-to-peer network to share with a brother or sister stationed at a military base in Afghanistan.

When the DMCA (Digital Millennium Copyright Act) law was passed, it struck a serious blow to the principle of fair use. Although the law makes ripping illegal, it has been controversial since its passage (Morris, Butler, & Band, 2018). In some cases, of course, copying an encrypted digital file may be legal according to fair use. But because the law unfairly criminalizes the legal fair use of copyrighted material, there is a special provision in the law to address fair use concerns. This special provision grants the Librarian of Congress the authority to exempt users who are, or are likely to be in the succeeding 3-year period, adversely affected in their ability to make noninfringing uses of a particular class of copyrighted works (Morris et al., 2018). To accomplish this, Section 1201 of the law mandates a rulemaking process that was expressly implemented to ensure that the public has the continued ability to engage in noninfringing uses of copyrighted works. So every 3 years, the US Copyright Office considers exemptions to the law for groups or individuals who can prove that the law adversely affects their ability to make lawful, noninfringing uses of copyrighted works. As part of the rulemaking process, the Copyright Office puts the burden on exemption seekers, requiring them to bring evidence of how the law limits their need to bypass DRM software. In general, the process begins with the submission of petitions detailing only the scope of the exemption requested. The Copyright Office groups the petitions into distinct classes and invites public comments on the proposed exemption classes through a Notice of Proposed Rulemaking. Supporters and opponents both provide written comments with legal and evidentiary facts in three rounds of comments, followed by public hearings.

In 2006, Professor Peter DeCherney of the University of Pennsylvania and his colleagues successfully argued before the US Copyright Office that film professors should be entitled to an anti-circumvention exemption. He showed that when teachers select clips by directly using a DVD, the players are slow to load content. Some DVDs automatically play trailers for other movies every time they are played. Some DVDs can't be easily cued up, which means teachers have to skim through all the chapters to find the precise scene they need. When teachers use multiple DVDs to show clips in class, this practice is time-consuming and often ineffective, which may lead to nonoptimal use of video in the classroom. DeCherney argued that possible alternatives to circumvention, such as using VHS cassettes, recording with a digital video recorder, or playing individual DVDs in succession, were inadequate instructional practices (DeCherney, 2012). For these reasons, the Register of Copyright granted the exemption to film professors to rip videos of audiovisual works included in the departmental library of a college or university's film or media studies program. Thanks to DeCherney's advocacy, the Copyright Office established the first ever educational exception to the DMCA's anti-circumvention provisions.

Through advocacy that follows the paradigm established by DeCherney, media literacy educators have expanded fair use to include the right to rip copy-protected movies and media through Section 1201 of the Digital Millennium Copyright Act of 1998. Because many elementary and secondary educators and learners depend on clips from film DVDs for use in both classroom teaching and student media production assignments, the law has had a negative impact on digital learning and, in particular, has discouraged educators from using film as a teaching resource. Few educators still use VHS tapes, as this equipment has become obsolete. Many have migrated their clip compilations to disk, while others use YouTube video clips, uploaded by others. But these are often of poor visual and sound quality, making it difficult to do the kind of close analysis required for media literacy education. In 2009, Renee Hobbs formally petitioned the Copyright Office to expand the law to include K-12 teachers and students as well as those who engage in media literacy education in libraries, museums, and other settings, but her petition was unsuccessful. In 2012, her second petition was successful and the law specified that college faculty as well as K-12 teachers may "rip" video from copy-protected DVDs or works distributed by online services for purposes of comment or criticism in noncommercial videos, documentary films, nonfiction multimedia e-books offering film analysis, and for certain educational uses. In 2015, her third petition enabled K-12 students to earn the right to legally create copies of copy-protected works using screen-capture technology (Hobbs, 2016). Continued advocacy may be needed to ensure that these fair uses of copyrighted material are available to educators and learners in the future.

The future of copyright

Rapid cultural changes resulting from widespread access to the Internet and other information technologies are opening up space for a vigorous discussion about the role of copyright and fair use in contemporary society.

But copyright law may not be meaningful or relevant if the free and open circulation of human creativity generates more financial rewards and social benefits than the practice of restricting access. Some creative people are choosing not to participate in the copyright system, a practice which developed in the 1980s and has become known as *copyleft*. Because there are licensing models like the open source movement, Creative Commons licenses, and the General Public License (GPL), contributors can share their contributions freely with others, enabling them to reuse and adapt them, sometimes with specific conditions, such as requiring that subsequent users also share their work freely.

Creative works are developed by people from all walks of life. At the same time, large technology platforms, media companies, and independent artists who are trying to make a living from their creative work are asserting their rights to control information and profit from it (Hyde, 2010). What are the implications for the future of copyright?

Some people believe that copyright law is currently interfering with innovation and the spread of knowledge and that removing the law would yield economic and social benefits. Legal scholar Yochai Benkler writes about the future of copyright in a networked society. He believes that nonproprietary information production (that is, the creation of information that is unencumbered by ownership rights) may be superior to the traditional industrial model that emphasizes exclusive rights. The economic model of information as a commodity, which copyright law embodies, might not be the best fit in the age of the Internet.

After all, as we have seen in this entry, information is a special kind of property. It's not like other kinds of property, because if one person consumes it, there is no effect on whether or not another person can consume it as well. Benkler (2006) argues that the current economic model of classifying intellectual property as a marketable product is inefficient. Right now, the current market system attempts to put a price on these resources and thereby restricts access to them. Those with an economic interest in controlling the production and dissemination of information and entertainment are trying to clamp down on people who wish to freely share information, culture, and knowledge.

The current copyright system attempts to make access to creative works more difficult and expensive for the general public to obtain. This may simply not be efficient from an economic standpoint or a cultural one. A nonproprietary production system that encourages the free flow of information, knowledge, and culture would intensify the spread of knowledge and innovation. After all, the cost of creating new material is typically much lower in a production model that relies on sharing information.

The Internet itself continues to be built upon the tremendous growth in the number of successful collaborative, peer production projects where creative products are developed outside of the traditional economic system. Open source software, social sharing, and other forms of peer production are widespread today. However, industries with an economic interest in maintaining the proprietary model of information dissemination (for example, Hollywood and the music industry) are working toward more restrictive copyright legislation that could shut down many peer production and information-sharing projects.

Perhaps copyright laws themselves are real obstacles to the free flow of information or perhaps the law will continue to evolve to better balance the rights of owners and users in ways that advance creativity, innovation, and the spread of knowledge. In a world in which information consumers are now users and creators themselves, knowledge of the changing nature of copyright law is a vital component of being a media-literate citizen.

SEE ALSO: Authorship and Participatory Culture; Digital Media and Information Rights; Media Access and Activism; Open Educational Resources; Policy Issues in European Media Literacy; Press Freedom for Student Journalists; Remix Culture

References

Adams, T., & Holland, C. (2017). Streaming media in an uncertain legal environment: A model policy and best practices for academic libraries. *Journal of Copyright in Education and Librarianship, 1*(2), 1–32. doi: 10.17161/jcel.v1i2.6550

Aufderheide, P. (2018). Codes of best practices in fair use: Game changers in copyright education. In R. Hobbs (Ed.), *The Routledge companion to media education, copyright, and fair use* (pp. 109–116). New York, NY: Routledge.

Aufderheide, P., Hobbs, R., & Jaszi, P. (2007). *The cost of copyright confusion for media literacy.* Retrieved from https://www.macfound.org/media/article_pdfs/MEDIALITERACYREPORT.PDF

Benkler, Y. (2006). *The wealth of networks: How social production transforms markets and freedom.* New Haven, CT: Yale University Press.

Cobia, J. (2008). The Digital Millennium Copyright Act takedown notice procedure: Misuses, abuses, and shortcomings of the process. *Minnesota Journal of Law, Science & Technology, 10*(1), 387–411. Retrieved from https://scholarship.law.umn.edu/cgi/viewcontent.cgi?article=1205&context=mjlst

Crews, K.D. (2002). New copyright law for distance education. The meaning and importance of the TEACH Act. Copyright Management Center at Indiana University—Purdue University-Indianapolis. Retrieved from https://alair.ala.org/handle/11213/9244

DeCherney, P. (2012). *Hollywood's copyright wars: From Edison to the Internet*. New York, NY: Columbia University Press.

Disclafani, C.B., & Hall, R. (2012). Stop saying no: Start empowering copyright role models. *Journal of Library & Information Services in Distance Learning, 6*(3–4), 251–264. doi: 10.1080/1533290X.2012.705151

Gillespie, T. (2007). *Wired shut: Copyright and the shape of digital culture*. Cambridge, MA: MIT Press.

Hobbs, R. (2010). *Copyright clarity: How fair use supports digital learning*. Thousand Oaks, CA: Corwin Press.

Hobbs, R. (2016). Lessons in copyright activism: K-12 education and the DMCA 1201 exemption rulemaking process. *International Journal of Information and Communication Technology Education, 12*(1), 50–63. doi: 10.4018/IJICTE.2016010105

Hobbs, R. (2017). *Create to learn*. Hoboken, NJ: John Wiley & Sons, Inc.

Hyde, L. (2010). *Common as air: Revolution, art, and ownership*. New York, NY: Farrar, Strauss and Giroux.

Kemp, J. (2016). Feature topic interviews: Media librarianship Q & A with Deg Farrelly. *Against the Grain, 25*(5), 11. Retrieved from https://docs.lib.purdue.edu/cgi/viewcontent.cgi?referer=https://www.google.co.uk/&httpsredir=1&article=6607&context=atg

Lessig, L. (2004). *Free culture*. New York, NY: Penguin Books.

Leval, P.N. (1990). Toward a fair use standard. *Harvard Law Review, 103*(5), 1105–1136. Retrieved from https://www.law.berkeley.edu/files/Leval_-_Fair_Use.pdf

Media Education Lab, Program on Information Justice and Intellectual Property, Center for Media and Social Impact. (2007). *Code of best practices in fair use for media literacy education*. Washington, DC: Center for Media and Social Impact.

Morris, C., Butler, B., & Band, J. (2018). Circumventing barriers to education: Educational exemptions in the triennial rulemaking of the Digital Millennium Copyright Act. In R. Hobbs (Ed.), *The Routledge companion to media education, copyright, and fair use* (pp. 52–64). New York, NY: Routledge.

Russell, C. (2004). *Complete copyright: An everyday guide for librarians*. Chicago, IL: American Library Association.

Samuelson, P. (2017). Justifications for copyright limitations and exceptions. In R. Okediji (Ed.), *Copyright law in an age of limitations and exceptions*. New York, NY: Cambridge University Press. Retrieved from https://www.law.berkeley.edu/files/Justications_for_Copyright_Limitations_and_Exceptions_-_Pamuela_Samuelson.pdf

Tushnet, R. (2004). Copy this essay: How fair use doctrine harms free speech and how copying serves it. *Yale Law Journal, 114*, 535–590. Retrieved from http://digitalcommons.law.yale.edu/ylj/vol114/iss3/2/

Further reading

Aufderheide, P., & Jaszi, P. (2011). *Reclaiming fair use: How to put balance back in copyright*. Chicago, IL: University of Chicago Press.

Benkler, Y. (2006). *The wealth of networks: How social production transforms markets and freedom*. New Haven, CT: Yale University Press.

Hobbs, R. (Ed.). (2018). *The Routledge companion to media education, copyright, and fair use*. New York, NY: Routledge.

Lessig, L. (2008). *Remix: Making art and commerce thrive in the hybrid economy*. New York, NY: Penguin Books.
World Intellectual Property Organization. (2016). Understanding copyright and related rights. Retrieved from http://www.wipo.int/edocs/pubdocs/en/wipo_pub_909_2016.pdf

Renee Hobbs is a professor of communication studies and Director of the Media Education Lab at the Harrington School of Communication and Media at the University of Rhode Island. Her research examines the conditions of media literacy education in elementary and secondary schools. She petitioned the US Copyright Office four times as part of the DMCA 1201 Triennial Review process. She has authored eight books and over 150 scholarly and professional articles. She has offered professional development programs in media literacy on four continents. She is the founding editor of the *Journal of Media Literacy Education,* an open-access, peer-review journal sponsored by the National Association for Media Literacy Education.

Creative Works

ALEXANDER SCHMOELZ
University of Vienna, Austria

Creative works: novel, meaningful, valuable, and sustainable

The term "creative works" refers to novel artifacts brought about through human activity. Creative ideas are a necessary but not sufficient element of creative works, as the ideas need to be implemented and turned into reality in order for creative works to be completed. The origin of the creative element in works has long been seen to reside in divine inspiration, but since the 1950s it has become evident that it resides at the intersection of the uniqueness of the individual, collaborative activity, and the broader cultural context.

Creative works are products or artifacts. They can be distinguished from creative persons and creative processes. Works are creative if they are *original* and *novel* by showing relative rarity. Creative works involve aspects that did not exist before or were not yet manifest. This includes novel transformations and modification of existing artifacts. The criterion of novelty and originality is constitutive of creative works. Novelty is fully and widely accepted and leads to the question: "Novel for whom?" Answering it gives us greater insight into this criterion.

- Creative works can be novel for all humanity or novel in a specific cultural context. In this sense, creative works are eminent and involve high or "big C" creativity (Gardner, 1993). Pablo Picasso was a great artist of his time and developed a new technique. Moreover, his creative work played a crucial role in the advent of cubism, a new form of painting.

- Creative works can be novel for the creator or for a specific group. In this sense, creative works are personal and involve everyday or "little c" creativity (Craft, 2001). In everyday situations and interactions, people can create artifacts and meanings that are new to them. In some cases, these creations may have life-changing consequences. Creative works can also be new ideas in which two thoughts are combined that have yet been unrelated.

This leads to a further criterion of creative works. Besides novelty, creative works need to be meaningful and (socially) valuable, as they demonstrate being comprehensible and useful—to a person, to a given group of reference, to a professional field, to a cultural context, or to humanity at large. Works might be novel and original but, if they are not valuable, appropriate for use, somehow practical, or appreciated by someone (sometimes not even by the creator herself), then they cannot be considered creative. More recently, the criterion of sustainability has been widely discussed as a constitutive element of creativity in works. Works are creative only if they are novel, meaningful, and valuable for a longer period and do not become meaningless, invaluable, or even destructive over time. These definitions also accentuate the relative use of the concept of creative works, because social value and sustainability are properties judged by individuals, groups, and society during a certain period of time.

The creative process

Novel and valuable works are the product of a creative process. Core to this definition is the process, which results in a novel work. This novel work is widely accepted as tenable, useful, or satisfying by a certain group at a certain point in time. The creative process, taken as a sequence of thoughts and actions that lead to a novel work, is supposed to consist of four stages: preparation, incubation, illumination, and verification. Preparation involves the construction, definition, and analysis of a problem as well as the conscious work that draws on a person's education, analytical skills, and problem-relevant knowledge. Incubation is the phase in which the person does *not* work intentionally and consciously on the given problem. Incubation may happen when working on other problems, during leisure time, or during play or dream. It is suggested that during the phase of incubation the mind rejects many ideas as useless, or as valuable in a nonreflective manner. Illumination is a period in which valuable ideas surface and become accessible to reflection. It appears to be some kind of sudden enlightenment, which, it is suggested, is preceded by the feeling of an emerging idea. Illumination is a delicate phase and cannot be rushed or pressed. After illumination, there is a phase of reflective work called verification. Here evaluating, refining, and reframing one's idea is key. This four-stage model of the creative process has been further developed by exploring subprocesses involved in creativity such as divergent thinking. Generally speaking it is becoming clear that the idea of a fixed sequence of four stages does not fit with the complexity and multidimensionality of creativity. The creative process is dynamic and allows for cycling between different processes, and it has been acknowledged that creativity might also involve the simultaneous presence of these processes.

More recent work shows that creative works stem from a creative process that presents individual, collaborative, and communal aspects (Craft & Chappell, 2016). At the individual level, the core drivers for producing creative works might be self-actualization, the human tendency to actualize one's potential (Maslow, 1974), and personality traits such as openness to experience, nonconformity, curiosity, and willingness to take risks. At the intersection between individual and collaborative levels there appears the aspect of thinking. As learning to think is a dialogic process, and given the relevance of external stimuli to core creative thinking, there are modes such as divergent thinking, lateral thinking, possibility thinking, and emotive lateral thinking. Thinking builds a bridge between individual and collaborative levels of the process of making creative works. At a collaborative level, different patterns of creative work have been identified, for example integrative, family, complementary, and distribute collaboration. At a communal level, values and thoughts about communal consequences of creative ideas and actions play a crucial role, and so do cultural criteria for judging and valuing creative works.

Moreover, creative works do not come from nothing, as creation *ex nihilo*, but evolve in social situations as creation *in situ*. Creative works emerge from something that is already given. The creative process needs to build on a given structure, routines, and materials in order to eventually deviate from the given patterns. It involves analyzing and disrupting given structures of thinking and action, identifying open issues and blind spots, having and reframing ideas, putting them into action, and making creative works a novel reality (Stenning et al., 2016).

This might happen through the process of co-creativity (Schmoelz, 2018). Stemming from studies on little c creativity carried out by Anna Craft (2001), wise and humanizing creativity (Craft & Chappell, 2016), and emotive lateral thinking (Scaltsas, 2016), the relevance of *co-creativity* becomes more and more visible when it comes to creative works. Co-creativity is novelty that has emerged through shared ideas and actions. Co-creative actors take the impact of that novelty into account (Walsh, Craft, & Koulouris, 2014). The process by which creative works emerge entails shared ideas and actions that are based on wise creativity. Wise creativity means that people think about the value of their creative works, discarding those ideas and actions that lack such value.

Creative works in various domains

Creative works can be found in business, politics, arts, humanities, science, and education. Even if creative works have long been associated with the arts, there are plenty of examples showing creative manifestations in various fields and professions. Gardner (1993) identifies Martha Graham and Pablo Picasso as big creators in the arts, but also mentions Albert Einstein and Sigmund Freud as creators in the sciences and humanities. Moreover, creativity is key to formulating and asking new questions, a key factor in the sciences and humanities. Scientific creativity also occurs at a collaborative level. Key creative inventions in quantum physics have been made in a social process, and yet

Nobel prizes are awarded to a limited number of people as a result of of the condition of three scientists, which often neglects the cumulative and collaborative process that leads to the manifestation of creative works in science.

Creative works manifest themselves even beyond arts and science. In the business world, creative works are becoming more and more essential. A constitutive element of market disrupters are their inherent creative works. Florida (2002) even argues that there has been a rise of the creative class, which is the core driver of economic development in postindustrial cities in the United States. This is a demographic segment—a supercreative core of creative professionals—of people whose work is knowledge-based and who are constantly finding and solving novel problems. More recently, the creative class has seemed to be globally expanding. This class is functional in terms of *creationist capitalism*, a mode of capitalism in which creativity is understood as labor and production is understood as creation. At its heart stands prosumption, in which creative works are directed at the *marketplace* alone.

Reckwitz (2017) goes beyond the domain-specific analysis of creative works. He unfolds how we live in a global regime of the aesthetically new and how we generate a creativity dispositive that permeates *all areas of life*. Among other factors, mass media and media production play a crucial role in intensifying the creativity dispositive. The creative individual and her relation to creative works have evolved alongside the transformation of structural conditions such as media technology. In the Renaissance, letterpress printing made creative artists visible and enabled them, whereas the modern star is embedded in the structural conditions of periodical celebrity journalism and in the distribution of visual and audio media technology. Stars and their creative works have become the core currency of *liberal individualism*, and creative works are driven by technological change.

Creative works seem to proceed from a regime of the aesthetically new that is underpinned by liberal individualism, creationist capitalism, and the structural conditions of media technology. The *novelty* of creative works has, however, become questionable.

Creative works in media education

The relation between creative works and the media reveals developments in the field of media education. Creative works proceed from an awareness of the cultural properties of the medium and from specific pedagogic practice, but not from the technology itself (Banaji & Burn, 2007). Even if some educators follow the imperative of mass media production in aiming for a noncritical reproduction of established media practices within the existing regime of liberal individualism (which is behind market-driven creative works), the essence of creativity in media education confronts aesthetical variations that go beyond existing routines and patterns of communication.

Facilitating media activism *in the classroom* might enable students to come up with creative media works that go beyond existing routines and patterns of communication in a twofold manner. First, creative media works might entail creative reframings of conventional technological practices. Second, they might critique and reframe existing normative practices of coercion, discrimination, and domination within and outside the media (Hug, 2011).

In literacy classroom practices, Walsh (2009) evidenced how students can critically reframe curricular knowledge through creative media works. First, students analyzed and questioned the knowledge of American history in their curriculum and critiqued the way Chinese immigrants are presented in history books. Second, they developed creative media works in which they reframed the representation of Chinese immigrants. A virtual exhibition of students' creative media works was then organized in a museum in New York City. The process of creating media works allowed students to disrupt and reframe the racist and exclusionary elements they encountered in school textbooks.

Other examples that go beyond existing routines illustrate the relation between creative media work in schools and the transformation of identity. Banaji and Burn (2007) exemplify how creative media works transform the creator by manifesting aspects of human identity in the form of multimodal texts and by making these aspects visible to other members of the community, inviting response and negotiation. In that manner, creative media works may enable students to change their own patterns of communication. These forms of creative work show that wisdom and creativity are interlinked, because they exemplify a concern for the practical problems of everyday life, especially interpersonal relationships. To be wise, creators must deal with people, not with things. Wise creativity means that agents take into account the impact and consequences of their creative ideas and works (Craft & Chappell, 2016).

Creative media works can also manifest "wise" aspects when it comes to empowerment *outside the classroom*. The project It Gets Better (http://www.itgetsbetter.org) was initiated in direct response to a number of students taking their own lives after experiencing homophobic bullying; but it aims to inspire hope in young people who face harassment in society as a result of their sexual orientation. The project uses creative media works, especially digital storytelling, as counternarratives of resistance and triumph from LGBT youths and their advocates.

Another example is the 1000Voices project (1000voices.edu.au). Creative media works are used for amplifying the voices of people with disability. Their authors are collecting and creating lifestory data and enable multimodal narratives by using the participants' preferred ways of representing, by incorporating creative abstract expression, and by valuing what is not said.

These examples represent the current decade of work on digital storytelling. Constructing creative media works with digital storytelling went from an educative decade, in which creative media works were related to the transformation of identity, to a social decade, in which they were seen to disrupt and reframe normative discourses by giving a voice to people who are currently not heard. The hallmark, the project that triggered the switch from educative to social in digital storytelling, was SilenceSpeaks (http://silencespeaks.org), coinitiated by Amy Hill in 1999. An example of a SilenceSpeaks project is Hill's (2008) study "Learn from My Story," which aimed to create spaces for silenced stories. This participatory media initiative for Ugandan women affected by obstetric fistula showed how digital storytelling and its creative media works can serve as a starting point for building leadership skills among women and can empower them to self-advocate by spreading the word about prevention and treatment.

In these projects, "ordinary" people became producers of creative media works and were able to be a vehicle for the voice of the silenced. Creative works in the sense of media productions by "ordinary" people are also present in the realm of cultural studies. Jean Burgess (2006) has used "vernacular creativity" as both an ideal and a heuristic device, to describe and illuminate creative practices that emerge from highly particular and nonelite social contexts and communicative conventions. Burgess illustrates how different creative media practices transform everyday *experiences* into a shared public culture.

Co-creative works in media education

Studies of co-creativity have shown that the process of making creative works has individual, collaborative, and communal (Craft & Chappell, 2016) dimensions. Creative persons and groups embody these different dimensions of the creative process and therefore constitute the idea of co-creativity, a kind of creativity that happens *in* and *between* us (Schmoelz, 2017). Creative works are generated in a process that happens both in *and* between us. Individual ideas are a necessary element, but collaborative actions and thinking about the communal consequences of those actions are equally important (Walsh et al., 2014). Thinking outside the box evolves through question-raising and active listening during dialogue. It has further been shown that co-creative works evolve through co-determined actions. These actions are determined by shared preferences and volition that precede the enactment of the means by which creative works are caused (Schmoelz, 2017).

With regard to co-creative works and media, Chappell et al. (2017) have studied virtual learning environments (VLE) and their potential for co-creativity. They have shown how VLEs that go beyond the competitive aspects of displaying creative media works can be about collective journeys of becoming by contributing to incremental, cumulative, and ethical group change. Moreover, digital stories have revealed themselves to be co-creative media works (Schmoelz, 2018), as they stem from individual, collaborative, and communal thinking and from actions that involve disruption and reframing and take the value of their impact into account. The process of co-creative digital storytelling led to co-creative flow, in which students experienced full immersion and enjoyment as well as the absence of control and rationality. Connected with the enjoyment of digital storytelling, they idolized and somehow humanized their co-creative media work, their digital story. Their co-creative media work became the highlight of their media education lessons.

(Co-)creative works in the future

Asking about (co-)creative works of the future and envisioning what may lie before us is not always an easy task. Future thinking and asking what probable, possible, and preferable futures might look like is one way to go. With regard to producing (co)creative works, a probable future is that creative persons will become more and more entangled in the diffuse and ambiguous schism between (i) noncritical reproduction of established media practices within the existing regime of liberal individualism of the market-driven creative works and (ii) being an agent of "wise" creative works that challenge the status quo and are mindful of the consequences of one's thinking and actions. A possible future is that these two processes become more and more extreme and constitute different paradigms for producing (co)creative works; or that one paradigm is destroyed by the other. The future could go both ways; there are convincing studies and reflections that suggest that creative works will become marketized and functional for capitalism alone, and therefore novelty as a necessary constitutive element of creative works will be questionable, because it is all "old wine in new bottles." Other studies suggest a "turn to life" (Heelas, 2002) for the creative industries. It is shown that claims for the demoralization of the creative and cultural industries may be premature and that individualization may offer spaces in which to reestablish noneconomic, "wise," and ethical values in creative works. A preferable future might be one in which unforeseeable new processes are created that lead to creative works, which are truly original, meaningful, valuable, and sustainable. This means that we may need to embrace ambiguity, contingency, empathy, and constructive conflict to create a kind of pluralism that does not lack a shared humanism.

SEE ALSO: Creativity and Media Production in Schools; Digital Storytelling; Media Education Research and Creativity; Media Production in Elementary Education; Understanding Media Literacy and DIY Creativity in Youth Digital Productions

References

Banaji, S., & Burn, A. (2007). Creativity through a rhetorical lens: Implications for schooling, literacy and media education. *Literacy, 41*(2), 62–70. doi: 10.1111/j.1467-9345.2007.00459.x

Burgess, J. (2006). Hearing ordinary voices: Cultural studies, vernacular creativity and digital storytelling. *Continuum: Journal of Media & Cultural Studies, 20*(2), 201–214. doi: 10.1080/10304310600641737

Chappell, K., Walsh, C., Kenny, K., Wren, H., Schmoelz, A., & Stouraitis, E. (2017). Wise humanising creativity: Changing how we create in a virtual learning environment. *International Journal of Game-Based Learning, 7*(4), 50–72.

Craft, A. (2001). Little-c creativity. In A. Craft, B. Jeffrey, & M. Leibling (Eds.), *Creativity in education* (pp. 45–61). London, England: Continuum.

Craft, A.R., & Chappell, K.A. (2016). Possibility thinking and social change in primary schools. *Education 3-13, 44*(4), 407–425. doi: 10.1080/03004279.2014.961947

Florida, R.L. (2002). *The rise of the creative class: And how it's transforming work, leisure, community and everyday life.* New York, NY: Basic Books.

Gardner, H. (1993). *Creating minds: An anatomy of creativity seen through the lives of Freud, Einstein, Picasso, Stravinsky, Eliot, Graham, and Gandhi.* New York, NY: Basic Books. Retrieved from http://www.loc.gov/catdir/enhancements/fy0830/92056172-b.html

Heelas, P. (2002). Work ethics, soft capitalism and the turn to life. In P. Du Gay & M. Pryke (Eds.), *Cultural economy: Cultural analysis and commercial life* (pp. 78–96). London, England: SAGE.

Hill, A.L. (2008). "Learn from my story": A participatory media initiative for Ugandan women affected by obstetric fistula. *Agenda, 22*(77), 48–60. doi: 10.1080/10130950.2008.9674957

Hug, T. (2011) Sondierungen im Spannungsfeld von Medienaktivismus und handlungsorientierter Medienpädagogik [Media activism and action-oriented media education]. *Medienimpulse: Beiträge zur Medienpädagogik, 2.* Retrieved from http://www.medienimpulse.at/articles/view/308

Maslow, A.H. (1974). Creativity in self actualising people. In T.M. Covin (Ed.), *Readings in human development: A humanistic approach* (pp. 46–53). New York, NY: MSS Information Corp.

Reckwitz, A. (2017). *The invention of creativity: Modern society and the culture of the new.* Cambridge, England: Polity.

Scaltsas, T. (2016). Brainmining emotive lateral solutions. *Digital Culture & Education, 8*(2), 106–118.

Schmoelz, A. (2017). On co-creativity in playful classroom activities. *Creativity: Theories—Research—Applications, 4*(1), 25–64. doi: 10.1515/ctra-2017-0002

Schmoelz, A. (2018). Enabling co-creativity through digital storytelling in education. *Thinking Skills and Creativity, 28,* 1–13. doi: 10.1016/j.tsc.2018.02.002

Stenning, K., Schmoelz, A., Wren, H., Stouraitis, E., Scaltsas, T., Alexopoulos, C., & Aichhorn, A. (2016). Socratic dialogue as a teaching and research method for co-creativity? *Digital Culture & Education, 8*(2), 154–168.

Walsh, C.S. (2009). The multi-modal redesign of school texts. *Journal of Research in Reading, 32*(1), 126–136. doi: 10.1111/j.1467-9817.2008.01385.x

Walsh, C.S., Craft, A., & Koulouris, P. (2014). Gameful learning design to foster co-creativity? In International Conference of the Australian Association for Research in Education *(AARE).* Fremantle, Australia. Retrieved from https://www.aare.edu.au/data/2014_Conference/Full_papers/Walsh_14_.pdf

Further Reading

Buckingham, D., & Willett, R. (2009). *Video cultures: Media technology and everyday creativity.* New York, NY: Palgrave Macmillan.

Craft, A. (2011). *Creativity and education futures: Learning in a digital age.* Stoke-on-Trent, England: Trentham.

Taylor, S., & Littleton, K. (2012). Contemporary identities of creativity and creative work. Farnham, England: Ashgate.

Alexander Schmoelz is lecturer and university assistant in the Department of Education at University of Vienna. He holds a PhD in educational science, an MA in political science, and a BA in media and communication studies. His research activities involve higher education development, teacher education, and school studies with a special focus on pedagogy and digital media that aim for co-creativity or inclusion. He has published numerous articles, acted as chair of various conferences, and is the reviewer for a number of academic journals. Since 2008, he has been managing national and European projects (COMENIUS, ERASMUS, FP7) on technology-enhanced learning, as a consultant for the Federal Ministry of Education and Gender Equality in Austria.

Creativity and Media Production in Schools

MARIA RANIERI
University of Florence, Italy

A common definition of media production is the ability to create messages in different media formats (including press, video, radio, comics, hypertext, webpages, podcasts, and social media) to express personal views and participate in community life. Together with critical understanding, media production is a fundamental component of media literacy and its relevance in recent years has even increased with a shift in emphasis from the critical to the creative dimension of media understanding. This shift has been influenced by several factors, among them new attitudes toward the relationship between production work and analytical work, which are increasingly seen as complementary in so far as media production itself may become a tool for critical analysis (Burn & Durran, 2006). But even more importantly, the rapid spread of accessible and affordable digital authoring tools is contributing to the development of a "participatory culture" (Jenkins, Clinton, Purushotma, Robinson, & Weigel, 2009), namely a culture where individuals are not just media consumers but also media producers able to share, remix, and create media. Creative media production today reflects the way in which people learn, work, and participate in society (Hobbs, 2017), although school is not yet fully prepared to foster children's media production skills and creativity or to manage media production projects in the traditional curriculum. In the following sections, we critically analyze the relationship between creativity and learning, the role that digital media tools may play in fostering creativity, and how creative media production may or may not fit into school curricula.

Creativity, learning, and education

The word "creativity" is widely used in many sectors of human activity and society. However, its meaning remains very often unclear, evoking implicit conceptualizations and naïve views (Runco, 2003). Just consider how common sense is full of convictions about creativity. For instance, creativity is commonly attributed to special individuals such as Michelangelo or Einstein, implicitly assuming that creativity is a personal ability pertaining only to outstanding people. Sometimes it is associated with a specific domain such as the arts, for example when people conceive of creativity as typical of great painters or filmmakers. Creativity is also viewed as a natural and innate feature of talented people, with the consequence that only those people can be creative, while the rest of humankind is condemned to be uncreative with no chance of education. These common views about creativity have sometimes been qualified as myths or misconceptions contrasting with the results of empirical studies. At other times they have been found as also reflected in literature (Ferrari, Cachia, & Punie, 2009). Indeed, looking at the research undertaken in this field, a rather complex and sometimes contradictory picture emerges. Although all agree that creativity entails originality, novelty, and value (Sternberg, 1999), scholars have provided different conceptualizations of this notion. Briefly, earlier studies on creativity were carried out within the psychometric approach, which considers creativity as a quality that can be measured and is possessed by everyone (Guilford, 1950). Though the idea of measuring creativity is highly arguable, this view has historically had the merit of broadening the scope of creativity by applying it not only to eminent people but to all individuals. In the psychoanalytical approach, the emphasis shifts to the origins of creativity, which is seen as a manifestation of the unconscious for artistic purposes (Eigen, 1983), while in the mystical approach, creativity is viewed as the result of divine inspiration. This last view is a recurring approach in the artistic domain and it has been influential in the field of education, since many parents and teachers conceive of children's creativity in terms of artistic talent, thus neglecting the relevance of creativity in other areas (Sharp, 2004).

A rather dominant approach is the focus on the end-product, where creativity is interpreted as a process resulting in a product and is viewed in opposition to reproductive experiences (Taylor, 1988). Here, "creativity" and "creations" very often overlap (Ferrari et al., 2009). However, in recent decades, a very prominent approach has been the cognitive one, which sees creativity as a cognitive and thinking skill or process and as a mental representation (Sternberg & Lubart, 1999). Recently, the collaborative approach has moved the emphasis from individuals to groups, teams, and organizations (Fischer, Scharff, & Ye, 2004), recognizing not only the role of individuals at the origins of creative ideas but also that of groups: since creativity results from interaction and collaboration with other individuals (Csikszentmihalyi & Sawyer, 1995), this can be referred to as "collaborative creativity" (Hermann, 2009). In these approaches, creativity is both individual and social; it is not limited to the mind of an individual but is a relational process that occurs in the interaction between individuals and society.

The idea of creativity as a social process has been theorized within the tradition of cultural psychology which conceives of social activity and cultural resources as key components of the creative process (Bruner, 1990; Engeström, 1996). This approach has its roots in Vygotsky (1978 [1931]), according to whom play is inherently creative since through the manipulation of culturally significant artifacts children develop the ability to understand and use symbols. The internalization of this ability and the combination of imagination with thinking in concepts generate true creativity, meant as a lifelong ability to transform cultural resources and one's own identity (Banaji, Burn, & Buckingham, 2010).

Given this plethora of definitions, several questions about creativity are still unanswered. In their extensive literature review on the (social, political, philosophical, and scientific) discourses relating to creativity, Banaji et al. (2010) identified four main themes which are currently under discussion, highlighting their implications for teaching and learning. First, there is fundamental disagreement among scholars as to whether creativity is an internal cognitive function, or an external social and cultural phenomenon. Second, the pervasive nature of creativity is also being debated: Is creativity a ubiquitous characteristic of human activity, or an exclusive ability of special individuals or groups in certain fields? Another issue concerns the impact of creativity on society: Does creativity inevitably produce social improvement, or can it generate disruption, conflict, and even antisocial effects? Finally, there are still debates about the relationship between creativity on the one hand, and teaching/learning on the other. In this respect, it must be pointed out that, similarly to other fields, the term creativity is often used in education but is rarely defined. For example, teachers may ask their students to be creative in their productions or evaluate their activities as creative, without providing any clarifications about the meaning of creativity, and this lack of explicit definition may lead teachers and students to identify creativity only with artistic talent and personal peculiarities (Beghetto, 2005). In addition, there are some tensions between creativity and formal education that must be considered. One of them relies on the "institutional grammar" of the school. For instance, Beghetto (2007) found that teachers prefer standardized answers rather than unique ones, partly because they associate creativity with nonconformity and disruptive behavior which can threaten teachers' authority and their control of the class. Another factor that may generate contrasting understandings of the relationship between creativity and teaching/learning refers to the way in which creative learning is related to play. As Banaji et al. (2010) explain, notions of creativity as skill-based to prepare students for work can be opposed to "game-based learning," which criticizes the idea of learning as mechanistic and joyless work and sees dynamic forms of learning in play. At the same time, many scholars underline the fundamental role of teachers in facilitating learners' creativity: they are seen as having the responsibility to assess students' creativity (Wyse & Spendlove, 2007), to build an appropriate climate for creative learning (Sharp, 2004) or find an adequate balance between structure and freedom of expression (Beghetto, 2005), or lastly, to respond to "unexpected curricular micro-moments" (Beghetto, 2013).

Creativity, digital media tools, school

When considering the relationship between creativity, media, and technologies, a fundamental question that generally comes to the fore is whether the use of technology is inherently creative. Loveless (2002) identifies some features of media technologies which can facilitate creativity and make people able to produce things that they would never have been able to produce without them. Among these features, he includes provisionality, interactivity, capacity, range, speed, and automatic functions which have to be seen as affordances of digital technologies, namely opportunities emerging in relation to human agency and purpose, rather than as determinants of creative expression. Indeed, when we look at the effects of technologies on creative practices, we cannot expect a standardized outcome, but we have to take into account a variety of factors such as the type of digital tool, the way it is used and its purpose, the context of use, and so on. Therefore, the capacity to use technological devices should be meant not only in terms of abilities to use particular technologies but also as the capacity to evaluate their appropriateness and be open to new developments.

Also in the educational field, the adoption of digital tools does not necessarily mean that teaching and learning become more creative, and what counts more is understanding their potential in specific social, cultural, and psychological circumstances (Banaji et al., 2010), rather than limiting oneself to their use for their own sake. Through information and communication technology (ICT), learners and teachers can engage in learning experiences which can support creativity by providing opportunities for exploration and play with materials and information, taking risks, and making mistakes in a nonthreatening atmosphere, enabling reflection, access to a resourceful environment, and flexibility in time and space.

Loveless (2002, 2007) suggests categorizing the activities which exploit digital technologies' affordances in relation to the elements featuring creative and learning processes. Digital media technologies can be used to develop ideas, both in supporting the early stage of thinking with tools for brainstorming and mapping, and in the trying out of ideas with the use of programming language, digital manipulatives, and simulations or in problem-solving tasks. Technologies can play an important role for learners in making connections with other projects and resources as well as in collaborating with others during the creative work in progress: blogs, wikis, social networks, and other services of Web 2.0 enable communication with individuals and groups external to classrooms in ways that were limited before the digital age. Technology also plays a distinctive role in creation and editing processes, allowing the development of multiliteracies: digital tools can sustain meaning expression through multimodality, providing the opportunity to trace the development and revise the production process. Lastly, media technologies can enable the publishing and presentation of works to different publics: an awareness of the audience is crucial for the creative process since it makes learners reflect more deeply on the level of originality and value of their work.

Another aspect to be considered is that digital technologies can support creativity both in traditional settings, such as classrooms and schools, and in online learning environments, such as virtual worlds or knowledge forums. An area of significant development is also represented by mobile technologies, which challenge our understanding of creative practices, bringing together both physical and virtual experiences of space and interactions. Indeed, in physical and/or virtual environments, creative activities carried out with new communication devices question traditional learning organizations in terms of pedagogy, curriculum, space, time, and staff. However, it is important to underline that while the use of technology for creative work is often perceived as a liberation from constraints, the emphasis should be on pursuing meaning-making in projects that enable pupils to develop their ideas over time, with opportunities to both complete carefully structured tasks and engage in open-ended experimentation. In order to create creative digital moments in school a crucial role is played by the teachers' capacity for improvisation and strategic risk-taking, which are the socioemotional and experiential competencies that teachers need "to create a learning experience from an unpredictable situation," especially when using digital media (Hobbs, 2013, p. 6). Very often the use of digital media in education (in and out of school) is seen by teachers as particularly challenging, since it generates a variety of classroom management issues such as "freedom, creativity and collaborative learning," that may not guarantee sufficient levels of "structure, scaffolding and support" (Hobbs, 2013). By pandering to such concerns, both creativity and technologies would be banned from education, should we fail to recognize teachers' capacity for risk-taking as a key component to transform unpredictable situations into opportunities for creative learning.

Teaching creative media production in schools

Although fostering creative media production in school may engender several risks, the capacity "to write" the media is relevant to the same degree as the ability "to read" the media. This seems quite obvious today. However, this was not the case a few decades ago, especially because teachers were afraid that students engaged with media production would end up by imitating mainstream media, reproducing dominant values and conventions rather than expressing themselves. To some extent media potential for creative expression was largely underestimated. This view had several limitations. First of all, according to the Social Learning theory (Bandura, 1986), models are an important source for learning new behaviors: learning is a cognitive process which happens in social contexts where individuals observe and imitate others. Therefore, imitation is an important mechanism for learning. When coming to media education, this does not mean that media production is just limited to reproduction. Indeed, all the media production process should be accompanied by acts of reflexivity. Before the media production process starts, students brainstorm ideas, discuss them, and decide which ideas to develop within their media project. At each stage of media production, learners take some decisions which bring them to analyze, compare, and reflect on the reasons for their decisions. During the design and implementation phase, learners will search for contents, compare sources, reflect on their target audience, decide the media format, and translate their ideas into an artifact. Again, learners take several decisions which entail reflection, awareness, and critical thinking. The opportunity to translate ideas into practice has particular relevance for learning in so far as through media production learners may publicly show what they have learnt, and this facilitates learning and understanding (Merrill, 2013). At the end of the process, a debriefing of the activity will lead learners to perceive in depth the challenges of media production in terms of context of production, audience, and effective communication. In particular, public self-evaluation plays an important role here (Buckingham, 2003): by evaluating their media products and those of their peers, learners are offered the opportunity to understand the relationship between the intention and the results, and therefore to glean the complexity of meaning production. Briefly, media production in school is not passive reproduction but critical imitation based on re-elaboration, remixing, and recombination; it does not have to do with technicalities but with questioning and reflecting; it is not an end in itself but an opportunity to learn.

Second, media production has to do with creativity and not with trivialized forms of communication and information retrieval. Creativity, as we have seen, is not a romantic or even mystic construct which characterizes outstanding individuals: creativity has a relational and social nature. This is why creative media production in school entails collaborative work, discussion, cooperation, and work in small groups with students playing different roles. Of course, we cannot take it for granted that learners know and master the "media grammar": although new generations are heavy users of media, this does not automatically translate into creative and expressive use, but specific educational interventions are required to enable learners to discover how media work. From Dewey onwards, learning by doing has been a main educational strategy to combine reflexivity and practice, and media education needs to keep together the analytical and communicative components of media literacy. Students should be engaged with tasks of gradually progressive difficulty, since managing too complex tasks may become a source of frustration due to the several elements that should be monitored.

Implementing media production projects requires a fair investment in time, but it can be motivating, especially for students at risk of drop-out who may suffer from poor concentration. Indeed, collaborative work may support them to develop an understanding of a topic, to feel part of a common project, and to acquire interpersonal and social skills. All of this is part of the pedagogical intervention.

If the equipment was a crucial condition for media production in school in the past, today the widespread availability of digital tools allows schools to overcome the technical and economic obstacles that previously prevented it. This is particularly true when thinking of students' personal devices, the use of which in school would expand the opportunities for media production. Just consider the widespread use of the so-called BYOD (bring-your-own-device) approach. The idea behind it is very simple: if students are already familiar with the particular device they usually use at home, it is reasonable and practical to allow them to bring it to school rather than duplicate the costs for the purchase of new technologies and waste time learning to use tools provided by the school. In addition to these practical benefits, some authors consider it a suitable approach for the school of the 21st century, as it is able to support personalized learning and to allow better integration between different learning contexts, from school to family and other places, in the context of seamless learning. In particular, Seipold (2011) emphasizes how such an approach can also benefit from the multiplicity of resources that students produce daily in everyday life and which may eventually link to learning experiences in formal contexts. Among the technologies that are best suited to be used in this context there are obviously mobile devices such as tablets or smartphones that, by virtue of their portability and availability always and everywhere, insinuate themselves strongly into the activities we carry out every day.

However, there are also critical issues to be considered. For example, students' mobile devices are not inherently suitable for learning and are often replaced with new models. Furthermore, the use of personal devices does not reduce connection costs, which must be considered during the design phase, together with the problems related to the diversity of devices. From a media education perspective, there are two main considerations to be taken into account. On the one hand, media education requires learners to take a distance from the media in order to better understand how media create and vehiculate meanings, values, ideologies, and so on. The familiarity of the personal device might prevail over the educational need for distancing the media and assuming a critical stance. On the other hand, beginning with learners' personal resources, such as the images or videos they have taken in their everyday life, may increase their interest and personal engagement. Today, finding a balance between familiarity and critical distance is a major challenge for media educators in the mobile individualized mass communication world. As an example, a creative activity of mobile storytelling (Ranieri & Bruni, 2013) in nine steps to train teachers is depicted below.

Step 1. To get started. The trainer introduces the topic through a presentation focused on how to create digital storytelling with mobile devices, focusing on storytelling, multimedia, mobile device affordability, storyboards, and storytelling apps.
Step 2. Show and try. Then, the trainer shows how to implement a digital story in a simple and immediate way with a digital storytelling app, involving five students in the production of a short mobile presentation of the course in five shots.
Step 3. What is your story? The trainees are organized in groups of 4–7 people and each group chooses the place to carry out the activity. To start working, each group undertakes a brainstorming activity on possible themes to be developed for the story.
Step 4. Link the ideas. Once the topic has been defined, each group defines the characters of the story, the setting, the times, the places, and the plot.
Step 5. Create the storyboard. The next step is creating a storyboard including texts and multimedia content that are necessary to create the multimedia product.
Step 6. Collect the multimedia materials. To collect multimedia materials, trainees can use their mobile devices. In some cases, they create new content, taking photos inside or outside the classroom or recording audio; in other cases, they can use images or music already stored on personal devices or searched online.
Step 7. Implement. Based on the storyboard and editing the multimedia content, each group develops its own story through the smartphone, tablet, or netbook.
Step 8. Log in. Finally, trainees share their multimedia products on a YouTube channel created by the trainer.
Step 9. Comment. Trainees visualize the products and discuss them, both to get ideas and to improve their work and that of others.

Acknowledgment

This entry is based on Ranieri and Bruni (2016).

SEE ALSO: Authorship and Participatory Culture; Creative Works; Hypertext and Hypermedia Writing; Meaning-Making; Media Education Research and Creativity; Media Production in Elementary Education

References

Banaji, S., Burn, A., & Buckingham, D. (2010). *The rhetorics of creativity: A literature review.* London, England: Creativity, Culture and Education.
Bandura, A. (1986). *Social foundations of thought and action: A social cognitive theory.* Englewood Cliffs, NJ: Prentice-Hall.

Beghetto, R.A. (2005). Does assessment kill student creativity? *The Educational Forum, 69*(3), 254–263. doi: 10.1080/00131720508984694

Beghetto, R.A. (2007). Does creativity have a place in classroom discussion? Prospective teachers' response preferences. *Thinking Skills and Creativity, 2*(1), 1–9. doi: 10.1016/j.tsc.2006.09.002

Beghetto, R.A. (2013). Expect the unexpected: Teaching for creativity in the micromoments. In M. Gregerson, J.C. Kaufman, & H. Snyder (Eds.), *Teaching creatively and teaching creativity* (pp. 133–148). New York, NY: Springer Science.

Bruner, J. (1990). *Acts of meaning*. Cambridge, MA: Harvard University.

Buckingham, D. (2003). *Media education: Literacy, learning and contemporary culture*. London, England: Polity Press.

Burn, A. and Durran, J. (2006). Digital anatomies: Analysis as production in media education. In D. Buckingham & R. Willet (Eds.), *Digital generations. Children, young people, and new media* (pp. 273–294). Mahwah, NJ: Lawrence Erlbaum.

Csikszentmihalyi, M., & Sawyer, K. (1995). Creative insight: The social dimension of a solitary moment. In R.J. Sternberg, & J.E. Davidson (Eds.), *The nature of insight* (pp. 329–363). Cambridge, MA: Bradford/MIT.

Eigen, M. (1983). A note on the structure of Freud's theory of creativity. *Psychoanalytic Review, 70*(1), 41–45.

Engeström, Y. (1996). Development as breaking away and opening up: A challenge to Vygotsky and Piaget. *Swiss Journal of Psychology, 55*(2/3), 126–132. Retrieved from http://lchc.ucsd.edu/mca/Paper/Engestrom/Engestrom.html

Ferrari, A., Cachia, R., & Punie, Y. (2009). *Innovation and creativity in education and training in the EU member states: Fostering creative learning and supporting innovative teaching*. Literature review on innovation and creativity in E&T in the EU member states (ICEAC). Seville: EC JRC-IPTS.

Fischer, G., Scharff, E., & Ye, Y. (2004). Fostering social creativity by increasing social capital. In M. Huysman & V. Wulf (Eds.), *Social capital and information technology* (pp. 355–399). Cambridge, MA: MIT Press.

Guilford, J.P. (1950). Creativity. *American Psychologist, 5*, 444–454. doi: 10.1037/h0063487

Hermann, T. (2009). Design heuristics for computer supported collaborative creativity. In *Proceedings of the 42nd Hawaii International Conference on System Sciences* (pp. 1–10). IEEE Computer Society. doi: 10.1109/HICSS.2009.144

Hobbs, R. (2013). Improvization and strategic risk-taking in informal learning with digital media literacy. *Learning, Media and Technology, 38*(2), 182–197. doi: 10.1080/17439884.2013.756517

Hobbs, R. (2017). *Create to learn. Introduction to digital literacy*. Hoboken, NJ: Wiley.

Jenkins, H., Clinton, K., Purushotma, R., Robinson, A., & Weigel, M. (2009). *Confronting the challenges of participatory culture: Media education for the 21st century*. Chicago, IL: The John D. and Catherine T. MacArthur Foundation.

Loveless, A. (2002). *A literature review in creativity, new technologies and learning: A report for Futurelab*. Bristol, England: Futurelab.

Loveless, A. (2007). *Creativity, technology and learning: A review of recent literature. Report 4: Update*. Bristol, England: Futurelab.

Merrill, M.D. (2013). *First principles of instruction: Identifying and designing effective, efficient, and engaging instruction*. San Francisco, CA: Pfeiffer.

Ranieri, M., & Bruni, I. (2013). Mobile storytelling and informal education in a suburban area: A qualitative study on the potential of digital narratives for young second generation immigrants. *Learning, Media and Technology, 38*(2), pp. 217–235. doi: 10.1080/17439884.2013.724073

Ranieri, M., & Bruni, I. (2016). Create, transform, and share: Empowering creativity and self-expression through mobile learning. In D. Parsons (Ed.), *Mobile and blended learning innovations for improved learning outcomes* (pp. 159–179). Hershey, PA: IGI Global.

Runco, M.A. (2003). Education for creative potential. *Scandinavian Journal of Educational Research, 47*(3), 317–324. doi: 10.1080/00313830308598

Seipold, J. (2011). *Mobiles Lernen. Theorien, Unterrichtspraxis und Analysemodelle der britischen und deutschsprachigen Mobile Learning-Diskussion* [Mobile learning. Theories, teaching practice and analysis models of the British and German mobile learning discussion] (Doctoral dissertation), University of Innsbruck, Austria. Retrieved from https://d-nb.info/1037455444/34

Sharp, C. (2004). Developing young children's creativity: What can we learn from research? *Topic, 32*, 5–12. Retrieved from https://www.nfer.ac.uk/publications/55502/55502.pdf

Sternberg, R.J. (1999). *Handbook of creativity.* Cambridge, England: Cambridge University Press.

Sternberg, R.J., & Lubart, T.I. (1999). The concept of creativity: Prospects and paradigms. In R.J. Sternberg (Ed.), *Handbook of creativity* (pp. 3–15). Cambridge, England: Cambridge University Press.

Taylor, C.W. (1988). Various approaches to and definitions of creativity. In R. Sternberg (Ed.), *The nature of creativity: Contemporary psychological perspectives* (pp. 99–121). New York, NY: Cambridge University Press.

Vygotsky, L.S. (1978 [1931]). *Mind in society.* Cambridge, MA: Harvard University Press.

Wyse, D., & Spendlove, D. (2007). Partners in creativity: Action research and creative partnerships. *Education 3–13, 35*(2), 181–191. doi: 10.1080/03004270701312034

Further reading

Banaji, S., & Burn, A. (2007). Creativity through a rhetorical lens: Implications for schooling, literacy and media education. *Literacy, 41*(2), 62–70. doi: 10.1111/j.1467-9345.2007.00459.x

Beghetto, R.A., & Kaufman, J.C. (2010). Broadening conceptions of creativity in the classroom. In R.A. Beghetto & J.C. Kaufman (Eds.), *Nurturing creativity in the classroom.* Cambridge, England: Cambridge University Press.

Cachia, R., Ferrari, A., Ala-Mutka, K., & Punie, Y. (2010). *Creative learning and innovative teaching. Final report on the study on creativity and innovation in education in the EU member states.* Seville: EC JRC-IPTS.

Craft, A. (2000). *Creativity across the primary curriculum: Framing and developing practice.* London, England: Routledge.

Davies, T. (1999). Taking risks as a feature of creativity in the teaching and learning of design and technology. *The Journal of Design and Technology Education, 4*(2), 101–108. https://ojs.lboro.ac.uk/JDTE/article/view/503

Fischer, G., Giaccardi, E., Eden, H., Sugimoto, M., & Ye, Y. (2005). Beyond binary choices: Integrating individual and social creativity. *International Journal of Human-Computer Studies, 63*(4–5), 482–512. doi: 10.1016/j.ijhcs.2005.04.014

Gauntlett, D. (2011). *Making is connecting. The social meaning of creativity from DYI and knitting to YouTube and Web 2.0.* Cambridge, England: Polity Press.

Lachs, V. (2000). *Making multimedia in the classroom: A practical guide.* London, England: Routledge.

Runco, M.A. (2007). *Creativity: Theories and themes: Research, development, and practice.* Amsterdam, Netherlands: Elsevier Academic Press.

Maria Ranieri is an associate professor of educational methods and technology at the University of Florence, Italy. Her main research areas include theory and methodology relating to media and technology in education. She has also worked on educational practices aimed at tackling different forms of intolerance, especially online hate speech and digital discrimination, through the promotion of critical media literacy skills. On these topics she has published several books and articles and coordinated European projects.

Critical Information Literacy

EMILY DRABINSKI and EAMON TEWELL
Long Island University, Brooklyn, USA

Critical information literacy (CIL) is a theory and practice that considers the sociopolitical dimensions of information and production of knowledge, and critiques the ways in which systems of power shape the creation, distribution, and reception of information. CIL acknowledges that libraries are not and cannot be neutral actors, and embraces the potential of libraries as catalysts for social change. Information literacy has been a large part of the academic library discourse internationally since the 1970s, as reflected in various professional standards and models. In 1989, the American Library Association convened a Presidential Committee on Information Literacy in order to develop a profession-wide approach to information literacy as an education domain for academic librarians. The committee's final report facilitated the growth of professional infrastructures that made information literacy central to academic librarian identity through the development of professional round tables, journals, task forces, and conferences. In 2000, this work culminated in a document from the Association of College & Research Libraries: the *Information Literacy Competency Standards for Higher Education*. From the perspective of CIL, the *Competency Standards* offered a decontextualized, skills-based approach to finding and evaluating information, and arguments against Standards-based teaching in libraries have formed a significant strand of CIL critique. The term information literacy itself has been observed to be comprised of two inherently contradictory terms connoting both freedom and control, and in this way may encourage a productive tension if engaged with critically by librarians (Pawley, 2003).

In many ways, critical information literacy can be seen as an approach to information literacy informed by critical theory, and oftentimes critical pedagogy. CIL ultimately seeks to identify and take action upon forms of oppression, and proposes to undertake this work by engaging with local communities. In addition, praxis is a concept central to critical information literacy in that it encourages the reciprocity between theory, reflection, and practice (Jacobs, 2008). Though not limited to teaching, critical information literacy is rooted in information literacy instruction and the educational efforts of librarians. CIL urges students to recognize and resist dominant modes of information production, dissemination, and use. Foundations of the critical information literacy literature include Elmborg's 2006 article on critical information literacy instruction and the edited volume *Critical Library Instruction: Theories and Methods* (Accardi, Drabinski, & Kumbier, 2010).

While these works and others find inspiration in Paulo Freire and the field of critical pedagogy, other researchers have emphasized the usefulness of critical theory as well as composition studies. Librarians incorporate queer, hip-hop, feminist, and critical race pedagogies into their instructional practice and document this work in conferences, books, and professional journals. CIL also engages the field of composition studies as librarians articulate information literacy through rhetorical frameworks. The field of CIL has grown significantly since 2000. Two notable works that expand upon and complement prior research include Higgins and Gregory's *Information Literacy and Social Justice: Radical Professional Praxis* (2013) and Downey's *Critical Information Literacy: Foundations, Inspirations, and Ideas* (2016). Tewell's (2015) literature review contains an introduction to the scholarship of CIL.

Critical information literacy overlaps considerably with critical media literacy, particularly concerning the teaching of knowledge structures and considerations of power and agency in both education and media creation and consumption. CIL tends to be more specific in its challenges to dominant information systems in that it frequently locates its critiques within and in relation to libraries and librarianship. Some proponents of CIL argue for expanding the literacies addressed in the library classroom to include visual literacies, media literacies, and metaliteracies, suggesting that the narrow focus on information constrains the critical potential of librarians. Still, information remains the focus for CIL practitioners. CIL and critical media literacy share many concerns, and additional research on the intersections between these fields could be of significant use to educators.

The theory and practice of critical information literacy continues to flourish, with the pace of scholarly interest showing no sign of slowing. Much of the early work in CIL centered on critiques of the Competency Standards adopted by the Association of College & Research Libraries (ACRL) in 2000. In 2016, the profession replaced the Competency Standards with the *Framework for Information Literacy for Higher Education*, a document that incorporates some ideas of the CIL literature. The *Framework* emphasizes concepts rather than competencies, and argues for contextual and self-reflective information literacy education that centers the needs of particular learners in particular situations. Since its adoption, the *Framework* has been the site of significant professional engagement, some of which expands the theory and practice of CIL.

As a document intended to shape both teaching practices in academic libraries and cross-disciplinary conversations about information and learning, the *Framework* is constituted primarily of six frames (ACRL, 2016). "Authority Is Constructed and Contextual," for instance, asks teachers and learners to consider context in assessing authority, as opposed to accepting more reductive indicators of authority such as an author's credentials or an article having undergone peer review (Drabinski, 2016). "Information Has Value" is a good example of the ways in which the *Framework* is both more open toward critical teaching and does not go far enough in its critique of information's production: the Knowledge Practices and Dispositions described include the examination of one's information privilege and recognizing the commodification of personal information, yet admit no contradiction when referring to the "information marketplace." Some have critiqued the *Framework* for not directly connecting social justice with information literacy, and have pointed to a need to move beyond the *Framework* for critical librarians (Battista et al., 2015). Ultimately, it is up to librarians to develop educational opportunities appropriate to their local contexts: a reality the *Framework* document acknowledges and encourages.

Current interest in CIL ranges from the theoretical to the practical, with the two-volume *Critical Library Pedagogy Handbook* (Pagowsky & McElroy, 2016), an article by Tewell (2017), and the recently established *Journal of Critical Library and Information Studies* being good examples of current directions and interests. Recent literature has engaged a number of theoretical orientations that range from classical Greek theories of time (Drabinski, 2014) to cyberfeminism (Schlesselman-Tarango, 2014). CIL is increasingly expansive in its consideration of useful theories and shared interests with other fields, particularly as it has matured.

With the intensifying corporatization of higher education across the world, CIL must continue to resist the encroachment of neoliberalism into new territories both digital and physical, as well as act to counter political regimes that attempt to stifle freedom of speech and sow confusion among citizens. CIL is fundamentally concerned with how some forms of knowledge and not others are produced as true. Making knowledge is a political project, one that critical library educators seek to surface and make evident to all kinds of learners. It is crucial that librarians and other educators not attempt to avoid politics, but instead engage directly with the major issues of violence towards women, people of color, queer people, and other marginalized populations, and with the systems of power that sanction and endorse these acts of violence. Connecting that violence to forms of knowledge production, dissemination, and use will continue to be a focus for CIL practitioners and theorists. Critical information literacy is one way that librarians can work with others to identify and resist forms of oppression, and it is imperative that this work continues.

SEE ALSO: Critical Pedagogy; Knowledge Structures

References

Accardi, M.T., Drabinski, E., & Kumbier, A. (Eds.). (2010). *Critical library instruction: Theories and methods.* Duluth, MN: Library Juice Press.

Association of College & Research Libraries. (2016). *Framework for information literacy for higher education.* Retrieved from http://www.ala.org/acrl/standards/ilframework

Battista, A., Ellenwood, D., Gregory, L., Higgins, S., Lilburn, J., Harker, Y.S., & Sweet, C. (2015). Seeking social justice in the ACRL framework. *Communications in Information Literacy, 9*(2), 111–125. Retrieved from http://www.comminfolit.org/index.php?journal=cil&page=article&op=view&path%5B%5D=v9i2p111

Downey, A. (2016). *Critical information literacy: Foundations, inspirations, and ideas.* Sacramento, CA: Library Juice Press.

Drabinski, E. (2014). Toward a Kairos of library instruction. *The Journal of Academic Librarianship, 40*(5), 480–485. doi: 10.1016/j.acalib.2014.06.002

Drabinski, E. (2016). Turning inward: Reading the Framework through the six frames. *College & Research Libraries News, 77*(8), 382–384. doi: 10.5860/crln.77.8.9537

Elmborg, J. (2006). Critical information literacy: Implications for instructional practice. *The Journal of Academic Librarianship, 32*(2), 192–199. doi: 10.1016/j.acalib.2005.12.004

Higgins, S., & Gregory, L. (Eds.). (2013). *Information literacy and social justice: Radical professional praxis.* Sacramento, CA: Library Juice Press.

Jacobs, H.L. (2008). Information literacy and reflective pedagogical praxis. *The Journal of Academic Librarianship, 34*(3), 256–262. doi: 10.1016/j.acalib.2008.03.009

Pagowsky, N., & McElroy, K. (Eds.). (2016). *Critical library pedagogy handbook.* Chicago, IL: Association of College & Research Libraries.

Pawley, C. (2003). Information literacy: A contradictory coupling. *The Library Quarterly, 73*(4), 422–452. Retrieved from http://www.jstor.org/stable/4309685

Schlesselman-Tarango, G. (2014). Cyborgs in the academic library: A cyberfeminist approach to information literacy instruction. *Behavioral & Social Sciences Librarian, 33*(1), 29–46. doi: 10.1080/01639269.2014.872529

Tewell, E. (2015). A decade of critical information literacy: A review of the literature. *Communications in Information Literacy, 9*(1), 24–43. doi: 10.15760/comminfolit.2015.9.1.174

Tewell, E. (2017). The practice and promise of critical information literacy: Academic librarians' involvement in critical library instruction. *College & Research Libraries, 79*(1), 10–34. doi: 10.5860/crl.79.1.10

Further reading

Bauder, J., & Rod, C. (2016). Crossing thresholds: Critical information literacy pedagogy and the ACRL Framework. *College & Undergraduate Libraries, 23*(3), 252–264. doi: 10.1080/10691316.2015.1025323

Beilin, I. (2016). Student success and the neoliberal academic library. *Canadian Journal of Academic Librarianship, 1*(1), 10–23. Retrieved from http://www.cjal.ca/index.php/capal/article/view/24303

Nicholson, K.P. (2015). The McDonaldization of academic libraries and the values of transformational change. *College & Research Libraries, 76*(3), 328–338. doi: 10.5860/crl.76.3.328

Schroeder, R. (2014). *Critical journeys: How 14 librarians came to embrace critical practice.* Sacramento, CA: Library Juice Press.

Seale, M. (2016). Enlightenment, neoliberalism, and information literacy. *Canadian Journal of Academic Librarianship, 1*(1), 80–91. Retrieved from http://www.cjal.ca/index.php/capal/article/view/24308

Emily Drabinski is Associate Professor and Coordinator of Library Instruction at Long Island University, Brooklyn. Emily is the recipient of the Ilene F. Rockman Instruction Publication of the Year Award for her 2015 article, "Toward a Kairos of Library Instruction." She is coeditor of *Critical Library Instruction: Theories & Methods* (2010).

Eamon Tewell is Assistant Professor and Reference & Instruction Librarian at Long Island University, Brooklyn. Eamon is the recipient of the 2016 Jesse H. Shera Award for Distinguished Published Research, awarded by the American Library Association's Library Research Round Table. His research interests are in critical information literacy, popular media in library instruction, and televisual representations of libraries.

Critical Pedagogy

TED KESLER
Queens College, CUNY, USA

Media texts are texts that are widely distributed and accessible, generate consumer culture, are in a wide range of forms and genres, and use digital technologies. They are pervasive and innately multimodal. For children aged 3 to 17, media texts comprise their popular culture, which they increasingly access online. The Child Trends Data Bank (www.childtrends.org/databank) reports that, by 2013, many of students' online activities outside school involved popular culture, including participating in gaming sites that have chat rooms and discussion boards, visiting popular culture websites, interacting on social media sites such as Instagram, and viewing videos on YouTube. Given the powerful interplay of youths with popular culture media, critical media literacy (CML) scholars contend that popular culture is a more significant, penetrating pedagogical force in young people's lives than schooling.

One reason why schools are wary of harnessing students' popular culture interests as pedagogical resources is that these texts might generate controversial and challenging ideological messages. Yet, precisely because of the ubiquitous nature and accessibility of popular culture media, schools might be exactly the sites where students could engage in critical analysis of these texts. After all, popular culture and mass media are part of the experiences that students bring with them to school and should be embraced and critiqued within the formal educational curricula. By analyzing how these texts construct readers and what these texts are doing and for what purposes, students could gain power over how to situate themselves as they interact with them.

Defining critical pedagogy

Freebody and Luke (1990) presented four reading resources that form the basis of critical pedagogy. These resources are code breakers, meaning-makers, text users, and text critics. Code breakers are able to decode words by putting sounds, symbols, and meanings together. Meaning-makers use strategies—including prior knowledge—to interpret meanings that are embedded in texts. Text users recognize and use various textual genres and structures in order to understand how texts work and how to use them for social purposes in specific contexts. Text critics are able to analyze and critique texts around issues of power, perspective, and social justice. They recognize how texts position them as readers and determine whether to accept or take an oppositional stance on the basis of what subjectivities they suppress or express. These four resources occur concurrently in a reading experience, although one may be foregrounded or backgrounded. Therefore competent readers build strong, expansive, and flexible repertoires across these four resources in order to navigate and negotiate all media texts.

To develop flexible and expansive competency across these four resources, critical pedagogy must be inherently dialogic. Freire (1970/2008) asserted: "I cannot think *for others* or *without others*, nor can others think *for me*" (p. 108). Dialogic pedagogy is generative and requires a genuine encounter between people, one mediated by social concerns about the world. The ultimate enactment of the dialogic curriculum is praxis, or "the reflection and action which truly transform reality" (p. 100). To achieve praxis, Freire advocated a problem-posing methodology. The teacher's role is to "re-present" the students' concerns about the world "not as a lecture, but as a problem" (p. 109) and to guide them toward developing critical perceptions and recognizing inherent contradictions that illuminate potential actions. Through dialogue, the teacher guides the students toward a state of *conscientizacao*—a level of awareness where they perceive both troubling situations and actions that will challenge "the obstacles to their humanization" (p. 110). In this dialogic pedagogy, students develop a sense of textual authority. They learn to recognize a multiplicity of perspectives; the contingency of composition and interpretation; and the ideological nature of all texts. Thus to teach critical literacy is to invite students to inhabit positions of textual authority, in which their work with texts is anchored in these recognitions.

Popular media texts are sites of pleasure, affiliation, and contestation. For youths, identities form and shift malleably as they strive to locate themselves on these sites. They both take on a text's assigned meanings of representations of identities (such as race, class, gender, age, ability, and ethnicity) and construct alternative meanings that are dependent on their interpretive communities, their beliefs, and their social networks. For example, youths' participation on social networking sites such as Twitter or Instagram is influenced by how many followers they have, how many "likes" or favorites or shares, and the kinds of comments their posts receive. School discourse privileges controlled, rational thought and logic over feelings of pleasure in learning, emphasizing an essential self. Consequently, students are locked into prescribed identities that value unity, conformity, and stability over individualization, multiplicity, and difference. However, young people experience multiple, fragmented, sometimes contradictory subjectivities as they engage with popular culture media and socially construct meaning with them. A critical media pedagogy therefore must be careful to honor youths' pleasure and affiliation on the sites they engage in, while also guiding them to challenge these sites for imposing who they might be and confining them to it.

One ubiquitous source of popular media texts for youths is gaming culture. In gaming culture, particularly socially networked online sites, youths become members of *affinity groups* as they participate in *affinity spaces* (Gee, 2004). Gee identified several core features of these spaces. Common endeavor is primary, so race, class, gender, or disability become irrelevant. Newbies and masters and all in between share common space. Some portals encourage participants to generate new ideas. Game organization is transformed through interaction. Both intensive and extensive knowledge are encouraged; both individual and distributed knowledge are encouraged. The site or space might encourage participants to seek and apply knowledge that they acquired elsewhere. Tacit knowledge is encouraged and honored. There are many different forms of and routes to participation. There are lots of different pathways to status. Finally, leadership is porous and leaders are resources (pp. 85–87). Gee asserted that these are powerful learning conditions to bring to school settings.

CML is critical pedagogy that focuses on popular media texts. CML applies concepts from media literacy, critical literacy, and cultural studies. CML begins with the premise that no text is neutral. Rather all texts, and particularly popular media texts, are steeped in an ideology with powerful historical, cultural, and political assumptions that, taken at face value, become naturalized values, beliefs, and agendas that serve to maintain dominant societal power structures and practices. As both theory and pedagogy, CML applies activist approaches of critical literacy that value a transformative, emancipatory pedagogy by uncovering the ideological meanings of texts and practices, in the interest of social justice. CML scholars such as Kellner and Share (2007) have developed conceptual frameworks designed to implement CML pedagogy in schools. A CML framework enables students to perceive and be critical of media texts that propagate normative ideological discourses—for example about class, gender, race, sexuality, religion, age—but also empowers them to use the media as modes of self-expression and social activism. This pedagogy is especially pertinent to groups that are often underrepresented or misrepresented in the media. These practices will prepare students to be active participants in a democracy.

One kind of action in response to injustice is composing. Composing is a more apt term than writing if we want to describe the process of creating a text by using one or more modes of expression within a critical pedagogy. Composing, then, is the deliberate use of signs, with the help of specific modes and media, to generate metaphoric meaning for what the sign maker intends to represent of the world. Composing, in this pedagogy, is always a situated response, an addressing of another in a particular time and place, a motivated making of words for some end; and "author," "editor," and "response" are situated, not generic. A good descriptor of this deliberate composing process is design work, or how people make use of the resources that are available at a given moment in a specific communicational environment to realize their interests as makers of a message or text. The New London Group (1996, p. 77) explained the meaning-making of multimodal texts as design work and described three elements to design: available designs (resources for meaning; available designs of meaning); designing (the work performed on/with available designs in the semiotic process); and the redesigned (the products of design work). They explained that "[d]esigning always involves the transformation of Available Designs; it always involves making new use of old materials" (p. 76). Moreover, the redesigned produces "new meaning, something through which meaning-makers remake themselves" (p. 76). Through the creative reappropriation of the world, designers generate new subjectivities, and this process constitutes learning.

CML scholars advise providing students with opportunities for alternative media productions that can challenge dominant media narratives. Constructing selves is especially powerful when students are given opportunities to produce *counternarratives*, or texts that challenge and transgress the taken-for-granted texts of popular culture. Students are able to apply, as acts of redesign, the multimodal understandings they gain from the analysis of multimedia texts. In 21st-century literacies, authorship is an act of bricolage (to extend Lévi-Strauss's use of bricoleur), of deliberately appropriating, assembling, and transforming diverse discursive fragments from popular culture.

A pedagogy that gives students opportunities to compose counternarratives also maintains respect for students' pleasure in popular culture media.

Research of critical media pedagogy and youth

Many seminal ethnographic studies of youths' literacy practices with popular culture texts map the complex terrain of students' out-of-school literacies, explore the disjuncture with school-based literacy, and indicate how embracing these literacies might foster students' in-school literacy development. These studies also reveal how these literacy practices shape and are shaped by particular social and cultural contexts. As examples of this complex terrain, researchers have analyzed adolescents' popular music fandom for the important literacy practices that might be incorporated in school settings, explored adolescent girls' use of instant messaging, showed the complex social worlds that were constructed through adolescent girls' reading of popular teen zines and through other unsanctioned literacy practices, analyzed the complexity of middle school girls' anime-inspired fan fiction, which repositioned them as capable literacy learners, investigated the literacy practices of adolescent males who identified as "gangstas," reframed adolescent students' engagements with school-sanctioned texts through hip-hop culture, and studied the naturally occurring digital literacy practices of mainstream youths who struggle with school-based literacy— naturally occurring, that is, on their smartphones.

Some researchers have used action research to directly teach students CML practices. Many of these studies take place in after-school programs. In these studies, researchers become teacher practitioners who guide students through dialogic inquiry toward critical understandings and analyze the critical understandings that students demonstrate. In one study, for example, the researcher provided an after-school writing workshop for adolescent girls. By deliberately weaving in popular culture texts, the researcher showed how much the girls developed in both their critical awareness and their writing skills. However, many of these studies reported on adolescents, highlighting the need for more studies of younger children's uses of popular media texts. Moreover, the fact that most of these studies documented marginalized literacy practices that occurred in after-school or out-of-school settings indicates that popular culture texts and CML are still not regular parts of literacy instruction in classrooms.

Critical media pedagogy studies in school settings

Some researchers have presented empirical studies of CML in school settings, for example, teaching fourth-grade students to write subtexts using blank speech bubbles to advertisements in children's popular magazines. Using a project-based curriculum, O'Brien (2001) described a four-year study in collaboration with two high school teachers who worked with at-risk adolescents in a media lab. Within a multiliteracies framework, O'Brien established the themes of *intermediality*—that is, ability to work with diverse symbol systems in an active way, where meanings are received and produced—and of *acuity* in using multimedia for artistic representation. In acting intermedially, the students in this study were able to channel their struggles with foundational literacy skills into the substance and intent of their expressions, into their finely tuned sense of audience, and into their ability to link their personal lives and feelings to the media and to the audience and use media to construct their own and others' worlds.

Share (2009) described a three-year federally funded program that focused on CML and created alternative media messages in an elementary school in downtown Los Angeles. Two years after the funding ended, Share interviewed some of the teachers who participated in the program. Because critical media pedagogy is multimodal and experimental, the four special-education teachers in Share's study reported high levels of engagement and learning by their students. Particularly effective was a dialogical problem-posing pedagogy that sought to turn students into subjects empowered to act on the world they are living in and learning about. Share also reported that in the two years since the funding had ended, standardization, starting with high-stakes accountability systems, prevented CML pedagogy in the school. This is a strong reason why so few CML pedagogical studies have occurred in school settings.

Implementing critical pedagogy in school settings

The New London Group (1996) called for a pedagogy that balances situated practice, overt instruction, critical framing, and transformative practice or opportunities to put transformed meanings to work in other contexts or cultural sites. Situated practice provides experiential learning and opportunities to use diverse discourses, including ones from students' lives and simulations of relationships in workplaces and public spaces. Regarding overt instruction and critical framing, teachers should not abrogate their pedagogical authority in situations where failure to intervene could be interpreted as condoning children's ill-informed or misguided ideas.

Assuming we are able to push past curricular restrictions in school settings, several educators have developed a curriculum for implementing critical pedagogy in classrooms, spanning grade levels from pre kindergarten through graduate school. In all these curriculum guides, one intention is to create what Dyson (2003) has called a permeable curriculum, which allows students' "recontextualization processes—processes of differentiation, appropriation, translation, and reframing of cultural material across symbolic forms and social practices" and across boundaries of official school literacy and out-of-school literacy practices (p. 24). All these guides describe an inherently student-centered pedagogy.

In Dyson's (2003) ethnographic studies of young children, the permeable curriculum was created with the following values: the teacher's responsive interactive style; a diversity of participatory structures; a breadth of official literacy practices; and explicitness about how to participate in these practices and in the classroom community (pp. 56–57). In *Literacy Moves On* (2005), each chapter describes the enactment of this permeable, critical curriculum across diverse media texts, embracing popular culture and new technologies in elementary classrooms. Books such as *For a Better*

World (Bomer & Bomer, 2001) and *Critical Literacy and Writer's Workshop* (Heffernan, 2004) describe the enactment of these values, emphasizing school-sanctioned texts and forms and genres of writing for advocacy in elementary classes.

One way for early childhood educators to create a permeable curriculum is through a problem-posing education based on Freire (1970/2008), in which students and teachers become coinvestigators of problems that arise organically from their daily experiences. With her first- and second-grade "peace classes," Cowhey (2006) enacted curriculum and classroom practices that were grounded in the lives of her students; critical, multicultural, antiracist, and pro-justice; participatory and experiential; hopeful, joyful, kind, and visionary; activist; academically rigorous; and culturally sensitive (p. 18). This critical pedagogy demands an inquiry stance and the willingness to get to the truth of things. For example, in Vasquez's (2014) negotiated curriculum, the author and her preschool students kept a growing audit trail on the classroom wall that traced the journey of their critical investigations during the year. The audit trail reminded students of the work they did, supported their making connections, and traced their progress.

Jones (2014) described three conditions that enable this kind of critical pedagogy in classrooms. The first condition is openness to unpredictability. By this Jones meant willingness to take risks with the curriculum and to be open to what might emerge beyond what has been in the past (p. 7). Concerning the second condition, Jones advocated an ethical stance of questioning, acting, and making sense rather than a moralistic stance of knowing right and wrong (p. 10). Finally, the third condition is a commitment to aesthetics and to the assumption that the production of beauty in the classroom and through writing is a gift worth the effort (p. 10). Through teachers' case studies, each chapter in Jones's book demonstrates the enactment of these conditions of critical pedagogy. Another example is the work that Kesler (2011) did with his third-grade students. He presented the story of Natasha—who created her family flower to replace the rigidity of the traditional family tree as a way to represent her family—and of Jackie, who told her grandfather's migration story and his service in World War II. For both students, these conditions created transformative possibilities that gave them access and agency in their social studies curriculum.

Some educators organize the implementation of CML pedagogy within a framework. For example, Janks (2014) provided critical explorations for adolescent students in areas of power, diversity, access, design, and redesign. Within the topic of power, various activities explored language and power, discourse and power, and diversity. Lewison, Flint, and Van Sluys (2002) advocated four dimensions of critical pedagogy: disrupting the commonplace, interrogating multiple viewpoints, focusing on sociopolitical issues, and taking action and promoting social justice. They noted that, with expert professional development support, newcomers and novice teachers were able to implement the first, the second, and perhaps the third dimensions, while only teachers with substantial experience in critical pedagogy were also able to guide students toward the fourth dimension. Hagood, Alvermann, and Heron-Hruby (2010) provided a trajectory of activities that guide adolescent students toward exploring how they use pop culture in their lives, how pop culture (mis)represents their multiple identities, and how integrations of popular culture literacies deepen their understanding of school-based literacy. These educators embrace turn-around pedagogies—that is, the substantive learning and teaching that occur when we connect students' interests in pop culture texts to the school curriculum.

Kellner and Share (2007) provided a conceptual framework based on CML theory for the study of popular media (see tinyurl.com/CMLFramework). Their framework is based on a model of radical democracy that promotes independence and interdependence but moves away from an uncritical dependency on media through dialogic inquiry. The framework presents five concepts, each with its own set of guiding questions for the critical analysis of texts. Briefly, these five key concepts are:

1. All media texts are socially constructed by authors.
2. All media texts are constructed using multimodal design with intricate semiotic meanings.
3. All media texts have intended audiences, and various audiences engage with the same media texts differently.
4. All media texts have inherent ideologies that are embedded in their total design.
5. All media texts are deeply connected to corporations, institutions, or other organizations with specific agendas or profit motives.

The Center for Media Literacy (http://www.medialit.org) provides this framework with guiding questions and other curricular materials for classroom implementation.

Kesler, Tinio, and Nolan (2016) implemented this framework with nine eighth-grade special education students, in a self-contained classroom in an urban public school. Through the use of screen capture software and think-aloud protocol, they were able to recreate each student's reading process, as they explored popular culture websites for critical understandings. They discovered that the multimodal elements of popular culture websites demanded an integration of multiple literacies, including digital literacy, CML, and foundational literacy skills, and these elements were generally supportive of students' CML analysis work. In addition, by producing counternarratives in the form of glogs, students were able to act like bricoleurs, orchestrating multiple modes and diverse design features, which had strong outcomes for their CML understandings. This study showed the need for more opportunities, especially for special-education students, to explore the constructed nature of media, authorship, intended audience, and ideology. Such exploration would empower them to challenge media messages and to produce alternative texts that improve society. Overall, this work has a great potential to purposefully engage the students in 21st-century literacies, establish their voices as authors, and construct identities.

Kesler (2014) also guided graduate students to use composition as a situated response for social action. He was not interested in mastery over any one genre of style, but rather in the capacity to negotiate contexts, to be socially and politically astute in discourse use. As a result, he opened up choices of audience, genre, form, and media, valuing students' cultural ways with words and trusting them to contribute to a better world. Graduate students consequently published a wide variety of genres, forms, and media, to diverse audiences, about diverse social justice topics that ranged from a nonfiction picture book for first graders about recycling to a comic strip for adult readers about the diamond industry, or to a video about preserving water and giving access to clean water to people in impoverished regions of the world. In this manner students realized composing as a way of addressing another in a particular time and place, a motivated making of words for some end. They were able to integrate a wide range of semiotic tools for expression and expanded their composing process repertoire. All told, writing for social action became more accessible and pertinent. As Cowhey (2006), Dyson (2003), Jones (2014), and Vasquez (2014) show, these results were possible only within a quieter branch of critical pedagogy, in a dignified classroom, where students lived in a collaborative coming together and where diverse genres and cultural traditions mingled in the classroom community.

Implications

While implementing critical pedagogy in school settings is clearly a challenge in our current era of standardization, it is imperative to provide this pedagogy for students. This is so for three reasons: the students' development as literate people; their situated and multiple identities; and their transformation and emancipation as citizens in a democratic society. Dyson (2005) defined literacy as "not a set of skills but a symbolic resource that mediates participation in varied kinds of practices for representing and communicating meaning" (p. xii). Students' school-based literate practices cannot, then, be confined to a narrow and regressive vision of literacy learning that privileges language as the only means of expression. Therefore Dyson (2005) implored: "we need curricula in which children and teachers use their cultural and symbolic resources to deconstruct and design texts of varied modalities, that is, curricula in which they make decisions about the symbolic tools and substance that might suit an ever widening, evolving network of communicative practices" (p. xii). Educators continue to create and implement curricula that prepare students in school to become competent with ever-evolving media texts that pervade their lives.

Critical pedagogy also explores how literacy inherently involves identity work. For students, this means exploration and expression of who they can be and hope to become. Always this work is situated response, propagated by communicative intentions, within deeply realized sociocultural contexts such as Cowhey's (2006) "peace class." These conditions are true for all our students, from the youngest (e.g., Vasquez, 2014) to the oldest (e.g., Kesler, 2014). A class exists as an interpretive community. Our charge as educators, then, is to guide students to realize how the interpretive community and the identities that members have for themselves within the community determine constructed meaning and text uses. This was the work achieved in Kesler's (2011) third-grade class, where Natasha and Jackie had opportunities to express oppositional readings of standard texts and to redesign such texts—for example a family tree or Ellis Island—for their own communicative intentions, which created space for who they could be in this interpretive community. Our responsibility is to prove to administrators and policymakers how rigorous this work is and that it ultimately has the capacity to meet—and indeed exceed—any standards frameworks, such as the Next Generation Learning Standards in the United States.

Finally, critical pedagogy in schools is imperative because it has the power to transform students' lives. Particularly for students who experience high levels of need and risks—our most vulnerable students—this work is emancipatory (e.g., Freire, 1970/2008; Janks, 2010; Jones, 2014). For Freire, *conscientizacao* is an awakening and a critical, dialogic problem-posing pedagogy is a humanizing pedagogy that leads to students' liberation. Janks (2010) explained that, because all texts are constructed with an inherent ideology, and especially because of the sophistication of digital technology, the public needs the ability to read media texts critically. With its emphasis on social justice, CML guides students to redesign these texts, through multiple modalities, by allowing meaning to determine form and by using discourses that they inhabit. A critical pedagogy in the school can guide students to realize how sanctioned genres and forms can offer even more access to networks of power and to a wider world—a world where they can belong and claim a space for themselves (e.g., Bomer & Bomer, 2001; Heffernan, 2004). Jones (2014) reminds us that critical pedagogy also provides a transformation for teachers. A dialogic, problem-posing pedagogy is messy and requires the willingness to live in ambiguity, with uncertain outcomes. Teaching within this uncertainty opens up transformative possibilities that enable us to "re-vision" our students. Critical pedagogy scholars concur that we must enter uncharted territory while we embrace the opportunities for students to reformulate texts and create countertexts, with the possibility of transforming their learning experience. The full participation of all our students in today's diverse classrooms and in our democratic society is at stake.

SEE ALSO: Authorship and Participatory Culture; Civic Activism; Critical Theory Applied to Media Literacy; Emancipatory Communication; Game Media Literacy; Hip-Hop Education; Meaning-Making; Media Access and Activism; Media Activism and Action-Oriented Learning; Media and Adolescent Identity Development; Mediatization; Popular Media on the Playground; Remix Culture; Social Action and Advocacy; Social Media as Media Literacy; Social Networking Skills

References

Bomer, R., & Bomer, K. (2001). *For a better world: Reading and writing for social action.* Portsmouth, NH: Heinemann.

Cowhey, M. (2006). *Black ants and Buddhists: Thinking critically and teaching differently in the primary grades.* Portland, ME: Stenhouse.

Dyson, A.H. (2003). *The brothers and sisters learn to write: Popular literacies in childhood and school cultures.* New York, NY: Teachers College Press.

Dyson, A.H. (2005). Foreword. In J. Evans (Ed.), *Literacy moves on: Popular culture, new technologies, and critical literacy in the elementary classroom* (pp. xi–xiii). Portsmouth, NH: Heinemann.

Freebody, P., & Luke, A. (1990). Literacies programs: Debates and demands in cultural contexts. *Prospect: An Australian Journal of TESOL, 5*(7), 7–16.

Freire, P. (1970/2008). *Pedagogy of the oppressed.* New York, NY: Continuum.

Gee, J.P. (2004). *Situated language and learning: A critique of traditional schooling.* New York, NY: Routledge.

Hagood, M.C., Alvermann, D.E., & Heron-Hruby, A. (2010). *Bring it to class: Unpacking pop culture in literacy learning*. New York, NY: Teachers College Press.
Heffernan, L. (2004). Critical literacy and writer's workshop: Bringing purpose and passion to student writing. Newark, DE: International Reading Association.
Janks, H. (2010). *Literacy and power*. New York, NY: Routledge.
Janks, H. (2014). *Doing critical literacy: Texts and activities for students and teachers*. New York, NY: Routledge.
Jones, S. (Ed.). (2014). Writing and teaching to change the world: Connecting with our most vulnerable students. New York, NY: Teachers College Press.
Kellner, D., & Share, J. (2007). Critical media literacy is not an option. *Learning Inquiry, 1*, 59–69. doi: 10.1007/s11519-007-0004-2
Kesler, T. (2011). Teachers' texts in culturally responsive teaching. *Language Arts, 88*(6), 417–426.
Kesler, T. (2014). Writing for social action in our digital age. In K.E. Pytash & R.E. Ferdig (Eds.), *Exploring technology for writing and writing instruction* (pp. 282–297). Hershey, PA: IGI Global.
Kesler, T., Tinio, P.L.V., & Nolan, B.T. (2016). What's our position? A study of critical media literacy with eighth-grade special education students. *Reading and Writing Quarterly, 32*(1), 1–26. doi: 10.1080/10573569.2013.857976
Lewison, M., Flint, A.S., & Van Sluys, K. (2002). Taking on critical literacy: The journey of newcomers and novices. *Language Arts, 79*(5), 382–392.
New London Group. (1996). A pedagogy of multiliteracies: Designing social futures. *Harvard Educational Review, 66*, 60–92. doi: 10.17763/haer.66.1.17370n67v22j160u?code=hepg-site
O'Brien, D.G. (2001). "At-risk" adolescents: Redefining competence through the multiliteracies of intermediality, visual arts, and representation. *Reading Online, 4*(11).
Share, J. (2009). *Media literacy is elementary: Teaching youth to critically read and create media*. New York, NY: Peter Lang.
Vasquez, V.M. (2014). *Negotiating critical literacies with young children* (2nd ed.). New York, NY: Routledge.

Further reading

Coiro, J., Knobel, M., Lankshear, C., & Leu, D.J. (Eds.). (2008). *Handbook of research on new literacies*. Mahwah, NJ: Lawrence Erlbaum.
Darder, A., Baltodano, M.P., & Torres, R.D. (Eds.). (2008). *The critical pedagogy reader* (2nd ed.). New York, NY: Routledge.
Evans, J. (Ed.). (2005). *Literacy moves on: Popular culture, new technologies, and critical literacy in the elementary classroom*. Portsmouth, NH: Heinemann.

Ted Kesler is associate professor in the Department of Elementary and Early Childhood Education at Queens College, City University of New York. His research interests include multimodal responses to literature, children's nonfiction, critical media literacy, reading processes, and action research. His work has appeared in a variety of journals, including *Reading and Writing Quarterly*, *Language Arts*, *Children's Literature in Education*, *Elementary School Journal*, *Journal of Literacy Research*, and *Reading Teacher*. His most recent book is *The Reader Response Notebook: Teaching Towards Agency, Autonomy, and Accountability* (2018).

Critical Processing of Idealized Beauty Images

SIÂN A. McLEAN
Victoria University, Australia; La Trobe University, Australia

ELEANOR H. WERTHEIM and SUSAN J. PAXTON
La Trobe University, Australia

A common element of many forms of media is the portrayal of idealized images of human beauty, also known as *appearance-ideal media images*, which typically involve a thin, toned ideal appearance for females and a lean, muscular ideal appearance for males. These idealized media images are often perceived as placing pressure on individuals to conform to those ideals and thereby as contributing to body dissatisfaction in children, young people, and adult men and women. Recognizing these concerns, theorists have begun to promote *critical processing* of appearance-ideal media images (and related media content) that reinforce cultural beauty standards, as a way to prevent the negative impact of the media on body image.

Body dissatisfaction refers to the negative evaluation of one's appearance, a fundamental component of which is concern about weight, shape, and size. In western cultures, the focus of dissatisfaction differs for males and females, females being typically concerned about being overweight or too large, whereas for males these concerns typically relate to being insufficiently lean and muscular. Body dissatisfaction is considered to be a serious public health problem due to its high prevalence, associated distress and low quality of life, and frequently negative psychological and physical health consequences. People of all ages, genders, and cultural or ethnic backgrounds are affected by body dissatisfaction. Children as young as primary school age have been shown to be dissatisfied with their weight, shape, or size; and, although body dissatisfaction does diminish somewhat with age, it is nevertheless still present through midlife and into older adulthood. Furthermore, body dissatisfaction is highly prevalent, especially among girls and women: substantial proportions of females (up to 60% of girls and 80% of women) express a desire to be thinner or to lose weight. The negative health consequences of body dissatisfaction have been well documented. Body dissatisfaction is associated with increased risk for the development of depressive symptoms and low self-esteem, increased engagement in health-risk behaviors such as smoking and unsafe sex practices, development of disordered eating, including unhealthy dietary restraint and binge eating, and risk of developing clinical eating disorders (Bucchianeri & Neumark-Sztainer, 2014). As a consequence of the high prevalence of body dissatisfaction and its potential for negative health outcomes, prevention and intervention are required.

One promising avenue for prevention is media literacy, which incorporates critical processing of media images and messages and, in relation to body dissatisfaction, includes a critique of appearance ideals. The media literacy approach is based on the premise that enhancing critical processing of how and why the media present appearance ideals may reduce the perceived credibility of media messages, thereby reducing the persuasive influence of the media and hence preventing the development of body dissatisfaction (McLean, Paxton, & Wertheim, 2016b).

Effects of media exposure and pressure on body dissatisfaction

To understand how critical processing may be a useful intervention approach for body dissatisfaction, it is important to first examine the ways in which exposure to appearance-ideal media contributes to experiences of body dissatisfaction. From a theoretical perspective, the sociocultural model of the development of body dissatisfaction offers a framework for understanding the interaction between the media and body image. The media are considered to be one source of influence and pressure, along with family and peers, which reflect and promote cultural ideals for appearance. Media depictions of women and girls emphasize the thin ideal, a body size that is unrealistically thin for most people to attain. Similarly, it is also unrealistic for most men to attain the extreme lean and muscular ideals emphasized in media depictions of men and adolescent boys. Exposure to these unachievable appearance ideals through the media and perceived pressure from the media to achieve them contribute to body dissatisfaction via two psychological processes: internalization of media appearance ideals and appearance-based social comparisons.

Internalization of media appearance ideals refers to a psychological process by which sociocultural ideals of appearance are adopted as personal standards to which individuals aspire. Thus individuals who endorse media appearance ideals take on the media ideals as standards against which they judge themselves. The internalization of appearance ideals enhances the likelihood of social appearance comparisons. *Social appearance comparison* describes the process by which individuals compare their appearance to that of others, as a means of self-evaluation and self-regulation. The targets of comparisons may be people in their personal network with whom they interact on a face-to-face basis, peers or friends with whom they interact online through social media, or celebrity or media figures who are viewed through traditional or new media platforms. Internalization of appearance standards, coupled with appearance comparison, is posited to result in body dissatisfaction. When an individual compares his or her appearance with media ideals that that individual aspires to meet and perceives that his or her own appearance is inferior to the internalized ideal appearance, body dissatisfaction results. Body dissatisfaction is more likely to be the outcome of comparison to media appearance ideals when the internalized appearance standards derived from media appearance ideals are unrealistic to achieve.

Exposure to appearance-ideal media images has been shown in experimental research designs to produce immediate increases in body dissatisfaction. These findings have been supported by meta-analyses where exposure to appearance-ideal media has been found to have small to moderate negative effects on body dissatisfaction (Want, 2009). Recent meta-analyses, however, have not supported these earlier findings but have concluded that effects on body dissatisfaction are not universal, exposure to media being suggested to affect only those with preexisting vulnerabilities (Ferguson, 2013). In particular, increased vulnerability to the negative impact of media exposure is conferred by heightened body dissatisfaction, internalization of media ideals, and appearance-comparison tendencies.

Theories of media effects and appearance norms

Cultivation theory (Morgan, Shanahan, & Signorielli, 2009) and social cognitive theory of mass communication (Bandura, 2009) may account for the creation of a sociocultural environment in which increased vulnerability to media exposure develops.

First, in accordance with *cultivation theory*, cumulative effects of media viewing occur through repeated exposure to consistent media messages that shape viewers' perceptions of social reality (Morgan et al., 2009). Viewing of contemporary western media repeatedly exposes consumers to content in which the thin ideal and the muscular ideal of appearance are portrayed as normative, desirable, and achievable. Furthermore, in such a culture, particularly for females but also for males, personal value is closely tied to the attainment of these appearance ideals, which further contributes to their desirability. In relation to appearance, an appearance culture or appearance norms that emphasize the desirability of thinness and muscularity, a culture created through repeated viewing of these messages comes to be perceived as the social reality.

Recurrent viewing of thin and muscular ideals of appearance in the media, accompanied by viewing messages that imply that thinness and muscularity are indicators of success and are associated with a range of social rewards, shapes body-related attitudes and behaviors of media consumers. Research supports this contention and the application of cultivation theory to body image, as media exposure appears to affect body dissatisfaction in a cumulative manner. Greater frequency of exposure to media content is associated with higher levels of body dissatisfaction and internalization of media ideals and with a stronger tendency to engage in appearance comparison. Furthermore, media-cultivated appearance norms may also contribute to the perceived pressure to adhere to sociocultural ideals of appearance. In support of this claim, perceived media pressure to attain appearance ideals has been shown to be related to body dissatisfaction in girls and boys, as well as in women and men.

Second, in agreement with *social cognitive theory*, individuals learn and acquire attitudes through the observation of social realities transmitted through mass media. As noted above, the media-portrayed social reality of appearance is discrepant with real-life experiences in that the image of women in the media is much thinner than the average woman and the image of men in the media is much more muscular than the average man. Under these circumstances, social learning through the observation of norms for appearance as portrayed by the media has the potential to create unrealistic appearance standards, which may be internalized or used as the basis for appearance comparison. Thus individuals who internalize unrealistic appearance ideals as personal standards and who choose to compare their appearance with media targets are likely to do so because media ideals of appearance are perceived as desirable, normative, and representative of social reality on account of repeated viewing and perception of media images as authentic.

In support of social cognitive theory of mass communication, exposure to media content that specifically depicts and reinforces appearance ideals as highly desirable has been shown to be related to body dissatisfaction (Tiggemann, 2005). Furthermore, this relationship between exposure to appearance-ideal media images and body dissatisfaction was found to be mediated by the internalization of media appearance ideals as well as by appearance schemas (beliefs about the importance and relevance of appearance to the self), which indicates that media exposure influenced individuals' perceived standards for appearance.

As noted before, negative effects on body image from exposure to media appearance ideals may be induced through repeated exposure to such ideals and through the creation of unrealistic standards for appearance. These effects are likely to be heightened in individuals with preexisting vulnerabilities. In a similar manner, it is probable that preexisting resilience impacts the relationship between exposure to media appearance ideals and body image outcomes. One factor that may confer resilience is critical processing of media—a key component of media literacy.

Critical processing of appearance-ideal images

Critical processing of media can protect against the negative outcomes of exposure to appearance-ideal media images and pressure from the media—both of which reinforce the desirability of unrealistic appearance ideals. The presence of protective factors can increase resilience to these negative outcomes by disrupting the action of risk factors. It is proposed that critical processing interrupts and prevents the internalization of, and social comparison with, appearance ideals presented in media, which in turn reduces the likelihood of body dissatisfaction resulting from media exposure.

What is critical processing?

Media-literate individuals possess skills that enable them to critically process media that they view or interact with. This involves thinking critically about the constructed nature of the media, for example by considering the underlying meaning and purpose of media creators, the positive and negative influence of media content on different audiences, and the extent to which media are a true reflection of social reality, including whether they distort or omit relevant information (Primack et al., 2006). Critical processing produces an evaluation of both the credibility of specific media content and the meaning of a media message for the individual. Media that are perceived as less credible and less personally meaningful are likely to have less influence on an individual.

In relation to appearance-ideal media images, which typically involve unrealistically slim, muscular, and attractive images and include contextual content that reinforces the desirability of appearance ideals, critical processing is thought to engage the viewer in an evaluation of the extent to which media images are realistic portrayals of social reality. This occurs through critical questions applied in a graded fashion, in order to promote consideration of simple through to more complex constructs. First, at the simplest level, one considers how the appearance of people in the media *reflects the social reality of the viewer*. This inquiry challenges the extent to which appearance-ideal media images are unrealistic, unnatural, or artificial. Second, one considers in what way the media present *a biased view of personal characteristics* according to appearance. This involves an evaluation of whether appearance-ideal media content conveys positive stereotypes of slim, muscular individuals such that they are shown as likeable, competent, successful, and so on. Such an evaluation would also consider whether nonideal appearance images—that is, less attractive, nonslim, nonmuscular images—convey negative stereotypes in that people with those physical characteristics are presented in media as lazy, incompetent, weak, and deserving to be blamed for their nonideal appearance. Third, at more sophisticated levels of critical processing, individuals will also recognize the *persuasive intent* of the media and the use of appearance-ideal images to promote an aspirational self-image. In such a manner, appearance-ideal images are associated with products or brands designed to increase the desirability of those products. This association not only promotes the products but also conveys the message that attaining an ideal appearance is a desired outcome.

Evidence supporting a role for the critical processing of the media and for effects on body image

Research investigating the effects of the critical processing of appearance media on body images emanates from four broad approaches. These approaches are qualitative research and quantitative research that uses cross-sectional designs, experimental designs examining the effects of exposure to appearance-ideal images, and experimental designs examining the outcomes of media literacy-based interventions designed to prevent negative effects of exposure to appearance-ideal media images.

Qualitative research

The potentially protective role of the critical processing of appearance-ideal images (protective, that is, against body dissatisfaction) has been recognized in findings from qualitative studies in which participants who were identified as having a positive body image have described using strategies akin to critical processing to protect their body image from exposure to appearance-ideal media. Both adolescent girls and young adult women with positive body image reported being critical of appearance ideals portrayed in media. Specifically, they noted that the images shown in media are unnatural and unrealistic portrayals of women and have achieved the "perfect" appearance only through artificial means, such as manipulation with photo-editing software. Teenage participants also recognized that the use of unrealistic appearance ideals is intended to convey a message that links thinness with positive characteristics (Holmqvist & Frisén, 2012). Further, the adult women described a process by which they actively filtered and rejected negative appearance-related messages from media (Wood-Barcalow, Tylka, & Augustus-Horvath, 2010). This process is likely to prevent appearance ideals portrayed in media from being internalized as standards to which the women aspire. Thus it seems that girls and women with a positive body image were aware of, and actively evaluated, the realism, the expectations of rewards from meeting appearance ideals, and the values associated with the appearance ideals depicted by the media.

Although these qualitative studies cannot contribute to conclusions about cause and effect relationships, the findings do allude to the possibility of a relationship between critical processing and body image. It appears that the natural practices engaged in by both adolescent girls and young adult women with positive body image to critically appraise, reject expectancies presented in the media, and filter media messages are akin to some of the processes defined by media literacy and may be related to higher body satisfaction. Such relationships can be examined through quantitative research.

Cross-sectional quantitative research

A small number of cross-sectional studies have attempted to examine whether more media-literate individuals—that is, those with greater skills or a higher engagement in critical appraisal and skepticism about appearance-ideal media images—have lower levels of body dissatisfaction and related outcomes. An early study examined critical thoughts that female college students generated in response to viewing appearance-ideal media. The number of critical responses generated by women, such as "I think she almost looks like a computer image and not a real person," was related to positive evaluations of participants' own appearance (Engeln-Maddox, 2005). Thus participants who were more critical of the appearance-ideal images they viewed were more likely to perceive their own appearance favorably.

More recent cross-sectional research has shown that, in adolescent girls, higher levels of critical processing related to skepticism about the realism of the media and their similarity to social reality was correlated with lower levels of body dissatisfaction, internalization of media ideals, and social appearance comparison (McLean, Paxton, & Wertheim, 2013). Similarly, adult women with a stronger tendency to process appearance-ideal media in a critical manner had higher levels of positive body image (Andrew, Tiggemann, & Clark, 2015). These findings are consistent with the description of the processes engaged in by women with positive body image described above and suggest that critical processing of the media is accompanied by more positive body image perceptions. Although such findings hint at the possible contribution of critical processing to protecting against the development of body dissatisfaction, the conclusions that can be drawn from them about causal relationships are limited by the qualitative and cross-sectional designs of these studies. It is necessary to turn to experimental designs that can offer information about the causal relationships between critical processing and body dissatisfaction.

Experimental studies of media exposure effects

The examination, through experimental designs, of the effects of critical media processing on body image has focused on distinct research questions. One area of research has asked whether more media-literate people, that is, people with higher levels of critical processing skills, are less likely to be negatively affected by exposure to appearance-ideal images than people with lower levels of critical processing skills. Research has also been concerned with understanding whether interventions that present information about the digital manipulation of appearance-ideal images are protective against the negative effects on body image of exposure to such images.

Research aiming to understand whether *exposure to appearance-ideal media images* produces different effects on body image for people with different levels of critical processing skills is in the early stages. To our knowledge, only one study has investigated this matter (McLean, Paxton, & Wertheim, 2016a). This study found that the body image of adolescent girls with preexisting high levels of critical thinking did not change after viewing appearance-ideal media images. In contrast, girls with low levels of critical thinking were not protected against media effects and experienced a reduction in body satisfaction after viewing the same images. This effect was amplified in girls who were vulnerable to the effects of media exposure on body image by way of having higher levels of internalized media ideals related to appearance. Further research is required to replicate these findings, although the preliminary results do suggest that the tendency to engage in critical thinking about the media mitigated the negative impact of exposure to appearance-ideal images on girls' body image, particularly for girls who had preexisting vulnerabilities.

Recently, public health initiatives have called for the media to display information pertaining to the digital manipulation of appearance-ideal images as an intervention against media effects on body image. The underlying assumption of such initiatives is that disclosure about the digital manipulation of images—achieved by means such as warning labels placed on those images—will prompt viewers to recognize the unrealistic nature of appearance-ideal media images, which in turn will reduce the likelihood of individuals comparing their appearance with those images and would lead to improved outcomes for body image.

A number of experimental studies have been conducted to examine the *effects of the use of warning labels* on body image and to gather empirical evidence for the assumptions underlying their proposed protective effects. Findings from this body of research have been mixed. A protective effect for body image that resulted from presenting appearance-ideal images with warning labels was found in an initial study. Participants who viewed images with a warning label had lower levels of body dissatisfaction after exposure than participants who viewed the same images without a warning label (Slater, Tiggemann, Firth, & Hawkins, 2012). However, follow-up studies have failed to replicate this effect (Ata, Thompson, & Small, 2013; Frederick, Sandhu, Scott, & Akbari, 2016). In addition, studies have failed to find evidence to support the assumption that warning labels alter viewers' perceptions of the realism of appearance ideals presented in the media, or that the presence of warning labels leads to lower levels of social appearance comparison than recorded after the viewing of unlabeled images (Tiggemann, Slater, Bury, Hawkins, & Firth, 2013). Taken together, these findings appear to indicate that the use of warning labels is ineffective as a protective strategy for body image. It may be that public awareness of the extent of digital manipulation is already high, hence warning labels do not alter the perceived realism of media images or the viewers' propensities to compare themselves with those images. Alternatively, warning labels may be insufficiently engaging, or insufficiently strong (e.g., are "low-dose" interventions), to influence the viewers' critical processing of appearance ideals in media. Furthermore, the studies have only looked at short-term outcomes. Repeated exposure to warning labels may have an impact over a longer follow-up period. Thus, more intense or engaging strategies may be needed to produce an alteration in realism or other critical thinking processes, to reduce the likelihood of appearance comparison, and ultimately to have an effect on body image.

Evaluations of brief interventions have attempted to determine whether stronger and more engaging strategies produce effective protection for body image against media exposure. In these studies, prior to viewing, participants were provided with a range of information—in written, audio, or audiovisual format—concerning the digital manipulation of appearance-ideal images; and this counteracted the negative effects on body image from the media exposure (e.g., Halliwell, Easun, & Harcourt, 2011). In addition, one study found that participants who received the intervention materials were more likely to react to the media images they viewed after the intervention with responses that questioned the realism of the images (Posavac, Posavac, & Weigel, 2001). This suggests that questioning the realism of images, which may be akin to engaging in critical processing of appearance-ideal media images, can be the mechanism that reduces the negative effects, on body image, of viewing such images. However, this mechanism requires further empirical testing.

In considering the outcomes obtained from these two types of intervention—display of warning labels accompanying images and presentation of multi-informational intervention materials before the viewing of appearance-ideal images—it is possible that the stronger dose of the latter type of intervention was more effective, although the two approaches have not been directly compared. Further, the enhanced specificity of content regarding the particular changes that can be made through digital editing may have contributed to the effects seen in the second type of interventions, whereas the nonspecific warning labels may not have provided sufficient information to produce a protective effect.

School-based media literacy interventions designed to prevent body dissatisfaction and eating disorder risks have been evaluated in different contexts. These have included single- and multisession programs, single-sex and coeducational audiences, and researcher delivery and teacher delivery of intervention activities. Programs that have included content designed to enhance students' critical processing so that they recognize the unrealistic nature of appearance-ideal media images, the biased perspectives presented through the media, and the persuasive intent of media content have been successful in reducing body dissatisfaction, disordered eating, and negative affect (Diedrichs et al., 2015; Dunstan, Paxton, & McLean, 2016; Wilksch & Wade, 2015). However, evidence to the effect that these positive outcomes are attributable specifically to the critical processing content of the programs is lacking. Media literacy approaches to body dissatisfaction and eating disorder risk prevention also typically address other components in addition to critical processing, such as media advocacy, social appearance comparisons, appearance conversations, and pressure to adhere to sociocultural ideals of appearance. Specific mediation analyses oriented toward identifying the mechanisms of change are required in order to isolate the active components of interventions that produce change. Further, few intervention evaluations have assessed whether students become more media literate or more proficient at critically processing media content after a program delivery. It is essential that these shortcomings are addressed in future research, if we are to understand the benefits of a critical processing of appearance-ideal media content on outcomes related to body dissatisfaction.

Gaps in knowledge

The body of qualitative, cross-sectional, and experimental research described above offers some preliminary conclusions about the role of critical processing in influencing outcomes for body image resulted from, or affected by, exposure to appearance-ideal media images. However, there are a number of gaps in the research literature—including in relation to measurement, promoting higher levels of sophistication in critical processing, and understanding when and what triggers people to engage in critical processing during media viewing—that are required to be addressed before we can more fully understand the role of critical processing in this area.

One essential component of research into critical processing that requires attention is related to the assessment of critical processing skills, both generic ones and skills that are likely to be pertinent to media that promote the thin and muscular appearance ideals. In relation to the latter in particular, the lack of valid and reliable self-report measures to facilitate research into the relationships between critical processing and body image outcomes limits the conclusions that can be drawn from current investigations. Although some instruments have been developed, for example the Media Attitudes Questionnaire (Irving, DuPen, & Berel, 1998) and the Critical Processing of Beauty Images Scale (Engeln-Maddox & Miller, 2008), further development of assessment measures focusing on idealized beauty images and based on media literacy theory is required to advance research into the critical processing of appearance-ideal media.

As described above, cross-sectional and experimental research has examined effects on body image of engaging in the simplest form of critical processing of appearance-ideal images, namely the extent to which media portrayals of appearance images are a reflection of social reality. However, critical processing in relation to body image is not limited to this form of processing. More sophisticated levels of processing include an understanding of biases presented in the media, particularly with regard to the presentation of positive and negative stereotypes associated with appearance, and also understanding and resisting the persuasive intent of media and how that intent shapes the desirability of appearance ideals. It is not yet known whether possession of skills in these more complex types of critical processes would be associated with better outcomes for body image in relation to the protective effects of critically processing the media at the simpler level.

Future directions

Recognizing the gaps in our understanding of how critical processing relates to body image as described above is crucial for setting the agenda for future directions of research. These gaps highlight the need to test an integrated model that establishes a framework for the role of the critical processing of media—alongside established predictors, mediators, and moderators of media effects—for attitudinal and behavioral outcomes. In addition, in the rapidly changing media environment, it will be necessary to examine the ways in which critical processing of media can be applied to social media networking.

Social media

The application of critical processing to social media engagement will be an important area for future research. Social media are a highly visual medium, in which a great deal of content is focused on the appearance of users. This appearance focus is associated with body image concerns. Furthermore, the social media environment provides a wealth of opportunities for appearance comparisons and for appearance-based feedback to be requested and received by users. Feedback in the form of "likes" of self-photos acts as a currency by which users assess their self-worth and their acceptance by peers. Critical processing of appearance images within this unique environment will need to be adapted from traditional settings so as to take into account the interactive and fast-paced nature of social media.

Theories of media effects

The findings, to date, on the role of critical processing in body image may be best understood by considering how they map onto a proposed model that combines the central elements of the *differential susceptibility to media effects* model, developed by Valkenburg and Peter (2013), and the basic framework of the sociocultural perspective on the development of body image described earlier in this entry. The proposed model offers an integrated structure for future research to examine relationships between exposure to appearance-ideal media images, critical processing, and body image. The broad principles underlying the differential susceptibility to media effects model are that media effects are conditional and that they are transactional. In relation to the first principle (the conditionality of media effects), responses to media exposure are not universal and outcomes are amplified or diminished by a range of moderator variables. In relation to the second principle (the transactional nature of media use), individuals seek out and tailor their media engagement to their personal preferences. In addition, the outcomes of media use continue to influence media choices in a feedback loop (Valkenburg & Peter, 2013). In relation to the sociocultural perspective, the effects of media exposure on body image are transmitted through the internalization of appearance ideals and through social appearance comparisons. These principles underlie the specific components of the proposed model, in which critical processing is proposed as a potential predictor, moderator, and mediator of the effects of media exposure on body dissatisfaction, as described below and also outlined in Figure 1.

First, preexisting variables that confer vulnerability, including media-ideal internalization, and preexisting variables that confer resilience, including critical processing skills, predict use and engagement with specific media. Second, media use or exposure

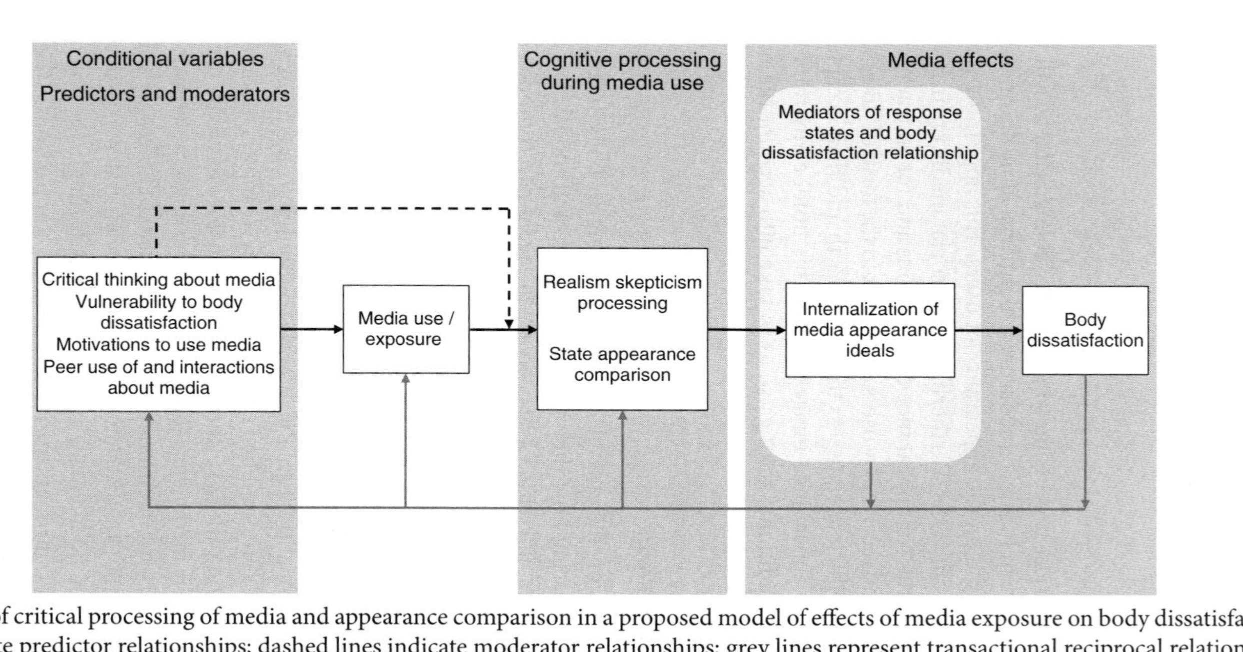

Figure 1 Role of critical processing of media and appearance comparison in a proposed model of effects of media exposure on body dissatisfaction. Note: solid lines indicate predictor relationships; dashed lines indicate moderator relationships; grey lines represent transactional reciprocal relationships. Source: Adapted from Valkenburg and Peter (2013): 226. Reproduced by permission of Oxford University Press.

to appearance-ideal media engages cognitive, emotional, and excitative (i.e., arousal) processes that occur during media use. Cognitive processing variables, which are of relevance to the proposed model, may include critical processing of the realism, biases, and persuasive intent of the media and comparison of one's own appearance with media images. Third, preexisting vulnerability or resilience variables may moderate the relationship between media exposure and cognitive processing. Fourth, the effects of media use on body dissatisfaction outcomes are mediated by the cognitive processing that occurs during media use. Negative outcomes are predicted by appearance-comparison processing and positive outcomes are predicted by critical thinking processing. Finally, internalization of media appearance ideals is proposed to mediate the relationship between cognitive processing and body dissatisfaction. Comparing one's appearance with the thin and muscular ideals presented in the media will lead to greater internalization of those ideals and, consequently, to greater body dissatisfaction. Conversely, critical thinking about appearance ideals in the media will reduce the internalization of appearance ideals, leading to lower levels of body dissatisfaction.

Research support exists for the individual elements of this model; however, the integrated model is yet to be tested. Advances in the measurement of critical processing and in the identification of how to promote the use of specific critical processing skills during media exposure will greatly enhance the ability to examine this model and our understanding of the role that a critical processing of idealized beauty images has on body image outcomes.

SEE ALSO: Children's Understanding of Persuasion; Media and Eating Disorders; Media Literacy Outcomes, Measurement; Resisting Persuasive Intent

References

Andrew, R., Tiggemann, M., & Clark, L. (2015). The protective role of body appreciation against media-induced body dissatisfaction. *Body Image, 15*, 98–104. doi: 10.1016/j.bodyim.2015.07.005

Ata, R.N., Thompson, J.K., & Small, B.J. (2013). Effects of exposure to thin-ideal media images on body dissatisfaction: Testing the inclusion of a disclaimer versus warning label. *Body Image, 10*(4), 472–480. doi: 10.1016/j.bodyim.2013.04.004

Bandura, A. (2009). Social cognitive theory of mass communication. In J. Bryant & M.B. Oliver (Eds.), *Media effects: Advances in theory and research* (3rd ed.). New York, NY: Routledge.

Bucchianeri, M.M., & Neumark-Sztainer, D. (2014). Body dissatisfaction: An overlooked public health concern. *Journal of Public Mental Health, 13*(2), 64–69. doi: 10.1108/JPMH-11-2013-0071

Diedrichs, P.C., Atkinson, M.J., Steer, R.J., Garbett, K.M., Rumsey, N., & Halliwell, E. (2015). Effectiveness of a brief school-based body image intervention 'Dove Confident Me: Single Session' when delivered by teachers and researchers: Results from a cluster randomised controlled trial. *Behaviour Research and Therapy, 74*, 94–104. doi: 10.1016/j.brat.2015.09.004

Dunstan, C.J., Paxton, S.J., & McLean, S.A. (2016). An evaluation of a body image intervention in adolescent girls delivered in single-sex versus co-educational classroom settings. *Eating Behaviors, Advance online publication.* doi: 10.1016/j.eatbeh.2016.03.016

Engeln-Maddox, R. (2005). Cognitive responses to idealized media images of women: The relationship of social comparison and critical processing to body image disturbance in college women. *Journal of Social and Clinical Psychology, 24*(8), 1114–1138. doi: 10.1521/jscp.2005.24.8.1114

Engeln-Maddox, R., & Miller, S.A. (2008). Talking back to the media ideal: The development and validation of the Critical Processing of Beauty Images Scale. *Psychology of Women Quarterly, 32*(2), 159–171. doi: 10.1111/j.1471-6402.2008.00420.x

Ferguson, C.J. (2013). In the eye of the beholder: Thin-ideal media affects some, but not most, viewers in a meta-analytic review of body dissatisfaction in women and men. *Psychology of Popular Media Culture, 2*(1), 20–37. doi: 10.1037/a0030766

Frederick, D.A., Sandhu, G., Scott, T., & Akbari, Y. (2016). Reducing the negative effects of media exposure on body image: Testing the effectiveness of subvertising and disclaimer labels. *Body Image, 17*, 171–174. doi: 10.1016/j.bodyim.2016.03.009

Halliwell, E., Easun, A., & Harcourt, D. (2011). Body dissatisfaction: Can a short media literacy message reduce negative media exposure effects amongst adolescent girls? *British Journal of Health Psychology, 16*, 396–403. doi: 10.1348/135910710x515714

Holmqvist, K., & Frisén, A. (2012). "I bet they aren't that perfect in reality": Appearance ideals viewed from the perspective of adolescents with a positive body image. *Body Image, 9*(3), 388–395. doi: 10.1016/j.bodyim.2012.03.007

Irving, L.M., DuPen, J., & Berel, S. (1998). A media literacy program for high school females. *Eating Disorders, 6*(2), 119–132. doi: 10.1080/10640269808251248

McLean, S.A., Paxton, S.J., & Wertheim, E.H. (2013). Mediators of the relationship between media literacy and body dissatisfaction in early adolescent girls: Implications for prevention. *Body Image, 10*(3), 282–289. doi: 10.1016/j.bodyim.2013.01.009

McLean, S.A., Paxton, S.J., & Wertheim, E.H. (2016a). Does media literacy mitigate risk for reduced body satisfaction following exposure to thin-ideal media? *Journal of Youth and Adolescence, 45*(8), 1678–1695. doi: 10.1007/s10964-016-0440-3

McLean, S.A., Paxton, S.J., & Wertheim, E.H. (2016b). The role of media literacy in body dissatisfaction and disordered eating: A systematic review. *Body Image, 19*, 9–23. doi: 10.1016/j.bodyim.2016.08.002

Morgan, M., Shanahan, J., & Signorielli, N. (2009). Growing up with television: Cultivation processes. In J. Bryant & M.B. Oliver (Eds.), *Media effects: Advances in theory and research* (3rd ed., pp. 35–49). New York, NY: Routledge.

Posavac, H.D., Posavac, S.S., & Weigel, R.G. (2001). Reducing the impact of media images on women at risk for body image disturbance: Three targeted interventions. *Journal of Social and Clinical Psychology, 20*(3), 324–340. doi: 10.1521/jscp.20.3.324.22308

Primack, B.A., Gold, M.A., Switzer, G.E., Hobbs, R., Land, S.R., & Fine, M.J. (2006). Development and validation of a smoking media literacy scale for adolescents. *Archives of Pediatrics and Adolescent Medicine, 160*(4), 369–374. doi: 10.1001/archpedi.160.4.369

Slater, A., Tiggemann, M., Firth, B., & Hawkins, K. (2012). Reality check: An experimental investigation of the addition of warning labels to fashion magazine images on women's mood and body dissatisfaction. *Journal of Social and Clinical Psychology, 31*(2), 105–122. doi: 10.1521/jscp.2012.31.2.105

Tiggemann, M. (2005). Television and adolescent body image: The role of program content and viewing motivation. *Journal of Social and Clinical Psychology, 24*(3), 361–381. doi: 10.1521/jscp.24.3.361.65623

Tiggemann, M., Slater, A., Bury, B., Hawkins, K., & Firth, B. (2013). Disclaimer labels on fashion magazine advertisements: Effects on social comparison and body dissatisfaction. *Body Image, 10*(1), 45–53. doi: 10.1016/j.bodyim.2012.08.001

Valkenburg, P.M., & Peter, J. (2013). The differential susceptibility to media effects model. *Journal of Communication, 63*(2), 221–243. doi: 10.1111/jcom.12024

Want, S.C. (2009). Meta-analytic moderators of experimental exposure to media portrayals of women on female appearance satisfaction: Social comparisons as automatic processes. *Body Image, 6*(4), 257–269. doi: 10.1016/j.bodyim.2009.07.008

Wilksch, S.M., & Wade, T.D. (2015). Media literacy in the prevention of eating disorders. In L. Smolak & M.P. Levine (Eds.), *The Wiley handbook of eating disorders* (pp. 610–624). Chichester, England: John Wiley & Sons, Ltd.

Wood-Barcalow, N.L., Tylka, T.L., & Augustus-Horvath, C.L. (2010). "But I like my body": Positive body image characteristics and a holistic model for young-adult women. *Body Image, 7*(2), 106–116. doi: 10.1016/j.bodyim.2010.01.001

Further reading

Bury, B., Tiggemann, M., & Slater, A. (2016). The effect of digital alteration disclaimer labels on social comparison and body image: Instructions and individual differences. *Body Image, 17*, 136–142. doi: 10.1016/j.bodyim.2016.03.005

Levine, M.P. (2016). Media literacy approaches to prevention. In T. Wade (Ed.), *Encyclopedia of feeding and eating disorders* (pp. 1–6). Singapore: Springer.

Perloff, R.M. (2014). Social media effects on young women's body image concerns: Theoretical perspectives and an agenda for research. *Sex Roles, 71*, 363–377. doi: 10.1007/s11199-014-0384-6

Rodgers, R.F. (2016). The relationship between body image concerns, eating disorders and Internet use, part II: An integrated theoretical model. *Adolescent Research Review, 1*(2), 121–137. doi: 10.1007/s40894-015-0017-5

Siân A. McLean is lecturer in psychology at Victoria University and honorary research fellow in the School of Psychology and Public Health, La Trobe University. Her research focuses on sociocultural and individual factors that contribute to body dissatisfaction in children, adolescents, and adults. She is highly experienced in school-based prevention and research investigating the role of media literacy as a protective factor in the development of body dissatisfaction. Dr. McLean's research on media literacy and body image has been recognized through the 2016 Peter Beumont Young Investigator Award.

Eleanor H. Wertheim is professor (personal chair) and head of the Department of Psychology and Counselling, La Trobe University, Melbourne. She is a clinical psychologist, a community psychologist, and a fellow of the Australian Psychological Society. She has conducted research on numerous topics related to body image and disordered eating across the lifespan, including aetiology, prevention, and treatment, using methods spanning from qualitative to prospective, and randomized controlled trials using group, classroom, and Internet modalities. Her focus is on biopsychosocial models that explore the effects of parents, peers, and media in influencing body dissatisfaction and disordered eating.

Susan J. Paxton is professor in the School of Psychology and Public Health, La Trobe University, Melbourne. Her research focuses on understanding risk factors for the development of body image and eating problems and the development and evaluation of prevention and therapy interventions based on the understanding of risk and maintaining factors. She is director of the Butterfly Foundation and past president of the Academy for Eating Disorders. In recognition of her research, she was awarded the 2013 Academy for Eating Disorders Leadership in Research Award.

Critical Theory Applied to Media Literacy

GIANNA CAPPELLO
University of Palermo, Italy

Being critical of the media has been one of the fundamental tenets of media literacy (ML). Earlier definitions of being critical—provided within the so-called "inoculative approach"—were centered around a moral and literary–esthetic notion of value that supposedly was being corrupted by the manipulative and commercial role of the media (Masterman & Mariet, 1994). Although these definitions were mostly popular from the 1930s to the 1960s, the idea that the media are agents of cultural and moral decline and that critical antibodies are needed for taking one's distance from them and for dismissing them as vulgar in comparison with "high culture" is still very common, especially among school teachers. According to this approach, ML was then essentially meant as an intervention to educate *against* the media. Eventually this radical rejection of all media gave way to a more "discriminatory" approach, by which the media were equaled to "popular arts" (Hall & Whannel, 1964). As a result, some media—such as the auteur cinema of the French Nouvelle Vague, Italian neorealism, and so on—could be included in the "high culture" canon. Therefore, while still calling for "protection" in general, ML was also interested in the study of some specific high-quality filmic productions. This was undoubtedly a step forward, thanks to which film studies courses started to be established in schools, colleges, and universities. ML, in this case, was meant to educate not against all media but *within* them. However, the discriminatory approach was still based on a disputable notion of cultural–esthetic value as a transcendental, decontextualized quality of the text itself, a value to be discovered by the "intelligent" reader. In fact the notion of being critical was ultimately originating from an elitist approach, the assumption being that students' cultural media tastes needed to be corrected and improved.

As it became apparent throughout the 1970s, to focus on film as a valuable "piece of art," dismissing as commercial and vulgar all the rest, narrowed down the field of ML, as it bracketed out the questions and issues raised by other media (such as television, newspapers, popular movies, advertising, etc.), by their increasing pervasiveness in people's everyday life, by their growing importance as social institutions interlaced with power (in fact a form of power themselves), and—last but not least—by the need to have a deeper understanding of the students' cultural tastes and consumption practices. The introduction of critical theory into the field of ML has not only provided a basis for addressing those questions and issues; it has also imbued ML with a political and civic orientation never experienced before. As a result of that, media literacy educators start questioning the manipulative role of the media from a standpoint quite different from that of literary criticism and its moral–esthetic rejection.

Critical theory refers to those German philosophers and social theorists—from Horkheimer and Adorno to Benjamin, Marcuse, and Habermas, to name but a few of them—who belong to the Western European Marxist tradition known as the Frankfurt School. Founded in 1923, the school was originally located at the Institute for Social Research. After 1933, the Nazis forced its closure, and the institute was moved from Germany to the United States, where it found hospitality at Columbia University in New York City. The biggest influence on the Frankfurt School is that of Marx's social and political thought. Other influences come from Freud and Weber. The spheres of inquiry of the Frankfurt School range from social and political theory, via psychology, to musical esthetics and literary criticism. Following this tradition, the aim of critical theory is to free human beings from all forms of oppression and domination. From this perspective, critical theory unites today a broad range of interdisciplinary approaches in the social sciences and philosophy that include feminism, postcolonial theory, and various strands of postmodern theories such as poststructuralism, critical discourse analysis, Marxist semiotics, and so on.

"What is theory?" was the very first question Horkheimer asks in his 1937 essay "Traditional and Critical Theory." Traditional theory is involved in "the critical examination of data with the aid of an inherited apparatus of concepts and judgments" (Horkheimer, 1989, p. 205). Following a Cartesian epistemology, it posits knowledge as grounded upon propositions that are based on self-evident truths and hence can be either confirmed or disconfirmed in empirical ways. According to this positivist epistemological model, knowledge is simply the mirror of an objective reality that exists per se. Critical theorists reject this model, maintaining that any valid, true form of knowledge about society and its phenomena needs to be aware not only of the object of knowledge but also of the subjective factors of cognition that determine the knowledge of that object. One cannot be a detached observer of an object of study, since society or history forges how reality is observed. To recognize the historical contingency of knowledge is of particular importance when one studies social phenomena, as this marks the ultimate difference between social studies and natural science. As Horkheimer (1989, p. 200) puts it in a famous sentence, "[t]he facts which our senses present to us are socially preformed in two ways: through the historical character of the object perceived and through the historical character of the perceiving organ. Both are not simply natural; they are shaped by human activity, and yet the individual perceives himself as receptive and passive in the act of perception." Critical theory characterizes itself as a method contrary to this "fetishization" of knowledge coming from traditional theory. It rather considers knowledge as something functional to ideology critique and social emancipation. As such, critical theory becomes social criticism and translates itself into social action, that is, into the transformation of reality, complying with Marx's much quoted dictum that philosophers should not simply interpret reality, but change it. Coupled with social emancipation, ideology critique has the function of unmasking all false representations of reality that, while presenting themselves as "natural," are in fact the result of human action and unequal power relationships.

With the advent of mass media, critical theorists start thinking about a new form of capitalist society, one based on an implicit form of domination and control, rationalized by new forms of state power and commodified forms of culture. It was getting clearer and clearer that capitalism was becoming more than a system of production, namely also—and, in many ways, more importantly—a disciplining force, securing forms of legitimacy and acceptance among the broader public. That explains, as Marcuse (1964) argues in his *One-Dimensional Man*, the lack of initiative for mass revolution to socialism in the capitalist world. Analyzing the postwar economic boom, Marcuse recognizes that capitalism was able to suppress all opposition not through overt repression but through affluence and consumerism, and by creating, through ideology, false needs in the public. "We are again confronted with one of the most vexing aspects of advanced industrial civilization: the rational character of its irrationality. Its productivity and efficiency, its capacity to increase and spread comforts, to turn waste into need, and destruction into construction, the extent to which this civilization transforms the object world into an extension of man's mind and body makes the very notion of alienation questionable. The people recognize themselves in their commodities; they find their soul in their automobile, hi-fi set, split-level home, kitchen equipment. The very mechanism which ties the individual to his society has changed, and social control is anchored in the new needs which it has produced" (Marcuse, 1964, p. 9).

Marcuse's critical stance toward mass media's ideological manipulative role follows the path established a few decades earlier by the work of Adorno and Horkheimer on the media as culture industry. "The Culture Industry: Enlightenment as Mass Deception" is one chapter in their *Dialectic of Enlightenment*, originally published in 1944 (see Adorno & Horkheimer, 1972), where Adorno and Horkheimer equalled the media to a factory producing standardized cultural commodities—films, radio programs, magazines, and so on—that are used to make profit and to manipulate mass society into passivity. In the culture industry, every single cultural good draws from the same stock of character types, plot structures, and modes of representation; indeed, this is a formulaic style that does not change over time but always remains the same. Therefore, while the surface content of popular culture may look different, its inner form constantly repeats itself. As a result, a kind of pseudo-individuation is produced whereby consumers are seduced into believing they are experiencing something unique when they are not. However, it is not simply the repetition itself, but also the manner in which it is perceived and consumed by the audience, that is so alarming for Adorno and Horkheimer. To encourage perpetual consumption, the culture industry must continually mask its repetitive formulas and deceive people into believing they are getting something new. It is this unconscious internalization of repetition that is instrumental to the dissolution of any critical capacity. Another major characteristic of the culture industry for Adorno and Horkheimer was the growing concordance between its products and everyday life. By erasing the distance between art and life, cultural representation and reality, the culture industry generates its most important ideological effect: its products do not misrepresent or distort the "truth" about reality but, more radically and worryingly, destroy the capacity of individuals to imagine anything different. In other words, the speculative and critical ability of art to reflect on social contradictions and tensions dissolves. In the end, the ultimate ideological effect of the culture industry is the establishment of a totalitarian system of cultural production that effectively and completely integrates individuals, their thoughts and activities, into prevailing social, economic, and political structures. This line of thought was brought back to the fore in the 1970s when, in the aftermath of Althusser's (1971) writings about ideological state apparatuses, the media appeared as a system through which dominant ideas and practices were imposed upon subordinated groups and this process resulted in "false consciousness"—that is, these groups' failure to recognize their own class interests and their submission to the dominant groups.

A more nuanced and less pessimistic theory of ideology—one that offered to media literacy educators more proactive views about the media and the audience in the classroom—came from the rediscovery, via British cultural studies, of Gramsci's writings about hegemony. Gramsci helped explain how a dominant class's leadership has to be gained and maintained over time through an endless struggle for consent with other social groups. Such struggle was to be fought over the cultural meanings that circulate in the society. Gramsci's concept of hegemony was an important one for British teachers, since it gave them the chance to work in the classroom with a much more "manageable" notion of the media's ideological power, one that allowed them to find ways to intercept the students' cultural tastes and practices. Media culture was no longer defined in the totalizing terms of a base–superstructure Marxist model, of Althusser's ideological state apparatuses, or of Adorno and Horkheimer's culture industry, but rather as a mobile ideological site where meanings are not imposed as false consciousness as they have to win people's consent, to speak to their interests and find a compromise with the existing dominant structures and ideas. When this is achieved, class interests no longer appear as such, but rather as either "national interest," "public interest," common sense or the taken-for-granted.

This brings us to the notion of myth developed by the French Marxist theorist Roland Barthes and to the critical theory produced by Marxist semiotics. Building on the work of the Swiss linguist Ferdinand de Saussure and on Marx, Barthes elaborated a complex system of semiotic analysis of media texts (Barthes 1973). His theory of the "myth" as the "falsely obvious" of the media provided media literacy educators with an important principle for action and reflection: to challenge the media's (especially television's) most powerful ideological weapon, that is, the naturalness of the image, its common-sense display of reality. Being critical now means to be able to decode the complex mythology of the media and understand that they do not simply reflect reality but rather represent it. For Barthes, the meaning of cultural products is conditioned by ideology and historically produced. Hence it is not eternal, but rather constantly mutating and reforming. Myth, under Barthes's Marxist perception, is always political, as it inevitably results from specific power structures and struggles in a certain society at a certain time. Its power resides precisely in concealing this historical specificity, presenting itself as objective and natural. By effacing politics and transforming history into "nature," myth forgets (Barthes's terms) that reality is far from "natural," as it is in fact forged dialectically by human activity and struggle. Similar notions can be found in Benjamin's (1936) study *The Work of Art in the Age of Mechanical Production*, and also in Marx's description of ideology as a *camera obscura* that inverts reality. In addition to that, Barthes's theories have helped media literacy educators overturn the question of value. As we have seen, previous approaches—namely the inoculative and the discriminatory one—had devalued popular cultural forms, their primary goal being in the first case to encourage appreciation of high culture and, in the second, to celebrate only certain movie productions, according to some esthetic criteria ultimately derived from the traditional literary canon. Value—that is, how "good" a certain media product is—was the central question for media literacy educators. Barthes chose instead to apply his complex semiotic analyses to phenomena (striptease, wrestling, toys, tour guides, a plate of fish and chips) that represented the utmost radical rejection of any idea of established cultural taste and value. According to him, they were all worthy of serious study, just like a poem or a melodrama, and any discrimination against them was in fact an expression of ideological power.

In arguing that every aspect of culture could be treated as "text" and hence subject to thorough scrutiny and analysis, Barthes was echoing Raymond Williams's (1977) notion of culture as "ordinary" and as "a whole way of life" that includes, then, not only the meanings and values residing in the text but also the practices that express them. Both Barthes and Williams based their cultural analysis on the recognition that all human activity has some cultural worth, as a process by which people identify and define themselves—and, by doing this, they conform and contribute to society's shared values. Ultimately both supported a notion of culture that is socially equalizing and rejected the elitist distinction between the highbrow and the lowbrow as a way to devalue mass participation in culture.

Along with the critical–semiotic study of media's ideological representations, throughout the 1970s and 1980s a massive number of studies were done on media as social institutions and economic organizations, on the professional practices and routines lying at the core of media productions (particularly with regard to the process of newsmaking), on media ownership and control, on advertising, on the relationship between media, the state, and the government, on media consumption practices and contexts, and so on. What these studies revealed was the complexity of the media communication process as it moves from the level of production to that of consumption. At the production end, they showed an increasing concentration of media ownership and a vast ramification of consumer and service industries (a capitalist chain, so to speak) that turn the media into multinational conglomerates. They also showed that media power does not operate as a monolithic force but is in fact the result of a complex series of professional, industrial, and personal relationships and constraints, often conflictual and contradictory. Similarly, at the consumption end, a vast array of empirical studies since the early 1980s started to scrutinize the audience as never before. In fact, the audience had long been taken for granted. Adopting a behaviorist and deterministic view, social scientists and communication scholars had long assumed that media effects depend mostly on the attributes of the message (or the medium, as McLuhan would say). A first attempt to have a more complex understanding of the audience was made in the 1970s, when the uses and gratifications approach posited that the audience actively interprets media texts, making choices among different media on the basis of how they, differentially, gratify certain needs and expectations. Additionally, in the 1980s another strand of audience research started to investigate the audience's interpretative activity using ethnographic methods; this strand was in search of empirical evidence derived not from individual psychologies, but from how such activity is systematically related to socioeconomic and subcultural positions of race, class, or gender. These studies marked a definite break with two traditional notions: first, the notion that different interpretations of the same text are necessarily "wrong" readings of the "true" meaning of that text, or the result of personal taste; second, the notion of the audience as a passive and easily manipulated entity. They also showed the importance of paying attention to the contexts within which texts are normally interpreted or experienced. Morley's studies, for example, showed that TV viewing is thoroughly integrated into (and conditioned by) a range of domestic and family routines (Morley, 1986, 1992). Despite the populist drift that many of these studies about the "active" audience have taken, to recognize the interpretive activism of the audience does not (should not) necessarily imply giving up the main goal of critical theory, which is to uncover the dominant meanings encoded in the text and the contextual–institutional conditions that brought them. Hall's (1980) encoding–decoding model shows clearly the dialectical tension between the encoding power of the media, that is, their power to inscribe certain dominant meanings, and the decoding power of the audience, that is, its power to interpret those meanings, negotiate between them and personal meanings, and even utterly oppose them.

Up until the early 1980s, audiences were of little or no interest to media literacy educators. This was due to a kind of legacy of traditional literary criticism by which readers were subordinate to the authority of both "authorship (justified by the transcendence of 'genius' or 'creativity') and the text itself (the transcendence of immanent 'meaning')" (Masterman & Mariet, 1994, p. 43). In consequence, interpretation was seen as a kind of ideologically innocent activity of uncovering "true" meanings taking place in a sociohistorical vacuum rather than a discursive construction resulting from the ideological position of the reader. With the advent of the ethnographic turn in audience research, media literacy educators, too, started to focus on the audience to help students develop a more critical understanding of how different audiences are addressed by different media productions, but also to make them reflect upon their being part of a targeted audience. While studying, for example, how fans are "cultivated" by the media industry, they can also critically look at their own fandom experiences. Institutional analysis, too, was part of this new season of ML. Take the example of studying how a newspaper is made. It has its own style and form, as these have developed over time. Through them it has established (and needs to maintain) constant loyalty and support from its readers, and then from its advertisers, upon which the profits of the newspaper largely depend. Additionally, it is subject to some kind of self-regulatory mechanisms and legal–deontological constraints; it values professional writing and thus needs to give its journalists respect and a certain degree of autonomy; and, of course, it needs to maintain good relationships with its more or less official and institutional sources of information. Indeed, a rather complex network of influences and interests are here at play, and it is the teacher's task to try to disentangle them together with their students in order to develop the latter's critical understanding of the "determinants" of media texts. In fact, as it has become clearer, it is quite difficult to find ways to connect these theoretical debates with the down-to-earth concerns of classroom practice.

Undeniably, when critical theory enters the ML classroom—in the varied forms briefly described above—at the heart of critical work in the classroom is not so much esthetic–moral value, as it used to, but the politics (and economics) of media representation. And yet, at the same time, some important limitations and problems emerge, as Williamson pointed out brilliantly in a much-quoted article (Williamson, 1981). As said, media literacy educators have always privileged critical thinking, which is the logical–cognitive dimension of social action (the interpretation of meanings), to the detriment of the irrational–bodily dimension of doing and affect based on play, sociability, and rituals. As a result, *reading the media* has long been the key teaching practice (especially in the 1960s and 1970s) and has prevailed over *writing the media*, on the assumption that media production in the classroom would simply amount to a mere technicality or an unreflective imitation of mainstream media practices, thus confirming the illusory and formulaic values of popular culture. This hypertrophy of the "critical" ignores that, in fact, media consumption occurs both at the cognitive and at the affective–social level. As Roger Silverstone (1999) suggests, pleasure is a very central aspect of media consumption and of social experience as a whole—pleasure of the body and the mind, where the "erotic" meets the "cerebral." To emphasize the cognitive aspects of reading the media means to underestimate how much cultural investments spring from social and emotional motivations as well (Cappello, 2009). It also means to uphold the questionable assumption that students are the "mystified" and the teacher is the "liberator." There is here a kind of "political evangelism" by which "the teacher reveals the truth and the students, once they witness it, automatically give their assent … a drastic oversimplification of the complex and messy realities of classroom practices" (Buckingham, 1996, p. 645), and one that ultimately polices out the students' experiences and pleasures by labeling them "false consciousness." Rationalistic forms of analysis may have the perverse and counterproductive effect of leading students to resist, or conform superficially to, their teachers' "politically correct" positions, ultimately hindering the occurrence of any real form of learning and change. In Buckingham's (1996) opinion, that is the risk run by the so-called "critical pedagogues" as they started to engage in the 1990s in the field of ML (Giroux, 1992, 1994; Giroux & McLaren, 1992; Giroux & Simon, 1988). What is it that students are actually learning by "doing" critical analysis? If we lead them to resist or conform to the "hidden curriculum" of the teacher, are we sure that a process of change in attitudes and behaviors has even just begun? Indeed, Williamson's (1981) nagging question is still there: "How does girl number twenty understand ideology?"

The adoption of more "playful pedagogies" (Buckingham, 2003a and 2003b), which allow introducing pleasure in the classroom, has increasingly appeared to be the precondition for answering those questions, together with the "rediscovery" of the pedagogical value of media production in the classroom. As a matter of fact, thanks also to the spreading of easy-to-use digital technologies, media literacy educators have realized that media production, far from being pedagogically irrelevant, may in fact be a space where students can explore and learn more about their cultural and affective investments in the media, without necessarily having to dismiss them as ideologically or commercially manipulative. However, that does not mean that we must throw the baby out with the bathwater. To recognize the limits of critical thinking does not imply that we no longer need it (Buckingham, 2003b). Quite the contrary, the need remains to find ways to connect critical analysis with media production (Cappello, Felini, & Hobbs, 2011). If taken alone, critical analysis may lead to abstract criticism with no connection to actual learning processes. At the same time, however, media production too, if taken alone, may lead to mere instrumentalism in search of "special effects" that try to mimic professional practices. It may also lead to a kind of populist call to listen to the students' self-authenticating voice as if the class were to be a kind of psychotherapeutic session where students express their "true" media experience in a sort of spontaneous flow of feelings. In fact, as Hall's encoding–decoding model shows us, any media experience is the result of a series of complex negotiations that take place in specific wider social, cultural, and institutional contexts. The point is, then, to try to make sure that students—by creatively engaging with media production—can also recognize these contexts and how they influence the formation of their identities and cultural investments. Ultimately, what critical theory as applied to ML should bring about is an *educative conception of politics*—one that does not merely consist of "unmasking … false ideas and replacing them by true ones" (Hall, 1994, p. 181); at the same time it should take us back to a *political conception of education*—one in which students come to realize that their own meanings and pleasures have a political dimension and that through education they can identify with it and tackle it. In so doing, ML will become a dynamic approach that "entails a constant shifting back and forth between different forms of learning, between action and reflection, between practice and theory, and between passionate engagement and distanced analysis" (Buckingham, 2003b, p. 154).

SEE ALSO: Active Audiences; Advertising Literacy; Awareness; Critical Information Literacy; Critical Pedagogy; Political Economy; Representation; Social Semiotics

References

Adorno, T.W., & Horkheimer, M. (1972). *Dialectic of enlightenment*. New York, NY: Continuum.

Althusser, L. (1971). *Ideology and ideological state apparatuses, Lenin and philosophy and other essays*. London, England: New Left Books.

Barthes, R. (1973). *Mythologies*. London, England: Paladin.

Benjamin, W. (1936). *The work of art in the age of mechanical production*. London, England: Penguin Books.

Buckingham, D. (1996). Critical pedagogy and media education: A theory in search of a practice. *Journal of Curriculum Studies, 28*(6), 627–650.

Buckingham, D. (2003a). Media education and the end of the critical consumer. *Harvard Educational Review, 8*(73), 309–327.

Buckingham, D. (2003b). *Media education: Literacy, learning and contemporary culture*. Cambridge, England: Polity.

Cappello, G. (2009). *Nascosti nella luce: Media, minori e media education*. Milan: FrancoAngeli.

Cappello, G., Felini, D., & Hobbs, R. (2011). Reflections on global developments in media literacy education: Bridging theory and practice. *Journal of Media Literacy Education, 3*(2), 66–73.
Giroux, H. (1992). *Border crossings: Cultural workers and the politics of education*. New York, NY: Routledge.
Giroux, H. (1994). Disturbing pleasures: Learning popular culture. New York, NY: Routledge.
Giroux, H., & McLaren, P. (1992). Media hegemony: Towards a critical pedagogy of representation. In J. Schwoch, M. White, & S. Reilly (Eds.), *Media knowledge: Readings in popular culture, pedagogy and critical citizenship* (pp. xv–xxxiv). Albany, NY: SUNY Press.
Giroux, H., & Simon, R. (1988). Critical pedagogy and the politics of popular culture. *Cultural Studies, 2*(3), 294–320.
Hall, S. (1980). Encoding/decoding. In Centre for Contemporary Cultural Studies (Ed.), *Culture, media, language: Working papers in cultural studies, 1972–1979* (pp. 128–138). London, England: Hutchinson.
Hall, S. (1994). Some "politically incorrect" pathways through PC. In S. Dunant (Ed.), *The War of the words: The political correctness debate* (pp. 164–184). London, England: Virago Press.
Hall, S., & Whannel, P. (1964). *The popular arts*. London, England: Hutchinson.
Horkheimer, M. (1989). *Traditional and critical theory in critical theory: Selected essays*. New York, NY: Continuum.
Marcuse, H. 1964. *One-dimensional man*. Boston, MA: Beacon Press.
Masterman, L., & Mariet, F. (1994). *Media education in 1990s Europe*. Strasbourg, France: Council of Europe Press.
Morley, D. (1986). *Family television*. London, England: Comedia.
Morley, D. (1992). *Television, audience and cultural studies*. London, England: Routledge.
Silverstone, R. (1999). *Why study the media?* London, England: SAGE.
Williams, R. (1977). *Marxism and literature*. Oxford, England: Oxford University Press.
Williamson, J. (1981–1982). How does girl number twenty understand ideology? *Screen Education, 40*, 80–87.

Further reading

Buckingham, D. (Ed.). (1998). *Teaching popular culture: Beyond radical pedagogy*. London, England: UCL Press.
Gramsci, A. (1971). *The prison notebooks*. New York, NY: International Publishers.
Stanford Encyclopedia of Philosophy. (2005). Critical theory. Retrieved from https://plato.stanford.edu/entries/critical-theory/#6
Thevenin, B.J. (2012). Critical media literacy in action: Uniting theory, practice and politics in media education. Journalism & Mass Communication Graduate Theses & Dissertations 6. Retrieved from https://scholar.colorado.edu/jour_gradetds/6

Gianna Cappello is associate professor at the University of Palermo, Italy, where she teaches undergraduate and graduate courses in digital media sociology and media education. She is cofounder and current president of the Italian Association of Media Education and codirector of MED's journal *Media Education: Studi, Ricerche e Buone Pratiche*. She is also cofounder and current vice president of the International Association of Media Education (IAME). Her research addresses issues in critical media theory, sociology of childhood, media literacy education, and digital media sociology.

Curation

SADIA KHAN
University of South Carolina, USA

IBRAR BHATT
Queen's University Belfast, UK

Curation is a practice of information gathering, management, and presentation. Whether carried out manually or computationally, the key feature of curation is the filtering process by which information is selected and shared. Through this process, curation intrinsically links information to knowledge and meaning-making. By making evaluative judgments about the validity and relevance of information, curatorship transforms information into knowledge based on awareness or belief about what is justifiably true. Thus, through the filtering process, knowledge can be said to be a by-product of curation. Because it links information to knowledge creation, the practice of curation is an important focus of inquiry in the fields of media literacy and education, as well as within the social sciences. The power of curation to inform and direct a conversation around a topic is another feature which makes it eminently useful.

Curation and controversy

Traditionally, curation has been the work of museum and library specialists, carefully and prodigiously selecting relevant materials to develop collections. Today, everyday acts of curation can look like selectively sharing content online, creating and maintaining a profile on any of the various social network platforms, and searching and compiling information for reporting. In each case, acts of information management create or add to a narrative around a topic. Curation describes the practices of harnessing preexisting content, transforming it through the application of criteria which assess and promote belief, and then directing the resultant packet of filtered information to a new audience.

In addition to library and media studies, online practices of curation have been discussed within the fields of information theory, literacy studies, and computer science. Curation's relevance across multiple fields stems from its particular characteristic of being able to tell a story through the choice of carefully selected and presented artifacts, the compilation of which collectively conveys meaning and knowledge not contained in the individual pieces of a collection. In this way, curation is an act of knowledge creation – the creation of a narrative which justifies its own relevance. The by-product of this as "created knowledge" makes curation a powerful tool, and also a topic of controversy. It also brings to bear the difference between human and computational forms of curation. Indeed, from these two modes of curation arise variances and disruptions in how curation is utilized and applied.

While they both perform the same task, manual (human) curation and computational (algorithmic) curation have different strengths, weaknesses, and consequences.

Computers and algorithms manage, filter, and report data more efficiently and thoroughly than humans can do manually. On the other hand, human processing offers impressionistic judgment, which is a defining factor of manual curation. In both cases, the reporting of filtered and selected information creates a unique narrative with its own meaning and its own reality.

Variations of curation, however, can not only look different, but also carry different implications. At its best, curation can have the effect of a masterful presentation which is well sourced and infused with creativity, utility, and meaning. It can present itself through products like innovative and life-saving research aided by a collaborative effort of scholars whose work is converged in a scientific report. Conversely, some forms of curation can create polarizing "bubbles" in which the only information one receives is filtered according to specific criteria set by the very consumers and/or producers of that information. In this scenario, the resultant "echo chamber" inevitably amplifies certain narratives while silencing others through the recirculation of partisan information – limiting the opportunity for a person to encounter conflicting views. Examples include Facebook friends' lists and Twitter feeds in which disagreeable information can be purged through "unfollow" and "block" options. Similarly, algorithmically determined newsfeeds decide on the information which is presented to a user based on personal habits, preferences, and usages. In both cases, filtered bubbles are created and maintained through a set of decisions and actions. The difference is in the nature of the filtering mechanisms.

Since curation is about information management, it becomes important to question *who manages these filters*. This question is critical because inherent in the filtering process are things like subjective evaluation, purpose, editorialization, summary, reduction, and approximation. A curated packet of information that results from this process is, therefore, imbued with these determinations.

To be a curator of information, awareness and discernment of the mediating factors is imperative – as is the ability to discriminate between sources and gauge authenticity and validity. Indeed, this is a critical requirement for the effective management and assessment of the troves of data available online, and also a requirement for detecting ineffectiveness and misguidance in what has been called "pre-curated" data (Bhatt, 2017) – or data which has already been filtered with some particular justification parameters.

The defining factors of curation

The use of information communications technologies (ICTs) has become ubiquitous in everyday life. As the amount of information on any topic immediately available to us has grown exponentially, and as we increasingly conduct our affairs online, much of the data that inform our life, behavior, and decisions are mediated by computers and the Internet. The consequences of this relate to curation; as such, curation has now come to encompass multitudinous and increasing forms of data-managing behavior. Curation as a term has therefore evolved to describe what is often done in digital environments and online in social, personal, educational, and commercial spaces.

This has been examined and documented in each of these areas through the study of such things as "remix" practices in music production, sharing content on social media, and writing and literacy in education. Each of these varied tasks involves curation outlined as: (i) problematizing an issue or topic; (ii) anthologizing and aggregating information relevant to a topic and enlisting filters to manage it; (iii) applying subjective, editorial discretion to appeal to and reach a target audience; (iv) adding value to preexisting content by contributing new or extended meaning and/or create a new narrative; and (v) presenting that data in the appropriately determined platform (Bhatt, 2017, p. 120).

Noticeably, computational and human curation are concurrent practices. While content aggregation manifests largely as algorithmically managed data, with little or no value placed on truth, accuracy, and morality, the remainder of the task lies in the hands of human curators who have a distinct role in making meanings out of the voluminous amounts of information that would overwhelm us otherwise. This discriminating behavior is about adding value, making meaning, and inspiring novelty. It is at the heart of content curation.

Indeed, the notion of meaning-making as a preeminent characteristic of curation is echoed widely. It is the factor that is most influential in making curation transformative. Adding meaning or expanding a narrative on a subject extends the relevance of that idea, that act of creativity, or that literacy event into the future, creating a new narrative, and, in a sense, a new reality.

This process of recombining preexisting content to fabricate new content has also been dubbed as "remix" and has been scrutinized for its paradoxically sequacious and innovative nature (Gunkel, 2016). In their investigation into the remixing practices of Internet bloggers and fanfiction writing, Lankshear and Knobel (2015) highlight the myriad social practices and conceptions of engaging in meaning-making which are enacted by searching, filtering, combining, repurposing, narrating, and sharing. These practices of creative decoding and encoding of information lend important insights into curation as a latent form of digital literacy.

Bhatt (2017), working in the field of literacy and education, documented practices of curation during his investigation into strategies of how college students searched for information, drew from previous texts, and handled a multitude of textual sources during their writing tasks. Mihailidis and Cohen (2013) and Barton (2017) also found similar practices in different contexts.

Mihailidis and Cohen investigated the online practices of students as they filtered and aggregated online information. Highlighting the need for students to be analytical and critical in their online life, they suggest a new set of pedagogical approaches which promote critical thinking and information filtering skills, and are centered around curation practices. Also examining curation as a digital literacy practice, Barton explored curation as part of social *tagging* in the photo-sharing site Flickr. Specific to how users utilized the tagging feature, he found that curation practices created a story not told by the pictures themselves, and not predicted by the site's designers. All three of these investigations reveal users/curators as active meaning-makers and agents of change.

Curators as agents of change

Curation is a subjective and inherently ideological process in which curators select existing objects to construct their own "truths." Through this production, curation becomes a creative expression of re-representation by which a curator can represent anything from empirical facts to information about oneself in a contextualized way. Embedded in the narrative that is created are the values of the narrator. In doing this, a narrator becomes the de facto author over a composition of voices, and by developing and employing skills which enable agency (Potter & Gilje, 2015), (s)he can also become an agent of change.

Barton's study of tagging practices on Flickr (mentioned above) is illustrative of this – showing how users of a platform perform curation practices *agentively*. By strategically recreating their online photo-narratives in order to demand change on the social media platform, users acted in a manner which was at odds with the intentions of the site's developers. Curation practices, therefore, are something that can allow power to be distributed a certain way. This potential is magnified when considering that the Internet itself is curated by millions of individual users making individual choices, effectively binding them together through shared practices.

Certainly, curation has the potential to be powerful. Millions of users coalescing around a narrative can effect change. This has been seen in social activism movements like the Occupy Movement, the Arab Spring, and other forms of political populism where a narrative is crafted, editorialized, shared, and continuously re-crafted – giving it a new reality when interpreted and acted upon by others.

But not all curation is the same. Where there is re-representation, there can be misrepresentation. And the difference can be as significant as the difference between knowledge creation versus a repeated circulation of misinformation and proliferation of ignorance. The former represents novelty, creativity, and innovation and is arguably the future of learning and scholarship; the latter, through the aggregation of people within increasingly partisan networks, has consistently been dubbed by the World Economic Forum as one of the main threats to human society and modern civilization (2013, 2018).

Discernment

The ability to transform ideas existing as data floating on the Internet into emergent concepts under the authorship of a curator is certainly significant, and it is aided and made more complex by the broadness of the Internet and the accessibility of its information. But effective curation requires thought and analysis applied through shrewd discernment, particularly at the aggregation and editorialization phases. There is simply too much information for humans alone to successfully harness. As such, the mediation of traditional *stewardship* (e.g., librarians, teachers, and even parents) has now had to give way to the work of computational curators.

Information searching now *requires* computer processors, search engines, and other tools of information management. Additionally, the Internet largely employs machine learning to organize itself and make things easier to find. While this delegation of curation work to machines is essential, its self-regulatory management has important implications. One consequence is that management filters can act as *pre-curators* (Bhatt, 2017). Search algorithms greatly affect the information we see and choose, and for that reason, search and social media executives hold the secrets to their algorithms tightly. Using data that is pre-curated according to algorithmic predictions about what we are looking for, or what others want us to see, think, or buy (into), will ultimately change the outcome of curation. More precisely, computational curation such as this affects the decisions and recommendations individuals, employers, and governments make for themselves and society. While this particular kind of curation is *considered* by many as more objective due to its mathematical formulation, those formulations are in themselves intrinsically biased by those who create the algorithms. These concerns are most often the subject of a nascent field known as critical algorithm studies (see Further reading), which investigates algorithms as social actors and objects of inquiry.

Algorithms now have increasing power over our lives due to their efficient information-harnessing and decision-making capabilities, but with an objectivity level that is questionable at best. For example, in 2009, a US school system applied an algorithmic teacher assessment tool which measured students' progress and calculated the extent to which their educational progress (or decline) was attributable to individual teachers. The teachers with the lowest calculated scores were fired each year, regardless of any positive evaluations and testimonials that they had received elsewhere. This demonstrates one of many ethical concerns with reliance on computational data management.

Equally important is the way computer algorithms promote and "sponsor" information based on corporate revenue maximization. Online search information is seen by many as objective and is then utilized in compiling investigative or academic reports. This has consequences. The facade of objectivity is important to recognize and it becomes important to ask: Who benefits when algorithms rank information? What role does the promotion or limiting of information have on decision-making, and why does it matter? Information theorists such as Clay Shirky, Tristan Harris, Luciano Floridi, and Frank Pasquale all point to the same thing: that credibility and authority are increasingly conveyed algorithmically.

Mindfulness of this exogenous arbitration is crucial for an effective human curator. This requires the ability to identify sources and filter information discriminately. But this is a skill set that has not had universal adoption; neither has it been applied with sufficient proficiency – leaving users susceptible to misguidance online. A 2016 executive summary research study conducted by Stanford University entitled *Evaluating Information: The Cornerstone of Civic Online Reasoning* found that even students at this highly selective university were largely unsuccessful in differentiating a reliable and factual website from a propagandist one (Wineburg & McGrew, 2016). The investigation saw similar findings across the educational spectrum, from middle school to college. What this suggests is that so-called digital nativism is not a predictor of judicious computer use.

Relevant to this problem is the field of study known as "agnotology" (Proctor, 2008). Agnotology examines how misinformation and ignorance are culturally produced.

Societal ignorance can manifest through neglecting to discern and discriminate between sources of information (as Wineburg & McGrew discovered), or as a result of deliberate and sponsored misrepresentation. An example of the latter includes the tobacco industry's marketing campaign to nurture doubt and ignorance about the detrimental health effects of smoking (Proctor, 2008, pp. 11–18). The proliferation of "fake," biased, or propagandist news articles which populate users' curated newsfeeds on social media sites is also a subject of concern for those studying agnotology and its relationship with curation.

Addressing these concerns in a 2010 executive summary to the Aspen Institute on media literacy, Renee Hobbs voiced a need to promote pedagogical tools to advance the principles of digital and media literacy, including analytical thinking, evaluation, and creative meaning-making. An informed society must encourage a kind of media literacy which fosters critical thinking to allow people to make informed decisions and avoid culturally induced ignorance through misinformation.

The permutations of the (mis-)use and (mis-)management of information which arise from a discussion of discernment matter when data floating on the Internet are transformed into works of curation. While the meaning-making and knowledge-producing aspects are what give curation its power to create and transform narratives around online content, the information management or data collection aspect is equally important. Without prudent filtering of information by its credibility, misinformation becomes infiltrated into curation work, thereby changing the meaning and knowledge that is produced. As misinformation becomes more pervasive, discernment and discrimination become increasingly difficult – and more necessary.

Addressing matters of information management necessitates updated skills, yet new requirements in research practices have not been coherently understood and applied across different fields. Researchers, institutions, and libraries struggle to delineate information management practices in the face of complexities added by metadata, algorithms, analytics, and evolving platforms for learning, teaching, and sharing. What may be needed are standards for information gathering generally and curation practices specifically which are commensurate with the kind of media literacy to which Hobbs refers. The field of library and information science (LIS) has an important part to play here – although the role of librarianship has been made more complex by the integration of data science into the traditional understanding of information gathering and preservation. Some of the implications of this hybridization have been discussed here in terms of media literacy and agnotology. As such, LIS scholars face the added task of establishing standards for the training of curation practices.

Efforts to address these issues of standardization and training have emerged from different contexts – mostly educational – with the goal of defining curation practice and establishing a reliable set of criteria by which to determine if information has been satisfactorily vetted. These efforts have been propelled by the requirements of government and university funding agencies and scholarly societies which judge outcomes by such things as credibility and reproducibility. However, there is still little coordination between groups working on this effort, and few LIS programs offer advanced classes or degrees in curation. This is despite researchers and research organizations voicing a need for training to deal with the evolving demands of research, the changed landscape of documentation and publication in the digital environment, and the need to comply with government requirements for the management of federally funded research data. The opening this leaves is felt throughout the educational spectrum, leaving researchers and students of all levels ill-prepared for the digital literacy requirements that curation demands and furthermore uncertain over what will be required to practice meaningful curation in the future, given the changes in data and information management.

Conclusion

The key feature that makes curation so consequential is the filtering process that links information to knowledge. When curators apply subjective and evaluative judgments about the relevance of information for a deliberate purpose, they create new knowledge. It is this knowledge production that makes curation relevant across multiple fields and can position curators as potential agents of change.

To capitalize on the potential for novelty and innovation requires both insight and skill. Because intermediating data filters and agents are not always transparent, such as in the case of algorithms, curation can easily and unknowingly be reincarnated as ignorance. How information is collated and circulated needs to be critically examined as part of any educationally viable approach to digital and media literacy. A critical approach is particularly important in learning environments where students are lauded as having "self-organized" their learning via web and computational sources. It is also pressing in light of recent research which finds that student web users are failing to sufficiently differentiate between sources of online information based on reliability.

As society grows skeptical of institutions marketing information and perceived to be biased and operating under agendas, perhaps it is not merely coincidental that over the last generation, museums have secured an increasing position of trust in society (Museums Association, 2013). Museums are acknowledged to have a crucial societal role that is broader than satisfying individual visitors. The role of museums as guardians of reliable information is due in large part to the role of museum curators as *stewards* of information and producers of knowledge. It is this type of stewardship which is relevant and required in online environments for the management of abundant information and knowledge production. Indeed, institutions of education, politics, and commerce can similarly benefit from securing a position of trust through the employment of prudent and transparent curation practices.

SEE ALSO: Authorship and Participatory Culture; Critical Information Literacy; Data Literacy; Digital Literacy; Meaning-Making

References

Barton, D. (2017). The roles of tagging in the online curation of photographs [Special issue]. *Discourse, Context & Media, 22*, 39–45. doi: 10.1016/j.dcm.2017.06.001

Bhatt, I. (2017). *Assignments as controversies: Digital literacy and writing in classroom practice*. Abingdon, England: Routledge.
Gunkel, D.J. (2016). *Of remixology: Ethics and aesthetics after remix*. Cambridge, MA: MIT Press.
Hobbs, R. (2010). *Digital and media literacy: A plan of action*. A White Paper on the digital and media literacy recommendations of the Knight Commission on the information needs of communities in a democracy. Washington, DC: The Aspen Institute.
Lankshear, C., & Knobel, M. (2015). Digital literacy and digital literacies: Policy pedagogy and research consideration for education. *Nordic Journal of Digital Literacy, 9*(4), 8–20.
Mihailidis, P., & Cohen, J.N. (2013). Exploring curation as a core competency in digital and media literacy education. *Journal of Interactive Media in Education, 2013*(1), 2. doi: 10.5334/2013-02
Museums Association. (2013). *The purposes of museums in society: A report prepared by BritainThinks*. London, England: Museums Association.
Potter, J., & Gilje, Ø. (Eds.). (2015). *Special Issue: E-Learning and Digital Media: Learners Identity and Curation, 12*(2), 123–258. doi: 10.1177/2042753014568150
Proctor, R. (2008). Agnotology: A missing term to describe the cultural production of ignorance (and its study). In L.L. Schiebinger (Ed.), *Agnotology: The making and unmaking of ignorance* (pp. 1–33). Stanford, CA: Stanford University Press.
Stanford History Education Group. (2016). *Evaluating information: The cornerstone of civic online reasoning* [Executive Summary Report]. Retrieved from http://sheg.stanford.edu/upload/V3LessonPlans/Executive%20Summary%2011.21.16.pdf
Wineburg, S., & McGrew, S. (2016, November). Why students can't google their way to the truth: Fact checkers and students approach websites differently. *Education Week, 36*(11), 22–28.
World Economic Forum. (2013). *Digital wildfires in a hyperconnected world*. Global Risks 2013: An Initiative of the Risk Response Network. Geneva. Retrieved from http://reports.weforum.org/global-risks-2013/risk-case-1/digital-wildfires-in-a-hyperconnected-world/
World Economic Forum. (2018). *The global risks report 2018*. Retrieved from http://www3.weforum.org/docs/WEF_GRR18_Report.pdf

Further reading

O'Neil, C. (2016). *Weapons of math destruction: How big data increases inequality and threatens democracy*. New York, NY: Crown.
Snyder, I.A. (2015). Discourses of "curation" in digital times. In R.H. Jones, A. Chik, & C.A. Hafner (Eds.), *Discourse and digital practices: Doing discourse analysis in the digital age* (pp. 209–225). Abingdon, England: Routledge.
Social Media Collective. (2017). *Critical algorithm studies: A reading list*. Retrieved from https://socialmediacollective.org/reading-lists/critical-algorithm-studies/

Sadia Khan is a graduate student studying rhetoric and composition in the Department of English Language and Literature at the University of South Carolina. As a freelance writer and editor, she has a diverse portfolio which includes work in digital literacy. Her academic background additionally includes studies in applied economics and third world development.

Ibrar Bhatt is a lecturer in education at Queen's University Belfast. His PhD was completed at the University of Leeds, and his research interests include digital literacy, writing, and how these relate to language education and knowledge production. He is author of the book *Assignments as Controversies. Digital Literacy and Writing in Classroom Practice* (2017).

Data Literacy

RAHUL BHARGAVA
MIT Media Lab, USA

The act of living our lives now involves the generation of vast amounts of data, stored in information systems across the world. This data is both qualitative and quantitative, spanning everything from videos of our children, to GPS (Global Positioning System) trails of our car movements, to logs of our web browsing habits. Some people can work nimbly with this data: gathering, analyzing, and finding stories in it with ease. Others don't have the awareness, knowledge, skills, or access to resources needed to do so. Data literacy generally refers to this ability to acquire, analyze, represent, and argue with this type of information. This is a relatively new term though, so an exact definition is actively debated by researchers and practitioners in the field (Letouzé et al., 2015).

Many domains leverage the idea of "literacy" to address their importance to society at large. At a high level, the hope is that literacies empower people to act and engage in the world from an informed and enabled point of view, letting them join in discussions that require said literacy, rather than being left behind due to a lack of basic understanding. With this in mind, literacies are often offered, and denied, to subpopulations based on entrenched social and political structures. The nascent concept of data literacy is no different.

The roots of data literacy can be traced to both historical and recent developments (Steen, 1999). It builds on a number of existing literacies, including:

- numerical literacy, which focuses on basic operations with numerical abstractions;
- information literacy, which emphasizes critical thinking about the source of information;
- scientific literacy, which highlights the role of scientific process for decision-making;
- statistical literacy, which argues for the use of statistical operations in everyday life;
- computational literacy, which pushes for algorithmic thinking and modeling as a problem-solving approach;

The International Encyclopedia of Media Literacy. Renee Hobbs and Paul Mihailidis (Editors-in-Chief), Gianna Cappello, Maria Ranieri, and Benjamin Thevenin (Associate Editors).

- digital literacy, which introduces how to operate computation tools and technologies related to the Internet.

These fields all offer basic skills that are part of data literacy. Proponents of its import offer that one of the things that make data literacy unique is how it combines all of these existing literacies.

The concept of "Big Data" has taken over much of the public and media narrative around data. Defining Big Data is debate of its own; a popular definition includes technology, analysis, and mythology (body & Crawford, 2012). A concept of Big Data literacy has not been well fleshed out in the field. Based on this inclusive definition it would require an understanding of the technologies used to gather large data sets, awareness of the algorithmic operations used to analyze them, and critical abilities to assess the aura of accuracy that surrounds them (D'Ignazio & Bhargava, 2015).

There is active debate about the exact definition of data literacy, with many potential capabilities mentioned. These often overlap with models of pipelines for working with data, creating an entanglement between product and process.

The ability to acquire data is often the first component mentioned. Acquiring data relates to the process of gathering data from sources, or in generating it oneself in the real world. Acquiring data often emphasizes digital literacy skills, focusing on how to search for and discover data sets online. To balance this, many educators in this realm add instruction on how to generate data about a topic oneself, or with an interest group. In the realm of Big Data the data itself is often gathered in the background of simply living our lives, leaving the people that generate the data unaware that it was even collected. Some definitions of data literacy include a related concept about knowing when data might be helpful. This meta-level argument ties into concepts of statistical literacy and scientific process.

A second piece of data literacy often included in definitions is the process of analyzing data. This refers to the ability to take a data set and perform algorithmic operations on it, both simple and complex. With small sets of data these manipulations can be simple, relying on basic numerical literacy. With Big Data, these operations rely on machine-assisted algorithms. Those two approaches require vastly different sets of background knowledge to perform, so many definitions of data literacy diverge when it comes to discussing which processes for analyzing data are most important to learn. In addition, many of these analytical processes are being shifted into software-driven black boxes, hidden behind the push of a button, leading to a very tool-focused approach by many to building analytical capacities of data literacy learners. Due to historical norms, this has introduced a deep-seated bias toward quantitative data. Qualitative analysis methodologies are seldom included in definitions of the core analytical approaches that make up data literacy. Big Data reintroduces qualitative data, but analyzes it through a quantitative lens: looking at words counts in text, or detecting face locations in images.

A common third piece of data literacy focuses in on the ability to represent data. This concerns how one transforms the data into a non-raw, non-numeric representation. Making charts and graphs is the most common approach to this. However, many practitioners are leveraging the creative capacities of new technologies such as computer-aided fabrication to introduce outputs such as physical manifestations of data. Others look to the arts for more participatory or performative approaches to representing data. Some definitions that focus on these types of creative representations often emphasize storytelling as a core piece of data literacy.

A fourth, more recent point of interest has been on how to structure reasoned arguments based on data. In lieu of emphasizing understanding analytical operations on data, this piece focuses instead on the larger context within which the data is being used. For many, this has become a core distinguishing factor of data literacy; that it includes a focus on using data to argue for change. This change could refer to anything from employees optimizing an operational efficiency in a corporation, to citizens advocating and creating change in a governmental program for their community. This requires an ability to draw conclusions from an analysis of data and link them to a larger context. Other definitions go further, including the idea of the desire to argue with data as part of the core definition. These definitions shift the meaning even more to think about awareness and context.

A fifth piece sometimes included in definitions of data literacy is an understanding of the mechanisms and motivations of data creation and use. This aspect includes a basic understanding of the ethical questions of permission and consent in regards to data collection practices. It also touches on the structures and exchanges used to trade vast amounts of data between companies and governments. These versions of the definition attempt to place the literacy in a societal and cultural context. Big Data is entangled with these ethical questions, due to the fact that it is often generated in extractive or hidden ways, and seldom shared with those that generate it.

There is no widespread agreement on which of these pieces are most critical to, nor even on which of these pieces should be included in, a definition of data literacy.

The question of who needs data literacy, and how much they need, is similarly open. Some governments have commissioned panels to suggest curricular standards that focus on data literacy. The United Nations (UN) has published about the need to increase data literacy (United Nations Data Revolution, 2014). Independent groups that work on workforce development have led surveys of the current offerings from higher education institutions for those wishing to pursue studies in this area. There is currently no common agreement on who needs data literacy, how much they need, nor who should provide it. However, it is clear that large groups across the world are working to increase data literacy, from both social-empowerment and workforce-development motivations.

In government, the question of who needs data literacy often overlaps with the issues of inclusion and empowerment. If a government is making data-driven decisions for its citizens, does it have an obligation to help them understand those processes? This question is at the core of many open data efforts, which attempt to publish official government data online in standard formats in order to ease the path to entry for citizenry using it.

A proliferation of digital tools has been created to support acquiring data literacy. These tools serve the diverse set of audiences interested in it. Simple aggregation tools are evolving to include higher-level analytic and visualization features. Graphic design tools now include data-centric capabilities that automate the generation of many standard, and less-often used, charts and graphs. This touches on many aspects of data visualization. Many are web-based tools that work on sample data, or that data users can upload. Some are focused on learning outcomes, while others focus on analytic and visual outcomes.

Educational programs have been created that focus on building data literacy. Some service organizations are looking to become more "data-centric" in their processes and technologies. Others introduce students in educational settings to playful and hands-on approaches to telling stories with data. Growth in educational programs has been driven by the perception that data literacy is a core skill needed for the next generation of workers in many industries. The role of "Chief Data Scientist" has been created in many organizations, highlighting the role data can play within their functioning. This, in turn, creates demand for data literacy skills in industries as diverse as healthcare provision, nonprofit advocacy, and logistics.

Ethical considerations play a central role in many introductions to data literacy. Questions about who gathers data, who is aware when data is being gathered, and who has access to it, all rest on ethical foundations. Governments, professional associations, and others are producing suggestions for new norms in the area, but there are no agreed-upon standards. These data practices will continue to evolve, but for now many refer to them as a "responsible" approach to data.

Many are experimenting with approaches for best learning data literacy skills. Online courses for individual learners use lecture videos and interactive exercises. In-classroom activities sometimes are focused on a singular piece of software, to build expertise in how it can be used to work with data. Others use hands-on activities with novel materials to make the acquisition of data literacy less intimidating to those who are wary of digital tools.

All of this attention and energy toward helping various audiences acquire data literacy is built on the presumption that society will continue to be data-driven. Some argue that the current surge in data-driven decision-making, which drives the growth in demand and supply for data literacy education, is a temporary phenomenon. The relevance of data literacy is closely intertwined with the availability of data, the capacity of digital tools to support operations on it, the centrality of data in our organizational and civic processes, and the motivation and drive to use it.

Here data literacy overlaps with media literacy, in that it focuses in on data and its representation as the media being accessed, analyzed, and created. Data is a media being used within society to represent, argue about, and affect the world.

SEE ALSO: Data Visualization; Media Literacy Foundations; Open Educational Resources

References

boyd, d., & Crawford, K. (2012). Critical questions for big data: Provocations for a cultural, technological, and scholarly phenomenon. *Information, Communication & Society, 15*(5), 662–679. doi: 10.1080/1369118X.2012.678878

D'Ignazio, C., & Bhargava, R. (2015). Approaches to building Big Data literacy. Paper presented at the Bloomberg Data for Good Exchange conference, New York, NY.

Letouzé, E., Noonan, A., Bhargava, R., Deahl, E., Sangokoya, D., & Shoup, N. (2015, September). *Beyond data literacy: Reinventing community engagement and empowerment in the age of data.* Data-Pop Alliance. Retrieved from https://datatherapy.files.wordpress.com/2015/10/beyond-data-literacy-2015.pdf/

Steen, L.A. (1999). Numeracy: The new literacy for a data-drenched society. *Educational Leadership, 57*(2), 8–13.

United Nations Data Revolution. (2014). *A world that counts: Mobilising the data revolution for sustainable development.* United Nations Independent Expert Advisory Group on a Data Revolution for Sustainable Development. Retrieved from http://www.undatarevolution.org/wp-content/uploads/2014/11/A-World-That-Counts.pdf

Rahul Bhargava is a research scientist at the Center for Civic Media at the MIT Media Lab. His work focuses on creative approaches to data literacy for novices and experts alike, encompassing digital tools and hands-on activities. Rahul blogs at datatherapy.org, publishes academically, teaches at MIT, and presents at international events.

Data Visualization

CATHERINE D'IGNAZIO
Emerson College, USA

Data visualizations are an increasingly powerful way to make knowledge claims about the world. While the visual display of quantitative information has a long history, data visualization has become a more mainstream form of communication than ever before. Data visualization can be defined as the graphic presentation of information that has been systematically collected. Forms of visualizations range from the familiar pie charts, timelines, and maps to more specialized forms such as treemaps, cartograms, streamgraphs, and chord diagrams. While much of contemporary data visualization is two-dimensional and distributed online, data visualization may also occur in print publications, motion graphics, or take on 3-D forms such as sculptures, public art, murals, and performances.

Whereas visualization was previously a niche form of communication for scientists, statisticians, and other professions, the past 20 years have witnessed a proliferation of data visualization more broadly in professional cultures as well as in popular culture. Data visualizations are routinely created by corporations, news organizations, nonprofit and nongovernmental organizations (NGOs), policymakers and government, independent designers and bloggers, and everyday people. Visualization has accompanied an increased interest in "data-driven decision-making" and it is often asserted that visualizations aid in gaining insight from large and complex data sets. Visualization publishers and designers often state that they are trying to make data more accessible and actionable to members of the general public and see data visualization serving a democratizing function, though scholars have questioned whether it truly does or not (Kennedy, Hill, Aiello, & Allen, 2016).

History of data visualization

While this entry focuses on visualization in the contemporary context, it is important to know and to teach learners that the form is not new. Scholars have shown that map projections date as early as Ptolemy (c. 85–c. 165) and there are examples of charts as early as the 10th century (Tufte, 1983). Data visualization witnessed a golden age in Europe from 1850 to 1900, with the growth of statistical theory, wide-scale systematic record-keeping by nation-states, and development of more sophisticated visual methods (Friendly, 2008). Until recently, however, data visualization was not seen as a single form or field of inquiry, with disciplines such as medicine, geography, statistics, and astronomy developing visual display methods independently of each other. There is much research to be done in this realm, for example, tracing the use of data visualization in a nonwestern context. Additionally, historians have challenged prior accounts of the evolution of data visualization, in particular in the way they write women's work with data out of the historical record (Klein, 2014).

Context of data visualization

There are three interrelated phenomena that have led to the popularization of data visualization. The first is the rise of "Big Data" defined as an interplay of technology, analysis, and mythology (boyd & Crawford, 2012). Because of advances in technological capacity and analytical methods, states and corporations are able to collect, store, and process more data than ever before. Data visualization is commonly seen as a path toward gaining insight from large and complicated data sets that would be impossible to understand in tabular form. It is worth highlighting the third part of boyd and Crawford's definition: "the widespread belief that large data sets offer a higher form of intelligence and knowledge that can generate insights that were previously impossible, with the aura of truth, objectivity, and accuracy" (2012, p. 663). Data visualization is often the visual enactment of this "aura of truth." Learning to be a critical reader and designer entails learning productive ways to challenge that aura.

The second phenomenon is the rise of the open data movement. Open data is the idea that certain data should be freely available to everyone to use and republish as they wish, without restrictions from copyright, patents, or other mechanisms of control. The movement started with governments in the United States and the United Kingdom but has now gone international with more than 50 nations across six continents committed to opening some of their data as well as the participation by some NGOs and corporations. The ideals of the open data movement include government transparency and accountability, increased trust, democratic access, faster scientific progress, economic development, and citizen empowerment. The practical outcome of the open data movement is that there are a proliferating number of ways to download data about everything from congressional voting records to agricultural statistics. For new learners these repositories can be both a tremendous realm of possibility and appear deceptively complete. Finding the data one *needs* remains a key challenge in data-driven inquiry projects.

The third and final phenomenon is "datafication," which can be defined as the transformation of social action into quantified data, thus allowing for real-time tracking and predictive analysis. For example, a personal health tracker uses an accelerometer to make a rough approximation of an individual's steps during the day. This constitutes "datafying" steps: counting and recording them through an analog-to-digital conversion process. Datafication is happening at many scales and becoming a norm in many industries, particularly as new economic models for successfully surveilling populations and monetizing data become apparent (van Dijck, 2014). For example, at the city scale, cities are experimenting with sensors in urban spaces to datafy traffic patterns, energy consumption, pedestrian activity, waste streams, and air quality, among many other things. Learning about data visualization entails understanding how and why institutions go about datafying various aspects of the world.

Examples of data visualization: personal, professional, public

Data visualization happens in a variety of contexts ranging from personal to professional to public. In the personal context, there have been a proliferation of self-tracking apps and personal health management technologies. Individuals can measure and track their steps, heart rates, GPS (Global Positioning System) location, posture, golf swing, income and spending, home climate control systems, and many more aspects of their everyday lives.

This data is presented back to the individual in the form of data visualizations that show current statistics, progression toward a goal, or compare data across time. For example, personal health trackers present users with a personal health dashboard, a series of small visualizations on one screen that are intended to be checked daily. On this dashboard, we see visualizations of heart rate, sleep patterns, weight, and weekly heart rate. From a critical perspective, it is important to remember that these visualizations have been designed to show some things and obscure others. Personal health trackers, particularly those used at scale, have access to aggregated health information of many people. Missing from the personal dashboard are the ways in which personal data is then stored, aggregated with millions of other records, sold to third-party brokers, and otherwise used by the corporate host to drive sales and revenue. This is not to imply malicious or exploitative intent. It is simply to state that visualizations, like many other media, obscure the material conditions of their making in favor of a localized experience.

Data visualizations are prevalent in a variety of professional contexts, too many to fully describe in detail in this entry. While financial and scientific professions have used data visualizations for a long time, they are on the rise in realms such as municipal government, food safety, and nonprofit management. Data visualizations are used for

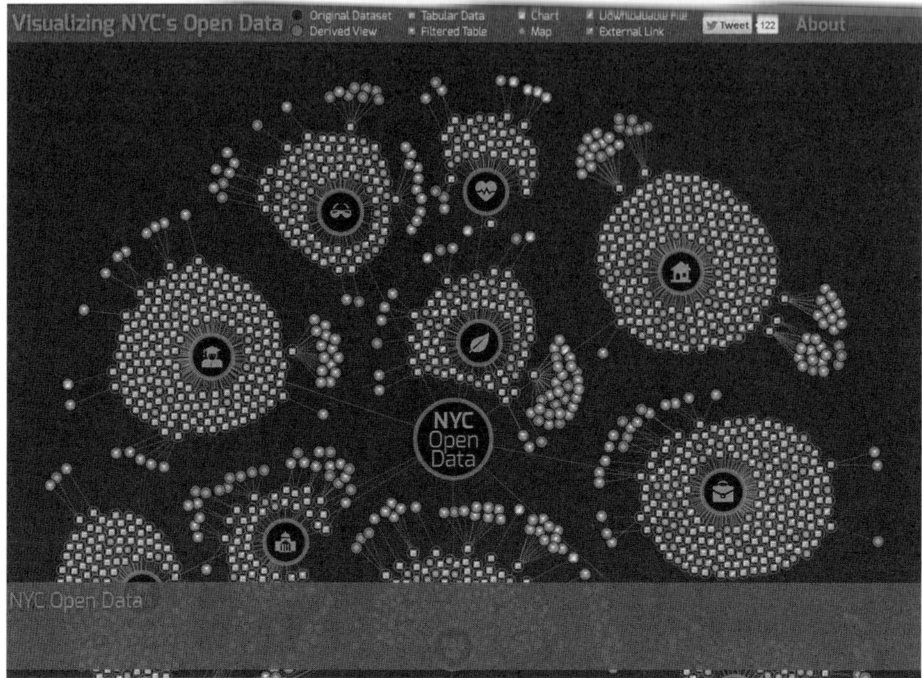

Figure 1 All of the data sets available on the NYC Open Data Portal. Source: nycopendata.socrata.com, October 2016.

internal monitoring and communication purposes as well as for external communication between an institution and its constituents or customers. For example, Figure 1 shows a network visualization of all of the data available via the New York City Open Data Portal. Each node is a single data set and the graphic icons allude to the data's general topic area, so a leaf icon represents environmental data. Further research is needed into the purpose, context, and reception of data visualization across extremely diverse professional contexts.

Finally, data visualizations have become extremely popular in more public forms of communication such as marketing, advertising, journalism, and social media. The "computer-assisted reporting" that took shape in the 1970s and 1980s now more often goes by the term "data journalism." This work takes numerous forms for the reader or end user. The most ubiquitous are simple, static charts that support news stories in print, on the web, or that are broadcast. More complex forms include interactive experiences that allow users to explore a question through visualizing data, such as "512 Paths to the White House" (Bostock & Carter, 2012) that explores alternate presidential outcomes depending on how US states vote in a national election. And news organizations are increasingly experimenting with hybrid forms that combine narrative storytelling with visualizations. The *Guardian* story in Figure 2 is a good example of this hybrid approach which uses short narrative statements punctuated by a series of visualizations to describe how Australian women won the 4×100 freestyle relay. The piece includes an animated graphic that demonstrates race order, a timeline showing when the record had previously been broken, and three photos annotated with data points.

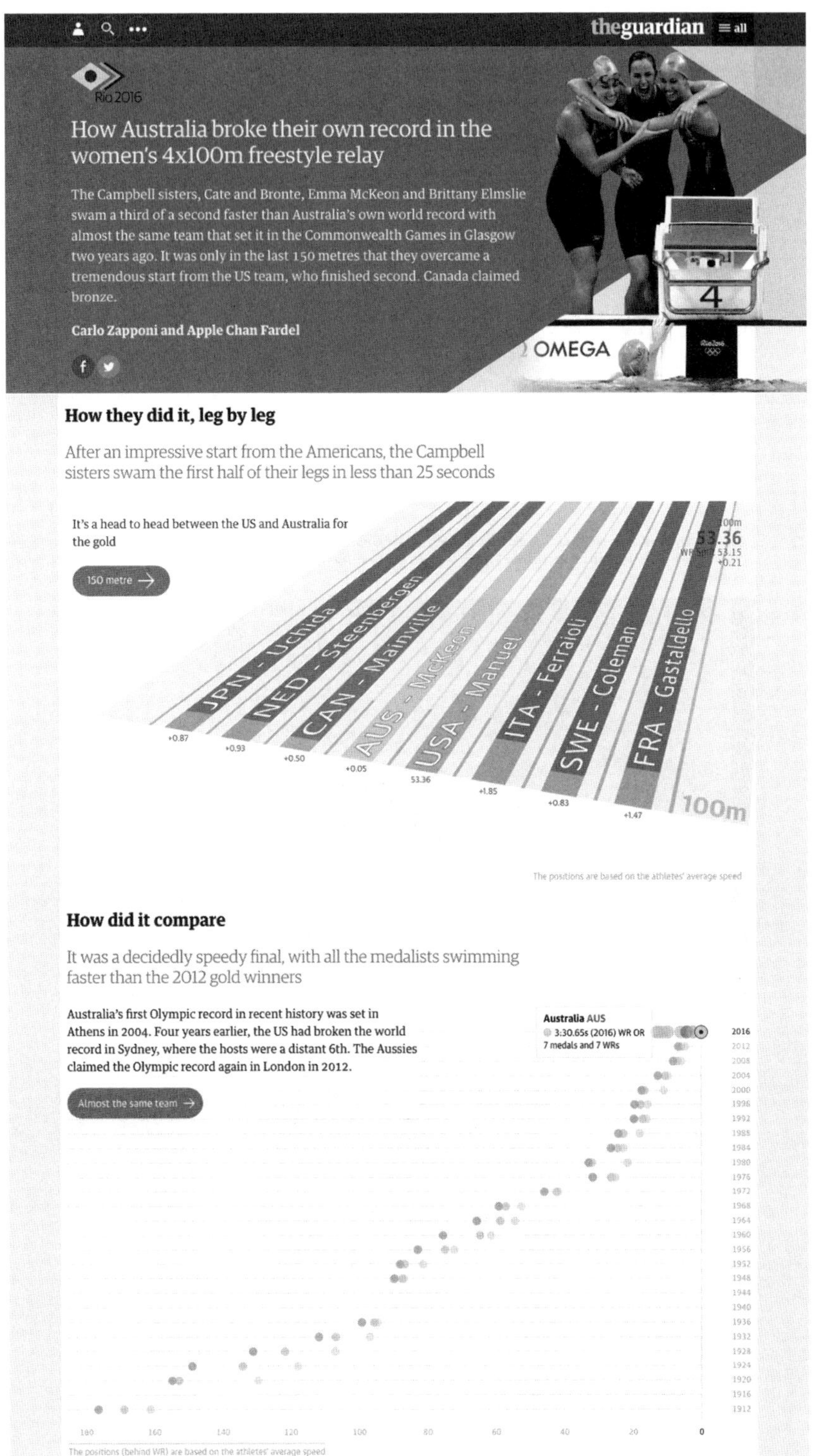

Figure 2 How Australia broke their own record in the women's 4×100m freestyle relay. Source: www.theguardian.com (Zapponi & Chan Fardel, 2016, August 7). *(continued overleaf)*

Coming from behind

Off the platform, only the Dutch were slower that the Aussies. Nonetheless Emma McKeon finished her leg only inches behind American Simone Manuel.

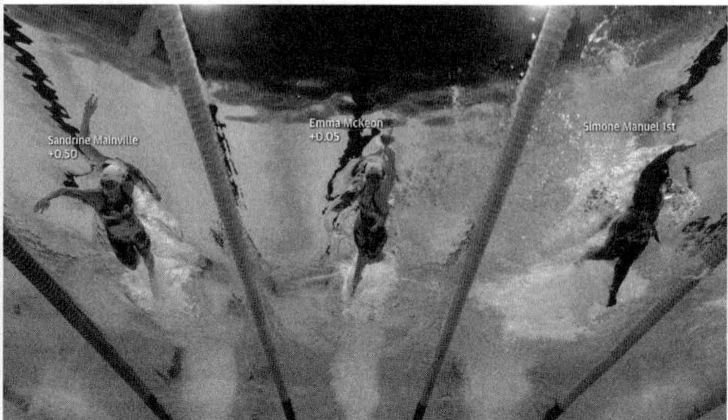

After Brittany Elmslie lost over half a second to Abbey Weitzeil, it was up to Bronte Campbell to swim faster than American Dana Vollmer. And she did, more than a second faster.

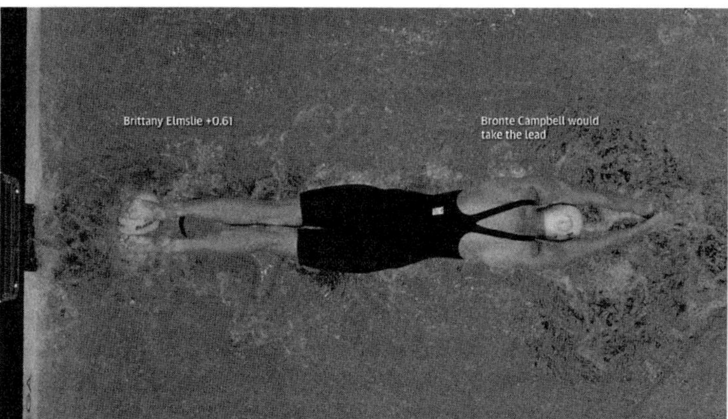

Big sister Cate was already half a body ahead of the world record when she jumped into the pool, she then swam her first 50 metres in just 24.15 seconds to lock it.

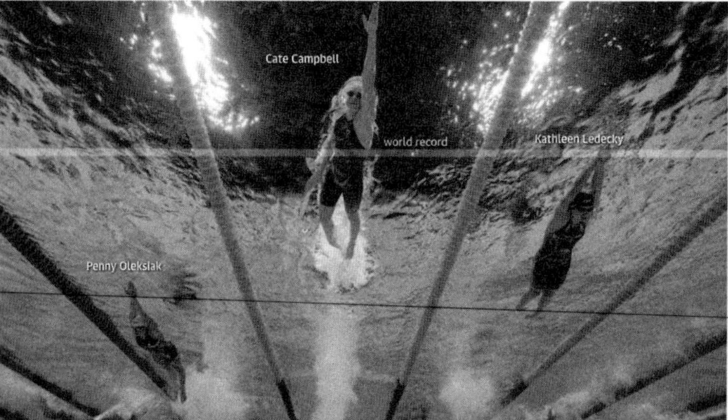

Figure 2 (*Continued*)

Knowledge domains

For the purposes of media literacy learners, there are five distinct knowledge domains that comprise learning about data visualization. They draw from creative and technical fields, so learners and instructors can often feel overwhelmed by the amount of disparate knowledge to assimilate. Learners need to understand basic principles of *graphic design*, including typography and visual relations such as color theory, contrast, balance, alignment, and repetition. *Interaction design and user experience* play a role when data visualizations are interactive. There are now established conventions for displaying summary views, zooms, and details (Kennedy et al., 2016; Shneiderman, 1996). Reading, interpreting, and creating data visualizations requires at least passing knowledge of *statistics* in order to characterize patterns from aggregated observations about the world. Learners find they can get rather far with descriptive statistics (e.g., mean, median, mode, max., and min.) but will be able to do more if they understand inferential statistics and advanced methods of data science such as building predictive models with machine learning. Basic understanding of *visual cognition* augments and integrates the prior three domains, as it deals with how the brain processes information, detects patterns, and uses visual search queries as part of its everyday architecture. Finally, data visualizations need to be assembled by some means. This is typically done through *software and web development*, that is, through writing code. Coding is not an absolute requirement because out-of-the-box software packages for data visualization are becoming more advanced; however, it does afford the ability to process data more effectively, tailor data visualizations to a particular project, and customize interactions.

Data visualization as process and product of inquiry

While data visualization is most commonly seen and considered as a polished communicative product, it is important to note that it is part of a broader process of inquiry, analysis, and communication. Learning data visualization is learning an inquiry process that is methodical and data-driven and setting expectations for what should be happening at each stage of the process. For this reason, many data visualization modules happen in research methods courses where students are learning how to formulate research questions and which methods are useful for which kinds of knowledge claims. Research methods courses introduce many of the critical skills that students need for working with data, including standardized methods for collecting data, designing surveys, and calculating uncertainty. Data visualization may be taught outside of the context of a formal research methods course, but educators may need to work harder to cultivate critical perspectives on data (as described below).

When data visualization is the goal of a data-driven inquiry project, it is important to note that visualizing data happens throughout the process, not just at the end as the product. While it is most common as a reader to encounter data visualizations as finished products of the data analysis process, data visualization creators will use visualization at every stage in order to understand questions like: Does my data answer my question? Where is the missing data? Do I need to find and combine another data set

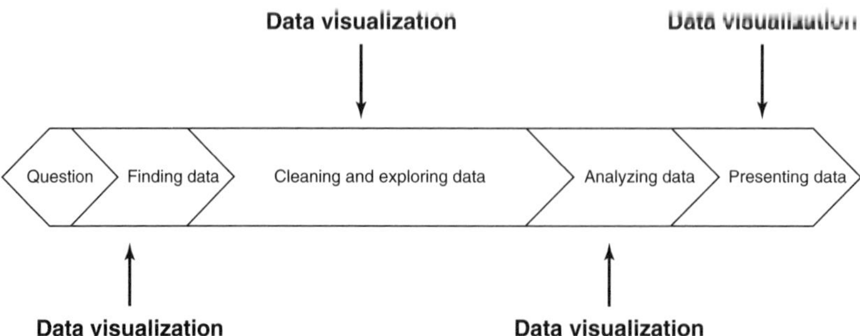

Figure 3 Visualization happens throughout the data exploration and analysis process, not just at the end. Source: The author.

to answer my question? Do I need to clean and standardize my data? What is the right method of analysis? (See Figure 3.)

Critical perspectives and metaskills

Because data visualization is a relatively new phenomenon as a form of popular communication, there is not a great deal of scholarship on critical analysis of these artifacts as media. Scholarship about visualization has tended to come from more technical fields such as *information visualization*, which concerns itself with the design of interactive systems that deal with large amounts of data, as well as *computer science* where the layout algorithms and methods for processing and displaying large amounts of data are invented. For this reason, data visualization has tended to have a more positivist inflection. But this is changing. In recent years, with the increasing attention to the intersection between data and society, scholars have borrowed from fields like *critical cartography*, *GIS*, *human–computer interaction* and the *digital humanities* to propose ways to critically read and create data visualizations. These proposals go by various names such as critical information visualization (Dörk, Feng, Collins, & Carpendale, 2013), public participatory GIS (Elwood, 2006), and feminist data visualization (D'Ignazio & Klein, 2016). In general, critical perspectives take issue with the way that data visualizations appear to present a neutral, objective "view from nowhere," note the inequalities in the data ecosystems from which these visualizations emerge, and highlight the power imbalances between who collects, stores, and analyzes data and who is collected, stored, and analyzed. Some designers have advocated incorporating other senses such as touch and even taste into experiential displays of data so that people might "feel" data, "visceralize" data, or "physicalize" data. Educators have asserted that these more creative methods can be used to inspire learners, help them feel less intimidated, and provide examples for designers to create more inclusive visualizations for particular audiences (Bhargava, 2014).

Learning about data visualization, therefore, represents an opportunity to become a critical reader and a critical data designer. These two roles go hand in hand. Informed reading of data visualization necessitates knowledge gained through hands-on experience of the data collection, analysis, and design process. While the section on *knowledge domains* described the fields that visualization draws from, those do not encompass the metaskills needed to operationalize this knowledge. These come from cultivating critical data literacy and include learning objectives such as (i) understanding what questions can be answered with data; (ii) understanding which aspects of the world data represents; (iii) understanding of institutional data collection and publication practices, including the role of data collection in surveillance, advertising, and corporate profit; and (iv) understanding that no data is "raw", that is, no data is an unfiltered representation of reality. Fostering critical data literacy should be seen as the core work of any process of teaching data visualization.

SEE ALSO: Critical Information Literacy; Data Literacy

References

Bhargava, R. (2014). Speaking data. Retrieved from https://datatherapy.org/2014/07/09/speaking-data/

Bostock, M., & Carter, S. (2012). 512 Paths to the White House. *New York Times.* Retrieved from http://www.nytimes.com/interactive/2012/11/02/us/politics/paths-to-the-white-house.html?_r=0

boyd, d., & Crawford, K. (2012). Critical questions for Big Data. *Communication & Society, 15*(5), 662–679. doi: 10.1080/1369118X.2012.678878

D'Ignazio, C., & Klein, L.F. (2016). Feminist data visualization. Retrieved from http://www.kanarinka.com/wp-content/uploads/2015/07/IEEE_Feminist_Data_Visualization.pdf

Dörk, M., Feng, P., Collins, C., & Carpendale, S. (2013). Critical InfoVis: Exploring the politics of visualization. *CHI '13 Extended Abstracts on Human Factors in Computing Systems* (pp. 2189–2198). doi: 10.1145/2468356.2468739

Elwood, S. (2006). Critical issues in participatory GIS: Deconstructions, reconstructions, and new research directions. *Transactions in GIS, 10*(5), 693–708. doi: 10.1111/j.1467-9671.2006.01023.x

Friendly, M. (2008). A brief history of data visualization. In C.-H. Chen, W. Härdle, & A. Unwin (Eds.), *Handbook of data visualization* (pp. 15–56). Berlin, Germany: Springer.

Kennedy, H., Hill, R.L., Aiello, G., & Allen, W. (2016). The work that visualisation conventions do. *Information, Communication & Society, 19*(6), 715–735. doi: 10.1080/1369118X.2016.1153126

Klein, L. (2014). Visualization as argument. Retrieved from http://lklein.com/2014/12/visualization-as-argument/

Shneiderman, B. (1996). The eyes have it: A task by data type taxonomy for information visualizations. *Proceedings 1996 IEEE Symposium on Visual Languages* (pp. 336–343). doi: 10.1109/VL.1996.545307

Tufte, E. (1983). *The visual display of quantitative information.* Cheshire, CT: Graphics Press.

van Dijck, J. (2014). Datafication, dataism and dataveillance: Big Data between scientific paradigm and ideology. *Surveillance and Society, 12*(2), 197–208.

Zapponi, C., & Chan Fardel, A. (2016, August 7). How Australia broke their own record in the women's 4×100m freestyle relay. *The Guardian.* Retrieved from https://www.theguardian.com/sport/ng-interactive/2016/aug/07/how-australia-broke-their-own-record-in-the-womens-4x100-freestyle-relay

Further reading

Bhargava, R. (2016). Data therapy – tips for empowering people with data. Retrieved from https://datatherapy.org/

Kirk, A. (2012). *Data visualization: A successful design process: A structured design approach to equip you with the knowledge of how to successfully accomplish any data visualization challenge efficiently and effectively*. Birmingham, England: Packt.

Meirelles, I. (2013). *Design for information: An introduction to the histories, theories, and best practices behind effective information visualizations*. Beverly, MA: Rockport.

Ware, C. (2008). *Visual thinking for design*. Burlington, MA: Morgan Kaufmann.

Catherine D'Ignazio is an assistant professor of civic media and data visualization at Emerson College, a principal investigator at the Engagement Lab, and a research affiliate at the MIT Center for Civic Media. Her work focuses on data literacy, feminist technology, and civic art. D'Ignazio has authored articles on critical data literacy as well as co-developed a platform called DataBasic.io. Her art and design projects have won awards from the Tanne Foundation, Turbulence.org, and the LEF Foundation. Her work has been exhibited at the Eyebeam Center for Art & Technology, Museo d'Antiochia of Medellín, and the Venice Biennial.

Denial of Service Action

MOLLY SAUTER
McGill University, Canada

Denial of service actions (DoS) and distributed denial of service actions (DDoS) are broad categories of actions in the online space that involve targeting a server or a service with the intention of rendering it inoperable. These actions generally fall within three broad categories: criminal actions, state-related or state-sponsored actions, and activist actions. They can be effected using a wide range of technological means. DDoS actions have become a popular tactic for digital activism, due to their ability to involve many casual participants and the relative ease with which they can be deployed. When employed for activist causes, DoS and DDoS actions are controversial, having been compared with widely respected tactics like sit-ins on the one hand and denigrated as "shouting down one's opponent" on the other. DDoS actions are likely to grow in popularity as a tactic of activism, criminality, and state aggression, as the Internet becomes progressively normalized as a zone of political action, and as the growth of the so-called Internet of Things (IoT) sector continues to provide millions of poorly secured Internet-connected devices to power botnets.

Technical description

At its core, a denial of service action is an action taken with the goal of rendering a given online service unavailable, typically through crashing or overwhelming the server or servers from which it operates. If this action comes from one source, it is a *denial of service action*; when it comes from several sources simultaneously or in sequence, it is a *distributed denial of service action.*

Traffic and exploit-based actions

There are many specific ways of mounting a denial of service action, so only the general theory behind these actions will be described here. Broadly speaking, there are two basic methodological paths a denial of service action can take: traffic-based or exploit-based.

A traffic-based action seeks to overwhelm a server through sheer volume of requests, sending hundreds or thousands of relatively simple requests in a short period of time. Though these may be something as innocuous as a "ping" request—a basic request wherein one computer asks another, essentially, "Are you there?"—a "ping flood" weaponizes its simplicity, sending thousands of pings a second to a targeted server. The sheer volume of traffic overwhelms the server, causing a bottleneck which impacts the server's ability to respond to legitimate traffic requests and maybe even causes it to crash. In the early days of the graphical web, it was possible to execute a successful traffic-based distributed denial of service action with a few dozen individuals manually reloading a specific webpage repeatedly at a coordinated time. However, from the early 2000s onward, successful traffic-based actions have tended to be automated, with scripts generating hundreds to thousands of requests per second.

An exploit-based action relies primarily on exploiting different systems or processes within the server to drain resources, rather than on just traffic volume. These might be repeated requests to load large image files, process-intensive search requests, or more specialized requests that rely on the specific eccentricities of a given server's architecture or programs. It is not unusual for traffic-based methodologies and exploit-based methodologies to be combined within a single action.

Botnets and independent actors

A distributed denial of service action occurs when multiple sources participate in a denial of service action in a coordinated manner. This coordination can take the form of independent individuals acting in scheduled, organized actions; volunteer botnets, made up of computers willingly linked to an external command-and-control server by their users; and nonvolunteer botnets, where those computers have been commandeered without the authorization of their users.

Activist DDoS actions, such as those powered by the Electronic Disturbance Theater's FloodNet tool in the late 1990s and early 2000s, have often relied on organized individuals acting according to coordinated schedules. These tactics, which required individuals to actively display commitment to an action by "showing up" online, allowed activist groups to maintain theoretical connections to street-based actions like sit-ins by requiring active commitment and real-time coordination, and maintaining a one-to-one relationship between an individual sitting at their computer and their digital "presence" at the action.

More recent activist DDoS tools, most notably the 2010 Anonymous tool LOIC (Low Orbit Ion Cannon), have included a functionality for volunteer botnets. Users can download a program that hooks their computer up to a command-and-control server, which directs the botnet remotely. Users do not need to track scheduling or organizing information, but can instead commit their computing resources to an activist botnet until such time as the action ends and the command-and-control server is decommissioned or the user deletes the DDoS program.

Criminal DDoS actions, such as those often used for extortion, harassment, or censorship, are usually powered by botnets made up of computers that have been illicitly enrolled without their users' knowledge, often through inadvertently downloading a piece of malware. Illicit botnets can contain computers from all over the world and can often be rented for a short period of time for DDoS actions, spam generation, or other criminal activities.

Non-PC botnets

The Mirai botnet, which crashed the Dyn DNS (Domain Name System) system in October of 2016, was at the time made up of nearly 500 000 IoT devices, or Internet-enabled objects that are not a traditional computing device such as a personal computer, tablet, or smartphone. As the number of IoT devices is expected to rapidly outpace that of traditional computing devices by 2020, botnets like Mirai which rely on these devices are expected to play a significant role in the makeup of future botnets, volunteer and otherwise.

Criminal actions, state actions, and activist actions

Not all DDoS actions can be considered to be criminal acts. As stated above, there are three broad categories that DDoS actions fall into: criminal actions, state-sponsored or state-related actions, and activist actions. While, at a technical level, all DDoS actions look basically the same, the stated motivations, the intended and actual effects, the power relationship between the perpetrator and the target, and the reception of DDoS actions can vary drastically. As such, it is essential to consider these factors when determining how to categorize a given action.

Criminal DDoS actions are often the teeth of an extortion campaign. These actions are usually powered by nonvolunteer botnets that have been temporarily rented for the purpose, or sometimes by purpose-assembled nonvolunteer botnets. These actions are perpetrated by criminal organizations or individuals against other individuals or online entities, for the purpose of driving them offline, silencing them, or extorting money from them. These actions are rarely publicly claimed or publicized by the perpetrators, and are only occasionally revealed by the targets.

Repressive governments have turned to DDoS actions as a way to silence minority media voices or political opponents or even engage in acts of cyberwar against other governments, as has been documented by Ethan Zuckerman and others. In these actions, the goal is to silence opposition voices or drive opponents offline by making maintaining an online presence financially and practically unsustainable. Often these actions entail a "denial of service by other means," in that frequently Internet service providers (ISPs) will decline to host an organization or publication that regularly attracts expensive and protracted DDoS actions, and minority or opposition media outlets will be unable to afford the large hosting bills that DDoS actions incur. These actions are often powered by rented nonvolunteer botnets, but have in some cases been at least partially powered by voluntary botnets or independent actors coordinated by state-related hackers or so-called patriotic hackers. In either case, the goal is silencing of critics or causing embarrassment or harm to a political opponent. These actions are rarely widely publicized, as the benefit of this tactic for states is the effectuation of censorship without appearing censorious.

Activist DDoS actions differ from criminal and state-sponsored/state-related DDoS actions in several key ways. These actions most frequently target the online presences of corporations or governmental entities, rarely those of individuals. The online presences are usually peripheral to the business of that entity: for example, the home page of Lufthansa Airlines, targeted during a 2001 action protesting Germany's immigration policies, is not integral to their primary business of flying planes. The goal is usually not exclusively to bring down content, silence opponents (who often have access to extensive public relations apparatuses), or simply break systems, but rather to effect a change in policy or behavior, or to draw attention to an event. These actions are publicized by the perpetrators, through press releases, social media, statements, and other public channels. This public claiming of responsibility sometimes occurs before or during an action as a tactic to recruit more participants. Sometimes these public claims are made using the activists' real names. Historically, these actions have been powered by independent actors and volunteer botnets, and have occasionally been augmented by nonvolunteer, rented botnets.

Notable actions and groups

1995: The Strano Netstrikes

Notable as one of the earliest identifiably activist DDoS actions, launched by Italian activist Tommaso Tozzi, these targeted French governmental sites to protest French nuclear policy. Powered by independent actors following a coordinated schedule, the series of "Netstrikes" lasted for only an hour at a time.

1997: Euskal Herria Journal/Institute for Global Communications

This was a popularly supported Spanish action intended to force the Institute for Global Communications (IGC), an ISP specializing in hosting vulnerable speech, to stop hosting *Euskal Herria Journal*, a Basque separatist publication. Primarily powered by independent actors manually reloading the site and sending large e-mail intended to tie up the ISP's e-mail servers, the action was initially supported by several Spanish newspapers, who later recanted their support due to free speech concerns. IGC ultimately did remove *Euskal Herria Journal*'s content from its server; however, it loudly protested what it saw as vigilante censorship. It is notable for being an edge case, as a popularly supported action not clearly related to the Spanish state that sought to silence a political minority.

1998: Electronic Disturbance Theater develops FloodNet

Electronic Disturbance Theater (EDT) members Carmin Karasic and Brett Stalbaum developed FloodNet as an automated DDoS tool for use during the group's pro-Zapatista "virtual sit-ins." The browser-based tool exploited Java's reload function, running in the background. It allowed participants to select targets from a predefined drop-down menu, and included a rough "message" function, whereby participants could enter text that would be inserted into a targeted server's error log. Though the tool automated the reload function, it required participants to actively select a target and launch the action according to an action schedule determined by the EDT. The EDT released the code for FloodNet in 1999, and adaptations of the tool were subsequently used by other groups in different actions.

1999: The electrohippies/World Trade Organization direct action campaign

During the 1999 World Trade Organization (WTO) meeting in Seattle, Washington, a British group called *the electrohippies* organized a two-stage activist DDoS action, targeting first the WTO's home page with an adapted version of the EDT's FloodNet tool, and then the organization's internal e-mail system, by encouraging participants to send thousands of e-mails with large attachments (the Kyoto Protocol on Climate Change was recommended) to several WTO-hosted e-mail addresses. The action succeeded in crashing the WTO's internal e-mail system for several hours. It was notable for being an identifiable direct action campaign, rather than one primarily oriented toward publicity or media attention.

1999: etoy/toywar/Twelve Days of Christmas

A joint action between the EDT, Swiss art group etoy, and the culture jamming group ®TMark , the "Twelve Days of Christmas" activist DDoS action was one part of the "toywar" campaign, launched to help defend etoy against a copyright lawsuit filed by US e-commerce company eToys. The "toywar" campaign involved physical world demonstration, publicity and letter writing campaigns, and a multiplayer online game. The DDoS action used a modified version of the EDT's FloodNet tool. It was notable for being one of the first activist DDoS actions broadly covered in the mainstream press as an activist action, rather than a criminal act, terrorist act, esoteric art project, or not at all.

2001: Kein Mensch ist illegal/Libertad!/deportation class action

Part of a multisited protest against German immigration policy, the deportation class action targeted the home page of Lufthansa Airlines, which at the time was the airline used by the German government to deport asylum seekers. The campaign included press releases, protest posters hidden on Lufthansa flights, and in-person actions at Lufthansa stockholder meetings. Using an adapted version of FloodNet, the action briefly crashed Lufthansa's home page, which at the time was one of the first to sell tickets directly to customers. Shortly after the campaign ended, Lufthansa stopped transporting deportees for the German government. The action is notable in that it resulted in a protracted court case. In 2006, a German higher court found that the action was not a coercive "show of force" but was rather a legitimate act of political protest intended to influence public opinion and, through public pressure, influence Lufthansa's policies.

2007: Estonia/Russia

Diplomatic tensions between Russia and the former Soviet republic of Estonia ratcheted up following an Estonian decision to move a statue memorializing Soviet forces who served during World War II. During this period, various Estonian websites, including those of the government, political parties, banks, media outlets, and news organizations, were hit with multiple DDoS actions. These actions persisted from early April through early May. The actions used a variety of methodologies, from ping floods to extensive rented botnets. Widely cited as one of the first acts of international "cyberwar," responsibility has been frequently assigned to Russian state-related hackers or independent "patriotic" hackers. It is notable as a major example of a state-sponsored or state-related "cyberwar" action.

2007: Anonymous/Operation Chanology

An extended activist DDoS campaign mounted by the semi-organized online collective known as Anonymous, this action initially targeted the Church of Scientology in response to perceived abuses of copyright regarding a leaked video of noted Scientologist Tom Cruise. The campaign later expanded in scope and focus to address Scientology's history of extensive alleged human rights violations, and to include physical world protests at multiple Scientology Centers internationally. The campaign used an early version of LOIC with an accessible graphical user interface that required active, coordinated participation on the part of those involved. It was notable as it represented the first time Anonymous, previously primarily infamous for their dedicated trolling and meme-making, shifted their focus to address recognized political issues and engage in physical world actions.

2008: Georgia/Russia

This was a series of actions that took place simultaneously with the Russo-Georgian War, wherein websites of various South Ossetian, Georgian, Russian, and Azerbaijani media and governmental organizations were targeted with exploit and botnet powered DDoS actions. The command-and-control servers were hosted by Russian hosting companies, and several Russian language sites offered automated DDoS tools for download. The actions were primarily powered by rented and purpose-assembled botnets, and accompanied other online actions, including website defacements. It was notable as an example of a state-sponsored or state-related DDoS action undertaken simultaneously with an international shooting war.

2009: Help Israel Win/Patriot DDoS Tool

This was an automated DDoS tool released during a period of Israeli–Hamas fighting in Gaza in January of 2009. A student group, Help Israel Win, developed the Patriot DDoS tool as a volunteer botnet tool that allowed users to join a botnet targeting several pro-Palestinian sites during the course of the hostilities. Help Israel Win claimed that at its largest, roughly 1000 computers were connected to the botnet. The Patriot DDoS tool was entirely automated, running in the background and offering no measure of control to users. It was notable as a state-related or paramilitary DDoS action.

2010: Anonymous/Operation Payback

This was a series of activist DDoS actions launched in December of 2010, targeting a number of different credit card processors, politicians, government websites, and others whom Anonymous saw as unfairly targeting Julian Assange and Wikileaks in the aftermath of the Cablegate release. Some sites, such as PayPal, EveryDNS, and the home page of Senator Joseph Lieberman, experienced significant downtime. The campaign was widely covered in the mainstream press, for multiple days, as an activist action, often embedding Anonymous calls to action and press release videos directly in articles. Though multiple tools were used, Anonymous IRC (Internet Relay Chat) channels specifically recommended a newer version of LOIC which included volunteer botnet capabilities, along with the accessible graphical user interface that allowed for independent targeting and deployment. The voluntary LOIC botnets were augmented by several different rented botnets over the course of the campaign.

2011: LiveJournal

In 2011, the community/blogging site LiveJournal was subjected to a series of botnet-powered DDoS actions that resulted in downtime and an exodus of users from the platform. LiveJournal was at the time the largest and most popular blogging platform in Russia, and was particularly popular among the educated middle class and dissident communities. It was notable as an example of a state-related or "patriotic" campaign to reduce the overall effectiveness of a community platform that was not initially constructed with political intentions in mind.

2016: Mirai/Internet of Things/Dyn DNS

On October 21, 2016, the DNS provider Dyn suffered a series of three extended, targeted, botnet-powered DDoS actions that temporarily disabled portions of the

Internet's DNS system, primarily in North America and parts of Europe. Major online companies such as Twitter, SoundCloud, Heroku, Amazon, Etsy, GitHub, Netflix, Reddit, Slack, among others, were impacted. The action was powered by a massive botnet of IoT devices that had been infected with the Mirai malware. The Mirai botnet contained nearly half a million such devices, and the DDoS action itself reached a throughput height of 1.2 terabits per second. It was notable for being the largest DDoS action of any kind at the time, for being the first to use a botnet primarily constructed from IoT devices, and for significantly crippling the global DNS infrastructure while it was in progress. (A previous action in 1992 had similarly downed some root DNS servers, but was not as significant in impact or scope as the Mirai action.)

Theory and criticism of activist DDoS actions

Groups like the EDT saw DDoS actions as an explicit gesture to street-based actions like sit-ins, occupations, and street marches. Their sense of the DDoS action was invested in establishing the Internet as a public space, similar to a public park or street, wherein individuals and groups could exercise their rights to speech and public assembly. This perspective conflicted with previous generations of digital activists, who often self-identified as hackers or hacktivists, and who saw the uninhibited movement of information as the Internet's highest goal. DDoS actions, regardless of their motivation, appeared to hacktivist groups like the Cult of the Dead Cow to be little more than excuses for censorship and attacks on the stability of the network, criticisms that echo those of disruptive street protests, and which have persisted as activist DDoS actions have grown in scope and notoriety.

More recent activist DDoS actions, such as those mounted by Anonymous, have repeated the EDT's "sit-in" theorizations of the tactic, and have similarly come under criticism for suppressing speech, disrupting business, compromising the network, or violating the sanctity of private property. These criticisms highlight core unresolved conflicts regarding the role of the Internet in the public sphere, the relative speech rights of individuals versus corporations, the primacy of corporations in the governance of the Internet and our world in general, and the concepts of private property, public property, and the commons in the online space.

Future of DoS and DDoS actions

Advances in Internet infrastructure have been a double-edged sword regarding DoS and DDoS actions. Entirely volunteer-based activist actions aimed at large corporate or government sites are unlikely to result in down time, due to the proliferation of DDoS mitigation services like Akamai and Arbor Networks. However, the popularity of IoT devices, which are expected to outnumber traditional computing devices by

2020, provides a rich new source of poorly secured machines from which powerful botnets may be constructed. DoS and DDoS actions will continue to be popular tactics of activism, state-related censorship and aggression, and criminal activity, due primarily to their ease of deployment and recruitment (of volunteers, patriotic hackers, and botnets). Identification and mitigation will continue to be a technical challenge. Future efforts in cyberwar and digitally focused social movement studies should focus on contextualizing DoS and DDoS actions in an analytical framework that reaches beyond the technological states at play, looking at power relations between organizers, participants, and targets, and intended effects and actual effects, as well as public framings and claims of responsibility. Though DoS and DDoS actions are "digitally native" tactics, it is useful to situate them analytically within histories of activism, state aggression, and criminality that include pre-Internet actions, offline actions, and nontechnical contextual factors.

SEE ALSO: Civic Activism; Civic Media; Civic Media Literacies; Copyright and Fair Use; Global Citizenship; Internet Safety; Media Access and Activism; Media Literacy and Social Activism; Mediated Communities; Messy Engagement; Representation of Politics; Social Action and Advocacy

Further reading

Coleman, G. (2014). *Hacker, hoaxer, whistleblower, spy: The many faces of Anonymous*. New York, NY: Verso.

Jordan, T., & Taylor, P. (2004). *Hacktivism and cyberwars: Rebels with a cause?* New York, NY: Routledge.

Nazario, J. (2009). Politically motivated denial of service attacks. Arbor Networks. Retrieved from https://ccdcoe.org/sites/default/files/multimedia/pdf/12_NAZARIO%20Politically%20Motivated%20DDoS.pdf

Raley, R. (2009). *Tactical media*. Minneapolis: University of Minnesota Press.

Sauter, M. (2014). *The coming swarm: DDoS actions, hacktivism, and civil disobedience on the Internet*. New York, NY: Bloomsbury.

Zuckerman, E., Roberts, H., McGrady, R., York, J., & Palfrey, J. (2010). Distributed denial of service attacks against independent media and human rights sites. Berkman Center for Internet and Society. Retrieved from http://www.refworld.org/pdfid/4d3025492.pdf

Molly Sauter is a Vanier scholar and PhD candidate in communication studies at McGill University, writing at the intersection of technology, history, politics, and philosophy. She is the author of *The Coming Swarm: DDoS Actions, Hacktivism, and Civil Disobedience on the Internet* (2014). Her writing on technology, politics, and society has been published in *The Atlantic*, *Los Angeles Times*, *Globe and Mail*, *National Post*, *Journal of Communication*, *American Behavioral Scientist*, *Case Western Reserve Law Review*, *io9*, *VICE Motherboard*, among other venues, and in collected volumes published by MIT Press and Peter Lang.

Digital Divide

JOY PIERCE
University of Utah, USA

Digital divide history

"Digital divide" is a term that began to be widely used in the mid-1990s to describe the disparity between households that have access to the Internet and households that do not have access to the Internet. Where and from whom the terminology originated is somewhat of a mystery. The concept of digital divide began in the early 1970s and journalists were credited with using this term in the mid-1990s (Gunkel, 2003). What is known is that the term became solidified by White House aide Albert Hammond and by Larry Irving, assistant secretary for communications and information, and administrator of the National Telecommunications and Information Administration (NTIA). A 1995 NTIA report brought attention to US household disparities in telephone subscribership—the delivery mode for dial-up Internet at the time. The document indicated that central city households generally had the lowest penetration for both telephones and computers, while rural households with computers consistently trailed urban areas and central cities in terms of modem penetration. The document also showed home computer ownership and Internet access based on race, education, and income. In short, households in rural and urban areas—racial minorities, undereducated and poor US citizens—were least likely to access information communication technologies (ICTs) or the Internet. By the time of the third NTIA report, the term "digital divide" was already in the document's title (National Telecommunications and Information Administration, 1998).

One of the catalysts for bridging the digital divide on what former US Vice President Gore called "the information superhighway" was the notion of ICTs as a global education and economic equalizer. Computers were in college classrooms around the world, and were making their way into primary and secondary schools in wealthy cities. Access to the Internet was seen as a way to change education in profound ways. Race, education, household income, [dis]ability, and age are variables often used in digital divide discussions. Another factor is location. Countries, cities, or institutions such as schools that do not have Internet access—whether due to topography or economy—are part of the digital divide conversation. The digital divide is a global phenomenon that affects nations differently according to context. Initially, physical access and connectivity was a concern in the Global West, infrastructure in developing nations, and economic struggles in underdeveloped nations. Each of these areas speaks to the discrepancies between wealthier nations and communities that are likely to have computer and Internet access and countries that cannot afford it or do not have the technical resources to provide their citizens with it.

Digital divide debates

Critics ask whether there is a digital divide. The arguments range from questionable data to partial data. A purely quantitative study may lack a qualitative component that could shed light on why a household does not have a home computer and Internet access. On the other hand, a qualitative study usually involves a small number of participants, which some argue makes the data invalid due to lack of generalizability. There are those who believe there is no need for a homogenous society, and therefore not having access to ICTs is not a problem worthy of study. As technology began to permeate all aspects of society—from communication to commerce and education—the digital divide proved real.

More than a decade after the digital divide was recognized, the term "digital inclusion" took hold globally among media and researchers, to describe digital disparities in hardware and broadband access; ICT knowledge and access in the home, the school, and the workplace; and the disparities in digital access that remained among poor, undereducated, and racial–ethnic minorities. The solution to inclusion is often described as community building, therefore grassroots organizations and community centers began offering access to ICTs through their facilities. Classes were often taught to community residents. Through these efforts and academic research, it became apparent that there were segments of the population that did not want to use a computer and access the Internet. These people were referred to as "choose-nots." Choose-nots were found to lack an interest because they had determined that ICTs were not important to their everyday lives or would not in any way enhance their lived experiences. This discovery prompts one into looking for ways to impress upon everyone that ICTs would become an integral part of global society.

Digital inclusion presupposes that people who are not connected to ICTs want to join the digital society and need assistance in understanding the importance of the technology. Rather than trying to find who was not connected, the notion put forward in digital inclusion was to work toward bringing underserved populations—people in underdeveloped and developing nations; poor, undereducated people and racial–ethnic minorities in the United States; and minority populations around the world—into the already existing digital society. The word "inclusion" is perceived as being more forward-thinking than the term "divide" when it comes to describing the state of digital affairs. Despite the shift in terminology and focus, a number of scholars and organizations around the world remain committed to the concept of digital divide. In doing so, they have discovered more nuanced approaches to understanding the digital divide.

Eszter Hargittai (2002) introduced the second wave of the digital divide by investigating user differences in ICT skills. This second wave interrogates access as both physical and intellectual, and usage as place and purpose. The questions asked were concerned with how people use digital tools; whether they are able to produce content and to complete a useful online search; and whether they know the difference between facts and opinions posted online. Another line of inquiry was whether and how underserved populations use technology for work and play. These questions are largely related to digital literacy. A turn to digital literacy has changed the meaning of access from physical or material ownership to one's ability to find meaningful information and to use technology in creative ways. Such literacy skills are believed to lead to educational, social, and economic empowerment. Scholars across disciplines such as communication, education, and sociology employ digital inclusion through use and effects as a means of discussing digital divisions. Whether they refer to digital inclusion or to digital divides, researchers are focused on the differential ability to use ICTs to evaluate information, gauge and solve complex problems, troubleshoot, and contribute to and communicate with a diverse online community.

Digital divide and the academy

The digital divide is studied across disciplines. Education scholars examine the ways in which knowledge is advanced and by whom using qualitative and quantitative methods. Sociologists employ a myriad of social theories to investigate why a particular population does not have access, as well as the ways ICT may empower it. The discipline focuses primarily on sociocultural aspects of ICT access. Research tools include surveys and interviews, which are used separately or in tandem. Library and information sciences look to physical access, hardware, software, and community needs when researching the digital divide. Many research studies take place in local libraries, government-sponsored community centers, and grassroots organization meeting places. Participant instruction is often part of the research process. Issues of power, race, class, and gender cut across all of the disciplines mentioned above. Some of the theoretical frameworks include contemporary social theory, critical cultural studies, critical race theory, feminist theory, history, and political economy. Methodologies range from structuralism to postmodernism, and the methods employed may include content analysis, ethnography, focus groups, participatory action research, participant observation, polls, questionnaires, rhetoric, and surveys.

Communication and media studies lean toward examining the interpersonal and organizational theories related to the digital divide. The focus is on the dialog between users or on how a user interacts with the technologies. As technology has taken hold in commerce, business scholars and economists have an interest in it and in how it is used (or not used) by individuals in their commercial practices. Over the past five years the medical field has recognized the impact that having access to ICTs makes. Computers and the Internet have enabled people in rural areas to communicate with medical staff hundreds or thousands of miles away. Scholars who measure a user's digital literacy may use specific sites to test knowledge. One of the subjects that have drawn the attention of medical and health scholars is medical information provided on the Internet. The researchers in medicine and health investigate what information patients are getting as well as what they are doing with that information. Another discipline that has a growing interest in digital divides and digital literacy is political science. Technology allows anyone who has access the ability to make political statements that stretch globally. There is also speculation that online voting may replace traditional ways of electing officials. Countries that limit citizens' ability to connect create a divide that is not physical, intellectual, or economic but rather informational. Political scientists may study what information citizens in those countries receive as well as in what ways they may gain knowledge through family and friends outside of their area. There is also interest in policy concerns. In the humanities, social scientists have long studied digital divides; however, there is growing interest among researchers in the field of medicine.

Academic units and professional organizations house digital divide divisions. The Oxford Internet Institute (OII), an interdisciplinary research and teaching department at Oxford in the United Kingdom, has founded the Connectivity, Inclusion, and Inequality Group. Scholars from around the world and in various disciplines study and congregate at OII to develop research, share information, and publish on the digital divide. The International Association for Media and Communication Research has a dedicated digital divide working group. Its annual conference brings digital divide scholars primarily from Africa, India, Mexico, and the United States. Partnership for Progress on the Digital Divide (PPDD) developed from a task force within the US National Communication Association. The PPDD connects research and policy and is the only professional organization of its kind in the world.

Connectivity across the globe

As technology advanced, more voices concerned with digital divides came to the fore. A discussion of inclusion presupposes that marginalized groups will benefit from the same hardware, software, and online uses as mainstream groups. As the United States made tremendous strides in advancing technology, world leaders saw other nations falling behind. The global digital divide was becoming wider. A UN Development Report (Annan, 2015) warned that new technological advances may broaden the gap in economic growth between developed nations and nations without skills, resources, and infrastructure to invest in ICTs. The authors of the report argued that the gap was creating parallel worlds. Such a gap would affect the world economy and would have long-term negative consequences for the underserved nations. The UN report indicated that when citizens in each world—haves and have-nots—are measured side by side, those with Internet access have an advantage and will further marginalize underserved and impoverished nations. Marginalization, according to the United Nations, may lead to the silencing of social and economic issues that are of concern to poorer nations. More than 15 years later, the United Nations' 193 member states agreed on a new set of sustainable development goals (SDG). Since the Internet has the potential to contribute to global development and empowerment, SDG Target 9c calls for universal and affordable access in the world's least developed countries by 2020. The network readiness index from the Global Information Technology Report assesses a country's preparedness for digital advances. Countries on the left are developed nations. The right column highlights the least prepared countries, which are also among the poorest countries in the world (Table 1).

The poorest countries face fundamental problems, as explicated by members of the United Nations in the statement above; but, for developing countries, access to information technologies has become important for integration into the global economy.

Table 1 Top and bottom 10 countries' preparedness for digital advances.

Top 10 Countries	*Bottom 10 Countries*
Finland	Tanzania
Taiwan, China	Cameroon
Iceland	Haiti
Norway	Burundi
United States	Malawi
Austria	Liberia
Sweden	Mauritania
Canada	Madagascar
Switzerland	Chad
Australia	Mali

Source: Baller, Dutta, & Lanvin, 2016.

Rodrigo Baggio founded the Center for Digital Inclusion in 1999. His goal was to assist in the fight against poverty, promote entrepreneurship, and develop avenues for people to empower themselves through the use of ICTs. The nongovernmental organization (NGO) continues that mission today. Leaders in developing and underdeveloped nations continue to work toward preparing for the next wave of digital advances. One means by which other nations anticipate growing closer to bridging the gap in the digital divide is the use of mobile devices. One such project was to provide hardware and connectivity in underdeveloped countries through a low-cost laptop program called One Laptop per Child (see OLPC, 2007). The laptops were distributed to children in Afghanistan, Kenya, Nicaragua, Peru, Rwanda, and Uruguay and in a few cities in the United States.

Connectivity speed is an aspect of the digital divide that may determine whether a user has access to the needed information. The initial method of connecting to the Internet came in the 1980s; connection was achieved via the telephone. Usage was limited to universities until 1992, when Sprint became the first Internet service provider (ISP). Anyone with a telephone connection could have access to the Internet. At about that same time, Tim Berners-Lee invented the World Wide Web—now known simply as the web. The web enabled users to see formatted texts and graphics. The ability to use a web browser to format text and upload images became widespread and these activities became popular; however, such creativity required significant bandwidth, which a telephone connection had difficulty processing. The graphics made the dial-up connection very slow. By the new millennium, a single-use line, called high-speed Internet (broadband), enabled users to access online data without the use of a telephone. The service was provided through cable companies at a fee. Broadband allows more information to transmit at a faster speed than dial-up. Today a person using dial-up may experience Internet transmission between 20 and 60 kilobits; but the average basic broadband speed is ten times faster. Accessing a color photograph using dial-up could take two minutes or longer, whereas it may take two seconds if the connection is made through broadband. This advancement became the catalyst for expanding digital divide data, while dial-up access is still available and used around the world where broadband does not exist. Web content is often created with broadband speeds in mind; therefore users with dial-up may be unable to access information as a result of slow connectivity. Much of the digital divide conversation—after the initial investigation concerning telephone penetration—begins with broadband access.

Developing and underdeveloped countries have chosen to focus on mobile phones as a way to close the gap in the digital divide. A 2014 Pew Research Center report surveyed seven countries in Africa and found that at least two thirds of the population in those countries own mobile phones (Pew, 2014). The report acknowledges that not all of the mobile units are smartphones, and the landline penetration in these countries is nearly 0 percent. India has the second largest penetration of smartphone use—surpassing the United States; yet, according to a 2012 UNESCO report (Huebler & Lu, 2012), it has the greatest number of illiterate adults. The factors in Africa and India indicate that the digital divide is in existence in another form too. Some scholars are skeptical about mobile phones and tablets as a means of digital inclusion. Technical skill in the workforce and infrastructure are digital divides that remain despite efforts to acquire more affordable devices. While mobile phone penetration has allowed the poorest people in off-the-grid locations to communicate with others, there is no indication that these people are able to access benefits like production, creativity, and economic growth, which are afforded to people who have access to mobile phones and computers with Internet connection. In addition, advanced mobile markets like Japan, South Korea, and the United States have the fastest speed and quality of access, which allows users to consume twice as many data as their counterparts in underserved countries. An aspect that is important to the use of mobile phones is the ability to travel to find connectivity.

Digital divides and the future

A growing amount of current research focuses on mobile device penetration and the benefits of using smartphones and tablets for online use among poor, undereducated, and minority populations. Digital divides are complex. Most scholars agree that the digital divide is not a binary concept. The nature of advancement in ICTs reveals the importance of physical access and infrastructure, as well as that of usability through digital literacy. Once hardware, software, and connectivity are provided, there are digital literacy concerns, namely about using ICTs to find relevant information for school, work, and play, to create new online possibilities, and to acquire skills in order to promote economic advancement. These three goals are suited to individuals as well as to institutions.

Mark Zuckerberg, founder and chief executive officer of Facebook, acknowledged that Internet access among poor and disadvantaged people is growing at a slow rate by comparison to the advances made in ICTs. He explains that some people have smartphones without data. He further argues there is no guarantee that most of the people on the planet will ever have Internet access. Closing the gap is important not only for citizens globally, but for future generations. Having ICTs in the school around the world is advocated for by scholars in education and sociology in particular. As the world becomes more connected, there is an awareness that allowing underserved nations to fall behind can cause matters of economic and policy concern.

The digital divide remains an important and powerful concept, which continues to shape and reshape the level and types of disparities among particular populations. While technology is always already moving at lightning speed and some are able to purchase the latest hardware, software, and mobile applications, there are others who cannot. The groups of people who lag behind remain the same: the poor, the undereducated, and racial–ethnic minorities. This triad holds true in any country at any time since the start of the digital revolution. Researchers continue to track data to see whether the digital divide is widening or closing. So far, if one gap narrows, another gap grows. Digital divides are not the product of one problem but of several entities, often connected to offline challenges. A systematic, concerted effort—comprised of grassroots organizations, national, state, and local government, community members, educators, and ICT developers—continues to work toward closing the digital divide gap.

SEE ALSO: Access; Digital Divide and Web-Use Skills; Digital Literacy; Health Media Literacy; Knowledge Structures; Literacy, Technology, and Media; Participatory Action Research

References

Annan, K. (2015). *Digital development: Report of the secretary-general.* Retrieved from http://unctad.org/meetings/en/SessionalDocuments/ecn162015d2_en.pdf

Baller, S., Dutta, S., & Lanvin, B. (Eds.). (2016). *The global information technology report.* Retrieved from http://www3.weforum.org/docs/GITR2016/WEF_GITR_Full_Report.pdf

Gunkel, D.J. (2003). Second thoughts: Toward a critique of the digital divide. *New Media & Society, 5*(4), 499–522.

Hargittai, E. (2002). Second-level digital divide: Differences in people's online skills. *First Monday, 7*(4). Retrieved from http://webuse.org/pdf/Hargittai-SecondLevelFM02.pdf

Huebler, F., & Lu, W. (2012). *Adult and youth literacy: National, regional and global trends, 1990–2015.* Montreal, Canada: UNESCO Institute for Statistics. Retrieved from http://unesdoc.unesco.org/images/0021/002174/217409e.pdf

National Telecommunications and Information Administration. (1998). *Falling through the net II: New data on the digital divide.* Washington, DC. Retrieved from http://www.ntia.doc.gov/ntiahome/net2

OLPC. (2007). One Laptop per Child: Mission. Retrieved from http://laptop.org/en/vision/index.shtml

Pew. (2014). *Mobile technology fact sheet.* Pew Research Center. Retrieved from http://www.pewInternet.org/fact-sheets/mobile-technology-fact-sheet

Further reading

Dolan, J.E. (2016). Splicing the divide: A review of research on the evolving digital divide among K-12 students. *Journal of Research on Technology in Education, 48*(1), 16–37. doi: 10.1080/15391523.2015.1103147

Regnedda, M., & Muschert, G. (Eds.). (2013). *The digital divide: The Internet and social inequality in international perspective.* New York, NY: Routledge.

Rennie, E., Hogan, E., Gregory, R., Crouch, A., Wright, A., & Thomas, J. (2016). *Internet on the outstation: The digital divide and remote Aboriginal communities.* Amsterdam, Netherlands: Institute for Network Cultures. Retrieved from http://networkcultures.org/wp-content/uploads/2016/06/TOD19-Internet-on-the-Outstation-INC.pdf

Younghoon, C., Hyerin, K., Siew, F., & Myeong-Cheol, P. (2015). A comparison of the digital divide across three countries with different development indices. *Journal of Global Information Management, 23*(4), 55–76.

Joy Pierce is associate professor in the Department of Writing and Rhetoric Studies at the University of Utah. She has published in communication, sociology, and qualitative research methods journals, and served as guest editor for a special issue of interdisciplinary journal *Social Identities.* Her research focuses on the digital divide at the intersections of race, class, education, and language. Dr. Pierce's recent book *Digital Fusion: A Society beyond Blind Inclusion* is an ethnographic work that spans 18 years and explores why poor and working-class minorities in two communities do not have home computers and/or Internet access.

Digital Divide and Web-Use Skills

REBECCA B. REYNOLDS and CHRISTOPHER LEEDER
Rutgers University, USA

In US society and worldwide, digital technologies have become ubiquitous in organizational, professional, communications, learning, and personal leisure contexts. Research indicates that uses of technology among the population are associated with social and cultural capital and social mobility (e.g., Livingstone, Van Couvering, & Thumim, 2005; Hargittai, 2010). Mastery of technology and of digital practices is seen as a threshold and point of entry for active participation in online cultures and contexts. Such mastery has been termed "digital literacy," and scholarship links digital skills to democratic participation (e.g., Mossberger, Tolbert & McNeal, 2007; Jenkins, 2009; Knight Commission on Information Needs of Communities in a Democracy, 2009; Hobbs, 2010; Horrigan, 2011).

To inculcate digital skill building and mastery in young people, US education leaders and policy decision-makers have called for an equitable delivery of digital technology interventions in schools. One example of such a US-based policy document is the Federal Communications Commission's National Broadband Plan of 2010, which asserts that broadband access at home is crucial for participation in the digital economy, and calls for wide-reaching digital literacy efforts in schools that should target children from an early age on and should aim to promote greater sophistication of technology uses among them (FCC, 2010; see also FCC, 2017). Another policy-level example is the US Department of Education's sweeping National Education Technology Plan of 2017 (Office of Educational Technology, 2017), originally drafted in 2010, which endorses a deep integration of technologies throughout the education system at all levels, including in the university. Further, national standards frameworks published by education associations such as the American Association of School Librarians (AASL, 2017) and the International Society for Technology in Education (ISTE, 2016) recommend that schools offer information and technology literacy-based programs and curricula that facilitate 21st-century skills, practices, and dispositions. Such national frameworks offer anchors of support for the integration of digital and information technology programs and guidelines toward obtaining the desired learning outcomes.

While policy frameworks and educational imperatives exhort educators to make available digital skills-based learning opportunities for US students, evidence nonetheless continues to support the persistent presence of a digital divide in the US population, which signals that, to date, any such educational efforts have fallen short of equalizing access and facilitating productive and constructive technology uses (e.g., NTIA 1999; Hargittai, 2002; Katz & Levine, 2015).

Given the implications of the digital divide for digital literacy, democratic participation, life, and livelihood outcomes for citizens, this entry addresses the following themes: (i) the various ways in which the digital divide has been defined over time, (ii) present-day empirical findings on the extent of the digital divide in US contexts since 2017, (iii) advances in theoretical conceptualization that expand our understanding of systemic forces at play, and (iv) one example of a solution to the problem of mitigating the digital divide that takes into account such systemic forces in its implementation strategy and includes measurable effects.

Digital divide

The digital divide is defined in simple terms as the gap between those who use computers and the Internet and those who do not (Katz & Levine, 2015, p. 7). The term was popularized in the *Falling Through the Net* reports that were released by the National Telecommunications and Information Administration (NTIA 1995, 1998, 1999). The digital inequality gap has been identified at two levels (Hargittai, 2002): level 1, which reflects inequalities stemming from access to technology (due to both infrastructure and economic cost); and level 2, which reflects inequalities stemming from variations in digital literacy—that is, in the types and sophistication of use and user expertise. Related to the digital divide is the "knowledge gap hypothesis" (Tichenor, Donohue, & Olien, 1970), which suggests that, as the infusion of mass media information into a social system increases, segments of the population with higher socioeconomic status tend to acquire this information at a faster rate than lower-status segments, increasing the gap in knowledge between these groups. Inequalities in technology access may result in knowledge gaps, educational opportunity barriers, and disparities in groups' socioeconomic potential, all of which run counter to the fulfillment of democratic goals and ideals (Bonfadelli, 2002).

Empirical findings supporting evidence of a digital divide in the United States

Here we report on some of the sociodemographic factors that indicate presence of a divide in access and uses around the time of writing. Broadly, as far as access and use go, data from the Pew Research Center indicate that 88% of US adults use the Internet as of 2016 (PRC, 2017). Roughly three-quarters of American adults (73%) have broadband Internet service at home (PRC, 2017). However, racial minorities, older adults, rural residents, and those with lower levels of education and income are less likely to have broadband service at home (PRC, 2017). According to one FCC report, 64.5 million people in the United States are still without high-speed broadband connectivity (FCC, 2016).

Race and ethnicity

Turner (2016) reports that systemic racial discrimination—for example discriminatory housing policies, credit, and lending practices—exacerbates market failures in the broadband market, leading to lower rates of adoption among racial and ethnic minorities, even when controlling for income. Among US adults, 78% of whites have home broadband access by comparison to 65% of blacks and 58% of Hispanics (PRC, 2017). Hispanics and blacks are less likely to own a computer or access the Internet than whites (Katz & Levine, 2015; Perrin, 2017b). Hispanic immigrant families are less digitally connected than other families: one in five (20%) immigrant Hispanic parents does not go online at all, by comparison to 4% of whites and US-born Hispanics and 2% of blacks (Rideout & Katz, 2016).

Age

With regard to age as a digital divide factor, research shows that older adults generally have more difficulty with technology than their younger counterparts and report more often being frustrated when using technology, less likely to regard cell phones and websites as user-friendly, and more likely to feel that the pace of technological innovation moves too fast (Van Volkom, Stapley, & Amaturo, 2014). Among US adults, 77% of people between the ages of 18 and 29 have home broadband access, by comparison to 81% of people aged 30–49, 75% of people aged 50–64, and 51% of people over 65 years old (PRC, 2017). One-third of the adults in this last category say they never use the Internet (Anderson & Perrin, 2017b).

Rural/urban

There has been a long-standing gap between rural and urban populations in their use of the Internet. Even as, overall, Internet use has increased dramatically, still in 2015 the rural/urban gap remained, 69% of rural residents reporting using the Internet compared to 75% of urban residents (Carson & Goss, 2016). Rural Americans are by 10 percentage points less likely than Americans overall to have home broadband (Perrin,

2017a). Along the community criterion, 73% of US adults in urban communities have home broadband access, by comparison to 76% of suburban adults and 63% of rural adults (PRC, 2017). Rural users are less likely than their urban counterparts to report using devices such as a desktop (29% for rural users to 35% for urban users) or a laptop (39% to 48%) and are also less likely to use the Internet from home (Carson & Goss, 2016).

Socioeconomic status

Citing technology maintenance theory, Gonzales (2016) finds that low-income users must work to maintain their access to technology, often experiencing cycles of dependable instability to such access. Lower-income households often retain older computers and devices, which may work slowly or intermittently; those in such households often make sacrifices in order to purchase smartphones and tablets (Katz & Levine, 2015). In terms of socioeconomic status, 53% of US adults who earn less than $30,000 have home broadband access, in comparison to 71% of those who earn $30,000–$49,999, 83% of those who earn $50,000–$74,999, and 93% of those who earn $75,000+ (PRC, 2017). Many low- and moderate-income families rely on mobile-only access (23%; see Rideout & Katz, 2016).

Gender

Regarding gender, among US adults, 74% of men and 72% of women have broadband access at home (PRC, 2017). There are no differences between men and women in the frequency of use of communication technologies, although male respondents in one study report greater ease of adaptation to technology than female respondents; women report more frustration when using technology than men in this study (Van Volkom et al., 2014).

People with disabilities

A digital divide is clearly present for people with disabilities. Significantly fewer people with disabilities (48%) use the Internet than do people without disabilities (80%). Americans with disabilities are more likely than Americans without a disability to say that they never go online (23% vs. 8%) and are roughly 20 percentage points less likely to say that they subscribe to home broadband and own a traditional computer, a smartphone or a tablet (Anderson & Perrin, 2017a).

Barriers to use

Of broadband nonusers in the US, 43% cite financial concerns (the cost either of the monthly service or of the computer itself) as their most important reason for not having broadband service (Horrigan & Duggan, 2015). However, the FCC's 2016 Lifeline Modernization Order, which proposes solutions to the national broadband affordability problem, also recognizes that nonmonetary barriers often impede digital inclusion, for example the lack of digital literacy and the lack of a perception of relevance (FCC, 2016). Other barriers to the adoption of broadband at home include reliance on a smartphone, the availability of alternative ways to access the Internet outside the home, and the lack of available service in rural areas (Horrigan & Duggan, 2015). Nearly half of those who do not have broadband at home—or 15% of all Americans—are in a "hard-to-reach" category, defined as less educated, older, and less connected to technology (Horrigan & Duggan, 2015). Other factors that influence nonuse include lack of comfort with computers and fear of negative experiences (FCC, 2010).

The second-level divide

In recent years, the focus of research on the digital divide has shifted away from physical access to the Internet to a "second level" of the divide, one related to discrepancies in Internet usage and skills (Hargittai, 2002; Lee, Park, & Hwang, 2015; Yu, Ellison, McCammon, & Langa, 2016). In the 1990s, research on the digital divide was focused on ownership, availability, and affordability of infrastructure (level 1), whereas today the focus is placed upon technology *users*, the frequency of their use, and their various types of uses (level 2: digital literacy; see Barzilai-Nahon, 2006). Scholars today call attention to differences in effective and efficient usage of the Internet even when people have gained access (Hargittai & Jennrich, 2016). Research shows that both *frequencies* and *types* of online participation vary by user background and by demographics such as gender, education level, and socioeconomic status (Hargittai & Jennrich, 2016; Van Deursen & Van Dijk, 2014). The second-level divide is also associated with a "democratic divide" between those who actively use the web for political information and activities and those who do not (Min, 2010). Being equipped with the skills to navigate and use the Internet is now seen by policymakers as critical to a meaningful adoption of broadband (FCC, 2017).

In the US context, even among those with moderate-to-high levels of technology access, more sophisticated forms of content creation, participatory engagement, and digital knowledge are associated with higher socioeconomic status and level of education. The higher the level of education, the greater people's self-reported digital skills, and those with higher levels of self-reported skill are more likely to visit the types of websites from which their human and financial capital may benefit. Hargittai (2010) finds that those from more privileged backgrounds use web-based technologies in more sophisticated and beneficial ways for a larger number of activities, with possible implications for social mobility. Approaches such as these indicate that outcome variables used in measuring the digital divide are expanding beyond simple access.

Complex research models

More complex scholarly models that incorporate social and economic theories to explain digital divides serve to further capture dynamic systems at play, at multiple levels of analysis. For example, Barzilai-Nahon (2006) proposes a hypothetical model that encompasses an integrative index of the digital divide and considers factors across levels, for example governmental and social supports/constraints, affordability, use, infrastructure access, accessibility, and sociodemographic factors. Katz, Moran, and Ognyanova (2017) argue that digital inequality be studied in the context of social relationships such as families, not as individualized experiences—and especially with great attention to parental mediation when studying children. Katz et al. (2017) investigate how multiple factors—including Internet connection type and parental mediation variables, such as parents' past experiences with technology and their perceptions and values for technology—when taken together, influence children's uses, in particular among low income families.

Van Dijk (2012) offers a framework for understanding the digital divide drawing upon "resources and appropriation theory," a materialist and relational theory that emphasizes positions and relations, instead of individual attributes. As elaborated in his book *The Deepening Divide* (Van Dijk, 2005), this framework applies resources and appropriation theory to understanding the diffusion, acceptance, and adoption of new technologies. Van Dijk (2012, p. 59) cites the following four concepts as the core of this theory:

1. a number of personal and positional categorical inequalities in society,
2. the distribution of resources relevant to this type of inequality,
3. a number of kinds of access to ICTs,
4. a number of fields of participation in society.

He states that 1 and 2 are held to be the causes and 3 is the phenomenon to be explained, 4 being the potential consequence of the whole process. He states: "4 feeds back upon 1 and 2, as more or less participation in several fields of society will change the relationships of categorical inequalities and the distribution of resources in society" (Van Dijk, 2012, p. 60). A fifth factor determining the type of inequality is also proposed: the special characteristics of information and communication technology. Van Dijk proposes that the core argument can be summarized as follows (p. 60):

1. Categorical inequalities in society produce an unequal distribution of resources.
2. An unequal distribution of resources causes unequal access to digital technologies.
3. Unequal access to digital technologies also depends on the characteristics of these technologies.
4. Unequal access to digital technologies brings about unequal participation in society.
5. Unequal participation in society reinforces categorical inequalities and unequal distributions of resources.

The article states that "the core part of the model is a number of kinds of access in succession. Here the multi-faced concept of access is refined and conceived as the total process of appropriation of a new technology" (p. 61). Van Dijk (2012) thus offers the schematic in Figure 1 as integral to the succession of technology appropriation during the ongoing evolution of the digital divide.

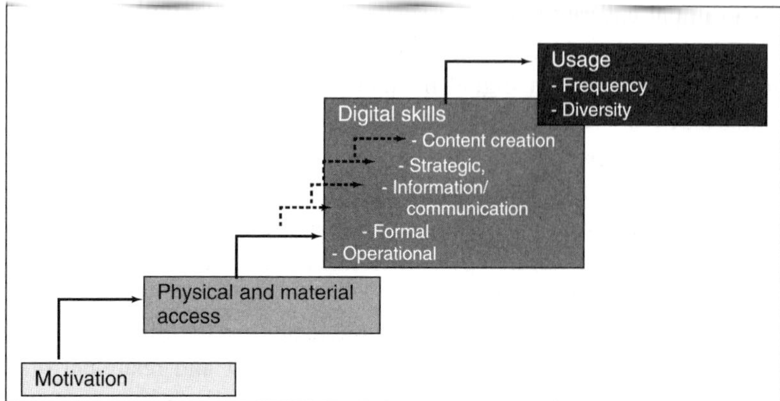

Figure 1 Four successive types of access in the appropriation of digital technology. Source: Van Dijk (2012): 61.

In this model, motivation must be developed sufficiently to access technology, which is mitigated by physical and material resources. Subsequently digital skills must develop, and these factors thereby play into the frequency and diversity of one's types of uses. Sociodemographic factors can interplay at all stages. Theory-based approaches to the study of the digital divide such as these offer important perspectives on how systems at multiple levels of analysis, from individual to structural, play into the entrenchment of digital inequalities in various societal contexts.

Solutions addressing the digital divide

Solutions to mitigate the digital divide would do well to take into account these dynamic systemic forces. One example of an educational program whose work touches multiple points of the Van Dijk model in its solution affordances is the Globaloria e-learning game design program. Globaloria offers an integrated instructional model for constructivist digital literacy development among young people, in which comprehensive introductory computer science educational opportunities are made available to partnering schools as formal classes, offered daily, for credit and a grade (Reynolds, 2016). Most participating schools reside in communities in which the majority of the student population comprises racial, ethnic, and socioeconomic groups that are underrepresented in the technology professions. This educational initiative can be seen to address socio-demographic barriers to motivation per Van Dijk's model, for instance, given that the program focuses on game design as an engaging context for learning deeper computing principles and allows students to participate in fun and purposeful uses of technology designed to raise their awareness of how technology can be useful to them in their lives. The program relies upon in-school infrastructure access such as high-speed Internet, and the availability of standard hardware and software, thus schools must meet these minimum resource thresholds (which is already the case in most US districts). Further, the organization asks for a seat-licensing fee on a per-student basis for the range of services offered, including teacher professional development. If these barriers at the institutional level can be met, then, once they are in place, the blended learning approach that Globaloria provides can activate and motivate students' personal agency across the range of learning dimensions that the program specifies as its objectives (Reynolds, 2016).

Thus far, more than 40,000 students have used Globaloria's computer science platform and courses over the past 12 years, and more than 1,100 teachers and education leaders were trained in the United States between 2006 and 2018. To date, Globaloria has worked predominantly within rural, low-income school communities in the states of West Virginia, Wyoming, and Oklahoma, as well as with Hispanic immigrant and English language learner (ELL) communities in Austin and Houston, Texas and in San Jose, California, and with black and Hispanic students in Queens and the Bronx, New York City. Reynolds (2017) explores the cultural responsiveness factors built into the program that help it to accommodate a successful and tailored implementation in a wide-ranging diversity of school communities with varying needs and conditions.

In conjecturing about the possible effects of student participation in this program, Reynolds and Chiu (2015) hypothesized that, if digital divide gaps such as those seen at the population level (e.g., gender, race, socioeconomics) exist among student participants in Globaloria before their participation, then it may be that those gaps narrow or disappear after students complete the program. Reynolds and Chiu (2015) investigate this line of inquiry in a study of 242 middle and high school student participants in this program, using a multilevel-analysis statistical model. Results show that indeed, while prior to participation the expected demographic inequities were present among students (as supported by past research in the general population), program participation eliminates gender effects and reduces parent education effects for students' computer uses. Further, students from schools with lower average parent education show greater increases in their frequency of technology engagement in school, which also supports the hypothesized gap closure. Program participation also weakens the relationship between students' prior school achievement and advanced technology activities. These results offer evidence that intensive school-based computing educational programs such as Globaloria, if offered at a higher level to diverse students, could measurably reduce digital divide gaps.

School-based settings as venues for equalizing effects

Collins and Halverson (2009) and Collins (2017) note the extent to which public education's funding inequities and variations can actually increase disparities among students and slow down even more the pace of change within school systems. The authors somewhat pessimistically propose that any potential equalizing effect played out through equitable school-based formal educational programs is quickly overridden by the unequal access of families with higher socioeconomic status to high-quality educational opportunities, which are often provided as supplements outside of school. According to these authors, such directed informal learning opportunities tend to favor those who have higher levels of education and socioeconomic advantage and thus awareness and means to participate, which will likely only serve to reinforce and reproduce societal inequalities (Collins & Halverson, 2009; Collins, 2017). However, studies and projects in smaller pockets and regions (e.g., the Globaloria research and other high-quality technology educational experiences directly targeted to diverse students; see Hobbs, 2010) demonstrate ways in which intensively focused educational efforts to support students' digital skills and participation have potential to play a crucial role for those who have the opportunity to encounter them.

This entry encourages readers to pursue intensive, comprehensive, well-designed and researched computing educational instructional experiences that have been developed using sound and rigorous research and development methods and that rely on an evidence base of effects studies backing up their impact. It encourages doing so especially with student populations whose socio-demographics fall in digital divide gap categories. And it advocates for public educational policies and reforms that create more and more viable and vigorous pathways for school district implementation of such experiences.

SEE ALSO: Access; Digital Literacy; Global Citizenship; Mediatization; Participatory Politics and the Civic Dimensions of Media Literacy

References

AASL (American Association of School Librarians). (2017). *Standards framework for learners.* Retrieved from http://standards.aasl.org

Anderson, M., & Perrin, A. (2017a, April 7). Disabled Americans are less likely to use technology. Pew Research Center. Retrieved from http://www.pewresearch.org/fact-tank/2017/04/07/disabled-americans-are-less-likely-to-use-technology

Anderson, M., & Perrin, A. (2017b, May 17). Tech adoption climbs among older adults. Pew Research Center. Retrieved from http://www.pewinternet.org/2017/05/17/tech-adoption-climbs-among-older-adults

Barzilai-Nahon, K. (2006). Gaps and bits: Conceptualizing measurements for digital divide/s. *Information Society, 22*(5), 269–278.

Bonfadelli, H. (2002). The Internet and knowledge gaps: A theoretical and empirical investigation. *European Journal of Communication, 17*(1), 65–84.

Carson, E., & Goss, J. (2016, August 10). The state of the urban/rural digital divide. National Telecommunications and Information Administration. Retrieved from https://www.ntia.doc.gov/blog/2016/state-urbanrural-digital-divide

Collins, A. (2017). *What's worth teaching? Rethinking curriculum in the age of technology.* New York, NY: Teachers College Press.

Collins, A., & Halverson, R. (2009). *Rethinking education in the age of technology. The digital revolution and schooling in America.* New York, NY: Teachers College Press.

FCC (Federal Communications Commission). (2010). Connecting America: The National Broadband Plan. Retrieved from https://www.fcc.gov/general/national-broadband-plan

FCC (Federal Communications Commission). (2016). Lifeline and Link Up reform and modernization [2016 Lifeline Modernization Order]. Retrieved from https://www.fcc.gov/document/fcc-modernizes-lifeline-program-low-income-consumers

FCC (Federal Communications Commission). (2017). Strategies and recommendations for promoting digital inclusion. Retrieved from https://www.fcc.gov/document/strategies-and-recommendations-promoting-digital-inclusion

Gonzales, A. (2016). The contemporary US digital divide: From initial access to technology maintenance. *Information, Communication & Society, 19*(2), 234–248.

Hargittai, E. (2002). Second-level digital divide: Differences in people's online skills. *First Monday, 7*(4). Retrieved from http://firstmonday.org/ojs/index.php/fm/article/view/942/864

Hargittai, E. (2010). Digital na(t)ives? Variation in Internet skills and uses among members of the "net generation." *Sociological Inquiry, 80*(1), 92–113.

Hargittai, E., & Jennrich, K. (2016). The online participation divide. In M. I. Lloyd. & L. Friedland (Eds.), *The communication crisis in America, and how to fix it* (pp. 199–213). New York, NY: Palgrave Macmillan.

Hobbs, R. (2010). Digital & media literacy: A plan of action. White paper issued by the Aspen Institute. Retrieved at http://mediaeducationlab.com

Horrigan, J.B. (2011). What are the consequences of being disconnected in a broadband-connected world? *Daedalus, 140*(4), 17–31.

Horrigan, J.B., & Duggan, M. (2015, December 21). Home broadband 2015. Pew Research Center. Retrieved from http://www.pewinternet.org/2015/12/21/2015/Home-Broadband-2015

ISTE (International Society for Technology in Education). (2016). *Standards for students.* Retrieved from http://www.iste.org/docs/Standards-Resources/iste-standards_students-2016_one-sheet_final.pdf

Jenkins, H. (2009). *Confronting the challenges of participatory culture: Media education for the 21st century.* Cambridge, MA: MIT Press.

Katz, V.S., & Levine, M.H. (2015). Connecting to learn: Promoting digital equity among America's Hispanic families. New York, NY: Joan Ganz Cooney Center at Sesame Street. Retrieved from http://joanganzcooneycenter.org/wp-content/uploads/2015/03/jgcc_connectingtolearn.pdf (downloadable from http://joanganzcooneycenter.org/publication/connecting-to-learn-promoting-digital-equity-for-americas-hispanic-families).

Katz, V.S., Moran, M., & Ognyanova, K. (2017). Contextualizing connectivity: How Internet connection type and parental factors influence technology use among lower-income children. *Information, Communication & Society.* doi: 10.1080/1369118X.2017.1379551

Knight Commission on Information Needs of Communities in a Democracy. (2009). *Informing communities: Sustaining democracy in the digital age* (Commission report). Retrieved from http://www.knightfoundation.org/research_publications/detail.dot?id=355939

Lee, H., Park, N., & Hwang, Y. (2015). A new dimension of the digital divide: Exploring the relationship between broadband connection, smartphone use and communication competence. *Telematics and Informatics, 32*(1), 45–56.

Livingstone, S., Van Couvering, E., & Thumim, N. (2005). *Adult media literacy: A review of the research literature.* London, England: Office of Communications (Ofcom). Retrieved February 1, 2005 from http://www.ofcom.org.uk/consumer_guides/media_literacy

Min, S. J. (2010). From the digital divide to the democratic divide: Internet skills, political interest, and the second-level digital divide in political Internet use. *Journal of Information Technology & Politics, 7*(1), 22–35.

Mossberger, K., Tolbert, C., & McNeal, R. (2007). *Digital citizenship: The Internet, society, and participation.* Cambridge, MA: MIT Press.

National Telecommunications and Information Administration. (1995). *Falling through the net: A survey of the "have nots" in rural and urban America.* Washington, DC: National Telecommunications and Information Administration. Retrieved from https://www.ntia.doc.gov/ntiahome/fallingthru.html

National Telecommunications and Information Administration. (1998). *Falling through the net II: New data on the digital divide*. Washington, DC: National Telecommunications and Information Administration. Retrieved from https://www.ntia.doc.gov/ntiahome/net2

National Telecommunications and Information Administration. (1999). *Falling through the net: Defining the digital divide*. Washington, DC: National Telecommunications and Information Administration. Retrieved from https://www.ntia.doc.gov/report/1999/falling-through-net-defining-digital-divide

Office of Educational Technology. (2017). National Education Technology Plan. Retrieved from https://tech.ed.gov/netp.

Perrin, A. (2017a, May 19). Digital gap between rural and nonrural America persists. Pew Research Center. Retrieved from http://www.pewresearch.org/fact-tank/2017/05/19/digital-gap-between-rural-and-nonrural-america-persists

Perrin, A. (2017b, August 31). Smartphones help blacks: Hispanics bridge some—but not all—digital gaps with whites. Pew Research Center. Retrieved from http://www.pewresearch.org/fact-tank/2017/08/31/smartphones-help-blacks-hispanics-bridge-some-but-not-all-digital-gaps-with-whites

PRC (Pew Research Center). (2017, January 12). Internet/broadband fact sheet. Retrieved from http://www.pewinternet.org/fact-sheet/internet-broadband

Reynolds, R. (2016). Defining, designing for, and measuring "digital literacy" development in learners: A proposed framework. *Educational Technology Research & Development, 64*(4), 735–762.

Reynolds, R. (2017). Adapting online blended E-learning solutions to diverse K-12 school contexts: Lessons learned and opportunities for future development. Paper presented at the Annual Meeting of the Association for Information Science and Technology, 2017, SIGUSE Workshop, Washington, DC.

Reynolds, R., & Chiu, M. (2015). Reducing digital divide effects through student engagement in coordinated game design, online resource uses, and social computing activities in school. *Journal of the Association for Information Science and Technology, 67*(8), 1822–1835.

Rideout, V.J., & Katz, V.S. (2016). *Opportunity for all? Technology and learning in lower-income families*. New York, NY: Joan Ganz Cooney Center at Sesame Workshop. Retrieved from http://joanganzcooneycenter.org/publication/opportunity-for-all-technology-and-learning-in-lower-income-families

Tichenor, P.J., Donohue, G.A., & Olien, C.N. (1970). Mass media flow and differential growth in knowledge. *Public Opinion Quarterly, 34*(2), 159–170.

Turner, S.D. (2016). Digital denied: The impact of systemic racial discrimination on home-internet adoption. Free Press. Retrieved from http://www.freepress.net/sites/default/files/resources/digital_denied_free_press_report_december_2016.pdf

Van Deursen, A.J., & Van Dijk, J.A. (2014). The digital divide shifts to differences in usage. *New Media & Society, 16*(3), 507–526.

Van Dijk, J.A.G.M. (2005). *The deepening divide: Inequality in the information society*. Thousand Oaks, CA: SAGE.

Van Dijk, J.A.G.M. (2012). The evolution of the digital divide. In J. Bus, M. Crompton, M. Hildebrandt, & G. Metakides (Eds.), *Digital enlightenment yearbook 2012* (pp. 57–78). Amsterdam, Netherlands: IOS Press.

Van Volkom, M., Stapley, J.C., & Amaturo, V. (2014). Revisiting the digital divide: Generational differences in technology use in everyday life. *North American Journal of Psychology, 16*(3), 557–574.

Yu, R.P., Ellison, N.B., McCammon, R.J., & Langa, K.M. (2016). Mapping the two levels of digital divide: Internet access and social network site adoption among older adults in the USA. *Information, Communication & Society, 19*(10), 1445–1464.

Further reading

Anderson, M. (2017, March 22). Digital divide persists even as lower-income Americans make gains in tech adoption. Pew Research Center. Retrieved from http://www.pewresearch.org/fact-tank/2017/03/22/digital-divide-persists-even-as-lower-income-americans-make-gains-in-tech-adoption

Dobransky, K., & Hargittai, E. (2016). Unrealized potential: Exploring the digital disability divide. *Poetics, 58*, 18–28.

Reynolds, R., & Chiu, M. (2012). Contribution of motivational orientations to student outcomes in a discovery-based program of game design learning. Paper presented at the International Conference of the Learning Sciences (ICLS), July 2012, Sydney, Australia.

Reynolds, R., & Chiu, M. (2013). Formal and informal context factors as contributors to student engagement in a guided discovery-based program of game design learning. *Journal of Learning, Media & Technology, 38*(4), 429–462.

Reynolds, R., & Harel Caperton, I. (2011). Contrasts in student engagement, meaning-making, dislikes, and challenges in a discovery-based program of game design learning. *Journal of Educational Technology Research and Development, 59*(2), 267–289.

Rebecca B. Reynolds is associate professor in the Department of Library and Information Science at Rutgers University's School of Communication & Information. Her work addresses the design, development, and deployment of e-learning systems in formal school settings in K-12 (primary and secondary education in the United States). Her work also investigates social constructivist human learning in naturalistic online participatory settings, including social media environments and massive open online courses (MOOCs). She has addressed in her work student digital literacy development, iterative design and development of educational technologies, and learning analytics, as well as educational problems and solutions related to the digital divide. She holds a PhD in mass communication with interdisciplinary studies in information science from Syracuse University, along with an MA from Syracuse University in Media Studies and BA from Tufts University in Sociology. Her work has been funded by an early career grant from the Institute for Museum and Library Services.

Christopher Leeder is postdoctoral research associate and instructor at the Rutgers School of Communication & Information. He completed his PhD at the University of Michigan. Publishing widely in the field of library and information science, he is a known researcher and teaching expert in the area of information-seeking and information literacy.

Digital Literacy

ROBERT J. BARON
Austin Peay State University, USA

Digital literacy describes the set of skills necessary for an individual to access, navigate, understand, and contribute to the modern digital information economy. Put another way, it is the skill set necessary for a person to be an active member of the modern Internet-mediated world. Like more general media literacy, developing digital literacy requires a person to learn how to "read," and understand, digitally mediated information; however, due to the interactive nature of many digital technologies, digital literacy also requires individuals to develop skills beyond being able to simply comprehend the messages they receive through digital media. To be considered digitally literate, a person needs to understand: (i) how to use modern digital technologies to access information, (ii) how to maneuver through the complex web of information made available by digital technologies, (iii) how to "read" and understand the messages on digital media, and (iv) how he or she can contribute to the digital information economy by using digital technology.

Unpacking digital literacy

Earlier conceptions of digital literacy often put a central focus on understanding computers as a new communication medium. For example, in one of the earliest formulations of the concept, Gilster (1997) defined digital literacy as: "The ability to understand and use information in multiple formats from a wide range of sources when it is presented via computers. The concept of literacy goes beyond simply being able to read; it has always meant the ability to read with meaning, and to understand. It is the fundamental act of cognition. Digital literacy likewise extends the boundaries of definition. It is cognition of what you see on the computer screen when you use the networked medium" (pp. 1–2).

In a similar vein, Gurak (1999) coined her own term for digital literacy, what she called "cyberliteracy," to describe "an electronic literacy—newly emerging in a new medium—that combines features of both print and the spoken word and it does so in ways that change how we read, speak, think, and interact with others" (p. 14). Both of these early formulations of digital literacy put specific emphasis on the "newness" of the Internet. They also show the roots of modern digital literacy's focus on understanding digital technology's role in changing and shaping the way users communicate.

It is important to note, however, that these and other, earlier works on digital literacy often focused on the Internet as a specific thing set apart from users' everyday lives. In the early days of the Internet, users would use their computers to "log in to the World Wide Web" or to "visit cyberspace." Today, one's digital media interactions seamlessly meld themselves into the fabric of everyday life. The rise of smart devices, wireless Internet access, Internet-integrated apps, and online services mean that modern Internet users are almost always "online" in some way. Today, instead of needing to "log in" to the Internet, users often need to make the conscious decision to "log out." The Internet's increased presence in daily life, in part, stems from the development of Web 2.0 as a digital design philosophy. O'Reilly (2005) outlined Web 2.0 as a series of design decisions made by technology companies in the early 21st century that put a greater focus on, among other things: using the Internet as a platform for services, harvesting user data, enabling collaboration and harnessing the power of that collaboration, and providing richer user experiences. The rise of Web 2.0 as an overall design philosophy has led to many of the integrated media experiences of modern digital life.

A key part of understanding the complexity of modern digital literacy is unpacking the Internet's dual role as both a communication medium and a more generalized technological platform. In certain cases, the Internet acts as a communication medium, enabling very specific kinds of digitally mediated exchanges and very particular kinds of digital communication. For example, two friends chatting over an instant messaging service or sharing photos through a social networking app like Snapchat are clearly examples of communication. In other cases, the Internet acts more as a generalized technology, allowing for digital versions of previously nondigital media experiences. For example, a person trying to access a TV program on a digital video streaming service like *Netflix* or *Hulu* or listening to music through an audio streaming service like *Pandora* or *Spotify* is using digital technology, but *not necessarily* digital technology as a medium. Buckingham (2006) notes that "digital literacy is much more than a functional matter of learning how to use a computer and a keyboard, or how to do online searches" (p. 267); rather, to be media literate a user needs "to be able to evaluate and use information critically if they are to transform it into knowledge. This means asking questions about the sources of that information, the interests of its producers, and the ways in which it represents the world; and understanding how these technological developments are related to broader social, political and economic forces" (p. 267).

Media scholars need to keep this distinction in mind as they work to make sense of the ways in which digital technology continues to change and shape the larger media.

Being digitally literate

Modern digital media users live and work in an atmosphere of digital information. Thus, trying to explain digital literacy is often like trying to explain air: one does not notice it until it is suddenly in short supply. Therefore, to better understand what it means to live in "a digital world," it is important to unpack each of the four parts of digital literacy outlined above.

Accessing digital media

Being digitally literate means understanding how to access information available through digital media technologies. Users need to know how to use digital technology to access information. The concept of access could also be thought of as basic "computer literacy." Unfortunately, the term computer literacy is often too limiting and calls to mind images of desktop home computers and "surfing the Internet." Understanding access as a part of digital literacy requires a more nuanced and complex understanding of just how digital the modern world has become. Today, digital technology is a broad category that encompasses everything from desktop computers, to mobile devices, to so-called "smart appliances," to wearable technologies. Thus, access, as related to digital literacy, is less about developing a specific set of skills with a specific device, and more about being able to access digital information and services from any number of interlinked devices. Learning how to access digital information means learning a multitude of technological skills.

Media literacy scholars need to understand the changing face of digital media access. For example, scholars increasingly need to consider the ways in which access to digital information is shaped by the design of online systems. Lessig (1999) highlighted the role that design and coding can play in shaping online interactions and behaviors. He noted that design decisions made by those in control of various digital systems' code can have huge impacts on the very nature of the Internet itself. As more information is made available online, and as technology companies work to make that information more "accessible" by streamlining and simplifying user interfaces, more and more subtle control is locked behind walls of code. Scholars also need to continue to examine key issues in access such as the ongoing "digital divide" between those who have access to the Internet and those who do not. While the rise of lower-cost computers, smartphones, and wireless Internet infrastructure have done much to alleviate the barriers to basic Internet access, the quality of that access remains an open question.

Navigating digital media

Being digitally literate means learning how to navigate the Internet. Being able to access the vast amount of information presented online is only the first step toward digital literacy. Once a person has developed the ability to access digital information, he or she must then learn how to move through the complex web of information presented by the modern Internet. These are two separate skills: just because a person has learned how to access the Internet doesn't necessarily mean that the same person knows what to do once he or she is online. Today's digital media users need to understand how to navigate a complex array of online technologies, information, and digitally mediated relationships to reach the information that they need. As an example of this distinction between access and navigation, consider danah boyd's (2014) discussion of youth digital culture. boyd argued that the assumption that certain Internet users are "digital natives," having an inherent understanding of how to use the Internet, is dangerous as "it allows some to eschew responsibility for helping youths and adults *navigate a networked world*. If we view skills and knowledge as inherently generational, then organized efforts to achieve needed forms of literacy are unnecessary" (p. 197, emphasis added). Once an Internet user has learned how to access digital media, he or she must additionally learn how to navigate the web of information that the modern digital media provide. In some cases, this navigation is as simple as learning how to sift through the results of an Internet search to find the information that is useful. In other cases, it might mean learning how to navigate between multiple topic-specific online spaces that offer more in-depth information.

Examining navigation as a part of media literacy also means understanding the social and cultural forces that shape the ways in which people use the Internet. Hargittai (2005) observes that "As the Internet spreads to an increasing portion of the population and as online services start permeating more and more parts of people's daily lives, nuanced measures of Internet use will gain importance for research on the social implications of information technologies" (p. 376). Digital media users' political views, ideological stances, and social networks can play a huge role in shaping which information those users find credible and valuable, and what information sources they regard as biased or trustworthy. In boyd's (2017) examination of the limits of media literacy education, she noted that much of the "tribalism" at play in modern American culture is caused by cultural forces like "our culture of doubt and critique, experience over expertise, and personal responsibility." She further noted that "media literacy asks people to raise questions and be wary of information that they're receiving. People are. Unfortunately, that's exactly why we're talking past one another." Scholars need to consider the powerful role that social networks play in shaping online actions. Users need to learn not only how to navigate between several sources of information, but also how to navigate the complex web of cultural assumption and social connections that guide their steps online.

Reading digital media

Being digitally literate means being able to understand and evaluate the information acquired from digital media. This aspect of modern digital literacy echoes the earlier definitions of digital literacy offered by Gilster (1997) and Gurak (1999) above. As more information is made available through the Internet, this skill requires greater development. Due to the proliferation of information on digital media platforms, understanding digital media also requires users to become proficient in evaluating the information they receive. In this way, digital media literacy is increasingly a practice in information literacy. Since so much information is available on the Internet, it is incumbent on users to learn how to be selective and critical of the information they choose to consume. For example, users need to evaluate the information they get from established media companies like *The New York Times*, the British Broadcasting Corporation (BBC), or *Le Monde* against information that comes from smaller news sources, alternative media, or even false sources of information that are circulated among their social groups on social media platforms like Facebook and Twitter.

While the core concept of users needing to "read" digital information hasn't changed much in the past 20 years, the context in which that information is read has changed. For one, scholars now need to consider the increasing importance of several new, fully digital, media experiences like video games, online social networking, and social media apps. Additionally, the proliferation of information has led to an increased need for critical awareness when looking at information online. Digital literacy scholars need to be mindful of the ways in which different kinds of information circulate online and the role that users' social networks play in promoting and distributing certain kinds of content. Additionally, digital media today are very often multimedia, combining multiple media formats, and thus multiple other forms of media literacy. Thus, being digitally literate means developing a multidimensional form of media literacy that often encompasses things like visual literacy and data literacy.

Creating digital media

Finally, being digitally literate means recognizing one's ability to make digital media and to participate in the digital information economy. One of the hallmarks for digital media literacy is the ability of users to harness the power of digital media to become media-makers themselves. Before the advent of digital media technologies, mediated communication was often unidirectional. To be a media producer required the ownership of expensive equipment and upfront material capital. With the advent of digital media technologies, the barriers to message production have become much lower. Users are increasingly empowered to make media with easy-to-use digital tools. Blogs are an example of this participatory potential. Before the advent of blogging, being able to distribute written language to the public required access to printing presses, publishers, and distributors. More recently, but none-the-less daunting, publishing online through a personal webpage would have required a web hosting service and knowledge of writing HTML (Hypertext Markup Language). Today, however, blogging is as simple as creating a page on a web hosting service or even creating a profile on a microblogging platform like Twitter or Wiebo.

In looking ahead to the future of production as a part of digital literacy, scholars are increasingly working to understand the ways in which digital technologies are changing the production–consumption dynamic at play in the larger media. As an example of this, consider the remix culture movement empowering users to "remix," and make, new media texts from the media they consume. Modern digital technologies put a host of powerful digital media creation tools at their users' fingertips (or in their pockets), and this has drastically reframed the ways in which users can interact with the media. Today, a digital media user can rip, record, edit, remix, upload, and share his or her own media creations through a host of apps on simple devices like smartphones. Digital literacy scholars need to understand the participatory nature of digital media if they hope to truly understand modern digital literacy.

SEE ALSO: Access; Data Literacy; Digital Divide; Digital Media in Higher Education; History of Media Literacy; Literacy, Technology, and Media; Media Literacy for the 21st Century Teacher; News Literacies; Online Reading; Participation through Public Media: Improving Media Literacy among Vulnerable Youth; Remix Culture; Visual Literacy; Web Television

References

boyd, d. (2014). *It's complicated: The social lives of networked teens*. New Haven, CT: Yale University Press.

boyd, d. (2017, January 5). *Did media literacy backfire?* Retrieved from http://points.datasociety.net/did-media-literacy-backfire-7418c084d88d

Buckingham, D. (2006). Defining digital literacy: What do young people need to know about digital media? *Digital Kompetanse: Nordic Journal of Digital Literacy, 4*(1), 253–276.

Gilster, P. (1997). *Digital literacy*. New York, NY: Wiley.

Gurak, L. (1999). *Cyberliteracy: Navigating the Internet with awareness*. New Haven, CT: Yale University Press.

Hargittai, E. (2005). Survey measures of web-oriented digital literacy. *Social Science Computer Review, 23*(1), 371–379. doi: 10.1177/0894439305275911

Lessig, L. (1999). *Code and other laws of cyberspace*. New York, NY: Basic Books.

O'Reilly, T. (2005, September 30). *What is Web 2.0?* Retrieved from http://www.oreilly.com/lpt/a/1

Further reading

Fuchs, C. (2017). *Social media: A critical introduction* (2nd ed.). Los Angeles, CA: SAGE.

Jenkins, H. (2006). *Convergence culture: Where old and new media collide*. New York, NY: NYU Press.

Lankshear, C., & Knobel, M. (Eds.). (2008). *Digital literacies: Concepts, policies and practices*. New York, NY: Peter Lang.

Shirkey, C. (2008). *Here comes everybody: The power of organizing without organizations*. New York, NY: Penguin Books.

Stephenson, N. (1999). *In the beginning ... was the command line*. New York, NY: Avon Books.

Robert J. Baron received his PhD in rhetoric, scientific, and technical communication from the University of Minnesota-Twin Cities in 2012. He is currently an assistant professor of communication at Austin Peay State University in Clarksville, Tennessee. He teaches classes in rhetoric and persuasive theory, social media, video game studies, and media literacy. His research looks at the intersection of rhetorical theory and digital technology. His past research has examined a diverse array of topics including digital architecture in online games, the development of ethos through online collaboration, and presidential rhetoric. His current research interests include topics such as the rhetoric of social media, social media storytelling, video game studies, and classical and contemporary rhetorical theory.

Digital Media and Information Rights

VALENTINA BAÚ
University of New South Wales, Australia

ENRICO CALANDRO
Research ICT Africa, South Africa

This entry advances theoretical reflections in the area of digital media access and citizen engagement and participation through digital communications. Specifically, it seeks to provide a conceptual framework to examine the relationship between economic development, civic and political participation, and access to digital media in countries where rights such as freedom of speech and information are not always upheld by governments.

What is observed is that improving access to digital media in a country by providing good quality, low-cost Internet service and IT (information technology) literacy does not necessarily facilitate a country's development when those media are subjected to government control. The issue this raises, in contrast, is that improved digital media access may result in increased control and restriction of freedoms in cases where telecommunications and Internet infrastructures are under government control. A rights-based approach to digital media access is therefore a crucial prerequisite in the formulation of developmental policy in this field.

The discussion is built around a number of examples from the African continent, belonging to contexts where access to digital media often rests on political interests and where compliance to human rights obligations such as access to information and freedom of expression is problematic. Particular emphasis is placed on two practical cases: the social media blackout during the 2016 Ugandan elections (Access Now, 2016) and the Internet shutdown during the elections in the Democratic Republic of Congo (DRC) that took place in 2015 (Bariyo, 2015) and in 2016 (Fox, 2016). In the Ugandan case, the population reacted to the social media shutdown by using encryption and Virtual Private Network (VPN) technologies (Atuhaire & Atuhaire, 2016), which allowed citizens to overcome limitations on freedom of expression and gave them access to information during the election period (Article19, 2016). In March 2016, during the presidential elections in the DRC, the government imposed a 48-hour shutdown of telecommunications services, attributing its actions to "reasons of security and national safety" and leaving the population without mobile network services, SMS (Short Message Service), and Internet on the day of the election (Global Voice Advocacy, 2016).

Digital media and society

Around the world, digital technology is seen as vital for economic development. In the United States alone, the Internet accounts for about 6% of the entire economy. Digital technology has expanded its role in the global economy in recent years, as both developed and developing nations have become increasingly reliant on the Internet (World Bank, 2016). The centrality of the Internet to social and economic life recently led the United Nations to enact a resolution supporting the "promotion, protection and enjoyment of human rights on the Internet." The resolution specifically condemns state efforts to intentionally inhibit or disrupt access to information online (United Nations General Assembly, 2016).

The growth of Internet use has a direct effect on the circulation of human rights principles and their application. As Kulnazarova (2014) explains, "[i]n the context of human interactions, the new and increasingly popular social media, such as Facebook, Weiboo, Twitter or LinkedIn, play a greater role—social media is a powerful instrument, which has a growing impact on shaping, changing and influencing public opinion through discussion and collective action" (p. 397). The role that these platforms have in encouraging a dynamic discussion in different directions can have a clear impact on public participation. This is demonstrated by the influence social media have on shaping government policies through comments, criticism, and responses provided by the public (Kulnazarova, 2014).

The Internet and the services that its infrastructure provides have created an ecosystem around which people's businesses and daily lives revolve. Internet infrastructure has permeated every aspect of people's existence, from social communications, information, and entertainment to health, commerce, education, and more. The Internet has made communications and information tasks for individuals and businesses fast, easy, and efficient. Despite the role of the Internet as a catalyst for economic activity, in recent times there have been a number of Internet disruptions instigated by public authorities. These have included temporary and complete shutdowns of Internet connectivity across several countries, and the blocking of specific messaging and social media services.

Governments attempt to justify Internet shutdowns by citing a variety of reasons, such as stopping people from sharing information, hindering the organization of protests during elections, or preventing unrest during public holidays, among others (Olukotun, 2016).

At the time of the Windhoek Declaration in 1991 on a free, independent, and pluralistic press, most African countries were only starting on a journey toward improved freedom of information. This was taking place after a number of decades that saw military regimes, one-party states, and the South African apartheid regime regularly perpetrating violations of media freedom. Those affected by these violations were mostly journalists, who were often detained, killed, arrested, sent to exile, or imprisoned. Along with these were the bombing of printing presses, closure of critical media houses, and state control of the broadcasting system and its regulation. Draconian laws were also passed preventing the normal functions of journalists (Kupe, 2016).

There is a wide range of tools that governments can draw on to limit a public use of the Internet that is politically challenging. The most widespread method involves the application of filters consisting of firewalls and proxy servers to the Internet traffic; this prevents users from accessing materials that can be regarded as morally or politically inconsonant. This type of censorship has, of course, its limits. There are many expert users who are able to circumvent the blockages and find their way into anti-government websites or access other material that is considered politically or culturally sensitive. Governments that are more fearful of or simply attentive to this practice of bypassing censored content enforce stricter methods such as public access restrictions to the Internet (Kalathil & Boas, 2003).

As well as manifest forms of control such as restricting access and applying censorship, authorities can also adopt more "subtle" strategies to disrupt Internet use when this is regarded as a threat. These consist of measures such as promoting self-censorship, which is usually backed by a series of high-profile arrests, and urging Internet companies to filter online content and be vigilant about their users' online behavior. These strategies allow the government to limit Internet access and communication without the use of firewalls or other technical means. Authorities in oppressive regimes ensure that users become promptly aware of what is considered an acceptable use of the Internet from a political standpoint; once this understanding is cemented, it becomes a useful avenue to sidestep blanket censorship. Where opposition parties exist, these have not been allowed to enjoy the benefits of online communication and Internet use more generally. On the whole, parties that have chosen to resist the regime have either been banned or made inoperable online through the use of political control (Kalathil & Boas, 2003).

Shutting down the web

From an economic perspective, a recent report from Deloitte (2016) explains that a temporary Internet shutdown has a significant impact on the GDP (gross domestic product) of a country. Specifically, the impact on GDP amounts to a loss of US$6.6 million for medium connectivity countries and to one of US$0.6 million for low connectivity economies. Even though, according to Deloitte (2016), the magnitude of the economic impact of temporary disruptions to the Internet ecosystem varies on the basis of the means, length, and target of the disruption, as well as of a country's existing levels of Internet connectivity, with specific reference to the economic context of most African countries, where both per capita GDP and level of connectivity are low, a temporary Internet shutdown can cause an estimated GDP loss of US$3 million per day. This amounts to 0.4% of the overall GDP of a country.

Internet shutdowns can have far-ranging consequences that go beyond the negative effects on the economy. Not only do they prevent citizens from connecting with family and friends and restrain them from accessing information and communications channels, but they can also make it difficult to request help in case of an emergency. If a country is already experiencing unrest, this can lead to serious human rights abuses. Internet shutdown obstructs the free flow of information and reporting. Cutting off communication and closing the medium for transmission of sensitive and crucial information from a crisis prone/inflicted area might prove to be detrimental rather than beneficial, as accurate and real-time reporting are necessary for relief and disaster management. Because the Internet has become a medium which caters for everyone's needs, irrespective of geographical, social, or economic boundaries, the unavailability of this channel has, for example, an impact on people's ability to access education and mobile phone money transaction services, especially in developing countries where large numbers of the population rely on these services. Also, across many African countries, social media have become the main gate of access to the Internet, and instant messaging services such as WhatsApp have substituted expensive SMS and voice call packages (Calandro & Chair, 2016).

Furthermore, Internet shutdowns restrict freedom of opinion and expression, which are cornerstones for the democratic functioning of a country, and therefore raise serious concerns about the motives of governments that resort to such measures when citizens are called to the polls. As the Internet makes possible both the consumption and the dissemination of information, its interruption represents a profound restriction on freedom of speech and expression for a country's population (Internet Governance Forum, 2016). The growing importance of the Internet has meant that its access has now become a significant public issue, not only in terms of promotion and provision, but also in relation to absence or limitation.

According to Duru Aydin (2016), Internet shutdowns are more likely to happen in countries where laws are outdated, overbroad, and not transparent, and when international standards do not disallow them. In India, for example, the government can use a telegraph law dating to 1885 to defend its decision to take over a provider's network. In other countries, governments can use telecommunications laws that were passed or updated before the Internet was recognized as an enabler of economic growth and social development. Other countries have very broad definitions of a "national emergency," which may leave the door open to misuse of the law. In addition, it has been acknowledged that the International Telecommunications Union (ITU) has provisions in its constitution that could be interpreted to justify an Internet shutdown (Duru Aydin, 2016). Article 34 on the Stoppage of Telecommunications gives permission to ITU member countries to block telecommunications "which may appear dangerous to the security of the State or contrary to its laws, to public order or to decency." Also, Article 35 on the Suspension of Services gives member states "the right to suspend the international telecommunication service" (Duru Aydin, 2016).

According to RightsCon (2016), "[I]nternet shutdown [is] an intentional disruption of Internet or electronic communications, rendering them inaccessible or effectively unusable, for a specific population or within a location, often to exert control over the flow of information." Although the African Declaration on Internet Rights and Freedoms (http://africaninternetrights.org/) emphasizes the importance of Internet Access and Affordability (Art. 2), Freedom of Expression (Art. 3), Right to Information (Art. 4), and Right to Development and Access to Knowledge (Art. 7), an alarmingly growing number of African states have shut down the Internet or social media to curb political dissent during presidential elections (Dahir, 2016a). After shut-downs in Egypt, Uganda, Burundi, Central African Republic, Mali, Zambia, Ethiopia, Chad, DRC, Congo Brazzaville, Gabon, Zimbabwe, Niger, and Togo, on November 30, 2016, Internet became inaccessible and international calls were blocked also in Gambia (Dahir, 2016a; Withnall, 2016). Both in the DRC and in Gambia, presidents came to power through military coups and later amended the constitution to remove limits to the presidential term. During presidential elections, both ordered the main telecommunication providers to cut services.

In Uganda, the presidential election of May 2016 saw the Ugandan president Yoweri Museveni sworn in for his fifth term in a climate of social media censorship. Journalists and nonprofit digital watchdogs in the country reported that from May 11, 2016, Twitter, Facebook, and WhatsApp were censored (Propa, 2016). A similar episode occurred in February 2016, when authorities blocked all access to social media and mobile phone money transfer services for three days during the presidential election, citing security concerns and a threat to public order and safety as the reasons for such a decision (Butagira, 2016).

In Uganda, again, restrictive measures to manage media information had already been adopted in 2013, when two media houses faced temporary closure due to the publication of articles that suggested that Museveni was already mentoring his son to take over the presidency. Prior to a presidential election, debate around presidential succession, accountability of public resources, governance, and other politically sensitive topics is typically constrained (Human Rights Watch, 2014). In 2013 the Public Order Management bill was passed, further restricting space for dissent and public critiques of governance. The law grants policymakers wide discretionary powers to permit or prohibit public meetings (Human Rights Watch, 2014). The Gambia, a country with a repressive history of murdering, jailing, or forcing dissidents into exile, recently banned the Internet and international calls as presidential elections were being held (BBC, 2016). Gabon has also experienced similar circumstances (Dahir, 2016b).

In the DRC, Interior Minister Raymond Zéphirin Mboulou ordered the two main telecommunications providers (MTN Congo and Airtel Congo) to cut Internet and telephone services for two days during the country's presidential elections in March 2016. The Congolese government indicated, once again, security as the main reason for its actions (Konviser, 2016).

These actions go against the United Nations resolution passed in July 2016, which condemns Internet shutdowns (United Nations General Assembly, 2016). Moreover, the cases presented here show how, despite the rapid increase of digital media access thanks to higher levels of competition and a reduction of prices for telecommunications services, the connection between increased access to digital media and social development may be disputable. In countries such as Uganda and the DRC, the enablement of participatory civil and political processes through access and use of digital media appears to be prevented by a digital media environment characterized by government control and censorship.

The impact of restricting online access

Authoritarian governments contribute significantly in defining a blueprint for the development of information and communication technologies such as the Internet in their countries, and in deciding how online platforms should serve economic, political, and even societal actors. Through the enforcement of targeted policies on electronic government (E-government) and the manipulation of key industries, despotic regimes put in place mechanisms that are set out to benefit primarily the state through the use of the Internet. By means of these schemes, the state is able to extend its reach significantly, despite the presence of users and content that want to challenge the authority. In addition to that, since both the physical and policy frameworks of the Internet are established by the state, the environment in which this technology is used is shaped from the top. As a consequence of this architecture, nongovernmental actors that engage in Internet use for their political action have very limited effects. Public Internet users may choose to refrain from browsing through politically sensitive material online, and businesses might find cooperation with the government more convenient than attempting to challenge its censorship (Kalathil & Boas, 2003).

Within this context, for groups that are typically outside the institutional sphere, such as activist groups, having their voices heard is too often a challenge. The asymmetrical dependency that characterizes the relationship between mainstream media and these alternative voices is one that sees the media at the center of the communication network and leaves activists on the side. Moreover, becoming engaged in a purposeful debate can only occur in a reality of freedom of expression and of participation in mainstream media deliberations. Hence, when mainstream media are state-owned, dictated by commercial imperatives, or subjected to other forms of repression, the impact of activist groups on the public discourse can be marginal. In order to gain media attention and produce a shift in this asymmetrical relationship, new creative ways must be sought that allow activists to reach the broader public (Pointer, Bosch, Chuma, & Wasserman, 2016).

It is not only activists who have reacted to Internet shutdowns. In the case of Uganda, the three-day social media ban in May 2016 did not stop nearly 15% of Internet users (approximately 1.5 million citizens) from circumventing the block and accessing social media platforms by means of VPN software. People chose to subvert the ban to express their political dissent, in spite of the risks of prosecution. VPN allows Internet connections to reroute and return to social media. VPN uses encryption and other security mechanisms to provide a secure and encoded channel that protects users' online activity and identity. On social media, users reported their views on a number of irregularities with the election process and sent reports about polling station results and vote-rigging, which occurred mostly in the form of pre-ticked ballot papers. Users also posted information about the location of strikes and roadblocks, and the location of police and their conduct toward protesters. The hashtag #Ugandadecides was used to share opinions and information on the election, and an informal business service to download VPN onto a smartphone for UGX5000 (US$1.5) emerged in Kampala. However, when the Uganda Communications Commission became aware of this subversive scheme, a statement was released through WBS TV Uganda (Wavah Broadcasting Services television) threatening to arrest VPN users for treason (Phillips & Atuhaire, 2016).

In the DRC, the activist group *Lucha* (Lutte pour Le Changement) pledged to carry out a "revolution with or without social networks," organizing protests and demanding the resignation of President Kabila. At the same time, in order to overcome the Internet blockage that was disrupting their activities, advocates shared tips on how to use neighboring countries' networks (Buchanan, 2016).

In other parts of the globe, such as India, Internet shutdowns have almost become the norm. Mobile Internet and broadband services have been cut during times of political unrest; during protests over jobs; to curtail election campaigning; and even to prevent cheating in examinations, which has been leading government officials to impose excessive restrictions (Bhattacharya, 2017; Human Rights Watch, 2017). The government has failed to explain shutdowns and to follow legal procedures, undermining stated objectives that sought to prevent violence fueled by rumors and by false information circulated on social media or mobile messaging applications.

In the region of Kashmir, in 2016, the Internet was deactivated for nearly two months. It was shut down by the Indian government in response to violent protests following the death of a local militant commander in a gun battle with the Indian military in early July. The absence of online social networks made it difficult for people to spread information and organize protests (Shah, 2017).

Yet, in other instances, such as in September 2016, when riots broke out in Bengaluru city, rather than resorting to a network shutdown, authorities used Twitter to send out regular announcements on the law and order situations, countering rumors and answering queries from concerned citizens (Human Rights Watch, 2017).

ICTs and censorship

The technological progress of information and communication technologies (ICTs) and their introduction into social life has gained a great deal of attention from governments and nongovernmental organizations alike at a policy level, as these technologies have shown both positive and negative effects in their adoption. ICTs have largely contributed to the growth of the global economy and the promotion of human rights issues worldwide, and they have provided political activists with powerful advocacy tools. They have also been instrumental in shifting power, changing regimes and contributing to a democratic future. At the same time, government censorship of these platforms has strongly limited public access to the Internet and led to significant violations of citizens' information rights. Moreover, governments have often steered the use of ICTs toward promoting policies that inculcate particular ideas and preclude free speech (Kulnazarova, 2014).

One cannot deny that there are a number of ways in which the Internet can be a serious threat for authoritarian regimes. Users living in repressed societies are now able to access news that is typically unavailable where both print and broadcast media are censored. In countries where the state or wealthy elites have full economic control, independent, alternative news providers can now have a voice online. ICT platforms can be a powerful channel to express dissent, facilitate communication, and enable groups to organize. These are all characteristics that expose them to scrutiny from the authorities. However, it is important to recognize that while the Internet has the capacity to challenge the status quo of authoritarian regimes, its impact is not so linear. The nature of the Internet is not intrinsically threatening for undemocratic regimes: the dissemination of new online technologies carries both opportunities and drawbacks. Aside from building a physical architecture that facilitates Internet control, many authoritarian governments have also been developing and implementing national ICT plans that define how the Internet will be used strategically to reach social, political, and economic goals determined by the state. Besides the online delivery of public services, a number of authoritarian governments have utilized the Internet for propaganda purposes. Newspapers run by the state can now be found online, alongside added features that allow users to interact on a particular topic. These tools are mostly used to hone ideological messages and shape the online political environment. In other words, the state can make use of these platforms to strengthen its position by means of a subtle influence rather than the traditional official rhetoric (Kalathil & Boas, 2003).

Control exerted by a government on online content carries major repercussions for freedom of expression and the ability to exercise censorship. In addition to the more evident damaging impact that this has on the political and civil rights of users, controlling or withholding information can also carry negative consequences for Internet access and use, leading to harmful economic results particularly for developing and middle income countries. Moreover, it is in these countries that Internet control by authoritarian regimes is especially a risk. What governments should really aim for is the creation of safe online environments for both citizens and businesses by preserving the Internet as a system for social and economic development. Hence, as Gruber, Jaume-Palasí, Leidel, and Spielkamp (2016) state, "an Internet policy should encourage and facilitate an open and competitive online landscape, reaffirming users' rights to free speech and expression and access to information" (p. 29).

The "right to communicate" as a human right

Citizen engagement is a process that allows government and nonstate actors to collaborate on joint decision-making in relation to policy planning and negotiation (Naidoo, 2008). The United Nations (2008, in Gaventa & Barrett, 2010) state that "engagement is regarded as an important governance norm that can strengthen the decision-making arrangements of the state and produce outcomes that favour the poor and the disadvantaged" (p. 12). It is for all these reasons that when ICTs began to emerge in the early 1990s, this was regarded as a new time for African democracy. This enthusiasm was driven by technologically determinist beliefs that had the introduction of new technologies, with the innovative elements of debate and interaction, identified as a catalyst for social change and stronger democratic participation (Pointer et al., 2016).

However, when citizen participation is neglected, an improvement in physical access to digital media does not necessarily lead to positive development outcomes. The arrival of these new platforms can certainly increase citizens' participation in political action. However, as previously discussed, on the negative side, it also offers greater opportunities to states to exert repression and surveillance on citizens by monitoring and tracking their activities online. As Pointer et al. (2016) highlight, this brings us back to the top-down modernization paradigm of development, which can also be adopted to theorize the African digital public sphere, as questions are being raised in relation to issues of inequality, access, and power that are embedded in these new technologies. In other words, some of the benefits of increased access to the use of digital media are not achieved in countries where citizens' information and communication rights are disregarded. Hence, besides the improvement of infrastructure, costs, and quality of Internet services, what is crucial in this context is the application of a rights-based approach to digital media access in the formulation of developmental policy.

Even though it does not formally exist as a provision of human rights law, the "right to communicate" has been strongly advocated by civil society organizations for a number of decades now. Two main arguments were first brought forward: the right to justification, which is essential for the recognition of human dignity; and the rights-discourse approach, which regards communication as a human need. The latter, in particular, makes a connection between the development of technologies and the necessity to expand rights in order to address the new reality created by those technologies: this is an environment where both established rights and the enactment of communication processes are faced with new threats. Even today, the ideal of a "right to communicate" continues to drive advocacy movements that strive to achieve a human rights-based approach to communication processes (Hamelink & Hoffmann, 2009).

Kulnazarova (2014) emphasises that "the freedom of expression [made explicit in the International Bill of Human rights] is invariably connected with the right to communication because the only way we can express our thoughts, opinions and views is in the process of deliberation and conversation with others, either in groups or between two individuals" (p. 402). All individuals have equal rights to produce, convey, and receive information, leading to an interaction with others that allows them to reach a mutually beneficial agreement. For this reason, the right to communication is a concept that must be placed at the center of human rights technology. It must also be further developed and adapted to the Internet era. It is not surprising that, with the occurrence of the technical revolution that is taking place, new forms of media have started to shape people's lives. Historically, both individual citizens and communities have always made use of a public space to share ideas and opinions connected to the public interest (Kulnazarova, 2014). In a large number of countries, both government and civil society organizations (CSOs) are trialing new information and communication technology platforms that invite and enhance citizens' voice. In Kenya, for example, the creation of the e-government strategy in 2004 has expanded the opportunity for citizens to participate in governance processes, which, combined with an increase in penetration of mobile broadband, has created opportunities for Kenyan citizens to participate in various processes online, including national and local budget preparation and plan formulation. This also enabled them to demand accountability from the political class on resource utilizations, or to submit complaints on poor governance and service delivery (Opiyo, Mwau, Mwang'a, & Mwaniki, 2017).

The objective of this effort is to achieve a better delivery of public services. An important distinction has been made between two types of ICT-enabled citizen voice: aggregated individual assessments of service provision and collective civic action. The first approach involves the gathering of users' feedback to provide decision-makers with real-time, accurate information that allows them to identify and tackle, at their discretion, service delivery problems. Collective civic action, on the other hand, encourages a higher degree of accountability from service providers, as this approach relies less on decision-makers' *arbitrium*: in essence, the public aggregation of citizens' views through ICT channels is much more likely to set the decision-makers' agenda when looking at broader policy priorities (Peixoto & Fox, 2016).

This demonstrates that the ability of citizens to express their views, reach out to their government constituents, and receive information from their institutions are all significant components of a functional and just public use of the Internet. It is also a way of strengthening governments' accountability. Similarly, the freedom of activist groups or individuals to have their voices heard over matters of social and political interest, to articulate their concerns, to let others know about injustice and manipulation, and to engage in a dialogue with those who share their views, are all crucial components of an effective social and economic development. A guarantee that digital media become free, accessible, and usable platforms for all at all times is necessary to recognize that connectivity and communication should be regarded as human rights principles that drive future developmental policies.

Conclusions

The debate on Internet access and Internet control has intensified over the past few years as governments have increased their watch on digital media and other information and communication technologies through Internet shutdowns and other forms of censorship or surveillance. In particular, in a growing number of African countries, governments have denied Internet access to their population during election times and have increased their control over the Internet. This has occurred despite the fact that Internet access and use, especially through mobile phones, have increased exponentially. A human rights-based approach to digital media access when regulating Internet policy in developing contexts is therefore crucial to emphasize the need for protection of fundamental rights such as freedom of expression, opinion, and access to information. A rights-based approach to the use of digital media is also at the heart of an open Internet and the essence of a "right to communicate." Therefore, one of the main challenges in development is now that of building states that are effective in incorporating human rights in national ICT planning and that remain accountable for their implementation. This is an important step toward the growth and strengthening of ICT literacy and use globally, and an opportunity for governments to enhance transparency, dialogue, and respect for human rights in their approach to digital communications regulation.

SEE ALSO: Civic Activism; Civic Media; Communication; Internet Safety; Media Access and Activism; Mediatization; Monitorial Citizenship

References

Access Now. (2016, February 23). Joint letter on Internet shutdown in Uganda. Retrieved from https://www.accessnow.org/joint-letter-on-internet-shutdown-in-uganda/

Article19. (2016, February 13). Uganda: Blanket ban on social media on election day is disproportionate. Retrieved from https://www.article19.org/resources/uganda-blanket-ban-on-social-media-on-election-day-is-disproportionate/

Atuhaire, P., & Atuhaire, G. (2016, February 24). How Ugandans overturned an election day social media blackout. *Motherboard*. Retrieved from http://motherboard.vice.com/read/uganda-election-day-social-media-blackout-backlash-mobile-payments

Bariyo, N. (2015, January 22). Democratic Republic of Congo extends Internet blockage. *The Wall Street Journal*. Retrieved from http://www.wsj.com/articles/congo-blocks-internet-access-amid-protests-against-president-kabila-1421938042

BBC. (2016, December 1). Gambia election: Internet and international calls banned. BBC. Retrieved from http://www.bbc.com/news/world-africa-38157127

Bhattacharya, A. (2017, February 9). Data show that India's reflexive reaction to politically stirring incidents is to shut down the Internet. *Quartz India*. Retrieved from https://qz.com/906737/indias-reflexive-reaction-to-politically-stirring-incidents-is-to-shut-down-the-internet/

Buchanan, E. (2016, December 15). DRC activists vow to carry out revolution "with or without social networks." *International Business Times*. Retrieved from http://www.ibtimes.co.uk/drc-activists-vow-carry-out-revolution-without-social-networks-1596748

Butagira, T. (2016, February 18). Museveni explains social media, mobile money shutdown. *Daily Monitor*. Retrieved from http://www.monitor.co.ug/News/National/Museveni-explains-social-media--mobile-money-shutdown/-/688334/3082990/-/rj5kk5z/-/index.html

Calandro, E., & Chair, C. (2016). Policy and regulatory challenges posed by emerging pricing strategies [CPRsouth Special Issue]. *Information Technologies & International Development, 12*(2). Retrieved from http://itidjournal.org/index.php/itid/article/view/1503

Dahir, A.L. (2016a, September 2). Gabon is the latest African country to shut down its Internet as election protests grow. *Quartz Africa*. Retrieved from http://qz.com/771996/gabon-is-the-latest-african-country-to-shut-down-its-internet-as-election-protests-grow/

Dahir, A.L. (2016b, December 1). Gambia's government has shut down the Internet on the eve of elections. *Quartz Africa*. Retrieved from http://qz.com/850002/gambias-government-has-shut-down-the-internet-on-the-eve-of-elections/

Deloitte. (2016). *The economic impact of disruptions to Internet connectivity. A report for Facebook*. London, England: Deloitte LLP. Retrieved from https://www2.deloitte.com/content/dam/Deloitte/global/Documents/Technology-Media-Telecommunications/economic-impact-disruptions-to-internet-connectivity-deloitte.pdf

Duru Aydin, D. (2016, May 25). The laws that let Internet shutdowns happen. *AccessNow*. Retrieved from https://www.accessnow.org/laws-let-internet-shutdowns-happen/

Fox, B. (2016, March 21). Internet blackout in Congo as government fears post-election unrest. *Euractiv.com*. Retrieved from http://www.euractiv.com/section/global-europe/news/internet-blackout-in-congo-as-government-fears-post-election-unrest/

Gaventa, J., & Barrett, G. (2010). *So what difference does it make? Mapping the outcomes of citizen engagement*. Brighton, England: Institute of Development Studies. Retrieved from https://www.ids.ac.uk/files/dmfile/Wp347.pdf

Global Voice Advocacy. (2016, March 23). Netizen report: Congo shuts down all communications on election day. *Global Voices Advox*. Retrieved from https://advox.globalvoices.org/2016/03/23/netizen-report-congo-shuts-down-all-communications-on-election-day/

Gruber, B., Jaume-Palasí, L., Leidel, S., & Spielkamp, M. (2016). *Guidebook Internet governance. Media freedom in a connected world*. Bonn: Deutsche Welle.

Hamelink, C., & Hoffmann, J. (2009). Communication as a human right: Picking up the challenge? In A. Dakrour, M. Eid, & Y.R. Kamalipour (Eds.). *The right to communicate: Historical hopes, global debates and future premises* (pp. 71–106). Dubuque, IA: Kendall/Hunt.

Human Rights Watch. (2014). World report 2014: Uganda. Events of 2013. Retrieved from https://www.hrw.org/world-report/2014/country-chapters/uganda

Human Rights Watch. (2017, June 15). India: 20 Internet shutdowns in 2017. Protection free expression online services public interest. Retrieved from https://www.hrw.org/news/2017/06/15/india-20-internct-shutdowns-2017

Internet Governance Forum. (2016). *Analysing the causes and impact of Internet shut downs* [Proposal background paper]. Retrieved from https://www.intgovforum.org/cms/igf2016/uploads/proposal_background_paper/IGF_InternetShutDown_Background_Paper.pdf

Kalathil, S., & Boas, T.C. (2003). *Open networks, closed regimes: The impact of the Internet on authoritarian rule*. Washington, DC: Carnegie Endowment.

Konviser, B. (2016, March 19). Congo orders telecom providers to shut down services for election day. DW. Retrieved from http://www.dw.com/en/congo-orders-telecom-providers-to-shut-down-services-for-election-day/a-19129396

Kulnazarova, A. (2014). Communication and new technology. In A. Mihr & M. Gibney (Eds.), *The SAGE handbook of human rights* (pp. 391–409). London, England: SAGE.

Kupe, T. (2016). Media freedom has come a long way in Africa, but it's still precarious. *Media Policy Project Blog*, The London School of Economics and Political Science. Retrieved from http://blogs.lse.ac.uk/mediapolicyproject/2016/05/05/media-freedom-has-come-a-long-way-in-africa-but-its-still-precarious/

Naidoo, K. (2008). Participatory governance, civic engagement and conflict resolution in the Southern African development community. *Conflict Trends, 1*, 32–40.

Olukotun, D.B. (2016). Internet shutdowns – an explainer. *DW Akademie*. Retrieved from http://www.dw.com/en/internet-shutdowns-an-explainer/a-36731481

Opiyo, R., Mwau, B., Mwang'a, K., & Mwaniki, D. (2017). Attaining e-democracy through digital platforms in Kenya. In T.M. Vinod Kumar (Ed.), *E-democracy for smart cities: Advances in 21st century human settlements*. Singapore: Springer.

Peixoto, T., & Fox, J. (2016). *When does ICT-enabled citizen voice lead to government responsiveness?* Washington, DC: The World Bank Digital Engagement Evaluation Team (DEET).

Phillips, G.S., & Atuhaire, G. (2016, February 24). How Ugandans overturned an election day social media blackout. *Motherboard*. Retrieved from http://motherboard.vice.com/read/uganda-election-day-social-media-blackout-backlash-mobile-payments

Pointer, R., Bosch, T., Chuma, W., & Wasserman, W. (2016). *Civil society, political activism and communications in democratisation conflicts* (MeCoDEM Series). Cape Town, South Africa: University of Cape Town.

Propa, J. (2016, May 11). Social media blocked in Uganda ahead of President Museveni's inauguration. *Global Voices Advox*. Retrieved from https://advox.globalvoices.org/2016/05/11/social-media-blocked-in-uganda-ahead-of-president-musevenis-inauguration/

RightsCon. (2016, March 30). No more Internet shutdowns! Let's #KeepItOn. *AccessNow*. Retrieved from https://www.accessnow.org/no-internet-shutdowns-lets-keepiton/

Shah, H. (2017, September 7). Where "digital India" ends. *Slate*. Retrieved from http://www.slate.com/articles/technology/future_tense/2016/09/india_champion_of_web_access_cuts_off_mobile_internet_in_kashmir.html

United Nations General Assembly. (2016). *The promotion, protection and enjoyment of human rights on the Internet*. Resolution A/HRC/32/L.20, July 1, 2016. Retrieved from http://digitallibrary.un.org/record/845728/files/A_HRC_32_L-20-EN.pdf

Withnall, A. (2016, December 1). Gambia election: Government shuts down Internet as President Yahya Jammeh faces threat to 22-year rule. *Independent*. Retrieved from http://www.independent.co.uk/news/world/africa/gambia-election-president-yahya-jammeh-shuts-down-internet-phones-polls-open-a7449371.html

World Bank. (2016). *World development report 2016: Digital dividends*. Washington, DC: The World Bank. Retrieved from http://www.worldbank.org/en/publication/wdr2016

Further reading

Monitoring Internet shutdowns in India: www.internetshutdowns.in/

Paradigm Initiative Nigeria. (2016). Choking the pipe: How governments hurt Internet freedom on a continent that needs more access. *Digital rights in Africa report 2016*. Retrieved from http://web.paradigmhq.org/download/digital-rights-in-africa-report-2016-lr/

West, D.M. (2016). Internet shutdowns cost countries US$2.4 billion last year. *Centre for Technology Innovation at Brookings*. Retrieved from https://www.brookings.edu/wp-content/uploads/2016/10/intenet-shutdowns-v-3.pdf

Valentina Baú works as a lecturer and researcher at the University of New South Wales (Sydney, Australia). Both as a practitioner and as an academic, her work has focused on the use of the media and communication in international development. She has completed a PhD at Macquarie University on the role of participatory media in conflict transformation and reconciliation after civil violence. Her present research explores different approaches and evaluation methodologies in the area of Communication for Development in Peacebuilding. In the past, Valentina has collaborated with international NGOs, the United Nations, and the Italian Development Cooperation, while working in different areas of the Global South. Her work has been published in established academic journals as well as on renowned online platforms.

Enrico Calandro is a senior research manager at Research ICT Africa, an information and communication technology (ICT) think tank based in Cape Town, South Africa. Enrico holds a PhD in business administration specializing in telecommunications policy from the Graduate School of Business, University of Cape Town, and his work explores the relationship between digital access and development with a focus on digital inequalities. Prior to joining Research ICT Africa, he worked as a technical advisor for the Southern African Development Community Parliamentary Forum's ICT program in Namibia, and as a trainee for the Information Society and Media Directorate General of the European Commission. He is a recipient of the Open Technology Fund fellowship on information controls, the Amy Mahan scholarship award for the advancement of ICT policy in Africa, and the United Nations Department of Economic and Social Affairs (UNDESA) fellowship for international cooperation.

Digital Media in Higher Education

NEIL SELWYN
Monash University, Australia

LUCI PANGRAZIO
Deakin University, Australia

Higher education is a distinct context in which digital media are used. As such, the use of digital media in higher education—and associated media literacy issues—certainly merit specific consideration in their own right. As far as this entry is concerned, "higher education" shall be taken to refer to university-level teaching and learning; that is, university students, teachers, and administrators engaged in pre-degree, undergraduate, and postgraduate courses. Of course, universities pursue other significant areas of work (such as academic research, commercial research and development, community engagement), all of which impact on their "education" provision. Nevertheless, it is university teaching and learning that will concern us for the remainder of this entry. In short, we will consider what digital media are present in higher education and, more importantly, what media literacy issues surround them.

It is worth foregrounding this discussion with a few notes on why higher education is a distinct educational context and, it follows, a distinct context of media use. First, many of the issues we shall go on to consider relate to *university students*, the majority of whom are young adults aged between 18 and 25 years. In one sense, this encyclopedia contains other entries analogous to the media literacy issues pertinent to university students; for example, entries on adolescent media uses; youth digital culture; and cyberbullying. Yet, university students differ significantly from adolescent and youth media users in terms of their characteristics and needs. These are not young adults per se, but young adults engaged in the role of "student." As such, these are individuals concerned with the scholarly requirements of being a student (e.g., attending classes, producing coursework, passing courses) and the social requirements of being a student (e.g., making friends, campus politics, sorority life, intermural and varsity sports). These young adults' media uses are *not* directly comparable with young adults who have entered the workforce. Neither are these "students" in the same sense as children and adolescents engaged in compulsory schooling. Indeed, growing numbers of university students study on a part-time basis, and even those who are enrolled "full-time" might be working one or more jobs to sustain their studies. Few university students are studying from 9 to 5, five days a week. These are people who have many other commitments and responsibilities besides their educational engagement.

Second, it is worth considering the distinctiveness of *university teaching and learning*. At first glance, much teaching and learning in universities is comparable to other education sectors. University courses are based around set curricula, classrooms, term times, examinations, and so on. Certainly, this encyclopedia features other entries relevant to university teaching and learning, not least entries on teaching with Twitter and YouTube; critical pedagogy; and teaching with media. Yet, higher education teaching and learning differs from high school, college, or workplace education in a number of important ways. First, most teaching and learning activities are not compulsory. Students' participation in university teaching is less coerced than in schools, and built around reduced expectations of direct contact with teaching staff. Indeed, university learning is often expected to take the form of "independent study"; that is, learning that is self-directed and self-responsibilized. Other differences are apparent in the form and function of university education. For example, universities rely on diverse modes of teaching delivery, with various forms of face-to-face teaching (large lectures, small labs, and individual tutorials) alongside "blended" digital provision (online lectures, massive open online courses, flipped classrooms, and so on). Of course, uses of digital media in university are defined differently by disciplines and fields; for example, engineers and nursing students will engage with digital media for learning in different ways than history or chemistry majors. Yet across all disciplines and fields, university teaching and learning is clearly highly specialized and "intellectual" in nature but is also more industry-orientated than might be the case in high school.

Third, we need to recognize the distinctiveness of *university teachers*. In one sense, teachers and tutors in higher education will often work along similar lines to school teachers. Certainly, parallels can be drawn with other discussions in this encyclopedia on teacher practice and teacher education. Yet, teachers working in higher education are distinct from school teachers or workplace trainers. For example, university "teachers" often are not professionals whose main job (or interest) is teaching per se. Instead, many people teaching in universities prioritize their work on academic research, publishing, and grant procurement. Other people employed to teach in universities are not tenured professionals, but adjunct, short-term contracted staff, teaching assistants, or postgraduate students. Alongside this lack of interest and/or permanence is a lack of pedagogic expertise. Many university teachers might be subject specialists with high levels of specific expertise, but are not trained teachers.

Fourth, it is worth noting the distinct nature of *universities* as educational institutions. Again, many aspects of universities are certainly comparable to other education institutions. As such, a few entries in this encyclopedia are relevant to university settings, such as the entries on K-12 (primary and secondary) schools and Massive Open Online Courses (MOOCs). Yet, universities differ from schools and colleges in a number of important ways. In a practical sense, universities are distinctly bounded locations. The campus is a location where many students live *and* learn, although universities have an ill-defined duty of care and tend not to act *in loco parentis* in the manner that schools are obliged to. Conversely, from a broader organizational point of view, universities are multibillion-dollar businesses that operate mostly on a profit-making basis with (relatively) little government funding and support. As with many other public services, university systems around the world have undergone extensive marketization and commodification of their services, alongside significant "massification" in terms of numbers of enrolments. All this has led to the emergence of the model "entrepreneurial university" that is focused on innovation, income generation, and addressing consumer demands.

Digital media use in higher education

As shall now be discussed, all of these factors make higher education a complex (and sometimes contradictory) context for digital media use. As such, it is perhaps useful to map out some of the prevalent digital media and digital practices in higher education. On the face of it, digital media are an integral feature of present-day universities in ways that would have been hard to imagine even a few years previously. Universities now operate on a "bring your own device" basis, with students and teachers using personal devices such as tablets, laptops, and smartphones to support a diversity of learning practices across campuses, at home, and at all points in between. Lecture theaters, seminar rooms, and other teaching and learning environments are awash with digital hardware and software, and a growing amount of pedagogic work is conducted on a "virtual" basis. Teaching and learning in most universities is predicated on institution-wide "learning management systems" supported by extensive digitalized resources. In addition, the day-to-day management and administration of courses is underpinned by software systems that support and structure the actions of students, teachers, and administrators in a variety of ways.

One way of making better sense of this digital milieu is to distinguish between digital media that are used *by* university students, and digital media that are used *on* university students. The notion of digital media that are used *by* students refers to the digital devices and applications that students make direct use of to support their studies. These include university systems and applications that students are required to use, alongside students' personally chosen digital media. In contrast, the notion of digital media that are used *on* students encompasses the growing number of institutional digital systems that students might not be aware of, yet are implicated with nonetheless.

In the first sense, then, are digital media used directly by students. Obviously, these include "institutionally imposed" media that students are compelled to use. Here universities provide a range of digital tools and systems in order for students to fulfill the requirements of their academic courses. Teaching in most universities is predicated on a specified learning management system. Students' work is uploaded through online submission applications, vetted by plagiarism detection software, and perhaps even automatically graded. Lectures are "captured" by video and audio systems, supported by the use of slideshow presentations, the in-lecture use of clickers, and live polling. Elsewhere, students are expected to participate in online discussion forums, quizzes, and examinations. Universities also make use of social media in the form of official Facebook pages in attempts to connect with their students.

Alongside this, we can also consider the digital media that university students choose for themselves. Here it is worth distinguishing further between digital media that students choose to use in their "real lives" as opposed to digital media they choose to use in their "university lives." In this sense, Kennedy, Judd, Dalgarno, and Waycott (2010) draw a useful distinction between "living" and "learning" media; that is, students' "everyday" uses of digital media as opposed to using media deliberately for academic studies and/or learning.

In terms of "learning" media, students rely on a personal array of digital media to engage in their studies. Clearly much of this is prosaic, such as the use of tools and applications to take notes, research information, and produce assignments. In this sense, some of the most prevalent digital media tools used by students are word processors, bibliographic databases, reference management tools, writing apps, and other tools of academic writing. Using digital technologies to "research information" through search engines such as Google and other popular resources such as Wikipedia also is a prominent practice. Content repositories such as YouTube, TED talks, and iTunes U are valuable sources of supplementary materials to corroborate or clarify what has been learned in classes. Social media are now a key means of communicating and collaborating with classmates: asking questions and exchanging information; working with peers; sharing ideas and preparing group work. Broader communities of students (particularly postgraduates) have formed on networks such as Academia.edu and ResearchGate to swap references, tips, and advice and engage in meaningful discussions about their work. All these digital media form a bedrock from which contemporary university students engage with their studies.

As noted above, students also use a range of "living" media to engage with the social requirements of university life. Personal uses of social media and mobile telephony are clearly integral elements of the everyday lives and interactions of university students. Social media applications such as Facebook, WhatsApp, Snapchat, and Instagram provide university students with extensive social information and communications environments. One important role that these digital media play is as a means of maintaining and sustaining social networks; with university peer groups, friends from previous stages of their lives (such as school friends), family members, and other acquaintances. Facebook is an important social tool used to aid the "settling-in" process at university, especially in terms of newly enrolled students as they adjust to university life and make tentative connections with an otherwise unfamiliar peer group on campus. Social media are an integral element of being connected with campus social life: receiving invitations, registering one's interest, and generally maintaining involvement in social activities. As reflected in the continued popularity of campus-specific online "StalkerSpaces," social media is an important site for frivolous, flirtatious, and sometimes unfriendly social interactions between students. Digital media are therefore an integral element of the contemporary university student experience.

Second, then, we also need to consider the digital media that are used *on* students; that is, digital systems and applications not used directly by students, but used by university authorities on their behalf. For example, many of the official teaching and learning media outlined earlier are increasingly integrated into overarching systems for broad areas of university administration. One such example is that of "student and administrative management systems" designed to cover every aspect of the university's official contact with a student. Indeed, online institutional systems are used to handle every contact that a student has with their university. These systems are used to handle initial admissions inquiries and applications from prospective students, enrolment, records of achievement, accounting and budgeting, and eventually graduation and alumni records. It is now common for a student's entire contact with the university organization to be administered through one "profile" on such a system.

One significant aspect of this institutional digital media involves the processing and reprocessing of student data. Complex systems are now used for processes such as "business intelligence," "learning analytics," "data mining," and "predictive analytics." In addition to formal grades and achievement indicators, universities are beginning to collate and combine data that arise "naturally" from students' interactions with course websites, library services, and face-to-face meetings with teaching staff. These "learning analytics" and "academic analytics" are being used to inform curriculum design, class planning, and targeted learning support offered to different groups of students. In addition is the growing institutional use of digital media and digital systems to ensure campus security. On-campus access systems use smart cards, remote tagging, facial recognition software and geospatial tracking of students' personal devices. Universities' security services provide safety apps to allow students to report crimes as well as track each other's movements. All told, digital media now play an important "behind the scenes" part in contemporary higher education.

Digital media problems and issues

In theory, then, nearly every aspect of higher education is entwined with digital media. However, this is not to say that media use is wholly beneficial and/or unproblematic. Indeed, there are a number of issues and problems that can be associated with the growing prevalence of digital media in higher education.

Student difficulties learning with digital media

Most students—especially those entering university directly from compulsory schooling—are assumed to be fully willing and able to use digital media during their studies. Yet students' engagements with digital media during their university studies are often complex, compromised, and problematic. Indeed, research studies often find that not *all* students are as inclined to integrate digital media into their studies as might be assumed. Recent surveys have tended to report varied and often educationally constrained uses of digital media. For example, one large-scale study of UK universities found students reported varying levels of digital confidence and skills, often reporting "initial surprise or confusion at the array of technologies that were available" (Jones, 2012). Moreover, students were found to be generally willing to conform to institutional requirements, university recommendations, and course requirements for their media use. Similarly, Kennedy et al. (2010) highlighted four distinct groups of student digital media users in Australian higher education, with the largest category of "basic users" comprising nearly 50% of students and "characterized by extremely infrequent use of new and emerging technologies and less than weekly or monthly use of standard web technologies" (p. 337).

Student difficulties with learning online

Concerns have also been raised over students' abilities to learn effectively in online educational contexts. Online learning requires specific aptitudes and abilities that differ from how students engage in traditional forms of education. In particular is what Terras and Ramsey (2015, p. 476) describe as "participatory literacy," that is "the collaborative and production-based skills that are required across a range of digital media that draws upon key abilities such as creativity, reasoning, focus, critical thinking and analysis." A key concept here is the ability of students to use technology as a means of "curating" their own learning; that is, researching and selecting new educational opportunities online that build upon their previous engagement. In all these ways, then, the individual is given responsibility for what Vistasp Karbhari terms as "sense making, way finding, and managing uncertainty" (2016, p. 3.4).

These observations highlight the risk that some students do not possess the skills and aptitudes required to engage successfully with digitally based education. As Mike Keppell (2014, p. 4) puts it, "we can't assume learners have the knowledge, skills and attitudes to be able to identify and effectively utilize appropriate learning spaces." This is reflected in the uneven outcomes which result from students' participation in MOOCs. Generally, these courses are found to be of most benefit to well-resourced students who already have successfully engaged in higher education, and are therefore well equipped to progress through university-level learning. As Hood, Littlejohn, and Milligan (2015) suggest, only a minority of students are best able to "self-regulate" the required "self-directed, non-linear nature of learning engagement in MOOCs, which requires individuals to determine and structure their learning largely independently."

Student difficulties with information literacy

These issues are echoed in concerns over the ability of students to seek and retrieve online information. Students—both at undergraduate and at postgraduate levels—have been found to be surprisingly ineffective in their use of the Internet and other research tools. Ian Rowlands and colleagues' (2008) study highlighted a range of limitations to many university students' uses of online information. These included a tendency to skim documents, "power browse" summaries of longer articles, or else "squirrel away" digital content without reading it at all. Recent studies have confirmed how university students, when using online sources of information, often struggle with issues of credibility, authority, relevance, and timeliness of information (Selwyn & Gorard, 2016). It has been reported that many students prefer visual/video-based content over text-based content, prioritizing ease and speed of consumption over authenticity and quality of information (Henderson, Selwyn, & Aston, 2017). In short, digital information resources are found to be rather *less* expansive and empowering for many university students than proponents of digital education would lead us to believe.

Student difficulties with online malpractice and cheating

Concerns have also been raised over growing rates of online plagiarism and other forms of digital "cheating." Now it is reckoned that substantial proportions of university students indulge in some form of plagiarism via online sources: from "cutting and pasting" a few unattributed sentences or paragraphs into an assignment through to purchasing ghost-written essays from Internet-based "contract cheating" services. Similarly, digital technologies now allow students to outsource difficult or unappealing aspects of their education work. The Internet has long been a source of "shadow" services that offer to complete student assessments and assignments for a fee. Students can now pay workers from companies such as No Need To Study to take their online courses: clicking through content, taking tests, and posting discussion forum comments where appropriate.

Narrowness of online interactions between students

In terms of student use of "living media" as opposed to "learning media," there are also increasing concerns over the limited nature of students' use of social media. On the one hand are concerns that students' social media use exacerbates social divisions and cliques among students. One recurring theme from studies of student media use is the tendency for online social networks to reinforce—rather than disrupt—differences in social contact. This is most noticeable in terms of race, class, and gender. Broadly, it is reported that white, middle-class, male students are most likely to maintain online networks of similar friends and acquaintances. Thus, Mayer and Puller's (2008) study of social network formation on US university campuses reported the strongest predictor of whether two students were "friends" on Facebook to be race, even after controlling for a variety of measures of socioeconomic background, ability, and college activities. Other studies have shown how social media can constrain social interactions for marginalized groups of university students, such as those from ethnic minority or dis/abled backgrounds (Marlowe, Bartley, & Collins, 2017; Seale, Georgeson, Mamas, & Swain, 2015).

Inappropriateness of online interactions between students

Also of concern is the popularity of divisive and demeaning student social media sites. This was apparent, for example, in the recent fad for UK students to create university-specific "Spotted" pages on Facebook where anonymous descriptions and comments on other students seen around the campus were posted and commented on. On the one hand, these pages could be seen as harmless "banter." Yet on the other hand, they could also be described as a form of predatory peer surveillance and verbal bullying. As Jaffer (2013) described, these sites were "meant to provide comic relief for procrastinating students. Inevitably, though, they have become a hotbed of sneering jibes and vicious gossip." Similarly, controversial but popular websites such as Uni-Lad in the United Kingdom provide spaces for students to engage in inappropriate misogynist, racist, and sexist behavior that both mirrors and also exceeds the rise of such cultures in offline campus spaces.

These concerns sit alongside instances of social media being used to promulgate dissent among students. This was illustrated in the much-publicized pushback on US campuses against geo-fenced social networks such as Whisper and Yik Yak (the latter of which allows anonymous interactions between users within a 5-mile radius). Here a number of US universities experienced instances of race hate, bullying, ostracizing, and harassment through these social media, leading to widespread campus bans. As Francesca Tripodi (2016, p. 21) notes, media such as Yik Yak act to marginalize and exclude students who do not "frequent the App from a privileged position."

Students' limited understandings of personal data

Less controversial, but no less significant, are concerns over students' lack of understanding of their personal data. As already outlined, higher education institutions generate a mass of personal digital data relating to students, learning, and the environments in which teaching and learning takes place. A wealth of data related to teaching and learning is generated by universities each academic year, usually in disparate, disconnected, and restricted forms. These data range from records of student satisfaction, online participation, and grades through to room bookings, class sizes, and demographics. "Trace" data is generated from students' interactions with online learning software and learning management software. This data tends to be inaccessible to students, often used only in a closed, "top-down" manner by university authorities to construct data profiles of students. Concerns, therefore, are raised over students' limited awareness and understanding of "their" data.

Digital media literacy solutions

So there is a question regarding what might be done to address these problems with student engagement with digital media in higher education. Clearly, many of the issues just outlined relate to issues of media literacy. More specifically, all of these issues point to an underlying shortfall in what might be termed students' "critical digital literacy." While definitions are contested and evolving, critical digital literacy could be described as a set of skills *and* a disposition toward digital media. This suggests the ability of students to analyze the specific multimodal features of digital media and manipulate these to achieve particular outcomes. Clearly, as the digital landscape is ever changing, these skills need to be flexible and transferrable so they can be applied over time and across contexts. Another important aspect of critical digital literacy relates to students' development and communication of "knowledge" or "how to assimilate the information, evaluate it and reintegrate it" (Gilster, cited in Pool, 1997, p. 9). Finally, in the age of social media, critical digital literacy also refers to students developing understandings of how context shapes behaviors, as well as the responsible management of online identities.

So there is a question regarding what examples we can point toward in terms of supporting the development of such critical digital understandings and practices in the context of higher education.

Improving students' digital skills

It is now widely recognized that universities need to provide opportunities for improving and expanding students' digital skills, rather than assuming that students already have these in place. This means not only the provision of guidance on how to use the official systems and information services at the university, but also the development of students' own digital skills. Jisc—the agency supporting digital services in the UK university sector—recommend embedding digital skills in a "connected curriculum" to encourage "authentic experiential learning" that will improve employability (Chatterton & Rebbeck, 2015, p. 11). Resources such as Jisc's "Developing Digital Literacies" wiki are designed to help university educators develop digital literacies through a "connected curriculum" approach.

Elsewhere, it has been argued that university educators and students need shared understandings of the digital literacies required for specific degree programs and courses. The University of Edinburgh's "Manifesto for Teaching Online" is a good example of teachers and students working together to develop shared understandings of what online learning should be. First initiated in 2011, the manifesto was made "open" so that all stakeholders could revise and rewrite it. Now, the 2017 version of the manifesto reaches well beyond online teaching to include more critical understandings on digital technologies, such as "Algorithms and analytics re-code education: Pay attention!"

Improving students' information literacy

This need for improved skills and understandings clearly relates to students' engagement with digitally based information. The Association of College & Research Libraries has renewed attention on information literacy by developing a *Framework for Information Literacy for Higher Education* (ACRL, 2016). This framework is based around six core concepts that organize many other ideas about information, research, and scholarship:

- authority is constructed and contextual,
- information creation as a process,
- information has value,
- research as inquiry,
- scholarship as conversation,
- searching as strategic exploration.

This framework encourages not only the development of skills, but also the adoption of a particular disposition toward the research process, which is underpinned by digital honesty and nonplagiarism. A good example of this has been efforts at University of Nevada Las Vegas to match the ACRL Standards to the undergraduate learning outcomes required of all students. Librarians mapped the curriculum and then integrated and scaffolded literacy learning throughout year levels.

It is also important for universities to acknowledge how popular digital information resources shift the textual practices of research. For example, Wikipedia might be better seen by university educators as a site for exploring critical understandings of the changing nature of textual authority and knowledge construction. Moreover, the issue of moving beyond the passive consumption of Wikipedia content needs to be foregrounded in the student consciousness. As such, there are clearly many ways in which universities need to engage more directly in supporting and enhancing the role that these online information sources are now playing in students' scholarship. For example, efforts are beginning to be made to integrate Wikipedia authorship and editing as part of class activities and even as part of assessed coursework. Clearly, universities now need to follow the lead of their students and actively engage with digital sources such as Wikipedia as accepted (but still contestable) sources of information and knowledge.

Improving students' data literacy

Improving students' understandings and skills regarding personal data remains a nascent area of digital media literacy work in higher education. Recent research by Selwyn, Henderson, & Chao (2017) involved giving university students "open" access to data being collected and collated in their university on their own academic performance and progress. This project worked with students to develop open data tools and techniques to explore alternate uses of this data, as well as developing students' awareness of the personal data being generated through their academic studies. The most insightful findings from this project related to the limitations of personal data within university contexts; in particular, the poor quality of data actually being collected by the universities, as well as the limited data awareness, skills, and "data imaginations" of students.

These findings echo those of Matzner, Masur, Ochs, & von Pope (2016, p. 280), who argue that a "crucial precondition" for critical data practices is an awareness of data generation and collection. One innovative approach to developing data awareness and agency was taken by the Our Data Ourselves project in the United Kingdom (Pybus, Cote, & Blanke, 2015). This involved the use of a data-gathering app that enabled students to examine and reclaim the data generated through their personal smartphone use. The researchers concluded that agency derived from students' ability to "work on, process and transform" (Pybus et al., 2015, p. 8) the materiality of data, which are typically beyond the user's knowledge or control. Developing similar applications that enable students to understand how data about them is collected and used in the university context would potentially help develop students' data literacies.

Improving students' critical understandings of digital media and social media

Finally, with regard to improving critical understandings of digital media, the consensus seems to be that this calls for educators to work with students in improving engagement with digital media. This can be seen in the ongoing turn toward transformative teaching with/about digital media. The University of Mary Washington's (UMW) Domain of One's Own is a good example of how universities can support the development of critical digital practices. While at UMW, students, faculty, and staff can register their own domain name and associate it with a hosted web space. Through the domain, users have the opportunity to create their own digital presence, while also learning skills of design and site management. This provides a meaningful way of developing a professional identity outside the realms of mainstream commercial social media.

To develop more responsible use of social media on campus many universities have now developed guidelines or policies for use; for example, see Boston University (2016) and UCLA (2016). While it seems reasonable that universities monitor and react to comments posted on official university forums, this is more complicated when it comes to social media sites beyond the university involving students and staff. A study by Rowe (2014) found that many students would *not* welcome contact from universities on their private social media sites, even if it were constructive. Universities therefore need to develop innovative approaches to social media that model critical and responsible use, rather than using more authoritarian measures.

This is a fraught area for universities to work through. As noted earlier, Yik Yak controversies prompted several US universities to ban the app from campus WiFi networks. However, this has been viewed by some commentators as an encroachment on freedom of speech, as well as being a response that targets the means of expression rather than the expression itself. In contrast, the University of Lincoln Students' Union developed a Show Your Best Side project designed by students to encourage "digital well-being" on social media. The project encourages students to develop more responsible online behaviors, highlighting the impact of online harassment, as well as the effect that negative attention can have on future career prospects. This work encouraged the use of "pinned pledges," which include preformatted anti-harassment slogans linked to mainstream social media platforms like Twitter and Facebook, therefore promoting the idea that online sexism, racism, and bullying have no place in university communities.

Conclusions

Higher education is a diverse context within which digital media are used by students. As such, university authorities and educators are continuing to explore the extent to which they are able and/or it is appropriate to support the development of students' digital media literacies. Clearly, universities have an important role to play in modeling good uses of digital media, as well as providing students with ample advice, support, and opportunities. Nevertheless, the exact nature of how university students engage with digital media falls ultimately to the students themselves. With this in mind, it seems sensible that universities pursue the kinds of programs and projects outlined toward the end of this entry, while encouraging students to remain critically engaged and aware of digital media use (be it for studying or socializing). Digital media literacy will continue to grow as a defining issue in higher education as the 21st century progresses. It is important that media scholars continue to remain engaged in these discussions.

SEE ALSO: Critical Information Literacy; Twitter in Education; University–School Partnerships for Media Literacy

References

Association of College & Research Libraries (ACRL). (2016). *Framework for information literacy for higher education*. Retrieved from http://www.ala.org/acrl/standards/ilframework

Boston University. (2016). *Social media guidelines*. Retrieved from https://www.bu.edu/tech/about/policies/info-security/social-media/

Chatterton, P., & Rebbeck, G. (2015). *Technology for employability: Study into the role of technology in developing student employability*. Bristol, England: Jisc.

Henderson, M., Selwyn, N., & Aston, R. (2017). What works and why? Student perceptions of "useful" digital technology in university teaching and learning. *Studies in Higher Education, 42*(8), 1567–1579. doi: 10.1080/03075079.2015.1007946

Hood, N., Littlejohn, A., & Milligan, C. (2015). Context counts: How learners' contexts influence learning in a MOOC. *Computers & Education, 91*, 83–91. doi: 10.1016/j.compedu.2015.10.019

Jaffer, S. (2013, February 4). Spotted at university. *The Guardian*. Retrieved from https://www.theguardian.com/education/2013/feb/04/spotted-at-university-misogyny-and-racism

Jones, C. (2012). Networked learning, stepping beyond the net generation and digital natives. In L. Dirckinck-Holmfeld, V. Hodgson, & D. McConnell (Eds.), *Exploring the theory, pedagogy and practice of networked learning* (pp. 27–41). New York, NY: Springer.

Karbhari, V. (2016). What is lost: The error of reducing complex higher education processes to metrics and singular narratives. In *Inspirational innovation* (pp. 3.1–3.6). Philadelphia, PA: Aramark. Retrieved from http://www.presidentialperspectives.org/pdf/2016/2016-Chap-3-What-is-Lost-Karbhari.pdf

Kennedy, G., Judd, T., Dalgarno, B., & Waycott, J. (2010). Beyond natives and immigrants: Exploring types of net generation students. *Journal of Computer Assisted Learning, 26*(5), 332–343. doi: 10.1111/j.1365-2729.2010.00371.x

Keppell, M. (2014). Personalised learning strategies for higher education. In K. Fraser (Ed.), *The future of learning and teaching in next generation learning spaces* (pp. 3–21). London, England: Emerald.

Marlowe, J., Bartley, A., & Collins, F. (2017). Digital belongings: The intersections of social cohesion, connectivity and digital media. *Ethnicities, 17*(1), 85–102. doi: 10.1177/1468796816654174

Matzner, T., Masur, P., Ochs, C., & von Pope, T. (2016). Do-it-yourself data protection. In S. Gutwirth, R. Leenes, & P. De Hart (Eds.), *Data protection on the move* (Vol. 24). Dordrecht, Netherlands: Springer.

Mayer, A., & Puller, S. (2008). The old boy (and girl) network: Social network formation on university campuses. *Journal of Public Economics, 92*(1–2), 329–347. doi: 10.1016/j.jpubeco.2007.09.001

Pool, C. (1997). A new digital literacy. *Educational Leadership, 55*(3), 6–11.

Pybus, J., Cote, M., & Blanke, T. (2015). Hacking the social life of Big Data. *Big Data & Society, 2*(2), 1–10. doi: 10.1177/2053951715616649

Rowe, J. (2014). Student use of social media. *Journal of Higher Education Policy & Management, 36*(3), 241–256. doi: 10.1080/01587919.2014.899054

Rowlands, I., Nicholas, D., Williams, P., Huntington, P., Fieldhouse, M., Gunter, B. … & Tenopir, C. (2008). The Google generation: The information behaviour of the researcher of the future. *Aslib Proceedings: New Information Perspectives, 60*(4), 290–310. doi: 10.1108/00012530810887953

Seale, J., Georgeson, J., Mamas, C., & Swain, J. (2015). Not the right kind of "digital capital"? *Computers & Education, 82*, 118–128. doi: 10.1016/j.compedu.2014.11.007

Selwyn, N., & Gorard, S. (2016). Students' use of Wikipedia as an academic resource. *The Internet and Higher Education, 28*, 28–34. doi: 10.1016/j.iheduc.2015.08.004

Selwyn, N., Henderson, M., & Chao, S. (2017). "You need a system": Exploring the role of data in the administration of university students and courses. *Journal of Further and Higher Education, 42*(1), 46–56.

Terras, M., & Ramsey, J. (2015). Massive open online courses: Insights and challenges from a psychological perspective. *British Journal of Educational Technology, 46*(3), 472–487. doi: 10.1111/bjet.12274

Tripodi, F. (2016). Reaffirmation and double marginalization: Yik Yak and community identity formation on college campuses. In J. Daniels, K. Gregory, & T. Cottom (Eds.), *Digital sociologies*. Bristol, England: Policy Press.

University of California Los Angeles (UCLA). 2016. *UCLA social media guidelines*. Retrieved from http://socialmedia.ucla.edu/

Further reading

Goodfellow, R., & Lea, M. (Eds.). (2013). *Literacy in the digital university: Critical perspectives on learning, scholarship and technology*. London, England: Routledge.

Henderson, M., Selwyn, N., & Aston, R. (2017). What works and why? Student perceptions of "useful" digital technology in university teaching and learning. *Studies in Higher Education, 42*(8), 1567–1579. doi: 10.1080/03075079.2015.1007946

Selwyn, N. (2014). *Digital technology and the contemporary university.* London, England: Routledge.

Neil Selwyn is a professor at Monash University, Faculty of Education. His research focuses on digital technology and education. Recent books include *What Is Digital Sociology?* (2018) and *Everyday Schooling in the Digital Age* (2018).

Luci Pangrazio is a research fellow at Deakin University's Research for Educational Impact (REDI) center. Her research interests include critical digital literacies, social media and young people, and critical responses to fake/junk news. Recent books include *Young People's Literacies in the Digital Age* (2018).

Digital News

ADAM MAKSL
Indiana University Southeast, USA

The Internet and digital technologies have upended the structures of many industries, especially those whose main focus is the collection and dissemination of information. In many cases, those individuals involved in the industries find their roles significantly changed and the expectations placed on them significantly broadened. This is certainly the case with digital news, for both digital news content creators and those who interact with the content—or, in past parlance, for both journalists and members of the audience.

In past eras, the role of the journalists was more clearly defined: to seek out and report truthful information. And the role of the audience members was to consume that information, largely trusting the institution of journalism and its public service mission. Information traveled primarily in a single direction, from journalists to the audience, with little feedback or interaction from the audience back to the journalist. Digital technologies in general—and the Internet and mobile devices in particular—have changed this model.

In a 2009 TED (technology, entertainment, and design) Talk, digital journalism scholar and New York University professor Clay Shirky contrasts the type of interaction supported by different media throughout history. He says, for example, that the phone allowed for one-to-one interaction and radio, television, newspapers, and books allowed for one-to-many interaction. The Internet gives us many-to-many interaction. In the context of journalism, that allows journalists and audiences to be both content creators and content consumers. And the interaction among them is bidirectional, allowing for constant feedback.

While this theoretically presents great opportunities for the democratization of news, it is challenging in the context of information abundance and lack of media literacy skills. The technology allows for the many-to-many interaction, and certainly the barriers to entry for content creation are less expensive. But the structural filters used in an era of information abundance may reduce the promise of a democratization of news and, more importantly, audiences' knowledge about those structural influences may work to maximize benefit and minimize potential harm.

Major dimensions

Within the context of media literacy, understanding digital news means understanding digital creation tools used by content creators; the differences between born-digital organizations and legacy organizations in adopting more digital strategies; and the role of artificial intelligence and algorithmic filtering of news content.

Digital technology has advanced the ability of journalists to tell stories using multimedia methods. Journalist Mark E. Briggs (2016) argues that "we are all web workers now" and that journalists must learn skills like blogging and microblogging, crowdsourcing, mobile reporting, digital photography, audio journalism, video, and data journalism. Journalists today produce content in all these forms, which are often consumed by the audiences concurrently or in integrated, increasingly mobile spaces.

Each new platform carries with it its own unique features and characteristics, and audiences should work to better appreciate the capacity of each platform and how each one is used by journalists. For example, journalists have used platforms like Twitter widely to disseminate news, especially breaking news, as well as to interact with sources and audiences. But Twitter limits its messages to 280 characters, which diminishes the ability to provide context to reporting. Journalists are increasingly publishing video on social platforms like Facebook, which are endowed with features that automatically play the video without sound. These characteristics can be viewed as both constraints on and expansions of a journalist's storytelling potential; but they do influence the content and the decisions that content creators make.

Social media sites like Facebook and Twitter have been primarily used by news organizations to simply link to news stories posted on websites. However, as newer social media tools require content to be created on their platforms or more readily serve to users content created on their platforms, news organizations have moved toward this distributed model. In 2015 and 2016, for example, Facebook introduced Instant Articles, a system that allows organizations to publish directly to the platform, benefiting users with faster-loading content on mobile platforms but giving the social network more power to control the environment in which the content is created and distributed.

Generally speaking, two types of news organizations exist in the modern online journalism ecosystem: born-digital organizations and legacy organizations that have adopted strategies that focus on the creation and distribution of digital content. Born-digital organizations were created in the Internet age and thus have no TV- or print-oriented routines or organizational structures. Legacy news organizations tend to be mostly broadcast or newspaper companies that retain TV and print production even while competing online. These differences are most stark when it comes to the business operations of news organizations.

The work of traditional legacy organizations is characterized by three elements (Nielsen, 2016). First, news is considered highly expensive to produce, especially in labor costs, though traditional organizations also have major capital expenses such as printing presses and broadcast transmitters. Second, news is considered nonrivalrous, which means that the consumption by one person does not affect the availability of the "good" to others. And, third, traditional news is produced is an environment with limited competition, owing in large part to high economic barriers to entry. Born-digital news organizations share the first two characteristics with their legacy counterparts—namely the high production costs, especially with labor (though other news production costs can be lower without print and broadcast infrastructures to build and manage), and the nonrivalrous nature of the news product. But the third point—that news exists in a market with limited competition—is no longer the norm for either born-digital organizations or the traditional legacy organizations that pivot to compete in the digital environment. There are simply more sources of information competing with one another for attention and sometimes shrinking advertising dollars. This increased competition for limited revenue has resulted in decreases in the resources spent on news production and has encouraged organizations to create content that is more likely to get attention, often through views and clicks.

Perhaps the most important dimension of digital news that is relevant to media literacy is the influence of social media. Hermida (2016) suggests that, as social media have become more popular and are part of an audience's daily routines, the context for journalism has changed rapidly, in some ways modifying the roles and practices of journalists. For example, the agenda-setting and gatekeeping roles of journalism change when everyone is one's own editor.

However, being one's own editor presupposes a high level of control and sophistication, and the increasing role technology companies play in filtering content affects the choices that a reader can make. In other words, a reader might be choosing the news stories he or she clicks on and reads from Facebook, but Facebook has already culled the list of content before it is ever presented to that reader. Although technology companies such as Facebook and Google have "become entwined in the distribution, circulation, and promotion of news and information" (Hermida, 2016, p. 89) in the 21st century, they do not create media. More importantly, these companies assert directly that they are not media companies but are just platforms. For example, when Facebook CEO Mark Zuckerberg was asked in August 2016 whether the company needed news editors, he said clearly: "No, we are a tech company, not a media company."

Early in Facebook's history—and for more of Twitter's history, though this has changed recently—the services would supply to users the most recent posts from accounts their users followed. However, now these services employ proprietary algorithms to choose the content that is presented to users, using factors such as how close the user is to the original poster; how many likes, clicks, or shares the post has received; the type of posts, whether photo, video, or text; the content of posts, where things like birthday celebrations and baby announcements seem to get more significant play; and whether the content of the post relates to a user's interests, what media the user has consumed in the past, and so on. The problem with eschewing the moniker of media company is that these so-called tech companies don't appreciate the humanness of the editorial decisions that go into what programmers and others resolve the algorithms will choose. Journalism—as an industry—is normatively interested in its public service mission, but there may be a disconnect between the public service ideals of journalists and those of designers and technologists at social media companies (Ananny & Crawford, 2015).

One major challenge social media companies face is how fake news is filtered through their platforms. This became a major issue during the 2016 presidential campaign and election, as stories from fake news sites were often shared on social media. Stories from sites that seem legitimate but offer fake stories that play directly into users' partisan preferences and biases have been shared widely on social media. Investigations from Buzzfeed and the *Guardian* found that the creators of these sites are attracted by the simple economics—that these largely false but highly partisan stories are widely shared and thus receive significant clicks, which produce advertising revenue. In November 2016, both Google and Facebook said they were restricting fake news sites' access to their vast advertising networks.

Finally, though the algorithms are proprietary, social media platforms do use "engagement" data to decide which content to serve, for example through the number of Facebook likes, shares, and comments a post receives. The concern, for many, is that heavily weighing engagement metrics in news judgments can create perverse incentives for journalists, for example leading to more sensational stories because those attract more clicks. Scholars have found that audience engagement does influence news judgment. However, editors' journalism training and strong role conception of the institutional obligations of journalism suppress some of the influence of engagement data.

A brief history of digital news

The first newspaper to offer its content online was the *Columbus Dispatch* in 1980, when it partnered with the Associated Press and the online service CompuServe. Although other newspapers were delivered through that service and others throughout the 1980s and early 1990s, it was not until commercial web browsers rose in popularity and use, in the mid-1990s, that online news really took off. Often content was "shovelware," a term used to describe situations where text and photos from newspapers and video from broadcast stations were simply copied and published online, largely in their original form. Although early online journalism and shovelware didn't change the routines of journalists and the substance of the journalism they created, they offered users a new way to organize content topically and a way to dig down further into the context of a story (Scott, 2005). Additionally, they allowed users to access news organizations' archives easily.

News organizations started to recognize that the online environment allowed them to cover breaking news quickly, which, with the advent of cable news, led to a 24-hour news cycle. The early days showed increased competition, as born-digital organizations started to compete with the legacy organizations.

News organizations started with shovelware, and many continued (and still continue) to focus on basic text, photos, and TV-style video on the web, even as more users use mobile devices for news consumption. Humprecht and Esser (2016) argue that the promise of digital journalism was threefold. First, it allowed for greater transparency, often by linking to original sources of reporting, such as databases or public documents. Second, it allowed for linking to background information or presenting information in nontraditional ways that can provide additional context, such as interactive maps or infographics. Third, it allowed audience members to participate in the news process, transforming the journalist–audience relationship from lecture to conversation. But simply being web-based did not promise that organizations use these tools effectively. Most organizations still rely primarily on text, with few hyperlinks, additional content, or participatory opportunities for readers beyond comment sections.

However, as social media have been integrated more into journalism processes, journalism organizations have more opportunities to realize the promise of digital journalism, especially in engaging with audiences. That said, many newsrooms still see social media as a risk to traditional journalism norms like accuracy and objectivity (Lee, 2016). Understanding the promise of digital news, as well as how news organizations assess the opportunities or risks of digital media technologies, is integral to understanding the environment in which audiences consume and engage with news. Media literacy scholars, in particular, must understand this environment, in which digital news is created to explore how audiences can be best equipped to consume such content. For example, as audiences are accustomed to opportunities to engage with others online, it might be useful for them to appreciate journalists' risk assessment of social media as a reason why the journalists do not fully engage. Such norms and behaviors of journalists would be useful in informing audience perceptions of news work.

Current and future directions in digital news scholarship

Journalism studies has long been thought to exist in an interdisciplinary space, borrowing theories and methodologies from humanities and social sciences. Research in journalism could largely be classified as normative, empirical, sociological, or comparative, with some historical progression from the former to the latter. However, scholars argue that theories established for old media may be somewhat inflexible in the digital age, so researchers should both adapt old theories and create new ones for a modern age (Steensen & Ahva, 2015). For example, some scholars have suggested that gatekeeping or hierarchy of influences theory may be outdated when journalists are no longer gatekeepers but participants in a reciprocal process of communication (Singer, 2016), or that at least the role of audiences needs to be expanded beyond that of being just one of many social–institutional influences (Vu, 2014).

Other scholars suggest that the influence of technology on journalistic practice has often focused on sociocultural factors, which include only human actors—primarily those involved in news work. This has missed humans and nonhumans involved in the technical side of journalism. Lewis and Westlund (2015) argue that journalism studies must take an integrated sociotechnical approach, in which both human and nonhuman actors, including audiences, are factored into how news is accessed, selected, processed, distributed, and interpreted.

The current directions of digital journalism scholarship have implications for media literacy research. For instance, critical media literacy scholars who focus on teaching knowledge of structural components of the media system and routines of media creators should better understand the role of both human and nonhuman agents in the process of media creation, selection, and distribution. Those who focus on media effects must understand the relational nature of journalism, where there are no easily defined or identified senders or receivers, and where journalism is created in an iterative and integrated environment. And those who focus on production and technical media creation skills must increasingly emphasize how audiences are integrated into the process and how messages are ubiquitous and multidirectional.

SEE ALSO: Adolescent Literacy in a Digital World; Digital Literacy; Digital Storytelling; News Literacies

References

Ananny, M., & Crawford, K. (2015). A liminal press: Situating news app designers within a field of networked news production. *Digital Journalism, 3*(2), 192–208.

Briggs, M.E. (2016). *Journalism next: The practical guide to digital reporting and publishing* (3rd ed.). Thousand Oaks, CA: CQ Press.

Hermida, A. (2016). Social media and the news. In T. Witschge, C.W. Anderson, D. Domingo, & A. Hermida (Eds.), *The SAGE handbook of digital journalism* (pp. 81–94). London, England: SAGE.

Humprecht, E., & Esser, F. (2016). Mapping digital journalism: Comparing 48 news websites from six counties. *Journalism, 19*(4), 500–518. doi: 10.1177/1464884916667872

Lee, J. (2016). Opportunity or risk? How news organizations frame social media in their guidelines for journalists. *Communication Review, 19*(2), 106–127. doi: 10.1080/10714421.2016.1161328

Lewis, S.C., & Westlund, O. (2015). Actors, actants, audiences, and activities in crossmedia news work. *Digital Journalism, 3*(1), 19–37. doi: 10.1080/21670811.2014.927986

Nielsen, R.K. (2016). The business of news. In T. Witschge, C.W. Anderson, D. Domingo, & A. Hermida (Eds.), *The SAGE handbook of digital journalism* (pp. 51–67). London, England: SAGE.

Scott, B. (2005). A contemporary history of digital journalism. *Television and News Media, 6*(1), 89–126. doi: 10.1177/1527476403255824

Singer, J.B. (2016). Transmission creep: Media effect theories and journalism studies in the digital age. *Journalism Studies, 19*(2), 209–226. doi: 10.1080/1461670X.2016.1186498

Steensen, S., & Ahva, L. (2015). Theories of journalism in a digital age. *Digital Journalism, 3*(1), 1–18. doi: 10.1080/21670811.2014.927984

Vu, H.T. (2014). The online audience as gatekeeper: The influence of reader metrics on news editorial selection. *Journalism, 15*(8), 1094–1110. doi: 10.1177/1464884913504259

Further reading

Gillespie, T. (2014). The relevance of algorithms. In T. Gillespie, P. Boczkowski, & K.A. Foot (Eds.), *Media technologies: Essays on communication, materiality, and society* (pp. 167–194). Cambridge, MA: MIT Press.
Reuters Institute for the Study of Journalism. (2016). Reuters Institute digital news report 2016. Retrieved from http://www.digitalnewsreport.org
Witschge, T., Anderson, C.W., Domingo, D., & Hermida, A. (Eds.). (2016). *The SAGE handbook of digital journalism*. London, England: SAGE.

Adam Maksl is associate professor of journalism and media at Indiana University Southeast, where he teaches and advises the multiplatform student news organization. Maksl's work—in teaching, research, and service—focuses primarily on youth media and news media literacy. His research has been published in *Journalism & Mass Communication Quarterly* and *Journalism & Mass Communication Educator*. Before entering academia, Maksl worked as a high school journalism teacher, and then as a university outreach coordinator for youth journalism programs. He holds a BS from Indiana University, Bloomington, an MA from Ball State University, and a PhD from the University of Missouri.

Digital Storytelling

BERNARD R. ROBIN and SARA G. MCNEIL
University of Houston, USA

Those who tell the stories rule the world.

Native American Proverb

Digital storytelling is the practice of creating a short movie by combining digital artifacts such as images, text, video clips, animation, and music using a computer-based program. Digital stories typically have narration in the form of recorded audio that provides an emotional element to the story. The digital story is saved in a digital format that can be viewed on a computer or other device capable of playing video files. Digital stories are usually uploaded to the web where they may be viewed through any popular web browser. As is the case with traditional storytelling, digital stories revolve around a chosen theme, often contain a particular viewpoint, and are typically just a few minutes long.

Despite its emphasis on computer technology, digital storytelling is not a new practice. One of the field's most noted pioneers is Joe Lambert, the cofounder of the Center for Digital Storytelling (CDS), now called StoryCenter, a nonprofit, community arts organization in Berkeley, California. The CDS has been assisting young people and adults in the creation and sharing of personal narratives through the combination of thoughtful writing and digital media tools since the early 1990s. Another pioneer in the field, British photographer, author, and educator Daniel Meadows has called digital stories "short, personal multimedia tales told from the heart." The beauty of this form of digital expression, he maintains, is that these stories can be created by people everywhere, on any subject, and shared electronically all over the world.

Many practitioners of digital storytelling believe that digital stories are distinct from, although often related to, other types of videos, such as interactive stories, narrative computer games, slideshows with images, and short narrated films. There may be diverse opinions on what constitutes a digital story, and there is no one perfect definition that fits all stories and all people, so it is ultimately up to individual viewers to determine what they consider a digital story to be or not be.

Basic elements of digital storytelling

Joe Lambert is known for disseminating the Seven Elements of Digital Storytelling (2003), which was first proposed in the early 1990s and is still cited as a useful starting point to begin working with digital stories. The seven elements are: (i) point of view (of the author), (ii) a dramatic question, (iii) emotional content, (iv) the gift of your voice (narration), (v) the power of the soundtrack (to support the storyline), (vi) economy (of length), and (vii) pacing of the story. Lambert (2010) later updated the Seven Elements to the Seven Steps of Digital Storytelling as shown in Table 1.

Categories of digital stories

Digital stories typically fall into three categories: personal narratives, historical documentaries, or stories that inform or instruct. Personal narratives usually revolve around a significant event in the creator's life and may include stories that honor the memory of specific people and places, deal with life's adventures, or share accomplishments, challenges, and recovery. Personal narratives have multiple benefits in an educational setting. Students who view the story learn about people from diverse backgrounds other than their own, and they can gain an appreciation of the types of hardships faced by others. Personal narratives can be used to facilitate discussions about current issues such

Table 1 The Seven Steps of Digital Storytelling.

1. Owning your insight	finding your story
2. Owning your emotions	identifying and conveying personal content
3. Finding the moment	identifying the moment of change in your story
4. Seeing your story	visualizing, locating, and understanding the images
5. Hearing your story	adding your voice, music, sound effects
6. Assembling your story	using structure, pacing, and economy
7. Sharing your story	presenting your story to an audience

as race, multiculturalism, and globalization and can be a positive way of dealing with emotional issues.

Digital stories can also be used to recount dramatic historical events that help viewers understand the past. In a classroom environment, students might use historical photographs, newspaper headlines, speeches, and other available materials to craft a story that adds depth and meaning to events from the past. Perhaps the most common use of digital stories is to inform or instruct. Teachers can use this type of digital story to present information to their students on subjects ranging from math and science, to art, technology, and medical education.

Benefits of digital storytelling in education, business, communities, and health sciences

Digital storytelling is currently being used in diverse ways around the world: in education and training; in business marketing; in organizations and nonprofits such as libraries, community centers, and museums; and in health science education. In education and training, digital stories are used to present new material, facilitate discussion, and make abstract or conceptual content more understandable. Research has shown that teachers' use of multimedia helps students retain new information and aids in the comprehension of difficult material. Students who create digital stories learn to organize their ideas, ask questions, express opinions, construct narratives, and present their ideas and knowledge in an individual and meaningful way (Ohler, 2007). In addition, when digital stories are published online, students have the opportunity to share their work with their peers and gain valuable experience in critiquing their own and other students' work, which can promote gains in emotional intelligence and social learning.

In business, digital stories are most often used in marketing to create connections between products and the audience on a deep emotional level and encourage a particular action. Nike's inspiring digital stories that began in 1974 with the theme "Just do it" are a good example. These stories continue to engage viewers because these emotional and innovative stories communicate across all generations and sports in a way a print advertisement cannot.

For community organizations and nonprofits, digital storytelling can be an effective way to engage audiences or gain support for a cause. Because digital storytelling is a universal way of communicating, museums can inspire visitors to connect with the artifacts and their own experiences and history. A 2014 report by the Rockefeller Foundation, *Digital Storytelling for Social Impact*, described how digital storytelling can help social impact organizations advance their missions and provided recommendations for skills, technologies, and metrics to evaluate the effectiveness of digital storytelling.

In health sciences, digital storytelling can be a tool for patients and health science professionals to share experiences, cope with illnesses, and add a human element to health problems. For example, community digital storytelling workshops can empower cancer survivors to create digital stories that reflect on their experiences as well as provide an authentic way for others to learn about the disease. Projects such as *Health*

Equity Change Makers (Office of Health and Human Resources, 2016) share personal stories about health disparities, and *We Are Healers* (University of Wisconsin-Madison Native American Center for Health Professions, 2016) provides stories and discussion resources about Native American people who have become health providers.

Research on the effectiveness of digital storytelling

Overall, a wide variety of research studies have shown that digital storytelling positively affects and supports teaching and learning in several ways. The process of creating digital stories has been shown to help learners organize and express their ideas, increase reading comprehension, and scaffold the development and formation of sociocultural identities and critical literacies. By sharing their own digital stories, learners can contribute to the development of a learning community and a positive classroom environment. As an instructional strategy, digital storytelling has been used by educators at all levels to reinforce and enrich traditional teaching methods and more effectively engage learners of all ages. Typical of the scope of research in this area, Smeda, Dakich, and Sharda (2014) explored the pedagogical benefits of digital storytelling. The main focus of their work was to assess the impact of digital storytelling on student learning and engagement. They found that digital storytelling can enhance a number of learning skills such as writing, research, use of technology, and communication. In addition, their results highlighted digital storytelling's ability to personalize learning experiences, support diversity, improve students' confidence, and enhance their social and psychological skills.

Challenges of digital storytelling

Creating an effective and engaging digital story is a challenging task. Creators must grapple with writing an effective script, respecting copyright for the multimedia elements included in the story, recording narration that communicates the story, choosing music that enhances but doesn't overpower the narration, and using feedback to improve the story. Teachers must find ways to guide the creative process, assess the stories, and model intellectual property use as well as protect students' safety when using online resources.

Some teachers may be reluctant to use digital storytelling in their classrooms because they do not know how to assess their students' work in a meaningful and practical way. Assessment of student-created digital stories can take place during the design process, during the development process, and after the digital story is completed. Each of these categories can be divided into self-assessment by the student who created the story, peer-assessment by fellow classmates, and educational assessment by the teacher. Story Circles allow students to share the rough drafts of their scripts in order to get peer feedback about their initial efforts at writing down their ideas. Story Circles can be a vital and integral part of story development in which a teacher can observe the interactions and also ask students to reflect about what they changed in their script after this peer feedback process. Story Screenings allow students to receive feedback from peers when a digital version of the story has been created. Other common assessment tools include checklists and rubrics, although more innovative approaches such as using a digital story as a reflective e-portfolio can be used for students to provide evidence of their learning.

The digital storytelling process

The design and development of a digital story is a multistep process that begins with the selection of the topic for the story and ends with the publishing of the completed digital file, with a number of steps in between. A 12-step process that is used in digital storytelling courses and workshops is presented in Table 2.

Hardware needed for creating digital stories

The basic hardware requirements for digital storytelling include a computing device to gather and assemble the media elements and a microphone to record audio narration. A digital camera, video camera, and a scanner are useful pieces of hardware that can be used to create still images and video clips. When digital storytelling first began, a Windows or Macintosh desktop or laptop computer, usually connected to the Internet, was needed. However, as computing devices have evolved, smartphones and tablet computers can now be used to download content from the web, take digital photos, record audio narration, and shoot full-motion video, all important tasks in creating a digital story.

Software programs for creating digital stories

Digital stories can be assembled with software installed on a desktop or laptop computer, with web-based tools, and with mobile apps for smartphones and tablets. The advantage of web-based software and mobile apps is that they employ simple, cross-platform interfaces and take advantage of cloud-based storage. Microsoft Movie Maker, Apple iMovie, and Adobe Premiere are examples of software programs that can be installed on a desktop or laptop computer. WeVideo is an example of digital storytelling software that can be used through a web-based interface. Smartphones and tablet apps that can be used for digital storytelling include Com-Phone Story Maker, Magisto, Splice, and Storyrobe.

To learn more

The Educational Uses of Digital Storytelling website (http://digitalstorytelling.coe.uh.edu/), created by educators at the University of Houston, serves as a comprehensive clearinghouse of information for those just starting to use digital storytelling as well as

Table 2 A 12-step process for digital storytelling.

Step	*Task*	*Recommendations*
1.	Choose a topic	Begin by thinking of the purpose of the story and define the audience.
2.	Conduct research on the topic	You can use online search engines, but don't forget that the library can also be a useful research tool.
3.	Write the first draft of the script	This will serve as the audio narration for your story. Read aloud what you have written. Make sure that the purpose of the story is clearly articulated and includes an identifiable point of view.
	Script tip 1: Keep your script small and focused	*You are writing a script for a digital story which is typically only a few minutes long. Focusing on a specific problem or topic will help you create a better digital story.*
	Script tip 2: Make it personal	*Your digital story is unique. It is your story, and the audience will want to hear it from your perspective. You may even need to reveal personal details in the story to reach an emotional depth, although it is up to you to decide what details you wish to share with others.*
	Script tip 3: Understand the story arc	*Most stories consist of three parts: a beginning, middle, and end. The beginning is where you set the scene and begin the plot. The middle is where you provide more details about the topic or problem you are trying to explain. The story should be building toward a climax or resolution. The end is where the questions are resolved. Will new knowledge make you stronger? Will you now be able to accomplish greater things? What happens next in your life? These questions will be answered and new insight will be revealed. The conclusion of your story should connect back to the beginning to form a thematic arc.*
4.	Receive feedback on the script	Share your script with others and ask them to give you feedback on what they thought might make your story clearer or more useful.
5.	Revise the script	Use the feedback you received to improve the next version of your script. Scriptwriting is an iterative process and it takes several attempts to get good results.
6.	Find, create, and add images	Use an online search tool specifically for images, such as Google Image Search. You can search for photographs, drawings, clip art, maps, charts, and more. Don't forget that you can use photos you take yourself with a digital camera.
7.	Respect copyrights	Look for material that is in the public domain or has a Creative Commons license.
8.	Create a storyboard	The storyboard is a written or a graphical overview of all of the elements you plan to include in the digital story. It serves as a blueprint or an advanced organizer as you plan to construct your digital story. Storyboards can help you visualize your story before it is created, when it is easier to make changes or add new content.

Table 2 *Continued*

Step	*Task*	*Recommendations*
9.	Record audio narration and add background music (optional)	Try to use a high-quality microphone or a voice recording app on a smartphone. Music that is appropriate to the theme of the story can add richness by complementing the narration. There are many great sites online that provide copyright-free music at no cost.
10.	Build the digital story	Select the software tool you will use to create your digital story.
11.	Give and receive feedback on the digital story	Participate in a Story Circle: Share your story with others and ask them to give you feedback on how to improve the digital version.
12.	Publish the digital story	Share your digital story online at locations such as YouTube, Google Drive, Microsoft OneDrive, Dropbox, etc.

for those who want to deeply explore the many facets of this educational technology practice. The site contains example digital stories, tutorials, links to e-books, websites, articles, and research studies about digital storytelling.

SEE ALSO: Creativity and Media Production in Schools; Hypertext and Hypermedia Writing; Literacy, Technology, and Media; Teaching with Media; Understanding Media Literacy and DIY Creativity in Youth Digital Productions

References

Lambert, J. (2003). *Digital storytelling cookbook and traveling companion*. Berkeley, CA: Digital Diner Press.

Lambert, J. (2010). *The digital storytelling cookbook*. Berkeley, CA: Digital Diner Press. Retrieved from https://wrd.as.uky.edu/sites/default/files/cookbook.pdf

Office of Health and Human Resources. (2016). *Health equity change makers*. Retrieved from http://www.minorityhealth.hhs.gov/ChangeMakers/

Ohler, J. (2007). *Digital storytelling in the classroom: New media pathways to literacy, learning and creativity*. Thousand Oaks, CA: Corwin Press.

Rockefeller Foundation. (2014). *Digital storytelling for social impact*. Retrieved from https://www.rockefellerfoundation.org/blog/digital-storytelling-social-impact/

Smeda, N., Dakich, E., & Sharda, N. (2014). The effectiveness of digital storytelling in the classrooms: A comprehensive study. *Smart Learning Environments, 1*(1), 1–21. doi: 10.1186/s40561-014-0006-3

University of Wisconsin-Madison Native American Center for Health Professions. (2016). *We are healers*. Retrieved from http://wearehealers.org/

Further reading

Lambert, J. (2009). *Digital storytelling: Capturing lives, creating community*. Berkeley, CA: Digital Diner Press.

Robin, B. (2008). Digital storytelling. A powerful technology tool for the 21st century classroom. *Theory into Practice*, themed issue on *New Media and Education in the 21st Century, 47*(3), 220–228. doi: 10.1080/00405840802153916

Robin, B. (2016). The power of digital storytelling to support teaching and learning. *Digital Education Review, 30*, 17–29. Retrieved from https://files.eric.ed.gov/fulltext/EJ1125504.pdf

Bernard R. Robin is an associate professor of learning, design, and technology in the College of Education at the University of Houston. Dr. Robin teaches courses on the integration of technology into the curriculum, educational uses of multimedia, and developing educational content for the web. Dr. Robin created the Educational Uses of Digital Storytelling website and has published extensively on the educational uses of digital storytelling. He was a member of a team of faculty and graduate students that created one of the University of Houston's first Massive Open Online Courses, *Powerful Tools for Teaching and Learning: Digital Storytelling.*

Sara G. McNeil is an associate professor in the College of Education at the University of Houston, where she serves as Coordinator for the Learning, Design and Technology Graduate Program. She teaches courses in instructional design, the collaborative design and development of multimedia, and digital presentations. She researches, publishes, and presents internationally about emerging technologies in education. Her multimedia projects include the design and development of Digital History, a comprehensive resource of high-quality, historical resources, and New Technologies, a website for K-16 teachers to help them select an appropriate Web 2.0 tool for a specific task.

Documentary Analysis and Production in Media Literacy

KATHERINE G. FRY
Brooklyn College of the City University of New York, USA

Exploring the dimensions of documentary analysis and production in media literacy necessarily begins with a discussion about what is understood to be documentary. On the surface a documentary is a distinct media genre, or unique set of storytelling conventions with accompanying audience expectations, like other media genres. Documentaries are a type of nonfiction media and, though they can be structured in many different ways, are typically informational accounts of issues, people, events, places, or ideas that are of broad interest or relevance, or are unique and considered worthy of documenting. Documentary styles vary greatly, but most often documentaries are assumed to be visually based, as in film or video documentary. However, they can also be audio, or sound-based. They are almost always a genre of electronic media, and not of print media.

Within the purview of media literacy it is necessary to reach beyond a surface definition to consider a much wider terrain for thinking about and using documentary to reach media literacy education goals. Three broad areas or parameters for considering documentary within media literacy education are included here. They are: (i) using documentary analysis to teach principles of media literacy of content and form, (ii) teaching documentary production as a means to teach components of media literacy, and (iii) teaching with and analyzing documentaries *about* media literacy education topics.

Teaching documentary analysis

The disciplines of communication and media education offer a rich history of using documentary as pedagogy. Some important works, from the 1970s into the 21st century, include Hendrix and Wood (1973) and Foss (1983) who examined the use of film to teach rhetoric. Robinson (1984) examined use of documentary to develop visual literacy skills for film students. More recently Edwards (2001) outlined the ways in which documentary production enhances a liberal arts education, while Margolis and Pauwels (2011) broadly examined the use of visual works, including documentary, as tools for higher education. Media literacy educators may draw on this rich foundation to develop core media literacy competencies.

One of the core principles of media literacy as laid out by the National Association of Media Literacy Education (NAMLE) (www.namle.net) in the US is teaching people to analyze media content on a number of dimensions. This core principle can be applied in teaching both visual and audio documentary. There are many dimensions to analyzing documentary content. Some key areas of focus, or key questions, are: How is the documentary content constructed? Who produced it and why? Who is the intended audience? How is the documentary distributed (through which channels)? And, finally, how is it used or interpreted by audiences?

To answer the first question about documentary construction one must examine the various informational and esthetic elements that are used. Documentaries are uniquely constructed forms that are purportedly informational and make use of facts as opposed to fiction. However, when analyzing a documentary it is important to note how facts or information are organized, and how audiences are encouraged to understand the topic. How does it unfold as a story? How is the story organized to create a particular focus? Who or what facts or ideas are included, and who or what is left out? What is the visual or audio style? Is there an on-camera or off-camera narrator? How do visuals and the use of the camera or sound components and editing techniques encourage a particular way of feeling about or understanding a subject? How do sounds, words, and text or other graphics employed in the documentary appeal to different senses, thus shape the information in different ways? What is the overall point of view (POV), and how do these production elements work together to create that POV? These are necessary questions that comprise the components of a media literacy-based analysis of documentary on the level of content itself.

Analyzing content necessarily includes analyzing the producer of the content, the channels of distribution, and the audience(s) for that content. An important part of understanding a documentary on a broader level is knowing who produced it and why. What relationship does the producer or production company or team have with the topic or subject? How does that explain the way the POV is constructed, or the style of production? From where did the funds come for producing the documentary? How does knowing that help one to realize what is at stake in getting across a particular version of a story or idea? Further, how does knowing that help one to better understand how to think about it as a whole?

Questions about ownership and production of a documentary constitute the political–economic realm of analysis, a crucial realm for deep critical evaluation. In other words, knowing the creator or producer is vitally important to understanding and evaluating it as viable information. For instance, a documentary about global warming produced by a for-profit energy company will offer a particular set of facts, production components, and framework for understanding what global warming is or is not, and the extent to which it is of concern both now and in the future. A documentary produced by a nonprofit environmental group will likely differ considerably. Both will work with their own particular set of facts, and both will use them in such a way as to create a unique POV because each is working to construct their own argument, hoping for a different audience interpretation, and perhaps a different outcome (see Center for Media Literacy, www.medialit.org, and PBS's *POV* website, www.pbs.org/pov, for more information and lesson plans for documentary analysis).

Just as with almost any kind of media content, producers envision an ideal audience for their work. It is the same with documentary production. Documentary producers imagine who their ideal audience is, then choose elements that will best reach that audience as well as the desired effect or outcome from that audience. The choices around documentary length, interview subjects, language choices, editing styles, and other post-production elements (music, effects, etc.) offer strong clues about what audience age group or other demographic is appealed to, or hailed, by a documentary. For example, Ken Burn's long-form documentaries *Baseball* and *The Men Who Made Radio* (www.pbs.org/kenburns/) were produced for an older adult audience, compared with the *We The Voters* series of short documentaries which were produced by Vulcan Productions (www.vulcanproductions.com) to reach an adolescent and young adult audience. The channels of distribution are also key components to understanding the audience and media–audience relationships. Ken Burns's documentaries were initially available via PBS television stations which traditionally skew to an older educated audience, while the *We The Voters* series were available first online, all at once, for on-demand viewing, which is a more useful distribution mechanism to a younger viewing audience (www.wethevoters.com).

Another important component of analyzing documentary from the purview of the audience is to recognize that audience members are active interpreters, and, even though a producer might have an expectation about what they want their ideal audience members to get from their work, a set interpretation is far from guaranteed. In fact, audience members vary greatly in the way they use documentaries, and in what they take away from their documentary viewing. Audience interpretation is guided by what individual audience members bring to their viewing experience, including their social, cultural, and economic background; their education level; their values;

their personal experience with the documentary topic; and a host of other complex factors that determine how they make sense of the world, which includes how they make sense of their media. A media-literate audience member will bring a wide range of critical viewing skills to the documentary viewing experience and will, by virtue of those skills, look more deeply into its construction. Ideally, this will result in a more educated critical interpretation and will recognize other possible interpretations. For all of these reasons, learning to analyze a documentary as a nonfiction media form is an important overall media literacy skill.

Teaching documentary production

While it is useful to teach analysis of documentary content and form as part of a student's media literacy training, it is also useful to teach students actual documentary production skills. Teaching how to produce documentaries is a crucial hands-on educational component in comprehensive media literacy education. It prepares students to then go on to produce documentaries *about* media literacy topics or about any other topics, giving voice to their specific concerns and interests, or allowing them to explore, learn, and engage with academic subjects or other subjects in entirely new ways. When students learn to produce documentaries from the media literacy framework they are learning several related skills, including decision-making, interviewing, collaboration, technical production, and the specific limitations, strengths, and characteristics of the medium or form within which they are working, including the biases and power of each form. Students are learning how to pull information together to create an argument or POV for an audience to achieve an expected outcome. This is nearly parallel to teaching them reading and writing skills in traditional literacy, but with the important added components of sound, visuals, and other effects with which they engage, usually via digital media, every day.

Typically, when learning documentary production in a media literacy workshop or classroom, the emphasis is on process instead of product. The end goal is not a tightly produced documentary, but an informational piece about something important to the students who have worked together to create it. Collaboration and enhanced understanding about the decision-making process in media content production, producing for and reaching an audience, and understanding distribution are important educational skills cultivated in learning documentary production. More specifically, students learn how words, sounds, and images (both still and moving) differently shape information, and can be uniquely combined via editing techniques for strategic ends.

Documentary production skills are empowering pedagogical techniques that help students learn content while developing their voice. Goodman (2003), Soep (2006), White (2012), and Daniels (2012) offer powerful examples of how students' use of sound and visual documentary productions skills have enhanced their ability to understand deeply their personal areas of interest, then create documentary works within those areas, with the goal of distributing them and making a difference within their communities. Chavez and Soep (2005) make the crucial point that this practice, the cultivation of "youth voice" and "youth empowerment," while often referenced in the youth media and media literacy worlds, needs to be problematized. That is, the terms and practices need to be examined from larger social and political contexts within which various youth are situated, and within which youth see themselves. Examples from Harris (2011) who worked with Sudanese refugees in Australia; Cavagnaro, Niles, Reiser, and White (2011) who worked with youth in Sierra Leone; and Prokhorov and Therkelsen (2015) who worked with youth studying abroad in Russia are broad cross-cultural examples of important contexts wherein youth learn documentary production skills in the context of their own cultures to both learn and teach others about their cultures.

A number of educators and youth media-oriented organizations successfully use documentary production pedagogy to help students learn academic disciplines such as natural history (Fink, 1997), or environmental education (Harness & Drossman, 2011). Documentary production has been used successfully by the New York City community-based media literacy organization The Learning About Multimedia Project, or The LAMP (www.thelamp.org), in classrooms to help students learn about science and social studies topics, and also in other workshop settings where student groups have gone on to produce short documentaries about cyberbullying or social media use.

In summary, the overall teaching goal of documentary production in a media literacy education framework is hands-on learning about each phase of the process of documentary production, from decision-making about the topic, to envisioning audience, to outlining the material or storyboard, to choosing all the production components, to editing, and to channels of distribution. Hands-on learning in all of these phases engages students deeply in the content with which they are working, and also with the process of media-making. If students are encouraged to critically evaluate each step in the process, they understand more deeply how informational content is creatively used to shape a message to reach certain goals. It helps them as both media creators and media users.

Teaching with documentaries about media literacy

The third broad area for considering documentary analysis and production in media literacy is using documentaries to teach about media literacy topics. The Media Education Foundation (MEF) in Massachusetts (www.mediaed.org) has for many years produced and distributed hundreds of documentaries about topics of interest to media literacy educators, most of them focused on media messages. A few examples include *Killing Us Softly*, by Jean Kilbourne, *Tough Guise*, by Jackson Katz, *Codes of Gender*, by Sut Jhally, and many, many others that cover a wide range of topics of concern for media literacy educators around media representation, media and consumerism, media genres, and the like. Likewise, media literacy-related documentaries have been produced for broadcast TV and aired on PBS's *Frontline* series, including Douglas Rushkoff's (www.rushkoff.com/film-TV) *The Persuaders*, about advertising and marketing, or *Generation Like*, which explores young people and their relationship with social media.

When teaching with documentaries about media literacy-related topics, it is helpful to guide students to critically engage on two levels with the documentaries: the level of content, which includes taking in and understanding the topics presented, and also the level of form, which includes analyzing the documentary as a documentary. For example, when a media literacy educator wants to raise awareness in students about mediated gender representations, they might engage students in a screening and discussion about the major themes in Katz's *Tough Guise*, as well as ask them to pursue probing questions about the visual, sound, and editing techniques used in that documentary to make points about men, media, and masculinity. The media literacy educator might also ask students to find out more about the producer—Katz, or the distributor—the Media Education Foundation. The educator ought to also ask how it was funded, how people access the video, who typically watches it, and how has it been interpreted. This sort of multilevel critique strategy is a sophisticated educational approach to teach students to learn from the documentary while also critiquing it as a documentary. Students should be encouraged to ask all the critical questions about all areas of content and form around a documentary in order to have a broad and deep media literacy engagement and understanding of it.

A final consideration of media literacy and documentary analysis includes probing the ethical dimensions of documentary production, more specifically, critiquing the ethical practices of documentary producers around, for example: (i) How information is gathered. Did the producers tell people they taped or interviewed what they were producing, and why?, or (ii) How topics are handled in a documentary. For example, if the documentary is cross-cultural or focuses on a very different culture than that of the producer(s), was it done sensitively and in context of the culture at large? (Danto, Hashmi, & Isabel, 2016). These are only a very few of the kinds of specifically ethical questions one might ask about how informational media such as documentaries are produced, distributed, and received.

The ethical dimension outlined above does not stand apart from the three broad areas of media literacy analysis and production developed earlier: (i) analyzing documentary form and content, (ii) teaching documentary production, and (iii) teaching media literacy-related documentaries. Additionally, one should not consider any one of these as sufficient stand-alone areas, but as deeply intertwined arenas of learning that, when combined and presented within an open and creative educational environment, create an immersive learning experience for many different age groups and, more specifically, create a comprehensive media literacy education effort around the informational genre called documentary.

SEE ALSO: Creativity and Media Production in Schools; Digital Storytelling; Educational Media, History; Learning from Media; Media Literacy and Visual Culture; Media Literacy as Contemporary Rhetoric; Media Production in Elementary Education; Political Economy; Representation; Teaching with Media; Visual Literacy; Youth Media

References

Cavagnaro, P., Niles, Z., Reiser, E., & White, B. (2011). This is our generation: Sierra Leonean youth viewing through film. *Youth Media Reporter, 5*, 1–4.

Chavez, V., & Soep, E. (2005). Youth radio and the pedagogy of collegiality. *Harvard Educational Review, 75*, 409–434.
Daniels, J. (2012). Digital video: Engaging students in critical media literacy and community activism. *Explorations in Media Ecology, 10*, 137–147.
Danto, A., Hashmi, M., & Isabel, L. (2016). *Think, point, shoot: Media ethics, technology and global change*. New York, NY: Routledge.
Edwards, E. (2001). To be rather than to seem: Liberal education and personal growth through documentary production. *Journal of Film and Video, 53*, 9–19.
Fink, L. (1997). Using video production in teaching natural history. *The American Biology Teacher, 59*, 142–147.
Foss, K. (1983). Celluloid rhetoric: The use of documentary film to teach rhetorical theory. *Communication Education, 32*, 51–61.
Goodman, S. (2003). *Teaching youth media: A critical guide to literacy, video production, and social change*. New York, NY: Teacher's College, Columbia University.
Harness, H., & Drossman, H. (2011). The environmental education through filmmaking project. *Environmental Education Research, 17*, 6.
Harris, A. (2011). Singing into language: Sudanese Australian women create public pedagogy. *Discourse: Studies in the Cultural Politics of Education, 32*, 729–743.
Hendrix, J., & Wood, J.A. (1973). The rhetoric of film: Toward critical methodology. *Southern Speech Communication Journal, 39*, 105–122.
Margolis, E., & Pauwels, L. (Eds.). (2011). *The SAGE handbook of visual research methods*. Los Angeles, CA: SAGE.
Prokhorov, A., & Therkelsen, J. (2015). Visualizing St. Petersburg: Using documentary production in a short-term study abroad program to enhance oral proficiency, media literacy and research skills. *Journal of Film and Video, 67*, 112–124.
Robinson, R. (1984). Learning to see: Developing visual literacy through film. *Top of the News, 40*, 267–275.
Soep, E. (2006). Beyond literacy and voice in youth media production. *McGill Journal of Education, 41*, 197–213.
White, T. (2012). Visual literacy and cultural production: Examining black masculinity through participatory community engagement. *Journal of Visual Literacy, 31*, 53–70.

Further reading

Tier, J. (2006). Exemplary introductory critical media literacy documentaries. *Journal of Adolescent & Adult Literacy, 50*, 68–71.

Katherine G. Fry is Professor and Chair of the Department of Television and Radio at Brooklyn College of CUNY, and cofounder and former education director of The Learning About Multimedia Project (The LAMP), based in New York City. A Fulbright Scholar to Turkey and international lecturer, Fry currently teaches and publishes in the areas of media ecology and media literacy. Her books include *Constructing the Heartland: Television News and Natural Disaster*, and co-editing of *Identities in Context: Media, Myth, Religion in Space and Time.* Her recent publications are in audience analysis of news, news literacy, and journalism education.

Ecomedia Literacy

ANTONIO LÓPEZ
John Cabot University, Italy

Ecomedia literacy bridges environmental issues and sustainability with media literacy. It is a framework that affirms the intrinsic relationship between media and the environment by highlighting the various ways in which the media affect the Earth's physical environment. Generally, an ecomedia literacy approach has two broad areas of inquiry: the ecological "footprint" of media technologies and the ecological "mindprint" of the knowledge and culture produced by media systems. This field includes the impact of communications technology on regional and global ecosystems, for example the environmental and human effects of "conflict minerals" mined in Africa; the environmental and human impact of gadget manufacturing; carbon emissions from coal-powered electricity generated to process data (especially server "farms" running the "cloud"); and toxicity from electronic waste (E-waste) that results from discarded and recycled media technologies, and from their planned obsolescence. It also explores media's impact on how humans understand their relationship with the ecosystems that sustain them. Finally, ecomedia literacy addresses pedagogy by developing ways for educators to incorporate environmental themes and concepts that also encourage sustainable cultural behaviors.

Ecomedia literacy (also referred to as "green" media education) is an emerging area of media literacy education, driven by a need to address the ecological crises of climate disruption, biodiversity loss, degraded food systems, clean water, deforestation, pollution, and ocean acidification (among many other environmental issues). Although the number of scholars concerned with sustainability in media, communications, and film studies increases every year, in 2017 the literature on media literacy education concerned with environmental issues was limited (see López, 2014 for a comprehensive study). This is not to say that individual media literacy practitioners have not taken up environmental themes in their work, but historically there has been no clearly

The International Encyclopedia of Media Literacy. Renee Hobbs and Paul Mihailidis (Editors-in-Chief), Gianna Cappello, Maria Ranieri, and Benjamin Thevenin (Associate Editors).

defined movement within media literacy education devoted entirely to promoting environmental approaches. Nonetheless, it is possible to identify major dimensions of the topic that have developed in previous years. Project Look Sharp developed several curricula around environmental themes, authoring several that were based on constructivist pedagogy (i.e., Sperry, 2011). Educators and scholars working in the area of critical media literacy connect a variety of social concerns—such as sexism, racism, gender identity, violence, and war—with environmental issues (Beach, Share, & Webb, 2017). Rauch (2018) promotes "slow media" literacy and "unplugging" as a way to encourage environmental awareness. Hadl (2016) penned a Japanese textbook on ecomedia literacy. López (2015) links ecomedia literacy and global citizenship with the Global Alliance for Partnerships on Media and Information Literacy Plan for Action and the UN Sustainable Development Goals. Though not explicitly identified as ecomedia literacy, a volume edited by Milstein, Pileggi, and Morgan (2017) addresses environmental communication, thereby proposing methods for combining the teaching of media and communications with environmental concerns.

One obstacle to greening media education is the confusion related to the use of environmental metaphors in media studies and media literacy. In the case of media ecology, which comes from medium studies, scholars use the ecology metaphor to describe media technologies as themselves a medium that produces deterministic "medium environments." Within the media ecology tradition, views range from "soft" to "hard" technological determinism; many of its scholars are neutral about the impact of media technology on society. In a different example, George Gerbner and Susan Sontag argued that mass media-produced image environments require a kind of "environmentalism"; and from this they inferred that the "media environment" is visually polluted and therefore requires intervention from activists, scholars, government regulators, and media educators. Currently the ecosystem metaphor is often used to describe particular operating systems, platforms, medium types, and gadgets (such as the Facebook ecosystem, the iPhone ecosystem, the Android ecosystem, or the newspaper ecosystem). What is common to all these metaphorical uses is that they eschew the actual environmental impact of media technologies on physical ecosystems. Moreover, they do not imply or explore environmental ideologies that influence how people believe they should act in relation to living systems. Consequently, ecomedia literacy not only reappraises the use of environmental metaphors but seeks to redress the absence of environmental concerns by repurposing the ecology metaphor to make it signify actually living, complex ecosystems embedded in physical environments.

Ecomedia literacy is coevolving with other emerging disciplines concerned with making the environment a broader subject of media and education scholarship. These fields can be divided into two broad categories. First is the area of media and communications studies that address the ecological dimension of media. Second is the group of pedagogical methods that promote environmental awareness. With regard to the first group, ecomedia studies is an interdisciplinary field examining the materiality, representation, and communication of media from an environmental perspective. Environmental communication (EC) combines ecocriticism with linguistic discourse analysis, rhetorical studies, political economy, and media studies to problematize the term "environment" when it is used to reinforce a separation between humans and living ecosystems; it combines approaches from humanities, environmental studies, and social and natural sciences. EC argues that environmental beliefs are culturally constructed and often reinforces a common conception that human activity is free from any consequences on physical health or environmental sustainability. EC contends that the concept of "nature" in literature and in the media often excludes humans, constructing the environment as something outside the realm of human activity. Like ecomedia studies, EC promotes the understanding that humans are also a part of living systems and are inherently ecological beings that depend on fresh air, water, and food to survive. EC positions itself as a "crisis discipline," and therefore promotes intervention into the status quo in order to promote sustainability and healthy living systems. Other fields that inform ecomedia literacy include media ecology, green media studies, ecocriticism, ecological economics, ecopsychology, technoliteracy, ecocinema studies, and environmental studies.

For a pedagogy of environmental change, ecomedia literacy draws on concepts and methods developed by ecoliteracy, critical media literacy, critical ecopedagogy, and education for sustainability. These methodologies start from the premise that environmental problems cannot be solved with the same kind of thinking (mental model, paradigm, or worldview) that created them. This entails a critique of the Euro-American epistemology based on the 18th- and 19th-century paradigm of technological progress, positivism, and mechanism that views humans as separate from their physical environment and assumes that the world operates like a machine with interchangeable parts. It is argued that these beliefs have created short-term benefits, but at the expense of environmental health. Consequently, ecologically oriented educational disciplines propose that unquestioned faith in positivism and the industrial and scientific revolutions are the root cause of the environmental crisis and therefore must be critically engaged. But, more importantly, they call for alternative forms of education, which do not reinforce the kind of mental models that drive environmental destruction. Thus an ecologically oriented education promotes an alternative paradigm, which is based on systems thinking and on a belief in the interconnectedness of life, humans, technology, and economics grounded in ecological ethics. Some methods include self-reflective practices (media "fasting," journaling, and mindfulness training); the use of a backward curriculum design based on problem-solving and solutions-generating outcomes (e.g., building a lesson or courses around answering essential questions, such as "What characterizes a healthy media ecosystem?"); scenario and world building to envision different futures; problematizing human–nature binaries; moving away from abstract knowledge to an experiential learning grounded in local ecosystems; transitioning to a model of political economy based on ecological economics; and "remediating" ecology metaphors to encourage learners to see media as embedded within living systems. These approaches seek to promote mental models that are "ecocentric" (Earth-oriented) as opposed to "anthropocentric" (human-oriented).

Like critical pedagogy, ecomedia literacy is not neutral or agenda-free: it actively acknowledges that our global ecosystems are in jeopardy and calls for intervention into media literacy practices in order to promote environmental sustainability. Consequently ecomedia literacy requires an environmental critique (also called "ecocriticism") of the media from several different perspectives, including those of materials economy, political economy, media systems, culture, and worldview. Borrowing from the tradition of media ecology and technoliteracy, ecomedia literacy demands a critical stance toward communications technology. It recognizes the way in which media technology and gadgets (cell phones, tablets, TV sets, computers, digital media tools, etc.) are products of the global system's political economy, and how technology companies, as expressed in economic theory, "externalize" the negative environmental costs to third parties (primarily workers and local ecosystems in developing countries). In addition, ecomedia literacy problematizes ubiquitous communication technology for producing a subjectivity that normalizes consumerism and displaces people's awareness of their living habitats. In particular, mobile media, the Internet, and television are believed to fracture time and space, thereby causing a loss of a "sense of place" (something valued by environmentalists), which leads to a broader sense of "placelessness."

Unlike digital literacy practices that often engage the material conditions of media gadgets uncritically, an ecomedia literacy framework considers how media gadgets are made and what their subsequent environmental footprint is. An ecomedia literacy analysis involves tracing the production chain of media gadgets—from the mining of "conflict minerals" in countries like the Congo to their manufacture and assembly in countries like China, then to distribution, consumption, and disposal. It also incorporates a discussion of the impact of carbon-powered server farms on climate change, and how renewable energy and "green IT" can be used to mitigate carbon emissions. This also necessitates an exploration of how energy policy is represented and promoted in the media. It also entails a critique of built-in obsolescence and consumerism as a driver of the ecological crisis. Data clouds are considered from the point of view of carbon extraction and pollution, but also from that of surveillance and privacy. Finally, the way in which communication technologies are promoted as empowering invites an ecocritical analysis of gadget marketing. In sum, all these approaches involve a holistic, intersectional analysis that is in alignment with the environmental and media justice framework that connects environmental destruction to income inequality, racism, sexism, violence, and militarism.

Following the tradition of environmental communication, ecomedia literacy also recognizes that the media entail symbolic action that can hinder or promote environmental sustainability. Symbolic action is the way in which discourses (visual, verbal, and textual) construct environmental problems and solutions. In studying how environmental discourses are constructed in the media, students actively participate in and engage with the public sphere. Youth media programs, service learning, and community engagement projects are important venues for bringing environmental issues to public attention (e.g., by engaging the media produced by indigenous groups involved in land struggles with energy companies and governments). Thus ecomedia literacy recognizes the generative power of media as a means of education and of raising awareness about environmental problems and solutions.

A number of areas already covered by media literacy practitioners can be tweaked so as to incorporate environmental themes. Such areas include critically analyzing news coverage of climate change and environmental justice movements; studying climate change disinformation; applying critical thinking and deconstruction techniques to advertising that specifically identifies environmental discourses; applying critical information literacy to determine the validity of environmental claims made in the media; learning to identify false environmental claims (i.e., greenwashing) in packaging and advertising; studying the role of social media in promoting and obfuscating climate change discourses; engaging in media-making practices that reflect real-world environmental problems and solutions; extending ethics and discussions of rights and responsibilities to biotic communities and workers; connecting the concept of the digital commons to environmental commons (air, water, etc.); applying alternative media practices to environmental change; analyzing media corporations and their sustainability policies; designing healthy media ecosystems; mapmaking of local environments and digital storytelling; and encouraging outdoor education by reducing screen time.

In terms of future directions in research, theory, and methodology for ecomedia literacy, there are a variety of opportunities for the framework to grow and evolve. To begin with, professional development and teacher training programs can start to incorporate an environmental studies component. Debates concerning education policy, common core standards, and testing can shift to recognize the economic and cultural dimension of environmental education, so that it is not just "siloed off" as science education. Media literacy educators can work toward advancing intercultural communication and respect for nonwestern epistemologies to incorporate an awareness of the environmental sensibilities of different cultures. In addition, media literacy organizations can promote environmental themes in curriculum development and during professional conferences. These approaches will necessitate more research and collaboration across disciplines, especially with practitioners of education for sustainability. Finally, with increased attention from media literacy practitioners to environmental themes, there needs to be research and resource sharing, in order to develop and refine curricula. As it is generally acknowledged that media are integral to environmental issues and the global ecological crisis intensifies, ecomedia literacy will likely become an integrated subject of media literacy.

SEE ALSO: Advertising Literacy; Civic Activism; Community Media; Critical Information Literacy; Critical Pedagogy; Critical Theory Applied to Media Literacy; Digital Literacy; Digital Media and Information Rights; Digital Storytelling; Global Citizenship; Learning about Materialism and Consumer Culture; Literacy, Technology, and Media; Meaning-Making; Media Activism and Action-Oriented Learning; Media Literacy and Social Activism; Media Literacy and Visual Culture; Media Literacy Education and 21st Century Teacher Education; Media Literacy for the 21st Century Teacher; Mediatization; Medium Theory; News Literacies; Political Economy; Representation of Nutrition and Food in the Media; Social Media as Media Literacy; Understanding Media Literacy and DIY Creativity in Youth Digital Productions; Youth Media

References

Beach, R., Share, J., & Webb, A. (2017). *Teaching climate change to adolescents: Reading, writing, and making a difference*. New York, NY: Routledge.

Hadl, G. (2016). *Kankyou media riterashii* [*Ecomedia literacy*]. Nishinomiya, Japan: Kwansei Gakuin University Press.

López, A. (2014). *Greening media education. Bridging media literacy with green cultural citizenship*. New York, NY: Peter Lang.
López, A. (2015). Ecomedia literacy for environmental sustainability. In J. Singh, A. Grizzle, S. J. Yee & S. H. Culver (Eds.), *Media and information literacy for the Sustainable Development Goals* (pp. 299–306). Göteborg, Germany: Nordicom.
Milstein, T., Pileggi, M., & Morgan, E. (Eds.). (2017). *Environmental communication and pedagogy*. New York, NY: Routledge.
Rauch, J. (2018). *Slow media: Toward a sustainable future*. Oxford, England: Oxford University Press.
Sperry, S. (2011). *Media constructions of sustainability: Food, water and agriculture*. Ithaca, NY: Project Look Sharp.

Further reading

Corbett, J.B. (2006). *Communicating nature: How we create and understand environmental messages*. Washington, DC: Island Press.
Louv, R. (2005). *Last child in the woods: Saving our children from nature-deficit disorder*. Chapel Hill, NC: Algonquin Books.
Maxwell, R., Lager Vestberg, N., & Raundalen, J. (Eds.). (2015). *Media and the ecological crisis*. New York, NY: Routledge.
Maxwell, R., & Miller, T. (2012). *Greening the media*. New York, NY: Oxford University Press.
Rust, S., Monani, S., & Cubitt, S. (Eds.). (2016). *Ecomedia: Key issues*. London, England: Routledge.
Walker, J., & Starosielski, N. (Eds.). (2016). *Sustainable media: Critical approaches to media and environment*. London, England: Routledge.

Antonio López, PhD, has a research focus on bridging sustainability with media literacy. He has written numerous academic articles and essays linking sustainability and environmental issues with media literacy, and also three books: *Mediacology: A Multicultural Approach to Media Literacy in the 21st Century* (2008); *The Media Ecosystem: What Ecology Can Teach Us About Responsible Media Practice* (2012); and *Greening Media Education: Bridging Media Literacy with Green Cultural Citizenship* (2014). He is currently associate professor of communications and media studies at John Cabot University in Rome, Italy.

Educational Media, History

MELDA N. YILDIZ
New York Institute of Technology, USA

The history of "Educational technology ... can be traced back to the time when tribal priests systemized bodies of knowledge, and early cultures invented pictographs or sign writing to record and transmit information" (Saettler, 2004, p. 4). Throughout human history, media have been used for educational purposes; sharing stories on the walls of the caves and in temples of worship. The earliest form of teaching was through speech and storytelling. Prior to writing, oral communication was crucial for learning. Through epic stories and poetry such as Homer's *Iliad* and the *Odyssey*, people learned through oral storytelling, memorization, and recitation. With the invention of paper, writing became as important as oral communication. This entry provides a timeline of events dividing educational media into three stages: (i) learn about media; (ii) learn from media; and (iii) learn with media.

Learn about media

The first stage in educational media is about studying the role of media in education. With the invention of the printing press, written materials became available to the public. Even though access to books was limited or impossible in medieval times, students learned from their religious leaders, scholars, and professors who had access to copies of the handwritten textbooks and they usually read or "lectured" it to the students. The term "lecture," which comes from the Latin meaning "reading, a text to read," changed English to mean "a long, serious educational speech."

In the 19th century, the advent of technological development and inventions including photography and the production of textbooks provided new educational media for schools in addition to slate boards and blackboards with chalks.

In 1904, during the World Fair in St. Louis, USA, the first school museum opened showcasing slides, charts, and other audiovisual instructional materials. The school museums "served as the central administrative units for visual instruction by distribution of portable museum exhibits, stereographs, slides, films, study prints, charts, and other instructional materials" (Reiser & Dempsey, 2018, p. 8).

In the 1900s, Thomas Edison was one of the first people who predicted the future of education going beyond the written text and using new media to revolutionize learning. The first documented media instruction started with the invention of motion pictures.

The 1920s signified the start of the "visual instruction movement," the time instructional films were being produced. By 1920, the focus of educational media shifted to audiovisual media. From 1914 through 1923, there was a rise of the visual instruction movement. The terms "visual instruction" and "audiovisual instruction" were used and the visual education (using slides and stereoscopes) movement started. The seminal book *Visualizing the Curriculum* was published in 1937 outlining the hierarchy of media with basic abstract concepts at the bottom to media that allow for concrete representations at the top. The writings of Edgar Dale, Charles F. Hoban, Jr., and James Finn argued the crucial role of audiovisual instruction in education to improve teaching and learning. At this time professional organizations for visual instruction were also established. Teacher education programs offered instruction on using visualization in teaching and schools regularly used films for instruction.

The 1920s and 1930s were the golden age for radio broadcasting and sound recordings. This era is considered the movement for "audiovisual instruction" and instructional radio. Radio was considered as the medium that revolutionized educational instruction; however, radio was not widely used in education due to poor radio signals.

Learn from media

In 1928, Alexanderson began testing television at an experimental station. Also in 1928 General Electric presented the first dramatic production on television.

The second stage is educational media focused on learning from media as a result of changes in technology that emerged during World War II. Following developments in audiovisual instruction, an era of instructional films (motion pictures) emerged. During World War II, the US army produced over a hundred training films and filmstrips. The US Federal Government established the "Division of Visual Aids for War Training."

In addition to motion pictures, other forms of audiovisual equipment were developed such as slide projectors and overhead projectors. Overhead projectors came into lecture halls first for military training and later into classrooms. Overhead projectors provided visuals and text using transparencies.

In the middle of the 20th century, television became the most popular instructional medium and, in 1939, DuMont made improvements in the cathode-ray picture tube and made the first television sets. In the US, the Federal Communication department set aside over 200 channels for educational use, thus initiating the use of television in media instruction.

The 1940s was the start of the instructional television era. Networks such as NBC and CBS aired their first official network television broadcast in the United States. Television recording tapes had replaced phonograph records. During the 1950s, interest in communication theories and media research began. The research focused on communication processes that involved a sender and a receiver of a message, and a channel, or medium.

Throughout this time the words "educational technology" and "instructional technology" were used. In the United States the Ford Foundation invested heavily in educational TV. Following the success of film and TV, computer aided instruction (CAI) became popular in public schools.

With the advent of CAI the movement of programmed instruction started in the 1950s with the use of new technologies for preparing instructional materials designed for children. In 1954, B.F. Skinner published *The Science of Learning and Teaching*. In his book he described ideas for improving learning through the use of effective instructional materials. He called these materials "programmed instructional materials." Sidney Leavitt Pressey was famous for having invented a teaching machine prior to Skinner. Pressey's machine administered multiple-choice questions and recorded the answers. Later, Skinner popularized the "teaching machines" which were one of the first forms of computer-based learning. These machines presented instruction in small steps, required an active response from the learner, provided immediate feedback, and control over learning.

The year after the launch of Sputnik in 1957, the National Defense Education Act (NDEA) was signed into law on September 2, 1958. The NDEA was influenced by the Soviet launch of the satellite Sputnik and prompted the United States to invest in educational institutions to improve primarily math and science education, which ultimately impacted educational media.

The 1963 definition produced by a commission established by the Department of Audiovisual Instruction focused on the design and use of messages in the learning process and emphasized the steps taken to design learning messages. "Audiovisual communication is that branch of educational theory and practice concerned primarily with the design and use of messages which control the learning process" (Ely, 1963, p. 18). This statement placed an emphasis on learning rather than instruction.

Sesame Street is an American educational children's television series which premiered on November 10, 1969. The organization that produces the program was formerly known as the Children's Television Workshop until June 2000. The program included short films, live action, animation, and puppetry. This highly rated, award-winning, research-based program reached not only over 90% of preschoolers but also was broadcast in more than 140 countries.

In the 1970s, educational media tools such as microcomputers became available for personal as well as classroom use. Instructional technology is considered as a process of educational media. In the later 1970s, access to microcomputers led to computer-assisted instruction.

In 1970, the Commission on Instructional Technology published a report providing two definitions of instructional technology. The term "instructional media" was defined as a means of instruction and included innovations in media and communications alongside teachers, textbooks, and blackboards with the pieces making up "instructional technology."

- Instructional technology is the media used for instructional purposes. This includes television, films, projectors, computers, and so on.
- Instructional technology is a systematic way of designing, implementing, and evaluating the process of learning and teaching. It uses specific objectives, is based on research, and uses human and non-human resources to create effective instruction.

The 1980s was the era of personal computers. As personal computers became relatively inexpensive and could fit on a desk, interest in using personal computers for instructional design tasks accelerated. Computers were increasingly being used in the 1980s for instructional purposes in primary and secondary education schools in the United States. When computers were first available in schools, they were mainly used for drills and practice of computer-related skills.

Learn with media

The third era of educational media started with the development of the information superhighway in the 1990s. The term "information superhighway" refers to globally connected digital communication systems and the Internet telecommunications network. Even though the Internet was developed in the late 1960s with the creation of the Advanced Research Projects Agency Network (ARPANET) funded by the US

Department of Defense, it was not available to the public at the time. When it became available the use of the Internet in education grew during the 1990s following the development of microcomputers in 1990s, and Internet-based educational media and technologies in Silicon Valley, USA, and around the world.

Access to and expansion of personal computers with Internet connectivity and application software increased the use of educational media in the schools. More educators and students started to use educational media such as personal computers, camcorders, and mobile devices not only for learning but also for developing new content. Personal computers connected to the Internet increased the number of distance education courses. Computer-based training, e-learning, flip learning, blended learning, and massive open online courses (MOOCs) were developed and continue to be integrated in the field of educational media.

Educational software such as Microsoft PowerPoint and Word were quickly adopted and used as part of the educational media. Today, educators and learners have access to a variety of educational media from e-mails to educational games, video, and multimedia production software. Technology developments in the 21st-century educational media technology resources allowed users to be producers of media as opposed to being simply consumers. The new generation increasingly depends on their mobile devices, seeking answers to their everyday questions through YouTube and Google, and sharing their stories on the digital walls of cyberspace.

Since the 1990s, there has been an increasing demand for the use of computers and other digital media (like blogs, social networks, online videos, and wikis) in instructional settings. The term "social media" and its use in the classrooms have been expanding for the millennials in the new millennium. Educators have been not only advocating the use of social media and integrating them into education but also rethinking the ramifications and challenges of social media. Blended learning and online instruction have been prevalent in educational institutions and industry settings. From primary and secondary education to higher education, growth in online teaching has led to many online institutions emerging that have provided new career opportunities in the field of instructional design and for technology professionals.

Educational media have been instrumental in providing "assistive technology" tools and resources for students with special needs. The field of assistive technologies has ben expanding. In the United States there are two major pieces of legislation for special education: (i) Section 504 of the Rehabilitation Act of 1973 and (ii) Individuals with Disabilities Education Act (IDEA). These legislative Acts govern the use of assistive technology within the school system. The National Instructional Material Access Center (NIMAC) has created a repository of accessible text and textbooks, braille readers, screen readers, and other digital text software for special education.

Assistive technology can be divided into three tech categories. Low tech encompasses equipment that is often low cost and does not include batteries or that requires charging (e.g., pencil grips for writing or masks and color overlays for reading). Mid tech supports used in the school setting include ergonomically designed keyboards for word-processing and handheld devices. High tech supports involve the use of tablet PCs and educational software including auditory feedback and speech to text functions.

Organizations

There are a growing number of educational media-related organizations, most of which reach international audiences. Here are a few selected organizations in the field of educational media.

International Technology and Engineering Educators Association (ITEEA)

The International Technology and Engineering Educators Association (ITEEA) was formerly known as the International Technology Education Association (ITEA), a nonprofit professional organization created in 1939. The association has been a constant advocate of strong teaching and learning methods used to advance curricula and instruction that keep pace with our rapidly advancing, highly sophisticated technological society. The association's name has been synonymous with major curriculum efforts that have spawned over decades of technology teaching, particularly during the 1960s during the launch of numerous curriculum efforts. These curriculum efforts were widely practiced until the advent of the standards movement (ITEEA, n.d.).

International Council for Computers in Education (ICCE)

The International Council for Computers in Education (ICCE) was founded in 1979. In 1989 ICCE changed its name to the International Society for Technology in Education (ISTE, see www.iste.org). ISTE is a nonprofit organization that serves educators interested in better use of technology in education. The organization provides books, journals, conferences, and workshops for educators and has established teaching and coaching standards formerly called National Educational Technology Standards (NETS).

Association for Educational Communications and Technology (AECT)

The Association for Educational Communications and Technology (AECT) provides standards, publications, and conferences in the field of educational media and technologies and has published several definitions of instructional technology. Details on the AECT website (aect.org) describe the evolutionary background of the organization since 1923.

The story of AECT is about a small band of educators passionate about finding better ways to help people learn and how they were eventually joined by tens of thousands of others in pursuit of that quest. What began in 1923 as the National Education Association's Department of Visual Instruction became an international association representing professionals in a broad range of occupations who have an interest in improving learning through the use of media and technology. AECT is the oldest professional home for this field of interest and has continuously maintained a central position in its field, promoting high standards, both in scholarship and in practice (AECT, n.d.).

In 1977, AECT adopted a new definition of educational technology. This new definition emphasized the systematic design process and included the analysis phase.

The definition also included terminology like human learning problems and solutions. "Educational technology is a complex, integrated process involving people, procedures, ideas, devices, and organization for analyzing problems and devising, implementing, evaluating and managing solutions to those problems involved in all aspects of human learning" (AECT, 1977). In the 1994 definition, AECT changed the term educational technology to instructional technology and wrote "Instructional Technology is the theory and practice of design, development, utilization, management, and evaluation of processes and resources from learning" (Seels & Richey, 1994, p. 9). In 2008, AECT rethought the role of educational media and technologies focusing on ethics, improving performance, and facilitating learning and changed the definition to, "Educational technology is the study and ethical practice of facilitating learning and improving performance by creating, using, and managing appropriate technological processes and resources" (Richey, Silber, & Ely, 2008, p. 24).

Association for the Advancement of Computing in Education (AACE)

The Association for the Advancement of Computing in Education (AACE) was founded in 1981, and is an international, not-for-profit, educational organization with the mission of advancing information technology in education and e-learning research, development, learning, and its practical application (see www.aace.org). The association publishes journals and books and provides conferences and workshops.

Conclusion

Educators have creatively used and will continue to use various types of media to improve their teaching: for example, historical photographs from the Library of Congress, political cartoons, magazine ads, online and TV commercials, and Facebook posts.

Most of today's educational media first created either for military or for business purposes are now used in classrooms. The field of education technology encompasses the analysis of learning theories, technological innovations as well as the design, development, implementation, evaluation, and management of instructional resources in a variety of settings, particularly educational institutions. As new media and technologies become cost effective and easy to use, educators have integrated them into their curricula. The crucial component of educational media integration into curricula is to provide time, resources, and professional development for teachers to experience the ever-growing number of educational media and software.

As the educational media enter into our classrooms, challenges such as Internet safety, cybersecurity, and cyberbullying follow. Librarians, also called information literacy specialists, continue to provide 21st-century skills such as media, information, and technology literacy skills which are the third pillar of the P21's Framework for 21st-century learning:

> To help practitioners integrate skills into the teaching of core academic subjects, the Partnership has developed a unified, collective vision for learning known as the Framework for 21st Century Learning. This Framework describes the skills, knowledge and expertise students must master to

succeed in work and life; it is a blend of content knowledge, specific skills, expertise and literacies. (Framework for 21st Century Learning, n.d.)

By providing professional development and training to teachers how to use new media and technologies in the classroom, they will continue to access, evaluate, and communicate the content and provide innovative instructions integrating new media and technologies.

SEE ALSO: Advertising Literacy; Digital Literacy; History of Media Literacy; Internet Safety; Network Neutrality

References

AECT (Association for Educational Communications and Technology). (n.d.). AECT in the 20th century: A brief history. Retrieved from https://aect.org/aect_in_the_20th_century_a_br.php

AECT (Association for Educational Communications and Technology). (1977). *The definition of educational technology.* Washington, DC: Association for Educational Communications and Technology.

Ely, D.P. (Ed.). (1963). The changing role of the audiovisual process in education: A definition and a glossary of related terms. [TCP Monograph]. *AV Communication Review, 11*(1, Supplement 6).

Framework for 21st Century Learning. (n.d.). P21 framework definitions. Retrieved from http://www.p21.org/storage/documents/P21_Framework_Definitions.pdf

ITEEA (International Technology and Engineering Educators Association). (n.d.). A brief history of ITEEA. Retrieved from https://www.iteea.org/

Reiser, R.A., & Dempsey, J.V. (2018). *Trends and issues in instructional design and technology.* New York, NY: Pearson Education.

Richey, R.C., Silber, K.H., & Ely, D.P. (2008). Reflections on the 2008 AECT definitions of the field. *TechTrends, 52*(1), 24–25.

Saettler, L.P. (2004). *The evolution of American educational technology.* Greenwich, CT: Information Age Publishing.

Seels, B.B., & Richey, R.C. (1994). *Instructional technology: The definition and domains of the field.* Bloomington, IN: Association for Educational Communications and Technology.

Further reading

Bates, T. (2014, December 10). A short history of educational technology. Retrieved from https://www.Tonybates.Ca/2014/12/10/A-Short-History-Of-Educational-Technology/

Hoban, C.F., Hoban, C.F., & Zisman, S.B. (1937). *Visualizing the curriculum.* New York, NY: Cordon.

Melda N. Yildiz is a global scholar, teacher educator, instructional designer, and author. Yildiz teaches in the School for Interdisciplinary Studies and Education at New York Institute of Technology. She served as a Fulbright Scholar in Turkmenistan (2009) and Azerbaijan (2016) teaching and conducting research integrating media education in preschool through college P16 classrooms. Yildiz coauthored, published, and presented on topics including media and information literacy, instructional technology, and multicultural and global education. She received an EdD from the University of Massachusetts, Amherst, in math and science and instructional technology, and an MS from Southern Connecticut State University in instructional technology. She majored in teaching English as a foreign language at Bogazici University, in Turkey.

Educommunication

IGNACIO AGUADED and AGUEDA DELGADO-PONCE
University of Huelva, Spain

Educommunication is a theoretical and practical field of study that has emerged from two converging disciplines, education and communication, once separate but now increasingly linked, with many aspects in common.

Etymologically, the verb "to educate" comes from the Latin *educare*, itself a derivative of *educere*, "to get from, extract, bring out"—for example, to bring into the open something that is inside us and, by extension, to produce, build up, expose knowledge and values to the world. In *comunicar*, "sharing" and "accessibility to all" are the underlying values. The convergence of the two disciplines—education and communication—is driven by the idea of forming critical, responsible, and participative citizens capable of comfortably inhabiting the ever-changing media ecosystem, using shared knowledge.

In 1979 UNESCO adopted the term *educommunication* in the sense of "education in communication," which includes "all ways of studying, learning and teaching at all levels (primary, secondary, higher, adult education, lifelong education) and in all circumstances, the history, creativity, use and evaluation of media as practical and technical arts, as well as the place occupied by media in society, their social impact, the implication of media communication, participation, modification of the mode of perception they bring about, the role of creative work and access to media" (UNESCO, 1984, p. 8).

Educommunication means knowledge of how the media function, of how they create meaning, how they are organized and construct reality, and how those who are media recipients understand this "reality." In this sense, Masterman (1993) insists on the importance of critical intelligence, and Kaplún (1998, p. 244) talks of "giving power to the students to act as broadcasters, arming them with possibilities, stimulus and the ability to generate their own messages, converting them into generators of dialogue in order to activate analysis, discussion and the participation of other students."

The concept of educommunication is implicit in numerous expressions that we use with their varied nuances: "education in media," "education in audiovisual communication," "information literacy," "media literacy," "audiovisual literacy," "literacy in information and communication technologies," "digital literacy" (ICT), "digital competence," and so on. Differences in definition are also evident in words such as "information," "digital," and "audiovisual," when matched with the terms "media" and "communication." Traditionally such terms are clearly demarcated: information deals with access to information, its treatment, and its conversion into knowledge; audiovisual relates to the mass media and audiovisual language; digital refers to skills in searching, processing, communication, creation, and dissemination through technology. Today, however, the term "media" is gaining ground as the one that best embodies convergence and integration, embracing both traditional media (press, radio, television, etc.) and recent arrivals (Internet, smartphones, etc.), as is also reflected in the terminology adopted by leading European and international bodies ("media literacy" at the European Commission and the Alliance of Civilizations; "media and information literacy" at UNESCO).

The first steps in educommunication were taken in the 1920s, in cinema and, later, in the print media.

In the 1950s and 1960s, France led the way in media education with the pedagogue Célestin Freinet, who promoted the use of the media in the classroom as a new way of thinking about expressivity. Vallet coined the expression *langage total* ("total language") to refer to the need to promote literacy in all languages. One stage, marked by its clearly protectionist nature in the face of media manipulation, was followed by another, which acknowledged popular art. It was no longer necessary to educate against the media but to differentiate and discriminate between a good film and a bad one (Masterman, 1993).

In the 1970s, McLuhan stated the importance of developing media literacy in the "global village." UNESCO echoed the need for education in media communication as a priority for the following decades. The focus at that time was on the receptor, on critical reception, and on the participant, especially in Latin America, which saw the development of one of the main currents in communication studies. In Europe, Cloutier introduced the concept of *emerec*, one who is both emitter and receptor, while in the United States Alvin Toffler presented the idea of the *prosumer* (producer and consumer). The new paradigm reinforces the role of producer of messages over that of passive receptor.

In the 1980s, the influence of information and communication extended to all aspects of social life, from general ones, for instance economic and political, to individual ones that affected everybody's values and lifestyles. In 1982, UNESCO's Grünwald Declaration urged the political and educational systems to "recognize their obligations to promote among their citizens a critical understanding of the phenomenon of communication" by promoting "a readjustment in educational priorities to promote the creation of mass critical awareness among viewers" (UNESCO, 1982, p. 1). Two years later, the same organism published *Media Education* (UNESCO, 1984), a compendium/compilation that proposed a critical analysis of the media by using their languages and techniques and defended the educational value of the media, which prepared the way for educommunication.

The emergence of technologies in education at the end of the 20th century and the arrival of the Internet on the media stage at the start of the 21st century provided educational centers with an infrastructure and stimulated an interest in the development of technological skills, which in turn led to the promotion of the idea of digital education. In Europe, this development was followed in 1996 by a "Learning in the Information Society" action plan for the period 1996–98 (visit http://aei.pitt.edu/1200), and in May

2000 by an "eLearning: Understanding the Future of Education" initiative communicated through the European Commission.

In 2002, after the UNESCO Sevilla Seminar on media education, media education ceased to be just a question of classroom activity; from that point on, media education became the responsibility of all. Regulatory authorities, state media, industry, parents, and citizens at large were to emphasize the media as an enriching experience rather than focusing on their negative effects.

The past 15 years have seen a boom in research and initiatives in educommunication, from assessment of levels of competence (Aguaded, 2013; Buckingham, Banaji, Carr, Cranmer, & Willett, 2005; Celot, 2015; Celot & Pérez-Tornero, 2009; Christ & Henderson, 2014; Ferrés, García-Matilla, Aguaded, Fernández, & Figueras, 2011) to education (Aguaded, 2014; Di-Croce, 2009; Grizzle & Torras-Calvo, 2013; Hobbs, 2010; Koltay, 2011; Livingstone, 2008; Moore, 2008), all with the aim of promoting a critical, creative, and participative citizenry.

Educommunication (or media education) has become a worldwide phenomenon, although its implementation varies from country to country. Lee (2010) classified countries into three groups to indicate the degree of implementation. The first group consists of states where media education is well developed, such as Australia, Great Britain, Canada (Ontario in particular), Finland, Denmark, Norway, the Netherlands, Sweden, France, and Switzerland. In these countries media education is firmly entrenched in the national or regional curriculum. The second category comprises states where media education is fairly well developed. However, advances in these countries depend more on individual initiatives taken by teachers or support groups, typical examples being the United States, Germany, and southern European nations. The third category contains countries and regions where media education development is still modest, for example Japan, Hong Kong, Taiwan, China, the Philippines, India, Russia, and some Latin American countries.

Australia, one of the pioneering nations in educommunication, has produced important studies on the subject—studies by Quin and McMahon, for example—and is home to the influential Australian Teachers of Media Queensland (ATOM QLD).

In Europe, despite encouragement from the European Union to incorporate media education into educational curricula (Recommendation 2009/625/CE of August 20, 2009), the implementation of educommunication policies and initiatives across the continent has been uneven. The integration of the media into school study plans has been effective in Scandinavian countries (Finland, Norway, Sweden) as well as in France and Great Britain, but less so in Portugal, Italy, and Spain, where initiatives in media education are largely the work of specific groups and organizations rather than being state-led. Recent times have seen the publication of numerous studies and projects that focus on different approaches, such as the use of and attitudes to the media, comparative analyses of media education in the curriculum, the level of citizens' media competence, practical work in media education, and the creation of resources for media literacy or the prevention of behaviors that put users at risk. In this sense, the journal *Comunicar: Media Education Research Journal* (www.comunicarjournal.com) acts a forum for such issues and is published in four languages: English and Spanish in its entirety, Chinese and Portuguese in abstracts.

Like Australia, Canada is one of the leading nations in media education, its motivation being a response to the concern about the media culture imported from the United States and the need to provide Canadians with a more analytical and reflective approach in the face of this challenge. Today all the country's provinces include media education in their study plans and recognize its value as a cross-curricular subject.

In the United States, media education—or *media literacy education*—was initially understood to be a "cognitive defence" against insidious forms of media sensationalism and propaganda. Later on it focused on developing citizens' practical critical thinking about the media. Media literacy education combines the approaches of protectionism, education, and enjoyment of the media. Today "the purpose of media literacy education is to help individuals of all ages develop the habits of enquiry and skills of expression that they need to be critical thinkers, effective communicators and active citizens in today's world" (NAMLE, 2009).

In China educommunication emerged in the 1990s, in particular in Hong Kong, where the development of media education took the form of the "network model": defenders of media communication education and interested organizations interacted to create an informal network designed to promote media education (Lee, 2010). Activity was centered on interactive and participative media, or *new media literacy*.

In Latin America, under Paulo Freire's influence, the predominant trend is educational communication and dialogue as a base for education and the practice of freedom, the emphasis being on the concept of the school as a forum for popular communication. This commitment to the collective, this interrelation between education and communication as a space for critical and creative knowledge, citizenship, and social empowerment characterize educommunication in Latin America, which is embodied in the idea of critical reception and has Orozco (2001, 2011) and Martín-Barbero (1987) as its leading exponents.

As digitalization is the current trend, it is necessary to consider the conceptual and terminological integration of digital and audiovisual literacy together with media literacy. Technological or media equipment does not make citizens competent in the field where the equipment operates. Educational training is required in order for someone to become competent, to be able to search for and discriminate information, to understand meaning and express oneself with and through the media, to participate and interact, to communicate. In consequence, it is necessary to deal with the procedures for accessing information, with the different languages that encode messages today, with the reception and comprehension of messages, with the technology that spreads this information, with the production, policies, and ideology of the media industry, with citizen involvement, and with the creative dimension of the media.

The effective integration of young people in society involves acquiring the skills and attitudes that allow them to handle technologies in the proper way, searching for information and then knowing how to assess its value, being capable of critical analysis, civic participation, and the creation, communication, and dissemination of knowledge; this is emphasized in several important studies on media competence (Celot & Pérez-Tornero, 2009; Ferrés et al., 2011; Hobbs, 2010; Jenkins, 2006; Lin, Li, Deng, & Lee, 2013). However, these requirements must be constantly updated and broadened, as the media evolves. The most relevant aspects concerning the development of educommunication involve three fields: knowledge (policies and media industry, production processes, technology, language and access to information); comprehension (reception and comprehension, ideology and values); and communication (creation and citizen involvement). In this sense, attention is now focusing on the emotional aspect, which is considered the driver of knowledge, according to the latest discoveries in neuroscience. At the same time, we need a form of education that enables us to control fluidity, the liquid (Bauman, 2000), that is to say, to control the constant and dynamic production of information and the unstable knowledge that technologies have entailed, where everything is in permanent change, where time and space no longer impose limits on learning. Educommunication is still an urgent necessity that demands the commitment of us all.

SEE ALSO: European Perspectives on Media Literacy; History of Media Literacy; Media Competence

References

Aguaded, I. (2013). Media programme (UE): International support for media education. *Comunicar, 40*, 7–8. doi: 10.3916/C40-2013-01-01

Aguaded, I. (2014). Research as a strategy for training educommunicators: Master and doctorate. *Comunicar, 43*, 7–8. doi: 10.3916/C43-2014-a1

Bauman, Z. (2000). *Modernidad líquida* [*Liquid modernity*]. Buenos Aires, Argentina: Fondo de Cultura Económica.

Buckingham, D., Banaji, S., Carr, D., Cranmer, S., & Willett, R. (2005). *The media literacy of children and young people: A review of the research literature on behalf of OFCOM*. London, England: University of London, Centre for the Study of Children, Youth and Media Institute of Education. Retrieved from https://www.researchgate.net/publication/253736824_The_Media_Literacy_of_Children_and_Young_People

Celot, P. (Ed.). (2015). *Assessing media literacy levels and the European Commission Pilot Initiative*. Brussels, Belgium: European Commission. Retrieved from https://eavi.eu/wp-content/uploads/2017/08/assessing.pdf

Celot, P., & Pérez-Tornero, J.M. (2009). *Study assessment criteria for media literacy levels: Final report*. Brussels, Belgium: European Association for Viewers' Interests. Retrieved from http://ec.europa.eu/assets/eac/culture/library/studies/literacy-criteria-report_en.pdf

Christ, W., & Henderson, J. (2014). Assessing the ACEJMC professional values and competencies. *Journalism & Mass Communication Educator, 69*(3), 229–242. doi: 10.1177/1077695814525408

Di-Croce, D. (2009). *Media literacy: Teacher resource guide*. Toronto, Canada: Canadian Broadcasting Corporation.

Ferrés, J., García-Matilla, A., Aguaded, I., Fernández, J., & Figueras, M. (2011). *Competencia mediática: Investigación sobre el grado de competencia en la ciudadanía en España* [*Media competence: Investigation into the degree of competence among the citizenry in Spain*]. Madrid, Spain: ITE/Ministerio de Educación.

Grizzle, A., & Torras-Calvo, M.C. (2013). *Media and information literacy: Policy and strategy guidelines*. Paris, France: UNESCO. Retrieved from http://goo.gl/HgzLYW

Hobbs, R. (2010). *Digital and media literacy: A plan of action*. Washington, DC: Aspen Institute.

Jenkins, H. (2006). *Convergence culture: Where old and new media collide*. New York, NY: NYU Press.

Kaplún, M. (1998). *Una pedagogía de la comunicación* [*A pedagogy of communication*]. Madrid, Spain: La Torre.
Koltay, T. (2011). The media and the literacies: Media literacy, information literacy, digital literacy. *Media, Culture & Society, 33*(2), 211–221. doi: 10.1177/0163443710393382
Lee, A. (2010). Media education: Definitions, approaches and development around the globe. *New Horizons in Education, 58*(3). Retrieved from https://www.learntechlib.org/p/111272
Lin, T.-B., Li, J.Y., Deng, F., & Lee, L. (2013). Understanding new media literacy: An explorative theoretical framework. *Journal of Educational Technology & Society, 16*(4), 160–170. Retrieved from www.jstor.org/stable/jeductechsoci.16.4.160
Livingstone, S. (2008). Engaging with media: A matter of literacy? *Communication, Culture & Critique, 1*(1), 51–62. doi: 10.1111/j.1753-9137.2007.00006.x
Martín-Barbero, J. (1987). *De los medios a las mediaciones* [*From media to mediations*]. Naucalpan, Mexico: Gustavo Gili.
Masterman, L. (1993). *Teaching the media*. London, England: Routledge.
Moore, P. (2008). *Teacher training curricula for media and information literacy*. Paris, France: UNESCO.
NAMLE. (2009). *Core principles of media literacy education in the United States*. Retrieved from https://nccas.wikispaces.com/file/view/NAMLE-CPMLE-w-questions2.pdf/263228724/NAMLE-CPMLE-w-questions2.pdf
Orozco, G. (2001). *Televisión, audiencias y educación* [*Television, audiences, and education*]. Bogota, Colombia: Norma.
Orozco, G. (2011). La condición comunicacional contemporánea: Desafíos latinoamericanos de la investigación de las interacciones en la sociedad red [The contemporary condition of communication: Latin American challenges in the investigation of interactions in the network society]. In N. Jacks (Ed.), *Análisis de recepción en América Latina: Un recuerdo histórico con perspectivas al futuro* [*Analysis of reception in Latin America: A historical record with a view to the future*] (pp. 377–407). Quito, Ecuador: Ciespal.
UNESCO. (1982). Grünwald declaration on media education. Retrieved from http://www.unesco.org/education/pdf/MEDIA_E.PDF
UNESCO. (1984). *Media education*. Paris: UNESCO.

Further reading

Masterman, L. (1984). La educación en materia de comunicación: Problemas teóricos y posibilidades concretas [Education regarding communication: Theoretical problems and concrete possibilities]. *Perspectivas, 13*(2), 191–200.

Ignacio Aguaded, PhD, is full professor at the Department of Education of the University of Huelva, Spain. He leads the fields of technology and innovation and is the chairman of Group Comunicar in Andalusia, a veteran in Spain in education through mass media. He is the editor of *Comunicar: International Media Education Research Journal*. He is also scientific advisor to several national and international scientific journals, as well as manager of Agora: Research Group in the Andalusian Research Plan, for which he develops various international investigation projects. He has participated in many investigation activities in the didactic use of mass media and has been the organizer and chairman of several scientific committees of international academic events.

Agueda Delgado-Ponce, PhD, is professor in the Department of Philology at the University of Huelva, Spain. She is a member of the research group Agora: Research Group in the Andalusian Research Plan; of Group Comunicar in Andalusia; and of the Euro-American interuniversity network Alfamed. Her research examines media competence and new languages of communication.

Emancipatory Communication

STEFANIA MILAN
University of Amsterdam, The Netherlands

Emancipatory communication indicates the creation of grassroots alternatives to existing media and communication infrastructure, whether analog or digital, commercial or state-owned. Examples include Internet servers and media platforms providing website hosting, e-mail accounts, and noncommercial social media services or blockchain technologies (Tréguer, Antoniadis, & Söderberg, 2016); community media such as low-power radio and micro-TV stations, which appropriate airwaves regardless of whether they have legal authorization to operate (Rennie, 2006); community-owned wireless networks for public Internet access (Powell, 2008); independent print media initiatives (Atton, 2002); social practices of horizontal knowledge production and critical pedagogy in the technology realm such as open source software and hacker communities (Coleman, 2013). By promoting first-hand engagement with infrastructure creation, emancipatory communication demystifies technology, whether digital or analog, unpacking its functioning and bringing it closer to the people's lived experience. By exposing the contradictions of the contemporary media landscape, it encourages critical thinking and public participation in the making of technology. By supporting the efforts of disempowered groups and individuals to obtain equality and freedom in their communications and content production, it opposes the profit-driven value system promoted by mainstream media and technology firms.

The group dynamics supporting infrastructure creation can be understood as "emancipatory communication practices": sociologically speaking, they represent ways of social organizing oriented to envisioning and crafting alternatives to the existing *mediascape*. At the core of these organizing efforts stands communication technology, and the belief that this is not neutral but rather the result of complex negotiations weighing sociopolitical values and economic interests. In addition, emancipatory communication activists share a mission, that of enabling individuals and groups to communicate in their own terms, outside of the logics of profit that characterize most contemporary media and communication outlets. In fact, by engaging in emancipatory communication practices, practitioners and users seek to circumvent the politics of enclosure and control enacted by states, regulators, and corporations.

A brief history of emancipatory communication

The history of emancipatory communication parallels that of social movements. One of the first examples of emancipatory communication dates back to the 1940s, when Bolivian miners set up community radio stations to, among other things, campaign for better wages. Often without a license to broadcast (the so-called pirate radios), locally owned stations mushroomed in various countries in Europe and Latin America from the 1970s onwards. Around the same time the first hacker communities appeared in North America. These early instances of emancipatory communication coexisted with the many advocacy efforts of the time, such as national media reform campaigns or the debate for a New World Information and Communication Order within the United Nations' Educational, Scientific and Cultural Organization in the 1970–1980s. However, policy advocacy and media reform remained fairly detached from the grassroots practices of infrastructure-making.

In the 1990s, the desire to create autonomous infrastructure independently of institutions and public policies met the Internet, which, lowering the skills and the costs of media production, stimulated the emergence of an unprecedented number of emancipatory communication projects. The Independent Media Center, or Indymedia, a global network of web-based independent reporting without editors, grew out of the global justice movement: three years after its foundation in Seattle in 1999, it counted over ninety nodes distributed in six continents. Recognizing the potential of the new information technologies for the promotion of social justice and development, in 1988 PeaceNet and GreenNet, two grassroots network operators, teamed up to create the first transatlantic digital communication network owned and operated by nongovernmental organizations. In many western countries, radical Internet service providers started offering noncommercial web hosting, mailing lists, and e-mail accounts. Traditional broadcasting experiments, however, did not surrender to the rule of the World Wide Web, with radio in particular continuing to thrive in the African continent, South-East Asia, and Latin America; micro-TV experiments emerged in Europe.

In the second half of the 2000s, emancipatory communication projects expanded also to social media networks, trying to create alternatives to Facebook and its monetization of user data. Activist developers experimented with wireless networks, encryption tools, and anonymization networks such as Tor, as well as blockchain technology, a decentralized and distributed computing system. Meanwhile, low-power radio was legalized in the United States in 2011. The availability of video-sharing platforms like YouTube, microblogging services like Twitter, and social networking sites such as Facebook and Instagram resulted in many activists and movements of the left migrating from self-organized services to commercial ones, which are used by the large majority of the population. While efforts at creating alternative infrastructure still thrive on the fringes of the system, this break has prompted activists to claim that "we need to talk about Facebook": "We see Facebook users as a real danger for our struggles. In particular, activists who publish important information on Facebook (often without knowing what they are doing), which is increasingly used by law enforcement agencies … For activists to allow this Trojan horse called

Facebook to be part of their everyday lives is a sign of ignorance on a critical level" (Nadir, 2012).

Infrastructure-making between emancipation and empowerment

Scholars have long acknowledged the crucial role of alternative communication infrastructure in the contemporary movement ecology. Over the years, different labels have been used to describe noncommercial grassroots media infrastructure, albeit with a focus on content production as opposed to infrastructure-making: among others, radical media (Downing, 2001), citizens' media (Rodriguez, 2001), alternative media (Atton, 2002), and autonomous media (Langlois & Dubois, 2005). Hackett and Carroll (2006) praised the "oppositional communication practices" aimed at cultivating alternative public spheres. Langlois and Dubois argued that autonomous media are "the vehicles of social movements" (Langlois & Dubois, 2005, p. 9). Uzelman spoke of "autonomous media practices," whose activists "encourage and help others to produce their own media products" and act as "teachers by way of the good examples they provide" (2005, pp. 23–24). Downing explained that radical media "express[ing] an alternative vision to hegemonic politics, priorities, and perspectives" tend to "break somebody's rules, although rarely all of them in every aspect" (Downing, 2001, pp. v–ix). Rodriguez stressed how these media are into "contesting social codes, legitimized identities, and institutionalized social relations"; the communication practices they support "are empowering the community involved, to the point where these transformations and changes are possible" (Rodriguez, 2001, p. 20).

Notwithstanding the burgeoning of infrastructure-making initiatives, however, the notion of emancipation has historically received little attention in media and communication studies. Enzensberger (1974) distinguished between the repressive use of media, where these are centrally controlled and promote passive consumption, and an emancipatory use of media, which goes along with a decentralized approach to media production, where media are collectively produced and can promote collective mobilization. By the same token, "emancipatory journalism" is a radical approach to journalism that seeks to "promote and contribute to human development" by encouraging practitioners to be fully involved in movements for social change (Shah, 1996, p. 146). Similarly to the notion of emancipatory communication, emancipatory journalism denies the neutrality of engagement with media, given the scarce freedom that characterizes today's media landscapes, and preaches involvement in social movements.

Here emancipation stands in for both positive and negative freedoms. On the one hand, it is intended as "freedom from" commercial and/or privacy-infringing logics and their constraints. From this perspective, emancipation resonates with the notion of self-determination as the free choice of individuals and groups with regards to their cultural and communicative future. Freeing people to communicate their own messages in ways that respect their values means providing the infrastructure and skills that are necessary to the task. On the other hand, emancipation evokes the "freedom for" affirmative action in the communication realm: emancipatory communication creates spaces for people to engage in communications and media production. As such, emancipation chimes with empowerment, or the process through which individuals and groups exercise control over their resources and messages by taking active part in the actions that reshape their communications. "Freedom for" thus points to the active exercise of control over technologies that empowers people, including average users. Paraphrasing Rodriguez (2001), communication infrastructure becomes a space for people to enact their democratic agency. In her view, "these practices and strategies of resistance constitute the politics of the quotidian": they expand and multiply spaces for political action, which is no longer confined merely to institutional spaces but becomes embedded in social life (2001, p. 21).

Features of emancipatory communication

Although emancipatory communication practices are varied and differentiated, they tend to share a number of features when it comes to reasons why people mobilize, modes of organizing, tactics they privilege, and their networking strategies. First, individuals decide to act upon a perceived sense of injustice that permeates the technology and media sphere and is believed to underpin and contribute to perpetuate other forms of inequality. For the most part, activists are concerned by the architecture of technology and the related institutional and industry arrangements and relations, which they deem obscure and deeply unfair. Conversely, they see communication infrastructure as a vehicle for social change: in the words of the activists, "we try to offer a liberating form of communication within the capitalist internet. We have always seen the internet as a resource for our struggles and at the same time recognised it as contested political terrain" (Nadir, 2012). Others explained: "the main motivation right from the start was the realisation that the so-called grass-roots 'social movements' needed new networks of communication that could not only work as a platform to project discourses and practices to the 'wider world', but also that the way these networks were created, run and developed, mirrored, as much as possible, the direct, participatory, collective and autonomous nature of the emerging social movement(s) themselves" (Milan, 2013, p. 58). Other motivating factors of emancipatory communication activists include the possibility to exercise freedom of expression and self-determination; the fascination for experimenting and learning in the technology realm; and the opportunity to act as service providers to other progressive social movements and causes.

Second, organizing forms are rooted in trust and loyalty. They are often an adaptation to political activism of familiar repertoires of interaction, like the group of friends or peers. Moreover, group dynamics are likely to reflect the medium around which activists organize, be it the Internet, with its decentralized networks of "equal" nodes, or broadcasting, with its orientation to the audience. For example, within the community radio sector there coexist a plurality of organization models, from semi-professional groups to grassroots organization with no formal structure, but all of them are opened to the community the station purports to serve. Participation, access, and locality are the main features of community radio groups. Groupings tend to be inclusive, and practitioners strive to keep access barriers low by, for instance, organizing regular training sessions for newcomers. Radical developers have a tendency to operate in an informal manner, often as "collectives" of equals rooted in the affinity of political values: "group[s] of people working together in a non hierarchical way, aiming to achieve goals all members of the collective agree upon … all the members of the project have the same status in the group. There are no formal hierarchies, no bosses or 'elders' that would have more formal authority than others" (Milan, 2013, p. 87). Individuals and individual expertise play a key role in the group, which functions through a "division of labor" model that values individual skills. Decision-making is supposedly reached by "rough consensus." More often than not, the group remains invisible, as a unit that exists mainly in function of service provision; the attempt to remain under the radar, however, is also a measure to protect the group activities from surveillance and repression.

Although building influence, lobbying, and campaigning might occasionally complement the direct engagement with infrastructure-making, emancipatory communication activists share a hands-on approach that privileges structural reform at the grassroots over policy advocacy work and institutional reform. In so doing, they seek to create parallel prefigurative realities establishing "temporary zones" for emancipation from state and corporate control (Downing, 2001). These prefigurative realities attempt at translating into practice here and now the activist ethics, including the values of egalitarianism, participation, and self-determination. In the words of the activists, "the political goal is to create counter-power, not to oppose [it] … Like in the Indymedia slogan: 'don't hate the media, become the media'" (Milan, 2013, p. 127). As an activist explained, "My main focus is not to become a player in the realm of the 'mainstream politics', but on the contrary, to by-pass the mainstream by creating living alternatives to it … Our job, as activists, is to create self-managed infrastructures that work *regardless of* 'their' regulation, laws or any other form of governance" (p. 130).

Finally, peer networking is key to the development and survival of emancipatory communication projects. Activists create connections with other like-minded groups for skill sharing and, in case of repression or institutional threats, self-defence purposes. Networks emerge at different levels, from national to transnational; some are institutionalized as membership-based associations providing services to their members, whereas others, more informal, emerge ad hoc or are activated in case of need.

SEE ALSO: Civic Media; Coding as Literacy; Community Informatics; Community Media; Critical Pedagogy; Media Access and Activism; Media Literacy for the 21st Century Teacher; Mediatization

References

Atton, C. (2002). *Alternative media*. London, England: SAGE.

Coleman, G. (2013). *Coding freedom: The ethics and aesthetics of hacking*. Princeton, NJ: Princeton University Press.
Downing, J.D.H. (2001). *Radical media. Rebellious communication and social movements*. Thousand Oaks, CA: SAGE.
Enzensberger, H.M. (1974). *The consciousness industry: On literature, politics and the media*. New York, NY: Seabury.
Hackett, R.A., & Carroll, W.K. (2006). *Remaking media. The struggle to democratize public communication*. New York, NY: Routledge.
Langlois, A., & Dubois, F. (Eds.). (2005). *Autonomous media: Activating resistance & dissent*. Montréal, Canada: Cumulus Press.
Milan, S. (2013). *Social movements and their technologies: Wiring social change*. Basingstoke, England: Palgrave Macmillan.
Nadir. (2012, October). We need to talk about Facebook. Retrieved from http://www.nadir.org/txt/We_need_to_talk_about_Facebook.html
Powell, A. (2008). Wifi publics: Producing community and technology. *Information, Communication & Society, 11*(8), 1068–1088. doi: 10.1080/13691180802258746
Rennie, E. (2006). *Community media. A global introduction*. Lanham, MA: Rowman & Littlefield.
Rodriguez, C. (2001). *Fissures in the mediascape. An international study of citizens' media*. Cresskill, NJ: Hampton Press.
Shah, H. (1996). Modernization, marginalization, and emancipation: Toward a normative model of journalism and national development. *Communication Theory, 6*(2), 143–166. doi: 10.1111/j.1468-2885.1996.tb00124.x
Tréguer, F., Antoniadis, P., & Söderberg, J. (Eds.). (2016). Alternative Internets. *Journal of Peer Production*, (9). Retrieved from http://peerproduction.net/issues/issue-9-alternative-internets/
Uzelman, S. (2005). Hard at work in the bamboo garden: Media activists and social movements. In A. Langlois & F. Dubois (Eds.), *Autonomous media: Activating resistance and dissent* (pp. 16–29). Montréal, Canada: Cumulus Press.

Further reading

Costanza-Chock, S. (2014). *Out of the shadows, into the streets! Transmedia organizing and the immigrant rights movement*. Cambridge, MA: MIT Press.
Dencik, L., & Leistert, O. (Eds.). (2015). *Critical perspectives on social media and protest: Between control and emancipation*. London, England: Rowman & Littlefield.
Downing, J.D.H. (Ed.). (2011). *Encyclopedia of social movement media*. Thousand Oaks, CA: SAGE.
Dunbar-Hester, C. (2014). *Low power to the people! Pirates, protest, and politics in FM radio activism*. Cambridge, MA: MIT Press.
Milan, S. (2016). Liberated technology: Inside emancipatory communication activism. In E. Gordon & P. Mihailidis (Eds.), *Civic media: Technology, design, practice* (pp. 107–124). Cambridge MA: MIT Press.

Stefania Milan is Associate Professor of New Media and Digital Culture at the University of Amsterdam. She is also the Principal Investigator of the DATACTIVE project (data-activism.net), funded with a Starting Grant of the European Research Council (ERC) and researching the evolution of activism vis-à-vis datafication, and of the ALEX-Algorithms Exposed project (algorithms.exposed), funded by a Proof of Concept grant of the ERC. Her research explores technology and participation, cyberspace governance, and emerging data epistemologies. Stefania is the author of *Social Movements and Their Technologies: Wiring Social Change* (2013/2016), and coauthor of *Media/Society* (2011).

Entertainment Information

CHRISTINA HICKS-GOLDSTON and JASON P. GOLDSTON
Austin Peay State University, USA

The concept of entertainment information can be formally explored as a method of relaying different forms of information to audiences, within specific platforms, in an entertaining manner or as information about the world of entertainment. In 1953 George Gallup, then director of the American Institute of Public Opinion, opined that one of the largest threats to America was "a citizenry which daily elects to be entertained and not informed" (Gallup, 1953, p. 473). Gallup noted that the difference in valuation between entertainment and information resided with the everyday choices of consumers, not with the choices of media organizations. To ensure revenue, media businesses will create the content that consumers want; and, overwhelmingly, consumers choose to be entertained over being informed. For Gallup, the issue is not with audiences' love of entertainment; instead, he noted that "there should be a better balance between entertainment and education" (Gallup, 1953, p. 473). He argued that a culture that values education values information. The responsibility for the balance rests with individuals, who change the valuation of the culture. When media businesses respond to a public's desire for more information entertainment rather than just for information, Gallup predicted cultural disintegration. Gallup lamented that a culture that continuously chooses entertainment over information may lead the culture to make us "kill ourselves laughing" (Gallup, 1953, p. 473).

Author and Internet activist Tristan Louis provided a further exploration of the content choices inherent in media organizations. According to Louis, the value of media is in the content, not in the delivery system; he presented three dimensions of media, each dimension representing a scale of opposites: entertainment versus information; directly purchased versus subsidized information; and mass-generated versus professional media-generated information (Louis, 2009a).

Dimension 1: entertainment versus information

Entertainment and information are important dividers in assessing media property, because there are different audience types for different kinds of information. According to Louis, all information is useful to someone, but most information is of no interest to most people. For example, financial facts are appealing to those individuals with business interests, or job-related information is appealing to individuals focused on specific careers or on changing careers. The two different styles of analysis when presenting information to the audience are (i) *in-depth*—which includes in-depth analysis with long and thorough information about a specific subject (e.g., the *New York Times*) and (ii) *scant*, which includes merely the main idea of a story in brief, without going into much detail (e.g., *USA Today*). Professionally created and vetted information is expensive, because formal investigation and analysis involve cost. While the discovery of factual information costs money in time and labor, inserting opinions is cheap. The result of the "cost factor" is a kind of "infotainment" relying heavily on opinion, as opposed to the information that relies heavily on facts. According to Louis (2009b), modern media organizations must attempt a balance between giving audiences the information they want and using entertainment to retain audience share. Audience share is important, because a media organization's value is linked to it. Many organizations emphasize the infotainment model because it is better than sole information at retaining audience share. Information media is actionable, and more valuable than entertainment. Information has value for the public good, but may not be actionable to most people; the consumer is left to evaluate the information on his/her own. Louis noted that, in the information age dominated by social media activity, consumers tend to lean toward the "wisdom of the crowds" or the self-correction of personal interest (which is conservative-leaning or liberal-leaning). Entertainment media is cheap to produce, but has less obvious community value; information media has value, but may be dependent on self-interest.

Dimension 2: subsidized versus directly purchased media

Subsidies from government or public bodies assist industry businesses in keeping the media cost low for consumers. Most media in the United States are subsidized by advertising or, in the case of public television, by the government. Advertising represents the largest revenue source for media organizations. Louis (2009c) stated that the negative side to a low-cost media commodity is that it results in the consumer treating media as disposable and as having little to no value. Digital media exacerbated the perception of media as a cheap commodity, as the cost for digital distribution and creation dropped to record lows. In the early days of the World Wide Web, traditional media outlets offered online content as a free incentive, creating the expectation that online media cost less. With search engine optimization and analytics advances, data-based online marketing became more valuable than traditional marketing. The lower-cost expectation traveled to traditional media, resulting in such organizations having to lower prices to remain competitive. One of three methods for subsidizing the lost revenue is pursuance of the advocacy media model. *Advocacy media* are subsidized by advocating a particular point of view or ideology, usually based in a political agenda. Another option, that of *noncore media*, is subsidized directly by a corporation, and the media exist to make the corporation look good. Noncore media are vulnerable to corporate buyouts, transitions in ownership, and the whims of the shareholders. Finally, *paid media* receive their revenue directly from the consumer rather than from the advertiser, usually in the form of "fair value" subscriptions. Paid media consumers are treated as customers rather than as commodities. Therefore paid media have an inherent value to the customer.

Dimension 3: mass-generated brands versus professional media brands

For Louis (2009d), *media brands* create professional content that requires many people for media creation. The people "band together" to create a media product. When the product was something that required writing, publishing, distributing, etc. the stages of production were lengthy and involved large groups of people (bands). Two of the main bands are the *content creation brand*—a name that refers to concept and delivery, and the *supply chain brand*—a name that refers to packaging, marketing, sales, and distribution. Professional content's packaged output is better known than the content creators. Content is in a very glossy, professional package, but the content is fixed and does not change over time. Professional subbrands, which are brands built around individuals such as author J.K. Rowling, director Steven Spielberg, or actor Tom Cruise, may evolve from other brands.

Louis (2009d) differentiated media brands as mass-generated media that emerge organically, usually free of cost. Brands can exist with or without specific contributors, as new contributors replace the old. Individuals who are not brands risk being forced out by other brands. Content is produced in unfinished form, updated as stories evolve. Content is malleable and collaborative. The editing process may be influenced by feedback from other sources, including audiences. Louis (2009d) theorized that the future of media will have larger sets of brands. Distribution costs will continue to decline to near zero. Traditional structures will be replaced by participatory models where brands curate inputs and individual curators become brands. The blurring of content curation and creation will create a new media model. Traditional media organizations must be ready and willing to evolve in order to survive.

Relaying information in education: pedagogy

Adults apply musical nursery rhymes to both entertain and teach or inform a child about living in the world. A study on children's exposure to nursery rhymes when they are as young as 3 and 4 years old revealed an "extremely robust" relationship between children's knowledge of nursery rhymes and their *phonological* (i.e., related to sounds in language) development (Maclean, Bryant, & Bradley, 1987). Early TV-era children's programs such as *Romper Room* (1953–1994) entertained children while also educating them. The show featured a hostess or teacher in a fictional preschool where small groups of children played games, shared songs and nursery rhymes, and learned how to treat others from the hostess and from characters such as "Mr. Doo Bee." *Romper Room* was unique in its format as a franchised program, allowing the show's originators in Baltimore to create content with resources that could be purchased by individual TV stations across the United States so as to be integrated with a local hostess and local children.

The "localized learning" model proved to be successful, and by 1957 22 stations were licensing the format and producing their own formats for the program (Moran, 2009). In 1971 F. Earle Barcus analyzed *Romper Room* as part of an Action for Children's Television (ACT) investigation for evidence that the program placed more emphasis on promoting toys than on educating children.

Romper Room was broadcast on commercial television, which allowed for a possible toy "sales pitch" within an episode. However, when *Sesame Street* premiered on public television in 1969, there were no commercials involved—just education via entertainment. Psychologist Gerald Lesser served as an adviser to the Children's Television Workshop, the team behind *Sesame Street*; Lesser's opinion was that television could capture children's attention through colorful characters and songs, while also teaching them daily. *Sesame Street* combined live action actors with muppets, some animation, and music while teaching arithmetic, language skills, and social competence.

Musical mnemonics are songs or rhymes to music designed to assist in the retention of learned material. One popular example is "The ABC Song" or "The Alphabet Song," which teaches children the alphabet by making them sing the letters. Between 1973 and 1985, children could watch the three-minute long *Schoolhouse Rock!* educational segments between Saturday morning programs and learn about a variety of subjects ("Multiplication Rock," "Grammar Rock," "Science Rock," and "America Rock," which explained American history). In 1982, "Computer Rock," which explained emerging computer technology, was added to the lineup, followed in 1994 by "Money Rock," which explained finances, and in 2009 by "Earth Rock," which explained ecology. Musical mnemonics have proven to be successful teaching and retention devices in higher education as well.

Video gaming, previously considered an exclusively entertaining pursuit, is also a recognized learning platform. An overview of gaming in education revealed five premises for the format: (i) digital games are built on sound learning principles; (ii) digital games provide more engagement for the learner; (iii) digital games provide personalized learning opportunities; (iv) digital games teach 21st-century skills; and (v) digital games provide an environment for authentic and relevant assessment (McClarty et al., 2012).

Relaying information in education: andragogy

Entertainment education (EE) is the process of purposely designing and implementing a media message that both entertains and educates, in order to increase audience members' knowledge of an educational issue, create favorable attitudes, shift social norms, and change overt behavior (Singhal & Rogers, 2002). Historically, EE has been used on popular broadcast programs for a variety of social issues. David O. Poindexter, former president of Population Communications International, discussed a combined effort between the Population Control Center and the three major broadcast networks in 1972 to incorporate a population control message into prime-time TV content. According to Poindexter, in the fall of 1972, the CBS programs *Maude*, *M.A.S.H.*, *Mary Tyler Moore*, and *All in the Family* carried the population issue (Poindexter, 2003). In 1986, at the height of the AIDS crisis, Linda Bloodworth-Thomason wrote an episode in the series *Designing Women* titled "Killing All the Right People," addressing the public's misconceptions about AIDS patients after her mother acquired the disease from a blood transfusion and subsequently died. In the fall of the 2005 TV season, both *ER* and *Gray's Anatomy* featured story arcs about the BRCA1 gene and links to breast cancer and possibly to ovarian cancer (Hether, Huang, Beck, Murphy, & Valente, 2008). Researchers at the University of Alberta analyzed 177 episodes of eight popular medical shows between 1990 and 2009 for possible facilitation in teaching medical information. Internationally, EE was used in Indian TV programs in 2000 to inform and educate the public about AIDS, and in Costa Rican radio in the mid-1970s for discussion of social topics such as sex, family planning, and contraception, which previously had been taboo. In the late 1970s Miguel Sabido's *Acompaname* was the first family-planning TV serial drama in Mexico. Sabido's methodology was transferred to India, Kenya, and Brazil (Poindexter, 2003).

According to Piotrow and de Fossard (2003), EE is most commonly used in radio and TV serial dramas, in films and videos, in songs, variety shows, and distance-learning formats. The challenges for EE are too much entertainment and not enough education; too much education and not enough entertainment; poor-quality entertainment; no credible urgency; routine recommendations; no immediate personal relevance; and controversies based on culture and tradition (Piotrow & de Fossard, 2003). The authors also referenced the nine Ps of EE for providing insight into effective use of the process. Piotrow argued that EE is an effective way to promote healthy behavior because it is:

- pervasive Everywhere, from street theater to national television, from songs and dances to community radio, entertainment is there, with some kind of message.
- popular People like entertainment, seek it out, and enjoy it.
- passionate Entertainment stimulates the emotions, so people remember, talk to others, and are more inclined to take action.
- personal People identify with dramatic characters as if they were personal friends.
- participatory People participate by singing, dancing, and talking about entertaining characters, stories, and activities.
- persuasive People can be persuaded to identify with role models and then see the consequences of sensible or foolish behavior and imitate what works.
- practical Entertainment infrastructures and performers are already in place and always look for good dramatic themes.
- profitable Good EE helps pay its own way and generates sponsorship, collateral promotions, and sometimes profit.
- proven effective Messages from entertainment can change the way people think, feel, and behave, as research has shown (Piotrow & de Fossard, 2003).

Relaying information in news reportage

The objective ideal of reporting news and information has not always been the dominant paradigm. Britain's broadsides of the 18th and 19th century were distributed among the masses at public executions. Such publications were largely sensationalist in nature and composed of lurid depictions or information about the criminal or crime printed on one side of the paper in large type; and they rarely cost more than a penny (visit http://broadsides.law.harvard.edu). The introduction of the American penny press newspapers in the 1830s offered larger audiences a lower-cost news source, and the newspapers at times included muckraking reports of social injustice or scandals (Harrower, 2013). However, the era of American yellow journalism began in the late 19th century as a product of the circulation war between Joseph Pulitzer's *New York World* newspaper and William Randolph Hearst's *New York Journal* newspaper. Yellow journalism was characterized by loud headlines, sensational stories about sin and sex, lavish use of "doctored" photos, and Sunday supplements of crowd-pleasing comics, features, and rumors disguised as news (Harrower, 2013). Modern-era journalism that is either fear-based or sensational in nature is a kind of entertainment information. Media analysts criticize fear-based journalism and sensational journalism as being profit-motivated rather than accurate; its goal is to achieve higher ratings and increased viewership (Serani, 2011).

Relaying information about entertainment: gossip

Entertainment reporting refers to information about celebrities and entertainment venues such as plays, films, television, radio, music, and popular culture. Historically, entertainment reportage included print media such as *Variety* (established 1905), an American trade magazine about the entertainment industry that began in the Vaudeville era, and early film-fan magazines such as *Photoplay* (established 1912) and *Motion Picture Story* (established 1911), which began in the silent film era, followed by other similar magazines such as the *Hollywood Reporter* (established 1930) in the golden age of Hollywood. Other entertainment publications through the years included *TV Guide* (established 1953), *Entertainment Weekly* (established 1990), *Rolling Stone* (established 1967), and *Billboard* (established 1894). Their content was largely industry- based and directed at fans of television, film, music, or theater. In 1981 the syndicated *Entertainment Tonight* TV program combined industry news with gossip in a half-hour format. In 1987 what is now known as E! (Entertainment Television) was launched as MovieTime. The channel extends information similar to that found on *Entertainment Tonight* (celebrity gossip, fashion, premieres, etc.) to an entire channel. Other publications involving celebrities or entertainment news are "gossip magazines" such as *People* (established 1974) or *Us* (established 1977). Before the rise of the gossip magazine, individuals such as Hedda Hopper, a former actress-turned-gossip columnist, provided information on celebrities' activities in her column for the *Los Angeles Times*. Hopper's rival was Louella Parsons, a columnist who began with the *Chicago Record Herald* before moving to the *Los Angeles Examiner*. Later on columnist Liz Smith began writing her "Cholly Knickerbocker" column in 1950, before becoming entertainment editor for *Cosmopolitan* and *Sports Illustrated* and for her self-titled column in 1976.

Relaying information online: entertainment gossip media

In the late 20th and early 21st century, as publications began moving to online formats, so did the entertainment publications, and some entertainment media are entirely online, for example the Internet Movie Database (imdb.com), Rotten Tomatoes, Metacritic, Vulture, Collider, or The Wrap. Just like print media, gossip magazines and reporters eventually became online fixtures, individuals such as Hopper, Parsons, and Smith being replaced by Perez Hilton or by websites such as TMZ (tmz.com), the Daily Mirror (mirror.co.uk), Page Six (pagesix.com), or NY Daily News (nydailynews.com).

SEE ALSO: Digital News; History of Media Literacy; Learning from Media; Media Literacy in Communication Education

References

Gallup, G. (1953). Mass information or mass entertainment. *Vital Speeches of the Day, 19*(15), 473–475.

Harrower, T. (2013). News in the 20th century: Yellow journalism. In T. Harrower (Ed.), *Inside reporting: A practical guide to the craft of journalism* (pp. 10–12). New York, NY: McGraw-Hill.

Hether, H.J., Huang, G.C., Beck, V., Murphy, S.T., & Valente, T.W. (2008). Entertainment-education in a media-saturated environment: Examining the impact of single and multiple exposures to breast cancer storylines on two popular medical dramas. *Journal of Health Communication, 13*(8), 808–823.

Louis, T. (2009a, October 3). Entertainment vs. information [Blog post]. Retrieved from http://www.tnl.net/blog/2009/10/03/entertainment-vs-information

Louis, T. (2009b, November 19). Media bands vs. media brands [Blog post]. Retrieved from http://www.tnl.net/blog/2009/11/19/media-bands-vs-media-brands

Louis, T. (2009c, October 26). Subsidized vs. directly purchased media [Blog post]. Retrieved from http://www.tnl.net/blog/2009/10/26/subsidized-vs-directly-purchased-media

Louis, T. (2009d, September 25). The three dimensions of media [Blog post]. Retrieved from http://www.tnl.net/blog/2009/09/25/the-three-dimensions-of-media

Maclean, M., Bryant, P., & Bradley, L. (1987). Rhymes, nursery rhymes, and reading in early childhood. *Merrill-Palmer Quarterly, 33*(3), 255–281.

McClarty, K.L., Orr, A., Frey, P.M., Dolan, R.P., Vassileva, V., & McVay, A. (2012). A literature review of gaming in education (Research report). Pearson. Retrieved from https://images.pearsonassessments.com/images/tmrs/Lit_Review_of_Gaming_in_Education.pdf

Moran, A. (2009). Global franchising, local customizing: The cultural economy of TV program formats. *Continuum, 23*(2), 115–125.

Piotrow, P., & de Fossard, E. (2003). Entertainment education as a public health intervention. In A. Singhal, M.J. Cody, E.M. Rogers, & M. Sabido. (Eds.), *Entertainment-education and social change* (pp. 39–60). New York, NY: Routledge.

Poindexter, D. (2003). A history of entertainment education, 1958–2000. In A. Singhal, M.J. Cody, E.M. Rogers, & M. Sabido. (Eds.), *Entertainment education and social change* (pp. 21–36). New York, NY: Routledge.

Serani, D. (2011). If it bleeds, it leads: Understanding fear-based media. *Psychology Today*, 7.

Singhal, A., & Rogers, E.M. (2002). A theoretical agenda for entertainment: Education. *Communication Theory, 12*(2), 117–135. doi: 10.1111/j.1468-2885.2002.tb00262.x

Further reading

Dying speeches & bloody murders: Crime broadsides collected by the Harvard Law School Library. (2013). Retrieved from http://broadsides.law.harvard.edu

Singhal, A., Cody, M.J., Rogers, E.M., & Sabido, M. (Eds.). (2003). *Entertainment-education and social change: History, research, and practice.* New York, NY: Routledge.

Christina Hicks-Goldston is an Associate Professor of Communication at Austin Peay State University. She is a critical cultural theorist and researcher, and her areas of research include race and gender in mass media, cultural context and media, and experiential learning. She is a certified Service Learning trainer and member of the Service Learning Advisory Board for her university. Her educational film, *Making the Connection: the Service Learning Revolution*, received eight awards for excellence and design following its August 2014 release. Last year, Dr. Hicks-Goldston wrote a chapter on media Service Learning projects involving senior citizens for the book *Culturally Engaging Service Learning in Diverse Communities.* Christina and her husband, Jason, are currently researching a project on augmented reality and transmedia as communication platforms.

Jason P. Goldston is a part-time undergraduate instructor of Communication at Austin Peay State University and a graduate instructor at Watkins College of Art, Design, and Film as well as a video/film editor and media management consultant. He coproduced, shot, and edited *Making the Connection: The Service Learning Revolution* with his wife, Christina, in 2013–2014. He also incorporates Service Learning and experiential learning into his courses, and has received commendation for his work with Volunteers of America and the Adventure Science Center in Nashville, TN. He and Christina are currently researching a project on augmented reality and transmedia as communication platforms.

Esthetics in Media Literacy

MICHELLE ZOSS
Georgia State University, USA

In a world of technologies and broad access to media, it seems fitting to take time to delve into the esthetics of media literacy. When the term esthetics comes up, some readers might be immediately put off. Esthetics may seem like an overbearing term that will lead to a discussion about whether or not something is beautiful. That argument might then devolve into disagreement about beauty being in the eye of one beholder over another. But esthetics is not simply about beauty. Rather, it is about relationships, how parts of a whole come together, and how the beholder takes on the media at hand.

To understand how esthetics and media literacy function, it is helpful to have working definitions for both concepts.

Aufderheide (1993) defines media literacy with actions requiring a person to "decode, evaluate, analyze and produce" texts in digital and print forms (p. 1). This definition makes the media-literate person one who not only consumes texts but also produces them in turn. Different from a more traditional term of literacy that may only include reading and writing of print and language-based texts, media literacy invites the production and consumption of texts that use visual, aural, musical, and linguistic elements. Thus media literacy opens up the idea of considering how to interact with texts to include everything from novels, poetry, and newspapers to social media posts, commercial advertisements, films, and other multimedia productions. In other words, media literacy opens up the conversation about how to read and compose in the world to the dynamic and ubiquitous tools now available on nearly any electronic device. With wide-ranging texts and practices, esthetics then can be a tool for grasping the particulars within media.

Esthetics as a relational concept dates back to the work of Baumgarten (1750/1961). He translated the ancient Greek term *aisthanesthai*, which means to perceive, into the modern term esthetics. To perceive in this sense requires particular action. Siegesmund (1999) pointed out that Greek verbs have three different forms of conjugation: one requires a person to do something to an object, the second requires the object to do something to a person, and the third requires an interplay of action between object and person. For example, in the first form of conjugation a person holds a book. In the second form, the book falls on the person's head. In the third form, a more complex transaction has to occur. Consider that a person could learn from the book and write commentary in response to it within its pages. The important point here is that the term *aisthanesthai* can only be conjugated in the third way; thus, perception requires a relationship. To perceive a text means that a person enters into a collaboration of sorts that may be brief or long, but it is an interaction nonetheless.

Perceiving in this sense requires a back and forth that provides room for the text to work on the person and the person to work on the text; Dewey (1934/1980) discussed this back and forth as the work of art. That is, the work of art is the relationship between the perceiver and the piece of art. Put another way, the *work* of art is in the perceiving and the meaning-making with an art work. The point here is that there is more going on than just seeing to recognize; instead, there is seeing to understand and make meaning. Perkins (1994) and Eisner (2002) both agreed that learning to perceive in this action-oriented way is an intellectual achievement. Extending the argument from art to media that include image, language, and sound turns the notion of perception, of esthetics, to a plethora of texts. Being media-literate, then, involves the work of attending carefully to the qualities of the media, understanding the relations among the qualities, and developing a sense of meaning about those qualities. It is in this relationship that esthetics come into play.

Qualities are the elements of design within a media text that, when brought together, give a sense of composition. Qualities in the arts include line, shape, color, sound, rhythm, movement, and more. When qualities come together, people make sense of the relations among qualities, a move that Reimer (2003) suggested was integral and distinctive to the arts. When considering media, the qualities are that which can be seen and heard within a text.

The benefit of an approach oriented toward esthetics is that there does not have to be a singular focus on language. Perceivers can focus on the properties of sound, music, image, and language qualities together. Reimer (2003) makes the case for understanding music. Perkins (1994) talks about the educated eye. Literacy specialists argued for decades about the importance of understanding language, but they also argued for the importance of acknowledging how and what is seen in a text (Flood, Heath, & Lapp, 1997/2005). Messaris (1998) pointed out the visual qualities of media support the ways in which the perceiver understands connections among qualities and therefore makes meaning of media texts. Within his argument, Messaris drew on the idea of visual language and used the grammar of language to describe the qualities of visual aspects within media. While his premise is stable, there is more to visual and musical qualities than can perhaps be accounted for in the ways that scholars have mapped out language. Eisner (2002) and Reimer (2003) both agree that there are features of visual art and music, respectively, which are difficult to express with words. Furthermore, they posit that having neologisms and other means of discussing, describing, and communicating about art and music may be necessary because words are sometimes simply not enough. Toward the goal of defining what is needed for keen perception of media, Siegesmund (1999) offered reasoned perception as a tool for teaching esthetics.

Reasoned perception refers to constructing meaning from the relations of qualities within a given text (Siegesmund, 1999). It is important, for instance, to understand sounds, music, moving and still images, and language as they relate to each other. Messaris (1998) gave useful examples related to the use of photographs in nature used in print advertisements for cigarettes. Imagine a print ad using a landscape image of a mountain or forest to make the implication that the cigarettes are as natural and healthy as the water, air, and plants in the image. The media-literate viewer of this ad might see the juxtaposition of nature with the cigarette brand and company logo as an opportunity both to consider the point of view of the corporation and to question the credibility of the implication. The importance of reasoned perception is that the viewer considers all the information at hand and the sociocultural, historical, and political knowledge that can also be brought to bear in perceiving that ad.

Contrast this scenic ad with current ads that have been court-ordered to appear on television: these 30-second spots require multiple tobacco companies to disclose information about how the companies have manipulated the paper, chemicals, and other elements within cigarettes that contribute to their addictive properties. These ads have white backgrounds with black text. A woman with a mid-Atlantic accent reads the text as three to four sections of text appear on the screen. There is no music. There is no scenic nature. There is a footnote at the bottom of the last screen showing that the commercial was paid for by the tobacco companies, again under court order. In this new ad, there is little left to the imagination, but there are still relations of qualities at play. The screen remains a white screen with a black sans serif font. The statements are declarative sentences and use the second person to describe the viewer. This is an ad that does not imply that cigarettes might offer a refreshing break like the print ad; rather, this ad makes it clear that cigarettes are deleterious to health and that the companies that made them did so knowing about the addictive and damaging properties. The implied message of the visual qualities is one of seriousness—there is nothing to distract from the words on the screen and the voice reading those words. Bookending the ad are statements about the federal court order requirements. These ads were made because an external authority told the companies they must be made, so there are no frills—no jingles, no product logos, no people using the products, no images at all. Instead, there is a reporting of information and a warning. Although warnings are often accompanied in media with bright red or orange colors used for fonts, backgrounds, and objects, this ad has none of these. Further, there are no warning sounds or music such as might be found in movies or television to show or forecast tension or danger.

Esthetics in media literacy is an opportunity for considering how a piece is constructed and perceived. In the case of a print ad for cigarettes with an image of a scenic lake, there is room within the perception of that ad to consider the product to be benign or even helpful. The difference with the television ad is the rather bland quality that leaves the information in simple form. Despite the court order, the intent of the ad may be to downplay the importance of the information or to simply report the information as a matter of routine. With both ads, it is the viewer who takes up the visual, verbal, and aural information to decide what to do next. The media-literate viewer who is also savvy with esthetics can further attend to the way in which the ads bring together colors, fonts, images and lack thereof, in addition to the language used. The work of making meaning about the ads thus requires the viewer to not simply see or hear the ads, but to perceive the nuances of what is included and not included in the ads.

Learning to attend to the relations of qualities in media, as well as the absence or presence of qualities, is a goal that Bruce (2009) contended is vital for adolescents. In his review of studies related to students producing and carefully viewing media, Bruce countered the myth that adolescents are merely passive recipients or consumers of media. Rather, he showed in multiple studies that adolescents can be taught and indeed do practice thoughtful relations with media both inside and outside of school settings. While the argument is not necessarily about esthetics alone, Bruce's discussion points to the important, transactional nature of media literacy. Furthermore, not only is this relationship vital for perceiving media in the wider world, it is also essential for learning in schools. Augustine and Zoss (2006) advanced additional evidence in a study of college students in a teacher education program. They found that teaching a curriculum with esthetics in the ways described here provided a key tool for helping novice teachers understand their own schooling experiences. Esthetics, then, offers a means for understanding the relations that perceivers develop with media as they work to understand the complexity and nuances of qualities in media texts.

SEE ALSO: Arts Education with iPads; Arts Literacies; Media Arts; Media Literacy and Visual Culture; Social Semiotics; Visual Literacy

References

Aufderheide, P. (1993). *Media literacy: A report of the National Leadership Conference on Media Literacy*. Aspen, CO: Aspen Institute.

Augustine, S.M., & Zoss, M. (2006). Aesthetic flow experience in the teaching of pre-service language arts teachers. *English Education, 39*, 72–95.

Baumgarten, A. (1961). *Aesthetica*. Hildesheim, Germany: G. Olms. (Original work published 1750)

Bruce, D. (2009). Reading and writing video: Media literacy and adolescents. In L. Christenbury, R. Bomer, & P. Smagorinsky (Eds.), *Handbook of adolescent literacy research* (pp. 287–303). New York, NY: Guilford.

Dewey, J. (1980). *Art as experience*. New York, NY: Perigree Books. (Original work published 1934)

Eisner, E.W. (2002). *The arts and the creation of mind*. New Haven, CT: Yale University Press.

Flood, J., Heath, S.B., & Lapp, D. (Eds.). (2005). *Handbook of research on teaching literacy through the communicative and visual arts*. Mahwah, NJ: Lawrence Erlbaum. (Original work published 1997)

Messaris, P. (1998). Visual aspects of media literacy. *Journal of Communication, 48*(1), 70–80.

Perkins, D.N. (1994). *The intelligent eye: Learning to think by looking at art*. Los Angeles, CA: The J. Paul Getty Trust.

Reimer, B. (2003). *A philosophy of music education: Advancing the vision* (3rd ed.). Upper Saddle River, NJ: Prentice Hall.

Siegesmund, R. (1999). Reasoned perception: Aesthetic knowing in pedagogy and learning. In L. Bresler & N.C. Ellis (Eds.), *Arts and Learning Research, 1998–1999. The Journal of the Arts and Learning Special Interest Group of the American Educational Research Association* (Vol. 15, pp. 35–51). Washington, DC: American Educational Research Association.

Further reading

Albers, P., & Sanders, J. (Eds.). (2010). *Literacies, the arts, and multimodality*. Urbana, IL: National Council of Teachers of English.

Christenbury, L., Bomer, R., & Smagorinsky, P. (Eds.). (2009). *Handbook of adolescent literacy research*. New York, NY: Guilford.

Flood, J., Heath, S.B., & Lapp, D. (Eds.). (2007). *Handbook of research on teaching literacy through the communicative and visual arts* (Vol. II). New York, NY: Lawrence Erlbaum Associates.

Michelle Zoss is Associate Professor of English Education at Georgia State University. She examines meaning-making of teachers and students in English classes that integrate visual arts. Her publications analyze student-made visual texts, teacher curriculum and pedagogy decisions, preservice teachers' understandings of esthetic experiences, and advocacy for integrating drawing and images throughout primary and secondary literacy education curricula. Her work appears in the journals *English Education, The Educational Forum, Curriculum & Teaching Dialogue,* and *International Journal of Education & the Arts*. She is co-chair of the Commission on Arts and Literacies, a special interest group in the National Council of Teachers of English.

EU Kids Online

SONIA LIVINGSTONE
London School of Economics and Political Science, UK

How are children using the Internet and mobile technologies in Europe, and what risks and opportunities arise that may influence their well-being? In 2010 the EU Kids Online network conducted detailed face-to-face interviews with 25 000 European 9- to 16-year-old Internet users and their parents in 25 European countries (see Livingstone, Haddon, Görzig, & Ólafsson, 2011). EU Kids Online is a pan-European research network that conducts and coordinates investigations into the way children use new media, with a particular focus on the conditions that shape online risk and safety. Its three phases of work were funded by the EC's Better Internet for Kids (originally, Safer Internet) program (visit www.eukidsonline.net). The survey was conducted in Austria, Belgium, Bulgaria, Cyprus, the Czech Republic, Denmark, Estonia, Finland, France, Germany, Greece, Hungary, Ireland, Italy, Lithuania, the Netherlands, Norway, Poland, Portugal, Romania, Slovenia, Spain, Sweden, Turkey and the United Kingdom. The publications that resulted, along with 1500 other recent studies, are summarized in EU Kids Online's European evidence database (visit www.eukidsonline.net). In 2013–14, Net Children Go Mobile replicated major parts of the EU Kids Online survey with 3500 European 9- to 16-year-old Internet users in seven countries (Belgium, Denmark, Italy, Ireland, Portugal, Romania, and the United Kingdom; see www.netchildrengomobile.eu), adding a focus on mobile devices (Mascheroni & Ólafsson, 2014). In that same year, EU Kids Online followed up its survey with a qualitative report on how 9- to 16-year-olds discuss their Internet use and their experiences of online risk (Smahel & Wright, 2014). This report was based on interviews and focus groups with nearly 400 children in nine countries (Belgium, the Czech Republic, Greece, Italy, Malta, Portugal, Romania, Spain, and the United Kingdom). All quotations in this chapter come from this qualitative research (Smahel & Wright, 2014).

This body of research was structured according to children's online access and use, risks and opportunities, and forms of mediation (by parents, schools, peers, industry, and culture). In what follows, the findings are reviewed in order to reveal the consequences of the risks that children encounter and the responsibilities of stakeholders as they manage these consequences, attempting to mitigate harm.

Changing conditions of access and use

Boy 1: I Skype on my phone a lot because it's just easier that way and usually a lot of people are online and it's just quick and you can actually see the person as well.

Boy 2: You don't have to pay.

Interviewer: You have to pay?

Boy 2: You don't have to pay for it.

Interviewer: So if you're using it on the Wi-Fi you've got at home or … ?

Boy 1: Yes, because like my sisters are away a lot.

Focus group with boys aged 13–14, UK

Since the advent of widespread Internet access some 20 years ago, children have been going online more, at younger ages (Holloway, Green, & Livingstone, 2013), and in more diverse ways with each passing year, which has resulted in "generation gaps" within the category of children and young people as well as between them as a whole and their parents and teachers. They prefer to go online with friends or when alone, often privately, in their bedrooms. This exemplifies the challenge for adults in guiding children online—whether to keep them safe or to encourage their exploration of new opportunities.

The comparison between the EU Kids Online 2010 survey and the Net Children Go Mobile 2014 survey found that, for the seven European countries included, going online in the bedroom rose from half of 9- to 16-year-olds who did this at all to two thirds who did this at least weekly (see Figure 1; Livingstone, Mascheroni, & Ólafsson, 2014). While there is little difference across gender, there are still big differences by age (one third of 9- to 10-year-olds vs. three quarters of 15- to 16-year-olds) and country (half of children in Belgium vs. nearly all in Denmark).

Yet—perhaps surprisingly, given the potential for usage anywhere, any time—Net Children Go Mobile also found that home remains the main location of Internet use, the bedroom being the main location for smartphone use; nearly half of 9- to 16-year-old Internet users rarely or never go online in other places, and three quarters never go online when "out and about." Further, in 2010, a shared PC was the most common way of accessing the Internet (58%), 31% using their phone. Today the balance has shifted: 46% use a laptop every day and 41% use a smartphone to go online. Such changes raise some key questions, many of which the EU Kids Online network has worked on:

- How can children's online opportunities and digital skills be further developed (Sonck, Livingstone, Kuiper, & de Haan, 2011)?
- What are the implications of these changes for the risk of harm to children, online and offline (Livingstone, 2013)?
- Are some children using the Internet in excess (Smahel et al., 2012)?
- What actions are needed from parents, schools, industry, children's organizations, and governments to maximize online benefits and minimize harm (O'Neill & Staksrud, 2014)?
- Are all countries facing similar challenges? If not, what differences really matter and what can we learn from them (Helsper, Kalmus, Hasebrink, Ságvári, & de Haan, 2013)?
- Are all families facing similar challenges, or are matters different for disadvantaged or vulnerable children (Livingstone, Görzig, & Ólafsson, 2011; Paus-Hasebrink, Sinner, & Prochazka, 2014)?

In addressing such questions, it is important to recognize that the Internet is not the cause of problems in children's lives in any simple sense, nor can it provide solutions

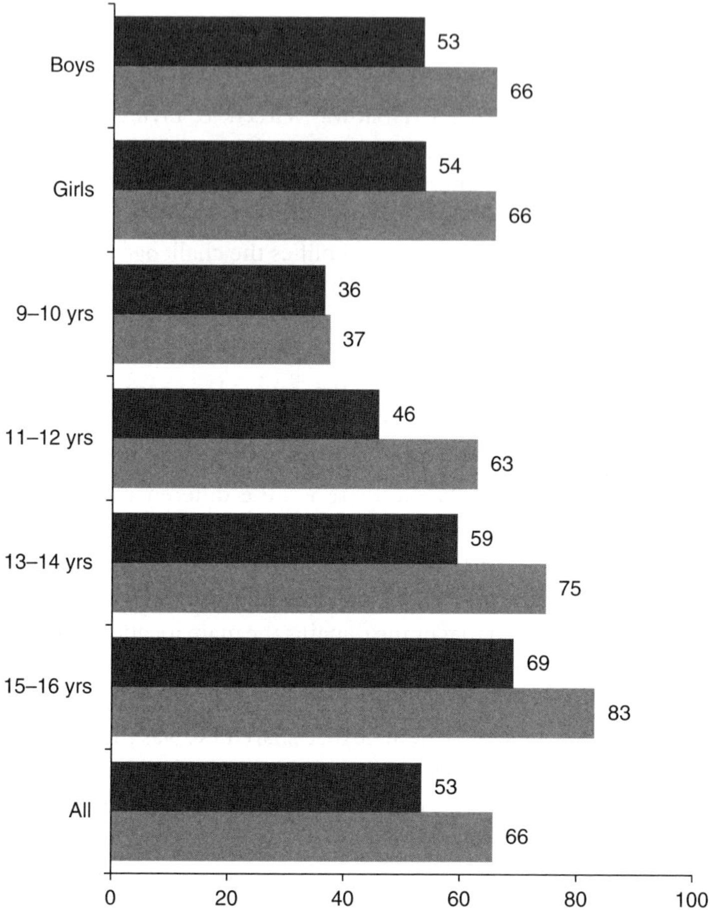

Figure 1 Children's use of the Internet in their own room. From Livingstone, Mascheroni, and Ólafsson (2014). Reprinted by permission of EU Kids Online.

in and of itself. The Internet is created by people, controlled by people, used by people—and it's they (we) who can change its consequences for our lives. But the Internet does make a difference—as a set of tools or environments that underpin everyday practices, a medium through which we engage with the world. That medium has particular qualities: rendering content persistent, replicable and remixable, scalable and searchable (boyd, 2014), all via decentralized, ubiquitous, interactive, near-instant networked exchanges (Lievrouw & Livingstone, 2009). For these reasons, the Internet can be said to be reconfiguring both our everyday interactions and the operation of the institutions and environments within which we act. But the consequences of Internet use, positive and negative, are always experienced by people as material bodies, geographically located.

New opportunities?

> Interviewer: How do you use the Internet?
>
> Girl 1: I use it every day; that's mainly just to check Twitter.
>
> Interviewer: Just to … ?
>
> Girl 1: Check Twitter and that's it, really.
>
> Girl 2: I'm not on Twitter. I can't see the point, and anyway, I don't want to, like, spend more time on social networks when I'm actually meant to be doing homework. I spend too much time on Facebook, anyway.
>
> Girl 3: Facebook, and like, do homework, and catch up with anything.
>
> Focus group with girls aged 13–14, UK

Although much is made of children's enthusiasm and pleasure in engaging with the Internet, our research leads us to conclude that the "ladder of opportunities" is still too steep (Livingstone & Helsper, 2007; Pruulmann-Vengerfeldt & Runnel, 2012): most children do not reach the level of creative, collaborative, or civic activities online. Moreover, there are considerable inequalities in age, gender, socioeconomic status, and country.

Data from 11- to 16-year-olds in 2010 and 2014 (for the same seven countries as before) show what these kids do online on a daily basis (see Figure 2). While they are, indeed, doing more every year, the ladder of opportunities remains as steep as ever. Children are most likely to engage with social networking sites, instant messaging, YouTube, and gaming. They are much less likely to create or upload content, read the news online, or participate in virtual worlds.

In a world where adults fear children who explore online widely—as they see risks rather than opportunities for making new contacts, for visiting unfamiliar sites, or for experimenting with one's identity—it seems that Internet use is often rather narrow and restricted. So, while it undoubtedly adds some resources to children's lives, these are far from transformative. The ambitions that many had in the early days of the Internet—that the Internet would stimulate the imagination and offer children new ways of picturing themselves and their future, or that it would fairly represent on the screen the huge diversity of children in front of the screen, or that it would provide opportunities for children to be taken seriously as they exercise their right to speak and be heard—all this is a far cry from a world of social networking with familiar friends and of laughing at witty YouTube clips, entertaining as these activities are (Livingstone, 2014b).

It is clear that the Internet has reconfigured the conditions under which children interact with their friends. It has shifted the meaning of "home" from its primary role as a retreat for the family to that of a networked hub for work and friendship. It has enhanced access to information and learning resources at any time—access no longer limited to schools or library visits. But it is less clear that, for most children, the Internet is significantly extending creativity, collaborative engagement with the wider world, or new forms of civic, community, or political participation. Any survey suggests that few children undertake such activities. Any interview with children generates some puzzlement that such possibilities could be open to or desirable for them.

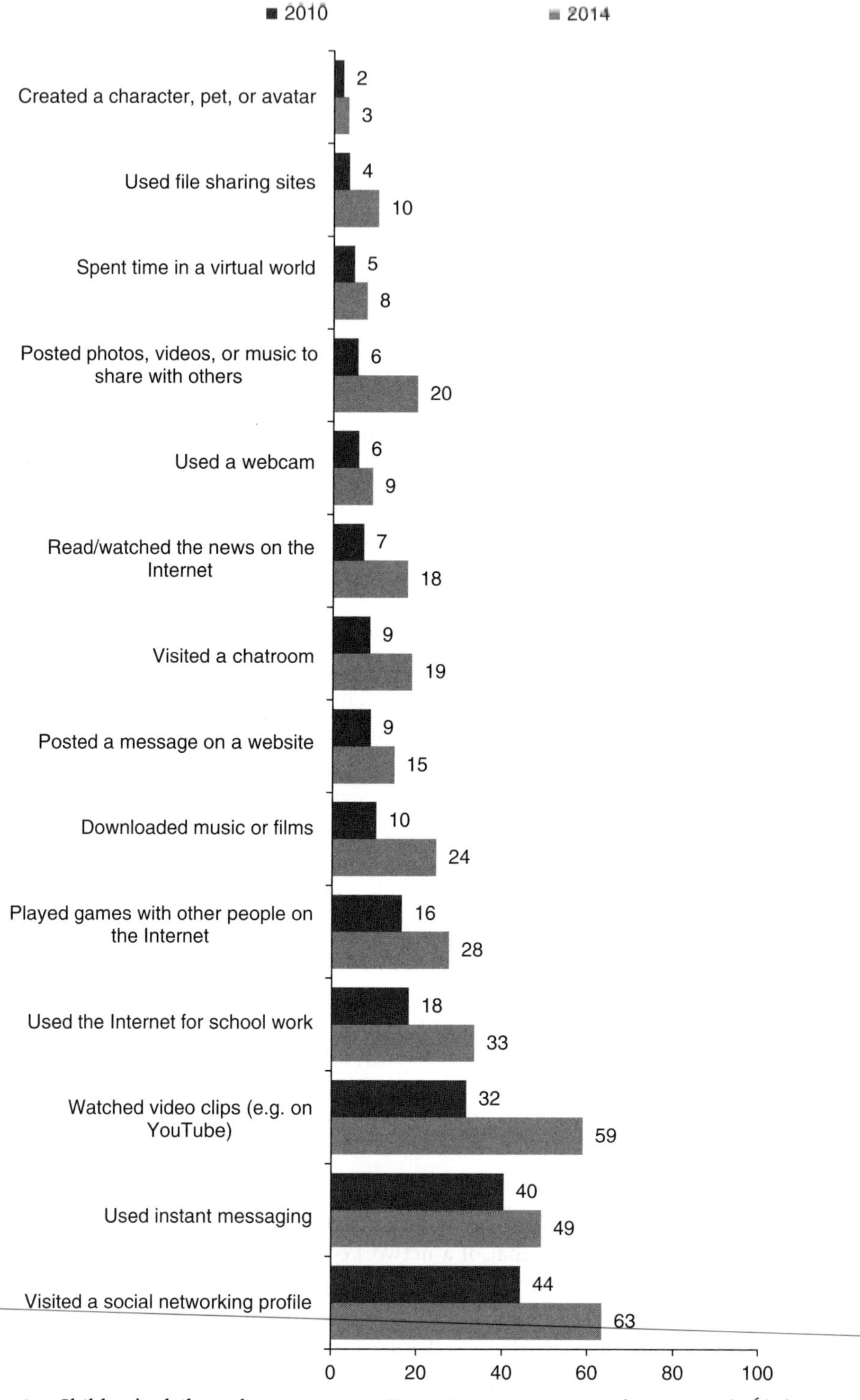

Figure 2 Children's daily online activities. From Livingstone, Mascheroni, and Ólafsson (2014). Reprinted by permission of EU Kids Online.

New risks?

> Some videos I see on the Internet make me scared. Filthy images don't frighten me! But they make me feel bad, because I don't like them. And frightening things stay in my mind.
>
> Boy, 10, Spain

> Once you read it, it can be deleted from the computer but not from your head!
>
> Girl, 15, Portugal

How many children encounter online risks? In our 2010 survey of children in 25 countries, we asked the 9- to 10-year-olds about just a few risks, for ethical reasons. We found that in the previous year 5% of Internet-using 9- to 10-year-olds said they had seen sexual images online, 3% had been sent bullying (nasty or hurtful) messages, 13% had met a new contact online, and 2% had met an online contact offline.

We asked more questions of children aged between 11 and 16. The most common risk they reported was making contact online with someone they did not know face to face. This finding—while meriting the efforts of safety awareness-raisers—illustrates the gap between risk and harm (Livingstone, 2013). While many children make such contacts, only a subset actually go on to meet such a person online, and nearly all of them report that the meeting turned out well (Barbovschi, Marinescu, Velicu, & Laszlo, 2012).

The next most common thing was seeing sexual images and receiving sexual messages. Exposure to pornography was reported more by boys and older children, and some (although not all) found this upsetting, intrusive, or inappropriate. Comparing across countries, exposure to sexual risks differentiated among countries the most clearly, being more typical of countries that we labelled "supported risky explorers" (Nordic countries and the Netherlands), where parents are more laissez-faire and children more free to explore the opportunities and risks online (Helsper et al., 2013).

Third came a set of risks related to user-generated content (UGC). These are likely to become more common over time as children increasingly engage with UGC, and yet such risks receive relatively little attention from policymakers (Livingstone, Kirwil, Ponte, and Staksrud, 2014). This is partly because, short of blocking YouTube, Facebook, and other UGC sites entirely, it is difficult to produce tools that filter such content. It is also because parents and educators seem reluctant to talk to children about content of this type, although a fair number of children have encountered hate content, pro-anorexia content (especially teenage girls), and sites where drug use, self-harm, or suicide are discussed.

Finally, being cyberbullied is reported by a small minority of 11- to 16-year-olds. This risk is the most likely to result in harm—half of these young people report being fairly or very upset by receiving nasty or hurtful messages online. Also interesting is that our analysis of cyberbullying revealed how a neat line cannot be drawn from perpetrators to victims, as there is considerable overlap, such that a substantial proportion of those who bully online have also been victims online, and vice versa (Görzig, 2011; Lampert & Donoso, 2012).

Is children's exposure to online risk changing? Again, we compared findings from our 2010 survey with the Net Children Go Mobile's 2014 survey. Figure 3 shows data

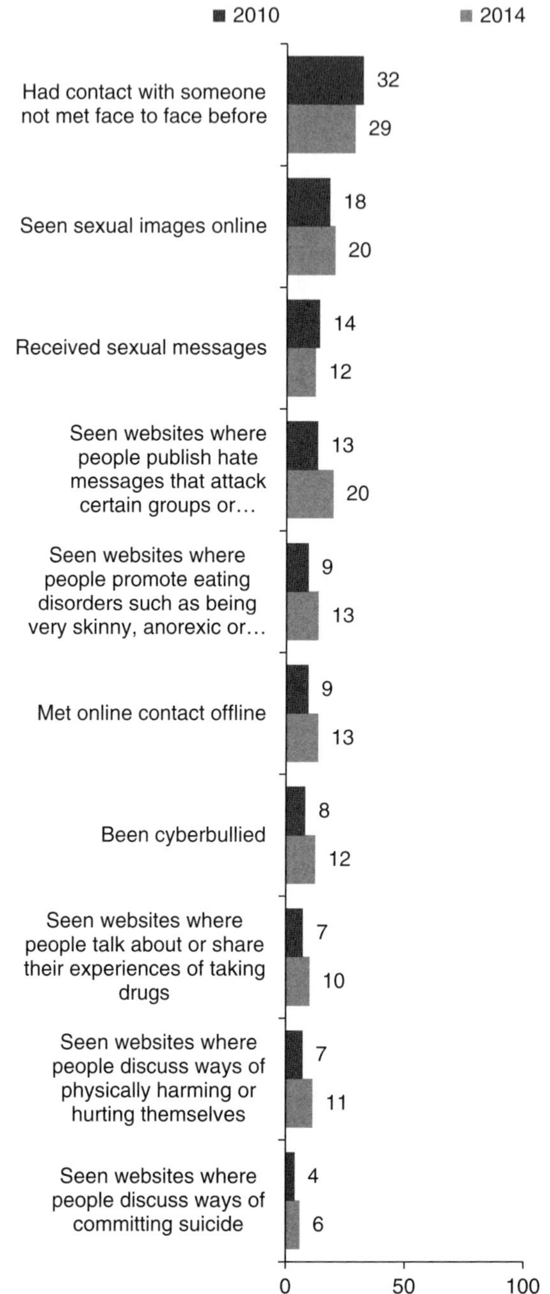

Figure 3 Children's encounters with online risk in the past year. From Livingstone, Mascheroni, and Ólafsson (2014). Reprinted by permission of EU Kids Online.

for 11- to 16-year-old Internet users in seven European countries, highlighting how children's exposure to online risk is changing.

Children are now more likely to be exposed to hate messages (from 13% to 20%), pro-anorexia sites (from 9% to 13%), self-harm sites (from 7% to 11%), and cyberbullying (from 8% to 12%). Although the incidence of meeting new contacts online has hardly changed, children are slightly more likely to meet an online contact offline (from 9% to 13%). Overall, online risk affects a significant minority but by no means a majority of young Internet users. The challenge of addressing negative UGC is, however, of increasing importance.

But not all risk results in self-reported harm. In our 2010 survey of 25 countries, one in eight of the 9- to 16-year-olds said that, in the past year, something had bothered or upset them on the Internet. This question was asked again by the Net Children Go Mobile survey in 2014 in seven countries. This revealed that fewer than one in five 9- to 16-year-olds said they were bothered or upset by something online in the past year. In the same seven countries, this figure had risen slightly since 2010 (from 13% to 17%). The increase is particularly striking among girls and teenagers. This matters, since much public anxiety centres on boys (for excessive or violent use) and on young children (for being vulnerable), which suggests a real need to target safety resources on girls and teenagers and to understand why they are particularly likely to experience harm linked to Internet use (Ringrose, Harvey, Gill, & Livingstone, 2013).

Overall, the incidence of harm online is lower than panicky media reports would suggest (Mascheroni, Ponte, Garmendia, Garitaonandia, & Murru, 2010). Nor is the increase as great as many have expected, given the rise of frequent, personalized Internet use. The many safety and awareness-raising initiatives are possibly proving effective. There are some country variations: the biggest increase in the percentage of upset online is in Denmark (from 28% to 39%), Ireland (from 11% to 20%), and Romania (from 21% to 27%). The percentages are fairly stable in the other countries. But it also seems that children are learning to cope with online risk, arguably by becoming more resilient as the Internet is more an ordinary part of daily life (Smahel & Wright, 2014), as discussed in the next section.

The more we delve into the complexities and contingencies of children's everyday Internet use, the more we see how difficult it is to say, simply, that the Internet is having this or that effect. Rather we need to ask subtler questions about how Internet use is reconfiguring the risk of harm in children's lives. For instance, our findings show little increase over time in the amount of bullying overall as Internet use increases. However, a growing proportion of bullying has an online dimension that reaches into many domains of a child's life, since much bullying consists of verbal or reputational attacks and bystanders online can amplify harm. Relatedly, researchers of child abuse argue less for an overall increase in the incidence of child abuse as Internet use increases, and rather for recognition of how the damage is compounded, since online images can be shared widely and are not easily removed, thereby perpetuating the victimization process (Webster et al., 2012). When it comes to the sharing of certain types of UGC, one may speculate that for today's teenagers it is easier to find others with similar problems; further, online message boards and chatrooms may "normalize" the thoughts and behaviours associated with mental health difficulties and to impede recovery (Bond, 2012).

Risky opportunities

> A stranger said that he liked me and that I was pretty. This was creepy, and I felt uncomfortable and weird about this.
>
> Girl, 11, Belgium

> She wrote to me that I am a bitch and so on … then she came to me with an older friend, I think she was 17 or so, they shouted at me and just kept writing and ugly things.
>
> Girl, 12, Czech Republic

Children's experiences are not to be neatly divided into ones that are clearly beneficial and ones that are harmful. Nor is it clear that, as is often claimed, children are "digital natives" equally at home online and offline, or that they therefore make no distinction between online and offline. On the contrary, our research suggests that children are grappling with the codes and conventions of the many and varied social situations they encounter—an ever more complex task, as these situations often occur online as well as offline. The consequences of such situations depend on a host of mediating factors—children's prior experience or resilience, for example, or the design and ease of use of particular social networking site interfaces, or the type of support children receive from their parents.

For most children, social situations online often take place on social networking sites such as Facebook. Comparing EU Kids Online 2010 findings with Net Children Go Mobile 2014 findings in seven European countries reveals that use of social networking sites continues to increase (from 61% to 68%), especially for boys and teenagers. Among users, the proportion of those who have Facebook accounts increased substantially (from over half to nearly all) in those few years (see Figure 4).

Although the number of "under-age" children on social networking sites has not changed much in the past few years (despite a fair amount of awareness raising and industry effort devoted to reducing this number), it remains substantial: 22% of 9- to 10-year-olds and 53% of 11- to 12-year-olds on Facebook. Interestingly, when parents ban their children from using social networking sites, this is often effective among 9- to 12-year-olds but less so among teenagers; in other words, it is far from being the case that children routinely ignore or evade parents' efforts to keep them safe online (Livingstone, Ólafsson, & Staksrud, 2011).

Children commonly describe online interactions as "weird" and as challenging their "social media literacy" (Livingstone, 2014a). Such interactions happen at the edge of their competence and are enticing, puzzling, and sometimes upsetting. Our report on risky communication online revealed that nearly half of 11- to 16-year-olds said it was easier to be themselves on the Internet than with people face to face; this points to the adolescent struggles for identity and autonomy that explain the huge popularity of social networking sites (Livingstone & Ólafsson, 2011). Possibly awareness-raising campaigns have been more successful at teaching children safety messages (such as "don't talk to strangers" or "don't disclose personal information") than at changing their

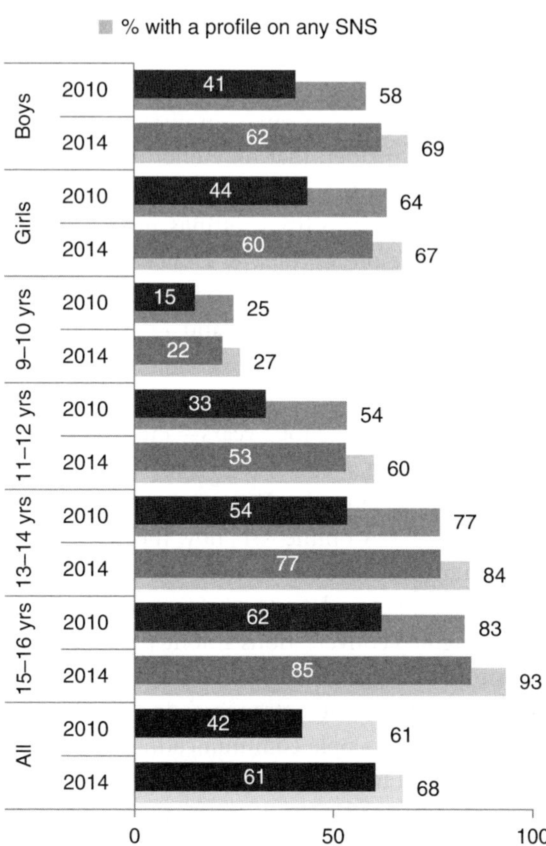

Figure 4 Children's use of social networking sites. From Livingstone, Mascheroni, and Ólafsson (2014). Reprinted by permission of EU Kids Online.

behavior, one reason being that children see the Internet less in terms of scary risks than in terms of risky opportunities (Livingstone, 2008; Kirwil & Laouris, 2012). After all, few really wish to meet strangers or disclose personal information to all and sundry. But they often do wish to make new friends, build close relationships, and widen their circle of contacts.

The result is that they do what their parents fear—exchange intimate details about themselves with people they do not know—but not from an attempt to be naughty or devious; arguably they must do this if they are to learn to manage trust and privacy in online situations that can be unfamiliar and difficult to manage. No wonder that research shows that the more opportunities children take, the more they are exposed to risks, and vice versa (Livingstone & Helsper, 2010). Nor should it be surprising that, as regards the use of social networking sites, the more digitally competent users are, the more likely they are to engage in "risky" practices such as having a public profile or a large number of online contacts (Staksrud, Ólafsson, & Livingstone, 2013). Problematically, however, finding it easier to "be yourself" online is more common among teenagers who say that they have problems with their peers, similarly, children are more likely to have a public profile or many online contacts if they have psychological difficulties, although this is also the case for those who lack the digital literacy to understand or manage privacy settings on social networking sites (Livingstone, Ólafsson, et al., 2011). Our report to the European Commission's CEO Coalition for a Better Internet for Children showed, further, that only one in seven among those upset by an online risk used the reporting tools provided—which suggests that the industry needs to make greater efforts to make privacy settings and reporting tools user-friendly for children (Livingstone, Ólafsson, O'Neill, & Donoso, 2012b). Variation by country where safety strategies are concerned has consequences. We found that in some countries—notably the United Kingdom and Ireland—the use of social networking sites is becoming "safer" (there is more privacy, fewer contacts, less under-age use). In other countries this is far from being the case. In Romania, the use of social networking sites has risen from 46% to 79% in the past four years—and 39% of those new users have over 300 contacts (vs. 18% average).

In 2013–14, EU Kids Online talked to European 9- to 16-year-olds, individually and in groups, about how they saw online risk, how they coped with it, and how they regarded the efforts of their parents and teachers to deal with it (Smahel & Wright, 2014). They had much to say about such matters, giving us a strong sense that our interviews were tapping into ongoing conversations among peers about what they called the "weird" but enticing world of Internet-mediated interactions. For instance, while adults distinguish between contact (from adult strangers) and conduct (peer-to-peer) risks, children didn't find this so easy: people communicating with them, whether more or less known to them, of varying (and often unknown) ages, presented both an opportunity and a risk to them. This led to lots of discussion among the children about what was and what wasn't safe in different situations.

Another theme concerned the difficulty of responding to inappropriate material produced by friends or peers. So, while adults often talk about "risks" as if they come from far away, for children risks can arise in their everyday chat with people from school; and, because this is so close to home, it can be much harder to deal with. Encouragingly, they had lots of ideas and strategies for how to respond to online risk. As one boy told us:

> It happened in our school. Someone took a picture of someone in a pose and then they edited the picture making a small comment and then … my schoolmate was pretty sad about it. Then I told everyone to delete the photo because I just asked them, if that was you, how would you feel? So they deleted the photo and everything's fine now.
>
> Boy, 11, UK

Children were keen to discuss how they try to avoid risky online problems and how they reflect on problematic situations afterwards, so as to be better prepared another time. But they prefer to discuss these situations with peers, because parents tend to criticize them for getting into the situation in the first place, and they fear that their parents will invade their privacy or limit their online freedoms (Smahel & Wright, 2014).

Children, and especially teenagers, have always pushed adult boundaries, transgressing norms overtly or "under the radar." Yet again, the Internet reconfigures the conditions under which this is possible. As public spaces are increasingly monitored or controlled, young people turn to online spaces for risky opportunities. But the nature of those online spaces means that their actions may persist over time and become visible to new or unanticipated audiences. boyd talks of "social steganography"—ways of "hiding in plain sight," which today mean using the particular features of social networking sites to communicate with peers in a way that observing adults do not notice or cannot decode (boyd, 2014). Yet, arguably, adults' recognition that they don't understand youth behaviour fuels their anxieties, and so young people's online activities become wrapped up in moral panics about morality, privacy, or risk in a way that is more intense now than it was before.

Conclusions

From the overall analysis of the many intersecting factors measured by our pan-European survey, EU Kids Online drew five broad empirically grounded conclusions (Livingstone, Haddon, & Görzig, 2012).

- The more children use the Internet, the more digital skills they gain, the higher they climb the "ladder of online opportunities" to gain the benefits.
- Not all Internet use results in benefits: the chance of a child gaining benefits depends on his or her age, gender, and socioeconomic status, on how parents support him or her, and on the positive content available to him or her.
- Children's use, skills, and opportunities are also linked to online risks: the more of these, the greater the risk of harm. Thus, as Internet use increases, ever greater efforts are needed to prevent risk from increasing proportionally.
- Not all risk results in harm: the chance of a child's being upset or harmed by online experiences depends partly on his or her age, gender, and socioeconomic status, and partly on his or her resilience and resources to cope with what happens on the Internet.
- Also important is the role played by parents, school, and peers along with the national provision for regulation, content provision, cultural values, and the education system.

Children's well-being in the digital age is presently undermined by a mix of innocence, ignorance, and something worse. Ideally, policymakers should now work to find ways to embed the importance of "the digital" into the policies and practices of the many organizations concerned with children's well-being and, conversely, to embed the importance of children's well-being and rights into the policies and practices of the many organizations concerned with the digital.

The pace of sociotechnological change is often thought to undermine such efforts, but at the same time it makes these efforts all the more urgent. Yet, although children's online activities are increasing year by year, this entry has shown that the patterns of children's lives are changing more slowly: age differences persist, socioeconomic inequalities still matter, and most children still don't reach very high on the ladder of opportunities. The same can be said about the risk of harm: while some risks are increasing, others are decreasing, and some are not changing much at all. It seems likely that the work of policymakers can slow or halt increases in more familiar risks, yet at the same time new risks continue to emerge.

EU Kids Online's report on explaining change—which analyzes the available longitudinal results—shows how change in children's lives depends on more than technological or policy change (Hasebrink, 2014). Also important are, first, increasing access to ever more online services, which results in a structural change in the online population. Then one must consider ongoing societal practices of incorporating and adjusting to new technologies in everyday contexts. Last, we are witnessing new cohorts (or "digital generations") of parents and children, each with changing knowledge and expectations. Some of these changes occur rather slowly and gradually (e.g., the gain in parental experience and expertise regarding the Internet, or changes in the school curriculum to teach digital skills). Some may be rather sudden (e.g., the takeoff of a new social networking service, or a fashionable practice among young people). The mass media's barrage of headlines claiming that everything is new may usefully call attention to the need for public awareness and resources, but it is misleading in terms of more fundamental processes of change. So, while up-to-date research is valuable, we must also consider the many factors that shape long-term trends over time, because, for children, the outcomes of Internet use depend on a host of individual, social, and cultural factors, all influencing each other and all changing according to different timescales.

EU Kids Online research shows that, in Europe, what happens offline will also be manifest online, that what happens online has consequences offline, and that we are witnessing a reconfiguring of risks and opportunities in children's lives. Yet, even with this wealth of evidence (our open-access European evidence database reviews some 1,500 recent studies published in many languages), there are key knowledge gaps (Ólafsson, Livingstone, and Haddon, 2014). These include uneven coverage by age, especially of young children, despite the rapid rise in their access to online devices; a focus on the fixed Internet, to the neglect of mobile, convergent, and emerging technologies; more research on risk than on opportunities, too little being known of children's developing skills or how they are gaining real benefit from the Internet; gaps regarding exposure to the full range of online risks, too little being known about which children are particularly vulnerable to harm; not enough on the role of parents and teachers and other mediators in determining which of their strategies really work toward empowering children online; and gaps in certain countries—while we can generalize across countries sometimes, for many purposes national and context-specific research is needed.

The EU Kids Online network is now mapping out its future research agenda (Livingstone, Mascheroni, and Staksrud, 2015). Our starting point is the argument that digital skills, literacies, and coping strategies are crucial in determining whether online activities turn out to be beneficial or harmful. We regard it as a priority to understand how these operate in relation to sociotechnological changes in online and offline environments. These environments can be conceived of in terms of specific domains of children's lives: information, education, and informal learning; health, advice, and well-being, with a focus on children with special needs or vulnerabilities; identity and relationships; and creative, collaborative, and civic engagement. Each of these, in turn, is shaped by relevant contexts of Internet use: parenting and communicative dynamics within families; social networks, peer support, and digital citizenship; schools, teachers, and places of informal learning; the industry's strategies and offers, including positive content, classification, tools, and safety by design; technological developments, including the Internet of Things, smart homes, wearable sensors, and more; and a host of wider societal norms and values, communication cultures, and regulatory frameworks.

We hope that researchers and research users around the world will continue to debate, extend, and complement these efforts in a sustained process of consultation, deliberation, and evidence gathering, in order to ensure that governments and governance processes around the world advance the best interests of children in the digital age.

Acknowledgment

This chapter draws on the work of the EU Kids Online network funded by the European Commission (EC) (DG Information Society) Safer Internet Programme (project code SIP-KEP-321803); see www.eukidsonline.net. The graphs in this chapter are reproduced with permission from Livingstone, Mascheroni, and Ólafsson (2014). Many thanks to colleagues in the network for their insights and collaboration during the EU Kids Online research.

SEE ALSO: Adolescent Literacy in a Digital World; Children and Media as a Discipline; Family Relationships and Media; Internet Safety; Media Literacy Foundations; Parental Mediation

References

Barbovschi, M., Marinescu, V., Velicu, A., & Laszlo, E. (2012). Meeting new contacts online. In S. Livingstone, L. Haddon, & A. Görzig (Eds.), *Children, risk and safety on the Internet: Research and policy challenges in comparative perspective* (pp. 177–190). Bristol, England: Policy Press.

Bond, E. (2012). *Virtually anorexic: Where's the harm? A6 research study on the risks of pro-anorexia websites.* Retrieved from http://www.thechildrensmediafoundation.org/wp-content/uploads/2014/02/Bond-2012-Research-on-pro-anorexia-websites.pdf

boyd, d. (2014). *It's complicated: The social lives of networked teens.* New Haven, CT: Yale University Press.

Görzig, A. (2011). *Who bullies and who is bullied online?* London, England: EU Kids Online. Retrieved from http://eprints.lse.ac.uk/39601

Hasebrink, U. (2014). *Children's changing online experiences in a longitudinal perspective.* London, England: EU Kids Online. Retrieved from http://eprints.lse.ac.uk/60083

Helsper, E.J., Kalmus, V., Hasebrink, U., Ságvári, B., & de Haan, J. (2013). *Country classification: Opportunities, risks, harm and parental mediation.* London: EU Kids Online, LSE. Retrieved from http://eprints.lse.ac.uk/52023

Holloway, D., Green, L., & Livingstone, S. (2013). *Zero to eight: Young children and their Internet use.* London, England: EU Kids Online. Retrieved from http://eprints.lse.ac.uk/52630

Kirwil, L., & Laouris, Y. (2012). Experimenting with self-presentation online: A risky opportunity. In S. Livingstone, L. Haddon, & A. Görzig (Eds.), *Children, risk and safety on the Internet: Research and policy challenges in comparative perspective* (pp. 113–126). Bristol, England: Policy Press.

Lampert, C., & Donoso, V. (2012). Bullying. In S. Livingstone, L. Haddon, & A. Görzig (Eds.), *Children, risk and safety on the Internet: Research and policy challenges in comparative perspective* (pp. 141–150). Bristol, England: Policy Press.

Lievrouw, L., & Livingstone, S. (2009). Introduction. In L. Lievrouw & S. Livingstone (Eds.), *New media: SAGE benchmarks in communication* (pp. xx–xl). London, England: SAGE.

Livingstone, S. (2008). Taking risky opportunities in youthful content creation: Teenagers' use of social networking sites for intimacy, privacy and self-expression. *New Media & Society, 10*(3), 393–411.

Livingstone, S. (2013). Online risk, harm and vulnerability: Reflections on the evidence base for child Internet safety policy. *ZER: Journal of Communication Studies, 18*, 13–28. Retrieved from http://eprints.lse.ac.uk/62278/

Livingstone, S. (2014a). Developing social media literacy: How children learn to interpret risky opportunities on social network sites. *Communications: The European Journal of Communication Research, 39*(3), 283–303.

Livingstone, S. (2014b). What does good content look like? Developing great online content for kids. In L. Whitaker (Ed.), *Children's media yearbook 2014* (pp. 66–71). Milton Keynes, England: Children's Media Foundation.

Livingstone, S., Görzig, A., & Ólafsson, K. (2011). *Disadvantaged children and online risk*. London: EU Kids Online, LSE. Retrieved from http://eprints.lse.ac.uk/39385

Livingstone, S., Haddon, L., & Görzig, A. (Eds.). (2012). *Children, risk and safety online: Research and policy challenges in comparative perspective*. Bristol, England: Policy Press.

Livingstone, S., Haddon, L., Görzig, A., & Ólafsson, K. (2011). *Risks and safety on the Internet: The perspective of European children. Full findings*. London, England: EU Kids Online. Retrieved from http://eprints.lse.ac.uk/33731

Livingstone, S., & Helsper, E.J. (2007). Gradations in digital inclusion: Children, young people and the digital divide. *New Media & Society, 9*(4), 671–696. Retrieved from http://eprints.lse.ac.uk/2768

Livingstone, S., & Helsper, E.J. (2010). Balancing opportunities and risks in teenagers' use of the Internet: The role of online skills and Internet self-efficacy. *New Media & Society, 12*(2), 309–329.

Livingstone, S., Kirwil, L., Ponte, C., & Staksrud, E. (2014). In their own words: What bothers children online? *European Journal of Communication, 29*(3), 271–288. doi: 10.1177/0267323114521045

Livingstone, S., Mascheroni, G., & Ólafsson, K. (2014). *EU Kids Online and Net Children Go Mobile: Comparative findings*. London, England: EU Kids Online. Retrieved from http://eprints.lse.ac.uk/60513/

Livingstone, S., Mascheroni, G., & Staksrud, E. (2015). *Developing a framework for researching children's online risks and opportunities in Europe*. London, England: EU Kids Online. Retrieved from http://eprints.lse.ac.uk/64470

Livingstone, S., & Ólafsson, K. (2011). *Risky communication online*. London, England: EU Kids Online. Retrieved from http://eprints.lse.ac.uk/33732

Livingstone, S., Ólafsson, K., O'Neill, B., & Donoso, V. (2012b). *Towards a better Internet for children: Findings and recommendations from EU Kids Online for the CEO Coalition*. London, England: EU Kids Online. Retrieved from http://eprints.lse.ac.uk/44213

Livingstone, S., Ólafsson, K., & Staksrud, E. (2011). *Social networking, age and privacy*. London, England: EU Kids Online. Retrieved from http://eprints.lse.ac.uk/35849

Mascheroni, G., & Ólafsson, K. (2014). *Net Children Go Mobile: Risks and opportunities* (2nd ed.). Milan, Italy: Educatt. Retrieved from www.netchildrengomobile.eu/reports

Mascheroni, G., Ponte, C., Garmendia, M., Garitaonandia, C., & Murru, M.F. (2010). Comparing media coverage of online risks for children in southern European countries: Italy, Portugal and Spain. *International Journal of Media and Cultural Politics, 6*(1), 25–44.

Ólafsson, K., Livingstone, S., & Haddon, L. (2014). Children's use of online technologies in Europe: A review of the European evidence database. London, England: EU Kids Online. Retrieved from http://eprints.lse.ac.uk/60221

O'Neill, B., & Staksrud, E. (2014). *Final recommendations for policy*. London, England: EU Kids Online. Retrieved from www.lse.ac.uk/media@lse/research/EUKidsOnline/EU%20Kids%20III/Reports/D64Policy.pdf

Paus-Hasebrink, I., Sinner, P., & Prochazka, F. (2014). *Children's online experiences in socially disadvantaged families: European evidence and policy recommendations*. London, England: EU Kids Online. Retrieved from http://eprints.lse.ac.uk/57878

Pruulmann-Vengerfeldt, P., & Runnel, P. (2012). Online opportunities. In S. Livingstone, L. Haddon, & A. Görzig (Eds.), *Children, risk and safety on the Internet: Research and policy challenges in comparative perspective* (pp. 73–86). Bristol, England: Policy Press.

Ringrose, J., Harvey, L., Gill, R., & Livingstone, S. (2013). Teen girls, sexual double standards and "sexting": Gendered value in digital image exchange. *Feminist Theory, 14*(3), 305–323.

Smahel, D., Helsper, E., Green, L., Kalmus, V., Blinka, L., & Ólafsson, K. (2012). *Excessive Internet use among European children*. London, England: EU Kids Online. Retrieved from http://eprints.lse.ac.uk/47344

Smahel, D., & Wright, M.F. (2014). The meaning of online problematic situations for children: Results of cross-cultural qualitative investigation in nine European countries. London, England: EU Kids Online. Retrieved from http://eprints.lse.ac.uk/56972

Sonck, N., Livingstone, S., Kuiper, E., & de Haan, J. (2011). *Digital literacy and safety skills*. London, England: EU Kids Online. Retrieved from http://eprints.lse.ac.uk/33733

Staksrud, E., Ólafsson, K., & Livingstone, S. (2013). Does the use of social networking sites increase children's risk of harm? *Computers in Human Behavior, 29*(1), 40–50.

Webster, S., Davidson, J., Bifulco, A., Gottschalk, P., Caretti, V., Pham, T., & Craparo, G. (2012). *European online grooming project: Final report*. Brussels, Belgium: European Commission Safer Internet Plus Programme.

Further reading

Byrne, J., Kardefelt-Winther, D., Livingstone, S., & Stoilova, M. (2016). Global Kids Online: Children's rights in the digital age: synthesis report. London, England: Global Kids Online.

Clark, L.S. (2013). *The parent app: Understanding families in the digital age*. Oxford, England: Oxford University Press.

Livingstone, S., Burton, P., Cabello, P., Helsper, E., Kanchev, P., Kardefelt-Winther, D., … & Yu, S.-H. (2017). *Media and information literacy among children on three continents: Insights into the measurement and mediation of well-being*. In *MILID Yearbook 2017*. Paris, France: United Nations Educational, Scientific and Cultural Organization.

Livingstone, S., Davidson, J., & Bryce, J., with Batool, S. Haughton, C., & Nandi, A. (2017). *Children's online activities, risks and safety: A literature review by the UKCCIS Evidence Group*. London, England: Department of Digital, Media, Culture and Sport.

Livingstone, S., Mascheroni, G., & Staksrud, E. (2018). European research on children's Internet use: Assessing the past, anticipating the future. *New Media & Society, 20*(3), 1103–1122. doi: 10.1177/1461444816685930

Livingstone, S., & Sefton-Green, J. (2016). *The class: Living and learning in the digital age*. New York, NY: NYU Press.

Livingstone, S., & Smith, P. (2014). Annual research review: Children and young people in the digital age: The nature and prevalence of risks, harmful effects, and risk and protective factors, for mobile and Internet usage. *Journal of Child Psychology and Psychiatry: Annual Research Review 2014, 55*(6), 635–654. doi: 10.1111/jcpp.12197

Livingstone, S., Stoilova, M., Yu, S.-H., Byrne, J., & Kardefelt-Winther, D. (2017). *Using mixed methods to research children's online opportunities and risks in a global context: The approach of Global Kids Online*. SAGE Research Methods Cases. London: SAGE.
Staksrud, E. (2013). *Children in the online world: Risk, regulation, rights*. Aldershot, England: Ashgate.
Uhls, Y.T. (2015). *Media moms and digital dads: A fact-not-fear approach to parenting in the digital age*. Boston, MA: Bibliomotion, Inc.
Unicef. (2017). *Children in a digital world*. New York, NY: UNICEF. Retrieved from: www.unicef.org/publications/index_101992.html
United Nations. (2016). *Ending the torment: Tackling bullying from the schoolyard to cyberspace*. New York, NY: Office of the Special Representative of the Secretary-General on Violence against Children.

Sonia Livingstone is professor in the Department of Media and Communications at the London School of Economics and Political Science. She researches children's and young people's risks and opportunities, media literacy, social mediations, and rights in the digital age. Her recent book is *The Class: Living and Learning in the Digital Age* (with Julian Sefton-Green; 2016). A fellow of the British Academy, British Psychological Society, Royal Society for the Arts, fellow and past president of the International Communication Association, and founder of the EU Kids Online network, she now leads the projects "Global Kids Online" and "Preparing for a Digital Future."

European Perspectives on Media Literacy

JOSÉ MANUEL PÉREZ TORNERO and TOMÁS DURÁN BECERRA
Autonomous University of Barcelona, Spain

Through legislation and programs granting access to funding, and as a consequence of the research and field-works, carried out by both universities and media education practitioners, in several European Union (EU) Member States, the EU has adopted a broad and highly inclusive approach to media literacy (ML). European authors have defended a wide understanding of media literacy that embraces the different skills needed to use the media critically and understand their structures as well as their content and languages, and thus acquire broader political, cultural, and critical views which, in turn, help develop more active citizenship and democratic societies.

Research done at a European level has in fact helped create a framework in which the European Commission (EC) has participated actively in terms of economic and political support (Pérez Tornero, Durán Becerra, & Tejedor Calvo, 2015). In 2011 the EC sponsored the creation of a Media Literacy Expert Group that gathers representatives from national public bodies, universities, and international organizations working in the field of media literacy. The group of experts (on media, information, digital, and audiovisual literacy) holds the responsibility of documenting and sharing good practices in the field of media literacy, which is understood as a discipline that integrates all the different forms of literacies. These literacies are related to cognitive processes as well as technical, social, and civic capacities needed to interact with the media and understand them critically. Actions that have taken place in Europe have resulted in a generalization and a reasonable acceptance of different media literacy-related actions supported by the EU within the EC's media literacy framework (set of actions, programs, and policies).

Milestones for media literacy in the EU

In tandem with the EC, the United Nations Educational, Scientific and Cultural Organization (UNESCO) developed important actions in the past two decades that have defined the future of media literacy in Europe. UNESCO's landmarks in the field of media literacy constitute also the foundation milestones for the EC's current framework. Media literacy thus assisted in a paradigm shift in which multiple actors were decisive.

The first grand encounter that marked the beginning of a common path between these two major players was the Gründwald Conference, in which UNESCO adopted an initial definition of media education based on definitions applied by edu-communicators and general media educators. Other encounters, such as the Toulouse conference (1990), Vienna (1999), and finally Seville (2002), provided evidence to the necessity of taking the media and digital literacy approaches to a level defined by the emergent—but already in place—knowledge society. Therefore, Seville is considered the moment when the frameworks of UNESCO and the EC began to merge in an evident way. Since then, the EC has strongly supported the development of media literacy within the Union.

Seville opened the debate that now supports the EC's approach to ML as well as UNESCO's media and information literacy (MIL) definition. It is based on the fact that digital societies do not just need a set of digital capacities/skills but a *meta-knowledge* necessary to understand both technological and media phenomena (Pérez Tornero et al., 2015). This means, to be able to comprehend in a savvy manner the media structures, their choices, and thus the possible biases in information at a time in which citizens must also be capable of understanding the technologies they use and the processes they mediate. After Seville, policymakers, and more specifically academicians and practitioners, started seeing media literacy as a set of digital and media skills needed to interact with information within the digital society. Participation and better decision-making were then set as priorities to be attended by media education. The objective behind these priorities since then has been the strengthening and enhancement of democracy and the empowerment of citizens.

EC's officials (on media-related units) used the Seville seminar to join efforts directed toward the definition of this new paradigm. By combining both media and digital skills within this new broad definition of media literacy, the Commission started supporting and setting the groundwork to generate media literacy-related programs and research projects. The objective was—and still is—to use the media, while acquiring media competencies (skills), as a means for learning and building better societies (with higher levels of participation and better understanding of information and content being consumed). These efforts had an impact on UNESCO's work too (e.g., conducting common research—MENTOR Project—or supporting common actions on MIL).

The EC displayed leadership in terms of policymaking between 2004 and 2010. Presenting recommendations, concepts, and even a directive by the Parliament (EP), as well as the creation of specific programs to fund research and practical actions of Member States, encouraged the strengthening of a Europe-wide movement on media literacy. This process is defined by three main characteristics: a continuous series of efforts to integrate and promote initiatives (new and in place); capacity to combine research, studies, and active lobbying (recommendations by the EC, national legislation in Member States); and creation of funding mechanisms (economic incentives, subsidies) accessible to researchers, practitioners, and governments. These lines have proven efficient to influence political will in several Member States which have, for instance, adopted the EC's 2009 recommendation to integrate media literacy into national curricula.

Media literacy policy

Europe has been very active in the field of policymaking with regards to media literacy. Although implementation of policies driven by the Commission and the EP has not been possible in all Member States, the standards set on these documents have contributed to shape a common understanding of media literacy in the continent. These efforts have taken place during the past decade, a period that constitutes the process of consolidation of a *European perspective* on media literacy (Pérez Tornero et al., 2015). Guidelines set within recommendations and directives issued by these European bodies have contributed to conceptualizing media literacy and have resulted in the creation of specific programs and aids aimed at generating both research and practical ML actions in the EU.

Several attempts to create awareness of the importance of media literacy at a European level have resulted in the issuing of specific communications and recommendations by the Commission and even direct mentions of the topic in the last two European Directives on Audiovisual Services (2007 and 2010). The first clear endeavor to define media literacy and create a framework for its development in the EU is the COM(2007) 833. Within this communication to the EP, the Council of Europe, the European Economic and Social Committee, and the Committee of the Regions, the EC established a first formal definition of media literacy. This very first definition aimed to contribute to the strategy set in Lisbon in the year 2000, which related media literacy to the digital environment and the fast emergence of information and communication technologies (ICT). The EC then recognized media literacy as "the ability to access the media, and to understand and critically evaluate different aspects of the media and media content. Media literacy also includes the ability to communicate in a variety of contexts" (European Commission, 2007).

In May 2008, the Council of Europe also issued a message in which support was given to the EC's communication of 2007 and encouragement to different stakeholders to sponsor the EC's framework was emphasized. In the message, the Council also asked the industry to support media literacy and to create actions for its development within the

EU. It also encouraged the promotion/enhancement of participation at the EU level, as well as the creation of opportunities related to social and political development through the acquisition of media literacy skills (Council of the European Union, 2008).

The message from the Council also took into consideration the responsibility that was set by the Audiovisual Media Services Directive (AMSD) of 2007 that—according to the AMSD of 2010—urges fostering media literacy in the different social sectors as well as monitoring the progress the Member States show in terms of inclusion and development of media literacy. According to the Council, the AMSD established a sort of obligation to assess and report levels of media literacy within the EU, as it demanded that the EP take into account those levels whenever a modification to the directive must be done (European Parliament; Council of the European Union, 2010).

In August 2009, the EC issued the recommendation C(2009) 6464 through which it called on the Member States to facilitate cooperation among the media industry and other stakeholders to support media literacy-related actions and asked them to include media literacy within their national curricula. Furthermore, the recommendation argued for the strengthening of the audiovisual industry by fostering media competence of citizens. Consistent with the recommendation, the improvement of media and digital skills and citizens' media competence can help improve the level of competitiveness of the audiovisual sector in the EU.

While "developing the guidelines for measuring levels of MIL [Media and Information Literacy], the EC and UNESCO worked simultaneously and in parallel on a theoretical-conceptual framework (UNESCO, 2013) which coincided with the findings submitted to the EC in 2009 (Pérez Tornero & Celot, 2009), which demonstrate the correlation between contextual factors and communication skills. Consensus shows that MIL development is better when there is a public policy in place that encourages these skills" (Pérez Tornero et al., 2015, p. 145). Tandem development between UNESCO and the European Commission described in UNESCO's *Media and Information Literacy and Intercultural Dialogue Yearbook 2015* is summarized as shown in Table 1.

Media literacy-related programs

The EC undertook several actions to consolidate a conceptual framework supported by legislative instruments. In order to set the foundations to a sustainable MIL movement in the region, better policy, more active research, and reliable indicators were supported and set by EU bodies, research groups, regulators, and practitioners.

The process to articulate a set of mechanisms to achieve this outcome is defined by a great variety of actions and programs sponsored by the EC since early 1990s. For instance, the first MEDIA Programme, launched in 1991, which initially aimed at strengthening the European audiovisual industry, realized that Europe's audiovisual audience and general public lacked capacities needed to support the industry. This last remark led progressively to the opening of the program to actors such as universities, research centers, and other types of organizations. Other programs were then launched taking into consideration the audiences and users. This is the case of Safer Internet, established in 1999. With the objective in mind of empowering citizens, the EC

Table 1 European and UNESCO MIL assessment frameworks

UNESCO (2013, p. 47)		*Pérez Tornero* (SC. Coord.) (2009, pp. 34–50)*	
Tier one: MIL country readiness	*Tier two: MIL competencies*	*Environmental factors (for ML)*	*Personal competencies*
1. MIL education 2. MIL policy 3. MIL supply 4. MIL access and use 5. Civil society	1. Access and retrieval 2. Understanding and evaluation 3. Creation and sharing	Media literacy context: 1. Media education (presence in curriculum; teacher training) 2. Media literacy policy (regulation) 3. Media industry 4. Civil society Media availability: (mobile phone; Internet; television; radio; newspapers; cinema)	Use: 1. Computer and Internet skills 2. Balanced use of media 3. Advanced Internet use Critical understanding: 1. Understanding media content and its functioning 2. Knowledge of media and regulation 3. User behaviour
MIL competency		Communicative skills	
Cognitive elements: attitudes (rights, principles, values, and attitudes), knowledge and skills. Which "together play an important role in the MIL Assessment Framework, as they do in the learning and teaching processes, and in relation to employment, for participation and empowerment in societal life" (2013, p. 47).		Social relations; Citizen participation; Content creation. "Social relationships demonstrate the potential for individual and group relationships via the media. (…) the media manages social groups and dictates the type of frequency of contact (…) [cooperation or conflict] among them" (2009, p. 44).	

**Study on Assessment Criteria for Media Literacy Levels* was coordinated by J.M. Pérez Tornero (scientific coordinator) and P. Celot (project coordinator and editor).

Source: Pérez Tornero et al. (2015, p. 145), drawing on information from UNESCO (2013) and Pérez & Celot (2009).

gradually integrated ML into its concepts, policies, projects, and priorities of funding in relation to the media sector.

These two major programs set the basis for actions that followed. Between 2004 and 2009 several initiatives were developed in the EU. Some examples are the European Charter for Media Literacy, which led to Euromeduc's conferences in 2004 and

2009 (European Media Education)—an encounter set to bring together European institutions, representatives from the industry, and MIL experts and educators—or the Media & Learning Conference, which takes place every year in Brussels. In general, events that have taken place in Europe have been sponsored both by the EC-MEDIA Programme (2007–2013) and by Creative Europe (2014–2020).

Another important institution that has played a significant role in the strengthening of media literacy in the EU is EACEA (the Education, Audiovisual and Cultural Executive Agency). It has been especially active in financing research programs such as Erasmus +, Europe for Citizens, and Creative Europe. It has also funded several educational activities (within the framework of Erasmus +).

In 2014, as a part of the EU 2020 Strategy, the European Digital Agenda emerged, with the aim of creating an appropriate environment for the development of the digital society and economy. Objectives within the Agenda seek to enhance educational, social, and economic-related processes and tasks through online services. Thus, the Agenda oversees the necessity of strengthening research and policy actions as a means to promote the use of digital services in a productive and safe manner (media-literate citizens).

MIL research in the EU

Different landmarks defined the emergence of media literacy in Europe. The first observation to take into consideration is the inclusion within the EU policy on information society of the promotion of digital literacy (Council of Lisbon, 2000). The second observation is related to the shift from digital to media literacy (Seville seminar, 2002), which resulted in the study *Promoting Digital Literacy* (Pérez Tornero, 2004). This study explores the processes Europe was undergoing at the time to effectively transit from a purely instrumental approach to the use of ICT to a more comprehensive understanding of media and their content, besides the opportunities and risks technologies create.

The need to systematize and focus on the regional development of ML is regarded as the third milestone in the consolidation of a European approach to media literacy. The EC, through the Media Programme, commissioned in 2007 the *Study on the Current Trends and Approaches to Media Literacy in Europe*, significant research that managed to identify the principal European initiatives and good practices in ML. In addition to the systematization achieved, this study generalized the term "media literacy" in Europe as a concept extended to all sorts of media and which incorporated the critical tradition largely explored by media education (Pérez Tornero, 2007).

At the time the study mentioned above was conducted, Europe had an already large tradition in ML. Some Member States, with different levels of development, had media literacy action/initiatives in place, which gathered concepts from digital and traditional literacy, and, in some cases, media education. The study showed that both critical approaches to the media and merely instrumental ones cohabited in the EU. This research served as a support document to the Commission to recommend the curricular implementation of MIL in all Member States.

In 2014 the EC commissioned the European Media Literacy Education Study (EMEDUS), which explored the implementation of the EC's 2009 Recommendation to

Member States for the curricular implementation of media literacy. The project also led to the creation of a European Media and Information Literacy Observatory (EMILO). EMILO was launched within the First Media and Information Literacy Forum, held at UNESCO's headquarters in Paris in May 2014.

This forum—sponsored by UNESCO and the EC, and which had a second meeting in 2016 in Riga—served as a platform to explore research being done in Europe. For instance, another European Project, TransLit (Frau-Meigs, 2012), which explored different definitions surrounding media and information literacy and their development and implementation in Europe, was presented. Like EMEDUS, the TransLit project showed major development in terms of ML policy in the region (Pérez Tornero et al., 2015).

A fourth landmark was also evidenced within the First European Media and Information Literacy Forum: the active participation of governmental bodies in ML initiatives (regulators, audiovisual authorities, educational departments). Participation of these types of institution—which have also commissioned delegates to represent their countries within the EC's Experts Group on Media Literacy—has led to the unification of goals and interests regarding media literacy and thus to the development of policy at different educational levels—also outside formal education—in Member States (UNESCO, 2014).

Project FilmEd—*Showing Films and Other Audiovisual Content in European Schools: Obstacles and Best Practices* (European Commission, 2015)—also confirmed the interest of the EC in building common approaches to media literacy and its defining elements. Commissioned in 2014 and published in 2015, this project analyzed the implementation of the AMSD (2010) in Member States in terms of rights and access to audiovisual content at schools, as well as the use of films and general audiovisual content by schools in the EU. Adding to previous research, such as Screening Literacy, conducted by the British Film Institute in 2012, FilmEd revealed that there are mechanisms to foster media- and audiovisual-related skills, which show progress in almost all Member States, but that there is still a way to go in terms of unification of policy.

Conclusion

Together with rights such as freedom of expression or access to information existent in Europe, ML constitutes one of the pillars of a broader right of communication. This consideration is backed nowadays by legislation and programs set by the EC and other EU institutions. The different actions that have shaped the European model of media literacy helped set a comprehensive approach to the field as well as an effective framework to generate policy to promote ML at both European and national levels. ML has thus gained space in laws, in general public policy, and within some regulatory authorities in the EU, making it co-substantial to communications development and regulation (Pérez Tornero et al., 2015, p. 148), which represents an example of policymaking in the field of ML that acts as a reference to other regions, understanding ML as a right linked to education, information, and freedom of expression.

SEE ALSO: Film Education in Europe; Media Literacy and Social Activism; Media Literacy in Spain; Media Literacy Outcomes, Measurement; Policy Issues in European Media Literacy

References

Council of the European Union. (2008, June 6). Council conclusions of 22 May 2008 on a European approach to media literacy in the digital environment. (C 140/8). *Official Journal of the European Union*. Retrieved from http://eur-lex.europa.eu/legal-content/EN/TXT/PDF/?uri=CELEX:52008XG0606(01)&from=EN

European Commission. (2007, December 20). Communication from the Commission to the European Parliament, the Council, the European Economic and Social Committee and the Committee of the Regions: A European approach to media literacy in the digital environment. *COM(2007) 833 final*. Retrieved from https://eur-lex.europa.eu/legal-content/EN/TXT/?uri=celex%3A52007DC0833

European Commission. (2015). Showing films and other audiovisual content in European schools: Obstacles and best practices. Retrieved from https://publications.europa.eu/en/publication-detail/-/publication/43f74b70-f099-484a-83d7-95369fd56f26/language-en

European Parliament; Council of the European Union. (2010, March 10). Directive 2010/13/EU of the European Parliament and of the Council of 10 March 2010 on the coordination of certain provisions laid down by law, regulation or administrative action in Member States concerning the provision of audiovisual media services. Audiovisual Media Services Directive. *Official Journal of the European Union*. Retrieved from http://eur-lex.europa.eu/legal-content/EN/TXT/PDF/?uri=CELEX:32010L0013&from=EN

Frau-Meigs, D. (2012). Transliteracy as the new research horizon for media and information literacy. *Medijske studije, 3*(6), 14–26.

Pérez Tornero, J.M. (2004). *Promoting digital literacy*. Brussels, Belgium: European Commission.

Pérez Tornero, J.M. (2007). *Study on the current trends and approaches on media literacy in Europe*. Brussels, Belgium: European Commission.

Pérez Tornero, J.M., & Celot, P. (2009). *Study on assessment criteria for media literacy levels*. Retrieved from http://ec.europa.eu/assets/eac/culture/library/studies/literacy-criteria-report_en.pdf

Pérez Tornero, J.M., Durán Becerra, T., & Tejedor Calvo, S. (2015). MIL policies in Europe 2004–2014: The uniqueness of a policy and its connection to UNESCO. In J. Singh, A. Grizzle, S.J. Yee, & S.H. Culver (Eds.), *MILID yearbook 2015. Media and information literacy for the sustainable development goals* (pp. 139–152). Gothenburg, Sweden: International Clearinghouse on Children.

UNESCO. (2013). *Global media and information literacy assessment framework: Country readiness and competencies*. Paris, France: UNESCO.

UNESCO. (2014). *Paris declaration on media and information literacy in the digital era*. Paris, France. Retrieved from Paris Declaration. Retrieved from http://www.unesco.org/new/fileadmin/MULTIMEDIA/HQ/CI/CI/pdf/news/paris_mil_declaration.pdf

José Manuel Pérez Tornero is a professor at the Department of Journalism and Communication Sciences at the Autonomous University of Barcelona (Universitat Autònoma de Barcelona, UAB) and the director of the research group of communication and education Gabinete de Comunicación y Educación. He is a member of the MILID (Media and Information Literacy and Intercultural Dialogue) Network (UNESCO and United Nations Alliance of Civilizations) and GAPMIL (Global Alliance for Partnerships in Media and Information Literacy). He has been a member of the Expert Group in "Media Literacy" in Europe since being invited by the European Commission in 2004. He has been the manager and coordinator of different research projects that involve the mapping and creation of a media and information literacy policy framework.

Tomás Durán Becerra is a researcher at the Department of Journalism and Communication Sciences at the Autonomous University of Barcelona (Universitat Autònoma de Barcelona, UAB). He is a political scientist from Universidad del Rosario (Colombia), with Master's degrees in information and communication (Université Panthéon-Assas, France) and communication and journalism (UAB). He has a PhD in communication and journalism (UAB). He works on MIL and ICT policy and MIL assessment schemes.

Faith-Based Media Literacy Education, History

ROSE PACATTE
Pauline Center for Media Studies, USA

At the beginning of the 21st century the Center for Media Literacy (CML, www.medialit.org) in Los Angeles, CA, described the discipline of media literacy education (MLE) as an educational imperative as well as a contemporary approach to education. The CML expanded on its earlier widely accepted definition of media literacy as "the ability to access, analyze, evaluate and create media in a variety of forms" which provides a framework to access, analyze, evaluate, create and participate with messages in a variety of forms – from print to video to the Internet ("What is Media Literacy," n.d.). Media Literacy builds an understanding of the role of media in society as well as essential skills of inquiry and self-expression necessary for citizens of a democracy.

In general differing faith traditions use these definitions as a premise for MLE. Shared theologies of communication and incarnation provide an entry point through which to consider entertainment and information media. These can often be uncomfortable topics for believers who are more at home "using" media to share, explain, and defend their beliefs and values. To include critical discernment of media messages and the culture they create, their role and influence in culture and society, to find God in media stories, are some of the key elements of what motivates faith communities to practice MLE in faith formation.

Converging theologies

The content of traditional or legacy entertainment media has long since been deemed problematic in the United States and other countries from a religious, moral perspective. The strong teaching authority of Christian churches in particular, whether Protestant and Bible-based or Catholic with its centralized teaching authority on faith

The International Encyclopedia of Media Literacy. Renee Hobbs and Paul Mihailidis (Editors-in-Chief), Gianna Cappello, Maria Ranieri, and Benjamin Thevenin (Associate Editors).

and morals, has led to movements that censor media productions such as the National Legion of Decency in the United States. Originally founded by concerned Catholics in late 1933, with Protestants and Jews invited to sign on as well, the Church was prepared to take on what Archbishop Amleto Giovanni Cicognani, speaking at the National Conference of Catholic Charities in New York on the authority of Pope Pius XI, denounced as "the incalculable influence for evil" exerted by the motion pictures. "Catholics are called by God, the Pope, the bishops, and the priests to a united front and vigorous campaign for the purification of the cinema, which has become a deadly menace to morals" (Doherty, 2007, p. 57). In 1933 a pledge against viewing immoral films was devised and taken yearly by the faithful in Catholic churches in the United States but with diminishing interest after World War II.

Despite the growing positive view of communication media and technology since the Catholic Church's Second Vatican Council (Eilers, 2011) and the World Association for Christian Communication, representing many Protestant denominations (Fore, 1990), the lingering vestiges of the theological traditions of Puritanism are a challenge to the consideration of media in a positive way. Pacatte (2007) takes this view a step further. She agrees that Puritanism for Protestants and Jansenism for Catholics continue to influence how faith communities form their views of media technology, stories and messages, and the entertainment they provide in countries like the United States and Canada. These attitudes can create a paradox. Conflicted audiences form negative judgments based on the content of entertainment and neglect the context of the stories media tell, while still partaking of them.

According to Tinker (2010) who compares the theories and practices of the Catholic-led Pauline Center for Media Studies (PCMS) in Los Angeles and the Presbyterian Media Mission (PMM) in Pittsburg, PA, understanding the relationship between media literacy and theology is no small task due to differing theological views of visual imagery, art in Church history, hermeneutics, language, and cross-cultural differences, to name a few. However, for both the PCMS and the PMM the primary understanding from which a consideration of media emerges is the relationship between the church and the "world," and its mission to the world. Hailer and Pacatte (2007) call MLE in faith formation "media mindfulness" because by anchoring media in the MLE universe, it is possible to mine its insights, its skill-building pedagogy, its theory and praxis, and integrate them into various ministries, especially education. This can happen when considering or teaching about media and values, virtue, spirituality, theology, Catholic social teaching, morality, intentional living, prayer, and worship.

In 2012 Stephanie Iaquinto and John Keeler wrote a history of the "subdiscipline" of MLE in faith communities in which they explore the challenges that MLE presents to religious educators in the United States and, to a limited extent, Canada. One of these is that of presenting fixed doctrine in a culture with fluid narratives. They refer to the work of Mary Hess, PhD, who asserts that MLE in the religious education context requires a pedagogical shift from a linear to a dialogic approach. They note, too, that there are positive signs amidst resistance stemming from differing theologies, visuals, and morality that can place the media in the basement of faith-based inquiry. They conclude that faith communities must be willing to engage in thoughtful discourse about media that is informed by both grace and humility. If that happens perhaps faith-based media literacy won't be relegated to the basement. Perhaps, instead, it will be to the dining room where engaging conversations take place and where community is renewed.

Pacatte (2005), a Catholic Christian, takes her cues from the theology of Jesuits Karl Rahner and John Staudenmeier: to love the world the way it is. This is a theology of incarnation approach to life and culture integrating faith and everyday reality. She paraphrases John 3:17, "For God did not send his Son into the culture to condemn it, but that the culture, through Christ, might be redeemed." Step one in the catechist's quest to articulate a media spirituality that is critical and affirming is to fall in love with the world, the culture, today not that of a century ago.

It is noteworthy that academia shows signs of research and reflection on MLE in faith communities. Tinker (2010), a Presbyterian, and De Azevedo (2015), a Catholic, wrote their graduate dissertations on MLE within their theological faith traditions.

Ecumenical and inter-religious media literacy education

The National Telemedia Council based in Madison, WI, founded for educators and parents, has promoted a media-wise, literate, global society since 1953. They take a positive, non-judgmental attitude and embrace a philosophy that values reflective judgment and cooperation rather than confrontation with the media industry. Representatives from several churches have been part of the educational organization since the beginning and continue to participate.

There is a significant sharing of ideas, resources, and activities among the churches, both Catholic and Protestant. The inter-religious dimension exists as well, through critical media awareness programs at the Museum of Tolerance in Los Angeles and the University of Southern California Shoah Foundation. Islam is organized differently than Christian churches and Judaism because with mosques it all depends on the place. Muslim efforts in MLE, while not directly related to any definition, share common themes. They take the form of advocacy and teaching the wider culture and audiences about Islam and its representation in media. Examples of this are the Muslim Public Affairs Council in Los Angeles, active in the entertainment industry since 1988, and the Council on American-Islamic Relations whose focus is to be a leading advocate for justice and understanding.

Since 1929 the inter-religious organization Religious Communicators Council (RCC) has promoted faith perspectives in public discourse and has recognized MLE efforts through its awards program. The RCC is highly diverse with members who are Hindus, Muslims, Christians, Jews, Scientologists, Buddhists, Sikhs, and Bahá'í. What unites all of these groups is a common dedication to fostering mutual respect for differences among people through communication, media, and education.

The Catholic Church, Catholics, and media literacy education

While two popes wrote about motion pictures, radio, and television in the first half of the 20th century it was the Second Vatican Council (Vatican II) held between 1962 and 1965, and its decree "Inter Mirifica" ("among the marvelous things") in 1963 that revealed a shift in how the official Catholic Church on a global level morphed from the consideration of communications media as a predominantly moral problem to an opportunity for good. In addition to using media for evangelization, the document recognized the powerful influence of the media in the modern world, and addressed media discernment, awareness, parental involvement, news, and the right to information, and called for Catholic schools to teach students about the media. This document established an annual commemoration of communications media and since 1966 the pope has issued a statement for World Communication Day. "Inter Mirifica" was only an introduction to the media world, however. It called for a follow-up document that would expand the theological, pastoral, and educational dimensions of communications.

Thus "Communio et Progressio" ("pastoral instruction on the means of social communication") was issued in 1971 and laid out a theological and pastoral premise for communications and media (Pontifical Commission on Social Communication, 1971). It marked a milestone in the development of Church teaching and its relation to the modern world through communications, though its influence has depended on local implementation. In addition, at least 12 Vatican and papal documents on aspects of the means of social communication have been issued as well. Most notable among them is "Aetatis Novae" ("the dawn of a new era") issued in 1992 that specifically called for MLE. This same document reiterated a theme that can be traced back to the otherwise negative papal document on movies "Vigilanti Cura" ("on motion pictures"), that the Church believes that the media are "gifts of God" and therefore worthy of our attention. Pope (now St.) John Paul II's final document published before his death in 2005 was *The Rapid Development* to commemorate, belatedly, the 40th anniversary of "Inter Mirifica." The pope wanted to make sure that people understood the import of the "global village" created by media and the opportunities media provide, especially the Internet. In two places he called for education in the responsible and critical use of media.

Pierre Babin and Crec-Avex

One of the great Catholic thinkers, writers, and teachers about religious meaning in global information and entertainment communications was Fr. Pierre Babin, O.M.I. (1925–1912) of Lyon, France. Inspired by "Inter Mirifica" and influenced by the Catholic-convert, media theorist, and communication philosopher Marshall McLuhan, he started a non-accredited school, Crec-Avex (the Center for Research and Education in Communication) in 1971 in Lyon to train faith leaders in a new way to communicate faith in the age of media. He called it the "the symbolic way" that required understanding the languages of the media and their messages (Babin, 1991) in order then to create media and discover media's spiritual dimensions. Hundreds of Catholics, Christians, Buddhists, and Muslims, mostly from Latin America, Asia, and Africa, trained at the center over a 30-year period. A critical methodology was not explicit but implied.

John J. Pungente, SJ, the Centre for the Study of Communication and Culture; the Jesuit Communication Project

In the 1980s a Canadian Jesuit priest and film educator, John J. Pungente, was assigned to the newly formed Centre for the Study of Communication and Culture (CSCC) in

London, England. One of the main interests of the center was in promoting research into media education. The CSCC created a program, "Adapting Jesuit Education to the Human and Spiritual Needs of the Information Society" because the Jesuits in secondary schools worldwide were in the process of renewing curricula. After sending out a survey, Pungente traveled from March to November 1984, covering 53 000 miles to 62 cities in 29 countries and interviewed over 170 teachers, students, media professionals, principals, headmasters, and parents to collect information about existing programs, curricula, and courses aimed at equipping students in Jesuit secondary schools with the critical tools needed to live in a media-rich culture (Pungente, 1985). He based his research on Masterman's (1982) premise for media education as a discipline that accepts that the media are pervasive and significant elements of our society, that they influence our perceptions in fundamental ways that need to be understood, and that they are worthy of close investigation.

The resulting report, "Media Education and The Jesuit Secondary School" (Pungente, 1985), was sent to the Jesuit Curia in Rome and to all the schools Pungente visited. It answered three questions: (i) What is the status of media education in Jesuit secondary schools around the world? (ii) What is the status of media education in other secondary schools? And (iii) What must be done to encourage media education in Jesuit secondary schools? While the data revealed that some schools taught or integrated MLE in the curriculum, most of the schools taught classes in specific media fields such as film, computer studies, popular music, and analysis of television. The concept of comprehensive critical media education, or MLE, was new to many. Pungente responded to the results with a primer and resource, *Getting Started on Media Education* (1985), that subsequently was sent to 400 Jesuit secondary schools around the world. Just how many schools have begun and sustained MLE since then, or if existing programs are related to Pungente's research, is not known with precision. However, the Jesuit Seattle Preparatory School has been teaching MLE since the early 1990s and Loyola University Baltimore, USA, also a Jesuit institution, has been teaching a graduate course in MLE to serving teachers since 2006. In March 2019, a new Media Literacy Curriculum on Media Literacy and Social Justice was launched, reflecting Catholic and Jesuit commitment to education and social justice.

In 1984, following his visit to Jesuit schools, Pungente founded the Jesuit Communication Project in Toronto to promote media literacy across Canada. He coauthored *Media Literacy*, a resource guide for the Ontario Ministry of Education in 1989, and other books and DVDs on MLE as well as on film and spirituality. He has also hosted two media literacy informed television series on cinema. Since 1985 Pungente has served as the executive secretary of the Ontario-based Association for Media Literacy and worked on the organization of the first and second North American Media Education conferences. In 1992 he was one of the founders of the Canadian Association for Media Education Organizations (CAMEO) and currently serves as its president.

The Jesuit-founded academic journal *Communication Research Trends* published by the CSCC, first in London then Santa Clara University in California, USA, has promoted research in communication and human values, social justice, theology, and media education since 1979. Paul Soukup, SJ, now heads the CSCC and edits the journal that as recently as 2013 published two issues on MLE.

Sister Elizabeth Thoman, HM, and the Center for Media Literacy

As a teacher in a Catholic high school in the 1970s Humility of Mary Sister Elizabeth Thoman realized that media played a dominant role in creating popular culture that influenced her students. She left teaching to pursue a graduate degree at the University of Southern California (USC) in search of a critical approach to media in education that would lead to the development of a skill set for teachers and students to interact with a mediated world. Thoman began publishing *Media&Values* through her Center for Media & Values in Los Angeles, CA, that became the Center for Media Literacy in 1989.

Though *Media&Values* was directed to all educators it often carried articles of interest to faith communities. Thoman's work and accomplishments in media literacy education over four decades brought media awareness to the attention of thousands of Catholic schools in the United States and beyond. In 1993, The Center for Media & Values, the National Catholic Educational Association, with the support of the US Conference of Catholic Bishops' (USCCB) Catholic Communications Campaign (CCC), produced a curriculum kit, *Catholic Connections to Media Literacy*, for Catholic schools. The video and guide booklet came packaged in a large oyster shell case that was sent gratis to every Catholic school in the US that together served over 7.5 million students at the time. It was the first formal attempt to integrate media literacy within the US Catholic school curricula and trainers from the CML traveled to Catholic schools across the US to prepare teachers. Thoman's work in MLE belongs in the annals of educational history. Her influence on MLE within and without the faith community in the United States and beyond is extensive and continues to bear fruit.

Today CML president Tessa Jolls consults with public and private educational entities around the world and its robust website on MLE is an extensive resource available to all.

Sister Angela Ann Zukowski, MHSH, the University of Dayton and Pastoral Communications

The Catholic University of Dayton's Institute of Pastoral Initiatives, directed by Sr. Angela Ann Zukowski, MHSH, DMin, included MLE in their summer Pastoral Communications and Ministry Institute (PCMI) for 10 years, 1990–2000, and bestowed certificates in MLE on dozens of catechists. Pierre Babin was often a member of the summer faculty as was long-time media educator Mary Byrne Hoffman who published a book with the Paulist Press in 2011 on media literacy and catechesis. Zukowski was also a consultant to the Vatican's Council on Social Communication and was a coauthor of the 1992 document "Aetatis Novae" that highlighted MLE for all Catholics. She also assisted in founding and continues to teach at the Caribbean School of Catholic Communication in Trinidad and Tobago where MLE is a core subject in the training of catechists and communicators. MLE is also a course that is offered by the university's online Virtual Learning Community of Faith Formation (VLCFF) that has hundreds of adult learners from about 45 dioceses in the USA, Canada, and Australia.

Roberto Giannatelli, SDB, and the Salesians

The Salesians of Don Bosco is an Italian-based international order of priests and brothers that has been doing significant MLE resource publishing since the 1980s in the US, India, and Italy. In the US the community published *Access Guides to Youth Ministry: Media and Culture* in the 1990s and Peter Gonsalves, a Salesian from India, wrote *Exercises on Media Education* in 1995 in which he lays down for Indian educators the key critical, discerning principles of MLE with almost 100 activities.

Perhaps the most prominent Salesian priest involved in media education in Italy was Professor Roberto Giannatelli (1932–2012). With a doctorate in pedagogy, he founded the Faculty of Communication at the Pontifical Salesian University in Rome where he served as rector from 1983 to 1989. He was president of the university's Institute of Social Communication Sciences from 1989 to 1995 when he became interested in MLE. Although he began to teach the subject in the communication department, the course was moved to the school of education. He was pivotal to the development of MLE in Italy and in 1996 cofounded MED, the Italian Association for Media Education. The Italian term for MLE, "Educomunicazione" ("Educomunicación" in Spanish and "Educomunicação" in Portuguese), seems to have come from Giannatelli and his colleagues as the term not only includes the concept of communication but simplifies what is otherwise a cumbersome translation.

The United States Conference of Catholic Bishops' Catholic Communication Campaign

The United States Conference of Catholic Bishops' (USCCB) Catholic Communication Campaign (CCC) created a 5-year program from 2000 to 2004 called *Renewing the Mind of the Media*. Like the Legion of Decency of old, it was pledged-based—for all ages, and all media, not just movies—but its educational goals were not clear. In 2013 the campaign created a *Faith and Safety* website and in 2014 *Social Media Guidelines* that also lacked a MLE dimension. However, the CCC's 1999 *Family Guide for Using Media* (USCCB, 1999) integrates MLE concepts and principles and is still online. This is also true of the USCCB's *National Directory for Catechesis* (2005.) Taking its cues from the Vatican's *General Directory for Catechesis* (1997) and adapting communications media and technology suggestions to parish and Catholic school faith formation programs in the United States, a section (Chapter 10, para. 69) is devoted to communications technology and catechesis. While the term MLE is not used in this section, the core concepts and principles of MLE are firmly implied. In fact, these are integrated throughout the entire volume. Five basic faith-based principles regarding all forms of media emerge: (i) become media-literate; (ii) use media in the classroom; (iii) create media; (iv) make media the subject of catechesis; (v) advocate for pro-social media.

The Daughters of St. Paul: The Pauline Institute of Communication in Asia and the Pauline Center for Media Studies, USA

The Daughters of St. Paul—Pauline Sisters—are an institute of Catholic religious women founded in Italy in 1915 and are now located in 52 countries worldwide.

Their express ministry is to use the media (initially print) to communicate the Word of God. The Second Vatican Council mandated that every institute of nuns, priests, and brothers was required to rewrite their rules or constitutions that govern them, replacing statutes derived from Canon Law with articles that authentically reflected the founding principles of the institute. The Daughters of St. Paul renewal journey lasted from 1969 to 1983; the first evidence of MLE exists in the Documents of their Special Chapter (1971). Their new rule (1984) draws from these and contains articles that specifically encourage MLE as a part of ministry to instruct the audience on how to discern critically the messages from all current forms of media and new technologies. Learning to be media aware and literate is called for within the initial training stages of new members yet after 30 years its inclusion in the curriculum is only now being formalized with some degree of standardization.

The Philippines

The first Pauline sister to begin MLE was Sr. Lucina Sarmiento (1933–1995) who pioneered MLE activities in the Philippines in the early 1970s. Together with representatives from 10 Catholic schools in Metro Manila, they organized the Philippine Association of Media Educators (PAME) under the National (Catholic) Office of Mass Media. In 1988, Sr. Lucina proposed to make MLE a regular mission activity of the Pauline sisters in the Philippines. The proposal was approved and included a long-range plan to systematize the training of MLE for sisters and pastoral workers.

In keeping with the plan, Sr. Consolata Manding earned a doctorate from the University of the Philippines in 2002 with a dissertation on *Media Literacy Education Among Pastoral Workers in the Philippines: Towards Building a Model Media Literacy Curriculum*. Sr. Clothilde de las Llagas earned a Master's degree in media literacy at the Appalachian State University, North Carolina, USA, in 2002 with the thesis *Communication and Media Education: A Curriculum Plan for Pauline's Communication Center in Metro Manila*. In 2010 she wrote the *A–Z Guide for Looking at Media: A Beginner's Companion to Media Literacy*.

Manding organized the Pauline Institute of Communication in Asia (PICA) in May 2002 that offers a MLE graduate program primarily intended for pastoral workers. The module-based program received government accreditation in 2005.

In addition to the graduate program, PICA also offers a MLE certificate and organizes MLE seminars to various groups: students, teachers, parents, pastoral workers in the dioceses and parishes, schools, religious institutions, and organizations.

Catholic educators and catechists in the Philippines who teach or integrate MLE into their curricula do so on their own initiative as Catholic schools are organized by diocese rather than a central educational authority, which is the reality in the Catholic world in general.

Public and private colleges that offer Bachelor of Science in mass communication degrees formed an association called the Philippine Association of Communication Educators (PACE) in the late 1980s. Members teach communication subjects and are learning how to integrate MLE in their respective courses.

The Philippine Department of Education 2016 curricula for primary and secondary levels include media information literacy. Training seminars are organized by respective private and public schools to integrate media information literacy across the curriculum. Despite the efforts to arrive at a common understanding and praxis, groups and schools define, interpret, and exercise MLE differently and this remains a challenge in both faith-based and public education.

The United States

Pauline sister Rose Pacatte of the USA/Toronto region of the institute first learned about MLE at a Catholic communications conference in Portland, OR, in 1990. Elizabeth Thoman presented on her work with *Faith & Values* magazine to an eager audience. Following this, Rose participated in the MLE conference held in Guelph, Ontario, and another Catholic communicator meeting in St. Louis, MO, in 1991. There she heard Thoman again speak about media literacy as well as Pierre Babin and determined to pursue a graduate degree in MLE. At the recommendation of John Pungente, SJ, Rose applied to the Institute of Education at the University of London where the first graduate degree in the subject ever was offered. She earned a Master of Arts in education in media studies and defended her dissertation on integrating MLE within initial formation (training) programs of women's religious communities of the Catholic Church (Pacatte, 1995).

That same year she returned to the US and founded the Pauline Center for Media Studies (PCMS, bemediamindful.org) in Boston and moved it to Culver City, CA, in 2002. The mission statement of the PCMS is: "To develop and encourage media mindfulness (MLE in faith communities) within the context of culture, education and faith formation." The methodology is one of theological reflection through access, reflection, analysis, evaluation, action, and dialogue about media productions and culture. In 2006, in collaboration with the Archdiocese of Los Angeles Office for Religious Education and Office for Secondary Education, she developed a 60-hour advanced certificate in media literacy program for teachers, clergy, parents, and catechists. Other dioceses recognize the certificate as a catechist specialization and so far more than 120 people from six US states, Canada, Italy, and Singapore have earned the certificate, including 25 of the Pauline sisters from four countries. Since 1995 Pacatte has traveled to numerous dioceses in countries around the world to teach about MLE. In 2015 she trained 30 African sisters from eight countries at the Pauline center in Nairobi, Kenya. Sr. Nancy Usselmann, MA in theology with a specialization in popular culture, became the director of the PCMS in 2016. In her graduate thesis Usselmann integrates MLE into the idea of becoming cultural mystics in a world permeated with media messages.

Sister Gretchen Hailer, RSHM, became involved in MLE in the 1970s and was an early trainer for Television Awareness Training (TAT), developed by the Protestant Media Action Research Center. She wrote *Believing in a Media Culture* in 1995 for St. Mary's Press which is owned and operated by the Christian Brothers. She devised the "Media Literacy Wheel" (Figure 1) as a *mindful* way to question media from a Catholic Christian faith perspective. In 2007 she teamed up with Sr. Rose Pacatte to write *Media Mindfulness: Educating Teens about Faith and Media*, also for St. Mary's Press, and in 2010 they wrote *Our Media World: Teaching Kids K-8 about Faith and Media* for Pauline

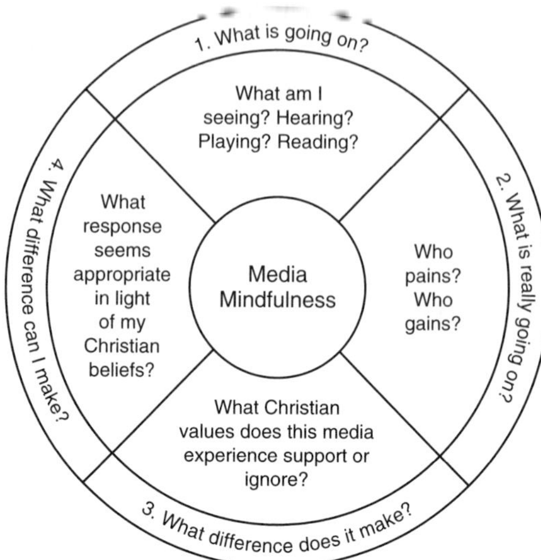

Figure 1 The Media Literacy Wheel. Source: Hailer & Pacatte (2007).

Books & Media. The methodology for all books is critical inquiry through the lens of faith and values, as well as theological reflection, by engaging in media and the popular culture they create.

In the 2000s two more Daughters of St. Paul earned graduate degrees in media education, Sr. Hosea M. Rupprecht at Webster University in St. Louis and Sr. Helena Burns at Appalachian State University. In 2011 Rupprecht authored *How to Watch Movies with Kids: A Values-Based Strategy* rooted in MLE.

In 2016 the Daughters of St. Paul in the United States/Toronto region of the institute fully institutionalized MLE within its mission as evidenced by the specialization of more sisters in communication and MLE, dedication of resources to the PCMS, and the development of the community's website to include the PCMS, including a speaker's bureau, as one of four visual pillars of the community's life and ministry. New members receive some media literacy training but it is not yet part of the initial curriculum.

In other countries

Since 2000 the Daughters of St. Paul in South Africa, England, Singapore, and India either give presentations on MLE or have sponsored Pacatte and others to give seminars on MLE in faith formation at their centers. In 2011, Sr. Noeline Razanatseheno in Madagascar, upon completion of her degree in communications, wrote *Ny haino aman-jery: Tontolo vaovao*, a book about MLE in Malagasy.

SIGNIS: The International Catholic Organization for Communication

Transcending these decades of the Catholic Church's media and media education activities are the activities of two lay-run Catholic media organizations, OCIC (the International Catholic Organization for Cinema) and Unda (the International Catholic Association for Radio and Television; Unda is Latin for "wave"). Both were founded in Brussels, Belgium, in 1928 by laymen who wanted to integrate their faith and professional lives. Eventually representatives from bishops' conferences worldwide became members. Their activities included producing media, promoting use of radio in mission lands, film criticism, and the recognition of accomplishments in cinema and television by participation in Catholic and ecumenical juries at international festivals. Media literacy education or something close to it was evident in the organizations' work from the 1950s. Unda's magazine *Educommunication* (1989–2001) was dedicated to media awareness. When the two groups merged into SIGNIS in 2001 (www.signis.net) the goal was to use media and communication for peace. A media literacy education desk was established at the headquarters and online to help young people especially to acquire an active attitude, a critical distance, and the freedom to make informed judgments about the media.

SIGNIS members have participated in several gatherings of the World Summit on Media and Children through panels and workshops on media literacy as carried out in Catholic schools, parish catechesis programs, and spirituality programs such as film retreats. Following the summit in Johannesburg, South Africa, in 2007, SIGNIS members from Argentina, Belgium, Malaysia, the Solomon Islands, the Philippines, the USA, and Italy formed the SIGNIS Media Education Project. While SIGNIS members want to join together to use resources more effectively to give a coherent response to the pervasive national and global media, the project aims to bring together worldwide experiences and achievements in this field. To accomplish this SIGNIS wants to build a world network of media educators and/or media education organizations, something that, as yet, does not exist.

Media literacy education, as outlined in Catholic Church documents, the World Day of Communication messages, the educational departments, and Catholic communities around the world, is a work in progress. Media literacy education, or media mindfulness, offer new ways to increase the relevance of the Catholic Church's work of evangelization by bridging faith and life that is influenced by information and entertainment media and the culture they create.

Protestant Churches, Protestants, and media literacy education

In the 1970s mainline communications professionals working in their church communication offices grew concerned at the influence of television on the communities and joined together to form the Media Action Research Center (MARC). Members included Stuart Hoover, PhD, a media education consultant to the Church of the Brethren, Ben Logan of United Methodist Communications, and Carolyn Lindekugel of the Lutheran Church of America. Their ecumenical efforts led to the development of the Television Awareness Training (TAT) program, a 10-part adult education course with goals to inform, discuss, and prompt positive action in churches and communities. In addition to Hoover, Logan, and Lindekugel authors included George Gerbner, Bob Keeshan ("Captain Kangaroo"), Aimee Dorr, Nicholas Johnson, Elizabeth Thoman, and Judge David Bazelon. TAT was the first comprehensive course about television published in the United States and hundreds of Protestant and Catholic religious educators were certified as "TAT trainers." Its popularity lasted well into the 1980s.

The Presbyterian Media Mission and the Electronic Great Awakening

The Presbyterian Media Mission (PMM) developed from the General Assembly of the Presbyterian Church of the USA (PCUSA) of 1980 that called for local churches to become involved in media ministry. This was in the era of the televangelists and the PCUSA did not find itself reflected in the politically charged "moral majority" of the Christian right or televangelism. At the PCUSA's general assembly in 1989–1990 the PMM was officially recognized as part of the Church's mission and focused on developing a media ministry outreach to launch people on their faith journey through media. Although a MLE curriculum was a goal of the PMM it was never forthcoming. The MLE work of the PMM is now tailored to the needs of individual churches upon request. This can take the form of presentations that guide churchgoers to theologize their relationship to the media so that media become less threatening. This allows them to live Christian spirituality and to find God and the good that are in media that can result in becoming co-creators of media as well.

In his history of the PMM, Andrew Tinker (2010) writes that the Electronic Great Awakening (EGA) media literacy project emerged from the PMM and is under its aegis. Its name is a nod to the evangelical great awakening that swept the USA and Great Britain in the 1700s. The EGA was started in the early 1990s to teach Christians to think critically about media in a faith-based way. Beth Merry was an early national coordinator for the EGA. When she first heard about media literacy at a PMM board meeting Merry remembers it being a eureka moment that combined her interests in religion, faith-based critical thinking, and communications. The specific purpose of the EGA is for Christians to become faith-empowered critics in a wired world. Tinker makes a distinction between the PMM that encourages individual reflection, even while not excluding other methods, and the dialogic MLE methodology used by the PCMS. Tinker also notes that theological tensions exist between the PCUSA's theology of Reformed Calvinism with its divide between the Church and the world, something Pacatte (2007) addresses as the influence of Puritanism and Jansenism as challenges to the comfort level of Christians with entertainment media.

As a member of the PMM, John Seibert developed "Principles of Media Literacy for People of Faith" for members of the PCUSA bringing together themes that are important not only to Christians but to other faith groups. In particular he notes human dignity, the common God, and the goodness of creation, themes that De Azevedo (2015) more recently explored in her doctoral dissertation on the link between Catholic social teaching and MLE. The PMM themes are:

1. Human beings are created in the image of God.
2. Artistic expression, like creative imagination, is a gift given by God.
3. The pursuit of the common good is the fundamental principle for the good of societies.
4. The power of the gift and act of the creative imagination and expression is rooted in human freedom.
5. The value of the human person is independent of material possessions or social status.
6. The whole world, and all that is in it, is the arena for God's activity.

These principles demonstrate the integration of incarnational theology and also common ground for Presbyterians and Christians in general to engage in MLE as a meaningful response to the influence of media in the faith lives of believers.

The Mormon Church

Brigham Young University of the Mormon Church of Jesus Christ of the Latter-day Saints teaches MLE in its theater and arts department. Dr. Benjamin J. Thevenin, a media scholar and researcher who is Mormon, studied under Stewart Hoover and his doctoral dissertation was on critical media literacy in action, uniting theory, practice, and politics in MLE. He spoke on a panel about Mormon media literacy at the 2013 National Association for Media Literacy Education (NAMLE, https://namle.net) conference in Torrance, CA. Thevenin also serves as an associate editor of the *Journal for Media Literacy* and is a member of the NAMLE board.

William F. Fore, PhD

William Fore is ordained in the United Methodist Church and contributed significantly to religious television programming beginning in 1953 and played a notable role in the founding of public television and radio. After serving as the chairperson on the advisory council of the National Organizations of the Corporation for Public Broadcasting from 1972 to 1975 he served as the chairperson of the World Council for Christian Communications from 1982 to 1988. After this he published *Mythmakers: Gospel, Culture and the Media* which became a staple textbook for Protestants and Catholics alike in bridging mediated culture and faith. The University of Dayton's VLCFF used it for several years starting in 2000 as the basis of its online courses "Media and Values" and "Introduction to Media Literacy" for catechist formation.

Teresa Blythe

Teresa Blythe is an ordained minister of the United Church of Christ who became interested in both media literacy and spiritual direction in the early 1990s while at seminary. After several years as a faith-based media educator she has moved into spiritual direction full time. She believes that media literacy is a spiritual issue and the key practices of media literacy are, in fact, spiritual practices.

Shared meanings and collaboration

The first national MLE organization in the US, the Partnership for Media Education (PME) began in 1997. From it came the National Association for Media Literacy Education (NAMLE) in 2008. MLE in faith-formation has always been part of the conferences sponsored by these groups and representatives from various faith communities have been and are welcome as active contributors to the proceedings and presenters. An example of this is the 2013 panel organized for the NAMLE conference and facilitated by Rose Pacatte, "Believing is Seeing—Religious Approaches to Media Literacy Education," which included representatives from Mormon, Protestant, Catholic, Islam, and Jewish faith communities or learning centers.

The history of the development of faith-based MLE shows how it emerged from different spaces to cross boundaries and unite educators from the public, secular, and religious spheres. There is a norm of respect and inclusivity that pertains to all of the organizations and persons named in this essay that demonstrates how MLE can be a common denominator for pro-social citizenship, co-existence, understanding, and collaboration in a mediated global village that is increasingly conflicted, diverse, yet connected.

SEE ALSO: Media Literacy in Canada

References

Babin, P., with Iannone, M. (1991). *The new era in religious communication*. Minneapolis, MN: Augsburg Fortress Press.

De Azevedo, M.R.T. (2015). *Media literacy and the common good: A link to Catholic social teaching*. Los Angeles, CA: Loyola Marymount University. Retrieved from http://digitalcommons.lmu.edu/etd/191

De las Llagas, C. (2010). *A–Z guide for looking at media: A beginner's companion to media literacy*. Manila, Philippines: Pauline Books & Media.

Doherty, T. (2007). *Hollywood's censor: Joseph Breen & the production code administration*. New York, NY: Columbia University Press.

Eilers, F.-J., SVD. (2011). *Communicating church: Social communication documents – an introduction*. Manila, Philippines: Logos.

Fore, W.F. (1990). *Mythmakers: Gospel, culture and the media*. New York, NY: Friendship Press.

Hailer, G., & Pacatte, R. (2007). *Media mindfulness: Educating teens about faith and media*. Winona, MN: St. Mary's Press.

Hailer, G., & Pacatte, R. (2010). *Our media world: Teaching kids K-8 about faith and media*. Boston, MA: Pauline Books & Media.

Iaquinto, S., & Keeler, J. (2012). Faith-based media literacy education: A look at the past with an eye to the future. *Journal of Media Literacy Education*, *4*(1), 12–31.

Masterman, L. (1982). *Media education: Theoretical issues and practical possibilities*. Article taken from a keynote lecture at the Australian National Media Education Conference, Adelaide, Australia, August–September. Retrieved from http://collections.infocollections.org/ukedu/uk/d/Jh1872e/3.1.html

NAMLE. (2015). The National Telemedia Council [Blog post]. Retrieved from https://namle.net/portfolio/the-national-telemedia-council

Pacatte, R. (1995). *Media education within initial formation programmes of women's religious communities of the Catholic Church*. London, England: University of London Institute of Education.
Pacatte, R. (2005). *To love the world the way it is: Integrating media messages and the spiritual life*. Catechetical Update, National Conference for Catechetical Leadership.
Pacatte, R. (2007). Shaping morals shifting views: Have the Ratings systems influenced how (Christian) America sees movies? In R.K. Johnston (Ed.), *Reframing theology and film: New focus for an emerging discipline*. Grand Rapids, MI: Baker Academic.
Pontifical Commission on Social Communication. (1971). *Communio et Progressio* [Pastoral Instruction on the Means of Social Communication]. Retrieved from http://www.vatican.va/roman_curia/pontifical_councils/pccs/documents/rc_pc_pccs_doc_23051971_communio_en.html
Pungente, J. (1985). *Getting started on media education*. London, England: CSCC.
Razanatseheno, N. (2011). *Ny haino aman-jery: Tontolo vaovao* [The media: A new world]. Antananarive, Madagascar: Pauline Books & Media.
Tinker, J. (2010). Analysis of the media literacy theories and practices of the Pauline Centre for Media Studies and the Presbyterian Media Mission (Master's dissertation, Edinburgh University, Scotland). Retrieved from https://www.era.lib.ed.ac.uk/handle/1842/4476
USCCB. (1999). *Family guide for using media*. Catholic Communications Campaign. Retrieved from http://www.usccb.org/about/communications/family-guide.cfm
USCCB. (2005). *National directory for catechesis*. Washington, DC: USCCB.
Vatican. (1997). *General directory for catechesis*. Retrieved from http://www.vatican.va/roman_curia/congregations/cclergy/documents/rc_con_ccatheduc_doc_17041998_directory-for-catechesis_en.html
Vatican Council II. (1963). *Inter Mirifica*. Retrieved from http://www.vatican.va/archive/hist_councils/ii_vatican_council/documents/vat-ii_decree_19631204_inter-mirifica_en.html
What is Media Literacy? A definition ... and more. (n.d.). Center for Media Literacy. Retrieved from http://www.medialit.org/topical-issue/def

Further reading

Communication Research Trends archive. Retrieved from http://cscc.scu.edu/trends
Keeler, J., & Iaquinto, S. (2012). Faith-based media literacy education: A look at the past with an eye to the future. *Journal of Media Literacy Education*, *4*(1), 12–31. Retrieved from http://files.eric.ed.gov/fulltext/EJ985676.pdf
Pungente, J., & Biernatski, E.E. (1993). Media education. *Communication Research Trends*, *13*(2).

Rose Pacatte, FSP, MEd in media studies, DMin, is a Catholic sister and the founding director of the Pauline Center for Media Studies in Culver City, CA. She has been working in media literacy education for more than 25 years and speaks on faith-based media literacy nationally and internationally, most recently in the United Arab Emirates. Rose has authored or coauthored eight books and is a coauthor of two award-winning books on media literacy in faith formation. *Lights, Camera, Faith: The Beatitudes and Deadly Sins*" is due out in 2019. She is a film critic for *St. Anthony Messenger* and the film and television contributor to the *National Catholic Reporter*. In 2007 she received the Jesse McCanse Award for individual contributions to media literacy from the National

Telemedia Council and the Dan Kane Award for religious communications from the University of Dayton in 2015. Rose received a Doctor of Ministry in pastoral communications in 2018 and received the Mother Theresa prize in spirituality and community service from the Graduate Theological Institute. She serves on the board of the SIGNIS Communicator Forum and is a past president of Catholics in Media Associates in Los Angeles.

Family Relationships and Media

LUCIE STASTNA
Institute of Communication Studies and Journalism, Czech Republic

Family, media, and technologies have all undergone dramatic changes throughout history. The nuclear family, consisting of a woman, a man, and their children, transformed during the second half of the 20th century into cohabitational arrangements of adults and children, in which the adults assume legal responsibility for the welfare and maturation of the children. Considering the various forms of family life present in western societies, it is difficult to conceptualize a family other than through the care and education of a new generation (Huston, Zillmann, & Bryant, 1994). Equally, the term "media" has changed and now represents a wide range of media devices and platforms. As new types of media or "technologically newest versions" of traditional media penetrate the market, households have become more media equipped. New devices rarely replace previous ones; instead, each finds its place and users within a family. Every new medium also raises a mixture of fears and hopes of how it will influence the life of a family and its members.

Family relationships can be characterized as ways in which family members are connected or as the state of this connection. By extension, this could include family members' emotional bonds, communication and interaction patterns, the requiring, negotiating, and setting of rules of behavior, the power structure within family, the requiring and keeping of family values and norms, and so on. The context of family relationships consists of social, cultural, political, economic, and media-technological conditions of family life. This entry uses the broader sense of the term.

The relation between media and family relationships can be seen from two basic perspectives. The first one examines modes of media use in a family and phenomena related to the "cohabitance" of family and media (two subtopics are discussed below: media use in relation to family norms and to issues of power and control). This stems from audience research, enriched by qualitative studies exploring media use in everyday family life. The second perspective focuses on the influence of media (use) on a family. It researches media effects that are related to a family, its members, and their relationships. This perspective is also linked to research on the representation of family in media content, which can inspire family members to establish expectations, values, norms, and behavior patterns related to family functioning.

Media use in relation to family norms and (dis)agreements

The prerequisite for mapping the connections between media and family relationships is uncovering *how media are used in a family*. Every family has its own system of rules, values, and norms, which influences how media are used (who can use them, when, for how long, and under what conditions, who decides what to watch together, etc.), what rules parents set for children's use of different types of media, if, how, and according to what criteria they regulate children's media use, how these rules are required, followed, or negotiated and redefined. The chosen parental mediation strategy is derived from the media environment of the family (Wartella, Rideout, Lauricella, & Connell, 2014), the overall style of parenting, and family communication and functioning. Chaffee, McLeod, and Atkin (1971) made note of family communication patterns: these patterns are related to family values. While some families emphasize the children's option to express their own opinion to the detriment of family harmony, others encourage their children to suppress their opinions to respect family harmony and cohesion. The connection between family values, communication, and parenting styles was also observed by Clark Schofield (2013), who defined two types of "parental ethics": the ethic of expressive empowerment and the ethic of respectful connectedness.

The expansion of the Internet and digital media brought about discussions on differences in digital media use by various family members, of different generations. Television is more accessible to children than books because literacy is not required; digital media seem to be even more accessible. Children grow up in a multimedia environment and use digital media intuitively from an early age. Contrarily, their parents and grandparents may have difficulties keeping up with the development of new media and technologies and availing themselves of all the related opportunities. Divergent skill and knowledge levels regarding digital media may lead both to tension and misunderstanding among family members and to common intergenerational "participative learning" (Clark Schofield, 2011). These differences can also affect parenting attitudes and related behaviors, as also mentioned below.

Media use in relation to issues of power and control

Research of media (especially television) use in families began in the 1950s, but the topic received more extensive focus in the 1970s and 1980s, when many qualitative studies explored everyday life with media in the context of the family system and its dynamics (Alexander, 1994). For example, David Morley's research (1986) on the context and dynamics of family TV viewing showed that it was usually the father who chose the TV program, who made plans for family TV viewing, and who held the remote control. And so the rules of TV use reflected the family power structure, power derived from the role of breadwinner. Mothers were more often those who adjusted to the needs of the others and watched programs they did not choose. While mothers took watching television as a social event or background for another activity, fathers perceived it as an opportunity to relax. This difference also caused conflict, as mothers preferred talking while watching television, while fathers did not want to be disturbed. The videocassette recorder (VCR) was a means of compromise, to record programs that could not be watched when broadcast.

According to other studies conducted in the 1980s (e.g., Bryce & Leichter, 1983; Lull, 1980), television can mitigate family tension or facilitate escape from everyday reality; it can provide topics for family conversation as well as decrease the amount of family communication. It can become a means for demarcating the borders between family members; it can be a companion in moments of loneliness or a kind of fireplace around which the family gathers. Some families use television to structure their daily schedule (planning other activities according to the TV program); others use television to fill their free time when they are not engaged in other, more important activities.

Other media have found their place in families as well. For example, mobile phones became indispensable for communication between family members. Despite the advantages of being in touch, parents can use mobile phones (and other digital media as well) as a means of total control and surveillance (see helicopter parents, e.g., in Clark Schofield, 2013) of their children, who lose not only their privacy, but sometimes experience mental health problems as well. Smartphones brought new possibilities to users (including an almost universal WiFi connection) together with new challenges for parenting: parental mediation is more difficult than it has ever been. According to recent research by Wartella et al. (2014), the vast majority of American parents (almost 70% of the representative sample, $n = 2326$) of children up to 8 years do not think that smartphones and tablets make parenting easier.

The ways in which people comment on their media use, how they actually use media, and how they explain their relationship to media, stem from their attitudes toward media and their perceived risks and opportunities. Parents also set rules of media use according to what influence they believe media have on their children and themselves (Hoover, Clark Schofield, & Alters, 2004). Wartella and her colleagues' research (2014) shows that parents more likely view a book, toy, or other activity as an educational opportunity than other, digital media. Nevertheless, they are more likely to find positive than negative effects of media and technology on their children's academic skills (the most negative effect is ascribed to video games).

Media as a potentially negative influence on family (relationships)

From the perspective of media effects on family, the presumption of socialization through media is the most interesting. While primary socialization occurs in the family at an early age, secondary socialization includes other socialization agents (school, peer group, media, church). While media can foster the influence of other socialization agents (family, church, school), they can also contrast and undermine their influence. Mass media differ from the other socialization agents because children encounter them informally, as they are part of the family environment; media content is not usually designed to socialize or educate, but to entertain and make a profit; and children are exposed to its influence from an early age (Huston, Zillmann, & Bryant, 1994). Besides mass media, present-day households are equipped with numerous digital media, which are usually accessible to preschoolers. In some families they even function as babysitters (Beyens & Eggermont, 2014; Wartella et al. 2014).

The possibility of media content disrupting the process of family socialization through its influence on the behavior, values, and attitudes of children and youths is often discussed in relation to portrayals of violence, sex and erotica, pornography, marketing communication (mainly because of its effect on children's consumer behavior), addictions and excessive media use, and so on. The influence of media on children can be mediated by parents; through diverse parental mediation strategies, they can mitigate negative and foster positive media effects on children. However, Vandewater, Lee, and Shim (2005) focus on violent media content and show that the influence of family and media content on children's behavior can be interrelated and reciprocally interdependent. According to their study, children in high-conflict families watched more violent television and spent more free time playing mildly violent electronic games than did those in less conflictual families.

In past decades, numerous theories were formulated regarding the form of media influence. The theory of social learning (Bandura, 1971) and the cultivation theory (Gerbner, 1998) can serve as examples of "old" theories applicable to the field of family relationships. While Bandura's theory explains how we learn new patterns of behavior through the observation of symbolic (media) or real (parental) models, which are demonstrated to us, Gerbner's theory clarifies how the intensive consumption of TV programming influences our ideas and conceptions of the real world. Both theories were introduced at a time when several TV channels dominated the media environment, nevertheless they are still influential. In the spirit of Bandura's theory, we can ask: to what extent do we use media content as symbolic models for our behavior and how contrasted could this content be in comparison to real models (e.g., from our family)? In relation to Gerbner's theory, the question remains as to how the intense, long-term consumption of TV (or other media) content can influence the concept of family, family relationships, and communication.

Other theorists concerned with media effects on the family and its members are characterized by a techno-deterministic approach. For example, according to Meyrowitz (1985), the use of electronic media (especially television) leads to the overlap of previously private social spheres and thus to the dissolution of borders between childhood and adulthood. The traditional, ongoing family socialization process is disturbed by television, which provides detailed insight into the backstage of adult life for children and reveals secrets that should have been hidden. As the Internet and digital media became widespread, supporters of technological determinism focused on the powerful effects they may have on their users.

As Buckingham (2013) summarized, digital media and the Internet were praised for the greater democratization of society, for the interconnection of its members and groups, for fostering more intensive and frequent communication between individuals and others, for ameliorating learning and self-development processes, and so on. On the other hand, media were accused of negative phenomena: various risks and cyberdangers, personal data abuse, superficialization of interpersonal communication, social isolation of individuals and groups, the development of various disorders (e.g., nomophobia, cyberchondria, addictions, digital dementia). The focus of discussion has shifted from "knowledge gaps," which were associated mainly with mass media, to "the digital divide": inequalities in access to digital media and new technologies among people from different geographical areas and social groups. Technological and social inequalities are also projected into family functioning and the ways in which media are used and how their use is controlled, regulated, and negotiated in a family, as demonstrated by Clark Schofield (2009), for example.

The influence of digital media on family and its functioning can be both positive and negative. As Lanigan (2009) summarized, they can be a means of communication that enables family members to keep in touch and can serve as a source of information for planning activities together or as a tool for co-use. The Internet has made many everyday tasks easier and quicker, and thus family members have more free time for their joint activities. On the other hand, home-based digital media can also have negative consequences: for example, conflicts among family members caused by excessive computer usage, the decrease in free time spent together as a result of isolated digital media use by some family members, and the reduction of family communication and emotional bonding. Lanigan's sociotechnological family model makes it possible to examine the aforementioned influences and represents an effort to capture the complexity of the impact of digital media on the family and its functioning. Other experts also call for a complex research approach to the study of family media use (e.g., Buckingham, 2013) because it could help overcome the limitations of optimistic and pessimistic perspectives.

SEE ALSO: Digital Divide; Family Strategies for Managing Media in the Home; Mobile Media and Parenting; Parental Mediation

References

Alexander, A. (1994). The effects of media on family interaction. In D. Zillmann, J. Bryant, & A.C. Huston (Eds.), *Media, children, and the family: Social scientific, psychodynamic, and clinical perspectives* (1st ed., pp. 51–59). Hillsdale, NJ: Lawrence Erlbaum.

Bandura, A. (1971). *Social learning theory*. New York, NY: General Learning Press.

Beyens, I., & Eggermont, S. (2014). Putting young children in front of the television: Antecedents and outcomes of parents' use of television as a babysitter. *Communication Quarterly, 62*(1), 57–74. doi: 10.1080/01463373.2013.860904

Bryce, J.W., & Leichter, H.J. (1983). The family and television: Forms of mediation. *Journal of Family Issues, 4*(2), 309–328. doi: 10.1177/019251383004002004

Buckingham, D. (2013). Making sense of the "digital generation": Growing up with digital media. *Self & Society, 40*(3), 7–15. doi: 10.1080/03060497.2013.11084274

Chaffee, S.H., McLeod, J.M., & Atkin, Ch.K. (1971). Parental influences on adolescent media use. *American Behavioral Scientist, 14*(3), 323–340. doi: 10.1177/000276427101400304

Clark Schofield, L. (2009). Digital media and the generation gap. *Information, Communication & Society, 12*(3), 388–407. doi: 10.1080/13691180902823845

Clark Schofield, L. (2011). Parental mediation theory for the digital age. *Communication Theory, 21*(4), 323–343. doi: 10.1111/j.1468-2885.2011.01391.x

Clark Schofield, L. (2013). *The parent app. Understanding families in a digital age*. New York, NY: Oxford University Press.

Gerbner, G. (1998). Cultivation analysis: An overview. *Mass Communication & Society, 1*(3/4), 175–194. doi: 10.1080/15205436.1998.9677855

Hoover, S.M., Clark Schofield, L., & Alters, D.F. (2004). *Media, home, and family*. New York, NY: Routledge.

Huston, A.C., Zillmann, D., & Bryant, J. (1994). Media influence, public policy, and the family. In D. Zillmann, J. Bryant, & A.C. Huston (Eds.), *Media, children, and the family: Social scientific, psychodynamic, and clinical perspectives* (1st ed., pp. 3–18). Hillsdale, NJ: Lawrence Erlbaum.

Lanigan, J.D. (2009). A sociotechnological model for family research and intervention: How information and communication technologies affect family life. *Marriage & Family Review, 45*(6–8), 587–609. doi: 10.1080/01494920903224194

Lull, J. (1980). Social uses of television. *Human Communication Research, 6*(3), 197–209. doi: 10.1111/j.1468-2958.1980.tb00140.x

Meyrowitz, J. (1985). *No sense of place: The impact of electronic media on social behavior*. New York, NY: Oxford University Press.

Morley, D. (1986). *Family television: Cultural power and domestic leisure*. New York, NY: Routledge.

Vandewater, E.A., Lee, J.H., & Shim, M.-S. (2005). Family conflict and violent electronic media use in school-aged children. *Media Psychology, 7*(1), 73–86. doi: 10.1207/S1532785XMEP0701_4

Wartella, E., Rideout, V., Lauricella, A., & Connell, S. (2014). *Revised parenting in the age of digital technology: A national survey*. Center on Media and Human Development, School of Communication, Northwestern University. Retrieved from http://cmhd.northwestern.edu/wp-content/uploads/2015/06/ParentingAgeDigitalTechnology.REVISED.FINAL_.2014.pdf

Lucie Stastna is a PhD candidate at the Institute of Communication Studies and Journalism at Charles University (Czech Republic). Her main focus is parental mediation and media education of adults. In 2012–2014, she led a research project titled Parents, Children, and Media, which explored parents' difficulties with parental mediation, and in 2015–2016, she co-led a national research study mapping media literacy among the Czech population. Since 2011, she has worked on various media education projects for schools.

Family Strategies for Managing Media in the Home

KELLY MENDOZA
Common Sense Education, USA

Parents and caregivers are the primary support system for children's engagement with media and technology. Parents are in an important position to guide children's media use because they are, typically, the decision-makers for purchasing devices, guiding media activities, setting behavioral norms, managing time spent, and overseeing media content. Yet many parents have concerns and challenges with their children's media use. A couple of decades ago, television was the main concern. But, as children and families have now increased access to digital devices and the Internet, and as the risks and benefits are more complicated, guiding kids in a digital age has become a bigger challenge for parents. The most comprehensive area of research on parent–child engagement with media in the home is *parental mediation*, which refers to any strategy parents use to restrict, supervise, or interpret media with children.

Parental mediation

The interest in parental mediation research, largely based in the United States, increased in the 1980s, when media deregulation was in effect and standards for children's television were low. Research continued in the 1990s with a focus on youth media interventions and parent media education efforts. Aligning with the rise of the Internet, from 2000 to the present, research on Internet mediation increased. These two areas—television and Internet—are the largest bodies of parental mediation research and will be the focus of this entry.

Most parental mediation research draws from developmental psychology and media effects frameworks, with a focus on how parental mediation could mitigate negative media effects on children's physical, psychological, and emotional well-being. Parental mediation can be thought of from two angles. Most consider "user-based" approaches, such as how parents guide children through restriction (rules and limits) or through instruction (interpreting media content). There is also a "system-based" approach, which consists of technical solutions within devices, for example blocking, filtering, and monitoring (Kirwil, Garmendia, Garitaonandia, & Martinez, 2009).

TV mediation

Watching television is still the most common media activity families do together. Televisions are still placed as the focal point of the living room or family room in homes, and access to shows is becoming more ubiquitous in an age of mobile digital screens and streaming services such as Netflix. On the basis of TV viewing behavior, researchers have identified three types of TV mediation: coviewing, restrictive mediation, and active mediation.

Coviewing

Coviewing refers to watching television together without discussion or commentary. Coviewing is not a deliberate form of mediation; simply by being present, parents who coview are engaging with the shows their children are watching. Coviewing is more commonly used than active mediation. Parents tend to coview more with younger than with older children, mothers coview more than fathers, and parents who have positive attitudes toward television often coview and encourage their children to watch specific programs because they see it as a tool that can reinforce positive lessons.

Coviewing increases children's enjoyment of programs because they often like viewing with their parents. However, parents who coview objectionable content (sex, violence, drugs, stereotypes, aggression) may encourage similar viewing habits and offer a "silent endorsement" of the messages (Nathanson, 1999). The common advice that parent advocacy groups give—"watch with your children"—may backfire if the parents don't discuss the messages portrayed.

Restrictive mediation

The term "restrictive mediation" refers to parents who manage children's media use through rules and limitations on devices, content viewed, and time spent. On average, between 50 and 75% of children and parents report having rules about watching television, and parents report more restrictions than children. Half of the kids who report having rules say that they can get around them. As children grow older, restrictive mediation decreases. Parents who restrict tend to watch less television and believe that certain content may have negative effects on children. Parents with younger children and girls, and low-income families, are more likely to restrict.

Evidence on the effectiveness of restrictive mediation is mixed. Restrictive mediation has been linked to slightly less TV viewing by children. Moderate and consistent restriction is related to less exposure to media violence and less aggression in adolescents. Restricting television has had a slight effect on mitigating the negative effects of advertising, though not as much as active mediation. Heavy restriction could backfire, as adolescents reported that they thought their parents did not trust them and, in turn, had more positive attitudes around restricted content (Nathanson, 2002). Nonetheless, parents rely on restrictive mediation as a useful and familiar parenting strategy. Restriction, rules, and limits—such as the advice to "set a media diet" or to "keep television out of kids' bedrooms"—are strategies commonly recommended to parents by advocates and parent media education programs. Restriction also has a history within a protectionist approach to media education that is based on mitigating negative health effects. The American Academy of Pediatrics has long recommended restrictions on screen time, particularly with infants and toddlers, who are experiencing rapid brain and social development. Furthermore, restrictive mediation can be assisted by technical tools designed to help the parents. In 1999 in the United States, the V-chip was the first technical control in place within televisions. The V-chip allows parents to block programming from children (on the basis of age and content ratings established by the TV industry). Today's digitally enabled televisions and devices offer more tools for parents to limit time and to keep children within parent-approved content.

Active mediation

Active mediation is a type of mediation where parents and children watch television together and parents engage in the discussion of programs, content, and advertising with children. As the least practiced type of mediation, it requires parental availability for discussion and parental engagement. Active mediation messages from parents can be negative, positive, or neutral in tone.

Active mediation has shown positive effects on promoting in children critical thinking skills about programs and commercials, learning more from educational television, increased pro-social behavior, increased skepticism toward TV news, increased engagement in political socialization, decreased aggression, decreased negative impact of advertising, increase in positive body image, and a decrease in the negative impact of violent and sexual content on teens.

Active mediation is also the type of parenting behavior most closely aligned with media literacy. If parents help their children ask questions about media messages, make their opinions known, and share their values, this in turn helps children think critically about the messages they receive. However, the effectiveness of active mediation may depend on the type of content viewed, on whether parents use negative, positive, or neutral active mediation, and on what exactly is communicated.

Factors that influence parental mediation

Several factors influence whether parents use mediation, why, and of what type that mediation is. A substantial contributing factor is parenting style; thus authoritative (more responsive and demanding than average) and authoritarian (high-control and low-warmth) parents are more likely to use restriction; permissive (warm and supportive but not demanding) parents are more likely to coview; and laissez-faire (uninvolved, low-demand, or neglectful) parents are more likely to not practice mediation at all.

Parents' mediation strategies are influenced by other factors such as their age, gender, culture, education, attitudes about media, availability, and communication style, as well as by the age, gender, and personality characteristics of their children. Mothers engage in mediation more than fathers, girls receive more mediation than boys, and restrictive and active mediation are used more with younger than with older children. In addition, the number and location of televisions and devices in the home influence mediation practices.

Internet mediation

As children have increased access to mobile devices and the Internet, guiding kids' media use has become more of a challenge for parents and caregivers. Digital technologies change quickly and offer a wider variety of options and activities (websites, apps, videos) beyond television. Parents may feel that their kids are more media savvy or skilled than they are and may worry about risks such as accessing worrisome content, talking to strangers, and sharing private or inappropriate information. Traditional strategies derived from TV mediation don't necessarily work the same way with mobile, individualized digital devices. These factors have resulted in a broader set of Internet mediation strategies. Researchers of Internet mediation are identifying different forms of engagement, supervision, and technical safety guidance. Researchers argue that parental mediation theory, rooted in television, needs to change and include specific activities related to interactive digital media, especially because the Internet poses different risks and benefits than television. Risks and benefits can each be thought of as having three Cs. Risks include *content* (pornography, violence, self-harm, pro-anorexia, drug use, hate speech, etc.), *contact* (communicating with and developing relationships with unknown others), and *conduct* (how children communicate online, whether they encounter mean messages and cyberbullying, and the information they share and post). However, benefits include *communication* (connecting with others in positive and beneficial ways) *collaboration* (sharing knowledge and interests), and *creativity* (digital media creation and self-expression).

The largest-scale study on Internet mediation is from the EU Kids Online survey. This survey examined 25 142 participants, who consisted of 9–16-year-olds and their parents in 25 European countries (EU Kids Online, 2014). On the basis of findings from this study as well as from related ones (Livingstone, Haddon, Gorzig, & Ólafsson, 2011; Livingstone & Helsper, 2008; Livingstone et al., 2017), there are five Internet mediation activities.

Active mediation

Active mediation refers to talking to or sitting with children as they go online and sharing activities together. This includes behaviors such as asking questions about what children are seeing and doing, explaining why certain websites are good or bad, and helping the child with something difficult to do or find. Approximately three fourths of parents prefer active mediation to restrictive mediation, technical controls, or monitoring alone as the top strategy practiced alongside safety mediation. Evidence is mixed as to whether active mediation reduces online risks, though the latest research shows that it is associated with risk reduction (EU Kids Online, 2014). Although active mediation allows kids to access online opportunities and develop digital skills, increased access can expose them to higher risks. However, children report appreciating their parents' interest and active mediation, while parents report confidence in their children's abilities.

Safety mediation

Safety mediation includes actively talking to children by advising them on Internet safety strategies. Alongside active mediation, safety mediation is widely used by parents. Although it can be preventive, safety mediation is often used as a reactive measure, such as after a child has experienced something upsetting online. Safety mediation is associated with reduced online risk, but allows fewer opportunities for children to develop their digital skills.

Restrictive mediation

Restrictive mediation refers to setting rules and restrictions about online safety behavior—for example whom kids can talk to online, what information they can post and share, what websites they can visit—and restrictions on uploading and downloading of information. As in the case of TV mediation, approximately half of parents report using the restrictive type of mediation for the Internet too. Parents are more likely to use restriction with younger children, if they have a negative view of the Internet and if they perceive their child as having low self-control. Restrictive mediation is associated with reduced online risk, but provides fewer opportunities for children to develop their digital skills. It can be useful if children are vulnerable to harm. However, children who receive restrictive mediation are less likely to solicit support from their parents, which may hinder their receiving the benefits of active mediation or safety mediation.

Technical controls

The term "technical controls" refers to the parents' use of control tools to filter, block, or monitor what children do online. These tools can limit children's access to certain websites, content, and overall time spent online; they can also track and monitor what children do online. Between one fourth and one third of parents report using technical controls. However, due to the variability in measuring the types, uses, and impact of technical controls, research is inconclusive on how effective these tools are in reducing children's online risks.

Monitoring

Monitoring consists of a parent's checking on a child's activities after use, for instance inspecting his or her browsing history and looking at chats or message history. Monitoring includes keeping an eye on the child while in the same room. Although over half of parents report using this method, it is unclear whether monitoring alone reduces online risk; besides, monitoring is difficult to measure, as it can be easily combined with active, safety, or restrictive mediation.

It is important to note that 10 to 15% of parents do not practice any form of mediation. Reaching these parents regarding the importance of being engaged in their kids' media use should be a priority.

Factors that predict Internet mediation

As with TV mediation, parents are more to mediate for younger children, mothers tend to mediate more than fathers, and parents' mediation choices are influenced by parenting style and cultural background. For instance, parents from individualistic cultures engage more in all types of mediation, while parents from collectivist cultures may not use any mediation or prefer restriction and technical solutions. Unlike in TV mediation, few differences have been found in Internet mediation between boys and girls. Parents who expect the Internet to have a positive effect are more likely to use active mediation. Parents from higher socioeconomic status (SES) homes, or who are confident about using the Internet, tend to make more use of active and safety mediation, but not of restriction. Restrictive mediation tends to be used by parents of lower SES, who have lower education and less confidence about using the Internet. Technical tools are most likely used with younger children and by parents who are worried about their child being online.

Internet mediation themes

Two important themes emerge from the research on Internet mediation. The first theme is that the Internet mediation strategies can be categorized into two types: *enabling mediation* and *restrictive mediation* (Livingstone et al., 2017). Enabling mediation, described as "empowered but safe" mediation, includes a combination of active mediation, safety mediation, technical controls, and monitoring. It includes activities that might be seen as both empowering and restrictive, but that set a foundation to encourage children to use the Internet in beneficial ways and to provide them with freedom and agency. Enabling mediation also keeps the door open for child-initiated support from parents. Although enabling mediation is associated with increased online opportunities and digital skills, it also poses higher risks for children. Restrictive mediation, the other type, is about relying on using rules and restrictions with children. This strategy is associated with fewer online risks, but also reduces children's opportunities to enjoy the benefits of the Internet and to develop digital skills. Restrictive mediation also reduces child-initiated support from parents, limiting parents' opportunities to guide children with active and safety mediation.

The second theme is a sort of conundrum: enabling mediation is a double-edged sword. Even though enabling mediation is recommended as an effective way to empower and protect children online, it does not mitigate children's exposure to online risks. However, the benefits of enabling mediation are seen to outweigh those of restrictive mediation; for, even though children may be exposed to risk, the goal is to help them, through guidance and support, navigate the risks and reap the benefits. They will also be exposed to situations in which they can build skills in decision-making, self-regulation, coping, and resilience. Recommendations for parents include supporting their kids' exploration of the Internet from an early age (including the benefits and risks), enhancing their online opportunities, focusing more on engaging activities and positive content, and communicating regularly with children about how to navigate risks online (EU Kids Online, 2014).

Future directions for parental mediation research

The era of TV mediation is decreasing, and research on Internet mediation—which inherently includes TV-viewing behavior—is increasing. Future research should continue exploring Internet mediation, looking at several key questions outlined below.

What factors predict Internet mediation?

More research needs to explore factors that predict mediation and how these factors differ across media types. For instance, how do parents mediate voice-activated speakers such as Amazon Alexa differently from a tablet? Furthermore, more research on parental mediation needs to examine characteristics of the child, for instance children with attention deficit hyperactivity disorder (ADHD) or autism. Research on the factors that predict mediation will contribute to developing more targeted approaches that can help parents mediate differently depending on device, characteristics of their child, context, and situation.

How can the media industry create better tools for kids … and support for parents?

Knowing that there is a need to support parents with Internet mediation—beyond technical tools—how can media producers and developers create better tools for kids—tools that keep them safe, but provide them with flexibility and freedom?

How can we best educate parents to guide their children's media use?

Parents are looking for help in guiding their children, whether from schools, the media, or friends and the community. We need to have a better understanding of how to best support parents in different ways, preferably when they need it. We also need to reach parents who do not engage in mediation at all, or who rely solely on restrictive mediation, on the value of active mediation for their children.

How do parents practice media literacy in mediation?

Surprisingly, parental mediation and media literacy are two fields that have not often crossed paths. As parental mediation is often situated in media effects, though media literacy practices are part of mediation, researchers are not making explicit connections or drawing on one another's work (Mendoza, 2009). Connecting the two areas, looking more closely at the actual content of parents' active mediation, would strengthen recommendations for parents.

SEE ALSO: Family Relationships and Media; Mobile Media and Parenting; Parent Advocacy Groups; Parental Mediation

References

EU Kids Online. (2014). *EU Kids Online: Findings, methods, recommendations*. London, England: EU Kids Online, London School of Economics.

Kirwil, L., Garmendia, M., Garitaonandia, C., & Martinez, G.-M. (2009). Parental mediation. In S. Livingstone & L. Haddon (Eds.), *Kids online: Opportunities and risks for children* (pp. 99–215). Bristol, England: Policy Press.

Livingstone, S., Haddon, L., Görzig, A., & Ólafsson, K. (2011). *EU Kids Online II: Final report*. London, England: EU Kids Online, London School of Economics.

Livingstone, S., & Helsper, E. (2008). Parental mediation and children's Internet use. *Journal of Broadcasting & Electronic Media, 52*(4), 581–599.

Livingstone, S., Ólafsson, K., Helsper, E.J., Lupiáñez-Villanueva, F., Veltri, G.A., & Folkvord, F. (2017). Maximizing opportunities and minimizing risks for children online: The role of digital skills in emerging strategies of parental mediation. *Journal of Communication, 67*(1), 82–105.

Mendoza, K. (2009). Surveying parental mediation: Connections, challenges, and questions for media literacy. *Journal of Media Literacy Education, 1*(1), 28–41.

Nathanson, A.I. (1999). Identifying and explaining the relationship between parental mediation and children's aggression. *Communication Research, 26*(2), 124–164.
Nathanson, A.I. (2002). The unintended effects of parental mediation of television on adolescents. *Media Psychology, 4*(3), 207–230.

Further reading

Buckingham, D. (1993). *Children talking television: The making of television literacy*. Washington, DC: Falmer Press.
Nikken, P., & Jansz., J. (2006). Parental mediation of children's videogame playing: A comparison of the reports by parents and children. *Learning, Media and Technology, 31*(2), 181–202.
Valkenberg, P., Krcmar, M., Peeters, A.L., & Marseille, N.M. (1999). Developing a scale to assess three styles of television mediation: "Instructive mediation," "restrictive mediation," and "social coviewing." *Journal of Broadcasting & Electronic Media, 43*(1), 52–66. doi: 10.1080/08838159909364474
Weaver, B., & Barbour, N. (1992). Mediation of children's televiewing. *Families in Society, 73*, 236–242.

Kelly Mendoza is Senior Director of Education Programs at Common Sense Education, where she oversees education program and content strategy for Common Sense Education, including digital citizenship curriculum, interactive games, and online professional development for K-12 schools. Her goal is to create curricula and programs that help schools create a positive culture around media and technology. She has also developed education resources and curriculum for teachers, students, and parents for Lucas Learning, the Media Education Lab, and PBS Frontline. Kelly has a PhD in Media & Communication from Temple University.

Film Education in Europe

MARK REID
British Film Institute, UK

This entry considers the range of European national film education policies in their relationship to national formal education structures, to indigenous film cultures, and to common understandings of pedagogy in film. It situates film education within both European policy structures, and the media education landscape in Europe. It concludes that a film education "culture of translation" between national and organizational settings is the most effective model for managing the competing national and supra-national demands and cultures in film.

In 1932, a Commission on Educational and Cultural Films in the UK produced its report *The Film in National Life*, concluding, in a paraphrase in *The Spectator* magazine, that "Every country ... sooner or later gets the films it deserves" (Gott, 1932). The issue framing this entry is the extent to which European countries have distinctive models and approaches to the film education (that is, "the film education they deserve") or alternatively whether a supra-national model of "European film education" might exist in competition with those national models.

An initial look at national film cultures in Europe supports the idea that what is possible in arts and cultural production is to some extent determined by nationhood: France, for example, proudly celebrates cinema as "the seventh art" and treats its favored directors as artists alongside painters and writers. It preserves cinema's elite position by decisive state intervention: a ban on screening film trailers and adverts and "film-free" Friday evenings on public service television, to encourage people to go to the cinema. The high valuation of film as art in turn is reflected in the character of French film education: unashamedly esthetic (though with room for a narrow vein of Hollywood populism); in love with the global and historical canvas of film; celebratory of the cinema as the pinnacle of film culture; dirigiste and elitist in its canonizing of certain film-makers and film.

In film cultural terms, France has the distinction of not being an English-speaking nation: by contrast, the UK film industry has since its inception both flourished and labored under the influence of Hollywood, under the misconception that both nations speak the same language. Some commentators have viewed this as a curse, with Nick Roddick pointing out that "if the USA spoke Spanish, the UK would have a film industry" (Roddick, 1985), while others can point to close and reciprocal artistic and industrial bonds and influences. The Hollywood influence on film education is felt keenly in the UK, with its plethora of film competitions, mock Oscar and BAFTA competitions, red carpet events, and close involvement of famous film actors and professionals.

A strong contrast with both UK and France is offered by a country like Lithuania. Its film culture, evolving as it did alongside political and cultural changes in the Soviet and post-Soviet orbit across the 20th century, can't help but mirror its social environment. As a small satellite region of the USSR, then a small independent nation, Lithuania had the capacity for only a small indigenous feature film industry. The documentary form had a greater impact, made as subversive culture before 1989 and as increasingly confident national expression after (see Meno Avilys, 2016). After the collapse of the Soviet Union in 1989, Lithuanian culture began a process of readjusting to its new political reality. Its emerging film education infrastructure was driven by a group of passionately enthusiastic young people behind the Skalvija Cinema Center or NGOs like Meno Avilys, who had studied or interned abroad. The relationship with Russia, and Russian film and media, continues as a strand in Lithuanian film education: important Lithuanian films are held only in the Russian state archives, and progress in reclaiming and restoring them is slow. And powerful Russian media interests are targeting the Baltic states, leading to calls for a strong media literacy to counter their messages and values.

All three of these nations—France, UK, and Lithuania—are (as of 2018) members of the European Union: an economic and political association of 28 nations, with more affiliated through the European Economic Area (for a full list see www.gov.uk/eu-eea), committed to economic, social, and cultural collaboration. The EU provides a political super-structure that fosters collaborative approaches to culture and trade, while simultaneously allowing for national self-determination. The EU to some extent defines what it is to be "European", in the arts and culture, and in media and film. The issue for this entry therefore is how "European-ness" is manifest in film culture and education, and how it plays out with national cultures, identities, and structures of film education.

The European Union and film education policy

It is the European Commission (EC)—the civil service of the European Union—that essentially manages the creation and circulation of "European" identity, in a range of Directorates General (DG) (full list can be found here: http://ec.europa.eu/about/ds_en.htm) that cover every aspect of trade and culture from agriculture to translation. Since 1991 the EU has taken an active interest in promoting media and film, under the twin drivers of industrial and cultural interests. Jacques Delors (Commission President 1985–1995) gave the audiovisual industries special status when he said "the audio-visual is not a merchandise like others, so it requires a specific regulation" (quoted in Hartlapp, Metz, & Rauh, 2014).

This "special status" was expressed in a series of MEDIA programs running from 1991, and, since the MEDIA program of 2007–2014, when the DG concerned was renamed Education and Culture, the MEDIA Unit has supported "media literacy" within a broader support for media industries, especially film and television. The Commission expresses its focus thus:

> Media literacy is vital for economic growth and job creation. Digital technologies are a key driver of competitiveness and innovation in the media, information, and communication technology sectors. (European Commission, 2016a)

Of the €755m allocated by the MEDIA program over the 7 years from 2007 to 2014, between 1 and 2% was spent on education. The rationale behind support for media literacy has always been explicitly to support the media industries, and to protect and nurture European audiovisual culture, as an expression of European heritage. In fact, for much of the time in EU MEDIA policy "media" has been read as "film": the money was to:

> support the development and distribution of thousands of films, as well as training activities, festivals, and promotional projects throughout the continent ... to strengthen the audio-visual sector; increase the circulation of European audio-visual works; and to strengthen competitiveness. (European Commission, 2016b)

In 2014, a merger of the EC's arts, cultural, and MEDIA programs became "Creative Europe": another 7-year fund, this time amounting to some €1.46bn. The "media literacy" component became explicitly a focus on "film literacy," being:

> activities aimed at promoting film literacy and at increasing audiences' knowledge of, and interest in, European audiovisual works, including the audiovisual and cinematographic heritage, in particular among young audiences. (EACEA, 2016)

The MEDIA program, and later Creative Europe, were and are explicitly transnational in emphasis: the EC outlaws national interventions in culture, education, business, or industry (so-called "state aid") while at the same time supporting broadly European heritage and culture (under the so-called "cultural exception"). The EC also cannot intervene in national or regional education jurisdictions. Europe is therefore saddled with a contradiction: on the one hand, seeking to support and sustain 30 nations and 400 languages (and many more ethnic groups and languages); on the other, proposing a single "European" identity.

The EC seeks to support film literacy through funding media/film education projects, usually 12 to 18 months in length, with a minimum of three different national partners, and three project languages, costing typically between €60k and €150k. Examples include a project to create a catalog of European feature films for children, along with screening notes and teaching resources; an exchange program for young people learning how to program "cultural cinema"; a website hosting archive materials that "open up" our understanding of classic European films. (Real examples of projects can be found at European Commission, 2013). While these funded projects are explicitly "transnational," as they feature multiple partners, whether they express a common "Europeanness" is a different question. Similarly debatable—or just not understood or explored—is whether, as a collection of competitive and time-limited projects, they have any lasting impact on film culture, either in participating countries, or in Europe more widely.

Without being formally adopted as European instruments, two projects over the last 10 years have attempted to set out some common European standards and principles in media and film education, and received some European endorsement in the form of funding. The *European Framework for Film Education* (BFI, 2015) was created by a group of 25 film educators from European countries, attempting to codify some of the varying and plural approaches to teaching and learning film across Europe. The focus was on identifying a common set of "learning outcomes", that is, those experiences, skills, and knowledge that could confidently be asserted happen as a result of specific types of activity. And the *European Charter for Media Literacy* (Euro Media Literacy, 2009) set out a simple definition of media literacy and then invited individuals, organizations, schools, and others to endorse it in the form of a signature as supporter, sponsor, or provider. To date both the charter and framework have had widespread endorsement, the charter in particular receiving many thousands of signatories and registrations. Both projects could be cited as examples of the power of grassroots, as opposed to top-down, transnational organizing.

Distinctions and definitions: media, film, and literacy

For some time the word "media" has been a catch-all of cultural activity that doesn't come under either traditional artforms or long-established communication practice. So "media" tends to include: anything digital or hosted on the Internet; advertising; radio; TV; and film, which can be any moving image product, found and experienced in a range of platforms from cinemas to YouTube files browsed on a mobile phone. These categories are slippery and overlapping: they mix symbolic meaning-making systems (film as a language and artform) with media of communication (mobile devices; binary code; radio broadcast signals) and with industrial sectors (advertising), while at the same time leaving out traditional meaning-making systems (speech; written language; music) even though these systems are completely integrated into contemporary digital media (one can't use Twitter without being able to write, for example). When one comes to define "media literacy," therefore, those confusions are transferred into classrooms, cinemas, and education and cultural policy.

The EC has attempted to achieve some degree of commonality over film and media literacy by publishing their own definitions:

> *Media literacy* refers to all the technical, cognitive, social, civic and creative capacities that allow us to access and have a critical understanding of and interact with media. These capacities allow us to exercise critical thinking, while participating in the economic, social and cultural aspects of society and playing an active role in the democratic process. (European Commission, 2016a)

And, working within the media definition, they have one for film literacy which reads:

> The level of understanding of a film, the ability to be conscious and curious in the choice of films; the competence to critically watch a film and to analyse its content, cinematography and technical aspects; and the ability to manipulate its language and technical resources in creative moving image production. (European Commission, 2016b)

Participants active in the field over the last 15 years have persistently argued that a media or film literacy properly and fully defined should be about *making* as well as *consuming* media (Buckingham, 2003; Burn & Durran, 2007). The 2013 definition of film literacy signifies a shift in the wider understanding of media and film education: that it should encompass equally the ability to both *read* and *write* in a meaning-making system. Up to that point, media and film education were understood as contributing only to the development of adventurous and discerning audiences, judicious in their choices of film content, but not active users and makers of media or film.

However, the overall notion of "literacy" is itself not so straightforward. A "literacy" is properly understood as the outcome of a learning process: in learning to read and write, one becomes literate. Narrower definitions of literacy tie the process of becoming literate to the acquisition of written language, the most socially powerful and sanctioned meaning-making system in most cultures. The social primacy of literacy in written language in European cultures can be traced to the Reformation in Europe, and the political struggles over translating the Bible into vernacular languages, and then printing it in mass editions. The consequence ever since, in northern European, or at least Anglophone, countries is that these societies are "mortgaged to the Word," and simultaneously suspicious of images. The corollary is that southern European countries, typically Catholic in religion, have been more tolerant of images and less "iconoclastic" (the word literally means to smash images).

There are writers and educators in Europe who are explicitly resistant to the "literacy" model of film. French theorist and critic Alain Bergala is one, arguing that to conceive film-as-language, as "readable object," reduces and "tames" the object of the film, negating its "radical impurity." He argues that film isn't like written language, a symbolic adaptation of the world into another semiotic system; rather, quoting Pasolini, he says film is a "language written from reality ... written in the total and natural language that is action in reality … representing reality by way of reality" (Bergala, 2003/2016, pp. 25–26).

A third conception of literacy can be derived from the work of the new literacy studies (e.g., Cope & Kalantzis, 2000) in which literacy is defined as being able to fully participate in society and culture. A "participatory" definition of literacy decouples it from single specific symbolic systems (like writing), and expresses it as a socially empowering process: being literate in this sense requires different experiences and skills in the 21st century than it did in the 16th or 19th. Today, with the ubiquity of YouTube, on-demand film and TV, tiny gifs and vines on social media, the moving image is an almost ubiquitous mode, so that social and cultural participation increasingly depends on one's ability to make, share, and comment on moving image texts.

In fact, the participatory definition of literacy has the capacity to encompass all of the other literacies. It doesn't implicitly valorize one meaning-making system above another, nor does it endorse different, "special" kinds of literacy. Instead literacy becomes a question of deciding which are the important meaning-making systems at play in a particular time, place, and culture, and how people can develop expressive and communicative capacities within them.

Screening literacy: surveying European film education

In 2012, the EC funded a consortium led by BFI (British Film Institute) to survey and map out the provision and practice of film education across 32 EU and EEA states, essentially asking and attempting to answer a set of questions: Who participates in, and who practices film education? Where does film education happen? How is film education pursued, funded, and organized? And most fundamental of all, why do people practice it at all? The following sections of the entry reproduce the findings of the survey as answers to these questions.

How is film education organized?

The data in *Screening Literacy* suggest three distinct settings for film education: formal education, mandated by national or regional education administrations; cultural spaces, funded and administered by the cultural sector (NGOs; cinemas, festivals, and archives; national film agencies); and a "third space" (Stevenson & Deasy, 2005): in school, but not in the curriculum, typically hosting after-school film clubs and projects.

The separation, or "relative autonomy," of these sectors from each other is striking: funding streams often come from separate ministries. For example, film education in the UK is majority funded by delegated National Lottery funding, via the Department of Culture, Media, and Sport, which is passed on to a national delivery body, Into Film (www.intofilm.org), supporting somewhere around a quarter of a million young people at around £5m per year, most of them in 8000 after-school film clubs. A separate program, reaching around 1000 16- to 19-year-olds aspiring to work in the film industry, is funded by the Department of Education to the tune of £1m per year. But access to film and media through the curriculum, in the form of high school qualifications for around 150 000 14- to 19-year-olds, is funded directly by the education ministry via schools, and there is overlap in provision. At the same time, cinemas around the UK offer programs for school students but only one, the BFI complex on the South Bank in London, directly engages with film and media students. Even though these three programs (funding for Into Film; the BFI Film Academy; and the BFI Southbank schools program) operate out of the same department of the BFI, there is little integration of their work.

Some nations in Europe have deliberately attempted to align or conjoin activity and provision in the formal education sector with that in the cultural sector, by using national strategies for coordinating resources: Denmark, Croatia, and Northern Ireland offer models of very close integration, with the latter justifying a closer focus.

In common with France and Germany, Northern Ireland can trace the emergence of a fully-fledged film education infrastructure to a postwar reconstruction, this time after the end of the "Troubles," a civil war that pitched different communities against each from the late 1960s until the Good Friday Agreement of 1998. The devolution of significant governmental powers in the same year led to control of cultural and educational policy, which created the opportunity for a Film Education Policy Working Group to create a strategy for film education in Northern Ireland. As one participant put it: "we got everyone who could say no into a room until they said yes."

The Group published its strategy in 2004 as *A Wider Literacy* (NIFTC/BFI, 2004). This report mandated a jointly owned film education strategy which included the explicit inclusion of film in the school curriculum framework; a formal film qualification for high school students; creative learning centers for film (and wider subject) training and delivery; a network of after-school film clubs; involvement of the official government education inspectorate (ETI, the Education and Training Inspectorate) in evaluating the effectiveness of the whole program; and access to heritage and global cinema both online and in cinema venues and film festivals (of which Northern Ireland has three). Northern Ireland's film education strategy is an example of a political–cultural–educational process that combined to create one of Europe's most robust and integrated film education infrastructures.

Elsewhere, other examples of close integration of film education functions can be found in Scandinavian countries, with Norway, Denmark, and Sweden's Film Institutes having a national remit and a "national strategy" supported by government. Denmark has a particularly strong interventionist structure whereby 25% of the public funding of film is directed straight to children's film production, distribution, exhibition, and education.

France follows a "dirigiste," more centralized approach to film education. Alain Bergala's *L'Hypothèse Cinéma* (2003/2016) recounts that development out of popular cultural education programs coming out of postwar reconstruction, all the way to the national program *Enfants de Cinéma* in which children from every level of schooling are taken to the cinema to see classic films old and contemporary, chosen by a committee of experts and cineastes. In 2015, *Ecole*, *Collège*, and *Lycée au Cinéma* worked with 11 000 schools, 1200 cinemas, and 750 000 children across the school year, around 12% of children at elementary and high school level (enfants-de-cinema.

com/). Another example, the international program *le Cinéma cent ans de jeunesse*, is discussed at the end of the entry.

Why is film education practiced?

Screening Literacy found very clear differences between the rationales followed in formal education and cultural settings respectively (see Table 1).

The emphasis on textual analysis in school-based film education perhaps reflects the common position of film study in mother tongue language and literature, and the lower ranked rationales for audience development (i.e., encouraging different choices in cinemas) and lesser focus on Europe's film heritage reflect the reluctance of the school sector to follow external drivers in curriculum practice. The higher ranking for audience development, heritage film, and wider viewing in the non-formal sector all reflect the cultural priorities of the cultural sector, and the welcome emphasis on enjoyment reminds us that watching films should after all be (some kind of) a pleasure.

Where does film education actually happen?

Is there a similar set of bifurcations where actual practice is concerned? Cultural bodies tend to emphasize the importance of visits to the cinema (the various "national schools film weeks"; UK's Into Film Festival; the network of Slovenian art house cinemas; a plethora of national cinematheques), and the importance of film festivals, especially those dedicated to children and young people (for example, BUSTER; BUFF; Giffoni; Olympia; Cinekids). The organization Europa Cinemas offers financial support for independent or arthouse cinemas that screen a proportion of non-native language European film, and have programs dedicated to young people (both in and outside school). This sector emphasizes the value of the cinema experience; shared, social, spectacular, "bigger than life," and the place where audiences meet film's heritage; national, global, and European. It tends to value film as art above film as communication, and values feature length, documentary, or short films where the cinematic esthetic is visible.

National film archives follow the imperative to understand the material basis and history of film, usually in a national context. For example, the Filmoteka Szkolna project in Poland circulated DVD box sets of key Polish films to thousands of schools, backed up with a CPD (continuing professional development) program for teachers and a website.

Table 1 Ranking of different rationales for film education in formal and informal settings given by 50 respondents.

Rationale	*Formal sector (%)*	*Non-formal (cultural) sector (%)*
Textual analysis	63	38 (and lowest ranked rationale)
Audience development	31	64
Wider viewing	51	77
Enjoyment	42	74
Heritage—world, European, national	34–42	51–61
Popular cinema access/understanding	22–28	42–48

Source: BFI (2013).

The Czech National Film Archive has created and distributed DVDs of classic Czech animations; the Cineteca di Bologna in Italy runs annual exchange and practice forums on archive film; and the Austrian Film Museum has an important education and publishing program.

On the other hand, in the formal education sector, schools across Europe tend to emphasize the incorporation of film into other subjects: mother tongue literacy, media education (which is rarely compulsory), information communication technologies, art, and history. Film is rarely studied in its own right as a compulsory subject. And there is another dimension to film education in schools: a focus in some nations on a wider range of film including more popular cinema (and television). In the UK this tradition has its origin in cultural studies and the work of Raymond Williams, emphasizing different conceptual underpinnings, the role of industry and institution in shaping film meanings, for example, or a focus on audience behavior, or on facets of representation.

Reflections by way of a conclusion: Europe and "translatable" film culture

The central conundrum of film education in Europe is a reflection of the tension between European and national identities introduced in the opening section of this entry. How can one reconcile the desire for national determination in all things alongside a political desire to align national cultures under a common European identity? The academic Alexis Nouss offers an elegant solution in his conception of "culture in translation," that is, a culture that subsists by virtue of continually reassembling, reimagining, recycling, and redistributing its stories, myths, ideas, and artifacts:

> A culture in translation means: a culture which exists not as a transmission of foundational elements, creating lines of tradition, as do the national traditions, but as a permanent translation of elements which, each time, recreate themselves, although keeping some common features. (Nouss, 2009)

Nouss's examples include the accordion, which has metamorphosed in a 500-year-long journey from Germany across the continent, and the cathedral, "translated" into iterations as different as Scandinavian Lutheran, or Scottish Calvinist, or Spanish Baroque, or Greek, or Eastern Orthodox examples. But one could also use football, food, or indeed film—and film education—as examples of "culture in translation."

Taking the notion of a "culture of translation" can help us better understand film education in Europe. First of all, maybe it can help us out of a compulsion to look for a definitive version of film education, that ought to apply to every setting, nationality, and culture. Film education will unavoidably reflect its cultural hinterland and provenance, whether that's the high esthetic seriousness of France, the communitarian pragmatism of Northern Ireland, Cyprus, Belgium, or other "divided" cultures, or the cultural and political reconstruction of the post-Berlin Wall former Soviet Bloc. Second, "translatability" can help us out of the cul-de-sac of dogmatic and normative versions of film: the moving image after all can be watched on mobile phones, computers and tablets, TV screens, all the way up to spectacular IMAX screens. In each presentation there is an irreducible core of what the moving image is (sound, picture, time), but the screening technology inflects the image, and its reception. In this version, there is no "better" or "worse" platform, no "film fetishism" (Buckingham, 2015), and no "gadgetisme" (Bergala, 2015).

The question of "translating" film education can be better understood through an actual example.

Le Cinéma cent ans de jeunesse is a 20+-year-old (and counting) program of "watching, making, and thinking film" (see Cinémathèque Française, 2016a, 2016b for full descriptions). Over time, it has built a "community of practice" (Wenger, 1998) that in 2017 reached across Europe (from France, to Lithuania and Bulgaria in the east, to Portugal and Spain, Italy, Belgium, Germany, and the UK), and beyond to Brazil, Cuba, and India. Groups of children, aged between 7 and 18, follow a different "theme" every year, which involves exploring a "question of cinema" (Bergala, 2015). Sample questions include "why move the camera?," "the role of the weather in film," the "long take," or "foreground/ background." Participant workshops are offered clips from the world and history of cinema, and a set of exercises that help explore the question: shooting "1-minute Lumiere" films, for example, or comparing the same action filmed in moving camera single takes, with fixed shots. The year culminates in the screening of a set of "film essais," 8-minute films shot and edited by children and young people on the year's theme.

The program is "translated" across nations and continents, age groups, languages, and settings (in school, out of school), while following a set of core precepts to do with film esthetics, children's experiences and views of the world, and the iterative relationship between watching, making, and "thinking" film. With a little push, the program can extend to include examples from YouTube, music video, and advertising, as it does in the UK version.

The program offers a vision of transnational cooperation through film that is not subject to jurisdiction, that is self-regulating, open access, generous, and tolerant, while still being coherent and critical. In its way, it offers a model for how Europe might express, celebrate, and encompass diversity, culture, and history within a kind of communitarian unity.

SEE ALSO: Educational Media, History; European Perspectives on Media Literacy; Media Arts; Media Literacy and Visual Culture; Policy Issues in European Media Literacy

References

Bergala, A. (2003/2016). *L'hypothèse cinéma* [The cinema hypothesis]. Vienna, Austria: Austrian FilmMuseum.

Bergala, A. (2015). An avant garde approach. In *Le Cinéma cent ans de jeunesse*. Retrieved from http://www.cinematheque.fr/cinema100ansdejeunesse/en/projet/an-educational-adventure.html

BFI. (2013). *Screening Literacy: A survey of film education in Europe*. London, England: BFI.

BFI. (2015). *The European Framework for Film Education*. London, England: BFI.

Buckingham, D. (2003). *Media education: Literacy, learning and contemporary culture*. Cambridge, England: Polity Press.

Buckingham, D. (2015). Keynote speech at Media Meets Literacy in Warsaw. Retrieved from http://mediameetsliteracy.eu/keynote/

Burn, A., & Durran, J. (2007). *Media literacy in schools: Practice, production and progression.* London, England: Paul Chapman Publishing.

Cinémathèque Française. (2016a). Retrieved from http://blog.cinematheque.fr/100ans 20152016/

Cinémathèque Française. (2016b). *A cinema education initiative.* Retrieved from http://www.cinematheque.fr/cinema100ansdejeunesse/en/

Cope, B., & Kalantzis, M. (Eds). (2000). *Multiliteracies: Literacy learning and the design of social futures.* London, England: Routledge.

EACEA. (2016). Creative Europe – Film Education 2017 – EACEA/25/2016. Retrieved from https://www.up2europe.eu/calls/creative-europe-film-education-2017-eacea-25-2016_1476.html.

Euro Media Literacy. (2009). *The European charter for media literacy.* Retrieved from http://www.euromedialiteracy.eu/charter.php

European Commission. (2013). *List of selected projects.* Retrieved from https://eacea.ec.europa.eu/sites/eacea-site/files/documents/publication_of_results_audev_2014_en.pdf

European Commission. (2016a). *Media literacy.* Retrieved from https://ec.europa.eu/digital-single-market/en/media-literacy

European Commission. (2016b). *MEDIA programme (2007–2013).* Retrieved from https://eacea.ec.europa.eu/creative-europe/actions/media_en

Gott, B.S. (1932). *The film in national life: Commission on education and cultural films.* London, England: Allen & Unwin.

Hartlapp, M., Metz, J., & Rauh, C. (2014). *Which policy for Europe? Power and conflict inside the European Commission.* Oxford, England: Oxford University Press.

Meno Avilys. (2016). *Anthology of Lithuanian documentary cinema* [DVD]. Available from http://www.menoavilys.org/en/294538/projects/anthology-of-lithuanian-documentary-cinema

NIFTC (Northern Ireland Film and Television Commission) and BFI. (2004). *A wider literacy: The case for moving image education in Northern Ireland.* Belfast, Northern Ireland: NIFTC.

Nouss, A. (2009). European Drift. Retrieved from https://www.academia.edu/1721965/European_Drift

Roddick, N. (1985). If the United States spoke Spanish, we would have a film industry. In M. Auty & N. Roddick. *British cinema now.* London, England: BFI.

Stevenson, L., & Deasy, R.J. (2005). *Third space: When learning matters.* Washington, DC: Arts Education Partnership.

Wenger, E. (1998). *Communities of practice: Learning, meaning, and identity.* Cambridge, England: Cambridge University Press.

Further reading

BFI. (2016). *BFI2022: Supporting the future of UK film.* Retrieved from http://www.bfi.org.uk/2022/

Buckingham, D. (2007). *Beyond technology: Children's learning in the age of digital culture.* London, England: Polity Press.

Burn, A., & Reid, M. (2012). Screening literacy: Reflecting on models of film education in Europe. *Nordic Journal of Digital Literacy, 7.*

European Audiovisual Observatory. (2016). *Mapping of media literacy practices and actions in EU-28.* Retrieved from https://rm.coe.int/media-literacy-mapping-report-en-final-pdf/1680783500

Hartai, L. (2014). *Report on formal media education in Europe.* Retrieved from https://eavi.eu/european-media-education-study/

London School of Economics. (2014). *Media Policy Project Planner.* Retrieved from http://blogs.lse.ac.uk/media-policy-planner/2014/03/20/media-literacy-in-the-uk-and-europe/

Reia-Baptista, V., Burn. A., Reid, M., & Cannon, M. (2014). Screening Literacy: Reflecting on models of film education in Europe. *Revista Latina de Comunicacion Social, 69*, 354–365. Retrieved from http://www.revistalatinacs.org/069/paper/1015_UK/RLCS_paper1015en.pdf

Reid, M. (2015). Le Cinéma cent ans de jeunesse: An integrated film education programme. *Media Education Journal, 58.*

Mark Reid trained as an English and drama teacher in 1991, before teaching English, media, and film for 6 years in a high school in south London, UK. He joined the British Film Institute as Teacher Training Officer in 1998, to establish distance learning MA modules for media and film teachers. In 2006 he re-established the learning program in the cinemas at BFI Southbank in London, where he has remained since. He has led a number of Europe-wide projects, including Screening Literacy (2012), and the Framework for Film Education (2015). He is currently Head of UK Learning Programs at BFI.

Game Design in Media Literacy Education

REBECCA B. REYNOLDS
Rutgers University, USA

Interactive games are one of the most popular and engaging media forms in use today. An array of communicative, narrative, filmic, ludic, and digital forms converge within games. In addition to serving as a platform for entertainment and interactivity, the promise and potential for games to be used as environments to elicit students' core curriculum domain learning, new literacy development, and computational thinking has also been recognized. Thus, games are growing in popularity for their purposeful didactic educational uses.

Scholars of gaming and learning have identified game play, production, design, and development as activities that merit the application of "literacy" perspectives. For instance, video game playing has been described as a form of "multimodal literacy," such that meaning, thinking, and learning are linked to words, images, actions, and sounds within games (Gee, 2007). Gee proposes that video game play can teach us how to situate and extract meaning in other multimodal spaces (2007, p. 40). Critical game studies approaches further explore the cultural aspects of gameplay and their effects.

Game *design* requires further technical knowledge of the programming code, design attributes, and game mechanics underlying game play interfaces. Contrasting game *play* with game *design*, Harel Caperton (2010) poses the question: "How can game players' system-understanding and literacy in the semiotic domain of videogame playing practices be complete, without providing them with the opportunity to learn how videogames are *made,* through engagement in the game production process?" (Harel Caperton, 2010). Harel Caperton (2010) points out that omitting game design when discussing gaming literacy is akin to omitting writing when considering traditional English language literacy instruction, and merely teaching students how to read. Her work adopts a constructionist pedagogical stance, stemming from earlier research and development at MIT Media Lab (e.g., Papert & Harel, 1991), placing value on the deep

The International Encyclopedia of Media Literacy. Renee Hobbs and Paul Mihailidis (Editors-in-Chief), Gianna Cappello, Maria Ranieri, and Benjamin Thevenin (Associate Editors).

learning that can emerge when one learns how to design and develop an interactive game for an audience to play.

Today's availability of a range of programming platform and curricular options (e.g., Unity, Javascript, Flash, GameMaker, Shiva, Unreal, Stencyl, GameSalad, Scratch, Globaloria, Taleblazer, Microworlds, and others) make game design an increasingly feasible endeavor for Primary, Intermediate, and Secondary Education, given professional development among educators. Game design has potential to enrich media literacy endeavors, allowing broadening of media production work to include more complex digital design and computer programming, along with conceptualization and application of interactivity. With the array of knowledge domains represented in game design, it may be a particularly efficient, albeit complex, vehicle for the delivery of a comprehensive form of media literacy instruction, one that incorporates computational thinking, a growing priority in the STEM (science, technology, engineering, and mathematics) educational agenda adopted by many policymakers.

Thus, this encyclopedia entry highlights game design pedagogy for its strong potential in building critical media and digital content creation dispositions, practices, and understandings, in today's students.

Gaming prevalence

Video gaming is on the rise. Sixty-three percent of US households are home to at least one game player who plays video games for >3 hours per week, and 65% of households own a device used to play video games (ESA, 2016). Twenty-seven percent of all gamers are under 18 years of age, and 29% are 18 to 35 years old, thus a majority of all players are 35 and under (ESA, 2016). Fifty-nine percent of gamers are male, 41% female (ESA, 2016). Consumers today access games on devices including consoles, PCs, mobile devices, and tablets; content is accessed through software, discs, online distribution, subscription or download services, mobile apps, and virtual or augmented reality peripherals (VR/AR) (DaSilva, Murray, & Lieberman, 2016). The social gaming sector is also growing rapidly. Fifty-four percent of the most active game players report playing games with others, and 48% of those most active play social games meant for multiplayers, indicating the social nature of the activity (DaSilva, Murray, & Lieberman, 2016). Social and casual games include e-sports, also growing in popularity, which involve competitive, sometimes professional-level video gaming tournaments in live stadiums or online spaces (DaSilva, Murray, & Lieberman, 2016).

Revenue growth for the video game industry is increasing faster than film entertainment and music sectors in North America, Asia Pacific, Latin America, Western Europe and the Middle East and North Africa (DaSilva, Murray, & Lieberman, 2016). The global video game industry has evolved to become a $100 billion industry as of 2016 (up 8.5% compared to 2015), and the industry is constantly innovating and bringing new applications to market, eclipsing other media forms such as film in revenues (Newzoo, 2016). For the first time, mobile gaming will take a larger share than PC games, with

$36.9 billion in revenues in 2016, up 21.3% globally (2016). Esports are primed to post earnings at around $621 million in 2016 (DaSilva, Murray, & Lieberman, 2016).

Critical game studies

Game play offers players the experience of simulated enactment and expression in a given immersive contextual environment. As a medium of expression, a cultural activity and industry, games and their development have potential to enrich societal engagement and discourse. "Critical game studies" is becoming an academic domain of importance in which scholars explore the rich cultural genre of games, and build critical theory around themes such as game narrative, character representation, discourse dynamics, design aspects, mechanics, and gameplay effects. Critical perspectives may involve Marxist, feminist, and/or racial justice frames of reference vis-à-vis game content, production, and play. This work is interdisciplinary, and often seen represented within academic disciplines of communication, media studies, and information science.

Adjacent to this scholarship, and intersecting with the learning sciences discipline, is research on the cognitive and learning processes that occur during video game play. One leading scholar of gaming literacy is James Paul Gee, who, with colleagues, launched the Games, Learning, and Society (GLS) conference in 2004 as a scholarly venue in this arena. Such work addresses the nature of cognitive and emotional development, literacy practices, and thinking and learning during gameplay in a range of gaming contexts including entertainment games, along with learning games that are developed with more explicit learning goals (e.g., Gee, 2005, 2007, 2008; Hayes, 2008; Shaffer, 2006; Squire, 2005, 2006; Steinkuehler, 2006, 2007).

While not the focus herein, critical game studies and gaming literacy research bear mentioning and consideration as additional areas of exploration for those interested in applying an approach that involves learners in game *play* with professionally designed gaming platforms (whether designed with educational and/or entertainment-oriented goals and objectives). Such approaches often invite teachers to develop curricular or pedagogical activities in an in-school or after-school context that augment and structure the central game play of a commercial gaming platform, to facilitate a greater extent of learning (beyond that which can be provided by the game's *play* alone).

Game design

Media literacy scholars such as Hobbs (e.g., 2010), Kellner and Share (e.g., 2005), Potter (e.g., 2004), and McChesney and Nichols (e.g., 2002) have long discussed the beneficial value of media production experiences for young people in offering epistemic learning opportunities that simulate the activities of media professionals in the cultural industries and that yield deeper understanding of a given medium through constructive creation. Practicing productive media content creation can cultivate more critical dispositions and knowledge about a given medium in those who practice creation. Constructive media production is a hallmark of media education. As games gain more prominence as popular media forms, game design as pedagogy grows in relevance and demand.

Constructionist perspectives

Much of the scholarly literature on educational game design emerges from the constructionist lineage of scholarship out of MIT Media Lab. In looking to the constructionist educational literature, we can identify key linkages between these works, and media literacy educational goals.

Constructionism is a teaching philosophy and framework for learning and educative action (diSessa & Cobb, 2004) that builds upon Vygotsky's (1962) social constructivist theory and Piaget's constructivist theory. In constructionist learning, students engage in conscious construction of a computational artifact in a workshop-style group educational environment (Papert & Harel, 1991). This approach holds that individuals learn best when actively engaging in a personally meaningful creative technological pursuit, while sensing that their work is valued as part of a larger enterprise (Barron & Darling-Hammond, 2008; Stager, 2001). Building upon social constructivist theory, constructionist interventions are designed to facilitate computational thinking and learning socially through dialogue, interaction, and mentoring with peers, teachers, and professional experts, along with information resources. Learners create a complex computational artifact of their own design, often through programming and coding, representing a concept or knowledge domain in the artifact.

In constructionist game design, students create games *about* topics and themes that they research and represent in the game dynamics or narrative, that have potential to build on their classroom learning. This is one area in which critical game studies perspectives may be relevant, in that messages and game concepts developed by learners have potential to subvert formulaic dominant paradigm themes and genres we often see in commercial entertainment type mainstream games. Nevertheless, more instructional design work is needed to support critical perspectives among learners in game design contexts.

Creating a game bearing thematic content of a learner's own device can also be motivating. Unlike traditional computer science (CS) curriculum, which has tended to focus on principles-first learning of CS, game design gives students a driving purpose for programming; publishing and sharing an interactive artifact that conveys meaning they have will to express (Harel Caperton, 2010).

Grover and Pea (2013) note that game design is "ideal" as a pedagogy for introduction to CS, in motivating and engaging, offering a means for active student exploration of computational thinking principles and practices. In the US, the National Science Foundation (NSF) has supported game design as one instructional design potential approach for addressing the need to expand the reach of CS and CT (computational thinking) educational opportunities into US schools, which means funding. For instance, with NSF support, Reppening, Webb, and Ioannidou (2010) developed a checklist for incorporating CT into public school settings as an additional subject domain, via game design.

Learning effects of game design

The learning effects of game design instruction have been studied rigorously. Kafai and Burke (2016) conducted a meta-analysis of this terrain, evaluating 55 research articles on game design. The authors found that the largest number of studies focus on learning programming, followed by the learning of other academic subjects. They noted that far fewer studies have focused on social and cultural dimensions of constructionist gaming, but note the importance of more work in this area (Kafai & Burke, 2016). Their article organizes the meta-analysis into consideration of: (i) personal dimensions of game design (such as learning coding, learning content, and learning how to learn); (ii) social dimensions of game design (such as collaborations and communities in which game making can take on various forms); and (iii) cultural dimensions of game design (e.g., who participates and can participate). In summarizing their conclusions, Kafai and Burke (2016) state that "children's capacity to create and modify digital games with and for each other offers them a tremendous advantage in understanding the ever-changing nature of digital media, public domain, and what it means to problem solve and participate." Informed by Grimes and Fields (2015), they position video game making "as a unique, early channel for children to comprehend the social, economic, and civil power of 'making' and 'sharing'" (Kafai & Burke, 2016). The authors emphasize that game design can enable students to grasp computational thinking through the creation of diverse user interfaces, and through understanding how these interfaces scale in complexity and must conform to a gameplayer's human needs and behaviors (Kafai & Burke, 2016).

Digital literacy perspectives on game design

Constructionist researchers tend to emphasize the CS and CT outcomes that have potential to be cultivated in game design. In an article entitled "Defining, Designing for, and Measuring, 'Social Constructivist Digital Literacy' Development in Learners: A Proposed Framework," Reynolds (2016) makes key linkages to digital and media literacy perspectives. This article presents a framework of six "contemporary learning practices" that have been identified in well-conceived, theoretically driven game design educational contexts. Her full article describes in detail the design of one such integrated educational solution called Globaloria, which offers a comprehensive game design curriculum, platform, and resources. More than 40 000 students have used Globaloria's computer science platform and courses over the past 12 years, and more than 1100 teachers and education leaders were trained in the USA between 2006 and 2018.

The article recommends that the framework of practices, when offered as a coordinated set through a comprehensive curriculum like Globaloria, comprises a particularly felicitous way of instilling "social constructivist digital literacy." Table 1 identifies the six main dimensions of learning practices.

Reynolds (2016) argued that the breadth of practices outlined is authentic to many real-world professional contexts involving digital media design and development. The framework's dimensions build upon social constructivist learning theory, proposing

Table 1 Six theoretically driven "contemporary learning practices comprising social constructivist digital literacy."

Contemporary learning practice domains	*Exemplary activities representing each practice domain*
1. Create	Invention, creation, and completion of a digital project stemming from an original idea
2. Manage	Project planning, project management, teamwork (e.g., role-taking, task delegation), problem-solving
3. Publish	Publishing, distribution of self-created digital artifacts to an audience, community of peers
4. Socialize	Giving and getting feedback about project through social interaction, participation, exchange
5. Research	Inquiry, information seeking, agentive use of resources to support the artifact's topic, message, design, execution
6. Surf/play	Surfing, experimentation, and play with existing networked web applications and tools

Source: Reynolds (2016).

that expertise within each of these practice dimensions is optimally cultivated *in coordination*; that is, within a game design course like Globaloria in which the learning objectives encompass *all of these practice domains*. In such a setting, students engage in contemporary learning practices (CLPs) 4–6 in service of CLPs 1–3. Creating a fully functioning game as a task-driven goal drives the purposive need to surf/play, research, socialize, publish, and manage. Key to the success of this integrated model are these factors (Reynolds, 2016): high quality pedagogy, teacher professional development, beneficial information resources such as programming tutorials, customization of online learning platform supports that afford students' social communication, sharing, and exchange, among others.

Reynolds (2016) proposes that when the CLPs are offered in coordination, allowing for ample time on task for students and teachers, such educational experiences will help prepare students for active participation and success in further computing education, future productive work environments, and, importantly, online digital cultures of democratic, civic, and societal participation.

Designing game design learning environments

Constructionist literatures on game design often include discussion of the workshop-based learning settings in which game design instruction is offered. Constructionist learning environments are explicitly designed to be workshop-based, and facilitative of students' social engagement and productivity driven expressive discourse, while also supporting their significant time on task, and affording time for learner reflection (Papert & Harel, 1991). John Seely Brown (e.g., 2005, 2006) advocates many of the same general learning principles as discussed in constructionism, in his scholarship on "communities of practice" and 21st-century learning. Such learning occurs in the context of high-density computer cultures, resembling the ways MIT (Massachusetts Institute of Technology) mathematicians, artists, musicians, and engineers collaborate on complex design problems. Seely Brown addresses the crucial value of learning through tinkering, preferably in a studio-like environment, and in a "learning-to-be" model of role-taking that emerges from joining and becoming a full participant in a learning community. This contrasts with "learning about" approaches to technology development, which are disconnected from how this work is completed in applied settings of innovation.

Seely Brown states,

> Today's students want to create and learn at the same time. They want to pull content into use immediately. They want it situated and actionable – all aspects of learning-to-be, which is also an identity-forming activity. This path bridges the gap between knowledge and knowing. (p. 6)

As students engage in teamwork and co-construction, they learn about productive roles, and then move on to a greater extent of role-taking. Facilitating role-taking in students requires experiential active educational opportunities. Seely Brown (2005) states that,

> since nearly all of the significant problems of tomorrow are likely to be systemic problems – problems that can't be addressed by any one specialty – our students will need to feel comfortable working in cross disciplinary teams that encompass multiple ways of knowing. (p. 2)

Game design offers the opportunity for young people to try on a number of different roles during game design, engaging in epistemic experiences that may allow them to imagine new possibilities for themselves.

Building in critical perspectives

A number of models for "culturally responsive teaching" (CRT) in computer science contexts have been developed, to encourage greater participation by underrepresented populations including girls and students of color, in computing. For instance, in the USA Globaloria has worked predominantly within rural low-income school communities in the states of West Virginia, Wyoming, and Oklahoma, as well as Hispanic immigrant and English language learner communities in Austin, TX, Houston, TX, San Jose, CA, and black and Hispanic students in Queens and the Bronx, NYC. CRT approaches employed include close consultative help provided to schools in developing a customized implementation plan attuned to their local needs, creation of a specialized bilingual game design CS curriculum for Spanish-speaking learners, extension of a mentor network of "help center coding coaches," employed full- and part-time, who are past Globaloria teachers and students who help schools and teachers onboard and manage the program.

Other related approaches include Scott, Sheridan, and Clark's work in culturally responsive computing (CRC) through game design which directly addresses questions of student identity development, intersectionality, and the role of a collaborative interdisciplinary team of students, teachers, families, and researchers (2015). There is no "one size fits all" solution for successful game design pedagogy; however, many resources exist for those who may wish to try this, and customize a solution uniquely situated to an education practitioner's local needs and context.

In the US, game development companies provide employment for growing numbers of professionals, especially on the West Coast, with companies in California and Washington leading the way, followed by Texas and New York (Newzoo, 2016). Career paths in the game industry include positions for animators, producers, audio engineers, creative directors, devops engineers, designers, programmers, artists, and editors, not to mention the usual business functions in marketing, sales, IT (information technology), HR (human resources), accounting, and management. Professionally, the information and technology sectors writ large are promising areas of economic growth toward which we must prepare the young.

Further, given the prominence of game play among young people, critical approaches to game literacies are needed, to cultivate discerning audiences of users. Game design educational experiences are emblematic of the longstanding media literacy traditions that invoke media production as a way to cultivate deeper understanding and critical literacies of media in learners. The research tradition and scholarly literature around game design is quite strong, as it intersects with computer science education, a growing priority as a "STEM" discipline of focus in national educational agendas. With effort on the part of educators and instructional designers, game design is well positioned as an activity to enable building of critical media and digital content creation dispositions, practices, knowledge, and understandings, in today's students, across a continuum of critical lenses.

SEE ALSO: Adolescent Literacy in a Digital World; Coding as Literacy; Computer Labs in Primary and Secondary Education; Creative Works; Digital Divide; Digital Divide and Web-Use Skills; Digital Literacy; Digital Storytelling; Game Media Literacy; Media Education Research and Creativity; Remix Culture; Social Media as Media Literacy; Understanding Media Literacy and DIY Creativity in Youth Digital Productions

References

Barron, B., & Darling-Hammond, L. (2008). Teaching for meaningful learning: A review of research on inquiry-based and cooperative learning. Edutopia. Retrieved from http://www.edutopia.org/pdfs/edutopia-teaching-for-meaningful-learning.pdf

DaSilva, A., Murray, B., & Lieberman, M. (2016). *2016 Top markets report: Media and entertainment*. Annual report of the International Trade Administration. Retrieved from http://www.trade.gov/topmarkets/pdf/Media_and_Entertainment_Top_Markets_Report.pdf

diSessa, A., & Cobb, P. (2004). Ontological innovation and the role of theory in design experiments. *Journal of the Learning Sciences, 13*(1), 77–103.

ESA (Entertainment Software Association). (2016). *Essential facts about the computer and video game industry*. Annual Report. Retrieved from http://essentialfacts.theesa.com/Essential-Facts-2016.pdf

Gee, J.P. (2005). Learning by design: Good video games as learning machines. *E-Learning, 2*(1), 5–16.

Gee, J.P. (2007). *What video games have to teach us about learning and literacy*. New York, NY: Palgrave Macmillan.

Gee, J.P. (2008). Learning in semiotic domains: A social and situated account. In M. Prinsloo & M. Baynham (Eds.), *Literacies, global and local* (pp. 137–149). Philadelphia, PA: John Benjamins Publishing Company.

Grimes S., & Fields D. (2015). Children's media making but not sharing. The potential and limitations of child-specific DIY media websites for a more inclusive media landscape. *Media International Australia, 54*(1), 112–122.

Grover, S., & Pea, R.D. (2013). Computational thinking in K-12: A review of the state of the field. *Educational Researcher, 42*(1), 38–43.

Harel Caperton, I. (2010). Toward a theory of game-media literacy: Playing and building as reading and writing. *International Journal of Gaming and Computer-Mediated Simulations, 2*(1), 1–16.

Hayes, E. (2008). Girls, gaming, and trajectories of technological expertise. In Y.B. Kafai, C. Heeter, J. Denner, & J. Sun (Eds.), *Beyond Barbie and Mortal Kombat: New perspectives on gender, games, and computing*. Boston, MA: MIT Press.

Hobbs, R. (2010). Digital & media literacy: A plan of action. White paper issued by the Aspen Institute. Retrieved from http://mediaeducationlab.com/

Kafai, Y.B., & Burke, Q. (2016). Constructionist gaming: Understanding the benefits of making games for learning. *Educational Psychologist, 50*(4), 313–334.

Kellner, D., & Share, J. (2005). Toward critical media literacy: Core concepts, debates, organizations and policy. *Discourse: Studies in the Cultural Politics of Education, 26*(3), 369–386.

McChesney, R.W., & Nichols, J. (2002). *Our media, not theirs: The democratic struggle against corporate media*. New York, NY: Seven Stories.

Newzoo. (2016). Global games market report. Annual report. Retrieved from https://newzoo.com/insights/articles/global-games-market-reaches-99-6-billion-2016-mobile-generating-37/

Papert, S., & Harel, I. (Eds.). (1991). *Constructionism*. Norwood, NJ: Ablex Publishing.

Potter, W.J. (2004). Argument for the need for a cognitive theory of media literacy: Media literacy in the future. *American Behavioral Scientist, 48*(2), 266–272.

Reppening, A., Webb, D., & Ioannidou, A. (2010). Scalable game design and the development of a checklist for getting computational thinking into public schools. *The 41st ACM Technical Symposium on Computer Science Education*. Milwaukee, WI: ACM Press.

Reynolds, R. (2016). Defining, designing for, and measuring "social constructivist digital literacy" development in learners: A proposed framework. *Educational Technology Research & Development, 64*(4), 735–762.

Scott, K., Sheridan, K., & Clark, K. (2015). Culturally responsive computing: A theory revisited. *Learning, Media and Technology, 40*(4), 412–436.

Seely Brown, J. (2005). *New learning environments for the 21st century*. Paper presented at the forum for the future of higher education, Aspen Symposium, Aspen, CO.

Seely Brown, J. (2006). New learning environments for the 21st century: Exploring the edge. *Change Magazine*, September/October.

Shaffer, D.W. (2006). *How computer games help children learn*. New York, NY: Palgrave Macmillan.

Squire, K.D. (2005). Educating the fighter. *On the Horizon, 13*(2), 75–88.

Squire, K. (2006). From content to context: Videogames as designed experience. *Educational Researcher, 35*(8), 19–29.

Stager, G. (2001). *Computationally-rich constructionism and at-risk learners*. Paper presented at the 2001 World Conference on Computers in Education, Copenhagen, Denmark. Retrieved from http://www.stager.org/wcce/index.html

Steinkuehler, C.A. (2006). Massively multiplayer online videogaming as participation in a discourse. *Mind, Culture, and Activity, 13*(1), 38–52.

Steinkuehler, C. (2007). Massively multiplayer online gaming as a constellation of literacy practices. *eLearning, 4*(3), 297–318.

Vygotsky, L.S. (1962). *Thought and language.* Cambridge, MA: MIT Press.

Rebecca B. Reynolds is Associate Professor in the School of Communication & Information at Rutgers University, and faculty affiliate of the Center for International Scholarship on School Librarianship. Her research addresses the development of e-learning systems for formal and informal learning in a broad range of affinity spaces. Publishing in the fields of information science, educational technology, and the learning sciences, she has received early career award grant funding from the Institute for Museum and Library Services, and has received two faculty department awards recognizing her research and teaching.

Game Media Literacy

CHRISTIAN J. SWERTZ
University of Vienna, Austria

Game media literacy can be defined as educational processes that specifically manifest themselves through the interaction with games. These processes include learning that takes place while playing games, education that happens while designing games, learning metalanguages to reflect games, and learning how to teach from gameplay. Applying games to teaching and learning content, as in serious games or edutainment products, is not included in the definition of game media literacy.

While the expression "game media literacy" is used by some scholars, most scholars use the term "game literacy." It seems to be obvious for most researchers that games are media, although the term "media" is seldom used. Instead, the word "text" is preferred as a synonym for "media" in game media literacy. Occasionally, "text" is replaced by "narrative," which leads to expressions like "digital multimedia narratives," a broader expression that refers to meaning-making. Sometimes, the term "gaming literacy" is also used. Since the different terms are not connected to fundamentally different concepts, but discuss different aspects of the same phenomenon, the term "game media literacy" can be employed as a synonym for the different expressions used in the literature.

The discussion on game media literacy started after the turn of the millennium. If there was a starting point, the book *What Video Games Have to Teach Us about Learning and Literacy* by James Paul Gee (2004) can be considered as such. Most papers refer in some respect to Gee's work. Since the discussion on game media literacy did not start before 2004, there are scarcely any substantial changes yet in the understanding of game media literacy.

Most papers highlight the common use of video games, mainly by young people, as a starting point that justifies researching and teaching game media literacy. All understandings of game media literacy are connected to definitions of text. The first element of contemporary definitions of text is most often a delimitation to narrow the definition of the term. Narrow definitions are assumed to restrict it to printed texts and to texts that are regarded as high culture. In contrast, the definition of text in the field of game media literacy includes multimedia and multimodal communication and popular culture. In turn, high-culture print artifacts are hardly considered. This is obvious for it is difficult to play with such things.

As it is connected to a broad understanding of text, game media literacy can be seen in the context of media literacy. With the term "media literacy," objectives for teaching and learning about media are addressed and consequences for pedagogies are derived. This includes a focus on the relation between making (as creative hands-on production) and critical reflection. Considering practices from certain media cultures is also part of both concepts. Still, the suggestion to learn how to teach from games is rejected as uncritical in some theories of media literacy. The uncritical tendency can be explained by the fact that theories of game media literacy are focused on online gamers and their culture. Refusing to play games is not considered as an option in these theories.

Playing games is understood as reading and creating games is understood as writing. In the discussion about game media literacy, four different perspectives can be distinguished:

- learning in games,
- learning about games,
- learning by game design,
- learning from games.

These perspectives are discussed in detail in the following sections.

Learning in games

Learning in games focuses on the skills gamers acquire while playing.

The assumption of a possible transfer of positive skills to people's lifeworlds (Habermas, 1985) is connected with the perspective of learning in games. In this respect there seems to be a contradiction to the widely accepted argument that violent behavior in games is not transferred to real life. While this argument is widely accepted by scholars of game media literacy, it is hardly explicitly discussed in game media literacy research. This missing discussion can be explained by the common assumption of players' reflective capacities. Due to their reflective capacities, game players are capable of distinguishing between violent pictures on screens and strategies they use to win games. Based on this distinction they transfer strategies, for example to win competitions in markets, but not the pictures that show weapons.

This is researched in a study by Witting (2007). She conducted qualitative interviews with 80 computer game players. The results of her texturing analysis, which is based on the comprehensive transfer model by Fritz (2005), show that violence is not transferred to actions in the real world, while patterns like precise observations and quick reactions are. In turn, values are transferred to the game world. Still, supporting critical reflection by media education is shown as effective for sustaining the boundary between virtual and real worlds.

The assumption of a possible transfer of positive skills is expressed in the development of specific pedagogies that foster the transfer of skills learned in games and by participating in the gaming culture. One pedagogy that fosters the transfer of skills is termed "epistemic games." In epistemic games, the transfer of skills is supported by combining action and reflection in contexts that simulate the way practitioners develop their epistemic frames (Shaffer, 2006).

Competencies that are developed in games also include spoken language literacy. Empirical evidence from the field of online gaming suggests that this applies to native speakers and to English-language learners of all ages. Other studies show a transfer of collaboration skills. This is connected to the fact that many games require collaboration. If a game requires collaboration, the educational objectives are expressed in the structure of the games. In this respect, the game mechanics, the game engine, and so on are considered as texts. In these texts game designers and producers express their ideas and thus become teachers for gamers.

Beside spoken language literacy and collaboration, identity development is discussed in the context of game media literacy. When critics argue that being an avatar in online games hardly helps to solve problems in real life, they assume a straight transfer from games to people's lifeworlds. In contrast to this assumption, game media literacy research shows that learning to play with identity is the crucial point here. In games, people can alter their identity without exposing their personality. If one identity fails, they just create a new one. By playing with online identities they can discover concepts that might be transferred to other parts of their lifeworlds.

Finally, the idea of learning from games includes learning content like history or economics while playing off-the-shelf video games that are not intended as serious games.

It is also argued that information ecology needs to be considered when discussing what is learned by playing games, because playing games is often connected with participation in online communities. This aspect is located between learning in games and learning about games, since online communication in a player community is not playing games but communicating about games. Additionally, it does not only take place while playing, and the communication is often not restricted to a particular game or playing games at all.

Learning about games

The second perspective is learning about games. In this perspective, game media literacy is connected to critical thinking, consideration of cultural contexts, creative actions, and the protection against the capacity of games to harm players. Learning objectives are not derived from games but from general theories, like theories of justice. Games are used as opportunities to facilitate learning objectives in a way that considers the common interests of learners.

Critical thinking is connected to the consideration of inequality, diversity, and ideology. To teach critical thinking, the importance of a metalanguage to analyze games is mentioned (Bogost, 2006). Thus, some papers discuss metalanguages and even meta-metalanguages that cover more than one type of text. Connected with the development of metalanguages, teacher training is mentioned as an issue (Apperley & Walsh, 2012). While teaching grammar as a metalanguage in lessons that focus on the printed text is common knowledge for language teachers, this is not the case for the grammar of games or other texts. This is connected to the fact that a commonly accepted metalanguage for games has not been developed yet. Sometimes, systemic functional linguistics is suggested as a background from which to develop such a grammar of games.

While the importance of a metalanguage is discussed, it is not assumed that players develop a metalanguage or critical thinking by just playing games. It is assumed that teaching about games through reflective postgame activities is necessary to reach these objectives. This is researched in a quantitative study by Treumann et al. They researched the media literacy of 3200 adolescents in a quantitative study based on the media literacy model by Baacke (1997). The results of a cluster analysis show that observed patterns of media literacy are connected to certain types of media use, ranging from 20.4% learning oriented through 20.3% uncritical naive, 19.1% clueless integrated, 12% all-rounder, and 7.8% loner to 3.2% creative maker (Treumann et al., 2007, 674ff). These results show that teaching a metalanguage can be effective.

To teach metalanguages, pedagogies are necessary. Suggestions for pedagogies range from analyzing games through Socratic dialogues to the development of games, with a clear preference for the latter. The same applies to the development of resources that protect players against possible harmful effects of games. As resources, the abilities to manage the effects of inertia, to reflect on the social-motivational dynamics of games, and to develop a psychological distance to game events are mentioned (Klimt, 2009).

Learning by game design

The third perspective, learning by game design, might also be understood as learning about games (Buckingham & Burn, 2007), while the instructional design changes from reflecting by theory to reflecting by doing. In literature, this perspective is sometimes addressed as game design literacy or gaming literacy. It starts with game mods (alterations that modify game design or gameplay) and continues to game making. Learning by game design implies a game perspective. In this perspective, game design shapes the way of understanding the world and being in the world (Zimmerman, 2009). This claim can in turn be understood as an implicit reaction to the use of digital electric Turing machines, which are toys and thus create a bias towards play (Swertz, 1999).

Studies show that game design literacy requires well-trained educational staff that not only have experience in playing, designing and implementing games, but also have adequate knowledge about video game theory. Benefits of teaching game design literacy are the development of critical thinking, collaboration skills, creativity, and an adult attitude toward games. This is sometimes connected to the necessity to learn and use a specialist game-maker language that allows for reflection in action. In a case study with some teenagers who used Gamestar Mechanics to learn how to develop games, Salen (2007) has shown that teenagers can learn how to develop games and develop a sound understanding of a design system while doing so.

Learning by game design has become a common practice for teaching computational thinking. As studies demonstrate, teaching computational thinking and critical thinking at the same time is quite possible. Still, the integration of both aspects is taken into account in some concepts only.

Learning from games

In the fourth perspective, learning from games is emphasized. In this perspective it is suggested that teaching and learning methods used in games to teach how to play them be transferred to real-life settings, especially in schools. Using elements of games like high-score lists, quests, the interactive structure of games, or the opportunity to play with identities in other contexts, is sometimes also labeled "gamification." Gamification theories are developed by analyzing games. Principles for learning, such as the achievement principle, the probing principle, and the insider principle (considering the learner as an insider and producer), are derived from analyzing games and observing gamers (Gee, 2007). They support the creation of engaging and immersive learning experiences (Squire, 2008).

In an experimental control-group study, Domínguez et al. (2012) researched this approach in a beginner course on information and computer technology with 80 participants. In the gamified version of the course, students scored better in activities and practical exercises but worse in the final examination. Overall, there were no significant differences, which is not astonishing since "no significant differences" has been a stable result of research about the introduction of digital media in teaching and learning processes since the 1970s.

It is also assumed that the widespread use of digital games has an impact on what is accepted as "literate" in society today. Thus we also have to learn from games what game media literacy might mean. In this respect, the term "game media literacy" needs to be understood as a temporal dialectical process that shapes gaming practices and is shaped by such practices.

Contexts of game media literacy

These four perspectives are theoretical distinctions that do not imply fundamental differences. On the contrary, they are all related to each other and can be connected in practice. One obvious example is a gamified game design project at school. Apparently, a gamified instructional design needs to apply gamification principles. These principles can also be discussed with the learners in an appropriate metalanguage so as to give a first opportunity for critical thinking, in this case about gamification.

Additionally, when designing games, the limitations and structures of the games need to be considered. When playing the designed games, learners learn what they invest in the game. They teach themselves and reflect on their own design decisions.

While most of the examples used to illustrate game media literacy are taken from digital games, game media literacy is not restricted to digital games. With the concept of game media literacy, board games, face-to-face role-play games, card games, and other types of games are included as well. This opens up the concept for teachers and learners not familiar with or not wishing to become familiar with digital games. One example is that of librarians who challenge students with knowledge quests. By doing so, they turn the library into a game. The rules of the library that determine where you can get gadgets or skills are interpreted as a game engine, and the librarians turn themselves into some sort of nonplayable artificial-intelligence-like characters.

As game media literacy is specific to games, it is assumed that the educational processes indicated by the term do not take place while people are using other media or while learning in other settings. A game is considered as an esthetic sphere in its own right. This can be connected to the famous words of Schiller: "Denn, um es endlich auf einmal herauszusagen, der Mensch spielt nur, wo er in voller Bedeutung des Worts Mensch ist, und er ist nur da ganz Mensch, wo er spielt [For, to finally speak it out at once, man only plays when he is in the fullest meaning of the word a human being, and he is only fully a human when he plays]" (Schiller, 1795), although this connection is hardly elaborated in game media literacy theories.

The discussion about game media literacy is connected to the discussion about dangers caused by video games. This connection is addressed by terms like "alternative literacy practices," which suggests a positive meaning of playing video games. In this respect, the term "game media literacy" is used as a combat term to defend video game culture against raiders from book culture and religious fanatic cultures, predominantly Christian religious fanatic cultures that consider games in general and video games in particular as the Devil's work. A reluctance to embrace games has a long tradition in Christian culture, while in the scientific discourse playing games has been shown as essential for human culture (Huizinga, 1949).

Based on discourse theory—the idea of respecting different discourses and rejecting the placing of bans on certain discourses—it is suggested to include gamer discourse in nongamer discourses and vice versa. An example is a dialogue about games that students play in class, with teachers as presumable representatives of a nongamer discourse. A dialogue like that can increase respect and allow reflection on cultural practices like social class or cultural values. It thus supports the development of critical thinking (Squire, 2005). This might include the consideration of inequalities among gamer cultures when designing game media literacy projects.

Good opportunities for learning something useful in and from games (where useful is not restricted to relevant in a competitive capitalistic economy, but might also mean relevant for personal development and the development of societies) justify games as relevant for informal learning. All scholars who research game media literacy argue that there are good opportunities for learning something useful in games and from games. The arguments range from theory of play through game analysis to empirical research.

The game media literacy discourse convincingly argues for the relevance of games for learning and the individuality of the esthetic of games. Thus game media literacy is relevant for society today.

SEE ALSO: Creative Works; Critical Pedagogy; Esthetics in Media Literacy; Faith-Based Media Literacy Education, History; Game Design in Media Literacy Education; Meaning-Making; Media Addiction among Children and Youths; Media Education Research and Creativity; Media Literacy Education and 21st Century Teacher Education; Media Literacy in Teacher Education; Video Games as Education

References

Apperley, T., & Walsh, C. (2012). What digital games and literacy have in common: A heuristic for understanding pupils' gaming literacy. *Literacy, 46*(3), 115–122. doi: 10.1111/j.1741-4369.2012.00668.x

Baacke, D. (1997). Medienpädagogik [Media education]. Tübingen, Germany: Niemeyer.

Bogost, I. (2006). *Unit operations: An approach to videogame criticism*. London, England: MIT Press.

Buckingham, D., & Burn, A. (2007). Game literacy in theory and practice. *Journal of Educational Multimedia and Hypermedia, 16*(3), 323–349. Retrieved from https://pdfs.semanticscholar.org/ce1e/11a6cb9b02236ac52f3b365371fe68611033.pdf

Domínguez, A., Saenz-de-Navarrete, J., de-Marcos, L., Fernández-Sanz, L., Pagés, C., & Martínez-Herráiz, J.J. (2012). Gamifying learning experiences: Practical implications and outcomes. *Computers & Education, 63*, 380–392. doi: 10.1016/j.compedu.2012.12.020

Fritz, J. (2005). Wie virtuelle Welten wirken. Über die Strukur von Transfers aus der medialen in die reale Welt [How virtual worlds work. About the structure of transfers from the medial to the real world]. Retrieved from http://www.bpb.de/gesellschaft/digitales/computerspiele/63699/wie-virtuelle-welten-wirken?p=all

Gee, J.P. (2007 [2004]). *What video games have to teach us about learning and literacy* (2nd ed.). New York, NY: St. Martin's Press.

Habermas, J. (1985). *Der philosophische Diskurs der Moderne* [The philosophical discourse of modernity]. Frankfurt am Main, Germany: Suhrkamp.

Huizinga, J. (1949). *Homo ludens: A study of the play-element in culture*. London, England: Routledge & Kegan Paul.

Klimt, C. (2009). Key dimensions of contemporary video game literacy: Towards a normative model of the competent digital game. *Eludamos. Journal for Computer Game Culture, 3*(1), 23–31. Retrieved from http://www.eludamos.org/index.php/eludamos/article/viewArticle/vol3no1-4/103

Salen, K. (2007). Gaming literacies: A game design study in action. *Journal of Educational Multimedia and Hypermedia, 16*(3), 301–322.

Schiller, F. (Ed.). (1795). *Die Horen. 2. Stück*. Tübingen, Germany: Cottasche Verlagsbuchhandlung.

Shaffer, D.W. (2006). *How computer games help children learn*. New York, NY: Palgrave.

Squire, K.D. (2005). Toward a media literacy for games. *Telemedium, 52*(1), 9–15.

Squire, K.D. (2008). Video game-based learning: An emerging paradigm for instruction. *Performance Improvement Quaterly, 21*(2), 7–36.

Swertz, C.J. (1999). Computer als Spielzeug [Computers as toys]. *Spektrum Freizeit, 8*(2), 112–120.

Treumann, K.P., Meister, D.M., Sander, U., Burkatzki, E., Hagedorn, J., Kämmerer, M., … & Wegener, C. (2007). *Medienhandeln Jugendlicher. Mediennutzung und Medienkompetenz – Bielefelder Medienkompoetenzmodell* [Media action of young people. Media usage and media literacy – Bielefeld media competency model]. Wiesbaden, Germany: VS-Verlag.
Witting, T. (2007). *Wie Computerspiele uns beeinflussen. Transferprozesse beim Bildschirmspiel im Erleben der User* [How computer games affect us. Transfer processes during screen play in the experience of the user]. Munich, Germany: kopaed.
Zimmerman, E. (2009). Gaming literacy: Game design as a model for literacy in the twenty-first century. In B. Perron & M.J.P. Wolf (Eds.), *The video game theory reader* (2nd ed., pp. 23–31). New York, NY: Routledge.

Further reading

Apperley, T., & Beavis, C. (2013). A model for critical games literacy. *E-Leaning and Digital Media, 10*(1), 1–12. Retrieved from http://journals.sagepub.com/doi/pdf/10.2304/elea.2013.10.1.1
Buckingham, D. (2007). Media education goes digital: An introduction. *Learning, Media and Technology, 32*(2), 111–119. doi: 10.1080/17439880701343006
Gee, J.P. (2008). *Social linguistics and literacies. Ideology in discourses* (3rd ed.). London, England: Routledge.

Christian J. Swertz has been head of the research unit for Media Education at the University of Vienna since 2004. His main research fields are media education, media literacy, media theory, video game studies, and technology enhanced learning. His publications cover the implementation of media in different sectors including game-based learning, educational metadata, and digital culture.

Girl Culture and Their Literacies

ELAINE J. O'QUINN
Appalachian State University, USA

History, gender, and literacy

Sometime in the late 1700s American families started to understand the necessity of play and toys as an important aspect of the learning process for children. This was mostly a result of the developmental ideas of John Locke (1632–1704), who continued to influence social practices of childhood throughout the 18th century and into the 19th century. Those views included his now much disputed belief of children as "tabula rasa" as well as his harsh notions of how children best achieve self-discipline. His ideas of play, though very gendered, did encourage parents and other adults to see recreational activity as a natural and acceptable part of growing up, if for no other reason than to help children further understand through different means the gendered roles they would have as adults: boys would be adventurous and act, and girls would passively nurture and care. As the centuries progressed and some of the toys of childhood became used by all children, the previously defined lines between play seen as acceptable for boys and that for girls, and the toys they might use, started to blur. Girls could exercise and use their bodies, as in the case of activities like sledding, skating, and jump rope, and boys could engage in what were considered more domestic enjoyments, like board games, music, and the arts. While many toys intended for use by only one gender still exist, others, especially those of the digital age, are seen as acceptable for all, though they may be and often are used differently by each group.

Because youths are known to test the boundaries of anything new made available to them (including traditional toys and forms of play and the more contemporary conception of toys such as technological devices and their intended purposes), a history of girls and their literacies and how they have "played" with those literacies can be traced through the literacies themselves and the kind of access girls have had to them. Understanding how girls have always "toyed" with literacy begins with early technologies as simple as paper, pencil, and print reading materials and ends with observations on the use of devices as complex as cell phones and media platforms as open-ended as the World Wide Web. There is a tendency to believe that boys will always be the first to use an evolving technology (be it traditional or "smart") as a toy to "play" with (as in creating games) and girls will simply reproduce that play or be shaped by it (as in baking in a miniature kitchen or mothering a doll), but there is ample evidence to suggest that girls also "play" in what may be more subtle ways as they form identity, make community, and even pursue issues of advocacy.

Anthropologist Margaret Mead (1949) was one of the first to note that even though children, as they grow, begin to compare themselves quite early to those around them, they are still able to experience themselves in critically complex ways. In the arena of gender, this is a very important observation to consider. Mead stressed that it was imperative that adults encourage children to deny the stereotypes of gender so easily fallen into in order that they might reach their own unique and full potential. In short, Mead flatly rejected some of the cultural ideals that many before her had used to divide and categorize by gender, claiming they did more harm than good. While some might disagree with Mead on other issues, it seems on this particular one she was certainly ahead of her time and helped pave the way for an expanded understanding of gender development, including that of psychologists like Carol Gilligan (1982), who helped pioneer the idea that when boys and girls come to different conclusions about certain issues and dilemmas it does not make one gender's answer or resolution more correct than the other. While it is true that Gilligan was mostly concerned with questions of moral reasoning and progress, her broader argument of how girls consider a "network of relationships" when determining a course of action is applicable to many aspects of their lives, including how they perceive issues of work and play and how they might use or even blend each to grow and achieve in somewhat different ways from boys. It is not a huge leap to see how Gilligan's research, and how it disrupts hierarchical categories, spills into other habits of being as well, including ones of literacy. In many ways,

Gilligan helps illuminate that literacy of any kind can never be, nor should it be, just one thing.

With that in mind, it becomes clear that literacy as it is now perceived is more than just an academic form of practice and development. Though historically it has been defined as an ability to read and write, researchers and cultural study theorists now understand it to be much broader and deeper in scope. Just as gender is no longer accepted as simple biology, so too has literacy come to be known as an inclusive action that encompasses social exercises, identity construction, perception and perspective, and a purposeful exploration of existing cultural divides. All of these aspects of literacy have informed and advanced the observations of researchers and theorists alike of the obvious: that gender lines and what constitutes personhood will be redefined, rejected, or repositioned when the interacting whole of a person is explored and considered. For girls, it means no longer being put in a simple box marked "pink." It follows then, that how literacy is used must also include a close look at purposeful choices and habits of tradition as a relevant and telling place to explore how girls make meaning of literacy practices and how those practices have evolved, as well as how they have remained unchanged over time. While some arenas of practice remain conventional and certainly controversial, it does appear that girls do and always have used their literacy in a variety of ways, including to "play" with their identity, independence, dreams, and desires, and with transformation of the world as they see it.

This difference in approach is, again, complicated through the work of researchers like David and Myra Sadker in their now famous report for the American Association of University Women (AAUW) entitled *How Schools Shortchange Girls* (1993). While specifically this report focuses on teacher–student interaction, it also points to a cycle of "learned helplessness" often associated with girls and leading to more contemporary phenomena such as "mansplaining" whereby men feel the need to jump in and tell girls (and women) what the "real" solution to a problem is or what the meaning of a situation is, resulting, to their mind, in a more "exacting" explanation of how and/or why something works as it should/does. While more recent studies suggest it is too difficult to determine if teacher responses to students do indeed promote or impede the learning of certain subject matter, there is evidence that in at least some subject areas gender bias does exists. The question is, does it exist because academic curriculums have promoted it or is it because of the way girls respond to and interact with certain material? Regardless of the answer, this bias has led to the "silencing" of girls or, at the very least, the perception that girls speak less authoritatively and are less likely to voice opinions in certain arenas than are boys, leading to messages that they deserve less respect for their insights and contributions when they do speak. Girls, aware of these messages and out of necessity, always have found ways to subvert academic systems of recognition which often become the framework for expected societal norms, and continue to do so.

While it is easy to dismiss 18th-, 19th- and possibly even 20th-century impressions of academic gender differences as revealed by the Sadkers as passé, the fact remains that even in the 21st century there is a widespread belief that girls fall short in their preparation for a fundamental curriculum built around certain literacies, a carryover, in part, from a curriculum that at one time intentionally excluded girls from even the most fundamental of literacies, reading and writing. Though clearly reading and writing have been available to girls for a much longer time, subjects like science, technology, engineering, and math are all areas from which girls were also once prohibited or to which they were allowed only limited access. It has only been fairly recently that they have been encouraged to pursue these fields in more aggressive ways, thus the ongoing push for science, technology, engineering, and mathematics (STEM) specifics for girls with upstart programs like GirlStart™, a Texas program offering free curriculum, summer camps, and after-school programs for girls to pursue STEM literacies. Lines may not be as clearly demarcated now as in the early days of STEM education, but they do still exist. The perception that girls are not as capable or as smart as boys when it comes to these fields is a stigma they still carry. Complicating the academic sensibilities surrounding girls and STEM are the social ones that are especially hyped and fixed in adolescence. A highly visible public example of this played out in 1992 when a talking Barbie™ doll famously reported that "Math class is tough," setting off a firestorm of protests that included everyone from the National Council of Mathematics Teachers to radical feminists to Lisa Simpson, a popular character in a TV cartoon show.

Again, in order to come to some understanding of difference not as something more or less than but as something that might offer additional value, it is important to explore at least some aspects of literacy and gender in terms of historical markers and pressures. Rather than blur the lines of young adulthood into one common experience, as so often happens, it is imperative to see what social forces, needs, desires, and experiences have influenced and acted on girls. Because the whole concept of adolescence and youth culture is still relatively new, beginning in earnest for the most part in the last few decades of the 19th century and coming more fully into the social conscience during the early 20th century, many of its issues, anxieties, and concerns have remained under an auspice of adult control with very little reporting out by girls of actual gendered experiences. Thankfully this has changed somewhat with more ethnographic studies and a field of methodology that is intended only for the study of girls (and not women). While it is not possible to go back in time and do actual interviews and observations of girls, their literacy habits, and what those habits suggest, some scholars have researched existing archived materials to try to piece together a picture of how girls have historically approached and considered literacy and applied it to their lives. Jane Greer is one of these scholars.

Girls writing

In her book *Girls and Literacy in America: Historical Perspectives to the Present* (2003) Greer outlines how the scripts of both girlhood and adolescence have not sufficiently allowed for the unique potential that girls and their ways of knowing contribute to personal and public domains. However, as she shows time and time again, that does not mean girls have not been charting their own course. One of her most intriguing examples of this is the one of high school student Dorothy Allen Brown, who in 1912 establishes a "secret society" of one, whereby she, through diary entries, records which women either in history or in her reading of fiction have influenced her by their desire and particular contribution to do good and help others. Brown calls this society

"The Order of the Scroll," and Greer shows how Brown uses it in part to construct a public identity from her personal affinity to women and characters such as Joan of Arc, Maid Marian, and Queen Victoria (Greer, 2003, p. 322). In essence, what Dorothy Allen Brown does is extend what she values in her literacy, both historical and literary, into her own persona. She does not merely determine these named women as good (a moral judgment), rather she uses her knowledge of them to help guide her own path and youthful journey. This is an excellent early example of how girls turn the "work" of literacy into the "play" that helps form their identity. It also resonates with what Gilligan discovered about girls and their development. They do not necessarily separate out the logistics of "what makes sense" (Brown is far from being a martyr, shepherdess, or queen) in their immediate situation from the ongoing consideration of something larger (a role model) that might be emerging.

Greer's look back at girls and what kinds of things they have always done with their basic literacy is essential because it holds the key to understanding how many girls continue to approach and respond to various forms of literacy. While reading and writing is a mainstay of Dorothy Allen Brown through a form that is considered to be the most rudimentary level of literacy, a diary entry, what it reveals is an ability and purposeful attempt to connect personal literacy to something larger and more enduring in the public domain. In other words, it appears as a gendered form of "play" that has meaning beyond the present, a notion that again connects to Gilligan's theory that girls desire to see past the confines of this instant and to the possibilities of tomorrow. Brown's "secret society" makes girls and their literacy habits visible in ways not always associated with the purpose of literacy, as advocates for something bigger than the self that in turn also improves and broadens the self.

Access

It is imperative that at this juncture there is a recognition of the differing life circumstances of girls and the role that disparity plays historically and currently in their use of literacy and how that may lead to different kinds of advocacy. While Dorothy Allen Brown may have had the "luxury" of attempting to construct a better self through an obviously large library, and thus build a better world based on her extensive readings and musings, those in less than ideal situations have in the past used, and continue to use, whatever limits to literacy they may have at hand to draw attention to and better the lot of those who surround them. It is a well-known fact that certain groups have been, and continue to be, denied literacy in various forms and for a multitude of reasons. Girls, people of color, immigrants, refugees, and the economically deprived have all at one time or another struggled to attain the highest levels of literacy, whether that be learning to read and write or simply having access to the devices necessary for ultimate literacy achievements.

Sociocultural, material, and economic status always influences literacy. Race, class, and representation are important considerations in understanding that girlhood in particular and literacy in general can be constructed very differently depending on life situation. If someone does not own or always have full access to the technologies of literacy, be that a pencil or a computer, then what they are able to do with those literacies is restricted. Because of inequalities like this, there is no such thing as "normal" when it comes to the literacy behaviors that girls, especially those who fall into one of more of these categories, might engage in or share. Since literacy for *all* girls has *not* always been viewed as necessary, these variations and what they represent are especially critical to recognize. Issues of ethnicity, economic resources, and social capital complicate conduct, and it is easy to see how girls, even if laws have occasionally been imposed to expect the contrary (there are many instances over the years of legislation requiring certain levels of literacies), may view their own literacy of any type differently than what might be expected and proceed at will. Laws may mandate what everyone learns, but girls will still appropriate what they actually do with what they learn.

Examples of groups using self-determined purposes of literacy beyond the expected that have led to advocacy would be Native American and African American girls, especially of the 19th century, whose exposure to reading and writing was limited to what was deemed only necessary to "civilize" them and to impart ascribed cultural beliefs that could be regurgitated. However, many girls moved beyond what was calculated as useful for them and independently decided to employ their skills to teach less fortunate others to read and write and to counter laws and federal regulations that would keep those others from becoming fully literate, contributing members of society in every sense. As the 20th century dawned, progressive movements did bring some pushback against such oppressive and limiting forces, but girls of color, as well as those who were immigrants, continued to suffer under the nationalistic metaphor of "melting pot," which seemed to malign any expansive view of literacy that might see unique circumstance and opportunity as a critical contribution rather than assume that national assimilation was in the best interest of all. These girls were some of the first to use their literacy as a tool of resistance and empowerment, but they were not the last.

Zines and advocacy

Another visible but more contemporary example of how girls have used their literacy to advocate for the interests of others as well as for causes that personally impact them can be seen in the creation and use of zines, an alternative form of publishing that often blends diary, editorial, collage, subversive language, and art. Zines are quite popular with girls for a variety of reasons: taking control of their sexuality; providing a space for creative endeavors; offering a place to connect with others who share similar interests; subverting political or social systems; highlighting alternative communities and lifestyles; critiquing the patriarchy; and addressing issues of sexism. As Margaret Finders discovered, girls use their literacy and play with practices like zines to engage in what she calls an "underlife" space (1997). Alison Piepmeier in *Girl Zines: Making Media, Doing Feminism* (2009) also noted that girls have come to use zines for everything from individual protests to organized activism, fueled in part by the radical punk fan efforts of the 1970s and continued into the 1990s by groups like Bikini Kill and the Riot Grrrls movement. Zines have a longer history of existence for other subgroups, but for girls, this is where the use of the medium begins in earnest. The move into the age of the Internet and computers (and personal copiers) has provided more extensive opportunities for those who have access to share zines and has enabled girls to print off and sometimes even sell their publications. It has made additional content easier to bring to the table while also inspiring a look at new subject areas, including more personalized accounts of experiences and beliefs.

These ongoing digital changes mean that many girls now have more access to a print subculture that previously was not always available to them. As the 1990s progressed, girls and the sheer number of their zines exploded as e-zines, blogs, and webzines became easier to create and easier to manage and distribute to a wider audience. Though many still see the web as a space controlled by males, girls (or gurrrls as they often identify themselves in these spaces) have certainly made their own claim in this arena. They network, produce, and communicate at rates never before seen and hardly consider themselves neophytes of the Internet, even if others do. Anita Harris (2003) and Mary Celeste Kearney (2006) have made valuable contributions to understanding how and why girls use this form of media literacy both to resist and reveal their worlds, and any online search of girls and their zines will quickly yield a large number of viable publications that may be readily viewed.

Magazines

A final note on zines is that at least in part they do grow out of the larger genre of commercial magazines and as such use them as models both in form and format. Without a doubt, magazines serve an entirely different purpose and continue to influence how girls perceive themselves and their world. It is important to note that while scholars from many fields have (and for a good variety of reasons) expressed serious concerns over the messages magazines send, there have been many positive changes in some of the ones currently marketed to girls. Teen and girl publications have always intended to entertain and socialize, and there is no question there have been serious consequences from images too often portraying who the ideal girl should be; however, some researchers now argue that girls are not always just the vulnerable consumer as traditionally pegged and are more media savvy than ever.

Over the years, numerous magazines targeted at girls have changed substantially in both image and text and have evolved to the point of recognizing that girls have agency and not only know how to use that agency but will use it. This has meant formatting that includes more than just celebrity gossip and idealized, Photoshopped™ body types, skin, and hair. Many contemporary magazines for girls include important health information, articles about world events, and advice columns that deal with real-life issues and are about more than just the male–female relationships that tended to be the focus in the past. Editors realize that many girls want reading material that provides avenues to self-actualization and the unlocking of personal potential, rather than a how-to manual on becoming a carbon copy of some unrealistic fashion model. In fact, many of the teen girl magazines now pride themselves as doing no Photoshopping™ at all and using models that are representative of all types of girls. One thing in particular that zines and current magazines do share is that they provide a space for real girls to self-express, whether that be through creative endeavors of writing or through other artistic modes; responding to each other; or asking questions about events and experiences that impact their daily lives. Thus, even in a very traditional medium, the literacy needs and habits of girls are being recognized, both in print and online, as something they must be able to constructively "play" with and use or there is a risk that they will actively reject the more traditional offerings of the past. Researchers like Sharon Mazzarella (2005) and Angela McRobbie (1991) are some of the latest generation of scholars who believe that media formats like magazines have changed in response to what girls expect and how they will react. Both unpack how media like zines and the Internet contribute to the evolving literacy identities of girls.

Clearly writing, once considered mostly a male domain for purposes of expediting work rather than "play," always has served girls in other capacities as well. Traditionally, while young men were learning how their skill could further serve their careers in areas such as business, politics, and law, girls were writing to understand themselves (journals and diaries), groom relationships (letters and cards), and express emotion and perspective while developing a fuller sense of personhood (speeches and editorials). Even when the way schools educated for writing changed, girls continued to use the medium for social, community, and personal gain as well as for academic mastery from which they have never shied away. Indeed, as Greer points out in an essay on girls' literacy performances both in and out of school, there is a history of girls using writing taught to them for academic purposes to express their own "transgressive opinions and views" (Greer, 2013, p. 17). Examples Greer gives demonstrate that many a girl in writing and speech for purposes of school has expressed authoritative resistance knowing the chance for backlash might exist.

Online journals and blogs

Other opportunities for writing that work for girls in varying ways include publication in online journals like *Teen Voices* (global), *Cicada*, and *Canvas*. These journals solicit and publish the work of young people. Girls especially have found outlets such as these beneficial not only for creative writing, but also for expository writing where they can express thoughts and views. Likewise, blogging, which can take the form of a diary, an opinion or idea piece, or a more formalized essay of factual information, remains highly popular with girls. Because blogs are online publications, they are generally interactive and may be open to the public or closed to a list-serve whereby the owner/writer controls access. As blogs have increased in popularity, girls have become more sophisticated in their use of them, often including links to similar topics, photographs that relate, and even videos that might be of interest to the readers. Personal websites and other social media formats like chat rooms (not without controversy because this is a subversive space in ways that can sometimes harm girls) have afforded girls public forums of expression that previously were constrained to much closer circles of friends and community. While it remains true that these literacy outlets can alienate those who do not participate, just as note passing, yearbook signing, and the like have done in the past, these newer forms of media communication have also opened doors and promoted friendships among girls with varying experiences and from a range of cultural groups.

Girls reading

Though writing has remained consistently a vehicle of resistance and action for girls, so too has reading. More access to reading materials both online and on other devices has certainly been a boon to their basic literacy, and with the advent of literature written specifically for them that includes both multicultural and multiethnic characters and cultures, as well as topics as diverse as sexual orientation, lifestyle differences, and physical, mental, spiritual, and emotional challenges, girls have been able to expand their views of self and the world in ways never before available to so many of them. While in the past reading for one's age group may have been considered simple entertainment done outside of school, the emergence of Young Adult Literature (YAL) with age-appropriate protagonists and stories of girls from all around the world has provided opportunities for girls aside from mere diversion. Long gone are the days when girls read books meant simply to inform them of their societal duties and learned place in the world as they matured. And while popular culture books considered "chick lit" like *Bridget Jones's Diary* (1996) or those dubbed "celebrity texts" like the *Gossip Girl* (2002) have always had a hardcore, pleasure reading audience, the very substantial number of books that fall into the YAL category have attained legitimacy both in school and with girls who are serious and informed readers.

Books for girls

Contemporary literature for girls always has been perceived as a threat to the adult world in that it generally has revealed girls for the independent and strong spirits that they are and has provided role models outside the realm of the domestic sphere, always a disruptive force for the dominant discourse. From *Little Women* (1880) to *The Hate U Give* (2017), girl protagonists who show any measure of acting outside the lines of what is deemed acceptable have caused concern and, in some cases, outrage over their behavior, no matter how minimally over the line it is or how unbelievable. Librarians, teachers, and parents alike have continuously expressed concern over the contemporary texts girls choose, fearful that their moral compass will permanently be diverted in the wrong direction should they get a taste of rebellious freedom.

Throughout the early 20th century the cultural influence of books intended exclusively for girls drew the ire of many adults who worried that books like the Nancy Drew series would encourage girls to lay down their sewing machines and baking pans and instead head off into the sunset in the infamous blue roadster driven by 16-year-old Nancy Drew, who appeared to have no domestic responsibilities and was set loose to explore a world in a way once only available to men. Though there was a slight deviation from this "frightening" trajectory in the postwar 1950s, when there was a national push to put women (and girls) back in the home where they "belonged," it was not long before the social movements of the 1960s and 1970s that were changing societal norms pushed back in reading material as well and cracked open the lives of girls in more ways than before, revealing them not only as independent beings, but as sexual (see *Mr. and Mrs. Bo Jo Jones* [1967] and *Forever* [1975]) and forward-thinking ones.

Ethnographic and psychological studies of girls' literacy habits across all domains, including reading, writing, media usage, and personal devices, to name the most obvious, have made it possible to better understand how girls make sense of their own lives and how they use those habits to make sense of the world they inhabit and also to express empathy for the lives of others. Meredith Cherland, in her popular and influential book *Private Practices: Girls Reading Fiction and Constructing Identity* (1994), looks at how the reading habits of girls can reflect the battles they have with the cultural norms that bind them, despite the fact that they often read fiction to gain agency. Scholars like Cherland note how difficult it is for girls to navigate identity in a culture that sends so many conflicting messages. Notwithstanding this fact, girls do understand the need not only to read about their lives but to also act upon them the best they can.

Mary Napoli, in her essay entitled "Girls Around the Globe as Advocates for Political, Cultural, and Social Literacy at Home" (2013, p. 71), found more recently that American girls in a summer book club reading stories of courageous girls in other parts of the world were eager not only to rethink some of the cultural messages of their own identities but also to transform their insights into acts of social justice and agency at home. After reading a variety of YAL texts, issues of poverty, hunger, gender inequities, education, power, and agency became more central to them than they had been in the past, leading them even to ask the facilitator if they could "do something to make a difference as a group" (p. 85). While the girls enjoyed the "play like" atmosphere of a group that could laugh and hang out together, their interest in the dilemmas of the characters they were reading about superseded the mere enjoyment of belonging to a "literacy club" (Smith, 1998). Just like Dorothy Allen Brown, the girls who have used literacy against social norms to help others be more educated, and the girls who author zines or blogs, these young women felt empowered to use their literacy in ways that moved beyond the level of self and into an arena of action.

Fanfiction

One final area of reading that intersects with writing and that girls are heavily involved in more than boys is that of fanfiction. Fanfiction extends the world and characters of popular texts. The texts can be representative of any medium (television and film qualify), but books are a major source, and many films, as well as some TV series (*Pretty Little Liars*, *Gossip Girl*), are indeed spinoffs of books. *Harry Potter*, the *Twilight* series, and *Lord of the Rings* are all examples of texts that girls write alternative endings for and "what ifs" about characters and their relationships. Some fanfiction engages in continuing the saga of a story once the officially published text has ended. In many ways, fanfiction combines literacies for girls who first read (or possibly view in the case of television or film) and then write. Because it happens in an online community, it is another way girls have learned to use their literacy to play, connect, interact, and just generally be social with each other.

Networking media

Because girls do enjoy being social, social networking media of the late 20th century and early 21st century like Myspace™, Facebook™, Snapchat™, and Instagram™ are a big part of the way a generation of girls has grown up with and interacted with technological advances. As media and computer technologies have become permanent fixtures of culture, they have brought both promise and problems to girls. The challenge of 21st-century technologies has not only been how to forge the tools of work and academics into devices of personal growth and achievement, but has included new struggles and an awareness of how these tools can harm girls in ways previously not experienced. While it is one thing to write a name and phone number on a bathroom wall that says "for a good time call …," in the era of new literacy technologies girls have become especially vulnerable to predators, cyberbullies, social intrusions, and subtle consumerism aimed at them that in the past did not have such easy access to their lives. Issues of safety are not to be dismissed and have been of paramount concern for parents and girls alike. Devices like cell phones with an ability to instantly text message, post pictures, and deliver video have brought about virtual situations that have given girls agency and autonomy that in some situations can end up hurting them. Sexting and the aforementioned chat rooms are an example of the kind of digital freedom that has ended up sometimes being harmful.

However, not all social networking works against girls, and there are many safe spaces that are valuable to them in terms of creativity and connection. Like other forms of literacy, they have learned to "play" with the web and what it can do for them. Discussion boards about issues that concern them and sites built especially for them are examples of ways girls use the web to expand their knowledge of self and other. Organizations from the American Library Association to corporations like Mattel™ and Seventeen™ have sponsored sites where girls are informed, educated, and entertained. They have access to interactive games, quizzes about important subject matter, and material that deals with issues of popular culture that concern them, all within the context of "play." While the traps for girls may vary with the site, there are many reputable sites that are built only with the good of the girl in mind.

Web 2.0

Included in the updated forms of the Internet that girls actively use to engage and create is Web 2.0. This has been of major interest to girls, and they have embraced it in powerfully individual ways. By combining the best of all Internet and computer technologies, it allows them to make the personal public by expression of identity in new formats. Again, girls have found a way not only to communicate but to play through the use of Web 2.0. Videoblogging, podcasting, webcams, screenplays, soundtracks, and other forms of media presence allow for virtual performances that are shared and used in a variety of ways, including further ways of networking, creating community websites, and promoting causes and advocacy. YouTube™ is probably the best-known Web 2.0 space of which girls have made use. Katie Kapurch, in her essay on "Girlhood, Agency, and Pop Culture Literacy," talks about the three-girl band who created online The Bella Cullen Project, based on the popular *Twilight* series. The girls managed to get over a million views on MySpace™ and even captured the attention of MTV (Kapurch, 2013, p. 118). Had it not been for an online presence, it is hard to imagine the girls would have made headlines in numerous magazines, including *Esquire*, been able to meet the author of the books, or met the cast from the movies that followed. The girls of The Bella Cullen Project are not the only ones to have attained fame (and sometime fortune!) from their escapades on social media sites. YouTube™ sensations Carly Rae Jepsen ("Call Me Maybe"), Alessia Cara ("Here"), and Tori Kelly ("Nobody Love") have all been led to venues as exciting as the Grammy's and late-night television, and to multiple record deals.

While initially the impetus for literacy as seen in the digital age appears to have been to decrease and aid in workload, as well as to provide an online arena for socialization and networking, it has not taken long for it to spill into the spaces where community, identity, and even careers are formed. I would argue that while girls have certainly responded to the advantages of media technology to make life easier for themselves in some capacity, they have also markedly considered ways that it enhances relationships and connections to others, displays their unique talents, and challenges them to represent the self as complex, evolving, and up to the task of breaking with mass depictions of who they are and who they can be.

Conclusion

Girls and their literacies is a complicated matter that is impacted by many points of entry. In many cases these entry points overlap and inform each other in ways that create something new. While reading and writing lie at the heart of literacy, learning how to read the world and the messages it sends in such a way as to know how to navigate it safely and respond to it positively and purposefully is a challenge that has become more difficult for girls in the face of so many technological advances. At the same time, it has also become more exciting. Society competes for the interest of the girl in many ways. Some of those competitions are healthy, and some are not. But girls will always see their way to use literacy as they see fit, either as a tool they can wield in the case of advocacy and resistance or as a toy to be "played" with that can report on, explore, or enhance their lives in multiple ways even while they fight against the forces that would use it against them.

SEE ALSO: Adolescent Literacy in a Digital World; Children's Culture; Community Media; Digital Literacy; Media Access and Activism; Media and Adolescent Identity

Development; Media Literacy Foundations; Online Reading; Performance Media; Sexting; Understanding Media Literacy and DIY Creativity in Youth Digital Productions; Youth Digital Culture

References

American Association of University Women. (1993). *How schools shortchange girls*. New York, NY: Marlowe.

Cherland, M.R. (1994). *Private practices: Girls reading fiction and constructing identity*. London, England: Taylor & Francis.

Finders, M. (1997). *Just girls: Hidden literacies and life in junior high*. New York, NY: Teachers College Press.

Gilligan, C. (1982). *In a different voice: Psychological theory and women's development*. Cambridge, MA: Harvard University Press.

Greer, J. (Ed.). (2003). *Girls and literacy in America: Historical perspectives to the present*. Santa Barbara, CA: ABC-CLIO.

Greer, J. (2013). The Order of the Scroll: Surveying girls' literacy performances in and out of school, 1885–2011. In E. O'Quinn (Ed.), *Girls' literacy experiences in and out of school: Learning and composing gendered identities* (pp. 11–26). New York, NY: Routledge.

Harris, A. (2003). gURL scenes and gurrrl zines: The regulation and resistance of girls in late modernity. *Feminist Review, 75*, 38–56.

Kapurch, K. (2013). Girlhood, agency, and pop culture literacy: The *Twilight* saga as exemplar. In E. O'Quinn (Ed.), *Girls' literacy experiences in and out of school: Learning and composing gendered identities* (pp. 107–122). New York, NY: Routledge.

Kearney, M.C. (2006). *Girls make media*. New York, NY: Routledge.

Mazzarella, S. (2005). *Girl Wide Web: Girls, the Internet, and the negotiation of identity*. New York, NY: Peter Lang.

McRobbie, A. (1991). *Feminism and youth culture: From Jackie to Just Seventeen*. Basingstoke, England: Macmillian.

Mead, M. (1949). *Male and female*. New York, NY: Quill.

Napoli, M. (2013). Girls around the globe as advocates for political, cultural, and social literacy at home. In E. O'Quinn (Ed.), *Girls' literacy experiences in and out of school: Learning and composing gendered identities* (pp. 71–89). New York, NY: Routledge.

Piepmeier, A. (2009). *Girl zines: Making media, doing feminism*. New York, NY: NYU Press.

Smith, F. (1998). *The book of learning and forgetting*. New York, NY: Teachers College Press.

Further reading

Baumgarder, J., & Richards, A. (2000). *Manifesta: Young women, feminism, and the future*. New York, NY: Farrar, Straus, & Giroux.

Brown, L.M. (1998). *Raising their voices: The politics of girls' anger*. Cambridge, MA: Harvard University Press.

Douglas, S.J. (1995). *Where the girls are: Growing up female with the mass media*. New York, NY: Three Rivers Press.

Gonick, M. (2006). Between "Girl Power" and "Reviving Ophelia": Constituting the neoliberal girl subject. *National Women's Studies Association Journal, 18*, 1–22.

Harris, A. (2004). *All about the girl: Culture, power, and identity*. New York, NY: Routledge.
Schrum, K. (2004). Some wore bobby socks: The emergence of teenage girls' culture, 1920–1945. New York, NY: Palgrave Macmillan.

Elaine J. O'Quinn is a professor of English and associate faculty member in Gender, Women's & Sexuality Studies at Appalachian State University where she teaches and helped organize a minor in girls' studies. She has published numerous articles and essays, guest edited a 2016 issue of *Gender Issues* devoted to girls' studies as an emerging field, and authored and edited a book entitled *Girls' Literacy Experiences In and Out of School: Learning and Composing Gendered Identities* (2013).

Global Citizenship

ROMAN GERODIMOS
Bournemouth University, UK

Global citizenship is an emerging concept that describes the status of a person as a member of the global community. Just like state citizenship, global citizenship has both formal and informal applications and is associated with a range of rights and responsibilities. However, while the conventional notion of citizenship, which is tied to the sovereign nation-state, is the product of centuries of legal, political, and social practice, global citizenship is a relatively recent development. As globalization poses unprecedented challenges for democratic representation, participation, and accountability, the idea of a form of citizenship that transcends national boundaries has been gaining traction among academics and policymakers. The role of the media in that process is fundamental, as they constitute both the space and the means through which citizens engage with one another and with public affairs. This is even more so at the transnational level. Thus media and media literacy are key components of the debate on global citizenship.

Citizenship as membership of a political community

Citizenship has traditionally been defined as membership of a political community within a finite geographic space, with all the privileges and duties that that membership entails. In the city-states of ancient Greece it indicated that one was a member of the *demos*—the decision-making populace of those early city-states (*poleis*). In ancient Rome, citizenship was associated with a series of privileges and legal protections. It was used as a tool of foreign policy and state expansion: colonies and allies were granted variable forms of citizenship through which they were both controlled and integrated.

Our modern idea of citizenship is intrinsically connected with the nation-state, which emerged as the sole legitimate and sovereign actor in the international system with the Treaty of Westphalia in 1648. As passports and border controls between states were introduced or tightened in the aftermath of World War I, citizenship became synonymous with nationality. Increased mobility, migration, and the emergence of diverse ethnicities within states have led to the decoupling of those two terms; but the legal, formal, and narrow definition of citizenship is, to this day, synonymous with being registered with the government of a country (usually the country of birth or permanent residence), mainly for the purposes of transnational identification.

The development of political theory in early modernity—and in particular the idea of democracy being based on a *social contract* between the state and the individual—gave citizenship a second layer of meaning at the domestic level. Citizenship became one side of the coin of democracy—the other being government *for* and *by* the people. From the late 18th century onward, the development of written constitutions and other foundational documents recognizing and protecting individual liberties, the expansion of suffrage and representation in government, and the growth of social movements (especially the labor and civil liberties movements) afforded the individual citizen *agency* as an empowered actor within the political system. Participating in elections, expressing one's voice through protest or industrial action, being subject to a common legal and constitutional framework, serving in the military, paying taxes, receiving the benefits of the welfare state (such as social security and universal healthcare coverage, where available) have been some of the formal duties and privileges associated with the status of being a citizen in modern liberal democracies.

Print and broadcast media—especially newspapers, radio, and television—were instrumental in bringing people together and in creating the national public spheres in which individuals identified themselves as members of the *body politic*, or what Benedict Anderson (1983) called "imagined communities." Identity is central to citizenship, both in the sense of being *identified by* others (as in the case of nationality) and in that of *identifying with* others, that is, being a member of a group that shares a geographic space and certain common traits (roots, language, religion, values, culture, etc.). *Community* is equally fundamental to the concept of citizenship, as a delineated space within which people reside and as a set of rules, norms, and practices that regulate that coexistence.

Cosmopolitanism and human rights

Cosmopolitanism (from the Greek words *cosmos* [world] and *polites* [citizen]), the idea that human beings are (or ought to be) citizens of the world, can be traced back to Greek philosophers (Diogenes the Cynic and the Stoics). It was later articulated and debated further by philosophers during the Enlightenment. Immanuel Kant's proposition of a "universal history with a cosmopolitan purpose" was particularly influential. However, until the middle of the 20th century, global citizenship remained either the subject of theoretical debate among philosophers or the reality of a small cosmopolitan urban elite. Diplomats and the upper classes, explorers and travel writers, artists and intellectuals moved across the world throughout the 19th century and during the interwar years, often fleeing from persecution.

The unprecedented horror of World War II constitutes a turning point—a historic break—in the evolution of the idea of citizenship. As a response to the trauma of the Holocaust and of the atomic bombings of Hiroshima and Nagasaki, and in order to ensure that similar atrocities would not be experienced again, the international community, within the framework of the newly founded United Nations, agreed on a set of fundamental liberties and rights to which human beings are inherently entitled, not by virtue of their membership of a particular state but by virtue of their membership of the *human race*. The Universal Declaration of Human Rights (UDHR; 1948) is the first document to formally articulate principles and values that are shared by citizens across a *global* community. Starting as an international *moral code*, these principles became the basis for a number of milestones that followed, such as the Geneva Conventions, the International Covenant on Civil and Political Rights, the International Covenant on Economic, Social and Cultural Rights, the International Convention on the Elimination of All Forms of Racial Discrimination, the International Convention on the Elimination of Discrimination Against Women, the United Nations Convention on the Rights of the Child, and the United Nations Convention against Torture.

By agreeing on these principles and values, sovereign governments surrendered some of their national sovereignty. Thus, in addition to the normative principles set out by the UDHR, a *legal code* of treaties, rules, and international judicial practice was also developed throughout the postwar era. The Nuremberg trials of prominent Nazi leaders formed the basis for jurisprudence on *international crimes* and, eventually, for the creation of the International Criminal Court, as well as of ad hoc tribunals and special panels (such as those created for the former Yugoslavia, Rwanda, and Sierra Leone). Genocide, war crimes, crimes against humanity, and crimes of aggression are now recognized as atrocities that transcend borders. The first three—along with ethnic cleansing—form the normative and legal basis of Responsibility to Protect (RtoP), an emerging commitment of the international community to assist states in protecting populations and, if all other measures fail, to intervene through the use of collective military force so as to protect affected citizens.

Therefore, for the first time in history, this framework based on global rules and norms affords individual citizens, by virtue of their common humanity and regardless of the rights or duties afforded to them by their *national* citizenship, certain inalienable *global* rights and liberties, as well as the obligation to refrain from certain types of mass crimes or else be in danger of facing prosecution by the international community outside of the territory of one's own country.

The scope of these rights and (especially) responsibilities is still very limited by comparison to that of state citizenship. Moreover, the means of regulating and enforcing them are fragile—prone to the limitations of the still highly state-centric nature of the global system. As there is effectively no independent mechanism of control and law enforcement across borders, this process still depends largely on the cooperation, participation, or consent of governments. Yet these are the first legal, formal, and universal applications of global citizenship beyond theory and normative discussions.

Global challenges and education for sustainable development

A second layer of practice around global citizenship is related to sustainable development and education. The postwar era saw the emergence of major environmental problems, such as the extinction of species and rainforests, extensive pollution of land, air, and water, toxic waste, vehicle emissions, ozone depletion, intensive industrial and farming practices, global warming, and limited clean water and energy resources. These issues were highlighted by scientists, educators, policymakers, and the environmental movement and led to important global milestones, such as the 1992 Earth Summit in Rio and the United Nations Framework Convention on Climate Change. Sustainability is now the top priority of the global community as articulated through the 2030 Agenda for Sustainable Development, which sets 17 global goals (SDGs) and 169 targets that cover a range of sustainability issues.

A crucial difference between the two forms of global citizenship outlined above is that, whereas the legal provision of fundamental liberties and human rights could be considered as a *passive* form of citizenship (the individual is automatically afforded these rights at birth and the international community is obliged to protect them), sustainability requires the *active* engagement of citizens. This engagement includes awareness of issues and targets, shifts in daily habits (e.g., use of sustainable sources of energy or ethical consumption), and participation in campaigns and schemes that are designed to turn the SDGs into reality.

One of the main outcomes of the 1992 Earth Summit was the realization that education is an essential mechanism of promoting sustainability. This led to the creation of Education for Sustainable Development (ESD)—a strategic campaign led by the United Nations with the purpose of integrating sustainable development issues into teaching and learning. ESD was the first comprehensive and coherent attempt to introduce global civics into the classroom around the world. It gradually evolved into global citizenship education (GCED); the two terms are now being used interchangeably, as the two fields share the common principles of peaceful coexistence, sustainable development, and respect for human rights. At the heart of global citizenship and GCED is demonstrating the interdependence between different global challenges, decision-makers, localities, and peoples, the links between the global and the local, and the role of citizens as stakeholders and active members of the community.

Global governance and the democratic deficit

The political agenda of the 21st century includes a series of highly complex and interconnected global challenges such as climate change, lack of food and clean water, poverty, terrorism and extremism, international organized crime, weapons of mass destruction, global epidemics, ethnic and religious conflicts, mass migration, and the practical and ethical implications of biotechnology, nanotechnology, and artificial intelligence. These issues are far bigger than individual states. While these global challenges have emerged over the past few decades, the executive power of national political systems has decreased, as multiple actors gain power both domestically and globally (multinational corporations, nongovernmental organizations, international organizations, policy networks, advocacy and interest groups, local authorities). The "hollowing out of the state" (Rhodes, 1997) has led to multilevel governance, as markets, bureaucracies, networks of experts, the voluntary or nonprofit sector, as well as digital publics and issue movements are becoming important actors.

As a result of those two forces—the scaling up of problems and the scaling out of decision-making—many scholars have argued that the institutions and processes of liberal democracies, which took shape in the 18th and 19th centuries, appear unable to maintain the social contract between citizens and the state. As decisions are made further and further away from the formal, visible outlets of republics, important questions of accountability, transparency, and representation emerge that in turn cast doubt over the legitimacy of political systems and the efficacy of citizenship as it has been conventionally conceptualized. This is known as the *democratic deficit*.

A similar problem exists at the global level. Decision-making networks and international organizations (both intergovernmental and nongovernmental) lack either the legitimacy or the resources needed to address the complex global challenges of the 21st century (Goldin, 2013). Globalization in the post-Cold War era has created unprecedented opportunities for mobility, trade, and communication across borders. However, as Malloch-Brown (2011) notes, this global revolution is "unfinished," as the current legal and political framework for democratic global governance, which would also include some kind of formal global citizenship, is not adequately developed. Conventional carriers of power and legitimacy, such as political parties within domestic systems, are in danger of becoming irrelevant, while unelected and unaccountable transnational networks of decision-makers are not subject to the checks and balances of representative government.

Media literacy as a means of enfranchising global citizens

The call for formalized global citizenship is not new. Supporters of cosmopolitan democracy have long called for various forms of global governance that would (i) extend the values, principles, and processes of democracy from the state to the international level by formally endowing global citizens with global rights and duties; (ii) ensure parity of representation and global enfranchisement through some form of world assembly or electoral process; (iii) protect universal humanitarian values by highlighting our common destiny; and (iv) enhance political legitimacy, global stability, and prosperity (see Archibugi & Held, 1995; Habermas, 2001).

Given the scale of the obstacles facing this effort—such as widespread public mistrust of globalization, a resurgence of nationalism in Europe and the United States, the crisis facing the European Union, and the salience of cultural, linguistic, and religious differences across the world—the prospect of democratic global governance in which citizens have a formal role seems theoretical at the moment. Yet, even if global citizenship does not exist in law (de jure), it exists in practice (de facto), as billions of people around the world engage with global current affairs, with one another, and with the global community. Global citizens today become aware of global issues via the media; they debate and interact with citizens from other countries in forums and social media; they express their voice through user-generated content; they participate in multiple forms of global civic activity such as protests, petitions, and fundraising campaigns; and they become emotionally and aesthetically invested in the symbolic and affective aspects of the global digital culture, through satire, memes, photographs, videos, hashtags, self-expression (see Mihailidis, 2014).

This wealth of activity constitutes the third empirical layer of global citizenship, not only because it is fundamentally political or because it takes place across national borders but also because it affects decision-making (through advocacy and the pressure of global public opinion), it socializes and influences others, and it creates political and media events in the same way in which civic action operates within national borders. Given the scale of the global community and the fact that a significant part of this activity takes place online, digital media are fundamental to the exercise of global citizenship, even more so than media have been within national public spheres. This poses profound challenges for democratic representation and participation and raises important questions.

If digital media are vital for an individual to enjoy his or her rights as a global citizen, then those who lack access to media—or who do not possess those resources, means, skills, and competencies needed to acquire and assess information and to meaningfully participate in digital culture—are effectively disenfranchised. Emerging challenges in the digital ecosystem, such as fake news, algorithmic personalization, surveillance, identity theft, and filter bubbles raise significant barriers to equal access to the emerging global public sphere. Media and digital literacy then provides citizens with the toolkit that enables them to access information, critically evaluate and produce content, develop empathy, have meaningful interactions (including with people and opinions that challenge them), experience a shared identity across borders, and fulfill their role as global citizens. Hence media and digital literacy is not peripheral to global citizenship; rather it is a fundamental mechanism of enfranchisement and inclusion in the global community.

SEE ALSO: Civic Activism; Civic Media; Media Access and Activism; Mediatization; Participatory Politics and the Civic Dimensions of Media Literacy

References

Anderson, B. (1983). *Imagined communities: Reflections on the origin and spread of nationalism.* London, England: Verso.

Archibugi, D., & Held, D. (1995). *Cosmopolitan democracy: An agenda for a new world order.* Cambridge, England: Polity.

Goldin, I. (2013). *Divided nations: Why global governance is failing and what we can do about it.* Oxford, England: Oxford University Press.

Habermas, J. (2001). *The postnational constellation.* Cambridge, England: Polity.

Malloch-Brown, M. (2011). *The unfinished global revolution: The limits of nations and the pursuit of a new politics.* London, England: Allen Lane.

Mihailidis, P. (2014). *Media literacy and the emerging citizen: Youth, engagement and participation in digital culture*. New York, NY: Peter Lang.
Rhodes, R.A.W. (1997). *Understanding governance: Policy networks, governance, reflexivity, and accountability*. Philadelphia, PA: Open University Press.

Further reading

Brown, G.W., & Held, D. (2010). *The cosmopolitanism reader*. Cambridge, England: Polity.
Held, D., & McGrew, A. (2007). *Globalization/anti-globalization: Beyond the great divide* (2nd ed.). Cambridge, England: Polity.
Johnston, R.J., Taylor, P.J., & Watts, M.J. (Eds.) (2002). *Geographies of global change* (2nd ed.). Oxford, England: Blackwell.
Scullion, R., Gerodimos, R., Jackson, D., & Lilleker, D. (Eds.). (2013). *The media, political participation and empowerment*. London, England: Routledge.
Seitz, J.K. (2008). *Global issues: An introduction* (3rd ed.). Oxford, England: Wiley Blackwell.
Slaughter, A.M. (2004). *A new world order*. Princeton, NJ: Princeton University Press.

Roman Gerodimos is principal lecturer in global current affairs at Bournemouth University and a faculty member at the Salzburg Academy on Media & Global Change. He is a Fellow of the Higher Education Academy and the recipient of the Arthur McDougall Prize awarded by the Political Studies Association for his research on online youth civic engagement. He has published in leading scholarly journals, has edited volumes, and is the coeditor of two books—on media and political participation and on the Greek crisis. His current research focuses on urban coexistence and public space and on the challenges facing democracy due to globalization and digitization.

Health Literacy

ANGELA COOKE-JACKSON
California State University, Los Angeles, USA

The intersection of health and literacy might seem obvious, yet it is only in the past four decades that scholars and practitioners have written about the two as a common construct—health literacy (Simonds, 1974). The term *literacy* was exclusively applied to reading and writing in the United States; but, as societal, cultural, and individual norms shifted, so did its definition. For instance, Nutbeam (2000) found that the definition was useful "to describe and explain the relationship between patient literacy levels and their ability to comply with prescribed therapeutic regimens" (p. 263). His definition was more specific to the patient–provider relationship. Conversely, the World Health Organization (see Nutbeam, 1998, p. 349) proposed a broader definition, according to which health literacy represents "the cognitive and social skills which determine the motivation and ability of individuals to gain access to, understand and use information in ways which promote and maintain good health." The WHO's definition and efforts toward agency and self-efficacy sought to move individuals beyond the capacity to read pamphlets or arrive at doctors' appointments on time. Basically it emphasized enriched individual experiences, as well as personal agency and knowledge of specific health disparities whereby a person received tools to steer through a complicated healthcare terrain.

A brief overview of health communication

The field of health communication has been instrumental to the development of health literacy, hence it is important to be aware of its origin and multilayered definitions. The field dates back to 1972, when a group of communication scholars gathered at the International Communication Association (ICA) conference in Chicago to form the

The International Encyclopedia of Media Literacy. Renee Hobbs and Paul Mihailidis (Editors-in-Chief), Gianna Cappello, Maria Ranieri, and Benjamin Thevenin (Associate Editors).

Therapeutic Communication Interest Group. This eclectic group of scholars sought to affirm the legitimacy of health and health-related activities and the importance of these activities to their research, particularly as it related to the field of communication. Over the course of the next 50 years the field would bear the name "health communication" as a title highlighting the idea that research in this field would seek to understand interpersonal-oriented communication as well as persuasion, mass communication, and communication campaigns. The definition emphasized the importance of the transactional process inherent in communication, in tandem with a specific focus on health information and on how and through what mechanisms the information is disseminated.

As in any multifaceted and multidisciplinary field, numerous definitions have emerged over time in health communication; all reflect the ways in which different health sectors address their primary goals and objectives, which focus on reaching different populations and groups. The goal is "to exchange health-related information, ideas, and methods in order to influence, engage, empower, and support individuals, communities, healthcare professionals, patients, policymakers, organizations, special groups and the public so that they will champion, introduce, adopt, or sustain health or social behavior, practice, or policy that will ultimately improve individual, community and public health outcomes" (Schiavo, 2007, p. 7).

As the field expanded and prominent organizations saw the importance and value of the research it produced, many adopted their own definitions, to reflect their specific goals. For instance, the National Cancer Institution (NCI) and the Centers for Disease Control and Prevention (CDC) see health communication as "the study and use of communication strategies to inform and influence individual and community decisions that enhance health" (US Department of Health and Human Services, 2008, p. 3). The definition reflects core values where the primary goal is to propose and design resources at numerous levels, including sources such as brochures or websites to communication campaigns.

The National Institutes of Health (NIH) defines health communication as "the study and use of communication strategies to inform and influence individual and community decisions that enhance health" (n.d., para. 2). NIH places specific emphasis on the importance of health literacy, noting the complexities of human communication and the need to promote individual understanding in information exchanges (National Institutes of Health, n.d.).

Fundamentally, the applied discipline of health communication seeks to understand health behaviors and to motivate behavior changes using messages that target specific populations and health disparities. As a result, an area in the field of health communication that has become increasingly visible is health literacy. The term *health literacy* is typically defined as "the degree to which individuals have the capacity to obtain, process, and understand basic health information and services needed to make appropriate health decisions" (Ratzan & Parker, 2000). The literature on health literacy is extensive. For instance, the National Academy of Sciences has reported on literacy, as it relates to medication usage and to the ability to read prescription labels. Additional research looks at health literacy and racial and ethnic inequalities in health outcomes. This work seeks to highlight health literacy alongside media literacy.

Understanding media and health literacy

Media literacy

Media literacy, which refers to the training of individuals in sharing information in integrated spaces of hypermedia activity, aims to engage people in more active civic lifestyles. Cooke-Jackson and Barnes (2013) observe that the concept is based on developing critical thinking skills and on being able to find, interpret, and evaluate relevant information. This foundation provides space for an individual to build skills around the generation of creative ideas, media production and promotion, and leadership through civic engagement. Moreover, fluency with information technology encourages critical thinking and judgment, as a result of which individuals can move from being media consumers to becoming engaged citizens. Basically fluency strengthens an individual's capacity not only to evaluate media around him or her but also to create his or her own media products with ease. To that end, understanding media literacy—the capacity to reason about media-based messages in relation to us, as a learned means of self-identification—is valuable for understanding health literacy. Health literacy, then, makes sense as an important means of disseminating health information while inviting people to inspect it and to acquire it. The more digitized communication we receive, the more reliant we become on our human application and analysis of these messages, where knowledge and the ability to scrutinize meanings and misgivings are crucial.

Health literacy

The rapid growth of our dynamic landscape in digital technology has changed how individuals communicate and interact within their families, communities, and societal structures. It has simultaneously increased the divide among low-literate, marginalized, and disparate populations. For instance, one study on web-based interventions for colorectal cancer screening acknowledged that the researchers not only made assumptions about their population's use of the web but also mistakenly believed that, when accessed, their innovative online health resources would be instrumental to removing confusion about cancer. In their conclusion, the authors of the study note that, while emerging technology can provide a fertile ground for growth, there are challenges that start with considering who is seeking health information on websites and about what (Fleisher et al., 2012).

Currently more than 90 million adults in the United States have low health literacy levels, hence the complex language used in healthcare has implications for families, communities, and national health systems. Notably, health literacy has implications for the individual as well as for policy, the environment, industry, and disease prevention. Moreover, health literacy does not just mean that an individual has the reading skills to understand the language used by health professionals and in health policies. To be health literate, individuals must be able to analyze general health information—text, charts, symbols, abbreviations, and so on—as it pertains to them and to their specific cultural and social norms and values. Basically, health literacy implies that individuals and communities can weigh risks and benefits and then make informed decisions and take action. For this reason, it seems obvious, as the US Department of Health and Human Services (n.d.) believes, that culture has major implications on how individuals communicate and understand health information. In consequence health practitioners must be culturally and linguistically competent, in order to make sure that positive health outcomes are accessible and useful among diverse populations.

When one investigates health literacy through the lens of the media, one finds other applications of the term as well. For instance, media advocacy and interactive health communication have strategically applied the term to explain mass access to information via mass media (television, radio, Internet) and via interactive technology (smart phones, tablets, augmented reality), to unpack how the larger public accesses messages, information, and services of interest in order to understand different health issues and disparities.

For instance, there has been a proliferation of research that investigates health and media literacy among adolescents and teens. This work makes the most sense when it seeks to increase agency and to enrich the lives of teens at an individual and societal level. More and more research attempts to understand the intersection of media literacy, health literacy, and health communication in relation to adolescents and young adults, especially on topics of sexual health, mental health, and gender. This body of research can be attributed to the rise in the use of new technology and the Internet among these age groups. Much of this work has been developed in order to help this population decipher and evaluate the content and the quality of health information.

On a global front, nurses and public health practitioners have acknowledged the importance of understanding low literacy in relation to birth rates among Aboriginal and Torres Strait Islander communities. Scholars investigated sleeping environments, parenting practices, and infant death rates, specifically the sudden unexpected death in infancy (SUDI) and its association with co-sleeping (i.e., the practice of sleeping alongside the baby instead of putting the baby back in the crib before and after breastfeeding). This ongoing research uses a model whereby Indigenous health workers (IHW)—who played full roles as community health educators—integrate PhotoStories on iPads into the day-to-day education of families, allowing them to visualize the implications of co-sleeping. This innovative use of technology lets mothers share their stories by offering personal narratives and instructions for co-sleeping care in digital format. Over time scholars observed a decrease in the number of sudden unexpected death in infants. Importantly, the culturally relevant strategy has been instrumental in improving health outcomes and in fostering long-term community resilience.

It is important to note that, as the concept of literacy shifts, so does the research on health literacy. At the outset, health literacy emphasized the individual and provided interaction within the healthcare system. Notably, scholars believe there is still room for growing and that there is still work to be done to reach an inclusive definition of health literacy. Furthermore, they realize that a person's literacy levels do not always reflect the complex health materials that that person receives; nor does the emergence of online communication explain how complex human skills make a literate citizen.

Conclusion

New directions and new growth in the area of health literacy are worth investigating. For instance, sexual health literacy on topics of sexuality and sexual health has emerged in gender identity and in negotiation work that challenges, specifically, heteronormative ideologies that marginalize LGTBQ people (Rubinsky & Cooke-Jackson, 2017). Mental health literacy, defined as "knowledge and beliefs about mental disorders which aid in their recognition, management or prevention," is also a promising emergent area of research (Jorm et al., 1997, p. 182). These are only a few of the new health literacy themes under investigation. To conclude, Ratzan (2001) poignantly observes that "communication alone is not a simple solution to the complex problem of health literacy"; instead, as he notes, "health literacy ought to be the common twenty-first-century currency we all share that values health as a central tenet of individual and community life" (p. 214).

SEE ALSO: Communication; Health Media Literacy; History of Media Literacy; Literacy, Technology, and Media; Media Literacy in Australia

References

Cooke-Jackson, A., & Barnes, K. (2013). Peer-to-peer mentoring among urban youth: The intersection of health communication, media literacy and digital health vignettes. *Journal of Digital and Media Literacy, 1*, 1–20.

Fleisher, L., Kandadai, V., Keenan, E., Miller, S., Devarajan, K., Ruth, K., … Weinberg, D. (2012). Build it, and will they come? Unexpected findings from a study on a web-based intervention to improve colorectal cancer screening. *Journal of Health Communication, 17*(1), 41–53.

Jorm, A.F., Korten, A.E., Jacomb, P.A., Christensen, H., Rodgers, B., & Pollitt. P. (1997). "Mental health literacy": A survey of the public's ability to recognise mental disorders and their beliefs about the effectiveness of treatment. *Medical Journal of Australia, 166*, 182–186.

National Institutes of Health. (n.d.). Clear communication. Retrieved from https://www.nih.gov/institutes-nih/nih-office-director/office-communications-public-liaison/clear-communication

Nutbeam, D. (1998). Health promotion glossary. *Health Promotion International, 13*(4), 349–364. doi: 10.1093/heapro/13.4.349

Nutbeam, D. (2000). Health literacy as a public health goal: A challenge for contemporary health education and communication strategies into the 21st century. *Health Promotion International, 15*(3), 259–267.

Ratzan, S.C. (2001). Health literacy: Communication for the public good. *Health Promotion International, 16*(2), 207–214.

Ratzan, S.C., & Parker, R.M. (2000). Introduction. In C.R. Selden, M. Zorn, S.C. Ratzan, & R.M. Parker (Eds.), *Health literacy* (pp. v–vii). Bethesda, MD: National Institutes of Health, US Department of Health and Human Services.

Rubinsky, V., & Cooke-Jackson, A. (2017). Where is the love? Expanding and theorizing with LGTBQ Memorable Messages of sex and sexuality. *Health Communication, 32*(12), 1472–1480.

Schiavo, R. (2007). *Health communication: From theory to practice.* San Francisco, CA: Wiley.

Simonds, S.K. (1974). Health education as social policy. *Health Education Monograph, 2*, 1–25.

US Department of Health and Human Services. (2008). Making health communication programs work. Retrieved from https://www.cancer.gov/publications/health-communication/pink-book.pdf

US Department of Health and Human Services. (n.d). Quick guide to health literacy fact sheet. Office of Disease and Prevention and Health Promotion. Retrieved from https://health.gov/communication/literacy/quickguide/Quickguide.pdf

Further reading

Berkman, N.D., Davis, T.C., & McCormack, L. (2010). Health literacy: What is it? *Journal of Health Communication, 15*(2), 8–19.

Nutbeam, D. (2008). The evolving concept of health literacy. *Social Science & Medicine, 67*, 2072–2078.

Sorensen, K., Van der Broucke, S., Fullam, J., Doyle, G., Pelikan, J., Slonska, Z., … & HLS-EU, Consortium. (2012). Health literacy and public health: A systematic review and integration of definitions and models. *BMC Public Health, 12*. doi: 10.1186/1471-2458-12-80.

Thoman, E., & Jolls, T. (2004). Media literacy: A national priority for a changing world. *American Behavioral Scientist, 48*(1), 18–29.

Young, J., Watson, K.L., Kearney, L. Cowan, S., & Craigie, L. (2014). *Safe sleep advice to safe sleep action: Pilot of the Pepi-Pod Program in Indigenous communities. Paper presented at the university research conference "Communication, Collaborate, Connect," Sunshine Coast, Australia, July, 14–18.*

Zarcadolas, C., Pleasant, A., & Greer, D.S. (2005). Understanding health literacy: An expanding model. *Health Promotion International, 20*(2), 195–203.

Angela Cooke-Jackson is associate professor of health communication and behavioral science at California State University, Los Angeles. She envisions her research at the nexus of culture, health disparities, and marginalized populations. Her cross-disciplinary scholarship and applied approach incorporate digital platforms, media literacy, and civic engagement to unpack health issues among at-risk urban youth and women of color. Her international research aspirations have taken her to Australia, Italy, Peru, and Hong Kong. Her travels to Australia were most enriching because they strengthened her understanding of the similar health disparities among indigenous Aboriginal, Torres Strait Islander, and people of color in the United States. Her work has been published in a number of books and in journals such as *Health Communication*, *Communication Teacher*, *Communication Studies*, the *Journal of Human Sexuality*, the *Journal of Intercultural Communication Research*, and *Qualitative Research Reports in Communication*.

Health Media Literacy

VANESSA E. GREENWOOD
Montclair State University, USA

Health media literacy (HML) is the enactment of media literacy within the context of health. It is particularly focused on how the understanding and enactment of health and health-related behaviors are influenced by, enacted through, and shaped by the rapidly changing technologically mediated environments in which humans live. HML requires accessing and understanding information, analyzing and evaluating its credibility and relevance, and actively applying new knowledge to enact healthy behaviors. Broadly conceived, HML implies the creation of healthy media environments for one's own individual benefit and for the benefit of society. HML has also been referenced internationally as media health literacy (MHL) and critical media health literacy (CMHL). The United Nations Educational, Scientific and Cultural Organisation (UNESCO) also refers to health literacy within the broad constellation of information and media literacy.

Conceptual origins

HML is an outgrowth from the concept of *health literacy* that originated more than two decades ago. The World Health Organization (WHO) defines *health literacy* as the ability to obtain, process, and understand health information and services necessary to make appropriate health decisions. The focus of health literacy is primarily the healthcare context relative to individualized patient treatment. Examples of this include navigating an illness, enacting (un)healthy behaviors, and making sense of healthcare policy. Common examples of health literate behaviors include the ability to treat a common illness at home; to schedule a doctor's appointment; to understand an informed consent document; to read a prescription label; to maintain oral health; and to prevent obesity. Health literate behaviors tap the individual's ability to speak, write, listen, compute, and to achieve conceptual understanding. From this perspective, health literacy has traditionally focused on print literacy and numeracy skills. Navigating the modern healthcare context requires an increasingly complex set of skills, such as understanding graphs or visual information, operating a computer, evaluating the credibility and truthfulness of health information, analyzing the risks and benefits of a particular treatment, and interpreting test results. Those who possess below-average health literacy are at added risk, as they are less likely to rely on written materials and more likely to rely on radio or television, healthcare professionals, family, friends, or coworkers for health information.

Given widespread print illiteracy, health illiteracy has emerged over the past two decades as "the silent epidemic" (Marcus, 2006, p. 339) that operates from a deficit model (e.g., solving a problem, treating an illness, and/or curing a disease). More recently, however, health literacy scholars and practitioners have called for an asset-based model (vs. a risk-oriented one) that integrates media literacy in critical analysis of health messages (Nutbeam, 2008; St. Leger, 2001). The constraints of relying on measures of print literacy, coupled with the significant increase in the mass mediation of health information over the past two decades, compel researchers, educators, and policymakers to find ways to draw on alternative forms of literacy, such as digital and media literacies.

There has recently emerged a "second wave" of health literacy research that emphasizes self-actualization while going beyond one's own self-centeredness to constitute a healthy populace of individuals and communities (Estacio, 2013). This evolutionary change in health literacy promotes empowerment and civic engagement. Along this vein, HML requires contextualizing choices and behaviors according to external factors of influence while also taking responsibility for one's own health and increasing the health of families and communities. This conceptual definition was recently crystalized by the work of Canadian scholars Joan Wharf Higgins and Deborah Begoray, who in 2012 conducted a conceptual analysis using the terms *health literacy*, *critical health literacy*, *media literacy*, *critical media literacy*, *media activism*, and *critical viewing*. They arrived at the construct of *critical media health literacy* to signify a right of citizenship that empowers individuals and groups "to critically interpret and use media as a means to engage in decision-making processes and dialogues; exert control over their health and everyday events; and make healthy changes for themselves and their communities" (p. 142). Drawing on this advocacy orientation, HML positions medical decision-making as merely one of its many goals, as it encompasses a broad constellation of sociocultural, political, and economic factors beyond the healthcare system.

Theoretical frameworks

HML offers an *ecological* approach to health media, positioning it as a complex message system that imposes on human beings certain ways of thinking, feeling, and behaving. Historically, media technologies have served as powerful communication channels to persuade the public in ways that can improve health and also to thwart it. Humans currently live within a vast ecology of media forms that include smart devices/computers, television, and other screen-based devices in addition to traditional broadcast media such as film, television, radio, newspapers, magazines, and books. Public health communication has morphed into an era of transmedia where oral, print, broadcast, and digital media converge. Mobile devices, including cell phones, and social media not only provide a public gateway for circulating health information, they also serve as a vehicle for health research by supplying portals for crowdsourced data that are fed back to the public. The use of modern media technologies to individually and collectively support positive health behaviors is groundbreaking. At the same time, our user-centered technologies result in more data than we know how to handle. The World Wide Web is a vast wilderness where prestigious research institutions coexist with highly commercial entities. Despite providing essentially free access to vast amounts of information, the Internet also poses a major challenge to the quality and reliability of health information. In this sense, HML is firmly grounded in symbolic interactionism where the media form (and its use) influence health and how audiences/consumers learn and live when it comes to health.

The convergence of media environments and the global proliferation of screen-based technologies raise questions as to the type of skills required for HML. At minimum, this implies an awareness of how the medium shapes the message and ideally a technological skill set aligned with that knowledge. This is particularly salient as humans currently learn about the world through devices and screens and less through direct lived experience. HML requires more than digital connectivity to information: it also requires social connectivity. In this sense, the theoretical framework most aligned with HML is social constructivism, which situates all humans as creators of their own understanding. Humans are both consumers and creators of information as they learn about health and act upon that knowledge. Not everyone agrees to what extent humans actively participate in this meaning-making process, however.

The convergence of *media* literacy with health literacy is a crucial dimension of HML, as it bridges the gap between knowledge and the health-related behavior. The connector is reflective inquiry; obtaining a personal understanding of the importance of critical analysis (of media messages, forms, and technologies) and what it reveals. In this sense, the key questions for HML seek a deeper understanding of the interpretation, constructions, ownership, values, and languages of media messages: How do humans interpret health messages? How is health constructed through mass media? How are media languages used to construct health? What values are associated with health through and across media? Who owns the media constructions of health? Answering these questions is not enough to achieve HML. Inquiry must lead to action. Along this vein, HML draws on a core principle of media literacy that individuals of all ages can and should also creatively *produce* media messages, share them, and then act upon them. No longer are health messages created, distributed, and received via a broadcast model. Globalization and democratization of media allow access and circulation of information in real time. Ultimately, however, those who have access to and control of the information environment will determine the purpose and quite possibly the outcome of health messaging.

By placing singular responsibility for health on the individual, we fail to hold accountable those institutional structures that disable individual agency and impede our ability to enact health behaviors. While HML is a set of individual skills, it cannot be accomplished without societal structures that allow individuals to conscientiously exercise their agency. HML is therefore influenced by cultural studies, which positions mass media as facilitators of top-down social, economic, and political oppression. However, a liberatory approach views media as tools for democratic practices for the purpose of resisting oppression. The WHO suggests that healthcare policies and practices are more likely to be successful if they modify both the physical and the social environments rather than simply rely on the limited success of changing individual behavior. When it comes to individual behavior, clinicians say that print literacy can be a stronger predictor of an individual's health status than income, employment status, education level, race, or ethnicity. On the other hand, others argue that print literacy isn't necessarily prerequisite to health literacy if individuals can speak, listen, and stand up for themselves. HML therefore must be inclusive of diverse cultural concepts of health that include economic, psychosocial, environmental, and spiritual attributes.

Since the 1940s the WHO and its member states have promoted good health as one of the fundamental rights of every human being. For decades, critical health literacy researchers and practitioners have intentionally included marginalized populations who lack access to health knowledge due to language barriers or illiteracy. However, assessing print literacy skills alone does not adequately address health as simultaneously shaped by historical, social, political, and economic forces. Like critical health literacy, HML borrows from critical theory and more specifically the liberatory philosophy of Paulo Freire. HML emphasizes what information is communicated, what information is withheld, and how individuals/populations use/create media in response to these messages. From a critical theoretical perspective, HML is a communal process where citizens become aware of oppressive issues, engage in critical dialogue, and become actively involved in health decision-making. Yet it is unclear in the research what constitute empowerment-based skills and how those can be cultivated.

Health is also not just the absence of illness or disease; it is a state of complete physical, mental, and social well-being. Yet there remain systemic and widespread stumbling blocks to achieving this ideal. Individuals are steeped in an environment of information that is brief, highly constructed, and often contradictory. Health information is produced and distributed by many different and often competing sources, including government, food and drug industries, and corporate marketers. The public health threats associated with sugary beverages, fast food, prescription drugs, and physical inactivity comprise what cultural critics call an "industrial epidemic" where corporations undermine public health through complex media campaigns and the strategic shaping of public policy (Moodie et al., 2013, p. 671). These competing priorities play out in public schools within the United States, as formal health curriculum defines and promotes nutritional standards while at the same time school cafeterias, vending machines, and advertisements provide children with easy access to junk food. Food marketing to children is a global public health problem and pervades North American, Latin American, and South American countries. The emergence of an unhealthy commodities industry in many countries and their financial and institutional relations with public health researchers, nongovernmental organizations, and national and international health agencies exacerbate an already heated conflict between global health and the profit motives of corporations. HML is concerned with identifying those structures that impair the agency of individuals in order to empower individuals and communities.

Research methods

There are currently no set standards for measuring the constructs, domains, dimensions, or levels of HML. Higgins & Begoray (2012) attribute this to the variety of definitions and numerous conceptual frameworks surrounding health literacy and media literacy. Conversations about health literacy have primarily consisted of voices of medical health professionals. Similarly, the contexts for studying health literacy have been patient–physician communication, healthcare, and health promotion. The methodology for studying health literacy is predominantly the measurement of reading ability (literacy) or self-report data, such as a pretest/posttest format to gauge critical thinking abilities. Ways of measuring health literacy have been limited to clinical screenings, reading comprehension, word recognition and numeracy, population literacy studies, or direct surveys that measure comprehension of health information. Health literacy indicators focus mainly on adult patients being able to decode written information and interpret information to comply with doctors' orders.

With the emergence of each new communications technology, the assumption also emerges that dissemination of correct information will produce a change in public health attitudes, values, and behaviors, for better and also for worse. While the goals of health literacy are improved health and well-being, scholars note that the bulk of research focuses on the negative effects of the lack of health literacy. More contexts outside clinical settings are much needed in developing measurements for HML. Public health researchers are investigating new approaches to quantifying health literacy levels. While these data can shed light on immediate interventions, researchers note that HML is a longer-term process requiring more longitudinal approaches.

Like media effects research, much of the research in public health education is grounded in the experimental hypothesis testing used in the natural sciences. A meta-analysis of research in the area of health-promoting media literacy indicates positive behavior-related outcomes as a result of media interventions (Jeong, Cho, & Hwang, 2012). The traditional approach to combatting health illiteracy (vs. fostering health literacy) is a top-down approach that assumes a direct causal relationship between health media and audiences. For nearly half a century, the dominant assumption has been that correct health information will produce a trigger-like reaction whereby new health facts lead to a change in health attitudes and values that will in turn bring about changes in health practices. The enduring assumption is that knowledge about diet, exercise, drugs, safety, oral health, sexuality, and relationships will develop certain attitudes that will lead to specific behavioral outcomes. The likelihood that public service advertising (PSA) campaigns will result in teens being less likely to use drugs, however, heavily depends upon how young people make sense of targeted media messages.

Based on the perceived effects of media on health, US agencies frame media literacy as a preventative measure or tool for reducing its negative effects. The US Department of Health and Human Services and the White House National Drug Control Policy have identified media literacy as a preventative measure for drug abuse. The American Academy of Pediatrics also advocates media literacy as a preventative measure for the negative effects of tobacco, alcohol, and food marketing. According to public health researchers, effective media campaigns focus on well-designed messages that are delivered to their intended audience with sufficient reach and frequency to be seen or heard and remembered (Bertrand, O'Reilly, Denison, Anhang, & Sweat, 2006). By far the most prevalent research on mass media effects is in the area of tobacco use prevention. One of the most successful public health media campaigns (i.e., the "truth" campaign) was responsible for 22% of the observed decline in youth smoking between 1999 and 2002 (Abroms & Maibach, 2008). If the priority is to influence behavior, then one might expect public media health campaigns to employ the same effective rhetorical devices used by advertisers, marketing professionals, and public relations specialists.

The challenge remains in the difficulty in measuring the success of such mass media interventions and their effectiveness.

Similar to the objectives of commercial media advertising, the objective of public health campaigns is to evoke cognitive and/or emotional responses that will lead to behavioral change. Scientific methodology does not fully explain human behavior, as humans are moral agents. Human behavior is complex and grounded in, among other things, cognition, skills, motivation, intentions, and demographic factors. More research is needed to understand the intersection of media and interpersonal communication and the general media ecologies of health. From this perspective, research that focuses exclusively on individual behaviors while ignorant of systemic forces may prove obsolete.

Conceptualizing public health as primarily the search for remedies or cures for ailments is a similar problem to defining media literacy as the search for audience protection from the perceived harmful effects of the media. Through and across the broadcasting era of the 20th century the focus has been the protection of audiences, especially young people, from the harms of media content and form(s). This inoculation approach has largely been ineffective in that it assumes that all audiences interpret media messages in essentially the same way. A more progressive approach is proactive rather than protectionist and empowers audiences and users within a media environment that is continuously evolving and increasingly complex.

A major challenge is that media literacy interventions have greater effects on knowledge about media and health than they have on attitudes and behavior. Health literacy, or even critical thinking about health, does not necessarily lead to behavioral change, which is a core function of the field of health promotion. Similarly, HML may cultivate media literacy skills but not necessarily lead to healthy behaviors. An agency approach to HML research, however, acknowledges the positive, negative, and unintended health effects of media use. For example, active video games that require players to physically move around may actually help to facilitate fitness and good health, although more research is needed to discover this potential. The media environment of humans also matters. Producers of children's media recognize this and tune into the interactions between player and platform. In this way, more research is needed with regards to the media ecology of media users, including the physiological, social, cultural, economic, and cultural factors that shape health behaviors and increase HML.

It is essential for all researchers and practitioners to acknowledge the constructed, owned, mediated, and technologized nature of health-related information. The commercialization of health communication is of particular concern. The United Nations Non-Communicable Diseases Action Group (UNNCDAG) has called for a new discipline of study to investigate industrial diseases "and the transnational corporations that drive them." Along this vein, the UNNCDAG recommends that researchers and educators refuse funding from tobacco, alcohol, and processed food and drink industries, or even those with which they affiliate. Future research must address the question, "What are the roles and responsibilities of corporations and governments in promoting HML?"

Ultimately, HML positions health not as an object to be acquired or a set of behaviors to imbue, but rather as a means of living within and seeing the world, which poses considerable challenges for identifying research methods. It is difficult to quantify HML, as it requires contextualizing choices and behaviors according to external factors of influence while also taking responsibility for one's own health and the health of families and communities. Community-based participatory research and "peer to peer messaging" where community members create (crowdsource) their own messages and catalyze civic engagement is one current methodology with promise. Ultimately, such qualitative yet empirical methods can empower researchers to more deeply understand the critical habits of mind and the skills of expression that in turn lead to knowledge about health and self-governance of the mind, body, and community.

SEE ALSO: Pediatric Perspectives on Media Literacy; Representation of Nutrition and Food in the Media; Representations of Gender, Sexuality, and Women in Popular Music

References

Abroms, L.C., & Maibach, E.W. (2008). The effectiveness of mass communication to change public behavior. *Annual Review of Public Health, 29*, 219–234. doi: 10.1146/annurev.publhealth.29.020907.090824

Bertrand, J.T., O'Reilly, K., Denison, R., Anhang, R., & Sweat, M. (2006). Systematic review of the effectiveness of mass communication programs to change HIV/AIDS-related behaviors in developing countries. *Health Education Research, 21*(4), 567–597. doi: 10.1093/her/cyl036

Estacio, E.V. (2013). Health literacy and community empowerment: It is more than just reading, writing and counting. *Journal of Health Psychology, 18*(8), 1056–1068. doi: 10.1177/1359105312470126

Higgins, J.W., & Begoray, D. (2012). Exploring the borderlands between media and health: Conceptualizing "critical media health literacy." *Journal of Media Literacy Education, 4*(2), 136–148. Retrieved from http://digitalcommons.uri.edu/jmle/vol4/iss2/4

Jeong, S.H., Cho, H., & Hwang, Y. (2012). Media literacy interventions: A meta-analytic review. *Journal of Communication, 62*(3), 454–472. doi: 10.1111/j.1460-2466.2012.01643.x

Marcus, E.N. (2006). The silent epidemic – the health effects of illiteracy. *New England Journal of Medicine, 355*(4), 339–341. doi: 10.1056/NEJMp058328

Moodie, R., Stuckler, D., Monteiro, C., Sheron, N., Neal, B., Thamarangsi, T., … & Casswell, S. (2013). Profits and pandemics: Prevention of harmful effects of tobacco, alcohol, and ultra-processed food and drink industries. *Lancet, 381*(9867), 670–679. doi: 10.1016/S0140-6736(12)62089-3

Nutbeam, D. (2008). The evolving concept of health literacy. *Social Science and Medicine, 67*(12), 2072–2078. doi: 10.1016/j.socscimed.2008.09.050

St. Leger, L. (2001). Schools, health literacy and public health: Possibilities and challenges. *Health Promotion International, 16*(2), 197–205. doi: 10.1093/heapro/16.2.197

Vanessa E. Greenwood is a full professor in the School of Communication and Media at Montclair State University in New Jersey. Dr. Greenwood is interested in how media technologies can support communicative and communal experiences among learners that ultimately lead to more democratic approaches to education and health. She is the author of *Rethinking Technology in Schools* (2009) and *Healthy Teens, Healthy Schools: How Media Literacy Education Can Renew Education in the United States* (2015).

Dr. Greenwood is the 2012 recipient of the Meritorious Service award from the National Association for Media Literacy Education (NAMLE) for her service as NAMLE Vice President and coeditor of the *Journal of Media Literacy Education*.

Hip-Hop Education

EMILY BAILIN WELLS
Columbia University, USA

The intellectual and sociohistorical contexts of hip-hop education

Hip-hop is most often defined as or associated with a genre of music, most notably for the linguistic style of rapping and the electronic beats that provide a rhythmic platform for expressing oneself and showcasing one's talents through wordplay, dance, music, and art. Hip-hop, however, is more than just a musical genre; it is a lifestyle, a culture, a knowledge base, and a platform for expression that emerged from building sociopolitical unrest in the South Bronx in the 1970s. It was an era in New York City characterized by deindustrialization, economic restructuring, and growing racial tensions (see Lipsitz, 1994). Hip-hop provided unprecedented outlets and platforms for marginalized populations, predominantly black and brown young people, to speak out and push back against the hegemonic ideologies, institutions, and systems that were oppressing communities and silencing injustices.

Hip-hop education, or hip-hop-based education, is education focused on the culture of young people of color whose realities are often discredited and disconnected from notions of success both in and out of the classroom. The pedagogical movement behind hip-hop education is responsive and emancipatory in nature, comprised of educators, scholars, activists, and teaching-artists committed to disrupting traditional conceptions of and approaches to education that have historically marginalized young people of color. The primary purpose and potential of hip-hop education is to authentically engage young people in their learning by working alongside them to forge stronger connections between their lived experiences outside of school and what they are learning in school. Hip-hop education is a type of culturally relevant and responsive pedagogy; it is a framework, a movement, and a mindset that positions young people as knowledge-holders and meaning-makers.

The historical roots and birth of hip-hop

There is an inextricable link between black music and the history and politics of black life (Asante, 2008). Foundational practices and causes for the emergence of hip-hop in the late 20th century can be traced back to song and storytelling traditions from Africa and the Caribbean West Indies up through the Civil War and the civil rights movement. The modes of song and storytelling over drum beats provided oppressed populations with ways to communicate with one another, to preserve memories and traditions of the past and pass them down to younger generations, and, most importantly, they were used to survive. Oral traditions provided life, love, and support in times of adversity, discrimination, and injustice.

Influenced by various musical genres such as blues, gospel, jazz, and reggae, there are four elements of hip-hop: DJ-ing (producers of music beats), MC-ing (individuals delivering messages through rapping or singing), breaking (dancing), and graffiti (creative and daring artwork). Clive Campbell, more famously known by his stage name, DJ Kool Herc, is credited with originating hip-hop music in the Bronx during the early 1970s. Using a two turntable system at parties, DJ Kool Herc would play two copies of the same funk record, isolating the instrumental portion of the song which emphasized the drum beat, or the "break," and elongated the song allowing for Herc to talk rhythmically over the beats, a practice that later came to be known as rapping. For Herc, the break was innately in the human. He aimed to create a spiritual and expressive space: an escape from reality. The MC, or master of ceremonies, later became synonymous with "rapper." Their job was to introduce the DJ, to get the crowd's energy up and keep it up, and eventually to deliver clever rhymes over the music. Break dancing, also known as "b-boying" (and later including "b-girling") was a style of street dance that would take place when the DJ would play with the breaks in songs. Breaking and graffiti became additional forms and outlets for young people to express themselves. The early years of hip-hop were about the music, looking and feeling good, and the social gatherings that brought the community together. In the mid-1980s and early 1990s—the golden age of hip-hop—the focus of hip-hop music turned to advanced lyricism with complex wordplay as well as the globalization of the music and culture. Throughout the 1990s, different sounds and styles of hip-hop music and culture continued to emerge across the country and around the world, becoming a global phenomenon.

There is a fifth element of hip-hop that is least discussed but arguably the most important: "knowledge of self," how people think about and construct who they are. Knowledge of self is less tangible than the other elements but the one that is most connected to the psychology of and history behind hip-hop. It is also the element that is most lacking in contemporary hip-hop culture and literature. Knowledge of self puts forth the idea of self as collective. It requires a deep command of hip-hop histories and traditions that convey largely unspoken but intuitive understandings of collectivity, history, and inherent cosmopolitanism, meaning that every individual is and should be connected to one another based on shared history, culture, and identity. Knowledge of self refers to how individuals view their identities and how they enact their authentic selves, a concept that has been an integrally foundational component of hip-hop education.

Because hip-hop and youth are inextricably linked, school has served as a foundational place where hip-hop culture has emerged and evolved. School, however, is also often a place of rules and structure that does not allow for young people to bring their lived experiences and personal interests and styles into the classroom. Young people use hip-hop as a mode to bring themselves, their culture, and the ways they understand the world around them into institutional settings, but these practices are often relegated to peripheral spaces like hallways, the cafeteria, and outside the school building. Hip-hop education seeks to center and cultivate these practices *within* classroom spaces: to celebrate the ways in which young people use hip-hop to construct "locally validated selves and senses of community" (Dimitriadis, 2001, p. 2).

The evolution and components of hip-hop education

Hip-hop education has experienced significant theoretical and pedagogical changes over the past 20 years. In the early 1990s, as hip-hop became a central component of youth culture and American popular culture, the emerging field of hip-hop studies primarily produced scholarship focused on historical analyses of hip-hop culture and descriptive explanations of the educational potential of rap lyrics (Hill & Petchauer, 2013). These early works also served as counternarratives to the images and messages in mainstream rap music that provided thin narratives of urban youth and urban culture. A commercialized subgenre of hip-hop known as "gangsta rap" emerged in the early 1990s, filled with images and messages that frequently glorified drugs and money, hypersexualized women, and focused on "making it." Getting out of the "hood" was often narrowly depicted as becoming a rap star or a professional athlete. It was at a similar time in the United States that media literacy was garnering attention and gaining traction as it offered perspectives and strategies for how to think critically about and challenge problematic images and messages in mainstream media and popular culture texts.

Young people often utilize images and messages that they receive through the media and dominant narratives of what it means to be an "urban youth" to create self-concepts, but these constructions of "self" do not always align with who they really are and who they want to be. Identity formation is a central task in adolescent development and membership and therefore must be taken into account when considering how other sociocultural influences such as race, class, gender, family, friends, and peer culture shape an individual's developmental path. Hip-hop has historically served as a space for young people to experiment with aspects of their identities and find their community by connecting with others who share understandings of what it means to be a person of color and marginalized in this country (Dimitriadis, 2001). The mainstream stories that are constructed about urban youths and urban youth culture oftentimes reinforce "deficit narratives" (academic failure, cultural and physical violence, lesser life chances, etc.) and leave little room for urban youths themselves to question, challenge, and talk back to these mainstream narratives and representations.

In the late 1990s and early 2000s, the focus of hip-hop scholarship shifted toward producing more tangible pedagogical practices and curricular strategies for integrating hip-hop texts into the classroom. Early hip-hop education largely focused on rap music texts: how to deconstruct them with young people and how to bring them into the classroom to better engage students and/or expand notions of what counts as "literacy" and "text" (see Hill & Petchauer, 2013).

Recent scholarship has challenged conventional notions of literacy by celebrating the unprecedented and fascinating multimodal literacy practices of young people (Vasudevan, Shultz, & Bateman, 2010). Recognizing how nontraditional literacies can provide young people with opportunities to share pieces of themselves, their lived experiences, and their perspectives can present unprecedented and unique access points to learning, engaging, and creating. Critical literacy practices are meant to foster community building through the creation of dialogues and listening opportunities through which participants work to develop critical stances and authentic voices. In the past decade, hip-hop education has gained depth and traction across the educational landscape, as greater emphasis has been placed on the importance of innovative, interdisciplinary approaches to teaching and learning.

The importance of listening to and incorporating student voice around issues of cultural relevance and inclusivity has become undeniable over the past decade as classroom populations have increasingly diversified in terms of race, ethnicity, socioeconomic status, and educational needs (Goodwin, 2010). Educational scholars argue that better connections must be made between what students are experiencing in their classrooms and in their outside lives. Young people have incredibly unique perspectives on the dynamics between their schools and communities, which must be recognized as promising catalysts for change. Students should be among those considered to have the "knowledge and position to shape what counts as education, to reconfigure power dynamics and discourse practices within existing realms of conversation about education," and to create new platforms and forums within which students can embrace the potential to exercise voice and agency (Cook-Sather, 2002).

In an historical sense, hip-hop education and media literacy education are tightly bound in that both fields work to challenge traditional conceptions of and approaches to literacy. Both are about expanding conceptions of literacy to include how we read both the word and the world (see Freire, 1970). Both work to demonstrate the validity of educational approaches and the incorporation of cultures that extend beyond the purview of traditional methods of schooling. Both advocate for the recognition of young people as possessors of significant and important social, symbolic, and cultural capital and knowledge. Hip-hop education draws from critical literacies and culturally relevant pedagogies. The field of critical literacies addresses imbalances of power and, in particular, pays attention to the voices of those less frequently heard. One of the most significant aspects of critical literacy education is that it begins with and remains tightly bound to one's lived experiences (Morrell, 2009).

Much like the 21st-century understandings of media and digital literacy education, hip-hop education focuses on deconstructing existing texts. In the past decade, however, these fields have placed greater emphasis on empowering young people to be active and critical consumers of mass media and popular culture texts through composition and production activities that position them as authors and meaning-makers. Critical media educators have encouraged youths to develop literacies that enable them not only to analyze structures of power, particularly with regard to race, class, gender, and sexual identity, and develop commitments to social transformation (Hill & Vasudevan, 2008), but to interrupt cycles of power and injustice by producing their own texts. Creating original multimodal texts provides young people with opportunities to express themselves, reflect on lived experiences, and respond to inaccurate or problematic images, messages, and representations in the media and popular culture. These experiences can also facilitate increased feelings of empowerment and self-worth among young creators.

Today, the pedagogical commitments of hip-hop education remain rooted in the necessity of acknowledging, incorporating, and celebrating the culture, history, and everyday experiences of young people. Hip-hop education is about emotion, empathy, self-care, belonging, and well-being. Much of the field of hip-hop education is focused on and committed to fundamentally rethinking what education and pedagogy might look like in increasingly diversifying 21st-century schools. Hip-hop education not only takes a culturally responsive approach to content, but constructs a different type of space in which young people can engage, explore, and create. Today's hip-hop education is also about conveying to young people—especially youths of color—that their histories, traditions, cultural roots, and perspectives are not only important but integral components of 21st-century learning and being a global citizen. Hip-hop education has played a significant role in illustrating the possibilities of rethinking what learning spaces can and should look like, as well as challenging traditional views of literacy.

Given that hip-hop is an inherently participatory culture, hip-hop education is inclusive by nature. Hip-hop educators incorporate aspects of hip-hop culture not only into curricular content, but also into their classroom spaces and practices, working to fundamentally rethink student engagement and disrupt traditional power dynamics between teacher ("knower") and student ("learner"). One example is the cypher. In a cypher, people stand in a circle at an equal distance from one another, someone might beatbox to provide a rhythm for pace and cadence, and one by one, members of the circle offer a rhyme, thought, question, or idea. Classroom cyphers can be used at the beginning of the day in homeroom, as a warm-up in class, or as a way to debrief following an activity or event, or at the end of the school day.

It is important to note that hip-hop education happens at various levels of schooling, although perhaps most frequently and easily in higher education as a result of fewer curricular restraints. As both hip-hop education and media literacy are rooted in commitments to expanding notions of literacy and better engaging students in their learning, however, there has been an increasingly sustained push to use hip-hop-based content and pedagogical practices in elementary and secondary schooling.

Current emphases in hip-hop education research and theory/ies

Reality pedagogy

Dr. Christopher Emdin (2016), a professor of urban science education, advocates for educators to connect students to science by using nonconventional means. He argues it is imperative for educators to consider and value students' lived experiences in school spaces. In his framework of reality pedagogy, a model of teaching and learning that extends culturally relevant pedagogy to include the educator and increase accountability for fundamentally changing the ways that both students and teachers learn and interact, Emdin translates ideas and practices from hip-hop into the "7 Cs" of effective teaching. They include: *cogenerative dialogue* (inspired by the hip-hop cypher where a group of people stand in a circle and take turns spitting free-style rhymes, it is a supportive and collaborative space aimed at building a shared experience; in a co-gen dialogue, students can engage one another in meaningful conversations about the lesson content and materials while connecting to their personal experiences and opinions); *coteaching* (having students be teachers in the classroom, where both adult teacher and peers are ready and willing to learn); and *cosmopolitanism* (having students develop responsibility for each other's learning both in and out of the classroom). Emdin suggests that teachers involve students in the classroom roles and spaces that adults traditionally occupy. He encourages teachers to have students help design lesson plans and activities; to have students think about and find examples of supplemental course readings or discussion prompts; to have students help research best practices for teaching; and to assign students the roles of interpreter, artist, or even teacher of a certain topic. In doing so, students become better connected to and more invested in what is being taught; they can begin to feel ownership over the material and their learning.

Critical hip-hop literacies

While it is paramount that hip-hop education continues to extend into various disciplines, given the inextricable ties to popular culture texts and the inherently critical nature of the field, spaces like English language arts (ELA) classrooms have and will continue to provide a productive and important space for hip-hop education. Dr. Lauren Kelly, for instance, a professor at Rutgers University and former high school ELA teacher in Long Island, New York, understands hip-hop education as a broad concept that encompasses a diverse set of theories and practices. Her research and pedagogy involve the development of critical hip-hop literacies, which she defines as critical engagement with hip-hop texts for the purpose of gaining a better understanding of self and society. She focuses on hip-hop rather than other cultural texts because hip-hop texts are explicitly classed, raced, gendered, sexualized, and laden with power relationships in addition to being prevalent and widespread in popular consumption. Her students read hip-hop lyrics as literacy texts through critical lenses, examining the apparent messages of the song, the artists' perspectives, and the social context from which the song was born. Kelly's pedagogical focus is on dialogic practices in the classroom, specifically, how discussion of hip-hop as literature and culture impacts young people's self-reflection and awareness, identity development, and understanding of the world. Living in an increasingly digital world where young people are both consumers and creators of media texts, Kelly argues it is imperative that we incorporate popular texts and media literacy education in the classroom in ways that are not only relevant to young people, but that challenge them to ask critical questions of the media and popular culture and encourage them to create their own texts that work to both resist and transform mainstream ideologies.

Meaning-making through hip-hop composition

Dr. Ian Levy, a former school counselor in the Bronx, uses hip-hop therapy to reach students in need of a type of counseling that falls outside the traditional approach. He works with high school students to articulate their feelings, process traumatic events, and express their hopes, dreams, and frustrations through the composition of hip-hop lyrics. "Too often schools don't teach students how to handle the explosive feelings that come with adolescence. By writing and sharing the 'raw core of feelings' that create havoc in their lives, they can practice a more effective way of handling their emotions" (Christensen, 2001, p. 129). Hip-hop therapy encourages students to name their daily struggles and works to demystify the negative stigmas associated with counseling and therapy. In addition to using hip-hop in his counseling sessions during the school day, Levy has also designed a hip-hop lyricism class in which students can get credit for the hip-hop texts they produce (lyrics, music compositions, and recordings, etc.) using equipment purchased from an online crowdfunding campaign, and he also runs a similar program after school.

Another example is educator Brian Mooney's breakbeat pedagogy (BBP), which revolves around the art of the *hip-hop event*. Extending from a traditional literacy event, the hip-hop event is multimodal and cross-curricular. BBP "involves the process of creating a poetry slam or Hip Hop event, alongside students, to initiate a democratic space for the elements to live and thrive within a school community" (Mooney, 2016, p. 52). Mooney argues that the spaces and platforms that poetry slams, hip-hop showcases, and open mics provide offer the most authentic representations of 21st-century literacies skills and practices.

Future directions in research, theory, and methodology

As illustrated, hip-hop education is dynamic, multifaceted, and constantly evolving. It holds great potential for helping researchers and educators continue to reimagine what pedagogy, knowledge, and school spaces can and should look like in ways that authentically reflect who students are and what they care about, and support continued explorations by students of themselves, others, and the world around them. In many respects, hip-hop education is still in its infancy, still being defined and developed, which is incredibly exciting. Above all else, to continue advancing scholarship and pushing hip-hop as a leading pedagogical orientation, the fifth element—knowledge of self—must remain at the center of teacher education, of learning practices, and of classroom spaces. Failing to support individuals in knowing and understanding one's self can make it difficult, if not impossible, to construct authentically inclusive and supportive school spaces and communities.

SEE ALSO: Creativity and Media Production in Schools; Critical Pedagogy; Global Citizenship; Meaning-Making; Media and Ethnic Stereotyping; Media Literacy and Visual Culture; Media Literacy Foundations; Media Literacy with New Immigrants; Participatory Action Research; Performance Media

References

Asante, M.K. (2008). *It's bigger than hip hop: The rise of the post-hip-hop generation.* New York, NY: Basic.

Christensen, L. (2001). *Reading, writing and rising up: Teaching about social justice and the power of the written word.* Milwaukee, WI: Rethinking Schools.

Cook-Sather, A. (2002). Authorizing students' perspectives: Towards trust, dialogue, and change in education. *Educational Researcher, 31*(4), 3–14. doi: 10.3102/0013189X031004003

Dimitriadis, G. (2001). *Performing identity/performing text: Hip hop as text, pedagogy, and lived practice.* New York, NY: Peter Lang.

Emdin, C. (2016). *For white folks who teach in the hood and the rest of y'all too: Reality pedagogy and urban education.* Boston, MA: Beacon Press.

Freire, P. (1970). *Pedagogy of the oppressed.* New York, NY: Seabury Press.

Goodwin, L. (2010). Globalization and the preparation of quality teachers: Rethinking knowledge domains for teaching. *Teaching and Education, 2*(1), 19–32. doi: 10.1080/10476210903466901

Hill, M.L., & Petchauer, E. (2013). *Schooling hip-hop: Expanding hip-hop based education across the curriculum.* New York, NY: Teachers College Press.

Hill, M.L., & Vasudevan, L. (2008). *Media, learning, and sites of possibility.* New York, NY: Peter Lang.

Lipsitz, G. (1994). *Dangerous crossroads.* London: Verso.

Mooney, B. (2016). *Breakbeat pedagogy: Hip hop and spoken word beyond the classroom walls.* New York, NY: Peter Lang.

Morrell, E. (2009). Critical research and the future of literacy education. *Journal of Adolescent & Adult Literacy, 53*(2), 96–104. doi: 10.1598/JAAL.53.2.1

Vasudevan, L., Schultz, K., & Bateman, J. (2010). Rethinking composing in a digital age: Authoring literate identities through multimodal storytelling. *Written Communication, 27*(4), 442–468. doi: 10.1177/0741088310378217

Further reading

Belle, C. (2016). Don't believe the hype: Hip-hop literacies and English education. *Journal of Adolescent & Adult Literacy, 60*(3), 287–294. doi: 10.1002/jaal.574

Chang, J. (2005). *Can't stop won't stop: A history of the hip-hop generation.* New York, NY: Picador.

Duncan-Andrade, J.M.R., & Morrell, E. (2008). *The art of critical pedagogy: Possibilities for moving from theory to practice in urban schools.* New York, NY: Peter Lang.

Hu, W. (2016). *Bronx school embraces a new tool in counseling: Hip-hop.* Retrieved from http://www.nytimes.com/2016/01/20/nyregion/bronx-school-embraces-a-new-tool-in-counseling-hip-hop.html?_r=0

Kelly, L.L. (2013). Hip-hop literature: The politics, poetics, and power of hip-hop in the English classroom. *English Journal, 102*(5), 51–56. Retrieved from https://pdfs.semanticscholar.org/1ad7/796b8f8d62c6d732e3bde1b8376c98dd9c91.pdf

Love, B.L. (2012). *Hip hop's lil' sistas speak: Negotiating hip hop identities and politics in the New South.* New York, NY: Peter Lang.

Love, B.L. (2016). Complex personhood of hip hop and the sensibilities of the culture that fosters knowledge of self and self-determination. *Equity and Excellence in Education,* (49)*4*, 414–427. doi: 10.1080/10665684.2016.1227223

Low, B.E. (2011). *Slam school: Learning through conflict in the hip-hop and spoken word classroom.* Stanford, CA: Stanford University Press.

Emily Ballin Wells holds a doctorate in communication and education from Teachers College, Columbia University. She is an educator committed to social justice and anti-racist pedagogies. Her work involves using critical media literacy and multimodal storytelling practices to engage young people and teachers in authentic identity work in order to create more inclusive and culturally relevant spaces and places of learning.

History of Media Literacy

MELDA N. YILDIZ
New York Institute of Technology, USA

Media literacy is a transdisciplinary concept that is intertwined with many fields such as education, communications, sociology, psychology, history, and politics. What it means to be literate, how one can attain media literacy, where it should be taught, and who needs it are matters connected to the history of media innovations, as these developed over time. This brief historical overview shows how the practice of critically analyzing media—and of creating it—developed over a long period.

Classical roots

The history of media literacy closely precedes the history of media technology. After the invention of radio and film in the late 19th and at the beginning of the 20th century, parents, scholars, politicians questioned the role of mass media and the use of media in education. Even in classical antiquity, Greek philosophers formulated concerns about how changes in communication and expression may influence human relationships and the nature of knowledge. Around 370 BCE, Plato discussed the role of writing in his dialogue *Phaedrus* and observed: "If men learn this [i.e., writing], it will implant forgetfulness in their souls; they will cease to exercise memory because they rely on that which is written, calling things to remembrance no longer from within themselves, but by means of external marks" (275a). In this dialogue Plato describes a conversation between his teacher Socrates and Phaedrus, an Athenian aristocrat; and writing emerges as the biggest problem in Greek society—one that may eliminate memory. Plato thought that, once the ideas get written down, someone else may use the writings against the person and miscommunicate the meaning. Only if you are there in person would you be able to defend your thoughts.

Literacy and the age of print

Prior to the invention of the moveable type printing press in 1452, attaining an education and becoming literate were available only to rich people and only through manuscripts, that is, texts in handwritten form—be they scrolls, codices, or papyri. People learned history through oral stories and religious murals, as well as by studying alongside a scholar or a master as an apprentice. Books were handmade and very time-consuming to produce, so very few people had the means to become educated and literate. Gutenberg's invention of moveable type changed the history of print media in 15th-century Europe. More and more people had access to written materials, became literate, questioned governments and religious leaders, and demanded more from their rulers. Just as Plato was wary of the written word, politicians and clergy were wary of the printed word. Those in power became gatekeepers of information and prevented media access and education until the beginning of the 20th century. Before the printing press was invented, people relied on interpretations of the religious books given by clergymen. The German theologian Martin Luther translated the Bible from Latin into German. People started to read and interpret the Bible for themselves, and this eventually led to the Protestant Reformation and to a democratization of religion and education.

Even though there were local news publications in ancient Greece, the mass production and distribution of news started in the 17th century. First, the government controlled most of the news. Later on the idea of a free press emerged through independence movements around the world; for instance, in the American colonies there was a movement to be free from the British.

Thomas Jefferson was critical of newspaper coverage during his presidency; however, he was one of the early supporters of free speech. He also underscored the importance of education. During his service as US minister to France in 1787, he wrote to Edward Carrington: "Were it left to me to decide whether we should have a government without newspapers or newspapers without a government, I should not hesitate a moment to prefer the latter, but I should mean that every man should receive those papers & be capable of reading them" (Founders Online, n.d.).

Awareness of media manipulation

In the 19th century, the penny press created a new competition between newspapers, and this led to the rise of public awareness of newspapers as a political force. As newspapers became popular and affordable, publishers made money from advertising revenue. To increase the revenue and to lower the cost, publishers started to choose profit over truth, sensationalism over ethical journalism and professionalism. At the very top of the first column on the front page of the *Sun*, the following was printed: "The object of this paper is to lay before the public, at a price within the means of everyone, all the news of the day, and at the same time offer an advantageous medium for advertisements" (Hamilton & Krimsky, 1997, p. 24). In the 1890s, Joseph Pulitzer and William Randolph Hearst both wanted to increase their sales and to attract advertisers. Their newspapers exaggerated the stories, focused on scandals, added sensationalized images and misleading headlines, and fabricated the interviews. Journalism of this era came to be known as "yellow journalism," and during this period the public grew more aware of media manipulation as a social phenomenon.

During the Spanish–American War of 1898, a New York newspaper headline read: "Maine Explosion Caused By Bomb or Torpedo?" This front-page story was about the sinking of a US battleship, the *Maine*, in Havana Harbor. Cuba was in the midst of its revolution against Spain's colonization. The USS *Maine* was there as a show of power, to protect US interests in Cuban independence and to ease the growing tension between the United States and Spain. The *Maine* sank, killing 260 men. Even today, the cause of the *Maine*'s sinking is unclear; either a mine in the harbor had exploded or the explosion was caused by internal coal fire. Without knowing exactly what happened, Pulitzer's paper speculated, sensationalized the story, and stoked tensions between the US and Spain. Since there were no photographs, the explosion was illustrated by pictures of bodies and flames shooting into the air; these were designed to grab the reader's attention and to spread rumors about enemy involvement in the sinking of the battleship. Such forms of yellow journalism fueled the need for a media-literate public. By reading between the lines, one can discover things such as what the story is about, who the target audience is, who benefits from the story, and who the sponsors are.

Film and radio attract interest from educators

Following the success of the penny press, another medium, motion pictures, started gaining popularity in the 1890s. According to film historian Dana Polan, the first college courses in film were taught at Columbia University, New York University, and Harvard University. These courses focused on the industry and craft of filmmaking, the nature of visual storytelling, and the practice of literary analysis of film. Soon after the motion pictures, radios started broadcasting news and music into homes at the beginning of the 20th century. During the 1930s, Edgar Dale, a professor at Ohio State University, published manuals on how teachers should use film and radio for learning purposes.

Listener associations affiliated with the Better Broadcasting movement helped people consider how to make active, responsible choices of what to listen to on the radio. The most well-known association of this kind is the National Telemedia Council (NTC), formerly known as American Council for Better Broadcasts (ACBB). ACBB started in 1935, as a small group of women in Madison, Wisconsin, part of the chapter of the American Association of University Women, and its publication, the *Journal of Media Literacy*, has been active since 1953.

Protecting youth from television

By 1950 TV sets were brought into homes. With this technological advancement, new opportunities and challenges to media literacy emerged. To make sense of television, it was thought that viewers required the mastery of the visual language of that medium. McLuhan and Carpenter (1960, p. xxi) argued: "Without an understanding of media grammars, we cannot hope to achieve a contemporary awareness of the world in which we live." After mass media came into our living rooms and schools in the 20th century, the concerns among educators, policymakers, and parents shifted from accessing to analyzing and evaluating media. As in the case of the media that preceded television, the first reaction to the explosion of television was that one should be fearful and cautious. Throughout the 20th century, in response to film, comics, radio, and television, some parents, teachers, and policymakers argued that children were in danger. This period of media literacy education was called *protectionism*. Protectionism comes in three forms: cultural, political, and moral defensiveness. In outlining the history of media education in England, David Buckingham (1998) explained the forms of cultural and political protectionism. As a result of cultural defensiveness, some media have been viewed as more valuable than others. The older generation often questions a new medium—for example, the social media today—and dismisses the newest media product. Political defensiveness focuses on the idea of protecting people from propaganda, false ideologies, and information. Finally, moral defensiveness outlines the effects of sex, violence, and consumerism on morality. The content of media such as violent video games and sexy music videos has been viewed as corrupting young minds, increasing violence in society, and contributing to the decline of moral values.

All this led to *moral panic*, a term coined by South African sociologist Stanley Cohen (2011) in his 1972 book *Folk Devils and Moral Panics*. Moral panic is the reaction of legislators, educators, and parents to a perceived threat to social norms, when a certain "condition, episode, person or group of people emerges to become defined as a threat to societal values and interests" (Cohen, 2011, p. 1). Moral panics have often surfaced when a new genre of music was first introduced in society—for example, jazz in the 1920s, rock 'n' roll in the 1950s, and rap music in the 1990s. Perceived threats related to the potential danger of the media raised fears among parents that these media would promote violence and sexualized behavior.

Many researches explored the role of the fear factor in the field of media education. George Gerbner from the University of Pennsylvania was the founder of cultivation theory and coined the term *mean world syndrome*. He measured how people who were frequent viewers of media violence had an exaggeration perception of the amount of violence in society. Media activist Danny Schechter (1999) described this idea in his book *The More You Watch, the Less You Know*.

Television's "critical viewing skills"

In the 1960s media literacy education shifted from protecting students from media to educating them, so as to make them able to deconstruct and analyze media messages and become productive citizens. Advertisements continue to be a powerful tool for the delivery of complex messages. During the 1964 presidential election, the iconic and haunting political ad used by Lyndon Johnson—the "Daisy" ad—demonstrated how media can change public opinion. Marshall McLuhan was one of the most influential media theorists. He first produced "Understanding New Media," a curriculum for high school students, in 1960; then in 1967 he wrote his famous book *The Medium Is the Message*. He theorized that the way we communicate is more important than what we communicate. Any new medium changes how we think, and its delivery changes our relationship with the outside world; "the personal and social consequences of any medium—that is, of any extension of ourselves—result from the new scale that is introduced into our affairs by each extension of ourselves, or by any new technology" (McLuhan, 1964, p. 1).

As the field of semiotics developed in Europe, Umberto Eco (1979, p. 15) emphasized the importance of media literacy: "A democratic civilization will save itself only if it makes the language of the image into a stimulus for critical reflection — not an invitation for hypnosis." Eco also argued for the role of media education: "If you want to use television for teaching somebody … you have first teach them how to use television" (Eco, 1979).

Around this time, Elizabeth Thoman founded the magazine *Media & Values* in 1977 and created the Center for Media Literacy in 1989. One of the pioneers of the media literacy movement in the United States, Thoman was also a high school journalism teacher, an award-wining still photographer, and the author of many media education articles. The London *Sunday Telegraph* acclaimed *Media & Values* as "the smartest magazine about media published in the US" (as quoted at https://www.medialit.org/founding-inspiration). Reaching over 10 000 readers, this magazine influenced a generation of teachers, parents, and religious leaders who recognized the need for media literacy education in and out of schools.

In a book titled *Teaching as a Subversive Activity*, Neil Postman first argued that education could be made more relevant by using inquiry to learn about real-world topics; and this included a focus on the role of the media in society. His prolific work as a writer and editor of the scholarly journal *ETC* introduced many teachers to the interdisciplinary study of general semantics, which postulated that knowledge and social relationships are shaped by symbol systems, including language and the visual media. In the mid-1980s Neil Postman wrote a seminal book called *Amusing Ourselves to Death* (Postman, 1985), claiming that television was at its most dangerous when it addressed "serious" topics such as news, politics, religion, and education.

Canadian educators, influenced by McLuhan, developed a knowledge community of high school teachers exploring how to integrate media literacy in the classroom. In 1987, a group of teachers from the Ontario Association for Media Literacy (AML) worked to draw the Key Concepts of Media Literacy for the Government of Ontario Media Literacy Resource Guide. With the active support of classroom teachers, media literacy had been mandated as part of the English curriculum for Grades 8 through to 13 in Ontario. Barry Duncan and a team of media educators collaborated on an invaluable Media Literacy Resource Guide by the Ontario Ministry of Education in 1989. The Guide was influenced by the work of Australian and British scholars, particularly that of Len Masterman, *Teaching about Television* (published in 1980) and *Teaching the Media* (published in 1985). Later the Guide was translated into French, Spanish, Japanese, and Italian.

Developing a knowledge community

A group of international educators, scholars, and media professionals gathered in Grunwald, Germany under the auspices of UNESCO, to make the first formal call for universal media literacy education. In 1989 a media literacy conference in Guelph, Ontario helped jumpstart the development of increasing contact between Canadian and American media literacy activists. MediaSmarts (formerly known as Media Awareness Network) was founded in 1990. It is a Canadian nonprofit charitable organization whose mission is to provide digital and media literacy programs and resources for Canadian homes, schools, and communities. Media Awareness Network was launched by the Canadian Radio-Television and Telecommunications Commission (CRTC) in response to media violence on television. Its vision is to promote critical thinking skills among youths and to engage them in becoming active and informed digital citizens.

In the 1990s a growing number of individuals and organizations were developing media literacy in the United States. Elizabeth Thoman worked with Charles Firestone of the Aspen Institute to create the National Leadership Conference on Media Literacy, which brought together 35 national leaders for a dialogue about the future of media literacy in the United States. Here the formal definition of media literacy was developed as "the ability to access, analyze, evaluate and create messages in a wide variety of forms" (Aufderheide, 1993, p. 1).

In 1992 Renee Hobbs created the first national-level teacher education program, the Harvard Institute in Media Education, located at Harvard University. American media literacy educators formed a coalition for hosting national conferences and for bringing together the growing community of educators, activists, and scholars. The Partnership for Media Education (PME) started in 1997, when Renee Hobbs, Elizabeth Thoman, Nancy Chase Garcia, and Lisa Reisberg began hosting annual conferences. This organization became the Alliance for a Media Literate America (AMLA) and later changed its name to the National Association for Media Literacy Education (NAMLE), a membership organization with over 4 000 members. These media educators and scholars have been organizing conferences and bringing media scholars from around the world into discussion and dialogue every 2 years. The organization sponsors an open-access peer-reviewed scholarly journal: the *Journal of Media Literacy Education*.

Among literacy scholars, an interest in media literacy was growing at the same time. The New London Group was formed in 1994 out of a group of academics who met at New London, Connecticut and used the term *multiliteracies* to challenge monocultural pedagogies and promote the value of relevance. They discussed the new media culture and the skills needed for the future and argued: "If it were possible to define generally the mission of education, it could be said that its fundamental purpose is to ensure that all students benefit from learning in ways that allow them to participate fully in public, community, and economic life" (New London Group, 2000, p. 9). This work reflected a growing interest in media literacy among literacy educators working in K-12 schools (i.e., primary and secondary education in the United States) and in teacher education programs.

Stakeholders in media literacy came from fields such as activism and social justice education. In 1993, Sut Jhally from the University of Massachusetts founded the Media Education Foundation (MEF), which produces educational documentary films that demonstrate the practice of critical reflection on and analysis of music video, entertainment, and news. In 2002 social justice activists developed an organization named the Action Coalition for Media Education (ACME). This group opposed the AMLA's efforts to secure funding from media companies in order to support media literacy education. It sought to create "an independently funded critical media literacy education network that teaches effective approaches to engage, challenge, and create media in ways that empower individuals and communities"; and it hosted conferences that emphasized critical perspectives on media literacy education (ACME, n.d.).

The strongest American media literacy program was developed in 2003 by Jim Steyer, who founded Common Sense Media, a San Francisco-based nonprofit organization that offers parents and educators strategies and resources to build media literacy skills in the home and in the school. They have developed media review services, educational curricula, and professional development programs. By 2016, the organization's website had over 65 million unique users and worked with over 275 000 educators in the United States.

There is a growing international community of media literacy educators. Italian media literacy educators established the Italian Association for Media and Communication Education (MED, https://www.medmediaeducation.it), a national membership organization that hosts an annual summer program of professional development in Italy. Under the leadership of Alton Grizzle, the Global Media and Information Literacy Week started in 2012 to bring together diverse scholars who are committed to promoting media and information literacy (MIL) as a way to foster social inclusion and intercultural dialogue.

In its current state, media literacy focuses on educating a new generation and on preparing it to analyze and create media. As technology makes media usage ubiquitous, in addition to accessing, deconstructing, and analyzing media messages, media literacy today seeks to empower people to create their own media messages, develop information and digital literacy skills, navigate a vast amount of knowledge, avoid spams, and gather trustworthy information. From health to politics, media literacy and its goals will continue to evolve, keeping pace with the changing times. Every new medium brings new challenges and concerns about media and their threat to safety, culture, and well-being and demands new skill sets. Today, in the age of "fake" websites, health information, and news sources, there are growing numbers of challenges for media educators. In addition to teaching about media, media educators have been teaching future generations how to take action on the media, what truth means, how to filter data and avoid spam, how to keep data safe and computers free from Internet viruses, how to develop netiquette, and how to eliminate media influence on lives, especially on democracy and free speech. Activists and scholars are fighting for net neutrality and industry regulations to ensure the free flow of information. As social media continue to take up more of our time and wearable technologies surround our bodies, media literacy education continues to be a crucial field of study, which encompasses multiliteracies and employs critical thinking skills and global competencies to prepare the next generation for the second half of the 21st century.

SEE ALSO: Advertising Literacy; Digital Literacy; Educational Media, History; Internet Safety; Network Neutrality

References

ACME.org. (n.d.). Smart media education for the 21st century: The Action Coalition for Media Education (ACME). Retrieved from https://acmesmartmediaeducation.net

Aufderheide, P. (1993). National leadership conference on media literacy. Conference report. Washington, DC: Aspen Institute. Retrieved from https://docs.google.com/viewer?url=http%3A%2F%2Ffiles.eric.ed.gov%2Ffulltext%2FED365294.pdf

Buckingham, D. (1998). Media education in the UK: Moving beyond protectionism. *Journal of Communication, 48*(1), 33–43.

Cohen, S. (2011). *Folk devils and moral panics: The creation of the Mods and Rockers*. London, England: Routledge.

Eco, U. (1979). *Can television teach? Screen Education*, Vol. 31, 15–24.

Founders Online. (n.d.). From Thomas Jefferson to Edward Carrington, 16 January 1787. Retrieved from https://founders.archives.gov/documents/Jefferson/01-11-02-0047

Hamilton, J.M., & Krimsky, G.A. (1997). *Hold the press: The inside story on newspapers*. Baton Rouge: Louisiana State University Press.

McLuhan, M. (1964). *Understanding media: The extension of man*. New York, NY: McGraw-Hill.

McLuhan, M., & Carpenter, E.S. (1960). *Explorations in communication: An anthology*. Boston, MA: Beacon Press.

New London Group. (2000). A pedagogy of multiliteracies: Designing social futures. In B. Cope & M. Kalantzis (Eds.), *Multiliteracies: Literacy learning and the design of social futures* (pp. 9–38). London, England: Routledge.

Postman, N. (1985). *Amusing ourselves to death*. New York, NY: Penguin.

Schechter, D. (1999). *The more you watch, the less you know: News wars/(sub)merged hopes/media adventures*. New York, NY: Seven Stories Press.

Further reading

Alvarado, M., Buscombe, E., & Collins, R. (1993). *The screen education reader: Cinema, television, culture*. Basingstoke, England: Macmillan.

Brown, J.A. (1991). *Television "critical viewing skills" education: Major media literacy projects in the United States and selected countries*. Hillsdale, NJ: Lawrence Erlbaum.

Eco, U. (1993). Can television teach? In (eds. M. Alvarado, E. Buscombe and R. Collins), *The screen education reader* (pp. 95–107) London, England: MacMillan.

Kubey, R., & Baker, F. (1999, October 27). Has media literacy found a curricular foothold? *Education Week*.

Mann, R. (2016, April 13). How the "Daisy" ad changed everything about political advertising. Retrieved from https://www.smithsonianmag.com/history/how-daisy-ad-changed-everything-about-political-advertising-180958741

Media Education Foundation. (n.d.). Films that inspire critical reflection on the social, political, and cultural impact of American mass media. Retrieved from http://www.mediaed.org

MediaSmarts.ca. (n.d.). Media literacy fundamentals: Canada's center for digital and media literacy. Retrieved from http://mediasmarts.ca/digital-media-literacy/general-information/digital-media-literacy-fundamentals/media-literacy-fundamentals

Ontario Ministry of Education. (Ed.). (1989). *Media literacy. Toronto*. Ontario, Canada.

PBS. (1999). Yellow journalism. Great Projects Film Company, Inc. Retrieved from http://www.pbs.org/crucible/frames/_journalism.html

RobbGrieco, M. (2014). Why history matters for media literacy education. *Journal of Media Literacy Education*, 6(2), 3–22.

Tyner, K. (1998). *Literacy in a digital world: Teaching and learning in the age of information.* Mahwah, NJ: Lawrence Erlbaum.

UNESCO.org. (n.d.). Global MIL week. Retrieved from https://en.unesco.org/global-mil-week-2016/history

Walsh, B. (n.d.). A brief history of media education. Retrieved from http://www.medialit.org/reading-room/brief-history-media-education

Melda N. Yildiz is a global scholar, teacher educator, instructional designer, and author. Yildiz teaches in the School for Interdisciplinary Studies and Education at the New York Institute of Technology. She served as a Fulbright Scholar in Turkmenistan (2009) and Azerbaijan (2016), teaching and conducting research that integrates media education into preschool through graduate school (P20) classrooms. Yildiz coauthored, published, and presented material on topics such as media and information literacy, instructional technology, and multicultural and global education. She received an EdD in math and science and instructional technology from the University of Massachusetts, Amherst and an MS in instructional technology from the Southern Connecticut State University. She majored in teaching English as a foreign language at Bogazici University in Turkey.

Hypertext and Hypermedia Writing

TROY HICKS
Central Michigan University, USA

Hypertext and *hypermedia* can be described as both technical and rhetorical concepts, born of the post-World War II imagination and finally enacted with the arrival of the public Internet in the late 1990s. While the terms have fallen out of the popular discourse related to digital composition (involving the study of written communication with networked computers) and have been replaced by concepts such as "multimodality" and "digital writing," both *hypertext* and *hypermedia* remain foundational concepts. As the capabilities of many web-based services improve, the barriers to produce hypertext and hypermedia decrease. Simultaneously, opportunities for a more sophisticated, rhetorical approach—in terms of timeliness, purpose, context, and audience awareness—are on the increase.

- The conceptual beginnings of hypertext/media can be found in Vannevar Bush's 1945 essay "As We May Think," yet practical applications were not present until Tim Berners-Lee introduced hypertext markup language (HTML) in 1989.
- At present, users of mobile devices, tablets, and personal computers are able to create and consume a variety of hypertext/media using free, open source software and web hosting, as well as with many paid services.

- As a topic of scholarly pursuit, interest in hypertext/media stretches across various disciplines including media and communication, composition and rhetoric, literacy and language, art and design, and teacher education and professional development.

Early history

First introduced by Ted H. Nelson in 1965, both *hypertext* and *hypermedia* entered the academic conversation. Nelson described *hypertext* as a combination of text and images connected in such a way that ink on paper—a medium fixed in both content and form—could not allow. *Hypermedia* was then distinguished by Nelson as being hypertext with additional audio and video material that could be arranged in a nonlinear format. Before Nelson introduced these terms, the potential for interlinked texts—with "texts" conceived broadly as alphabetic characters arranged into words, sentences, and paragraphs, as well as media such as images, video, and audio—had been discussed, yet not fully realized, for two decades.

First, Vannevar Bush had penned an essay in 1945 for *The Atlantic*, "As We May Think." In this monumental essay, Bush envisioned the *memex*, a machine in which individuals could store media and personal communications on accessible microfilm—stitched together into useful sequences—as a tool to supplement the memory. Then, in the 1960s, Douglas Engelbart and his team working for the United States Air Force had developed an "online system," abbreviated as NLS, with capabilities for sharing text, image, and video through one device and interface. Designed as a means to communicate across their labs, the NLS also introduced the concept of synchronous video conversations. It was first demonstrated publicly in December 1968.

Thus, by the time the terms *hypertext* and *hypermedia* became popularized, the concept of rich, interactive texts had been established in both theory and practice. However, two limitations remained: first, personal computing technology had not caught up with the potential for these systems; second, the network architecture upon which such exchanges could occur had not been built.

In 1969 and throughout the 1970s, the Advanced Research Projects Agency Network, or ARPANET, was being developed by the Department of Defense and included collaborators from multiple universities and other agencies. In the early incarnations of ARPANET, text was able to be transferred, but hypertext and hypermedia were still not an accessible form of communication—for readers or writers—due to the ways in which information was encoded and shared across the network using packets and protocols such as TCP/IP (Transmission Control Protocol/Internet Protocol). Yet, human emotion and intention through textual characters—if not yet hypertext or hypermedia themselves—were introduced through ASCII (American Standard Code for Information Interchange) art, Multi-User Dungeons/Domains (MUDs), Gopher, and other early Internet tools. Opportunities for collaboration, creativity, and communication flourished in the textual version of the Internet; however the promise of an open, accessible set of hypertexts and hypermedia that would be created for and used by the general public was still elusive.

Recent history

Perhaps the most significant innovation that led to the popularization of hypertext and hypermedia, then, came in 1989 when Tim Berners-Lee, a computer scientist at CERN, the European Organization for Nuclear Research, created and implemented "hypertext transfer protocol" (HTTP), making the countless numbers of digital domain names into human-readable addresses, or Uniform Resource Locators (URLs), and moving away from TCP/IP protocols. With the HTTP protocol, documents coded in "hypertext markup language" (HTML) could be formatted and shared across the network, readable by humans and computers. An HTML document from one server could be accessed through the network and—rather than being rendered in a completely textual presentation—it would show the document as the original designer had encoded it in HTML with appropriate formatting, colors, embedded images and media and, most importantly, hyperlinks to yet more documents. Berners-Lee's innovation led to the development of initial versions of HTML and other web standards that have, since that time, been managed by the team at the World Wide Web Consortium (W3C). It was at this critical turning point right after Berners-Lee developed HTML that Marc Andreessen and Eric Bina—then working together at the National Center for Supercomputing Applications (NCSA) at the University of Illinois—designed the Mosaic web browser (which ultimately became Netscape Navigator), and the ability for a user to both consume and create hypertext/hypermedia was popularized. Metaphors such as the "information superhighway" were used to describe the ability for a user to get "on" the Internet and then be transported to other virtual spaces.

While these technical standards were the foundation of the early web, there were community norms and rhetorical practices coming into play as well. In these earliest days of the public Internet, the concept of net neutrality was born: anyone, anywhere in the world—with sufficient access to the network and hardware to create a website—could post content on the Internet. This assumption also led to the idea that participation on the Internet could—and, indeed, *should*—be open to all without heed for nationality, gender, (dis)ability, or other aspects of the physical self. These possibilities to engage more fully within and across texts also amplified calls for advocacy and civic engagement, both locally and globally, with overtones of a more open, egalitarian space for participation. Hypertext and hypermedia, it was imagined, could serve to democratize information.

At the same time these unhindered ideals were taking form, the late 1990s and early 2000s saw an immediate commercialization of the World Wide Web, and hypertexts and hypermedia were developed for the full range of communicative purposes, including buying and selling goods and services. HTML and a series of additional web-based technologies—most notably Flash and Java—allowed professional web developers and amateurs alike the opportunity to compose hypertexts and hypermedia. Webpages were generally considered to be relatively static or unchanging in the sense that, in order to update the content of a site, a user would have to edit the source code and repost the content to the web server through File Transfer Protocol (FTP). Web content was not delivered dynamically, at least not in the sense that it could be easily changed or updated without the use of specialized programs for editing HTML and transferring files. Rather than requiring users to create HTML code from scratch, save the text file, and then view their creations in a web browser, an updated version of Netscape Communicator also included a "what you see is what you get" (WYSIWYG) text editor. However, different browsers sometimes required different nuances in HTML; thus, a document that worked well on Netscape would not necessarily work well on Internet Explorer. An additional, significant challenge remained: HTML did not allow for much flexibility because the writing itself was encoded in the programming language. However, this would change soon. Extensible markup language (XML), cascading style sheets (CSS), and, eventually, HTML5 became new web standards, allowing users to create documents and have them delivered dynamically to different web browsers and to make content accessible to users of all (dis)abilities.

Capabilities for creating hypertexts and hypermedia expanded, too, with other types of computer programs that didn't involve the Internet. In K-12 (primary and secondary) education, for instance, hypertext and hypermedia writing can be traced most directly to the program Hypercard, a program developed for Apple computers and first made available in 1987. With Hypercard, users could create individual notecards that included text, images, and buttons that could then link to additional cards; all the cards together comprised one "stack." In later editions of Hypercard, Quicktime movie files could also be embedded within a card. One challenge that Hypercard posed came from the fact that stacks were unique sets unto themselves, and not hyperlinked through the Internet. While there were stacks available for download, some critics would argue that Hypercard was not truly a hypermedia authoring system because it did not make use of independent links to various other resources on the web.

While technologies for producing hypertexts were being developed, significant improvements in other software programs that encouraged creativity were emerging as well. Other commercial products including Microsoft's Front Page and MacroMedia's Dreamweaver came to the market, and the ability to create hypertext documents expanded. Adobe's Photoshop, for instance, sparked a revolution in photo-editing that even the best photographers and editors had not been able to accomplish in the darkroom and with other lighting or camera tricks. Adobe's entire creative suite—including video editing and desktop publishing platforms—allowed users to engage in the full process of production for various forms of media. Apple, too, presented a variety of tools that would become staples of professional (Final Cut Pro) and amateur (iMovie, iDVD, Garageband) media production. Open source tools, fueled by communities like GitHub, became increasingly available (Audacity for audio editing, OpenShot for video editing, and GIMP for photo editing). With increasingly faster access speeds, users were able to share their productions universally, leading to new understandings of authorship and participation on the web, ultimately leading to more substantive understandings of how children, teens, and adults envision themselves as "prosumers" of hypertext and hypermedia. This led to even greater participation. The Pew Internet and American Life Project (Pew Research Center, 2018a) reported, in 2015, that the number of American adults who regularly used the Internet grew from 14% in 1995 to 68% in 2005 and, most recently, 89% in 2018. Hypertext and hypermedia became more popular as ways for users to read, view, and listen to a variety of forms of information.

Implications for scholarship in education, media, writing, and communication studies

From the perspective of writers, new literary forms enabled by hypertext and hypermedia as both fiction and poetry began appearing in venues such as the Electronic Literature Organization (https://eliterature.org) and the Electronic Poetry Center (https://writing.upenn.edu/epc/). These works are characterized by their use of images, sounds, videos, and, of course, hyperlinks. Authors worked to create immersive, interactive experiences that would—quite often—utilize a combination of media that would require a reader/viewer to engage by reading text, listening to music or narration, viewing video, and clicking on links. Digital storytelling, for instance, involves the combination of media elements such as words, images, video, and sound (typically, music and narration) and is often shared through hypermedia texts such as blog posts or webpages.

At the same time these new forms of fiction and poetry emerged, so too did hypertext and hypermedia become the new norm for traditional sources of news media, academic publishing, and other forms of nonfiction. Journals created to both feature and study hypertexts and hypermedia began, including examples such as *Kairos: A Journal of Rhetoric, Technology, and Pedagogy* (http://kairos.technorhetoric.net/) and *Digital Literary Studies* (https://journals.psu.edu/dls). News organizations began regular publishing online, as did academic journals, raising questions about their business models, many of which required individual or institutional subscriptions to access premium content, thus subverting the idea that information online should be readily accessible, for free, by all. Still, hypertext and hypermedia allowed for infinite combinations of new materials to be produced and published. And, as the technology evolved, web browsers and services have been able to record users' habits; specific websites would serve up content that was customized based on their past browsing history, location, computer brand, and other signals.

The shift in the production of hypertext and hypermedia was not without significant concerns to many educators, as numerous websites have emerged, providing misleading or entirely false information produced and published on the web. At the same time, librarians and other educators worked to develop resources that would, in turn, help students evaluate these illegitimate hypertexts and hypermedia works through information literacy and strategic searching skills. One notable example, martinlutherking.org, proved to be a common case, as it was a website registered to the white supremacist group Stormfront and claimed to tell the revisionist "truth" about a heroic African American hero, requiring special attention to the evaluation of credibility. These underlying challenges facing both consumers and creators of hypertext and hypermedia became myriad, including Internet filtering, digital citizenship, Internet safety, and teaching youth to be digitally literate. Issues of equity and the digital divide are still of significant concern.

As these concerns about the credibility of web-based texts grew, a substantial shift in the way that hypertext and hypermedia were produced and distributed occurred. Rather than having a single webpage with the content of the document enmeshed with the HTML code, a new generation of tools—and conceptual changes in the ways that users would consume and produce content—moved the ways in which hypertexts and hypermedia were used. In 2005, Tim O'Reilly published his essay describing this phenomenon, "What Is Web 2.0?," documenting a number of technical adaptations in website design and function that were allowing users to more readily create, publish, share, and collaborate via the Internet. New technologies that were driven by a database-backed web allowed users even more freedom and flexibility in terms of design and publishing. For instance, blogs could be produced quickly and allowed users the opportunity to write with a WYSIWYG interface as well as highly customizable themes. Changing a hypertext's look and feel before the advent of Web 2.0 tools was a significant undertaking; with the power of a database-backed web, the design of a website could be changed with the push of a button and the content would remain intact. Rich Site Summary/Really Simple Syndication (RSS) allowed content to be delivered through a variety of means to users within the web browser on the existing domain, as well as through RSS readers such as NewsGator and Google Reader. Additional technologies introduced in the Web 2.0 era included wikis, social bookmarking/curating tools, podcasts, and photo sharing. No longer did users require access to their own server space; instead, content became hosted on the web, or "in the cloud."

Because the use of hypertextual and hypermedia writing allows users to create, link, and remix materials in ways previously unknown or unavailable, it contributes to the ability of amateurs to take existing content—words, images, sounds, and video—and alter that source material in significant ways. Additional challenges to fair use and copyright emerged as hypertexts and hypermedia became easily accessible with a simple cut/copy/paste command. Larry Lessig refers to this idea as "remix" (2008), and it was significantly enhanced by the use of hypertexts and hypermedia as a way to find initial texts, as well as to distribute work. The creation of digital texts, as Lessig noted, was also facing more and more legal challenges. Creative Commons, a licensing system in which the copyright holder can maintain their rights on a continuum of preferences, has been developed. Creators can choose from "attribution only" all the way through options for commercial or noncommercial reuses of their work, as well as the ability to edit the original material, or leave it in an unmodified state.

Since the introduction of WYSIWYG editors, the ability of casual users of the Internet to create hypertext and hypermedia has increased dramatically. Nearly ubiquitous in web-based publishing platforms and in word processors today, examples such as the "hyperlink" feature in Microsoft Word and the ability to embed images and videos into a PowerPoint slide deck are now normal features. As more and more web-based services have been introduced for broad use, and for the educational market in particular, the ability to produce hypertext and hypermedia has become more widely available on a variety of platforms. For instance, the production and publishing of a website can now be accomplished quickly and easily without the purchase of a domain name using a service such as Google Sites, WordPress, Weebly, or Wix. Users are able to collect and edit images with websites such as Pixlr, and edit video with services such as WeVideo. The technical capabilities of smartphones, tablets, desktops, and laptop computers continue to improve, as do the software programs that come in their standards configurations. For instance, all Apple devices running the OSX operating system (laptops and desktops) as well as iOS devices (iPhone and iPad) come standard with iMovie and Garageband. Hyperlinks and hypermedia are easily embedded within social media with shortened URLs and animated GIFs or brief videos.

Future directions

The requisite conditions for producing hypertext and hypermedia have changed significantly over the past 20 years, and participation has increased. This increase can be attributed directly to the rise of broadband and mobile Internet access, as well as the increasing influence of social networks. According to the Pew Research Center (2018b), in 2005, 8% of adults stated that they had produced content on social networks and this percentage had grown to 69% in 2018. This increase in content production clearly demonstrates that most users, amateur and professional, are interested in creating content and sharing it online, even if it is not necessarily hypertextual. As the technical capabilities for producing and publishing hypertext and hypermedia became more widely available, so too did opportunities for writers of all genres to express themselves. Additionally, readers/viewers of hypertexts and hypermedia often experienced a type of cognitive dissonance as they transferred linear, print-based skills to documents that were available digitally, infinitely searchable, and hyperlinked. Thus, a great deal of scholarship related to "new literacies," "multimodal composition," or "multimodality," "transmedia," and "digital writing" began to emerge, and educators have become more active in creating and sharing open educational resources.

Researchers interested in hypertext/media writing will want to consider in what ways hypertext/media composition will continue to change as it relates to:

- ongoing debates about copyright and fair use,
- alternative copyright licensing such as Creative Commons,
- available software and web-based apps—as well as open source alternatives—across mobile, tablet, and desktop platforms
- available input devices such as cameras, styluses, touch screens, and trackpads;

in what ways we will support, discourage, or otherwise influence users who are interested in consuming and creating hypertext/media as it relates to:

- emergence and cost of new consumer technologies,
- use of open source software,

- policies that enable and/or restrict Internet access,
- innovative approaches to teaching/learning;

and in what ways hypertext/media will itself continue to change as it relates to:

- location-based services enabled by the Global Positioning System (GPS),
- temporal aspects of social networking applications such as Snapchat,
- the quality and quantity of data that can be stored remotely ("in the cloud").

SEE ALSO: Authorship and Participatory Culture; Copyright and Fair Use; Digital Divide; Digital Literacy; Educational Media, History; Participation through Public Media: Improving Media Literacy among Vulnerable Youth; Visual Literacy

References

Bush, V. (1945, July). As we may think. *The Atlantic*. Retrieved from https://www.theatlantic.com/magazine/archive/1945/07/as-we-may-think/303881/

Doug Engelbart Institute. (n.d.). Doug's great demo: 1968. Doug Engelbart Institute. Retrieved from http://www.dougengelbart.org/firsts/dougs-1968-demo.html

Lessig, L. (2008). *Remix: Making art and commerce thrive in the hybrid economy*. London, England: Penguin Books.

Nelson, T.H. (1965). Complex information processing: A file structure for the complex, the changing and the indeterminate. In *Proceedings of the 1965 20th National Conference* (pp. 84–100). New York, NY: ACM. doi: 10.1145/800197.806036

Pew Research Center. (2018a, February 5). Internet use over time. Retrieved from http://www.pewinternet.org/data-trend/internet-use/internet-use-over-time/

Pew Research Center. (2018b, February 5). Social media use over time. Retrieved from http://www.pewinternet.org/data-trend/social-media/social-media-use-all-users/

Further reading

Baron, D. (2001). From pencils to pixels: The stages of literacy technology. In E. Cushman, E.R. Kintgen, B.M. Kroll, & M. Rose (Eds.), *Literacy: A critical sourcebook* (pp. 70–84). Boston, MA: Bedford/St. Martin's. Retrieved from http://www.english.illinois.edu/-people-/faculty/debaron/essays/pencils.htm

Bolter, J.D. (2001). *Writing space: Computers, hypertext, and the remediation of print* (2nd ed.). London, England: Routledge.

Charney, D. (2001). The effect of hypertext on processes of reading and writing. In E. Cushman, E.R. Kintgen, B.M. Kroll, & M. Rose (Eds.), *Literacy: a critical sourcebook* (pp. 85–103). Boston, MA: Bedford/St. Martin's. Retrieved from http://www.dwrl.utexas.edu/~charney/homepage/Articles/Charney_hypertext.pdf

Cope, B., Kalantzis, M., & New London Group. (2000). *Multiliteracies: Literacy learning and the design of social futures*. London, England: Routledge.

Dalton, B., & Proctor, C.P. (2008). The changing landscape of text and comprehension in the age of new literacies. In J. Coiro, M. Knobel, C. Lankshear, & D.J. Leu (Eds.), *Handbook of research on new literacies* (pp. 635–669). New York, NY: Taylor & Francis.

Lankshear, C., & Knobel, M. (2011). *New literacies: Everyday practices and social learning* (3rd ed.). Maidenhead, England: Open University Press.

Leu, Jr., D.J., Kinzer, C.K., Coiro, J.L., & Cammack, D.W. (2004). Toward a theory of new literacies emerging from the Internet and other information and communication technologies. In R.B. Ruddell & N.J. Unrau (Eds.), *Theoretical models and processes of reading* (pp. 1570–1613). Newark, DE: International Reading Association.

National Writing Project, DeVoss, D., Eidman-Aadahl, E., & Hicks, T. (2010). Because digital writing matters: Improving student writing in online and multimedia environments. San Francisco, CA: Jossey-Bass.

Spiro, R.J., DeSchryver, M., Hagerman, M.S., Morsink, P.M., & Thompson, P. (Eds.). (2015). *Reading at a crossroads?: Disjunctures and continuities in current conceptions and practices.* New York, NY: Routledge.

Thompson, C. (2013). *Smarter than you think: How technology is changing our minds for the better.* New York, NY: Penguin Books.

Troy Hicks, PhD, is Professor of English and Education at Central Michigan University (CMU). He directs both the Chippewa River Writing Project and the Master of Arts in Educational Technology degree program. A former middle school teacher, he collaborates with K-12 (primary and secondary) colleagues and explores how they implement newer literacies in their classrooms. In 2011, he was honored with CMU's Provost's Award for junior faculty who demonstrate outstanding achievement in research and creative activity, in 2014, he received the Conference on English Education's Richard A. Meade Award for scholarship in English Education, and, in 2018, he received the Michigan Reading Association's Teacher Educator Award. Dr. Hicks has authored numerous books, articles, chapters, blog posts, and other resources broadly related to the teaching of literacy in our digital age.

I

Informal Learning on YouTube

PATRICIA G. LANGE
California College of the Arts, USA

An oft-heard saying is: "You can learn anything on YouTube." From the content of its videos to its interactivity through comments, YouTube offers numerous ways in which viewers may engage in processes of informal learning that are socially oriented, engaging, and self-paced. Launched in 2005 by former PayPal employees, the site enables participants to create and share videos online. According to YouTube's website, people from around the world watch hundreds of millions of hours of video on a daily basis, generating billions of views for YouTube's videos. Approximately 400 hours of video are being uploaded to the site every minute, with steady increases in viewership forecast for the foreseeable future (Robertson, 2015). YouTube combines an array of videos from the novice to the professionally produced, a collection that is said to be part of its appeal. Its varied content attracts viewers and encourages participants to interact, such as by providing tips and suggestions to video makers and fellow viewers on a vast variety of subjects.

Informal learning is generally conducted outside of formal educational channels, is not strictly planned, places control of learning in the hands of learners, and facilitates varying degrees of awareness that a participant is engaged in learning (Drotner, 2008). Informal learning is often associated with qualities such as being surprising, interpersonal, and pleasurable (Sefton-Green, 2004). Other qualities include being "open-ended," "explorative," "enjoyable," and exhibiting a "perception of choice" (Boekaerts & Minnaert, 1999). Given that its vast array of content demands that participants identify and choose what they will engage with, YouTube facilitates a sense of fun and self-paced exploration of numerous topics.

Informal learning arguably exists on a continuum with formal education (Sefton-Green, 2004). In certain circumstances learning in schools may be fun and interpersonal, and instances of informal learning may at times exhibit planned and serious qualities (Sefton-Green, 2004). Within this continuum, YouTube offers material that

The International Encyclopedia of Media Literacy. Renee Hobbs and Paul Mihailidis (Editors-in-Chief), Gianna Cappello, Maria Ranieri, and Benjamin Thevenin (Associate Editors).

may supplement formal learning environments. Yet, because learning occurs outside of classrooms and is frequently conducted at the users' pace, such engagements may be considered types of informal learning. For example, supplementary material from formal classes may appear on YouTube, for instance in the form of video lectures. Such materials may assist in projects such as massive open online courses (MOOCs) and flipped classrooms in which one-to-many instruction may be incorporated into materials such as video lectures outside the classroom, while more interactive and interpersonal exercises may be conducted within the classroom (Bishop & Verleger, 2013). Conversely, material in YouTube videos may be brought into formal classrooms for discussion and exercises.

In addition to supplementing formal education, a great deal of attention is being paid to how people learn through digital spaces on their own. Of particular interest is exploring how people engage in peer-to-peer forms of informal learning that do not draw on authority figures such as teachers and are conducted in environments outside of classrooms. Spaces of learning may greatly influence how particular types of instruction are interpreted. Researchers have found that more organic interactive learning is occurring in everyday digital environments of sociality and play between people in similar age cohorts or within multigenerational spaces of shared interests. On YouTube informal learning may take many forms, for example learning from the content of videos and learning through interactions with others, or learning from viewers and learning through self-assessment of one's work.

Proponents of participatory types of informal learning acknowledge that the site has the potential to promote peer-to-peer connections that facilitate learning in socially oriented ways. Through the sharing of common interests, video creators and viewers may circulate interesting and informative ideas that would otherwise be difficult to access. Not all local mentors such as teachers in schools or community centers share the same interests, passions, and abilities as those required by learners. However, informal learning is not without difficulties, which include the vulnerabilities of learning in public, experiencing challenges to identity formation, dealing with harassment and negative feedback, and uncertainty in assessing the mentors' abilities and the learners' progress. Learning in public may mean risking one's reputation, as one reveals ignorance when developing new information or skills. In addition, scholars studying informal learning rarely address assessment, or the degree to which a third party might rate the quality of instructional videos or the learners' abilities after engaging in informal learning on YouTube. Although interactive feedback is seen as an important aspect of informal learning, assessment has traditionally been associated with modes of formal learning (Hofstein & Rosenfeld, 1996). Further, not all observers are capable of assessing what has been learned during processes of informal engagement. For example, nontechnical parents who see their children as digitally accomplished may not always have sufficient skill to make accurate assessments about the degree to which their children have actually mastered specific digital literacies and skills.

Despite such concerns, scholars are increasingly investigating the range and types of informal learning that are occurring on YouTube. Having a strong sense of enjoyment and a sense of choice prompts individuals to learn by making, sharing, and viewing videos online. YouTube's videos and interaction also facilitate spot-learning on specific, circumscribed subjects that do not require a lengthy formal course; they then help viewers solve an immediate problem or explore new knowledge or skill such as learning how to accomplish a specific video editing technique. The degree of self-conscious learning that occurs on YouTube varies, with some videos, for instance tutorials, guiding knowledge and skill acquisition in directed and planned ways, while at other times YouTubers learn by simply being exposed to content that they might not otherwise encounter in their daily lives. YouTube's open-ended structure and the vast array of its content encourage self-directed exploration and a sense of sometimes unexpected discovery, which facilitates learning on the basis of shared interests and passions.

Experiments in learning on YouTube

Scholars in media studies and anthropology have engaged in high-profile experiments in bringing elements of the classroom into the informal learning environment of YouTube. In addition, teachers have brought aspects of YouTube into the classroom, in part by encouraging students to evaluate videos and to make their own. These experiments have met with mixed results, but they all tend to illustrate how YouTube may be used at various points on a theoretical continuum between strictly formal and informal learning.

Media scholar Alexandra Juhasz and anthropologist Michael Wesch launched two separate, well-publicized experiments in 2007 that sought to interact with YouTube and facilitate informal learning. Juhasz taught a class entitled "Learning from YouTube." Later she also produced a video book of the same title that explored, among other subjects, the tension between entertainment and education. In the class, students' class sessions and homework were posted to YouTube, in an effort to interact with broader audiences that could engage with the material at their own pace and interact with it in their own way. Juhasz observed that students largely received mocking public commentary on their work. In addition, YouTube's technical features—such as difficulties in linking relevant material—complicated the ability of the class to create a feeling of community on the site or to connect with audiences outside the classroom. Nevertheless, Juhasz has argued that students learned valuable meta-lessons about how learning on YouTube works, as well as about its technical and social limitations (Juhasz, 2009). The exercise itself supplemented learning about media literacies by helping students to understand how the commercial parameters of an online platform influence opportunities for in-depth exchange.

Adopting a different tactic, anthropologist Michael Wesch created a video called *The Machine Us/ing Us*, which was posted on January 21, 2007 and has since garnered more than 11 million views. The video demonstrates that people with various levels of media expertise can create video messages and link to other people. It invites viewers to reflect on important concepts such as copyright, authorship, and identity (Ryan, 2010). Wesch also worked with students to create a video for YouTube called *A Vision of Students Today*, which was posted on October 12, 2007 and has received more than 5 million views. The video discusses technological changes that have occurred in student learning due to cellphones and the Internet. The video takes a critical stance at the degree to which students are struggling to connect to formal learning contexts. Wesch also launched a digital ethnography program in which students were encouraged to create online communities and share their perspectives through blogs and videos (Ryan, 2010). These materials enliven learning, provide meta-lessons and critiques about institutions of higher learning, and create an opportunity for students to develop digital media-making skills by engaging in spaces of informal learning such as YouTube.

Both experiments attempted to bring students into contact with a wider population online and to explore how YouTube and video making might spur wide-scale discourse on learning about media. Although the results were uneven, each experiment provided meta-lessons about the challenges of both formal and informal learning environments. They all offered insights into the opportunities and difficulties that emerge from experimenting with hybrid, interactive forms of learning. Juhasz's work suggested that much needs to be done before classroom and online hybrid models will likely promote connected and deeply engaged forms of community. Conversely, Wesch's experiment showed the importance of pursuing alternative technical forms and social spaces for learning, given students' increased reliance on technology and on social media.

Teachers have also attempted to bring a sense of fun and engagement from YouTube into formal classroom settings in creative ways. For instance, mathematics teachers have used videos of young children singing algebra equations to popular tunes. Another tactic involves watching videos with news stories that facilitate classroom discussions about how the media transmit particular messages through their structure and form (Lange & Parker, 2010). An increasing number of teachers are encouraging students to make their own media and to post them to YouTube, as part of classroom exercises and assignments such as making documentaries on important topics. Instructors report that students not only learn about content or overt subjects of school reports and documentaries but also become more media-literate by learning how videos and the stories in them are technically crafted and received. Experiments on creating media as alternatives to written work suggest that more hybrid digital models of informal and formal learning will increase in the foreseeable future.

Learning about content

On YouTube, video lectures may be posted as supplements to institutional learning at schools and museums. In addition, participants may engage in do-it-yourself forms of instruction. A popular method of informal learning is the video tutorial, which allows peer-to-peer exchange of information that learners can engage with at their own pace. Video tutorial makers set out to explain a concept, provide information, or demonstrate a process. Tutorials have appeared across an extremely broad range of activities that assist in improving media-making skills such as incorporating special effects, using lighting equipment, sound mixing, storyboarding, and editing. In addition to tutorials, video makers and viewers may also learn from the feedback that is posted to videos, as additional tips and critiques may be provided.

Assessing the total number of tutorial videos and their viewership on YouTube is difficult. At a minimum, one set of researchers identified and studied 300 video tutorials across 30 channels on YouTube (Gruffat, 2015). At the other end of the spectrum, simply typing in the word "tutorial" on the site yields over 100 million results, which suggests that tutorials on a wide range of topics are a popular genre on YouTube. Statistics from Pew Research Center's Internet and American Life Project suggest a growing popularity of educational videos online in general. Pew surveyed just over 1000 adult users online (18 years of age and older) and found that, of the 18% of US adult Internet users who post their own videos online, 30% say they post educational or tutorial videos (Purcell, 2013). In terms of viewership, according to Pew, 50% of adults who are online say they watch educational videos, which represents an increase from 38% in 2009 and 22% in 2007. Further, video users online who are under the age of 50 are more likely to watch "how-to" videos than older viewers. Across all age groups, 72% of the viewers surveyed said they were likely to watch "how-to" videos (Purcell, 2013).

Video tutorials on YouTube provide information and instructions for learning information, demonstrating a process, or acquiring new skills. Several types of tutorials have been observed to exist online (Perkel & Herr-Stephenson, 2008). The first form is the more traditional type of tutorial, in which a person provides visual step-by-step instructions and tips for how to do something, for example how to add a particular special effect to a video. The second type may be classified as a walk-through, in which a video maker demonstrates or performs a replica of how they did something—say, completing a task successfully in a video game. A third form is known as a guide, in which a person might address a whole subject and talk about it in general terms rather than specifically demonstrate a process. In these examples, learning may occur as viewers watch and attempt to replicate the instructions in these videos. Tutorial makers often claim that the major impetus for creating such instructional material comes from viewers who would like to replicate an effect seen in a video maker's work.

Tutorials enable learners to access information and resources that are not always available to them locally. These include not just the material artifacts of the videos themselves, but in some instances tutorials become a social resource, as viewers may use them to identify and connect to potential mentors, who may further guide learners or engage in collaborative forms of learning and in accomplishing activities (Perkel & Herr-Stephenson, 2008). Once a video tutorial is created, it arguably becomes a "socially encoded" artifact, in that it materializes a set of information that either has been deemed by particular individuals as important for others to know (Lange, 2014) or is created at the request of viewers who seek information and assistance. In the area of music learning and education, researchers have used the term "pedagogical syncretism" to refer to how learners use a mixture of strategies such as combining the viewing of videos and the study of online resources (e.g., discussions on forums) to learn how to play songs (Waldron, 2013). The term may be applied to refer to how YouTube in general might be used in syncretic ways, in combination with multiple learning methods. Watching video tutorials may offer one channel in a mix of learning strategies.

Learning through interaction

Informal learning may occur on YouTube through interaction that takes place both on and off the site. Viewers and video makers may learn through feedback, in the form of commentary that is posted to videos, or by privately communicating with mentors either through YouTube's messaging system or through other online or offline back channels. A famous example that well illustrates interactive, participatory learning dynamics was that of Peter Oakley, a 79-year-old Englishman who was known on YouTube as Geriatric1927. Oakley began experimenting with video blogging and eventually posted over 60 videos on his channel. His autobiographical videos discussed being a widower, his pre-World War II experiences, and his views on England's class system (Sørenssen, 2009). In his videos he admits that he needs assistance when it comes to vlogging. Viewers responded by critiquing the technical aspects of his videos, advising him to add music, and providing tips on how to change the color and font of text. Oakley incorporated these tips, and scholars observed how his media literacy improved over the course of his interactions with YouTubers. Despite the statistical claim that YouTube is dominated by younger viewers, the interactions also showed potential opportunities for intergenerational learning exchanges through video. Reports suggest that 91% of US teens (13–17-year-olds) and 81% of millenials (often defined as comprising young people in their late teens and up to their early thirties) watch YouTube. Scholars argue that Oakley's popularity on YouTube stemmed in part from a need for a "grandfather" figure, given current sociological trends in which young people decreasingly have immediate access to grandparents (Sørenssen, 2009).

In addition to enabling the acquisition of technical skills, interactions on the site prepare video makers to learn how to participate in video-based social media environments. By interacting with others and engaging with feedback, video makers can learn how to deal with efforts at community building and joint media-making and how to respond to "haters" or viewers who post unnecessarily harsh criticism. By operating a channel and by posting videos, video makers create for themselves an opportunity to learn about multiple and complex dimensions of participation, including monetizing videos, promoting videos through social channels, and interacting with fans and mass media organizations.

Commentators may provide suggestions and mentorship to video makers. Their commentary may also be seen by other viewers. Informal learning through interactivity may thus occur bidirectionally. Video tutorials may have an effect of "flattening" pedagogical structures such that people teach each other nuanced information by interacting at a variety of levels with the video and the surrounding discourse. For example, an expert may post a video on how to accomplish a video-editing technique, and viewers may provide feedback on the legibility of the video both in terms of how content was explained and in terms of how clearly the video was technically executed. Viewers may call out, for instance, a video tutorial with poor lighting, or they may show appreciation for instructional techniques such as inclusion of samples of how a special effect should look in a video once it is executed properly. In this way a video maker who is expert enough to make a tutorial may also learn important lessons on how to improve the quality of tutorials—a dynamic that illustrates bidirectional opportunities for informal learning.

Video makers who create tutorials may themselves learn in a variety of ways, such as by seeking assistance through Google searches, by engaging in trial and error, and by watching others' videos as well as their own in order to discover and assess areas of improvement. Video makers report that simply watching their work when it is posted and situated in the context of YouTube often exposes problems or areas that require improvement, from technical to social aspects of video creation. In the field of music learning, the term "purposive listening" means employing active listening to music with the purpose of putting what is heard to practical use (Green, 2002). This term may also be applied to viewing videos: there creators may engage in "purposive viewing" in order to learn techniques and tips that may be gleaned from videos and applied to one's own work (Lange, 2014). Viewers may learn about technical video-making techniques as well as get participatory lessons on style, on what constitutes appealing content, and on how to interact with participants in order to increase viewership. Finally, Green's concept might also be applied to explore the possibilities of "purposive commenting," in which participants view comments with the goal of actively reviewing, critiquing, and learning about appropriate participation in terms of comment content and form (Lange, 2014). What constitutes productive online participation is gleaned by observing interactions between video makers and viewers and among commenters.

Incidental learning

In addition to planned video tutorials and other forms of direct commentary and critique, learning may be accomplished through casual forms of participating on YouTube. Experts argue that informal learning as a general category includes various levels of planned guidance and overt consciousness that a participant is actually engaged in learning. Experts have thus distinguished between informal and incidental learning, the latter referring to instances that are strictly unintentional and serendipitous and often result as a by-product of another activity (Marsick & Watkins, 1990). Incidental learning typically occurs in an unplanned way, when a person is engaged in another interaction or task. As a subset of informal learning, incidental learning may prompt learners to reevaluate tacit assumptions, recognize mistakes, and reconsider their interpretations of others' actions. Ideally, for incidental learning to take root, it must eventually move from being tacit to a state of recognized awareness, through processes of self-reflection.

YouTube offers an environment for such forms of incidental learning, as when it becomes possible to glean tips inadvertently, while watching a video for entertainment. For example, a funny pranking video that casually explains how sound effects are achieved may be seen as an incidental type of informal learning, as the instruction emerged for the viewer in an unplanned and serendipitous way. In addition, participants have reported developing an increased understanding of other cultural groups as they learned about their experiences through YouTube. Posting controversial political videos that express a point of view may attract commentary from multiple perspectives, which provides additional information both to a video maker and to the viewers who read the commentary. Contrary to fears about online interactants simply operating in echo chambers with regard to political positions, studies suggest that young people online tend to be exposed to viewpoints other than their own when engaging in everyday activities online. For example, drawing on a survey of youth civic engagement in California from 2005 to 2009, researchers found that, when participating on blogs and social media in general, youths tended to report being exposed to views that both aligned with and diverged from their own (Kahne, Middaugh, Lee, & Feezell, 2011). Such observations are consistent with the experiences of case studies on YouTube, in which participants report receiving supportive as well as hostile commentary of disagreement on their videos.

Informal learning challenges

YouTube has received harsh criticism for the supposed lack of quality of its vernacular videos (Sherman, 2008). Yet other scholars have argued that it is precisely the uneven quality of videos on the site that encourages novice video makers to begin creating and sharing videos (Gauntlett, 2011). The massive number of videos and comments related to improving work on video creation demonstrates that there is a "discourse of quality" on the site in which participants of various abilities, from the novice to the professional, dialogically discuss ways to improve their work in both technically conventional and socially emergent participatory ways (Müller, 2009). However, these opportunities for informal exchange also produce a "participation dilemma" (Müller, 2009). This term captures the fact that vernacular media makers are often encouraged to participate on sites like YouTube but are criticized rather than celebrated for their supposed rejection of craftsmanship, aesthetic quality, and participatory ethics. To avoid being exploited or mocked, novice participants are encouraged by scholars, educators, and cultural critics to improve their digital and media-making literacies in conventional rather than individualistic or democratizing ways. Discourses of quality and the abundance of video tutorials on a range of media literacy subjects challenge, however, the assumption that ordinary media makers remain unconcerned about quality.

The participation dilemma also places novices in the potentially awkward position of trying to learn in public. Engaging in collaborative types of informal learning online includes posting work in order to gain feedback from viewers and fellow media makers. But posting work as one is acquiring a new skill reveals a creator's potential weaknesses and areas that require improvement. While some scholars see spaces like YouTube as celebrating connected and collective acts of learning, others are concerned about the site as creating a space of vulnerability for learners who experiment with the development of new skills.

Video tutorials also carry a stigma with some creators, who espouse technical identities that privilege certain forms of learning over others. Scholars have found that, for some learners, tutorials are legitimate forms of learning, while for more technically oriented participants tutorials represent a less valuable or socially legitimate way of acquiring new media skills (Perkel & Herr-Stephenson, 2008; Lange, 2014). Technical participants often tend to privilege trial and error forms of learning over the use of artifacts such as tutorials for gaining in-depth and socially acceptable forms of knowledge. Posting a tutorial itself becomes a way of creating a visible identity as an expert vis-à-vis one's viewers. For example, in the area of online art communities, scholars found that tutorial makers might post video tutorials as a response to viewers' queries, but they might also be motivated by a wish to capitalize on a genre that is known to gain views and enhance one's reputation, and hence by a wish to become publicly recognized as an expert in a particular area. Further, tutorial makers may be dismissive of viewers who need tutorials, as more technically oriented participants believe that watching tutorials amounts to a low-status form of learning by "copying" and thus potentially stunts rather than encourages improvement (Perkel & Herr-Stephenson, 2008). Although helpful to many, video tutorials and other informal videos may also function to enhance viewership and boost the personal reputation of certain creators.

Feedback versus assessment

Scholars have often associated the term "assessment" with teachers' appraisal of students' work. The term also applies to evaluations of educators by formal, institutional, accrediting bodies. However, it has also been observed that resources may be of uneven or even questionable quality. Although YouTube tutorials abound, little information is available about third parties who might wish to assess whether an individual resource such as a YouTube video walk-through is providing the ideal—or even an acceptable—pedagogical tactic for particular learners. At the same time, tutorial makers may distribute videos in a one-to-many model but may not necessarily connect with a student as mentors, which leaves open the question of how well a student has actually mastered a particular knowledge terrain or has acquired a technique or skill from using videos or combinations of learning methods on and off of the site.

Studies of informal learning tend to use the term "feedback" as opposed to "assessment" when discussing the dialogical ways in which learning occurs in creative, online spaces such as YouTube. As noted, feedback can be extremely important not only for the video maker but also for other viewers, who are exchanging information about a particular topic. In some cases, important feedback in the learning process may even consist principally of encouragement rather than of specific assessments on technical execution. However, it has also been observed that participants on YouTube endure hostility, unnecessarily harsh commentary, and even threats, which complicates participants' enthusiasm for learning in public. While scholars in formal education tend to express concern about YouTube's lack of systematic assessment and hostile learning environments, scholars who support YouTube emphasize its varied content, the availability of distributed mentors, and collaborative forms of interaction as potential ways to conduct self-paced and playful modes of informal learning.

SEE ALSO: Connected Learning; Entertainment Information; Media Literacy in Portugal; Participation through Public Media: Improving Media Literacy among Vulnerable Youth; Social Networking Skills; Video Composition in Secondary School

References

Bishop, J.L., & Verleger, M.A. (2013). The flipped classroom: A survey of the research. Paper presented at the 120th ASEE Annual Conference & Exposition, June 23–26, 2013.

Boekaerts, M., & Minnaert, A. (1999). Self-regulation with respect to informal learning. *International Journal of Educational Research, 31*, 533–544.

Drotner, K. (2008). Informal learning and digital media: Perceptions, practices and perspectives. In K. Drotner, H.S. Jensen, & C. Schrøder (Eds.), *Informal learning and digital media* (pp. 10–28). Newcastle, England: Cambridge Scholars.

Gauntlett, D. (2011). *Making is connecting*. Cambridge: Polity.

Green, L. (2002). *How popular musicians learn: A way ahead for music education.* Aldershot, England: Ashgate.

Gruffat, C. (2015). Tutorials on YouTube: A study from the perspective of digital humanities. *Social Media Studies, 1*(2), 143–149.

Hofstein, A., & Rosenfeld, S. (1996). Bridging the gap between formal and informal science learning. *Studies in Science Education, 28*, 87–112.

Juhasz, A. (2009). Learning the five lessons of YouTube: After trying to teach there, I don't believe the hype. *Cinema Journal, 48*(2), 145–150.

Kahne, J., Middaugh, E., Lee N., & Feezell, J.T. (2011). Youth online activity and exposure to diverse perspectives. *New Media & Society, 14*(3), 492–512.

Lange, P.G. (2014). *Kids on YouTube: Technical identities and digital literacies.* Walnut Creek, CA: Left Coast Press/Routledge.

Lange, P.G., & Parker, J.K. (2010). YouTube: Creating, connecting and learning through video. In J.K. Parker (Ed.), *Teaching tech-savvy kids* (pp. 37–64). Thousand Oaks, CA: Corwin.

Marsick, V.J., & Watkins, K.E. (1990). *Informal and incidental learning in the workplace.* New York, NY: Routledge.

Müller, E. (2009). Where quality matters: Discourses on the art of making a YouTube video. In P. Snickars & P. Vonderau (Eds.), *The YouTube reader* (pp. 126–139). Stockholm, Sweden: National Library of Sweden.

Perkel, D., & Herr-Stephenson, B. (2008). Peer pedagogy in an interest-driven community: The practices and problems of online tutorials. Paper presented at the MEDIA@LSE Fifth Anniversary Conference, September 21–23, 2008.

Purcell, K. (2013). Online video 2013. October 13. Washington, DC: Pew Research Center. Retrieved from http://www.pewinternet.org/files/old-media//Files/Reports/2013/PIP_Online%20Video%202013.pdf

Robertson, M.R. (2015). 500 hours of video uploaded to YouTube every minute [Forecast]. Tubular Insights, November 13, 2015. Retrieved from http://tubularinsights.com/hours-minute-uploaded-youtube

Ryan, D. (2010). Media review: Technology and professor Michael Wesch of Kansas State University. *Journal of Student Affairs Research and Practice, 47*(2), 267–269.

Sefton-Green, J. (2004). *Literature review in informal learning with technology outside school.* Future Lab Report 7. Retrieved from https://www.nfer.ac.uk/publications/FUTL72/FUTL72.pdf

Sherman, T. (2008). Vernacular video. In G. Lovink & S. Niederer (Eds.), *Video vortex: Responses to YouTube* (pp. 161–168). Amsterdam, Netherlands: Institute of Network Cultures.

Sørenssen, B. (2009). Breaking the age barrier in the internet age: The story of Geriatric1927. In P. Snickars & P. Vonderau (Eds.), *The YouTube reader* (pp. 140–151). Stockholm: National Library of Sweden.

Waldron, J. (2013). User-generated content, Youtube and participatory culture on the web: Music learning and teaching in two contrasting online communities. *Music Education Research, 15*(3), 257–274.

Further reading

Juhasz, A. (2011). *Learning from YouTube* [Video book]. Cambridge, MA: MIT Press. Retrieved from http://vectors.usc.edu/projects/learningfromyoutube

Lange, P.G., & Ito, M. (2010). Creative production. In M. Ito, S. Baumer, M. Bittani, d. boyd, R. Cody, B. Herr-Stephenson, H.A. Horst, ... L. Tripp (Eds.), *Hanging out, messing around, and geeking out: Kids living and learning with new media* (pp. 243–293). Cambridge, MA: MIT Press.

Tan, E. (2013). Informal learning on Youtube: Exploring digital literacy in independent online learning. *Learning, Media and Technology, 38*(4), 463–477.

Waldron, J. (2013). Youtube, fanvids, forums, vlogs and blogs: Informal music learning in a convergent on- and offline music community. *International Journal of Music Education, 31*, 91–105.

Patricia G. Lange is an anthropologist and associate professor of critical studies (undergraduate program) and visual and critical studies (graduate program) at California College of the Arts in San Francisco. Her work focuses on technical identity performance, online communication, and the use of video to express the self. She is the author of *Kids on YouTube: Technical Identities and Digital Literacies* (2014). She also produced and directed the film *Hey Watch This! Sharing the Self through Media* (2013), which provides a diachronic look at the rise and fall of YouTube as a social media site.

Internet Safety

LIES DE KIMPE
University of Antwerp and Ghent University, Belgium

MICHEL WALRAVE
University of Antwerp, Belgium

KOEN PONNET
Ghent University, Belgium

JORIS VAN OUYTSEL
University of Antwerp, Belgium, and University of Texas Medical Branch, USA

The term "Internet safety" encompasses a set of issues that are, either directly or indirectly, related to the physical and psychological well-being of Internet users. Also referred to as "online safety," "digital safety," or "e-safety," this concept is associated both with the risks individuals face online and with the ways they can protect themselves against those risks. A large body of research within this domain is dedicated to the safety of children and adolescents. One reason for this specific focus is the fact that young people are the most active Internet users. Being online offers them a whole range of opportunities, but at the same time this may confront them with several risks. Adolescents may be particularly vulnerable when facing those online risks as compared to adults, because they are, among other things, more stimulated by short-term rewards than by long-term prospects and because they have a higher tendency to take part in risky behaviors than adults. An additional concern related to this age group is that the way in which they access the Internet differs from previous generations. Most devices that are used to go online have become portable and, therefore, young people spend more and more time alone with their laptops, smartphones, and tablets, in their bedrooms for example. In consequence, children's Internet use is often free of parental supervision.

That most studies focus on young people's online behavior does not mean, however, that adults are insusceptible to online risk. Just like children and adolescents, they are connected to the Internet. They may be less vulnerable to some risks and less prone to taking risks in general, but they are not immune to the potentially negative consequences related to risky Internet use, such as reputational damage or losing money through online scams. Furthermore, some research points out that older Internet users (65- to 90-year-olds) tend to have less experience with various types and functions of technology (Olson, O'Brien, Rogers, & Charness, 2011), implying that older users may be just as vulnerable online as their younger counterparts in some situations.

Over the years, academic researchers from different disciplines (e.g., communication studies, psychology, law), educators, media outlets, and governmental institutions have voiced concerns about the risks people face online on a daily basis and have expressed the need for appropriate interventions in order to minimize the harm some online activities might cause, especially to children. More recently, however, some academics have started to label this increased worry as "moral panic." They claim that the Internet is not as dangerous as generally assumed by public opinion, since not every risk Internet users face will inevitably result in a negative outcome or harm. Nonetheless, they do not deny that some Internet users have negative experiences which result in harm. Therefore, it is important to address these issues so the risks Internet users encounter are minimized without limiting the opportunities the World Wide Web has to offer.

A number of different categorizations are used to classify online risks. One frequently applied categorization is created within the framework of the project EU Kids Online and distinguishes aggressive, sexual, commercial, and value-related risks (Livingstone, Haddon, Görzig, & Ólafsson, 2011). In a second categorization, a distinction can be made between risks related to online content and those related to online contact (Youth Protection Roundtable, 2009). Contact risks assume a direct connection or interaction between offender and victim, while this kind of connection is absent or less visible when facing content risks. Based on the framework derived from EU Kids Online and the Youth Protection Roundtable Toolkit, a categorization is proposed in Table 1 that will be used in the remainder of this entry. It is important to note that overlap may exist between some of these categories (e.g., between aggressive content and some value-related risks). Moreover, some risks may co-occur in specific online contexts (e.g., hate speech could lead to cyberbullying). As such, it is not the scope of this entry to present an exhaustive overview of all risks Internet users may encounter.

Aggression risks

The freedom and anonymity the Internet offers can be used to hurt others through spreading hateful or violent messages, images, and/or videos. Although many types of

Table 1 Categorization of online risks.

	Content risks	*Contact risks*
Aggression	Violent or hateful content	Cyberbullying Cyberstalking
Sexual	Pornography	Sexting Sextortion Online grooming
Value-related	Incorrect or harmful information on • suicide • self-harm • anorexia • racism • hate speech • …	Incorrect or harmful advice on • suicide • self-harm • anorexia • racism • hate speech • …
Commercial	Gambling Copyright infringement Hybridization of commercial content and entertainment	Harvesting personal data Spam Phishing Identity theft

Source: Based on Livingstone et al. (2011); Youth Protection Roundtable (2009).

cyberaggression exist (e.g., flaming, outing, (in)direct harassment), the umbrella term most often used to talk about this variety of online aggression is *cyberbullying*. No consensus exists on the definition of this term, but it can be understood as aggressive or cruel acts carried out by an individual or group against a victim by means of the Internet or other digital technologies (Tokunaga, 2010). Some definitions stress the power imbalance between the victim and the perpetrator, while others emphasize the repetitive nature of the aggressive acts.

Although everyone can become a victim of cyberbullying, research is mostly conducted among children and teenagers. Because differences in both definition and measurement exist, it is difficult to estimate the prevalence of cyberbullying within this age group. On average, between 20% and 40% of young people have been cyberbullied at least once (Tokunaga, 2010). The number of cyberbully victims has even increased during the past decade (Jones, Mitchell, & Finkelhor, 2012). This is not very surprising, since young people have become active users of social media and the Internet. As a result, an important part of their social life now occurs online. The increase in the number of cyberbully victims should thus be seen as a shift in or expansion of the bullying context, rather than as an increase in the number of bullied children. The majority of cyberbully victims are upset by this experience. Depending on the frequency, length, and severity of the aggressive acts, experiencing cyberbullying is associated with psychological problems (e.g., depression, social anxiety), affective disorders (e.g., detachment), and academic problems (e.g., drop in grades, increased absences). On a more aggregated level, cyberbullying is linked to negative school climate. It is suggested that the harm caused by cyberbullying is potentially more severe when compared to offline bullying as it can easily happen anonymously, may be witnessed by a wider audience, and can occur at any time, 24 hours a day. It should be mentioned, however, that apart from the latter, these features are not unique to the cyberbullying context (e.g., spreading rumors is a form of anonymous offline bullying) (Heirman et al., 2016).

A specific form of cyberbullying is *cyberstalking*, or the repeated and unwanted pursuit of an individual using electronic devices. These digital technologies can be used by stalkers both to collect information about their victim and to reach out to him or her. The difference between cyberbullying and cyberstalking is that stalkers do not by definition wish to cause harm, although they usually do. It is assumed that the perpetrator often wants to initiate a love relationship or friendship with the victim. Other possible motivations are jealousy and revenge. Stalking victims may suffer from psychological (e.g., inner unrest, anger, depression) and social problems (e.g., mistrust toward others). In contrast to offline stalking, cyberstalking has been barely examined. One study showed that 6.3% of people stated to have been a cyberstalking victim for at least 2 weeks (Dreβing, Bailer, Anders, Wagner, & Gallas, 2014).

Next to interpersonal forms of aggression, Internet users may be confronted with *violent content*. In this case, the aggressive message is not directed straight at the user. Violent and hateful images, videos, or texts can be a depiction of reality but can also be displayed within forms of entertainment, such as games. The latter have been studied quite extensively in the past, especially since gaming is very popular among youths. For instance, research has demonstrated that violent video game play is associated with aggression, both in the short and long term (Willoughby, Adachi, & Good, 2012). Therefore, it is not unthinkable the same link exists between other types of online violence and aggressive behavior or, for example, between online violence and radical ideologies (see below).

Sexual risks

The Internet also serves as a platform for the distribution of sexually explicit content, such as online *pornography*. When (young) Internet users face this potentially age-inappropriate and/or unsolicited content, this can be upsetting. One study found that 14% of young people (9- to 16-year-olds) were confronted with sexual content within the 12 months prior to the survey (Livingstone et al., 2011), while other research indicates that 23% (10- to 17-year-olds) saw pornography unwillingly in the past year (Jones et al., 2012). The older teenagers get, the more likely it is they have seen sexual images online. A fifth to a quarter of them reported to have been very upset after seeing this explicit content (Livingstone & Smith, 2014). Younger children are more likely to be bothered than older children.

Teenagers and adults can also produce sexual content themselves. When they send these self-produced sexualized texts, photos, or videos to each other via cell phones or the Internet, this is called *sexting*. Because a variety of definitions and measurements of sexting exist, estimates of prevalence differ widely. The rates depend highly on the nature of the content (nearly nude, nude, or explicit; text, photo, or video), the role the individual takes on (receiver or creator), and the age of the sample. Results therefore range from 2.5% to 25% for minors and from 30% to 54% for adults (Döring, 2014). Although some consider sexting to be a normal part of sexual experience, individuals who engage in sexting should be aware of the risks linked to this specific online contact. Once a sexual message or image is sent, it is difficult to control what happens with it and who will be able to see it. When a sexting message reaches unintended audiences, this content can cause reputational damage or can be abused by (cyber)bullies. In addition, sexting can put individuals at risk of *sextortion*. This is a type of blackmail in which the offender obtains sexually explicit material created by the victim and uses it to pressure him or her to perform sexual acts or to pay a certain amount of money. By threatening to reveal this intimate content to friends or family, offenders try to achieve their goals. Because it is assumed a lot of sextortion cases stay unreported, it is difficult to estimate its prevalence.

Similar to sextortion are concerns related to adults approaching children online with the intent to sexually abuse them, also known as *online grooming*. Social media platforms and mobile applications offer sexual predators a whole range of new and easy tools to contact young people. Although this risk should be taken seriously, the moral panic surrounding this topic may not be in proportion to the number of online grooming victims. First of all, it is assumed that children are more frequently groomed by acquaintances in an offline setting than by strangers on the Internet (Livingstone & Smith, 2014). It is further true that young people do not always know who they are chatting with online, but according to the EU Kids Online study only 9% of young people actually arrange a face-to-face meeting with a stranger. It happens even less frequently that youngsters go to such meetings alone or without telling another person. Over half of these meetings are with people related to their own friendship circle. When meeting an unknown person face-to-face, 11% of the European youths claimed this encounter made them feel upset or uncomfortable. This equals about 1% of all young Internet users (Livingstone et al., 2011), which indicates that only a relatively small proportion of youths experience real harm as a result of meeting strangers.

Value-related risks

While risks related to digital forms of aggression and sexual risks have received ample research attention, less is known about value-related risks. These risks are related to the harmful content and untrustworthy information that can easily be found online and that can negatively affect the values a person holds regarding him- or herself, a group of individuals, or society as a whole. For example, there are numerous sites available on *suicide* and *nonsuicidal self-injury* (NSSI), respectively depicting and discussing different ways to end one's own life and ways to inflict self-harm. These sites are easily accessible. The majority do not explicitly encourage harmful behaviour, however, but use a neutral tone (Lewis & Knoll, 2015). Some even promote help-seeking (Mok, Ross, Jorm, & Pirkis, 2016).

Still, it should be considered that being confronted with information on suicide methods or self-injury may pose a risk to vulnerable individuals, although this is not the case by default. Research has shown that suicide-related Internet use is associated with an increase in suicidal thoughts (Mok et al., 2016). This result may imply that processing tips and advice on suicide and NSSI indeed leads to an increase in destructive thoughts or can even reinforce harmful behavior. However, this observation may just as well suggest that the Internet is used as a tool to seek help when suffering from suicidal ideation or self-harm tendencies. The interactive features of suicide and NSSI websites, such as chatrooms, may offer individuals who seek help a virtual space where they can give each other emotional support. More research is necessary to fully understand the motivations of the Internet users who visit these types of webpages.

"Pro-ana" sites, which portray anorexia as a lifestyle choice instead of a disease, have the same twofold nature. They may offer support to people with an eating disorder, but this doesn't mean the websites are completely beneficial and that they cannot be potentially harmful to the site's users. One study on pro-anorexia sites, for example, (Bardone-Cone & Cass, 2007) showed that respondents who viewed a pro-ana website perceived themselves as heavier than those exposed to other websites. These findings suggest that taking part in this type of unsafe community can be perceived as harmful.

Research discussing value-related risks is scarce. Therefore it is difficult to gauge how many people visit websites with such content. The EU Kids Online survey offers some insight into this topic by showing that up to 5% of teenagers have already visited a suicide site, 7% have been confronted with a self-harm site, and 10% have seen pro-ana websites (Livingstone et al., 2011). Little is known, however, about other ways in which unhealthy messages are spread, for instance through social networking sites. It is equally unclear what kind of short- and long-term effects being exposed to value-related risks might have on Internet users.

The Internet is also used by violent ideological groups to spread *hateful or even aggressive messages.* Within these groups, a set of beliefs is shared that considers violence as a justified way to achieve group goals. Often their hate is directed toward people with a different race, religion, or sexual orientation. With their ideology, these groups offer a clear framework that makes sense of the world and reduces ambiguity, which makes membership very attractive to some individuals. Believed to be especially vulnerable to this type of reasoning are (young) people in search of an identity and a sense of belonging. Depending on how often and how long certain messages are consulted, exposure to hateful or racist content can shape belief systems. Moreover, it is feared that exposure will in some cases lead to the mobilization of supporters to become involved in extreme actions, online or even offline. In this respect, it is worrying that in Finland 67.4% of 15- to 18-year-olds (Näsi, Räsänen, Hawdon, Holkeri, & Oksanen, 2015) and in the United States 65.4% of 18- to 36-year-olds were exposed to hate materials online in the 3 months prior to the study (Costello, Hawdon, Ratliff, & Grantham, 2016). One fifth of the latter group was even confronted with content calling for violence. Time spent online and specific attitudes like (a lack of) trust in the government were closely related to their likelihood of exposure. In this regard, it is remarkable that there is still a lot of uncertainty about a possible connection between exposure to hateful online content and the engagement in violent extremism or the adoption of a radical ideology.

Commercial risks

Businesses and other commercial actors have developed several ways to *harvest personal data* from Internet users. Cookies, for example, which are web-tracking and information-gathering tools, are used to save personal data from the users of a specific website (e.g., which buttons are clicked, which pages are visited). On the one hand, these data can be used to personalize advertisements and other content, which makes them more relevant for the consumer. On the other hand, however, this data collection often takes place in a (for the Internet user) nontransparent way. Although it is sometimes possible to decline cookies, this may result in the inability to consume (some of) a website's content. Consumers are thus left with little choice. The same holds for social network sites (SNS): without the disclosure of at least some personal information it is impossible to enjoy the benefits related to SNS. These practices can be perceived as an invasion of consumers' privacy. Moreover, people are often uninformed about how the collected data are used exactly.

A specific concern exists surrounding the collection of personal data from young people. Since children and teenagers influence family purchase decisions and often have pocket money of their own to spend, they are an attractive demographic for advertisers. The fact that young people are avid Internet users makes it easy for commercial actors to target them online and collect their personal details. It is questioned, however, to what extent young people are able to assess whether they are consuming advertisements and whether their personal data are being collected. This may be problematic, especially when they are confronted with *hybridizations between marketing content and entertainment*, such as "advergames" or online games containing brand communication. Because the persuasive intent of these games is less obvious, the games might make young people more susceptible to the commercial messages as compared to other forms of advertising. It might also affect their decisions regarding the disclosure of personal data.

If individuals do not carefully manage personal data, this can have unwanted consequences. For instance, one may receive *spam*, which can be defined as all unsolicited e-mail communication, ranging from unsolicited advertising, through inappropriate (sexual) content, up to fraudulent messages. The latter can be part of a *phishing attack*, in which dishonest individuals or criminal organizations try to collect personal financial information (e.g., passwords, credit card numbers), often while pretending to be a trusted company. If Internet users fall for this con, this can result in *identity theft* and the loss of large amounts of money.

Lastly, some commercial risks directly resulting from Internet users' own conduct should be discussed. One of them is the usage of *illegal copies of software and media files*, that is, the illegal downloading or streaming of copyrighted music, movies, games, or e-books. Although those copyright infringements negatively affect the financial situation of individual creators and the creative industry as a whole, some consider illegal downloading, sharing, and streaming an acceptable practice. In theory, however, digital piracy is a crime and copyright violators risk fines or even imprisonment.

Also, *gambling sites* can have negative consequences for their users. This relatively new branch within the gambling industry, which encompasses all forms of wagering and gambling through devices connected to the Internet, has proven to be rather hard to study. As online gamblers are not easy to reach, most research uses purposive sampling strategies to collect information. Therefore, the prevalence rate of online gambling is difficult to estimate. One survey in the United Kingdom, however, indicated that 14% of the respondents had gambled online in the past year (Wardle, Moody, Griffiths, Orford, & Volberg, 2011). It is noteworthy that younger people are more likely to use online gambling methods. This might be explained by the fact that some websites do not ask for a user's age. Moreover, studies show that problem gambling appears more frequently among those who use the Internet to gamble compared to those who do not. In practice, problem gambling can have several negative consequences: evidently it can cause financial problems, but it can also lead to interpersonal and mental health problems (e.g., stress, anxiety).

Intervention

While a growing body of literature focuses on specific online safety issues, evidence-based interventions are lacking to successfully reduce online risks and harm. Several possible approaches have, however, been developed. Most often, *awareness campaigns* created by (inter)national governmental organizations are used (e.g., ThinkUKnow, an online safety campaign launched in the United Kingdom and Australia). Campaigns offer the option to reach both minors and adults and can stimulate public debate and raise awareness about Internet safety. At the same time, it isn't always clear to what extent these campaigns also contribute to behavioral change.

Additionally, *legislative initiatives* have been taken in the past to enforce a decrease in online risks. An important part of these initiatives deals with the regulation of data collection and privacy. A well-known example in this context is the Children's Online Privacy Protection Act (COPPA), created in the United States to regulate the online collection of personal data from children. The European Union has similar data protection rules. These do not specifically focus on online data collection, however, but are applicable in a digital context. Moreover, legislation is also issued on hate speech, violent content, or pornography that can be implemented in the online environment.

Other stakeholders, such as *teachers and schools*, can contribute to the online safety of youths in particular. Since the Internet is often used for educational purposes, both at school and at home, it is appropriate that educators pay attention to children's online safety. A first approach schools have been using is technical mediation in the form of filtering software that aims to block unwanted or harmful content. It should be taken into account, however, that these tools aren't capable of removing Internet risks completely. Moreover, filtering software cannot serve as a substitute for teaching young people how to use the web responsibly. Also, single-session lectures in schools dedicated to improve children's knowledge on online safety are claimed to have rather little effect (Jones & Finkelhor, 2011). Most of these programs are implemented without any evaluation of their effectiveness. More integrated and evidence-based approaches are thus needed. An important example in this context is the Finnish KiVa Program. This program, aimed at the reduction of bullying, considers bullying a group phenomenon. It encourages bystanders to speak out and to support bully victims. In this way, bullies do not gain status within the peer group, which discourages further bullying behavior. The program provides lessons and exercises, an online learning platform, and a guide for parents. This approach has proven its effectiveness in reducing both traditional bullying and cyberbullying. It is suggested that the implementation of similar evidence-based programs to tackle other online risks, such as sexting, might be interesting. These programs can aspire to prevent specific risks, but can also teach young people how to react when they have a negative online experience. Two coping strategies might be interesting for children and adolescents in this regard: communicating (e.g., talking to someone trustworthy about the problem) and problem-solving (e.g., reporting the problem, blocking the sender). The latter coping strategy, in particular, appeals to children who feel harmed by an online experience (Vandoninck, d'Haenens, & Roe, 2013). Other authors suggest that it might be interesting to adopt a more general approach, instead of developing specific Internet safety education. They assume that stressing general life skills like empathy, emotional intelligence, and conflict management might be beneficial. An example of such an approach is the Fourth R program, which focuses on the development of healthy friendly and romantic relationship skills. This program has proven its effectiveness in decreasing several offline risk behaviors, hence the same might hold true in an online context.

Efforts made to create a safer online environment for young people don't stop after school. Since young people most often go online at home, *parents* in particular can contribute to the online safety of their children. Two broad types of parental mediation can be distinguished: restrictive and active mediation. The former implies that parents try to control or limit the amount of time spent online, the content that is consulted (e.g., by using blocking or filtering software), and the online activities their children are involved in. This approach is perceived rather critically, since restrictions might motivate young people to use avoidance techniques. Additionally, some state that this form of mediation is indeed linked to less exposure to risks, but at the same time limits the opportunities the Internet has to offer (e.g., entertainment, communication, learning). With active mediation these problems may not arise, since in this case parents do not try to limit children's Internet use. Instead they share online activities with their children, teach them how to avoid certain online risks, and discuss their Internet use. In this way, children are able to explore the online environment by themselves, but with the guidance of an adult. It is claimed that this may improve children's learning process.

Apart from parents and teachers, peers are also an important source of influence in adolescents' lives. However, little is known about peer influence and peer support in relation to online safety. It might be interesting for future research to explore how peers can be taught skills to help each other avoid Internet risks. Moreover, future studies should address the lack of knowledge on the risks faced by relatively new Internet users, such as very young children and the elderly. Since these demographics have become more and more present online, it is imperative to develop a better understanding of their Internet use and how they cope with online risks. At the same time, academics should attentively follow the development of new modes of access to the Internet, as well as the emergence of new online risks.

SEE ALSO: EU Kids Online; Sexting

References

Bardone-Cone, A.M., & Cass, K.M. (2007). What does viewing a pro-anorexia website do? An experimental examination of website exposure and moderating effects. *International Journal of Eating Disorders, 40*(6), 537–548. doi: 10.1002/eat.20396

Costello, M., Hawdon, J., Ratliff, T., & Grantham, T. (2016). Who views online extremism? Individual attributes leading to exposure. *Computers in Human Behavior, 63*, 311–320. doi: 10.1016/j.chb.2016.05.033

Döring, N. (2014). Consensual sexting among adolescents: Risk prevention through abstinence education or safer sexting. *Cyberpsychology, 8*(1), 1–18. doi: 10.5817/CP2014-1-9

Dreßing, H., Bailer, J., Anders, A., Wagner, H., & Gallas, C. (2014). Cyberstalking in a large sample of social network users: Prevalence, characteristics, and impact upon victims. *Cyberpsychology, Behavior, and Social Networking, 17*(2), 61–67. doi: 10.1089/cyber.2012.0231

Heirman, W., Walrave, M., Vandebosch, H., Wegge, D., Eggermont, S., & Pabian, S. (2016). Cyberbullying research in Belgium: An overview of generated insights and a critical assessment of the mediation of technology in a Web 2.0 world. In *Cyberbullying Across the Globe* (pp. 169–191). Berlin, Germany: Springer.

Jones, L.M., & Finkelhor, D. (2011). Increasing youth safety and responsible behavior online: Putting in place programs that work. Washington, DC: Family Online Safety Institute. Retrieved from http://scholars.unh.edu/ccrc/56/

Jones, L.M., Mitchell, K.J., & Finkelhor, D. (2012). Trends in youth Internet victimization: Findings from three youth Internet safety surveys 2000–2010. *Journal of Adolescent Health, 50*(2), 179–186. doi: 10.1016/j.jadohealth.2011.09.015

Lewis, S.P., & Knoll, A.K. (2015). Do it yourself: Examination of self-injury first aid tips on YouTube. *Cyberpsychology, Behavior, and Social Networking, 18*(5), 301–304. doi: 10.1089/cyber.2014.0407

Livingstone, S., Haddon, L., Görzig, A., & Ólafsson, K. (2011). *Risks and safety on the Internet: The perspective of European children. Full Findings.* London, England: EU Kids Online. Retrieved from http://www.lse.ac.uk/media-and-communications/assets/documents/research/eu-kids-online/reports/D4FullFindings.pdf

Livingstone, S., & Smith, P.K. (2014). Annual research review. Harms experienced by child users of online and mobile technologies: The nature, prevalence and management of sexual and aggressive risks in the digital age. *Journal of Child Psychology and Psychiatry, 55*(6), 635–654. doi: 10.1111/jcpp.12197

Mok, K., Ross, A.M., Jorm, A.F., & Pirkis, J. (2016). An analysis of the content and availability of information on suicide methods online. *Journal of Consumer Health on the Internet, 20*(1–2), 41–51. doi: 10.1080/15398285.2016.1167579

Näsi, M., Räsänen, P., Hawdon, J., Holkeri, E., & Oksanen, A. (2015). Exposure to online hate material and social trust among Finnish youth. *Information Technology & People, 28*(3), 607–622. doi: 10.1108/ITP-09-2014-0198

Olson, K.E., O'Brien, M.A., Rogers, W.A., & Charness, N. (2011). Diffusion of technology: Frequency of use for younger and older adults. *Ageing International, 36*(1), 123–145. doi: 10.1007%2Fs12126-010-9077-9

Tokunaga, R.S. (2010). Following you home from school: A critical review and synthesis of research on cyberbullying victimization. *Computers in Human Behavior, 26*(3), 277–287. doi: 10.1016/j.chb.2009.11.014

Vandoninck, S., d'Haenens, L., & Roe, K. (2013). Online risks: Coping strategies of less resilient children and teenagers across Europe. *Journal of Children and Media, 7*(1), 60–78. doi: 10.1080/17482798.2012.739780

Wardle, H., Moody, A., Griffiths, M., Orford, J., & Volberg, R. (2011). Defining the online gambler and patterns of behaviour integration: Evidence from the British Gambling Prevalence Survey 2010. *International Gambling Studies, 11*(3), 339–356. doi: 10.1080/14459795.2011.628684

Willoughby, T., Adachi, P.J., & Good, M. (2012). A longitudinal study of the association between violent video game play and aggression among adolescents. *Developmental Psychology, 48*(4), 1044–1057. doi: 10.1037/a0026046

Youth Protection Roundtable. (2009). Youth protection roundtable toolkit. EC Safer Internet Programme. Retrieved from http://www.yprt.eu/yprt/content/sections/index.cfm/secid.11

Further reading

Livingstone, S.M., Haddon, L., & Gorzig, A. (2012). *Children, risk and safety on the Internet: Research and policy challenges in comparative perspective*. Bristol, England: Policy Press.

Valcke, M., De Wever, B., Van Keer, H., & Schellens, T. (2011). Long-term study of safe Internet use of young children. *Computers & Education, 57*(1), 1292–1305. doi: 10.1016/j.compedu.2011.01.010

Walrave, M., Ponnet, K., Vanderhoven, E., Haers, J., & Segaert, B. (Eds.). (2016). *Youth 2.0: Social media and adolescence. Connecting, sharing and empowering*. Berlin, Germany: Springer.

Lies De Kimpe is a PhD student at the Department of Communication Studies of the University of Antwerp (MIOS) and at Ghent University (imec-mict). Her main research interests are online risk behavior and cybercrime victimization.

Michel Walrave is a professor at the Department of Communication Studies of the University of Antwerp and Chairman of the research group MIOS (Media and ICT in Organisations and Society). His research is centered around online self-disclosure and privacy. He investigates adolescents' and adults' online disclosure of personal information to other individuals or companies, and related opportunities and risks.

Koen Ponnet a professor at Ghent University (imec-mict). His main research interests are the determinants of risk and problem behavior of adolescents and adults, both offline and online.

Joris Van Ouytsel is a researcher at the Department of Communication Studies of the University of Antwerp. His research focuses on cyberdating abuse and sexting. His work is supported by the Research Foundation—Flanders.

Investigating TPACK as Professional Knowledge for Australian Literacy Teachers

LYNDE TAN and JINNAT ALI
Western Sydney University, Australia

The evolving nature of literacy necessitates new bodies of professional knowledge that equip literacy teachers for effective teaching in the digital age. Identifying *technological pedagogical content knowledge* (TPACK) for literacy teaching is defensibly crucial to teacher education programs. While recommendations for new literacies have been put forward by literacy researchers, less is reported about the knowledge that literacy teachers need to develop students' metalanguage for responding to and composing multimedia and multimodal texts. Critical investigations of what constitutes literacy teachers' TPACK for negotiating a range of texts across modes, mediums, and contexts with their students warrant further research to inform reforms in literacy education.

Literacy reforms across countries are driven by the changing culture of learning and communication landscape. In the context of Australia, the new *Australian Curriculum: English* (2015) has placed multimodal literacy at the core of its classroom practices, that is, an explicit knowledge about language and how it interacts with other modes of meaning-making in a range of text types and mediums of communication. In addition, it also expects teachers to seamlessly integrate the teaching of language and literacy together with other curricular demands such as integrating technology and cross-curriculum priorities. The *Australian Professional Standards for Teachers* (Australian Institute for Teaching and School Leadership, 2017), a framework that describes quality teaching across various domains of teaching and career stages, expect the teaching profession to demonstrate uses of information and communication technology (ICT) when meeting three specific standards:

1. Standard 2: Know the content and how to teach it (e.g., a graduate teacher is expected to implement teaching strategies for using ICT to expand curriculum learning opportunities for students: standard 2.6).
2. Standard 3: Plan for and implement effective teaching and learning (e.g., a graduate teacher is expected to demonstrate knowledge of a range of resources, including ICT, that engage students in their learning: standard 3.4).
3. Standard 4: Create and maintain supportive and safe learning environments (e.g., a graduate teacher is expected to demonstrate an understanding of the relevant issues and the strategies available to support the safe, responsible, and ethical use of ICT in learning and teaching: standard 4.5).

In essence, it can be argued that demonstration of quality teaching constitutes strong evidence of integrating content, pedagogy, and technology, and understanding the complex interdependence of contextually bound factors that influence teachers' effectiveness in literacy teaching.

Competing discourses of literacy

With the changing times, there are increased demands on learners. The ubiquitous influence of technology implies that to be literate today, it is indispensable for learners to respond to and compose texts creatively and confidently using a range of media and modalities (Tan & Zammit, 2016). Current debates on literacy education strongly suggest that the notion of literacy should be expanded and that it is more appropriate to understand literacy as a pluralistic term. Many national curricula have widely accepted literacy beyond reading and writing print-based texts. Burgeoning lists of multiple literacies such as information literacy, media literacy, and ICT literacy are commonly advocated as key skills for the 21st century. The key thrust of multiple literacies is to ensure schools remain relevant in equipping learners with the knowledge and skills necessary for them to actively participate in the globalized economy.

While broadening notions of literacy to embrace multiple ones, the models of literacy adopted by many educational authorities remain rooted in the *autonomous model*, that is, literacy is understood as discrete and measurable skills which are independent of their social and cultural context (Street & Lefstein, 2007). From this perspective, literacy is learned and taught as a form of individual development along a carefully charted and predictable trajectory. It can be argued that understanding literacy based on the autonomous model is a narrow viewpoint. Street and Lefstein (2007) advocate that literacy entails ideological work when people interact with one another to define what is and is not reading and writing; it imbues values in how and what they read and write and, over time, sanctions some ways of reading and writing and marginalizes others. The ideological model of literacy does not deny the development of skills for socioeconomic and cognitive gains, but perceives it as a contested term encapsulated within power structures. The ideological model of literacy posits *literacy as social practice*, that is, its forms, uses, purposes, and outcomes vary according to social and cultural groups (Street & Lefstein, 2007).

The New London Group's (NLG) (Cope & Kalantzis, 2000) argument for multiple literacies, or multiliteracies, bears the ideological model of literacy to address the cultural and linguistic diversity in various social and cultural contexts. It is noteworthy that the NLG's notion of multiliteracies emphasizes the multiple forms of literacy associated with semiotic modes found in the multiplicity of communication channels and media, or multimodal literacy. The proliferation of new digital media and multimodal texts in literacy practices calls for a distinction between media and literacies. This raises the issue of the new wine in old wine skin symptom when technology is integrated into literacy education. Although new media are used for teaching and learning, teachers continue to use them to propagate old literacy skills. Conversely, it can also be argued that new literacies may produce skills that promote traditional literacies related to the printed media. The use of technology does not necessarily guarantee effective teaching and new literacies. For effectiveness to be demonstrated, Mishra and Koehler (2006) argue that "good teaching requires an understanding of how technology relates to the pedagogy and content" (p. 1026).

Importance of TPACK in literacy education

With the intent of advancing technology integration at theoretical, pedagogical, and methodological levels, Mishra and Koehler (2006) built on Shulman's (1986) notion of *pedagogical content knowledge* (PCK) and proposed a framework known as technological pedagogical content knowledge (earlier known as TPCK). Shulman (1986) contended that pedagogical knowledge and content knowledge are not mutually exclusive: effective teaching requires teachers to understand the relationships between the two domains of knowledge and represent the subject matter in ways that can be understood by the learners.

A review of Shulman's (1986) notion of PCK is essential when technology is used as a teaching resource. Mishra and Koehler (2006) argue that "knowledge about technology cannot be treated as context-free and that good teaching requires an understanding of how technology relates to the pedagogy and content" (p. 1026). They propose the TPACK framework to describe the domains of knowledge and their interrelationships as a requisite form of knowledge crucial for teachers to integrate technology into teaching.

- content knowledge (CK): topical knowledge related to the subject matter;
- pedagogical knowledge (PK): methods of teaching and learning the subject matter and their educational values;
- pedagogical content knowledge (PCK): knowledge of adopting appropriate approaches to represent the content knowledge in an effective order;
- technological knowledge (TK): knowledge of the range of technology available and how to use it;
- technological content knowledge (TCK): knowledge of using technology to represent the content knowledge;
- technological pedagogical knowledge (TPK): knowledge of how teaching is influenced by the way technology is used;
- technological pedagogical content knowledge (TPACK): integrated knowledge of using technology to represent, teach, and facilitate the learning of the content knowledge.

Successful integration of technology in literacy education necessitates a clear understanding of TPACK in practice. Research has shown that providing teachers with technology without developing their TPACK is not efficacious. Chai, Tan, Deng, and Koh (2017) argue that although preservice teachers' beliefs about the culture of learning do change with an increase in their TPACK, their design capacities in appropriating a new culture of learning for formal learning remain lacking. What is clear from the existing body of research is that curricular and pedagogical reforms must be accompanied by the development of teachers' TPACK in order for teachers to be able to meet expected standards for teaching new literacies. Mere use of technology is insufficient to develop a new ethos of learning and literacies. Developing teachers' TPACK capacities is necessary to reconstruct meaningful relationships among technology, content, and pedagogy as they develop students' understandings toward the changing of text, literacy, and meaning-making processes in a range of texts across modes, mediums of communication, and contexts.

TPACK in literacy education: trends in current research

Empirical studies on TPACK shows that great attention has been paid to: (i) applying TPACK in specific contexts of practice, (ii) validating the research instrument to measure TPACK, (iii) theoretical debates on the TPACK framework, and (iv) exploring the use of TPACK for assessment. Despite the accelerating adoption of TPACK in integrating technology across diverse settings and disciplines, there are also research studies that have reported its limitations. A common thread through the criticisms is related to the distinction of the knowledge domains in practice: first, it is not always possible and necessary to differentiate the various knowledge domains in the TPACK model when developing teachers' capacities to integrate technology; second, there is an assumption that teachers have the capacities to differentiate these knowledge domains and use the TPACK model for self-assessment; third, the importance of teaching and understanding the TPACK metalanguage is overrated to the extent that the role of teachers' tacit knowledge in integrating technology has been under-acknowledged (Brantley-Dias & Ertmer, 2013; McGrath, Karabas, & Willis, 2011). Dobozy and Campbell's (2016) central question of "what do teachers actually do with TPACK?" (p. 125) remains unanswered and point out that alternative models are emerging.

As the development and adoption of the TPACK model continues, recommendations put forth for future research in TPACK point to the increasing need for developing TPACK in specific subject matters as well as customizing and validating instruments to measure it (Koehler, Shin, & Mishra, 2012). TPACK is situated in a particular context of practice and as such, any mindless application of or overreliance on one TPACK measure over another should be circumvented. Moreover, from an ideological perspective, what counts as literacy is context-bound and governed by social institutions and power relationships. Literacies change over time and they are embedded in the social and cultural contexts which make some literacies more dominant and privileged than others.

The ideological nature of literacies and the situated nature of TPACK warrant a review of TPACK in literacy education, especially for countries that have already reframed literacy in their national curriculum. For example, in 2012, the Board of Studies, Teaching and Educational Standards (BOSTES) New South Wales (NSW) in Australia, currently known as the NSW Education Standards Authority (NESA), published the new *NSW Syllabus for the Australian Curriculum: English K-10* (Board of Studies NSW, 2012). This is a syllabus that places multimodal literacy or meaning-making through language and other semiotic modes as its key focus; learning across the curriculum is infused in its content, including ICT capability (Tan & Zammit, 2016).

To assess the extent of TPACK research done in light of the new *NSW Syllabus for the Australian Curriculum: English K-10* (Board of Studies NSW, 2012), a review of papers on TPACK in the field of teacher education between 2012 and 2016 was conducted.

The review showed that out of 101 studies, most of them were conducted in Australia (37.6%, n = 38), followed by Asia (33.6%, n = 34), and then Europe (13.9%, n = 14), and America (12.9%, n = 13). TPACK research in Africa contributed the remaining 2.0% (n = 2) within the same period. Of these studies, 45.5% were about preservice teachers, 8.9% were about initial teachers, and 5.0% included both preservice and initial teachers. A central theme in the TPACK research on preservice and inservice teachers was on measuring the teachers' perceptions of TPACK in the context of teaching a specific subject. Of the 38 TPACK studies in Australia, only six included a clear focus on literacy in the context of the English curriculum, and of these six studies, two studies were conducted in NSW, three focused on preservice teachers, two on practicing teachers, and one on teacher education in general. Table 1 shows the themes of these six studies related to language and literacy in Australia from 2012 to August 2016.

It is apparent that in the context of Australia, the inception of the new Australian curriculum for the various key learning areas, including language and literacy, has led to a growing interest in developing teachers' TPACK capacities. ICT capacity is a general capability integrated across all key learning areas. According to the Australian Curriculum, Assessment and Reporting Authority (ACARA) (n.d.), ICT capability is an important component of the *Australian Curriculum: English* as students are expected to use ICT to access, analyze, modify, and create hybrid, digital, and multimodal texts for conducting research online and digital publishing, independently and with others. These are also skills needed to understand and interpret how text producers construct meanings in digital, media, and other texts to achieve some intended purposes using specific techniques to mediate the target audience's perceptions.

The review suggests that both educational researchers and practitioners are in search of frameworks to address the complexities of infusing technology in teacher education programs, both in the universities and in schools. Of note is the *Teaching Teachers for the Future (TTF) Project* (Heck & Sweeney, 2013; Parr, Bellis, & Bulfin, 2013) that attempts to build teachers' TPACK capacity while supporting them to meet the Australian Professional Standards for Teachers in the context of implementing the new Australian curriculum across the key learning areas, including English. Although Mishra and Koehler's (2006) TPACK model serves as a useful framework to codify the domains of knowledge teachers need to use technology to teach effectively, Parr et al. (2013) contend that "contemporary English classrooms are not spaces where knowledge can be neatly defined before, during or after students 'get to work'" (p. 19). Underpinning the *Australian Curriculum: English* is a social view of language and literacy which emphasizes that textual meanings are constructed by an individual and that they are shaped by the social interactions in which one engages (Tan & Zammit, 2016). Meaning-making choices and social negotiations of meanings enable students to make text-to-text, text-to-world, and text-to-self connections which can not always be reified by predetermined outcomes. Each semiotic mode carries meaning that needs to be unpacked, both as a single entity and as a whole multimodal unit. Engagements with a range of texts across modes, media, and contexts in particular problematize the content knowledge when employing Mishra and Koehler's (2006) TPACK framework to build teachers' capacities in infusing technology in literacy teaching.

Table 1 TPACK in Australia literacy education (2012–August 2016).

	Key themes related to preservice teacher education	*Relevant literature*	*States in Australia*
1	**Becoming multimodal authors: preservice teachers' interventions to support young children with autism** The two case studies argued that when preservice teachers were cognizant of their TPACK and developed clear understanding of students' learning needs, they were capable of designing appropriate interventions that enabled students with autism to be effective multimodal authors.	Oakley, Howitt, Garwood, & Durack (2013)	Western Australia
2	**Teaching English teachers for the future: speaking back to TPACK** The authors provided a critique of TPACK and reacted against a reductionist approach when initial teachers attempted to develop their TPACK while using ICT for English teaching to meet both the standards for quality teaching and curriculum outcomes.	Parr, Bellis, & Bulfin (2013)	Victoria
3	**Using Most Significant Change Stories to Document the Impact of the Teaching Teachers for the Future Project** With respect to teaching English, the study showed that there was a strong correlation between the knowledge/understanding and attitudes/beliefs of teacher educators with those of the preservice teachers. The study also showed that the reported change in the knowledge/understanding and attitudes/beliefs of preservice teachers did not result in a reported increase in the preservice teachers' confidence in using ICT to teach English.	Heck & Sweeney (2013)	Queensland
4	**Technology integration and High Possibility Classrooms** Drawing on TPACK, the author developed the High Possibility Classrooms model which she argued to be an effective pedagogical scaffold for supporting teachers in integrating technology across subjects, including English.	Hunter (2015)	New South Wales

(*continued overleaf*)

Table 1 (Continued)

	Key themes related to preservice teacher education	Relevant literature	States in Australia
5	**High Possibility Classrooms: using an Australian framework to enhance learning using technology in high schools** The author argued that while existing frameworks like TPACK were useful for developing teachers' capacity in technology integration, the High Possibility Classrooms framework, which was developed based on exemplary teachers' knowledge of technology integration in Australia, was more congruous with NSW teachers' praxis of integrating technology across key learning areas, including English.	Hewes (2016)	New South Wales
6	**Creativity, visualization, collaboration, and communication** The author argues that developing teachers' TPACK capacities is integral in infusing digital technologies into the various key learning areas in the Australian curriculum.	Finger (2015)	(Not specific to any state in Australia)

Based on the review, it is also evident that in the move toward implementing the new *Australian Curriculum: English*, teachers are in search of exemplary practices of integrating technology into literacy teaching. The two studies by Hewes (2016) and Hunter (2015) seem to suggest that understanding TPACK in practice necessitates a model that is drawn on TPACK but appropriated to fit the situated nature of integrating technology into the local context of curricular reforms. These studies, including Heck and Sweeney (2013), also indicate the importance of having more than one mechanism to measure TPACK. Narratives or case studies of exemplary practices of using technology for teaching serve as beacons for the fraternity of literacy educators as teachers at the various career stages seek to design solutions that are responsive to their students and specific learning contexts (Mishra & Koehler, 2006).

Future directions

Previously, it was argued that there is a distinction between media and literacies. New media do not spontaneously lead to new literacies; it is widely acknowledged that digital media create new practices while making old practices easier. It is hard to ignore the affordances of technology when the advent of technology has proliferated the production of multimedia and multimodal texts in everyday and classroom practices. The digital environment has necessitated the understanding of modal affordances and how meaning-making occurs across modes and mediums of communication. In articulating the multiliteracies or multiple literacies needed for the digital age, information, media, and technology skills are commonly emphasized in many 21st-century skills. The United Nations Educational, Scientific and Cultural Organization (UNESCO, 2011) has developed a list of media and information literacy (MIL) competencies for teachers which include the following:

1. understanding the role of media and information in democracy;
2. understanding media content and its uses;
3. accessing information effectively and efficiently;
4. critically evaluating information and information sources;
5. applying new and traditional media formats;
6. situating the sociocultural context of media content;
7. promoting MIL among students and managing required changes. (pp. 29–34)

Skillful teachers are expected to demonstrate competencies in these aspects in order to develop their students to be effective, critical, and creative consumers and producers of a wide range of texts. In response to the evolution of new media and changes in young people's literacy practices, the often-cited work of Jenkins, Clinton, Purushotma, Robison, and Weigel (2006) is of note. Jenkins et al. (2006) argue for a new understanding of media literacies that are crucial for the digital age, namely:

1. play: the capacity to experiment with one's surroundings as a form of problem-solving;
2. performance: the ability to adopt alternative identities for the purpose of improvisation and discovery;
3. simulation: the ability to interpret and construct dynamic models of real-world processes;
4. appropriation: the ability to meaningfully sample and remix media content;
5. multitasking: the ability to scan one's environment and shift focus as needed to salient details;
6. distributed cognition: the ability to interact meaningfully with tools that expand mental capacities;
7. collective intelligence: the ability to pool knowledge and compare notes with others toward a common goal;
8. judgment: the ability to evaluate the reliability and credibility of different information sources;
9. transmedia navigation: the ability to follow the flow of stories and information across multiple modalities;
10. networking: the ability to search for, synthesize, and disseminate information;
11. negotiation: the ability to travel across diverse communities, discerning and respecting multiple perspectives, and grasping and following alternative norms. (p. 4)

Jenkins et al. (2006) put forward their notion of new media literacies in the context of young people's participatory culture with digital media. However, their notion of new media literacies may not fit all contexts of technology use, and it can be argued that some of these new media literacies are better achieved in specific learning environments. For example, in game-based learning, play, performance, simulation, multitasking, and distributed cognition are pedagogical affordances in such a learning environment.

Nonetheless, UNESCO's (2011) MIL competencies for teachers remain critical for developing these new media literacies. Before teachers design learning opportunities to develop their students' new media literacies, they themselves are expected to know the relationship between media and information literacy as well as other aspects such as citizenship and democracy. They need to equip themselves with a repertoire of strategies for developing the metalanguage to deconstruct meanings in a wide range of texts such as examining representations in media. Teachers themselves are expected to demonstrate ICT and information literacies for effective search for information and teach their students to do so similarly with clear standards of assessing the credibility and value of the information found. In short, using ICT for new media literacies requires deep levels of TPACK from teachers.

Describing teachers' TPACK for new media literacies is not a straightforward task as young people's engagement with media and multimodal texts is constantly changing. Tan (2013) argues that when teachers do not understand their students' literacy practices, literacy activities that are perceived as educational may be in fact redundant for the students. Extending Tan's (2013) argument, it can also be contended that when teachers' TPACK capacity is limited, they do not understand that "experimentation is an indispensable way of participating in digital media production" (p. 93) and students' engagements with digital and media texts are shaped by the technical affordances of the digital media they use. The development of TPACK and the development of an understanding of young people's digital cultures are inseparable; to engage students in literacy learning, teachers play a role in connecting with the history of their practices and allowing them to flow and fuse between their school and out-of-school literacies.

New literacies engage students in constant (re)creating of their meaning-making resources beyond language. The focus of literacy teaching is to engage students as producers of texts where they are expected to be cognizant of the modal affordances of meaning-making resources and exhibit a clear understanding of how transduction or shifts across modes occur in text productions. In essence, literacy teaching has to consider ways of scaffolding students to deconstruct and construct a wide range of texts using technology as they pay attention to the meaning-making processes in the social negotiations and construction of texts. Further research is needed to measure and develop TPACK in literacy education to develop both teachers and students to be competent, critical, and creative users of technology in literacy. Surveys developed to measure TPACK in literacy education need to appropriate the definitions of Mishra and Koehler's (2006) TPACK constructs in order for it to find its fit with the subject matter. For the TPACK construct, factors such as the following are possible ones for consideration in teacher surveys.

1. Using technology, I can draw out students' initial concepts about the topic of inquiry.
2. Using technology, I can build students', understandings to prepare them for a writing task.
3. Using technology, I can facilitate students' deconstruction of the multimodal meanings of the mentor (exemplary) text.
4. Using technology, I can lead students in composing a multimodal text.
5. Using technology, I can support students in their independent construction of a multimodal text.
6. Using technology, I can sequence the teaching and learning activities to facilitate students' multimodal meaning-making.

Effecting major changes in curriculum and pedagogical practices in the digital age requires building teachers' capacities in TPACK. Research on TPACK in literacy education and standards of quality teaching clearly should not be conducted in a mutually exclusive manner. While teachers' dispositions and perceptions of technology use have been widely researched in educational research, further research is needed to understand the relationships between TPACK and expanded notions of literacy associated with semiotic modes of meaning-making across mediums of communication. Moving forward, more research on the relationships between TPACK and multimodal literacy should be undertaken to better prepare our teachers to nurture students who are multiliterate.

SEE ALSO: Digital Literacy; Literacy, Technology, and Media; Media Literacy Education and 21st Century Teacher Education; Media Literacy in Australia; News Literacies; Social Semiotics; Teaching with Media; Youth Digital Culture

References

Australian Curriculum, Assessment and Reporting Authority. (2015). *Australian Curriculum: English*. Retrieved from https://australiancurriculum.edu.au/f-10-curriculum/english/?strand=Language&strand=Literature&strand=Literacy&capability=ignore&priority=ignore&elaborations=true

Australian Curriculum, Assessment and Reporting Authority. (n.d.). *General capabilities in the Australian Curriculum: English*. Retrieved from http://www.acara.edu.au/_resources/English_-_GC_learning_area.pdf

Australian Institute for Teaching and School Leadership. (2017). *Australian professional standards for teachers*. Retrieved from https://www.aitsl.edu.au/teach/standards

Board of Studies NSW. (2012). *NSW syllabus for the Australian Curriculum: English K-10 syllabus*. Sydney, Australia: Author.

Brantley-Dias, L., & Ertmer, P.A. (2013). Goldilocks and TPACK: Is the construct "just right?" *Journal of Research on Technology in Education, 46*(2), 103–128. doi: 10.1080/15391523.2013.10782615

Chai, C., Tan, L., Deng, F. & Koh, J. (2017). "Examining pre-service teachers' design capacities for web-based 21st century new culture of learning." *Australasian Journal of Educational Technology, 33*(2), 129–142. doi: 10.14742/ajet.3013

Cope, B., & Kalantzis, M. (2000). *Multiliteracies: Literacy learning and the design of social futures.* London, England: Routledge.

Dobozy, E., & Campbell, C. (2016). The complementary nature of learning design and TPACK. In J. Dalziel (Ed.). *Learning design: Conceptualizing a framework for teaching and learning online* (pp. 96–116). New York, NY: Routledge.

Finger, G. (2015). Creativity, visualisation, collaboration and communication. In M. Henderson, & G. Romeo (Eds.), *Teaching and digital technologies: Big issues and critical questions* (pp. 89–103). Melbourne, Australia: Cambridge University Press.

Heck, D., & Sweeney, T. (2013). Using most significant change stories to document the impact of the Teaching Teachers for the Future Project: An Australian teacher education story. *Australian Educational Computing, 27*(3), 36–47.

Hewes, B. (2016). High Possibility Classrooms: Using an Australian framework to enhance learning using technology in high schools. *ACEL e-Publications: e-Teaching, 9.* Retrieved from http://www.acsp.catholic.edu.au/pdf%20uploads/6%20e-Teaching_2016_09.pdf

Hunter, J. (2015). *Technology integration and High Possibility Classrooms.* New York, NY: Taylor & Francis.

Jenkins, H., Clinton, K., Purushotma, R., Robison, A., & Weigel, M. (2006). *Confronting the challenges of participatory culture: Media education for the 21st century.* Chicago, IL: The John D. and Catherine T. Macarthur Foundation.

Koehler, M.J., Shin, T.S., & Mishra, P. (2012). How do we measure TPACK? Let me count the ways. In R.N. Ronau, C.R. Rakes, & M.L. Niess (Eds.), *Educational technology, teacher knowledge, and classroom impact: A research handbook on frameworks and approaches* (pp. 16–31). Hershey, PA: Information Science Reference.

Mishra, P., & Koehler, M. (2006). Technological pedagogical content knowledge: A framework for teacher knowledge. *Teachers College Record, 108*(6), 1017–1054. doi: 10.1111/j.1467-9620.2006.00684.x

McGrath, J., Karabas, G., & Willis. J. (2011). From TPACK concept to TPACK practice: An analysis of the suitability and usefulness of the concept as a guide in the real world of teacher development. *International Journal of Technology in Teaching and Learning, 7*(1), 1–23.

Oakley, G., Howitt, C., Garwood, R., & Durack, A. (2013). Becoming multimodal authors: Pre-service teachers' interventions to support young children with autism. *Australasian Journal of Early Childhood, 38*(3), 86–96.

Parr, G., Bellis, & Bulfin, S. (2013). Teaching English teachers for the future: Speaking back to TPACK. *English in Australia, 48*(1), 9–22.

Shulman, L.S. (1986). Those who understand: Knowledge growth in teaching. *Educational Researcher, 15*(2), 4–14. doi: 10.3102/0013189X015002004

Street, B., & Lefstein, A. (2007). *Literacy: An advanced resource book.* London, England: Routledge.

Tan, L. (2013). Production-on-the-go practice: Storyboarding as a retrospective and redundant literacy activity. *Learning, Media and Technology, 38*(1), 86–101. doi: 10.1080/17439884.2011.638928

Tan, L., & Zammit, K. (2016). *Teaching writing and representing in the primary school years.* Melbourne, Australia: Pearson Australia.

United Nations Educational, Scientific and Cultural Organization. (2011). *Media and information literacy curriculum for teachers.* Paris, France: Author.

Further reading

Chai, C.S., Koh, J.H.L., & Tsai, C.C. (2013). A review of technological pedagogical content knowledge. *Journal of Educational Technology & Society, 16*(2), 31–51.

Schmidt, D., & Gurbo, M. (2008). TPACK in K-6 literacy education: It's not that elementary! In American Association of Colleges for Teacher Education, Committee on Technology Innovation (Ed.), *Handbook of technological pedagogical content knowledge (TPCK) for educators* (pp 61–86). New York, NY: Routledge.

Voogt, J., Fisser, P., Pareja Roblin, N., Tondeur, J., & van Braak, J. (2013). Technological pedagogical content knowledge – a review of the literature. *Journal of Computer Assisted Learning, 29*(2), 109–121. doi: 10.1111/j.1365-2729.2012.00487.x

Lynde Tan is a Lecturer in English language and literacy curriculum and pedagogy in the School of Education at Western Sydney University. Her research focuses on pedagogical issues pertinent to the use of digital media for formal and informal learning. She has published extensively in several international refereed journals and currently serves on the Editorial Review Boards for the *Journal of Adolescent & Adult Literacy* and *E-Learning and Digital Media.*

Jinnat Ali is a research officer at the School of Education, Western Sydney University. His doctoral research was completed at Western Sydney University in 2007 and focused on developing a theoretically based, psychometrically sound, multidimensional measure of student motivation for use in diverse cultural settings. His research interests are in student motivation, self-concept, engagement, information and communication technology education, and well-being in cross-cultural settings, and instrument design and validation.

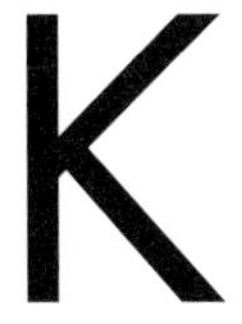

Knowledge Structures

IRENE ANDRIOPOULOU
EKOME SA – National Centre of Audiovisual Media & Communication, Greece

> *The first problem of the media is posed by what does not get translated, or even published in the dominant political languages.*
>
> J. Derrida

Setting up an infrastructure for measuring media and information literacy in national contexts

It is a fact that the exponential growth of the information society, with all its digital-related parameters, has put media in the front row of the intermediated public sphere. Media, nowadays, act as a Newtonian "centripetal force" that sets the rules for an active public discourse and sustainable democratic societies. Using communication skills as a main vehicle, every citizen today has the indisputable right to seek/access information, exchange ideas and beliefs, and to interact with media procedures through a multitude of media platforms and mechanisms, cultivating thus an active digital citizenship, a main ingredient to building knowledge societies. According to the United Nations Educational, Scientific and Cultural Organization (UNESCO), knowledge societies must build around four pillars: freedom of expression; universal access to information and knowledge; respect for cultural and linguistic diversity; and quality education for all.

Defining media and information literacy

The key premise in this rapidly changing environment of knowledge structure is the acquisition of a critical set of competencies that formulate media and information

The International Encyclopedia of Media Literacy. Renee Hobbs and Paul Mihailidis (Editors-in-Chief), Gianna Cappello, Maria Ranieri, and Benjamin Thevenin (Associate Editors).

literacy, acting as a catalyst for a mindful approach and critical management of all information and media messages that citizens are challenged with, through traditional and new media forms. As the late media theorist Eco (Fedorov & Kolesnichenko, 2013) stipulates, in the near future (or, it is already happening) our knowledge society will be divided into two citizen categories: the *haves* and *have-nots*, that is, those who know how to filter and critically assess media messages toward creating a self-conscious media identity and those who receive a swelling media and information flood but do not know how to deal with it. According to the European Commission approach (EC Communication 2007/833, EC Recommendation 2009/6464, AVMSD 2010/13/EC, MLEG), *media literacy* is the ability to access the media and understand and critically evaluate different aspects of media contents and media themselves, as well as the ability to create communications in a variety of contexts (user-generated content). It relates to all types of media, including television and film, radio and music, print media, Internet, virtual reality, and all other digital communication technologies. It thus combines a set of technical, cognitive, and social skills that, when used correctly and ethically, lead to user empowerment. In another context, it may be also used as a means to social activism, exerting social, economic, and political influence on the media industry and challenging the status quo. According to this polyprismatic approach, *media and information literacy* (UNESCO) as a composite concept lies in the complex multiliteracies that emerge from media convergence between broadcasting, telecoms,

Figure 1 Elements of media and information literacy ecology. Source: Wilson, Grizzle, Tuazon, Akyempong, & Cheung (2011, p. 19).

and new technologies and engages multiple stakeholders from a wide range of scientific fields that sometimes complement and at other times contradict each other. Having said that, depending on the medium in question, it encompasses television/audiovisual literacy, news literacy, commercial literacy, digital literacy, information literacy, and so on (see Figure 1).

In any case, media and information literacy shapes our behavioral attitude and, according to Gerbner (1999), the stories the media tell us "weave the seamless web of the cultural environment that cultivates most of what we think, what we do, and how we conduct our affairs."

The main challenge that every citizen is faced with in developed societies from this "data smog" (Shenk, 1997) is adopting a critical "antilepsis" (from Greek, meaning comprehension and appreciation) and effective management of the incoming messages and media content. To this end, there is a need for balancing between two somewhat conflicting goals: maximizing the potential of media and digital technologies and minimizing the risks they entail (Carlsson, 2013, p. 8). Indicative questions are: What are the main mechanisms and prerequisites that the modern-day media user-consumer-producer needs to have in order to acquire in-depth knowledge and media wisdom? What are the tools that may be used in order to distinguish between quality information and low-quality/fake content? And what is the editorial responsibility of the media service providers in this nonlinear communicative procedure?

Indicators: a key tool for promoting media and information literacy and ensuring media pluralism

It is a fact that there's an increasing mobility of media and information literacy initiatives globally that pave the way for empowered citizen expression and sustainable development. However, this activity is not (always) seconded by relevant measurement tools, such as indicators and assessment mechanisms, that are key constituents for a pluralistic media dynamics *for all*.

This is where the need for media and information literacy indicators comes in, to ensure the smooth operation of media mechanisms and safeguard basic citizen rights, simultaneously. These indicators create the conditions under which individuals and societies may question the function of media and information providers, at the same time evaluating the quality of their content and actively taking part in social activism for better services and content. On this premise, indicators may have a tremendous impact on the pluralistic nature of public information and communication policies, creating the infrastructure for a healthy and knowledgeable society. By the term "indicator" we refer mainly to the quantitative and qualitative measuring tool that has as its core function—in our case—the monitoring of media and information literacy levels and competencies in a variety of contexts in the public sphere in order to offer a thorough insight. According to the EAVI (European Association for Viewers Interests) Study on Assessment Criteria for Media Literacy Levels in Europe (EAVI, 2009), commissioned by the European Commission, indicators are "a unit of measurement for the evaluation of data and the subsequent conceptualization of media and information literacy from a holistic perspective." Indicators may be simple or more complex, using data from different variables, and may be new or based on alterations of already existing ones (e.g. social, economic, and educational indicators, etc.). For example, an indicator for media literacy policies may be the outcome of a national communication and information policy and/or closely interrelated with the digital policy. A number of experts are requested to take part in the formation and evaluation of indicators, in the case of media and information literacy, from multiple scientific fields (media, education, ICT, academia, regulation, etc.). By and large, media indicators record the existing situation and level of progress and development of a country in media in order to advise and support policymakers on future steps. At the same time, they act as a magnifying mirror on problematics and possible "ellipses," in order to enable better focus on these areas and take the necessary steps toward improvement.

Conditions for setting up indicators

Taking into account the various challenges for formulating media indicators in a state/region, we should primarily focus on the necessary conditions that act as common denominator for media and information literacy.

1. Critical overview of existing indicators (e.g. digital indicators such as DESI [Digital Economy and Society Index], GDP [gross domestic product] level, Eurobarometer, education indicators such as the Programme for International Student Assessment [PISA]) and evaluation of their functionality, impact, and effectiveness.
2. Definitional orientation of media literacy in the field of communication and information, through deconstruction of its content. This originates from the fact that the term "media literacy" has, thus far, proved to be rather resistant to a fully consensual definition. However, in order to implement media and information literacy indicators, we need to have a clear idea of what they consist of. This context also encapsulates existing technical infrastructure (digital policy), understanding of the main players and stakeholders involved, and fair competition rules in the digital market.
3. Pilot use on a limited social sample within a SWOT (Strengths, Weaknesses, Opportunities, Threats) analysis of the related environmental parameters.
4. Harmonization of indicators with the regulatory framework of a region or country on media development, operated within an enlarged digital and communication policy. This is of crucial importance since state legislation is future-proof and acts as a protectionist shield for democratic performances.

Challenges, risks, and impediments for enforcement

Arguably, it is not easy to establish media and information literacy indicators from scratch, since they are firmly allied to the cost of implementation and other risk-related issues. The multidimensional nature of media literacy also makes it more complex. For

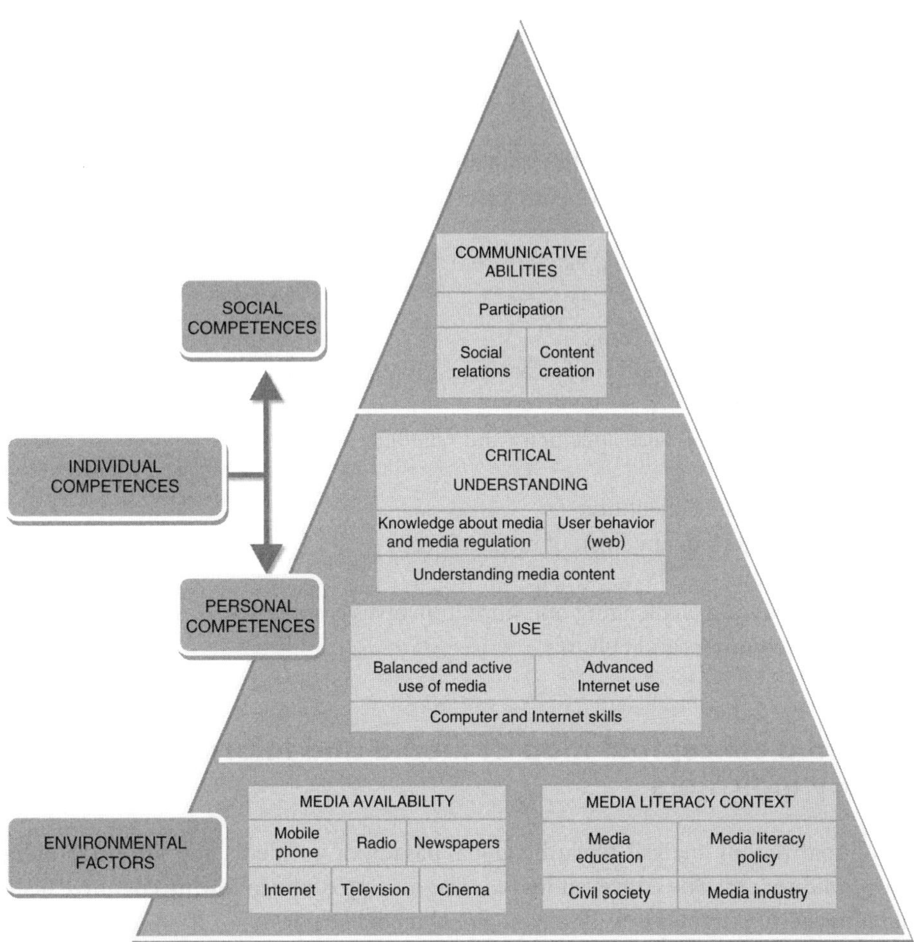

Figure 2 Structure of media literacy assessment criteria. Source: European Association for Viewers Interests (2009, p. 8).

example, how do we measure critical understanding and awareness of media messages among citizens? How do we evaluate creativity and original thought and action among different age groups? Media (and information) literacy is not only about technical competencies and skills, and we certainly do not want our approach to be limited to that.

The focal point for formulating indicators shall be a division between definitional and practical dimensions. *Definitional indicators* refer to the conceptual framework of media and information literacy competencies, individual, social, and communication skills. *Practical indicators* have to do more with public policies on digital infrastructure, access to information and digital technologies, access to media content through linear and nonlinear service platforms, and exercise and choice among a variety of resources that ensure media diversity and pluralism. A more detailed approach may be studied on the pyramid of assessment criteria (see Figure 2) for the development of media literacy within a society (EAVI, 2009).

The graphic shows the fields within which indicators have been chosen. The base of the pyramid illustrates the necessary preconditions for media literacy development and the environmental factors which facilitate or hinder it. The second level illustrates the personal competencies to facilitate technical and cognitive skills which, in turn, facilitate communicative ability, at the apex of the pyramid, which permits full engagement with the media literacy society.

In addition, the quality and functionality of indicators may be affected by a wide range of factors that form the 12 basic principles.

- *Pertinence* and data relevance;
- *Timeliness*, need for up-to-date data;
- *Accuracy* on data reporting;
- *Frequency*, a very important factor since it offers long-term data analysis;
- *Cost-effectiveness*;
- *Validity*, combined with specificity and *reliability*;
- *Consistency*;
- *Economy* in data collection;
- *Independence* from any form of interference;
- *Transparency*;
- *Comparability*, a challenging one since it involves comparison of same data among different countries and cultures.

Toward a conceptual map of media and information literacy indicators

To summarize, our analysis toward a global paradigm for media and information literacy indicators may be conveyed in a *conceptual map* of the following cognitive fields that interact in a circular way, based on global media ecology.

1. *Presence of a sustainable and concrete regulation on media and information literacy, both in typical education and the lifelong learning field.* State regulation may issue national recommendations and directives, comply with EU and global regulatory policy, encourage co- and self-regulation among media players, ensure digital infrastructure for all citizens, and also gear media literacy policies toward gender-specific issues and social minorities. To this end, it is also important to shift away from child protectionist laws and place an emphasis on user empowerment through media and information literacy. The focus on user empowerment rather than on limiting protectionist laws is twofold: first, it is in alliance with the relevant Conventions on Freedom of Expression and Information (Art. 19 of the Universal Declaration of Human Rights, Art 13. of the Convention of the Rights of the Child); and second, it applies better to children when they are grown up as adults since they have already acquired media and information literacy competencies and thus are not susceptible to potential negative influence.
2. *Presence of a national (public or private) entity on media and information literacy* that will be assigned to draw the national public policy and coordinate all relevant actions, networking, and synergies within the country and in the European

Union and the global scene. Due to multiple intersecting fields, this authority may engage all forms of media, archives, information bodies, libraries, educational sectors, ICT markets, and relevant cultural bodies. A typical example of EU networking is the EC Media Literacy Expert Group (MLEG) DG Connect (Directorate-General for Communications Networks, Content and Technology), launched by the European Commission in 2006, that contains national-assigned experts on media literacy. The aim of the Expert Group is to identify, document, and extend good practices, facilitate networking between different stakeholders, with the aim of cross-fertilization, explore synergies between different EU policies, and support programs and media literacy initiatives.

3. *Availability of independent media authorities with advanced duties on media literacy.* The independent media authority may act as a media literacy "watchdog" that will promote active (awareness campaigns, toolkits, measures) and passive (labeling, monitoring regulatory framework) actions on media and information literacy.
4. *Co- and self-regulation actions initiated by the media industry, information service providers, and Internet intermediaries.* Such initiatives may involve: enacting tools for minors' protection from harmful content on the media platforms (such as encryption, filtering, parental control), adapting program classification for both audiovisual and Internet content, taking Internet neutrality measures, advancing fair competition and advertisement in media, combating hate speech and radicalization on digital platforms, promoting news literacy against fake news, ensuring freedom of expression and media pluralism, actions toward protection of copyrights, encouragement of public broadcasting campaigns from public and private media, and more.
5. *Concrete presence of media and information literacy in typical education.* Innovative approaches may be present cross-sectorally or through autonomous objects of study and certainly supported within lifelong learning mechanisms. Embedding media literacy into the curriculum means that this indicator shall not be limited to acquiring ICT skills but delve into the real and complex nature, rules, and messages of all media.
6. *Lifelong learning training actions and initiatives for educators* (students, tutors, practitioners, supervisors, inservice teachers). These initiatives may involve the use of Massive Open Online Courses (MOOCs) as well as a wide range of Open Educational Resources (OERs), such as open libraries, repositories of media content, and index networking platforms. They may also engage synergies of media/digital creativity awards, seminars, workshops, conferences, and other target-group-related activities that offer a greater insight to teachers wishing to study media literacy in depth.
7. *Advanced and up-to-date research on media and information literacy.* This indicator is closely related to the previous one, since it focuses on the availability of ample methodological research from assigned bodies and the academia that will help demystify the digital trends and measure media impact on human behavior and within society norms. Such research may involve, for example, regular statistical monitoring of media access and use among certain target groups, such as

the annual reports issued by Ofcom in Britain that offer a national overview of media preferences and upcoming trends. Or, it may focus on qualitative analysis and national reports within greater networking platforms and online libraries. A recent example of mixed research on a pan-European level is the new study "Mapping of Media Literacy Practices and Actions in EU-28" (Cappello, 2017) by the European Audiovisual Observatory of the Council of Europe. The study collects and analyses media literacy initiatives and policies on a national and international level in order to provide an overview of media literacy in Europe. The study was financed by the European Commission and provides a detailed analysis of the main trends, based on a selection of 547 projects involving 939 stakeholders across the European Union.

8. *Strong presence of social activism and civil society actors.* In the context of active citizenship and user empowerment, both as a means and an end, an extra indicator is that of monitoring the level of civil society initiatives run by nongovernmental organizations, cultural foundations, parental unions, media and journalism associations, and educational bodies. As pinpointed by relevant EU studies, sometimes it is easier to develop voluntary action on media literacy that may serve as pressure for more concrete, state-driven decisions.
9. *Clear division of the target group involved and addressed per se.* As has already been stipulated, media and information literacy addresses *all* citizens of *all* ages. However, when trying to measure certain media and information literacy actions, it is good to have a specific idea of to whom it is targeted and what other social variables are engaged. To be more specific, different approaches and criteria need to be used with target groups of children and minors (of preschool, primary, secondary level), social minorities (immigrants, refugees), senior citizens, less versus highly educated populations, and people with disabilities, as well as with other social and economic factors.
10. *Sufficient operation of media and information platforms for the promotion of activities, policies, and research results through open society mechanisms.* This last indicator is of equal importance to the previous ones since it emphasizes the fair and easy distribution of all actions taken on media and information literacy. Distribution channels may be enforced by public service media, through open government initiatives and platforms, and through special campaigns on social media and other digital tools. An all-inclusive and pragmatic approach on media literacy cannot exist and go further unless it is followed by corresponding promotion and availability of all data and perspectives. Thus, an open and wise information society cannot progress without the acquisition of the relevant procedures.

Conclusions

The aforementioned suggested indicators attempt to canvass the main rationale behind the operability of media and information literacy policy on a national context. At the same time, in some cases, the presence of media and information literacy indicators may function as a potential barometer for the less developed fields and thus lead to new, more focused and effective policies. Arguably, enforcement and smooth operation of indicators does not come easily. Controversies arise constantly that deal with the cost of implementation, the systematic monitoring of statistical data, the digital gap (social, geographical) per country, GDP level, and constant reforms of education, media, audiovisual, and digital policies.

It is a fact that indicators alone cannot capture impact; nonetheless, they need to be tailored to the particular context in which they are being used. Media and information literacy indicators need thus to be aligned with the universal knowledge and information indicators that are connected with critical thinking and management of resources, problem-solving , creativity, and active citizenship in 21st-century societies.

Yet, the greater challenge remains the realization that pursuing media and information literacy in the form of indicators and metric levels not only secures a prominent place for the country in the global public sphere, but constitutes a fundamental socioeconomic convention toward the welfare of sustainable and knowledge democratic societies, where human capital is on top.

SEE ALSO: European Perspectives on Media Literacy; Media Literacy Outcomes, Measurement; Mediated Communities; Policy Issues in European Media Literacy

References

Cappello, M. (2017). *Mapping of media literacy practices and actions in EU-28*. Council of Europe. Strasbourg, France: European Audiovisual Observatory. Retrieved from https://rm.coe.int/media-literacy-mapping-report-en-final-pdf/1680783500

Carlsson, U. (2013). Preface. In A. Grizzle & M.C.T. Calvo (Eds.), *Media and information literacy policy and strategy guidelines* (p. 8). Paris, France: UNESCO. Retrieved from http://unesdoc.unesco.org/images/0022/002256/225606e.pdf

European Association for Viewers Interests. (2009). *Study on assessment criteria for media literacy levels*. Brussels, Belgium: EAVI. Retrieved from http://ec.europa.eu/assets/eac/culture/library/studies/literacy-criteria-report_en.pdf

Fedorov, A.V., & Kolesnichenko V. (2013). Marshall McLuhan and Umberto Eco as theorists of media education. In A.I. Kubyshkin (Ed.), *Representations of Canada* (Vol. 8, pp. 74–82). Volgograd, Russia: Volgograd State University. Retrieved from https://psyfactor.org/t/Fedorov_Kolesnichenko_2013_McLuhan_and_Eco.pdf

Gerbner, G. (1999). Foreword: What do we know? In J. Shahaha & M. Morgan (Eds.), *Television and its viewers: Cultivation theory and research*. Cambridge, England: Cambridge University Press.

Shenk, D. (1997). *Data smog: Surviving the information glut*. San Francisco, CA: Harper Collins.

Wilson, C., Grizzle, A., Tuazon, R., Akyempong, K., & Cheung, C.-K. (2011). *Media and information literacy curriculum for teachers* (p. 19). Paris, France: UNESCO. Retrieved from http://unesdoc.unesco.org/images/0019/001929/192971e.pdf

Further reading

Ellis, S., & Lau, J. (2008). *Towards information literacy indicators*. Paris, France: UNESCO. Retrieved from http://unesdoc.unesco.org/images/0015/001587/158723e.pdf

Grizzle, A. (2012). *Gender-sensitive indicators for media*. Paris, France: UNESCO.
IPDC. (2008). *Media development indicators: A framework for assessing media development*. Paris, France: UNESCO.
Media Pluralism Monitor, Monitoring Risks for Media Pluralism. Centre for Media Pluralism and Media Freedom—Robert Schuman Centre for Advanced Studies—European University Institute (http://monitor.cmpf.eui.eu/).
Moeller, S., Joseph, A., Lau, J., & Carbo, T. (2010). *Towards media and information literacy indicators*. Bangkok, Thailand: UNESCO. Retrieved from https://www.ifla.org/files/assets/information-literacy/publications/towards-media-and-Information-literacy-indicators.pdf
Tornero, J.M., Paredes, O., Giraldo, S., & Fernàndez, N. (2010). *Indicators for assessing the critical understanding of media in the European model of media literacy*. Barcelona, Spain: UAB. Retrieved from https://santiagogiraldoluque.files.wordpress.com/2012/11/2-indicators-for-assessing-the-critical-understanding-of-media-in-the-european-model-of-media-literacy.pdf

Irene Andriopoulou is a media researcher/analyst with an expertise in media literacy. She has worked with UNESCO Media & Information Literacy Unit as the Greek editor of *Media and Information Literacy Curriculum for Teachers* (2014). As member of the EC Media Literacy Expert Group (2006–2018) she contributed to many EU studies and groups on media literacy, such as the study *Mapping of Media Literacy Practices and Actions in EU-28* (2017) as well as drafting EC policy papers (AVMSD 2010/13, Rec. 2009/6464). Since 2017, she has been the media expert of Fest of Fests network. She is the Greek coauthor of *DIMLE, Keys to Interpreting Media Literacy Messages* (2017). She works at the Audiovisual Education Department of the National Centre of Audiovisual Media & Communication, EKOME SA, the new public entity for the Greek audiovisual industry.

L

Learning about Materialism and Consumer Culture

SUZANNA J. OPREE
Erasmus University Rotterdam, The Netherlands

Capitalism and its associated concerns

Insights from developmental psychology and sociology have long predicated that the values and behaviors of individuals are shaped and determined by their environment. More specifically, individuals are influenced by the microsystem (i.e., their direct social environment, consisting of family, friends, and colleagues), the exosystem (i.e., their extended social environment, consisting of indirect social ties—for example, friends of family and friends—and neighbors, and the mass media), and the macrosystem (i.e., society at large, consisting of political systems, economics, and the ideologies of the culture). Notably, these systems are nested. The capitalistic ideology which is dominant in many contemporary societies oozes down from the macrosystem, to the exosystem, the microsystem, and—finally—the individual (Kasser & Linn, 2016).

According to Kasser and Linn (2016, p. 124), the capitalistic ideology contains three important features. At the societal level, it (i) stimulates private ownership, (ii) encourages the pursuit of self-interests (i.e., wealth and possessions), and (iii) presumes that market competition will result in high-quality goods for low prices. At the individual level, people living in capitalist societies tend to value success, ambition, authority, status, and wealth more than harmony, equality, honesty, social justice, curiosity, and intellectual autonomy. Though part of the same macrosystem themselves, many parents and caregivers in capitalistic societies do worry that their society puts too much emphasis on the acquisition of goods, and too little emphasis on the importance of interhuman relationships.

Parents and caretakers in capitalistic societies are particularly concerned about the influence of advertising on children, claiming it is "'exploitative', 'in your

The International Encyclopedia of Media Literacy. Renee Hobbs and Paul Mihailidis (Editors-in-Chief), Gianna Cappello, Maria Ranieri, and Benjamin Thevenin (Associate Editors).

face', 'insidious', 'too powerful', and 'excessive'" (Oates, Newman, & Tziortzi, 2014 pp. 117–118). Oates and colleagues (2014) conducted their research in the United Kingdom but provide ample evidence that similar sentiments exist across the globe, referring to studies conducted in Australia, Belgium, China, Cyprus, Hong Kong, New Zealand, Sweden, and the United States. Parents' and caretakers' main apprehensions relate to the amount of advertising children are exposed to, the type of products that are promoted, and the appeals that are being used to do so, as well as children's ability to recognize and truly understand the nature of advertising, and the adverse effects advertising may ultimately have on children's behavior: stimulating pester power (i.e., the nagging for advertised goods) and causing conflict within the family.

Whereas parents and caretakers consider children to be a vulnerable consumer group, many marketers would claim that children are quite savvy at understanding brands and advertising (Spotswood & Nairn, 2016). However, while the research on children's vulnerability may have been inconclusive several years ago (see DCSF/DCMS, 2009, in Spotswood & Nairn, 2016), the evidence on children's limited capacity to recognize and understand advertising as well as advertising's undesired effects is mounting. Children's advertising exposure has been linked to unhealthy eating, body and eating disorders, violence and aggression, use of alcohol and tobacco, and—most relevant for this entry—materialism (Kasser & Linn, 2016). Childhood materialism, in turn, has been linked to increased risk of overspending and debt later in life, as well as a series of unfavorable character traits such as self-centeredness, entitlement, possessiveness, and disdain.

Defining materialism and consumer culture

The intensifying concerns about the spiraling effects of capitalism and advertising on the population's materialism inspired researchers to study materialism from both a theoretical and an empirical angle. Richins and Dawson (1992) compared classic and contemporary conceptualizations of materialism and found that they focused on three aspects. The first aspect is acquisition centrality (i.e., living a lifestyle in which consumption is perceived as a goal in itself), the second acquisition is the pursuit of happiness (i.e., consumption is perceived as a means to achieve the goal of increased happiness and/or well-being), and the third is possession-defined success (i.e., consumption is perceived as a means to improve one's self-image and one's ability to signal status).

Up to this day, the material values scale of Richins and Dawson (1992), which was built on the previous insights, remains a popular instrument for empirically measuring respondents' materialism, and it has been successfully implemented across the globe. The fact that materialism scores have been found to fluctuate across the globe has been explained by the notion that different nations have different consumer values. Capitalistic countries, where materialism flourishes, tend to have a strong consumer culture. A consumer culture is denoted by a surplus of goods and two commonly shared and deeply rooted consumer values/beliefs. The first belief is that continuous consumption is of vital importance to both the well-being of the country (i.e., without continuous consumption its economy would collapse) and the well-being of the individual (i.e., without continuous consumption he/she would become unhappy). The second belief is that goods and services can take on a significance beyond their practical value (Hovland & Wolburg, 2010).

The belief that goods and services can take on symbolic meaning is often utilized in advertising. Products are "sold" on the merit of providing a means to acquire the good life (e.g., luxury, comfort, status, and fun) or the so-called body perfect. With more and more advertisers using a "360-degree strategy," targeting consumers via a variety of media, the consumer values in advertising are hard to escape (Kasser & Linn, 2016). Even parents of preschoolers are worried about the amount and type of advertising their kin are exposed to. When asked whether they would support a ban for TV advertising aimed at preschool children, only 17% disagreed, 27% were neutral, and as many as 56% agreed (Watkins, Aitken, Robertson, & Thyne, 2016).

Consumer socialization

Unmistakably, the media—and advertising in particular—play a role in children's consumer socialization. Consumer socialization has long been defined as the "process by which young people acquire skills, knowledge, and attitudes relevant to their functioning as consumers in the marketplace" (Ward, 1974, in McNeal, 2007). This process is generally believed to consist of five stages, each connected to a different age group.

Stage 1: Observation (0–6 months)

The first stage of consumer socialization is the stage of observation (0–6 months). Between the age of 0 and 2 months, children are in the substage of random observation. In this substage consumption patterns are fully instinctive and based on reflexes (e.g., the child wants to drink milk because it is hungry). Between the age of 2 and 6 months, children are in the substage of voluntary observation. In this substage habits start to form based on preferences (e.g., after eating fruit, the child may prefer that due to its sweet taste).

Stage 2: Requesting/seeking (6–24 months)

The second stage is the stage of requesting/seeking (6–24 months). Between the age of 6 and 14 months, children are in the pre-language/pre-legs substage. Although children in this substage cannot verbalize their consumption preferences, they are able to reach for products when they are in close proximity (e.g., rather than being fed, a child can eat small pieces of bread by itself). Between the age of 15 and 24 months, children are in the post-language/post-legs substage. Despite a frequent use of incorrect labels, children in this substage are able to utter small words/expressions and use them to ask for specific products (e.g., "bana" for a banana), and they can also venture off and reach for products outside of their immediate reach (e.g., crawl or walk to the other side of the room when a toy or food product draws their attention).

Stage 3: Selecting/taking (24–48 months)

The third stage is the stage of selecting/taking (24–48 months). In this stage, children learn to formulate specific requests for the products they long for (e.g., "want banana!"). These requests can relate to products their parents introduced them to, but also to products advertised in the media. Children may respond to products they see in advertising, either during ("want that!") or after the fact (e.g., in store, responding to products from licensed characters they recognize, such as Dora the Explorer). Parents tend to want to resist this so-called pester power as much as they can. Still, because hearing "no" quite often is frustrating to children, they soon learn how to ask politely (e.g., "banana please!"), and how to successfully bargain and plead whenever their requests are declined.

Stages 4 & 5: Co-purchase (48–72 months) and independent purchase (72–100 months)

The fourth stage is the co-purchase (48–72 months). Children have learned that the products in store are not up for grabs, but up for sale. They want to have their own money and make small purchases. Parents typically supervise their children's first purchase and the first series of purchases after that. The fifth and final stage is the independent purchase (72–100 months). The first independent purchases tend to be supervised too, but rather than standing right next to their children (i.e., at the counter), parents will be in close proximity (i.e., the next shop-shelf).

According to Valkenburg and Cantor (2001), children have matured in their consumer development once they are able to "(1) feel wants and preferences, (2) search to fulfill them, (3) make a choice and a purchase, and (4) evaluate a product and its alternatives" (p. 61). Rather than describing the phases in consumer socialization in months, these authors describe it in years. The previous classification stops at 100 months, thus around 8 years of age. However, according to Valkenburg and Cantor (2001), children's consumer socialization continues between the ages of 8 and 12 years.

Children's consumer development between the ages of 8 and 12 years is characterized by a changing relationships with peers and a changing relationship with brands and advertising (Valkenburg & Cantor, 2001). Children's ability to recognize and understand other people's emotions and thoughts improves rapidly, and the opinions of others matter to a greater extent. Children want to fit in with the peer group, tend to conform to the group norm, and become more critical of brands and advertising. They are loyal toward the brands they like, but reject brands and products that are perceived as inferior by their peers. Children start to lose interest in toys and start to become interested in objects with a social function, making them susceptible to materialism: they start to consume products because they believe they make them happy, and because they can increase their peer group status and popularity.

Though some would argue that peers function as a "filter" for advertising (Valkenburg & Cantor, 2001, p. 68), others claim that children remain vulnerable to the effects of advertising throughout their adolescent life because adolescents' persuasion knowledge is yet to fully mature. Recently, for instance, the growing use of muscular male actors in commercials led to increased body-anxiety among teenage boys (i.e., because they were falsely led to believe that such a body structure is "normal" and attainable) and, subsequently, extremely frequent and intense training sessions at the gym (jeopardizing their physical and mental health). Adolescence is also a phase of insecurity and exploration, making teenage girls and boys gullible to the messages and products portrayed in advertising. For example, previously, many teenage boys bought and excessively used Axe deodorant (also known as Lynx), because they felt anxious about their body odor and wanted to attract girls (i.e., obtain "the Axe effect").

Commercialized content

Children and teenagers are frequently targeted by marketers because they represent three different types of market (McNeal, 2007). First, they represent a primary market. Children and teens today have more pocket money and purchasing power than ever before. In the United Kingdom, for instance, the average amount of pocket money received by children between the ages of 8 and 15 years increased from £1.13 in 1987 to £6.55 in 2016, an increase of 480% in the past 20 years (Halifax, 2016). Second, children represent a secondary market or so-called market of influencers. They influence family purchase decisions by asking for specific goods themselves, and by announcing their preferences at the request of their parents and caregivers. Children's influence is large in the child-specific treats and family entertainment categories (more than 50% of children have a considerable influence), but also in the children's clothing and dining out categories and food choices at home (20–50%) (Marić, 2016). Finally, children represent a future market. By influencing children's brand familiarity and brand preferences, advertisers hope to create lifelong loyal customers.

Television remains the most prominent way in which advertisers target children. Children are estimated to view between 10 000 and 40 000 TV commercials per year. Still, it must be acknowledged that children's advertising exposure through other media is growing rapidly. Children's use of and advertisers' presence on websites and apps is increasing (Opree, 2014). Popular children's website and mobile apps are saturated with advertising, which can be presented in the form of "dull" banners yet is often presented in the form of branded pictures, branded videos, branded websites, advergames, branded games and virtual worlds, social marketing, and/or branded contests (Hurwitz, Morales, Montague, Lauricella, & Wartella, 2016). Compared to children who are exposed to TV advertising, children who are exposed to interactive advertising content are more likely to stay fixated for extended periods of time, develop favorable brand attitudes, and ask for the advertised brand. Importantly, even between the ages of 8 and 12 years, many children who engage with such interactive advertising content often do not realize that they are being targeted.

Persuasion knowledge and advertising literacy

Children's ability to recognize and understand advertising has often been referred to as persuasion knowledge and/or advertising literacy. For a long time, these two concepts have been used interchangeably. However, a seminal paper by Rozendaal, Lapierre, van Reijmersdal, and Buijzen (2011) has shifted the field. It is now commonly accepted that persuasion knowledge (i.e., knowledge about advertising's tactics and intent) is part of children's advertising literacy, but that advertising literacy encompasses more than just that. Within the old cognitive defense view, researchers assumed that increasing children's persuasion knowledge would shield them from the effects of advertising. However, given the fun and enticing nature of contemporary interactive advertising, children are likely to process such content without much thought. The only way to increase their defenses for interactive advertising content is by making them more negative toward advertising in general. In its new conceptualization, advertising literacy consists of three dimensions each with multiple components (see Rozendaal et al., 2011, and the text below). Previous research studied the development of children's advertising literacy on the following specific dimensions and components (for ages 8–12, see Opree & Rozendaal, 2015).

Conceptual advertising literacy

The first dimension of children's advertising literacy, conceptual advertising literacy, consists of six components: though children's overall conceptual advertising literacy and recognition of advertising improve significantly between the ages of 8 and 12 years, no significant age differences have been found in their ability to recognize advertising's source and intended audience and/or in their ability to understand advertising's selling intent, persuasive intent, and use of persuasive tactics.

Attitudinal advertising literacy

The second dimension is attitudinal advertising literacy and consists of three components: understanding of advertising's bias, skepticism toward advertising, and disliking of advertising. Both children's overall attitudinal advertising literacy and their performance on all three dimensions increase significantly between the ages of 8 and 12 years. These findings can be explained by the filtering function of peers referred to by Valkenburg and Cantor (2001). However, intuitively, they may also be attributed to children's building consumer experience. Advertising portrays products and brands in very favorable manners: toys look bigger, are animated with impressive movements or sounds, and so on. The consumption of the advertised products may not—more often than not—live up to the high expectations, causing consumer discontent and increasingly negative attitudes toward future commercial utterances.

Advertising literacy performance

The third dimension is children's advertising literacy performance. In essence, this dimension captures the extent to which children activate their conceptual and attitudinal advertising literacy when confronted with advertising (Rozendaal et al., 2011). In the past, it has been measured with one or more of seven components. Children's overall advertising literacy performance increases significantly between the ages of

8 and 12 years, and the same holds for children's tendency to employ selective exposure, counterarguing, attitude bolstering, negative affect, and assertions of confidence techniques when faced with advertising: as they grow older, children become more likely to actively divert their attention from advertising, refute advertising's claims, boost their own preexisting attitudes, get annoyed by or angry with advertising, and assert that advertising does not influence them. Children's tendency for source derogation and source validation (i.e., to dismiss the validity of the source and to compare the validity of the source to that of their direct social environment), however, does not increase between the ages of 8 and 12 years.

Consumer empowerment: theory and practice

The United Nations has recommended to "prohibit all forms of advertising to children under 12 years of age, regardless of the medium, support or means used, with the possible extension of such prohibition to children under 16 years of age." In practice, child-directed advertising is forbidden in only a few countries and regions (e.g., Norway, Sweden, and Quebec), and restricted in most (Verdoodt, Lambrecht and Lievens, 2016). The level of restriction differs greatly by country, but one common approach is that advertising should be recognizable as such to children. For instance, commercials blocks on television should be announced as such, and online advertising should contain a disclosure such as "sponsored" or "advertising."

Legislation on disclosures is often presented as a means for consumer empowerment: consumers (i.e., both children and adults) are provided with the tools that allow them to take active control over their decision-making process. In theory, by easing the recognition of advertising, disclosures enable consumers to activate their persuasion knowledge and to shield themselves from advertising's effects. In practice, though, it appears that even though disclosures facilitate the activation of persuasion knowledge, they seldom lead to critical processing and/or reduced susceptibility to advertising's effect on brand liking and purchase intentions (Boerman & van Reijmersdal, 2016).

For children and adults alike, the effectiveness of disclosures is bound to strict conditions. Research among adults has indicated that, due to their signaling function, disclosures lead to *increased* brand recall (Boerman & van Reijmersdal, 2016). If this increased brand recall is not accompanied with *decreased* brand liking and purchase intentions, the use of disclosures backfires and actually benefits the advertisers. In order to fulfill their original purpose, disclosures should aim not only to facilitate consumers' recognition of advertising and activate their conceptual advertising literacy, but also to activate their attitudinal advertising literacy. Whether or not disclosures are effective in increasing critical processing and reducing consumers' susceptibility to advertising's effect on brand liking and purchase intentions depends largely on—among other factors such as their timing and duration (for a detailed discussion, see Boerman & van Reijmersdal, 2016)—their content.

Research among children has indicated that disclosures that simply warn children about advertising and its commercial intent (i.e., "Now it's time for the commercials, but pay attention: commercials want you to like and buy their products") do not activate their persuasion knowledge or increase their advertising literacy performance. Disclosures that warn children about advertising's manipulating intent (i.e., "Now it's time for the commercials but pay attention: commercials are not always fair; sometimes they tell you things that are untrue"), however, do (Rozendaal, Buijs, & van Reijmersdal, 2016, p. 4). In line with these findings, Hudders, Cauberge, and Panic (2016) found that advertising literacy interventions are only successful when they aim to increase children's attitudinal advertising literacy.

Past research has confirmed that children's conceptual advertising literacy and advertising literacy performance are unrelated, but that children's attitudinal advertising literacy and advertising literacy performance are related: children with greater insight into advertising's bias, greater skepticism, and more negative attitudes toward advertising are more likely to activate their advertising literacy when being confronted with advertising (Opree & Rozendaal, 2015). Combined with the fact that their attitudinal advertising literacy lags behind their conceptual advertising literacy (Opree & Rozendaal, 2015), it seems of vital importance that future advertising literacy training programs focus on increasing children's attitudinal advertising literacy in order to help reduce the effects of advertising.

Socioeconomic status differences and the effects of family income

The links between advertising exposure and materialism, and between exposure to commercial media and materialism, have been well documented in the literature. Still, consumers' (i.e., both children's and adults') susceptibility to the effect of advertising and commercial media on materialism may differ greatly between individuals, and not only because of differences in their persuasion knowledge. Consumers' exposure to media and their susceptibility to its effects depend on their *dispositional susceptibility* (i.e., personality, identity, and mood), *developmental susceptibility* (i.e., cognitive and emotional development), and *social susceptibility* (i.e., social contexts at the macrosystem, exosystem, and microsystem). Unhappy children, for instance, are found to be more susceptible to the effects of advertising on materialism than happy children (Opree, 2014). And as discussed in the previous section, children with higher levels of attitudinal advertising literacy are less susceptible to the effects of advertising than children with lower attitudinal advertising literacy (e.g., Hudders, Cauberge, & Panic, 2016). Differences in the effects of advertising and commercial media between social classes, however, have been largely unexplored, even though researchers have identified clear links between inequality and materialism.

Social class is usually assessed through people's socioeconomic status (SES), being their level of education, occupation, and income. Differences in SES are thought to reflect differences in access to both financial and social resources. As explained in the introduction to this entry, the capitalistic ideology and the consumer values it represents are present in society at large, as well as in people's extended and direct social environments. It seems that children from low-SES families are more likely to engage in conspicuous consumption in order to address a disconnect between their ideal self and their actual, attainable self and to deal with insecurities that can result from poverty. Though qualitative-oriented research also suggests that children from low-SES families show a heightened interest in commercials (Lawlor, 2009), it is unknown whether this interest increases children's awareness of and susceptibility to the values in advertising.

Future directions

Directions for future research can be derived from each of the sections in this entry. First, the history on the capitalistic ideology indicates that the rise in consumer culture has been accompanied by increasing worries from parents and caregivers about the effects of advertising on their children. The level of capitalism varies among countries across the globe, and some countries have only recently begun their transition. There is a need for research exploring how such societies can benefit from the capitalistic ideology without suffering from its proven side effects.

Second, more and more advertisers seem to be using a "360-degree strategy," leaving no space to escape advertising. The current generation of children is exposed to advertising at an increasingly young age. Parents seem to be in favour of bans on child-directed advertising, but such legislation exists in just a few countries. More research is needed about other ways parents can protect their kin. There is a rich research tradition on the success factors of parental generic *media* mediation strategies, yet there is an increasing need for studies examining the effectiveness of parental *advertising* mediation: do the same principles apply? For instance, is active mediation (i.e., talking with children about advertising's content) better than restrictive mediation (i.e., taking measures reducing children's advertising exposure which, as a side effect, may prevent them from learning how to deal with it)?

Third, it is important to realize that not only online advertising but also online shopping is commonplace in contemporary society. The current-day framework on children's consumer socialization needs to be updated with insights into children's first online purchases, as well as information about the timing and procedures of learning online shopping scripts. With offline shopping children learn the scripts (i.e., picking an item, bringing it to the counter, and paying for it) through observation of their parents' behavior. When and how do parents educate their children about online shopping? Without the proper guidance, children's first online purchases and learning of scripts could be the result of trial and error (e.g., accidently purchasing items in an online game using their parents' credit card information).

Fourth, current research about advertising literacy has primarily focused on whether or not it can be used to reduce the intended effects of advertising (i.e., effects on brand recall, brand liking, and purchase intentions). Little to nothing is known about its ability to reduce advertising's unintended effects: would disclosures and/or enhancing children's advertising literacy empower them as consumers by making them less vulnerable to advertising's effects on materialism and all other outcomes mentioned by Kasser and Linn (2016)?

Finally, earlier studies on the relation between family income and children's general media use indicated that children's media use is higher, and parents' perceived and actual media mediation skills are lower, in low-SES than in high-SES families (Livingstone, Mascheroni, Dreier, Chaudron, & Lagae, 2015). Consequently, children in low-income families are at higher risk of experiencing adverse media effects, and this may apply to advertising and commercial content too. Given the global increase in income equality, it seems of vital importance for future research to investigate whether children from low-SES families are more exposed to advertising and more vulnerable to its effects than children from high-SES families.

SEE ALSO: Advertising Literacy; Children's Understanding of Persuasion; Learning from Media; Media and Adolescent Identity Development; Parental Mediation; Preschool Children and Media; Representation of Health, Body, (Dis)Ability; Representation of Nutrition and Food in the Media; Resisting Persuasive Intent

References

Boerman, S.C., & van Reijmersdal, E.A. (2016). Informing consumers about hidden advertising. A literature review of the effects of disclosing sponsored content. In P. de Pelsmacker (Ed.), *Advertising in new formats and media: Current research and implications for marketers* (pp. 115–146). London, England: Emerald Group.

Halifax. (2016, June 3). *Ker-ching! Children's pocket money hits nine-year high* [Press release]. LLoyds Banking Group. Retrieved from http://www.lloydsbankinggroup.com/Media/Press-Releases/2016-press-releases/halifax/ker-ching-childrens-pocket-money-hits-nine-year-high/

Hovland, R., & Wolburg, J.M. (2010). *Advertising, society, and consumer culture.* Armonk, NY: M.E. Sharpe.

Hudders, L., Cauberge, V., & Panic, K. (2016). How advertising literacy training affects children's responses to television commercials versus advergames. *International Journal of Advertising, 35*(6), 909–931. doi: 10.1080/02650487.2015.1090045

Hurwitz, L.B., Morales, E.D., Montague, H., Lauricella, A.R., & Wartella, E. (2016). Mobile marketing to children: A content analysis of food and beverage company apps. *Public Health, 141*, 241–244. doi: 10.1016/j.puhe.2016.09.025

Kasser, T., & Linn, S. (2016). Growing up under corporate capitalism: The problem of marketing to children, with suggestions for policy solutions. *Social Issues and Policy Review, 10*(1), 122–150. doi: 10.1111/sipr.12020

Lawlor, M.-A. (2009). Advertising connoisseurs: Children's active engagement with and enjoyment of television advertising. *Irish Marketing Review, 20*(1), 23–24.

Livingstone, S., Mascheroni, G., Dreier, M., Chaudron, S., & Lagae, K. (2015). *How parents of young children manage digital devices at home: The role of income, education, and parental style.* London, England: EU Kids Online, LSE.

Marić, D. (2016, April 12). *Consumers in training: How children in the Americas are influencing the purchasing decisions of their parents.* Retrieved from https://www.linkedin.com/pulse/consumers-training-how-children-americas-influencing-purchasing

McNeal, J.U. (2007). *On becoming a consumer: Development of consumer behavior patterns in childhood.* Burlington, MA: Butterworth-Heinemann.

Oates, C., Newman, N., & Tziortzi, A. (2014). Parents' beliefs about, and attitudes towards, marketing to children. In M. Blades, C. Oates, F. Blumberg, & B. Gunter (Eds.), *Advertising to children. New directions, new media* (pp. 115–136). London, England: Palgrave Macmillan.

Opree, S.J. (2014). *Consumed by consumer culture? Advertising's impact on children's materialism and life satisfaction* (Doctoral dissertation). Amsterdam School of Communication Research, Netherlands. Retrieved from http://dare.uva.nl/search?metis.record.id=410142

Opree, S.J., & Rozendaal, E. (2015). The advertising literacy of primary school aged children. In I.B. Banks, P. de Pelsmacker, & S. Okazaki (Eds.), *Advances in advertising research series (Vol. V): Extending the boundaries of advertising* (pp. 191–202). Wiesbaden, Germany: Springer Gabler.

Richins, M.L., & Dawson, S. (1992). A consumer values orientation for materialism and its measurement: Scale development and validation. *Journal of Consumer Research, 19*(3), 303–316. doi: 10.1086/209304

Rozendaal, E., Buijs, L., & van Reijmersdal, E.A. (2016). Strengthening children's advertising defenses: The effects of forewarning of commercial and manipulative intent. *Frontiers in Psychology, 7*(1186), 1–11. doi: 10.3389/fpsyg.2016.01186

Rozendaal, E., Lapierre, M.A., van Reijmersdal, E.A., & Buijzen, M. (2011). Reconsidering advertising literacy as a defence against advertising effects. *Media Psychology, 14*(4), 333–354. doi: 10.1080/15213269.2011.620540

Spotswood, F., & Nairn, A. (2016). Children as vulnerable consumers: A first conceptualization. *Journal of Marketing Management, 32*(3), 1–19. doi: 10.1080/0267257X.2015.1107616

Valkenburg, P.M., & Cantor, J. (2001). The development of a child into a consumer. *Journal of Applied Developmental Psychology, 22*(1), 61–72. doi: 10.1016/S0193-3973(00)00066-6

Verdoodt, V., Lambrecht, I., & Lievens, E. (2016). *Mapping and analysis of the current self and co-regulatory framework of commercial communication aimed at minors. A report in the framework of the AdLit research project*. AdLit. Retrieved from http://www.adlit.be/output

Watkins, L., Aitken, R., Robertson, K., & Thyne, M. (2016). Public and parental perceptions of and concerns with advertising to pre-school children. *International Journal of Consumer Studies, 40*(5), 592–600. doi:10.1111/ijcs.12304

Further reading

Buckingham, D. (Ed.). (2011). *The material child: Growing up in consumer culture*. Cambridge, England: Polity Press.

Dittmar, H. (Ed.). (2008). *Consumer culture, identity, and well-being: The search for the "good life" and the "body perfect."* Hove, England: Psychology Press.

Mayo, E., & Nairn, A. (2009). *Consumer kids: How big business is grooming our children for profit*. London, England: Constable.

Schor, J.B. (2005). *Born to buy: The commercialized child and the new consumer culture*. New York, NY: Scribner.

Tatzel, M. (Ed.). (2014). *Consumption and well-being in the material world*. Dordrecht, Netherlands: Springer.

Suzanna J. Opree is Senior Assistant Professor of Quantitative Research Methods at the Erasmus School of History, Culture, and Communication at the Erasmus University Rotterdam, The Netherlands. Her research examines the effects of advertising on youths' materialism and well-being and has been published in renowned journals such as *Communication Research*, *Media Psychology*, and *Pediatrics*. A recent article on advertising's effects on children's psychological well-being and happiness, coauthored by Professor Moniek Buijzen and Dr. Eva A. van Reijmersdal, received the top paper award of the Children, Adolescents and Media Division at the 2016 annual conference of the International Communication Association.

Learning from Media

HEATHER L. KIRKORIAN
University of Wisconsin-Madison, USA

Learning from media takes many forms, the most obvious of which entails gaining explicit knowledge from educational media (i.e., curriculum-driven media that have a deliberate goal of teaching) such as educational television programs, video games, and mobile applications. Other types of learning from media may be less obvious (e.g., learning how to collaborate in multiplayer games) or less desirable (e.g., acquiring scripts for aggressive behavior from violent content). While historical debates may have focused on global media effects on learning, the extant empirical literature clearly demonstrates that it is media content, rather than the platform or device per se, that is most likely to determine media effects on learning (see Clark, 2012). Thus, the focus has shifted from questions about *whether* children and adults learn from media to questions about *how, for whom, and under what conditions.*

The majority of controlled, empirical research on learning from media examines children's learning from educational television, with a growing body of literature on digital games. Thus, the focus of this entry will be learning from media across childhood. Additionally, the current entry focuses on learning from media in informal contexts (e.g., at home).

Media that are created for learning in informal contexts by young children are intended to be perceived as entertainment, not as education. Such "edutainment" for young children was first introduced in the middle of the 20th century (Wartella & Robb, 2008). The most notable early example is *Sesame Street,* which has relied on developmental and learning science since its inception and is still in production today. Educational content has greatly expanded since the 1960s, with many more titles on many different platforms. The target audience for educational media has also expanded over the past several decades: videos with educational claims have targeted infants as young as just a few months old, and the majority of mobile applications that are marketed as "educational" are intended for use by young children (Shuler, Levine, & Ree, 2012). Each new wave of educational media carries with it hopes for cost-effective, scalable educational interventions as well as concerns over the potential negative effects of media on cognition, social skills, and health. While there is evidence that some types of media content can result in negative outcomes for some individuals (e.g., violent video games increasing aggressive behavior for certain children), research predominantly demonstrates that high-quality, evidence-based educational media can produce positive outcomes (Anderson & Kirkorian, 2015).

Some educational media are informed by research and theory in the developmental and learning sciences. The most widely used theories for educational media are based on principles for how children and adults learn in the real world. One such theory is Fisch's capacity model (see Fisch, Kirkorian, & Anderson, 2005). The capacity model is grounded in information-processing theories of human cognition, particularly as it relates to a limited capacity for processing information. Fisch proposed that in order to understand educational television, viewers must process both the narrative (i.e., the story) and the educational content (i.e., the lesson to be learned). In order to support comprehension and learning, the program should contain a clear educational lesson that is integrated seamlessly with a simple narrative. Such integration reduces competition between processing the narrative and processing the educational content. Similarly, Strommen (1993) proposed an information-processing model related to the difficulty of interactive media devices; that is, one's ability to learn from interactive media such as digital games will depend partly on the cognitive demands of using the device itself. Complementing theories of learning from television and interactive media, Mayer (2001) proposed a theory for how learners integrate information across media platforms. While these theories consider the extent to which individuals comprehend educational content in educational media, other theories address the degree to which viewers can transfer what they learn from media to real-life situations. In order to maximize the likelihood of such transfer, media creators should not only integrate educational and entertainment content, but also present educational lessons using many different examples in a variety of contexts. This strategy helps viewers to create flexible representations of a lesson, and therefore more easily see the connection between that lesson (e.g., in a TV program) and a situation they face in the real world (Fisch et al., 2005).

Educational media that implement these theoretical frameworks have the potential to promote learning. In fact, there is extensive empirical research on the impact of educational television, particularly during early and middle childhood. Programs that are designed to promote early learning can be effective. Specific educational outcomes include those related to early literacy, vocabulary, and problem solving (see Anderson & Kirkorian, 2015). This early learning appears to boost school readiness, insofar as young children who watch more educational television during the preschool years are better prepared for entering first grade. In turn, these children go on to earn higher grades, engage in more leisure book reading, and participate in more extracurricular activities in high school compared to peers who watched less educational television as a preschooler. The benefits of high-quality educational television for preschoolers appear to be universal: Mares and Pan (2013) conducted a meta-analysis of research on international coproductions of *Sesame Street* in 15 countries around the globe. They found positive effects of the program for knowledge in cognitive, social-emotional, and health domains among low-, middle-, and high-income countries.

There are fewer explicitly educational television programs for school-age children and adolescents. However, as with programming for preschoolers, empirical evidence demonstrates that educational television for older children can reach its intended learning goals. Although some studies suggest that children's total amount of time using media in a typical day is negatively correlated with academic achievement, studies that consider not just how much children watch but also *what* they watch typically find that different types of content lead to different outcomes. This includes randomized control trials demonstrating positive effects of educational media in a wide range of domains, such as mathematics, science, literacy, and social studies (see Anderson & Kirkorian, 2015). Indeed, the quality of instructional content is a key determinant of learning across the lifespan, regardless of the instructional modality (Clark, 2012).

Although educational media can be effective for children and adults alike, children younger than about 3 years of age typically benefit more from real-life experiences. Dozens of studies have documented a *video deficit* among infants and toddlers, such that these young children learn more readily from real-life demonstrations than from the same demonstrations on a video screen. For instance, 24-month-olds are less likely to learn words or find hidden objects using demonstrations that they see via closed-circuit video versus in person. There are several complementary hypotheses for why the video deficit exists (Kirkorian, Pempek, & Choi, 2017). For instance, video is perceptually impoverished in comparison to real-life scenarios, such as lacking some visual cues about the three-dimensionality of objects and their relation to each other in space. This means that infants may recognize objects more slowly when they are depicted in two-dimensional images. Once infants are able to recognize the images in video, they must also realize the symbolic relation between images and real objects; that is, they must understand that a picture is both an object in itself and also a symbol that represents an object in the real world. Such symbolic reasoning appears to develop during the third year of life. Finally, if toddlers are able to recognize the symbolic relation between images and real objects, they must then be able to overcome differences between the context in which they initially learned the information (e.g., a television program) and the context in which they apply that information (e.g., a playground). Younger children have particular difficulty transferring memories across contexts, even if there are only subtle differences between those contexts.

Although infants and toddlers appear to learn less from screen media than from real-life demonstrations, they can learn from media under some circumstances (Kirkorian, Pempek, & Choi, 2017). For instance, infants are more likely to imitate actions that they see on video if they have repeated exposure to the video demonstration, which supports the hypothesis that infants process video more slowly than they process real-life events. Because repetition helps toddlers to learn information from media, this strategy also helps toddlers transfer to situations that are different from those seen in media. Other research demonstrates that toddlers are more likely to imitate the actions of familiar people and beloved characters than those of unfamiliar characters. Additionally, toddlers are more likely to learn from screens when the experience is socially interactive, as during video chat. Non-social interactivity that is contingent on the child's own behavior, as in the case of computer games and mobile applications, has also been shown to increase learning among some young children. However, such interactivity may not support learning if the game mechanics are particularly difficult (Strommen, 1993).

Once children can readily transfer knowledge between screens and real-life scenarios, their learning from media further depends on the extent to which they understand the intended lesson and the narrative through which the lesson is delivered (Anderson & Hanson, 2010). For instance, many educational television programs contain complex video editing techniques that represent transitions in space and time (e.g., cuts between scenes). Toddlers appear to become sensitive to such transitions around 18 months of age, insofar as they look longer during shot sequences presented in their original order versus a random order. However, comprehension of video editing techniques develops throughout early childhood. More complicated techniques (e.g., flashbacks) can be confusing for children through the elementary school years. Children demonstrate adult-like comprehension of lengthy narratives during the middle school years.

While research on television has a much longer history than research on video games and other interactive media, there is a growing body of literature on games for learning in both formal and informal contexts. This literature indicates that video games that are designed around a specific educational goal can be effective in reaching that goal. In addition to specific knowledge gains for drill-and-skill games, research demonstrates that some types of games may also enable players to develop and practice more general cognitive skills that support learning and academic achievement across domains. Such games are most likely to lead to improvement on tasks that are highly similar to the games themselves (e.g., mentally rotating shapes to fit into empty spaces), but some games have produced broad transfer of perceptual learning and cognitive skills. For instance, adults who are trained with first-person action games show gains in visual processing and attentional control (see Anderson & Kirkorian, 2015). With only a few exceptions, such research is limited to adult participants, and none have been conducted with young children. Further research is needed to establish whether such effects are seen in young children and, if so, whether such effects are lasting and alter long-term academic outcomes.

Another important area for future research will be the identification of individual viewer characteristics (other than age) that moderate learning from media. Fisch's capacity model (see Fisch et al., 2005) posits several characteristics that will help children to comprehend both narrative and educational content, including their familiarity with narrative structure in general and the media content in particular, their prior knowledge of the educational content, and their cognitive abilities. A few studies have provided empirical support for this aspect of the capacity model as it relates to television. However, such research is limited and has yet to be conducted with educational games and mobile applications. Thus, researchers still know relatively little about the types of experiences and abilities that help individuals learn from different types of media. Such information is critical for identifying whether, how, and *for whom* media can promote learning.

There has also been renewed interest in examining the impact of context on learning from media. Such investigations consider not only how to create media for learning, but also how to capitalize on the social context of media use (e.g., interactions with co-viewers) to help support that learning (Kirkorian & Anderson, 2015). For instance, adult mediation can help young children comprehend both narrative and educational content. Similarly, young children are more likely to transfer learning from screens to real-life scenarios if adults draw connections between media content and the child's own experiences.

SEE ALSO: Digital Media in Higher Education; Educational Media, History; Media Use in the Science Classroom; Preschool Children and Media; Teaching about Media Violence; Teaching with Media; Video Games as Education

References

Anderson, D.R., & Hanson, K.G. (2010). From blooming, buzzing confusion to media literacy: The early development of television viewing. *Developmental Review, 30*, 239–255.

Anderson, D.R., & Kirkorian, H.L. (2015). Media and cognitive development. In R.M. Lerner, L.S. Liben, & U. Mueller (Eds.), *Handbook of child psychology and developmental science* (7th ed.). Hoboken, NJ: Wiley.

Clark, R.E. (2012). *Learning from media: Arguments, analysis, and evidence* (2nd ed.). Charlotte, NC: Information Age Publishing.

Fisch, S.M., Kirkorian, H.L., & Anderson, D.R. (2005). Transfer of learning in informal education: The case of television. In J.P. Mestre (Ed.), *Transfer of learning from a modern multidisciplinary perspective* (pp. 371–393). Greenwich, CT: Information Age Publishing.

Kirkorian, H.L., Pempek, T.A., & Choi, K. (2017). The role of online processing in young children's ability to learn from interactive and non-interactive media. In R. Barr & D. Linebarger (Eds.), *Media exposure during infancy and early childhood: The effect of content and context on learning and development*. New York, NY: Springer.

Mares, M.L., & Pan, Z. (2013). Effects of *Sesame Street*: A meta-analysis of children's learning in 15 countries. *Journal of Applied Developmental Psychology, 34*, 140–151. doi: 10.1016/j.appdev.2013.01.001.

Mayer, R.E. (2001). Cognitive theory of multimedia learning. In R.E. Mayer (Ed.), *Multimedia learning*. New York, NY: Cambridge University Press.

Shuler, C., Levine, Z., & Ree, J. (2012). *iLearn II: An analysis of the educational category of Apple's app store*. Joan Ganz Cooney Center. Retrieved from www.joanganzcooneycenter.org

Strommen, E. (1993). Preschoolers: A cognitive model of device difficulty. In M.R. Simonson & K. Abu-Omar (Eds.), *Proceedings of the 15th Annual Selected Research and Development Presentations, AECT '93, New Orleans, LA*. Washington, DC: Association for Educational Communications and Technology.

Wartella, E., & Robb, M. (2008). Historical and recurring concerns about children's use of the mass media. In S.L. Calvert & B.J. Wilson (Eds.), *The Blackwell handbook of children, media, and development* (pp. 319–360). Boston, MA: Blackwell.

Further reading

Barr, R., & Linebarger, D. (2016). *Media exposure during infancy and early childhood: The effect of content and context on learning and development*. New York, NY: Springer.

Fisch, S.M., & Truglio, R.T. (2001). *G is for growing: Thirty years of research on children and Sesame Street*. Mahwah, NJ: Erlbaum.

Gee, J. (2007). *What videogames have to teach us about learning and literacy* (2nd ed.). New York, NY: Palgrave Macmillan.

Kirkorian, H.L., Wartella, E., & Anderson, D.R. (2008). Media and young children's learning. *Future of Children, 18*, 63–86.

Mayer, R.E. (2001). *Multimedia learning*. New York, NY: Cambridge University Press.

Heather L. Kirkorian is Associate Professor of Human Development and Family Studies at the University of Wisconsin-Madison. Her research addresses (i) how young children process screen media, (ii) how young children learn from different sources of information, and (iii) the impact of screen media on play and parent–child interactions. She has published in top journals in developmental psychology including *Psychological Science, Child Development,* and *Developmental Psychology.*

Literacy, Technology, and Media

MARIA RANIERI
University of Florence, Italy

From literacy to literacies

Since the second half of the last century, the debate on the concept of literacy has developed around two main lines, one defining literacy as a set of cognitive abilities, including reading and writing, the other as a socially situated practice (Cappello, 2017). According to the first perspective, the development of reading and writing skills has significant implications both on the individual level, with the emergence of new forms of thought such as analytical thinking, and on a socioeconomic, political, and cultural level (Goody & Watt, 1963; Ong, 1982), to the point that the transition from oral to written culture has been referred to as the "big gap" (Scribner & Cole, 1981). However, at the end of the 1970s, this model of literacy entered a crisis and a new vision emerged, solicited by new literacies studies (NLS): in this view, far from being an independent neutral psychological skill, literacy is seen as a situated practice, that is as a practice incorporated in the specific contextual conditions in which it is defined, institutionalized, and practiced (Street, 2003). NLS advocates, in fact, consider literacy as a repertoire of changing practices for intentionally communicating in a variety of social and cultural contexts.

Practices are seen as constructions of particular social groups rather than as individual cognitive capacity: for example, one of the first studies carried out in the wake of this tradition was the ethnographic study of Street (1984), who investigated the way in which commercial discourses were developed within an Iranian community to conclude that literacy practices gain meaning mainly through their rooting in specific cultural values and orientations. Parallel to the emergence of this new vision of literacy, a revival of Vygotsky's work (1962) occurred in the same years. As is well known, Vygotsky attributed an essential function to language in the interaction with the social and material environment, and this view has been clearly recognisable, from the late 1980s, in socioconstructivist theories of learning such as situated cognition (Brown, Collins, & Duguid, 1989), communities of practice (Lave & Wenger, 1991), and NLS (Street, 2003).

Moving toward the end of the 1990s and the early 2000s, the most significant change in this area was certainly what Mills (2010) defined as the "digital turn," that is, the greater attention paid to the new literacy practices taking shape in digital environments in a variety of social contexts, such as workplaces and training, economics, and leisure. The digital turn is a consequence of globalization and the growing variety of technologies available today to circulate information and support communication. Research in the field of NLS has obviously reflected this shift of emphasis from the study of paper-based reading and writing practices to the analysis of new textual practices mediated by digital technologies. Particular attention has been paid to the innovative and productive potential of literacy practices implemented in digital environments by children and adolescents both outside and inside schools (Gee, 2003; Lankshear & Knobel, 2003; Sefton-Green, 2007; Street, 2003).

The emergence of new digital textualities through wikis, blogs, databases, and online news requires new text comprehension skills along with new capacities for producing, processing, and transmitting electronic texts. This new extension of the concept of literacy has led the same NLS proponents to wonder about how to circumscribe this notion in a continuously changing communication environment. This difficulty is not just about NLS. A call for reconceptualizing the notion of literacy for the new era was also launched in the 1990s by the New London Group (1996) who coined the expression "multiliteracies" to address two main issues: on the one hand, the need to develop a new pedagogy of literacy to face the multiplicity of contemporary forms of communication, which require the ability to understand multimodal texts (Kress, 2000); on the other hand, the need to promote a pedagogy of literacy to respond to the cultural and linguistic diversity that is now permeating our societies as a consequence of globalization (New London Group, 1996).

The theorists of NLS, multiliteracies, and multimodal semiotics (Jewitt & Kress, 2003) have argued that traditional views of reading and writing are no longer adequate to describe literacy practices that develop in today's society, where new multimodal textualities are practiced. Therefore, extending the concept of literacy to include non-paper-based reading and writing practices does not entail any imprecision: on the contrary, it is a justified attempt not to exclude literacy practices transformed by the growing diffusion of digital technologies for communication.

Briefly, from the 1970s onwards we have witnessed a twofold expansion of the concept of literacy, the first in a sociocultural sense aimed at interpreting literacy no longer, or not only, as individual cognitive ability, but as a social practice; the second in the media-digital sense, aimed at including in literacy not only the textual production practices related to paper but also those produced under the form of multimodal texts. This expansion does not involve replacing traditional, "paper" literacy, but as Hobbs explains (2010, p. 16), recognizing that "because today people use so many different types of expression and communication in daily life, the concept of literacy is beginning to be defined as the ability to share meaning through symbol systems in order to fully participate in society." The following text specifically focuses on the concepts of media and digital literacy, in order to deepen the assumptions and implications of the "digital turn" for current reflection on literacy.

Media literacy for critical understanding and citizenship

The expression "media literacy" began to circulate in the 20th century, especially in the United States where curricula on television literacy were implemented in schools. Until recently, the use of this formula was rare in Europe, Canada, or Australia, where alternative labels like "media education" or "*éducation aux médias*" were preferred. Currently the term media literacy has largely been adopted in the European lexicon, as evidenced by several sources such as institutional documents, conferences, scientific publications, and so on. According to Buckingham (2003), media literacy is the result of media education which is defined as the teaching and learning process through which the ability to "read" and "write" the media and make active and aware use of it is promoted. That said, despite the good will of researchers to define terms and concepts, looking at the documentation available on this construct, we can note that media literacy refers to a broad and varied semantic universe and, at the same time, different formulas are used as equivalent to it. Moreover, there is no internationally agreed definition of media literacy: the concepts related to media literacy appear to be unstable and expanding.

Nevertheless, there is a certain consensus on defining media literacy according to the following four categories: access, analysis, evaluation, and communication and creative production (Celot & Tornero, 2008).

- *Access*: this concerns the ability to use the media, including both the material access and the immaterial one, meant as the cognitive ability to adequately use them. Specifically, in terms of abilities it refers to a set of skills ranging from the basic skill to read and write the media to the ability to use research and consultation tools. The conditions for access, encompassing the material and immaterial component, are not the same for all people, but rely on factors such as age, geographical context, sociocultural background, and so on.
- *Analysis*: this refers to the ability to read and understand media content and opportunities. Reading the media entails being able to decode a message in relation to a specific communicative situation, while understanding the media means being able to relate a meaning to a concrete context. The analysis involves a deep understanding of the messages and requires knowledge of appropriate concepts and categories (taken from semiotics), the use of logical links (before/after, cause/effect), the ability to determine the genre of a text, the point of view and the socioeconomic interests that it expresses, the intention of the author, the esthetic principles and its poetics, and the contextualization of the text in the historical-cultural environment in which it was produced.
- *Evaluation*: this consists of the ability to classify media content and opportunities; it also includes judgments on the value that a message has for each reader, also in terms of meaning; it entails the ability to identify the ethical, esthetic, and cultural values underlying a certain message and the comparison between these and the set of values of the evaluating subject. Various subdimensions are included in the analysis and evaluation area, among which is the individual's ability to search and select information and to evaluate it considering its reliability, credibility, and truthfulness. This is the area of critical thinking, an area of major interest for media literacy. Being able to evaluate and appropriately use different sources is of crucial importance, including verifying their reliability and value, contextualizing them according to the context where they were produced, highlighting their ideological dimensions, and evaluating their structure and coherence.
- *Communication and creative production*: this includes the skills that are necessary to create and produce messages, using a variety of expressive codes (from written to audiovisual or digital codes), and to disseminate them. Other skills related to this area are: understanding the characteristics of the audience to whom the message is addressed and being able to adapt the message to the audience in order to capture and maintain the attention; being able to organize a sequence of ideas in an effective and attractive discourse storyline. This area is further enriched

by the 20th-century theoretical reflection on the notion of communication and its ethical-political implications. Specifically, Habermas stressed the pragmatic nature of the communication capacity, pointing out that it represents the necessary universal component that allows people to interact according to shared rules. As such, this skill allows citizens to be active and participate in the public sphere, and therefore must be equally distributed.

To sum up, the development of media literacy skills involves a process which can be depicted in three main phases. At a first level, the material and cognitive access to the media prevails as a necessary, still not sufficient, condition for media literacy. At a second level, a media-literate citizen must be able to critically and deeply understand the mechanisms that govern the media landscape, and this requires a commitment to the analysis and evaluation of media content and contexts as well as their opportunities and limitations. Finally, as a last step we find the productive-creative component: the new digital media have enormously increased the opportunities for creating and producing messages, but there is no deterministic relationship between media diffusion and increase in creative production and active participation. Media education should promote learning opportunities aimed at encouraging both the development of critical understanding for the building up of an aware public and the active participation of citizens in the new digital landscapes.

What's new about digital literacy

The expression "digital literacy" or "digital competence," according to the lexicon of the European Union, which most likely adopted the term "competence" rather than "literacy" for the difficulty of translating the word "literacy" in neo-Latin languages, is more recent than the term media literacy, although the cultural origins of digital literacy can be traced back to concepts that have emerged since the 1960s. Digital literacy was first used by Gilster (1997), who, in the context of a broader reflection on the potential of the Internet for our societies, defined this competence as "the ability to understand and use information in multiple formats from a wide variety of sources when it is presented via computers" (p. 1). This definition emphasizes critical thinking skills and information assessment rather than technical skills. Ten years later, the definitions have multiplied and, although there is no univocal definition of this literacy, all researchers agree that other literacies related to ICT (information and communication technologies) converge in this concept and are more generally related to the media (Tornero, 2004; Martin, 2005), including media literacy, computer literacy, and information literacy. Computer literacy and information literacy have had a certain fortune since the 1960s, and over time their meaning has also evolved, especially that of computer literacy. In fact, if the early definitions of computer literacy mainly included technical-procedural skills, from the 1990s onwards the emphasis has gradually shifted to cognitive aspects. For example, in the definition of the Educational Testing Service (ETS, 2002) the reflective nature of ICT literacy is highly underlined: "ICT literacy cannot be defined primarily as the mastery of technical skills. […] the concept of ICT literacy should be broadened to include both critical cognitive skills as well as the application of technical skills and knowledge. These cognitive skills include general literacy, such as reading and numeracy, as well as critical thinking and problem solving" (p. 1). As far as information literacy is concerned, it dates back to the 1970s and is defined as the set of skills necessary for individuals to recognize their information needs and to locate, evaluate, and effectively use information (Association of College and Research Libraries, 2000). Again, the critical, cognitive, and evaluative dimensions are stressed.

Focusing on digital literacy, some authors point out that it is the result of a stratified and complex combination of skills, abilities, and knowledge. With this in mind, Tornero stated (2004, p. 31): "Digital literacy merges capacities: purely technical aspects, intellectual competences and also competences related to responsible citizenship. They all allow an individual to develop him or herself completely in the information society." Martin (2005, pp. 135–136) also defined digital competence as "the awareness, attitude and ability of individuals to appropriately use digital tools and facilities to identify, access, manage, integrate, evaluate, analyse and synthesise digital resources, construct new knowledge, create media expressions, and communicate with others, in the context of specific life situations, in order to enable constructive social action; and to reflect upon this process." Another interesting model is the holistic framework provided by Eshet-Alkalai (2004), who identified different literacies taking into account the historical evolution of technologies and their impact on the progressive reformulation of the concept of literacy. Stressing how digital literacy is not to be understood as the pure ability to physically use a computer program, he pointed out that digital literacy is characterized by five types of literacies, namely: the ability to read instructions from graphical interfaces (photovisual literacy), the ability to use digital reproduction to create new and creative products (reproduction literacy), the cognitive flexibility necessary to build nonlinear hypertextual knowledge (branching literacy), the ability to critically evaluate the quality of digital information (information literacy), and the ability to understand the rules which regulate the sociorelational connections innervating cyberspace (socioemotional literacy).

Another important definition was provided by the European Union (2006): digital competence includes the ability to critically use ICT for work, leisure, and communication. It involves a good knowledge of the nature, the role, and the opportunities that ICT offer in everyday life, private, social, and working spheres, and in particular the potential of the Internet for the exchange of information and online collaboration, learning, and research. The EU definition also emphasizes that the use of ICT requires a critical and reflective attitude, that is, an attention to problems related to the validity and reliability of information and an interest in engaging in communities and networks for cultural, social, and/or professional purposes.

Other authors, moving from the theoretical perspectives of media education, shifted the emphasis to the critical understanding of the media and their social, economic, and cultural implications (Buckingham, 2007; Pietrass, 2007). Buckingham (2007), for example, suggested defining digital literacy in relation to the four main dimensions of media analysis, referring to representation, language, production, and audience. Still from the media education perspective, Hobbs (2010, p. 17) talked about media and digital literacy, defining it as "the full range of cognitive, emotional and social competencies that include the use of texts, tools and technologies; the skills of critical thinking and analysis; the practice of message composition and creativity; the ability to engage in reflection and ethical thinking; as well as active participation through teamwork and collaboration."

Considering this variety of perspectives and the necessarily stratified nature of the construct, Calvani, Ranieri, and Fini (2009) proposed defining digital competence as the ability to explore and deal with new technological situations in a flexible way, analyze and critically evaluate information, and use the potential of technologies for the representation of and solution to problems and for the shared and collaborative construction of knowledge, keeping an awareness of personal responsibilities in the relation with the other through mutual rights/duties.

More recently, the JRC-IPTS (European Commission–Joint Research Centre–Institute for Prospective Technological Studies) research center has developed DIGCOMP, a framework for digital competence which is based on the main dimensions evoked in the Recommendations of the European Union (2006), while integrating them with contributions offered by various scholars in the field (Ferrari, 2013). The model describes digital competences in terms of knowledge, skills, and attitudes, paying attention to citizens' needs in the information society, namely: the need to be informed, to interact, to express themselves, to feel safe, and to be able to manage problem situations related to technological tools and digital environments.

DIGCOMP identifies 21 skills related to five main areas.

- Area 1: information literacy. This area covers all the knowledge and skills related to the search, selection, evaluation, storage, and retrieval of information.
- Area 2: communication and collaboration. This area is about the ability to interact responsibly with technologies, to share content, and to collaborate with others.
- Area 3: creation of digital content. This area is about the ability to create, modify, and recombine digital content creatively and in compliance with copyright.
- Area 4: security. This area covers all the knowledge and skills necessary to secure their devices and to protect their personal data, their physical and psychological well-being, and the environment.
- Area 5: problem-solving. This area covers the skills useful to face technological problems, identify innovative solutions with technologies, and update their digital skills.

Later versions of the DIGCOMP framework reflect the evolution of the ICT world, particularly referring to mobile technologies, and open the door to the concept of data literacy (included in area 1), a new component that is gradually gaining prominence with the explosion of Big Data.

Media literacy and digital literacy: differentiating elements and converging areas

So far, we have concentrated on the new forms of literacies solicited by the development of media and digital technologies. But what are the relationships existing between these various forms of literacy? For example, should we consider digital literacy an evolution of media literacy, or are these different areas? These questions are highly relevant insofar as we are dealing with skills and contents potentially or desirably linked to the school curriculum. Greater clarity on these issues should lead to better planning and evaluation of teaching and learning practices of media and digital literacy.

The authors who come from media education generally tend to highlight how the concept of media literacy is conceptually broader than that of digital literacy and to identify the latter with more markedly technical-informatics skills. Celot and Tornero (2008), for example, distinguish four main stages in the history of literacy, including digital literacy in the broader field of media education:

- traditional literacy that deals with reading and writing: it is the first and most ancient form of literacy that we have known and that saw primary school play an essential role in the process of promoting reading and writing skills;
- audiovisual literacy, typical of electronic media (cinema and television): it has developed with particular attention to the analysis of images; it has produced some changes in educational policies, but has never translated into formal policy formulations;
- digital literacy, linked to the development of new digital media: it is a rather recent concept, prompted by the appearance of new technologies and the need to train useful skills to better use them; it is usually used to indicate mastery of the technical skills necessary to use new digital tools;
- media education: solicited by media convergence, including both electronic media for mass communication and digital media characterized by multimedia communication, it represents the advanced stage of development of the information and knowledge society and entails the mastery of previous literacies.

In this perspective, media literacy belongs to the final stage of literacy processes and requires, by including them, the previous literacies. Digital literacy is identified in particular with the technical component. Buckingham (2007) also claims a similar position and assimilates digital literacy to computer literacy, which is as a set of skills allowing users to effectively use computer programs or perform basic information search operations. After all, the main contexts in which digital literacy has been discussed in Europe have been those of the assessment of "ICT skills" at school with the ECDL (European Computer Driving Licence) and those of online security. However, as previously shown, recent studies tend to distance themselves from the approaches to digital literacy that emphasize only procedural aspects, and above all they highlight the critical-reflective components: in these perspectives, promoting digital competence means fostering individuals' metacognitive skills related to the use of the media in terms of their technological potential, their use as a source of information and knowledge, and their ethical and social implications. In other words, even the concept of digital literacy has gradually been enriched with critical, cultural, ethical, and cognitive values. At the same time, it is legitimate to ask whether this multiplication of literacy makes sense, whether it is really necessary to speak of different literacies, especially in the light of convergence (Buckingham, 2007). In fact, ICT should be seen as media: the media increasingly combine different modes of communication and operate through multiple technological platforms. For this reason, it seems senseless to distinguish so many literacies. So, what can we conclude on this variety of literacies related to media and digital technologies? It would certainly be hasty to draw conclusions; however, it is possible to identify some differentiating elements and converging areas between media and digital literacy as discussed below.

Differentiating elements

- *Cultural origins*: media and digital literacy have different cultural backgrounds, with media literacy coming from semiotics, cultural studies, and critical theory, and digital literacy coming from computer literacy and research privileging the instrumental value of technologies. This diversity obviously influences the way in which these concepts are represented with relevant implications: for example, the tendency to identify digital literacy with technical and procedural skills remains dominant, and this contributes to creating barriers that make it difficult to find common ground, which is particularly important when coming to the need for introducing these literacies into the school curricula.
- *Optimism versus caution*: generally speaking, a generous, warm, and optimistic attitude prevails in those scholars or supporters of computers and new media in education: the term "digital" sounds like something positive and powerful, creative and revolutionary. On the contrary, in the tradition of media education, a substantial distrust toward the media, together with a greater emphasis on the critical component, prevails, although attenuated when compared to the past. In this context, "digital" is not necessarily a synonym of "good" or "inclusive" or "participatory" or "creative" and so on. The "digital," no less than the "analogical," is not neutral/natural and as such it requires to be analyzed critically.

Converging areas

- *Access*: a first converging area between media and digital literacy can be identified in the attention paid to access. Indeed, in both cases, as a first step, the accent is on being technically equipped and having adequate skills to use the technical tools. However, the procedural components should be deemphasized to shift the focus to more advanced aspects linked to the ability to engage with technological problem-solving or to understand the mechanisms which regulate how technologies work, taking into account that they are not neutral. This could be assimilated to a form of "metatechnological" or even "metadigital" awareness.
- *Critical understanding*: a second possible converging area between media and digital literacy could be identified at the critical and metacognitive level. Although optimistic attitudes toward everything digital dominate, research on digital literacy underscores the ability to understand and evaluate information meaning, reliability, and relevance as a key element of digital literacy. It is a crucial issue on which media

and digital literacy can find fertile areas of intersection, influencing and enriching each other.

Areas of mutual integration

- *Categories of analysis*: over time, media education has developed a rich repertoire of techniques for the analysis of media contents, texts, and contexts, as well as of the different forms of fruition and consumption. For example, the four categories of Production, Representation, Language, and Audience, proposed by Buckingham (2003) for media analysis, entail questions that can also be used to analyze and critically evaluate online information and content. Therefore, it is a question, on the one hand, of renewing this repertoire considering the evolution of media themselves and, on the other hand, of recovering the critical instances and dimensions incorporated by these analytical tools.
- *Topics and issues*: although we must be careful not to fall into today's traps of bewitching discourses around the potential of new digital technologies, it is true that the Internet is a more open and interactive information and communication system than traditional media like radio and television, and therefore it is potentially more suited to favoring and supporting forms of social participation. At the same time, this potential has also highlighted its limitations in terms of unequal distribution of digital media. Studies on the digital divide have shown how inequalities are reinforced rather than mitigated by the diffusion of digital technologies, and this is a major challenge for contemporary societies. The debate around digital literacy, since its very beginning, has also led scholars and policymakers to reflect on issues related to media and social inclusion, media and participation. A contamination on these themes seems to be not only desirable but also fertile for the developments of media literacy.
- *Contexts for intervention*: the school has always been a privileged field of intervention for media literacy. The current reflection on digital literacy pushes us to consider other contexts and to look at the processes of literacy in terms of lifelong learning. For example, the European Union evokes "digital competence" in the context of lifelong learning skills, namely those skills necessary for continuous training and not just for compulsory education. From this point of view, this sounds like an important reminder to promote media and digital literacy also in settings that are not exclusively linked to the school.
- *Theory and practice*: as pointed out above, digital media offer increased opportunities for media production. In this respect, digital environments and digital literacy can provide opportunities to reinforce the dialectic between theory and practice, reflexive analysis and creative production, thought and action, which is so important for learning. To some extent, these unprecedented opportunities for media production may help in overcoming the traditional critique of media education as being too concentrated on abstract concepts, thus recovering creativity as a tool for critical analysis and thinking.

SEE ALSO: Access; Digital Literacy; European Perspectives on Media Literacy; History of Media Literacy

References

Association of College and Research Libraries. (2000). *Information literacy competency standards for higher education*. Chicago: IL: American Library Association.

Brown, A., Collins, J., & Duguid, P. (1989). Situated cognition and the culture of learning. *Educational Researcher, 18*(1), 32–42. doi: 10.3102/0013189X018001032

Buckingham, D. (2003). *Media education: Literacy, learning and contemporary culture*. London, England: Polity Press/Blackwell.

Buckingham, D. (2007). Digital media literacies: Rethinking media education in the age of the Internet. *Research in Comparative and International Education, 2*(1), 43–55. doi: 10.2304/rcie.2007.2.1.43

Calvani, A., Ranieri, M., & Fini A. (2009). Assessing digital competence in secondary education – issues, models and instruments. In M. Leaning (Ed.), *Issues in information and media literacy: Education, practice and pedagogy* (pp. 153–172). Santa Rosa, CA: Informing Science Press.

Cappello, G. (2017). Literacy, media literacy and social change. Where do we go from now? *Italian Journal of Sociology of Education, 9*(1), 31–44. doi: 10.14658/pupj-ijse-2017-1-3

Celot, P., & Tornero, J.M.P. (2008). *Media literacy in Europa. Leggere, scrivere e partecipare nell'era mediatica*. Roma, Italy: Eurilink, Eurispes.

Educational Testing Service. (2002). *Digital transformation: A framework for ICT literacy*. Princeton, NJ: Educational Testing Service. Retrieved from https://www.ets.org/Media/Tests/Information_and_Communication_Technology_Literacy/ictreport.pdf

Eshet-Alkalai, Y. (2004). Digital literacy: A conceptual framework for survival skills in the digital era. *Journal of Educational Multimedia and Hypermedia, 13*(1), 93–106. Retrieved from https://www.openu.ac.il/personal_sites/download/Digital-literacy2004-JEMH.pdf

European Union. (2006). Recommendation of the European Parliament and the Council of 18 December 2006 on key competences for lifelong learning. *Official Journal of the European Union* (2006/962/EC), L394/10–18.

Ferrari, A. (2013). *DIGCOMP: A framework for developing and understanding digital competence in Europe*. Seville, Spain: European Commission–Joint Research Centre–Institute for Prospective Technological Studies. Retrieved from http://publications.jrc.ec.europa.eu/repository/bitstream/JRC83167/lb-na-26035-enn.pdf

Gee, J. (2003). *What video games have to teach us about learning and literacy*. New York, NY: Palgrave Macmillan.

Gilster, P. (1997). *Digital literacy*. New York, NY: John Wiley & Sons, Inc.

Goody, J., & Watt, I. (1963). The consequences of literacy. *Comparative Studies in Society and History, 5*(3), 304–345. doi: 10.1017/S0010417500001730

Hobbs, R. (2010). *Digital and media literacy: A plan of action*. Knight Commission on the Information Needs of Communities in a Democracy. Washington, DC: Aspen Institute.

Jewitt, C., & Kress, G. (2003). *Multimodal literacy*. New York, NY: Peter Lang.

Kress, G. (2000). Multimodality. In B. Cope & M. Kalantzis (Eds.), *Multiliteracies: Literacy learning and the design of social futures* (pp. 182–202). South Yarra, Australia: Macmillan.

Lankshear, C., & Knobel, M. (2003). *New literacies: Changing knowledge and classroom learning*. Philadelphia, PA: Open University Press.

Lave, J., & Wenger, E. (Eds.). (1991). *Situated learning: Legitimate peripheral participation*. Cambridge, England: Cambridge University Press.

Martin, A. (2005). DigEuLit – a European framework for digital literacy: A progress report. *Journal of eLiteracy, 2*, 130–136. Retrieved from http://citeseerx.ist.psu.edu/viewdoc/download?doi=10.1.1.469.1923&rep=rep1&type=pdf

Mills, K.A. (2010). A review of the "digital turn" in the new literacy studies. *Review of Educational Research, 80*(2), 246–271. doi: 10.3102/0034654310364401

New London Group. (1996). A pedagogy of multiliteracies: Designing social futures. *Harvard Educational Review, 66*(1), 60–92. doi: 10.17763/haer.66.1.17370n67v22j160u

Ong, W.J. (1982). *Orality and literacy: The technologizing of the word.* New York, NY: Routledge.

Pietrass, M. (2007). Digital literacy research from an international and comparative point of view. *Research in Comparative and International Education, 2*(1), 1–12. doi: 10.2304/rcie.2007.2.1.1

Scribner, S., & Cole, M. (1981). *The psychology of literacy.* Cambridge, MA: Harvard University Press.

Sefton-Green, J. (2007). *Literature review of informal learning with technology outside school.* Bristol, England: Futurelab.

Street, B. (1984). *Literacy in theory and practice.* Cambridge, England: Cambridge University Press.

Street, B. (2003). What's "new" in the new literacy studies? Critical approaches to literacy in theory and practice. *Current Issues in Comparative Education, 5*(2), 77–91. Retrieved from https://www.tc.columbia.edu/cice/pdf/25734_5_2_Street.pdf

Tornero, J.M.P. (2004). *Promoting digital literacy.* Final Report EAC/76/03. Retrieved from http://www.gabinetecomunicacionyeducacion.com/sites/default/files/field/adjuntos/comprender_dl.pdf

Vygotsky, L. (1962). *Thought and language.* Cambridge, MA: MIT Press.

Further reading

Calvani, A., Fini, A., Ranieri, M., & Picci, P. (2012). Are young generations in secondary school digitally competent? A study on Italian teenagers. *Computers & Education, 58*(2), 797–807. doi: 10.1016/j.compedu.2011.10.004

Cope, B., & Kalantzis, M. (2000). *Multiliteracies: Literacy learning and the design of social futures.* South Yarra, Australia: Macmillan.

Gee, J. (1996). *Social linguistics and literacies: Ideology in discourses* (2nd ed.). New York, NY: Routledge and Falmer.

Jenkins, H., Clinton, K., Purushotma, R., Robison, A.J., & Weigel, M. (2006). *Confronting the challenges of participatory culture: Media education for the 21st century.* Chicago, IL: The John D. and Catherine T. MacArthur Foundation. Retrieved from https://www.macfound.org/media/article_pdfs/JENKINS_WHITE_PAPER.PDF

Jewitt, C., & Kress, G. (2003). *Multimodal literacy.* New York, NY: Peter Lang.

Knobel, M., & Lankshear, C. (2009). Remix: The art and craft of endless hybridization. *Journal of Adolescent & Adult Literacy, 52*(1), 22–33. doi: 10.1598/JAAL.52.1.3

Lankshear, C., & Knobel, M. (2003). *New literacies: Changing knowledge and classroom learning.* Philadelphia, PA: Open University Press.

Maria Ranieri is an associate professor of educational methods and technology at the University of Florence, Italy. Her main research areas include theory and methodology relating to media and technology in education. She has also worked on educational practices aimed at tackling different forms of intolerance, especially online hate speech and digital discrimination, through the promotion of critical media literacy skills. On these topics she has published several books and articles and coordinated European projects.

Local Public Access Centers

ISABELLA REGA
Bournemouth University, UK

Definitions and typologies

Local public access centers, often referred to as telecenters, are public venues used to access information and communication services and resources through (digital) technologies. They are set up to contribute to digital inclusion and to support citizens and local communities in acquiring information and digital literacy skills. This type of initiative has taken different forms in different parts of the globe. In the Global North, public libraries usually embrace the role of promoting digital inclusion and digital and information literacies among the local public. In the Global South, this role has been taken up by venues, often created on an ad hoc basis, to address the information and communication needs of disadvantaged communities and with an emphasis on development-related activities in domains such as health, education, and agriculture. Local public access centers in the Global South are labeled differently according to their geographical location and the initiative or institutions which set them up; alternative names for telecenters are community technology centers, community communication centers, and eCenters (Gomez & Camacho, 2011). It is important to notice that while telecenters are often standalone facilities, they can also be placed in existing locations, such as public libraries, schools, or community centers. Some authors argue that cybercafés, operating for-profit initiatives and open for the public to access usually a computer with an Internet connection for a fee, also fall within the local public access places definition (Gomez & Camacho, 2011). Nevertheless, this last kind of local public access center is not taken into consideration in this encyclopedia entry, which will focus on initiatives funded and set up by public organizations (e.g., national and local government) or a third sector organization (e.g., international organizations and nonprofit-making entities), each of which have an explicit aim to foster socioeconomic development through digital inclusion.

Several authors have suggested classifications of local public access centers based on criteria such as location, size, services offered, and hosting organizations (Roman & Colle, 2002; Townsend, Espitia, Jorge, & Lee, 2001). From the different typologies and definitions presented in the literature, there are few recurring pillars: the goal of local public access centers is to provide universal access to information and communication technologies (ICTs), to be community-oriented (vs. business-oriented), and to aim at supporting the socioeconomic development of the served community via a variety of services. These services range from basic training on computers and the internet to more sophisticated services such as information and education services related to matters of interest for the local community and community-based services such as library or meeting place facilities (Colle & Roman, 2001; Rega, 2010).

History and stakeholders

According to (Molnár & Karvalics, 2002), the first community technical center was opened in Harlem, USA, in 1983, with the primary aim of bridging the growing digital divide between social classes; these centers offered free access to technologies and placed great emphasis on teaching digital skills. Another pivotal initiative, aiming at giving access to ICT to two entire communities, can be traced back to 1985 in the villages of Vemdalen and Harjedalen in Sweden (Molnár & Karvalics, 2002; Parkinson, 2005; Short, 2001).

Molnár and Karvalics (2002) distinguish between two telecenter models in Europe, the Scandinavian model with a specific social and developmental aim and the more profit-oriented Anglo-Saxon model having emphasis on production and employment. Telecenters of both types were soon imitated by the governments of Canada, Australia, Great Britain, and Hungary. The adoption of the Scandinavian model aimed to give disadvantaged communities new educational and economic opportunities through ICT. For example, the Western Australia Telecenter Network (Short, 2001) aimed to give rural communities access to higher education and the Telework, Telecottage, and Telecenter Association aimed to meet the employment needs of rural and economically disadvantaged communities in Britain (Latchem & Walker, 2001). By 1994, there were more than 230 telecenters in Australia, Austria, Canada, Denmark, Finland, Germany, Ireland, Japan, Norway, Sweden, the UK, and the USA, according to Latchem & Walker (2001). In the 1990s, international organizations led the nonprofit organizations in beginning to adopt the Scandinavian model also in developing countries. In the early 2000s, authors started to refer to this development as the so-called incubation phase of the telecenter movement around the world (Rega, 2010). In the Global North, ad hoc local public access places gradually joined public libraries in embracing the mission of spreading digital and information literacies. Nevertheless, a powerful network of digital competence centers still existed in Europe, gathering 25 000 local public access centers, aimed at supporting Europeans lacking digital skills (all-digital.org). In the Global South, the telecenter model prospered through UNESCO (United Nations Educational, Scientific, and Cultural Organization), the ITU (International Communication Union), the USAID (United States Agency for International Development), the IDRC (International Development Research Center), and the FAO (Food and Agriculture Organization) being the main international funders of pivotal initiatives and programs. In the early 2000s, governments, often supported by private sector foundations and multinational companies and nonprofit-making organizations, joined the telecenter movement, and enabled local public access centers in urban and rural disadvantaged communities to bloom. In the first decade of the 21st century, telecenter networks operating in different continents, such as Somos@Telecentros and the Asia-Pacific Telecenter Network, started to be formed and, in 2005, IDRC, Microsoft Corporation, and the Swiss Agency for Development and Cooperation funded telecenter.org, a global initiative that brought together most telecenters, regional and national networks, and hundreds of non-networked telecenters around the globe, with more than 550 000 affiliated centers.

There are a few recurrent elements in the history of public access places, both in the Global North and in the Global South. These include the importance of *developing content and services pertinent and tailored to local needs*, the importance of having *staff trained periodically* and able to work as *infomediaries within the community*, and a structure *networked with other local public access places*. Furthermore, one matter mainly concerns public access places in the Global South, which is sustainability, a crucial issue in countries where public policies concerning public centers, such as libraries or community centers, struggle to reach underserved and rural communities.

Sustainability

Local public access places around the world are struggling to survive and academics and practitioners have been debating over the last 15 years how telecenters can achieve sustainability. If we consider sustainability as a mere financial issue, there are two main schools of thought. The first claims a telecenter should find a way to be financially independent and self-supporting as a business (Fuchs, 1998; Townsend et al., 2001), whereas the other claims a telecenter should be considered in the same way as other public information services (e.g., libraries) and sustained by local and national authorities (Dagron, 2001). More recently, researchers have tended to consider sustainability as more complex and multidimensional, including social, political, and technological dimensions (Ali & Bailur, 2007; Bailey, 2009; Kumar, 2004).

Figure 1 summarizes the most salient factors contributing to sustainability (Best & Kumar, 2008; Colle & Roman, 2001; Etta & Parvyn-Wamahiu, 2003; Roman & Colle, 2002) by forming three macro categories, which are the local public access center and its internal organization, the local public access center and its local context (i.e., the local community), and the local public access center and its national or international context (Rega, 2010).

The case for community multimedia centers

A particularly relevant initiative in the field of media literacy is the case of UNESCO Community Multimedia Centers (CMCs). UNESCO (with the support, inter alia, of SDC, Swiss Agency for Development and Cooperation) created the CMC model, which combines community radio managed by locals broadcasting in local languages and community telecenter facilities. A CMC's primary aim is to foster equitable access to information and knowledge for development, reduce the digital divide, promote social inclusion and civil participation, and promote the circulation of content that supports communities in improving their daily life conditions (Creech, 2006). The official documents for the CMC model emphasize the dimensions of information

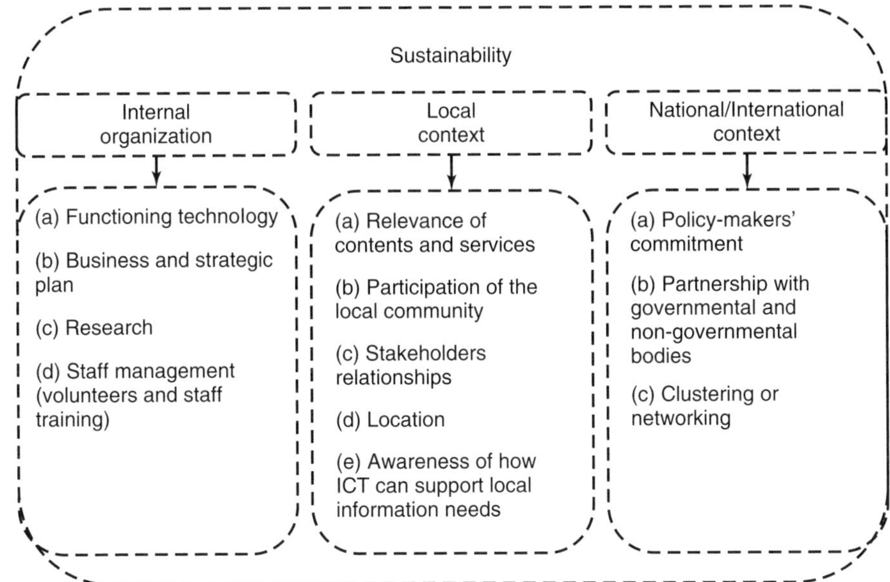

Figure 1 Sustainability factors. Source: Rega (2010).

and communication among its grounding aspects and underline how information and communication should be catalyzed and reinforced by the synergy of the two components of the radio and the telecenter (UNESCO, 2004). Through CMCs, local community members can access and use a number of different ICTs, such as computers, the Internet, digital libraries, fax and photocopy machines, and so on, and can listen to and participate in a local radio station managed by local people and broadcasting community-relevant information in native and national languages (Rega, 2010).

The program got off the ground in 2001 with 40 CMCs being set up in more than 15 countries in Africa, Asia, and the Caribbean during the pilot phase. The scale-up phase was launched at the World Summit of the Information Society of Geneva in 2003 and it began in 2004 with three countries in Africa (Mali, Mozambique, and Senegal) being selected for the development of a national network of 50 CMCs (IISD, 2006).

In 2010, the Mozambican Ministry of Science and Technology (MCT) took charge of the program, with the goal of creating one CMC in each of the 128 districts of the country in the following 5 years. This program comprised CMCs making a strategic contribution to achieving the national development and ICT goals of the country. In 2013, 43 CMCs were in place all over the country (Rega et al., 2011). Despite inconsistencies in the resources and services offered, CMCs remain the prevailing typology of local public access places in Mozambique.

The synergies with mobile technologies and the future

After initial enthusiasm in the late 1990s and early 2000s, local public access places, especially in the Global South, suffered criticism due to issues related to sustainability and a high risk of failure (Toyama, 2015). Recently, the rapid and pervasive adoption of mobile technologies has called into question the necessity of continued investment in this kind of initiative (Chigona, Lekwane, Westcott, & Chigona, 2011; Roman, 2003). Nevertheless, local public access places continue to receive considerable attention from both practitioners and academics (Gomez & Camacho, 2011) and the number of telecenters has continued to grow. Additionally, more recent studies show how they serve different needs than those met by private, mobile technologies (Bailey & Ngwenyama, 2011; Martin & Abbott, 2011; Sey et al., 2013; Unwin, 2009). Users and relevant stakeholders are shaping new ways for access (Cheng, Kao, & Ying-Chao Lin, 2004; Rega, Vannini, Raimilla, & Fauró, 2013; Vannini, Nemer, & Rega, 2017). Studies and evidence of how local public access places and mobile technologies can benefit from one another and coexist are still at an initial stage (Vannini et al., 2017) and it will be interesting to see the conclusions. Currently, one of the most promising areas of synergy concerns mobile information literacy and the relevant skills, concepts, and attitudes of people using mobiles, rather than computers, to access the internet (Clark, Coward, & Rothschild, 2017).

SEE ALSO: Access; Adolescent Literacy in a Digital World; Civic Media; Community Informatics; Community Media; Computer Labs in Primary and Secondary Education; Digital Divide; Digital Literacy; Literacy, Technology, and Media; Mediatization

References

Ali, M., & Bailur, S. (2007). The challenge of "sustainability" in ICT4D: Is bricolage the answer? In *Proceedings of the 9th International Conference on Social Implications of Computers in Developing Countries*. São Paulo, Brazil.

Bailey, A. (2009). Issues affecting the social sustainability of telecentres in developing contexts: A field study of sixteen telecentres in Jamaica. *The Electronic Journal on Information Systems in Developing Countries, 36*(4), 1–18.

Bailey, A., & Ngwenyama, O. (2011). The challenge of e-participation in the digital city: Exploring generational influences among community telecentre users. *Telematics and Informatics, 28*(3), 204–214. doi: 10.1016/j.tele.2010.09.004

Best, M.L., & Kumar, R. (2008). Sustainability failures of rural telecenters: Challenges from the sustainable access in rural India (SARI) project. *Information Technologies & International Development,* 4(4). Retrieved from http://itidjournal.org/itid/article/view/309/141

Cheng, J.M.S., Kao, L.L.Y., & Ying-Chao Lin, J. (2004). An investigation of the diffusion of online games in Taiwan and application of Rogers' diffusion of innovation theory. *Journal of American Academy of Business, 5*(1/2), 439–445.

Chigona, W., Lekwane, O., Westcott, K., & Chigona, A. (2011). Uses, benefits and challenges of public access points in the face of growth of mobile technology. *The Electronic Journal of Information Systems in Developing Countries, 49*(1), 1–14. Retrieved from doi: 10.1002/j.1681-4835.2011.tb00349.x

Clark, M., Coward, C., & Rothschild, C. (2017). *Mobile information literacy: Building digital and information literacy skills for mobile-first and mobile-centric populations through public libraries*. 2nd AfLIA Conference & 4th Africa Library Summit proceedings, 14–20 May 2017: Yaoundé, Cameroon.

Colle, R.D., & Roman, R. (2001). The telecenter environment in 2002. *The Journal of Development Communication, 12*(2), 15.

Creech, H. (2006). *Evaluation of UNESCO's community multimedia centres.* United Nations Organization for Education Science and Culture. Retrieved from http://unesdoc.unesco.org/images/0014/001456/145629e.pdf

Dagron, A.G. (2001). Prometheus riding a Cadillac? Telecentres as the promised flame of knowledge. *Journal of Development Communication, 12*(2), 803–824.

Etta, F.E., & Parvyn-Wamahiu, S. (2003). *The experience with community telecentres.* Ottawa, ON, Canada & Dakar, Senegal: International Development Research Centre (IDRC) & Council for the Development of Social Science Research in Africa. Retrieved from http://www.idrc.ca/EN/Resources/Publications/Pages/IDRCBookDetails.aspx?PublicationID=195

Fuchs, R.P. (1998). *Little engines that did.* IDRC Study/Acacia Initiative. Retrieved from http://web.idrc.ca/en/ev-10630-201-1-DO_TOPIC.html

Gomez, R., & Camacho, K. (2011). Users of ICT at public access centers: Age, education, gender, and income differences in users. *International Journal of Information Communication Technologies and Human Development, 3*(1), 1–20. doi: 10.4018/jicthd.2011010101

IISD. (2006). Evaluation of UNESCO's community multimedia centres. Final report. Retrieved from http://unesdoc.unesco.org/images/0014/001456/145629e.pdf

Kumar, R. (2004). eChoupals: a study on the financial sustainability of village internet centers in rural Madhya Pradesh. *Information Technologies & International Development, 2*(1), 45–73. Retrieved from http://itidjournal.org/itid/article/view/192

Latchem, C., & Walker, D. (Eds.). (2001). *Perspectives on Distance education: telecentres: case studies and key issues.* Vancouver, BC, Canada: The Commonwealth of Learning - COL. Retrieved from http://dspace.col.org/handle/11599/116

Martin, B.L., & Abbott, E. (2011). Mobile phones and rural livelihoods: Diffusion, uses, and perceived impacts among farmers in rural Uganda. *Information Technologies & International Development, 7*(4), 17.

Molnár, S., & Karvalics, L.Z. (2002). Two models and six types of telecentres: A typological experiment. *Prolissa,* 327–332.

Parkinson, S. (2005). *Telecentres, access and development: Experience and lessons from Uganda and South Africa.* IDRC.

Rega, I. (2010). *What do local people think about telecentres? A key issue for sustainability* [Doctoral dissertation]. Università della Svizzera italiana – USI, Lugano, Switzerland. Retrieved from https://doc.rero.ch/record/17990/files/2010COM001.pdf

Rega, I., Cantoni, L., Vannini, S., David, S., Baia, A., & Macueve, G. (2011). *Community multimedia centres in Mozambique: A map.* (White Paper No. 1.0). Lugano: NewMinE Lab. – USI. Retrieved from http://www.newmine.org/publications-2/working-papers/white-paper-community-multimedia-centres-in-mozambique-a-map

Rega, I., Vannini, S., Raimilla, M., & Fauró, L. (2013). *Telecentres and mobile: An initial overview* (Working Paper No. 1.0). Associazione seed. Retrieved from http://seedlearn.org/telecentres-and-mobile-technologies-global-pilot-study/

Roman, R. (2003). Diffusion of innovation as a theoretical framework for telecenters. *Information Technologies & International Development, 1*(2), 53–66.

Roman, R., & Colle, R.D. (2002). *Themes and issues in telecentre sustainability* (Development Informatics Working Paper No. 10). Manchester, England: Institute for Development Policy and Management, University of Manchester. Retrieved from http://unpan1.un.org/intradoc/groups/public/documents/NISPAcee/UNPAN015544.pdf

Sey, A., Coward, C., Bar, F., Sciadas, G., Rothschild, C., & Koepke, L. (2013). *Connecting people for development: Why public access ICTs matter.* Seattle, WA: Technology & Social Change Group, University of Washington Information School. Retrieved from http://tascha.uw.edu/publications/connecting-people-for-development

Short, G. (2001). Lessons learned in pioneering telecenters in Australia. *The Journal of Development Communication, 12,* 2.

Townsend, D.N., Espitia G.D., Jorge, S.N., & Lee, C.B. (2001). *Telecenters and telecommunications development: Options and strategies*. DNTA. Retrieved from http://www.share4dev.info/kb/documents/4230.pdf

Toyama, K. (2015). *Geek heresy: Rescuing social change from the cult of technology*. New York, NY: PublicAffairs.

UNESCO. (2004). *Scale up initiative for community multimedia centres in Mozambique* (UNESCO document). United Nations Organization for Education Science and Culture.

Unwin, T. (Ed.). (2009). *ICT4D: Information and communication technology for development* (1st ed.). Cambridge, England: Cambridge University Press.

Vannini, S., Nemer, D., & Rega, I. (2017). *Integrating mobile technologies to achieve community development goals: The case of telecenters in Brazil*. Proceedings of the 8th International Conference on Communities and Technologies (pp. 115–124). ACM.

Further Reading

TwineSocial: Social Hub for Telecentre Foundation. (n.d.). Retrieved October 26, 2017, from http://www.twinesocial.com/KatrinaWalker

Isabella Rega is Principal Academic in Digital Literacies and Education and Deputy Head of the Center for Excellence in Media Practice at Bournemouth University, UK. Her research interests lie at the intersection between digital media and their role in promoting socioeconomic development in the Global South. Isabella is also cofounder of a Swiss nonprofit organization, named Associazione seed, that promotes the use of educational technologies in the nonprofit sector in Switzerland and abroad. She has an extensive track record of awarded competitive research projects, the last one being the UK AHRC International Network *e-Voices: Redressing Marginality*.

Meaning-Making

THOMAS DEVERE WOLSEY
American University in Cairo, Egypt

DIANE LAPP
San Diego State University, USA

Making-meaning is an act of building knowledge through interaction and analysis, the conceptualizations of information being shared through the universe of discourse. Meaning-making involves constructing knowledge by interpreting and interacting with written text and other visual and sense-based information sources (such as a spoken word, photographs, icons, or symbols). While there are many lenses through which one can view the act of making meaning (e.g., cultural studies), this entry takes a pedagogical approach because the act of teaching is built on the foundation of helping students to make meaning.

Meaning-making requires conceptual change on the part of the meaning-maker. Conceptual change requires existing mental models to shift or change in some way, as a result of an encounter with new experiences. It may be possible to acquire knowledge about a topic without making meaning of it. Persons capable of reciting game scores for a favorite baseball pitcher have not necessarily made meaning of those scores; they have merely identified them or broken the initial code of information (Luke & Freebody, 1997). To make meaning, the reciter must also combine that entry-level literal knowledge with other information about how to interpret game scores. Simple knowledge acquisition is not sufficient to count as meaning-making.

For the purposes of this entry, meaning-makers are those who converse, read, view video online, listen to podcasts, and interact with other modes of communication in order to understand and construct ideas not previously understood by them or whose previous understanding is subject to further scrutiny. Similarly, meaning-makers use their command of language, understanding of cultures (their own or others), and their experiences to express new or reimagined meanings that others may also

The International Encyclopedia of Media Literacy. Renee Hobbs and Paul Mihailidis (Editors-in-Chief), Gianna Cappello, Maria Ranieri, and Benjamin Thevenin (Associate Editors).

come to understand through art, written text, and design (e.g., architecture, software, webpages). Finally, meaning is often constructed without conscious effort. For example, a 7-year-old boy may read superhero comic books for the sake of adventure, but he is also constructing conceptions of masculinity and noteworthy character traits.

A making-meaning model

Several factors or conditions lend themselves to meaning-making encounters (see Figure 1). Such factors interact with one another, but not all are necessary for meanings to be made. These include global meanings, autonomy and authority, signifiers, and events and experiences as perceived by the potential meaning-maker. While these conditions vary depending on the meaning-making event or experience, they do tend to intertwine (this is represented by the crossing arrows on the left of the model) as the meaning-maker attempts to impose order and meaning. For scholars studying media literacy, the notion of the postmodern world figures prominently for meaning-makers. In postmodernism, change from existing models is a central lens for making meaning (e.g., Taylor, 2005).

A visual model of a meaning-making process may provide additional clarity. Various factors or conditions affect how people make meaning of events and experiences. Events may be thought of as a unitary happening at a particular point in time, while an experience may expand over time to include observations, encounters with text, and interactions with other meaning-makers. This entry uses the term "experience" with reference to both events and experiences, somewhat interchangeably. How meanings are made depends on the state of the conditions along the left-hand side of Figure 1. These inform global meanings held or constructed by an individual meaning-maker and various experiences encountered. Where a discrepancy exists between global meanings and the perceived meaning of a given experience, there is a possibility of making-meaning. Several possible products or meanings made are suggested along the right-hand side of the model. These are representative but not exhaustive. An explanation of the meaning-making model follows.

In this model, the affordances (e.g., authority) interact with the signs generally accepted within a community and with the perceptions and mediating factors (distractions, noise) that lead to the possibility of a discrepancy. Global and existing meanings held by the meaning-maker are compared with the events and experiences currently in play. The result is a new or adjusted meaning or the absorption of the new event or experience into the global meaning.

Global meaning

Global meanings (see Park, 2010) are the general systems people use to orient themselves toward their experiences. These include the culture to which the meaning-maker belongs, core beliefs about the way the world operates (beliefs related to such concepts as "justice," "religion," and "social norms"), and the identity the person has

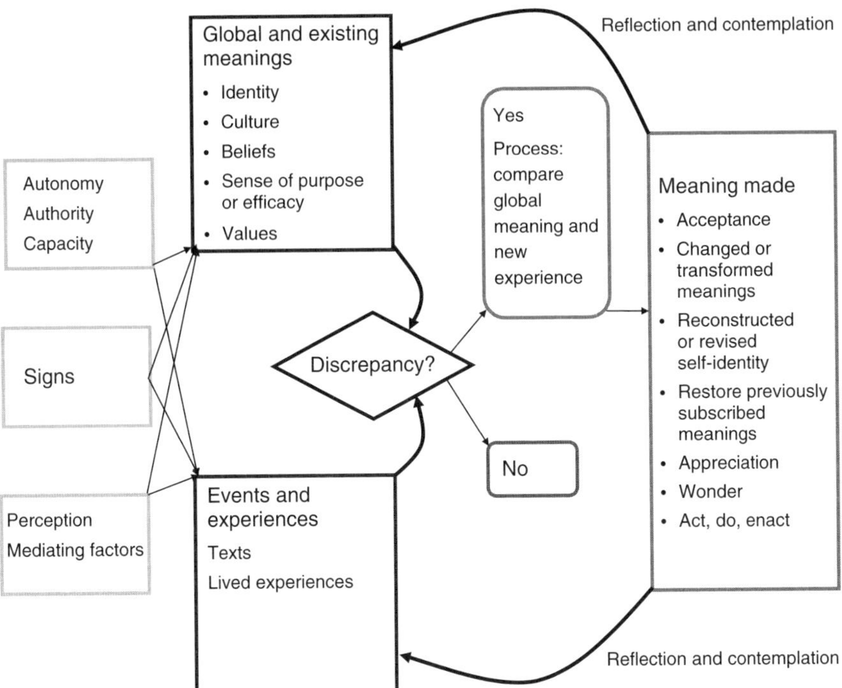

Figure 1 A meaning-making model.

constructed over time. Intertwined with these meanings are the values that assist the meaning-maker in the construction of new meanings from events and experiences.

From a survey of over 100 000 individuals each year of the study, researchers at the Cheskin Added Value marketing research firm (Diller, Shedroff, & Rhea, 2008) synthesized a list of 15 meanings that people believe figure significantly in their lives. The list, the authors suggest, is not exhaustive but appears to be representative of the most common meaningful experiences. It includes such global meanings as accomplishment, beauty, and security, which frame how people take action in the world, respond to events and experiences, and enact the meanings they have built in their own lives and for others. These may be interpreted as global meanings.

Specific events and experiences

An event or experience provides the counterpoint to global meaning. When an experience leads the meaning-maker to notice a discrepancy between what is learned through that experience and the global meanings that make up part of the maker's identity, the potential for making new meaning arises. Discrepant events include those that expose a previously unfilled need, which results in innovation. Experiences and events include a wide variety of possibilities that lead humans to build new meanings. A life event, such as the death of a loved one, can cause one to reexamine global beliefs. Stressful situations at work or in the home may also have the same result. Encountering new ideas by reading a text, viewing a movie, or experiencing a work of art is frequently intended to move meaning-makers to expand the global meanings that inform their lives. Travelers to unfamiliar places, to illustrate this point, often encounter overwhelming stimuli that cause culture shock; how the culture-shocked traveler responds on the basis of his or her global meanings can lead to a discrepancy, and thus to an opportunity for new meanings to be made.

When something occurs that may lead to new meanings being made, the experience is filtered through the senses. It can be argued that it is not possible to know anything were it not for the senses. In many ways, the conceptualizations people treat as reality are the result of organizing things, mainly linguistically, in their minds. "We know that 'nature' never repeats or standardizes. We do it [in our minds]" (Postman & Weingartner, 1969, p. 91). In other words, the reality humans create is based on perceptions through the senses translated into categories and classifications expressed as language.

Affordances

The meaning that can be constructed is dependent to some degree on the autonomy the meaning-maker has to shape it. Imposed meanings are less likely to become part of an individual's orientation toward experiences and concepts. Coupled with autonomy is authority, which involves one's capacity to take control of the meaning-making experience or to participate in it toward the making of future meanings. Put another way, students and other would-be meaning-makers need to value their lives and believe that the meanings they construct have value to others.

Meaning-makers who fail to acquire the authority to make meaning that is relevant to themselves or to others may also fail to discover something that has not been said or something they need to express. A student, as the term is used here, means any person who attempts to find or make meaning from the interaction with others through writing, images, video, and cultural symbols. For this reason, meaning-making tasks that are imposed are frequently less than successful in the transformative process of making meaning. In formal schooling, instructional scaffolding by a skilled teacher may help overcome this difficulty. A traditional example is the student in an English literature course who is directed to read in order to understand a novel from the canon. Due to lack of experience with similar novels, he may not make the necessary connections that more experienced readers may make.

Banking models of education in which a teacher imparts knowledge to passive students (Freire, 1993) tend to work against meaning-making. Where a culture based on relative power exists, some potential makers of meaning may not be, or feel, invited to participate in the endeavor. Instead, Freire proposed a dialogic approach in which teachers learn *with* students and those working to overcome oppression. He further proposes that, when humans recognize that the "seat of their decisions" (p. 99) is in themselves and in their relations with the world at large, they encounter "limit-situations" [sic] or obstacles against which they can push to create meaning.

Media literacies require meaning-makers to carefully examine inputs for bias, spin, or other misinformation. The prevalence of socially or politically oriented memes in social media spaces, for example, suggests that meaning-makers understand how marketing strategies, social media, and persuasive techniques are employed to shape individual views and cultural norms. Like other pedagogies, meaning-making is a skill acquired over time and as messages develop as technology and popular trends change with time. In other words, meaning-makers can exert control over the information and messages conveyed by media.

Signs

Signifiers are containers of meaning. Written texts, images, colors, sounds, speech, gestures, and other forms of communication may all count as signifiers. These, coupled with the things signified (the referent), constitute a sign and involve one in taking a critic stance as a listener, reader, or viewer. In short, signifier + signified = sign. From those, meaning can be derived or made. In terms of media that, by their various characteristics relative to the medium, employ text, color, video, and images frequently, the signifiers used require meaning-makers to work with many of them at once, creating richer meanings or excessive noise. Semiology (or semiotics) is the study of signs and of how they function in human lives. If the signifier stands in for the meaning intended, then the signified is the actual thing. To illustrate, "automobile" is a word serving as a signifier for a real thing in the world, in this case, a transportation device with four wheels and a motor. The actual transportation device is the signified. The signifier and the signified combine as a mental construct to become the sign (Barthes, 1964). Similarly, the color white or the word "white" are signifiers for the signified absence of pigmentation. As a sign, the signifier and the signified combine and may also connote, in some cultures, notions of purity or cleanliness as a mental construct.

The signifier and the signified need have no direct connection with each other. A *heart* in English is *corazón* in Spanish, yet both words stand for the same organ that pumps blood through the body. Knowing the manner in which humans communicate through signs and the ability to use those signs to construct new meanings offers additional possibilities as digital environments become more egalitarian. In this way, symbols can act as a very powerful sign that contributes to meaning-making processes. Symbols and icons create connections in the mind of the meaning-maker by calling up past experiences and cultural capital. Constructed through metonymy (an associated idea that represents something else; for example, "crown" might substitute for the king who wears it), synecdoche (a part of a thing that represents the entire thing; for example, "hired hands" might represent people who work for others), or cultural associations (for example, a national flag might stand for a country and the values it cherishes), symbols help meaning-makers with the task of finding and building meaning.

Beyond tropes that are commonly used literary themes or devices that facilitate meaning-making, signs that one can combine using a system or a structure result in meaning if the maker has the capacity to understand the agreed-upon references to the signs and to understand and manipulate the system so as to combine signs in a meaningful way. A system is a nonrandom, organized approach that constitutes a whole of something. A neighborhood is a system comprising many homes and the people who occupy them. An automobile relies on electrical and mechanical systems in order to function. Language is a system that permits communication between members of a society through combinations of words into sentences. Language and other signs (such as color, images, and icons) operate as a system to organize content.

The meaning-maker must determine how to combine the content in order to transform it into a meaning-making process. The determination may be deliberate or partially automatic, based on prior experience and global meanings (i.e., previously held beliefs and knowledge). As 21st-century literacies rely more and more heavily on imagery (for example, memes), the role of signs such as a flag or trope also increases. A poorly chosen metaphor, such as those that characterize immigrants as "not at their best," can quickly become an unexamined stereotype.

Other cognitive activities lead to greater understanding. Metaphors are so prevalent in the lives of humans that they often become transparent. Not just the province of poetry and other literature, metaphors undergird cultures in subtle ways. Time is often thought of in terms of money, for example: "How will you *spend* the summer?" "I *invested* a lot of time in that project." "The traffic accident *cost* me several hours yesterday." Because time and money are both valuable and limited in supply, their pairing helps convey meaning even when the meaning-maker doesn't realize it. Metaphors are useful ways to make comprehensible something that is unknown or less well understood by mapping it to the attributes of another, better-known subject. They can highlight critical attributes or shade less important ones. An argument is often characterized militarily, in that the person representing a contrary point of view may be the *opponent*, the speaker may *win* points or *attack* a weak point in the opposing argument. In a battle metaphor for argument, the competitive aspects are foregrounded while the cooperative aspects of the debate may be hidden or deemphasized.

Making connections between ideas leads to greater meanings being made. The capacity of the human mind to make inferences fuels new meaning. Moreover, as one engages more with ideas, the possibility of building new meaning increases exponentially. Inferences fall into two categories. Textually implicit inferences require a meaning-maker such as a reader to make connections within a single text. Scriptally implicit inferences require the meaning-maker to make connections and notice patterns between different texts or between a text and the maker's own experiences. In general, writers imply while readers infer, and the principle extends to the creators and perusers of graphics, images, video, and other multimedia representations. In the study of literature, meaning may be made through the literary device of intertextuality, by noting the way one text influences another text; similarly, an allusion in one text to another is a helpful device for assisting the meaning-making process. Mary Shelley's *Frankenstein*, for example, demonstrates intertextuality by making a connection to the story of Prometheus from Greek mythology.

Meanings made

Transformation and interpretation are critical to any attempt at constructing meaning. Without transformation, meaning may be recognized but not made. Interpretation requires the meaning-maker to find or apply knowledge of signs in communication in order to identify meaningful patterns or to create them. The possibility for transforming existing thought arises when an obstacle or discrepancy (Park, 2010) causes a need to reconcile global meanings with a new event or experience.

Events and experiences may include encounters with written text, images, and other modes of communication. Furthermore, the stance one takes during and after reading, for example, can change or shape the meaning made from the written work. The transactional theory of reading (Rosenblatt, 1994) suggests that readers adopt a stance along a spectrum or continuum from the efferent to the esthetic. Accordingly, the reader must bring to the reading event interpretations that may result in conceptual transformations of meaning. The efferent stance suggests that a reader's purpose is to take something away from the reading event, a bit of knowledge or wisdom that might serve a purpose once the reading is complete. Rosenblatt proposes that efferent reading leaves a "residue" (p. 22) of information to be obtained, a solution to a problem, and so on.

At the other end of the spectrum, readers may adopt an esthetic stance. From this stance, they engage in meaning-making during the reading event. They read for an experience that involves imagery being called up, attitudes toward the text, emotions, and associations with other texts. The transactional theory of reading may also be applied to other types of texts, such as video, images, and multimedia. Rosenblatt is careful to point out that readers may read for purposes that lie somewhere between the two poles of efferent and esthetic reading. The same text can be read efferently or esthetically, or somewhere along the continuum. In terms of meaning-making, the theory also suggests that, depending on how readers (or viewers, or listeners) direct their attention, the meaning they construct from the text will change as well.

Closely allied with meaning-making is comprehension, particularly in relation to how readers understand written text. Meaning-making and comprehension are not interchangeable, but the two concepts do map together nicely. Comprehension spans a spectrum from understanding the text literally, at a denotative level, to evaluating and appreciating a text. As noted above, what the meaning-maker brings to the equation is vitally important; however, that doesn't mean that anything the reader thinks a text means is acceptable. A means of determining the reliability of perceptions as translated into understanding or comprehension is necessary if communication is to result. Comprehension can be said to occur at several levels when a reader:

- literally recognizes what has been experienced or perceives what actually is,
- associates meanings from within the text and from prior experience (see the discussion of inference above), and
- is cognizant of the relationship between perception or experience and other modalities that are similar or different (evaluative or applied comprehension).

When readers or potential meaning-makers cannot or do not differentiate between their perceptions and the meaning or purpose of the text on the page (or in some other medium), meaning breaks down and comprehension does not occur. Indeed, misconceptions that arise from observations from a single vantage point, or from a misreading of the text, can hinder the meaning-making process. Not only is that knowledge incorrect, but it must also be unlearned if another meaning is to be built in its place. Science teachers encounter this problem quite often. Students, on the basis of their observations or of what they have been told, may believe that the moon only rises at night, that dinosaurs and cavemen occupied the planet at the same time, or that blood is blue. With those misunderstandings, new meanings are built on a rickety foundation.

Attention directed intentionally toward a meaning-making purpose may not be essential, but purposeful attention can nurture the making of meanings made in a way in which serendipitous events cannot. While moments of inspiration, when the right combination of signs and thoughts emerges spontaneously, are iconic in human history (for example, x-rays were discovered accidentally, when Röntgen was working with visible light), most meanings that are made are intentional and the product of an investment of effort.

The focus of attention similarly changes how meanings are made and how others make meaning within a community of learners, professionals, and parties with an interest in a particular subject. Students and professionals in various disciplines approach meaning-making in agreed-upon ways, usually through incremental change and growth within the community. Scientists, for instance, tend to read back and forth between the written text and graphics or charts to verify information. Historians look closely at the source of an artifact, while mathematicians are mostly interested in the accuracy of the math rather than in the source. Through commonly held constructs within a disciplinary community, participants can construct new knowledge within the bounds of those constructs, while occasionally challenging the constructs themselves on the basis of new understandings (Wolsey & Lapp, 2016). An example of how new knowledge is constructed by changing constructs is the designation of Pluto, formerly considered the ninth planet in the solar system. The discovery of similar-sized objects beyond Pluto's orbit caused scientists to reevaluate their classificatory system, to establish new meanings for what they term "planet," and to add a new meaning for bodies in space like Pluto, now a dwarf planet. Note that this example also illustrates the notion that signifiers are only arbitrarily connected to the signified, the actual thing in the world (in this case, solar system) they represent.

Technology and the making of meaning

Activity theory (e.g., Engeström, 1999) offers a particularly useful lens for considering the role of technology in meaning-making endeavors. Activity theory postulates an object of human action, a subject who carries out the action, and a mediating artifact. Mediating artifacts can be conceptual or material, and frequently a combination of both. Technologies work as mediating artifacts of human activity. For example, a simple technology such as a pen (the artifact) permits the subject to write (the object of the activity). Writing is itself a technological artifact, a system that includes the code of a given language; and it depends on material artifacts, the technologies of paper, pen, printing press, computer, and so forth. Without the material technologies, the idea of writing cannot function.

Some theorists suggest that a society's technology shapes the development of its structure and values (see Ong, 2002). A few suggest that it is the society that shapes the technology that emerges, while others assert that technologies are neutral in terms of the values they carry. An example of the neutral viewpoint is the position advocated by proponents of gun ownership, who assert that the weapon has no inherent value; rather the value is dependent on what humans do with the guns. A more likely view is that technology and societies are intertwined as parts of a complex cultural interchange. This view suggests that all technologies carry cultural value in some manner. A printing press carries the cultural value that what is written should not be solely the province of a few elites who can read and write. Digital technologies increase the possibility that more people will value, access, and create texts that transcend the words alone and incorporate multimedia—video, audio with voice and music, artwork, photography, and graphics.

Digital technologies increase people's capacity to make connections with one another through various types of networks, often through social media. Through these connections, meaning-making is possible. On the other hand, meanings can also be ossified or overly biased if appropriate care and critical reflection are not taken. Research released by the Stanford History Education Group (2016) with over 7800 participants from middle school, high school, and college reported that a disappointing number of students had difficulty reasoning in digital spaces. They struggled to identify the credibility of news sources or disinformation in social media feeds. By contrast, digital environments may also permit the collective wisdom of the crowd to build new meanings. In this instance, a crowd is any group that shares a common interest but may lack cohesion beyond that interest.

Social contexts are amplified or muted, depending on the media source and its stance toward the topic at hand. Context always imputes a social aspect (see Kellner & Share, 2005). Social aspects may include being unaware, or partially aware, of new research or features of given phenomena. As a result, interpretation suggests frameworks for considering the information provided as well as the manner in which it is conveyed.

A good example of how technology stimulates crowdsourced meaning is Wikipedia. Instead of relying on one or two experts to construct the online encyclopedia, Wikipedia depends on many contributors from the public at large. The more contributors there are and the more revisions occur to Wikipedia entries, the less biased the articles become. Another example can be found in the Arab Spring uprisings in the Middle East beginning in 2010. Although the results of the Arab Spring were in the end disappointing for participants, the movement permitted disaffected protesters across several countries to build a collective meaning, founded on the discrepancy between their expectations of supporting human rights and of opposing oppressive regimes. Social media played a significant role in uprisings in many countries, allowing protesters to organize and build collective understandings of purpose. Open-source initiatives allow users across the planet to build and refine software or to share content for anyone else to use as they mash up media or create entirely new content.

Meanings made

As meaning-makers move through a process of constructing meaningful insights and new understandings, meanings made may result. Park (2010) explains: "Meanings made refers to the products of meaning-making processes. That is, meanings made are end results or changes derived from attempts to reduce discrepancies or violations between appraised and global meaning" (p. 260). Referring to meaning as a "product" or "result" is problematic in some ways, in that these terms imply something complete or finished; however, these terms are useful in that they provide a waypoint for people whose natural disposition is to make meaning out of challenging or intriguing experiences. Meanings made should still be subject to contemplation and reflection, as the paths toward meaning cycle, spiral, and grow with new experiences.

Outcomes or products of the meaning-making process include acceptance of a discrepant event (for example, when a stressful experience such as loss of a loved one occurs). A change or transformation of a mental construct may be another result. At times, the restoration of a previously held meaning is possible. In many cases the meaning made can transform how the meaning-maker views her or his identity or helps reconstruct that identity. Meaning-making through engagement with art and literature frequently engenders appreciation for the form or theme of the work or inspires a sense of wonder. For many, making-meaning means doing something, acting on the meaning (see Freire, 1993), seeing how the new understanding is interpreted or affects others, or enacting a principle derived from the meaning in their identities or lives in the wider world.

Readers who read a novel or some other work over and over again often find new meaning with each subsequent rereading, as their experiences expand and life circumstances change. Thomas Edison made numerous attempts to find a workable filament for his incandescent light bulb, learning from experience and building understanding toward a successful solution. Many authors and artists discover meaning during the creation process, fusing meaning-making events with meanings made. Illustrating this point is a quotation attributed to E.M. Forster: "How do I know what I think until I see what I say?"

Makers, as part of the maker movement, are individuals who join other individuals online and in real space to collaborate, share ideas, and pool resources. They are inventors, students, teachers, tinkerers, marketers, and hackers who make meaning through their do-it-yourself (DIY) and do-it-with-others (DIWO) engagement with various technologies, to create a wide variety of products. Autonomy and authority to create are built into the maker culture.

From these examples and the model of meaning-making (see Figure 1), principles for teaching and learning emerge. The process works best when the meanings made cycle back to inform global meanings and singular events and experiences through reflection and contemplation, which are represented by the arrows arcing to the left in the graphic representation. These principles apply in educational settings from professional development work to the kindergarten classroom and to the weekend workshop at the hardware store. Autonomy and authority are primary motivators as learners make meaning from their experiences. Meanings made tend to be spiral and cyclical when reflection and contemplation are integral to the process. Rich meaning develops from a vast network of global meanings that are built from the meaning-maker's values, culture, and identity. Spaces that promote a sense of reliability foster meaning-making that people can push against or choose to stay within. Instructional leaders may be able to encourage meaning-making by curating instructional resources rather than by mandating them. A set of novels from which students might choose can be more meaningful for them than a single text that all are required to read. Seeding topics from which students might select for their inquiries or problem-based projects is more likely to result in engagement, and thus in meanings made.

Psychiatrist Victor Frankl, who survived 3 years in a German concentration camp, reminds his readers in 1946 that there is no single meaning in life; rather, meaning is found in the moments and the circumstances of life. Along with freedom, meaning is found through responsible conduct.

SEE ALSO: Coding as Literacy; Curation; Social Semiotics; Understanding Media Literacy and DIY Creativity in Youth Digital Productions

References

Barthes, R. (1964). *Elements of semiology* (A. Lavers & C. Smith, Trans.). New York, NY: Hill and Wang.

Diller, S., Shedroff, N., & Rhea, D. (2008). *Making meaning: How successful businesses deliver meaningful customer experiences*. Berkeley, CA: New Riders.

Engeström, Y. (1999). Activity theory and individual and social transformation. In Y. Engeström, R. Miettinen, & R.L. Punamäki (Eds.), *Perspectives on activity theory* (pp. 19–38). Cambridge, England: Cambridge University Press.

Frankl, V.E. (1946). *Man's search for meaning: An introduction to logotherapy* (4th ed.). Boston, MA: Beacon Press.

Freire, P. (1993). *Pedagogy of the oppressed: 30th anniversary edition* (M.B. Ramos, Trans.). New York, NY: Continuum.

Kellner, D., & Share, J. (2005). Toward critical media literacy: Core concepts, debates, organizations, and policy. *Discourse: Studies in the Cultural Politics of Education, 26*(3), 369–386.

Luke, A., & Freebody, P. (1997). Shaping the social practices of reading. In S. Muspratt, A. Luke, & P. Freebody (Eds.), *Constructing critical literacies: Teaching and learning textual practice* (pp. 185–225). Cresskill, NJ: Hampton Press.

Ong, W.J. (2002). *Orality and literacy*. New York, NY: Routledge.

Park, C.L. (2010). Making sense of the meaning literature: An integrative review of meaning making and its effects on adjustment to stressful life events. *Psychological Bulletin, 136*(2), 257–301. doi: 10.1037/a0018301

Postman, N., & Weingartner, C. (1969). *Teaching as a subversive activity*. New York, NY: Dell.

Rosenblatt, L.M. (1994). *The reader, the text, the poem: The transactional theory of the literary work*. Carbondale, IL: Southern Illinois University Press.

Stanford History Education Group. (2016). Evaluating information: The cornerstone of civic online reasoning [Executive summary]. Retrieved from https://ed.stanford.edu/news/stanford-researchers-find-students-have-trouble-judging-credibility-information-online

Taylor, B.C. (2005). Postmodern theory. In S. May & D.K. Mumby (Eds.), *Engaging organizational communication, theory, and research: Multiple perspectives* (pp. 113–140). Thousand Oaks, CA: SAGE.

Wolsey, T.D., & Lapp, D. (2016). *Literacy in the disciplines: A teacher's guide for grades 5–12*. New York, NY: Guilford.

Further reading

Bruner, J. (2002). *Making stories: Law, literature, life.* New York, NY: Farrar, Straus and Giroux.
Hughes, T.P. (2004). *Human-built world: How to think about technology and culture.* Chicago, IL: University of Chicago Press.
Lakoff, G., & Johnson, M. (1980). *Metaphors we live by.* Chicago, IL: University of Chicago Press.
Shedroff, N. (n.d.). Making meaning. Retrieved from http://nathan.com/making-meaning

Thomas DeVere Wolsey is the founder of an educational consulting firm and professor of literacy education. Dr. Wolsey currently teaches at the Graduate School of Education at the American University in Cairo, Egypt. He has taught English and social studies in public schools for 20 years. His research on the topics of visual literacy, writing, technology's intersections with traditional literacies, and the meanings people make of the human-built environment are represented in several books and peer-reviewed journal articles.

Diane Lapp is a distinguished professor of education at San Diego State University, where her work continues to be applied to schools. Diane is also an instructional coach at Health Sciences Middle School and Health Sciences High and Middle College in San Diego, California.

Media Access and Activism

CLAUDIA RIESMEYER
Ludwig-Maximilians-University of Munich, Germany

Media access and activism, defined as civic and political engagement and participation, are directly associated with media literacy and media socialization. Media literacy, expressed in a reflective media usage, on the one hand, is essential for civic and political engagement as well as participation, since "empowerment of people through media and information literacy (MIL) is an important prerequisite for fostering equitable access to information and knowledge and free, independent and pluralistic media and information systems" (UNESCO, 2016). On the other hand, the dissemination of media literacy is a task of the media socialization process in which different media socialization agents are involved (Arnett, 1995), and where "skills necessary to function as members of their social group" (Grusec, 2002, p. 143) should be learned.

Defining media literacy is still a challenge within communication studies. Many different definitions of media literacy exist, resembling a "patchwork of ideas" (Potter, 2010, p. 676; Potter & Thai, 2016), all having in common that they describe media access as a central component of media literacy. Hobbs and Moore (2013, p. 16) define media literacy as the ability "to access, analyze, compose, reflect, and take action in the world" (see also Livingstone, 2004; Pfaff-Rüdiger, Riesmeyer, & Kümpel, 2012).

Media access is composed of the following skill sets: "listening skills, reading comprehension, using appropriate technology tools, asking questions, gathering information using multiple sources, applying information solving problems" (Hobbs & Moore, 2013, p. 16) and is considered a dynamic and social process (Livingstone, 2004). Hobbs and Moore (2013) understand "taking action in the world" as the ability to perceive problems and to take responsibility for problem-solving, to thereby participate in civic and political processes (Pfaff-Rüdiger & Riesmeyer, 2016).

With this understanding of media literacy, two meanings of the construct are associated. First, media literacy is an ability to protect recipients in general, and children and adolescents in particular, from dangers and enables a reflective media usage. These skill sets (of media literacy) should be disseminated within the framework of the media socialization process as an elucidation of possible opportunities, risks, and consequences of media usage. Studies such as EU Kids Online (2014) show how the usage period of mobile media has developed toward "always on." With the increasing usage of digital and mobile media, as well as a growing multitude and variety of channels and content, the need for media literacy is growing, in order to be able to perceive, select, receive, and evaluate content in a need-oriented way (Hobbs, 2011a, 2011b).

Second, media literacy is linked to a civic and political perspective. The hope is that those who use media competently will be aware of their rights and duties, and will demand and exercise these through media access (Livingstone, Mansell, Couldry, & Carr, 2015). Competent media usage could help in the understanding of digital inequalities and possibly even overcome them (Zillien & Hargittai, 2009), since the more media literate a recipient is, the more they can benefit from their media usage, and fulfill developmental tasks as well as basic needs. Furthermore, with media literacy the hope is to enable cultural citizenship as cultural participation (Klaus & Lünenborg, 2012) and to acquire civic competence (European Council, 2006) through literate media usage. This means that media literacy is understood not only as a cultural concept, but also as a component of lifelong learning that affects all generations equally (European Council, 2006; Hobbs & Moore, 2013).

Therefore, all media socialization agents are required to have the appropriate skills, or to acquire them if necessary, in order to be able to impart them to learners. It is discussed in the literature whether these are general social skills (life skills) which can be applied to the respective situation, media environment, and usage (such as reflexive skills; Pfaff-Rüdiger & Riesmeyer, 2016).

Links between the use of digital media and civic and political engagement and participation (*access*) have been widely researched (inter alia Gil de Zúñiga, Jung, & Valenzuela, 2012). The basic assumption is that some characteristics of social media can be suitable to encourage someone to engage in civic and/or political engagement (Kahne, Lee, & Feezell, 2012), as they provide, among other things, the possibilities for sharing content with others and the mobilization of others through the exchange of information and opinions. In the literature, the link between media access and activism is characterized by two perspectives (Norris, 2001; de Vreese, 2007).

1. *Mobilization*: The mobilization hypothesis as an Internet-optimistic view and is based on the assumption that the use of social media not only strengthens the

engagement and participation of those who are already interested in politics, but also initiates or intensifies the involvement of those who have not yet participated in civic or political processes.

2. *Reinforcement*: The reinforcement hypothesis is a more pessimistic view of the Internet and expects that especially those who are already politically active and involved offline will utilize the opportunities offered by social media and be encouraged to (further) participate. If someone has been strengthened in his or her attitude, the online engagement could also stimulate the offline participation.

However, the question is what factors determine who is civically or politically active. Not all recipients are equally active; for instance, education and income positively influence political online participation: the more educated someone is and the higher their income, the more likely they will civically or politically engage and participate. Gender and age also have an influence. Men use social media more for political participation than women, and younger more so than elder, whereby these findings correlate with the use of mobile media per se. "Even among youth, male, higher status, and better educated citizens are more engaged online than their female, lower status, and less educated counterparts" (Livingstone, Bober, & Helsper, 2005). The results illustrate that an increased use of digital and mobile media does not necessarily have to lead directly to an increased civic and/or political engagement. The results rather coincide with the findings of the digital divide or participation divide (Hoffmann, Lutz, & Meckel, 2015; Norris, 2001).

From these findings, two challenges can be identified which concern the scientific research process, on the one hand, and the media socialization process, including all agents involved, on the other. Communication studies should use more concise terminologies and reveal the understanding of the analyzed constructs: How are central terminologies defined and operationalized for empirical studies? In this way, argumentations would be intersubjectively comprehensible, so that drawn conclusions could be understood and one's own conclusion could be derived. For example, what does engagement mean? Is it enough to recognize an online petition in order to be considered engaged, or does the petition have to be formulated and disseminated? The same applies to concepts in politics. When attention is drawn to young people, their political disinterest and thus their political nonengagement are criticized. This criticism, however, can also be traced back to the underlying construct in politics, which is often based on an institutional political understanding (de Vreese, 2007). However, if the policy terminology is broadened and extended, for example to include civic, individual, and collective agents (such as environmental and consumer protection organizations), then young people are interested and engaged, and demonstrate this by participating in petitions on social media, also possibly formulating them themselves, and by taking part in demonstrations.

The scientific disclosure of the terminology is directly linked with the second challenge, which affects all media socialization agents. Media socialization, as a process of lifelong learning and of media literacy dissemination, creates the prerequisite for civic and political engagement and allows participation. Within this process, not only should the dissemination of technical knowledge (technical access to media) and the elucidation of the dangers of media usage occur, but the chances of media usage and a reflection of media contents should also be emphasized. Media literacy comprises, in addition to expertise, self- and social competence (Pfaff-Rüdiger et al., 2012). These competences include reflexive and participatory skills. If these components are emphasized in the media socialization process, this will not only help raise awareness of the basic needs and enable the use of media analogously toward them (Jordan, 2017), but it will also make it clear that media content should, on the one hand, be evaluated and classified (keywords: source criticism, credibility). On the other hand, such media socialization would illustrate that the use of media can involve opportunities for engagement and participation, if media is consciously used to achieve the developmental needs (Jordan, 2018). The challenge for the media socializing agents is to generate this attention for conscious media usage and the conscious application of media within civic and political engagement and participation. In order for this to be successful, it is necessary to strengthen the recipients' belief and confidence in their self-efficacy (Bandura, 1997; Hoffmann et al., 2015). Here a particular focus can be on those groups who are not yet politically engaged and participating to the extent described above. More than ever, media literacy is a key skill for civic and political engagement and participation if activism is to emerge from media access.

SEE ALSO: Access; Civic Activism; Media Literacy Foundations; Mediatization

References

Arnett, J.J. (1995). Broad and narrow socialization: The family in the context of a cultural theory. *Journal of Marriage and the Family, 57*(3), 617–628. doi: 10.2307/353917

Bandura, A. (1997). *Self-efficacy: The exercise of control.* New York, NY: W.H. Freeman.

de Vreese, C. (2007). Digital renaissance: Young consumer and citizen? *The Annals of the American Academy of Political and Social Science, 611*(1), 207–216. doi: 10.1177/0002716206298521

EU Kids Online. (2014). *EU Kids Online: Findings, methods, recommendations.* London, England: LSE. Retrieved from http://eprints.lse.ac.uk/60512/1/EU%20Kids%20onlinie%20III%20.pdf

European Council. (2006). *Key competences for lifelong learning.* Retrieved from http://eur-lex.europa.eu/legal-content/HR/ALL/?uri=uriserv:c11090

Gil de Zúñiga, H., Jung, N., & Valenzuela, S. (2012). Social media use for news and individuals' social capital, civic engagement and political participation. *Journal of Computer-Mediated Communication, 17*(3), 319–336. doi: 10.1111/j.1083-6101.2012.01574.x

Grusec, J. (2002). Parental socialization and children's acquisition of values. In M. Bormstein (Ed.), *Handbook of parenting* (pp. 143–168). Mahwah, NJ: Lawrence Erlbaum.

Hobbs, R. (2011a). The state of media literacy: A response to Potter. *Journal of Broadcasting and Electronic Media, 55*(3), 419–430. doi: 10.1080/08838151.2011.597594

Hobbs, R. (2011b). *Digital and media literacy: Connecting culture and classroom.* Thousand Oaks, CA: Corwin.

Hobbs, R., & Moore, D.C. (2013). *Discovering media literacy: Teaching digital media and popular culture in elementary school.* Thousand Oaks, CA: Corwin.

Hoffmann, C.P., Lutz, C., & Meckel, M. (2015). Content creation on the Internet: A social cognitive perspective on the participation divide. *Information, Communication & Society, 18*(6), 696–716. doi: 10.1080/1369118X.2014.991343

Jordan, A. (2018). Growing up online: Media use and development in early adolescence. In P. Vorderer, D. Hefner, L. Reinecke, & C. Klimmt (Eds.), *Permanently online, permanently connected: Living and communicating in a POPC world* (pp. 165–175). New York, NY: Routledge.

Kahne, J., Lee, N.-J., & Feezell, J.T. (2012). Digital media literacy education and online civic and political participation. *International Journal of Communication, 6*, 1–24. Retrieved from https://dmlhub.net/wp-content/uploads/files/International_Journal_Communication.pdf

Klaus, E., & Lünenborg, M. (2012). Cultural citizenship: Participation by and through media. In E. Zobl & R. Drüeke (Eds.), *Feminist media. Participatory spaces, networks and cultural citizenship* (pp. 197–212). Bielefeld, Germany: transcript Verlag.

Livingstone, S. (2004). Media literacy and the challenge of new information and communication technologies. *The Communication Review, 7*(1), 3–14. doi: 10.1080/10714420490280152

Livingstone, S., Bober, M., & Helsper, E. (2005). Active participation or just more information? *Information, Communication & Society, 8*(3), 287–314. doi: 10.1080/13691180500259103

Livingstone, S., Mansell, R., Couldry, N., & Carr, J. (2015). *Children's rights in the digital age.* Retrieved from http://www.lse.ac.uk/website-archive/publicEvents/pdf/2015-LT/20150211-Sonia-Livingstone-PPT.pdf

Norris, P. (2001). *Digital divide: Civic engagement, information poverty, and the Internet worldwide.* Cambridge, England: Cambridge University Press.

Pfaff-Rüdiger, S., & Riesmeyer, C. (2016). Moved into action. Media literacy as social process. *Journal of Children & Media, 10*(2), 164–172. doi: 10.1080/17482798.2015.1127838

Pfaff-Rüdiger, S., Riesmeyer, C., & Kümpel, A.S. (2012). Media literacy and developmental tasks: A case study in Germany. *Media Studies, 3*(6), 42–56. Retrieved from https://www.researchgate.net/publication/285583511_Media_Literacy_and_Developmental_Tasks_A_Case_Study_in_Germany

Potter, W.J. (2010). The state of media literacy. *Journal of Broadcasting and Electronic Media, 54*(4), 675–696. doi: 10.1080/08838151.2011.521462

Potter, W.J., & Thai, C. (2016). Conceptual challenges in designing measures for media literacy studies. *International Journal of Media and Information Literacy, 1*(1), 27–42. doi: 10.13187/ijmil.2016.1.27

UNESCO. (2016). *Media and information literacy.* Retrieved from http://www.unesco.org/new/en/communication-and-information/media-development/media-literacy/mil-as-composite-concept/

Zillien, N., & Hargittai, E. (2009). Digital distinction: Status-specific types of Internet usage. *Social Science Quarterly, 90*(2), 274–291. doi: 10.1111/j.1540-6237.2009.00617.x

Further reading

Havighurst, R.J. (1948). *Developmental tasks and education.* New York, NY: Longman.

Hobbs, R., & Moore, D.C. (2013). *Discovering media literacy: Teaching digital media and popular culture in elementary school.* Thousand Oaks, CA: Corwin.

Jenkins, H. (2007). *Confronting the challenges of participatory culture: Media education for the 21st century.* Chicago, IL: The John D. and Catherine T. MacArthur Foundation.

Livingstone, S. (2004). Media literacy and the challenge of new information and communication technologies. *The Communication Review, 7*(1), 3–14. doi: 10.1080/10714420490280152

Pfaff-Rüdiger, S., & Riesmeyer, C. (2016). Moved into action. Media literacy as social process. *Journal of Children & Media, 10*(2), 164–172. doi: 10.1080/17482798.2015.1127838

Potter, W.J. (2013). *Media literacy.* Thousand Oaks, CA: SAGE.

Claudia Riesmeyer is a research associate at the Department of Communication Studies and Media Research, Ludwig-Maximilians-University of Munich, Germany. Her research focuses on media literacy, journalism and public relations, political communication, and methods.

Media Activism and Action-Oriented Learning

THEO HUG
University of Innsbruck, Austria

Neither media activism nor action-oriented learning are precisely defined concepts nor are they considered as equally relevant in discourses of media literacy or media education. While in many countries concepts of "action-oriented learning" are widely used in educational discourses, concepts of "media activism" are more used in political discourses, informal learning contexts, and, more recently, in media theory. However, relationships between both terms and corresponding practices need to be clarified in view of manifold interpretations and valuations.

As a first approximation, media activism can be described as an umbrella term for various forms of activist practices making use of media as well as information and communication technologies for different purposes including social or economic change, policy change, uncovering power structures or illegal activities, empowering disadvantaged groups, or highlighting questionable developments and future prospects. Action-oriented learning can be characterized as a blanket term that encompasses holistic understandings of dealing with meaningful tasks in learning environments, at the same time fostering integrated developments of learning strategies and problem-solving techniques, building and sharing of knowledge, and methodological and social competences as well as communication skills and abilities for teamwork. Thus, methods and principles of teaching and learning are based on different theoretical traditions ranging from pragmatism, reform pedagogy, learning psychology, and educational theory to social phenomenology, critical social theory, constructivist theory, media theory, and cultural ecology. According to specifications of the key terms being discussed in this entry, their relationship appears as incompatible, contrary, conflicting, complementary, compatible, or even synonymic.

Over the past two decades, we have seen an increasing interest in concepts and practices of media activism. Along with the arrival of networked "do it yourself" media, social media platforms, mobile communication services, and the Internet of Things, contemporary forms of media activism gradually attracted attention in media studies, and to a relatively lesser extent also in media education and critical literacy studies. Still, this should not detract from the fact that people have always found ways and tools to communicate critical issues by way of circumventing control bodies of the prevailing normative and political systems throughout history. This applies from cultural activities with masks in pre- and protohistoric times, ancient Greek practices of *parrhesia* and early graffiti, insubordinate and indecent forms of the European medieval carnival cultures, illegal pamphlet printing and use of leaflets, to radio activism and hacking computer networks.

So far, most definitions of media activism do not consider such a wide range of phenomena. Lasar (2007), for example, who supports his account with examples from the

United States since the 18th century, defines the term as two related types of activity, one with regard to creating media "that challenge the dominant culture, structure, or ruling class of a society" and the other advocating "changes within that society intended to preserve or open up space for such media" (p. 925). Meikle (2010) focuses on more recent perspectives as related to activist practices and the Internet. He puts a special emphasis on challenges for closed systems in view of dynamics of openness as related, for example, to open source, open society, and open content developments. In so doing, he distinguishes four dimensions of Net activism, namely intercreative texts (in the sense of Tim Berners-Lee), tactics, strategies, and networks.

In contrast, Sützl (2011) outlines the theme historically, from the perspective of carnival cultures as media of resistance since the Middle Ages, criticizing narrow views often suggested by effective tactical media interventions in the 1990s and other viewpoints which eliminate "the existence of a disobedient, oppositional media culture potentially different from a 'normal' use that is adjusted to the circumstances" (p. 3). Such a broader historical approach to media activism allows for highlighting "media history *as* the history of resistance" in terms of content and also as a "mode of media history which facilitates the comprehension of media activism in its political dimension" (p. 9).

Both historical and systematic analyses can be done in nonreductionist ways if we understand the different forms of media activism as variations of relevant aspects which allow for diverse exemplifications (*sensu* Nelson Goodman) of the subject. Such aspects include

- unconventional use of media in the context of creative reframings or social orientations;
- medial forms aiming at strengthening minorities as well as questioning mainstream developments, structural constraints, power relations, or cultural hegemony;
- cognitive autonomy in oppositional or alternative cultures toward established media institutions (see Hug, 2012).

This applies to historic forms of media activism *avant la lettre* and also to contemporary forms including culture jamming, alternative media, tactical media, hacktivism, electronic civil disobedience, electronic street theater, citizen journalism, knowledge commons, swarming and anti-corporate saboteurs, and media interventions questioning the workings of biopower. Many activists who witnessed the emergence of so many politically, culturally, or artistically driven forms of "activism" using digital media would agree that educational media ecologies and social learning environments are important in order to empower active citizenship and democratic attitudes. Nonetheless, concepts of action-oriented learning as discussed in institutionalized educational contexts are barely considered explicitly in media activist discourses.

While mainstream media activist concepts and practices are attracting little attention in mainstream discourses on action learning or action-oriented learning, there is a long tradition of action-oriented learning especially in media pedagogy and media literacy education (Tulodziecki & Grafe, 2012). There has also been hardly any interest in media activism in these discourses. While we find distinctions like action-oriented, learning-oriented, and balanced action learning in a systematic review on action learning research (Cho & Egan, 2009), both media and media activism can be regarded as blind spots.

This is all the more surprising since demands for critical thinking and responsible action play an important role in the context of action-oriented learning, too. At least democratically organized societies committed to the tradition of the Enlightenment share ideals of a critical attitude toward dogmatic or opportunistic thinking. Admittedly, understandings of "critical thinking" do vary a lot. The spectrum extends from autonomous, skeptical, logical, methodical, systematic, science-oriented, critical of society, networked, systemic, contextualist, self-reflective, poly-logical, postcolonial, metacognitive, and metacritical thinking to critique of ideological assumptions and skillfully conceptualizing, analyzing, synthesizing, applying, and evaluating information and its sources. Yet, since the 1970s we can observe repeated affirmations of claims and general principles for critical thinking as well as reorientations from conservative protection-oriented toward action-oriented concepts and practices in (post-)modern educational systems. Especially in the context of media (literacy) education, a strong emphasis has been put on fostering abilities to critically analyze and reflect media messages as well as to take action, create content, disseminate one's messages, and participate in public spheres of mediated cultural life. In this sense, media literacy education can be understood as a form of action-oriented learning.

On the one hand, the social, political, emancipatory, and aesthetic demands in the field of action-oriented learning and (media) education suggest parallels to media-activist orientations. On the other hand, these orientations and related practices shed light on opportunities and challenges for action-oriented learning and media work both inside and outside of schools as related to

- rethinking educational designs, pedagogical and psychological routines, and demands for critical thinking;
- options for enhancements of didactical thinking and acting;
- principles of action-oriented learning and their relation to dynamics of self-cultivation, self-determination (*Selbstbestimmung*), and heteronomy (*Fremdbestimmung*);
- exploring possibilities and limitations for institutional self-reflection, openness in education, and education for all;
- questioning basic assumptions of learning cultures and media use as well as educational trance phenomena on individual and institutional levels.

Broadly speaking, concepts and practices of media activism and action-oriented learning can be considered as different forms of intervention in society and as more or less contrasting fields in which (media) educational endeavors can be positioned. Related spheres are disjunctive or similar depending on whether we conceive them broadly or narrowly. Basically, there are three options (see Hug, 2012).

1. Media activism and action-oriented learning turn out to be *largely disjunctive spheres* if we understand action-oriented concepts and practices mainly as part of outcome-based education and training or learning-objective-oriented approaches

in which acting is conceptualized as performing in line with expectations toward a predetermined goal. The two spheres conflict or are incompatible if, for example, concepts of instructional design that focus on learners dealing increasingly independently with given tasks and problems in self-organized ways play a major role, whereas educational efforts, concerned with unmasking the shortcomings of democracy, practicing civil disobedience, and promoting moral courage and resistance opposite problematic mainstream developments, play a minor role or no role at all.

2. Conversely, the two spheres can be described as *largely identical* if we think of (media) education and action-oriented learning as the epitome of socio-critical pedagogical interventions and initiatives as well as the promotion of self-determination and self-empowerment. If we define action-oriented learning as transformative learning fostering simultaneously individual competence development, personal growth, and social change for improving social justice and economic development toward a more egalitarian society, the two spheres can barely be distinguished from one another. Moreover, if educational activities are taken as a form of cultural politics aiming at social and emancipatory transformation, promoting disadvantaged groups as well as the cultivation of human agency and the creation of a counterpublic, corresponding transformative activities are compatible or even synonymous with politically motivated media activism.
3. *Partial overlaps of the spheres* can be described inasmuch as media-critical motives, enhancement of scopes of action and activities, and partial overcoming of hegemonic tendencies and power interests can play an important role in both spheres. Especially if we recognize the value of learning by doing (John Dewey) and informal and nonformal educational dimensions, for example, of hackerspaces, makerspaces, or extracurricular historical-political education work, the two spheres and related learning contexts appear as complementary or at least partially compatible.

The three options show that a simple comparison between two contrasting fields would be too short-sighted. A superficial comparison of critical media activism and well-behaved action learning, effective grassroots interventions and ineffective action-orientations in educational institutions, or sociocultural revolution promoted in educational hacking contexts and restricted codes of criticism in action-oriented learning is overly narrowly considered. Claims of critical and democratic orientations are significant in both areas, albeit in different respects.

So far, mutual exchange and encounters between the two spheres are rare. Current research shows that thoughts about enhancements of action-orientations are given in critical pedagogy, digital commons networks, and the open education movement rather than in learning sciences, educational psychology, or studies on human resource development.

A clear assignment of the indicators shown in Table 1 to media activism (left column) and action-oriented learning (right column) may seem possible at first sight. On closer examination, it quickly becomes clear that such a strict separation only applies in the context of a juxtaposition of particular contrary understandings of the two spheres.

Table 1 Media activism (left) and action-orientations (right) in learning and education: fields of tension and conflicting priorities worthy of discussion (see Hug, 2014, p. 124).

destabilization		*stabilization*
discontinuity	–	continuity
short-term intervention	–	long-term intervention
revolution	–	evolution
transform	–	reform
subversion	–	transparency
disobedience	–	obedience
self-will, obstinacy	–	solidarity
resistance	–	adaption
refusal	–	participation

In particular, action-oriented media education does not only deal with differentiated perception, interpretation, analysis, and reflection but also with hands-on activities and change-oriented forms of intervention.

However, there are also differences connected to aspects such as temporality and scopes of action, institutional responsibility and legal mandate, significance of cultural resources and autonomy of people, data and media, and reach of claims for education for some, many, or all. Additionally, educational paradoxes should be taken into account. This applies both to traditional polarities and educational contradictions between freedom and open space for development, on the one hand, and to constraints and enforcement, on the other, and to contemporary paradoxical aspects such as:

- assertions of decision-makers in educational and political institutions regarding the relevance of critical thinking and action-orientations in education at the same time as most of the money goes in support of technological developments or public relations offices, and only very little in support of media (literacy) education studies and respective applications research;
- schooling as long-term intervention and promotion of instant knowledge related to traditional teaching subjects;
- new forms of mobile communication and mobile activism, but mainstream education in many places is still treating digital mobility as an outlier if not banning mobile devices from educational institutions;
- new media dynamics, cultural convergence, instability of platforms, and the hidden work of algorithms, as well as educational policies with a focus on knowledge architectures from a predigital or "typographical" age, hardly taking notice of changing lifeworlds, mediated lifestyles, systemic perspectives of offline–online relations, or interrelations of global public spheres and their relevance for education;
- calls for solidarity in view of increasing social inequality, migration flows, and climate change, and educational politics of ignorance and learning practices forgetting relevant connections.

Regardless of all difficulties related with such paradoxes, post-democratic conditions, and lack of funds for action-oriented projects in education, there is an increasing number of examples of educational practices at the crossroads of media activism, media literacy, and action-oriented learning. Corresponding initiatives often refer to theories and concepts of openness, constructivist learning, democratic education, economies of the commons, and the work of Freire (1996) or Giroux (2001). Respective educational practices relate to a broad spectrum of areas including commons-based peer production, community media, open education and the free software movement, ethical hacking, collaborative peer-to-peer networks developing and conducting campaigns and social media strategies, media contributions on perspectives of minority groups or "forgotten" themes, open innovation and free culture, social learning and civic education, transformative and embodied learning, environmental awareness, health education (Piran, Levine, & Steiner-Adair, 1999), and critical information literacy reflecting on issues of personalization and tracking when using commercial search engines or library services based on matching technologies which originally were meant for supporting consumer cultures and monetary profit.

Neither media activism nor action-oriented learning are values per se. Related concepts and practices are relevant in sociocultural and discursive contexts and dependent on criteria of actors, groups, and communities. Thinking together, ongoing developments in both fields can support human agency, structural change, and self-reflective empowerment beyond the opposition between technophobic humanities and techno-euphoric engineering sciences. Nevertheless, no clever assemblage of media activism, action-oriented learning, media literacy, and critical literacy skills adds up to wisdom. For one thing, deep understanding and successful dealing with complex mediated constellations require thinking beyond literacies and opening up toward relations of literacy, numeracy or mathemacy, oracy, and picturacy. This implies (i) a critical assessment of the epistemological, cultural, and educational relevance of corresponding multimodal and multicodal forms and (ii) a rethinking of media literacy education if we want to avoid dead ends of the "literacification" of everything. Then again, limitations of affirmative ways of action-oriented learning which are blind to power relations ought to be considered.

Furthermore, paradoxes of truth-telling and critique should not be underestimated as, for example, endeavors of degovernmentalization show when they turn into activities of regovernmentalization under other auspices. And last but not least, successful learning and education is not only related to action-oriented concepts but also to going without deliberate action, not trying to make things happen or "not doing" (*wu wei*). Bringing together creative thinking, living learning, and research that matters remains ambivalent. However we deal with media activism and action-oriented learning in terms of designing, structuring, arranging, organizing, shaping, forming, framing, molding, enabling, and so on, playing by established or innovative rules, there is always a tension between bringing something to life deliberately and letting something come alive.

SEE ALSO: Citizen Journalism; Civic Activism; Community Media; Creativity and Media Production in Schools; Critical Information Literacy; Critical Pedagogy; Data Literacy; Media Access and Activism; Media Competence; Media Education Research and Creativity; Media Literacy and Pragmatism; Media Literacy and Social Activism; Media Literacy for the 21st Century Teacher; Mediated Communities; Mediatization;

Mobile Media and Parenting; Open Educational Resources; Participatory Action Research; Participatory Politics and the Civic Dimensions of Media Literacy; Social Action and Advocacy; Teaching with Media

References

Cho, Y., & Egan, T.M. (2009). Action learning research: A systematic review and conceptual framework. *Human Resource Development Review, 8*(4), 431–462. doi: 10.1177/1534484309345656

Freire, P. (1996). *Pedagogy of the oppressed*. London, England: Penguin Books.

Giroux, H.A. (2001). *Theory and resistance in education: Towards a pedagogy for the opposition*. Westport, CT: Bergin & Garvey. (Original work published 1983)

Hug, T. (2012). Explorations in the tension between media activism and action-oriented media pedagogy. *Journalism and Mass Communication, 2*(3), 457–463.

Hug, T. (2014). Media form school: A plea for expanded action orientations and reflective perspectives [Special issue]. *MedienPädagogik* [MediaPedagogy], *24*, 114–135. doi: 10.21240/mpaed/24/2014.09.25.X

Lasar, M. (2007). Media activism. In G.L. Anderson & K. Herr (Eds.), *Encyclopedia of activism and social justice* (Vol. 3, pp. 925–927). Thousand Oaks, CA: SAGE.

Meikle, G. (2010). Intercreativity: Mapping online activism. In J. Hunsinger, L. Klastrup, & M. Allen (Eds.), *International handbook of Internet research* (pp. 363–377). Dordrecht, Netherlands: Springer.

Piran, N., Levine, M.P., & Steiner-Adair, C. (Eds.). (1999). *Preventing eating disorders: A handbook of interventions and special challenges*. Philadelphia, PA: Brunner/Mazel.

Sützl, W. (2011). Medien des Ungehorsams: Zur Geschichtlichkeit von Medienaktivismus [Media of disobedience. On the historicity of media activism]. *Medienimpulse, 1*, 1–11. Retrieved from http://www.medienimpulse.at/articles/view/290

Tulodziecki, G., & Grafe, S. (2012). Approaches to learning with media and media literacy education—trends and current situation in Germany. *Journal of Media Literacy Education, 4*(3), 44–60. Retrieved from http://digitalcommons.uri.edu/cgi/viewcontent.cgi?article=1082&context=jmle

Further reading

Choudry, A. (2015). *Learning activism: The intellectual life of contemporary social movements*. Toronto, Canada: University of Toronto Press.

Lievrouw, L.A. (2011). *Alternative and activist new media*. Cambridge, England: Polity Press.

Ollis, T. (2012). *A critical pedagogy of embodied education: Learning to become an activist*. New York, NY: Palgrave Macmillan.

Sützl, W., & Hug, T. (Eds.). (2012). *Activist media and biopolitics: Critical media interventions in the age of biopower*. Innsbruck, Austria: Innsbruck University Press.

Ziccardi, G. (2013). *Resistance, liberation technology and human rights in the digital age*. Dordrecht, Netherlands: Springer.

Theo Hug is professor of educational sciences at the University of Innsbruck (Austria) and coordinator of the Innsbruck Media Studies research forum. His areas of interest include media education and philosophy of education, mobile learning and microlearning, research methodology and theory of knowledge, medialisation and philosophy of science. He is the author and/or editor of several books on various aspects of media, communication, and education, and together with Josef Mitterer he is literary executor of the Ernst von Glasersfeld archive. Since 2015 he has been a member of the European Academy of Sciences and Arts (EASA).

Media Addiction among Children and Youths

DANIJEL LABAŠ
University of Zagreb, Croatia

Children, youths, and media

Today's children and young people are exposed to various media content, and have access to the content on the Internet, radio, television, and in newspapers. Sensational news is often used to attract users to make the media profit and strengthen consumerism in young users of media content which can lead to media addiction in various forms. "In today's digital world, there seems to be a thin line between technology use and abuse. Many people's Internet habits may seem excessive: sleeping with a smartphone under the pillow, texting one person while having a face-to-face conversation with another, or tweeting from a funeral. But some people cross that thin line even one step further, going from Internet use and abuse to Internet addiction" (Perdew, 2014, p. 25). But, this phenomenon is still called by different names: Internet addiction, problematic use of the Internet, compulsive Internet usage, virtual addiction, pathological Internet usage, and Internet abuse (Carlisle, Carlisle, Polychronopoulos, Goodman-Scott, & Kirk-Jenkins, 2016).

However, we are aware that the modern world is unthinkable without mass media. Calling them the "fourth estate" or "extensions of the man" as they were called by Marshall McLuhan (Labaš & Vizler, 2005), mass media undoubtedly affect individuals and their thoughts, ideas, and attitudes (Kunczik, 2014). Thanks to the mass media, there is a lot of information in the world that is created, changed, transmitted, bought, and sold (Malović, 2014).

Furthermore, mass media today are also a means of conveying the expression of popular culture. Mass media "allow multiple consuming of the same forms of popular culture—newspapers and magazines can be read over and over again, the same music videos broadcast on music programs several times a day, television shows rewrite popular series and movies, and mass media are spreading popular culture" (Labaš & Mihovilović, 2013, p. 107). Music programs, series, movies, newspapers, and magazines are just some of the parts of popular culture that entertain many children and young people during their free time.

In fact, mass media, besides informing, educating, and entertaining, increasingly manipulate, impose their views, form opinions, and impose certain daily topics, encourage aggression, violence, and fear. By creating entertaining and manipulative content, media negatively affect children in their everyday life, for example, by advertising and spreading consumerism, tabloidization, sensationalism and other trends, exposure to violence and child pornography (Labaš, 2015). Zlatko Miliša, Mirela Tolić, and Nenad Vertovšek point out the most significant media manipulations: "Superficiality is easier than the depth of content, a shorter subject is easier to convey than deeper and complex information, bizarre attracts more attention than ordinary, media sends messages of consumption as a primary human need" (Miliša & Vertovšek, in Miliša, Tolić, & Vertovšek, 2010, p. 40). Since the media have become so inevitable and their content can harm users we have to defend ourselves from them and their influence on our behavior, ideas, attitudes, and thinking. Many people become addicted to them, which of course applies to both children and young people (Carlisle et al., 2016).

Different research has shown that today's children and youths worldwide are to a great extent exposed to and consume media. Research shows that the world's children spend more than six hours per day on media use (Leggett, 2013). If consumed in an appropriate fashion, the media can enrich children's lives, although excessive use of the media from an early age and exposure to violent and other inappropriate content can adversely affect children's development, thinking, attitudes, and behavior (Common Sense Media, 2013). Many research studies have revealed that even before they start school, children spend several thousand hours on media use, during which they are exposed to tens of thousands of instances of violent content and hundreds of thousands of advertisements (Common Sense Media, 2013; Strasburger, Wilson, & Jordan, 2009; Trend, 2007). W. Potter states that "children's cognitive, emotional and moral reasoning abilities are not developed well enough for them to process … messages in a way that it protects them from harm" (Potter, 2013, p. 416), which has been shown, among others, in an international comparative study of the media habits of children and the attitudes of their parents and the experiences and safety of children on the Internet in Europe and in Croatia (www.eukidsonline.net, hrkids.online). The overall aim of the research conducted in 33 European countries was to gain a better insight into the habits of children using the Internet and contemporary technologies, to examine the frequency and forms of exposure of children to disturbing content and violence, and to examine protective factors and the role of the environment in the protection and education of children and young people on challenges and dangers on the Internet. "In digital society, like ours, it is difficult to find an area of individual or social life where there is no media, and this fact will also determine the direction of the future development of society. ... The media are no longer just the means, they are our cultural environment and the atmosphere. Therefore, education must deal with the media – and this is a kind of media education that will educate and be aware of and critical citizens from the earliest age" (Labaš, 2015, p. 105). The fact is that today's children and young people are not living in some other time and space than this digital one. This was confirmed by the research of the Kaiser Family Foundation (Kaiser Family Foundation, 2011). It was the third piece of research titled "Generation M2: Media in the lives of 8 to 18 year olds," focused on how much young people use the media. The research found that children between the ages of 8 and 18 today spend on average 7 hours and 38 minutes a day on the media, mostly using IT (information technology) tools. Total media use is 53 hours a week. But we have to add that this research does not take into account that many young people use more than one form of media at once. If we only count the use of the media separately, then we could reach usage of 10 hours and 45 minutes a day. The relationship is based on a survey conducted in the United States on a representative sample of 2002 pupils between the third grade of primary school and the last school year, aged 8 to 18. In addition, a group of 702 volunteers spent seven days using electronic means to calculate multitasking use of media.

Media use and addiction as an educational challenge

In this context, it is true that new media and new digital technologies are a challenge from an educational point of view (Ciboci, Kanižaj, & Labaš, 2014) because new technology can lead to new addiction (Perdew, 2014, p. 25). On the one hand, at the anthropological level it can be seen that the (new) media can harm relationships between human beings and immediate interpersonal communication. On the other hand, on a cognitive level the problem of "excessive information" or "congestion of information" is often evidently confused with knowledge, whereby the loss of "specific weight" of information is visible because of the irrefutable fact that in this "flood of information" (Kunczik, 2014) that we are plagued by every day across a variety of media, especially through the webpages—where everyone can be a "journalist"—it is very difficult to distinguish what is important and what is completely irrelevant.

Apart from the irrelevant, there is morally and humanly harmful information about racism, religious intolerance, terrorism, pornography, pedophilia, and violence or the promotion of different political and economic ideologies, some of which have their "reflection" in the so-called "digital gap" not just between information rich countries and those who do not have access to the information (Labaš, 2011) but between children and parents, too ("Preliminary results," 2017).

In fact, children and young people, being socialized by media, have developed ways of using media that are completely different from those used by their parents. They do not make the distinction between "the world" and "the world of the media." They are children in the world of the Internet and the Internet is part of their "real–virtual" world. However, more research that has shown that adolescents are active and self-confident media users, also warns of their marked naivety ("Children's exposure to newer forms of risk behavior," 2018; Buckingham, 2000).

Excessive use of the media and illiteracy or ignorance about the role and influence of the media can lead to various problems, especially in the younger population: from the classic problem of addiction to the isolation of oneself, and the problems of aggression or violence among children stimulated by the use of the Internet and the absorption of its content. Maletzke defines "influence" as "all the processes of behavior and experience that can be reduced to the fact that the person is a recipient of mass communication" (according to Kunczik & Zipfel, 2006, p. 156). Although at the time when Maletzke mentioned the influence of the media he did not think about future media—the Internet and its influence—it is clear that the Internet today strongly influences its users and their thinking, and also influences personality development. The problems mentioned by different scholars and researchers (Labaš, 2011, pp. 37–38), related to the use of the media, especially of the Internet by children and youths, are: exposure of children to violence and inappropriate content because of the impossibility of legal regulation of all Internet sites, but also the alienation of children, cyberbullying, violence, sexualization, and addiction (hrkids.online; Hinduja & Patchin in Bilić, Buljan Flander, & Hrpka, 2012, p. 305; "Experiences and attitudes," 2015).

Given that children are increasingly surrounded by media, we cannot ignore their influence on the behavior and performance of these children. It is important to note once again that children are consciously exposed to media, listen to radio stations, read newspapers or magazines, listen to music, watch television series. We must remember that children are active users of mass media and consume them to meet their needs for entertainment, information, and social development as they are trying to interpret and value media contents, attributing to them various meanings (hrkids.online; Labaš & Vizler, 2005).

Media use and the question of addiction

In this place it is necessary to highlight the fact that research carried out in the United States in 2003 shows that children already spent 1023 hours looking at TV screens, and in school benches 900 hours (Kanižaj & Ciboci, 2011, p. 12). Given the development of media in past years, as we just mentioned before, this ratio has been surely increased (Common Sense Media, 2013). When considering such data, it is not strange or wrong to say that the media are kind of educators of children. An even older 1992 survey concluded that children in their elementary school education saw about 8000 murders and 100 000 other forms of violence in the media. In real life, however, they do not even experience 1% of what is seen in the media (Kanižaj & Ciboci, 2011, p. 11). The media can easily become addictive, whether it is playing video games, watching television, communicating via smartphones, or surfing the Internet (Weinstein, Curtiss Feder, Rosenberg, & Dannon, 2014). But, it is not so easy to reveal and perceive those kinds of problems and even deal with them using various detachment techniques. Due to too much screen exposure (which has become a part of everyday life, to the extent that the dependence cannot be identified), the term "screen time" was introduced. Apart from addiction, attachment to screens affects children and youths in different ways (Nakaya, 2015). As the EUKids Online Croatia 2017 survey showed, almost one in three children aged 9 to 17 communicated online with people whom they did not meet offline. This information suggests that children, even younger ones, focus on socialization and communication with others on social networks, including with people unknown to them ("Preliminary results," 2017).

In the research on the behavior of children on the Internet and Facebook, on the website of the Zagreb Children's Clinic for the Protection of Children, the majority of children visit Facebook many times a day and spend up to several hours a day on the

Internet (Poliklinika za zaštitu djece Grada Zagreba, 2017). When asked about how they spend their free time, 5% said it was on the Internet, while the rest of the time the children spent more time with some other free activities. Nevertheless, in reality 26% of surveyed children spend their free time on the Internet. Is this about creating addiction or the lack of potential free activities that kids love away from the Internet? Of nearly 1500 children surveyed, 30% think that they should spend less time on social networks and the Internet.

The 2013 survey conducted in the United States included teens, generations Y and Z (Madden, Lenhart, Duggan, Cortesi, & Gasser, 2013). The study was carried out with more than 800 children and parents aged 13 to 17 years. The results showed that 95% of teenagers use the Internet on a daily basis, of which about 75% have Internet access on cell phones or tablets. As a comparison, it is claimed that about 50% of adults use the Internet, thus showing a certain gap and the "technological superiority" of younger generations. The study states that 93% of young people have access to a computer, and the differences between them are apparent depending on their social status, race, and age. A little less than 40% of the children surveyed in the research had a smartphone. The authors point out that compared to 2011 this percentage has increased considerably. Two years earlier, in 2011, 23% of children were using smartphones, and by 2013 the percentage had risen to 37%. "Over the past ten years, teens and young adults have been consistently the two groups most likely to go online, even as the internet population has grown and even with documented larger increases in certain age cohorts (e.g. adults 65 and older)" (Lenhart, Purcell, Smith, & Zickuhr, 2010, p. 4). Young Americans between 13 and 17 years of age in 2015 were mostly using the following social media: Facebook (71%), then Instagram (52%), Snapchat (41%), Twitter (33%), Google+ (33%), and the least Vine (24%) (Madden et al., 2013, p. 3). And in the same year children and young people between the ages of 8 and 18 used their smartphones for social networking (40%), listening to music (40%), gaming (23%), visiting websites (22%), and watching videos online (22%) (Common Sense Media, 2013, p. 60).

Internet addiction and its symptoms

As different research has shown, electronic media have become an integral part of the child's everyday life (Ofcom, 2017). They use them during meals, before bedtime, just after waking up, and during time with friends. The consequences of excessive and uncontrolled exposure to electronic media may be slower development, obesity, aggressiveness, lack of concentration and attention, sleep disturbances, and other psychological disturbances. Excessive exposure to electronic media may develop into addiction (Kuss & Griffiths, 2012; Lin & Lei, 2015): "The first person to publicly use the phrase "Internet Addiction disorder" meant it as a joke. In 1995, psychiatrist Ivan Goldberg posted a humorous entry about Internet addiction on PsyCom.net. He crafted it to read like an entry in the *DSM*. In his post, Goldberg describes symptoms such as 'a need for markedly increased amounts of time on Internet to achieve satisfaction' and 'involuntary typing movements of the fingers.' … While Goldberg may have been joking, other professionals began seriously questioning whether there may in fact be such a disorder as Internet addiction" (Perdew, 2014, pp. 25–26).

Scientists still do not agree on the definition of Internet addiction today. But "whether recognized officially or unofficially, Internet addiction seems to be affecting lives in the United States and across the globe. Surveys in the United States and Europe indicate as many as 8.2 percent of the population may be affected by compulsive computer use that results in social, psychological, and neurological problems" (Nakaya, 2015; Perdew, 2014, p. 13).

Starting with the diagnostics of pathological gambling Kimberly S. Young has drawn up the diagnostic internet addiction questionnaire (IADQ, Internet Addiction Diagnostic Questionnaire). "Since then, many researchers have studied compulsive use of the Internet" (Perdew, 2014, p. 27). Mark Griffiths and other doctors saw the similarities between Internet addiction and other addictive behaviors, noting physical problems and symptoms associated with Internet addiction such as: carpal tunnel syndrome, dry eyes, migraines, back aches, poor eating habits, poor hygiene, and irregular sleep (Perdew, 2014, p. 27). "For Internet addicts, being online becomes the most important part of their lives. The Internet consumes thoughts, behaviors, and feelings. But then users begin to need increasingly more time online to get the same high" (Perdew, 2014, p. 29). Young writes that "screen addiction is an impulsive-control problem that can be divided into various subtypes." There is an increasing number of children and young people subject to some of these forms of addiction, as Kimberly Young states: "1. Sexting and Online Sex Addiction – Individuals who suffer from this are typically engaged in viewing, downloading, and trading online pornography or involved in adult fantasy role-play chat rooms, social media, and sexting. 2. Internet Infidelity and Online Affairs – Individuals who suffer from an addiction to chat rooms, social networking, or texting become over-involved in online relationships or may engage in virtual adultery. ... 3. Video Games and Gaming Addiction – Anyone who has experienced it knows all too well – video game addiction is real. Although gaming addiction is not yet officially recognized as a diagnosable disorder by the American Medical Association, there is increasing evidence that people of all ages, especially teens and pre-teens, are facing very real, sometimes severe consequences associated with compulsive use of video and computer games. ... Of course, all gamers are not screen addicts – many teens can play video games a few hours a week, successfully balancing school activities, grades, friends, and family obligations. But for some, gaming has become an uncontrollable compulsion. ... 4. Net Compulsions – Screen Addiction can be generalized compulsive behavior to Internet gambling, shopping, or eBay. These focus on winning and often cause financial problems, relationship problems, and work-related problems among addicts. Gamblers will be mesmerized as they play slot machines, craps, blackjack and roulette on tablets and phones. Millions of Americans play various gambling games on the Internet, even though the businesses are typically illegal, unregulated, and offer no consumer protections. ... Problem gamblers typically deny or minimize the problem. They also go to great lengths to hide their gambling. ... 5. Information Overload – The wealth of data available has created a new type of compulsive behavior regarding excessive Internet and database searches. Screen addiction in this case results in spending greater amounts of time searching and collecting data from the web and organizing information. Obsessive compulsive tendencies and reduced work productivity are associated with this behavior" (http://netaddiction.com/kimberly-young/, 2018; Weinstein et al., 2014). As Laura Perdew explains, "while many experts insist Internet addiction is a legitimate mental disorder, that belief is not universally held in the industry .... Despite these opposing views, many professionals are working to establish Internet addiction as a disorder in its own right. To this end, experts cite parallels between Internet addiction and other forms of addiction" saying that "approximately 86 percent of those supposedly addicted to the Internet are ultimately diagnosed with other disorders, such as depression, anxiety, or learning disabilities" (Perdew, 2014, pp. 34–35, 87).

In addition to the aforementioned problems with addiction, the problems of obesity, insomnia, hyperactivity, or memory problems are often associated with children's use of the media. To the effects we just presented, we need to add the effects of phone addiction by children and young people ("digital natives") who are neglecting face-to-face communication and conversations (Turkle, in Perdew, 2014, pp. 52–56), and the loss of privacy by "sharing too much" on social networks and in "virtual life" (Perdew, 2014, pp. 57–65).

Conclusion

Given the large number of young media and Internet users and given all possible open questions on addiction and the dangers mentioned, it is important to learn how to use the Internet, because "it is necessary to wake and strengthen the awareness that prevention is the best solution" (Flego, 2009 in Labaš, 2011, p. 43). The results of different research presented in this paper tell us that children are active media users, so they should be media-literate in order to know how to use the media properly, to get information about media issues, and to understand the importance of the media in their everyday life and thus in the educational system (Kanižaj & Car, 2015; Labaš, 2015). The fact is that the Internet has a number of positive effects with a certain amount of risky and harmful content for a healthy psychosocial development of children and young people, however, there are still quite unexplored issues that require additional and continuous research insight (Li, O'Brien, Snyder, & Howard, 2015). Also, excessive use of the media can lead to social isolation, which could create addiction. Therefore, it is important to work to increase awareness of this issue, along with the inclusion of children and young people as active participants (Bilić et al., 2012). "Digital culture generates new competencies, skills and behaviors" (Pasqualletti & Nanni, 2005, p. 259), but equally can also lead to new problems and addictions in children and young people with whom we have to interact in the educational field.

SEE ALSO: Adolescent Literacy in a Digital World; Communication; Critical Pedagogy; Digital Literacy; Media and Adolescent Identity Development; Media Competence; Media Literacy in Croatia; Preschool Children and Media; Representation of Children and Youths in Media; Sexting; Teaching about Media Violence

References

Bilić, V., Buljan Flander, G., & Hrpka, H. (2012). *Nasilje nad djecom i među djecom*. Jastrebarsko, Croatia: Naklada Slap.

Buckingham, D. (2000). *After the death of childhood, growing up in the age of electronic media*. Cambridge, England: Polity Press.

Carlisle, K.L., Carlisle, R.M., Polychronopoulos, G.B., Goodman-Scott, E., & Kirk-Jenkins, A. (2016). Exploring internet addiction as a process addiction. *Journal of Mental Health Counseling, 38*(2), 170–182.

Children's exposure to newer forms of risk behavior in the virtual world. (2018, February 15). *Predstavljanje rezultata o izloženosti djece novijim oblicima rizičnog ponašanja u virtualnom svijetu*. Retrieved from http://hrkids.online/post/third-press/

Ciboci, L., Kanižaj, I., & Labaš, D. (2014). Media education from the perspective of parents of preschool children: Challenges and trends in free time media use. *Medijska istraživanja, 20*(2), 53–67.

Common Sense Media. (2013). Zero to eight: Children's media use in America 2013. Retrieved from http://www.commonsensemedia.org/research/zero-to-eight-childrens-media-use-in-america-2013

Experiences and attitudes of children, parents and teachers towards electronic media. (2015). Iskustva i stavovi djece, roditelja i učitelja spram elektroničkih medija [Experiences and attitudes of children, parents and teachers towards electronic media]. Retrieved from https://www.unicef.hr/wp-content/uploads/2015/09/Izvjestaj_-_Iskustva_i_stavovi_djece_roditelja_i_ucitelja_prema_elektronickim_medijima.pdf

Kaiser Family Foundation. (2011, February 11). Generation M2: Media in the lives of 8 to 18 year olds. Retrieved from https://www.kff.org/other/report/generation-m2-media-in-the-lives-of-8-to-18-year-olds/

Kanižaj, I., & Car, V. (2015). Hrvatska: nove prilike za sustavan pristup medijskoj pismenosti. In V. Car, L. Turčilo, & M. Matović (Eds.), *Medijska pismenost – preduvjet za odgovorne medije* [Media literacy – a prerequisite for responsible media] (pp. 19–38). Sarajevo, Bosnia and Herzegowina: Fakultet političkih nauka Univerziteta u Sarajevu.

Kanižaj, I., & Ciboci, L. (2011). Kako je nasilje preko medija ušlo u naše domove. Utjecaj, učinci i posljedice nasilja u medijima na djecu i mlade. In L. Ciboci, I. Kanižaj, & D. Labaš (Eds.), *Djeca medija. Od marginalizicije do senzacije* [Children of the media. From marginalization to sensationalism] (pp. 11–34). Zagreb, Croatia: Matica hrvatska.

Kunczik, M. (2014). Masovni mediji i njihov utjecaj na društvo. In S. Malović, (Ed.), *Masovno komuniciranje* [Mass communication] (pp. 15–39). Zagreb, Croatia: Golden marketing-Tehnička knjiga – Sveučilište Sjever.

Kunczik, M., & Zipfel, A. (2006). *Uvod u znanost o medijima i komunikologiju* [Introduction to media science and communication]. Zagreb, Croatia: Friedrich Ebert Stiftung.

Kuss, D.J., & Griffiths, M.D. (2012). Internet and gaming addiction: A systematic literature review of neuroimaging studies. *Brain Science, 2*(3), 347–374.

Labaš, D. (2011). Djeca u svijetu interneta – zatočenici virtualnog svijeta. Pedagoški modeli i otvorena pitanja. In L. Ciboci, I. Kanižaj, & D. Labaš (Eds.), *Djeca medija. Od marginalizacije do senzacije* [Children of the media. From marginalization to sensationalism] (pp. 35–64). Zagreb, Croatia: Matica hrvatska.

Labaš, D. (2015). "Djeca medija" – mladi obrazuju mlade. In V. Car, L. Turčilo, & M. Matović (Eds.), *Medijska pismenost – preduvjet za odgovorne medije* [Media literacy – a prerequisite for responsible media] (pp. 109–121). Sarajevo, Bosnia and Herzegovina: Fakultet političkih nauka Univerziteta u Sarajevu.

Labaš, D., & Vizler, A. (2005). Odgovornost primatelja i medijska etika [Media ethics and responsibility of the recipient]. *Nova prisutnost, 3*(2), 277–295.

Labaš, D., & Mihovilović, M. (2013). Rodni stereotipi u Cosmpolitanu i Kliku [Gender stereotypes in Cosmopolitan and Klik]. *Kultura komuniciranja, 2*(2), 113–174.

Leggett, S. (2013). *Children and their media 2013. Childwise.* Retrieved from https://prezi.com/6spkttfivlhp/children-and-their-media-2013/

Lenhart, A., Purcell, K., Smith, A., & Zickuhr, K. (2010). *Social media & mobile internet use among teens and young adults.* Washington, DC: Pew Research Center. Retrieved from http://www.pewinternet.org/files/old-media//Files/Reports/2010/PIP_Social_Media_and_Young_Adults_Report_Final_with_toplines.pdf

Li, W., O'Brien, J.E., Snyder, S.M., & Howard, M.O. (2015). Characteristics of Internet addiction/pathological internet use in U.S. university students: A qualitative-method investigation. *PLoS One, 10*(2), e0117372, https://www.ncbi.nlm.nih.gov/pmc/articles/PMC4315426/

Lin, F., & Lei, H. (2015). Structural brain imaging and internet addiction. In C. Montag, & M. Reuter (Eds.), *Internet addiction: Neuroscientific approaches and therapeutical interventions* (pp. 21–42). Cham, Switzerland: Springer International Publishing.

Madden, M., Lenhart, A., Duggan, M., Cortesi, S., & Gasser, U. (2013). *Teens and technology 2013.* Pew Research Center's Internet and American Life Project. Retrieved from http://www.pewinternet.org/files/old-media/Files/Reports/2013/PIP_TeensandTechnology2013.pdf

Malović, S. (2014). Masovno komuniciranje [Mass communication]. In S. Malović (Ed), *Masovno komuniciranje* (pp. 41–132). Zagreb, Croatia: Golden marketing-Tehnička knjiga – Sveučilište Sjever.

Miliša, Z., Tolić, M., & Vertovšek, N. (2010). *Mladi – odgoj za medije: priručnik za stjecanje medijskih kompetencija* [Youth, media education: a manual for the acquisition of media competences]. Zagreb/Zadar, Croatia: M.E.P./Udruga CINAZ.

Nakaya, A.C. (2015). *Internet and social media addiction.* San Diego, CA: ReferencePoint Press.

Ofcom. (2017). Children and parents: Media use and attitudes report. Retrieved from https://www.ofcom.org.uk/__data/assets/pdf_file/0020/108182/children-parents-media-use-attitudes-2017.pdf

Pasqualetti, F., & Nanni, C. (2005). Novi mediji i digitalna kultura. Izazov odgoju [New media and digital culture: Challenge for education]. *Kateheza, 27*(3), 244–265.

Perdew, L. (2014). *Internet addiction.* North Mankato, MN: Abdo Publishing.

Poliklinika za zaštitu djece Grada Zagreba. (2017). Istraživanje o iskustvima i ponašanjima djece na internetu i društvenoj mreži Facebook [Research about the experiences and behaviors of children on the internet and on the social network Facebook]. Retrieved from http://www.poliklinika-djeca.hr/istrazivanja/istrazivanje-o-iskustvima-i-ponasanjima-djece-na-internetu-i-na-drustvenoj-mrezi-facebook-2/

Potter, W.J. (2013). *Media literacy.* Thousand Oaks, CA: SAGE.

Preliminary results of national research on child and youth safety on the internet. (2017, November 21). *Preliminarni rezultati nacionalnog istraživanja sigurnosti djece i mladih na internetu.* Retrieved from http://hrkids.online/post/second-press/

Strasburger, V.C., Wilson, B.J., & Jordan, A. (2009). *Children, adolescents and the media.* Thousand Oaks, CA: SAGE.

Trend, D. (2007). *The myth of media violence.* Malden, MA: Blackwell.

Young, K.S. (2018). *Screen addiction.* Retrieved from http://netaddiction.com/compulsive-surfing/

Weinstein, A., Curtiss Feder, L., Rosenberg, K.P., & Dannon, P. (2014). Internet addiction disorder: Overview and controversies. In K.P. Rosenberg & L. Curtiss Feder (Eds.), *Behavioral addictions* (pp. 99–117). Retrieved from http://scitechconnect.elsevier.com/wp-content/uploads/2014/10/Internet-Addiction-Disorder.pdf

Further reading

Bilić, V. (2016). The net-generation methods of learning, online activities and upbringing outcomes. *Croatian Journal of Education, 18*(1), 259–277.

Chen, Q., Quan, X., Lu, H., Fei, P., & Li, M. (2015). Comparison of the personality and other psychological factors of students with internet addiction who do and do not have associated social dysfunction. *Shanghai Archives of Psychiatry, 27*(1), 36–41.

Ciboci, L., Kanižaj, I., & Labaš, D. (2015). Public opinion research as a prerequisite for media education strategies and policies. In S. Kotilainen & R. Kupiainen (Eds.), *Reflections on media education futures* (pp. 171–182). Gothenburg, Sweden: The International Clearinghouse on Children, Youth & Media Nordicom, University of Gothenburg.

Kuss, D.J., Griffiths, M.D., Karila, L., & Billieux, J. (2014). Internet addiction: A systematic review of epidemiological research for the last decade. *Current Pharmaceutical Design,* 20(00), 1–26. Retrieved from https://pdfs.semanticscholar.org/1682/7c8aa80f394a5117126e1ec548fd08410860.pdf

Won Jin, S., & Berge, J. (2015). An emerging global concern of internet addiction: Sociocultural influences on immigrant families. *The Global Studies Journal, 9*(1), 15–34.

Younes, F., Halawi, G., Jabbour, H., El Osta, N., Karam L., Hajj A., & Rabbaa Khabbaz, L. (2016). Internet addiction and relationships with insomnia, anxiety, depression, stress and self-esteem in university students: A cross-sectional designed study. *PLoS ONE, 11*(9), e0161126. doi: 10.1371/journal.pone.0161126

Young, K.S., & Nabuco de Abreu, C. (2011). *Internet addiction: A handbook and guide to evaluation and treatment*. Hoboken, NJ: John Wiley & Sons, Inc.

Danijel Labaš, PhD, Associate Professor, studied philosophy and theology in Zagreb and Rome (Pontificia Università Gregoriana) and in 1996 earned his PhD in communication sciences at Università Pontificia Salesiana in Rome. Dr Labaš has been a faculty member at the University of Zagreb Center for Croatian Studies continuously since 2007. He was the head lecturer of different courses on communication science, semiotics of mass communication, journalism ethics, media pedagogy, media and children, and media and violence. He has participated in numerous scientific conferences at home and abroad and has published several books and collections, as well as scientific papers. He is president of the Association for Communication and Media Culture.

Media and Adolescent Identity Development

ELLEN MIDDAUGH
San José State University, USA

Media have long been considered an important resource for adolescent identity development. Print and TV media provide opportunities to learn about various ways of life and roles people play within them. Sharing media preferences (movies, music, etc.) is a common method by which teens assert identity. These uses of media have potential positive and negative consequences, depending on the media and a given adolescent's interaction with them. For example, media can serve as a window into alternative possible futures, which is particularly important for teens marginalized in their face-to-face communities. On the other hand, lack of representation, presentation of harmful stereotypes, or unrealistic standards can lead teens to undervalue or distance themselves from certain aspects of their identities.

With the rise of the Internet and digital media, theory and research have identified new dimensions to the relationship between media and adolescent identity development. One line of research builds on the early predictions that the Internet would provide increased opportunities to use media for identity exploration, and has begun to unpack the relationship between different kinds of digital media use and identity development as a global construct. Additional lines of research focus on the relationship between media and particular domains of identity development—gender, ethnic or racial, civic or political, LGBTQ, and disability—paying attention to a range of media formats but with considerable attention on digital and social media.

While the research on media and adolescent identity development crosses cultural settings (United States, China, Netherlands, Israel, etc.) much of the work focuses on industrialized nations where an extended adolescence is common and the media environment is technologically advanced.

Media and global identity development

Developmental psychologists view adolescence as a critical period for identity development. The combination of increasing cognitive capacity for introspection and hypothetical thinking, an expanding social world, and physical changes prompts the questions, "Who am I? Where do I belong? Where am I going?" in multiple domains (Steinberg, 2017, Ch. 8). The development of a coherent and stable sense of identity is considered to be an important aspect of successful development. Key to the process is a phase of purposeful searching in which adolescents try on different aspects of identity and get feedback, especially from peers. This phase is described as moratorium and is viewed as a useful stepping-stone toward identity achievement, which is associated with greater well-being than other identity states. Less productive states include foreclosure (identify formed without exploration in deference to authority) and diffusion (shifting identity based on context with little purposeful searching) (Steinberg, 2017, Ch. 8).

Earlier research on broadcast and print media suggests that seeing multiple ways of living through media may support identity exploration (Subrahmanyam & Šmahel, 2011). Current research seeks to better understand the role of digital media (text, video games, social network sites, etc.) in supporting adolescent identity development. One view is that by allowing youths to produce and share media easily with peers and the public or at times to create alternate identities in anonymous settings, digital media create opportunities for identity exploration and experimentation, particularly for those who are in situations that limit opportunities for exploration in their physical communities (Manago, 2015). This view was first rooted in early observations that the anonymity provided by online chat rooms provides opportunities for people to try on different personas with little risk.

Those who are shy or lonely in their face-to-face communities may feel more confident trying out different aspects of their identity in the comfort of an anonymous setting or through a game avatar where they get feedback from other group members or players. There is evidence that some teens do engage in identity experimentation by pretending to be different online than they are in real life, particularly shy or lonely teens. What is more common, however, is identity expression in which adolescents and emerging adults manage their identity by portraying an aspirational or ideal self (Manago, 2015; Subrahmanyam & Šmahel, 2011). The positive interpretation of this is that digital media provide opportunities for adolescents to create a self that can serve as a guide as they resolve identity conflicts.

An alternate view is that the increased opportunities through digital media to present aspects of identity to a range of audiences in a series of brief exchanges encourages identity fragmentation (similar to a state of diffusion) because teens avoid rather than learn to resolve conflicts in their identity. Findings related to problematic gaming and rates of Internet addiction among the very types of teens who are likely to use the Internet for identity exploration, those who are shy or have large discrepancies between their actual and ideal selves, support this hypothesis (Manago, 2015).

Research that directly tests the impact of social media use on adolescent self-concept tends to support the fragmentation hypothesis as well. Teens who use the Internet for identity exploration tend to have less coherent self-concepts (Davis, 2013). However, at this point, the research is entirely cross-sectional. Longitudinal studies would be needed to determine whether online identity exploration is causing identity distress or less coherence in self-concept or whether teens in this identity state are more likely to engage in such identity exploration. Longitudinal studies would also be able to provide information as to whether the combination of exploration and weakened self-concept at one time point is a period of productive exploration that is later followed by a stronger and more coherent identity or whether it is indicative of long-term problems in identity.

Other concerns include the potential for the adoption of negative or extreme identities, for example over-identification with violent video game characters or identification with extremist movements, which have previously been found to explicitly target adolescents with youth-friendly media through music, videos, social media, and so on. It is worth noting, however, that the impact of such efforts is difficult to establish (see Middaugh, Schofield-Clark, & Ballard, 2017).

A final mechanism through which social media is believed to support adolescent identity development is through the management of relationships. With social media, teens are able to maintain relationships across settings (school, hobbies) or transitions (high school to college), which may encourage greater identity integration as all these relationships are being conducted in the same "place" (i.e. the social network site) (Manago, 2015). Peers also play an important role in adolescent identity development, so to the extent that social media can facilitate and help with maintaining relationships, as several studies suggest it can, then such media use can indirectly support identity development (Davis, 2013).

At this point, research has identified multiple forms of identity work that can happen through digital media (experimentation, exploration, expression) in a variety of settings (social media, games, anonymous online communities) and through varied pathways (directly or indirectly through friendships). Additionally, the teens who use media vary in their own initial identity states (foreclosure, diffusion, moratorium, achievement), which may impact how they use media for identity work. In order to resolve conflicting findings and conclusions, in addition to longitudinal research, research will likely need to take into account and systematically explore how these different forms of identity work, settings, and initial states interact to produce more or less positive identity outcomes for adolescents.

Media- and domain-specific identity development

Identity development has also been studied through the lens of specific areas of identity, asking whether and how teens come to understand the role of gender, sexuality, race, ethnicity, religion, work, and so on as part of their identity.

Racial and ethnic identity

Ethnic identity development is considered to be a particularly important aspect of identity development for minority youths who must resolve the awareness of discrimination or lack of representation with a positive affiliation with their own race or ethnicity (Steinberg, 2017, Ch. 8). A substantial body of research finds that a positive racial or ethnic identity leads to higher self-esteem and a sense of well-being and lower rates of personal distress and mental health problems (Smith & Silva, 2011). US media portrayals of racial and ethnic minority youths, which have been well documented as both under-representing and presenting harmful stereotypes of Black, Latino, Asian American, and Native American individuals, may present barriers to the development of a positive ethnic identity (Tukachinsky, 2015). The potential harm to self-concept is a common argument for more inclusive media, but there is a surprisingly small amount of research that directly tests the impact of such media on adolescents' identity and self-concept. This is an area where additional research is needed.

There is also evidence that media can play a positive role in racial and ethnic identity development. First- and second-generation immigrant youths can use movies, television, and music to connect to their native culture and express cultural identity. There is also evidence that minority youths use social media to explore their racial or ethnic identity with peers and are often more comfortable doing so in that setting (Subrahmanyam & Šmahel, 2011) and engage in media production to counter negative stereotypes (Jenkins, Shresthova, Gamber-Thompson, Kugler-Vilenchik, & Zimmerman, 2016).

Gender and sexual identity

Media also play an important role in gender identity development. Much of this influence happens before adolescence, when children receive messages through television, books, and movies about the activities, careers, and behaviors that are associated with being male or female. During adolescence, as biological changes create more pronounced physical differences between genders, the awareness of gender identity becomes more pronounced. At this point in development, media serve to provide information about dating and sexual behavior and gender roles within such relationships, often reinforcing traditional conceptions of gender roles and portrayal of females as objects rather than subjects of sexual interest (Steinberg, 2017, Ch. 7).

Overall, exposure to television, film, magazines, and music videos is associated with increased body dissatisfaction, particularly for females, which may complicate the development of a positive gender identity. There is also evidence that digital and social media reinforce these trends, though it is not clear whether such media have a different or stronger effect than traditional forms of media.

For LGBTQ youths, media provide important opportunities for gender and sexual identity exploration (Pascoe, 2011). Such youths are less likely to have access to related peers and role models in their face-to-face life than other groups, thus media provide opportunities for youths to explore and develop positive sexual and gender identities. As with racial and ethnic identity, exposure to stereotypes or negative portrayals may present challenges to positive sexual or gender identity development. However, LGBTQ individuals also often cite media as a critical source of support in understanding and accepting their gender and/or sexual identity. Not only do television and film provide access to a limited but potentially greater number of role models than teens have access to in their local communities, but the Internet has been cited as a critical support for finding information and access to community for LGBTQ youths.

Disability and identity

As with race, gender, and sexual orientation, youths with disabilities must grapple with lack of representation or misrepresentation in the media as they come to an understanding of how their disability fits into their personal and public identities. Additionally, media, and particularly digital media, can provide opportunities for youths to take a more active role in constructing their public identity (Ginsburg, 2012). Through blogs, YouTube videos, and social media, youths with a range of disabilities are able to share how they see themselves and present a positive identity to a larger public. The multimedia format may also be particularly valuable for youths who are nonverbal as it allows for public expression of identity and personality that may be overlooked in face-to-face life (Ginsburg, 2012).

Additionally, social media provide opportunities for individuals with disabilities to connect with each other and form community identity, as has been noted among individuals with Autism Spectrum Disorder (ASD) (Pinchevsky & Peters, 2016). Peer communication is a critical component of identity development, but for adolescents with ASD, face-to-face communication can present challenges that are not present in an online setting, such as the need to read facial cues or make eye contact. Thus social media may provide a particularly good setting for identity exploration through peer interaction.

Civic and political identity development

Civic identity is the extent to which adolescents clarify their sense of belonging and commitment to participation in a larger community through participation in civic life (Youniss & Yates, 1997). Broadcast and print media convey to adolescents who (and who is not) an elected official and the types of personality characteristics elected officials have. While there are many factors that contribute to youth disinterest in political engagement, one category of reason has to do with conceptions of the type of person who is cut out for politics (someone who likes to argue or tell other people what to do). Some of these dynamics may simply be replicated or exacerbated through digital media as video clips and tweets provide youths with images of politicians.

Research on civic identity development suggests that opportunities to explore civic issues, connect with the community, and develop civic skills help to counteract some of these influences and are supportive of immediate and continued civic and political participation (see Middaugh, Schofield-Clark, & Ballard, 2017). Case studies of young activist groups find that in some cases, such as the Harry Potter Alliance, media can play a role in bringing groups of young people together in a community that then inspires a range of actions (Jenkins et al., 2016) providing the kinds of experiences that are supportive of civic identity development typically found in face-to-face communities. Research also finds a relationship between youth participation in a range of online communities and civic and political engagement, reinforcing (though not directly testing) the idea that such communities support the development of civic identity (see Middaugh, Schofield-Clark, & Ballard, 2017).

Conclusion

The overall landscape of research on media and adolescent identity development suggests that the growing variety of media with which adolescents interact and the expanded role of social media in the life of the teen play a significant role in adolescent identity development. At this point research has identified significant opportunities for identity exploration, particularly for marginalized youths. However, these opportunities must also be examined in light of the risks of fragmentation, reinforcing of stereotypes, and adoption of negative identity, among others. Several recommendations for future research have been made throughout this entry, with an emphasis on the need for longitudinal studies and more direct empirical tests of the impact of different areas of identity work and media participation on adolescent outcomes. Additionally, research examining how media literacy and media literacy education may moderate the impact of media participation on adolescent development is needed.

SEE ALSO: Adolescent Literacy in a Digital World; Civic Activism; Mediatization; Representation of Politics; Representation of Race; Representations of Gender, Sexuality, and Women in Popular Music; Youth Media

References

Davis, K. (2013). Young people's digital lives: The impact of interpersonal relationships and digital media use on adolescents' sense of identity. *Computers in Human Behavior, 29*, 2281–2293. doi: 10.1016/j.chb.2013.05.022

Ginsburg, F. (2012). Disability in the digital age. In H. Horst & D. Miller (Eds.), *Digital anthropology*. London, England: Berg.

Jenkins, H., Shresthova, S., Gamber-Thompson, L., Kugler-Vilenchik, N., & Zimmerman, A. (2016). *By any media necessary: The new youth activism*. New York, NY: NYU Press.

Manago, A. (2015). Identity development in the digital age: The case of social networking sites. In K. McLean & M. Syed (Eds.), *The Oxford handbook of identity development*. Oxford, England: Oxford University Press.

Middaugh, E., Schofield-Clark, L., & Ballard, P. (2017). Digital media, participatory politics and positive youth development. *Pediatrics, 140*(Suppl. 2), S127–S131. doi: 10.1542/peds.2016-1758Q

Pascoe, C. J. (2011). Resource and risk: Youth sexuality and new media use. *Sexuality Research and Social Policy, 8*(1), 5–17.

Pinchevsky, A., & Peters, J. (2016). Autism and new media: Disability between technology and society. *New Media & Society, 18*(11), 2507–2523. doi: 10.1177/1461444815594441

Smith, T., & Silva, L. (2011). Ethnic identity and personal well-being of people of color: A meta-analysis. *Journal of Counseling Psychology, 58*(1), 42–60. doi: 10.1037/a0021528

Steinberg, L. (2017). *Adolescence* (11th ed.). New York, NY: McGraw-Hill.

Subrahmanyam, K., & Šmahel, D. (2011). *Digital youth: The role of digital media in development*. New York, NY: Springer.

Tukachinsky, R. (2015). Where we have been and where we can go from here: Looking to the future in research on media, race, and ethnicity. *Journal of Social Issues, 71*(1), 186–199. doi: 10.1111/josi.12104

Youniss, J., & Yates, M. (1997). *Community service and social responsibility*. Chicago, IL: University of Chicago Press.

Further reading

boyd, d. (2014). *It's complicated: The social lives of networked teens*. New Haven, CT: Yale University Press.

Gardner, H., & Davis, K. (2014). *The app generation: How today's youth navigate identity, intimacy, and imagination in the digital world*. New Haven, CT: Yale University Press.

Middaugh, E., & Kirshner, B. (2015). *#youthaction: Becoming political in the digital age*. Charlotte, NC: Information Age Press.

Ellen Middaugh, PhD, is an assistant professor of child and adolescent development in the Lurie College of Education at San José State University. Her research focuses on the influence of varied social contexts on youth civic identity development and on the implications of digital media for positive youth development. Recent publications include "U Suk! Participatory Media and Youth Experiences with Political Discourse" in *Youth & Society* (2016), "The Social and Emotional Components of Gaming" in *Democracy & Education* (2016), and "Youth Comprehension of Political Messages in YouTube Videos" in *New Media & Society* (2015). She previously served as research director for the Mills College Civic Engagement Research Group.

Media and Eating Disorders

RACHEL F. RODGERS and JENNIFER L. O'FLYNN
Northeastern University, USA

SIÂN A. McLEAN
Victoria University, Australia

In western societies, the mass media, including print but also increasingly screen forms of media, contribute to the marketing of appearance concerns and body shape and weight policing through the creation and mass broadcast of unrealistic appearance ideals, the advertising of products aiming to change appearance, and the presentation of body shape as highly malleable and controllable. In addition, it has been suggested that media promote the commodification of bodies and simultaneously encourage (over)consumption while glorifying restraint of food intake and leanness. Together, these messages create a discourse that has been suggested to increase the likelihood of individuals engaging in extreme weight-control behaviors, such as inappropriately restricting food intake, over-exercising, or engaging in purging behaviors (compensatory behaviors to attempt to counteract food consumption and to prevent weight gain), that may result in eating disorders.

Here, we will provide an overview of the ways in which media create this discourse, followed by an examination of the evidence supporting the association between media consumption and exposure and eating disorders with specific focus on social media as an emerging form of media. Finally, directions for future investigation and implications will be presented.

Media content

Appearance ideals

The bodies represented in the media are, in the vast majority, very lean and toned, with an emphasis on extreme thinness for women, and hypermuscularity for men. These bodies represent a very small proportion of the range of shapes and sizes found among the general population, and the discrepancy between the average body size depicted in the media, and that of the general US population in particular, has been increasing dramatically over the past decades. In fact, increasingly, the women depicted both in print and screen media have body weights that are unhealthily low, thus normalizing and glamorizing underweight.

In addition to the portrayal of a somewhat singular body type presented as ideal, media images are almost without exception digitally manipulated in ways that to a smaller or greater extent modify the body shapes depicted to render them even more unrealistic. In this manner, body shapes are manipulated to be thinner, or to be leaner and more muscular, appearance of skin is digitally altered to be flawless and perfect, and facial attractiveness enhanced. This manipulation of media images may amplify the gap between bodies and appearance presented in media images, and those lived in by most individuals. Importantly, although manipulated, these images are presented as real and attainable, which potentially increases the likelihood that individuals will strive to attain such an appearance.

The creation of positive expectations associated with appearance ideals

In addition to the depiction of individuals with unrealistic bodies, and the creation of appearance ideals that are largely unattainable by healthy means, the media reinforce the desirability of such body shapes by associating them with positive life outcomes including success, happiness, health, and popularity. This is achieved through a discourse transmitted through the text in media products as well as the images that equate slenderness with socially valued personal attributes such as self-discipline as well as positive achievements and outcomes. For example, luxury brands depict extremely slender women in their advertisements, implying that the achievement of such an appearance is associated with the lifestyle depicted in these advertisements and the capacity to purchase their products. These implicit messages embedded in media content increase the positive expectations of achieving appearance ideals.

Expectations of attaining personal goals in the professional and personal sphere may make an important contribution to an individual's striving for appearance ideals. Worryingly, such messages regarding the benefits of thinness and socially prescribed attractiveness can be found in children's media content including books but to an even greater extent in television and cartoons. Similarly, high rates of weight-stigmatizing content occur in various types of media, in the form both of humor at the expense of large individuals and as commentary around their shape and weight. Such messages also contribute to emphasizing the importance placed on thinness and weight control. In this way, the media increase the desirability of unrealistic body shapes and sizes by creating the expectation that achieving such an appearance will result in social rewards and prevent social exclusion or stigma.

Controllability of appearance

Associated with the discourse emphasizing the rewards of attaining media ideals is an emphasis on the controllability of weight, and a presentation in media of shape and weight as being highly malleable and amenable through strategies such as dieting and exercise. In recent years, an increasing amount of media content has been devoted to weight management and weight loss, for example through reality television and infomercials, and it has been suggested that such content exacerbates unrealistic expectations regarding the degree to which significant weight loss and body shape changes are possible. In addition, consistent with other types of appearance-related media, such content generally targets and depicts women to a greater extent than men, and greater emphasis is placed on modifying eating patterns, mostly through restriction, as opposed to exercise as a strategy for achieving weight loss. Thus, the increasing focus on individual responsibility and capability to control weight is another important aspect of media discourse.

Media, capitalism, consumerism, and commodification

A critical underpinning of the points outlined above is the consumer culture in which this media discourse evolves. The setting up of the body as a site for ongoing improvements occurs within a context in which appearance is a highly lucrative market (beauty, diet, fitness, etc.) and the media participate in both creating body "problems" and promoting a variety of products promising to alleviate them. In this way, for example, the term "cellulite" first appeared in the magazine *Vogue* in 1968 and has since opened the doors to a huge market for cosmetic products and procedures. Furthermore, as capitalism is in essence a growth model, new body problems and their accompanying solutions must constantly be created to sustain the economic model, and therefore individuals are prey to the media continuously creating new and unattainable appearance criteria and standards that they fail to meet. Similarly, the increasing presence of male bodies in media has been accompanied by the identification of men as a valuable appearance-market, and has been accompanied by a rise in the promotion of personal care and grooming products for men, as well as a wide array of muscularity enhancing products.

From a critical standpoint, capitalism, and through it the media, can be viewed as having largely commodified the body, that is, appropriated the body as a form of merchandise. Technology has had an important role to play in this by enabling the rearrangement, modification, removal, and fragmentation of body parts in the service of appearance improvement. Cosmetic surgery represents a more extreme form of this commodification, and the surgical transformation of bodies with the aim of attaining socially constructed appearance ideals reflects the lengths to which society has normalized the undergoing of extreme medical procedures in the pursuit of appearance ideals.

In addition, it is important to consider the role played by another important stakeholder; that is, the food industry. Contemporary western societies are characterized by an overabundance of food, and, notably, carefully engineered foods that are designed to be difficult to eat in moderation. Advertising constitutes one of the most effective ways for the food industry to maintain or increase their "stomach share," which is essential to growth within a capitalist structure (Moss, 2013). Thus, the media contribute to the creation of an environment that is saturated in food cues and invitations to consume calorically dense foods, while simultaneously promoting an ultra-slender appearance ideal. In a capitalist consumer society, social participation is enacted through consumption, and identity is defined and developed through a similar process. As a result, this juxtaposition has been argued to create a double-bind for individuals who are caught between these two extremes, and who may develop a "bulimic" style of interacting (oscillating between restriction and over-consumption) within this environment (Bordo, 2004).

Empirical evidence for the relationship between media exposure and eating disorders

Definition of eating disorders

Eating disorders are serious mental health conditions marked by preoccupation with weight and shape manifesting in disordered eating and weight-control behaviors that result in medical problems, severe impairments in functioning, emotional distress, and, in extreme cases, death. The *Diagnostic and Statistical Manual of Mental Disorders* (5th ed.; DSM-5; American Psychiatric Association, 2013) contains five diagnostic categories of eating disorders, including Anorexia Nervosa (AN), Bulimia Nervosa (BN), Binge Eating Disorder (BED), Other Specified Feeding or Eating Disorders (OSFED), and Unspecified Feeding or Eating Disorders (UFED). AN symptoms include an extreme fear of fat and weight gain that leads to eating restriction and low body weight. Individuals with BN often fall within normal weight ranges and engage in binging episodes, during which they consume an unusually large amount of food followed by inappropriate compensatory behaviors such as self-induced vomiting, use of laxatives, or excessive exercise to attempt to prevent weight gain. BED is characterized by binging episodes during which individuals report a loss of control and consume a large amount of food in a discrete time period, but these episodes are not followed by purging or other forms of compensation. OSFED and UFED include disordered eating behaviors and symptoms that do not meet full criteria for AN, BN, or BED. Disordered eating encompasses a wide variety of abnormal and unhealthy eating behaviors that do not meet full criteria for an eating disorder diagnosis, but may include many of the same features such as restriction, binging, or purging. Common among all eating disorders are negative feelings related to weight and body shape, with AN, BN, and several forms of OSFED marked specifically by preoccupation with one's body and obsession with weight-control behaviors.

Prevalence, morbidity, and mortality

Eating disorders are prevalent within adolescent populations, with the average onset of eating disorders between 14 and 19 years old. While lifetime prevalence of AN, BN, and BED are estimated to be 0.6%, (0.9% for females), 0.6% (0.5% females), and 2.8% (3.5% for females) respectively (Hudson, Hiripi, Pope, & Kessler, 2007), rates of individuals meeting criteria for subthreshold AN (meeting most but not all criteria for diagnosis) are estimated to be higher, and recent surveys have revealed escalating rates of eating disorders, with 5.6–6.9% of the population sampled in a 2015 study having met criteria for BED and subthreshold BED within the past three months (Hay, Girosi, & Mond, 2015). Further, research among college samples highlights the alarming rates of eating disorder symptoms in this population, with 54.2% of students having reported criteria for some type of eating disorder or pathology (Quick, Berg, Bucchianeri, & Byrd-Bredbenner, 2014) and 30.2% reported engaging in compensatory behaviors to control weight after eating in the past month (Lipson & Sonneville, 2017). Overall, the prevalence of eating disorders has continued to increase in recent years.

Eating disorders, specifically AN, have the highest mortality rate of any mental health disorder due to their high comorbidity with medical complications and other mental health conditions, including suicidal ideation and behaviors. Eating disorders have high comorbidity with several medical conditions, including heart complications that may lead to cardiac arrest, skin and teeth damage (BN), biochemical imbalances and abnormalities, and gastrointestinal alterations and damage. Eating disorders are also strongly associated with other mental health conditions, including anxiety, depression and obsessive-compulsive disorder, general impairment in functioning, and suicidality (ideation, plans, and attempts).

Evidence of influence of traditional media on eating disorders

Disordered eating and eating disorders often begin with dieting and weight-control behaviors aimed at losing weight or increasing muscle mass, resulting from sociocultural pressures to attain an ideal body shape that is slender with little body fat, or highly muscular with little body fat. As described above, dieting, weight loss, and muscle enhancing pressures and images endorsing the thin or muscular ideal are pervasive in modern media. Thus, exposure to, followed by endorsement of, these ideals, that is, internalization of media ideals, may lead to dissatisfaction with one's appearance, and increased efforts to attain appearance ideals.

In support of this process, longitudinal research demonstrates that internalization of the thin ideal promoted by the media, body dissatisfaction, and perceived pressure to be thin are risk factors for eating disorders in females (Rohde, Stice, & Marti, 2015). In addition, consumption of traditional media, such as television, movies, and magazines, has been identified as a risk factor for eating disorder development. Time spent viewing television, music videos, and magazines focused on beauty and appearance has been correlated with body dissatisfaction, drive for thinness, and internalization of the thin ideal and symptoms of BN, particularly for individuals under the age of 18 (Grabe, Ward, & Hyde, 2008). In addition, endorsement of media appearance ideals has been shown to predict onset of eating disorder behaviors. Specifically, adolescent girls who reported trying to look like girls or women they see in media had higher likelihood of onset of frequent binge eating (Field et al., 2008). Similar effects have been found among boys and men, with media consumption associated with the internalization of media ideals, dissatisfaction with appearance, the pursuit of both leanness and muscularity, and disordered eating behaviors (Rodgers, Ganchou, Franko, & Chabrol, 2012).

An intriguing naturalistic experiment conducted in the Pacific island nation of Fiji has provided additional evidence for the effect of consumption of traditional media on development of disordered eating attitudes and behaviors. A comparison of levels of disordered eating between cohorts of adolescent girls was conducted immediately following, and three years following, the introduction of western media to Fiji through television. It was found that the latter cohort had significantly greater prevalence of disordered eating and purging (self-induced vomiting). Further, qualitative data directly linked media consumption to endorsement of and the desire to look like western media appearance ideals (Becker, Burwell, Herzog, Hamburg, & Gilman, 2002). Thus, these findings also support the media influence model described above, such that exposure to traditional media leads to internalization of media appearance ideals, which in turn contributes to the development of body dissatisfaction and disordered eating.

The contention that the media promotion of the association between appearance ideals and expectancies of positive rewards contributes to body image and eating concerns is also supported by research findings. The extent to which young women hold positive expectations about the consequences of achieving an appearance similar to media ideals has been associated with levels of endorsement of these ideals as well as body image dissatisfaction. Furthermore, expectancies of rewards from thinness have been found to predict increases in binge eating over time in adolescent girls (Smith, Simmons, Flory, Annus, & Hill, 2007). These findings support the role of the expectancies set up by media content in the relationship between media exposure and body image and eating concerns. Experimental research has also documented the immediate effect that exposure to appearance-focused media can have on individuals' body image, resulting in negative thoughts and feelings about one's body and self. Similar effects exist among men, with increases in body image concerns and pursuit of leanness and muscularity in response to exposure to media images.

In terms of the mechanisms thought to account for the effects of experimental exposure to media images on body image, social comparison has been identified as playing an important role, and contributing to explaining why some but not all individuals who are exposed to media ideals experience body dissatisfaction. Social comparison can be defined as the tendency to compare one's appearance to that of others. The conjunction of unattainable appearance ideals and the discourse of the body as highly malleable in media may increase the likelihood of appearance comparisons with media images. Such comparisons are generally unfavorable, and highlight the extent to which an individual is not only divergent from media ideals but is also a failure for being so, thus contributing to body dissatisfaction. Consistent with this, the negative effects on body image from exposure to appearance ideals in media are amplified following appearance comparison with the ideal figures. Thus appearance comparisons play an important role in accounting for the detrimental effect of media exposure on body image.

Notably, some media literacy interventions that increase consumers' awareness about the intent of industries' messaging and the alteration of images in media, aim to reduce comparisons with media and can mitigate some immediate negative effects of appearance-focused media. These findings support the relationship between media exposure and elevated risk for eating disorders. Further, they provide hope that eating disorder prevention efforts, such as media literacy programs, can help reduce the influence of media as a risk factor for eating disorder development.

Emerging evidence with social media

Emerging research on the impact of social media on body image has suggested that social media may be more strongly associated with eating disorder risk factors and development than traditional media. Much like traditional media, social media is laden with appearance-related content that promotes body image concerns and drive for thinness, but social media includes the added complexity of user-edited images, engagement with the media content, and inability at times to discern user generated versus industry-generated content. In addition, the social media environment has the capacity to tailor itself to the interests of the user, through targeted advertising and machine learning, meaning that individuals who are interested in appearance-related content may be exposed to such content at a much higher rate, thus increasing their risk for eating disorders. An association between social media use and risk for eating disorders has been supported, and research comparing the effect of traditional media exposure to magazines and television to exposure to Internet images and social media sites has found that there is a stronger association between Internet exposure and eating disorder risk factors when compared to traditional media exposure (Tiggemann & Miller, 2010).

In addition, social media presents various platforms that host highly appearance-focused content, including "thinspiration" and "fitspiration" content. Such content promotes engagement in extreme appearance-oriented behaviors and even highly risky weight-control behaviors, while normalizing their content. Empirical research supports the hazard these sites create as engagement with them is associated with increased dieting, body dissatisfaction, and negative affect, and may increase existing risky behaviors or promote development of eating disorder symptoms (Rodgers, Lowy, Halperin, & Franko, 2016).

In addition, social media platforms are highly interactive and enable users to modify and comment on images. Negative comments on profile updates of social media sites are associated with increased shape and weight concerns. The ability of users to edit and comment on extreme images amplifies the potential for negative thoughts about one's self and one's body, potentially increasing risk factors for eating disorders. Research on the effect of social media on eating disorder development is still emerging. While theoretical models of the influence of social media have been developed (Figure 1), more research is needed to understand the effect of this new media platform on risk factors for eating disorders and the mechanism underlying the association between exposure to and engagement with social media and eating disorder development.

Future directions and implications

The media contribute to increasing the risk for eating disorders by promoting unattainable appearance ideals, creating unrealistic positive expectations around achieving appearance ideals, and normalizing risky weight and appearance-changing behaviors. In addition, social media is emerging as a highly appearance-focused form of media that may also contribute to increasing eating disorder risk. More research is needed to help clarify the mechanisms through which media contribute to eating disorder risk, as well as which individuals are most vulnerable to these effects. Furthermore, more work is needed to develop programs that can provide skills to buffer the deleterious effects of media exposure.

In addition, it is important to consider opportunities for encouraging the creation of media content that is less appearance focused, and does not contribute to the creation

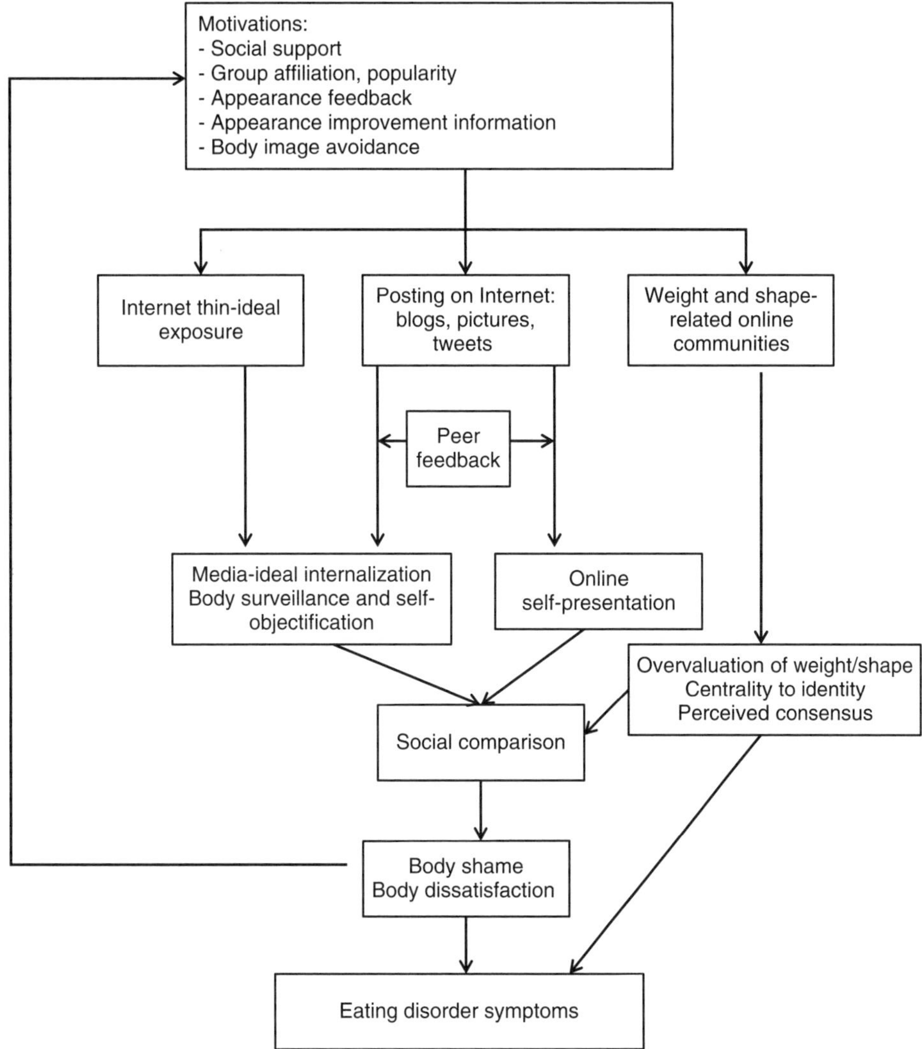

Figure 1 An integrated model of the influence of Internet on body image concerns and eating pathology. Reproduced from Rodgers (2016, p. 121) by permission of Springer.

of unattainable appearance ideals. In recent years, a small number of corporations have modified their advertising campaigns in an effort to promote a more realistic body image and thus decrease the negative impact of their advertisements. To some extent, such strategies may be successful and it will be important to continue to explore ways of creating less harmful media content. Public policy and legislation may provide an impactful means of changing the media environment to decrease eating disorder risk.

SEE ALSO: Critical Processing of Idealized Beauty Images; Representation of Health, Body, (Dis)Ability; Representation of Nutrition and Food in the Media; Self-Objectification

References

American Psychiatric Association. (2013). *Diagnostic and statistical manual of mental disorders* (5th ed.; DSM-5). Washington, DC: American Psychiatric Press.

Becker, A.E., Burwell, R.A., Herzog, D.B., Hamburg, P., & Gilman, S.E. (2002). Eating behaviours and attitudes following prolonged exposure to television among ethnic Fijian adolescent girls. *The British Journal of Psychiatry, 180*(6), 509–514. doi: 10.1192/bjp.180.6.509

Bordo, S. (2004). *Unbearable weight: Feminism, western culture, and the body*. Berkeley: University of California Press.

Field, A.E., Javaras, K.M., Aneja, P., Kitos, N., Camargo, C.A., Taylor, C.B., & Laird, N.M. (2008). Family, peer, and media predictors of becoming eating disordered. *Archives of Pediatrics and Adolescent Medicine, 162*(6), 574–579. doi: 10.1001/archpedi.162.6.574

Grabe, S., Ward, L.M., & Hyde, J.S. (2008). The role of the media in body image concerns among women: A meta-analysis of experimental and correlational studies. *Psychological Bulletin, 134*(3), 460. doi: 10.1037/0033-2909.134.3.460

Hay, P., Girosi, F., & Mond, J. (2015). Prevalence and sociodemographic correlates of DSM-5 eating disorders in the Australian population. *Journal of Eating Disorders, 3*(1), 19. doi: 10.1186/s40337-015-0056-0

Hudson, J.I., Hiripi, E., Pope, H.G., & Kessler, R.C. (2007). The prevalence and correlates of eating disorders in the National Comorbidity Survey Replication. *Biological Psychiatry, 61*(3), 348–358. doi: 10.1016/j.biopsych.2006.03.040

Lipson, S., & Sonneville, K. (2017). Eating disorder symptoms among undergraduate and graduate students at 12 US colleges and universities. *Eating Behaviors, 24*, 81–88. doi: 10.1016/j.eatbeh.2016.12.003

Moss, M. (2013). *Salt, sugar, fat: How the food giants hooked us*. New York, NY: Random House.

Quick, V., Berg, K.C., Bucchianeri, M.M., & Byrd-Bredbenner, C. (2014). Identification of eating disorder pathology in college students: A comparison of DSM-IV-TR and DSM-5 diagnostic criteria. *Advances in Eating Disorders: Theory, Research and Practice, 2*(2), 112–124. doi: 10.1080/21662630.2013.869388

Rodgers, R.F. (2016). The relationship between body image concerns, eating disorders and Internet use, part II: An integrated theoretical model. *Adolescent Research Review, 1*(2), 121–137. doi: 10.1007/s40894-015-0017-5

Rodgers, R.F., Ganchou, C., Franko, D.L., & Chabrol, H. (2012). Drive for muscularity and disordered eating among French adolescent boys: A sociocultural model. *Body image, 9*(3), 318–323. doi: 10.1016/j.bodyim.2012.03.002

Rodgers, R.F., Lowy, A.S., Halperin, D.M., & Franko, D.L. (2016). A meta-analysis examining the influence of pro-eating disorder websites on body image and eating pathology. *European Eating Disorders Review, 24*(1), 3–8.

Rohde, P., Stice, E., & Marti, C.N. (2015). Development and predictive effects of eating disorder risk factors during adolescence: Implications for prevention efforts. *International Journal of Eating Disorders, 48*(2), 187–198. doi: 10.1002/eat.22270

Smith, G.T., Simmons, J.R., Flory, K., Annus, A.M., & Hill, K.K. (2007). Thinness and eating expectancies predict subsequent binge-eating and purging behavior among adolescent girls. *Journal of Abnormal Psychology, 116*(1), 188–197. doi: 10.1037/0021-843X.116.1.188

Tiggemann, M., & Miller, J. (2010). The Internet and adolescent girls' weight satisfaction and drive for thinness. *Sex Roles, 63*, 79–90. doi: 10.1007/s11199-010-9789-z

Further reading

Bordo, S. (1993). *Unbearable weight: Feminism, western culture, and the body* (10th anniversary ed., 2003). Berkeley: University of California Press.

Levine, M.P., & Murnen, S.K. (2009). "Everybody knows that mass media are/are not [pick one] a cause of eating disorders": A critical review of evidence for a causal link between media, negative body image, and disordered eating in females. *Journal of Social and Clinical Psychology, 28*(1), 9–42. doi: 10.1521/jscp.2009.28.1.9
Wykes, M., & Gunter, B. (2005). *The media and body image*. London, England: SAGE.

Rachel F. Rodgers, PhD, is an associate professor in the Department of Applied Psychology at Northeastern University and the Director of the APPEAR research lab. Her research interests focus on the understanding of sociocultural risk factors for body image, eating, and food-related concerns, and the development of successful prevention programs. In addition, her work strives to inform public policy as a means of universal prevention.

Siân A. McLean, PhD, is Lecturer in Psychology at Victoria University and an honorary research fellow in the School of Psychology and Public Health, La Trobe University. Her research focuses on sociocultural and individual factors that contribute to body dissatisfaction in children, adolescents, and adults. She is highly experienced in school-based prevention and research investigating the role of media literacy as a protective factor in the development of body dissatisfaction. Dr. McLean's research on media literacy and body image has been recognized through the 2016 Peter Beumont Young Investigator Award.

Jennifer L. O'Flynn, EdM, is a PhD candidate in counseling psychology at Northeastern University. She earned her Master's in human development and psychology at the Harvard Graduate School of Education. She has experience working with young adults in both university and outpatient clinical settings. Her primary research interests relate to eating disorder prevention, educating emerging adults about mental health issues, and reducing barriers to professional help seeking in college-aged populations.

Media and Ethnic Stereotyping

SRIVIDYA RAMASUBRAMANIAN and ALEXANDRA SOUSA
Texas A&M University, USA

While media remain an important tool for disseminating information and connecting people, they are also a site of harmful racial and ethnic stereotyping. Scholars have recognized the role that the media play in the creation and perpetuation of stereotypes for many groups, both in the United States and around the world. These stereotypes not only contribute to how members of minoritized groups negotiate their identities, self-worth, and belongingness, but also impact how majority groups manage their own perceptions of racial–ethnic minorities and make race-based decisions and social judgments. Understanding the implications of media messages can help audiences recognize harmful ethnic stereotyping and begin to construct ways to counteract it. Media literacy and participatory media initiatives are some of the methods through which these harmful stereotypes are being challenged.

Effects of racial and ethnic media stereotyping

Media narratives provide significant information about race and culture across ethnic groups and powerfully shape ideas about interethnic and interracial relations (Tukachinsky, Mastro, & Yarchi, 2015). One of the first steps toward countering ethnic stereotypes in the media is becoming conscious of the fact that the media represent these groups in biased ways. Racial and ethnic minority groups are often positioned as "the other," exotic, and mediocre counterparts designed to further bolster white characters and storylines. Between sensationalized media coverage of incidents of police brutality and the disproportionate number of black characters who are cast as criminals, representations of ethnic minority groups remain limited and harmful (Dixon & Linz, 2000). Black women are confined to a restricted set of roles, which range from the boisterous "mammy" to the stereotypical welfare queen and the hypersexualized jezebel. Latino males find themselves posited as "macho" criminals of limited intelligence, while Latinas become oversexualized and are depicted as loud and threatening to their non-Latina rivals. Even though these characters are becoming more visible, stereotypes do get more engrained if they are not challenged (Mastro, Behm-Morawitz, & Kopacz, 2008). Historically, Asians are portrayed in mainstream media as the perpetual foreigner, the exotic geisha or the China doll, the yellow peril, or hardworking, polite, model minorities (Mok, 1998). Representations of the third world and of the Global South in western narratives similarly take a Eurocentric, orientalist approach by presenting people from these areas as wild, uncivilized, and exotic and contrasting them to western characters depicted as heroic saviors (Shohat & Stam, 1994). Because of these stereotypical representations, youths from minority or marginalized groups are left without sufficient role models in the media.

Ethnic stereotyping in the media can impact identity formation for members of underrepresented groups; it also skews the perception of minorities by dominant groups, which are exposed to the same limited representations. Scholars have used the priming perspective to suggest that racial and ethnic stereotypes in the media can prime majority-white audiences to have negative stereotypes, social judgments, prejudicial feelings, and even lower race-based policy support (Gilliam & Iyengar, 2000; Oliver & Fonash, 2002). Youth and adolescents are particularly susceptible to the harmful effects of media stereotyping because they are in a period of identity development. Bandura's *social cognitive theory* has defined these effects and has helped scholars explore how mediated characters affect their young real-life viewers. Media have a tangible effect on how people perceive the real world and on the judgments they develop about certain groups of people as a result of the mental models that they create (Mastro et al., 2008). Because the media have become central tools in helping adolescents shape and negotiate their identities, the effects of limited and negative representations of race and ethnicity in the media can be detrimental. If minorities continue to be marginalized and tokenized, these representations and images will contribute to youths' perception of how they should act—not only by virtue of their race, but also by virtue of their gender. Recent research suggests that exposure to positive portrayals and counterstereotypes can help negate the effects of harmful media stereotypes. Vicarious positive mediated contact with ethnic and racial minorities is able to bring about more sympathetic and supportive attitudes towards them. Specifically, exposure to positive or admirable media celebrities from racial and ethnic outgroups can lead to a lowering of racial–ethnic prejudice and can increase people's support for policies such as affirmative action (Ramasubramanian, 2015).

While most of the research on the effects of racial and ethnic stereotypes in the media is focused on majority-white audiences, some other studies also examine how they shape ethnic minority audiences. Script theory also becomes applicable to studying the effects of media in this scenario. Scripts are knowledge and memory structures that present to us different people and which teach us what is normal and comfortable for them. People are drawn to familiar ideas and images, which create scripts they use to respond to similar situations. These ideas are often tied to deeply rooted cultural and social scripts. Repeated exposure to the same scripts and stereotypes therefore becomes hard to resist and helps set the scripts we create for ourselves. These perceptions help maintain harmful stereotypes in social hierarchies and work against our efforts toward racial equality.

Media literacy and racial–ethnic stereotype reduction

Although there are multiple avenues for addressing these types of abuses in the media, media literacy remains one of the most effective and least controversial solutions. Media literacy is widely defined as "the ability to analyze, access, and produce media in a variety of forms" (Livingstone, 2004, p. 5). Media literacy assumes that messages are constructed for persuasive purposes and are interpreted differently as a result of the values embedded within particular groups. Engaging in media literacy education teaches audiences to be more responsible and conscious consumers. Countering the negative effects of racial and ethnic media stereotyping is one of the goals of media literacy training. Often such media literacy interventions start by encouraging audiences to question and critically engage with media stereotypes.

Some scholars have made a distinction between the production aspects of media literacy, with their benefits, and intervention-oriented media literacy education initiatives. Using a cultural studies approach, production aspects focus on what audiences do with media, while education initiatives take a media effects approach that is concerned with what media do to audiences. Scharrer (2007, p. 35) synthesizes the media effects and cultural studies approaches and defines media literacy as fostering "critical thinking and discussion of media-related issues, including how media messages are created, marketed, distributed as well as their potential influence (or how they are received)." In practice, media literacy initiatives combine both of these approaches to create alternative spaces that counter mainstream media. Ramasubramanian (2007) proposes a two-pronged method that combines a message-centered approach (such as exposure to counterstereotypical narratives) and an audience-centered approach (such as motivating audiences to develop critical thinking skills) to effectively combat implicit racial and ethnic stereotypes.

Research on the effects that media literacy initiatives have on reducing and combating racial and ethnic stereotypes is sparse. Scharrer and Ramasubramanian (2015) provide an overview of quantitative and qualitative research on media literacy initiatives of this type. For instance, Cole and colleagues (2003) conducted a study using positive *Sesame Street* video clips to reduce ethnic stereotypes between Israeli and Palestinian youths, while Gorn, Goldberg, and Kanungo (1976) examined the effects of a similar clip, in a study of the willingness of white kids to play with nonwhite characters in a Canadian context. Hobbs, Cabral, Ebrahimi, Yoon, and Al-Humaidan (2010) show that children are able to develop visual literacy skills and conduct their own research in order to counter ethnic stereotypes of Arabs and Middle Easterners in popular films such as *Aladdin*. In a rare study that involved older adults, Moffitt and Harris (2014) conducted focus group discussions with black girls and their mothers to understand sexist and racist portrayals of African Americans in the *Princess and the Frog*. Researchers working with Latino/a youths show that participation in media literacy programs helps them recognize media stereotypes of their group; it also makes them feel motivated to engage in specific actions to counter those stereotypes (Vargas, 2006; Yosso, 2002).

Some researchers offer guidelines on how to effectively incorporate popular media such as hip-hop, music videos, and video games into their existing curriculum in order to highlight racism and ethnic discrimination (Childs, 2014). Others have incorporated media literacy education into after-school programs such as the Media Minds curriculum (Owusu, 2010). At the college level, Kavoori (2007) describes the Thinking Television project, which uses research methods and critical media literacy to systematically engage students in conversations about how to deconstruct media texts about African Americans and link them to historical conditions and to wider sociological issues such as capitalism. In terms of transcultural media literacy initiatives, some studies demonstrate that wishful identification with popular characters in Japanese anime and Korean soap dramas helps break down ethnic stereotypes entertained by American fan audiences (Kim, 2015).

Participatory media and alternative storytelling

As the definition of media literacy also reveals, understanding the effects of media goes beyond analyzing their content; it extends to producing content. Scholars such as Nakamura (2007) suggest that, instead of creating democratic spaces for equal participation, a color-blind Internet tends to replicate real-world hegemony. Therefore critical participatory media initiatives have to collectively resist such hegemonic racial discourses online by creating alternative stories, positive and diverse, and by building social connections for greater solidarity (Santoy, 2013). Participatory media empower individuals to construct portrayals that better represent them, foster social equity, and allow youths to become engaged citizens. Examples include blogs, podcasts, digital storytelling, and sharing music, photos, and video. By putting media tools into the hands of those groups that traditionally have been silenced in the mainstream media, participatory media counteract not only the negative representations that are prevalent, but also the detrimental effects that result from them. This concept has become the foundation for many organizations and initiatives that use media to counteract and challenge harmful racial and ethnic stereotypes perpetuated by mainstream media. Participatory media set the stage for producing counterstereotypes as well as fresh and accurate representations. Certain organizations are adhering to the principles of media literacy and participatory media and are addressing ethnic stereotyping head-on, through the critique and creation of media. These initiatives illustrate how media literacy can be used to make a difference and to change the media landscape.

Participatory media give marginalized groups the ability to challenge and resist common cultural stereotypes. This is the central mission of the Philadelphia-based initiative FAAN Mail, a media literacy and activism project designed to give women of color a voice. The project recognizes not only that accurate and diverse representations of black women are often missing from the mainstream, but also that important issues that affect these groups are missing from the general conversation that goes on in the media. FAAN Mail has even piloted a youth media program for girls, Sisters Action Media. Similarly, Santoy (2013) describes how three Chicana bloggers use online spaces to assert their ethnic identities through active participation that celebrates the creativity of women of color. Latinitas, an Austin-based initiative, is a nonprofit that empowers young Latinas through the use of media and technology. The organization began by creating the first online magazine produced *by* and *for* Latina girls; now it has workshops on technology and media tools, an interactive blog, conferences, and a strong presence on social media. Question Bridge is another example of a transmedia, community-based, participatory project that uses multiple media formats, such as geolocation hotspots, videos, and art installations, to resist and redefine black masculinity (Ramasubramanian, 2016). Central to this collaborative participatory art initiative are video-based dialogic exchanges among all those who self-identify as black males. This type of identity mapping that uses self-generated tags leads to a unique visual mapping of the dynamic and diverse nature of black masculinity.

Conclusion

Media are often the source of harmful racial and ethnic stereotypes, which can negatively impact intergroup relations and attitudes between majority and minority ethnic groups. However, media literacy and participatory media can be used to promote responsible consumption and production of racial and ethnic representations. Media initiatives in the United States and around the world are using media to empower under-represented and misrepresented groups by giving them the ability to engage in, and create, media that express the true scope of their diverse experiences.

SEE ALSO: Critical Pedagogy; Digital Divide; Digital Storytelling; Emancipatory Communication; Representation of Ethnicity; Representation of Race; Stereotype Threat

References

Childs, D.J. (2014). "Let's talk about race": Exploring racial stereotypes using popular culture in social studies classrooms. *Social Studies, 105*(6), 291–300.

Cole, C., Arafat, C., Tidhar, C., Tafesh, W.Z., Fox, N., Killen, M., & Richman, B. (2003). The educational impact of Rechov Sumsum/Shara'a simsim: A Sesame Street television series to promote respect and understanding among children living in Israel, the West Bank, and Gaza. *International Journal of Behavioral Development, 27*(5), 409–422. doi: 10.1080/01650250344000019

Dixon, T.L., & Linz, D. (2000). Overrepresentation and underrepresentation of African Americans and Latinos as lawbreakers on television news. *Journal of Communication, 50*(2), 131–154. doi: 10.1093/joc/50.2.131

Gilliam, F.D., & Iyengar, S. (2000). Prime suspects: The influence of local television news on the viewing public. *American Journal of Political Science, 44*(3), 560–573.

Gorn, G.J., Goldberg, M.E., & Kanungo, R.N. (1976). The role of educational television in changing the intergroup attitudes of children. *Child Development, 47*(1), 277–280. doi: 10.2307/1128313

Hobbs, R., Cabral, N., Ebrahimi, A., Yoon, J., Al-Humaidan, R. (2010). *Combating Middle East stereotypes through media literacy education in elementary school*. Paper presented at the annual meeting of the International Communication Association.

Kavoori, A. (2007). Media literacy, "thinking television," and African American communication. *Cultural Studies/Critical Methodologies, 7*(4), 460–483. doi: 10.1177/1532708607305038

Kim, G.M. (2015). Transcultural digital literacies: Cross-border connections and self-representations in an online forum. *Reading Research Quarterly, 51*(2), 199–219.

Livingstone, S. (2004). Media literacy and the challenge of new information and communication technologies. *Communication Review, 7*, 3–14.

Mastro, D.E., Behm-Morawitz, E., & Kopacz, M.A. (2008). Exposure to television portrayals of Latinos: The implications of aversive racism and social identity theory. *Human Communication Research, 34*(1), 1–27.

Moffit, K.R., & Harris, H.E. (2014). Of negation, princesses, beauty, and work: Black mothers reflect on Disney's *The Princess and the Frog*. *The Howard Journal of Communications, 25*(1), 56–76.

Mok, T. (1998). Getting the message: Media images and stereotypes and their effect on Asian Americans. *Cultural Diversity and Mental Health, 4*, 185–202.

Nakamura, L. (2007). *Digitizing race: Visual cultures of the Internet*. Minneapolis: University of Minnesota Press.

Oliver, M.B., & Fonash, D. (2002). Race and crime in the news: Whites' identification and misidentification of violent and nonviolent criminal suspects. *Media Psychology, 4*(2), 137–156.

Owusu, S. (2010). Using media literacy to combat racism. *Youth Media Reporter, 4*, 15–18.

Ramasubramanian, S. (2007). Media-based strategies to reduce racial stereotypes activated by news stories. *Journalism & Mass Communication Quarterly, 84*(2), 249–264.

Ramasubramanian, S. (2015). Using celebrity news to reduce racial/ethnic prejudice. *Journal of Social Issues, 71*(1), 123–137. doi: 10.1111/josi.12100

Ramasubramanian, S. (2016). Racial/ethnic identity, community-oriented media initiatives, and transmedia storytelling. *Information Society, 32*(5), 333–342. doi: 10.1080/01972243.2016.1212618

Santoy, J.J. (2013). Chicana bloggers: Creating diversity online via participation. *Journal of Adolescent & Adult Literacy, 56*(5), 361–367.

Scharrer, E. (2007). Closer than you think: Bridging the gap between media effects and cultural studies in media education theory and practice. In A. Nowak, S. Abel, & K. Ross (Eds.),

Rethinking media education: Critical pedagogy and identity politics (pp. 17–35). Cresskill, NJ: Hampton Press.
Scharrer, E., & Ramasubramanian, S. (2015). Intervening in the media's influence on stereotypes of race and ethnicity: The role of media literacy. *Journal of Social Issues, 71*(1), 171–185. doi: 10.1111/josi.12103
Shohat, E., & Stam, R. (1994). *Unthinking Eurocentrism: Multiculturalism and the media.* New York, NY: Routledge.
Tukachinsky, R., Mastro, D., & Yarchi, M. (2015). Documenting portrayals of race/ethnicity on primetime television over a 20-year span and their association with national-level racial/ethnic attitudes. *Journal of Social Issues, 71*(1), 17–38.
Vargas, L. (2006). Translational media literacy: Analytic reflections on a program with Latina teens. *Hispanic Journal of Behavioral Sciences, 28*(2), 267–285. doi: 10.1177/0739986305285823
Yosso, T. (2002). Critical race media literacy: Challenging deficit discourse about Chicanas/os. *Journal of Popular Film & Television, 30*, 52–62. doi: 10.1080/01956050209605559

Further reading

Hancock, Q., Jolls, T., & Jolls, P. (2013). Racism and stereotypes in electronic media. *Public Library Quarterly, 32*(4), 333–344.
Rheingold, H. (2008). Using participatory media and public voice to encourage civic engagement. In W. L. Bennett (Ed.), *Civic life online: Learning how digital media can engage youth* (pp. 97–118). Cambridge, MA: MIT Press.

Srividya Ramasubramanian earned her PhD from Penn State University and is associate professor in the Department of Communication at Texas A&M University. Her interests are cultural diversity, media literacy, and stereotyping processes.

Alexandra Sousa is a doctoral student in the Department of Communication at Texas A&M University. Her research is focused on diversity and inclusion, especially in the higher-education context. She is also interested in issues of conflict management, representation, and facilitating dialogue about diversity.

Media and Public Engagement with Science

JOANNA NURMIS
University of Maryland, College Park, USA

Familiarity with basic scientific facts, a trustful attitude toward the scientific community, and a capacity to follow scientific reasoning are critical elements of citizens' participation in a democracy. Many policy decisions that are put to a vote either directly through referenda or indirectly through elections rely on an understanding of the underpinning scientific facts: for example, climate change mitigation policies, vaccination regulations, or menu options in schools.

Media play a critical role in keeping the public abreast of scientific information and current scientific developments. Indeed, most adults do not come across scientific information after high school or college, except through news articles, videos, or radio broadcasts – the media thus bear a significant responsibility in engaging the public with science, even as scientists are increasingly reaching out to the public in more direct manners. Interestingly, the public's trust in media is much lower than its trust in the scientific community (38% vs. 76%). This means that even though members of the public express a high level of trust in scientists, they are much less likely to trust the scientific content presented to them in the distilled form of a news report. One interesting solution to this problem has recently been found in applied research: the highly successful *Climate Matters* program equips weathercasters, a particular section of local journalism professionals who do enjoy high levels of trust, with climate-relevant background information to better inform the public about the links between day-to-day weather extremes and the unfolding phenomenon of climate change (Maibach et al., 2016).

Civic scientific literacy was defined by Miller (1983) to mean "the ability of a citizen to find, make sense of, and use information about science or technology to engage in a public discussion of policy choices involving science or technology." Yet, scientific literacy rates in a highly developed country like the United States are low: over two thirds of the adult population do not understand the basic scientific process, have scant knowledge of scientific facts that underpin everyday life, and are not able to make well-informed policy decisions on matters ranging from food security to climate policy (Miller, 2016). However, it is important to note that merely focusing on increasing the rate of scientifically literate people does not automatically translate into better public engagement with science. On the contrary, it has been shown that especially at higher levels of education, where scientific literacy is high, approaches to polarizing scientific issues are informed mostly by personal beliefs, party affiliation, and other values that have nothing to do with rationality or science. Similarly, the problem at hand does not seem to be a lack of trust in scientists, as this has remained stable and high throughout the past three decades. Over 75% of the American public trust scientists at least a fair amount, according to Pew (Funk & Kennedy, 2016), yet that does not help to explain the vast gaps between the public and scientists on several important issues, such as the existence and causes of climate change. In this last case, 97% of scientists agree that climate change does exist and is caused by humans (Cook et al., 2016), but only 70% of US adults believe it exists and 58% believe it is human caused (Leiserowitz, Maibach, Roser-Renouf, Rosenthal, & Cutler, 2017). Such gaps are largely due to the fragmentation of the media landscape; audiences have less and less contact with one mainstream media narrative about scientific findings, and are more frequently exposed instead to those news outlets that present science news in a way congruent with that particular audience's beliefs and values. Another major factor has been the pervasive emphasis in newsrooms on objectivity as balance, which compelled news outlets to present two sides of any scientific debate even when the overwhelming majority of scientists stood on one side (Boykoff, 2007; Hiles & Hinnant, 2014). Although this standard is now evolving toward an approach that weighs the evidence and gives more credence in a news report to the side that most peer-reviewed scientific publications support, the problem of balance as bias still exists because it is both more cost-effective and more entertaining to present both sides as embroiled in conflict, rather than to carefully weigh the available evidence.

Whereas from the 1970s the dominant approach in science communication rested on the assumption that merely conveying more information to the public at large would suffice, this so-called knowledge deficit model has recently been reconsidered. The knowledge deficit model, sometimes called the information deficit model, failed to account for other factors beyond rational thought in how people process scientific information, especially when it brings to bear on policy relevant issues that they already have an opinion on. For example, in the aforementioned case of climate change, research has found that preexisting values and political leanings are a better predictor of one's beliefs about climate change than the level of scientific literacy and numeracy (Funk & Kennedy, 2016; Kahan et al., 2012). In fact, Kahan et al. (2012) discovered that polarization on the subject of climate change increased, rather than decreased, at higher levels of science literacy. In addition, as Scheufele and Lewenstein (2005) established, individuals tend to use a heuristic information processing model when presented with new scientific information, rather than analytical thinking which requires more focus and intellectual effort. A complicating and related factor is the development of information silos, which allow members of the public to only encounter information about scientific developments framed in a way that will fit in with their prior beliefs. Indeed, empirical research has shown that in the case of climate change, one is less likely to trust climate scientists and more likely to harbor doubts about the existence of climate change if one consults only conservative news media (Hmielowski, Feldman, Myers, Leiserowitz, & Maibach, 2014).

Because straightforward transmission of scientific facts as prescribed by the deficit model was shown to be ineffective in engaging the public with climate change, the concept of public engagement with science, also called the "dialogue" model, has become more widely used. The idea of engagement differs from the previous goal of "understanding" in two ways. First, it parts with the assumption that people process scientific information in a purely rational manner, drawing from empirical research that reveals the role of motivated reasoning in the way people assimilate scientific facts. It also strives for a deeper connection between people and science that goes beyond mere education of a passive public and strives to foster an emotional connection and attitude change, as well as behavioral adjustment (Lorenzoni, Nicholson-Cole, & Whitmarsh, 2007). Public engagement with a scientific topic or issue thus goes beyond simply knowing about something; it implies having a personal connection that leads to a change in attitude and, if necessary, taking action.

This approach has led to more research into the potential of non-text-based media to foster public engagement with scientific topics, such as visual storytelling, virtual reality experiences, and video games (Metag, Schäfer, Fuchslin, Kleinen-von, & Barsuhn, 2016; O'Neill, 2013; O'Neill & Smith, 2014). A major finding occurring repeatedly in current science communication research is the fact that raising awareness of a particular risk (e.g., health or climate related) without providing any information about how people can respond to the issue leads to an attitude of defeatism and abandonment of responsibility on the public's part (O'Neill & Nicholson-Cole, 2009; Witte, 1992). In addition, while journalists are more aware of the need for a public engagement approach rather than a simple recounting of the latest published studies, staffing resources devoted to science reporting in newsrooms are diminishing (a case in point was the 2008 decision by CNN to cut its entire science, environment, and technology news team).

Despite the fact that scientists have consistent and fruitful relationships with journalists, and despite the overall trust and goodwill between these two communities, overwhelming differences between the scientific and journalistic communication practices continue to make public engagement with science a difficult task for media professionals. First, the dominant style of news, which favors episodic frames and definite headlines, stands wholly at odds with the scientific method: scientists are traditionally wary of disclosing research results before a publication has been accepted, which may take years; and when they do present results, they emphasize limitations, caveats, and the necessity to conduct replication studies. Quite often, scientific studies are reported in a simplified fashion by research institutions' press releases, and are simplified or distorted even further by media professionals. Second, despite the recognition of the limitations in the knowledge deficit model, many scientists themselves continue to follow the knowledge deficit model because they are not trained in public communication or the social sciences (Simis, Madden, Cacciatore, & Yeo, 2016): thus, they continue to approach their role as top-down educators and popularizers of science (Peters, 2013). Third, scientists are careful to preserve their reputation for neutrality and very rarely, if ever, allow themselves to make pronouncements on policy that would be beneficial for the common good based on their findings. This in turn allows controversy around the desirable policy to continue playing out in media reports, even when the evidence points clearly in the direction of one particular policy; however, more and more scientists realize that expressing their informed views on policy does not have to infringe on credibility, as experimental research by Kotcher, Myers, Vraga, Stenhouse, and Maibach (2017) has shown. While scientists have become more willing to communicate directly with the public and employ the diverse web-based media to that end, journalists still bear the main role in mediating between scientists and the public, especially on issues that have policy implications for the public good. The responsibility of journalists in science communication is double: both in actively weighing the evidence behind diverging scientific claims, and in ensuring that audience members' risk perceptions are based on actual scientific findings rather than the preexisting culturally formed views. This seems a tall order in a context of dwindling resources for science and environmental news. Both scientists and journalists need to develop a higher awareness of recent findings in empirical social science that can help understand the role of motivated reasoning and cultural cognition in how the public processes science information (Scheufele, 2014).

SEE ALSO: Ecomedia Literacy

References

Boykoff, M.T. (2007). Flogging a dead norm? Newspaper coverage of anthropogenic climate change in the United States and United Kingdom from 2003 to 2006. *Area, 39*(4), 470–481. doi: 10.1111/j.1475-4762.2007.00769.x

Cook, J., Oreskes, N., Doran, P.T., Anderegg, W.R.L., Verheggen, B., Maibach, E.W., ... & Rice, K. (2016). Consensus on consensus: A synthesis of consensus estimates on human-caused global warming. *Environmental Research Letters, 11*(4), 48002. doi: 10.1088/1748-9326/11/4/048002

Funk, C., & Kennedy, B. (2016). The politics of climate. Pew Research Center. Retrieved from http://www.pewinternet.org/2016/10/04/the-politics-of-climate/

Hiles, S.S., & Hinnant, A. (2014). Climate change in the newsroom: Journalists' evolving standards of objectivity when covering global warming. *Science Communication, 36*(4), 428–453. doi: 10.1177/1075547014534077

Hmielowski, J.D., Feldman, L., Myers, T.A., Leiserowitz, A., & Maibach, E. (2014). An attack on science? Media use, trust in scientists, and perceptions of global warming. *Public Understanding of Science, 23*(7), 866–883. doi: 10.1177/0963662513480091

Kahan, D.M., Peters, E., Wittlin, M., Ouellette, L.L., Slovic, P., Braman, D., & Mandel, G. (2012). The polarizing impact of science literacy and numeracy on perceived climate change risks. *Nature Climate Change, 2*(10), 732–735. doi: 10.1038/nclimate1547

Kotcher, J.E., Myers, T.A., Vraga, E.K., Stenhouse, N., & Maibach, E.W. (2017). Does engagement in advocacy hurt the credibility of scientists? Results from a randomized national survey experiment. *Environmental Communication, 11*(3), 415–429. doi: 10.1080/17524032.2016.1275736

Leiserowitz, A., Maibach, E., Roser-Renouf, C., Rosenthal, S., & Cutler, M. (2017). *Climate change in the American mind: May 2017*. New Haven, CT: Yale Program on Climate Change Communication.

Lorenzoni, I., Nicholson-Cole, S., & Whitmarsh, L. (2007). Barriers perceived to engaging with climate change among the UK public and their policy implications. *Global Environmental Change, 17*, 445–459.

Maibach, E., Woods Placky, B., Witte, J., Seitter, K., Gardiner, N., Myers, T., ... & Cullen, H. (2016). TV meteorologists as local climate change educators. In H. van Storch (Ed. in Chief), *Oxford research encyclopedia of climate science*. Oxford, England: Oxford University Press.

Metag, J., Schäfer, M.S., Fuchslin, T., Kleinen-von, K.K., & Barsuhn, T. (2016). Perceptions of climate change imagery: Evoked salience and self-efficacy in Germany, Switzerland, and Austria. *Science Communication, 38*(2), 197–227. doi: 10.1177/1075547016635181

Miller, J.D. (1983). Scientific literacy: A conceptual and empirical review. *Daedalus, 112*(2), 29–48.

Miller, J.D. (2016). Civic scientific literacy in the United States in 2016: A report prepared for the National Aeronautics and Space Administration by the University of Michigan. Retrieved from http://home.isr.umich.edu/files/2016/10/NASA-CSL-in-2016-Report.pdf

O'Neill, S.J. (2013). Image matters: Climate change imagery in US, UK and Australian newspapers. *Geoforum, 49*, 10–19. doi: 10.1016/j.geoforum.2013.04.030

O'Neill, S.J., & Nicholson-Cole, S. (2009). "Fear won't do it." *Science Communication, 30*, 355–379. doi: 10.1177/1075547008329201

O'Neill, S.J., & Smith, N. (2014). Climate change and visual imagery. *Wiley Interdisciplinary Reviews: Climate Change, 5*(1), 73–87. doi: 10.1002/wcc.249

Peters, H.P. (2013). Gap between science and media revisited: Scientists as public communicators. *Proceedings of the National Academy of Sciences, 110*, 14102–14109. doi: 10.1073%2Fpnas.1212745110

Scheufele, D.A. (2014). Science communication as political communication. *Proceedings of the National Academy of Sciences of the United States of America, 111*, 13585–13592. doi: 10.1073/pnas.1317516111

Scheufele, D.A., & Lewenstein, B. (2005). The public and nanotechnology: How citizens make sense of emerging technologies. *Journal of Nanoparticle Research, 7*(6), 659–667. doi: 10.1007/s11051-005-7526-2

Simis, M.J., Madden, H., Cacciatore, M.A., & Yeo, S.K. (2016). The lure of rationality: Why does the deficit model persist in science communication? *Public Understanding of Science, 25*(4), 400–414. doi: 10.1177/0963662516629749

Witte, K. (1992). Putting the fear back into fear appeals: The extended parallel process model. *Communications Monographs, 59*(4), 329–349. doi: 10.1080/03637759209376276

Further reading

Brossard, D. (2013). New media landscapes and the science information consumer. *Proceedings of the National Academy of Sciences, 110*(Suppl. 3), 14096–14101. doi: 10.1073/pnas.1212744110

Schäfer, M. (2009). From public understanding to public engagement. *Science Communication, 30*(4), 475–505. doi: 10.1177/1075547008326943

Schneider, S.H. (1988). The greenhouse effect and the US summer of 1988: Cause and effect or a media event? *Climatic Change, 13*(2), 113–115. doi: 10.1007/BF00140564

Joanna Nurmis holds a doctorate in journalism studies from the University of Maryland. Now residing in the Bay Area, she continues to pursue research in environmental communication while working as a digital content creator at the Stanford Woods Institute for the Environment. Her dissertation investigated the role that photojournalism plays in public engagement with climate change, and she has published book chapters as well as articles on this and related topics.

Media Arts

BENJAMIN THEVENIN
Brigham Young University, USA

Media arts is an artistic and educational discipline that understands media principally as platforms for creative expression. Media arts draw upon (and often overlap with) traditions within the arts and humanities including visual arts, music, theater, literature, and so forth, making particular use of contemporary media, including digital, networked, and interactive technologies. Areas within media arts may include:

- film, video, and animation;
- graphic and digital arts and effects;
- sound design and music production;
- scenic, costume, and make-up design for screens;

- performance involving media technologies;
- video games;
- interactive, web-based, and networked media;
- virtual and augmented reality.

As both an artistic and educational discipline, media arts emphasize creative expression and critical analysis of multiple media forms, walking a line between arts, humanities, communications, and technology. Given that the discipline makes use of various media and draws upon a range of artistic traditions, media arts are not informed by a single, unified theoretical or esthetic tradition. Analyses of media arts may draw upon frameworks and terminology developed in fields such as cinema studies, cultural studies, media studies, semiotics, critical theory, and so forth.

In the context of media education, media arts are a historically significant tradition, though their perspectives and pedagogies differ somewhat from those that dominate the field of media literacy. Media arts education has been critiqued for its emphasis on technical competence and personal expression at the expense of social or political relevance. However, media arts initiatives commonly make an effort to highlight the integration of theory, production, and politics.

Recently, the media arts have been designated within educational policy as a fifth arts discipline (along with music, dance, theater, and visual arts). This positions media arts education between discourses of "arts literacies" and "media" or "digital literacies." Also, as new media technologies—including, for example, virtual and augmented reality—develop, media arts studies, education, and creative practice attempt to make sense of and make use of these emerging media.

Creative expression

Perhaps one of the most significant characteristics of media arts—especially in the context of other approaches to studying and teaching media and culture—is the emphasis placed on creative expression. Media are understood not simply as channels or networks through which individuals send and receive messages comprised of information, but rather as sites where artists can use deliberate narrative and/or esthetic elements to express their emotions, share their experiences, and explore concepts in conversation with some kind of audience.

While no single understanding of creativity is used across the field of media arts education, the creative process engaged in by scholars, educators, and artists typically includes some of the following.

Cultivation of creative capacities

Media arts initiatives commonly emphasize the value of the creative process as being equally important as the completed work. Within media arts education, objectives include helping student artists identify sites of creative inspiration, including personal experience, existing creative work, esthetic or conceptual traditions within the arts, various techniques, styles, or themes, and cultural, historical, or political context. Studies of historical, theoretical, and esthetic traditions of media and arts disciplines often play a role in this stage. So, for example, preparatory to a screenwriter conceiving of a story for a horror film, she may examine the use of the "final girl" archetype in the genre, study the influence of gothic literature or German Expressionism on early Hollywood monster movies, or reflect on her own experiences with fear or trauma. Media artists learn to draw upon these sources and develop processes for translating this inspiration into the conceptualization of their own work.

Conceptualization of creative work

Drawing upon various sources of inspiration, media artists then develop a central concept for their own work. This "brainstorming" phase is commonly addressed in media arts education contexts, where students are encouraged to record ideas for their creative work, seek feedback from others, create connections between ideas they find compelling, and begin to create some sort of overarching idea that the work will explore. During this stage, media artists may familiarize themselves and experiment with different ways of ways of conceiving, organizing, revising, and connecting creative ideas as a means of developing these fragments into something unified. So, for example, a graphic artist might use a sketchbook to doodle ideas or a Pinterest board to archive visuals they find compelling or the Sketch app to create multiple iterations of a single design as they work toward a final concept. This process of conceptualization of creative work often requires an understanding of the affordances and limitations of the technologies and the media artist's experience with said technologies.

Acquisition of technical skills

Not unlike artists working in other artistic disciplines, in order to practically realize the concept they have developed, media artists must have some understanding of the tools with which they will craft their work. In the creation of a web series, for example, the process may require media artists to have an understanding of the tools and processes of elements such as lighting, sound recording, video-recording, data transfer, video editing, sound mixing and editing, color correcting, creating special effects, uploading, sharing, and marketing via social media, and so forth. Successful media artists, whatever their specialization, often familiarize themselves with various tools that correspond with their area of emphasis, for example, a cinematographer will learn about different cameras and lenses and know which will best serve a particular project. Also, media artists, especially those working on smaller productions like a web series, often take on multiple roles and are required to have some technical competence in various aspects of the process, for example, an editor might be responsible for and must have a working knowledge of transferring the footage, editing audio and video, generating special effects, and exporting and uploading the final piece onto social media. And as new media tools and technologies are constantly being developed, media artists are often continually learning new technical skills and processes, in contrast with, for example, a cellist or an oil painter who, while developing and practicing new techniques, is typically working with the same set of instruments and/or materials. The acquisition of technical skills goes hand in hand with the media artists' development of a conceptual understanding of esthetic conventions and practical experience with technique.

Familiarization with language and conventions

Depending upon the specific medium in which a media artist chooses to create their work, there are corresponding conventions or languages with which the artist must become familiar in order to successfully realize their concept. Studies of semiotics—whether it is of composition or color theory in design, juxtaposition or narrative construction in film or video, and so forth—often play a part in this stage of the creative process. Media arts programs (similar to media literacy education) emphasize the constructedness of media texts, how an artist makes use of specific processes of signification as a means of effectively expressing their concept in their chosen medium. So, not unlike a poet who masters the use of different rhyme schemes or meters, uses of metaphor, or other literary devices, a successful media artist deliberately employs different forms or styles in the creation of their work.

Deliberate development of form and content

As media artists become proficient in the language of their particular craft or medium, they are able to make deliberate decisions about the relationship between form and content of their creative work. This typically involves understanding how a convention of a particular form has been used in context; to tell specific stories, express certain emotions, or explore particular ideas. Examples of this type of study might include examining the use of narration in documentary to communicate an authoritative perspective on the subject or examining the use of a "retro" pixelated visual esthetic in a mobile game to elicit a feeling of nostalgia from the player. As media artists become familiar with the tools and techniques, languages and conventions of their form, and as they understand the significance of these traditions to explore certain ideas, they are able to create work in which there is a unity of form and content.

Revision and refinement

A significant part of the creative process involves revising and refining the work so that it serves as a successful realization of the artist's vision and reaches and resonates with its intended audience. Media arts initiatives typically devote a large amount of time and effort to this stage of the process, as peers and mentors provide feedback on each other's work. The production of multiple drafts, cuts, or versions is typical of the production of many media arts, though the iterative development process in game design provides an especially effective example of this stage. The development of a video game is substantially comprised of repeated processes of building and testing. Through these play-tests, developers are able to understand what the game communicates to the player (how to play, for example), how the player understands and interacts with the game (what choices players make), whether the game successfully achieves its creator's intentions (whether it is fun, challenging, etc.), and, perhaps most importantly, whether it works (what bugs need to be fixed). Also, this process of revision and refinement often positions the work not simply as the realization of the creator's vision, or a unified work of art but something with which the audience will engage and interact.

Audience engagement

The ultimate goal of most media artists is to share their work with others, though, depending on the media used in the work and the context in which this work is engaged with by the audience, this experience can vary widely. Regardless of the specifics of the presentation/performance of the final work, though, media arts education often emphasizes the significance of this experience as the site where creator, work, and audience can interact. Conversations concerning (and even studies of) audience reception or interpretation often play a part in media arts education. Whether it is a fan-video distributed via YouTube watched on a mobile phone or an installation making use of virtual reality in a museum space, the experience of the audience engaging with the work of a media artist is of special significance.

Critical analysis

In addition to the production of creative work, media arts—and media arts education specifically—often include a component of critical analysis. Theoretical frameworks are introduced and applied in analyses of creative works, with various objectives including esthetic appreciation, ideology critique, examinations of genre, authorship, and so forth. As discussed, given that media arts draws upon multiple artistic disciplines, philosophical and esthetic traditions, there is a multitude of analytical approaches employed in media arts education including, but not limited to: semiotics, narratology, auteur theory, various esthetic theories, Marxist critical theory, various psychoanalytic theories, media ecology, various critical cultural theories including postcolonial theory, feminist criticism, queer theory, eco-criticism, as well as examinations of media genres, history, industries, and technologies. Oftentimes, critical analysis of media arts serves to prepare student artists to understand and effectively employ a particular esthetic or theoretical concept in the creation of their own work. In other cases, the objective of this critical engagement is to develop an understanding and/or appreciation of a particular tradition, form, concept, and so on.

Media arts and media literacy

Within the context of media education, media arts are a historically significant tradition. Disciplines that are commonly associated with media arts—such as film studies, visual communication, and cultural and media studies—developed over the 20th century and informed the discourse around media literacy (Hobbs & Jensen, 2009). Along with disciplines like democratic education, critical pedagogy, digital citizenship, youth media, news literacy, and so forth, media arts is a vital part of the field of media literacy, sharing some key concepts and approaches with these other disciplines, while also differing from them in some significant ways.

As discussed, central to many media arts initiatives is the integration of media analysis and production, a perspective shared by media literacy scholars and educators. As demonstrated in the discussion above, media arts education shares the media literacy movement's emphasis on questions of:

- authorship ("Who made this?");
- context ("When was this made?");
- purposes ("Why was this made?");
- content ("What ideas, values, information, points of view are [represented]?");
- technique ("What techniques are used and why?");
- responses ("How does this make me feel and how do my emotions influence my interpretation of this?");
- interpretations ("How might different people understand this message differently?") (Rogow & Scheibe, 2007).

However, as the field of media literacy is dominated by perspectives emerging from communications and education traditions, some of the terminology, analytical frameworks, and theoretical perspectives employed in the field are not often included within media arts education. Commonly absent from most media arts education are discussions regarding, for example, institutions, economics, effects, and credibility. This is not to suggest that media artists and media arts educators are unaware of issues regarding the political economy of the media and cultural industries, the potential power of media to influence attitudes and behaviors, and so forth. Rather, media arts education—due to its roots in the fields of arts and humanities—understand media texts primarily as esthetic objects and artistic expressions rather than cultural products or media "messages." Some have argued that this difference in perspective, though, positions media arts education as a "marginalized discourse" within the field of media literacy education (Lopez, 2014).

In addition to understanding media in slightly different ways than much of the field of media literacy, media arts education has been critiqued by media literacy scholars for its emphasis on personal expression, esthetic appreciation, and skill acquisition at the expense of critical engagements with media's role in larger ideological, social, and political issues. Kellner and Share (2007) write:

> Many of these programs tend to unproblematically teach students the technical skills to merely reproduce hegemonic representations with little awareness of ideological implications or any type of social critique. (p. 61)

While this argument might be overstated—as the pedagogical approaches in media arts initiatives vary widely—it is not without some justification. The objective of many media arts programs is career development and job placement; thus, an emphasis is placed on the acquisition of technical skills and the understanding of particular conventions, processes, and practices. Also, the link between video production, graphic design programs, and advertising—an industry that is often the subject of scrutiny in media literacy education—may further validate this critique.

However, it may also be pertinent to acknowledge that while media arts education may emphasize personal expression or esthetic technique, many initiatives make an effort to situate these discussions within broader social, cultural, and political contexts. Not unlike its sister disciplines the youth media and "maker" movements, media arts education frequently frames creative expression as integrated with cultural participation, civic engagement, and even political activism. In the same publication, Kellner and Share (2007) acknowledge the potential political significance of increased emphasis on media arts in public education, writing:

> Incorporating the arts and media production into public school education holds important political benefits for making learning more experiential, hands-on, creative, expressive, and fun. Media arts education can bring pleasure and popular culture into mainstream education, thereby making school more motivating and relevant to students. (p. 7)

Media arts education's emphasis on creative production often allows for more self-directed learning. Its engagement with popular culture allows educators to connect the curriculum to students' everyday lives, validate their interests and experiences, as well as challenge the understanding of legitimate knowledge in traditional education. And media arts' emphasis on personal expression invites students to exercise agency not just as artists, but potentially as citizens and activists. As student artists produce "alternative media"—from "block-umentary films" to "games for change"—they are expressing themselves, sharing their experiences, but also participating in civic discourse.

Additionally, on closer examination, the contrast articulated by Kellner and Share between media arts education and critical media literacy reveals false dichotomies between theory and practice, esthetics and politics. Nearly any study of esthetic traditions will reveal that historically, esthetic techniques have been developed and employed in the arts (and media arts specifically) not simply to achieve some conception of "beauty" or "unity," but rather as means of effectively communicating specific ideas or emphasizing particular perspectives. The esthetics are practical demonstrations of the theoretical concepts, and their underlying political philosophies.

For example, within the tradition of cinema, the integration of media theory, production, and politics is exemplified by filmmaker and theorist Sergei Eisenstein.

Eisenstein is among the most prominent Soviet filmmakers and is credited for the development of the "montage method" of filmmaking. His films *Battleship Potemkin* (1925), *October* (1927), and *Alexander Nevsky* (1938) (among many others) practice the juxtaposition of strikingly dissimilar images as a means of producing specific responses in the audience and advocating for particular ideological perspectives. This technique is probably most famously demonstrated in the Odessa staircase sequence from *Battleship Potemkin* in which shots of marching Cossack soldiers are cross-cut with scenes of fatally injured peasants and crying children. Eisenstein wrote extensively—in his books *The Film Sense* (1942) and *Film Form: Essays in Film Theory* (1949) and numerous essays—about the use of visual language to communicate revolutionary ideology.

It follows, then, that while media arts' principal interest may not be in, for example, the political implications of works of art, the subject of ideology has been and remains an important concern within the tradition. The scholarship surrounding "visual literacy"—often associated with media arts education—while emphasizing the process of signification in contemporary media, acknowledges the importance of examining texts in relation to context (Messaris, 1998). Zettl (1998), for example, advocates for an approach to visual literacy that allows for "contextual media aesthetics" (p. 84), which includes an understanding of *esthetic elements and structures of screen images,* how these elements and structures are processed by our own *mental maps*, and how those mental maps function within larger *intellectual and cultural frameworks.*

Media arts, literacies, and technologies

As of 2014, the United States' National Core Arts Standards identifies media arts as an arts discipline. The identification of media arts with the disciplines of music, dance, theater, and visual arts, signals an important development in media arts education. While media arts has and continues to have a presence in educational disciplines as varied as communications, technology, arts, and humanities, this institutional acknowledgment of media arts as an arts discipline may signal a shift in how media artists, scholars, and educators understand their work and position themselves within artistic, academic, and educational contexts. For example, the extent to which media arts educators will continue to approach their pedagogy with the principles of media literacy (access, analyze, evaluate, and create) as opposed to the standards of arts education (creating, performing/presenting/producing, responding, and connecting) will be determined by the scholars and artists, teachers and students working in the discipline (Jensen & Draper, 2015; National Association for Media Literacy Education, 2007; National Coalition for Core Arts Standards, 2014).

And last, as media arts already integrates multiple media forms, utilizing a variety of tools and technologies, the discipline will likely continue to creatively engage with emerging media platforms and technologies, so that in addition to film and video, games, and graphics, media artists in the years to come will draw upon holographic technologies, biometric media, and mixed reality in their creative work.

SEE ALSO: Arts Education with iPads; Arts Literacies; Authorship and Participatory Culture; Creative Works; Digital Storytelling; Documentary Analysis and Production in Media Literacy; Film Education in Europe; Game Design in Media Literacy Education; Media Education Research and Creativity; Performance Media; Production in the Pedagogic Project of Media Literacy; Remix Culture; Understanding Media Literacy and DIY Creativity in Youth Digital Productions; Visual Literacy; Youth Media

References

Eisenstein, S. (1942). *The film sense.* New York, NY: Harcourt, Brace and Company.

Eisenstein, S. (1949). *Film form: Essays in film theory.* New York, NY: Harcourt, Brace and Company.

Hobbs, R., & Jensen, A. (2009). The past, present and future of media literacy education. *Journal of Media Literacy Education, 1*(1), 1–11.

Jensen, A., & Draper, R.J. (2015). *Arts education and literacies.* New York, NY: Routledge.

Kellner, D., & Share, J. (2007). Critical media literacy, democracy, and the reconstruction of education. In D. Macedo & S.R. Steinberg (Eds.), *Media literacy: A reader*. New York, NY: Peter Lang.
Lopez, A. (2014). Back to the drawing board: Making comics, making media literacy. In B.S. de Abreu, P. Mihailidis, A.Y.L. Lee, J. Melki, & J. McDougall (Eds.), *International handbook of media literacy education*. New York, NY: Routledge.
Messaris, P. (1998). Visual aspects of media literacy. *Journal of Communication, 48*(1), 70–80.
National Association for Media Literacy Education. (NAMLE). (2007). *The core principles of media literacy education in the United States*. Retrieved from http://namle.net/publications/core-principles/
National Coalition for Core Arts Standards.(2014). *National core arts standards media arts*. Retrieved from http://www.nationalartsstandards.org/
Rogow, F., & Scheibe, C. (2007). *Key questions to ask when analyzing media messages*. National Association of Media Literacy Education (NAMLE).
Zettl, H. (1998). Contextual media aesthetics as the basis for media literacy. *Journal of Communication, 48*(1), 81–95.

Further reading

Albert, D. (2016). An interview with Richard Burrows about the media arts standards: A pathway to expression and knowing the world. *Arts Education Policy Review, 117*(3), 146–152.
Hobbs, R. (1998). The seven great debates in the media literacy movement. *Journal of Communication, 48*(1), 16–32.
Martens, H. (2010). Evaluating media literacy education: Concepts, theories and future directions. *Journal of Media Literacy Education, 2*(1), 1–22.

Benjamin Thevenin is an assistant professor of media arts at Brigham Young University. His studies focus on the relationships between youth, media, and politics, and in particular how we can better prepare young people to become thoughtful citizens, consumers, and creators of media. Thevenin teaches classes on creativity, children's media, new media, and media education. He serves on the Leadership Council of the National Association of Media Literacy Education. Benjamin lives with his wife Emily and three boys in the beautiful Wasatch mountains.

Media Competence

GERHARD TULODZIECKI
University of Paderborn, Germany

SILKE GRAFE
University of Würzburg, Germany

Media competence comprises the two conceptual components *media* and *competence*. Depending on the underlying concepts, the term *media competence* can have very different meanings. Therefore, it is necessary to consider for each concept of media competence which meaning of media and of competence has been taken as a basis.

Concepts of media as an educational issue

The term *media* can be understood as having diverse meanings. On the one hand, it may be used for all modes in which facts or feelings can be experienced and ideas can be formed, for example, language, music, models, signs, or symbols in general. On the other hand, the term may be restricted to forms and experiences by which contents are mediated with technical support, for example, photo, book, film, radio, television, and computer. For media pedagogy, it seems functional to follow the second meaning and to limit the term *media* to modes of experience which are technically conveyed and technically available. This means that the correspondent opportunity for experience relies on technical support and can generally be processed with technical means and without the author or the original issue. Such an understanding of media offers a unique opportunity to analyze the characteristics of technically conveyed and available experiences and contents and to formulate correspondent scientific statements. At the same time, other modes of experience—in contrast and comparison to technically conveyed and available experiences—can and should be kept in mind and included in any analysis (Tulodziecki, 2013). Moreover, this meaning is in accordance with the historical development of media education as it is connected with mass media like the press, radio, and television. Against this background, it seems appropriate in the context of the term *media competence* to understand media as agents through which potential signs in communicative contexts are recorded or created and processed, transmitted, saved, reproduced, or presented and are available. This assumes that media contents, in conjunction with their form, influence individuals and society and are seen in the context of the technical, legal, economic, personal, and further institutional and social conditions influencing their production and distribution (Tulodziecki, Herzig, & Grafe, 2010).

Concepts of competence in relation to media competence

The term *competence* originates from the Latin *competentia*, which can be translated as *encounter*. The Latin term implies that the encounter is aspired to but cannot be enforced. Based on its origin and also on daily usage the term states that *responsibility* (in the widest sense) is given for a certain field and that this responsibility coincides with the ability and readiness of acting persons (Tulodziecki, 2013). However, if the term *competence* is used in science, other conceptual ideas apply. In an attempt to classify the multifaceted scientific discourse on the term *competence*, four concepts can be differentiated: (i) a language theoretic concept, (ii) a socio-critical concept, (iii) a functional–pragmatic concept, and (iv) a concept from the viewpoint of action theory and pedagogy. These concepts must not be understood as accurate separations but as perspectives with diverse references.

The language theoretic concept is based on Chomsky's approach (1968) for human language acquisition. He assumed a general cognitive device that allows for the development of a suitable system of rules when learning a language, which, for example, enables children not only to repeat sentences they hear but also to create new sentences or to express thoughts at will. In this context, Chomsky understood the ability to speak as an innate human potential which constitutes human competence. According to his understanding of competence, a difference between a non-visible cognitive system and a visible performance in linguistic behavior was assumed. Hence, he made a distinction between competence and performance. Strictly speaking, considering differing competence between individuals is superfluous because competence is understood as a cognitive base of linguistic acts, which is common to all human beings. Assessing differences is only relevant on the level of performance. According to this concept, media competence would have to be understood as a general cognitive base for acting in the field of media which devolves to all humans by nature. Empirically proven differences would not stem from differing competence but from personal or situational factors influencing the performance.

The language theoretic concept of competence was an important starting point for Habermas (1971) who extended and used it to develop his concept of a socio-critical approach differently. He generalized Chomsky's term of competence with his term of *communicative competence* by referring competence not only to verbal utterances but also to all kinds of communicative expressions. In this sense, communicative competence is granted to every human and enables the arrangement of communicative situations. Likewise Habermas (1971), having socio-critical intentions, understood competence on the one hand as a precondition of discourses that are free of domination (as ideal speech situations), and on the other hand as the goal of development and socialization aimed at truth and communication. In a similar sense, Baacke (1973) conceived the term *competence* as a human ability that must be presumed and also as a skill that has to be aspired to and facilitated in its development by learning.

Another concept of competence, which can be characterized as functional–pragmatic, was focused on by media education, due to a demand for models of media competence. The functional–pragmatic competence model has its background in a view of education that is basically at the bottom of international comparative studies such as the Programme for International Student Assessment (PISA) and can be described by the term *literacy*. Originally, this term signified reading and writing skills. *Literacy* is associated with the idea that contents should be learnt and taught in such a way that they are of practical value for learners in their lives and jobs. With regard to philosophy, this concept is based on a pragmatism which favors human actions and their consequences over mere ideas. Hence, key criteria for learning contents are their usefulness and the success of actions based on these contents, while usefulness and success should be indebted to living together democratically and to human welfare. Concerning the socioeconomic context, the concept of literacy is based on the claim to meet the need for qualification, which changed in the context of globalization, and at the same time to develop a modern educational concept adequate for the knowledge society. In this sense, media competence should essentially be understood as a means for realizing media-related, professional, and societal tasks.

Alongside the concepts of competence, an understanding of competence from the perspective of action theory and pedagogy plays a vital role in the discourse about media competence. An early approach to understanding competence from such a perspective can be found in Roth's work (1971). Roth puts the term *competence* in the context of guiding principles for education. Later, Weinert (2001) presents an intermediate position on Roth's concept of competence with his pedagogical–psychological understanding of competence. He discriminates between subject-specific, interdisciplinary, and action competences, whereby action competences comprise cognitive skills and competences for solving problems as well as motivational, volitional, and moral competences. Against this background and with regard to media, the concept of competence can be characterized as follows: competence in media-related contexts refers to proficiency, skills and readiness, knowledge, capability, and attitudes (including value orientations) that are considered as dispositions for self-dependent, media-related judgment, and acting. The dispositions include issue-related, motivational or self-regulatory, and social–communicative components. They can be acquired in educational processes, facilitate a reflexive coping of diverse situational tasks or requirements in the field of media and are directed toward autonomy or self-reliant acting.

Different concepts of media competence

The concepts of competence and their relations to the term *media competence* are general and basic positions. Further and more concrete explanations of the term *media competence* can be found in various approaches. In Germany, this has been subject to notably intense discussion. Many references have been made to Baacke's (1997) understanding of media competence in this context where he significantly influenced the discussion about media competence in German-speaking countries.

Baacke (1997) attempted a clarification based on his earlier considerations about communicative competences. He distinguished four fields of media competence: (i) media criticism (with an analytic, reflexive, and ethical focus), (ii) media knowledge (with an informative, instrumental, and qualification dimension), (iii) media use (which can happen receptively or interactively), and (iv) media creation (which should be understood as innovative or creative) (Baacke, 1997). This differentiation was also used for comprehensive empirical research on media-related actions by youths.

In comparison to Baacke, Tulodziecki (1997) focuses more strongly on referring media competence to generic educational objectives in the information and knowledge society and on the dimensions of action and content fields of media competence. On the first level, he describes media competence as the readiness and ability to act appropriately in a self-determined manner which is creative and socially responsible in media contexts. On a second level, he distinguishes two main fields of activity (using appropriate types of media for a variety of purposes and creating own media messages) and three fields of contents: design of media messages, media influences and conditions of media production, and media distribution. This way, he attains five task areas for the development of media competence: (i) selecting and using appropriate types of media for a variety of purposes, (ii) creating and disseminating own media, (iii) understanding and evaluating media messages, (iv) becoming aware of and dealing with media influences, and (v) identifying and evaluating conditions of media production and media dissemination.

Compared with Baacke and Tulodziecki, Aufenanger (2001) stresses which basic capability is necessary to act in an environment where media are natural constituents.

He defines six dimensions of media competence: (i) a cognitive dimension which refers to knowledge, understanding, and analysis in media contexts, (ii) a moral dimension that points to the consideration and assessment of media from an ethical perspective, (iii) a social dimension that calls attention to the fact that realizing cognitive and moral dimensions depends on the domain of social and political acts, (iv) an affective dimension that includes a perspective on media in their role of entertainment and enjoyment, (v) an esthetic dimension which considers media as a means of expression with a certain esthetic potential, and (vi) an action dimension which is perceivable in the self creation of media and in their use as a means of expression and information with experimental possibilities.

In the context of the mentioned aims, fields, tasks, and dimensions of media competence, other authors emphasize special or further aspects of media competence, as the following examples indicate:

- Groeben (2002) draws attention to the assumptions that media competence is an important precondition for the ability to act in social contexts, that media and media institutions also have to be considered as instances of socialization, and that chances for social participation given by media should be taken.
- Schorb (2005) describes media communication as a constitutive element for the development of society as a living environment for human beings, and he understands media competence as a precondition for social participation, with media competence comprising three main categories: knowledge of media in a functional and structural as well as orientational sense; assessment of media as a critical reflection and as a qualification on an ethical and cognitive basis; and interacting with media as use of media and participation in media as well as creation of media.
- Spanhel (2006) considers processes of media use in the light of the self-directed development of adolescents. He understands media competence as a complex combination of patterns of perception, feeling, thinking, acting, and judging, based on the human ability for interpreting symbols. In this context, he stresses three basic anthropological functions of media: constitution and shaping of social relationships; constitution and shaping of personal environments; and communication and agreement about contents.
- Wagner (2013) describes media particularly as tools of appropriating the world. He considers them as relevant for education primarily because they broaden our horizon of experience and communication and because they are essential tools of the production, presentation, and dissemination of knowledge. Moreover, he includes a historical perspective and emphasizes the relevance of media for the development of culture and society. On the basis of this understanding of media, he particularly stresses the awareness of mediality in its relevance for media competence and media education.

All approaches described have in common that the term *media competence* is used for knowledge and skills as well as for attitudes or individual patterns of acting. Furthermore, all of the approaches assume that human beings are able and ready to interpret and create potential signs in a manner relevant for action. Thus, so far, in all approaches media competence is generally understood as human ability and readiness to act in media contexts. The term *ability* conveys the assumption that the correspondent skills are connected to an elementary potential or human predisposition. The term *readiness* refers to motivational or volitional aspects of competence. The term *acting* is associated with the conception of an active subject who is able to take charge of their own life and develop their skills. All in all, these approaches to media competence are, broadly speaking, close to the concept of competence from the perspective of action theory and pedagogy, and partly include explicit or implicit references to other concepts described.

References to different concepts of competence, however, can lead to a certain ambiguity of the term *media competence* in discussions on media education. For example, the term may be used both for referring to a universal human potential and for indicating a certain level or a target level as an aim for media education. Moreover, references to different concepts were the main reason for criticizing the term *media competence* in the first decade of the 21st century. Among other things, critics also said that media competence would aim at: (i) a social–technological assimilation rather than at the ability to accept criticism and a reflexive attitude, (ii) knowledge for the sake of action rather than at knowledge for the sake of orientation, (iii) the relationship between human being and medium rather than at the relationship between human being and the world, and (iv) directed learning processes rather than at self-directed developmental and educational processes. But this criticism was based on the suggestion of a mere functional–pragmatic or functional–technological understanding of competence. Such an understanding may be encountered outside the field of media education but does not do justice to the media education discourse. Media education approaches are dominated by an understanding of competence that also pays attention to the ability to accept criticism, reflexive attitudes, knowledge for the sake of orientation, the relationship between human beings and the world imparted by media, and self-direction.

In an international context, issues of media competence are often discussed under the term *media literacy*, which puts special emphasis on the aspect of literacy (consider the general term *competence* reviewed previously). In the USA, *media literacy* has been defined as “the ability to access, analyze, evaluate and communicate messages in a wide variety of forms” since a conference on media literacy was held in 1993 (Hobbs, 2008). In Europe, Buckingham (2007) points out that there are three key concepts that apply to all kinds of literacy: representation, language, and production. With regard to media, *representation* is about the way reality is represented in the media and about the reliability and trustworthiness of media information; *language* is about the language of media and its functionality; *production* is about the conditions and background of producing media messages, which also includes the question of how certain target groups are addressed, and which attempts at manipulation accompany this. Accordingly, in the international discussion about media literacy there are several important fields of action for media competence, for example, access, analysis, evaluation, and creative production, as well as meaningful fields of content, for example, media language, media influences, and conditions of media production.

Standard models of media competence

If competence is to be used as an objective or reference point for educational processes, it is necessary to concretize it in terms of targets for different age groups or target groups. In the educational system, formulating educational standards, which should rely on explicit competence models, is a well-established procedure for such demands.

Educational standards have been claimed in media education. They are attributed with important functions for the development of media pedagogical practice and for reformatting the educational system. For example, the standards are highly significant for orientation, curriculum development, qualification and professionalization for pedagogical activities, and for the evaluation of teaching and learning processes. Thus, standards basically offer an orientation for learners and educators and for educational institutions regarding the knowledge, skills, abilities, or attitudes that are to be achieved by learners. This way, standards can also stimulate revisions of existing curricula or the development of new curricula to reach the standards. Furthermore, they are helpful for answering the question of which competencies educators need to be able to stimulate to facilitate the acquisition of target knowledge and skills. Furthermore, standards offer the opportunity to measure and evaluate the results of learning and teaching processes.

In order to realize such functions for media education, special standard models of competences have been developed. Examples are the *Zurich standard model* (cf. Moser, 2007) and the *Paderborn competence standard model* (cf. Tulodziecki et al., 2010). The *Zurich standard model* explicitly refers to Baacke's (1997) media pedagogical approach with its orientation toward action theory and its establishment in the concept of communicative competence. The *Paderborn competence standard model* is based on an understanding of competence that highlights acting adequately, in a self-determined manner, creatively, and being socially responsible in a world shaped by media as a key idea for education in the knowledge and information society.

The following examples demonstrate which decisions are necessary to develop a competence standard model. The examples have been selected because they particularly fulfill the claim to describe educational standards for different levels of competence based on a competence model. Moreover, both models are more established in the media education discussion than other models.

The *first decision* in the development of a competence standard model concerns the question of which areas and aspects of competence should be included as structural leading points. Using the background of the approaches to media competence previously described, the following methods of structuring are suitable:

- Structuring according to fields of action: aspects like the reception and production of media offerings, the choice and use of media alternatives, the creation and dissemination of own media contributions and/or media-based communication and cooperation could be used for the structure.
- Structuring according to fields of contents: important fields of content could be ways to design media or their *language*, the impacts media have on individuals and social or societal contexts, as well as conditions of media production and media design (including technical, economic, institutional, and political conditions).

- Structuring according to dimensions: such as cognitive, ethical–moral, emotional, affective–motivational, social, esthetic, and an action dimension can be distinguished.
- Structuring according to functions: in this way, the significance of media for information and learning, for presentation and entertainment, for game and simulation, for cooperation and exchange, and for social presence could be emphasized.
- Structuring according to subskills or key competencies: for example, having knowledge at one's disposal, handling technology, understanding, analyzing, evaluating, and creating could be called subskills. Potential key competences could be, for instance, professional competence, methodological competence, learning competence, and social competence.
- Structuring according to different kinds of media: in this context, media could be differentiated as picture or photo, print media, audio media, video or film, and other audio media as well as computer-based media (offline and online).

Against the background of these options, the *Zurich standard model* determines three fields of action in the context of media as structuring elements. The three fields are: use and creation of media products, exchange and mediation of media messages, and reflection and criticism of media. Moreover, since *media education* or *school information technology* has been identified as an interdisciplinary subject in the curriculum of the Swiss canton Zurich which has to be integrated into other subjects, Moser (2007) considers an orientation toward the following general competences: professional competences; methodological competences; and social competences. These should then be focused with regards to media suitable for connecting to the determined fields of action. This way, a matrix is created which comprises nine cells, each with one educational standard for different target levels.

In the *Paderborn competence standard model* different ways of structuring are combined. As areas of competence, two fields of action and three fields of content are connected. This way, the media education task areas were chosen as areas of competence: (i) selecting and using appropriate types of media for a variety of purposes, (ii) creating and disseminating own media messages, (iii) understanding and evaluating media messages, (iv) becoming aware of and dealing with media influences, and (v) identifying and evaluating conditions of media production and media distribution. Moreover, the areas of competence are connected to different competence aspects, which leads to an emphasis on additional ways of structuring on the level of competence aspects. For example, the first area of competence—selecting and using appropriate types of media—is structured according to the functions: selection and use of available media for information, for learning, entertainment, and gaming, for communication and cooperation, as well as for analysis and simulation; and the second area of competence—creating and disseminating media—is structured according to different kinds of media: pictures or photos, print media, audio media, video clips or films, and computer-based interactive media. Within the framework of this structure educational standards are formulated for each competence aspect. The structure of the competence standard model is presented in Table 1.

Table 1 Structure of the Paderborn competence standard model. The competence expectations serve as an orientation guide for the end of the "Sekundarstufe I" (school age: approximately 15 years old).

Field of competence	**Selecting and using appropriate types of media for a variety of purposes**				
Competence expectation	Different media and possibilities not involving media can be used with regard to intended functions (information and learning, entertainment and game, communication and cooperation, analysis and simulation). Pupils should be able to compare and evaluate them with regard to chosen criteria. They should be able to choose them according to a certain situation giving reasons and be able to use them with regard to social and societal responsibility.				
Differentiation of level	Aspects and levels of development with regard to affective–motivational, intellectual, and social–moral dimension of media competence.				
Aspects of competence	Information	Learning	Entertainment and game	Communica-tion and cooperation	Analysis and simulation
Standards of level X					
Field of competence	**Creating and disseminating own media messages**				
Competence expectation	Pupils are able to create media messages using a reasonably chosen scope for the design of pictures, written texts, audio and video clips, as well as interactive contributions. They should be able to use the respective technique in an appropriate way. They are able to plan and create own media messages with regard to social and societal responsibility and they are able to disseminate them to individuals, certain groups, and in public.				
Aspects of competence	Pictures or photos	Print media	Audio media	Video clips	Computer-based interactive media
Standards of level X					
Field of competence	**Understanding and evaluating media messages**				
Competence expectation	Media messages can be designed in different possible ways, e.g., representational systems, design techniques, types of media, structure of course, and types of programs. Pupils should be able to illustrate different possibilities of media design with regard to different criteria. They should be able to analyze and reflect the different means of design with regard to media and own media messages. They should be able to estimate their relevance for media messages and be able to evaluate the divide between form and content as well as other aspects.				

Table 1 (*Continued*)

Field of competence	**Selecting and using appropriate types of media for a variety of purposes**				
Aspects of competence	Representa-tional systems	Techniques of design	Types of media	Structure of course	Types of programs
Standards of level X					
Field of competence	**Becoming aware of and dealing with media influences**				
Competence expectation	Media messages can influence emotions, beliefs, behavior and value orientations as well as social conditions which can have different consequences. Pupils should be able to describe and evaluate the different influences and possible consequences using different criteria. They should be able to analyze problematic influences of using media and creating own media messages, review them in appropriate ways and take countermeasures.				
Aspects of competence	Emotions	Beliefs	Behaviors	Values	Social contexts
Standards of level X					
Field of competence	**Identifying and evaluating conditions of media production and media distribution**				
Competence expectation	Pupils should be able to explain different technological, economic, legal, personnel and other political and societal conditions of media production and media distribution. They should be able to connect such conditions with different media and their use. They should be able to evaluate the conditions with regard to desirable conditions for society and they should be able to describe and make use of ways to influence them by their own media use.				
Aspects of competence	Technical conditions	Economic conditions	Legal conditions	Personnel and other institutional conditions	Political and other societal conditions
Standards of level X					

Source: Tulodziecki et al. (2010).

The *second decision* in developing a competence standard model is to be made regarding the number of levels or age groups for which educational standards will be defined in the competence standard model.

- In the Zurich model, four levels of competence are fixed in reference to the Swiss educational system: (i) end of the basic level (when children are approximately

7 years old), (ii) end of the "Mittelstufe" (approximately 11 years old), (iii) end of the 8th grade (approximately 13 years old), and (iv) end of the 11th grade (approximately 17 years old) (Moser, 2007). For example, a standard for the field of action *use and creation of media products* and the competence aspect *professional competence* on the fourth level is described as: uses media for own learning and working on the basis of differentiated knowledge (Moser, 2007).

- In the Paderborn model, three levels are differentiated with regard to the German education system: (i) end of elementary school (when children are approximately 9 years old), (ii) end of sixth grade (approximately 11 years old), and (iii) end of "Sekundarstufe I" (approximately 15 years old). For example, the standards for the third level of the competence area *selecting and using appropriate types of media for a variety of purposes* and the competence aspect *learning* reads: "Comparing and evaluating different media offerings and non-media learning opportunities according to various criteria/Choosing different learning opportunities appropriately/with good reason, handling them properly, and using them responsibly" (Tulodziecki et al., 2010, p. 371).

In connection with the differentiation between levels of competence, there should be a reflection on criteria for the advancement from the first to the last level of competence. For instance, the educational standards for different levels of competence in the Paderborn model have explicitly been formulated with regard to theories of needs and motives, which particularly relate to affective–motivational development, theoretical approaches to cognitive complexity, which particularly refer to issues of intellectual development, and theoretical approaches to the level of social–ethical judgment, which aim at the development of value orientations in particular. This procedure should guarantee educational standards formulated with regards to development. At the same time, a formulation of educational standards not achievable at the end of the respective educational section should be avoided.

The *third decision* when constructing a competence standard model is necessary with regard to the question of how concrete or abstract the very formulations of standards should be. This entails further questions if one attempts to describe and measure facets of media competence.

The formulations in the Zurich model seem more general and less concrete than the ones in the model from Paderborn. These differences in the level of concretion or abstraction also relate to the attempt in the Zurich model to describe every competence level using only nine standards. As a consequence it is necessary to concretize the educational standards using indicators for implementation. In contrast to this, the Paderborn model comprises more educational standards, but indicators are not needed. The educational standards are formulated in a manner that shows what concrete tasks for proving the standards could look like, without anticipating these tasks in detail (Tulodziecki, 2007).

Current discussions about competence models and standard models for media education also include discussion about decisions necessary for developing competence standard models. However, the suitability of the areas and aspects of competence that, until now, have been selected for use in the models to encompass the latest developments, for example, in the fields of datafication and *big data*, is increasingly problematic, and so are potentially necessary additions or amendments. In this context, the question arises of which media-related and IT knowledge and skills are indispensable if responsibility, a capability to act, and readiness to act should also be regarded as key ideas for education in a mediatized, digitalized, and networked world.

In any case, competence standard models are important instruments of quality development and quality assurance in connection with their functions of orientation, curriculum, professionalization, and evaluation. Regarding quality development, they offer various stimuli and aids for reflection on and improvement of existing recommendations and measurements for media education instruction and the according initial and continuing education of pedagogical staff. Regarding quality assurance, standards allow for evaluating learning achievements and for planning further measurements to facilitate the achievement of target standards. This way, standards can contribute to providing high-quality media education instruction.

Assessment of media competence and learning processes

If standards are to come into effect in educational practice, it will be necessary to think over ways of proving whether certain standards are achieved or not. For this, rating scales, tests with respective tasks or performance records with an accompanying reflection, such as portfolios, can be used. It is also possible to combine different methods. With each method, success can generally be either self-assessed or assessed by others.

Rating scales allow for assessment for the standards themselves or for single indicators on whether a standard has been reached or not. If tests are to be developed, appropriate tasks have to be formulated. When working with a portfolio, learners can compile media products they have created, demonstrate other achievements, and can reflect on them with regard to educational standards.

For the development of tests, it has to be considered which criteria the tasks should meet with respect to the understanding of media competence represented here. First, the solution of the task has to allow for a conclusion regarding whether or not the standard was achieved. In this context, the tasks should have a meaning for the adolescents (that is, meet their interests), they should be situated (that is, refer to their living circumstances), and they should be practice-oriented (that is, be relevant for present or future actions). Ideally, the solution should indicate ways for further support where required.

Types of tasks which fulfill these criteria are exploration tasks, meaningful problems, cases that require a decision, tasks that require something to be created, or tasks that demand a judgment. Such tasks cannot only be used for the assessment of educational standards as they may also serve as starting points for learning processes aiming at media competence. Focusing on exploration, problems, decisions, creating, or judging could also reduce the risk connected with orientation on educational standards. Such a risk could be that proceeding with a focus on standards might give aspects of objectives and of the test itself too high a priority in comparison to process-related considerations. But if learning processes are stimulated by tasks which provoke exploration, problem-solving, decision-making, creating a product or judgment, and challenge the intellectual and social–moral capacities of learners, the process itself becomes very significant. This way, an action-, need-, and experience-oriented as well as a situation-specific and development-adequate learning can take place. In the context of corresponding process-related considerations, educational standards function as an aid for reflection rather than as a means of regulation.

Against this background, a core task for media education and educational policy now and in the future is to facilitate and make obligatory the systematic integration of media competence and media education into curricula or the educational programs of pedagogical institutions. A very important precondition for this is to ensure that acquiring pedagogical media competence becomes a core component in the context of teacher or educator preservice and in-service training.

SEE ALSO: Digital Literacy; Learning from Media; Media Literacy in Germany

References

Aufenanger, S. (2001). Multimedia und medienkompetenz [Multimedia and media competence]. In S. Aufenanger, R. Schulz-Zander, & D. Spanhel (Eds.), *Jahrbuch Medienpädagogik 1* [Annual book of media pedagogy 1] (pp. 109–122). Opladen, Germany: Leske & Budrich.

Baacke, D. (1973). *Kommunikation und Kompetenz* [Communication and competence]. München, Germany: Juventa.

Baacke, D. (1997). *Medienpädagogik* [Media pedagogy]. Tübingen, Germany: Niemeyer.

Buckingham, D. (2007). Schooling the digital generation. Popular culture, new media and the future of education. *Medienimpulse, 15*(59), 5–20.

Chomsky, N. (1968). *Language and mind*. New York, NY: Harcourt.

Groeben, N. (2002). Dimensionen der medienkompetenz [Dimensions of media competence]. In N. Groeben & B. Hurrelmann (Eds.), *Medienkompetenz. Voraussetzungen, dimensionen, funktionen* (pp. 160–197). Weinheim, Germany: Juventa.

Habermas, J. (1971). Vorbereitende überlegungen zu einer theorie der kommunikativen kompetenz [Preliminary considerations on a theory of communicative competence]. In J. Habermas & N. Luhmann, *Theorie der gesellschaft oder sozialtechnologie – was leistet die systemforschung?* (pp. 101–141). Frankfurt, Germany: Suhrkamp.

Hobbs, R. (2008). Debates and challenges. Facing new literacies in the 21st century. In K. Drotner & S. Livingstone (Eds.), *Children, media and culture* (pp. 431–447). Los Angeles, CA: SAGE.

Moser, H. (2007). Standards als instrument der medienbildung [Standards as an instrument of media education]. In J. Winkel (Ed.), *Standards in der medienbildung* (pp. 35–51). PLAZ-Forum, 16. Paderborn, Germany: University of Paderborn, Teacher Education Center.

Roth, H. (1971). *Pädagogische anthropologie* [Pedagogical anthropology]. Vol. 2. Hannover, Germany: Schroedel.

Schorb, B. (2005). Medienkompetenz [Media competence]. In J. Hüther & B. Schorb (Eds.), *Grundbegriffe medienpädagogik* (4th ed., pp. 257–262). München, Germany: Kopaed.

Spanhel, D. (2006). *Medienerziehung* [Media education]. Stuttgart, Germany: Klett-Cotta.

Tulodziecki, G. (1997). *Medien in erziehung und bildung* [Media in education] (3rd ed). Bad Heilbrunn, Germany: Klinkhardt.

Tulodziecki, G. (2007). Medienbildung – welche kompetenzen schülerinnen und schüler im medienbereich erwerben und welche standards sie erreichen sollen [Media education – media-related competencies students acquire and standards they are to reach]. In J. Winkel (Ed.), *Standards in der medienbildung* (pp. 9–33). PLAZ-Forum, 16. Paderborn, Germany: University of Paderborn, Teacher Education Center.

Tulodziecki, G. (2013). Medienkompetenz [Media competence]. In D. Meister, F. von Gross, & U. Sander (Eds.), *Enzyklopädie erziehungswissenschaft online*. Fachgebiet: Medienpädagogik (pp. 1–33). doi: 10.3262/EEO18130313

Tulodziecki, G., Herzig, B., & Grafe, S. (2010). *Medienbildung in schule und unterricht* [Media education in school and in lessons]. Bad Heilbrunn, Germany: Klinkhardt/ UTB.

Wagner, W.-R. (2013). *Bildungsziel medialitätsbewusstsein* [The educational objective of mediality awareness]. München, Germany: Kopaed.

Weinert, F.E. (2001). Vergleichende leistungsmessung in schulen – eine umstrittene selbstverständlichkeit [Comparative performance measurement at schools – a controversial matter of course]. In F.-E. Weinert (Ed.), *Leistungsmessungen in den schulen* (pp. 17–31). Weinheim, Germany: Beltz.

Further reading

Hobbs, R. (2011). *Digital and media literacy: Connecting culture and classroom*. Thousand Oaks, CA: Corwin.

Martens, H. (2010). Evaluating media literacy education: Concepts, theories and future directions. *Journal of Media Literacy Education, 2*(1), 1–22.

Tulodziecki, G., & Grafe, S. (2010). Developing a competence standard model for media education. *Recherches en Communication, 33*, 53–67.

Gerhard Tulodziecki is Professor Emeritus of Education at the University of Paderborn. He was director of the Institute for Media Education at the Research and Development Center for Educational Technology in Paderborn. His research interests include principles of teaching and learning, media literacy education, and teacher education. Gerhard Tulodziecki was a member of various committees, for example, the steering group on educational technology (Council of Europe), the advisory board of the German Institute for Audio-Visual Aids in Science and Education (FWU), and the Project Group of Media Education of the German Joint Commission for Educational Planning and Research Funding (BLK).

Silke Grafe is Professor of Education at the University of Würzburg. Her research interests include media education from an international and intercultural perspective, teaching and learning with and about media in the classroom, media pedagogy in teacher education and professional development, developing and validating measures of pedagogical media competencies of students in initial teacher education, and virtual and augmented reality in education. Silke Grafe was a member of the expert group of media literacy of the German Federal Ministry of Education and Research and a member of the EMEDUS European Expert Group of Media Literacy Education.

Media Diaries as Pedagogy

MATTHIAS BERG
University of Bremen, Germany

Media diary is an umbrella term for a wide range of techniques for individuals gathering information on their use of and experience with media. In media and communication research, media diaries serve as a method for generating standardized as well as non-standardized data, whereas in education, media diaries are a tool for training media literacy. Thereby, media diaries range from detailed, time-oriented reports of media-related activities to more qualitative reflections of the appropriation and meaning of media in everyday life along with various context information. Furthermore, they may refer either to the contact with media content and specific messages (reception of, e.g., news or entertainment programs) or the use of certain media technologies (e.g., television, gaming console, smartphone). While the degree of reflection may vary, a high level of participant involvement is common to all forms of media diaries, due to the ego-centered and self-reporting nature of the method.

These characteristics of the media diary relate back to the offspring of the diary as literary practice, which has largely developed in modernity. It belongs to the self-narratives and aims at the self as an object of description and analysis (Chang, 2008, p. 35). Accordingly, observations of the self as well as its relations to the outer world are formulated from an ego-centered and subjective perspective. In research, original diaries have been used as primary sources, for example in literary studies, history, or psychology, and thus can be methodologically characterized as a non-reactive research method. In social sciences, solicited diaries are purposefully produced by research participants in order to receive data from individual perspectives.

Diaries in media education and literacy research

In the field of education in general, diaries are predominantly applied as learning diaries serving different purposes: next to the stabilization and retention of the actual learning content, students' reflections aim at making the learning processes transparent. The focus on the metalevel of learning is intended to ultimately improve individual techniques of knowledge acquisition. Furthermore, such documents can serve as feedback loops for educators as well as sources for the evaluation of pedagogical practices and educational research (Glogger, Schwonke, Holzäpfel, Nückles, & Renkl, 2012, pp. 452–455).

When it comes to the media diary as a specific tool for teaching media literacy, diaries are applied as instructional practice and often combined with subsequent discussions. The accomplishment of the goals of (critical) media (Kellner & Share, 2005) as well as information literacy (Livingstone, van Couvering, & Thumin, 2008) presupposes a certain understanding of today's media societies and environments. A means of reaching this understanding is present in approaches which employ observation and self-observation on the part of the individual. Due to their reflexive nature, diaries help to raise awareness of the importance and various influences of media. Consequently, keeping a solicited media diary as a means of reflecting one's personal media use (Rosenbaum, Beentjes, & Konig, 2008, p. 335) contributes, for example, to revealing the temporal structures established through the use of media. Thus, routines, individual patterns of usage, and experiences related to media can be detected and compared, giving an impression of shared as well as individualized media practices. Lloyd-Kolkin, Wheeler, and Strand (1980), for instance, designed a curriculum for teaching critical TV viewing to high school students that includes logging personal television habits in order to discuss them in class or within the family.

In addition to their practical application as a tool in media education, media diaries also function as a research method contributing insights to media literacy research. As a versatile academic field, media literacy research depends on current empirical findings in order to perform its key tasks, which include defining and measuring media literacy as well as developing and evaluating corresponding programs. In such a perspective, insights into children's and adolescents' lifeworlds, which are increasingly pervaded by various forms of media communication, are indispensable. Here, media diaries have proven to be a helpful method of gaining access to children's everyday media experiences. Scantlin (2008, p. 58), for example, mentions accuracy, multiplicity, and absence of distortions as advantages of the diary method for measuring the amount of time children spend with media. Following a more qualitative approach, Hartung, Reißmann, and Schorb (2009) had children and adolescents report on their consumption of music and the corresponding emotions.

As those latter examples suggest, the full diversity as well as the potentials of media diaries as a research method also become apparent when looking at their application in media and communication research in general.

Diaries in media and communication research

In social sciences, the application of solicited diaries as a research method goes back to the 1920s (Gersbuny & Sullivan, 1998, p. 69). Especially in time-use studies, the diary as a standardized approach is well established as a method of shedding light on the many activities people spend their time on throughout the day. Against the background of a temporally structured grid (e.g., 15 minutes), participants are asked to report in detail on their daily activities, provided with an often extensive list of pre-coded activities. Due to the connected effort and expense, large-scale time-use studies are regularly used for secondary analyses. In media and communication research, such datasets are interpreted concerning the duration and contextual embeddedness of media use, including phenomena like media multitasking or shifting time budgets connected to the diffusion of new media technologies.

Besides secondary analysis of time-use studies, standardized diary data are also distinctly collected by media and communication scholars dealing with interpersonal media communication, digital media, as well as classical mass media use (Gunter, 2000, pp. 93–134). The latter, in particular, also comprises commercially oriented research, such as readership, viewing, or listening diaries carried out by publishers or broadcasters.

Standardized media diaries are comparable to time-use diaries in the sense that respondents are provided with temporally structured sheets or notebooks in which the use of or exposure to respective programs, channels, media content, or technologies is reported. Subsidiary information may refer to details on locality, social situation, parallel activities, or individuals' emotional constitution in order to reconstruct the context of media use in the subsequent analysis of statistical data. In a very broad perspective, approaches such as survey questionnaires, yesterday interviews, or the experience sampling method, where self-reports of media use are randomly stimulated by electronic devices, are all subsumed under the term media diaries.

In addition to standardized forms, media diaries are also used in qualitative research designs. Next to interviews and observations, diaries belonged to the instruments used in domestication research from its very beginnings in the 1990s (Gunter, 2000, p. 130). Even in contemporary research, the application of qualitative media diaries often bears witness to a certain orientation toward media ethnographic perspectives. Instead of the researcher carrying out observations, self-observation in and reflection of activities related to media content and technologies are stimulated. Focusing on the appropriation of media in everyday life, qualitative diaries have been applied in areas such as personal relationships, diasporic communities, political or public participation, and the relation between media and community life.

With qualitative media diaries the means of reporting range from handwritten entries in notebooks to the use of online media such as e-mail, blogs, or specific diary apps. Consequently, the mode of reporting may be totally open, featuring narrations in running text and keywords, respectively, or combine pre-structured elements with fields for open entries.

Furthermore, in qualitative media research, diaries are mostly used as one component in multi-method designs and triangulated with other types of empirical data like interviews or network maps (Hepp, Roitsch, & Berg, 2016). Accordingly, the analysis of qualitative media diaries may include approaches such as content analysis or visualization techniques of discovered patterns expressing the process dimension of media use.

Compared to standardized diaries, in an open manner of use they show more traits of the diary in the original sense of the word, such as reflexivity or self-analysis. Common to standardized as well as non-standardized media diaries, however, is a high degree of involvement on the side of the research participants. Thereby, media diaries deliver valuable insights owing to their richness concerning context and subjective impressions of media-related actions and experiences. And since they are conducted over time, diary data enable an analysis of communicative process patterns, where other methods mostly retrieve data at a particular point in time.

Methodological criticism concerning media diaries mostly refers to the issue that the quality of the data obtained is hard to assess. This point is particularly applicable to the level of the individual diarist and can have several reasons. For one, the media diary is to be characterized as a reactive research method so that one cannot rule out the possibility of changes in behavior due to the act of self-observation and reporting. Furthermore, relevant instances of media communication may be intentionally omitted or unintentionally forgotten, especially if the diary keeping is not realized immediately (Gunter, 2000, pp. 96–97). Despite those potential problems, aggregated data of standardized diary studies have proven to be more accurate than recall surveys, especially when single media are focused (Gunter, 2000, p. 116; Scantlin, 2008, p. 58). In terms of qualitative studies, possible weaknesses can be compensated through data triangulation. Finally, a major challenge of diary studies is connected to the aforementioned involvement, which also may cause a low response rate from the start or fatigue on the diarist's side. Corresponding adjusting screws of the research design are factors such as the duration of data elicitation (from a single day up to several weeks), the complexity of pre-coded categories, and the comprehensiveness of retrieved context information.

Future developments and potentials of media diaries as pedagogy

As has been shown above, the media diary is applied as a research method with a wide range of different approaches as well as a pedagogical tool in media education. In the sense of a method, the collection of self-reported data on media use is the central aim. However, some studies working with feedback discussions after the period of self-observation mention that research participants talked about the revealing nature of media diaries as a side effect (Berg & Düvel, 2012, p. 85). This awareness of personal media practices, in turn, is what diaries are aiming at when applied in media education and poses a fundamental prerequisite for acquiring further media literacy. One possible way of extending the present potentials of media diaries might exist in combining the two features of awareness-raising and generating solid data material. In addition to specific types of media or certain kinds of messages, more open self-observations may prove valuable to discuss similarities and differences of individual media repertoires. Besides the abundance of devices and services for media communication regularly appropriated at the individual level, such comparisons of diaries could also be used for analytic discoveries of the richness and complexity of today's media environment on the whole.

In this regard, the role of media as technologies is becoming ever more relevant, especially since recent developments also alter the opportunities for media diaries as tool as well as method. For one, this has already been implied with the reference to digital media as new means of diary keeping. Using a smartphone app to report on media activities is likely to be closer to the mediatized as well as mobilized lifeworlds of especially younger respondents than a paper and pencil journal. Furthermore, some diary studies and training programs have already experimented with video and audio recordings. Since technological convergence and portability of devices have led to the constant availability of various instruments for media production, this can also be seen as a way to expand opportunities in the sense of multimedia diaries as media products in their own right (which potentially contributes to the development of practical media-related skills). It is also conceivable to collect and integrate personal digital "found pieces," which again can stimulate further reflections. Altogether, this might allow for more detailed specifications of communicative context in order to comprehend the density of today's media experience. Finally, the media diary as personal reconstruction of activities could be extended with less reactive metadata of communication such as logfiles, protocols, or other digital traces. This can be as easy as reviewing and reflecting on the personal browser or chat history. Such combined approaches might help to overcome the dichotomy of individual-centered perspectives on media use on the one hand and abstract aggregations of "big data" on the other hand. This again stresses the need for the contextualization of huge amounts of communication metadata produced by each and every use of digital media. In sum, digital media diaries offer new opportunities for standardized as well as non-standardized research approaches. Taking their transmedial capacity as a central characteristic of media diaries, this research method and tool for media pedagogy, respectively, allows for a very broad perspective on the comprehensive cosmos of mediated communication ranging from traditional analog or electronic mass media to the latest developments in digital communication.

SEE ALSO: Acceptable Use Policies; Children and Media as a Discipline; Digital Literacy; Family Strategies for Managing Media in the Home; Reflection

References

Berg, M., & Düvel, C. (2012). Qualitative media diaries: An instrument for doing research from a mobile media ethnographic perspective. *Interactions: Studies in Communication & Culture, 3*(1), 71–89. doi: 10.1386/iscc.3.1.71_1

Chang, H. (2008). *Autoethnography as method*. Walnut Creek, CA: Left Coast Press.

Gersbuny, J., & Sullivan, O. (1998). The sociological uses of time-use diary analysis. *European Sociological Review, 14*(1), 69–85.

Glogger, I., Schwonke, R., Holzäpfel, L., Nückles, M., & Renkl, A. (2012). Learning strategies assessed by journal writing: Prediction of learning outcomes by quantity, quality, and combinations of learning strategies. *Journal of Educational Psychology, 104*(2), 452–468. doi: 10.1037/a0026683

Gunter, B. (2000). Media research methods: Measuring audiences, reactions and impact. London, England: SAGE.

Hartung, A., Reißmann, W., & Schorb, B. (2009). Musik und Gefühl. Eine Untersuchung zur gefühlsbezogenen Aneignung von Musik im Kindes- und Jugendalter unter besonderer Berücksichtigung des Hörfunks. [Music and emotion. A study on the emotion-related appropriation of music by children and adolescents with particular consideration of radio]. Berlin, Germany: Vistas.

Hepp, A., Roitsch, C., & Berg, M. (2016). Investigating communication networks contextually: Qualitative network analysis as cross-media research. *MedieKultur, 32*(60), 87–106. doi: 10.7146/mediekultur.v32i60.21614

Kellner, D., & Share, J. (2005). Media literacy in the US. *MedienPädagogik*, 11. doi: 10.21240/mpaed/11/2005.09.15.X

Livingstone, S., van Couvering, E., & Thumin, N. (2008). Converging traditions of research on media and information literacies: Disciplinary, critical, and methodological issues. In J. Coiro, M. Knobel, C. Lankshear, & D.J. Leu (Eds.), *Handbook of research on new literacies* (pp. 103–132). New York, NY: Routledge.

Lloyd-Kolkin, D., Wheeler, P., & Strand, T. (1980). Developing a curriculum for teenagers. *Journal of Communication, 30*(3), 119–125.

Rosenbaum, J.E., Beentjes, J.W., & Konig, R.P. (2008). Mapping media literacy: Key concepts and future directions. In C.S. Beck (Ed.), *Communication Yearbook 32* (pp. 312–353). New York, NY: Routledge.

Scantlin, R. (2008). Media use across childhood: Access, time, and content. In S.L. Calvert & B.J. Wilson (Eds.), *The handbook of children, media, and development* (pp. 51–73). Chichester, England: Blackwell.

Further reading

Kaun, A. (2010). Open-ended online diaries: Capturing life as it is narrated. *International Journal of Qualitative Methods, 9*(2), 133–148. doi: 10.1177/160940691000900202

Zimmerman, D.H., & Wieder, D.L. (1977). The diary: Diary-interview method. *Urban Life, 5*, 479–498.

Matthias Berg is a research associate at the ZeMKI, Center for Communications, Media, and Information Research, University of Bremen, Germany. His research interests are communication and media studies, with a focus on mediatization research, the interrelations of communication and mobility, as well as media and community-building, and media generations. Recent publications include: *A Processual Concept of Media Generation* and *Investigating Communication Networks Contextually* (both together with Andreas Hepp and Cindy Roitsch).

Media Education Research and Creativity

ALBERTO PAROLA
University of Turin, Italy

We define media education (ME) as a vast area of knowledge at the intersection of the two great worlds of education and communication. ME abandons the idea of protection as abstinence and is oriented toward protection as proactive behavior. The difference is subtle but significant, since self-protection allows the development of individual awareness and coparticipation, unlike the problematic approach based on prohibition. The most fruitful approach is to use the media as opening a formative, creative, and professional opportunity for the whole of life (Masterman, 1985; Giannatelli and Rivoltella, 1995; Rivoltella, 2001; Buckingham, 2003; Hobbs, 2011). Currently the "digital" is bringing out new and complex problems. The practices related to them (privacy defense, writing skills, empathic approach, risk perception, construction of one's own identity, and so on) must be understood in depth, given the remarkable acceleration of all the informal learning processes of the last three decades. These are issues that confront us with unknown ontological and epistemological questions. The theme of creativity, declined in its various forms, can be a key to developing remarkable skills and competences. In this sense, it is necessary to ensure that the individuals' biology is better matched to the screen's mediation and the cognitive and emotional difficulties of managing relationships. We have observed creativity connected to media in different historical moments, in individual or social situations, in significant proposals of the digital citizen, and in the use of different languages such as comics, photography, music, video, and so on, thanks to original mash-up forms. In general all these languages tend to hybridize and create new modalities of communication and expression, also through remediation attempts (Bolter & Grusin, 1999). Furthermore, creativity occurs when we reflect and make observations and research on thought, intelligence, cognitive processes, knowledge approach, language itself, mental images, interface and objects design, learning spaces, and so on (the list is by force partial). Not being able to address all the issues here, this entry will limit itself to providing some theoretical–practical categories that can better represent the relationship between ME and creativity.

The relationship between ME and creativity

If imagination is essentially an immaterial personal mental experience, creativity is free thought and concrete behavior. Lehrer (2012) states that the reality of the creative process requires perseverance, the motor of the ability to complete a given task. The "creativity question" is one of the most long-lived on which man has tried to reflect. Already the first philosophers questioned for a long time this mysterious gift entrusted to human beings. After thousands of years, it continues to be a complex concept that no one has yet been able to fully define: at the moment it continues to escape attempts at scientific explanation. From the birth of psychology in the middle of the 19th century, and then shortly after, with the first experimental research in the educational field, creativity was brought closer to the concept of intelligence. These two aspects can be partly assimilated (those who are creative are also intelligent), partly perceived as opposites (those who are intelligent, in the sense of convergence, could be not very creative, in the sense of divergence). If creativity has been subjected to numerous investigations, this is thanks to 20th-century studies related to the works of Binet and Simon (intelligence tests), Piaget (evolutionary stages), Guilford (factorial theory), Sternberg (the metaphors of the mind and the triarchic model)—and one should not forget Vygotsky (the relationship between thought and language), Bruner (cultural psychology), and, more recently, Gardner (multiple intelligences). The first useful indications in terms of creativity come from those who have observed the *gifted* (Terman, Bartlett, and Monks among others), but also from the acute analysis of extraordinary characters, great artists and scientists such as Leonardo and Einstein, who used creativity as the instrument of their works and discoveries (think of the studies of Wallace and Gruber). Every creative individual is a *unique product* that describes a cross between individual processes and cultural situations within a specific historical period. In different moments and situations, creativity has been conceived of as consisting of different factors linked to thought: we can mention, besides Guilford's *divergent thinking* and Bruner's *narrative thinking*, Bartlett's *original and adventurous thinking* (which is similar to Morin's "systemic thinking"), Wertheimer's *productive thinking*, Norman's cognitive artifacts idea, or the research on the collective and connective intelligence carried out respectively by Levy and De Kerchkove. Creativity, of course, is also expressed through interfaces, objects, and space design, an increasingly significant element in the digital field (one may think, in this sense, of Munari's pioneering analogical work, which still has contemporary relevance). After an initial phase linked to intelligence, flexibility, and originality, studies on creative thinking moved toward personality aspects, which until then had remained on the margins: this is, in particular, the risk acceptance, humor, nonconformity and the ability *to play with ideas*. Of course, all these aspects find (and have found in the past) a fertile ground in media education activities carried out in schools. From here comes the double role of the teacher-researcher who allows students to apply creativity in media education. For example, we need to know that, if the "fixation factor" (that is, the formula or rigid model that prevents you from leaving standardized schemes) can negatively affect creativity, a sufficient period of "incubation of ideas" can favor it. The two concepts at work here are the concept of organization (creativity depends on a flexible operating context) and the concept of time (creativity requires tranquility, freedom, silence, and long periods of time). The mind must be able to wander, as stated by Corballis (2015). Not by chance, with the advent of the web, the moments of confrontation in relation to the "maker movement," the meaning and the *start-up* process and the constant evolution of the Internet of Things, are increased significantly: this means that the *media* and the *digital* automatically inspire a union (*coniunctio*) between creativity and intelligence, between divergent and convergent thinking, waiting for useful solutions. The school suffers from organizational problems and time management. We know well that the current school is no longer sustainable, since it is rigid and *fixed* on narrow schematisms and does not allow incubation periods for the students' and their teachers' good ideas. ME allows us to abandon the fixation model and to proceed toward a different didactic and a better management of space and time. The good practices of the last three decades certify this clearly. The model proposed by Urban (1995) in Table 1, which is dated but still effective and complete, highlights the richness of the components of the construct "creativity" and places the concept in a social context.

In relation to media education research (MER), it is very important to rely on effective theoretical models with reliable indicators, since in many media education areas it is easy to confuse creativity with a simply animating activity. Thinking of congenial solutions, creativity must creep into many original digital situations, such as the themes

Table 1 Urban's creativity model.

General concept	*Indicators*
General knowledge	Memory, reasoning
Specific knowledge	Skills, special skills
Dedication to the task	Concentration, persistence
Grounds	Curiosity, need for news, game, communication
Openness to the experience	Availability to new, risk, adaptability, nonconformism
Divergent thinking	Flexibility, fluidity, originality

Adapted from Urban (1995).

of competence, play, and risk, which are very similar to the attitudes and behaviors of prosumers or participative citizens. This also applies to optimal teaching methods designed to reach the competences goals. Among other things, we can cite the simulation methods and the serious games: media creativity, in this case, can manifest itself both as a teacher's project and as a project, also didactic and self-evaluative, of the student. Other very important aspects are those related to visual thought and metaphor: with the advent of the digital, especially mental images (over time studied above all by Kosslyn, Shepard, Pylyshyn, and Paivio) are once again at the center of the interest of pedagogues and psychologists—given the hypothesis that the children of today can no longer imagine precisely because, partly paradoxically, they receive too many visual stimuli as a result of the elaboration of a great quantity of images. Not only cognitive aspects and appropriate soft skills guide us toward a model of creativity that must be adapted to contemporaneity, but also psychodynamic aspects (and, in some cases, various elements referable to psychopathology) such as regression, openness to the world, equilibrium breakdown, and everything that competes with the coexistence of primary and secondary processes. These aspects are also connected with Goleman's (1995, 2007) emotional and social intelligence, Berthoz's (2013) concept of *vicariance* (as *simplex principle* and creative deviation), and Mallgrave's (2013) studies of *space empathy*, which refer to the theme of classrooms and formal and informal learning environments.

Buckingham (2003) argues that historically the media materials production at school has always been criticized, due to fear of a vague imitation of the "mass formats" by children and young people. The production of creative potential was strictly subordinated to the demonstration of the message's comprehension, necessarily directed against the dominant ideologies. Today the scenario is different, because the opposition should eventually be directed against the "giants of the web," but this attitude would represent a paradox ("How can I criticize Google and Facebook for what they offer me for free?"). The sure fact is the importance of simulation in creative production that, as already mentioned, requires rigorous work and a good dose of persistence. A final theme to be addressed is that of the relationship between MER and evidence-based education (EBE). The work of Hattie (2009) about "visible learning" leads us to reflect very carefully on the factors that really affect school education. For example, in a compendium of more than 60 research studies and meta-analyses, Deasy (2002) analyzed the possibility of transferring skills from art (visual arts, dance, theater, music) to learning in other school areas (reading skills, problem-solving, motivation, linguistic development, writing, mathematics, science), but also noted changes related to the motivation to attend school and self-confidence.

In short, if we compare the concept of "creativity" to the media, we can think of the former in the following ways:

- as fuel to ME and to the development of different categories of thought and media skills;
- as facilitator of a balanced relationship between biological reality and digital reality (complexity and "simplexity");
- as epistemic writing (Bereiter & Scardamalia, 1987) and production through the various languages and their recoding transcoding;

- as observation of the *invisible* thanks to the production and recognizability of mental images that, for example, allow us (e.g., by means of media educative coding activities) to shed light on often unexplained cognitive processes;
- as an essential element for Hattie's (2009) visible learning;
- as the integration of "deep learning," understood not only in a cognitive and metacognitive sense, but as a meta-quality, the result of the encounter with one's own self, as many psychodynamic theories suggest.

Therefore we can argue that the triangulation ME–MER–creativity can act as an engine to plan, observe, and evaluate paths oriented to the goals of competences. Therefore, in order to achieve organizational change, it is necessary to disassemble and restructure the school and its schematisms in large areas of the world.

Creativity and media education research

The relationship between creativity (media and digital) and media and MER is productive only within an organized and virtuous partnership. We define MER as the sum of cognitive, comprehensive, and change-oriented research strategies in a recursive perspective on data interpretation and the design of good media education practices, oriented toward a participatory research based on different and repeated cycles of action. This continuity allows a perpetual process of exchange between theory and practice and an upgrade of the teacher's professionalism that, in this sense, as already mentioned, also assumes the role of observer-researcher (Parola, 2008). This can be accomplished within a system designed beforehand, which provides for the harmonious interconnection between subsystems such as research, educational contexts in schools and territories, the public and the citizens, and the world of media production (TV, editorial, cinematographic, digital, crossmedia, etc.). We can call it media education research system (MERS). As can be seen in Figure 1, the scheme has four main dimensions and these activities annex other subdimensions as they connect to one another. In short, we can reason on different axes that connect keywords in reciprocal bidirectional mode, with research at the center (in our case, MER): the result will be composed of the activities arising from such links.

The link Re-Pr (the relationship is between research and production)

The production (of TV programs, animation shorts, apps, video games, media in general) can stimulate the design and carrying out of a research, as a product can be considered of interest for an in-depth study, or because a publisher may request advice from a research group in order to evaluate their product. The Re environment sends feedback to Pr, which collects information to improve or adapt the product itself. This happens only through Pr's "educational" availability. Vice versa, Re can ask Pr to check and document the quality of its products with a view to producing in line with an educational minor's needs, for example through a system of quality indicators. We assume that the ME can't evolve and develop by renouncing the support of media education research. The hypotheses regarding the effectiveness of a given intervention,

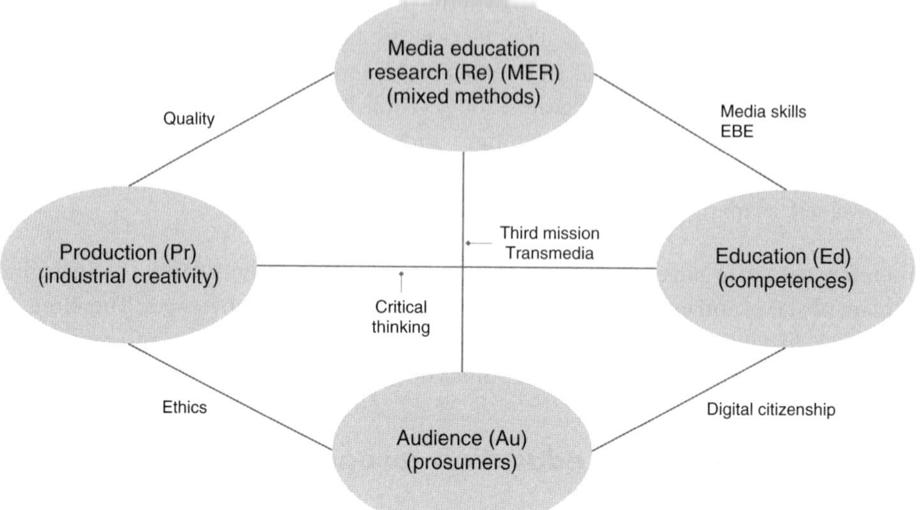

Figure 1 Media education research systems (MERS).

the observation of the contexts in which the experiences take place, the experimental research on the fruition behaviors, the learning, the emotions, and so on represent the basis on which the individuals' education can be built. The keywords are therefore observation of processes, assessment of skills (supported by divergent thinking), and experimentation in educational contexts: they represent a methodological strategy of research in ME, which should be considered particularly urgent. A close collaboration between Re and Pr allows the producer herself to be able to reflect during the creative phase and to fine-tune the product; and this establishes a dialogue between researcher, producer, and public (audience, or Au) prosumer. *The goal is to know how to observe and understand creative ideas.*

The link Ed-Au (the relationship is between education and the public or citizenship)

Teachers, educators, parents, and children, faced with media use, ask a series of questions, expressing a need for knowledge and training: for example, educators and parents worry about the relationship between children and the media (especially smartphones), teachers question their teaching (in an unstable balance between skills and creativity), while the boys, more open to media experiences, reflect on questions about their future with the media and how they can exploit them in their favor, even in their free time, from a personal and creative, relational and professional point of view. They can thus become good users, but also effective media readers and writers, taking on greater critical autonomy and enhancing their chances of communicating effectively and in an original way. The two main drivers of the relationship between the keywords are:

1. the *network*, that is, the relationships that are established—must be established—between the different actors of ME through their "doing cognitive and relational network" (ME can not disregard a constant and meticulous work of this kind);

2. *training*, intended as a double level of activation of ME paths, in a given context (school or territory) and as training of trainers (teachers, educators).

The goal is to develop teaching and parenting creativity via divergent thinking.

The link Re-Ed (the relationship is between research and educational and training contexts)

Training or education designate the traditional mission of educational institutions, new initiatives at school, and university-level, local, and territorial initiatives, in collaboration with the world of associations. The research identifies the critical dimensions in terms of ME and invites the partners to fill any gap, thanks to training courses or educational interventions (school, family, territory, etc.). Furthermore, the research suggests the paths to be taken (the curricula) and tests them through the educators' collaboration. Here creativity is expressed in terms of scientific divulgation or third mission (Re translates paradigmatic thought into narrative thought), while Ed makes creativity a pillar of the ME, provided that, as already said, it does not turn into an animating activity that is an end in itself. *The objective is the cyclicity of actions, the recurrence of reflections, the design of good practices informed by empirical evidence.*

The link Re-Au (the relationship is between research and audience)

This ratio is the weakest, by definition and tradition. Even if the publication of the research carried out in the academy often does not reach users in a direct and effective way, it is possible to involve the passive listener or reader and the prosumer, questioning him or her and stimulating that person to learn more and better (think about fake news), to provide opinions, formulate judgments, suggest modifications and elaborate observations of what he or she sees, reads, and listens to every day in relation to the media. Research will restore the conditions for a better interaction and relationship between the person and the media system. Also in this case, the prosumer presents the discourse linked to the "third mission," understood as an ability to disseminate information and research among citizens. However, while Ed can actively deal with it, Au still tends to live it passively: in this sense, the prosumer should develop more skills around the relationship between information, thought, and behavior. If the prosumer understands what Re says, he or she is not able to ask him- or herself: "How can I translate scientific concepts into something understandable and return a shareable product to my network?" The initial input can come from Re, when the researcher, for example, is interested in making a study of the relationship between teenagers and smartphones; from Pr if it is the medium itself to express, for example, a need for quality monitoring and requests self-evaluation; from Au if, for example, an association of parents raises a problem or makes a fear known; from Ed if teachers express opinions or design media education courses. Once the circuit has been activated, this can take on different forms: the important thing is that each "node" has sufficient propulsive energy, thanks to the assumption of responsibility, the presence of resources, and the skills of all the actors of the system, at the local level and, more generally, at the institutional level. *The goal is to conceive of creativity as the engine of planning and understanding the close relationship between narrative thinking and paradigmatic thinking.*

The link Pr-Au (the relationship is between production and the public)

Here we introduce the theme of the quality of media production, including the creative aspect. Today as in the past, media production tends on one hand to homologate styles (old television), on the other to foster children's creativity (various apps and software, YouTube, and much more). Therefore we risk that the personal expressive capacity is less creative and the languages less articulate and more rigid; then the hybridization of styles and the contamination of genres through the original bricolage form makes the scenario open to a great many ideas. From the point of view of the reflective ability of the student who learns informally, having available a *mental scheme* of good quality and a well-established *culture of quality and beauty* would allow him or her to manage and govern a series of cognitive operations that can also be exercised at school, thanks to the techniques learned through continuous experimentation. The media are psycho-technologies (De Kerckhove, 1991) and those who use them must know the relationship between their psychology and that of the interface with which it is interacting (and therefore the designer). Others speak of these aspects from a sociosemiotic approach. This also applies to the link Ed-Pr: if the producer (or publisher) is open to a training project within the educational environments, negotiating the main guidelines, teachers and students will be able to acquire skills that go well beyond the paths made in the *institutional enclosures. The goal is a possible consolidation of the relationship between critical thinking and divergent thinking, thanks to transmedia paths that envisage a project based on the past–present–future process structure with reference to knowledge and skills useful to the competence development.*

The link Pr-Ed (the relationship between production and education)

From a creative point of view, one must free oneself from the one-sidedness of this relationship. There should be a more collaborative attitude that nurtures young people's creativity, avoiding standardized models. Effective training is needed to highlight the potential of the "algorithm" as an enemy of creativity and imagination.

SEE ALSO: Awareness; Digital Literacy; Family Relationships and Media; Game Design in Media Literacy Education; Game Media Literacy; Health Media Literacy; Hypertext and Hypermedia Writing; Media and Adolescent Identity Development; Media Competence; Media Literacy Education and 21st Century Teacher Education; Participatory Action Research; Performance Media; Video Games as Education; Web Television

References

Bereiter, C., & Scardamalia, M. (1987). *The psychology of written composition*. Hillsdale, NJ: Lawrence Erlbaum Associates.

Berthoz, A. (2013). *La vicariance: Le cerveau créateur de mondes*. Paris, France: Odile Jacob.

Bolter, J.D., & Grusin, R. (1999). *Remediation: Understanding new media*. Cambridge, MA: MIT Press.

Buckingham, D. (2003). *Media education: Literacy, learning, and contemporary culture*. Cambridge, MA: Polity/Blackwell.
Corballis, M.C. (2015). *The wandering mind: What the brain does when you're not looking*. Chicago, IL: University of Chicago Press.
De Kerckhove, D. (1991). *Brainframes: Technology, mind and business*. Utrecht, The Netherlands: Bosch & Keuning.
Deasy, R.J. (2002). *Critical links: Learning in the arts and student achievement and social development*. The Arts Education Partnership: Washington, DC.
Giannatelli, R., & Rivoltella, P.C. (1995). *Le impronte di Robinson: Mass media, cultura popolare, educazione*. Rivoli, Italy: Elle Di Ci.
Goleman, D. (1995). *Emotional intelligence*. New York, NY: Bantam Books.
Goleman, D. (2007). *Social intelligence*. London, England: Harrow.
Hattie, J.A. (2009). *Visible learning: A synthesis of over 800 meta-analyses relating to achievement*. London, England: Routledge.
Hobbs, R. (2011). *Digital and media literacy: Connecting culture and classroom*. Thousand Oaks, CA: Corwin/SAGE.
Lehrer, J. (2012). *Imagine: How creativity works*. Boston, MA: Houghton Mifflin Harcourt.
Mallgrave, H.F. (2013). *Architecture and embodiment: The implications of the new sciences and humanities for design*. London, England: Routledge.
Masterman, L. (1985). *Teaching the media*. London, England: Routledge for Comedia/New York, NY: MK Media Press.
Parola, A. (2008). *Territori mediaeducativi*. Trento, Italy: Erickson.
Rivoltella, P.C. (2001). *Media education: Modelli, esperienze, profilo disciplinare*. Rome, Italy: Carocci.
Urban, K.K. (1995). Different models in describing, exploring, explaining and nurturing creativity in society. *European Journal for High Ability, 6*, 143–159.

Further Reading

Arieti, S. (1979). *Trattato di psichiatria*. Turin, Italy: Bollati Boringhieri.
Bartlett, F. (1958). *Thinking: An experimental and social study*. London, England: G. Allen.
Bateson, G. (1972). *Steps to an ecology of mind*. New York, NY: Ballatine Books.
Bronfenbrenner, U. (1979). *The ecology of human development: Experiments by nature and design*. Cambridge, MA: Harvard University Press.
Bruner, J. (2003). *Making stories: Law, literature, life*. Cambridge, MA: Harvard University press.
Buckingham, D. (2009). Creative visual methods in media research: Possibilities, problems and proposals. *Media, Culture & Society, 31*(4), 633–652.
Creswell, J.W., & Plano Clark, V.L. (2011). *Designing and conducting mixed methods research*. Thousand Oaks, CA: SAGE.
Gardner, H. (1984). *Frames of mind: The theory of multiple intelligences*. London, England: Heinemann.
Guilford, J.P. (1956). The structure of intellect. *Psychological Bulletin, 53*, 267–293.
Hobbs, R., & Jensen, A. (2009). The past, present, and future of media literacy education. *Journal of Media Literacy Education, 1*, 1–11.
Kosslyn S. (1980). *Image and mind*. Cambridge, MA: Harvard University Press.
Livingstone, S. (2002). *Young people and new media: Childhood and the changing media environment*. London, England: SAGE.
Mezirow, J. (2000). *Learning as transformation: Critical perspectives on a theory in progress*. San Francisco, CA: Jossey-Bass.
Morin, E. (2001). *Seven complex lessons in education for the future*. Paris, France: UNESCO.
Norman, D.A. (2013). *The design of everyday things*. New York, NY: Basic books.

Parola, A., & Ranieri M. (2010). *Media education in action.* Florence, Italy: Florence University Press.
Sternberg, R.J. (1980). *Handbook of intelligence.* Cambridge, England: Cambridge University Press.
Trinchero, R. (2013). *Costruire, valutare, certificare competenze.* Milan, Italy: Franco Angeli.
Wertheimer, M. (1966). *Productive thinking.* London, England: Social Science Paperbacks in association with Tavistock.

Alberto Parola is associate professor of educational research at the Department of Philosophy and Education Sciences, University of Turin. His main areas of interest are research methods in education, media education, and learning technology. He authored and coauthored *Regia educativa* (2012), *Media education in action* (with M. Ranieri; 2010), and *Scritture mediali* (with L. Denicolai, 2017)—among many other books. Currently he is codirector of the journal *Media Education: Studi, ricerche, buone pratiche* and president of Cinedumedia (Interdepartmental Research Centre on Digital Education) at the University of Turin. He was vice president of Media Education Italian Association and has collaborated with RAI Italian television, the Ministry of Education, and different institutions in European projects.

Media Impact on Refugee Children

JODY LYNN McBRIEN
University of South Florida, Sarasota-Manatee, USA

Since 2015, media reports on refugees and refugee children have created diverse responses from international media consumers. Certainly the media stories about 3-year-old Alan Kurdi, a Syrian boy washed ashore on a Turkish coast, led to an empathetic response from the world. But it was short-lived, disrupted by reports of terrorist attacks in the US, France, Germany, and the Netherlands, which resulted in 658 deaths in Europe and the Americas between January 1, 2015 and July 16, 2016 (Gamio & Meko, 2016); and which many have equated with refugees, in part due to populist speeches and fears. These are the deaths publicized in western nations. However, an additional 28 000+ deaths have resulted from terrorist attacks in the Middle East, Africa, and Asia in the same time period. As a result, many more flee their countries as refugees in hopes of staying alive. The BBC reported that by fall 2015, 8000 new refugees were entering Europe every day.

The United Nations High Commissioner for Refugees (UNHCR) reported an estimated 65.3 million people—one person out of every 113—were displaced (within their own country, or as a refugee or asylum seeker) due to conflict and persecution in 2015. This included 21.3 million refugees and 3.2 million asylum seekers. To break this down to more comprehensible terms, 24 people fled their homes *every minute*. The UNHCR found that 51% of this number were children and youth under 18 years old. Through a complex process, only about 1% of refugees are designated annually for permanent resettlement in one of 33 countries that have agreed to abide by UN resettlement procedures. The majority of refugees are in temporary shelter in either refugee camps or urban settings, 86% of whom are in "developing countries."

The topic of refugees has gone from one outside common parlance to a frequently used term in recent years. However, in spite of increased usage, the term remains mired in misunderstandings. In 2005, the word was used to describe the thousands who fled their homes as a result of Hurricane Katrina in the United States. This use is in contrast to the definition provided in the 1951 Convention related to the Status of Refugees and its 1967 Protocol, and to the US 1980 Refugee Act; namely,

> owing to well-founded fear of being persecuted for reasons of race, religion, nationality, membership of a particular social group or political opinion, is outside the country of his nationality and is unable or, owing to such fear, is unwilling to avail himself of the protection of that country; or who, not having a nationality and being outside the country of his former habitual residence as a result of such events, is unable or, owing to such fear, is unwilling to return to it. (OHCHR, 1951)

In particular, in 2016, popular usage of the word "refugee" tied people fleeing persecution or death to those conducting terrorist acts, both in Europe and the United States, as some politicians have melded the concepts. More specifically, Muslim refugees have been targeted as potential terrorists, especially by conservative media sources. Simultaneously, statistics from the FBI (Federal Bureau of Investigation), the Global Terrorism Database, and even the conservative CATO Institute have contradicted these assumptions. FBI reports to 2005 indicated that over 90% of terrorist attacks in the United States were committed by non-Muslims. The Global Terrorism Index (Institute for Economics & Peace, 2016) reported that while terror attacks worldwide have increased by 80% since 2000, less than 1% of deaths in the West occur from such attacks. Additionally, 80% of terror attacks in the West are *not* committed by Islamic fundamentalists. Finally, a fall 2016 policy analysis on terrorism and immigration produced by the CATO Institute concluded that Americans have a 1 in 3.64 *billionth* of a chance per year of being killed in a terrorist attack by a refugee (Nowrasteh, 2016).

Even prior to the recent allegations equating refugees with terrorism, refugees have been equated with immigrants. Many Americans think of immigrants as illegal, not being aware of distinctions. United States President Donald Trump has even questioned the security of allowing legal migration, bringing that message to millions of Americans. Refugees are technically immigrants, as immigrants are defined as people moving from one place to another, whether nationally or internationally. However, refugees, as defined by the Geneva Convention, are a very small portion of this category.

In addition to negative media about refugees, there are media stories about positive ways in which nations are supporting refugee children and families. However, reader responses typically include many negative comments. For example, an online press report about support for refugee families in Ann Arbor, USA (Stanton, 2016) accumulated 770 reader responses in less than 24 hours accusing liberals and conservatives of bigotry, assuming that refugees all go on welfare, and expecting dismal results. Reader comments indicated beliefs that the refugees oppressed and raped women and children, beheaded or burned people alive, killed LGBT people, enslaved people, committed honor killings, and would soon be in charge of the local city council. The insinuation is clearly that refugees are criminals and terrorists.

Refugee youth portrayed by media

As mentioned, roughly 50% of refugees are 18 years of age and under. As such, many are struggling to learn the language and culture of their resettlement country, as well as attempting to meet the academic standards in their new countries. Academic expectations vary widely between countries. For instance, when asked the time period for taking major tests in New Zealand, a teacher responded that they take them when they are ready (McBrien, 2014). In contrast, resettled refugee students in the United States may be expected to take standardized exams one year or less from the time at which they begin in a US school.

There are media pieces that provide a human face of refugee and asylum-seeking children. *The Guardian* (Gentleman, 2016) interviewed some of the 600+ unaccompanied children living in the Calais, France, camp, who spoke of their fears of rats and police who spray teargas at them. Twelve-year-old children are responsible for 9-year-old siblings; French authorities closed a café that fed the children for free. Gentleman concluded that more unsuitable homes for children were hard to imagine. The reporter described their dwellings as tents and poorly constructed huts, not waterproof, and typically bug-infested. Their close proximity made fire a hazard.

Makepeace's 2007 documentary, *Rain in a Dry Land*, follows the first 18 months of two Somali Bantu refugee families resettled in the United States—one in Springfield, Massachusetts; the other in Atlanta, Georgia—after many years in the Kakuma refugee camp in Kenya. Aden and Madina's oldest son dreams of becoming a doctor. But the steep challenges he faces with language in his new school and frustrations from teachers that do not have the skills to help him cause him to drop out. In Atlanta, single mother Arbai and her daughters face racism and xenophobia as they struggle to adapt from their life of subsistence farming to that of a consumer culture. In a struggle for acceptance, her daughter Sahara chooses subculture characteristics, taking an older lover and becoming defiant, spurning her native culture and respect for her mother. Scenes of both families illustrate a dire need for teacher and staff training to help refugee children succeed.

Other well-documented challenges are issues of prejudice and discrimination that refugee children encounter at the hands of not only native-born children, but also teachers. Researchers have examined the challenges faced by Somali refugee youth in the United States as they maintain Somali and Muslim identities while trying to fit into their new society. Others have identified numerous findings of prejudice and bias by teachers and students toward resettled refugee students. Likewise, academic research in the United Kingdom and Australia has concluded that media have negatively influenced popular opinion about refugees and asylum seekers (Gale, 2004; Leuder, Hayes, Nekvapil, & Baker, 2008).

Negative reports and insinuations about resettled refugees exacerbate the challenges faced by students, as they are included in reports about refugees and asylum seekers in general. A report by the Information Centre about Asylum and Refugees (ICAR, 2012) in Great Britain concluded that much of the media coverage about refugees and asylum seekers was based on sensationalism and inaccuracies. The ICAR report also questioned whether asylum seekers were, in fact, threats or under threat as a result of inaccurate media reporting about them and ensuing bias.

Refugee youth in control of media

In the latter years of the 20th century, media witnessed a major change from a passive audience to one that can create its own media messages. This ability has increased tremendously in the 21st century with social media sites such as Facebook, Twitter, YouTube, Instagram, Pinterest, and more. As a result, refugee youth are able to access media to respond to messages against them. For instance, in 2015, a group of Somali teen girls created a video entitled "What's Up with the Hijab?" to explain Islam and the veil. It also presents the suggestion that wearing hijab can serve the purpose of resistance.

Resettled refugees in New York City worked together to create three award-winning films about ways in which they survived war, connected with their families, and became activists (The Documentary Project, n.d.). Resettled youth have participated in photography projects and exhibits to connect with their host societies and provide accurate descriptions of why they have resettled in their new communities. Refugee youth in Baltimore participate in Artworks, using social media to support their products and programs. PREP, the Pinellas (Florida) Refugee Education Program, has engaged its resettled refugee students in creating two films: *The Long Road Home* (PREP, 2013), about families who have resettled in the Tampa area; and *Refugees: Roads to Success* (Popp, 2015), about how several of their students have overcome obstacles to reach academic success. Professors at the Free University of Brussels have joined with community organizations to create videos about cooperative projects in Belgium to support refugee and migrant integration. Projects like these occur throughout resettlement countries to provide leadership and participant opportunities for resettled refugee youth, including the creation of videos shared online.

Conclusions

Refugee youth are certainly affected by media, especially negative reports and reader responses inferring that refugees are potential criminals and terrorists rather than the truth; namely, that they are fleeing from their countries to save their lives and the lives of family members. Xenophobic repetitions of these themes by well-known politicians only serve to increase public fears, resulting in less support and more challenges presented to refugees trying to establish themselves in countries of resettlement. Even in media stories that humanize refugees, reader responses indicate the fears and prejudice that are stirred by negative publicity.

At the same time, options for refugees to participate in media-making allow them to present an alternative perspective of people grateful for resettlement, but struggling to find acceptance and support in their new lands. Much of their media shows not only challenge, but also success in creating positive new lives in resettlement.

SEE ALSO: Adolescent Literacy in a Digital World; Authorship and Participatory Culture; Meaning-Making; Media and Adolescent Identity Development; Media and Ethnic Stereotyping; Media Literacy, Terrorism, and Fear; Media Literacy with New Immigrants; Youth Media

References

The Documentary Project (n.d.). Retrieved from http://thedocumentaryproject.org/

Gale, P. (2004). The refugee crisis and fear: Populist politics and media discourse. *Journal of Sociology, 40*(4), 321–240. doi: 10.1177/1440783304048378

Gamio, L., & Meko, T. (2016, July 16). How terrorism in the West compares to terrorism everywhere else. *The Washington Post* online. Retrieved from https://www.washingtonpost.com/graphics/world/the-scale-of-terrorist-attacks-around-the-world/

Gentleman, A. (2016, August 2). Hungry, scared, and no closer to safety: Child refugees failed by Britain. *The Guardian*. Retrieved from https://www.theguardian.com/world/2016/aug/02/child-refugees-calais-failed-by-britain

ICAR. (2012). *Asylum seekers, refugees, and media*. Retrieved from http://citeseerx.ist.psu.edu/viewdoc/download?doi=10.1.1.694.5340&rep=rep1&type=pdf

Institute for Economics and Peace. (2016). *Global Terrorism Index 2015*. Retrieved from http://economicsandpeace.org/wp-content/uploads/2015/11/Global-Terrorism-Index-2015.pdf

Leuder, I., Hayes, J., Nekvapil, J., & Baker, J.T. (2008). Hostility themes in media, community, and refugee narratives. *Discourse & Society, 19*(2), 187–221. doi: 10.1177/0957926507085952

Makepeace, A. (Producer & Director). (2007). *Rain in a dry land* [Documentary]. United States: Anne Makepeace Productions, Inc.

McBrien, J.L. (2014). *I orea te tuatara ka patu ki waho*: Competing priorities in the New Zealand refugee resettlement strategy. Fulbright New Zealand. Retrieved from http://www.fulbright.org.nz/publications/2014-mcbrien/

Nowrasteh, A. (2016). Terrorism and immigration: A risk analysis. CATO Institute. Retrieved from https://www.cato.org/publications/policy-analysis/terrorism-immigration-risk-analysis

OHCHR (Office of the High Commissioner of Human Rights). (1951). Convention relating to the Status of Refugees. Article 1. Retrieved from http://www.ohchr.org/EN/ProfessionalInterest/Pages/StatusOfRefugees.aspx

Popp, M. (Director). (2015). *Refugees: Roads to success*. Pinellas refugee education program. Retrieved from https://www.youtube.com/watch?v=T-bfJxRoGoc&feature=youtu.be

PREP. (2013). The long road home: Tampa Bay refugee stories. Retrieved from https://www.youtube.com/watch?v=T-bfJxRoGoc&feature=youtu.be

Stanton, R. (2016, September 22). Ann Arbor community coming together to welcome hundreds more refugees. MLive Media Group. Retrieved from https://www.mlive.com/news/ann-arbor/index.ssf/2016/09/ann_arbor_community_coming_tog.html

Further reading

McBrien, J. (2005). Educational needs and barriers for refugee students in the United States: A review of the literature. *Review of Educational Research, 75*(3), 329–364. Retrieved from http://www.jstor.org.ezproxy.lib.usf.edu/stable/3515985

McBrien, J.L., & Day, R. (2012). From there to here: Using photography to explore perspectives of resettled refugee youth. *International Journal of Child, Youth and Family Studies, 3*(1), 546–568. Retrieved from https://search.proquest.com/openview/3343f2bb331db3ff0859780b51428b12/1?pq-origsite=gscholar&cbl=2046194

Philo, G., Briant, E., & Donald, P. (2013). Impacts of media coverage on migrant communities in the United Kingdom. In *Bad News for Refugees* (pp. 131–164). London, England: Pluto Press. doi: 10.2307/j.ctt183p4bm.9

Saunders, D. (1997). Invisible youth reappear! A review of two youth produced videos. *Social Justice, 24*(3), 100–104. Retrieved from http://www.jstor.org.ezproxy.lib.usf.edu/stable/29767024

Willis, M., & Fernald, C. (2004). A view of Sudanese refugee resettlement through Nebraska's print media. *Great Plains Research, 14*(2), 271–292. Retrieved from http://www.jstor.org.ezproxy.lib.usf.edu/stable/23779482

Jody Lynn McBrien, PhD, is a Professor in the College of Liberal Arts and Social Sciences at the University of South Florida, Sarasota-Manatee campus, teaching courses in international and comparative education, social foundations of education, and international human rights. She was a 2014 Ian Axford Fellow in Public Policy examining refugee resettlement policy in New Zealand; and a 2017 visiting professor at Soka University, Tokyo, Japan, teaching international education while researching refugee policy in Japan. She was a founding member of the American Media Literacy Association. Her publications include numerous journal articles and book chapters on supporting the cultural integration of refugee students.

Media Industry Involvement in Media Literacy

RENEE HOBBS
University of Rhode Island, USA

The rise of the Internet and social media has intensified the need to build people's knowledge and competencies in using technology and in accessing, analyzing, creating, and sharing media. People also need opportunities to reflect upon media influence on individuals and society and take appropriate forms of social and political action using media texts, tools, and technologies. Today, stakeholders in the media literacy movement include parents, librarians, technologists, educators, public health professionals, artists, cultural critics, and political activists. Some are motivated by the impulse to protect people from the potential risks and harms associated with exposure to mass media and digital media; others are motivated by the empowerment opportunities created by the use of mass and digital media.

But individuals working in public broadcasting, journalism, advertising, public relations, film and television, publishing, and digital and social media also care about media literacy. Why is it important to them? Two forms of self-interest seem to explain their motivation: the potential to increase demand for quality and the potential impact on the future workforce. Today's press leaders sometimes still suggest that formal training in news literacy will increase the demand for quality journalism, even as the Internet has contributed to a significant loss of local journalism in the United States. This perspective is not new. For nearly 50 years, media industry stakeholders have stated that they recognize the potential of media literacy to increase demand for quality media. As far back as the 1960s, public broadcasters, filmmakers, and news media organizations around the world appreciated the value of an educated audience and they have taken steps to advance the knowledge and skills of media users to advance appreciation of quality media productions. The history of the British approach to media education reveals that it was rooted to the critical analysis of literature. Analyzing media was understood as a means of helping people become discriminating readers and viewers (Buckingham, 1998). By the middle of the 20th century, creating media became understood as a part of media literacy education, and scholastic journalism programs developed with assistance from community journalists and professional industry organizations.

Media literacy programs, as developed by the media industry, have taken on distinct forms with a focus on creating demand for media products and services; providing information about content, structures, or production processes; offering consumer protection or minimizing risks associated with media use; promoting creative self-expression and active participation in media culture; and challenging media industries to address problematic or ethically questionable practices. As we will see below, although support from media industry stakeholders has been controversial, the programs that they have supported have been a source of innovation in advancing the media literacy competencies of citizens.

One of the "great debates" in media literacy

The media industry support of media literacy initiatives has been controversial. During the 1990s, American educational practitioners split into two factions, largely due to the controversy associated with a media literacy professional membership association's decision to accept monies from media companies to support the cost of conference gatherings (Heins & Cho, 2003). Among the "great debates" of the media literacy education community, Hobbs (1998) identified the question, "Should media organizations provide support for media literacy?" Proponents have argued that the good that media organizations can do by contributing their funding outweighs the potential dangers of the program's use as part of a public relations campaign or as a shield against government regulation. Critics have feared that media companies are effectively "taking the anti-media stand out of the media literacy movement to serve their own goals: co-opting the media literacy movement and softening it to make sure that public criticism of the media never gets too loud, abrasive or strident" (Hobbs, 1998, p. 26).

By far the hottest and most controversial issue in the history of the media literacy movement was the decision by the Alliance for a Media Literate America (later renamed the National Association for Media Literacy Education) to accept a donation of $25 000 from Channel One, a company owned by Chris Whittle that had launched a program of current events news into American high schools. The daily news program was funded by commercial advertising and provided supplemental educational resources that reached 5 million young people across the United States. Channel One's commercial content was hated by some media literacy advocates because they perceived that students were forced to watch ads. Others noted that ads enabled the news and current events program to be available for free to schools, who also received access to video playback equipment that could be used for noncommercial educational programming (Greenberg & Brand, 1993). Channel One provided media literacy education to teachers in the form of curriculum resources and video segments showing media literacy in action, including analysis of both news and advertising that aired on Channel One.

By the end of the first decade of the 21st century, however, the debate about commercialism in schools had largely dissipated due to the increasing variety of projects supported by media industry stakeholders. And although critics have voiced their fears and frustrations about media industry involvement in media literacy education, the role of the media industry in media literacy education has not been monolithic. In fact, media industry stakeholders have played significant roles in media education over the course of 100 years. But the tension between the business community and the education community has remained consistent over time. For example, when the Society for Visual Education was established in 1919 by professors from the University of Chicago and other distinguished educational institutions, the group foundered and failed after only a few years (Saettler, 2004). Other organizations of the time rose up, including the National Academy of Visual Instruction, the Visual Instruction Association of America, and the Division of Visual Instruction of the National Education Association. During the first half of the 20th century, there were four publications devoted to the topic: *Moving Picture Age*, *Educational Film Magazine*, *Visual Education*, and *The Screen*. But the effort to bring films into the classroom failed over a period of 20 years.

What happened? Tensions between education and business leaders contributed to the failure of the visual education movement. Educators resisted the slick promotional propaganda used by film companies promoting their wares. Fragmentation among the interests of educators was another challenge: some educators were interested in creating educational films, while others were interested in using existing commercial films as teaching tools, and still others were interested in adult education. The educators with interests in the newest technologies tended to dominate the community because of the business community's interests in selling projectors, screens, films, support materials, and ancillary equipment to schools. When the Rockefeller Foundation studied the problem, they determined that "both educators and business men [sic] developed the notion that entertainment, commercialism and education do not mix" (Saettler, 2004, p. 106). Despite this history, the continuing rise of educational technology shows that educators have been well able to coordinate their work with the business community. Venture capitalists invested $8.1 billion in ed tech start-ups in 2017, with China and India ramping up their focus on digital learning. But few of these resources are directed at media literacy per se.

Today, a variety of media literacy organizations receive substantial support from media industry firms but none has been more successful at attracting corporate funding than Common Sense Media in San Francisco. This San Francisco-based nonprofit organization founded by Jim Steyer advocates for child and family issues associated with media and technology. They provide media literacy curriculum materials and professional development to K-12 (primary and secondary) educators and offer reviews of TV shows, movies, games, and apps for parents and families. Media companies like AOL, Netflix, and Yahoo! buy licenses to use Common Sense Media reviews, generating nearly 50% of their $19 million annual budget. Amazon and Comcast, two of the largest media companies in the world, are among the dozens of media and technology firms that have a multiyear partnership agreement with the nonprofit organization. By partnering with media, retail, and technology companies, Common Sense Media resources (including reviews, articles, and videos) are provided to parents and educators at the point when they are deciding what kinds of media to use in the family.

In part because of their active engagement with dozens of major media industry stakeholders, Common Sense Media has the lobbying power to pressure the media industry to address issues of concern to parents and families. For example, their advocacy for children's privacy has resulted in the "Do Not Track" bill, which would require Internet companies to obtain consent from teens and from parents of children under 13 before collecting their personal or location information or sending targeted advertising. They also have advocated for more effective policies to limit the distribution of sensitive information about students to noneducational, commercial media organizations and other third parties. In the United States, no other media literacy organization receives as much financial support from the media industry or the philanthropic community, so Common Sense Media's power dwarfs that of the membership organization, the National Association for Media Literacy Education (NAMLE).

Among the many different types of industry involvement in media literacy, six groups have had significant investment over time: public broadcasting, journalism, broadcast and cable TV industry, the advertising industry, the film industry, and the digital platform industries. While some initiatives have reached a wide audience, others have received less attention. Many initiatives have served the strategic needs of media organizations; they are not developed merely for goodwill purposes. Unfortunately, few of these initiatives have been formally studied in the context of academic scholarship in media studies or education. But in general, industry-sponsored initiatives in media literacy have had a significant impact on increasing the visibility of media literacy to educational stakeholders and members of the general public.

Public service broadcasters as media literacy educators

Across the United States and around the world, public service media have pioneered initiatives in media literacy as part of their public service mission. Public service broadcasters have long supported professional development programs to advance the knowledge and skills of current teachers in elementary and secondary education. For example, at the 2018 SXSWedu conference, PBS (Public Broadcasting Service) and KQED, the public media station serving the San Francisco Bay Area, announced a partnership to offer PreK-12 teachers free certification in media literacy.

The PBS Media Literacy Educator Certification by KQED recognizes educators who excel in creating and implementing instruction with media, and provides support to help all teachers accelerate these skills. Teachers who participate in the program submit evidence of their competencies through an online portfolio, and free media literacy courses are available on the KQED Teach platform to help teachers improve their skills in specific areas. The focus is on helping educators develop competencies, including the ability to create original content using multiple media production techniques. Available courses include: Finding & Validating Information Online; Understanding Copyright & Fair Use; Video Storytelling Essentials; Designing Presentations; Safety and Privacy in a Participatory Culture; How to Manage and Assess Media Projects; and more.

In Europe, public service broadcasters have also embraced the opportunity to help increase the visibility of media literacy. When the European Broadcasting Union issued its first viewpoint on media literacy, they demonstrated the strategic position of public service media in promoting media literacy in bridging the digital divide, empowering citizens to democracy, and creating a trusted space. For example, in Great Britain, the need to promote media literacy is outlined in the 2006 BBC (British Broadcasting Corporation) Charter Agreement, and emphasizes helping people to "build their confidence and skills, and encourage audiences to move from passive consumption to active participation and constructive engagement" (BBC, 2006). The BBC's Media Literacy Strategy (2013) shows three strands: Get Connected, Get Smart, and Get Creative. According to the German public service broadcaster ZDF (Zweites Deutsches Fernsehen), it uses the concept of *Medienkompetenz*, which divides media literacy into four basic components: use, knowledge, critical understanding, and creativity. Most of ZDF's initiatives focus on media literacy promotion, where messages emphasize the importance of protecting minors from potentially inappropriate content. In case studies of public broadcasters in Great Britain, Germany, and Italy, Radoslavov (2014) examined how public value is differentially defined in relation to the media literacy missions of these national public service broadcasters and how they reflect the need to validate the continuing but marginal relevance of public service media in the 21st century.

Film industry and media literacy

The film industry has supported film and media education for many years, but media industry leaders have an ambivalent perspective on the value of formal education in helping to prepare the workforce of the future. Certainly, the tech industry has valued how digital media tools, when used in school, can promote student interest in science, technology, engineering, and mathematics (STEM) opportunities. But since the so-called creative media industry has long had an oversupply of potential new entrants because the industry is seen as glamorous and exciting, it is unlikely to engage with the formal education sector in the same way as tech firms do. After all, most entrants to the media industry begin through voluntary or unpaid working jobs (called internships). Plus, the creative media industries use an increasingly high proportion of freelancers, especially those areas most closely involved in the production process. A UK report revealed that freelancers are used in 80% of film production jobs, for example. Radio production, photo imaging, animation, and independent production for television, including camera/photography, make up/hairdressing, lighting, costume/wardrobe, and audio/sound/music, are freelance jobs (Petrie & Stoneman, 2014).

A few film industry initiatives move beyond industry training to incorporate principles of media literacy education that target wide audiences, not just people preparing to become media professionals. Most notable among them is the Film Foundation's media literacy curriculum, The Story of Movies, developed by Catherine Gourley and funded by filmmaker Martin Scorsese. The initiative has an explicit focus on film appreciation and on critical analysis of classic American cinema. The Story of Movies materials were commissioned and created by The Film Foundation in partnership with IBM (International Business Machines Corporation) and TCM (Turner Classic Movies). The program targets middle school students and includes instructional support for the careful study of three classic American films: *To Kill a Mockingbird* (1962), *The Day the Earth Stood Still* (1951), and *Mr. Smith Goes to Washington* (1939). The program includes a DVD (digital video disc) of each film for in-depth study, a teacher's guide, and a student activities booklet. The champion of this program, Martin Scorsese (2013, p. 9), has been articulate on his vision of film media education: "Now we take it for granted—reading and writing are taught in schools—but the same kinds of questions are coming up around moving images: Are they harming us? Are they causing us to abandon written language? We're face to face with images all the time in a way that we never have been before. And that's why I believe we need to stress visual literacy in our schools. Young people need to understand that not all images are there to be consumed like fast food and then forgotten, we need to educate them to understand the difference between moving images that engage their humanity and their intelligence, and moving images that are just selling them something. In fact, as Steve Apkon, the film producer and founder of The Jacob Burns Film Center in Pleasantville, NY, points out in his new book *The Age of the Image*, the distinction between verbal and visual literacy needs to be done away with, along with the tired old arguments about the word and the image and which is more important. They're both important. They're both fundamental. Both take us back to the core of who we are."

Some Hollywood celebrities have advocated for media literacy education. Academy Award-winning actor Geena Davis founded the Geena Davis Institute on Gender and Media in 2004 as a research-based organization working within the media and entertainment industry to engage, educate, and influence content creators, marketers, and audiences about the importance of eliminating unconscious bias, highlighting gender balance, challenging stereotypes, creating role models, and scripting a wide variety of strong female characters in entertainment and media that targets and influences children ages 11 and under (Smith, Choueiti, Prescott, & Pieper, 2012). With funding from Google, they are developing a software tool to measure screen and speaking time without the need for human coding or content analysis. As female characters are vastly underrepresented in film, the software tool confirms continuing gender disparities.

Some Hollywood leaders have talked about visual and media literacy within the larger context of K-12 school reform. For example, the George Lucas Educational Foundation has focused on project-based learning. They aim to increase awareness of project-based learning in classrooms, which occurs when students and teachers explore real-world problems and challenges. Although the Foundation has offered little focus on media literacy or media education, the broad goals of project-based learning are aligned with an inquiry pedagogy (Baines et al., 2015).

Journalists and media literacy

A need for media literacy education has long been positioned with the argument that people with higher levels of media literacy will prefer quality media content over sensationalism and junk entertainment. Globally, newspapers and news media have recognized the significance of the education market and have provided educational materials to increase the use of their products and services in schools. More than 50 countries around the world have some form of "newspaper in education" program, generally involving the provision of workshops and educational programs for educators and sometimes the creation of specially prepared materials designed to introduce students in elementary and secondary schools to news and current events (Claes & Quintellier, 2009). In the United States, the Newspaper in Education movement helped support the shift in teaching not just about the past, but about the present. For example, during and after World War II, nearly 50% of American high schools offered a civics course entitled "Problems in Democracy" that included regular reading of newsmagazines like *Time*. By the 1950s, representatives of the newspaper industry had met with the National Council for the Social Studies and the National Council of Teachers of English to develop a program on how to use the daily newspapers in the classroom. In general, from the 1940s to the 1990s, the news media industry has emphasized the role of information about current events, politics, health, and science in the practice of learning to become a citizen in a democratic society.

The *New York Times* is perhaps the best example of a contemporary news organization that is emphasizing the value of demystifying the practice of journalism and helping students build critical reading skills. They offer media literacy resources to teachers at the New York Times Learning Network (n.d.), a website with daily lesson plans that encourage students to read, critically analyze, and respond in writing to news and opinion articles. Each week during the school year, in Film Club, a short nonfiction video is provided and learners post and share responses. Many educational materials and resources on the website contain a focus on learning to examine both the form and the content of news stories. This approach to media literacy emphasizes understanding specific characteristics of the form and the variety of news genres within a daily newspaper. One typical lesson plan helps students understand the distinction between news and news analysis, explaining how news analysis, columns, and opinions adhere to standards that differ from straight news and op-ed pages and encouraging students to make these distinctions as they read the paper.

Interest in news literacy has grown with support from philanthropies founded from previous newspaper fortunes made by large conglomerates from earlier eras. The McCormick Foundation and the John S. and James L. Knight Foundation support news literacy initiatives in the United States even as the revenue of newspapers in the United States has continued to decline. They have supported projects including the News Literacy Project and the news literacy undergraduate course at the University of New York at Stony Brook. These news literacy programs focus on the importance of helping young people and educators to appreciate quality journalism, reflecting the assumption that people need to be taught to respect the norms of professional journalism like fairness, accuracy, and balance. Often developed and taught by former journalists, the overall message to learners is rooted in a focus on rebuilding trust for mainstream news media. Through stimulating and renewing consumer demand for quality journalism, the press can perform its historic function in democratic societies.

Broadcast and cable TV support media literacy

In the United States, media industries have made efforts to educate the public about what they do and why it matters, especially when doing so insulates them from unwanted potential government regulation. Since the rise of special interest politics in the mid-1970s, alliances between government and businesses have been highly effective in addressing policy and perception issues in the area of media, children, technology, culture, and youth.

Historically, the television industry has advanced media literacy education in a variety of important ways. One example of the media industry's involvement in media literacy is the work developed by Roy Danish of the Television Information Office at the National Association of Broadcasters, who created a curriculum in 1961 entitled Television in Today's Society, which offered a program of instruction to more than 1000 teachers in the New York City area. The materials included a binder with scripts of 13 lectures, other print materials, and instructions on how to deliver a course explaining the new medium of television (Danish, 1961). The program was designed as an inservice training program for teachers or as part of an adult education or college-level course in communications, mass media, or broadcasting. In distributing the curriculum materials to educators across the country, it was expected that the local organizer would find suitable local experts on the topics explored in the curriculum. Presumably, local experts would review the printed script or lecture notes as a guide to their own presentations. Each session was planned for about 80 minutes and included a detailed written summary of lectures, a suggested reading list, a quiz-questionnaire, a set of slides, and recommendations for appropriate supplemental 16 mm educational films. The diversity of materials ensured that the program could be flexibly used with different types of high school and adult audiences. This approach set the stage for conceptualizing media literacy as the provision of knowledge about the economic, regulatory, and institutional functions of the mass media industry.

Broadcasters also provided opportunities for media literacy educators to demonstrate their craft. In 1976, Neil Postman taught a college-level course called "Communications: The Invisible Environment," on Sunrise Semester (CBS-TV, 1976), between September 1976 and January 1977. The course consisted of three 30-minute lectures per week. On the third lecture each week, Neil brought on camera a panel of so-called colleagues, but actually, they were graduate students at New York University. Peter Haratonik, Marcia Rock, Mel Elberger, and Paul Levinson participated in some of these programs. In one program, they debate the value of TV advertising and entertainment as a form of art and commerce. Serious academic discussion of media, as part of educational television, has been seen infrequently on commercial television since that time.

By the 1970s, as concerns voiced by parents and teachers increased about television's impact on children's behavior, social science researchers measured the impact but few proposed practical strategies for addressing the potential risks and harms resulting from exposure to problematic media content that included propaganda, violence, sexuality, and racial and ethnic stereotypes. Child development specialists were approaching the study of media as a factor in the cultural environment that was having a negative influence on children's behavior, including their aggressive impulses, imagination, and social skills. In 1980, when Jerome and Dorothy Singer, developmental psychologists at Yale University, received financial support from ABC, an American television network, to develop and disseminate "Creating Critical Viewers," the concept of media literacy and critical viewing became more visible nationwide. This set of lesson plans was designed to teach children media vocabulary words to understand the constructed nature of media messages and help children identify stereotypes, recognize media genres, and discriminate between entertainment, information, and persuasion (Singer & Singer, 1991). The subsequent national effort, supported by the National Association for Television Arts and Sciences (NATAS) and launched during a key period of congressional debates about the social responsibilities of broadcasters, contributed to the growth of the media literacy movement, and the resulting publicity for the program showed that academics could work with television networks to be part of the solution in addressing parental concerns about the negative impact of television on children (Cherow-O'Leary, 2014).

The cable television industry has supported media literacy, too. Cable in the Classroom, formed in 1989 with a group of cable companies pooling resources to provide public service programming, offered 500 hours of commercial-free quality educational programming. Since the programming was copyright-cleared, educator and school districts were encouraged to build libraries of relevant programming. Over a 10-year period, the organization offered media literacy training to 7500 teachers per year. They hosted an annual gala event in Washington, DC, to acknowledge teachers and educational leaders who were using cable television programming in innovative ways. Their magazine, *Cable in the Classroom Magazine*, edited by Al Race, offered numerous examples of media literacy education by elementary and secondary teachers.

By the early 1990s, the term media literacy was becoming more familiar to those in the broadcast and cable television industry, and they recognized it as an opportunity to "wear the white hat" in the face of increasing public criticism about the increasing levels of sex and violence on American television (Montgomery, 2007). KNOW TV was a 1995 initiative developed by Renee Hobbs in collaboration with The Learning Channel, which is owned by Discovery Communications, Inc. As part of the channel's launch, a curriculum kit was developed that demonstrated nine critical questions for analyzing documentary and nonfiction television. Questions included the following.

- What is a documentary?
- What is the purpose?
- How does the purpose shape the content?
- How are language, sound, and image used to manipulate the message?
- How do different viewers interpret the same message?
- What techniques are used to enhance the authenticity of the message?

- What techniques are used to enhance the authority of the message?
- What techniques are used to involve or engage the viewer?
- Who makes money from this message?

Although the program focused on analyzing historical and cultural documentaries traditionally used in school, KNOW TV curriculum was notable for its time in offering explicit inclusion of docudrama, fictional film depictions of historical events, and even the earliest forms of reality television, including shows like *Cops*, as artifacts for in-school analysis. The curriculum included a VHS (Video Home System) clip compilation tape and a binder with activities that included reading, writing, discussion, role-playing, and simulation, and these resources were combined with a day-long professional development program. The initiative was awarded the Golden Cable ACE Award, the cable industry's highest award for public service.

Only a few years later, after the massacre of high school students and a teacher at Columbine High School in Littleton, Colorado, Discovery Communications contracted with Hobbs to create *Assignment: Media Literacy*, a statewide initiative in Maryland, developed in coordination with the media company at the Maryland State Department of Education. The program used a similar structure, with a binder of curriculum resources, a VHS clip compilation tape, and a day-long teacher education program. Additional support from the National Cable Telecommunication Association enabled some program elements to be used in the State of Texas for inservice teacher education, supported by the state education agency in Texas.

More recently, broadcasters have seen media literacy as a way to attract media-savvy viewers to new broadcast channels and services. Pivot was a cable television network developed by Participant Media, a film and media production company founded by Jeff Skoll in 2004 to create entertainment that inspires and creates social change. The company adopted media literacy as a part of their campaign to invite audiences to make a difference in the world through social action campaigns associated with their entertainment products. Their Eyes Wide Open campaign, developed in 2013, sought to educate young adults about the power and pitfalls of media, offering tips on the importance of considering the sources of information they consume, recognizing their own role in producing and sharing content, and exploring the trade-offs inherent in giving personal information online.

Advertisers and media literacy

Critical analysis of advertising has been a popular and enduring feature of media literacy theory and practice as it enables robust dialogue about aesthetics, language, production, audiences, meaning, and economics. However, support from the advertising industry has been sporadic and minimal. During the 1950s, Canadian philosopher and literary critic Marshall McLuhan began suggesting strategies for reading advertising using techniques of literary analysis. His book, *The Mechanical Bride*, demonstrated how values messages were embedded in ads for toothpaste, deodorant, and food products. The practice of critically analyzing advertising as a means to support the development of critical thinking skills became popular during the 1960s and 1970s and was influenced by McLuhan's claim that popular culture, advertising, film, and television are forms of art akin to literature.

Although the advertising industry in the United States has never supported media literacy initiatives, in Great Britain, the industry has been more proactive, in part because of the opportunity provided by the World Health Organization's work in food marketing to children that has positioned media literacy as an alternative to government regulation (Buckingham, 2009). When UK candy advertisers supported the development of the Media Smart curriculum in the United Kingdom in 2002, they enlisted the support of media literacy experts in the creation of the educational resource materials and lessons for children ages 6 to 11. With video clips, teacher notes, and activity sheets, the curriculum used compelling pedagogical methods to introduce children to how advertising works, methods used to persuade children including celebrity appeals, and the function of public service advertising. Independent research with teachers and students revealed that children learned about the concept of target audiences and the intersection between peer culture and brand culture (Buckingham, Willett, Banaji, & Cranmer, 2007). The success of this initiative encouraged educators to see media literacy as a means of demystifying media by "pulling back the curtain" on how media messages are created and why they have impact on consumers.

Technology companies and media literacy

When Internet and technology industries develop media literacy initiatives, they tend to position their work in relation to the power of creative expression or as a means of socializing youth and setting norms about appropriate online behaviors when texting, sharing image files, or interacting on social networks. Some Internet services firms support important, high-visibility work in media literacy education that has had a transformative impact on the lives of underserved children and youth, both across the United States and around the world.

One example is Adobe Youth Voices, a philanthropic program which provides grants, computer software, and stipends to a variety of youth media and media literacy organizations. The goal of the Adobe program is to give underserved and "at-risk" students access to digital technologies, like Premiere and Photoshop, so that they can educate people about social issues (like violence, sexual health, immigration, and health care) in their own communities. Thousands of young people in the United States, India, and around the world have participated in this program and learned to make short films that address their lived experience and social reality. The visibility of this initiative has positioned media literacy as an outlet for creative expression by children and youth, especially from underserved communities.

Technology firms are also interested in digital and media literacy as a means to minimize the potential risks and harms of Internet use. When the public hears the phrase online safety, they may think about predators, sexting, and some of the more lurid and sensational media stories about the harms and risks that may befall children and youth in the new realms of the Internet and social media spaces. One might expect the online safety community to be dominated by the perspectives of concerned parents and law enforcement officials. But since the mid-2000s, the online safety community has been significantly influenced not by the voices of frustrated and angry parents, but by the interests of Internet and technology industries who seek to reassure citizens that the Internet is a fine place for their children to play, interact, and learn.

The Internet Keep Safe Coalition (iKeepSafe) is a nonprofit international alliance of more than 100 policy leaders, educators, law enforcement members, technology experts, public health experts, and advocates. In 2011, iKeepSafe introduced the Google Digital Literacy and Citizenship Curriculum. The program, which targets middle school students ages 11–13, consists of a set of three short animated YouTube videos with lesson plans and handouts. This approach to media literacy is designed to influence students' perception of online behaviors, being socially appropriate in interactions with people online, and avoiding scams. The learning goals are oriented around increasing knowledge about the tools offered by Google/YouTube to protect oneself from inappropriate content when using the Internet and the importance of making appropriate choices to minimize personal risk. For example, learning goals state that students will understand that not everything they see on the web is true; how to recognize online scams; how to protect themselves from scams; and how to take action if they find themselves being scammed. Vocabulary words include terms like *spyware*, *phishing*, *firewall*, and *pop-up contest*. The videos show specific features of YouTube designed to help users identify and address problematic content, including the "flagging" feature and the ability to erase negative comments about one's own posted videos. After viewing the videos, teachers are instructed to review the main ideas presented. Then learners participate in a quiz-assessment activity, where, in one lesson, teachers are encouraged to use the format of the popular television quiz show "Who Wants to be Millionaire" to engage students in answering comprehension questions about Internet scams. Students can use Lifelines or Phone a Friend when answering these questions.

The curriculum has a focus on increasing awareness, emphasizing the value of being skeptical about information provided on the Internet and about the motives of people who use the Internet for social relationships. The tone of the curriculum conveys a sense of warning about those who use the Internet and positions learners as potential victims who may be taken advantage of. The curriculum explicitly offers a list of "dos and don'ts," including an admonition to not post private information like addresses or phone numbers or to engage in sexual talk online. In other similar curricula, such as the materials created by Common Sense Media, this framing is often called "digital citizenship," and it explicitly refers to a focus on teaching social norms of relational politeness and online safety with an emphasis on ethics and social responsibility. Students are not invited to ask "how" and "why" questions about the Internet and social media. These approaches are about defining normative social behavior, not about providing learners with information to help them understand how the Internet works, how it is (un)regulated, why scams are so common online, or how consumer protection laws apply to the Internet.

Finally, in a return to the time-honored tradition of educational television, YouTube's most famous digital content creators, John and Hank Green, have developed a nine-part series of YouTube videos under the Crash Course brand. In a course called "Media Literacy" they use a fast-paced mix of animation with a direct address from hip-hop cultural commentator Jay Smooth (Siede, 2018). The series of 10-minute episodes was produced by Nick Jenkins and includes topics such as the history of media, media ownership, media policy, online advertising, and media economics.

Conclusion

The media industry has used a variety of approaches to advance media literacy by creating demand for media products and services; providing information about content, structures, or production processes; offering consumer protection or minimizing risks associated with media use; promoting creative self-expression and active participation in media culture; and challenging media industries to address problematic or ethically questionable practices. The media industry's involvement in media literacy is part of a wider cultural trend as people shift from passive spectators to active participants in an increasingly mediated world.

The media industry's involvement in media literacy is part of a wider cultural trend that is occurring as deregulation of media industries places more responsibility on the shoulders of individuals. Although media industry stakeholders have helped to advance media literacy education, media literacy should not be conceptualized as a substitute for media regulation (Silverstone, 2004). In the United States, NAMLE has acknowledged that media literacy educators "share with media owners, producers, and members of the creative community responsibility for facilitating mutual understanding of the effects of media on individuals and on society" but that media literacy education "does not excuse media makers from their responsibility as members of the community to make a positive contribution and avoid doing harm" (NAMLE, 2010, p. 1).

In the future, media industry stakeholders must move to address some newly emerging and significant gaps in public understanding in advancing media literacy for children, youth, and families. One major unexplored issue concerns Big Data and privacy. Today, every device we own generates data that are used by companies to improve their sales; the rise of data warehouses has enabled companies to gather information about our airline flights, job applications, insurance plans, credit card usage, and GPS (Global Positioning System) locations. Most people, young and old, are unaware of how information they provide becomes commodified. The rise of digital marketing and the surge in Big Data represent significant shifts in the relationship between the audience, author, media industry, and advertiser, but there have been few efforts to explain these shifts to ordinary citizens. This is a ripe topic for digital and media literacy education, and the media industry has an important role to play in addressing it.

SEE ALSO: European Perspectives on Media Literacy; Media Literacy for the 21st Century Teacher; Policy Issues in European Media Literacy

References

Baines, A., DeBarger, A.H., De Vivo, K., Warner, N., Brinkman, J., & Santos, S. (2015). *What is rigorous project-based learning?* San Rafael, CA: George Lucas Educational Foundation.

BBC. (2006). *Building public value: Renewing the BBC for a digital world.* Retrieved from http://downloads.bbc.co.uk/aboutthebbc/policies/pdf/bpv.pdf

BBC. (2013). *BBC media literacy strategy.* Retrieved from http://www.bbc.co.uk/learning/overview/about/assets/bbc_media_literacy_strategy_may2013.pdf

Buckingham, D. (1998). Media education in the UK: Moving beyond protectionism. *Journal of Communication, 48*(1), 33–43.

Buckingham, D. (2009). *The impact of the commercial world on children's wellbeing.* Retrieved from https://www.academia.edu/679743/The_Impact_of_the_Commercial_World_on_Childrens_Wellbeing

Buckingham, D., Willett, R., Banaji, S., & Cranmer, S. (2007). Media Smart *Be Adwise 2*: An evaluation. Media Smart. Retrieved from https://www.academia.edu/2748245/Media_Smart_Be_Adwise_2_an_evaluation

CBS-TV. (1976). Sunrise Semester with Neil Postman [Video file]. Retrieved from https://youtu.be/RusSZHPz6Xc

Cherow-O'Leary, R. (2014). Creating critical viewers. *Journal of Media Literacy Education, 6*(2), 87–92. Retrieved from http://digitalcommons.uri.edu/jmle/vol6/iss2/8/

Claes, E., & Quintellier, E. (2009). Newspapers in education: A critical inquiry into the effects of using newspapers as teaching agents. *Educational Research, 51*(3), 341–363. doi: 10.1080/00131880903156922

Danish, R. (1961). *Television in today's world.* Washington, DC: National Association of Broadcasters, Television Information Office.

Greenberg, B.S., & Brand, J.E. (1993). Television news and advertising in schools: The "Channel One" controversy. *Journal of Communication, 43*(1), 143–151. doi: 10.1111/j.1460-2466.1993.tb01252.x

Heins, M., & Cho, C. (2003). Media literacy: An alternative to censorship. The Free Expression Policy Project. Retrieved from https://ncac.org/fepp-articles/media-literacy-an-alternative-to-censorship

Hobbs, R. (1998). The seven great debates in the media literacy movement. *Journal of Communication, 48*(1), 16–32.

Montgomery, K. (2007). *Generation digital: Politics, commerce, and childhood in the age of the Internet*. Cambridge, MA: MIT Press.

National Association for Media Literacy Education. (2010). Core principles of media literacy education in the United States. Retrieved from http://namle.net/publications/core-principles/

New York Times Learning Network. (n.d.). Retrieved from http://learning.blogs.nytimes.com

Petrie, D.J., & Stoneman, R. (2014). *Educating film-makers: Past, present and future.* Chicago, IL: Intellect Books.

Radoslavov, S. (2014). Media literacy promotion as a form of public value? Comparing the media literacy promotion strategies of the BBC, ZDF and RAI. In G. Lowe & F. Martin (Eds.), *The value of public service media.* Gothenburg, Sweden: Nordicom.

Saettler, P. (2004). *The evolution of American educational technology*. Greenwich, CT: Information Age Publishing.

Scorsese, M. (2013). The persistence of vision: Reading and the language of cinema. National Endowment for the Humanities lecture. Retrieved from https://www.neh.gov/about/awards/jefferson-lecture/martin-scorsese-lecture

Siede, E. (2018, February 22). Crash Course is launching a series all about media literacy. Boing Boing. Retrieved from https://boingboing.net/2018/02/22/crash-course-is-launching-a-se.html

Silverstone, R. (2004). Regulation, media literacy and media civics. *Media, Culture & Society, 26*(3), 440–449. doi: 10.1177/0163443704042557

Singer, J., & Singer, D. (1991). *Creating critical viewers: A partnership between schools and television professionals.* New York, NY: ABC Television. Retrieved from https://depts.washington.edu/nwmedia/sections/nw_center/curriculum_docs/ccv.pdf

Smith, S.L., Choueiti, M., Prescott, A., & Pieper, K. (2012). *Gender roles & occupations: A look at character attributes and job-related aspirations in film and television.* Geena David Institute on Gender in Media. Retrieved from https://seejane.org/wp-content/uploads/full-study-gender-roles-and-occupations-v2.pdf

Further reading

Cruse, E. (2006). Using educational video in the classroom: Theory, research and practice. Library Video Company. Retrieved from https://www.safarimontage.com/pdfs/training/UsingEducationalVideoInTheClassroom.pdf

Lewis, J., & Jhally, J. (1998). The struggle over media literacy. *Journal of Communication, 48*(1), 109–120. doi: 10.1111/j.1460-2466.1998.tb02741.x

RobbGrieco, M. (2014). Why history matters for media literacy education. *Journal of Media Literacy Education, 6*(2), 3–20. doi: 10.23860/JMLE-2016-06-02-2

Tigga, R. (2009). *Rise, decline, and re-emergence of media literacy education in the United States: 1960–2000* (Unpublished doctoral dissertation). Marquette University, Milwaukee, WI.

Renee Hobbs is a professor of communication studies and Director of the Media Education Lab at the Harrington School of Communication and Media at the University of Rhode Island. Her research examines the conditions of media literacy education in elementary and secondary schools and she has authored eight books and over 150 scholarly and professional articles. She has offered professional development programs in media literacy on four continents. She is the founding editor of the *Journal of Media Literacy Education,* an open-access, peer-review journal sponsored by the National Association for Media Literacy Education.

Media Literacy among the Elderly

LEOPOLDO ABAD ALCALÁ
Universidad CEU San Pablo, Spain

Media literacy among older people has to be addressed in tandem with the great challenge of demographic ageing facing future societies, and linked with targets of active ageing and personal and social empowerment, in order to facilitate senior citizens' participation in the opportunities offered by the information society. This requires effective and appropriate training initiatives within the framework of the new communications media and information technology allowing real media literacy of older persons, and avoiding placing them at a disadvantage or leaving them technologically vulnerable. These initiatives must take into account the personal and social peculiarities of this section of the population, which will involve the need for changes to and adaptation of the proposals in this area.

Media literacy of older people must be linked to the process of demographic change in modern societies. According to the United Nations *World Population Ageing* report of 2015, between 2015 and 2030 the number of people worldwide over 60 years of age will increase by 56%, while in 2050 the global elderly population will more than double the 2015 percentage, reaching around 2.1 billion. In terms of the number of people over 80 years of age, this growth is even faster, in 2050 reaching triple the 2015 percentage. By region, the increase in the number of people over 60 years of age in the 2015–2030 period will be 71% in Latin America and the Caribbean, 66% in Asia, 64% in Africa, 47% in Oceania, 41% in North America, and 23% in Europe.

In these societies that will tend to be made up of mostly older people, the skills to access information in its various forms, to process it in context, and to use it advantageously according to the person's characteristics will become essential for social participation and personal fulfilment. One of the main obstacles to the proper development of media literacy of older persons is the trend—especially in governments and public institutions—to address this more from a quantitative perspective (use of and access to media, especially digital) than a qualitative perspective (skills and abilities for profitable use of media depending on personal circumstances). Critical thinking, rather than technical competence, is the central element of literacy. In short, it is so-called critical knowledge that must be strengthened, which includes understanding media content and their function, knowledge of the media, their regulation, and their use by users (Celot & Pérez Tornero, 2009).

These approaches are changing, and we can see that the current European Union *Data and Indicators* of the *Digital Scoreboard* include those relating to digital skills where the various skills regarding the use of information and communication technology (ICT) are assessed according to different criteria (age, education, socioeconomic status, gender, disability, environment, professional status, etc.). Meanwhile, in its report *Digital Readiness Gaps* (Horrigan, 2016), the Pew Research Center addresses digital skills, dividing and categorizing citizens into five categories in descending order of digital skills: "Digitally Ready," "Traditional Learners," "The Reluctant," "Cautious Clickers," and "The Unprepared."

One of the key issues to be addressed when looking at the achievement of media literacy among older people is the recent and rapid change of the media paradigm. As the United Nations Educational, Scientific and Cultural Organization (UNESCO) indicates in the *2014 Paris Declaration on Media and Information Literacy in the Digital Era*, continuous technological developments create and mediatize an ever-growing amount of content and information as well as new online spaces. They introduce new issues, challenges, and possibilities such as the new Internet scenario becoming mobile, ubiquitous, and multiplatform. Individuals gain more control over their roles as media creators and critics, and not only as consumers. Social media and social network sites take on added significance, as they serve as references to new forms of social interaction.

The uniqueness of education for this group is that instead of being focused on competitive tasks it should be linked to the acquisition and learning of skills to reinforce their sense of self-fulfillment, associated with the promotion of active aging. It tends to be unconnected with job-related training and voluntary, and its aims are personal (individual development, self-realization), social (interpersonal relationships, participation in and involvement with the environment), and cultural enrichment. Citizens who are not intellectually and emotionally qualified to use ICT are more likely to be culturally marginalized in the 21st century. This digital illiteracy will undoubtedly cause greater difficulties in accessing the opportunities offered by the media, helplessness and vulnerability when handling information, and an inability to use digital communication resources.

To avoid this situation, achieving media literacy among older persons should start with its consideration as a multiple, comprehensive, and integrated learning of the various forms and languages of representation and communication—textual, sound, iconic, audiovisual, hypertextual, three-dimensional—through the use of various technologies—printed, digital, and audiovisual—in different social interaction situations and contexts. Thus, the literacy needed for the 21st century must necessarily be "media" literacy—given the current importance of the media—"digital" literacy—since most of the information handled is digitalized—and multimodal—due to the convergence of text, sound, image, video, and animation (Area Moreira, 2012, p. 24).

For this group, a critical understanding should be fostered of the media as one of the most powerful social, economic, political, and cultural institutions of our time. Changes in the environment of the communications media are altering our understanding of literacy, and they require new mental habits, new ways of processing culture, and new methods of interacting with the world around us. We are beginning to identify and assess these emerging sets of social skills and cultural competencies (Jenkins, 2008, p. 38).

These competencies and skills covering media literacy basically involve taking responsible decisions regarding the access to and sharing of information, understanding, analyzing, and assessing information in context, reflecting critically on our communicative behavior from an ethical standpoint, and participating socially through various communicative actions by producing content disclosed publicly and privately (Hobbs, 2010, vii–viii).

Given all of the above, dealing with media literacy of older persons requires a multiple plan which assesses the different circumstances of this age group and of each particular individual, avoiding reducing media education to the development of digital competence focusing on a more technological and instrumental dimension, in the procedures for using and handling devices and programs, while not taking into account attitudes and values. Aspects such as education, aptitude, social background, socioeconomic status, gender, ethnicity, career, or the family situation shape the manner in which older people interact with the media (Prendergast & Garattini, 2015). When it comes to considering the methodological proposals for the media literacy training of senior citizens, a series of physical, psychological, and social determinants that influence their learning processes must be taken into consideration (Livingstone, Van Couvering, & Thumim, 2005).

Among the above, account must be taken of the existence of limitations that may hinder media literacy processes, such as a loss of vision or hearing, functional restrictions, or neurological impairment. One of the problems facing senior citizens in this new media landscape is that the media's multitasking trends tend to rely on similar neural networks and cognitive functions that decline with age (Ziegler, Mishra, & Gazzaley, 2015, p. 5).

Among the psychological determinants there is evidence of the existence of so-called technological anxiety, understood as fear or apprehension felt by older people when they have to work with or learn to use computers. This anxiety is one of the main causes limiting the possibilities of senior citizens to take full advantage of the various forms of technology available to them. Another fundamental aspect of the media literacy process for older persons is its perceived usefulness in their daily lives. For this group of people, learning that is geared toward achieving specific aims which reap clear benefits in their daily lives is key to any media literacy initiative.

On the other hand, research has demonstrated the existence of certain social contexts that benefit the media literacy of senior citizens: socioeconomic status (the better the economic situation, the higher the levels of media literacy), education (older people with higher levels of education have higher levels of media literacy), the family situation (families with high levels of media literacy—children, grandchildren, nieces and nephews, spouses, etc.—foster the development of media literacy among older members), and past professional experience (those who have worked—albeit tangentially—with new information and communication technology are more likely to successfully accept and acquire media literacy).

Age-appropriate education is critically important to the adoption of new media by older persons given that there is an abundance of evidence that, although age-related changes have a negative impact on technological learning, these negative effects can be at least offset by training materials and teaching methods designed to adapt to these changes. In fact, there is empirical evidence that the success of ICT learning programs for senior citizens is primarily determined by the quality of the program design rather than by age or personality.

Recommendations for these media literacy initiatives for older people include most notably (Mayhorn, Stronge, McLaughlin, & Rogers, 2004; Xie & Bugg, 2009): (i) class sizes must be small and be organized by level of skill and experience; (ii) the initial stage must involve positive and successful experiences to promote commitment and avoid frustration and abandonment; (iii) teachers' empathic attitude has been shown to be fundamental, encouraging questions to be asked, avoiding the use of technical jargon and creating a kind (almost family-like) environment; (iv) educational materials must be clearly structured, gradually increasing in complexity without providing too much information in each session; (v) such materials must be adapted to compensate for the percentage reduction in motor and cognitive skills; (vi) there must be a causal link between the objectives proposed and achievements made; (vii) practice must be encouraged at home by self-guided and self-led systems that allow the use of the skills and competencies worked on in the classes.

Media literacy adapted to the social and personal circumstances of older people is necessary in ever-more aging societies and in view of the technological omnipresence of the media.

SEE ALSO: Digital Divide; Digital Divide and Web-Use Skills; Digital Literacy; Health Media Literacy

References

Area Moreira, M. (2012). La alfabetización en la sociedad digital [Literacy in the digital society]. In M. Area Moreira, A. Gutiérrez Martín, & F. Vidal Fernández (Eds.), *Alfabetización digital y competencias informacionales* [Digital literacy and information skills] (pp. 3–42). Madrid, Spain: Fundación Telefónica/Editorial Ariel.

Celot, P., & Pérez-Tornero, J.M. (2009). *Study on assessment criteria for media literacy levels: A comprehensive view of the concept of media literacy and an understanding of how media literacy levels in Europe should be assessed*. Brussels, Belgium: European Commission. Retrieved from http://ec.europa.eu/assets/eac/culture/library/studies/literacy-criteria-report_en.pdf

Hobbs, R. (2010). *Digital and media literacy: A plan of action*. Washington, DC: The Aspen Institute & Knight Foundation. Retrieved from https://www.knightfoundation.org/media/uploads/publication_pdfs/Digital_and_Media_Literacy_A_Plan_of_Action.pdf

Horrigan, J.B. (2016, September 20). *Digital readiness gaps*. Pew Research Center. Retrieved from http://www.pewinternet.org/2016/09/20/2016/Digital-Readiness-Gaps/

Jenkins, H. (2008). *Confronting the challenges of participatory culture: Media education for the 21st century*. Chicago, IL: The John D. and Catherine T. MacArthur Foundation.

Livingstone, S., Van Couvering, E., & Thumim, N. (2005). *Adult media literacy: A review of research literature*. London, England: Ofcom & London School of Economics.

Mayhorn, C.B., Stronge, A., McLaughlin, A.C, & Rogers, W.A. (2004). Older adults, computers training, and the systems approach: A formula for success. *Educational Gerontology, 30*(3), 185–203. doi: 10.1080/03601270490272124

Prendergast, D., & Garattini, Ch. (2015). Introduction. In Ch. Garattini & D. Prendergast (Eds.), *Aging and the digital life course. Life course, culture and aging. Volume 3: Global transformations* (pp. 3–15). Oxford, England: Berghahn.

UNESCO. (2014). *Paris declaration on media and information literacy in the digital era*. Retrieved from http://www.unesco.org/new/fileadmin/MULTIMEDIA/HQ/CI/CI/pdf/news/paris_mil_declaration.pdf

Xie, B., & Bugg, J.M. (2009). Public library computer training for older adults to access high-quality Internet health information. *Library & Information Science Research, 31*(3), 155–162. doi: 10.1016/j.lisr.2009.03.004

Ziegler, D.A., Mishra, J., & Gazzaley, A. (2015). The acute and chronic impact of technology on our brain. In L.D. Rosen, N.A. Cheever, & M.L Carrier (Eds.), *Psychology, technology and society* (pp. 3–19). Chichester, England: Wiley-Blackwell.

Further reading

Abad Alcalá, L. (2014). Media literacy for older people facing the digital divide: The e-inclusion programmes design. *Comunicar, 42*(21), 173–180. doi: 10.3916/C42-2014-17 http://eprints.rclis.org/21159/

Eshet-Alkalai, Y., & Chajut, E. (2010). You can teach old dogs new tricks: The factors that affect changes over time in digital literacy. *Journal of Information Technology Education, 9*(3), 173–181. Retrieved from http://www.jite.org/documents/Vol9/JITEv9p173-181Eshet802.pdf

Gilster, P. (1997). *Digital literacy.* New York, NY: Wiley.

Hamelink, C.J. (2000). *The ethics of cyberspace.* London, England: SAGE.

Hargittai, E., & Hinnant, A. (2008). Digital inequality differences in young adults' use of the Internet. *Communication Research, 35*(5), 602–621. Retrieved from http://www.eszter.com/research/pubs/A25.Hargittai.Hinnant-DigitalInequality.pdf

Leopoldo Abad Alcalá graduated in journalism (Universidad Complutense de Madrid, UCM) and law (Universidad Nacional de Educación a Distancia) and has a PhD in information sciences (UCM). He is principal investigator of the project "Digital divide and older people: Media literacy and e-inclusion" (CSO2012-36872) and of the project "Elderly people, E-commerce and electronic administration" (CSO2015-66746-R), both part of the Spanish National I + D + i Plan. He is author of more than 30 publications (including "Media Literacy for Older People Facing the Digital Divide: The e-Inclusion Programmes Design") and is a guest lecturer at European, US, and Ibero-American Universities. Currently, he is an associate professor at CEU San Pablo University (Madrid).

Media Literacy and Alcohol Abuse Reduction

BRUCE E. PINKLETON and ERICA W. AUSTIN
Washington State University, USA

Young people develop their attitudes and expectancies toward drinking through a variety of factors. These include normative assumptions concerning their peers' drinking, observations of others' drinking behaviors, and messages presented in digital and traditional mass media. Adolescents consume a surprising amount of media, much of it containing exaggerated and misleading portrayals of alcohol, tobacco, sex, and other potentially harmful substances and behaviors. As young people have migrated their media use to include larger amounts of digital and social media, marketers have evolved their marketing efforts to include substantially greater amounts of digital and social media (Hoffman, Pinkleton, Austin, & Reyes-Velazquez, 2014). As a result, traditional media such as television and movies—and now digital and social media—provide adolescents with nearly unrestrained access to an overabundance of alluring but distorted and potentially unsafe media content, much of it directly or indirectly encouraging alcohol consumption, other forms substance use, sex, and a variety of unsafe behaviors.

The result of exposure to these mediated portrayals can contribute to negative outcomes for both individuals and society. Scholars and other experts have conducted a variety of research addressing the associations between consumption of misleading media messages and negative health-related outcomes in a variety of contexts including alcohol abuse and substance use. While the results of this research do not offer definitive proof, a large number of empirical studies provide compelling evidence supportive of the negative influence of media exposure on adolescents' decision-making and behaviors (e.g., Brown & Bobkowski, 2011). Ultimately, these research findings emphasize the need for interventions that can disrupt the flow of incorrect and idealized messages about substance use to adolescents and increase their ability to detect and use correct, realistic information in their decision-making.

In contrast to negative outcomes resulting from exposure, media messages can produce constructive outcomes to the extent that users are able to distinguish between accurate, beneficial information and information that is deceptive or harmful. As a result, many experts have suggested that media literacy is a potentially effective way to equip young people with the critical thinking skills necessary to distinguish truthful information from unhealthy or deceptive information and to develop healthy skepticism toward media messages. Even so, gaps exist in researchers' current understanding concerning media literacy including its effects on young peoples' decision-making and its effectiveness as a health promotion strategy. As a result, this entry examines the current state of research concerning media literacy and its role in alcohol- and substance-use reduction. The entry concludes with a discussion of the state of research and the critical informational needs in our understanding of media literacy and its effectiveness.

Media exposure and the use of alcohol and other substances

Alcohol abuse among young people is a public health crisis. The Centers for Disease Control and Prevention (CDC) reports that excessive drinking results in more than 4,300 deaths among underage youths each year and that youths drink 11% of all alcohol consumed in the United States. In addition, 90% of the alcohol consumed by young people is consumed in binge drinking (CDC, 2017). For college students, the problem is particularly acute. Research indicates that 80–90% of all underage college students drink, 44% of college students binge drink, and more than 65% of college students report instances of intoxication (Johnston, O'Malley, Bachman, & Schulenberg, 2012). Research results indicate that alcohol abuse among college students associates with violence, health problems, social problems, financial problems, unlawful behavior, and a host of other negative consequences, including death (CDC, 2017).

While the causes and contributors to underage drinking are complex, research indicates that young people are exposed to a large volume of alcohol advertising. This exposure associates with increases in their initiation of drinking and higher levels of alcohol consumption (Anderson, de Bruijn, Angus, Gordon, & Hastings, 2009). Young people who report more positive responses to alcohol advertising also report more positive expectancies toward drinking, approve of drinking greater amounts of alcohol, express stronger normative beliefs concerning alcohol consumption, and report greater intentions to drink than those with less positive responses to alcohol advertising (Hoffman et al., 2014).

Marketers carefully design alcohol advertising to maximize its persuasive influence on audience members. Alcohol advertising succeeds by relying on well-designed social cues that include the use of attractive models, demonstrable social rewards, and desirable features such as colors, music, humor, and action (Chen, Grube, Bersamin, Waiters, & Keefe, 2005). In addition, because alcohol advertising enjoys substantial design and exposure frequency advantages over media messages recommending drinking in moderation, it overwhelms well-intended but poorly designed logic-based health promotion efforts that rely on donated media time. In fact, research by Siegel and colleagues (2016) found evidence of a robust relationship between underage youth exposure to alcohol advertising and past 30-day brand consumption among study participants.

In addition, research by Primack, Sidani, Carroll, and Fine (2009) found independent links between adolescents' exposure to movies and their use of alcohol. Media portrayals containing alcohol typically present its use as normative in fictitious portrayals that are exciting, glamorous, and free of negative consequences. Storylines and related portrayals demonstrate the benefits of alcohol use as a good way to fit in with others and/or relax and relieve stress after a hard day at work. Ultimately, media serve as what researchers have called a glorified peer, serving to socialize adolescents and shaping their attitudes and expectancies toward alcohol and other substances.

Why is this important? Research indicates that young peoples' positive affect toward highly desirable media messages and the portrayals they contain may help bypass more logical aspects of their decision-making. Even when marketing messages contain obviously fictitious storylines and events, young people may learn to appreciate and interpret messages concerning alcohol so they encourage pro-consumption attitudes and behavior. Ultimately, young people's exposure to alcoholic beverage advertising and their positive responses toward those ads influence underage drinking and the emergence of related problems. Given the influence of media messages on young people's substance use, researchers have recommended media literacy as a way to help individuals develop the critical thinking skills necessary to better understand media and potentially avoid negative media effects.

The ability of media literacy to help negate misleading media messages

While scholars and others continue to discuss and develop definitional aspects of media literacy, the term typically refers to individuals' ability to access, analyze, evaluate, and communicate messages in a variety of forms (Aufderheide, 1993). Programs promoting media literacy education typically attempt to provide individuals—often young people—with the skills necessary to analyze the accuracy of media messages, and media literacy education typically results in a more thoughtful approach to media message processing. The ultimate outcome of this process is the development of healthy skepticism and logic-based message processing, which helps to diminish the negative impact of media messages on decision-making and behavior.

To sell alcoholic beverages, tobacco, and other products to consumers, marketers develop and test creative advertising appeals containing attractive images, appealing features, and other perceived benefits that link consumption with desirable social rewards and impact young peoples' decision-making and alcohol consumption. An informed, thoughtful approach to consuming media messages requires individuals to distinguish between beneficial, truthful information and deceptive information that is unhealthy. As a result, many public health experts have recommended media literacy as a developmentally appropriate instructional tool that can help young people develop the critical thinking skills necessary to better understand media messages that are misleading or unhealthy.

Decision-making is a learned skill that incorporates both logic and emotion. To understand why media literacy training can help reduce alcohol abuse, it helps to understand how young people make decisions. Research indicates that young people do not absorb media messages in a passive, uniform manner. Instead, they actively process messages and progress through a number of steps as they receive and respond to them, ultimately leading to behavioral outcomes (Austin, Pinkleton, Hust, & Cohen, 2005; Pinkleton, Austin, Cohen, Chen, & Fitzgerald, 2008). While logic is an important part of individuals' responses to media messages, affective—or emotional—reactions can alter logical decision-making processes. The degree to which advertising messages seem desirable to young people, for example, can encourage them to seek the benefits advertising promotes through imitative behavior. Adolescents' likelihood of engaging in risky behaviors increases when they identify with and desire to be like the characters in media portrayals and develop expectancies and efficacy for engaging in similar behavior (Austin, Pinkleton, Chen, & Austin, 2015). Strengthening key aspects of adolescents' logic-based decision-making through media literacy can help negate the allure of glamorized, misleading media messages (Jeong, Cho, & Hwang, 2012).

Taking this decision-making process into account, media literacy interventions aim to strengthen the ways audience members make sense of messages according to their own personal experience, ability, and need. Empirical evaluations of media literacy curricula, for example, generally indicate that children and adolescents who are aware of advertisers' motives are more likely to be skeptical of media messages and report less inclination to emulate behaviors they view on television. Evaluations of media literacy-based interventions have shown that media literacy training can help reduce positive expectancies regarding risky behavior and increase self-efficacy to resist peer pressure. Researchers also have found that higher levels of skepticism toward messages can help curb young peoples' desire to emulate behaviors and help to counter negative message outcomes (Austin & Pinkleton, 2016). By enhancing young people's understanding and awareness of media techniques, media literacy helps to increase their scrutiny of and critical thinking about media messages and can enhance their skepticism toward advertising for alcohol and other products. Ultimately, when young people have improved critical thinking skills, they have an improved ability to understand and deconstruct media messages as well as a better understanding of the intentions of message producers. This will help reduce unhealthy message effects and produce more realistic expectancies regarding media messages.

The effectiveness of media literacy training

Often media literacy programs focus on developing or activating skepticism toward media messages in young people, with even modest interventions showing positive effects on individuals' ability to critically analyze media messages. The effectiveness and influence of media literacy education should be most evident through assessments of individuals' understanding and beliefs related to decision-making processes because an increased understanding of media messages should alter their decision-making influence. In their meta-analysis of media literacy research, Jeong and colleagues (2012) concluded that media literacy interventions typically produce effects on outcomes they classify as relevant to either media or behavior.

Outcomes relevant to media include measures of media-related knowledge and assessments of individuals' understanding of the persuasive intent of advertising, their awareness of media influence, their skepticism toward media messages, and similar variables. Outcomes relevant to behavior include individuals' normative perceptions and their expectancies and attitudes toward engaging in behaviors, along with their perceived self-efficacy to perform behaviors such as refusing to use tobacco or alcohol. As a result of their research, Jeong and colleagues (2012) suggest that media literacy programs generally are effective at producing desired outcomes on most media- and behavior-relevant outcomes. In addition, the authors note that media literacy education may have greater effects on media-relevant outcomes than on behavior-relevant outcomes. These authors conclude that media literacy curricula can equip individuals to resist potentially harmful media message effects.

Consistent with this perspective, public health experts, health campaign practitioners, scholars, and others generally report that media literacy education provides an effective strategy for substance-abuse prevention by examining the influence of media literacy on relevant attitudes, self-efficacy, and behavior. For example, research concerning anti-smoking media literacy educational programs indicates that media literacy programs can provide significant benefits to young people including increasing participants' knowledge, correcting their misperceptions regarding peer norms, increasing their critical thinking and skepticism, and increasing their perceived efficacy. In a comparison of a media literacy-based anti-smoking education program to a typical anti-smoking educational program, for example, Primack, Douglas, Land, Miller, and Fine (2014) found that students in the media literacy program experienced improved media literacy skills and normative understanding related to smoking when compared to other participants in the typical program. In addition, the results of a survey of 3,600 college students by Primack and colleagues (2009) indicated that higher media literacy skills concerning smoking independently associated with lower incidence of smoking behavior.

Research concerning young people and alcoholic beverage advertising indicates that media literacy training can have both immediate and delayed effects on children's decision-making and behavior. In terms of immediate outcomes, study participants demonstrated an increased understanding of the persuasive intent of advertising and expressed lower desirability, operationally defined as a desire to be like characters they see in alcoholic beverage advertising (Gordon, Jones, Kervin, & Lee, 2016). Participants also expressed lower expectations of positive consequences from drinking alcohol, and were less likely to select an alcohol-related product in a merchandise-selection exercise. In addition, participants indicated that TV programming was less realistic and indicated more accurate views of social norms related to alcohol use. Effects of media literacy training also were evident in participants' expectancies and behavior at delayed posttest (Austin and Johnson, 1997a, 1997b).

Ultimately, the preponderance of research evidence indicates that media literacy has the potential to provide a variety of benefits to participants tied to health-related decision-making, self-efficacy, and behavior. Individuals who have received media literacy training have demonstrated improved critical thinking skills and an improved ability to understand and deconstruct media messages, as well as a better understanding of the intentions of message producers, leading to strengthened decision-making and positive behavioral outcomes related to health.

The future of media literacy education in alcohol abuse reduction

Research indicates that well-funded and professionally produced alcohol marketing efforts—including digital media marketing tactics—and other alcohol portrayals in social media are among a variety of factors that contribute to alcohol abuse among young people (Jernigan, Noel, Landon, Thornton, & Lobstein, 2017). In their work, health promotion experts typically contend with a large volume of professionally created messages promoting alcohol consumption, and research indicates that alcohol advertisements receiving the highest marks for likeability are associated with greater intentions to purchase specific brands and the related products they promote (Chen et al., 2005). When well-intended but poorly produced and/or poorly targeted public health programming competes with highly desirable alcoholic beverage advertising, health education programming is likely to be marginally effective at best. This is especially true when adolescents have determined that the use of alcohol and other substances is normative and develop expectancies that it is rewarding.

As a result, researchers, educators, and health promotion experts have recommended and tested media literacy education as a novel approach in helping to counter misleading portrayals of alcohol in traditional and social media. Generally, current research indicates that, while media literacy is not a panacea for young people inundated by negative media content, it does have the potential to equip individuals with the decision-making skills necessary to resist the allure of fictional and potentially harmful media messages. Educational programs featuring media literacy appear to have promise as part of a health communication intervention resulting in better decision-making through participants' development of skepticism toward media messages. As health promotion experts increasingly turn to media literacy to help promote healthy decision-making, there are a variety of questions and issues still unresolved in the research literature. Successfully addressing these questions and issues will potentially help improve the effectiveness of media literacy-based health campaigns and help continue to move the field forward through an improved understanding and evaluation of media literacy programming.

To be effective in reducing alcohol abuse, health educators and scholars should note the importance of fully understanding the attitudes and behaviors of targeted audience members in order to reach them with successful media literacy programming. Well-intended health campaigns of all kinds are likely to fail when experts neglect to thoroughly research their targeted audience members. The incredible uptake in digital media use by young people and the ongoing evolution of social media provide a regularly moving target for health promotion experts attempting to address adolescents' media use. Especially at younger ages, for example, the decision-making and developmental differences among members of different age groups often are significant. In addition, as young people age, their understanding of norms and peer group influences typically change. When practitioners fail to understand targeted audience members, their programming may be ineffective or produce unintended and poorly understood outcomes that make it difficult to evaluate the effectiveness of media literacy training.

Some evaluations of media literacy, for example, have provided counterintuitive results. In some instances, participants have reported increased message desirability as a result of media literacy training (Pinkleton, Austin, Chen, & Cohen, 2012, 2013). This created a need to consider whether or not participants' responses to media literacy training reflected an improved awareness of message design techniques—and, therefore, a successful intervention—rather than a mixed or negative outcome. An analysis of data from two media literacy evaluations by Austin and colleagues (2015) indicated that media literacy treatments negated the effect of perceived desirability on participants' attitudes and reduced the effects of desirability on participants' expectancies among other outcomes. These results supported what the researchers deemed the "double-edged desirability hypotheses," that media literacy education can diminish the influence of desirable but largely fictional media messages regardless of its effects on participants' message affinity (Austin et al., 2015).

In addition, it is possible for media literacy training to contribute to an increase in some detrimental attitudes in young people, while also providing decision-making benefits likely to help reduce the influence of fictional media portrayals. Some scholars have suggested that when media literacy material is not carefully matched to the developmental sophistication of young targeted audience members or if researchers do not pretest materials interactively, participants in media literacy programming might take away incorrect messages (e.g., Byrne, Linz, & Potter, 2009). As a result, understanding targeted audience members well, while not a new concept in health promotion, is critical in the development of successful media literacy campaigns.

Next, as researchers work to understand and assess the effectiveness of media literacy training in reducing substance abuse, it is important for them to distinguish critical thinking, which involves the process of critical message evaluation—from skepticism—which is the result of critical thinking and results in more careful processing and message scrutiny. Research indicates that media literacy programming is likely to succeed when it helps young people engage in critical thinking regarding media messages (Lee, Cheung, & Cheung, 2016). When young people think critically about media messages as a result of media literacy training, their media-related cognitions should reflect skepticism, a sense of incredulity resulting in more purposeful and thoughtful message processing (Austin, Muldrow, & Austin, 2016). Research concerning the processing of media messages indicates that individuals do not exert purposeful, thoughtful control over all of their responses to media messages. This is of potential concern because entertaining media messages, digital marketing games, and other forms of immersive marketing environments potentially tap into young people's affective decision-making processes. In this instance, these messages might bypass systematic processing responses reflective of critical thinking. In addition, individuals may recall information without recalling its source or context, putting them at risk for believing inaccurate or untruthful content.

Because people do not apply systematic message processing to every media encounter, it is important to study the role of media literacy training in individuals' critical thinking about messages concerning alcohol use and their development of skepticism toward these messages. Ultimately, a key focus of media literacy evaluations should be a greater understanding of participants' development of healthy skepticism toward the messages they see in traditional and digital information sources. Understanding more about individuals' critical thinking skills and their development of skepticism will help researchers develop more effective media literacy-based health communication programming.

The parameters of effective media literacy training, including the potential role of individual differences in decision-making and media literacy outcomes, also require additional study. Message processing and the effectiveness of media literacy education likely is affected by a number of individual, sociocultural, developmental, and environmental differences among those receiving media literacy training (Pinkleton et al., 2013). As a result, the individual benefits accrued from media literacy education will likely depend on these and other variables. Researchers need to examine how differences in a range of participants' individual characteristics alter their ability to gain more or less from media literacy education and also how best to bridge these differences to develop more effective programming. Some research findings indicate, for example, that young people who are lower in terms of their media literacy-related understanding or are younger and in need of greater cognitive development may gain more from media literacy intervention than others (Austin & Pinkleton, 2016).

In addition, research results concerning media literacy and gender indicate there may be important gender-based differences in response to media literacy training. In particular, Chen (2013) found that a negatively valenced media literacy lesson helped to reinforce logic-based decision-making in adolescent males' interpretations of alcohol advertising, reducing their perceptions of realism and expectancies for drinking. Adolescent females, conversely, already had developed an understanding of the ways in which alcohol advertising uses attractive characters and unrealistic settings. The females in this study benefited more from a balanced media literacy lesson which contributed to their skepticism toward media messages (Chen, 2013). Research by Austin and colleagues (2016) indicates gender also may be an important consideration in understanding the role of personality characteristics on wishful identification, a decision-making variable typically affected by media literacy.

Ultimately, a variety of individual differences are likely to play a role in responses to media and to media literacy training concerning alcohol. As a result, researchers examining media literacy and ways to increase its effectiveness should further examine a range of individual differences in personality, sociocultural development, and environmental and other factors affecting media use and decision-making and behavior, and their role in responses to media literacy training. It will be important for scholars to continue working to understand message receivers' decision-making processes and the role of individual differences in learning and responses to media to improve the effectiveness of media literacy programming.

Next, researchers need to conduct additional research regarding the influence of specific pedagogical aspects of media literacy programming on learning and other relevant outcomes. There are a number of studies examining the effectiveness of a media literacy curriculum taught by either an adult or a peer educator, for example, without directly comparing the same curriculum taught by both an adult and a peer educator. It may be that lessons taught by peer educators are more effective because of participants' perceptions of source–audience similarity, for example. Conversely, the effectiveness of media literacy training may increase when education professionals or other relevant adults teach curricula because of their perceived expertise and authority. It also is possible that other instructor variables influence the effectiveness of media literacy curriculum training and that these variables potentially apply to all curriculum instructors in different ways.

In addition, Jeong and colleagues (2012) determined that the impact of media literacy curricula on decision-making outcomes increased as a function of the number of media literacy lessons participants received. This indicates that the success of media literacy training may be linked to lesson reinforcement. As a result, researchers evaluating media literacy training should examine curriculum specifics including message reinforcement, both as part of a regular series of lessons and as part of a delayed, booster reinforcement lesson or series of lessons. Clearly, additional research should address these and related issues that, while apparently relatively simple, could make an important difference to the success of media literacy programming.

In addition, researchers should consider the role of specific contents within media literacy curricula. Different lessons serve different intended purposes within a series of media literacy lessons. How do changes in the curriculum translate into different training outcomes? Is a general media literacy curriculum as effective as a curriculum created to address a specific issue or context such as alcohol abuse? Is it possible to take a series of lessons created for one context and, with some content editing, successfully apply it to other contexts? It will be important for researchers and health promotion practitioners to examine and understand the answers to these questions as they attempt to use media literacy to address a greater range of media-related concerns with a broader range of participants.

Finally, it also will be important to continue to use more sophisticated research designs and to continue to refine construct measurement in the evaluation of media literacy intended to reduce substance abuse. One of the biggest limitations of previous media literacy evaluations has been the cross-sectional nature of evaluation data which makes it impossible to draw conclusions about causality. In addition, evaluation findings typically are limited to single samples. Because decision-making models typically hypothesize that media message interpretations contribute to decisions over time, it is important for researchers to replicate and extend evaluation studies in a longitudinal, repeated-measures design.

The preponderance of research evidence indicates that media literacy education has tremendous potential to help reduce substance abuse and to strengthen other forms of health-related decision-making. Research findings indicate media literacy training can provide an improved understanding of the persuasive intent of advertising and improved critical thinking skills to help young people resist the allure of fictional messages concerning alcohol and other substances. Media literacy also helps correct young people's norm misperceptions and contributes to an increase in their skepticism, critical thinking skills, and efficacy to control their choices related to substance use. In order to more fully realize the benefits of media literacy, researchers must continue working to answer existing questions and extend the methods they use to include longitudinal, repeated-measures research designs. This will allow health promotion experts to tailor media literacy programs to the specific needs of audience members and take full advantage of the benefits media literacy training provides.

SEE ALSO: Advertising Literacy; Children's Judgment of Reality and Fantasy; Children's Understanding of Persuasion; Digital Literacy; Health Media Literacy; Learning from Media; Media Competence; Media Literacy and Smoking; Media Literacy in the Primary Grades; Media Literacy Outcomes, Measurement; Representations of Gender, Sexuality, and Women in Popular Music; Representations of Risky Behaviors

References

Anderson, P., de Bruijn, A., Angus, K., Gordon, R., & Hastings, G. (2009). Impact of alcohol advertising and media exposure on adolescent alcohol use: A systematic review of longitudinal studies. *Alcohol and Alcoholism, 44*(3), 229–243. doi: 10.1093/alcalc/agn115

Aufderheide, P. (1993). *National leadership conference on media literacy.* Conference report. Washington, DC: Aspen Institute.

Austin, E.W., & Johnson, K.K. (1997a). Immediate and delayed effects of media literacy training on third graders' decision making for alcohol. *Health Communication, 9*(4), 323–349. doi: 10.1207/s15327027hc0904_3

Austin, E.W., & Johnson, K.K. (1997b). Effects of general and alcohol-specific media literacy training on children's decision making about alcohol. *Journal of Health Communication, 2*(1), 17–42. doi: 10.1080/108107397127897

Austin, E.W., Muldrow, A., & Austin, B.W. (2016). Examining how media literacy and personality factors predict skepticism toward alcohol advertising. *Journal of Health Communication, 21*(5), 600–609. doi: 10.1080/10810730.2016.1153761

Austin, E.W., & Pinkleton, B.E. (2016). The viability of media literacy in reducing the influence of misleading media messages on young people's decision-making concerning alcohol, tobacco, and other substances. *Current Addiction Reports, 3*(2), 175–181. doi: 10.1007/s40429-016-0100-4

Austin, E.W., Pinkleton, B.E., Chen, Y., & Austin, B.W. (2015). Processing of sexual media messages improves due to media literacy effects on perceived message desirability. *Mass Communication & Society, 18*(4), 399–421. doi: 10.1080/15205436.2014.1001909

Austin, E.W., Pinkleton, B.E., Hust, S.J.T., & Cohen, M. (2005). Evaluation of an American Legacy Foundation/Washington State Department of Health media literacy pilot study. *Health Communication, 18*(1), 75–95. doi: 10.1207/s15327027hc1801_4

Brown, J.D., & Bobkowski, P.S. (2011). Older and newer media: Patterns of use and effects on adolescents' health and well-being. *Journal of Research on Adolescence, 21*(2), 95–113. doi: 10.1111/j.1532-7795.2010.00717.x

Byrne, S., Linz, D., & Potter, W.J. (2009). A test of competing cognitive explanations for the boomerang effect in response to the deliberate disruption of media-induced aggression. *Media Psychology, 12*(3), 227–248. doi: 10.1080/15213260903052265

CDC (Centers for Disease Control and Prevention). (2017). *Fact sheets – underage drinking.* Retrieved from https://www.cdc.gov/alcohol/fact-sheets/underage-drinking.htm

Chen, M.J., Grube, J.W., Bersamin, M., Waiters, E., & Keefe, D.B. (2005). Alcohol advertising: What makes it attractive to youth? *Journal of Health Communication, 10*(6), 553–565. doi: 10.1080/10810730500228904

Chen, Y. (2013). The effectiveness of different approaches to media literacy in modifying adolescents' responses to alcohol. *Journal of Health Communication, 18*(6), 723–739. doi: 10.1080/10810730.2012.757387

Gordon, C.S., Jones, S.C., Kervin, L., & Lee, J.K. (2016). Empowering students to respond to alcohol advertisements: Results from a pilot study of an Australian media literacy intervention. *Australian and New Zealand Journal of Public Health, 40*(3), 231–232. doi: 10.1111/1753-6405.12459

Hoffman, E.W., Pinkleton, B.E., Austin, E.W., & Reyes-Velazquez, W. (2014). Exploring college students' use of general and alcohol-related social media and their associations to alcohol-related behaviors. *Journal of American College Health, 62*(5), 328–335. doi: 10.1080/07448481.2014.902837

Jeong, S., Cho, H., & Hwang, Y. (2012). Media literacy interventions: A meta-analytic review. *Journal of Communication, 62*(3), 454–472. doi: 10.1111/j.1460-2466.2012.01643.x

Jernigan, D., Noel, J., Landon, J., Thornton, N., & Lobstein, T. (2017). Alcohol marketing and youth alcohol consumption: A systematic review of longitudinal studies published since 2008. *Addiction, 112*(Suppl. 1), 7–20. doi: 10.1111/add.13591

Johnston, L.D., O'Malley, P.M., Bachman, J.G., & Schulenberg, J.E. (2012). *Monitoring the Future national survey results on drug use, 1975–2011: Volume II, College students and adults ages 19–50.* Ann Arbor: Institute for Social Research, the University of Michigan.

Lee, A.Y.L., Cheung, C.-K., & Cheung, M. (2016). Bringing media literacy education into the school curriculum: A trilevel adoption of innovation model. In C.-K. Cheung (Ed.), *Media literacy education in China* (pp. 31–45). Singapore: Springer.

Pinkleton, B.E., Austin, E.W., Chen, Y., & Cohen, M. (2012). The role of media literacy in shaping adolescents' understanding of and responses to sexual portrayals in mass media. *Journal of Health Communication, 17*(4), 460–476. doi: 10.1080/10810730.2011.635770

Pinkleton, B.E., Austin, E.W., Chen, Y., & Cohen, M. (2013). Assessing effects of a media literacy-based intervention on U.S. adolescents' responses to and interpretations of sexual media messages. *Journal of Children and Media, 7*(4), 463–479. doi: 10.1080/17482798.2013.781512

Pinkleton, B.E., Austin, E.W., Cohen, M., Chen, Y., & Fitzgerald, E. (2008). Effects of a peer-led media literacy curriculum on adolescents' knowledge and attitudes toward sexual behavior and media portrayals of sex. *Health Communication, 23*(5), 462–472. doi: 10.1080/10410230802342135

Primack, B.A., Douglas, E.L., Land, S.R., Miller, E., & Fine, M.J. (2014). Comparison of media literacy and usual education to prevent tobacco use: A cluster-randomized trial. *Journal of School Health, 84*(2), 106–115. doi: 10.1111/josh.12130

Primack, B.A., Sidani, J., Carroll, M.V., & Fine, M.J. (2009). Associations between smoking and media literacy in college students. *Journal of Health Communication, 14*(6), 541–555. doi: 10.1080/10810730903089598

Siegel, M., Kurland, R.P., Castrini, M., Morse, C., Groot, A. de, Retamozo, C., & Jernigan, D.H. (2016). Potential youth exposure to alcohol advertising on the Internet: A study of Internet versions of popular television programs. *Journal of Substance Use, 21*(4), 361–367. doi: 10.3109/14659891.2015.1029023

Further reading

Austin, E.W., Pinkleton, B.E., Austin, B.W., & Van de Vord, R. (2012). The relationships of information efficacy and media literacy skills to knowledge and self-efficacy for health-related decision making. *Journal of American College Health, 60*(8), 548–554. doi: 10.1080/07448481.2012.726302

Austin, E.W., Pinkleton, B.E., Chen, Y., & Austin, B.W. (2015). Processing of sexual media messages improves due to media literacy effects on perceived message desirability. *Mass Communication & Society, 18*(4), 399–421. doi: 10.1080/15205436.2014.1001909

Bergsma, L.J., & Carney, M.E. (2008). Effectiveness of health-promoting media literacy education: A systematic review. *Health Education Research, 23*(3), 522–542. doi: 10.1093/her/cym084

Chang, F., Miao, N., Lee, C., Chen, P., Chiu, C., & Lee, S. (2016). The association of media exposure and media literacy with adolescent alcohol and tobacco use. *Journal of Health Psychology, 21*(4), 513–525. doi: 10.1177/1359105314530451

Chen, Y., Porter, K.J., Estabrooks, P.A., & Zoellner, J. (2017). Development and evaluation of the sugar-sweetened beverages media literacy (SSB-ML) scale and its relationship with SSB consumption. *Health Communication, 32*(10), 1310–1317. doi: 10.1080/10410236.2016.1220041

Jernigan, D.H., Padon, A., Ross, C., & Borzekowski, D. (2017). Self-reported youth and adult exposure to alcohol marketing in traditional and digital media: Results of a pilot survey. *Alcoholism: Clinical and Experimental Research, 41*(3), 618–625. doi: 10.1111/acer.13331

Pinkleton, B.E., Austin, E.W., & Van de Vord, R. (2010). The role of realism, similarity and expectancies in adolescents' interpretation of abuse-prevention messages. *Health Communication, 25*(3), 258–265. doi: 10.1080/10410231003698937

Primack, B.A., Kraemer, K.L., Fine, M.J., & Dalton, M.A. (2009). Media exposure and marijuana and alcohol use among adolescents. *Substance use & misuse, 44*(5), 722–739. doi: 10.1080/10826080802490097

Bruce E. Pinkleton (PhD, Michigan State University) is Dean of the Edward R. Murrow College of Communication at Washington State University. His research focuses on media literacy, media and health, and decision-making in the digital era. His work has been published in tier-one journals in communication, health communication, and public health. His research has been funded by the National Institutes of Health,

ABMRF/The Foundation for Alcohol Research, the Washington State Department of Health, and other organizations.

Erica W. Austin (PhD, Stanford University) is Vice Provost for Academic Affairs and Founding Director of the Murrow Center for Media & Health Promotion Research at Washington State University. Her research focuses on how media literacy skills and family communication practices about media contribute to health behaviors and civic involvement.

Media Literacy and Pragmatism

LANCE E. MASON
Indiana University Kokomo, USA

One can arguably trace the origins of media literacy to the pragmatism of Charles S. Peirce and his work on signs (see Peirce, 1958). Peirce's triadic theory examines signs, or the *representamen*, in relation to what the sign stands for, its object or *referent*, and what sense is made of the sign, it signified or *interpretant*. This trifold conception forms the basis of contemporary semiotic theory, which continues to inform contemporary media literacy. Peirce's classification of signs into three broad types has also been influential. *Icons* are the first category; they signify through resemblance and include photographs, maps, and diagrams. Signs of the second type are known as *indexes*, which signify by indication. Examples include gestures such as pointing, or sending smoke that indicates fire. *Symbols* are the final category. These have an arbitrary character and signify through rules and conventions—a category with examples such as formal language and other abstract symbol systems. These groupings have implications for media literacy because meaning-making is at least partly dependent on the characteristics of the signs that one is interpreting.

When we look at the early pragmatists, John Dewey's influence should also be considered. What media theorist James Carey (1989) later characterized as the Dewey–Lippmann debates of the 1920s were early attempts to ascertain how democracy could survive in a pervasive media culture that included the newly emerged technologies of radio and sound movies in addition to print. Walter Lippmann (1922/2010) declared that the power of what he called *stereotypes*, which were transmitted through the media, had replaced the direct, contextual experience citizens needed to intelligently participate in democratic matters. John Dewey (1927/1946) acknowledged Lippmann's insights, but insisted that, by bolstering the elements of direct experience for citizens in combination with a renewed emphasis on participation at the local level, democracy could thrive despite massive technological and social changes. This "debate" began what is still an ongoing discussion in American culture about the proper role of the media in a democratic society, which is a consistent consideration in contemporary media literacy discourse.

Dewey's conception of engagement between humans and their environments is also a formative factor in pragmatist conceptions of media literacy. Dewey's collaborator and fellow pragmatist, George H. Mead, first identified the anticipatory structure of communication, which is based upon what one expects to hear from the other. From this perspective, communication is irreducibly interactional and rooted in linguistic and cultural commonalities, while also requiring a degree of imaginative empathy from participants. Mead theorized that one comes to understand the self as a distinct entity by participating in the communicative process with others.

Dewey appropriates Mead's articulation of communication and extends it to all environmental engagement, which he eventually labels *transactions* (see Dewey & Bentley, 1949). This conception posits a mutual constitution between humans and their environments, which include the objects, tools, technologies, and other people therein. This term codifies in Dewey's social theory what was a long-standing emphasis on environments in his educational philosophy, in which he argued that the environment was the sole factor under control of the teacher and the main variable that should be modified in order to alter educational results.

The aforementioned insights from Peirce, Mead, and Dewey form the primordial stew for an approach to media education that expands beyond mere content analysis by emphasizing the lived experiences created by media environments and their consequences for individuals, social life, and democratic culture. Proponents include Neil Postman and Marshall McLuhan who, both in unique ways, apply pragmatism's concerns with embodiment and perception, along with its embrace of open-ended, fallible inquiry and its focus on consequences, to middle-to-late 20th-century concerns about electronic media. Both were also advocates of what has come to be known as media literacy education, even though they are better known as theorists than as pedagogues.

Although Neil Postman pulls from a vast range of sources in his work, he clearly draws upon the semiotic tradition of Peirce, along with the focus on lived experience and embodied perception from Dewey. He also shares Dewey's belief that democracy requires particular attitudes and behaviors from citizens, although Postman connects this concern more specifically to media technologies and the environments they foster.

For Postman as well as for McLuhan, the most important understanding for media literacy is that different forms of media create unique environments for experience, and each of these environments has inescapable biases that affect user perception, content creation, and ultimately the broader society, owing to altered individual and social practices. In Postman's book cowritten with journalist Steve Powers (see Postman & Powers, 1992/2008), the authors argue that media education should begin by considering how particular media are created. In the book's example of TV news, this involves examining who decides what is broadcast and what interests they represent. The authors also recommend paying close attention to the language employed on TV news by having students evaluate the descriptive, evaluative, and inferential statements made by anchors and reporters; and this should be followed by analyzing the connotative meanings of the statements.

Postman and Powers (1992/2008) contend that media literacy should foster an understanding of the perceptual meaning-making differences between pictures and language. Pictures communicate in particulars, whereas language is abstract and thus offers generalized ideas about the world. For example, one can view a picture of a rock, but it requires language to classify the object into a category known as rocks. Thus screen technologies such as television and video require language in order to communicate with any degree of precision about the world, yet the authors argue that images dominate the content of television, including TV news. They support this point by noting how lead stories in local TV news broadcasts often involve fires or other active carnage, because television favors images that change. The same story of a fire would likely be found deep within the pages of the next day's local newspaper, because moving images play no role in the print medium. The authors compare TV coverage of a fire with that of the national budget, which is an important matter of public interest but is not visually appealing and thus only receives momentary coverage. This demonstrates how media forms drive media content; it also highlights some concerns with the societal shift to screen-based news and information that the authors believe media-literate citizens should consider. In addition, TV news can only cover one story at a time, which, in conjunction with the profit-making motive, compels an emphasis on superficial coverage of matters that have broad appeal. By contrast, newspapers are able to cover a much wider range of events, some of which may only appeal to a small subset of readers because of the individualized nature of the medium.

Postman and Powers (1992/2008) also examine TV commercials, although their primary concern is not the content of any one advertisement but rather the collective message embedded in commercials. They argue that commercials are modern-day parables that instruct people in proper ways of living and, as a whole, contain the implicit yet incessant message that life's troubles can be quickly and effectively solved through the purchase and consumption of consumer goods, which the authors argue are displacing timeless virtues such as piety, restraint, and humility. This overarching criticism sidesteps media debates about user agency, as the authors acknowledge that viewers are not likely to fall victim to any particular advertisement. Their concern is, rather, that long-term exposure to such altered conceptions of the good is slowly shifting the social norms over time, with little conscious awareness. From this perspective, media literacy education can be conceived of as a process of bringing these matters to conscious attention and reflective examination by students.

Mason (2015) applies some of these insights on screen media and advertising directly to media literacy education, asserting that commercials exemplify screen media conventions in a compressed form, which can be used to understand more complex creations such as TV shows, movies, or documentaries. Taking a perceptual focus, the author suggests isolating each dimension of the ad—which includes images, sound, and written text—so as to analyze it discretely, which allows students to examine how screen media technologies combine perceptual elements in ways that often override sensory inputs and leave viewers with mere impressions. This process has severe implications for politics, as campaigns have learned how to exploit the medium to craft specific impressions of their candidate (or of their opponent) while offering little in the way of substantive policy positions. The author suggests transposing the commercial's spoken language into written form, thereby separating it from the imagery while exposing it to careful, reflective analysis. Mason (2015) states that students can begin to form conclusions about the subtle and pervasive influence of commercials by analyzing several examples and making generalizations across them.

While Marshall McLuhan does not fit neatly into the pragmatist tradition, his "probes" into perceptual changes in relation to the media expand lines of inquiry begun by classical pragmatists into electronic media and their broader societal effects. In 1977, Marshall McLuhan, Kathryn Hutchon, and Eric McLuhan published a book titled *City as Classroom: Understanding Language and Media* that provides a curriculum for exploring perception in relation to media changes (McLuhan, Hutchon, & McLuhan, 1977). Exercises set students upon an exploration of various environments using what the authors call *figure–ground analysis*. Simply stated, *figure* is what one notices within an environment, whereas *ground* consists of the things one ignores. What emerges as figure to one's perception depends upon the mediating factors of the environment. The authors have students begin by examining the school building and surrounding campus, then continue by investigating a plethora of items and technologies such as cars and money, along with traditional media like newspapers, magazines, books, radio, and television, each of which mediates human environments and thus alters figure–ground relationships when present. One exercise has students change the date of an older newspaper to a newer date; the purpose is to see whether this changes perception of the paper's relevance. This is followed by a comparison of newspaper and literary writing styles. The authors ask students to choose some literary tales such as "Little Red Riding Hood" and rewrite passages in newspaper style, which brings the techniques of both writing genres to the students' attention.

The authors of *City as Classroom* maintain that one way to understand the individual and social effects of media technologies is to imagine life without them. Drawing upon this insight, Mason (2016) asserts that figure–ground analysis can be useful in helping 21st-century students become more aware of the ways in which digital mediation structures their lives by employing such techniques to examine smartphones and social media platforms. Students could consider how interacting with friends or coordinating social activities would change and what other aspects of personal recreation and interpersonal interactions would be altered as a result. A powerful extension of this exercise, according to Mason (2016), would be to have students live without a particular piece of media or with all electronic media for a set amount of time, for example one 24-hour period.

Mason and Metzger (2012) insist that pragmatism, as an open-ended and holistic approach to inquiry, can provide a foundation for a media literacy pedagogy that incorporates elements from various approaches to media education. These range from the aforementioned analysis of media forms, exemplified by Postman and McLuhan, to a more conventional focus on analyzing media messages or the ideological emphasis of critical media literacy. The authors contend that a pragmatist conception of media literacy would integrate these approaches while stressing their various dimensions in particular contexts. This is largely consistent with Postman's and McLuhan's own perspectives. While Mason's and Metzger's investigations into media forms offer unique contributions to media literacy pedagogy, their inquiries also include critical examinations of content and ideology that tend to be more commonly articulated features of media literacy education.

Future work from this perspective could conceivably be used to further consider the uniqueness of new media environments, including by examining the individualized nature of news and entertainment on social media that are deeply influenced by algorithms. It could also contribute to considering how media literacy education should respond to what has become an increasingly polarized culture, in which citizens have little exposure to divergent lifestyles or perspectives, owing in large part to greater immersion in new media environments.

SEE ALSO: Civic Activism; Civic Media Literacies; Creativity and Media Production in Schools; Critical Pedagogy; Global Citizenship; Media Literacy Education and 21st Century Teacher Education; Media Literacy in Teacher Education; Media Production in Elementary Education; Teaching with Media

References

Carey, J. (1989). *Communication as culture: Essays on media and society.* New York, NY: Routledge.

Dewey, J. (1927/1946). *The public and its problems.* Athens, OH: Swallow Press.

Dewey, J., & Bentley, A. (1949). *The knower and the known.* Boston, MA: Beacon Press.

Lippmann, W. (1922/2010). *Public opinion.* Blacksburg, VA: Wilder Publications.

Mason, L.E. (2015). Analyzing the hidden curriculum of screen media advertising. *Social Studies, 106*(3), 104–111. doi: 10.1080/00377996.2015.1005284

Mason, L.E. (2016). McLuhan's challenge to critical media literacy: The *City as Classroom* textbook. *Curriculum Inquiry, 46*(1), 79–97. doi: 10.1080/03626784.2015.1113511

Mason, L.E., & Metzger, S. (2012). Reconceptualizing media literacy in the social studies: A pragmatist critique of the NCSS position statement on media literacy. *Theory and Research in Social Education, 40*(3), 436–455. doi: 10.1080/00933104.2012.724630

McLuhan, M., Hutchon, K., & McLuhan, E. (1977). *The city as classroom: Understanding language and media.* Agincourt, ON: Book Society of Canada.

Peirce, C. (1958). *Selected writings.* New York, NY: Dover Publications.

Postman, N., & Powers, S. (1992/2008). *How to watch TV news* (Rev. ed.). New York, NY: Penguin Books.

Further reading

Cherryholmes, C.H. (1999). *Reading pragmatism.* New York, NY: Teachers College Press.

Postman, N. (1979). *Teaching as a conserving activity.* New York, NY: Delacorte Press.

Postman, N. (1985/2003). *Amusing ourselves to death: Public discourse in the age of show business.* New York, NY: Penguin Books.

Postman, N., & Weingartner, C. (1969). *Teaching as a subversive activity.* New York, NY: Dell Publishing.

Lance E. Mason is associate professor of education and Senior Mosaic Faculty Fellow at Indiana University Kokomo, Indiana, where he teaches courses in social studies education and foundations of education. His research explores the foundations of media and democratic education and has appeared in prominent education journals, including *Curriculum Inquiry, Theory & Research in Social Education, Education & Culture: The Journal of the John Dewey Society, Dewey Studies: An Online Journal of the John Dewey Society, Social Education, Contemporary Issues in Technology and Teacher Education,* and *Social Studies.*

Media Literacy and Smoking

BRIAN A. PRIMACK
University of Pittsburgh School of Medicine, USA

MICHELLE S. WOODS
University of Pittsburgh Center for Research on Media, Technology, and Health, USA

JANIS B. KUPERSMIDT
Innovation Research & Training, USA

MELINDA C. BIER
University of Missouri, St. Louis, USA

ERICA W. AUSTIN
Washington State University, USA

Despite declines in smoking in recent decades, tobacco use remains the leading cause of preventable morbidity and mortality in the United States (US Department of Health and Human Services, 2014). Because 90% of all adult smokers begin smoking in their teens—two thirds becoming daily smokers before the age of 19 (US Department of Health and Human Services, 2014)—feasible and effective prevention programs that target adolescent smoking are urgently needed.

Media exposure is associated with adolescent tobacco use. Notably, among high school students, media-related cognitions significantly predict descriptive norms (i.e., perceptions of the prevalence of tobacco use) and students' perceptions of the social desirability of tobacco use (Elmore, Scull, & Kupersmidt, 2017). The magnitude of the effects of media exposure on adolescent cigarette smoking may be equal to or even greater than that of traditional risk factors such as sensation seeking and peer smoking (Primack, Longacre, Beach, Adachi-Mejia, & Dalton, 2012).

To address the influence of media exposure on tobacco use, organizations such as the Centers for Disease Control and the American Academy of Pediatrics endorse the use of media literacy (Centers for Disease Control and Prevention, 2003; Strasburger & Hogan, 2013). Media literacy aims to improve a participant's ability to analyze, evaluate, and produce media messages in a broad range of forms (Aufderheide & Firestone, 1993). These objectives may provide a framework in which adolescents become discerning consumers of media related to tobacco, which may subsequently make them feel empowered to make choices from a more informed perspective and less likely to base decisions on attractive but unrealistic or misleading media portrayals (Hobbs, 2004).

While media literacy programs have been frequently used to address adolescent health risks such as eating disorders, there have been comparatively fewer studies related to the impact of media literacy on smoking. For example, a meta-analysis identified 51 media literacy interventions, 6 of which were related to tobacco use (Jeong, Cho, & Hwang, 2012). Research examining the effectiveness of media literacy interventions on smoking outcomes has included both quasi-experimental and experimental designs.

Early studies in the field of media literacy focused on the feasibility, acceptability, and initial efficacy of school-based tobacco prevention programs that incorporated the teaching of media literacy skills. For example, a quasi-experimental study assessed changes in tobacco-related knowledge and attitudes among 10th-grade students who received a curriculum intervention (Gonzales, Glik, Davoudi, & Ang, 2004). The authors reported that the media literacy curriculum could be conducted and that students enjoyed it. They also found that students in the intervention classrooms had stronger anti-tobacco attitude changes at follow-up than students in comparison classrooms.

A second quasi-experimental study evaluated the effectiveness of a media literacy intervention among high school and college students (Pinkleton, Austin, Cohen, Miller, & Fitzgerald, 2007). The authors used a pretest/posttest one-group design to assess the effectiveness of a theory-based media literacy curriculum based on the message interpretation process (MIP) model (Austin, 2007). They found significant increases in reflective thinking around tobacco-related media messages and changes in the ability and motivations to resist smoking-related influences. A key aspect of this work was the finding that increased media literacy skills can diminish the influential effects of desirable media messages, perceived realism and peer norms, peer influence, and attitudes about advertising.

An evaluation using a similar design demonstrated the feasibility, acceptability, and initial efficacy of a multidimensional tobacco media literacy program with middle school students using a pretest/posttest design (Bier, Schmidt, & Shields, 2011). Results indicated that students' general and smoking-specific media literacy attitudes increased significantly over the course of the intervention; however, pro-smoking attitudes also increased. Despite this, students enjoyed the program, actively participated, and reported that the program would be effective for reducing youth smoking. These complex findings may be interpreted in light of the fact that there was no control or comparison group, and the effects may be a function of maturation. Alternatively, the curriculum might require modification to align more strongly with theoretical models regarding the mechanisms of media message influence.

Studies such as these indicate that media literacy programs are feasible to teach, acceptable to conduct, and can be learned. However, when there is no control group, it is unclear whether outcomes improve directly as a result of the intervention or because of other factors such as maturation or social desirability biases. Establishing that media literacy knowledge and skills have increased also needs to be combined with evidence that this knowledge and these skills predict targeted attitudes, beliefs, and behaviors. For these reasons, conducting randomized studies with control groups and carefully conceptualized outcome measures have made important contributions to this field.

Some early anti-tobacco programs incorporating concepts related to media literacy were not specifically identified as media literacy programs. For example, with the Hazards on Tobacco program, researchers reported small but significant improvements in understanding the role of tobacco advertising among middle school students in the intervention group by comparison to the control group (Beltramin & Bridge, 2001). While the overall program addressed multiple content areas, the researchers had particular interest in "the coverage of the informational and persuasive role of tobacco advertising meant to help students understand the potential impact of tobacco advertising on individual choice" (p. 270), which may be interpreted as related to media literacy.

One study assessed the effectiveness of an intervention designed to prevent smoking initiation among middle school students randomly assigned by classroom through comparison to a control group or to one of two different intervention conditions (Banerjee & Greene, 2007). While one intervention condition focused only on the analysis of tobacco-related content in media messages, the second combined activities related to both analysis and production (students developed their own anti-smoking advertisements). Results revealed that the combined analysis and production condition was generally most successful in reducing students' pro-smoking attitudes and intentions to smoke.

Media Detective, a media literacy substance abuse prevention program based on the MIP model, was designed to reduce children's intentions to use tobacco and alcohol products by improving critical thinking skills about media messages (Kupersmidt, Scull, & Austin, 2010). In a short-term randomized controlled trial (RCT), intent-to-treat analyses revealed that, by comparison to control participants, students who received the program significantly increased their media literacy skills. For example, they had a better understanding of the persuasive intent of advertising and less interest in alcohol-branded merchandise. Also, intervention participants demonstrated significantly better critical thinking skills, assessed using a performance-based, media deconstruction task. Finally, at posttest, students in the intervention group who had previously used alcohol or tobacco reported significantly greater feelings of self-efficacy to refuse substances in the future. These findings suggest the potential efficacy of media literacy education (MLE) for universal intervention as well as for selected prevention targeted at higher-risk youth.

Media Ready, another MLE program based upon the MIP model, was evaluated in a short-term efficacy trial with middle school students using a RCT design (Kupersmidt, Scull, & Benson, 2012). As in the findings of the evaluation of the Media Detective program, in the intent-to-treat analyses students in the intervention group significantly improved their media literacy attitudes and skills by comparison to the control group. Specifically, high-risk students in the intervention group who had previously used tobacco reported significantly lower intentions to use tobacco in the future than high-risk students in the control group. These analyses also supported the MIP model as a mechanism of change in MLE: the intervention changed media literacy attitudes and skills, and these changes mediated the reduction in intentions to use tobacco in the future.

Other researchers found mixed results for the use of MLE for tobacco prevention in a small sample of elementary school- and middle school-age students. Participants were randomized to media literacy lessons or a matched-contact creative writing program. Results suggested that, by comparison to the control group, the media literacy group improved during the course of the intervention; however, the authors also found that expectations of smoking increased in participants aged 10 and younger (Kaestle, Chen, Estabrooks, Zoellner, & Bigby, 2013).

AD IT UP, an anti-tobacco media literacy program used with ninth-grade students randomized by classroom to a media literacy curriculum or a standard educational program, was evaluated using a cluster-RCT design to analyze program efficacy and to strengthen the assessment of acceptability in terms of methodology (Primack, Douglas, Land, Miller, & Fine, 2014; Primack, Fine, Yang, Wickett, & Zickmund, 2009). In an intent-to-treat analysis, smoking media literacy changed more among intervention participants than among control participants. Intervention students exhibited a greater reduction in descriptive norms for smoking (i.e., in their perceptions of the prevalence of smoking). Independently coded data revealed that in open-ended questions intervention participants had more responses that rated the program as compelling than did students in the control group.

On the basis of the success of AD IT UP, a web-based adaptation was developed to minimize barriers to accessibility and sustainability in terms of cost, teacher training, and standardization of delivery. The web-based version was evaluated using a crossover randomized trial design (Shensa, Phelps-Tschang, Miller, & Primack, 2015). Analysis revealed a significant effect for intervention on improved smoking media literacy attitudes for students in the intervention condition.

Another recent study explored whether an online MLE program, Media Detective Family (MDF), completed by parents with their elementary school-age children, could be an effective approach to substance abuse prevention (Scull, Kupersmidt, & Weatherholt, 2016). In a small RCT that included an active control group in a pretest/posttest and three-month follow-up, children who received the MDF program reported a significant reduction in their use of tobacco and alcohol by comparison to children who did not receive the MDF program. These findings are important in that they demonstrate that convenient web-based programming completed with a parent can teach media literacy skills and prevent smoking in elementary school children.

One important direction for future intervention and research will involve using additional study designs. For example, most prevention programs have been relatively brief and do not include booster sessions for sustaining change in cognitions and behavior over time. Thus there is a great need for studies using longer-term longitudinal randomized controlled trial designs to examine the efficacy of MLE programs for reducing and preventing tobacco use.

Another direction for future research will involve continued exploration into the mechanisms behind MLE. Many studies were developed on the basis of the MIP model and suggest its applicability. However, mediating variables may differ across different developmental age groups. For example, media literacy cognitions may be more highly developed in older groups of youth (e.g., high school and college students) and other substance-related cognitions, such as descriptive norms, may be essential targets for intervention that reflect the profound influence of the peer group on behavior—as found in a recent evaluation of the effectiveness of the Media Aware program for high school students (Kupersmidt & Scull, 2013).

Another challenge for media literacy programming will be to optimally determine the most effective format for interventions. For example, in-person programs are valuable because of the personalized attention they can provide, while web-based programs can be associated with greater implementation fidelity. Retention rate and selection bias should also be taken into consideration for establishing the validity of intervention studies.

Finally, another important direction for future research will be to examine the potential value of MLE around alternative forms of tobacco use. Recent reports indicate that the 30-day prevalence of E-cigarette use and waterpipe (also known as hookah) smoking is now greater than the 30-day prevalence of traditional smoking. While it is understandable that prior research has focused on traditional smoking, it will be important for interventions to adapt to a changing landscape of tobacco control.

SEE ALSO: Advertising Literacy; Health Literacy; Health Media Literacy; Literacy, Technology, and Media; Pediatric Perspectives on Media Literacy; Representations of Risky Behaviors

References

Aufderheide, P., & Firestone, C. (1993). *Media literacy: A report of the national leadership conference on media literacy*. Queenstown, MD: Aspen Institute.

Austin, E.W. (2007). Message interpretation process. In J.J. Arnett (Ed.), *Encyclopedia of children, adolescents, and the media* (Vol. 1, pp. 535–536). Thousand Oaks, CA: SAGE.

Banerjee, S.C., & Greene, K. (2007). Antismoking initiatives: Effects of analysis versus production media literacy interventions on smoking-related attitude, norm, and behavioral intention. *Health Communication, 22*(1), 37–48. doi: 10.1080/10410230701310281

Beltramin, P., & Bridge, R. (2001). Relationship between tobacco advertising and youth smoking: Assessing the effectiveness of a school-based, antismoking intervention program. *Journal of Consumer Interests, 35*(21), 263–277.

Bier, M.C., Schmidt, S.J., & Shields, D. (2011). School-based smoking prevention with media literacy: A pilot study. *Journal of Media Literacy Education, 2*(3), 185–198.

Centers for Disease Control and Prevention. (2003). *Designing and implementing an effective tobacco counter-marketing campaign*. Atlanta, GA: Centers for Disease Control and Prevention. Retrieved from http://www.webcitation.org/6dJCGMBKb

Elmore, K.C., Scull, T.M., & Kupersmidt, J.B. (2017). Media as a "super peer": How adolescents interpret media messages predicts their perception of alcohol and tobacco use norms. *Journal of Youth and Adolescence, 46*(2), 376–387. doi: 10.1007/s10964-016-0609-9

Gonzales, R., Glik, D., Davoudi, M., & Ang, A. (2004). Media literacy and public health: Integrating theory, research, and practice for tobacco control. *American Behavioral Scientist, 88*(2), 189–201. doi: 10.1177/0002764204267263

Hobbs, R. (2004). The seven great debates in the media literacy movement. *American Behavioral Scientist, 48*(1), 42–59. doi: 10.1111/j.1460-2466.1998.tb02734.x

Jeong, S.H., Cho, H., & Hwang, Y. (2012). Media literacy interventions: A meta-analytic review. *Journal of Communication, 62*(3), 454–472. doi: 10.1111/j.1460-2466.2012.01643.x

Kaestle, C.E., Chen, Y., Estabrooks, P.A., Zoellner, J., & Bigby, B. (2013). Pilot evaluation of a media literacy program for tobacco prevention targeting early adolescents shows mixed results. *American Journal of Health Promotion, 27*(6), 366–369. doi: 10.4278/ajhp.120221-ARB-105

Kupersmidt, J.B., & Scull, T.M. (2013). An evaluation of the efficacy of media literacy education for substance abuse prevention in high school students. Paper presented at the annual meeting of the Society for Prevention Research, San Francisco, CA, May.

Kupersmidt, J.B., Scull, T.M., & Austin, E.W. (2010). Media literacy education for elementary school substance use prevention: Study of Media Detective. *Pediatrics, 126*(3), 525–531. doi: 10.1542/peds.2010-0068

Kupersmidt, J.B., Scull, T.M., & Benson, J.W. (2012). Improving media message interpretation processing skills to promote healthy decision making about substance use: The effects of the middle school Media Ready curriculum. *Journal of Health Communication, 17*(5), 546–563. doi: 10.1080/10810730.2011.635769

Pinkleton, B.E., Austin, E.W., Cohen, M., Miller, A., & Fitzgerald, E. (2007). A statewide evaluation of the effectiveness of media literacy training to prevent tobacco use among adolescents. *Health Communication, 21*(1), 23–34. doi: 10.1080/10410230701283306

Primack, B.A., Douglas, E.L., Land, S.R., Miller, E., & Fine, M.J. (2014). Comparison of media literacy and usual education to prevent tobacco use: A cluster randomized trial. *Journal of School Health, 84*(2), 106–115. doi: 10.1111/josh.12130

Primack, B.A., Fine, D., Yang, C.K., Wickett, D., & Zickmund, S. (2009). Adolescents' impressions of antismoking media literacy education: Qualitative results from a randomized controlled trial. *Health Education Research, 24*(4), 608–621. doi: 10.1093/her/cyn062

Primack, B.A., Longacre, M.R., Beach, M.L., Adachi-Mejia, A.M., & Dalton, M.A. (2012). Association of established smoking among adolescents with timing of exposure to smoking depicted in movies. *Journal of the National Cancer Institute, 104*(7), 549–555. doi: 10.1093/jnci/djs138

Scull, T.M., Kupersmidt, J.B., & Weatherholt, T.N. (2016). The effectiveness of an online, family-based media literacy education program for substance abuse prevention in elementary school children: Study of the Media Detective Family program. *Journal of Community Psychology, 45*(6), 796–809. doi: 10.1002/jcop.21893

Shensa, A., Phelps-Tschang, J., Miller, E., & Primack, B.A. (2015). A randomized crossover study of web-based media literacy to prevent smoking. *Health Education Research, 31*(1), 48–59. doi: 10.1093/her/cyv062

Strasburger, V.C., & Hogan, M.J. (2013). Children, adolescents, and the media. *Pediatrics, 132*(5), 958–961. doi: 10.1542/peds.2013-2656

US Department of Health and Human Services. (2014). *The health consequences of smoking: 50 years of progress: A report of the Surgeon General.* Atlanta, GA. Retrieved from http://www.webcitation.org/6dJFmoRUa

Further reading

Phelps-Tschang, J.S., Miller, E., Rice, K., & Primack, B.A. (2015). Web-based media literacy to prevent tobacco use among high school students. *Journal of Media Literacy Education, 7*(3), 29–40.

Primack, B.A., Gold, M.A., Switzer, G.E., Hobbs, R., Land, S.R., & Fine, M.J. (2006). Development and validation of a smoking media literacy scale for adolescents. *Archives of Pediatrics & Adolescent Medicine, 160*(4), 369–374. doi: 10.1001/archpedi.160.4.369

Primack, B.A., Sidani, J., Carroll, M.V, & Fine, M.J. (2009). Associations between smoking and media literacy in college students. *Journal of Health Communication, 14*(6), 541–555. doi: 10.1080/10810730903089598

Salgado, M.V, Perez-Stable, E., Primack, B.A., Kaplan, C.P., Mejia, R.M., Gregorich, S.E., & Alderete, E. (2012). Association of media literacy with cigarette smoking among youth in Jujuy, Argentina. *Nicotine & Tobacco Research, 14*(5), 516–521. doi: 10.1093/ntr/ntr240

Brian A. Primack, MD, PhD, is professor of medicine, pediatrics, and clinical and translational science, Bernice L. and Morton S. Lerner Endowed Chair, Dean of the Honors College, and director of the Center for Research on Media, Technology, and Health at the University of Pittsburgh. He has written multiple peer-reviewed articles on media literacy and smoking, including publications in the *Journal of School Health*, *Pediatrics & Adolescent Medicine*, the *American Journal of Health Behavior*, the *Journal of the National Cancer Institute*, and the *Journal of Health Communication.*

Michelle S. Woods, BA, is communications officer at the Center for Research on Media, Technology, and Health at the University of Pittsburgh. She has coauthored an article on media use in education published in *Advances in Health Sciences Education.*

Janis B. Kupersmidt, PhD, is president and senior research scientist at Innovation Research & Training. She has developed or codeveloped and evaluated the effectiveness of five media literacy education, substance abuse prevention programs: Media Detective, Media Detective Family Night, Media Detective Family, Media Ready, and Media Aware. Her articles on substance abuse prevention, media literacy, and social cognition have been published in *Pediatrics*, the *Journal of Youth and Adolescence*, *Prevention Science*, the *Journal of Health Communication*, the *Journal of Media Literacy Education*, and *Psychological Assessment.*

Melinda C. Bier, PhD, is associate director of the Center of Character and Citizenship and senior research fellow in the Division of Educational Psychology, Evaluation, and Research of the College of Education at the University of Missouri, St. Louis. Dr. Bier is the principal investigator for Youth Empowerment in Action, which develops and assesses strength-based positive youth development interventions, including research on tobacco education and media literacy. She has written articles on media literacy and smoking published in journals such as the *Journal of School Health* and *Health Promotion Practice.*

Erica W. Austin, PhD, is vice provost for academic affairs at Washington State University. She has also served as director of the Edward R. Murrow Center for Media and Health Promotion Research in the Edward R. Murrow College of Communication. Her research on media messages and substance use has been published in *Health Communication*, the *Journal of American College Health*, *Current Addiction Reports*, *Mass Communication and Society*, *Communication Research*, and the *Journal of Health Communication.*

Media Literacy and Social Activism

KYOKO MURAKAMI
Hosei University, Japan

Media literacy is generally understood to be the set of knowledge, competencies, and skills needed to be an active citizen in a media and information pervaded society. Achieving "literacy" involves a learning process for gaining not only the basic skills and knowledge necessary to read, interpret, and produce various types of media text and messages, but also competencies which are needed to take part in a process of social and cultural change (Hobbs, 2015; Kellner & Share, 2005). Social activism, on the other hand, can be defined as socially and culturally motivated action for change that goes beyond conventional forms and behaviors. With the rapid changes that have occurred over recent decades in digital communication environments around the globe, various interdisciplinary scholarships relevant to media literacy have emerged in the realms of education, mass media, critical cultural studies, and media production (Hobbs, 2015), and some elements of social activism are inherently linked with these distinct disciplinary communities related to media literacy (Kellner & Share, 2005). As a result of this process, media literacy has become interconnected with social activism.

Activism is a process of social change (Hallahan, 2010), or "action on behalf of a cause, action that goes beyond what is conventional or routine" (Martin, 2007, p. 19). It involves a set of processes, forms, and approaches that promote social and political participation, movements, campaigning, advocacy, and engagement so as to bring about change in social, cultural, and political norms and values through individual and collective action. There are a wide variety of socially, culturally, and politically motivated actions and movements for change with themes such as human rights, the environment, world peace, or opposition to particular social systems or beliefs. The term *activism*, however, is not well defined and continues to morph and change depending on one's conception and value system (Martin, 2007).

There are three characteristics of social activism that can be associated with media literacy. First, activism in itself is not considered to be "good" or "bad," because its value depends entirely on the cause and the actions of the participants (Martin, 2007); the value of a particular act of social activism depends completely on one's judgement and beliefs as to which causes are worthwhile, noble, urgent, unrealistic, misguided, or even dangerous. Regarding media representation in relation to race, class, gender, and disability, for instance, those who enjoy dominant and prestigious status or positive representation may reinforce it as a social and cultural norm by exercising a number of media and power channels, while those who are marginalized, or negatively or passively represented, may protest against those representations, or may promote revised, positive images by utilizing media. Therefore, activism can be considered as a result or outcome of media literacy, depending on how one defines fundamental concepts of media literacy such as authors and audiences, representation and reality, and messages and meaning.

Second, although activism sometimes involves violent action against physical objects, such as defacing a website (Martin, 2007), almost all social activism related to media literacy as a part of civic engagement involves non-violent action. Gene Sharp (2005) identified the following three types of non-violent social action: (i) protest and persuasion, such as public speeches, slogans, banners, parades, or public assemblies including teach-ins; (ii) non-cooperation, including numerous types of social, economic, and political strikes and boycotts; and (iii) intervention, including psychological, physical, social, economic, and political intervention such as fasting, sit-ins, guerrilla/street theater, stay-in strike, or setting up alternative communication systems.

Finally, there are many more grassroots or oppressed social activists engaged in social activism than members of the power elite, which instead uses the mainstream media and advertising to promote their interest. Although there have been a wide variety of approaches to social change through media literacy, both historically and recently, most social activism associated with media literacy is, needless to say, non-violent, grassroots or oppressed activism. Thus, we will limit our examination to the three types of non-violent social action identified by Sharp (2005), and issues of media-, digital-, and cyber-related extremism, such as hacktivism, cyberterrorism, criminal hacking, and hate speech will be outside the scope of this entry.

New approaches in media literacy and social activism

Reflecting a growing interest in media literacy education around the globe, there has been much controversy as to the best methods of teaching it (Hobbs, 1998), a controversy which has had a significant impact on social activism. The four leading theoretical and conceptual approaches to media literacy (Kellner & Share, 2007) reflect diverse interests and methodologies, and as far as social activism or social activists in media literacy are concerned, these distinct approaches confront the questions of who is the vehicle delivering a message, and how and why they join activist groups or choose to participate in social activism.

Protection approach

The first approach to media literacy aims to protect audiences from the dangers of media effect and manipulation. The protection approach has been one of the most influential frameworks, not only for media literacy researchers, particularly those in the media effect tradition, but also for activists. According to the protection paradigm, parents and teachers are the most powerful agents of social activism, while researchers and scholars seldom engage in this type of activism directly. Those who believe in the power of the media's negative and positive effects often consider media audiences, particularly children and young adults, as vulnerable and passive (Potter, 2004), and advocate protection approaches to educators and parents in order to minimize the potentially negative and harmful effects of images and messages presented by the mass media and entertainment industries, especially those that relate to violence, stereotypes, consumerism, or biases based on race, ethnicity, or gender. There have been countless examples of protection activists around the globe who have had an impact by influencing legislation, learning environments, or technology use related to vulnerable audiences, particularly children. In the United States for instance, the Children's Television Act of 1990 required the television broadcasting industry to produce educational programming with a limited number of commercial messages.

Critical media literacy approach

The second approach is based on the belief that there is a complex set of hierarchical assumptions that one gender, race, class, or sexuality is superior to others. Shaped by several different philosophical orientations, such as postmodern and liberation pedagogy, feminist theory, multiculturalism, and cultural and media studies, the critical media literacy approach makes no attempt to be neutral in its struggle against oppression. Like the protection approach, the critical media literacy approach sees the mainstream media as the main source of denial of the inequities and injustices of society; thus, it also has the embedded assumption that mass media audiences are passive consumers of the cultural industries. Nevertheless, unlike the protection approach, this approach encourages teachers, students, and citizens to be active agents by critically analyzing media culture, representations, and discourses as social and cultural products or struggles, and by emphasizing the importance of learning how to use media as methods of self-expression and social activism (Kellner & Share, 2005). The critical media literacy approach, which is grounded on an inquiry-based, student-centered, bottom-up paradigm, has been employed by media literacy activists in a number of initiatives related to representation and messages, in an effort to confront social and cultural injustices, and disseminate principles of equality and social justice. Using examples of the creation of digital narratives and media products, Haddix et al. (2016) demonstrated the process of identity construction by contrasting typical representations of marginalized groups with authentic members of these groups, instilling students with a sense of agency and activism.

Media arts education approach

Influenced by both the critical media literacy approach and media literacy/education programs that encourage media production by students, media art educators try to cultivate students' sense of the esthetic qualities of media and the arts. They also encourage students to utilize their creative knowledge and skills as media producers to critically examine the dominant representations of the media while reflecting on their own esthetic experiences, and to transform their cultural and esthetic reality into arts and media. Although some scholars have noted a tendency for media arts education approaches to favor individual self-expression over social and cultural critiques of dominant narratives, or alternative media production (Kellner & Share, 2007), there have also been a wide variety of examples of social activism inside and outside of schools, as well as community-based programs, inspired by this approach. By examining the power of logos in visual and media communication, as well as the concepts of "subvertising" (making critical parodies of commercial advertisements), "culture jamming" (subverting media culture and institutions for progressive social change), and media activism, these projects have raised public awareness regarding important social issues related to inequality and injustice. Simultaneously, students experienced a sense of empowerment by examining cultural constructs and producing alternative media which challenged the hegemony of mainstream social and cultural representations, transforming the reality of their own world into an alternative context (Chung & Kirby, 2009). The media art education approach is probably the most radical approach among the four discussed here, in respect to social activism.

Media literacy education movement

The final approach is the media literacy education movement as a whole in the UK, Australia, Canada, and the United States. In these countries, many significant fronts of media literacy education have emerged, leading to the creation of a movement over the last three decades. Influenced by the action-oriented education ideas of Dewey and Freire, mainstream media literacy education leaders have advocated social and civic action through the asking of critical questions and the encouragement of reflection, in order to foster a sense of empowerment and citizenship. Although there are diverse ideas and approaches to media literacy education as a whole, three distinct characteristics of this approach as a form of social activism can be identified. First, most of the media literacy education movement that has been led by academics and teachers has occurred in the realm of education. Unlike the protection paradigm, which focuses on cultural and political defense against the negative effects of media messages, many media literacy education scholars have introduced interdisciplinary theoretical frameworks and implementations that are based on pedagogical values and practices. Second, both agents and audiences in this paradigm are viewed as fundamentally active, and most of them are even assumed to be choosing to consume mainstream media and cultural production and entertainment. Third, unlike the other approaches, the media literacy education movement approach is not always based on specific assumptions, such as a particular interpretation of social and cultural power dynamics, as in the media effect tradition. This affords ample scope for students' own spontaneous discovery and for the formulation of problem-solving strategies.

Limitations of media literacy and social activism and their future from global perspectives

Broad access to the Internet has enabled individuals to access, analyze, collaborate, interact, create, and act in highly networked communities where physical, geographic, and space–time boundaries do not seem to exist. Some scholars are urging young people to utilize digital and social media as tools for civic participation (Hobbs, 2010; Jenkins, Clinton, Purushotma, Robison, & Weigel, 2007), and to become democratically engaged, media-literate citizens who are critical thinkers, creators, and communicators, and thus agents of social change or social activism (Mihailidis, 2014). While there can be no doubt that the acquisition of media literacy competencies is essential for youth and citizens to become full participants in the civic life of our current media-saturated societies, or to become agents of social change or social activism, we are confronted by three general limitations of media literacy and social activism in regards to who can be a media-literate citizen, how we judge media literacy and social activism, and which knowledge and skills are required to be a media-literate citizen.

The first limitation is the demographic issue of the "digital divide," which refers to the geographical, economic, social, cultural, and generational imbalance in the use of information communication technologies. On one hand, the 2011 Arab Spring movement is a good example of social and political activism involving many young people who made extensive use of social and mobile communication tools, performed collective actions, and had significant impacts regionally and globally. On the other hand, the protesters were disproportionally young, media-literate or well-educated males, although the political participation of females was greater than in the past. Media literacy and social activism could be extended to all ages, classes, and genders, particularly women and less educated people, who may have fewer opportunities to practice media literacy in less developed regions or where communication technologies are limited.

The second limitation to be considered is that media literacy and social activism can face severe challenges if government, society, or cultural or religious norms restrict people's freedom of speech or freedom of the press. In countries and regions where these freedoms are tightly restricted by governments, or in which there are strict social and religious norms, citizens may have very limited freedom to express ideas about diverse alternatives to existing social, cultural, religious, and political perspectives. Therefore, engaging in critical thinking, one of the most important elements of media literacy, may be restricted, as well as any type of social activism which could result.

The incomplete perception of diverse and multicultural points of views is the third element limiting media literacy and social activism. Although there are enormous amounts of information and messages on the Internet, we typically search only for what we want to find and seldom search for other information. In addition, the major search engines that most of us use, such as Google, Bing, and Yahoo, employ so-called "search engine optimization" algorithms which rank webpages and content. This means that as more and more people use and search the Internet, they are likely to obtain value-laden representations from the most popular websites, and are less likely to be exposed to reality, to more diverse alternatives, or to information from other cultures. Without media literacy competencies, it is extremely difficult for youth and citizens to understand these biases when seeking information, and to participate in civic life or become agents of social change or social activism.

Concerning global perspectives, there are positive trends nevertheless. Although media literacy movements have occurred mainly in the developed countries of regions such as North America and Europe, there have been a number of regional, national, and international stakeholders that have promoted media literacy around the world. For instance, the United Nations Educational, Scientific, and Cultural Organization (UNESCO), one of the most influential supporters of media literacy activism, has been involved in creating various multinational and transnational networks and partnerships, and has published many teaching and policy-related books for the promotion of media and information literacy, both locally and globally, particularly in countries and regions where the concepts of media and information literacy are less widely understood.

Is an active, media-literate citizen a social activist? The answer is somewhat ambiguous, but it is safe to say that open-mindedness for social activism can be seen as a barometer of the maturity level of a democratic society. As people obtain better educations and have greater exposure to and understanding of social and political issues, they tend to become less acquiescent to authority. When systems do not work well, media-literate citizens may be more willing to take action for change by bringing a wide variety of social and mobile communication tools into action. Regardless of what one's position or perception is, it is clear that citizens need to acquire media literacy competencies in order to better understand the reality of their societies, and that media literacy has become embedded in the process of social and cultural change.

SEE ALSO: Active Audiences; Civic Activism; Media Access and Activism; Media Activism and Action-Oriented Learning; Media Industry Involvement in Media Literacy; Mediatization

References

Chung, S.K., & Kirby, M.S. (2009). Media literacy art education: Logos, culture jamming, and activism. *Art Education, 62*(1), 34–39.

Hallahan, K. (2010). Public relations media. In R.L. Health (Ed.). *The SAGE handbook of public relations* (pp. 623–642). Los Angeles, CA: SAGE.

Haddix, M., Garcia, A., & Price-Dennis, D. (2016). Youth, popular culture, and the media: examining race, class, gender, sexuality, and social histories. In K.A. Hinchman & D.A. Appleman (Eds.), *Adolescent literacies: A handbook of practice-based research* (pp. 21–37). New York, NY: The Guilford Press.

Hobbs, R. (1998). The seven great debates in the media literacy movement. *Journal of Communication, 48*(1), 16–32.

Hobbs, R. (2010). *Digital and media literacy: A plan of action*. Washington DC, WA: Aspen Institute Communications and Society Program. John S. and James L. Knight Foundation. Retrieved from http://knightcomm.org

Hobbs, R. (2015). *Media literacy*. Oxford Research Encyclopedia of Communication. doi: 10.1093/acrefore/9780190228613.013.11

Jenkins, H., Clinton, K., Purushotma, R., Robison, A., & Weigel, M. (2007). *Confronting the challenges of participatory culture: media education for the 21st century*. Chicago, IL: The John D. and Catherine T. MacArthur Foundation.

Kellner, D., & Share, J. (2005). Toward critical media literacy: core concepts, debates, organizations, and policy. *Discourse: Studies in the Cultural Politics of Education, 26*(3), 369–386.

Kellner, D., & Share, J. (2007). Critical media literacy, democracy and the reconstruction of education. In D. Macedo & S. Steinberg (Eds.), *Media literacy: A reader* (pp. 3–23). New York, NY: Peter Lang.

Martin, B. (2007). Activism, social and political. In G.L. Anderson & K.G. Herr (Eds.), *Encyclopedia of activism and social justice* (pp. 19–27). Los Angeles, CA: SAGE.

Mihailidis, P. (2014). *Media literacy and the emerging citizen: Youth, engagement and participation in digital culture*. New York, NY: Peter Lang.

Potter, W.J. (2004). *Theory of media literacy: A cognitive approach.* Los Angeles, CA: SAGE.
Sharp, G. (2005). *Waging nonviolent struggle.* Boston, MA: Porter Sargent.

Further reading

De Abreu, B.S., & Mihailidis, P. (Eds.) (2014). *Media literacy education in action: Theoretical and pedagogical perspectives.* New York, NY: Routledge.
Hobbs, R. (2015). *Media literacy. Oxford Research Encyclopedia of Communication.* doi: 10.1093/acrefore/9780190228613.013.11
Kellner, D., & Share, J. (2007). Critical media literacy, democracy and the reconstruction of education. In D. Macedo & S. Steinberg (Eds.), *Media literacy: A reader* (pp. 3–23). New York. NY: Peter Lang.

Kyoko Murakami, PhD, University of Kansas, is director of the Asia-Pacific Media and Information Literacy Education Center, program manager of CultureQuest Japan, and lecturer at Hosei University in Japan. She is also director and among the founding members of the Global Alliance for Partnerships on Media and Information Literacy (GAPMIL). Her research interests include children/students' collaborative activities and cross-cultural/inter-cultural understanding, media and information literacy and civic participation, and media and gender policy and representation in education.

Media Literacy and Visual Culture

SUSAN D. MOELLER
University of Maryland, USA

What is visual culture?

"Visual culture" encompasses all that we literally "see."

What is visual culture? It depends. What we consider to be visual culture changes in response to social and economic disruptions, technological shifts, alterations in networks of exchange, and upheavals in ways of thinking.

Visual culture is the brand recognition of McDonald's arches, Nike's swoosh, and a president's red trucker hat. Visual culture is the Standing Buddhas of Bamiyan, destroyed by the Taliban in 2001, but resurrected more than a decade later with 3-D light projection. Visual culture is Rudolf Nureyev's choreography of *Swan Lake* that privileged the beauty of the dancing of the male ballet lead as forcefully as that of the lead female. Visual culture is the outfitting of police and security services with body-cameras that act both as deterrents to abusive behavior and as records of violence and injustice after an attack. Visual culture is the story of the Koh-i-Noor diamond found in Andhra Pradesh that tells of the bad luck that befalls men who wear it—so the stone has become part of the Queen *Mother's* Crown of the United Kingdom. Visual culture is IKEA creating an app that uses augmented reality, so customers can see how the furniture will look and fit in their homes. Visual culture is artist Ai Weiwei's elegant Beijing Bird's Nest stadium that despite its iconic Olympic status was afterwards abandoned. Visual culture is a doctor who picks up a surgical instrument to operate on a patient hundreds of miles away, via a robot surgeon that cuts, removes, and stitches a patient's colon or hernia. Visual culture is Marcel Ophuls's film *The Sorrow and the Pity* that combined the narrative of contemporary interviews with the authority of documentary footage to get at the truth of the Nazi occupation of France—but left audiences themselves to judge who should be blamed. Visual culture is a Silicon Valley T-shirt with a graphic that mashes up the pixelated computer icon of a pointing finger with Michelangelo's hand of God reaching across the Sistine Chapel ceiling.

Visual culture is all that and more. Visual culture encompasses cereal box design and the shape of chicken nuggets, animé cosplay and toilets that are designed differently depending on the country.

Visual culture is also the sucking black hole of digital and visually intensive interfaces: Facebook and Sina Weibo, AirBnB and Yelp, the *New York Times* online and World of Warcraft, Skype and WhatsApp, Instagram and Minecraft, Fantasy Football and Pinterest. Visual culture is fans posting YouTube videos of themselves dancing to Bollywood music, Snapchat pushing get-out-the-vote messages to its users, riders choosing five stars when rating their Uber drivers, and digital natives checking their texts as well as their heart rates on their Apple watches.

Twenty-first century media are remaking visual culture, shaping it by algorithms, remixing it across economic and education strata, manufacturing it out of pixels, and dispersing it digitally. Critics used to sort visual culture into distinct categories: culture for elites with refined tastes and that for the masses in search of distraction. A Shakespeare play, high culture. A hip-hop video, low culture. Renaissance frescos? High culture. Sayings on T-shirts? Low culture. Yet ever since Lawrence Levine's pivotal work in 1988, *Highbrow/Lowbrow: The Emergence of Cultural Hierarchy in America*, scholars have recognized that "high" culture has always been shaped by "low" audiences, and vice versa. Moves to silo visual culture have simply been plays for cultural, social, and political appropriation.

In theory, aesthetics are the signature element of visual culture. Most often—as the tools of media literacy make evident—politics, economics, and technology are the central drivers of visual culture.

Control and power

Visual culture is a crowded and contested space. The range of actors and institutions with an investment in controlling what and how the public sees has always been wide … and it's widening. Every person has a right to access and participate in visually dense and rich culture(s), but media literacy trains audiences to recognize that not all can equally access that right. Visual culture is like water to a fish: we all swim in visual culture, but are usually unaware of our surroundings. Individuals can contribute to their visual surroundings. Indeed, media literacy gives audiences the tools to participate in visual culture—to imagine, create, construct, collect, curate, and commemorate their culture. Yet individuals do not control their culture. Individuals exercising freedom of expression may help shape visual culture, but their visual experience of the world is more thoroughly directed by the habits of the communities in which they live, corporate insights about what they as customers want, and the dictates of their governments. The tools learned from media literacy help observers track visual culture as it enters the global marketplace. Media literacy gives audiences the tools to evaluate the messages of visual culture and deduce what influences culture.

Visual "culture" is a plural experience, rather than a singular one. Visual culture may be liberating but it is also imposed. It is both shared and discrete, uniquely expressive and slavishly derivative. There have been moments when visual culture appears to celebrate a diversity of peoples coming to sing "in perfect harmony," as in Coke's 1971 ad of singers on a mountaintop or Apple's 1997 "Think different" campaign with its ad highlighting "the rule-breakers and trouble-makers who pushed humanity forward," such as Martin Luther King Jr., Maria Callas, and Mahatma Gandhi. And then there have been dark eras, of totalitarian enforcement, when the Hitlers of the world have suppressed the visual culture(s) they consider to be "degenerate." Audiences that are media literate recognize those who are invested in enhancing access to visual culture as well as those committed to circumscribing participation in culture—those who restrict the ability of groups and individuals to have a voice, who stoke biases and inculcate prejudices.

Visual culture can be accessible—or at least visible—across languages and literacies. But media literacy teaches that what individuals are able to see and what they are able to do about what they see may be a matter of human rights and justice. We take for granted when we wake up in the morning that we can influence our own environment, but media literacy reminds us what could happen if we woke up in a John Rawls "veil of ignorance" world and our situation in life had changed. As a member of the 1%, our windows would still have a wonderful view. As a have-not, we would wake up on the street, in a grey world controlled by others.

What is visual culture's relationship to media literacy? Three metaphors

The window

Visual culture, at its most basic, is framed by four questions (Figure 1): (Q1.) *How do we see—by means physiological, intellectual, and mechanical?* (Q2.) *What are the occasions, places, people that we see?* (Q3.) *How do we transmit what we see?* (Q4.) *What audience is doing the seeing?* Media literacy is a means by which these four questions can be considered and the space opened by them explored.

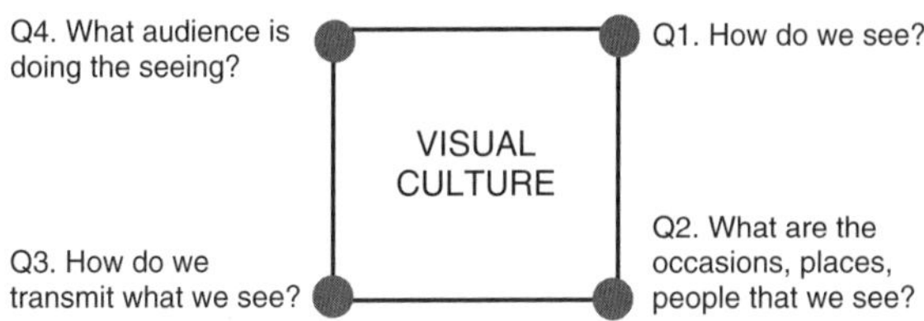

Figure 1 Window visualization.

Figure 2 NASA figure of a "normal" spider web (L) and a web by a spider given caffeine (R). As noted MentalFloss.com: "Caffeinated spiders made smaller, but wider webs, characterized by threads meeting at wide angles, disorganized cells and a lack of the normal 'hub and spoke' pattern." Sources: https://en.wikipedia.org/wiki/Effect_of_psychoactive_drugs_on_animals#/media/File:Caffeinated_spiderwebs.jpg and http://mentalfloss.com/article/51967/what-does-marijuana-do-spiders

The web

But conceiving of a window is not sufficient to describe all the parameters of visual culture. Visual culture is also a locus for engagement in the world, a locus that is less a simple connected geometry than a messy set of nodes. Imagine those webs created by spiders that are fed flies soaked in caffeine and that as a consequence dizzily repeat the toing-and-froing between one node and another while leaving additional sets of intersections inexplicably untraveled (Figure 2). The world's encounters with and creation of visual culture(s) are like those of the drugged spiders: audiences may be frantic in their concern with one node, while oblivious—and seemingly unconnected—to other expressions of visual culture. The tools of media literacy are valuable for those wanting or needing to investigate all the nodes of our culture—as well as valuable for alerting audiences to the hiccup of spaces in between.

The contrails

Throughout recorded history, visual culture has flowed from individuals and groups as they insistently describe themselves and participate in their worlds. Yet we are only beginning to teach the information and the skills that students—and adults—need to understand visual expressions. We teach toddlers to sing their ABCs. We teach children their times tables. We teach adolescents how to critique Shakespeare's plays. We teach

Figure 3 The contrails of an Airbus A340 jet, over London, England. Source: https://en.wikipedia.org/wiki/Chemtrail_conspiracy_theory#/media/File:Contrail.fourengined.arp.jpg

young professionals how to read a spreadsheet. But we are only beginning to teach the upcoming generations about how to access and make sense of visual culture. Media literacy training can help the public evaluate the contrails of visual data that are streaming past us in our ever more hyper-visual and visualized world (Figure 3).

The circular reciprocity of visual media and visual culture

Picasso is once said to have mused, "If I paint a wild horse, you might not see the horse … but surely you will see the wildness." Picasso knew that the visual arts don't slavishly reproduce what an artist is looking at; at their best, the arts illuminate deeper truths.

Media literacy tools help decode visual culture, assisting audiences to understand what has been visible as well as what has been invisible to them. And if one reflects that visual culture is not just an expression of the arts but of the sciences too, media literacy tools can help audiences understand how the sciences also aid the world to "see more" and "see differently." Galileo supposedly insisted "*E pur si muove*" ("And yet it moves") after being forced by the Roman Inquisition to recant his observation that the Earth revolves around the sun, a confirmation of the Copernican Revolution that remade how the public saw the heavens. In our time, NASA has shown truths invisible to human eyes, but made visible through new technologies of sight, such as its eXtreme Deep Field (XDF) image of the universe that stitched together the light from ancient as well as youthful galaxies into a "flattened" moment of time.

When audiences are media literate, they are more aware of what they see—and why they see what they see. American author and philosopher Henry David Thoreau wrote in his journal in July 1857: "Many an object is not seen, though it falls within the range of our visual ray, because it does not come within the range of our intellectual ray, i.e. we are not looking for it. So, in the largest sense, we find only the world we look for." What we see is shaped not solely by visual clues, but by expectations of what we are seeing or should see.

Media past and the new mobile and digital technologies present and future have framed and will continue to frame "our" cultural reality. Media, of all kinds, on all platforms, have always *reflected* as well as *affected* how we see and understand our world. Our visual reality is expressed and preserved in part through artifacts—tangible artifacts as well as fleeting virtual ones, meaningful in their time and illuminating in hindsight. In turn, those artifacts are reproduced for broad(er) recognition in and through media, interpreted and disseminated by media, and often themselves products of what we might call "the media." In short, *visual media* as a term of reference is not synonymous with *visual culture*, but media both shape visual culture and are the signifiers of it.

Today's Venn diagram that maps the zones of visual culture and of media would find a great deal of overlap—even beyond what Walter Benjamin envisioned in his 1936 essay on "The Work of Art in the Age of Mechanical Reproduction." Many media are part of the world's visual culture; many media report on visual culture. But a static Venn diagram would miss the trend line that has been long in the making. The trend has perhaps been obscured by an ahistorical understanding of the collective noun "media," which in many instances has been used as a synonym for "the news." Media are more than listserv updates, nightly newscasts, multimedia presentations, or weekly podcasts. Media are everything that is made to carry an idea or a bit of news.

Journalism and the authority of "seeing"

"Vision is the art of seeing things invisible," wrote Jonathan Swift, the author of *Gulliver's Travels*, in 1745. From Homer's coining of the phrase: "out of sight, out of mind" to Caravaggio's depiction of the Gospel of John's story of Doubting Thomas to Margaret Bourke-White's photos of the Buchenwald death camp, writers and artists and photographers have wrestled with the tensions between sight and recognition, looking and belief, seeing and witnessing. Their works have helped the world recognize what is there to be *seen*, as well as what has been present but has been *not-seen*.

Seeing is the 21st century's essential sense. "Sight" and "vision" are critical to the future of a plethora of fields and professions (Figure 4). Neurologists are learning about humans' phenomenal visual faculties, such as our ability to distinguish roughly 10 million different colors. Computer scientists are building on our physiological capabilities by creating new ways for us to interact with and process the world. Data *visualization* has become a means to track and curate what society is up to; the trends buried in the data are saving patients from cancer, improving just-in-time retail decisions, and finding the better ways through traffic bottlenecks. Physical seeing can now be mediated by augmented reality and supplemented by computer-generated information such as GPS (Global Positioning System) data, manipulated in real time through the simulated environments of virtual reality. Media literacy will increasingly be needed to guide audiences through the technological challenges, the economic opportunities, and the ethical and philosophical implications of our "seeing more" by our ceding aspects of our "sight" to the AI (artificial intelligence), digital, and robotic versions of ourselves.

"Seeing" is never just about "sight." "Therefore speak I to them in parables," the King James Bible reports Jesus saying to the multitudes, "because they seeing see not; and

Figure 4 Political cartoon by James Gillray, 1803, of George III peering through a telescope at a miniature Napoleon, after the King of Brobdingnag and Gulliver. Source: https://www.metmuseum.org/art/collection/search/391822

hearing they hear not, neither do they understand." The concept of "seeing" has moral force and moral implications. When one "sees," one understands. "Words are never enough," *Life* magazine wrote in a 1943 editorial defending its publication at the depths of World War II of a photograph of three dead American soldiers on the beach in Papua New Guinea. Nine years later, in 1952, *Life* published an essay of photographs of the dying and the dead from Hiroshima and Nagasaki taken in the hours after the atomic blasts. Again, *Life*'s editors wrote an accompanying editorial defending their publication of grim photos. They repeated a line they had written in the earlier essay: "Dead men have indeed died in vain if live men refuse to look at them." Only if one sees the world, does one understand the world. Twenty years after that Hiroshima editorial, on December 29, 1972, the weekly *Life* magazine published its last issue.

For the next several decades photographers struggled to support themselves; there were few publications that emphasized photojournalism. Revenue, even for the premier photo agencies, plummeted as the magazine outlets for their images shut down. Then came the Internet. While it took years for photo-intensive sites and platforms to work through their design and bandwidth issues, today it is rare to see a major news, entertainment, or retail site that is not led by its photos. And repeated studies concur that images drive traffic and frame how audiences see content. Images are once again recognized to be integral to the public's understanding of the world.

Seeing has always been more than verification, and visual culture more than a translation of what is seen, but at times those are their most potent functions. What is seen, and even the verbal description of things seen, can connect people and ideas and influence actions. That then is a role for media literacy: to help audiences investigate the authority of seeing, the credibility of being an eyewitness, the seductiveness of looking. Media literacy helps audiences consider how to communicate what has been seen and consider the responsibilities and the ethics of what they are seeing.

Pedagogy: media literacy and visual culture in the classroom and beyond

Media literacy is a core competency in the 21st century. The tools of media literacy are needed to assist students' understanding of the visual inundation of today's world, and address concerns of cultural responsibility, fairness, tolerance, and charity. Courses and class modules on media literacy help students decode the power and meaning(s) of the visual artifacts of the past as well as the present.

The growing insidiousness and intrusiveness of "seeing" has led to a greater need for media literacy training both of the young and of adults. Social media sites such as Facebook and Twitter that enable users to post photos, videos, and memes have short-circuited years of civic behavior, with the consequence that the direct-to-the-audience images are enabling trolling and the dissemination of fake news. The expansion of visual technologies has led to an erosion of privacy and enabled under-age sexting as well as governments' photo surveillance of their citizens. Individuals are using visual input to make conscious and unconscious decisions across the spectrum of their personal lives, swiping through apps such as Tinder that are shaping who people are attracted to, and apps such as Yelp that are changing where and how people eat.

As the public's need for media literacy skills has grown, media literacy "training" is increasingly occurring outside schoolrooms, through outlets such as satirical websites and late-night TV talk shows. Media literacy training also occurs via watchdog sites that fact-check the assertions of politicians and through public service announcements and advertising that address social issues and challenge viewers to (re)consider their assumptions. Even TV entertainment shows are teaching their viewers to be media literate, especially those shows that expose the foibles of modern culture.

The theory (and the expansion) of visual culture

In the 1990s and early 2000s, years before Twitter and Facebook launched, those in the "new" field of visual culture acknowledged that the definition of the discipline was a moving target. Nicholas Mirzoeff wrote in his edited book of essays, *An Introduction to Visual Culture,* that came out in 2000: "During this volume's compilation, visual culture has gone from being a useful phrase for people working in art history, film and media studies, sociology and other aspects of the visual to a fashionable, if controversial, new means of doing interdisciplinary work, following in the footsteps of such fields as culture studies, queer theory and African-American studies." He noted that "Postmodernism is visual culture," explaining that "While print culture is certainly not going to disappear, the fascination with the visual and its effects that was a key feature of modernism has engendered a postmodern culture that is at its most postmodern when it is visual" (2009, p. 4).

Three years later, in 2003, James Elkins, in his book *Visual Studies: A Skeptical Introduction*, tried to further define visual culture. As a discipline, he said, visual culture was "preeminently an American movement … younger than cultural studies by several decades." It was also "less Marxist, further from the kind of analysis that might be aimed at social action, more haunted by art history, and more in debt to Roland Barthes and Walter Benjamin than the original English cultural studies" (p. 2). Elkins noted that "The best brief definition I know is George Roeder's, which he borrows from Gertrude Stein. 'Visual culture is what is seen,' Roeder says, and continues: 'Gertrude Stein observes that what changes over time is what is seen and what is seen results from how everybody's doing everything. What is seen depends on what there is to see and how we look at it.' Given that a definition of visual culture would go against the grain of visual culture's ambition to remain fluid, Roeder's paraphrase of Stein does a good job: it is no more rigid than Stein's abstract grammar permits, and it hints at the viewer's share and the work that images do in culture" (p. 4).

A discipline, therefore, birthed out of the British cultural studies movement, excited by new theoretical approaches in art history and film studies, became cross-pollinated not only by material culture and media studies but by discourses of race and gender and growing interest by the humanities in examining the influence of political, corporate, and economic institutions on culture. Then the Internet exploded, and so too digital and mobile technologies.

Ten years after Elkins wrote his *Skeptical Introduction*, he returned to write another "introduction" to visual culture, this time to the field as the past decade had changed it beyond recognition. He again noted that many academics continued to make distinctions between "visual culture" and "visual studies," saying that "In general those who favor *visual culture* want to emphasize that the subject in question is culture and not vision, and those who favor *visual studies* want to stress the generality of the field and its commitment to visuality" (Elkins, Burns, McGuire, Chester, & Kuennen, 2013, p. 8). In this work, *Theorizing Visual Studies*, Elkins recognized more geographic and academic progenitors of the discipline, especially noting the *Bildwissenschaft* in German-speaking countries. Despite his careful timeline of the historiography of the field to date, however, he noted that the field of visual culture had undergone expansions so rapid that "no scholar has been able to trace" them. The book's most significant contribution, by many estimations, was his opening introduction observing the contributions of such theorists, authors, and journals as Michel Foucault, Jacques Lacan, W.J.T. Mitchell, Mieke Bal, and the *Journal of Visual Culture*.

The "field" of visual culture remains somewhat an artifact of its early years, variously defined, taught, and housed depending on its originating academic home on individual campuses, now scattered across the globe. Yet the field continues to change. Elkins's book, *Farewell to Visual Studies*, published in 2015, began with a searing critique of the field, in part arguing that for all its "blending" of different academic departments, for all that visual studies is "effectively a laboratory for thinking about relations between fields that address the visual," "visual studies remains a university discipline, and its spaces are seminar rooms, lecture halls, and libraries...." Among the great failings of visual studies, he observed, is that the field "is undecided about how it engages politics"; it does not "include theories of making; ... it has a disproportionate interest in contemporary fine art; ... its attachment to images is unclear"; and most damningly, "it uses images too cursorily, as illustrations or information; its images continue to merely illustrate or exemplify theories ... " (p. 9).

It is in those critiques that media literacy tools can be most helpful to the field of visual culture.

Cross-disciplinary engagement with visual culture

There are and have been a plethora of art historians and philosophers, scientists and public policy experts who have written on topics related to visual media and visual culture. Fifteen years into the 21st century an author in the academic journal *Mass Communication and Society* wrote: "The rise of visual communication as a field of academic research ... remains largely fragmented, preventing easy access for scholars, researchers, and students who seek a quick guide to visual media analysis" (Fahmy, Bock, & Wanta, 2014, p. 216). A summary of the literature that has contributed to an understanding of the visual in society, politics, and culture ranges from works in communication, journalism and science, history and art history, medicine, public policy, literature, and philosophy.

As notions of what visual culture *is* have expanded over the past several decades, *what* humans see and *how* humans see have become preoccupations beyond the originating field of cultural studies. Interest in visual culture and visual studies is evident among neuroscientists interested in unraveling the secrets of the brain, philosophers interested in unpacking the inclinations of the mind, and entrepreneurs interested in facilitating and monetizing how publics visually construct their environments. What humans (are able to) see has further become a preoccupation among astrophysicists searching for the universe's first light, molecular biologists advancing genome editing using artificially engineered nucleases known as "molecular scissors," and, perhaps more prosaically, among art historians interested in changing presentations of the self and literary critics interested in how one's mind's eye imagines verbal descriptions.

Among the leaders in the field of visual culture since the 1980s have been the prolific writers W.J.T. Mitchell, a professor at the University of Chicago, and James Elkins, a professor at the School of the Art Institute of Chicago. Elkins, Mitchell, and others based in the United States helped create and shape the field of visual studies in the United States, and in doing so, have drawn extensively on European theorists (especially German and French speakers, such as Freud and Wittgenstein, Derrida, Foucault, and Lacan) as well as on the robust American history of theoreticians. Many locate Walter Benjamin's influential essay "Art in the Age of Mechanical Reproduction," in 1936, as the beginning of the field of visual studies and culture, and credit writers of the 1950s and 1960s as the immediate "grandfathers" of the discipline—authors such as Marshall McLuhan, Rudolf Arnheim and E.H. Gombrich. Also pivotal in the conceptualization of the field of visual culture have been those writing specifically on photography, especially Susan Sontag and Roland Barthes. Sontag's later works, which also dealt with the impact of the visual on the public's perception of the world, have also been influential, especially *Illness as Metaphor and AIDS and Its Metaphors* (2001), and *Regarding the Pain of Others* (2002).

Other fields too have found deep interest in the intersection of visual culture and media literacy. They have included:

1. *Books in political communication and journalism that have considered the ethics and authority of images.* The discipline of political communication has long overlapped with the field of visual studies and culture, first as it investigated the role of television in the public space, and more recently as it has turned to examine social media and audiences. Early and still important voices in political (including visual) communication have included Neil Postman, Shanto Iyengar, Todd Gitlin, Kathleen Hall Jamieson, Robert Entman, Lance Bennett, Doris Graber, Stuart Ewen, Noam Chomsky, George Lakoff, and others.

   Within the profession of journalism, the concerns of visual culture arise in textbooks on journalism ethics, such as those by Paul Lester, as well as in texts teaching multimedia and broadcasting skills. In the specific field of international affairs and journalism, authors, including Barbie Zelizer, Susan Moeller, Daniel Pearlmutter, Lina Khatib, and Sonia Livingstone, have addressed the role photojournalism plays in the shaping and understanding of global news and policy options. There has also been a significant body of work considering journalistic images of the other; influential works on images of race and religion have included very personal investigations, by authors such as Ta-Nehisi Coates, and investigations of cultural representation, such as the books of Edward Said. Other researchers on visual culture have mined the history of how race has been visually constructed. John Stauffer and Zoe Trodd's book *Picturing Frederick Douglass: An Illustrated Biography of the Nineteenth Century's Most Photographed American* noted, for instance, that Douglass intentionally sat for so many photographic portraits to ensure a more accurate portrayal of black Americans. In an era of racist caricatures, such as blackface minstrelsy, Douglass believed the camera would show the true dignity of the black man. By contrast, other authors have traced how in the hands of many, photography became a tool to reinforce economic and racial distinctions; the Belgians in Rwanda, for instance, created photo ID cards in order to rigidly stratify the colonial population into tribes, categorizing them according to "scientific methods" such as measuring their "nose and skull size."
2. *Books in natural history and neuroscience that explain the science of how the brain sees, including how visual information is processed, and those in the field of neuroaesthetics and other disciplines that use science to examine and explain art.* A surprising number of scientists and doctors have written books for general audiences about vision and the brain: such works run the gamut from *New Yorker*-style pieces, featuring case studies of patients (neurologist Oliver Sacks's essays for example), to works authored by experts in computer science or computational psychology, such as those by James Stone and Donald David Hoffman, whose 1998 book *Visual Intelligence: How We Create What We See* explained that human eyes are not passive recorders of what is seen, but are instead "constructing" the visual experience.

Other authors—including neurobiologist Margaret Livingstone, neuroscientists Anjan Chatterjee and Vilayanur S. Ramachandran, ophthalmologist James Ravin, and Michael Marmor, an expert in retinal physiology—have become fascinated with the convergence of art, science, and technology, writing on the science of aesthetics and illusions and the role of vision and eye disease in the creation of art and the perceptions of the artists. Still others, including Sean Cubitt and Philip Ball, have written about how technologies have shaped why artists create what they do, or have written historically based accounts, such as those by Simon Ings and Mark Smith.

3. *Books on philosophy and literature, including those that consider perception, including how humans prioritize and represent sensory, including visual, experiences.* Elaine Scarry's signal work *The Body in Pain* (1985) set the stage for the past decades of cross-disciplinary investigations of how experiences are represented, and her later books, *Resisting Representation* (1994), and *On Beauty and Being Just* (1999) continued to expand the field. Works in this category also include literary critiques of individual books, authors, and/or schools or themes in literature: for example, examinations of Toni Morrison's and Gabriel García Márquez's literary depictions of sight and seeing.
4. *Books from art history: artists' biographies or books on themes or schools, and so on, of painting or photography or film or architecture, and so on.* It is difficult to pick up an art, architecture, photography, or film book that doesn't address the notion of "visual culture" or that doesn't exhaustively use the words "seeing," "sight," "vision," and so on. Quite a few deal with issues of "seeing," such as Glenn Most's book on the construct "seeing is believing" inherent in the Biblical texts on and paintings of Doubting Thomas. And there have been countless authors and museum exhibits (consider the many books of Svetlana Alpers, Simon Schama, T.J. Clark, and Neil MacGregor of the British Museum) that have emphasized the power and impact of artists' visions and the freighted relationships among artists, subjects, donors, and audiences that turn around the idea of visual culture. Public television too has repeatedly produced movies relating to how "we" see, using art as the experience with which to explore the core issue of culture: see, for example, various BBC series, including John Berger's films and book *Ways of Seeing*, Sister Wendy's *Story of Painting*, and Simon Schama's *Power of Art*.
5. *Books on technology and design.* Many of the books addressing contemporary design and technology seek to explain the emergence of the 21st century's visually dominated culture, including considerations of how people look at (e.g. eye-tracking) and process (cognition) information. As design and "design-thinking" have moved to the fore of product creation (thanks in many ways to Apple, and such design studios as frog design, Pentagram, and IDEO), "human-centered" design has both formed a philosophy of design and become a driver of the technology industry. What a product "looks" like matters, but is only one part of the form-and-function equation, as the seminal works by John Maeda and Don Norman identify. Many of the books from the design field are how-tos for designers and entrepreneurs, but some of the best (including those written by professors attached to MIT's Media Lab or to various centers at Stanford)

ground their discussions of design technology on cognition studies and other human-subject research. Then there are resources relating to the explaining of data, including considerations of data visualization. Many works representing this field are also how-tos, an approach perhaps expected in a young discipline, where making sense of visual data remains a significant challenge, although industries such as the tech and security industry that are investing heavily in such visually critical technologies as facial recognition and artificial intelligence are also represented by books considering both science and ethics.

SEE ALSO: Arts Literacies; Civic Media Literacies; Critical Information Literacy; Data Visualization; Learning from Media; Meaning-Making; Media Competence; Media Literacy, Terrorism, and Fear; News Literacies; Teaching with Media

References

Benjamin, W. (2008). *The work of art in the age of its technological reproducibility, and other writings on media*. M.W. Jennings, B. Doherty, & T.Y. Levin (Eds.). Cambridge, MA: Belknap Press.

Elkins, J. (2003). *Visual studies: A skeptical introduction*. London, England: Routledge.

Elkins, J., Burns, M., McGuire, K., Chester, A., & Kuennen, J. (Eds.). (2013). *Theorizing visual studies: Writing through the discipline*. New York, NY: Routledge.

Elkins, J., Frank, G., & Manghani, S. (Eds.). (2015). *Farewell to visual studies*. University Park, PA: Penn State University Press.

Fahmy, S., Bock, M.A., & Wanta, W. (2014). *Visual communication theory and research: A mass communication perspective*. New York, NY: Palgrave Macmillan.

Hoffman, D.D. (1998). *Visual intelligence: How we create what we see*. New York, NY: Norton.

Mirzoeff, N. (2009). *An introduction to visual culture* (2nd ed.). London, England: Routledge.

Scarry, E. (1985). *The body in pain*. New York, NY: Oxford University Press.

Scarry, E. (1994). *Resisting representation*. New York, NY: Oxford University Press.

Scarry, E. (1999). *On beauty and being just*. Princeton, NJ: Princeton University Press.

Further reading

Arnheim, R. (2004). *Visual thinking* (2nd ed.). Berkeley, CA: University of California Press.

Barthes, R. (2010). *Camera lucida: Reflections on photography* (Richard Howard, Trans.). New York, NY: Hill and Wang.

Berger, J. (1990). *Ways of seeing: Based on the BBC television series*. London, England: Penguin Books.

Bleiker, R. (Ed.). (2018). *Visual global politics*. Abingdon, England: Routledge.

Gombrich, E.H. (2000). *Art and illusion: A study in the psychology of pictorial representation* (Millennium ed.). Princeton, NJ: Princeton University Press.

Ings, S. (2008). *A natural history of seeing: The art and science of vision*. New York, NY: Norton.

Lester, P.M. (2018). *Visual ethics: A guide for photographers, journalists, and filmmakers*. New York, NY: Focal Press.

Livingstone, M.S., & Hubel, D. (2014). *Vision and art: The biology of seeing* (Expanded, rev. ed.). New York, NY: Harry N. Abrams.

Maeda, J. (2006). *The laws of simplicity*. Cambridge, MA: MIT Press.
Mirzoeff, N. (2016). *How to see the world: An introduction to images, from self-portraits to selfies, maps to movies, and more*. New York, NY: Basic Books.
Mitchell, W.J.T. (2018). *Image science: Iconology, visual culture, and media aesthetics*. Chicago, IL: University of Chicago Press.
Moeller, S. (2008). *Packaging terrorism: Co-opting the news for politics and profit*. Chichester, England: Wiley-Blackwell.
Schama, S. (2012). *The power of art*. London, England: The Bodley Head.
Sontag, S. (2001). *On photography*. New York, NY: Picador.
Stone, J.V. (2012). *Vision and brain: How we perceive the world*. Cambridge, MA: MIT Press.
Zelizer, B. (2010). *About to die: How news images move the public*. New York, NY: Oxford University Press.

Susan D. Moeller is the director of the International Center for Media and the Public Agenda (ICMPA), and Professor of Media and International Affairs at the University of Maryland, College Park, USA. She is cofounder of the Salzburg Academy on Media & Global Change in Austria. Her books include *Shooting War: Photography and the American Experience of Combat* (1989), *Compassion Fatigue: How the Media Sell Disease, Famine, War and Death* (1999), and *Packaging Terrorism: Co-opting the News for Politics and Profit* (2009). Moeller was formerly the director of the journalism program at Brandeis University, a senior fellow at the Kennedy School of Government at Harvard University, and a Fulbright professor in Pakistan and in Thailand. In 2008, she was named a Carnegie Scholar for her work on Islam and also named a Teacher of the Year by the State of Maryland. Moeller received her PhD and AM from Harvard and her BA from Yale.

Media Literacy as Contemporary Rhetoric

RICHARD BEACH
University of Minnesota, USA

The need for a contemporary rhetorical theory

Classical Greek and 19th-century rhetorical theory defined strategies for analyzing people's use of language in order to persuade audiences to adopt certain claims or beliefs. These strategies had three basic components: ethos—an ethical appeal to an audience that made it perceive a speaker or writer as credible; pathos—an appeal to emotion; and logos—an appeal to use of language and argument, components that focused primarily on the speaker's or writer's own rhetorical strategies.

In the 20th and 21st centuries, as people increasingly employed multimodal and digital tools for rhetorical purposes, there emerged a need for a contemporary rhetorical theory to explicate uses not only of language, but also of these multimodal and digital tools for engaging audiences. This explicating involved going beyond speakers' and writers' strategies for persuading audiences through the use of ethos, pathos, and logos to also consider how speakers and writers employ both language and multimodal and digital tools to gain audience identification with their beliefs or stances (Burke, 1969). Audiences are more likely to identify with a speaker or writer when that speaker's or writer's needs, beliefs, and goals are aligned with their own needs, beliefs, and goals, so that they perceive him or her to be knowledgeable and believable about their topic or issue (Head, 2016).

Tools for applying contemporary rhetorical analysis

The use of images, videos, and audio or music has resulted in increased analysis of the use of visual rhetoric strategies to engage audiences. Such analysis involves a focus on the use of artistic or cinematic techniques to appeal to or position audiences. For example, a close-up shot on a certain person or object establishes a connection between an audience and that person or object. Nazi propaganda films used to position audiences through camera angles as looking up at Hitler in order to portray him as a powerful figure.

Visual rhetoric analysis also focuses on the use of equivalences between a belief, a brand, or a product and certain status markers that may appeal to audiences. For example, advertisements for expensive cars portray their owners as living in upper-middle-class settings, thereby equating ownership of such cars with owners' class status. Fostering students' critique of how audiences are positioned to accept these equations involves encouraging them to resist being positioned as consumers on the basis of these equations. Students could identify how they were positioned as gullible through disparities between the use of a product they may not need and their life without that product (Begoray, Higgins, Harrison, & Collins Emery, 2013).

Contemporary rhetorical theory also builds on critical discourse analysis to examine how speakers and writers employ discourses defined as certain ways of knowing and thinking that serve to gain audience identification (Gee & Handford, 2013). Speakers or writers employ these discourses to invite their audiences to accept or reject their particular way of knowing or thinking about a topic. In online interactions, they construct a "discoursal self" based on use of discourses to project a certain identity to gain audience identification (Burgess & Ivanič, 2010). A politician may adopt a conservative political discourse to critique the control of "big government" as "encroaching" on "people's freedom" in order to construct his or her identity as a true conservative and to appeal to and gain identification from conservative voters. The news media or social media may frame certain topics or events on the basis of certain political, economic, or scientific discourses, which results in the creation of media "filter bubbles" that serve only to reify audiences' existing beliefs, limiting the degree to which these audiences are open to entertaining alternative perspectives on a topic or issue (Stewart, 2005).

Students also engage in cross-cultural virtual interactions that require a cosmopolitan openness for accepting differences in audiences' cultural and economic perspectives (Hull & Stornaiuolo, 2014). Analysis of online interactions between students in New

York City and students in India found that, through exposure to different cultural and economic perspectives, students recognized the limitations of their own cultural and economic perspectives (Hull & Stornaiuolo, 2014).

The need for students to employ rhetorical analysis and media production

Contemporary rhetorical theory serves a useful purpose in identifying the problem of audiences being overwhelmed by multiple, competing messages and images. In order to gain audience identification, speakers and writers employ attention-transaction practices designed to make something stand out in the midst of alternative multiple messages to capture attention (Lanham, 2007), and such practices result in increased use of sensationalized content or misinformation. This points to the need for instruction in rhetorical analysis of the attempts to gain audiences' attention through sensationalized content or misinformation.

Given the increased dissemination, on social media, of news stories with misinformation or disinformation, researchers have examined students' ability to engage in critical analysis of these news stories. In one study, 82% of middle-school students were not able to distinguish between an ad labeled "sponsored content" and an authentic news story on a website (Stanford History Education Group, 2016). These findings have led educators to adopt instruction to support critical analysis rhetorical practices in the media (Ashley, 2012). For example, the News 4 Literacy Project (http://www.thenewsliteracyproject.org) developed the "checkology virtual classroom" tool (http://tinyw.in/Ezpa) for analyzing examples of use of "fake news" stories.

There has also been an increased recognition that students are more likely to be motivated to learn to employ effective rhetorical strategies through civic engagement projects to instigate change on issues that concern them (Martens & Hobbs, 2015). In one project, students identified problematic mainstream media representations of issues in their schools to then create videos critiquing those representations (Garcia, Mirra, Morrell, Martinez, & Scorza, 2015). In creating their videos, students had to consider their audiences' potential responses or uptake, which led to an increased awareness of the importance of gaining audience identification.

Current and needed future research

There is a need for future research on the benefit and limitations of how social media create and foster relations with others. Given a focus on the use of social media to gain audience identification, one survey indicated that 57% of teens have met a new friend through social media and online game play (Lenhart, 2015); while they may prefer to interact with friends face to face, they often do not have the time or safe spaces to do so (boyd, 2016). Other research indicates that participation on social media serves to strengthen personal face-to-face relationships by maintaining connections through the online sharing of personal information (Davis, 2013). In using Facebook, students seek to identify with their "friends" by posting or sharing material they assume will be of interest to them, as well as "likes" or comments on the posts of their "friends" (Head, 2016). It is also the case that online sharing with peers serves as an outlet or relief valve—relief, that is, from the pressures of school work, given that "they aren't addicted to the computer; they're addicted to interaction, and being around their friends" (boyd, 2016, n.p.). On the other hand, adolescents' increased use of social media since 2012 has led to a decline in their psychological well-being (Twenge, Martin, & Campbell, 2018), which suggests the need for research on the limitations of excessive social media use.

There is also need for research on how speakers or writers create meanings associated with their audiences' responses to and participation in interactions. Such research includes analysis of speakers' or writers' projection of a certain persona or ethos, which may or may not appeal to audiences. In an online college composition course, Laura Ewing (2013) had her students reflect on creating an online persona perceived to be believable and credible by contrasting their persona adopted on a class blog with their persona on Facebook, Flickr, and Twitter. She found that her students were highly aware of the need to monitor their postings on social media, as they were concerned that these postings could be accessed by parents, relatives, or potential employers.

Given this focus on projected persona or ethos, researchers have examined how people construct online identities in which they portray themselves only in positive ways that preclude presentations of more complex aspects of their identities. One critique of Facebook noted that social media encourage "an identity that is extroverted, outgoing and even sometimes narcissistic; most importantly, one that would be approved by their peer group" (Pangrazio, 2013, p. 39).

There is also a need for research contrasting communication in lived world contexts versus virtual rhetorical contexts. When communicating face to face, or even when writing with others, users are relatively familiar with components of their rhetorical context, particularly their audience(s). When communicating in virtual spaces such as on social media sites, users often have limited knowledge as to the nature of their local or global audiences, so they may not know how to contextualize or frame their postings to achieve a certain (desired) audience response. Students may experience instances of what dana boyd (2014) defines as "context collapse" when they experience being simultaneously in digital rhetorical contexts with different audiences, for example when they share the same personal occurrences with both intimate peers and parents, on the same social media site.

Researchers have also examined students' ability to transfer their use of alternative digital and multimodal practices across different rhetorical contexts; for example, they have examined how students draw on their online writing experiences for use in formal academic writing (Anson & Moore, 2017). While students employ more informal language in online writing, they need to employ more formal language for writing essays in schools, and this requires an ability to determine differences in registers between their uses of language in these contexts.

Conducting the research associated with assessing students' rhetorical production requires the development of new criteria, based on not only use of language but also analysis of visual rhetoric. One useful set of criteria for assessing multimodal production was formulated by the National Writing Project's Multimodal Assessment

Project (MAP), which identified criteria from five domains: artifact (finished product), context, substance (content, quality, and significance of ideas presented), process management and skills, and habits of mind (Eidman-Aadahl et al., 2013). This assessment focuses not only on students' final productions, but also on their reflection on the processes employed in their analysis and production; and it does so in order to assess these students' awareness of addressing certain rhetorical contexts. For example, a student may reflect on how she employed certain processes, skills, and habits of mind to create a video in relation to the rhetorical context. For providing feedback on students' uses of videos as visual rhetoric, researchers and educators can employ annotation tools such as Video Ant (https://ant.umn.edu), which will help them identify specific rhetorical uses of cinematic techniques designed to produce audience identification.

To determine the relationship between knowledge of media literacy practices and media production, researchers can employ the new media literacy skills (NMLS) questionnaire, which is based on Jenkins's (2006) list of media literacy practices (play, performance, simulation, appropriation, multitasking, distributed cognition, collective intelligence, judgment, transmedia navigation, negotiation, visualization). This tool will help them find, for example, connections between scores on this assessment and higher consumption and production of new media (Literat, 2014).

In summary, contemporary rhetorical theory provides useful perspectives for an examination of rhetorical uses of both language and multimodal texts that are directed at gaining audience identification for the purpose of fostering change in audiences' beliefs and ideas. There is a need for instruction and further research on students' critical analysis of speakers' and writers' effectiveness in engaging their audiences.

SEE ALSO: Children's Understanding of Persuasion; Civic Activism; Resisting Persuasive Intent

References

Anson, C.M., & Moore, J. (Eds.). (2017). *Critical transitions: Writing and the question of transfer*. Fort Collins: Colorado State University Open Press.

Ashley, S. (2012). Exploring message meaning: A qualitative media literacy study of college freshmen. *Journal of Media Literacy Education, 4*(3), 229–243.

boyd, d. (2014). *It's complicated: The social lives of networked teens*. New Haven, CT: Yale University Press.

Begoray, D., Higgins, J.W., Harrison, J., & Collins Emery, A. (2013). Adolescent reading/viewing of advertisements. *Journal of Adolescent & Adult Literacy, 57*, 121–130. doi: 1002/JAAL.202

Burgess, A., & Ivanič, R. (2010). Writing and being written: Issues of identity across timescales. *Written Communication, 27*(2), 228–255.

Burke, K. (1969). *A rhetoric of motives*. Berkeley: University of California Press.

Davis, K. (2013). Young people's digital lives: The impact of interpersonal relationships and digital media use on adolescents' sense of identity. *Computers in Human Behavior, 29*(6), 2281–2293.

Eidman-Aadahl, E., Blair, K., DeVoss, D.N., Hochman, W., Jimerson, L., Jurich, C., … Wood, J. (2013). Developing domains for multimodal writing assessment: The language of evaluation, the language of instruction. In McKee & DeVoss (Eds.), *Digital writing: Assessment and evaluation*. Logan, UT: Utah State University Press. Retrieved from http://ccdigitalpress.org/dwae/07_nwp.html

Ewing, L.A. (2013). Rhetorically analyzing online composition spaces. *Pedagogy, 13*(3), 554–561.

Garcia, A., Mirra, N., Morrell, E., Martinez, A., & Scorza, D. (2015). The Council of Youth Research: Critical literacy and civic agency in the digital age. *Reading & Writing Quarterly: Overcoming Learning Difficulties, 31*(2), 151167.

Gee, J.P., & Handford, M. (Eds.). (2013). *The Routledge Handbook of Discourse Analysis*. New York, NY: Routledge.

Head, S.L. (2016). Teaching grounded audiences: Burke's identification in Facebook and composition. *Computers and Composition, 39*, 27–40.

Hull, G.A., & Stornaiuolo, A. (2014). Cosmopolitan literacies, social networks, and "proper distance": Striving to understand in a global world. *Curriculum Inquiry, 44*, 1544.

Jenkins, H. (2006). *Confronting the challenges of participatory culture: Media education for the 21st century*. Chicago, IL: MacArthur Foundation. Retrieved from http://tinyw.in/xB75

Lanham, R. (2007). *The economics of attention: Style and substance in the age of information*. Chicago, IL: University of Chicago Press.

Lenhart, A. (2015). *Teens, technology and friendships*. Washington, DC: Pew Research Center. Retrieved from http://tinyw.in/0G6p

Literat, I. (2014). Measuring new media literacies: Towards the development of a comprehensive assessment tool. *Journal of Media Literacy Education, 6*(1). Retrieved from http://digitalcommons.uri.edu/jmle/vol6/iss1/2

Martens, H., & Hobbs, R. (2015). How media literacy supports civic engagement in a digital age. *Atlantic Journal of Communication, 23*(2), 120–137.

Pangrazio, L. (2013). Young people and Facebook: What are the challenges to adopting a critical engagement? *Digital Culture and Education, 5*(1), 34–47.

Stanford History Education Group. (2016). *Evaluating information: The cornerstone of civic online reasoning*. Palo Alto, CA: Author. Retrieved from http://tinyw.in/crPc

Stewart, C.O. (2005). A rhetorical approach to news discourse: Media representations of a controversial study on "reparative therapy." *Western Journal of Communication, 69*(2), 147–166.

Twenge, J.M., Martin, G.N., & Campbell, W.K. (2018). Decreases in psychological well-being among American adolescents after 2012 and links to screen time during the rise of smartphone technology. *Emotion, 18*(1), n.p. doi: 10.1037/emo0000403s

Further reading

Delagrange, S.H. (2011). *Technologies of wonder: Rhetorical practice in a digital world*. Logan, UT: Computers and Composition Press.

Duggan, M., & Smith, A. (2016). The political environment on social media. Washington, DC: Pew Research Center, October 25. Retrieved from http://tinyw.in/ddlL

Eyman, D. (2015). *Digital rhetoric: Theory, method, practice*. Ann Arbor: University of Michigan.

Gries, L. (2015). *Still life with rhetoric: A new materialist approach for visual rhetorics*. Logan, UT: Utah State University Press.

Kuypers, J.A. (2016). *Rhetorical criticism: Perspectives in action*. Lanham, MD: Rowman & Littlefield.

Sellnow, D. (2010). *The rhetorical power of popular culture: Considering mediated texts*. Thousand Oaks, CA: Sage.

Richard Beach is professor emeritus, University of Minnesota. He has published books on teaching media literacy and digital writing as well as on teaching about climate change to adolescents, with attention to representations of climate change issues in the media. His current research focuses on use of languaging as social action for creating relations in the English language arts classroom. He served as president of the Literacy Research Association.

Media Literacy Education and Second Language Acquisition

HAIXIA HE
Ningxia University, China

In recent years, with the emergence of diversified new media and the development of fourth-generation (4G) networks, videos, websites, blogs, podcasts, Facebook, WeChat, mobile client, and so on have profoundly transformed the ways in which young people entertain, learn, communicate, and get connected to the world. Although the "anywhere, anytime" access to the Internet yields amazing benefits in education and brings students convenient access for their learning and daily lives, some of them become Internet, laptop, and smartphone addicts. Thus students need to be educated to be fully aware of the influence of media on their lives and on society. Strategies should be developed and applied to permit students to critically analyze the media, become independent from their influence, and open up their minds to embrace and experiment with new tools of learning provided by the information age. In a century like ours, the world needs not only a generation of specialists in English but also a generation of intelligent thinkers. In the context of developing modern information technology, it becomes a trend for the teacher to use new media to reform the teaching pattern of English in order to develop students' media literacy and stimulate their second language (L2) acquisition.

Media literacy education

The notion of literacy has expanded well beyond books and magazines, to include a wide range of multimedia concepts and forms such as graphic novels, comics, web pages, online fiction, e-books, reality programs, and advertising content (Vize, 2011, p. 78). Media literacy is a process of accessing, analyzing, evaluating, and creating messages in a wide variety of forms. It uses an inquiry-based instructional model that encourages people to ask questions about what they see and read. It is an extension of traditional literacy (listening, speaking, reading, and writing), which involves people's ability to analyze all kinds of information transmitted by media such as television, radio, web, newspapers, and magazines, as well as the ability to produce various kinds of media information with information technology.

Media literacy education has been an interest in the United States since the early 20th century, when high school English teachers first started using film to develop students' critical thinking and communication skills. During the 1970s and 1980s, attitudes to mass media and mass culture began to shift. Educators began to be aware of the need to guard against the prejudice of taking print as the only real medium that the English teacher has a stake in. By the early 1990s media literacy education began to appear in state English education curriculum frameworks as a result of increased awareness of the central role of visual, electronic, and digital media. It is gaining momentum in the United States because of the increased emphasis on 21st-century literacy, which incorporates media and information literacy, collaboration and problem-solving skills, and a stress on the social responsibilities of communication.

Media literacy education aided mainly by media technology provides a vast, updated linguistic resource of accents, vocabulary, grammar and syntax, and all kinds of discourse, which shows us language in most of its uses and contexts—something that neither course books nor classrooms can do (Sherman, 2009, p. 2). Many teachers of English as second language (ESL) introduce media literacy in their classes in order to bring real life into the classroom and provide a life-like context for learners to learn the language. Many media literacy-inspired activities can be designed to enhance students' critical thinking skills; and these can also greatly facilitate L2 acquisition.

L2 acquisition

L2 acquisition refers to the process of acquiring another language consciously or unconsciously. The American linguist Stephen D. Krashen (1981) frames language learning in two ways: (i) the learner naturally learns the form and function of the language through contact with it; (ii) the learner learns the form and function of language in a classroom environment. Krashen believes that consciously learning language rules in the classroom does not have much effect on language acquisition. Since the learner tends to directly construct a new relationship between language and thinking in a natural environment, there is no need for the learner's mother tongue to play an intermediary role in the process. On the other hand, language contact in a natural environment can greatly facilitate learners' practical language skills. Inspired by Krashen's theory, many English teachers try their best to create a classroom environment that comes as close as possible to a natural environment. Their goal is to motivate the learner through much L2 input and output aided by media technology that minimizes native language interference.

Language learners can improve if they experience the target culture and language in the classroom as a rehearsal for the real life. Thus media that present native speakers of English and contain abundant cultural information through videos, movies, songs, newspapers, magazines, live newscasts, advertisements, Internet, radio and TV programs could be broadly used in English classrooms to introduce students to authentic language learning. Since thinking and expressing oneself in English are crucial components in the process of learning English, it is better to foster and strengthen students' language skill of listening, speaking, reading, and writing by analyzing media with critical questions. To introduce critical media literacy in the ESL classrooms, teachers should not only consider the presence of media artifacts but also endeavor to teach about the media. It is by questioning these media that ESL students find the opportunity to engage in a critique of the culture while learning how the language works.

The implications of media literacy for language teaching: a case study in the United States

ESL teachers are beginning to explore the approaches to analyzing print, radio, web, and TV advertisements with the purpose of developing students' analysis, critical thinking, and literacy skills in ways that support English language learning (Hobbs, He, & Robb-Grieco, 2014, p. 7). Quinlisk (2003) framed media literacy as a way to pull back the curtain on media's power of shaping reality, as she described her own work with L2 learners in analyzing advertising, news, and issues of representation. Park (2011) used articles from the *New Yorker* with English language learners in South Korea in order to promote critical reading.

A case study observed by the author in a city of the United States can be a good example. This study was researched and examined by an experienced high school English teacher who taught ESL to new immigrants aged between 14 and 20 at a public high school. The research was designed to establish whether analyzing ads with critical questions could improve new immigrants' critical thinking skills and English language skills in a nurturing environment. A range of media and technology were used, including copies of print ads, library magazines, and a class website where students could view ads and write their comments on their own wiki pages. Focusing on strategies that involved the use of key critical questions on students' handout to analyze advertising, as shown in Table 1 (Hobbs et al., 2014, p. 11), the participating teacher used four instructional practices.

The technique of cloze

Students were asked to listen to an audio recording of the participating teacher reading a short passage that analyzed a print ad with the key critical questions, but omitted several key words. While listening, students were required to choose from a group of words provided in a box the correct words for filling in the blanks. In the process of inserting the correct word into the incomplete sentence, students had to use the meaning and the pronunciation of every word and sentence and to complete the exercise with the help of online dictionaries and translations, which enhanced their vocabulary.

The approach of generating questions

While viewing an ad provided by the participating teacher, students were asked to read the answers, which were sections of an analysis of the ad done by the participating teacher; then they were asked to match each answer to the key critical question on their handout. This approach deepened critical questions in students' mind as "tools" for analyzing all media texts that they may encounter in daily life. To generate questions,

Table 1 Key questions for analyzing media messages.

Audience and Authors	Author's Purpose	A1. Who made the media text? A2. What is the purpose? Why was this made? A3. Who is the target audience?
Messages and Meanings	Content Techniques Interpretations	M1. What is this about? What is the main idea? What are the messages? M2. What techniques are used to attract attention? What techniques communicate the message(s)? M3. How can different people understand the messages differently? M4. What is left out of the message(s)?
Representations and Reality	Context Representations Credibility	R1. When, where, and how was this shared? R2. What lifestyles, values, and points of view are represented? R3. Is this fact, opinion, or something else? R4. How does the message relate to reality? Are the messages true and correct?

Source: Hobbs et al. (2014, p. 11).

students had to read every sentence of the analysis carefully and understand it well, which was a useful way to practice their reading skills.

The practice in analyzing ads with critical questions

After analyzing some ads with the given answers, students were required to produce their own answers and analyze several ads by using the key critical questions. They were encouraged to express their ideas from any perspective by observing visual ads on a smartboard, which greatly improved their speaking skills.

The activity of collaborative writing on Wiki page

Students were required to choose and bring their own ad from a magazine for analysis with the key critical questions and to write full paragraphs. Once checked and corrected by the participating teacher on their homework, students were asked to discuss and type up several analysis paragraphs on ads to be posted on the Wiki website with their partner; then group presentations were made in the class, which created opportunities for students to practice writing and speaking skills.

An online pretest and posttest done by the participating students demonstrated that they did learn the key questions and concepts and could apply them to new advertisements as well as to different genres of media text, including newspapers and magazines. By examining improvement in students' advertising analysis, the study also showed that these instructional activities provide a meaningful opportunity for students to develop their critical thinking and practice their skills of speaking, listening, reading, and writing in English.

Media literacy instructional practices for WeChat-based activities in L2 Learning in China

Currently, new media are changing the ways in which teaching and learning have been done for centuries; and the traditional English teaching model in China has been greatly affected. In this new age of electronics, many schools are being transformed by a fleet of laptops, smart phones, and connectivity for 24 hours a day. More and more English learners can access a large number of vivid and authentic language learning resources through the web. Some social networks, such as WeChat in China and Facebook or Twitter in the United States can be used as platforms for designing activities that develop students' skills of critical thinking and language learning.

Taking as an example WeChat, a Chinese social media mobile application software, this application can be used to explore media literacy education activities with critical questions meant to develop English learning in China. From sending quick voice messages to posting videos and previously saved or live pictures and making online payment, WeChat is an all-you-can-use mobile service and the mobile phone software that is most popular in China and most frequently used by people of all ages. It is believed that, by using audio and visual media through WeChat and with effective critical thinking support, students can develop their language skills while practicing the sorts of critical thinking they will need to analyze texts. Hobbs and colleagues (2014, p. 7) have agreed with Barthes's claim that reading a text—whether it be verbal, visual, auditory, or interactive—depends on our ability to make the symbols mean something through the mobilization of a set of cultural codes. ESL instructors can send English audio and video materials related to the textbook to WeChat group platforms, for students to download them in a limited time. After listening, watching, and reading these materials, students can use text messaging, hold-to-talk voice messaging, and walkie-talkies to discuss the materials through the key critical questions, as shown in Table 1, to train their mouths and their thinking in a fixed time. To improve speaking skills, instructors can also encourage students to express their ideas from any perspective, to say anything relevant that comes to their mind, and to extend their thinking through broadcast messaging or videoconferencing from WeChat to the whole class.

At the beginning, the activities should be introduced and taught in class in order to help students become familiar with all the questions. Teachers can ask students some simple questions about their first reactions to the videos, for example, "What do you think when you see this? How do you feel? What made you think or feel that?" Then teachers can ask students to connect their thoughts to key media literacy concepts; they go on to ask the key questions and lead students to expand their answers. Finally students are required to write full paragraphs or texts, analyzing the video with the help of the key questions, so as to practice their writing skills and develop their vocabularies. Teachers can release reading material through the WeChat platform, which helps students improve their reading efficiency and grammar level.

Researchers believe that, by making it possible to analyze the media through key critical questions, WeChat can be used as a training platform for L2 listening, speaking, reading, writing, and critical thinking. More specific activities need to be explored and practiced later.

Expectation

The new ideas, means, technology, and platforms brought about by new media thanks to the continuous development of science and technology require students to timely grasp and make full use of knowledge resources and constantly enhance their foreign language knowledge and professional skills in order to become better persons for a new era. The use of new media on the teaching and communication platform can better promote teaching and learning and facilitate communication between teachers and students. The examples of media resources that can be introduced into ESL classrooms are numerous and the methods and instructional strategies described in this entry will be beneficial to students in practicing critical thinking, developing media literacy, and acquiring English. The case study with key critical questions designed in instructional activities and in WeChat-based L2 teaching discussed in this entry will give other instructors a concrete example of what is reasonable to implement in L2 teaching while developing students' critical thinking.

SEE ALSO: Literacy, Technology, and Media; Media Literacy and Visual Culture; Media Literacy with New Immigrants; Teaching with Media

References

Hobbs, R., He, H., & RobbGrieco, M. (2014). Seeing, believing, and learning to be skeptical: Supporting language learning through advertising analysis activities. *TESOL Journal, 6*, 447–475. doi: 10.1002/tesj.153

Krashen, S. (1981). *Second language acquisition and second language learning*. Oxford, England: Pergamon.

Park, Y. (2011). Using news articles to build a critical literacy classroom in an EFL setting. *TESOL Journal, 2*, 24–51. doi: 10.5054/tj.2011.24413

Quinlisk, C.C. (2003). Media literacy in the ESL/EFL classroom: Reading images and cultural stories. *TESOL Journal, 12*, 35–40.

Sherman, J. (2009). *Using authentic video in the language classroom*. Beijing, China: Foreign Language Teaching and Research Press.

Vize, A. (2011). Engaging ESL students in media literacy. *Screen Education, 61*, 78–81.

Further reading

Barthes, R. (1975). *S/Z*. New York, NY: Macmillan.

Barthes, R. (1983). *Empire of signs*. New York, NY: Hill and Wang.

Bremer, E. (2011). Unit plan for introduction to media and advertising: Cultivating critical thinking skills. Retrieved from http://teachingfilmandmedia.wikispaces.com/Unit+Plan+for+Introduction+to+Media+and+Advertising+Cultivating+Critical+Thinking+Skills

Hobbs, R. (2004). Analyzing advertising in the English language arts classroom: A quasi-experimental study. *Studies in Media and Information Literacy Education, 4*(2), 1–14. doi: 10.3138/sim.4.2.002

Hobbs, R. (2007). *Reading the media: Media literacy in high school English*. New York, NY: Teachers College Press.

National Association for Media Literacy Education. (2007). *Core principles of MLE*. Retrieved from http://namle.net/publications/core-principles

Wikipedia. (2017). Media literacy. *The free encyclopedia*. Retrieved from http://en.wikipedia.org/wiki/Media_literacy

Wikipedia. (2017). WeChat. *The free encyclopedia*. Retrieved from https://en.wikipedia.org/wiki/WeChat#cite_note-23

Haixia He teaches English in the School of Foreign Languages and Cultures at Ningxia University in western China and specializes in the design of media- and video-based language activities and curriculum to advance second language learning while enhancing students' critical thinking. Her recent projects focus mainly on the use of new media, especially massive open online courses (MOOCs) and micro-lessons as pedagogical tools designed to promote language acquisition and culture awareness. She has published over ten articles, coauthored more than two books, and done four research programs.

Media Literacy Education and 21st Century Teacher Education

ELLEN YEH
Columbia College Chicago, USA

GUOFANG WAN
University of West Florida, USA

During the past decade, media literacy education (MLE) in teacher education has changed dramatically. The focus has expanded from exploring ways to use media and technology as tools in teaching to integrating meaningful MLE into curricula (Hobbs & Jensen, 2009; Jolls, 2015). The main focus of MLE in 2007 was on pedagogy and practice in K-12 (i.e., US primary and secondary education) settings and on the relationship between MLE and content matter in cross-disciplinary subjects (Hobbs & Jensen, 2009). In 2010 the US Department of Education proposed a national education technology plan (see Hobbs, 2010), stating that, in order to adapt to the rapidly changing world, students must obtain 21st-century skills that comprise media literacy and knowledge across various content areas and disciplines, as well as the connections among them.

The 2010 plan encouraged educators to apply pedagogical strategies and approaches in guiding their students to interact with media content, popular culture, and social media communities as methods or tools for their learning (Hobbs, 2010). However, whether preservice and inservice teachers have the media literacy skills to guide their students remains controversial. In the past, educators were considered the "window of the world" and possessed the authority to provide knowledge and information, whereas now students are exposed to various multimedia sources in the digital world from an early age (Jolls, 2015). Students learn not only from their teachers but also from their peers and from various online platforms. Introduced in 2007, the *Core Principles of Media Literacy Education in the United States* (National Association for Media Literacy Education [NAMLE], 2013) reported that media literacy educators need to develop creative approaches in order to change traditional educational practices and enhance students' media literacy knowledge and skills (Hobbs & Jensen, 2009). To carry out these core principles, teacher educators and media literacy educators should not only continue to establish MLE in K-12 settings but also include teacher education programs that reach out to educators, share resources in various disciplines, and develop new relationships with community and media partners.

Given the importance and value of MLE, teacher preparation programs should include systematic, consistent, measurable, and scalable professional development opportunities for MLE at the global level. The United Nations Education, Science, and Cultural Organization (UNESCO) has developed and promoted MLE locally and globally. Education systems in other countries are fully aware of the importance of MLE (Jolls, 2012). For instance, the Office of Communications, the government agency responsible for broadcasting and telecommunications in the United Kingdom, provides resources and research for media literacy to educators across the country. Finland also adopted a national strategy and advocated for MLE (Finnish Ministry of Education and Culture, 2013; Jolls, 2015).

According to UNESCO's *Media and Information Literacy* (Grizzle & Calvo, 2013), the Canadian government was a pioneer and Canada itself was the first English-speaking country in the world to address and mandate MLE in the K-12 curriculum. The Canadian Teachers' Federation and Canada's Centre for Digital and Media Literacy supported a National Media Literacy week around the country. During this event, educational institutions and communities promoted and celebrated the works of students and teachers and offered a series of professional development trainings. The Ministry of Education in Ontario also sponsored the Teacher Learning and Leadership Program (TLLP) to promote teaching and learning strategies to support student achievement in MLE. Ontario provided additional qualification and certificate courses for educators in media literacy. Participants received a Specialist Certification in Media Literacy after attending the program. In Alberta, Athabasca University provided media literacy online courses not only for educators but also for parents and students (Grizzle & Calvo, 2013).

Defining media literacy and its role in the 21st century

In today's information and knowledge societies, people's lives are saturated with diverse forms of media and information technology and affected by the changes brought upon by these channels of media and technologies. To successfully and effectively participate in the 21st century, individuals need a new set of critical competences, related to locating, analyzing, evaluating, and producing information using a variety of media (Aspen Media Literacy Leadership Institute, 1992). Media literacy, determined by UNESCO

(2003) to be "a prerequisite for participating effectively in the Information Society, and part of the basic human right of lifelong learning," is defined succinctly by the Aspen Media Literacy Leadership Institute (1992) as the ability to access, analyze, evaluate, and create media, from print to video and the Internet.

Becoming a 21st-century citizen requires not only consuming and accessing information offline and online but also full participation in contemporary media culture. Therefore media literacy skills should be taught as part of formal education, especially in K-12 and teacher preparation programs (Hobbs, 2010). Incorporating media literacy into formal education has the potential to narrow the gap between digital divides, to bridge diverse cultural groups, to motivate learners to make connections across various disciplines, and to offer more equitable opportunities in multimedia environments (Hobbs, 2010; Meehan, Ray, Walker, Wells, & Schwarz, 2015).

Media literacy is one of the most crucial skills in this information-rich, rapidly growing digital world. MLE refers to teaching students the skills to (i) access and comprehend information in multiple forms (e.g., paper-based texts, digital texts, graphic designs, images, sound); (ii) analyze and examine ways in which online content is formed by identifying the sources and by evaluating the credibility and accuracy of the content; (iii) create content through the use of various media materials; (iv) reflect on one's behaviors and communication on the basis of social and ethical norms (e.g., appropriate use of language, images, sound); (v) participate as a member of a community by taking social action and responsibility as well as by working collaboratively to solve problems and share knowledge (Aybek, 2016; Hobbs, 2010); (vi) become culturally relevant in media literacy content (Gay, 2000); and (vii) understand fully critical media literacy and how to engage in the social contexts around individuals through issues of inequality and injustice (Kellner & Share, 2007), human rights and freedom of expression (Morrell, 2005), and participatory democracy (Mihailidis & Thevenin, 2013).

Statistics show that being an active participant in contemporary online culture is continually increasing. For example, more than 2.5 billion people—approximately one-third of the world's population—are registered on some form of social media (Statista, 2016). The Pew Research Center reported that more than 90% of teens in the United States log online daily, three-quarters of them actively using social media (Lenhart, 2015) and nearly two thirds creating content such as YouTube videos and posting pictures and texts on social networking sites (Lenhart, Madden, Smith, & Macgill, 2007). Other international survey data were collected from 65 experts in 20 countries to investigate MLE curriculum development in school settings (Fedorov, Levitskaya, & Camarero, 2016). Survey respondents included MLE experts from countries such as Armenia, Australia, Belgium, China, Germany, Hungary, Mexico, Russia, Thailand, Turkey, and the United States. Findings showed that experts ranked items associated with *participatory culture* as the most important learning outcomes among those listed. Unlike consumer culture, participatory culture involves making and sharing individual creations and productions on various online platforms such as social media. Additionally, participatory culture has fewer obstacles to personal expression and civic engagement (Jenkins, Clinton, Purushotma, Robison, & Weigel, 2006). This form of cultural involvement supports online media users as actively contributing agents rather than mere receivers of media content ("Participatory culture," n.d.). Fedorov et al. (2016, p. 329) found that "creating a media text for self-expression" (36.9%) and "creating a media text for participation in social/political life" (30.8%) are the most important media literacy learning outcomes that should be included in the K-12 curriculum. Teens are actively engaged in participatory culture, but how to teach teens to appropriately use and critically evaluate information online is crucial.

Since participatory culture shifts the emphasis of media literacy from individual activities to global community engagement, MLE must include social skills and intercultural competencies that need to be developed in addition to traditional literacy. Therefore, to improve these new skills, a systematic curriculum of MLE that includes more than just traditional traditional literacy is required. Inservice and preservice teachers play a critical role in preparing children and youths to acquire these skills so that they may be able to participate in the digital society fully. To understand better these concepts and obtain the media literacy skills, teacher preparation programs need to integrate MLE into the curriculum and to incorporate measurable and scalable media competency assessment tools and methods that understand inservice and preservice teachers' learning processes, challenges, and needs.

Reflection on needs and challenges in fostering media literacy in teacher education

During the last decade, MLE has grown rapidly, as policymakers and teacher educators advocated for its integration into teacher-training programs and K-12 curricula (Meehan et al., 2015). In 2009, Senator Jay Rockefeller proposed the Twenty-First-Century Skills Incentive Fund Act. This $100 million fund sought to offer students more curriculum options, including fostering information, digital, and media literacies. Its goal was to encourage students to go beyond the traditional academic context and to develop 21st-century skills such as critical thinking, problem-solving, communication, creativity and innovation, collaboration, contextual learning, and information and media literacy skills (Hobbs, 2010). Similarly, Congress supported the Healthy Media for Youth Act and offered $40 million to sponsor the development of MLE (Hobbs, 2010). These funding sources, however, are woefully inadequate when it comes to implement MLE successfully into K-12 teacher-training programs across the United States.

Despite teacher educators' efforts to push for MLE in teacher-training programs, media literacy content is often excluded from undergraduate teacher education curricula, especially in elementary education courses (Meehan et al., 2015). This absence (or only minimal presence) of media literacy in teacher preparation programs stems from myriad reasons, including national and state standards that primarily focus on core subjects such as English language arts, mathematics, sciences, social studies, and history. For example, technology standards are mentioned in Standard 1.5 of the Council for the Accreditation of Educator Preparation (CAEP) standards, but no media literacy criteria are included (Meehan et al., 2015). Additionally, inadequate access to technology equipment presents another obstacle for MLE (Gruszczynska, Merchant, & Pountney, 2013). Fedorov et al. (2016) suggest that the main challenges for implementing and developing media literacy curricula are a lack of communication and collaboration with administrative offices, curricula already filled with core content, a lack of systematic, fully developed teacher-training programs on media literacy, and insufficient research and funding support.

While both research and policy emphasize media literacy at the K-12 level, Schmidt (2013) suggests that, in order to narrow the gap between experienced media users ("digital natives") and novice media users ("digital immigrants"), professional development that builds MLE knowledge and experience for educators is the predominant factor that would motivate educators to teach media literacy. To date, unlike the majority of preservice and inservice teachers, who are digital immigrants, most K-12 students are digital natives who have been exposed to digital media (e.g., social media, pop culture, films, music) from a young age (Prensky, 2001). MLE aims to ensure that these children and youths, who are familiar with media and digital environments, understand the structure and functions of mass media and acquire the knowledge to critically evaluate media content (Aybek, 2016).

In spite of the importance of teaching media literacy in schools and of providing professional development materials that demonstrate how MLE can be integrated into school curricula (Wan, 2006), previous studies reported that preservice and inservice teachers lack confidence to effectively incorporate MLE into their curricula and feel unprepared to teach media literacy (Lauri, Borg, Gunnel, & Gillum, 2010; Stein & Prewett, 2009). In a study conducted by Aybek (2016), prospective teachers demonstrated low critical thinking-disposition scores in media literacy. Media literacy levels also vary significantly according to gender, age, and content across subject groups (Hargittai, 2010; Jones, 2013; Lauri et al., 2010). Given these research findings, it is important to integrate MLE into higher-education curricula, and especially into K-12 teacher preparation programs.

As MLE has yet to be fully incorporated into mainstream education, little systematic research has been conducted to investigate ways to implement media literacy effectively into K-12 settings and teacher preparation programs (Jolls, 2015). The Center for Media Literacy (CML) offered multiple teacher-training workshops for K-12 teachers, ranging from short introductory training sessions in media literacy to one-week intensive programs with mentoring and take-home assignments. Center data revealed different learning outcomes for participants: some teachers, who acquired media literacy skills immediately, applied them to their current curricula, whereas others required at least a year of transition (Jolls, 2015; Jolls & Grande, 2005). The CML also conducted a longitudinal evaluation of the program Beyond Blame: Challenging Violence in the Media (see Webb & Martin, 2012), which further demonstrated the importance of media literacy in K-12 teacher education. Students taught by the teachers who participated in a one-day workshop demonstrated better understanding of the content knowledge and more positive attitudes and behavior changes (Webb & Martin, 2012). Hence one can say that preservice and inservice teachers would benefit from professional development and additional resources; however, until media literacy teacher-training programs are fully developed and delivered in ways that are accessible and comprehensible to educators, sustained transformation in MLE will be difficult (Jolls, 2015).

Teacher education training models for media literacy education

Across the globe, teacher education programs offer various types of media literacy training in terms of consultation, workshops, partnerships, mentoring, seminars, and intensive summer courses. However, few training programs address the overall aspects of MLE, and existing ones mainly target fields related to communication studies and technological education (Hobbs, 2007). Furthermore, the lack of a systematic and consistent professional training for inservice and preservice teachers is problematic. One case study in Australia showed that teachers received media literacy training and information from informal sources such as media artists, technology professionals, leaders of NGOs, local organizations of voluntary teachers, and a wide range of short workshops and courses (Hobbs, 2007; Kress, 2003). This inconsistency occurs across the globe; one finds it in the United States, in Holland, in Italy, in the United Kingdom, and in other countries (Hobbs, 2007). Hobbs (2010) summarized various approaches to media literacy teacher education and provided recommendations, hoping to raise awareness among stakeholders such as teacher educators, media-related professional community members, and government institutions that are motivated to support and sustain these programs. Here are four models that Hobbs (2010) proposed, as a framework for MLE teacher-training programs, professional development training, curriculum and instruction approaches, partnerships and mentoring, and university coursework.

The first model is that of professional development training. The most common formats for MLE along this model are conference workshops and short courses that target not only educators but also staff and youth service workers. The model offers basic introductory media literacy content and approaches in the form of analysis of media content, discussion, and modeling of media production. However, this model is most effective at delivering approaches and strategies designed to analyze media but weaker when it comes to media production, which is emphasized in modern, online participatory culture. On the basis of participants' needs, some short courses outline specific topics such as pop culture, music, media violence, film, critical media literacy, and website credibility. As mentioned above, the program Beyond Blame: Challenging Violence in the Media (for which see Webb & Martin, 2012), which strengthened the importance of both long-term and short-term professional development training in MLE, is an example of a professional development program. The program evaluation indicated that teachers who attended the workshop positively influenced their students' attitudes, behaviors, and content knowledge across subject areas.

The second model, curriculum and instruction approaches, primarily focuses on inservice and preservice teachers and provides a variety of curricular materials and resources for MLE. For instance, a reference book for teachers to use in their classrooms (Wan & Cheng, 2004) was designed to help elementary school teachers develop their students' media literacy skills. This curriculum resource offered a series of 20 thematic units that demonstrate how to integrate MLE into the existing school curricula. The ready-to-go lessons include rationale, student learning outcomes, materials, procedures, grade-appropriate adaptations, and assessment tools. In addition, there has been other research conducted around curriculum and instruction approaches. Laughter (2015) applied the framework of critical media literacy (Kellner & Share, 2007) by developing action research and by using music videos and mash-ups to involve preservice teachers in teaching social justice. The findings of Laughter's (2015) study show that this action research enhanced students' motivation to learn new ways of becoming their own educational advocates and connected course content to students' lives. Another study, from Redmond (2015), bridged common core standards with learners' media experiences. Redmond (2015) proposed the benefits of integrating a literacy model into middle school curricula and illustrated how the government, through the Common Core State Standards (CCSS), provided funding opportunities for educators to incorporate media literacy into their curricula. On the basis of Redmond's approach, educators develop culturally responsive middle school education practices and promote 21st-century skills. The findings of this study show how educators employed various multimedia texts and engaged the learners, making them interact with these texts actively. Furthermore, through this literacy model, educators came to value the learners' needs and integrated meaningful, culturally responsive content into the curricula. Lastly, the educators who had committed to MLE were more motivated than others to help students develop 21st-century skills.

The third model proposed by Hobbs (2010) is partnerships and mentoring. Hobbs suggested three types of partnerships in teacher education: (i) building interdisciplinary connections that bring teacher educators and inservice and preservice teachers together, for collaboration and learning; (ii) supporting MLE across K-12 districts that collaborate with local community and media partners; and (iii) collaborating with media-related companies to connect local and national news media with teacher education programs and to raise awareness and civic engagement. For the first recommendation, Hobbs suggested collaboration between communications or media studies majors; she also suggested teacher preparation programs designed to develop community-based MLE, or certification programs in media literacy. The second recommendation involved collaborating with local community and media partners in order to support MLE across K-12 schools. States should provide funding and scholarships (when available) for school districts to promote MLE. An example at the national level was (or is, if still active) a partnership between the Department of Education and a television production company, the Discovery Channel, that offered the curriculum "Assignment: Media Literacy" in Maryland (Hobbs, 2004). This curriculum provided materials and MLE content to thousands of educators. More partnerships with media-related professional communities should be encouraged, as well as the infusion of media literacy concepts into state curricula. Hobbs (2007) also suggested collaborating with media-related companies in order to heighten awareness of civic engagement. For instance, the New York Times Learning Network offers over 3000 media literacy curriculum materials (lesson plans, activities) to help educators incorporate meaningful and current content into their curricula. Red Lasso, News Trust, and NBC Learn are other media organizations that provide materials for MLE. Well-developed and sustainable mentoring and partnership programs offer real-time support from experienced mentors and experts, which could lead to more successful teacher-training experiences in the long term (Hobbs, 2007).

The final model addressed is university coursework. Hobbs (2010) notes that few university-level courses are offered in the area of media literacy. In spite of the growing number of MLE courses in communications, media studies, higher-education programs (Hobbs, 2007), and other media literacy-related elective courses offered in new doctoral programs, the implementation of media literacy into K-12 teacher preparation programs remains underdeveloped. A small number of research studies have introduced ways to integrate media literacy into university curricula across majors. Robertson and Hughes (2012) developed a four-year study of a teacher preparation course based on socioconstructivist theory. In an English language arts course for preservice teachers, critical media literacy and social justice that included the use of digital technologies were explored. Findings showed that preservice teachers who reported using digital media in their classrooms were motivating, engaging, and innovative. In addition, preservice teachers showed more confidence and were reportedly more comfortable about applying new technologies and digital media skills to teach and articulate deep concepts, such as critical media literacy and social justice issues. More media literacy courses need to be offered in teacher preparation programs or as university-level electives. Given the inconsistent nature of access to formal MLE and expertise for teachers, it is crucial to understand which media literacy curricular elements are beneficial for learners and what methods are conducive to integrating meaningful MLE content into learning.

Curriculum and instruction for media literacy education

This section contains a review and critique of the current challenges of fostering media literacy through standards-based instruction, followed by a discussion of culturally relevant and critical media literacy curricula in teacher preparation programs. Current research evidence of effective curriculum and instruction for MLE is then explored.

Fostering media literacy through standards-based instruction

With the increasing prevalence of digital media in all aspects of life, media literacy needs to be integrated into mainstream formal education (Hobbs, 2010). However, as noted previously, the primary challenge for MLE is the lack of systematic and standardized practices for the incorporation of MLE across cultures and institutions (Fedorov et al., 2016). In response, leading researchers and scholars in the field created guidelines for MLE across the globe (Hobbs, 2010; Jolls, 2015; Potter, 2014; Silverblatt, 2014). For instance, UNESCO (Grizzle & Calvo, 2013; Grizzle & Wilson, 2011; Pérez & Varis, 2010; and see UNESCO, 2013) and the European Association for Viewers' Interests (Celot, 2015; EAVI, 2011; Fedorov et al., 2016; Jolls, 2015) created guidelines for media literacy and information literacy curricula. In the United States, the importance of infusing media literacy into standards-based instruction has also been recognized by many professional associations and institutions such as the National Council of Teachers of English (NCTE), the National Council for Accreditation of Teacher Education, International Reading Association (see Hobbs, 2010), the National Association of Media

Literacy Education (NAMLE), the CML (see Meehan et al., 2015), and the National Council for Social Studies (NCSS).

Examples of infusing media literacy into standards-based instruction in K-12 curricula were referenced to studies by Meehan et al. (2015) and Wan (2006). Meehan et al. proposed applying the key questions and core principles of media literacy as the main learning outcomes and instructional guidelines of their two teacher preparation courses, *Introduction to Secondary Education* and *Secondary Social Studies Practicum*. The key questions and core principles were developed by the CML and NAMLE Media Lit Kit (visit http://www.medialit.org), both of which covered discussions of authorship, purpose, economics, impact, content, technique, and credibility of media literacy content (Meehan et al., 2015; NAMLE, 2013). Wan (2006) explained to teachers who were concerned about adding a new subject (MLE) to an already overcrowded (or packed) curriculum that, by its nature, media literacy encourages an interdisciplinary approach to education and teachers can make connections across content areas by teaching with media and about media. Wan (2006) also demonstrated how MLE can be integrated into every school subject. For instance, to provide MLE for elementary school children through the reading of nonfiction, Capstone Press published a set of media literacy books in 2007 (Andersen, 2007a, 2007b; Wan, 2007a, 2007b; Baker, 2007; Botzakis, 2007). This entertaining series embraces music, television, Internet, video games, movies, and print media, while simultaneously giving young readers the systematic knowledge and skills required to question pop culture and to recognize the influential nature of media messages.

In addition to advocacy by professional associations and institutions, the Common Core State Standards Initiative (CCSSI) (2010) emphasizes that educators need to help students obtain the skills required to access, analyze, evaluate, create, reflect, and react to media content. These indispensable skills need to be introduced and addressed in the MLE curriculum in order for students to be prepared to attend college, apply for jobs, and live in a digital world (Hobbs, 2010). In response, teacher preparation programs have already begun to instruct preservice teachers by enhancing their media and digital literacy. The National Council of Teachers of English (NCTE) (2003) encourages preservice and inservice teachers—as well as staff members—to attend professional development programs that emphasize the new literacies (i.e., media literacy, technology literacy, digital literacy, and information literacy). The National Council for the Accreditation of Teacher Education (NCATE) (2007) standards, which are now replaced by CAEP, also strengthen this notion and claim that educators need to acknowledge the important impact of media and to assess how the latter influence individuals' behaviors, values, and cultures. Educators are responsible for teaching children and youths new ways to create and interact with multimedia forms, including film, video, graphics, audio, and photography. As the new trend for curriculum development continues, CCSS is believed to allow for a more consistent curriculum across the nation (Jolls, 2015).

While educators around the United States try to connect media literacy with the CCSS, challenges have occurred because the standards of CCSSI do not explicitly address media literacy (Meehan et al., 2015). Drew (2012) analyzed the CCSSI content and found that the standards make use of disconnected and inconsistent concepts of 21st-century literacies. Thus, too many terms for new literacies (e.g., changing from visual literacy to multimodal or transmedia literacies) have been misleading and confusing for educators. Another issue is that the CCSS narrows the concepts of literacies. For example, the materials and content that the CCSS promote focus on getting technological tools and hardware into students' hands, so they can apply these tools for standardized tests associated with CCSS (Heitner, 2013; Laughter, 2015).

Simply updating standards and composing documents are not enough to change MLE in K-12 and higher education. Providing media literacy materials and lesson plans can assist educators with ideas and strategies for use in teaching; however, these effects alone are insufficient. If the goal is to transfer media literacy knowledge and skills from educators to students, systemic expansion of media literacy curricula across the United States needs to happen (Hobbs, 2010). Explicit and convincing instructional practices and substantial professional development programs of MLE are needed to support and promote media literacy across the nation.

Culturally relevant curriculum

The heterogenous population that can be found in K-12 settings across the United States has been rapidly growing and embraces diverse languages, races, ethnicities, and cultures. In 2014, the percentage of nonwhite public school students enrolled in elementary and secondary schools increased to 50.5%; this was the first time that nonwhite students exceeded half of the total enrollment (National Center for Education Statistics [NCES], 2017). Between 2004 and 2014, the white student population decreased from 28.3 million to 24.9 million. Conversely, the Hispanic student population increased from 9.3 million to 12.8 million (19% to 25%) during this same time period. The Asian and Pacific Islander student population also increased from 2.2 million to 2.6 million (i.e., 4% to 5%) (NCES, 2017). According to NCES (2017), the nonwhite student population is projected to increase to 55% in 2026, of which 29% will be Hispanic, 6% Asian–Pacific Islander, 15% black, 1% American Indian–Alaska Native, and approximately 4% from biracial or multiracial groups.

The multicultural student population requires support from teachers with special training. Research indicates that integrating culturally relevant curricula into teacher education programs will allow preservice teachers to obtain intercultural competence (Garrett-Rucks, 2016; Sleeter, 2010) and to be better prepared for multicultural and multilingual classroom settings. Gay (2000) proposed the concept of "culturally relevant teaching" and claimed that preservice and inservice teachers need to be ready for the diverse classrooms, so that they may be able to provide democratic and inclusive learning environments for their students (Meehan et al., 2015). Meehan et al. (2015) support Gay's (2000) culturally relevant teaching and learning approach, and agree with Cortés that multicultural and multilingual education needs to be taught and learned through the lens of media literacy: "Enveloping media multicultural curriculum guarantees that school educators do not have the power to decide if multicultural education will occur. … Rather, school educators can only decide whether or not they will consciously participate and how they will participate in the inevitable process of teaching and learning about diversity" (Cortés, 2000, p. xvi).

Challenges have been identified for effectively integrating culturally relevant curricula into MLE (Fedorov et al., 2016). Sara Gagai, a scholar involved in the Digital International Media Literacy eBook Project (DIMLE), which is an international collaboration with participants from over 40 countries, explained that the aim of DIMLE is to provide teacher educators with the latest relevant, culturally sensitive, and context-sensitive media literacy materials and curricula. Unfortunately, the main obstacles to developing these curricula are a lack of practice in MLE across cultures and institutions and a lack of culturally relevant media literacy content in the curricula for learners with diverse cultural backgrounds. Fedorov et al. (2016) recommends that the DIMLE offer opportunities for educators and scholars to share their media literacy resources and pedagogical approaches worldwide.

Another way to engage students in culturally relevant learning is through discussions on the themes of race, gender, class, and sexuality through media, in the classroom (Laughter, 2015; Kellner & Share, 2007; Luke, 2012; Mihailidis & Thevenin, 2013). As demonstrated by one of the thematic units in Wan and Cheng's (2004) media literacy textbook, identifying and discussing cultural stereotypes and biases in the media allow children to see that media portrayals are not necessarily neutral. Exposing students to these stereotypes can be an effective way to introduce the young to critical media literacy.

Critical media literacy curriculum

In today's world we encounter media at every turn, and young people's lives are increasingly spent online. This would not be an issue if media simply reflected reality and were unbiased and neutral. However, each medium shapes reality in unique ways, and we can no longer trust the veracity of every message we encounter, whether it is in the format of text, video, or photograph. The information we encounter in the media may contain values, beliefs, and behaviors that are shaped by economic, social, and political factors. Becoming literate in the 21st century means being capable of understanding the influence of media on society, developing strategies to critically analyze the media, and becoming independent from the influence of media. In the study conducted by Fedorov et al. (2016), findings showed that critical media literacy was rated as one of the most important learning goals for teacher training. Participants who are experts in the field of MLE claimed that "demonstrating understanding of the role and functions of media in democratic societies" (52.3%) and "analyzing and critically evaluating media representations of people, issues, values, and behaviors" (58.5%) are the most important learning outcomes that should be incorporated into MLE curricula (Fedorov et al., 2016, p. 330).

Critical media literacy, an important aspect of MLE, not only comprises the concepts of media literacy skills but also emphasizes civic engagement, specifically social justice. According to Kellner and Share (2007, p. 62), "[c]ritical media literacy thus constitutes a critique of mainstream approaches to literacy and a political project for democratic social change." Previous studies have investigated the relationships between critical media literacy and issues of social justice and participatory democracy (Flores-Koulish & Deal, 2008; Laughter, 2015; Kellner & Share, 2007; Luke, 2012; Mihailidis & Thevenin, 2013). For instance, Flores-Koulish and Deal (2008) applied the framework of Blythe

Clinchy and Jill Tarule's popular 1992 *Women's Ways of Knowing* to investigate 55 MA students' perspectives of a course in critical MLE in the United States. The results reveal new approaches to engage students in critical media literacy discussion and teach us a constructed way of comprehending critical media literacy (Flores-Koulish & Deal, 2008). Flores-Koulish and Deal (2008) emphasize that exposing students to literature and research in social justice and multicultural education allows them to get a deeper understanding of critical media literacy. Therefore educators should learn new ways to teach media literacy and acknowledge that this is a powerful means of introducing the concept of critical media literacy to their students (Flores-Koulish & Deal, 2006).

Learning critical media literacy allows students to establish their own stance, challenge media production and narratives, and critically analyze the connections between media and audiences, information, and power (Kellner & Share, 2007). The primary purpose of learning critical media literacy is to understand and analyze the power structures in a society through the lens of its media. For instance, media users need to understand the politics and symbolic representations of gender, class, race, and sexuality through media ("Media literacy," n.d.). The framework of Kellner and Share (2007) delineates five core concepts in critical media literacy: all media messages are "constructed"; media messages are constructed using a creative language with its own rules; different people experience the same media message differently; media have embedded values and points of view; and media are organized for the sake of gaining profit and power. Also contributing to teaching critical media literacy, the media literacy series at Capstone Press (Andersen, 2007a, 2007b; Wan, 2007a, 2007b) encourages students to ask the following five questions about each piece of media they encounter: "Who made the message and why? Who is the message for? How might others view the message differently? What is left out of the message? How does the message get and keep my attention?" (Andersen, 2007a, p. 5).

By asking these questions, students start to view media and popular culture through a critical lens and will not take issues in the popular culture for granted. For instance, Flores-Koulish (2010) investigated how graduate students in a MLE course and in a race, class, and gender in education course explore critical media literacy and express transformation during their learning process. The results indicate that critical media literacy can in principle trigger students to question issues they have been taking for granted in the popular culture. The study also shows that collaborative projects in media literacy analysis offer students eye-opening experiences. Collaborating with their peers as a community to discuss media literacy topics enhances understanding and shows that practices of collective interrogation can be healthy and productive.

There is limited empirical research on critical media literacy in teacher education. Thus far, the majority of studies have emphasized ways to engage new digital tools in the curriculum rather than deepen the practice of social justice (Laughter, 2015). Therefore more studies are needed to examine critical media literacy in K-12 teacher preparation programs. Such studies should (i) cover ways to critically analyze the curriculum and apply constructivist pedagogical methods in preservice classroom practicums (Flores-Koulish & Deal, 2008; Meehan et al., 2015), (ii) offer a critical media literacy framework for teacher preparation programs (Flores-Koulish, 2010; Laughter, 2015), (iii) apply critical media analysis to teacher education (Chamberlin-Quinlisk, 2012;

Meehan et al., 2015), (iv) introduce popular culture narratives through the lens of critical media literacy (Fuxa, 2012; Staples, 2013), and (v) select meaningful materials and contents for effective MLE (Fuxa, 2012).

Preservice and inservice teachers are required to understand various ways to teach critical media literacy to their students so as to render these students able to critically consume and create contents in the digital world (Botzakis, 2011; Laughter, 2015; Kellner & Share, 2007). Alvermann and Hagood (2000, p. 199) claimed that critical media literacy offers a framework to "deconstruct several aspects of established school discourse: the space of school, the pedagogy and practices of literacy instruction, and relations between students and teachers." Therefore critical media literacy in teacher education should aim at engaging students in the social contexts around them through issues of inequality and injustice (Alvermann & Hagood, 2000; Laughter, 2015; Kellner & Share, 2007), human rights and freedom of expression (Morrell, 2005), and participatory democracy (Mihailidis & Thevenin, 2013).

Ethical use of information online

Early adoption of technology has changed the ways in which children play, interact with others, learn, and use information. There is no doubt that academic integrity is fundamental to every aspect of teaching, learning, and educational research (Bretag, 2016). Cyberplagiarism is at an all-time high among school students, and computers and the Internet have played a major role in facilitating it (Parker, Lenhart & Moore, 2011). The Josephson Institute of Ethics (2012) found that 16% of the 23 000 US high school students surveyed admitted to having copied an Internet document for a classroom assignment. According to Wan and Scott (2016, p. 1), "[t]echnology has provided opportunities without boundaries to children, enabling them to do things that their parents had not even dreamt of at their age. Children take virtual tours around the world even before they set foot in their neighborhood." When this unprecedented access to information is in place, it is not fair to expect adults, let alone children, to know what an ethical and fair use of information is without being educated on expectations and consequences.

Two major approaches to dealing with the ethical and proper use of digital information in schools have been identified: legislation and education (Wan & Scott, 2016). Legislation focuses on setting up rules that guard against and penalize plagiarism, while education focuses on instructing students on why plagiarism is wrong and how to avoid it. Regarding the educational approach, Wan and Scott stated that, "if students are educated about how to interact with online information within the ethical and legal framework, i.e., armed with information literacy, early on, and if they grow up in a culture of ethical use of information, many potential future problems may be prevented" (Wan & Scott, 2016, p. 2). Many school student handbooks give a description of plagiarism such as this: "Plagiarism includes using or copying the language, structure, idea, and/or thought of another and representing it as one's own original work" (Henrico County Schools, 2014); and the consequences of plagiarism follow. However, little advice on how to deter students from performing such acts is offered (Lathrop & Foss, 2005). The best way to develop ethical practices in students is to integrate the ethical use of information into various subjects—English, science, and mathematics classes—as well as into classroom technology and library practice (Wan & Scott, 2016).

Other aspects of critical media use—such as safe surfing, anti-cyberbullying, and proper online behaviors and use of information—should be addressed in the K-12 curriculum (Wan, 2006; Wan & Cheng, 2004). Studies investigating the digital media behavior of young adolescents and children suggest that appropriate use of the Internet can be beneficial to children's development of self-identity, as well as of their cognitive and social skills (Liu, Fang, Deng, & Zhang, 2012; Wan, Yeh, & Cheng, 2016). To date, pathological Internet use is a severe problem, especially for digital natives. Children who use the Internet excessively frequently struggle with health problems, low achievement in academic settings, family relationship issues, social problems, and depression (Wan, Yeh, & Cheng, 2016). Introducing the concepts of cyberbullying and creating safe online surfing environments are two factors crucial for preventing children from being exposed to cyberviolence, pornographic content, materialism, and problems in social life (Wan & Gut, 2008). Studies show that young adolescents who lack quality children–parent communications and family support are more likely to develop pathological Internet use (Liu et al., 2012). Therefore, in addition to teaching students media literacy at school, educators should communicate with parents and encourage them to provide support at home, so that students may develop positive social connections online (Liu et al., 2012). Liu et al. (2012) also support Wan and Gut's (2008) three stages of MLE principles: making wise choices and managing the amount of time spent; critically analyzing and questioning the truth of information; and exploring the deeper issues of who produces the media and for what purposes. Chang and Liu (2011) validated the importance of MLE and encouraged educators to address these principles while teaching media literacy.

MLE in teacher preparation programs provides future educators with a deeper understanding of media literacy, critical media literacy, culturally relevant curricula, and integrated approaches that promote media literacy in standards-based instruction. Moreover, teacher preparation training programs can help narrow the gap between pedagogical theories and practices of integrating meaningful media literacy into curricula. It is essential for teacher educators, policymakers, administrative staff, and community and media partners to work together and understand that MLE is a core component of effective teaching and learning. MLE should be introduced in the context of critical media literacy and of the culturally relevant curriculum, so that educators can raise students' awareness around civic engagement and the importance of becoming active 21st-century citizens in online participatory cultures.

SEE ALSO: Authorship and Participatory Culture; Media Literacy Education and Second Language Acquisition

References

Alvermann, D.E., & Hagood, M.C. (2000). Critical media literacy: Research, theory, and practice in "new times." *Journal of Educational Research, 93*, 193–205.

Andersen, N. (2007a). *At the controls: Questioning video and computer games*. Bloomington, MN: Capstone Press.

Andersen, N. (2007b). *Music madness: Questioning music and music videos*. Bloomington, MN: Capstone Press.

Aspen Media Literacy Leadership Institute. (1992). Media literacy: A definition and more. Retrieved from http://www.medialit.org/media-literacy-definition-and-more

Aybek, B. (2016). The relationship between prospective teachers' media and television literacy and their critical thinking dispositions. *Eurasian Journal of Educational Research, 63*, 261–278.

Baker, F.W. (2007). *Coming distractions: Questioning movies*. Bloomington, MN: Capstone Press.

Botzakis, S. (2007). *Pretty in print: Questioning magazines*. Bloomington, MN: Capstone Press.

Botzakis, S.G. (2011). Using nonprint media and texts to support marginalized readers. In L.A. Hall, L.D. Burns, & E.C. Edwards (Eds.), *Empowering struggling readers* (pp. 161–177). New York, NY: Guilford Press.

Bretag, T. (Ed.). (2016). *Handbook of academic integrity*. Singapore: Springer Science+Business Media. Retrieved from https://link.springer.com/content/pdf/bfm%3A978-981-287-098-8%2F1.pdf

Celot, P. (2015). *Assessing media literacy levels and the European Commission: Pilot initiative*. Brussels, Begium: EAVI.

Chamberlin-Quinlisk, C. (2012). Critical media analysis in teacher education: Exploring language-learners' identity through mediated images of a non-native speaker of English. *TESL Canada Journal, 29*(2), 42–57.

Chang, C., & Liu, E. (2011). Exploring the media literacy of Taiwanese elementary school students. *Asia-Pacific Education Researcher, 20*(3), 604–611.

Common Core State Standards Initiative (CCSSI). (2010). *English language arts standards*. Retrieved from http://www.corestandards.org/wp-content/uploads/ELA_Standards1.pdf

Cortés, C. (2000). *The children are watching: How the media teach about diversity*. New York, NY: Teachers College Press.

Drew, S. (2012). Open up the ceiling on the Common Core State Standards. *Journal of Adolescent and Adult Literacy, 56*, 321–330.

EAVI. (2011). *Testing and refining criteria to assess media literacy levels in Europe: Final Report*. Brussels, Belgium: EAVI.

Fedorov, A., Levitskaya, A., & Camarero, E. (2016). Curricula for media literacy education according to international experts. *European Journal of Contemporary Education, 17*(3), 324–334.

Finnish Ministry of Education and Culture. (2013). *Good media literacy: National policy guidelines*. Retrieved from http://minedu.fi/en/publication?pubid=URN:ISBN:978-952-263-222-7

Flores-Koulish, S. (2010). Practicing critical media literacy education: Developing a community of inquiry among teachers using popular culture. Retrieved from https://files.eric.ed.gov/fulltext/ED509928.pdf

Flores-Koulish, S.A., & Deal, D. (2006). Media literacy for reading master's students. *Academic Exchange Quarterly, 10*(3), 159–163.

Flores-Koulish, S.A., & Deal, D. (2008). Reacting to change: Critical media literacy for United States reading teachers? *Simile, 8*(3), 1–14. doi: 10.3138/sim.8.3.001

Fuxa, R. (2012). What "Dirty Dancing" taught me about media literacy education. *Journal of Media Literacy Education, 4*(2), 179–183.

Garrett-Rucks, P. (2016). *Intercultural competence in instructed language learning*. Charlotte, NC: Information Age Publishing.

Gay, G. (2000). *Culturally responsive teaching: Theory, research, and practice*. New York: Teachers College Press.

Grizzle, A., & Calvo, M.C. (2013). *Media and information literacy: Policy and strategy guidelines.* Paris, France: UNESCO.

Grizzle, A., & Wilson, C. (2011). *Media and information literacy: Curriculum for teachers.* Paris, France: UNESCO.

Gruszczynska, A., Merchant, G., & Pountney, R. (2013). Digital futures in teacher education: Exploring open approaches towards digital literacy. *Electronic Journal of E-Learning, 11*(3), 193–206.

Hargittai, E. (2010). Digital na(t)ives? Variation in Internet skills and uses among members of the "net generation." *Sociological Inquiry, 80*(1), 92–113.

Heitner, E. (2013). The trouble with the common core. *Rethinking Schools, 27*(4). Retrieved from http://www.rethinkingschools.org/archive/27_04/edit274.shtml

Henrico County Schools. (2014). *Code of student conduct.* Retrieved from http://www.henrico.k12. va.us/Pdf/Instruction/CodeOfConduct.pdf

Hobbs, R. (2004). A review of school-based initiatives in media literacy. *American Behavioural Scientist, 48*(1), 48–59.

Hobbs, R. (2007). Approaches to instruction and teacher education in media literacy. Retrieved from http://unesdoc.unesco.org/images/0016/001611/161133e.pdf

Hobbs, R. (2010). *Digital and media literacy: A plan of action.* Washington, DC: Aspen Institute.

Hobbs, R., & Jensen, A. (2009). The past, present, and future of media literacy education. *Journal of Media Literacy Education, 1*(1), 1–11.

Jenkins, H., Clinton, K., Purushotma, R., Robison, A.J., & Weigel, M. (2006). Confronting the challenges of participatory culture: Media education for the 21st century. *MacArthur Foundation Publications, 1*(1), 1–68.

Jolls, T. (2012). Media literacy: A system for learning anytime, anywhere. Los Angeles Center for Media Literacy. Retrieved from http://www.medialit.org/reading-room/media-literacy-system-learning-anytime-anywhere-part-1-change-management

Jolls, T. (2015). The new curricula: How media literacy education transforms teaching and learning. *Journal of Media Literacy Education, 7*(1), 65–71.

Jolls, T., & Grande, D. (2005). A road to follow. *Arts Education Policy Review, 107*(1), 25–30.

Jones, C. (2013). The new shape of the student. In R. Huang & J.M. Kinshunk Spector (Eds.), *Reshaping learning: The frontiers of learning technologies in global context* (pp. 91–112). New York, NY: Springer.

Josephson Institute of Ethics. (2012). 2012 report card on the ethics of American youth. Retrieved from https://charactercounts.org/wp-content/uploads/2014/02/ReportCard-2012-DataTables.pdf

Kellner, D., & Share, J. (2007). Critical media literacy is not an option. *Learning Inquiry, 1*, 59–69.

Kress, G. (2003). *Literacy in the new media age.* London, England: Routledge.

Lathrop, A., & Foss, K. (2005). *Guiding students from cheating and plagiarism to honesty and integrity: Strategies for change.* Westport, CT: Libraries Unlimited.

Laughter, J. (2015). ELA teacher preparation 2.0: Critical media literacy, action research, and mashups. *Contemporary Issues in Technology and Teacher Education, 15*(3), 265–282.

Lauri, M.A., Borg, J., Gunnel, T., & Gillum, R. (2010). Attitudes of a sample of English, Maltese and German teachers towards media education. *European Journal of Teacher Education, 33*(1), 79–98.

Lenhart, A. (2015). *Teens, social media and technology overview, 2015.* Washington, DC: Pew Research Center, Internet and Technology. Retrieved from http://www.pewinternet.org/2015/04/09/teens-social-media-technology-2015

Lenhart, A., Madden, M., Smith, A., & Macgill, A. (2007). *Teens and social media.* Washington, DC: Pew Internet and American Life Project. Retrieved from http://www.pewinternet.org/files/old-media/Files/Reports/2007/PIP_Teens_Social_Media_Final.pdf.pdf

Liu, Q., Fang, X., Deng, L., & Zhang, J. (2012). Parent–adolescent communication, parental Internet use and Internet-specific norms and pathological Internet use among Chinese adolescents. *Computers in Human Behavior, 28*(4), 1269–1275.

Luke, A. (2012). Critical literacy: Foundational notes. *Theory into Practice, 51*(1), 4–11.

Media literacy. (n.d.). Retrieved August 14, 2017 from https://en.wikipedia.org/wiki/Media_literacy#Critical_media_literacy

Meehan, J., Ray, B., Walker, A., Wells, S., & Schwarz, G. (2015). Media literacy in teacher education: A good fit across the curriculum. *Journal of Media Literacy Education, 7*(2), 81–86.

Mihailidis, P., & Thevenin, B. (2013). Media literacy as a core competency for engaged citizenship in participatory democracy. *American Behavioral Scientist, 57*, 1611–1622.

Morrell, E. (2005). Critical English education. *English Education, 37*, 312–321.

National Association for Media Literacy Education (NAMLE). (2013). *Core Principles of Media Literacy Education*. Retrieved September 6, 2017 from http://www.namle.net/publications/core-principles

National Center for Education Statistics (NCES). (2017). *Racial/ethnic enrollment in public schools, 2017*. Washington, DC: Institute of Education Sciences.

National Council for the Accreditation of Teacher Education (NCATE). (2007). *Professional standards for the accreditation of teacher preparation institutions*. Retrieved from http://www.ncate.org/public/standards.asp?ch=4

National Council of Teachers of English (NCTE). (2003). *Position statement on multimodal literacies*. Retrieved from http://www.ncte.org/positions/statements/multimodalliteracies

Parker, K., Lenhart, A. & Moore, K. (2011). *The digital revolution and higher education*. Pew Research Center. Retrieved from http://www.pewinternet.org/2011/08/28/the-digital-revolution-and-higher-education

Participatory culture. (n.d.). Retrieved August 9, 2017 from https://en.wikipedia.org/wiki/Participatory_culture

Pérez, J.M., & Varis, T. (2010). *Media literacy and new humanism*. Moscow, Russia: UNESCO Institute for Information Technologies in Education.

Potter, W.J. (2014). *The skills of media literacy*. Santa Barbara, CA: Knowledge Assets.

Prensky, M. (2001). Digital natives, digital immigrants. *On the Horizon, 9*(5), 1–6.

Redmond, T. (2015). Media literacy is common sense: Bridging Common Core Standards with the media experiences of digital learners. *Middle School Journal, 46*(3), 10–17.

Robertson, L., & Hughes, J. (2012). Surfacing the assumptions: Pursuing critical literacy and social justice in pre-service teacher education. *Brock Education: A Journal of Educational Research and Practice, 22*(1), 73–92.

Schmidt, H. (2013). Media literacy education from kindergarten to college: A comparison of how media literacy is addressed across the educational system. *Journal of Media Literacy Education, 5*(1), 295–309.

Silverblatt, A. (2014). *The Praeger handbook of media literacy*. Santa Barbara, CA: Praeger.

Sleeter, C.E. (2010). Culturally responsive pedagogy: A reflection. *Journal of Praxis in Multicultural Education, 5*(1), 116–119.

Staples, J.M. (2013). Reading popular culture narratives of disease with pre-service teachers. *Teacher Education Quarterly, 40*(4), 27–40.

Statista. (2016). Leading social networks worldwide as of April 2016, ranked by number of active users. Retrieved from http://www.statista.com/statistics/272014/global-social-networksranked-by-number-of-users

Stein, L., & Prewett, A. (2009). Media literacy education in the social studies: Teacher perceptions and curricular challenges. *Teacher Education Quarterly, 36*(1), 131–148.

UNESCO. (2003). Towards an information literate society: The UNESCO Prague Declaration. Retrieved from http://www.unesco.org/new/fileadmin/MULTIMEDIA/HQ/CI/CI/pdf/PragueDeclaration.pdf

UNESCO. (2013). *Global media and information literacy assessment framework: Country readiness and competencies.* Paris, France: UNESCO.

Wan, G. (2006). Integrating media literacy into the curriculum. *Academic Exchange Quarterly.* Retrieved from https://www.questia.com/read/1G1-155568005/integrating-media-literacy-into-the-curriculum

Wan, G. (2007a). *TV takeover: Questioning television.* Bloomington, MN: Capstone Press.

Wan, G. (2007b). *Virtually true: Questioning online media.* Bloomington, MN: Capstone Press.

Wan, G., & Cheng, H. (2004). The Media-savvy student: Teaching media literacy skills, grades 2–6. Chicago, IL: Chicago Review Press. Retrieved from https://www.amazon.com/Media-Savvy-Student-Teaching-Literacy-Skills/dp/1569761701

Wan, G., & Gut, D. (2008). Roles of media and media literacy education: Lives of Chinese and American adolescents. *New Horizons in Education, 56*(2), 28–42.

Wan, G., & Scott, M. (2016). Start them early and right: Creating a culture of academic integrity in elementary schools. In Tracey Bretag (Ed.), *Handbook of academic integrity* (pp. 1–13). Springer. doi: 10.1007/978-981-287-079-7_50-1

Wan, G., Yeh, E., & Cheng, H. (2016). Digital media use by Chinese youth and its impact. In C.K. Cheung (Ed.), *Media education in China* (pp. 47–64). Hong Kong, China: Springer.

Webb, T., & Martin. K. (2012). Evaluation of a US school-based media literacy violence prevention curriculum on changes in knowledge and critical thinking among adolescents. *Journal of Children and Media, 6*(4), 430–449.

Further reading

Deal, D., Flores-Koulish, S., & Sears, J. (2010). Media literacy teacher talk: Implementation, interpretation, and frustration? *Journal of Media Literacy Education, 1–2,* 121–131.

Hobbs, R. (2011). *Digital and media literacy: Connecting culture and classroom.* Beverly Hills, CA: Corwin/SAGE.

Hobbs, R., & Moore, D.C. (2013). *Discovering media literacy: Digital media and popular culture in elementary school.* Thousand Oaks, CA: Corwin/SAGE.

Ellen Yeh holds a PhD in curriculum and instruction with a specialization in second language education from Ohio University. She is an assistant professor in the English and Creative Writing Department and serves as a director of the English as an Additional Language Program at Columbia College, Chicago. Her research interests include media literacy education, computer-assisted language learning, intercultural studies, and the education of diverse populations. Her nationally recognized research has appeared in chapters and refereed journal articles—for example the article entitled "Teaching culture and language through the multiple intelligences film teaching model in the ESL/EFL classroom" (2014), published in the *Journal of Effective Teaching.*

Guofang Wan joined University of West Florida as a professor and chair of the Department of Teacher Education and Educational Leadership. Her research interests range from the education of diverse populations and media literacy education to

English as a second language. She has authored and edited several books, including *The Media-Savvy Student: Teaching Media Literacy Skills* (coauthored with Hong Cheng; 2004). Among Wan's recognitions are the Margaret B. Lindsey Award for Distinguished Research in Teacher Education, awarded by the American Association of Colleges for Teacher Education (AACTE), and the Fourth Annual Media Literacy Award, awarded by the National Council of Teachers of English (NCTE).

Media Literacy for the 21st Century Teacher

DENISE L. SAUERTEIG
KQED, USA

MARIA F. CERVERA GUTIERREZ
Independent scholar, USA

BRIT TOVEN-LINDSEY
California State University East Bay, USA

INGRID HU DAHL
Capital One, USA

In the context of increasingly affordable devices, Internet in every school, and a constant flow of news and information, the vast majority of American youths are using computers and the Internet to support their academic, personal, and social endeavors. According to the Pew Research Center, 92% of teens report going online daily, and nearly a quarter are online "almost constantly" (Lenhart, 2015). Nearly three quarters of teens have access to a smartphone, and more than 70% are regularly using multiple social media platforms such as Facebook, Instagram, and Snapchat. Yet despite their confidence and comfort in navigating online spaces and interacting on social media, research indicates that young people do not have high levels of media literacy, and the majority struggle to evaluate the credibility of new sources and identify misinformation (e.g., Wineburg & McGrew, 2016; Wineburg, McGrew, Breakstone, & Ortega, 2016). In addition, the majority of young people are media consumers and are not contributing to media production in any meaningful way.

Young people are socialized from an early age in the use of computers and digital technologies to accomplish specific tasks and to interact in online spaces (e.g., Sims, 2014). This socialization happens primarily at home, among peer groups, and in school. Schools, and teachers in particular, have become an important component of the conversation about helping young people develop relevant skills for engaged citizenship and career success in the 21st century. Researchers and nonprofit organizations have developed various frameworks and definitions to articulate the types of skills that young people need to thrive and prepare for a full participation in society. According to the Partnership for 21st Century Learning (2015), students should develop a range of skills and competencies that include creativity and innovation, critical thinking, communication and collaboration, flexibility and adaptability, cross-cultural competence, and global awareness, along with core academic subjects such as English, math, and science. Among these essential skills is also the development of information, media, and ICT (information and communication technology) literacies that allow individuals to create, evaluate, and effectively engage with information, media sources, and digital technologies.

Similarly, the International Society for Technology in Education (ISTE, n.d.), a non-profit organization supporting educators, established standards for student technology use and skill development in schools (www.iste.org). The standards focus on four main areas including, creativity and innovation, communication and collaboration, research and information fluency, and critical thinking, problem-solving, and decision-making. According to ISTE, students should be able to use technology to develop innovative products and processes, gather, evaluate, and use information, communicate effectively and collaborate with others, and use critical thinking skills to solve problems and conduct research.

In the context of the rapid expansion of personal computing and the Internet, researchers began to examine the ways that these new digital technologies were influencing language and literacy practices (e.g., Belisle, 2006; Coiro, Knobel, Lankshear, & Leu, 2008; Funk, Kellner, & Share, 2016; Gee, 2008). From a sociocultural perspective, literacies are embedded in social practices and are therefore constantly evolving to meet the needs of contemporary life. More than a simple set of skills to be gained, new literacies, or multiliteracies, involve applying specialized knowledge for particular purposes and are situated within social, cultural, and historical contexts. Therefore, literacies are connected to social identity and are an integral part of the everyday experiences of individuals engaged in oral, written, and computer-mediated interactions.

Young people are developing these new literacy skills through everyday communication and interactions such as blogging, texting, pinning, tweeting, podcasting, photographing, and videoing. Digital texts are often multimodal, hyperlinked, and interactive. Digital communications can also reach a diverse audience when posted on social media or even shared directly with peers through advanced online archives, searchability, and easy replication. In the context of this unprecedented access to flows of news and information, the networked nature of communications, and the proliferation of biased and unchecked online materials, young people need support and guidance to develop high levels of information and media literacies.

In the Common Core State Standards (2010), developed by the Council of Chief State School Officers (CCSSI) and the National Governors Association, media literacy is featured among the key design considerations. Specifically, the standards state that students need the ability to "gather, comprehend, evaluate, synthesize, and summarize information and ideas, to conduct original research to answer questions or solve problems, and to analyze and create a high volume and extensive range of print and non-print texts in media forms old and new" (CCSSI, 2010, p. 4). Students who are college and career ready according to these standards are able to use technology to enhance their communication skills in reading, writing, speaking, and listening. They should also be able to use technological tools to support their learning and deepen their understanding of core concepts.

In recognition of the changing landscape of digital communication and the role of technology in teaching and learning, media literacy is embedded directly into the standards and the ability to "produce and consume media is embedded into every aspect of today's curriculum" (CCSSI, 2010, p. 4). By expanding the definition of traditional literacy to include reading and writing with digital media, and stressing the use of digital texts, the Common Core Standards indicate a shift forward in the cultural penetration and educational legitimacy of online texts and platforms. Similarly, this shift points to a recognition of the importance of youths as makers and producers in the digital space and the role of teachers and schools in supporting the advancement of these skills as a central component of the curriculum. However, many educational systems and actors are not equipped to make this shift in the classroom.

Media literacy in the classroom

The Common Core Standards are designed to prepare students for entry-level careers, college courses, and workforce training programs, and have received considerable buy-in from education stakeholders across the country. At the same time, they represent a significant change from past state standards and assessment measures (Porter, McMaken, Hwang, & Yang, 2011). In the past, one of the biggest problems with incorporating media literacy into the curriculum was the struggle to fit it within the standards. While teachers wanted to incorporate media into the classroom, many worried that there was no room for it with all of the other content they were tasked with covering. With the new standards, media literacy should now be embedded throughout the curriculum, which can be equally challenging for teachers who lack the skills and confidence with media creation and analysis to effectively incorporate these practices into their teaching.

At this point, most public school districts are using some form of digital learning to support instruction, ranging from fully online courses to enhancements to classroom instruction (Evergreen Education Group, 2015). Yet, there is significant variability in the ways that teachers and schools are able to use digital technologies to support instruction and student learning. Numerous factors impact the differential usage of technology in schools, including the presence of stable staff and support systems, the number of English-language learners and other at-risk students, pressure to improve standardized test scores, and students' level of experience with ICT and access to computers at home (Warschauer & Matuchniak, 2010). National statistics on teachers' use of education technology also indicate differences among schools with low and high levels of poverty concentration (Gray, Thomas, & Lewis, 2010). Teachers in low-poverty schools were more likely than their counterparts at high-poverty schools to report that their students sometimes or often used education technology to prepare written text (66 and 56%, respectively), and develop and present multimedia presentations (47 and 36%, respectively). By contrast, teachers at high-poverty schools reported greater usage of technology tools for learning or practicing basic skills (83% compared to 61% for low-poverty schools).

Digital technologies are also changing the teaching profession and placing new demands on teachers to gain expertise in various programs and applications as well as developing strategies for incorporating technology into curriculum and pedagogy. Many school districts are also implementing some form of blended learning and/or competency-based instruction with their students, citing a range of benefits such as extending learning beyond the school day, personalized learning for students, and increased engagement among students (Blackboard, 2016). A national survey of nearly 2500 Advanced Placement (AP) and National Writing Project (NWP) teachers found that for 92% of participants the Internet has a major impact on their ability to access content, resources, and materials for teaching (Purcell, Heaps, Buchanan, & Friedrich, 2013). The majority also reported that the Internet had a major impact on their ability to collaborate with other teachers (69%), interact with parents (67%), and interact with students (57%). At the same time, 75% of teachers reported that the Internet and other digital tools added new demands on the range of content and skills they needed to be knowledgeable about for their profession, and 41% reported that these advances created more work in an effort to be effective teachers.

Meeting teachers where they are

Advances in the accessibility and ease of use of a wide range of digital communication tools has led to increased opportunities for teachers to incorporate media-making and critical literacies into the curriculum for students of all ages. Yet, professional development and training for teachers who are less familiar and confident with these activities is limited and can leave many educators feeling overwhelmed. Unfortunately, this skills gap perpetuates the persistent digital use divide for both students and teachers in the United States, with those in higher resourced communities benefiting from more robust training and support. In other words, teachers who are unable to access resources and training lack the necessary media literacy skills to bring these types of opportunities into their classrooms

Acknowledging this dearth of high-quality training and support for educators related to digital media literacy, KQED Education created an online professional learning platform and community to provide teachers with training, resources, and support to advance their media-making skills. This platform, KQED Teach, aims to provide a community of practice for teachers at all skill levels to gain new competencies, to provide a forum for discussion and community building, and to offer concrete examples for incorporating media-making into their teaching to support student learning and engagement across the curriculum. The following sections will provide a brief overview of the mission and goals of KQED Education and KQED Teach, as well as lessons learned from the first year of implementation. The final section will offer recommendations to support ongoing discourse and future research.

KQED Education

KQED is a public media organization based in Northern California that provides a community-supported alternative to commercial media. KQED Education is a distinct and critical contributor to KQED's public service mission focused on creating and disseminating unique and engaging educational content. Education resources are designed to cultivate a deep interest in engagement with learning, accompanied by an expanded worldview and sense of possibility in relation to college, career, and community for young people aged 11–24. The organization believes that a major accelerant of these outcomes is the development of new media literacies, as defined by Jenkins (2009).

According to Jenkins (2009), new media literacies are the ability of students to understand and interpret media and also to engage with it through critical dialogue and media-making. This definition of media literacy—and especially digital media literacy—represents a set of fundamental capabilities for every student as they prepare for meaningful participation in society, both as a citizen and as a worker. Jenkins (2009) argues that young people need to gain core cultural competencies and social skills to engage in the new media landscape, to move beyond individual activities to community engagement, and to build on the traditional literacy skills to incorporate the practices of participation. The 4 Cs, or practices of participation, include the ability to create media, to circulate them to various audiences, to collaborate with others to complete tasks and form new knowledge, and to connect in both physical and online spaces. Focusing on this robust definition of media literacy capitalizes on the ways that digital media and associated participatory learning attributes can serve as a powerful, efficient, and, in many cases, superior vehicle for improving educational experiences and outcomes.

KQED Education aims to support the development of media literacy in its fullest sense. Namely, the ability to critically consume media content, to express an opinion about it, and to create one's own digital media as the deepest expression of media engagement and learning.

With these clear objectives in mind, KQED Education designed a collection of participatory educational resources and curricula for educators. Ultimately, KQED Education aims to elevate the ways that media-making is incorporated into school curriculum and teaching practices, and to provide opportunities in formal education contexts for students to engage civically in online spaces and become creators rather than just consumers of media. These activities offer youths the chance to explore personal assumptions about media and the forces that control them.

What is KQED Teach?

KQED Teach (teach.kqed.org) is a free, online learning platform that helps teachers learn and practice 21st-century digital media literacy skills. Participants are invited to demonstrate their ability to create effective media in a variety of formats, to learn how digital media can be used effectively to promote learning in various academic content areas, and to develop strategies for transforming their learning environments. Courses range from digital foundations to making infographics to video storytelling, with new courses and experiences being continually developed. Courses and modules can be taken individually or in sequence as part of a cohort or professional learning experience. Educators at all levels of experience and expertise can utilize the resources to advance their skills, whether they're looking to make small adjustments or rethink and transform their teaching practice.

Content on KQED Teach is designed to be both platform- and device-agnostic. Smartphones are the preferred recording device, which allows teachers to capitalize on the technology they already have in their learning environment. As previously stated, nearly three quarters of teens have access to smartphones (Lenhart, 2015), a device powerfully equipped to make most media content and post online. KQED Teach aims to take a democratic approach to media-making, utilizing everyday technology to get media creation into all classrooms. The model also emphasizes the teacher as the producer of media by encouraging teachers to create and post "Make and Shares" to demonstrate their new media skills gained in a particular module. These products, or examples of different digital media content, become part of a teacher's online portfolio, help to build teachers' confidence in creating their own media, and contribute to the community of practice. In addition, the practice of sharing their own work empowers teachers to learn, share, and analyze, mirroring the pedagogical practice they will implement with their students. The online community of practice supports further learning through communication with peers and sharing of resources, lesson plans, and viewing of media content creation, and teachers have the possibility of becoming mentors to other teachers.

Lessons learned from the first year of KQED Teach

When launching KQED Teach, KQED Education wanted to capitalize on the opportunity to continually improve the Teach platform and resources, to deepen our understanding of the ways that teachers are addressing digital media literacy in classrooms, and to develop best practices for supporting teachers in an online professional learning community. The following sections will highlight some of the major findings from initial user experience research that accompanied the launch of KQED Teach as well as insights from an external evaluation of educator perceptions and uses of the KQED Teach platform conducted during the first year. The user experience research was designed to gain a better understanding of KQED Teach users' motivations, behaviors, and needs, while the external evaluation aimed to explore the implementation and impact of the online learning community.

Limited consensus about media literacy

The results of initial user experience research highlighted the fact that the formal educator community lacks a common understanding of media and digital media literacy. Teachers conflated the meaning of terms such as educational technology, digital media, and media literacy, indicating that many teachers are unclear about these fundamental concepts. Further, a significant proportion of teachers indicated that they were interested in media literacy as a concept but were unclear on how to apply it in their classroom. While many teachers are drawn to learning communities such as KQED Teach with the hope of learning new digital skills to apply in their classrooms, they may have a limited understanding of the benefits of media creation for student learning and engagement. Without this fundamental understanding of how media literacy and creation can empower students and help to prepare young people for engaged citizenship and academic success, many teachers may lack the motivation to gain these new skills or develop best practices for implementation in their curriculum and teaching (e.g., Kim, Kim, Lee, Spector, & DeMeester, 2013).

KQED Teach participants also consistently indicated that they viewed media literacy as the reading or interpretation of media as text. This assumption is reinforced by the pervasive focus on deconstructing media texts within media literacy education, to the detriment of encouraging young people to leverage digital tools to create and share their own content. This limited view of media literacy is problematic considering the proliferation of biased and opinion-based news and information that students interact with online that requires a more nuanced understanding of the current media climate. Being an informed and critical consumer of media by interpreting sources, understanding bias, and being cognizant of the various forces driving media production is of central importance. As previously discussed, the majority of young people struggle to navigate the increasing complexities of online resources to find well-sourced and reputable sources of information (Wineburg et al., 2016). At the same time, contributing to the discourse by not only researching and analyzing information but also documenting and sharing a well-formed opinion and new knowledge can be a powerful tool to help young people connect to the issues on a personal level and gain a deeper understanding of the complex challenges faced by our society.

Community support encourages engagement and persistence

One of the key findings from the external evaluation of KQED Teach was the critical role that the online community played in supporting individual learning and engagement. For many users, the ability to post messages and communicate with peers enhanced both their learning and their motivation. As one teacher put it, "Your peers are the best source to learn from. You've got people who are first year teachers and people who are veteran teachers and they all bring their strengths. We can all learn from each other's strengths." Supportive comments from other learners were viewed as a reward and recognition that helped to alleviate feelings of isolation that many online learners encounter. Another user commented, "I think an aspect of teaching that sometimes happens is that people feel very alone in their classroom … The KQED Teach platform is really nice because it provides the opportunity to share and collaborate." Even if other users provided only minimal feedback, such as a "thumbs up" or other emoji, users appreciated knowing that there were other teachers engaged in the community and learning alongside them.

At the same time, users were discouraged when they did not receive feedback from the community or encountered an empty discussion thread. Data from the external evaluation indicated that most conversation threads were relatively brief, that online forum participants did not often respond to moderator prompts or questions, and that participants generally limited their online conversations to a single module or course. Some learners were also hesitant to post Make and Shares or comments to the online forum without spending considerable time preparing their materials or making sure it was their best effort. In this sense, most learners reported that the online forum and community personalized the learning experience and significantly contributed to their learning, yet many were also limiting their participation and not fully contributing to the community by posting and commenting as they moved through the modules and courses.

The online community was also viewed as an important component of the professional development process. "There are very few professional development programs where you can get collaborative and see how other teachers have taught something, and where you can see what materials they used, their notes, and how multiple teachers commented on the same lesson," said one participant. Many teachers appreciated the example lesson plans and curriculum components that other users shared, and wanted more concrete examples of how to translate these new skills into their own classrooms. Some users even suggested that moderators could introduce discussion topics and guide the online discussion, similar to the role of an instructor or facilitator in more formal online courses and activities. These findings align with previous research that highlights the importance of effective and open communication among participants and a sense of community based on common purpose and inquiry in developing an effective online professional learning community (e.g., Aragon, 2003; Garrison, 2007; Lock, 2006).

Conclusions and recommendations

Advancing a shared definition of media literacy and emphasizing the importance of preparing teachers to incorporate digital media skills in every aspect of the curriculum, as the Common Core State Standards suggest, is a critical first step in preparing young people to engage in the new media landscape in thoughtful and critical ways. It is imperative that young people gain more advanced skills to navigate online spaces and critically evaluate information from diverse sources, and helping teachers develop the necessary skills to engage in this work can go a long way to advancing this cause. Online professional learning communities, such as KQED Teach, can help to equip teachers with relevant resources to advance their digital media skills and find innovative ways to leverage digital tools to enhance their teaching.

In addition, online professional learning communities provide educators with a virtual space to connect and collaborate with colleagues grappling with the same challenges, to share victories, and to build momentum for continual growth. Yet, among Teach users, many learners were not taking full advantage of the online forum and learning community despite reporting that this was of central importance to their engagement with the platform. Teachers indicated that posting Make and Shares or commenting on the posts of fellow teachers felt more challenging, or was more intimidating, than sharing personal photos or opinions on other social media because it was related to their professional practice. Further, many learners are content to "lurk" in online communities, benefiting from the posts and conversations of others without personally contributing. These findings highlight a challenge for curriculum and product designers attempting to provide an engaging and welcoming online community for learners that will help them overcome this hesitation to actively engage. In addition, research from online courses indicates that teaching presence, or knowledgeable moderators and designers, encourages higher levels of participation among online learners (e.g., Garrison & Arbaugh, 2007). Finally, providing learners with certificates or badges may be another tool to encourage higher levels of engagement in the online community and forum (e.g., Gibson, Ostashewski, Flintoff, Grant, & Knight, 2015).

By embracing a critical media literacy pedagogy that emphasizes production rather than consumption, teachers can equip students with the mindset needed to help shape their culture and challenge existing media paradigms, to cultivate a more informed and media-literate generation (Campbell, 2006). As participation online eases for students, the diversity of voices that can be heard increases, bolstering civic engagement in a democratic society. In addition, thoughtful design of online learning communities coupled with the use of ongoing data collection and analysis to inform best practices, including more robust use of data analytics and Big Data tools, can provide new opportunities to broaden the reach and impact of online professional learning communities to all educators.

SEE ALSO: Media Industry Involvement in Media Literacy; Media Literacy Education and 21st Century Teacher Education

References

Aragon, S.R. (2003). Creating social presence in online environments. *New Directions for Adult and Continuing Education, 2003*(100), 57–68. doi: 10.1002/ace.119

Belisle, C. (2006). Literacy and the digital knowledge revolution. In A. Martin & D. Madigan (Eds.), *Digital literacies for learning* (pp. 51–67). London, England: Facet Publishing.

Blackboard. (2016). *Trends in digital learning: How K-12 leaders are empowering personalized learning in America's schools.* Retrieved from http://www.tomorrow.org/speakup/2016-digital-learning-reports-from-blackboard-and-speak-up.html

Campbell, G. (2006). Education, information technologies, and the augmentation of human intellect. *Change: The Magazine of Higher Learning, 38*(5), 26–31.

Coiro, J., Knobel, M., Lankshear, C., & Leu, D.J. (2008). Central issues in new literacies and new literacies research. In J. Coiro, M. Knobel, C. Lankshear, & D.J. Leu (Eds.), *Handbook of research on new literacies.* New York, NY: Taylor & Francis.

Common Core State Standards Initiative (2010, June). *Common Core State Standards for English language arts and literacy in history/social studies, science, and technical subjects.* Retrieved from http://www.corestandards.org/wp-content/uploads/ELA_Standards.pdf

Evergreen Education Group. (2015). *Keeping pace with K-12 digital learning: An annual review of policy and practice* (12th ed.). Retrieved from https://www.inacol.org/wp-content/uploads/2015/11/Keeping-Pace-2015-Report-1.pdf

Funk, S., Kellner, D., & Share, J. (2016). Critical media literacy as transformative pedagogy. In M.N. Yildiz & J. Keengwe (Eds.), *Handbook of research on media literacy in the digital age* (pp. 1–30). Hershey, PA: Information Science Reference.

Garrison, D.R. (2007). Online community of inquiry review: Social, cognitive, and teaching presence issues. *Journal of Asynchronous Learning Networks, 11*(1), 61–72.

Garrison, D.R., & Arbaugh, J.B. (2007). Researching the community of inquiry framework: Review, issues, and future directions. *The Internet and Higher Education, 10*(3), 157–172. doi: 10.1016/j.iheduc.2007.04.001

Gee, J.P. (2008). *Social linguistics and literacies: Ideology in discourses* (3rd ed.). New York, NY: Routledge.

Gibson, D., Ostashewski, N., Flintoff, K., Grant, S., & Knight, E. (2015). Digital badges in education. *Education and Information Technologies, 20*(2), 403–410. doi: 10.1007/s10639-013-9291-7

Gray, L., Thomas, N., & Lewis, L. (2010, May). *Teachers' use of educational technology in US public schools: 2009. First look.* Washington, DC: National Center for Education Statistics. Retrieved from https://nces.ed.gov/pubs2010/2010040.pdf

International Society for Technology in Education. (n.d.). ISTE standards for students. Retrieved from http://www.iste.org/standards/iste-standards/standards-for-students

Jenkins, H. (2009). *Confronting the challenges of participatory culture: Media education for the 21st century.* Chicago, IL: The John D. and Catherine T. Macarthur Foundation. Retrieved from http://files.eric.ed.gov/fulltext/ED536086.pdf

Kim, C., Kim, M.K., Lee, C., Spector, J.M., & DeMeester, K. (2013). Teacher beliefs and technology integration. *Teaching and Teacher Education, 29*, 76–85. doi: 10.1016/j.tate.2012.08.005

Lenhart, A. (2015). *Teens, social media, and technology overview 2015.* Washington, DC: Pew Research Center. Retrieved from http://assets.pewresearch.org/wp-content/uploads/sites/14/2015/04/PI_TeensandTech_Update2015_0409151.pdf

Lock, J.V. (2006). A new image: Online communities to facilitate teacher professional development. *Journal of Technology and Teacher Education, 14*(4), 663–678.

Partnership for 21st Century Learning. (2015). *Framework for 21st century learning.* Retrieved from http://www.p21.org/our-work/p21-framework

Porter, A., McMaken, J., Hwang, J., & Yang, R. (2011). Common Core Standards: The new US intended curriculum. *Educational Researcher, 40*(3), 103–116. doi: 10.3102/0013189X11405038

Purcell, K., Heaps, A., Buchanan, J., & Friedrich, L. (2013, February 28). *How teachers are using technology at home and in their classrooms.* Washington, DC: Pew Research Center. Retrieved from http://pewinternet.org/Reports/2013/Teachers-and-technology

Sims, C. (2014). From differentiated use to differentiating practices: Negotiating legitimate participation and the production of privileged identities. *Information, Communication & Society, 17*(6), 670–682. doi: 10.1080/1369118X.2013.808363

Warschauer, M., & Matuchniak, T. (2010). New technology and digital worlds: Analyzing evidence of equity in access, use, and outcomes. *Review of Research in Education, 34*(1), 179–225. doi: 10.3102/0091732X09349791

Wineburg, S., & McGrew, S. (2016, November 1). Why students can't Google their way to the truth: Fact-checkers and students approach websites differently. *Education Week.* Retrieved from http://www.edweek.org/ew/articles/2016/11/02/why-students-cant-google-their-way-to.html

Wineburg, S., McGrew, S., Breakstone, J., & Ortega, T. (2016). Evaluating information: The cornerstone of civic online reasoning. *Stanford Digital Repository.* Retrieved from http://purl.stanford.edu/fv751yt5934

Denise L. Sauerteig is the Learning & Evaluation Manager for KQED. She leads all evaluation efforts for KQED, focused on the reach, engagement, and impact of educational resources produced by KQED. Prior to KQED, her research interests included digital media and learning, learning in informal environments, teacher professional development, and STEM education. Denise holds an MA in international education policy analysis from Stanford University.

Maria F. Cervera Gutierrez was formerly the Associate Director of Curriculum and Online Learning for KQED Education. Before working for KQED, she created and wrote multiple children's TV shows for Canal Once, Mexico's public media station. Her work focuses on designing experiences that make meaningful use of technology to advance learning. She holds a BA in communications from Universidad Iberoamericana and an MA in learning design and technology from Stanford University.

Brit Toven-Lindsey is a postdoctoral researcher in the College of Education and Allied Studies at California State University East Bay. Her research interests include assessment and evaluation of innovative teaching practices, access and equity in STEM fields, and undergraduate career preparation and pathways. She holds a PhD in education from the University of California, Los Angeles.

Ingrid Hu Dahl is the Director of Learning Experiences at Capital One, cultivating and co-creating leadership, influence, and strategic design experiences. Dahl was previously the Managing Director of KQED's Learning initiative where she oversaw the development of products, platforms, and content. Prior to KQED, she was the Senior Director of Education and Field Building at Bay Area Video Coalition where she designed programs to bridge underrepresented young professionals to the tech sector. She was also a program officer at the Academy for Educational Development in New York City.

Media Literacy Foundations

RENEE HOBBS
University of Rhode Island, USA

The concept of media literacy has been circulating in the United States and Europe since the beginning of the 20th century; but it continues to morph and change as a result of changes in education, technology, media, popular culture, and society. Media literacy is widely understood as the knowledge, competencies, and life skills needed to participate in contemporary society by accessing, analyzing, evaluating, and creating media messages in a wide variety of forms. Media literacy can be understood as the outcome of the practice of media literacy education. In some contexts, the broader term "media education" is used to refer to all the contexts in which learning about media occurs.

The most widely used definition of media literacy emerged from the Aspen Institute, which brought together a group of media literacy experts in 1993 to define media literacy as a "movement to expand notions of literacy to include the powerful post-print media that dominate our informational landscape," noting that it "helps people understand, produce and negotiate meanings in a culture made up of powerful images, words and sounds" (Aufderheide, 1993, p. 1). This definition has been used in most scholarly and practitioner discourse on media literacy education in the United States. In parts of the world, the term media education is used to refer to the knowledge and the analytical tools that empower consumers to function as autonomous and rational citizens (Tyner, 2004).

There are a number of approaches to media literacy now in wide circulation around the world. As RobbGrieco (2015, p. 5) notes in his history of media literacy in the United States, "the conceptual contours of meaning, theory, and application of the basic definition and the terms within it have been continuously contested and employed in very different ways by scholars and practitioners with different disciplinary and institutional interests." Scholars have identified how different stakeholder groups seek distinctive names to represent their understanding of the competencies for using media and technology. A variety of terms have been promulgated that aim to capture the full constellation of habits of mind, knowledge, attitudes, and skills necessary for full participation in contemporary, media-saturated society. Some of these include media competence, cyberliteracy, new literacies, digital literacy, web literacy, transliteracy—and more.

To understand the dynamic concept of media literacy, it is necessary to appreciate its theory, history, and pedagogy as well as some of the ongoing controversies and challenges in the field. As we will see in this encyclopedia and in the pages that follow, media literacy has entered the education and cultural system in four distinct ways: as an expanded form of literacy; as an intervention to address potential harms of media exposure; as an approach to integrate digital technology into education; and as a dimension of global citizenship.

Theories of media literacy

Because of its transdisciplinary nature, media literacy has been conceptualized in relation to four primary theoretical positions: as a means to counter the negative effects of mass media; as a way to counter the hegemonic power of mass media; as a way to recognize the structure and constructed nature of media messages; and as a way to acknowledge the role of play, identity, voice, and subjectivity in the practices of consuming and creating media. Each of these four traditions has its adherents and its detractors, which has contributed to some of the "great debates" in the field (Hobbs, 1998).

The rhetorical tradition, developed by scholars in the humanities, has long recognized the importance of language and other symbol systems as a structuring tool for human thought and action. For 2500 years, beginning with the transition from oral to written culture, people have been debating whether media emancipate us or are forms of social control. The argument goes back to ancient times, with questions like these: How does our use of symbol systems like language and images shape social relationships? What is gained and what is lost with the strategic use of language and other symbols as tools for expression, persuasion, and advocacy? How can symbol systems be used to express, distort, or misrepresent our sense of personal identity, the value of social relationships, and our understanding of reality? During the 20th century, the rise of structuralism and poststructuralism created renewed interest in these questions, exploring the relationship between language and other symbol systems as they connect to perception, cognition, and meaning-making. In the field of communications, Marshall McLuhan was perhaps the foremost scholar within this tradition. By practicing an inquiry approach to media, McLuhan theorized that learners might shift the perspective on the media environment in order to assess what is gained and lost through our uses of media technologies— ultimately in order to act more strategically about media use (Strate, 2016).

The media effects tradition has also been aligned with media literacy, as researchers who examine the impact of media on attitudes, beliefs, and behaviors conceptualize media literacy as a means to minimize the potentially negative consequences of media violence, cyberbullying, stereotyping, or consumer culture. Media literacy is positioned as a way to solve the problem of children and young people, who can be duped or misled by media messages from advertising, news, and Hollywood. In this view, audiences are vulnerable to negative media messages and media users must gain knowledge and skills in order to resist media influence and attain a critical distance from the overwhelming, symbolic environment of the media. It's been claimed that this theoretical framework presents a deficit model of learners. But advocates of this position say that it is responsive to the real needs of parents and educators, as they see children's active imitation and uncritical acceptance of the values presented in mass media and popular culture. In a comprehensive meta-analytic assessment of 51 studies, Jeong, Cho, and Hwang (2012) found a substantial overall effect size of media literacy interventions on outcomes such as media knowledge, criticism, perceived realism, influence, behavioral beliefs, attitudes, self-efficacy, and behavior. Researchers found that the magnitude of intervention effects did not vary by agent, target age, the setting, audience involvement, topic, country, or publication status.

The critical cultural studies tradition has embraced media literacy as a means to theorize the audience of mass media as made up of passive dupes of the culture industries. In this view, the mass audience consumes the products of the culture industries, which reproduce power relations in favor of those who control the means of production, and finds the products of this culture (movies, music, and the like) both irresistible and inescapable; it cannot help delighting in seeing itself reproduced in the endless variation of representations of capitalist mass production. But media products alienate the masses from the means of production of their own culture and suppress critical thinking on the part of the audience by creating a spectacular demand for automatic cognitive processing. Audiences may like the pleasure of feeling superior to mass media and popular culture. It makes them feel like experts. But critical theorists scorn this pleasure, positing that it produces a false consciousness in the mass audience. Media literacy education that pulls back the curtain on the political economy of the media helps audiences become capable of resisting dominant discourses through oppositional meaning-making (Cappello, 2016). Assuming that corporate media institutions perpetuate injustices, students are encouraged to identify sexist, racist, heteronormative, and class-biased media messages and representations and to create their own media messages to counter these representations. They are also offered opportunities to access information and entertainment that is produced by nonmainstream independent and diverse producers (Kellner & Share, 2005).

In the American cultural studies tradition, audiences are conceptualized as active, not passive, engaged in the creative work of meaning-making. Media literacy competencies include those related to play, identity, voice, and subjectivity in the practices of consuming and creating media (Jenkins, Clinton, Purushotma, Robison, & Weigel, 2007). Research on highly engaged audiences, including fans, has been critical to the development of this line of argument. In this tradition, media fans are a perfect model of the active audience; theorists emphasize the idea that culture is produced by the people, from the bottom up, as well as from the top down, by powerful institutions like mass media. The rise of user-generated content and the use of digital platforms for creating and sharing ideas have validated this approach (Bulger & Davison, 2018). Thus educators engage learners through the use of tools for accessing and responding to popular culture, including blogging, message boards, and video production. The engagement that results from interest-driven learning is thought to promote lifelong learning skills (Ito et al., 2013).

To synthesize ideas from these four theoretical traditions, a set of key concepts and core principles has developed among the knowledge community, as the latter expanded and developed through contact at scholarly and professional conferences and through publication of ideas in books, journals, monographs, and videos. Originally developed by the Center for Media Literacy (Thoman & Jolls, 2005), as part of the Aspen Institute Leadership Conference on Media Literacy in 1992, and further refined by a variety of scholars over time, the key concepts include these five ideas:

1. All media messages are constructed.
2. Media messages use medium- and genre-specific codes and conventions.
3. Different people interpret media messages differently.
4. Media have embedded values and points of view.
5. Media messages have political, economic, and social power because they influence perceptions, attitudes, and behavior.

In addition, the National Association for Media Literacy Education (NAMLE) (2007) identified a few key principles of media literacy: (i) media literacy education requires active inquiry and critical thinking about the messages we receive and create; (ii) media literacy education expands the concept of literacy to include all forms of media (i.e., reading and writing); (iii) media literacy education builds and reinforces skills for learners of all ages—skills that, like print literacy, necessitate integrated, interactive, and repeated practice; (iv) media literacy education develops informed, reflective, and engaged participants, essential to a democratic society; (v) media literacy education recognizes that media are a part of culture and function as agents of socialization; and (vi) media literacy education affirms that people use their individual skills, beliefs, and experiences to construct their own meanings from media messages.

Some history

The history of media literacy is complex and contextual, as each country and region has an account of how these ideas and practices developed over time and historical accounts are situated in personal and collective memory (Hobbs, 2016). Film viewers recognized the importance of talking about film within the first years of exposure. Between 1915 and 1934, educators and parents around the world engaged in community film discussions and dialogues, redefining notions of spectatorship. One example of a local cinema club devoted to the study of film was the Cleveland Cinema Club, founded in 1915. In Europe, cinema clubs existed across the United Kingdom, France, and Italy, influencing how a generation of educators conceptualized film and media education. Researchers have also described the historical origins of youth cinema clubs in Russia, noting that the form and structure of these clubs made them serve as a precursor to contemporary media literacy education programs (Federov & Friesem, 2015).

During this time, the concept of active film viewing also became a part of the serious study of film in the context of university and higher education; and, as Polan (2007) has observed, there were three distinct threads to teaching about film that focused on (i) the industrial craft of film production; (ii) the aesthetic form and content of film stories; and (iii) the cultural influence of film on social norms, attitudes, and behaviors.

During the 20th century, the press, radio, and television began to be understood as shaping culture and society, generating a significant level of interest around the world in understanding how new tools of expression and communication affected children and youths. In the United States, the Payne Fund studies represented a first attempt to investigate the media's influence in public life using principles of social science to measure film's impact on knowledge, behavior, and socialization. Some of the Payne studies explored the frequency of movie viewing as well as the influence of films on children's sleep habits and on their attitudes toward racial and ethnic groups. Other studies showed that children and adults acquire considerable general information about school subjects, including English, history, and geography from movie viewing. It was hypothesized that movies could revolutionize the means by which traditional academic subjects are taught in the classroom, especially for those who were not academically gifted. As a result of pioneering media educators, educational media began to be produced in a number of countries around the world.

The culminating volume in the Payne Fund Studies was Edgar Dale's (1938) *How to Appreciate Motion Pictures*, a book intended for high school teachers and students. This work stood in distinct contrast to the dominant discourse of the other Payne Fund studies, which in general characterized children and young people as being seduced by the overwhelming visual spectacle of films into adopting questionable moral values. Dale wrote about the practice of *film appreciation*, which, even then, had some early advocates among high school teachers, social workers, youth advocates, parents, and the clergy. He believed that film viewers could analyze cinematography, study the narrative representations of race and wealth, assess historical accuracy, and relate a character's behavior to their own personal lives (Dale, 1938). Such methods of viewing were thought to produce discriminating viewers who would serve as new types of consumers, enticing Hollywood to create quality films. Advocates of film appreciation thought they could produce a new generation of filmmakers, who might reform Hollywood either by working within the film industry or by competing with Hollywood in alternative venues devoted to educational and documentary filmmaking.

Media reform and media advocacy have long been comingled with media literacy. All across the United States, "Better Broadcast" groups were formed in the 1930s, often co-sponsored by organizations such as the American Association of University Women. By the 1950s, with the advent of television, in the United States these groups came together at a national level, to form the American Council for Better Broadcasts, with representatives from 18 national organizations and 18 state groups and with delegates from 93 cities in 34 states. Their mission was to stimulate the broadcasting of good radio and TV programs; to study in order to arrive at a standard for judging the programs; and to encourage stations in fulfilling their obligations to serve the public interest, convenience, and necessity. The monthly newsletters of this particular organization morphed into the *Telemedium*, a publication of the National Telemedia Council in Madison, Wisconsin.

In England, early government support for media education was an important source for funding and visibility. The British Film Institute, a government agency, actively supported a discourse community of educators by disseminating publications, journals, curriculum resources, and conferences, as Bolas (2009) has chronicled in his history of the rise of screen education in England. In the 1950s the British Society for Education in Film and Television published the journal *The Film Teacher*, edited by Derek J. Davies, which aimed to explore how to immunize children from negative media influence and help children practice discrimination in evaluating film quality. Other journals promoting audiovisual education also proliferated, and the British Film Institute promoted instructional strategies for teaching film through the dissemination of film extracts, which were made available to teachers. The topic of media violence also attracted substantial attention, as British educators were concerned about films "in which vicious behavior is disguised, presented in a form in which audiences can enjoy it with a clear conscience" (Mackendrick, as quoted in Bolas, 2009, p. 74).

British students could take a film appreciation class in some schools, but they did so as an additional subject superimposed upon an already full schedule and with no academic credit to be acknowledged. By the mid-1950s, the book *Teaching Film*, by Grace Greiner, identified five approaches to teaching film to high school students through discussion, namely moral, sociological, critical, technical, and historical approaches. During this time, it was relatively rare to engage children and young people in film production; but one article, published in *Film Teacher* in 1955, describes a program where children created short film and learned that the process involves a lot of planning, collaboration, and hard work.

Often considered the grandfather of the North American media literacy movement, Canadian philosopher Marshall McLuhan created a media literacy syllabus for high school students under the rubric of a new approach to language and literature, emphasizing the practice of interpretation not through an expert transmission model, but through probing, deconstruction and close reading and using advertising and other popular culture texts for literary analysis (Strate, 2016). Terms such as genre, language, audience, message, medium, meaning, form, content, and context were central to this approach. As a result, Canadian English educators took the early lead in developing curriculum resources to extend these ideas into classrooms.

At a time when media education was generally conceptualized as teaching *with* film and media, McLuhan's emergence in the 1960s offered educators fresh perspectives on educating the TV generation by teaching *about* media. In his view, societies have always been shaped more by the nature of the media with which individuals communicate than by the apparent content of the communication. His dictum "the medium is the message" came to embody the historical view that the means by which human beings communicate have always structured their actions. He also introduced the idea that the mass media were turning the world into a "global village," shrinking the world in terms of shared experience.

By the mid-1970s there was a growing discourse about television's impact on children and youths and increasing public awareness that media literacy could support media reform initiatives, educational innovation, and assistance for parents and caregivers. Elizabeth Thoman created *Media&Values* as a magazine for the Center for Media and Values, which became the Center for Media Literacy. As the most influential nonprofit organization promoting media literacy in the United States in the 1980s and 1990s, the Center helped formulate media literacy concepts and educational practices and inspired cross-disciplinary conversations between stakeholders in media studies, education, and the public sphere that contributed to the current field of media literacy education. Over 16 years, the *Media&Values* magazine reflected the shifts in media literacy education, from a mostly protectionist paradigm concerned with helping individuals mitigate negative media effects to an empowerment paradigm seeking to help people use media for their benefit (RobbGrieco, 2015).

During the 1970s, some schools in the United Kingdom were actively involved in teaching about media. In 1980 Len Masterman wrote *Teaching about Television*, which offered a comprehensive philosophy and overview of pedagogical methods that represented best practices among educators. At the time, a distinct tension was evident between educators who focused on the analysis of media and educators who made students engage in creating media. In some US communities, school-based programs in media production developed in the 1970s, but were eventually cut owing to budget shortfalls; as a result, afterschool and summer youth media programs sprang up to provide children with media production learning experience. When Neil Postman popularized the idea of media literacy through books like *Amusing Ourselves to Death* (published in 1985), he emphasized the ways in which media discourses were reshaping politics, education, religion, and the news and positioned media literacy as an empowering solution to the cultural problems brought on by television. His longstanding support for media literacy spurred interest from college faculty and educators in K-12 (i.e., US primary and secondary education) schools.

A national and international community developed by the 1980s, as schools were actively experimenting with media literacy in Canada, the United States, the United Kingdom, Germany, and other nations. In 1987, Ontario was the first Canadian province to mandate media education, publishing *Media Literacy*, a resource guide for middle school and high school learners. In 1998 a national organization was formed to support the work of media literacy educators and became the National Association for Media Literacy Education. During this time a scholarly and professional literature began to emerge.

All over the world, media literacy education shifted greatly during the second decade of the 21st century as a result of increased access to digital technology in schools. Digital technology enabled new forms of pedagogy as the Internet entered the classroom. By 2005, many states and provinces in North America included a media literacy strand in English language arts education, which gave media literacy equal status with traditional areas of interest and emphasis such as oral communication, vocabulary, reading, and writing. In Turkey, a media literacy elective course was developed for middle-school students in 2007. By 2015, more than 350 000 children would enroll in the course each year (Hobbs & Tuzel, 2017).

The rising public concern about fake news and disinformation has also had an impact on public interest in media literacy. Although measuring media literacy has proved contentious, especially as regards the development of comparable, standardized indices, policymakers and citizens recognize the value of a well-educated population whose members have the habits of mind needed to critically analyze and create media in a wide variety of forms (Bulger & Davison, 2018). For these reasons, media literacy has entered the education and cultural system in four primary ways: as an expanded form of literacy; as an intervention designed to address potential harms of media exposure; as an approach designed to integrate digital technology into education; and as a dimension of global citizenship.

Media literacy as literacy

Educators and artists understand media literacy as aligned with the practice of creative expression, interpretation, and meaning-making. Terms such as author, text, audience, message, meaning, and representation have also expanded from their earlier semantic areas, which were focused on writers and writing, toward the inclusion of forms of expression and communication that incorporate visual, audiovisual, sound, interactive, and digital formats and modes.

Although literacy has traditionally been understood as the sharing of meaning through spoken and written language, the concept is expanded to include a wider variety of symbolic forms, for example images, graphic design, and multimedia. New forms of expression and communication are displacing the primacy of print language. Because social media tools and platforms have enabled group collaboration and community dialogue, audiences have become producers, and the gap between productive literacies and receptive literacies has narrowed.

In this view, literacy is no longer confined to the domain of printed language. Literacy educators have also begun to rediscover the role of media literacy in reading and writing instruction. There are important connections between visual production and alphabetic reading and writing, as writing teachers used the instructional strategy of producing media to encourage critical analysis, promote creativity and invention, consider the relationship between image and word, and destabilize concepts of linearity and originality through the application of concepts such as assemblage and remix.

Although print-based text is in no way endangered, it now "interacts with digital technologies and multimodality to create more complex texts" (Carrington & Robinson, 2009, p. 5). Learners' engagement with media is explored through the examination of various interpretive communities and affinity groups, which develop as those who have similar interests learn from one another with digital texts, tools, and technologies.

Literacy practices are embedded in situational contexts. The widespread availability and circulation of texts creates opportunities for many different forms of shared cultural participation, and yet also demands increased levels of intellectual curiosity, critical analysis, and creative expression. Inspired by Vygotsky's work on apprenticeship, literacy scholars acknowledge intellectual interdependence between learners and teachers in a particular culture, as learners do not merely absorb messages in the cultural environment but actively co-construct them (Lee & Smagorinsky, 2000). Thus literacy practices are shifting from a focus on individual behavior to a focus on collaborative, social activity.

As an expansion of traditional literacy education, some people see media literacy education as a distinct set of pedagogical practices such as close analysis of media texts, cross-media comparison, keeping a media diary, and multimedia composition (Baker, 2018). These instructional practices help learners in many ways: they build awareness of the constructedness of the media and technology environment, deploy strategies useful in the meaning-making process, increase knowledge about the economic, political, and historical context in which media messages circulate, and appreciate the ways in which messages influence attitudes and behavior (Wilson, Grizzle, Tuazon, Akyempong, & Cheung, 2011).

Support among literacy educators for the practice of media literacy education has been a major factor in the rise of media literacy education around the world. In some European countries, media literacy education has developed in informal learning contexts, owing to the absence of media literacy frameworks in the national curriculum. Although France, Finland, and some other countries have media education authorities as government agencies, media education is generally not embedded in ministries of education but is thought to have a broader focus that embraces culture, community, and business stakeholders. In the United States, with its decentralized education system, support for digital and media literacy education exists in many of the over 15 000 local school districts. It is not known how many students receive exposure to media literacy education, but one study with a representative sample of California young adults found that nearly one third claimed to have had such exposure in school (Kahne & Bowyer, 2017). Although nearly all states include media literacy learning outcomes in their state education standards, each of the school districts must decide whether and how media literacy education is implemented.

Media literacy education in schools generally happens as a result of initiatives taken by enthusiastic individual teachers or school leaders (Hobbs, 2011). University departments may advance media literacy in K-12 education by using school–university partnership models, which bring undergraduate and graduate students into schools to support the integration of media literacy into the curriculum (Scharrer, 2006). Motivated practitioners advocate for, implement, and develop programs on the basis of their own interests in and motivations about media literacy and in relation to the unique needs of their communities. This results in a highly varied practice (which may have a focus on the Internet, advertising, news, or entertainment media), generally paired with some form of production activities (e.g., video production).

Media literacy interventions

Extending from the media effects tradition, there have been a number of empirical investigations of media literacy interventions carried out by social science researchers from the disciplines of psychology, communication or public health, and many of these demonstrate meaningful effects on targeted attitudes and behavior (Jeong et al., 2012). Most interventions approach media literacy as a means to address problematic dimensions of media culture that stem from the content or usage of mass media, digital media, and popular culture. Often labeled protectionist media literacy, these interventions address issues such as media violence, stereotypes in the representation of gender and race, materialism and consumer culture, the glamorization of unhealthy behavior, for example drinking and smoking, the practice of sexting and cyberbullying, and the like.

Media literacy is associated with increased resilience in children and youths, which is a key factor in health and human development. Media literacy has been found to be effective in a wide variety of contexts and learning environments. Some programs consist of only one or two short sessions; others last for a semester or more. Some focus on one issue (violence, advertising, alcohol); others address many different topics (for a review, see Martens, 2010). For example, researchers have found that adolescents with higher levels of media literacy education (as measured on an 18-item Smoking Media Literacy scale) showed lower levels of smoking behavior and intent to smoke (Primack, Gold, Land, & Fine, 2006). They have tested whether children's fears about terrorism could be mitigated through a three-session media literacy program that targeted their mothers, who learned about how news is constructed in order to be able to calm children who might witness violence on TV news (Comer, Furr, Beidas, Weiner, & Kendall, 2008).

Some media literacy interventions might not be truly educational, however. Researchers have explored how to reduce children's exposure to television and TV violence. In one study, researchers implemented a 28 lesson classroom based media literacy intervention on 496 children aged 6–10. These children were persuaded to develop critical attitudes to TV violence and the program was successful in decreasing the amount of time during which they watched media violence, an effect that lasted up to 8 months (Rosenkoetter, Rosenkoetter, & Acock, 2009). Such approaches to media literacy, while potentially valuable, have been criticized as essentially coercive and not truly embodying the core principles of media literacy education, which respect the autonomy of the individual viewer to make independent and well-informed choices.

The rise of digital literacy and learning

Among educational practitioners and scholars, the rise of digital technologies in education provided an impetus for an interest in media literacy pedagogy to develop. The term *digital literacy* is beginning to be used to designate the technical, cognitive, and social competencies, knowledge, and skills needed to communicate effectively and to participate in the contemporary knowledge economy. Digital literacy draws fresh attention to issues of identity in a networked world; multimodality, hypertexts, mash-ups, and remixing; games, learning, and literacy; and collaboration and peer production (Jones & Hafner, 2012). The American Library Association (2013) has defined digital literacy as "the ability to use information and communication technologies to find, understand, evaluate, create and communicate digital information. Basic reading and writing skills are foundational; and true digital literacy requires both cognitive and technical skills."

The use of mobile media, social media, and new technologies for teaching and learning is creating new opportunities for digital and media literacy education in the context of elementary and secondary education; but there are some concerns about what actual learning outcomes may result from the use of technology tools for transmission-based (and not inquiry-based) learning. This is why media literacy educators have long sought to differentiate their work from that of information and communication technology (ICT) experts or educational technologists. The rise of digital media and learning runs the risk of resurrecting "an old and well-established confusion between teaching about media and teaching through media" (Buckingham, 2009, p. 6). Media literacy educators also differentiate between using media to merely engage learners, as a delivery system, and using them as a teaching aid. When media are used in these functional or instrumental ways, critical questions about cultural, political, and economic contexts tend to be marginalized or ignored.

Media literacy educators use digital technology to cultivate student agency and voice by creating media. Studies of media production in and out of schools have demonstrated how these instructional practices capitalize on children's knowledge and familiarity with media culture (Burn & Durran, 2007). Such work is thought to represent authentic learning, which connects classroom and culture. However, in some schools and communities, the norms and routines of the school culture may interfere with media literacy. Analyzing and creating media in the classroom takes up valuable classroom time and teachers struggle with the "messy engagement" that occurs when students are able to use their popular culture knowledge and creative media production skills (Hobbs & Moore, 2013). For these reasons, in many European and American schools, digital media production stands as a challenge to the traditional academic curriculum. Its novelty as an in-school activity can make it difficult to create organic connections between school learning, everyday life, and digital media.

Talk about mass media, entertainment, and popular culture in the language arts classroom can even be perceived suspiciously by students, as they ask: "What does this have to do with school?" The traditional, content-focused framing of knowledge in the traditional school curriculum contributes to a social reality in which children accept the truth that school knowledge falls within the logical space of the school world, rather than expecting school activities to have any relevance to life outside school (Pérez Tornero, Celot, & Varis, 2007).

With support from charitable foundations, a research and practice area known as *digital media and learning* has developed. The group of scholars behind it advocates broadened access to "learning that is socially embedded, interest-driven, and oriented toward educational, economic, or political opportunity" (Ito et al., 2013, p. 1). For example, a young person who is able to pursue a personal interest or passion with the support of friends and caring adults, and is then able to link this learning and interest to academic achievement, career success, or civic engagement is demonstrating a form of connected learning. This kind of learning is conceptualized as resilient, adaptive, and effective because it is built on the foundation of the individual person's interests, where social support from others helps overcome adversity and provide recognition. Connected learning taps into the opportunities provided by digital media to link more easily home, school, community, and peer contexts of learning; to support peer and intergenerational connections that are based on shared interests; and to create more connections with nondominant youth, drawing from the capacities of diverse communities.

In one project, researchers developed a 3-year longitudinal study to examine a learning environment intentionally designed to provide urban youths with tools that allowed them to create, collaborate, and communicate with new media production technologies. The program offered a series of after-school clubs in graphic design, digital broadcasting, movie making, music recording and remixing, and video game development. Results show that, with effective mentoring, students were able to shift their sense of identity to position themselves as authors (Barron, Gomez, Martin, & Pinkard, 2014). Scholarly inquiry into the practices that contribute to youth empowerment is a vital part of research in digital and media literacy education.

Media literacy and citizenship

Media literacy is increasingly recognized as a tool for strengthening young people's participation in civic and political life. It has the capacity to enable young people to seek out information on relevant issues, evaluate the quality of the information available, and engage in dialogue with others in order to form coalitions. The rise of interest in media literacy education has emerged from a need to respond better to globalization and citizenship in contemporary society (Mihailidis, 2014).

A global approach to media literacy and global citizenship has emerged, spurred by increasing contact between scholars globally, as well as by cross-national studies of media literacy in Europe, Asia, and around the world (Livingstone, 2004). Scholars understand media literacy in relation to a complex interplay of issues, including differential access to technology, democratic political systems and the rise of populism, xenophobia and nationalism (Ranieri, 2016), and the cultural milieu of various nations as they advance media literacy education into formal, informal, and tertiary education (Frau-Meigs and Torrent, 2009).

Media literacy educational initiatives are also becoming cross-national, as programs like the Salzburg Academy on Media and Global Change offer summer learning opportunities to students, teachers, and experts from multiple countries (Mihailidis, 2018). UNESCO has developed a global teacher education program, the Media and Information Literacy Curriculum for Teachers, a resource designed to support member states in their continuing work toward achieving the objectives of the Grünwald Declaration (1982), the Alexandria Declaration (2005), and the UNESCO Paris Agenda (2007)—all related to media and information literacy. Acknowledging the convergence of radio, television, Internet, newspapers, books, digital archives, and libraries, the curriculum is designed for integration into the formal teacher education system.

Although some critics have questioned the value of teaching students to discriminate between fact and opinion in the so-called post-truth world, the general consensus among educators and scholars continues to be to emphasize the value of giving students multiple and varied opportunities to analyze and create media messages, especially in relation to community, social, and cultural issues that they themselves perceive to be relevant.

Research has shown media literacy education to be effective in supporting the habits of mind associated with citizenship in democratic societies. One study found that nearly half of the high school students from 21 high schools in California had engaged in various classroom activities designed to support media literacy competencies, including critically analyzing the trustworthiness of websites, using the Internet to get information about political or social issues, and creating content for the web. These activities are associated with higher rates of online politically driven participation (Kahne, Lee, & Feezell, 2012), and other research has shown that students who received media literacy education were better at analyzing critically media messages that were aligned with their existing beliefs, thus countering natural tendencies toward confirmation bias. In a quasi-experimental design study with a large sample of California youth, those with greater levels of exposure to media literacy education outperformed others in the ability to recognize the bias embedded in a political media message that aligned with their preexisting beliefs (Kahne & Bowyer, 2017).

Governments have also approached media literacy largely in relation to issues of deregulation, economic development, and cultural preservation. As part of the Communications Act of 2003, the British broadcast regulator OFCOM is building public awareness of media literacy to promote the interests of all citizens and to protect them from harm. When the agency was established, its focus was on media industry deregulation; it removed obstacles to cross-media ownership and to global media companies operating in the UK market. As a policy, media literacy is thought to be more important in a deregulated, market-driven economy, where people need to be responsible for their own behavior as consumers (Buckingham, 2009). In this view, then, the global media industry is a stakeholder in advancing the goals of media literacy. However, in the US, the media sector has supported some forms of media literacy, but not others. Companies such as Time Warner, Google, and other large companies provide financial support to Common Sense Media, a San Francisco-based media literacy organization that caters to the needs of parents and educators. Private philanthropies associated with journalism have supported the growth of news literacy by providing financial support to nonprofit organizations such as the News Literacy Project.

Some people consider media literacy to be a type of advocacy or social movement, aimed particularly at young adults, children, and parents. Social movements arise in response to changing social norms and values, as a form of political participation whereby people engage in a sustained public effort to make social change by using communicative action to raise awareness, to build strategic alliances, and ultimately to challenge and reform some aspects of contemporary culture. Those who see media literacy as a social movement are generally motivated by their awareness that changes in audience behavior can bring about changes in the media industry. This is sometimes conceptualized as demand-focused media reform. A wide variety of small groups, nonprofit organizations, and other individuals advocate media literacy at the local and community levels. While this approach to media literacy has been roundly criticized as a form of moral, cultural, or political defensiveness (Buckingham, 2003), it continues to have traction in the United States and some other countries, especially in relation to the ever-changing forms of contemporary digital technology, mass media, and popular culture. A number of youth and media advocacy groups are allied with the social movement conceptualization of media literacy. For example, as part of their advocacy efforts for media literacy, Girl Scouts USA conducted survey research with girls aged 11–17, finding that about half of the sample are regular viewers of reality TV shows and that regular viewers accept and expect a higher level of drama, aggression, and bullying in their own lives (Girl Scouts USA, 2011).

One grassroots policy issue that has been directly addressed by media literacy educators is the issue of copyright and fair use. Media literacy educators rely on the ability to use copyrighted materials for learning purposes. In Europe, national copyright laws have created some confusion about basic pedagogical practices like using images in PowerPoint slides or remixing digital content. When American media literacy educators experienced a generalized climate of fear, uncertainty, and doubt about the legal use of copyrighted materials for teaching and learning, they worked collaboratively, with support from expert legal scholars, to develop a Code of Best Practices in Fair Use for Media Literacy Education. As a result of advocacy carried out by media literacy educators, the US Copyright Office has extended fair use to include the ability to "rip" videos from DVDs for media literacy education in the context of higher as well as elementary and secondary education (Hobbs, 2010).

Media regulators themselves may engage in media literacy in countries like Singapore or Turkey, where the media regulator (MDA or RTUK) takes responsibility for curriculum development and teacher training in media literacy programs offered in the elementary and secondary schools. Frau-Meigs and Torrent (2009) catalogued these practices in a book titled *Mapping Media Education Policies*, which outlined activities in Austria, Brazil, Spain, South Korea, Finland, Argentina, Turkey, and other countries. At the Education, Youth and Culture meeting held in Brussels in 2009, the Council of the European Union formally adopted a policy on a European approach to media literacy in the digital environment that was "embedded in a package of measures to ensure an effective European single market for emerging audiovisual media services" (O'Neill, 2010, p. 328).

In some countries, media literacy policy aims to build national audiences for the audiovisual economic sector and to protect cultural heritage against the encroachment of Hollywood. Long an advocate for the use of critical inquiry in media literacy teacher education, the British Film Institute shifted gears in 2012, advancing a new strategy called Film Forever, a plan to nurture business growth and cultural vibrancy across the United Kingdom. Thus the British Film Institute promotes media education in after-school programs largely because of an interest in supporting the British film industry. The program is designed to support a prosperous film business sector by cultivating audiences. Funded by a significantly increased lottery allocation and government grants, fundraising, and new entrepreneurial activity, the Film Forever program relies on collaboration with the United Kingdom film industry as well as on nonprofit cultural and educational partners.

The European Commission has invested millions of euros in supporting European nations to develop the media and information literacy competencies of its citizens. This reflects an increasingly global awareness of the need to empower citizens by providing them with the competencies necessary to engage with traditional media and new technologies. Key elements include understanding the role and functions of media in democratic societies; understanding the conditions under which the media can fulfill their functions; critically evaluating media content; engaging with media for self-expression and democratic participation; and developing the skills needed to produce user-generated content.

Access to quality media and information content and participation in media and communication networks are necessary to realize Article 19 of the Universal Declaration of Human Rights regarding the right to freedom of opinion and expression. Recognizing the increasingly competitive environment of the audiovisual sector that results from an inclusive knowledge society, the Council of Europe has noted that the education system must get better at supporting people's ability to access, understand, evaluate, create, and communicate media content as part of lifelong learning. It noted: "The responsible and informed use of new technologies and new media requires citizens to be aware of risks and to respect relevant legal provisions, but most literacy policies should address such questions in the context of a generally positive message" (Council of Europe, 2007, p. 2). The Council recommended the progressive development of criteria intended to assess the levels of media literacy in member states from 2011 on, a task that has been initiated by a number of federal agencies with support from key European scholars. Some scholars question, however, the extent to which European media literacy education will balance the "consumer" orientation (promoting the use of media) with the "citizenship" orientation (empowering critical analysis and active participation), especially given the recalcitrance of the formal education sector in many European nations (O'Neill, 2010).

The UN–Alliance of Civilizations Media Literacy Education Clearinghouse is a global repository of media literacy education, research, media education policy, and youth media. Nordicom and UNESCO have also established a clearinghouse to collect research on youth and media with the goal of broadening the public's knowledge and awareness of media literacy. Policy work continues to raise awareness and to mobilize all stakeholders involved, including high-level political decision-makers, for maximum impact. These organizations collaborate with others, international and national, on launching initiatives such as public awareness campaigns on media literacy, helping to set up national and international meetings with key decision-makers.

Finally, both government policymakers and charitable foundations have explicitly addressed the need for media literacy for the wider population, not just for children and youths. For example, the Federal Communications Commission's Future of Media initiative sought public comment on this question: What kinds of digital and media literacy programs are appropriate to help people both use new information and communication technologies effectively and to analyze and evaluate the news and information they are receiving? The Knight Commission's influential report *Informing Communities: Sustaining Democracy in the Digital Age* identifies media literacy in relation to enhancing the information capacity of individuals, particularly in the area of citizenship. And it is impossible to overstate the influence of the John D. and Catherine T. MacArthur Foundation, which from 2007 to 2016 invested more than $120 million in research on digital media and learning, supporting a variety of diverse research and practical projects that are transforming the field.

The future of digital and media literacy

The future of media literacy will be shaped by the practices of the present era. There are a number of strategies that could help if they were more readily available to all learners, for example intensifying the focus on the young (Bazalgette, 2011). But substantial obstacles exist. Consider this. When the testing company that administers the high-stakes scholastic assessment test (SAT) required for admission to American colleges used a question that invited students to critically analyze the genre of reality TV, it asked them to write an essay in response to the following prompt: "Reality television programs, which feature real people engaged in real activities rather than professional actors performing scripted scenes, are increasingly popular. These shows depict ordinary people competing in everything from singing and dancing to losing weight, or just living their everyday lives. Most people believe that the reality these shows portray is authentic, but they are being misled. How authentic can these shows be when producers design challenges for the participants and then editors alter filmed scenes? Do people benefit from forms of entertainment that show so-called reality, or are such forms of entertainment harmful?" (Strauss, 2011, p. 1).

While media literacy educators cheered at the news and students may have valued the chance to critically examine reality TV as part of the testing experience, some educators who prioritize the need to transmit core knowledge were less than satisfied. Some objected to any educational emphasis on activating students' prior knowledge from their experience with mass media and popular culture, seeing it as "dumbing down" the curriculum.

The biggest obstacle that faces the future of global media literacy concerns attitudes and perceptions that media literacy is not a "serious" subject. Among the elites who control and set educational policy, this is perhaps the most substantial and well-entrenched attitude about media literacy that persists today: in Britain, a recent empirical analysis of British newspaper coverage found that media studies was represented and framed as a "soft" or "Mickey Mouse" subject and 61% of news stories depicted the academic program as having little educational value (Bennett & Kidd, 2017). Such long-standing attitudes continue to limit the application of digital and media literacy in elementary and secondary educational institutions around the world. In the future, it will be important to address these attitudes and align the ever-changing conceptualizations of media literacy, so that it continues to be relevant to the growing intersections of technology, mass media, education, digital and social media, and popular culture.

SEE ALSO: Creativity and Media Production in Schools; Media Literacy among the Elderly; Media Literacy and Alcohol Abuse Reduction; Media Literacy and Pragmatism; Media Literacy and Smoking; Media Literacy and Visual Culture; Media Literacy as Contemporary Rhetoric; Media Literacy Education and Second Language Acquisition; Media Literacy in Communication Education; Media Literacy in Teacher Education; Media Literacy in the Primary Grades; Media Literacy in the Social Studies NCSS; Media Literacy, Terrorism, and Fear; Media Literacy with New Immigrants; Media Production in Elementary Education

References

American Library Association. (2013). Digital literacy, libraries and public policy. Office of Information Technology Policy. Retrieved from http://www.districtdispatch.org/wp-content/uploads/2013/01/2012_OITP_digilitreport_1_22_13.pdf

Aufderheide, P. (1993). *Media literacy: A report of the national leadership conference on media literacy*. Washington, DC: Aspen Institute, Communications and Society Program.

Baker, F. (2018). *Close reading the media*. New York, NY: Routledge/Middle Web.

Barron, B., Gomez, K., Martin, C.K., & Pinkard, N. (2014). *The digital youth network: Cultivating digital media citizenship in urban communities*. Cambridge, MA: MIT Press.

Bazalgette, C. (2011). The entitlement project: Manifesto for media education. Retrieved from http://www.manifestoformediaeducation.co.uk/wp-content/uploads/Manifesto-Cary-Bazalgette.pdf

Bennett, L., & Kidd, J. (2017). Myths about media studies: The construction of media studies education in the British press. *Continuum, 31*(2), 163–176.

Bolas, T. (2009). *Screen education: From film appreciation to media studies*. Bristol, England: Intellect.

Buckingham, D. (2003). Media education and the end of the critical consumer. *Harvard Educational Review, 73*(3), 309–327.

Buckingham, D. (2009). The future of media literacy in the digital age: Some challenges. *Medienimpulse, 2*. Retrieved from http://medienimpulse.erz.univie.ac.at/articles/view/143

Bulger, M., & Davison, P. (2018). *The promises, challenges and futures of media literacy*. New York, NY: Data and Society Institute. Retrieved from https://datasociety.net/pubs/oh/DataAndSociety_Media_Literacy_2018.pdf

Burn, A., & Durran, J. (2007). *Media literacy in schools: Practice, production and progression*. London, England: Chapman.

Cappello, G. (2016). Gianna Cappello on Theodor Adorno. In R. Hobbs (Ed.), *Exploring the roots of digital and media literacy through personal narrative* (pp. 107–125). Philadelphia, PA: Temple University Press.

Carrington, V., & Robinson, M. (2009) *Digital literacies: Social learning and classroom practices*. New York, NY: SAGE.

Comer, J.S., Furr, J.M., Beidas, R.S., Weiner, C.L., & Kendall, P.C. (2008). Children and terrorism-related news: Training parents in coping and media literacy. *Journal of Consulting and Clinical Psychology, 76*, 568–578.

Council of Europe. (2007). Recommendation CM/REC-2007–11 of the Committee of Ministers to member states on promoting freedom of expression and information in the new information and communications environment. Strasbourg, France: Council of Europe.

Dale, E. (1938). *How to appreciate motion pictures*. New York, NY: Macmillan.

Federov, A., & Friesem, E. (2015). Soviet cineclubs: Baranov's film/media model. *Journal of Media Literacy Education, 7*(2), 12–22.

Frau-Meigs, D., & Torrent, J. (2009). *Mapping media education policies in the world: Visions, programmes and challenges.* Paris, France: UNESCO.

Girl Scouts USA. (2011). Real to me: Girls and reality TV. Retrieved December 1, 2011 from http://www.girlscouts.org/research/publications/girlsandmedia/real_to_me.asp

Hobbs, R. (1998). The seven great debates in the media literacy movement. *Journal of Communication, 48*(1), 16–32.

Hobbs, R. (2010). *Copyright clarity: How fair use supports digital learning*. Thousand Oaks, CA: Corwin/SAGE.

Hobbs, R. (2011). The state of media literacy: A response to Potter. *Journal of Broadcasting and Electronic Media, 55*(3), 419–430.

Hobbs, R. (2016). *Exploring the roots of digital and media literacy through personal narrative.* Philadelphia, PA: Temple University Press.

Hobbs, R., & Moore, D.C. (2013). *Discovering media literacy: Digital media and popular culture in elementary school.* Thousand Oaks, CA: Corwin/SAGE.

Hobbs, R., & Tuzel, S. (2017). Teacher motivations for digital and media literacy: An examination of Turkish educators. *British Journal of Educational Technology, 48*(1), 7–22. doi: 10.1111/bjet.12326

Ito, M., Gutiérrez, K., Livingstone, S., Penuel, B., Rhodes, J., Salen, K., … Watkins, C. (2013). *Connected learning: An agenda for research and design.* Digital Media and Learning Research Hub, Irvine, CA. Retrieved from https://dmlhub.net/wp-content/uploads/files/Connected_Learning_report.pdf

Jenkins, H., Clinton, K., Purushotma, R., Robison, A., & Weigel, M. (2007). *Confronting the challenges of participatory culture: Media education for the 21st century.* Chicago, IL: MacArthur Foundation.

Jeong, S.-H., Cho, H., & Hwang, Y. (2012). Media literacy interventions: A meta-analytic review. *Journal of Communication, 62*(3), 454–472.

Jones, R., & Hafner, C. (2012). *Understanding digital literacies.* New York, NY: Routledge.

Kahne, J., & Bowyer, B. (2017). Educating for democracy in a partisan age: Confronting the challenges of motivated reasoning and misinformation. *American Educational Research Journal, 54*(1), 3–34.

Kahne, J., Lee, N.J., & Feezell, J.T. (2012). Digital media literacy education and online civic and political participation. *International Journal of Communication, 6*, 1–24.

Kellner, D., & Share, J. (2005). Toward critical media literacy: Core concepts, debates, organizations, and policy. *Discourse: Studies in the Cultural Politics of Education, 26*(3), 369–386.

Lee, C., & Smagorinsky, P. (2000). *Vygotskian perspectives on literacy research: Constructing meaning through collaborative inquiry.* New York, NY: Cambridge University Press.

Livingstone, S. (2004). Media literacy and the challenge of new information and communication technologies. *Communication Review, 7*(1), 3–14.

Martens, H. (2010). Evaluating media literacy education: Concepts, theories and future directions. *Journal of Media Literacy Education, 2*(1), 1–22.

Mihailidis, P. (2014). *Media literacy & the emerging citizen: Youth, engagement and participation in digital culture.* New York, NY: Peter Lang.

Mihailidis, P. (2018). Civic media literacies: Re-imagining engagement for civic intentionality. In E. Gordon & P. Mihailidis (Eds.), *Learning, Media and Technology, 43*(2), 152–164.

National Association for Media Literacy Education. (2007, November). Core principles of media literacy education in the United States. Retrieved from http://namle.net/publications/core-principles

O'Neill, B. (2010). Media literacy and communication rights: Ethical individualism in the New Media environment. *International Communication Gazette, 72*(4–5), 323–338.

Pérez Tornero, J.M., Celot, P., & Varis, T. (2007). *Current trends and approaches to media literacy in Europe*. Brussels, Belgium: European Commission. Retrieved from http://ec.europa.eu/culture/media/literacy/docs/studies/study.pdf

Polan, D. (2007). *Scenes of instruction: The beginnings of the US study of film*. Berkeley: University of California Press.

Primack, B.A., Gold, M.A., Land, S.R., & Fine, M.J. (2006). Association of cigarette smoking and media literacy about smoking among adolescents. *Journal of Adolescent Health, 39*(4), 465–472.

Ranieri, M. (Ed.). (2016). *Populism, media and education: Challenging discrimination in contemporary digital societies*. New York, NY: Routledge.

RobbGrieco, M. (2015). *Media for media literacy: Discourses of the media literacy education movement in* Media & Values *magazine, 1977–1993*. Unpublished dissertation, Mass Media and Communication Program, Temple University, PA.

Rosenkoetter, L.I., Rosenkoetter, S.E., & Acock, A.C. (2009). Television violence: An intervention to reduce its impact on children. *Journal of Applied Developmental Psychology, 30*, 381–397.

Scharrer, E. (2006). "I noticed more violence": The effects of a media literacy program on knowledge and attitudes about media violence. *Journal of Mass Media Ethics, 21*(1), 70–87.

Strate, L. (2016). Lance Strate on Marshall McLuhan. In R. Hobbs (Ed.), *Exploring the roots of digital and media literacy through personal narrative* (pp. 49–65). Philadelphia, PA: Temple University Press.

Strauss, V. (2011, March 15). SAT question on reality TV stirs controversy. *Washington Post*. Retrieved from https://www.washingtonpost.com/blogs/answer-sheet/post/sat-question-on-reality-tv-stirs-controversy/2011/03/15/ABjNyCY_blog.html?noredirect=on&utm_term=.b35c0209051d

Thoman, E., & Jolls, T. (2005) Media literacy education: Lessons from the Center for Media Literacy. *Yearbook of the National Society for the Study of Education, 104*(1), 180–205.

Tyner, K. (2004). Beyond boxes and wires: Literacy in transition. *Television and New Media, 4*(4), 371–388.

Wilson, C., Grizzle, A., Tuazon, R., Akyempong, K., & Cheung, C. (2011). *Media and information literacy curriculum for educators*. Paris, France: UNESCO.

Further Reading

Beach, R. (2007). *Teaching media literacy*. Thousand Oaks, CA: Corwin/SAGE.

Bennett, W.L. (2008). *Civic life online: Learning how digital media can engage youth*. Cambridge, MA: MIT Press.

Buckingham, D. (2003). *Media education: Literacy, learning and contemporary culture*. Cambridge, England: Polity.

Felini, D. (2014). Quality media literacy education: A tool for teachers and teacher educators of Italian elementary schools. *Journal of Media Literacy Education, 6*(1), 3–25.

Masterman, L. (1985). *Teaching the media*. London, England: Polity.

Nichols, J. (2006). Countering censorship: Edgar Dale and the film appreciation movement. *Cinema Journal, 46*(1), 3–22. doi: 10.1353/cj.2007.0003

Pérez Tornero, M., & Varis, T. (2010). *Media literacy and new humanism*. Moscow, Russia: UNESCO Institute for Information Technologies in Education.

Renee Hobbs is professor of communication studies and director of the Media Education Lab at the Harrington School of Communication and Media at the University of Rhode Island. Her research examines the conditions of media literacy education in elementary and secondary schools and she has authored eight books and over 150 scholarly and professional articles. She has offered professional development programs in media literacy on four continents. She is the founding editor of the *Journal of Media Literacy Education,* an open-access, peer-review journal sponsored by the National Association for Media Literacy Education.

Media Literacy in Australia

MICHAEL DEZUANNI
Queensland University of Technology, Australia

Australia's promotion of media literacy originated in public concerns about the influence of cinema on children in the 1920s. Indeed, social and moral anxiety about children's interactions with popular culture and media and the need to impart civic values to the child as future citizen have laid the foundation for education about various forms of media for the past 80 years, particularly within the Australian schooling system. Accompanying this concern for young people's welfare has been an ongoing recognition of the possibilities for the transformation of education through media technologies, both to make education more engaging and to allow students to communicate in various modes, including through media production. The change in young people's ability to successfully negotiate the media has been reflected in the evolution of media literacy in Australia. Media literacy education has moved from being a specialist pursuit for a relatively small number of teachers and students in secondary schools to being a more general goal of education. Most recently, media literacy education has started to gain a foothold in primary schools owing to the widespread availability of digital devices and the implementation of the media arts strand of the Australian curriculum.

Historical background

The 1927 Australian Royal Commission into the Moving Picture Industry in Australia was central to the development of media literacy education in Australia (Dezuanni & Goldsmith, 2015). This national public commission travelled to all Australian states and territories to gather testimony from film producers and exhibitors, but also from teachers, concerned citizens, law enforcement authorities, court representatives, church leaders, and medical professionals. A key function of the commission was to explore the role of cinema in children's lives. The commission drew attention to the role the moving image could play in education as a technology for delivering content into the classroom in new, engaging ways. Teachers who were already using cinema in their classrooms spoke about its ability to transform the way they taught. A significant number of "witnesses" from a variety of school, church, and community organizations also argued that cinema might be used to expose young people to good-quality productions with a positive message. However, many who appeared before the commission expressed deep concerns about the harmful effects of cinema on children and young people, especially when these were exposed to non-Australian or British content with adult themes. Many also expressed concern about the physical effects of attending cinema on children's eyesight (owing to sitting too close to the screen), on their concentration at school after watching late-night films, and on the spread of illness at close quarters, in the cinema. The commission's focus on the positive and negative consequences of cinema for children established parameters for the gradual introduction of film appreciation and production in Australian schools (Dezuanni & Goldsmith, 2015).

It was not until after World War II, however, that film education started to gain momentum in Australia. Two individuals played an important role in the development of film appreciation from the 1940s to the 1960s: William Herbert Perkins in Tasmania, through the University of Tasmania, and Newman H. Rosenthal in Melbourne, through the University of Melbourne. Both Perkins and Rosenthal were trained teachers who learned about film projection and the educational potential of film while educating troops during World War II (Hooper, 2012; Scrivener, 2012). Both men were film enthusiasts and both used their postwar university roles to promote the use of cinema in education. Perkins had a significant influence on the development of the English curriculum in Tasmania through his role within Tasmania's Department of Education, which led to the inclusion of film texts in the senior English curriculum and in public examinations as early as 1946. Perkins' books *Learning the Liveliest Art* (published in 1968) and *Learning the Liveliest Arts* (published in 1972; this latter included television) influenced an emerging generation of Australian media teachers. In the 1960s, Perkins also spent time in London at the British Film Institute and wrote about the development of 'screen education' in Australia. Upon return to Australia, Perkins established an Australian version of the Society for Education in Film and Television (SEFTV)—the ASEFTV.

The British influence on film education in Australia was also evident in Rosenthal's work. In 1953 he published a book called *Film in our lives: An approach to film appreciation*, which included a reprint of a section of the United Kingdom's *Report of the Departmental Committee on Children and the Cinema*, popularly known as the "Wheare Committee." "Educating Children's Taste in Films" focused on school film-club activities in the United Kingdom in which children and young people viewed and critically discussed films. While the Wheare report explicitly stated that film appreciation should not become part of the formal curriculum, which it asserted was already overcrowded, it encouraged its take-up in clubs and societies with the aim of promoting discrimination in viewing (Rosenthal, 1953, p. 66). As foundation president of the Victorian Council for Children's Films and Television, Rosenthal headed a delegation to the Royal Commission on Television in 1953. Echoing the objectives of the 1927 commission, the TV commission was appointed, in part, in response to "the genuine fear felt by a large section of the Australian community that an unregulated introduction of television would have unfortunate social effects" (Commonwealth of Australia, 1953, p. 52). Rosenthal argued, though, that television should not be made "a scapegoat for the social sins of omission and commission of the community" and that "[t]he effect of television on the child, like that of the film, will depend largely on what he [*sic*] brings to it" (Commonwealth of Australia, 1953, p. 40).

During the 1960s, film appreciation and production developed in Australia's southern states, particularly in Victoria, Tasmania, and South Australia. For instance, in South Australia, a film study committee was constituted in 1965 by the State Department of Education: 18 schools initially implemented a film curriculum, which by 1970 had expanded to 86 secondary schools (Sharman 1971, p. 12). In 1963, the first issue of the *Film Appreciation Newsletter* was published in Victoria by the Australian Teachers of Film Appreciation (ATFA; see Burton, 1982). In 1974, the ATFA changed its name to the Association of Teachers of Media (ATOM), which subsequently became the Australian Teachers of Media, with representation in most Australian states. This early period in the development of media literacy education in Australia was represented in the proceedings of an influential five-day conference in Melbourne in 1970, hosted by UNESCO with keynote speakers from the United Kingdom and the United States. This event was attended by media literacy advocates and education department representatives from all Australian states, and reports were presented about developments in "screen education" in each state. These reports indicate a steady development of media literacy in most Australian states in the 1960s (UNESCO, 1971).

Throughout the late 1970s and into the 1980s, the Australian Teachers of Media became a significant national organization for the promotion of media literacy education, with strong connections to the "media education" movement in the United Kingdom. ATOM chapters in each state advocated for media literacy to be represented in official curriculum documents and educational policy. In Queensland, this led to the introduction of a senior course in film and television in 1979, which continues through to the present day under the name Film, Television and New Media—a university entrance course studied by over 4000 students in almost 200 secondary schools across the state. In Western Australia, in 1979, the Department of Education released the *Primary Media Studies Teachers' Resource Book* (Education Department of Western Australia, 1979). In 1981 the New South Wales Department of Education published a *Mass Media Education* policy (Mass Media Sub-Committee, 1981); and in 1984 it published *All about Mass Media: K-12* (NSW Department of Education, 1984). Also in 1984, the South Australian Department published the *8–12 Media Lab*. Beginning in the 1970s, ATOM began hosting the influential National Media Education conference, which continues to the present day.

Australian media literacy approaches

Media literacy in Australia from the 1940s to the 1960s was largely characterized by its focus on teaching young people about quality cinema. Perkin's and Rosenthal's books aimed to promote "appreciation" as the ability to analyze films (and eventually television) to indicate the features of quality in filmic style, characterization, and thematic treatment. The implication of the appreciation discourse was that some films and television programs were of higher cultural value than others. Discriminating between higher and lower forms of culture, including popular culture, was a specific approach within film and media analysis in the United Kingdom, and was taken up by Australian teachers. A focus on the need to discriminate about the quality of popular culture is evident in Richard Hoggart's (1957) *The Uses of Literacy* and in Stuart Hall and Paddy Whannel's (1964) *The Popular Arts*, both of which are foundational texts for media education. In Australia, several books were published in the early 1970s that were clearly influenced by the discrimination approach, including Dwyer, Milliss, and Thompson's (1971) *Mastering the Media* and T.V. Cooke's (1972) *Understanding Television*.

Ongoing developments in media and cultural studies in both the United Kingdom and Australia in the 1970s and 1980s had a significant impact on media literacy education in Australia. The "cultural turn" and European "theory" drew attention away from cultural value and toward questions about power relations, ideology, representation, audience practices, and institutional factors. UK media education scholar Len Masterman's work was particularly influential in Australia, bolstered as it was by his presentations for the ATOM National Conference in 1982. Drawing on Marxist structuralism, Masterman argued that the goal of media education was to lead students to "critical autonomy," principally by teaching them techniques of "demystification" designed to enable them to identify the hidden ideological influences within a text and within production processes (Masterman, 1985). In addition, Masterman was suspicious of students who mimicked popular cultural forms through media production, because he believed that this approach merely reinforced the dominant ideological and commercial agendas of the media corporations.

In Australia, several media, communications, and cultural studies scholars were also particularly influential during this period. Graeme Turner's (1988) book *Film as Social Practice* was widely used in the 1990s with undergraduate film and communications students, many of whom went on to complete teaching qualifications. This book took a "conceptual" approach that drew heavily on British cultural studies through chapters on film language, narrative, culture and ideology, and audience. Turner also worked with Stuart Cunningham to write a highly influential book titled *The Media in Australia*, which was published in 1993. This publication brought the industry and institutional aspects of Australian media into particular focus, rounding out the triad of industry, text, and audience as a framework for studying media. John Fiske and John Hartley's (1978) *Reading Television* and Ien Ang's (1985) study of *Dallas* promoted cultural and social readings of television that recognized the central role audiences play in active meaning-making. The industry, text, and audience approach to media study resonated with the British Film Institute's "key concepts" approach (Bazalgette, 1992), which came to underpin school-based media courses in most Australian states from the 1990s to the present day.

Media literacy in Australia in the 2010s

The past two decades in media literacy education in Australia have been characterized by an increasing focus on media production as an important accompaniment to critical analysis, as technologies have become more accessible. All Australian states with the exception of New South Wales offer an upper-secondary school elective in media production and analysis. In addition, there has been increasing focus on media literacy education at all levels of schooling, both through the English curriculum and within arts education. Media literacy education has had a presence in the English curriculum at most levels of schooling since the 1960s, and in the 2010s media texts are often used in English classes from about the middle years of primary school (i.e., with students from the age of 8 years on). In New South Wales, Australia's most populous state, media curricula do not exist outside the English curriculum as a separate entity at any level of schooling. The focus within the English curriculum, however, is typically on textual analysis and rarely accounts for contextual factors such as institutional impact and audience practices. Furthermore, media production is seldom a feature of students' creative practice in the English classroom in Australia.

Media literacy education involving media production has primarily been located in the arts curriculum of Australia since the early 1990s. In 1994, media was identified as one of five arts areas in the national curriculum statements on the arts (Australian Education Council, 1994). In 2008, the Australian government announced that a new Australian curriculum would be created; thus, for the first time, curriculum development was made both a state and a federal government responsibility. The national curriculum made some content mandatory for all children in the primary years of education (foundation to year 6) and strongly recommended for secondary schools. Australian Teachers of Media successfully lobbied for the media curriculum to be included in the Australian curriculum, and "media arts" content was developed for students from pre-school to year 10; this content underpinned by five key concepts (media languages, representations, audiences, institutions, and technologies) and by making (production) and responding (critical analysis; see ACARA, 2016). The media arts curriculum is unique internationally because it outlines a curriculum scope and sequence for 5–15-year-old children, placing emphasis on both production and analysis. Media arts provides students with opportunities to use digital images, sound, and text to tell stories. The curriculum states: "Media arts involves creating representations of the world and telling stories through communications technologies such as television, film, video, newspapers, radio, video games, the internet and mobile media. Media arts connects audiences, purposes and ideas, exploring concepts and viewpoints through the creative use of materials and technologies" (ACARA, 2016).

The implementation of media arts for primary schools in Australia has coincided with a dramatic increase in the availability of technology in classrooms, including tablet computers that enable media production. A key policy of the Australian federal government has been to encourage "bring your own device" (BYOD) strategies to enable widespread use of computing in schools (DEAG, 2013, p. 7). The focus on BYOD has not been universally implemented in Australian schools and there are issues with children's equitable access to resources; however, where technologies like tablet computers are available, media production is accessible even to young children. A national study conducted from 2014 to 2016 (Cunningham et al., 2016) showed that most children and young people reported that they had been asked at least once during their primary and lower secondary schooling to make video content as part of their learning. Media literacy education in Australia, then, is moving from being a specialist concern in secondary schools to becoming a more general part of the curriculum, as educational policy and technological development promote multimodal communication in classrooms. The challenge for educators is to find ways to enable children and young people to critically engage with media content as they participate in its production and consumption in ever more complex ways.

SEE ALSO: Film Education in Europe; History of Media Literacy; Media Arts; Media Literacy in Canada; Media Literacy in England; Media Literacy in New Zealand

References

Ang, I. (1985). *Watching Dallas*. New York, NY: Methuen.

ACARA. (2016). *Australian curriculum, the arts: Media arts*. Australian Curriculum, Assessment and Reporting Authority, Sydney. Retrieved from https://www.australiancurriculum.edu.au/f-10-curriculum/the-arts/media-arts

Australian Education Council. (1994). *The arts: A curriculum profile for Australian schools*. Melbourne, Australia: Curriculum Corporation.

Bazalgette, C. (1992). Key aspects of media education. In M. Alvarado & O. Boyd-Barratt (Eds.), *Media education: An introduction* (pp. 199–219). London, England: British Film Institute.

Burton, L. (1982). *Editorial. Metro, 58*, 3.

Commonwealth of Australia. (1953). *Report of the Royal Commission on television*. Canberra, Australia: Australian Government.

Cooke, T.V. (1972). *Understanding television: A course in English for Australian schools*. Sydney, Australia: Reed Education.

Cunningham, S., Dezuanni, M., Goldsmith, B., Burns, M., Miles, P., Henkel, C., Ryan, M., & Murphy, K.(2016). *Screen content in Australian education: Digital promise and pitfalls*. Retrieved June 18, 2018 from https://eprints.qut.edu.au/101132

DEAG. (2013). *Beyond the classroom: A new digital education for young Australians in the 21st century*. Digital Education Advisory Group, Australian Government, Canberra, Australia. Retrieved November 3, 2016 from https://docs.education.gov.au/documents/digital-education-advisory-group-final-report

Dezuanni, M., & Goldsmith, B. (2015). Disciplining the screen through education: The Royal Commission into the Moving Picture Industry in Australia. *Studies in Australasian Cinema, 9*(3), 298–311. doi: 10.1080/17503175.2015.1087133

Dwyer, B., Milliss, R., & Thompson, B. (1971). *Mastering the media*. Sydney, Australia: Reed Education.

Education Department of Western Australia. (1979). *Primary media studies teachers' resource book*. Perth, Australia: Education Department of Western Australia.

Fiske, J., & Hartley, J. (1978). *Reading television*. New York, NY: Methuen.

Hall, S., & Whannel, P. (1964). *The popular arts*. Boston, MA: Beacon Press.

Hoggart, R. (1957). *The uses of literacy: Aspects of working class life*. London, England: Chatto & Windus.

Hooper, C. (2012). Rosenthal, Newman Hirsh (1898–1986). In *Australian dictionary of biography*. Retrieved from http://adb.anu.edu.au/biography/rosenthal-newman-hirsh-15929

Mass Media Sub-Committee. (1981). Mass media education: Guidelines and suggestions for implementing mass media programs in schools. NSW Department of Education, Hunter Region Language Curriculum Committee, Adamston, New South Wales, Australia.

Masterman, L. (1985). *Teaching the media*. London, England: Comedia.

NSW Department of Education. (1984). *All about mass media: K-12*. New South Wales Department of Education, Sydney, Australia.

Rosenthal, N. (1953). *Film in our lives*. Melbourne, Australia: F.W. Cheshire.
Scrivener, L. (2012). Perkins, William Herbert (1910–1988). In *Australian dictionary of biography*. Retrieved from http://adb.anu.edu.au/biography/perkins-william-herbert-15083
Sharman, E. (1971). *State report: South Australia*. In Australian National Advisory Committee for UNESCO (Ed.), *Developing in schools a critical study of film and television* (pp. 6–8). Canberra, Australia: Australian Government Publishing Service.
Turner, G. (1988). *Film as social practice*. London, England: Routledge.
UNESCO. (1971). *Developing in schools a critical study of film and television*. Canberra, Australia: Australian Government Publishing Service.

Michael Dezuanni undertakes research and teaching in the field of digital cultures and education, which includes film and media education, digital literacies, and arts education. He is appointed by the Film, Television and Animation Discipline in the Creative Industries Faculty and is a member of the Queensland University of Technology's Digital Media Research Centre. Michael explores the most effective, productive, and meaningful ways for individuals to use and understand the media and technologies in their lives.

Media Literacy in Austria

BRIGITTE HIPFL
University of Klagenfurt, Austria

First attempts: film education and protecting audiences from "bad" influences

As Edith Blaschitz and Michael Seibt (2008) point out in their review on the historical roots of media literacy in Austria, public concern regarding the "low quality" of literature and the "reading mania" of children and adolescents was already addressed by the intellectual elite, in particular, by teachers, at the end of the 19th century. It became important to restrict and supervise what children read. Similarly, popular entertainment in cinematographic theaters at the beginning of the 20th century was credited with offering an illusory world, resulting in an overexcitement of children's phantasies and possibly in violent and/or criminal behavior. As a consequence, a preventive and normative approach toward media became the dominant public discourse. At the same time, several institutions were established to deal pedagogically with the then new media. In 1921 the Austrian Photograph and Film Service was founded by the Austrian Ministry of Education to support the use of appropriate photographs and films in educational contexts. In the 1920s, more than a dozen so-called school-cinemas were established, while guidelines for the didactic use of films were developed by the Viennese Pedagogical Society in 1925, and a few years later, the Austrian Ministry of Education offered courses to educate directors of school-cinemas.

Besides institutionalized education in schools, political parties and the Catholic Church (which was the dominant faith at the time and remains so) became involved in educational work with media. The social democrats established a Workers Radio Alliance (Arbeiter-Radiobund) in 1924 in which members had a say regarding the programming of public radio, which was dedicated to public education and good entertainment, and included workers' issues. Another main goal was to acquire technical knowledge that would enable the members to construct their own radio apparatus so that everybody should be in possession of a radio without having to buy the then very expensive commodity (Weblexikon der Wiener Sozialdemokratie, n.d.). Film became more and more important in the workers' education movement, materializing into two strands. First, there was the critique of films as commodity, as well as the critique of films that were either propagandistic or representationally idyllic. Second, "good" films that addressed working lives were shown, but also advice and information regarding "good" films was offered. A film rental service was institutionalized by the social democrats' Central Office for Education. Even an Alliance of Socialist Worker-Film Makers (Bund der sozialistischen Arbeiterfilmer) was founded (see Weidenholzer, 1981). In a parallel move, the Catholic Church began its film education with film reviews published in a Catholic-oriented newspaper, warning the readers of films that did not comply with Catholic values, suggesting "good" films instead. In 1934 the Institute for Film Culture was founded which, in the authoritarian regime of the Austrian corporate state, became the Central Office of National Film Education (Hauptstelle für volkserziehliche Filmarbeit). This office also published the magazine *The Good Film* (*Der gute Film*) (Blaschitz, 2005). The main intention was to argue against the "smut and dross" (Schmutz und Schund) deployed in so many movies that would result in the deterioration of morality and Christian values. In National Socialism, radio and film were used for political propaganda intended to reach everybody in private households and schools (radio receivers were installed in larger schools), via radio and moving cinemas. Even nurseries were addressed (Blaschitz, 2005). Not listening to the national socialist radio programs and listening instead to another foreign channel (like Radio London) was seen as a form of resistance, not carrying out one's duty.

After World War II, when Austria was occupied by the Allies (Soviet, American, British, and French troops) and declared the "first victim" of the Third Reich, the Allies started a politics of reorientation, intended to "insure the institution of a progressive long-term educational program designed to eradicate all traces of Nazi ideology and to instill into Austrian youth democratic principles" (Heer, 1983, quoted in Blaschitz, 2005, p. 15). This also included the airing of US educational films about concentration camps. During this time, the Austrian Federal Ministry of Education became very active in campaigns against smut and dross as a way to control and protect youths. Films were categorized and certified according to their permissibility for certain age groups. Additionally, following the model of US youth book clubs, the Austrian Youth Book-Club (Österreichischer Buchklub der Jugend) was institutionalized, intended not only to pursue "good" books but also to prevent youths from reading comics, which were considered "bad" (Blaschitz, 2014). Later, in the 1950s, the "Good Film" initiative (Aktion "Der gute Film") was started by the Federal Ministry, which then became a well-established institution by itself, continuing the work that had started before World War II with the Institute for Film Culture. In these years, educational endeavors related to film usually involved discussions after film screenings. These were in place in almost all educational institutions from the church, the federation of labor unions, and provincial youth units to adult education institutions. In school, a decree of film education was introduced by the Federal Ministry in 1958 (Blaschitz and Seibt, 2008).

In the 1960s, pedagogical interest also took print media and television into consideration as part of mass media. Austrian television, which started as public television in the late 1950s, was not seen as a problem; rather, because of its educational mandate, television was highly appreciated and special programs for education (so-called educational television, Schulfernsehen) were developed (Schludermann, 1981).

As this short review illustrates, the first half of the 20th century in Austria is characterized by attempts to control and censor and thus to protect youths from what were understood as morally problematic influences from media like film and comics. This is also the context for new developments that started with academic explorations of issues of media literacy.

Media literacy in the academy: communication education, media didactics

Teacher education was the primary field where a more scientifically grounded approach to media began to develop. Franz Zöchbauer, a teacher at the Salzburg College of Education in the 1960s had been active in the Catholic film education tradition of protecting minors. In his doctoral thesis on youth and film, he carried out one of the first empirical studies on film reception in Austria. Zöchbauer collected around 3000 questionnaires from students aged 10 to 18 years in Salzburg, and based his discussion on the smut and dross approach that was still valid at that time (Blaschitz, 2014). Later, he expanded film education to include television as a medium that needed to be critically explored. Zöchbauer was the first in the Austrian context to make a connection between pedagogy and media and communication studies that focused on journalism at that time. For Zöchbauer, this resulted in making communication the key concept, with media use comprising three forms of communication: each encounter with a medium is seen as an example of mass communication, followed by intrapersonal communication when the person processes what she or he has encountered. It then ends with interpersonal communication when the person converses with other people. Subsequently, Zöchbauer advocated "communication education," intended to increase communicative competencies and autonomous, self-defined communication (Zöchbauer, 1974).

In the 1970s, educational technology was another approach that became prominent in Austria. In the newly founded College of Educational Sciences in Klagenfurt, which then became the University of Educational Sciences, one of the first five research and teaching areas was in educational technology and media pedagogy, chaired by Adolf Melezinek. Here the key questions were how new technological developments and media could be used to facilitate and improve learning and processes of communication in educational settings. Media were approached as means for didactic purposes, to support educators and their educational objectives. At the same time, partly influenced by developments in Germany introduced by Dieter Baacke, a broader approach pointed toward critical reflections on media and media representations, as well as using media to express one's interests as a form of democratic citizenship. This approach emerged at the universities of Innsbruck, Klagenfurt, Salzburg, and Vienna, each having their respective specific focus. First, classes on issues of media pedagogy (this was the general term used at the time, covering four different fields: knowledge regarding the organization, structure, and economic principles of media; the critical-reflective approach; media production: like students' radio, for example; and the didactic use of media) were offered to students in education in the late 1970s and the 1980s. Graz University started an extracurricular training course on journalism and media; Hans Heinz Fabris in Salzburg initiated what now would be called community media (Fabris, 1979). In 1980, Thomas Bauer was the first academic in media and communication studies (and so far, the only one in the Austrian context) to focus in his habilitation thesis explicitly on media pedagogy from a communication perspective (Bauer, 1980).

Conceptually, in the following years, media competence prevailed as the key term and foundation of media pedagogy, with communication becoming the superordinate concept (Schludermann, 1999). The Klagenfurt group chaired by Klaus Boeckmann referred to Immanuel Kant's characterization of enlightenment as an individual's departure from immaturity, and coined the term "media maturity" to characterize the intended goals of media education (Schludermann, 1999). This was one way to broaden the then-dominant understanding of media literacy as the materialization of certain skills (like being able to analyze and use media, for example) toward "media mature" citizens. In the past decade, the term "Medienbildung" has become the preferred term to stress that media literacy is more than certain skills and competencies; it comprises individuals' critical reflections on continuous encounters with their changing media cultures, so as to become active citizens in a mediatized world.

With the development of digital media in the 1990s, questions of educational technology reemerged. New possibilities of e-learning, blended learning, and distance learning were discussed, in particular by Peter Baumgartner, who became the chair of the Department of Interactive Media and Educational Technology at Krems University in 2006 (a new university for further education that offers vocational courses), and Theo Hug from Innsbruck University, who extended the discussions to include questions of mobile learning, microlearning, and media literacy and e-education. In 2004, at Vienna University, Christian Swertz started a subdepartment on media pedagogy with a special focus on "e-learning in university didactic" within educational sciences (Paus-Hasebrink and Hipfl, 2005).

The theoretical foundations for teaching and research in the broad field of media education have become fairly widespread, reaching from expansions of educational theories to the use of concepts from psychology, sociology, philosophy, and culture theory, and working within critical theory traditions such as cultural studies, critical pedagogy, and gender studies and, most recently, referring to media theories as well as to concepts from science and technology studies and affect theory.

As this overview illustrates, courses on media literacy, as well as research in the field at the university level, were for the longest time defined by and dependent on the interests and commitments of a few singular people. This changed with several initiatives starting at the turn of the 21st century, which were intended to create networks comprised of academics, engaged teachers, teacher educators, social workers, and media practitioners to pool their expertise for interventions into public discussions, and toward the consideration of media education in policy decisions. One such initiative was the establishment of a division of media education in the Austrian Society for Educational Research and Development in 2004. The Austrian Society of Communication has not been big enough to be differentiated into several divisions, but has included issues of media literacy on a regular basis in its journal *Medien Journal*, and made it a topic in its bi-annual conferences. However, most Austrians interested in media literacy also join the media education division of the German Communication Association, the media education division of the German Society for Educational Sciences, and/or the Society for Media Education and Culture of Communication, also located in Germany.

Institutionalizing media education in Austrian schools

The most systematic approach toward media education was adopted by the Austrian Ministry of Education when it issued the media education policy decree in 1973 to integrate media education in compulsory schooling. The decree, which was updated in 1994, 2001, and most recently in 2012, asks all teachers to make media literacy an integral part of their regular teaching. Instead of establishing a new subject like media studies, for example, every teacher should not only use media as didactic means, but should also reflect and analyze the constructedness of media, the commercial interests involved in media products, and the differences in individuals' reactions to the same media messages. Although the decree exemplarily points to possibilities where teaching media could be interwoven into the curriculum of certain school subjects, to actually practice media education in their day-to-day teaching became quite a challenge for the teachers as they themselves had not undergone any formal training in media education. Consequently, Susanne Krucsay, the very engaged head of the media pedagogy department of the Federal Ministry of Education, cooperated with the Klagenfurt group around Klaus Boeckmann to start an inservice program in the early 1980s so that teachers would become multipliers of media education. Due to the fact that further education of teachers functions on a voluntary base, neither this model nor attempts to institutionalize media education on the provincial level of advanced teacher training proved to be successful. To not give up on the goal to make media education an indispensable part at school, Krucsay started accompanying measures to support teachers with materials that would motivate and inspire them to do media education (Krucsay & Zuna-Kratky, 1991). All of these initiatives have become most useful and easily accessible resources for teachers and educators. In the late 1980s, brochures, which comprised background information as well as pedagogical ideas on how to work with students, were printed with a focus on certain topics such as media violence, gender issues, or advertisements. Now these brochures and continuously added materials are available at the website mediamanual (www.mediamanual.at/), which was installed by the Federal Ministry of Education in 2001. Mediamanual also lists activities and events related to media literacy and invites European schools to compete with projects for the yearly *Media Literacy Award*. The journal *Medienimpulse*, offering teachers access to the discussions on media literacy within the scientific community, was funded by the Ministry in 1992 and has recently changed from a printed journal into an online journal (www.medienimpulse.at).

Unfortunately, when it comes to compulsory training of teachers in media education, no fundamental changes have taken place since the 1980s. With the establishment of Krems University and its specialization in further education in 1994, advanced training courses in media education have been offered for those who take them voluntarily. Only recently have the first serious attempts to integrate media education in the curriculum of teacher education started in the process of the restructuring of Austrian teacher training.

Current developments and challenges

Currently, the focus on digital media dominates discussions about what literacy means under contemporary conditions. In which ways digital media should be implemented and dealt with at school and in college and university programs, and what kind of research is seen as essential, is also being discussed. The Austrian Ministry of Education started an initiative called School 4.0 (Austrian Ministry of Education, n.d.) to improve and support digital competencies. This initiative, which consists of measures like the implementation of basic digital education at all school levels, courses for advanced teacher training, and the development of teaching material, resembles early attempts in media literacy. Interestingly, the relationship between the newly proposed digital literacy and what already is covered by the media education decree, which in its last version included digital media, is not addressed. Within the scientific community, the discussions are much more differentiated, pointing toward the challenge to grasp conceptually what has been characterized as the mediatization of all aspects of life, and what this means for teaching and learning, but also for becoming a critical citizen (see *Medienimpulse*, 2017, issues 1 and 2).

SEE ALSO: Communication; Critical Pedagogy; Digital Literacy; Educational Media, History; Film Education in Europe; Media Competence; Media Literacy Education and 21st Century Teacher Education; Media Literacy Foundations; Media Literacy in France; Media Literacy in Germany; Media Literacy in Teacher Education; Reflection

References

Austrian Ministry of Education. (n.d). School 4.0. Retrieved from https://www.bmb.gv.at/schulen/schule40/index.html

Bauer, T. (1980). *Medienpädagogik. Einführung und Grundlegung* [Media education. Introduction and foundation]. Vienna, Austria: Böhlau.

Blaschitz, E. (2005). *"Denn Österreich ist in dir, Jugend!" Schule und Medien als Mittler von Österreich- und Demokratiebewusstsein bei Kindern und Jugendlichen (1945–1955)* ["Because Austria is in you, youth!" School and media as agents of creating an awareness of Austria and democracy (1945–1955)]. Vienna, Austria: Bundesministerium für Bildung, Wissenschaft und Kultur.

Blaschitz, E. (2014). *Der "Kampf gegen Schmutz und Schund"* ["Fighting smut and dross"]. Vienna, Austria: LIT.

Blaschitz, E., & Seibt, M. (2008). Geschichte und Status Quo der Medienbildung in Österreich [History and status quo of Medienbildung in Austria]. In E. Blaschitz & M. Seibt (Eds.), *Medienbildung in Österreich. Historische und aktuelle Entwicklungen, theoretische Positionen und Medienpraxis [Medienbildung in Austria. History, recent developments, theoretical positions, and media production]* (pp. 11–25). Vienna, Austria: LIT.

Fabris, H.H. (1979). *Journalismus und bürgernahe Medienarbeit. Formen und Bedingungen der Teilhabe an gesellschaftlicher Kommunikation* [Journalism and participatory media production. Forms and preconditions of social participation]. Salzburg, Austria: Neugebauer.

Krucsay, S., & Zuna-Kratky, G. (1991). Media education in primary schools in Austria: Teaching materials. *Educational Media International, 28*(2), 57–62. https://doi.org/10.1080/0952398910280202

Medienimpulse. Beiträge zur Medienpädagogik. http://www.medienimpulse.at/ausgaben

Paus-Hasebrink, I., & Hipfl, B. (2005). Medienpädagogik in Österreich: Perspektiven. Potenziale und Probleme – Ein Kaleidoskop in acht Bildern [Media education in Austria: Perspectives – potentials – problems. A kaleidoscope with eight patterns]. *MedienPädagogik.* Retrieved from http://www.medienpaed.com/article/view/72.

Schludermann, W. (1981). *Schulfernsehen aus mediendidaktischer Sicht* [Educational television from the perspective of media didactics]. Bamberg, Germany: Leuchtturm Verlag.

Schludermann, W. (1999). Media maturity. The pedagogical return to basics of media pedagogy. In Austrian Federal Ministry of Education and Cultural Affairs (Ed.), *Educating for the Media and the Digital Age* (pp. 244–250), proceedings of UNESCO international conference. Vienna, Austria: Federal Ministry of Education.

Weblexikon der Wiener Sozialdemokratie. (n.d.). Arbeiter-Radio-Bund Österreichs. Retrieved from http://dasrotewien.at/seite/arbeiter-radio-bund-oesterreichs-araboe

Weidenholzer, J. (1981). *Auf dem Weg zum 'Neuen Menschen'. Bildungs- und Kulturarbeit der österreichischen Sozialdemokratie in der Ersten* Republik [Towards the "New Human Being." Educational and cultural work of Austrian social democrats in Austria's First Republic]. Vienna, Austria: Europaverlag.

Zöchbauer, F. (1974). Von der Medienerziehung zur Kommunikationserziehung [From media education to communication education]. *Jugend, Film, Fernsehen, 1*, 9–13.

Brigitte Hipfl is Associate Professor of Media Studies in the Department of Media and Communication Studies at the University of Klagenfurt, Austria. Her research interests are media and gender, subject formations, media education, the affective labor of media, and postcolonial Europe. Currently, she is exploring how migration is addressed in Austrian cinema and television. Among her recent English publications is a book co-edited with Kristín Loftsdóttir and Andrea L. Smith, *Messy Europe: Crisis, Race, and Nation-State in a Postcolonial World* (2018).